KB220941

# YBM 실전토익 RC 1000

# 1

발행인 허문호
발행처 YBM

문항 개발 Marilyn Hook
편집 윤경림, 정유상, 이진열
디자인 김현경, 이현숙
마케팅 정연철, 박천산, 고영노, 김동진, 박찬경, 김윤하

초판인쇄 2024년 12월 10일
2쇄발행 2025년 4월 1일

신고일자 1964년 3월 28일
신고번호 제1964-000003호
주소 서울시 종로구 종로 104
전화 (02) 2000-0515 [구입문의] / (02) 2000-0305 [내용문의]
팩스 (02) 2285-1523
홈페이지 www.ybmbooks.com

ISBN 978-89-17-23963-8



낙장 및 파본은 교환해 드립니다.
구입철회는 구매처 규정에 따라 교환 및 환불처리 됩니다.

# 최신 토익 경향 완벽 반영!
# 100% 전면 개정!

**최신 토익 경향 반영**

토익 시험 최신 출제 경향 및 난이도 완벽 반영!
새로운 문제들로 구성한 최신 개정판!

**고품질, 고난도 문제로 실전 대비**

고품질, 고난도 문제로 엄선된 모의고사 10세트 수록!
OMR 답안지 마킹까지 실전처럼 연습!

**상세하고 명쾌한 해설**

모든 문제 정답 및 오답 이유 + 핵심 출제 포인트 상세히 설명!
문제 유형 표시, 패러프레이징 및 핵심 어휘 선별 정리!

**맞춤 학습 가이드**

테스트 맞은 개수에 따라 앞으로의 공부 방향을 제시!
현재 실력에 따라 점수를 더 빠르게 올릴 수 있는 가이드 제공!

**부가 학습자료 무료 제공**

YBM 1등 강사 동영상 강의 + 단어장 + 단어 암기용 MP3 모두 무료 제공!
단어장 및 MP3: www.ybmbooks.com ▶ MP3·학습자료

# 토익의 구성 & 수험 정보

**TOEIC 소개**

Test of English for International Communication(국제적 의사소통을 위한 영어 시험)의 약자로서, 영어가 모국어가 아닌 사람들을 대상으로 커뮤니케이션 능력에 중점을 두고 일상생활 또는 국제업무 등에 필요한 실용영어 능력을 평가하는 글로벌 평가 시험이다.

**시험 구성**

| 구성 | Part | 내용 | | 문항수 | 시간 | 배점 |
|---|---|---|---|---|---|---|
| 듣기 (L/C) | 1 | 사진 묘사 | | 6문항 | 45분 | 495점 |
| | 2 | 질의 & 응답 | | 25문항 | | |
| | 3 | 짧은 대화 | | 39문항 | | |
| | 4 | 짧은 담화 | | 30문항 | | |
| 읽기 (R/C) | 5 | 단문 빈칸 채우기(문법/어휘) | | 30문항 | 75분 | 495점 |
| | 6 | 장문 빈칸 채우기 | | 16문항 | | |
| | 7 | 독해 | 단일 지문 | 29문항 | | |
| | | | 이중 지문 | 10문항 | | |
| | | | 삼중 지문 | 15문항 | | |
| Total | 7 Parts | | | 200문항 | 120분 | 990점 |

**TOEIC 접수**

TOEIC 접수는 한국 토익 위원회 사이트(www.toeic.co.kr)에서 온라인 상으로만 가능하다. 사이트에서 매월 자세한 접수 일정과 시험 일정 등의 구체적 정보 확인이 가능하니, 미리 일정을 확인하여 접수하도록 한다.

**TOEIC 성적 확인**

성적 확인은 TOEIC 홈페이지에 안내된 성적발표일에 인터넷 홈페이지, 어플리케이션을 통해 확인이 가능하다. 최초 성적표 발급은 우편 또는 온라인을 통해 수령이 가능하며 재발급은 성적 유효기간(2년) 내에만 가능하다. 단, 공공기관에 한하여 2023년 4월부터 5년으로 유효기간이 연장되었다.

## 시험장 준비물

| | |
|---|---|
| 신분증 | 규정 신분증만 가능<br>(주민등록증, 운전면허증, 기간 만료 전의 여권, 공무원증 등) |
| 필기구 | 연필, 지우개 (볼펜이나 사인펜은 사용 금지) |

## 시험 진행 시간

| | |
|---|---|
| 09:20 | 입실 (09:50 이후는 입실 불가) |
| 09:30 - 09:45 | 답안지 작성에 관한 오리엔테이션 |
| 09:45 - 09:50 | 휴식 |
| 09:50 - 10:05 | 신분증 확인 |
| 10:05 - 10:10 | 문제지 배부 및 파본 확인 |
| 10:10 - 10:55 | 듣기 평가 (Listening Test) |
| 10:55 - 12:10 | 독해 평가 (Reading Test) |

## TOEIC 점수

TOEIC 점수는 듣기 영역(LC) 점수, 읽기 영역(RC) 점수, 그리고 이 두 영역을 합계한 전체 점수 세 부분으로 구성된다. 각 부분의 점수는 5점 단위이며, 5점에서 495점에 걸쳐 주어지고, 전체 점수는 10점에서 990점까지이며, 만점은 990점이다. TOEIC 성적은 각 문제 유형의 난이도에 따른 점수 환산표에 의해 결정된다.

# 토익 경향 분석 & 고득점 전략

## PART 5 단문 빈칸 채우기 Incomplete Sentences

총 30문제

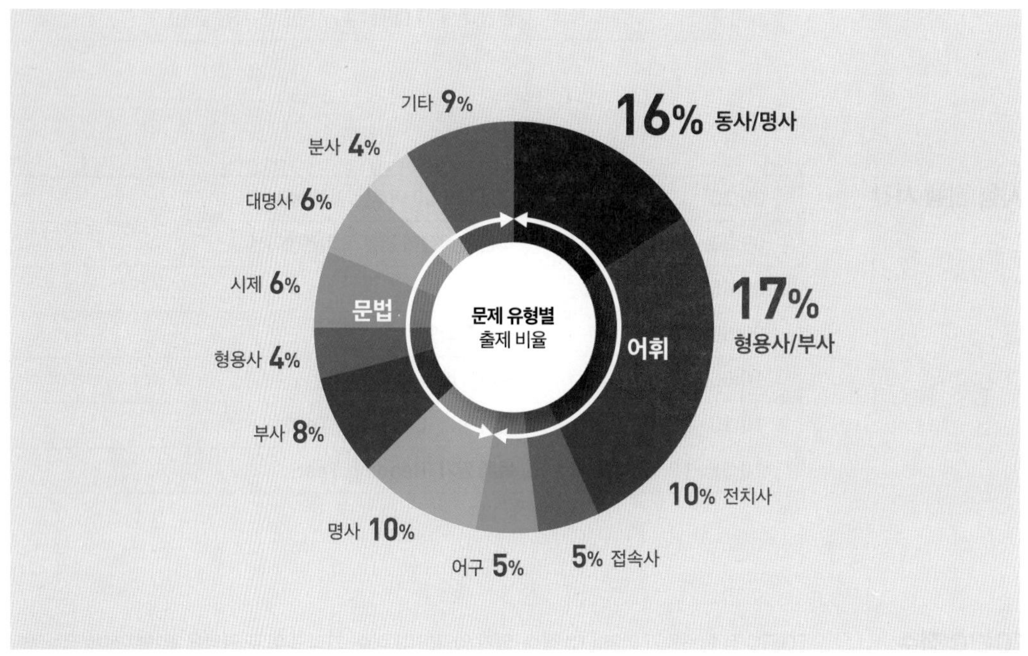


고득점 전략

**보기를 먼저 보고 문제 유형을 파악한다**

보기가 다양한 품사로 구성되어 있으면 문법 문제이고, 동일한 품사의 다양한 어휘로 구성되어 있으면 어휘 문제이다. 문제 유형을 먼저 파악하여 문제를 훨씬 더 빠르고 정확하게 해결할 수 있다.

**어휘는 같이 쓰이는 표현과 함께 콜로케이션으로 익힌다**

같이 쓰이는 어휘들을 묶어서 콜로케이션(collocation)으로 익혀 두면 어휘 문제뿐 아니라 문제 문제를 해결하는 데도 큰 도움이 된다.

# PART 6 장문 빈칸 채우기 Text Completion

총 4지문 16문제 (지문당 4문제)

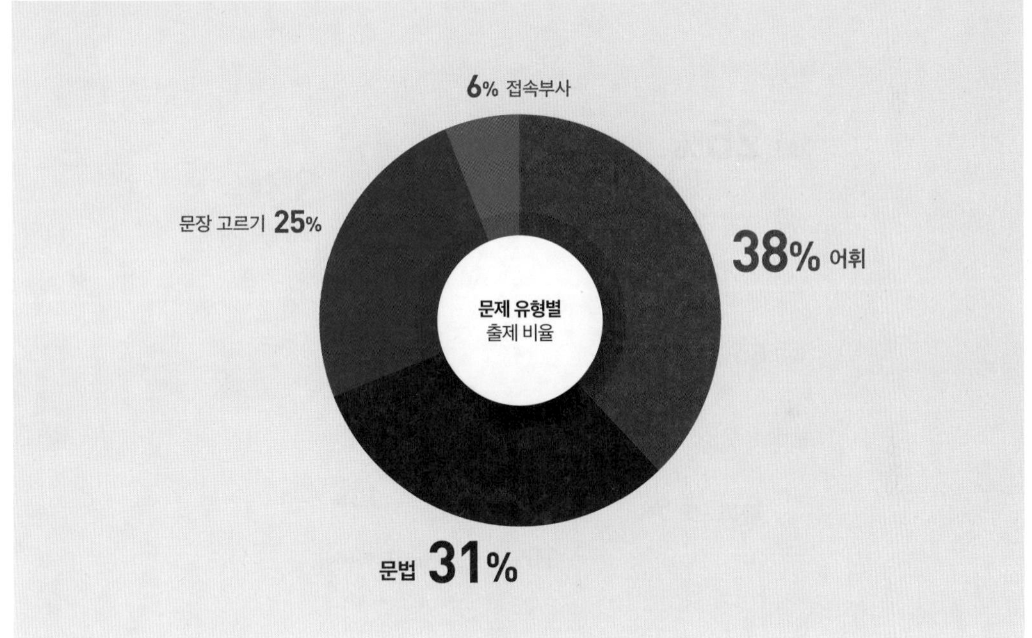


**고득점 전략**

**전체 지문을 읽으면서 문제를 푼다**

Part 6는 전체 지문의 내용 흐름을 파악해야 해결할 수 있는 문제가 대부분이다. 빈칸이 있는 문장만 보고 오답을 고르지 않도록 전체 지문을 읽으면서 문제를 푸는 연습을 해야 한다.

**시간 표현을 확인한다**

Part 6에서는 시제 문제가 많이 나온다. 앞뒤 문장의 시제와 시간 표현도 단서가 될 수 있다. 때로는 메일을 보낸 시간, 기사의 작성 일자 등도 정답의 단서가 될 수 있으니 확인해야 한다.

# PART 7 독해
Reading Comprehension

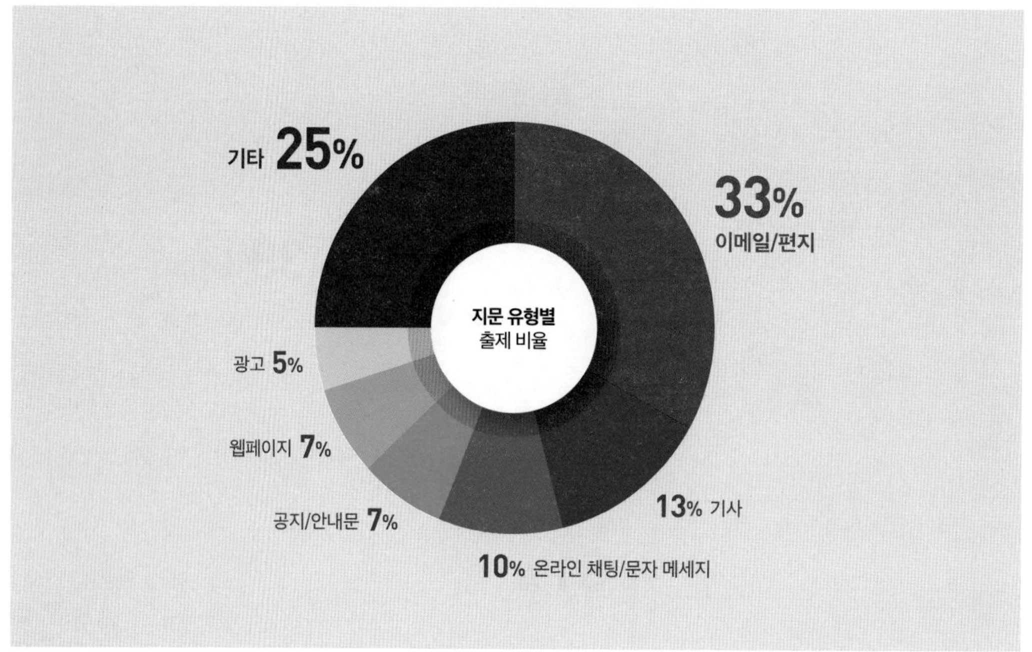


고득점 전략

**시간을 최대한 확보한다**

Part 7은 늘 시간이 부족하므로 전략적으로 시간을 분배해야 한다.
Part 1과 Part 2 디렉션이 나오는 시간을 활용하면 Part 5를 몇 문항은 풀 수 있다.
Part 5는 시간을 최소한으로 사용하고, Part 7에서 시간을 충분히 쓰는 것이 유리하다.

**뒤에서부터 푸는 것이 좋다**

Part 7은 대체로 뒤로 갈수록 지문의 길이가 길고 어렵다. 그리고 이중 지문과 삼중 지문은 문제 푸는 데 시간이 더 걸린다. 앞에서부터 풀다가 시간이 얼마 안 남은 상황에서 이중/삼중 지문 문제를 풀려면 마음이 조급해져서 지문에 딸린 문제 전체를 놓치기 쉽다. 따라서 뒤에서부터 푸는 것이 도움이 될 수도 있다.

총 15지문 54문제(지문당 2~5문제)

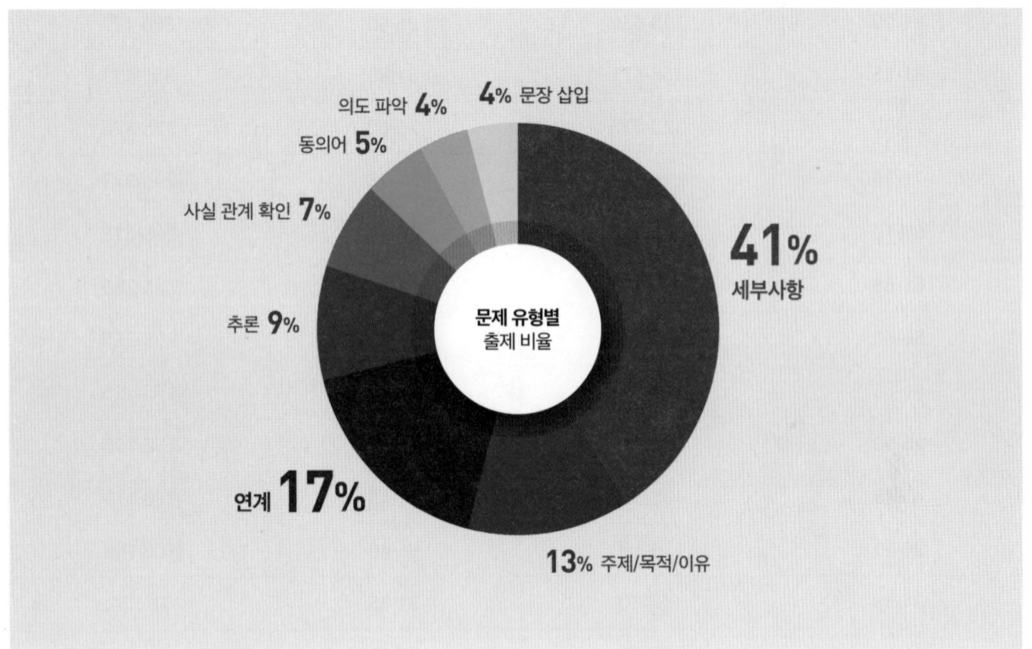


**문항당 1분씩 할애한다**

Part 7 문제 푸는 시간은 대략 문항당 1분 정도로 생각하면 된다.
다만, 앞쪽에 배치된 비교적 쉽고 짧은 단일 지문 문제는 1분 이내로 풀어야 한다.
여기서 시간은 줄이면 그만큼 어려운 문제에 시간을 더 할애할 수 있다.

**잘 풀리지 않는 문제는 과감히 넘어가라**

잘 풀리지 않는 문제는 잡고 있지 말고 넘어 가도록 한다. 그 문제 때문에 풀 수 있었던 문제를 놓치게 되는 일이 생길 수 있기 때문이다. 시간이 남으면 다시 돌아와서 천천히 읽어보도록 한다.

# 점수 환산표

| LISTENING Raw Score (맞은 개수) | LISTENING Scaled Score (환산 점수) | READING Raw Score (맞은 개수) | READING Scaled Score (환산 점수) |
|---|---|---|---|
| 96-100 | 480-495 | 96-100 | 460-495 |
| 91-95 | 435-490 | 91-95 | 410-475 |
| 86-90 | 395-450 | 86-90 | 380-430 |
| 81-85 | 355-415 | 81-85 | 355-400 |
| 76-80 | 325-375 | 76-80 | 325-375 |
| 71-75 | 295-340 | 71-75 | 295-345 |
| 66-70 | 265-315 | 66-70 | 265-315 |
| 61-65 | 240-285 | 61-65 | 235-285 |
| 56-60 | 215-260 | 56-60 | 205-255 |
| 51-55 | 190-235 | 51-55 | 175-225 |
| 46-50 | 160-210 | 46-50 | 150-195 |
| 41-45 | 135-180 | 41-45 | 120-170 |
| 36-40 | 110-155 | 36-40 | 100-140 |
| 31-35 | 85-130 | 31-35 | 75-120 |
| 26-30 | 70-105 | 26-30 | 55-100 |
| 21-25 | 50-90 | 21-25 | 40-80 |
| 16-20 | 35-70 | 16-20 | 30-65 |
| 11-15 | 20-55 | 11-15 | 20-50 |
| 6-10 | 15-40 | 6-10 | 15-35 |
| 1-5 | 5-20 | 1-5 | 5-20 |
| 0 | 5 | 0 | 5 |

이 환산표는 본 교재에 수록된 Test용으로 개발된 것이다. 이 표를 사용하여 자신의 실제 점수를 환산 점수로 전환하도록 한다. 즉, 예를 들어 Listening Test의 실제 정답 수가 61~65개이면 환산 점수는 240점에서 285점 사이가 된다. 여기서 실제 정답 수가 61개이면 환산 점수가 240점이고, 65개이면 환산 점수가 285점임을 의미하는 것은 아니다. 본 책의 Test를 위해 작성된 이 점수 환산표가 자신의 영어 실력이 어느 정도인지 대략적으로 파악하는 데 도움이 되긴 하지만, 이 표가 실제 TOEIC 성적 산출에 그대로 사용된 적은 없다는 사실을 밝혀 둔다.

# RC 학습 기록표

테스트별로 맞은 개수를 기록하세요. 학습 성취도와 취약한 PART가 어디인지 알 수 있습니다.

| | 맞은 개수 | | | | 환산 점수 |
|---|---|---|---|---|---|
| | PART 5 (총 30문제) | PART 6 (총 16문제) | PART 7 (총 54문제) | 맞은 개수 합계 | 총점 |
| TEST 1 | | | | | |
| TEST 2 | | | | | |
| TEST 3 | | | | | |
| TEST 4 | | | | | |
| TEST 5 | | | | | |
| TEST 6 | | | | | |
| TEST 7 | | | | | |
| TEST 8 | | | | | |
| TEST 9 | | | | | |
| TEST 10 | | | | | |

TEST의 환산 점수를 점( • )으로 표시해서 점수 변화를 확인해보세요.

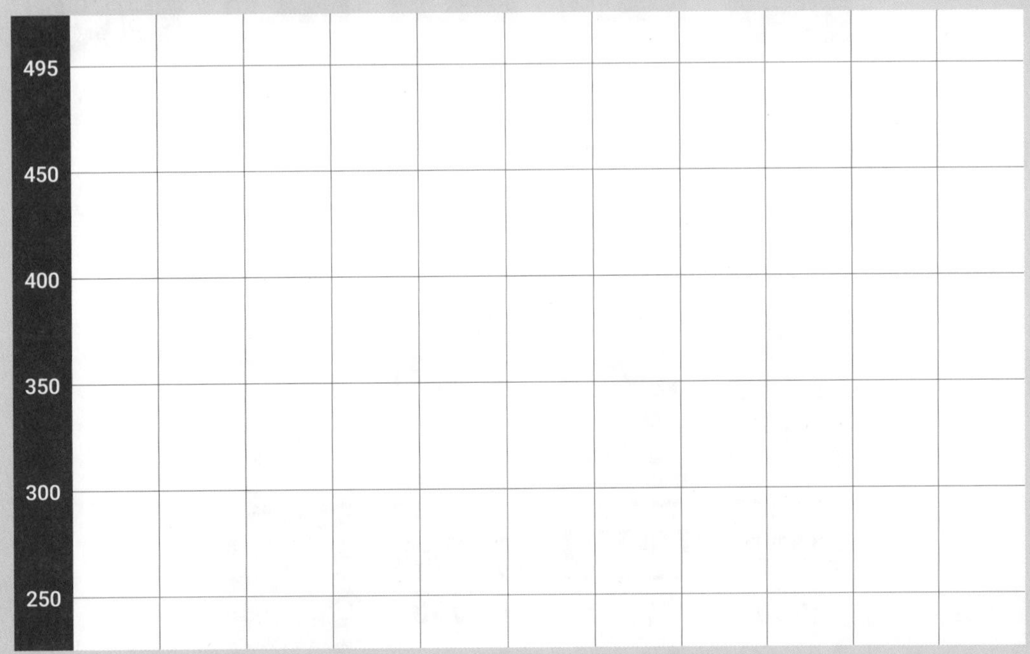

# 점수대별 학습 가이드

## 토익 초급 LEVEL

맞은 개수 50개 미만

**성적 진단** 실전 문제를 풀이하기엔 기본기가 부족합니다. 입문서를 통해 필수단어와 빈출표현을 암기하면서 기초를 다지는 것이 좋습니다.

**학습 POINT** 어휘 / 빈출표현 / part별 문제 유형 학습

**연계 교재**

## 토익 중급 LEVEL

맞은 개수 50~70개

**성적 진단** 기본기는 갖췄지만 기복이 큰 점수대입니다. 전략서를 병행하면서 자주 틀리는 유형에 대한 풀이 전략을 익혀 보세요. 자주 등장하는 오답의 유형도 함께 기억해두면 정답을 찾을 때 고민하는 시간을 크게 줄일 수 있습니다.

**학습 POINT** 풀이 전략 학습 / 오답 유형 확인 / 다양한 문제 풀이

**연계 교재**

## 토익 고급 LEVEL

맞은 개수 70개 이상

**성적 진단** 중간 휴식 없이 실제 시험처럼 풀이하면서 집중력을 유지하는 훈련을 하는 것이 좋습니다. 틀린 문제 위주로 검토하면서 약점을 보완해 나간다면 고득점은 문제없을 겁니다.

**학습 POINT** 연습은 실전처럼 / 집중력 유지 / 오답 피드백

**연계 교재**

# CONTENTS

# YBM 실전토익 RC1000

## 테스트 전 체크리스트

- 중간 휴식 없이 제한 시간을 지켜서 풀이하세요.
- 제한 시간은 답안지에 마킹하는 시간도 포함시켜야 합니다.
- 찍은 문제는 번호 옆에 꼭 체크해 주세요.
- 시간 안에 풀지 못한 문제는 틀린 것으로 채점해 주세요.

# RC TEST 1

## READING TEST

In the Reading test, you will read a variety of texts and answer several different types of reading comprehension questions. The entire Reading test will last 75 minutes. There are three parts, and directions are given for each part. You are encouraged to answer as many questions as possible within the time allowed.

You must mark your answers on the separate answer sheet. Do not write your answers in your test book.

## PART 5

**Directions:** A word or phrase is missing in each of the sentences below. Four answer choices are given below each sentence. Select the best answer to complete the sentence. Then mark the letter (A), (B), (C), or (D) on your answer sheet.

**101.** The town council must be given advance notice of ------- to official historic structures.

(A) modifications
(B) modifying
(C) modified
(D) modifies

**102.** Upon its founder's retirement, the magazine published a special article on ------- achievements.

(A) he
(B) him
(C) his
(D) himself

**103.** Many restaurants have ------- been using mobile apps to manage their staff work schedules.

(A) successfully
(B) succeeding
(C) succeeded
(D) successes

**104.** Mena Hotel has prospered mainly because its management understands ------- to create comfortable spaces for guests.

(A) yet
(B) how
(C) about
(D) that

**105.** Ms. Cox's computer is ------- old that it cannot run the new teleconferencing software.

(A) too
(B) soon
(C) enough
(D) so

**106.** Focus group participants are instructed ------- the group's discussions confidential.

(A) keeping
(B) keeps
(C) to keep
(D) having kept

**107.** Visit our Web site to learn the sources of the ingredients used ------- our products.

(A) from
(B) to
(C) in
(D) up

**108.** Donors to nonprofit organizations receive ------- tax benefits under the province's new tax policy.

(A) dominant
(B) generous
(C) enthusiastic
(D) respective

**109.** ------- the renovation of its office is completed, most Montes Corporation employees will be working remotely.

(A) Finally
(B) During
(C) Around
(D) Until

**110.** The Steppville Star Award honors citizens who have made ------- contributions to the community.

(A) meaningful
(B) mean
(C) meaning
(D) meaningfully

**111.** The Drayton supermarket chain claims that the ------- of its frozen foods is carried out via state-of-the-art refrigerated trucks.

(A) variety
(B) transport
(C) appraisal
(D) freshness

**112.** The Lytleton Historical Archives prohibits the ------- of its collection by visitors.

(A) photocopier
(B) photocopying
(C) photocopied
(D) photocopy

**113.** Even though the company has been outperformed by competitors in recent years, it is still -------.

(A) profit
(B) profited
(C) profitably
(D) profitable

**114.** Market research shows that most people ------- Hardwood Gym's membership fee pricing very reasonable.

(A) appreciate
(B) consider
(C) agree
(D) view

**115.** Regardless of ------- goods are being stored there at the moment, the warehouse must be secured at night.

(A) either
(B) while
(C) whether
(D) following

**116.** The social media platform Connectra deletes all of the data associated with ------- user accounts after one year.

(A) inactive
(B) indirect
(C) unlikely
(D) unmistakable

**117.** The ability to broadcast live video through Showvia is the platform's most ------- requested feature.

(A) potentially
(B) sharply
(C) perfectly
(D) heavily

**118.** An efficiency consultant could help us ------- parts of our production process that should be simplified.

(A) identify
(B) prevent
(C) ensure
(D) excel

**119.** There is ------- more skilled at attracting positive media attention than our new head of public relations.

(A) other
(B) anyone
(C) whoever
(D) no one

**120.** ------- the projector in the conference room broke down, the IT team was able to fix it before the meeting was scheduled to start.

(A) Unless
(B) Besides
(C) Although
(D) Amid

*GO ON TO THE NEXT PAGE* →

**121.** Ms. Cardenas is trying to improve her career ------- by earning additional qualifications.

(A) intentions
(B) prospects
(C) selections
(D) obstacles

**122.** Many reviews of *Silver Sword* give special praise to its director for the thrilling action scene ------- the end of the film.

(A) near
(B) except
(C) like
(D) upon

**123.** The interior decorator explained that measuring the lobby's dimensions ------- was an important part of her planning process.

(A) highly
(B) precisely
(C) extremely
(D) identically

**124.** ------- its limited collection of artworks, the Zielinski Museum consistently attracts remarkable numbers of visitors.

(A) Among
(B) Along with
(C) In spite of
(D) Rather than

**125.** Now that Mr. Jo ------- from the firm, another attorney at South Bay Law Group is overseeing our legal affairs.

(A) departing
(B) has departed
(C) to depart
(D) depart

**126.** The state environmental agency has made ------- progress in reducing air pollution.

(A) impressively
(B) impressed
(C) impressive
(D) impressions

**127.** Please draw up a list of alternative dinner venues ------- the clients do not want to go to the Italian restaurant.

(A) after all
(B) apart from
(C) which
(D) in case

**128.** ------- the popularity of the résumé writing workshop, the library will decide whether to hold other events for job seekers.

(A) Depending on
(B) Just as
(C) Not only
(D) Provided that

**129.** No other salesperson at Jinkwang Laboratories can speak ------- about the advantages of its medical devices than Vincent Cobb.

(A) persuasive
(B) persuasively
(C) most persuasive
(D) more persuasively

**130.** Whitlow Engineering ------- a summer internship program for university students for the past five years.

(A) is conducting
(B) will be conducting
(C) has been conducting
(D) would have been conducting

## PART 6

**Directions:** Read the texts that follow. A word, phrase, or sentence is missing in parts of each text. Four answer choices for each question are given below the text. Select the best answer to complete the text. Then mark the letter (A), (B), (C), or (D) on your answer sheet.

**Questions 131-134** refer to the following article.

(May 19)—Meat substitutes, which are plant-based foods with meat-like tastes and textures, are currently enjoying a boom nationwide. The market for such products grew nearly 50% in the past year, and they can now be found in a ------- **131.** range of settings, from supermarket shelves to fast-food restaurants.

A major reason for this trend is changing consumer ------- **132.** affected by concern about the environmental impact of livestock farming. According to Ivan Ortega, spokesperson for the Plant Based Food Association, the lower prices and better taste of newer meat substitutes have contributed ------- **133.** . Mr. Ortega believes that this sector of the industry will only continue to grow in the future. ------- **134.** .

**131.** (A) total
(B) broad
(C) constant
(D) numerous

**132.** (A) to prefer
(B) preferably
(C) preferring
(D) preferences

**133.** (A) as well
(B) already
(C) so far
(D) mainly

**134.** (A) Furthermore, his health has improved since the removal of meat from his diet.
(B) His association also includes makers of dairy alternatives such as soy milk.
(C) Therefore, he feels the process for making meat substitutes is too complex.
(D) In fact, he predicts that substitutes will equal meat in popularity within 15 years.

*GO ON TO THE NEXT PAGE* →

**Questions 135-138** refer to the following letter.

5 February

Lou Spellman
Senior Project Manager
North Perth Developers
349 Doyle Street
North Perth WA 6006

Dear Mr. Spellman,

Thank you for your invitation to bid for the contract for Stonefield Apartments. Enclosed you will find our bid, which ------- (**135.**) the price for which we could install the desired plumbing and a prospective timeline. I believe you will find it to be a very attractive ------- (**136.**).

------- (**137.**). We are currently finishing up the installation of all plumbing in the four-story Nowlin Hotel on schedule and under budget. ------- (**138.**) that, we equipped all 32 restrooms of the Rishley Center with reliable touchless sinks and toilets.

It would be my pleasure to speak with you about our bid or the Packard & Bowers crew. I can be reached at 9291 4998.

Sincerely,

Bella Packard
Packard & Bowers Plumbing
Encl.

**135.** (A) specify
(B) specified
(C) specifies
(D) is specifying

**136.** (A) design
(B) proposal
(C) building
(D) appliance

**137.** (A) The bid invitation said that the deadline for submissions is 6 February.
(B) The computer-generated image of the complex on your Web site is stunning.
(C) I would also like to highlight our recent work on similar projects.
(D) My business partner is familiar with your company.

**138.** (A) Prior to
(B) After
(C) Instead of
(D) Concerning

**Questions 139-142** refer to the following e-mail.

To: Nate Hopkins <nate.hopkins@genmail.com>
From: Akari Kaneko <a.kaneko@flurry.com>
Date: July 27
Subject: Announcement

Dear Mr. Hopkins,

I am sorry to announce that the Flurry app will cease ------- (139.) on September 1. From that date, it will not be possible to stream, download, or listen to podcasts through Flurry. Also, you will no longer have access to data associated with ------- (140.) Flurry account, such as downloaded episodes, lists of favorite shows, and listening preferences. If you would like to save this information and export it to another podcast app, please ------- (141.) the instructions at www.flurry.com/help/394. ------- (142.). Questions may be directed to the Flurry customer service center, which will remain open through September 1. We apologize again, and thank you for using Flurry until now.

Sincerely,

Akari Kaneko
President, Flurry, Inc.

**139.** (A) operate
(B) operated
(C) operative
(D) operations

**140.** (A) my
(B) their
(C) your
(D) our

**141.** (A) unveil
(B) consult
(C) refer
(D) contact

**142.** (A) Otherwise, no action is necessary on your part.
(B) Afterward, Flurry should run more smoothly.
(C) Our new parent company offers its own podcast app.
(D) We see you have not downloaded the most recent update.

*GO ON TO THE NEXT PAGE*

**Questions 143-146** refer to the following article.

OAKRIDGE (November 22)—Oakridge authorities were notified yesterday that intercity express bus operator Swiftbus ------- (143.) service to its stop in the city. The company specified December 1 as the effective date of the change. Located in front of Oakridge Plaza, the soon-to-be ------- (144.) stop was added to the line running between Bealett and Knappton earlier this year. ------- (145.). In the notice, Swiftbus cited low ridership as the reason for the decision. ------- (146.) also expressed a willingness to reestablish service to the city if there is an increase in demand in the future.

**143.** (A) will be halting
(B) has been halting
(C) has halted
(D) is halted

**144.** (A) granted
(B) inspected
(C) expanded
(D) discontinued

**145.** (A) The route has been served up to twice daily, depending on the day.
(B) Oakridge officials are seeking more ways to improve its transit services.
(C) The plaza has since become the cultural center of Oakridge.
(D) Both destinations have strong manufacturing industries.

**146.** (A) He
(B) It
(C) Some
(D) We

## PART 7

**Directions:** In this part you will read a selection of texts, such as magazine and newspaper articles, e-mails, and instant messages. Each text or set of texts is followed by several questions. Select the best answer for each question and mark the letter (A), (B), (C), or (D) on your answer sheet.

**Questions 147-148** refer to the following notice.

***STATON GRILL CORPORATE HEADQUARTERS***

**UPCOMING WEBINAR**

**Topic:** Customer Satisfaction

**Speaker:** Manuel Rios, founder of Rios Restaurant Consulting and author of *Front of House: The Importance of Hospitality in Restaurants*

**Date:** 19 September, 10:00 A.M.

**Venue:** www.v-meet.co.uk (Event ID: 093 657 893)

This Webinar is mandatory for Staton Grill employees who interact directly with patrons. Computer access is required. Please join by 9:55 to prevent delays.

**147.** Who will most likely attend the Webinar?
(A) Kitchen staff
(B) Menu developers
(C) Servers and cashiers
(D) Potential franchise owners

**148.** What are attendees asked to do?
(A) Use a company computer
(B) Read a book beforehand
(C) Provide a personal ID code
(D) Enter the Web venue early

GO ON TO THE NEXT PAGE

**Questions 149-150** refer to the following e-mail.

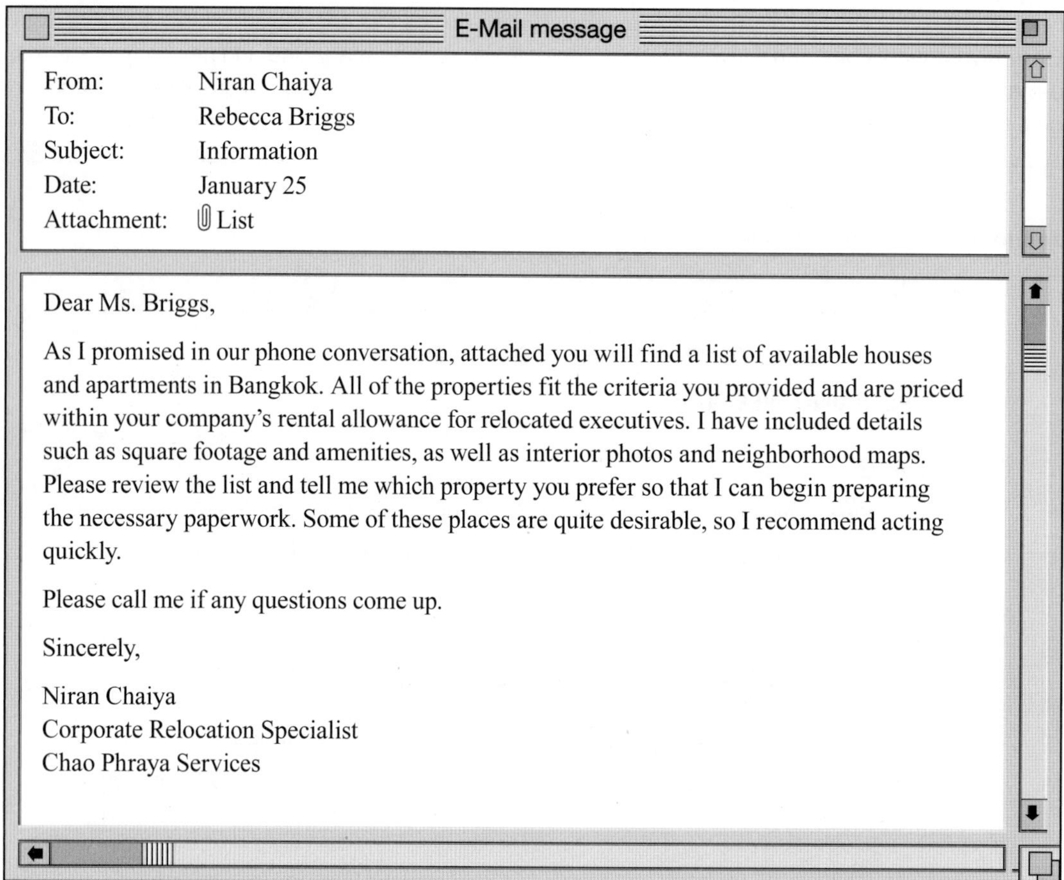

E-Mail message

From: Niran Chaiya
To: Rebecca Briggs
Subject: Information
Date: January 25
Attachment: List

Dear Ms. Briggs,

As I promised in our phone conversation, attached you will find a list of available houses and apartments in Bangkok. All of the properties fit the criteria you provided and are priced within your company's rental allowance for relocated executives. I have included details such as square footage and amenities, as well as interior photos and neighborhood maps. Please review the list and tell me which property you prefer so that I can begin preparing the necessary paperwork. Some of these places are quite desirable, so I recommend acting quickly.

Please call me if any questions come up.

Sincerely,

Niran Chaiya
Corporate Relocation Specialist
Chao Phraya Services

**149.** What is one purpose of the e-mail?

(A) To describe some of the difficulties of relocation
(B) To promote a new benefit for executives
(C) To arrange payment of an allowance
(D) To supply information on housing options

**150.** What is Ms. Briggs asked to do?

(A) Confirm a timeline
(B) Communicate a preference
(C) Visit some properties
(D) Collect some documents

**Questions 151-152** refer to the following instructions.

Don't have time to go to your local Songmin clinic for a minor medical issue? E-visits are a convenient way to get help wherever you are. Simply follow these steps:

1. Go to our Web site (www.songminhealth.com) and sign in.
2. Hover your mouse over the "E-visits" tab and select "Start an E-visit" from the drop-down menu.
3. Answer the questions on the resulting form about your symptoms and concerns. Be as clear and specific as possible. Submit the form.
4. Check your e-mail inbox for the response from a Songmin doctor. It may include advice, a referral for testing, or a prescription for medication.
5. If you do not receive a response within two business hours, or if there is a change in your symptoms, please call our assistance line at 1-800-555-0138.

SONGMIN HEALTH

**151.** Who are the instructions most likely intended for?

(A) Healthcare patients
(B) Clinical doctors
(C) Medical records clerks
(D) Technical support providers

**152.** What is the reader asked to do?

(A) Give clear recommendations
(B) Respond to an e-mail message
(C) Fill out a document online
(D) Make an appointment in advance

*GO ON TO THE NEXT PAGE*

**Questions 153-154** refer to the following text-message chain.

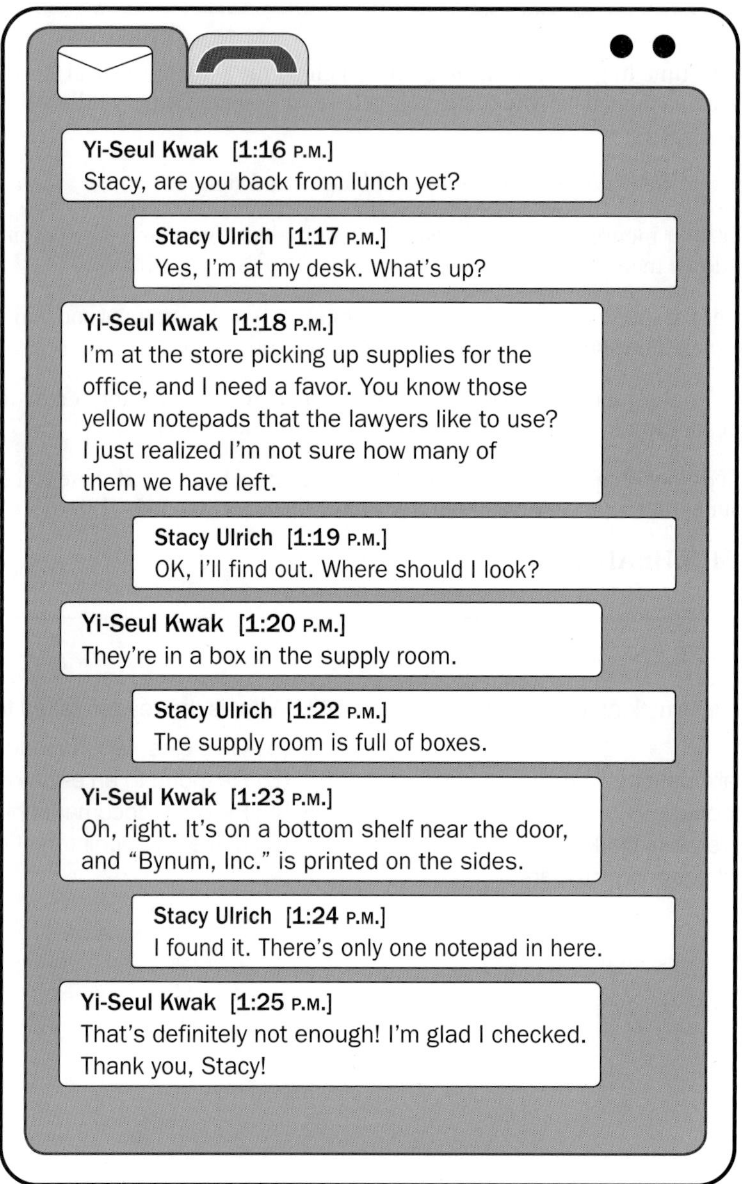

Yi-Seul Kwak [1:16 P.M.]
Stacy, are you back from lunch yet?
Stacy Ulrich [1:17 P.M.]
Yes, I'm at my desk. What's up?
Yi-Seul Kwak [1:18 P.M.]
I'm at the store picking up supplies for the office, and I need a favor. You know those yellow notepads that the lawyers like to use? I just realized I'm not sure how many of them we have left.
Stacy Ulrich [1:19 P.M.]
OK, I'll find out. Where should I look?
Yi-Seul Kwak [1:20 P.M.]
They're in a box in the supply room.
Stacy Ulrich [1:22 P.M.]
The supply room is full of boxes.
Yi-Seul Kwak [1:23 P.M.]
Oh, right. It's on a bottom shelf near the door, and "Bynum, Inc." is printed on the sides.
Stacy Ulrich [1:24 P.M.]
I found it. There's only one notepad in here.
Yi-Seul Kwak [1:25 P.M.]
That's definitely not enough! I'm glad I checked. Thank you, Stacy!


**153.** What problem does Ms. Kwak have?
- (A) She will be unavailable to accept a delivery.
- (B) She is uncertain about an inventory level.
- (C) She cannot locate some supplies.
- (D) She is unable to use her desk.

**154.** At 1:22 P.M., what does Ms. Ulrich imply when she writes, "The supply room is full of boxes"?
- (A) She needs a more detailed description.
- (B) Ms. Kwak should not make a purchase.
- (C) She cannot find space for some objects.
- (D) Ms. Kwak will have to organize the room.

**Questions 155-157** refer to the following job posting.

## Trail Ride Associate Needed

Morris Falls Guest Ranch is seeking a horseback riding enthusiast to assist with our popular trail ride program for guests. Duties of this full-time position include teaching guests how to prepare horses for rides, leading small groups of riders along trails on and near the ranch, and handling general horse-care tasks in our barn.

Applicants must be able to demonstrate high-level horseback riding skills. Other qualifications include having done at least six months of paid or volunteer work in a horse barn and possession of a cheerful, friendly personality. Weekend availability is a must, and the successful candidate should expect to be scheduled for at least one weekend shift per week.

To apply, send an e-mail entitled "Trail Ride Associate Application – (your name)" to contact@morrisfalls.com with your résumé and a short cover letter attached.

For details and photographs of our horse barn and horseback-riding trails, visit www.morrisfalls.com/riding.

**155.** The word "handling" in paragraph 1, line 4, is closest in meaning to
(A) touching
(B) performing
(C) training
(D) selling

**156.** What is NOT mentioned as a requirement for the job?
(A) A special physical ability
(B) Familiarity with a certain region
(C) Experience with some of its duties
(D) Specific character traits

**157.** According to the job posting, why should readers visit the ranch's Web site?
(A) To learn about its facilities
(B) To submit an application
(C) To see other job listings
(D) To read about its history

**Questions 158-160** refer to the following form.

**RESERVATION CONFIRMATION**

AUTRY CAR RENTAL
1200 Weaver Street, Stolton
www.autrycarrental.com
Customer Service Line: 1-800-555-0176

| | |
|---|---|
| Customer: | Russell Lam |
| Mobile Phone: | 1-314-555-0141 |
| Address: | 450 Spring Drive, Huntley |

**Rental Details**

| | |
|---|---|
| Vehicle: | Clavince C70 Sedan |
| Rental Branch / Date: | Branham / December 8 |
| Return Branch / Date: | Lucasville / December 10 |
| Mileage Cap: | 450 miles (150 miles/day) |
| Driver: | Russell Lam |

**Charges**

| **Description** | **Amount** |
|---|---|
| Vehicle rental | $168.72 ($56.24/day x 3 days) |
| Delivery of vehicle to customer's home | $30.00 |
| **Total:** | $198.72 |
| Deposit Paid Upon Reservation: | $59.62 |
| Balance Due Upon Vehicle Return: | $139.10 |

**158.** What is indicated about the rental terms?

(A) The price per day varies.
(B) Two customers are allowed to drive.
(C) There is a limit on the driving distance.
(D) There is a charge for last-minute reservations.

**159.** Where will a customer begin driving the vehicle?

(A) In Stolton
(B) In Huntley
(C) In Branham
(D) In Lucasville

**160.** What amount will Autry Car Rental receive on December 10 ?

(A) $59.62
(B) $139.10
(C) $168.72
(D) $198.72

**Questions 161-163** refer to the following press release.

FOR IMMEDIATE RELEASE

Contact: Alberto Gutierrez, a.gutierrez@viga.com

VANCOUVER (13 July)—VIGA is proud to announce the purchase of eight Noonan N250 airplanes. — [1] —. The planes' delivery in approximately two years will bring the company's total fleet size to 156 aircraft, the third largest among Canadian carriers.

The deal is the latest in VIGA's long and successful relationship with Noonan. — [2] —. At the same time, it marks the addition of a new and exciting model to the carrier's fleet, as well as a step towards its sustainability goals.

The Noonan N250 features the sophisticated TF8 turbofan engine, which provides excellent fuel efficiency and emits little carbon dioxide. The TF8 also has a lower noise footprint than other engines, affording travelers a peaceful in-cabin experience. — [3] —. A single-aisle plane, each N250 can carry a total of 130 passengers.

VIGA intends to use the planes to add new international service routes between its hub in Vancouver and airports in the United States. — [4] —. Depending on demand, it may also increase the frequency of existing flights.

**161.** What most likely is VIGA?

(A) A commercial airline
(B) An airplane manufacturer
(C) An airport management company
(D) A pilot training facility

**162.** What is indicated about the airplanes?

(A) They are built in overseas plants.
(B) They were recently delivered to a buyer.
(C) They are relatively quiet in flight.
(D) They use a particular type of fuel.

**163.** In which of the positions marked [1], [2], [3], and [4] does the following sentence best belong?

"The specific destinations to be involved have not yet been determined."

(A) [1]
(B) [2]
(C) [3]
(D) [4]

GO ON TO THE NEXT PAGE

**Questions 164-167** refer to the following article.

**The Power of Solar Canopies**
By Leslie Rodgers

Solar canopies are arrays of solar panels that rise high enough above the ground to allow people and vehicles to pass beneath them. They are most commonly built over parking areas, and are suitable for any type of place with such a facility, from universities to shopping malls. — [1] —. Installing a solar canopy brings advantages such as lower electricity bills and a reputation for being environmentally conscious, in addition to making the parking area more pleasant for drivers by providing shade and shelter from rain and snow.

Those who are interested in adding a solar canopy to their parking area will need to start by determining a few conditions. — [2] —. These include the budget for the project, the ideal area the canopy would cover, and the height at which it must be set.

Next, decisions must be made about the particular solar technologies that will be used. — [3] —. A solar energy consultant can explain the advantages and disadvantages of the options available. In addition, anyone considering investing in a solar canopy should check a database of renewable energy incentives for helpful public policies such as sales tax exemptions or installation subsidies. — [4] —.

**164.** For whom is the article mainly intended?

(A) Aspiring entrepreneurs
(B) Makers of public policy
(C) Property owners
(D) Landscape architects

**165.** What is NOT a stated benefit of solar canopies?

(A) They offer protection from weather conditions.
(B) They reduce consumption of fossil fuels.
(C) They decrease energy expenses.
(D) They positively affect an establishment's reputation.

**166.** According to the article, what can a consultant discuss?

(A) The steps in an installation process
(B) The best way to use a database
(C) Possible locations for a solar canopy
(D) Characteristics of some technologies

**167.** In which of the positions marked [1], [2], [3], and [4] does the following sentence best belong?

"For example, buyers currently have a choice of three types of battery for storing the captured energy."

(A) [1]
(B) [2]
(C) [3]
(D) [4]

**Questions 168-171** refer to the following e-mail.

E-Mail message

| | |
|---|---|
| **To:** | All Staff |
| **From:** | Sherry Cohen |
| **Subject:** | CEO visit |
| **Date:** | Monday, April 21 |
| **Attachment:** | Doc_1 |

Hello everyone,

I am sorry to announce that this week's branch visit from our CEO, Mr. Saito, has been shortened to just one day, Wednesday. It seems an urgent matter has come up that will require him to stay at headquarters tomorrow.

Obviously, this means I've had to make adjustments to the itinerary for the visit; see the highlighted sections of the attachment. Most notably, the on-site reception for Mr. Saito will be held at 5 P.M. instead of during working hours. Please make an effort to attend, even if it means rescheduling an after-work commitment. Additionally, several of our planned presentations will need to be condensed, and the one on the market for staffing services in the hospitality industry has been cancelled altogether.

I apologize for the difficulties arising from these last-minute changes. Still, let's make a good impression on Mr. Saito by accepting them with professionalism and flexibility.

Sherry Cohen
Director, Averton Branch
Dunstad

**168.** What is suggested about the CEO's visit?
(A) It will be the first at this branch.
(B) It was supposed to begin tomorrow.
(C) There is an urgent reason for it.
(D) It was announced suddenly.

**169.** What does Ms. Cohen ask employees do on Wednesday?
(A) Stay past their usual finishing time
(B) Attend a preparatory meeting
(C) Help set up an event site
(D) Present some market research

**170.** What is most likely included with the e-mail?
(A) An updated schedule
(B) An executive profile
(C) An edited slide show
(D) A list of food options

**171.** What kind of business most likely is Dunstad?
(A) A hotel chain
(B) A medical clinic
(C) An insurance agency
(D) A job-placement firm

*GO ON TO THE NEXT PAGE*

**Questions 172-175** refer to the following online chat discussion.

| | | |
|---|---|---|
| **Malik Hassan** | **[10:00 A.M.]** | Good morning, everyone! I know we're meeting later to plan out the March issue, but I wanted to share some good news with you now: Lila Bernardi has agreed to film a "10 Questions for a Star" video for the magazine's Web site. |
| **Amanda Qiu** | **[10:01 A.M.]** | Wow, that's great! Judging from other interviews she's given, I'm sure that she'll have fun answers to the questions. |
| **Brian Cook** | **[10:01 A.M.]** | Wonderful! That should really increase awareness of the Web site. |
| **Amanda Qiu** | **[10:02 A.M.]** | Definitely. She has fans in countries all over the world. |
| **Malik Hassan** | **[10:03 A.M.]** | I hope this leads her recording company to consider collaborating on features for the magazine, too. |
| **Brian Cook** | **[10:04 A.M.]** | Regalement has so many great performers on its roster. |
| **Malik Hassan** | **[10:06 A.M.]** | You know, the band High Tide has an album coming out in the summer that they'll want to promote. If the Bernardi video goes well, I may be able to convince Regalement to let us do a print interview with High Tide's members. |
| **Amanda Qiu** | **[10:07 A.M.]** | Great idea, Malik. |
| **Malik Hassan** | **[10:07 A.M.]** | OK, I'll let you both get back to work. I'm looking forward to hearing some exciting article proposals this afternoon, though. |
| **Brian Cook** | **[10:08 A.M.]** | You certainly will! I just received a very interesting one from Sonya Aguilar, the freelance journalist we worked with a couple times last year. |

**172.** What does Mr. Hassan announce to the other writers?

(A) The theme for a magazine issue
(B) A change to a meeting agenda
(C) Some feedback on a recent project
(D) A positive development for their business

**173.** At 10:02 A.M., what does Ms. Qiu mean when she writes, "Definitely"?

(A) Some content should be translated into other languages.
(B) The Web site is a valuable marketing tool for the magazine.
(C) A celebrity's past interviews were entertaining.
(D) The Web site will achieve greater fame.

**174.** What industry is Regalement in?

(A) Publishing
(B) Web design
(C) Music production
(D) Fashion

**175.** What will Mr. Cook most likely do in the afternoon?

(A) E-mail a previous collaborator
(B) Oversee the filming of a promotional video
(C) Share an idea suggested by a freelance journalist
(D) Proofread an article written by Ms. Aguilar



*GO ON TO THE NEXT PAGE*

**Questions 176-180** refer to the following information and e-mail.

# AIM

### The Staley Foundation

The Staley Foundation is proud to support the growth of small businesses through AIM, its mentorship program for small business owners. Mentees in the program are matched with volunteer mentors who then give ongoing expert advice at no cost. This advice focuses on general matters such as business planning and human resources, though efforts are made to find mentors with insight into the mentee's specific field, whether it be technology or food service. Mentees are also eligible to participate in AIM's frequent educational events and access its library of resources. Applications to receive mentorship through AIM are accepted on a rolling basis. Applicants must reside in the Hamrick City metropolitan area and have launched their business within the past 12 months. Visit www.staleyfoundation.org/aim to learn how to apply.

### About the Staley Foundation

The Staley Foundation was established in honor of Rosaline Staley by her daughter, Emily Barrett. Ms. Staley was a groundbreaking economist and author whose works are still frequently read in university classrooms today. The foundation's mission is to improve the quality of life of Hamrick citizens through economic empowerment.

***E-Mail***

| | |
|---|---|
| **To:** | Aaliyah Williams |
| **From:** | Min-Woo Ma |
| **Subject:** | Re: Problem |
| **Date:** | April 4 |

Dear Ms. Williams,

I am sorry to hear that you are having trouble arranging your first meeting with your AIM mentor. Keep in mind that spring is a busy time for landscapers. Still, one of our staff members will speak to Mr. Finn about the issue, and if necessary, we will assign you another, more responsive mentor.

Whatever happens, I hope you will attend a workshop on brand-building that we just scheduled for May 1. The leader, Molly Tate, ran a successful interior design firm for years. Of course, the workshop itself is intended for a general audience, but you could approach Ms. Tate afterwards about providing some extra guidance specific to your field. Let me know if you are interested.

Sincerely,

Min-Woo Ma
The Staley Foundation

**176.** What is the purpose of the information?

(A) To publicize a local opportunity for mentorship
(B) To seek donations for a charitable cause
(C) To report on the success of an economic initiative
(D) To recruit volunteer workers for an organization

**177.** Who is Ms. Barrett?

(A) The writer of a textbook
(B) The founder of an organization
(C) A previous participant in a program
(D) An economics professor

**178.** What is one reason Mr. Ma sent the e-mail?

(A) To ask for details about a problem
(B) To give his opinion on some branding
(C) To refuse a request for reassignment
(D) To issue an invitation to an event

**179.** What can be concluded about Ms. Williams?

(A) She inquired about Ms. Tate's qualifications.
(B) She has been unable to reach Mr. Ma by phone.
(C) She started a business less than a year ago.
(D) She will have more free time next month.

**180.** In what industry does Ms. Williams most likely work?

(A) Technology
(B) Food service
(C) Landscaping
(D) Interior design



*GO ON TO THE NEXT PAGE*

**Questions 181-185** refer to the following Web page and review.

https://www.crowdview.com/search

**User:** Gwyneth Lim

*Best Providers of Laundry Services Near Me*
**My Location:** 680 Central Avenue, Lanham (change)
**Distance Limit:** 10 miles

---

**Greenworld Cleaners**
★★★★⯪ 4.5 (18 reviews)
Special services: dry cleaning; pickup/delivery

180 Pruitt Street
Embryville, OK
**Distance:** 4.5 miles

**Champion Cleaning**
★★★★⯪ 4.5 (23 reviews)
Special services: dry cleaning; clothing alteration/repair

455 First Street
Lanham, OK
**Distance:** 1.4 miles

**Barger Family Cleaners**
★★★★☆ 4.0 (16 reviews)
Special services: dry cleaning; household linens

2400 Oak Avenue
Chisholt, OK
**Distance:** 5.2 miles

**Greenworld Cleaners Lanham**
★★★⯪☆ 3.5 (27 reviews)
Special services: dry cleaning; pickup/delivery

48 Pearl Road
Lanham, OK
**Distance:** 0.8 miles

**Milburn Laundry Services**
★★★☆☆ 3 (9 reviews)
Special services: dry cleaning; next-day turnaround; clothing alteration/repair

364 Chester Street
Embryville, OK
**Distance:** 3.9 miles

---

**User:** Gwyneth Lim

*My Latest Reviews*

**Category:** Laundry Services
**Posted:** January 14

I recently inherited a beautiful ivory silk dress from my grandmother that had become yellowed with age in some areas and had a small tear in the skirt. Another Crowdview user's detailed review said that Champion Cleaning had fixed similar issues with one of her silk items, so I brought my dress there. I am glad I did! They were able to remove the discoloration and mend the tear so delicately that you can only notice the stitches from a few inches away. The staff member at the counter also took the time to explain how to store the dress properly in the future. My only complaint about Champion Cleaning is that their excellent work comes at a high price. I would not be willing to pay that much for care of an item that was less precious to me.

**181.** How are the first two businesses in the list similar?

(A) They are part of the same corporate chain.
(B) They are located in the same town.
(C) They share the same average rating.
(D) They have received the same number of reviews.

**182.** According to the Web page, what could Barger Family Cleaners most likely do?

(A) Dry clean some clothing within 24 hours
(B) Wash a set of window curtains
(C) Transport cleaned items to a customer's house
(D) Shorten the sleeves of a shirt

**183.** What does Ms. Lim say about her dress?

(A) Its color is the result of a special dyeing technique.
(B) It has been stored in her closet for a long time.
(C) Some of its original stitching was done by hand.
(D) It used to belong to one of her relatives.

**184.** How far from Ms. Lim's location is the business she chose?

(A) 0.8 miles
(B) 1.4 miles
(C) 3.9 miles
(D) 4.5 miles

**185.** According to the review, what disappointed Ms. Lim?

(A) The prices that were charged for some services
(B) The advice provided by an employee
(C) The accuracy of a review on Crowdview
(D) The persistence of a problem after a cleaning

*GO ON TO THE NEXT PAGE* →

**Questions 186-190** refer to the following article, schedule, and e-mail.

## Improvements to Bellamy Parkway Scheduled

(March 10)—Over the next several weeks, the Grovert Department of Transportation will oversee improvements to some of Bellamy Parkway's major intersections between Colwell Street and Hines Creek Drive. The parkway will be widened around each intersection to create turn lanes for both left and right turns, and dedicated stoplights will be added to control the left-turn lanes.

"Separate turn lanes will allow traffic to flow smoothly instead of building up behind cars that are waiting to make a turn," explained Rod Thornton, the department's director. "As the city's population has grown, this has become a problem, particularly during rush hour and near Rock Hills Elementary School." Frustrated Grovert voters approved a short-term increase in the city's property taxes to pay for the $1.8 million project.

During the improvements to each intersection, two of the parkway's four lanes will be closed to traffic in the relevant area to provide space for work crews and equipment. Drivers who take Bellamy Parkway frequently should visit the Department of Transportation's Web site to check the roadwork schedule.

### BELLAMY PARKWAY IMPROVEMENTS SCHEDULE

- March 14–March 25: Colwell Street intersection
- March 28–April 8: Hines Creek Drive intersection
- April 11–April 22: Newton Street intersection
- April 25–May 6: Silva Boulevard intersection

Delays or other changes to this schedule will be announced on the homepage of the Department of Transportation's Web site.

**E-Mail message**

| | |
|---|---|
| **To:** | Lillian Magano |
| **From:** | Yuriko Fujita |
| **Date:** | April 7 |
| **Subject:** | Roadwork reminder |

Hi Lillian,

I was just looking over the school calendar and noticed that the roadwork on the turnoff to our street starts next Monday, the eleventh. Before you leave work today, could you send out an additional reminder to parents about it? Since it will be taking place so close by, I think it will cause more inconvenience to the school than the upgrades to other sections of the parkway have. We should warn the parents that school buses may be a little behind schedule in the afternoons, and that those who drive may see delays during pick-up and drop-off.

Thanks,

Yuriko Fujita
Vice Principal

**186.** According to the article, what is true about the planned improvements?
(A) They are part of a pilot program.
(B) They include repairs of some damage.
(C) They will relieve traffic congestion.
(D) They are required by new safety laws.

**187.** What does the article mention about the cost of the project?
(A) It will be covered by tax revenue.
(B) It will be higher than initially expected.
(C) It has not been made public.
(D) It is reasonable.

**188.** What will happen on March 14 ?
(A) Citizens will vote on a proposal.
(B) Some lanes of a street will be closed.
(C) Revisions to a schedule will be announced.
(D) A city department will host an information session.

**189.** Why did Ms. Fujita write the e-mail?
(A) To explain the meaning of a calendar entry
(B) To list some transportation alternatives
(C) To assign a communication task
(D) To suggest delaying a pick-up time

**190.** What is implied about Ms. Magano?
(A) She subscribed to a mailing list.
(B) She will meet with Ms. Fujita next week.
(C) Her child attends elementary school.
(D) Her workplace is on Newton Street.

GO ON TO THE NEXT PAGE

**Questions 191-195** refer to the following brochure and e-mails.

## The Egmont

Situated in Wellington's Central Business District, The Egmont is one of the city's most popular venues for private celebrations, corporate meetings, fund-raisers, and more. Its convenient location is just a short walk away from numerous hotels, several bus stops, and a train station.

The Egmont offers two spacious multi-purpose event rooms. The Manuka Room is best for groups of between 100 and 200, while our grandest space, the Kauri Room, can hold up to 300 guests comfortably. We also have two dedicated conference rooms, the Rata Room and the Pikao Room, which have maximum capacities of 35 and 70 people, respectively.

State-of-the-art projectors, speakers, and other multimedia equipment are available for all of our rooms, supported by convenient in-house technical assistance. In addition, The Egmont's catering service can make delicious, custom fare for a variety of situations, from light refreshments to multiple-course dinners.

First-time clients who reserve rooms for certain days and times are eligible for a 10% discount. Visit www.theegmont.co.nz for details.

To: Aaron Jones
From: Ruth Henare
Date: 12 October
Subject: Awards dinner venue

Hi Aaron,

This morning I called The Egmont about hosting our annual awards dinner. They do have the space and catering capacity to accommodate our entire guest list, which has grown beyond 200 people. However, the room we'd need is already booked for every Saturday evening in November, so 11 November is no longer an option. That Sunday, 12 November, is open, though, as is Friday, 17 November. Also, Thursday, 16 November is available at a discounted rate.

I think we should take it. Our attendees will understand the date change if we explain that our original venue shut down unexpectedly. I hope you'll let me know your decision soon, as all of these dates are approaching quickly and there are many preparations still to be made.

Thanks,

Ruth

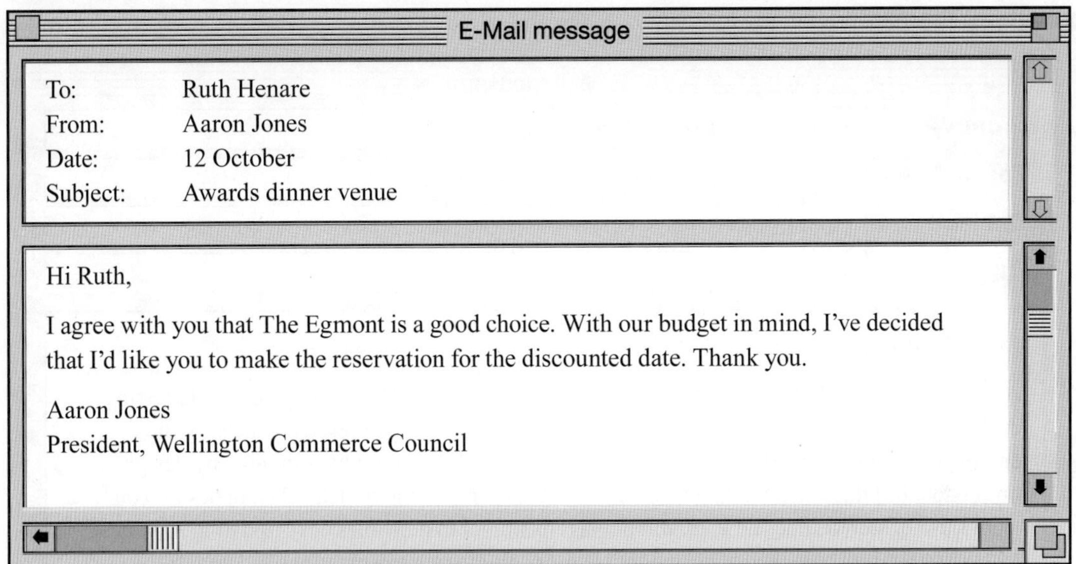

E-Mail message

To: Ruth Henare
From: Aaron Jones
Date: 12 October
Subject: Awards dinner venue

Hi Ruth,

I agree with you that The Egmont is a good choice. With our budget in mind, I've decided that I'd like you to make the reservation for the discounted date. Thank you.

Aaron Jones
President, Wellington Commerce Council

**191.** What does the brochure suggest about The Egmont?

(A) It is a short train ride from Wellington.
(B) Its staff includes an audiovisual technician.
(C) It recently added a second restaurant.
(D) It is the site of a large yearly fund-raiser.

**192.** What does Ms. Henare indicate about the awards dinner?

(A) It will feature a buffet meal.
(B) It will honor a hotel manager.
(C) She will be unable to attend it.
(D) She is seeking a new location for it.

**193.** Where will the organization most likely hold its awards dinner?

(A) In the Manuka Room
(B) In the Kauri Room
(C) In the Rata Room
(D) In the Pikao Room

**194.** Why is Ms. Henare concerned?

(A) Many people have declined an invitation.
(B) There is not much time to prepare for an event.
(C) A catering service is more expensive than expected.
(D) She has never seen a venue in person.

**195.** On which date will the Wellington Commerce Council's awards dinner most likely take place?

(A) November 11
(B) November 12
(C) November 16
(D) November 17

GO ON TO THE NEXT PAGE

**Questions 196-200** refer to the following e-mails and survey excerpt.

**E-Mail message**

**From:** Slide Ace <contact@slideace.com>

**To:** Roy Thornton <roy.thornton@gannitt.com>

**Subject:** Opportunity

**Date:** July 10

Dear Mr. Thornton,

As valued users of Slide Ace 2.2, you and your staff are invited to participate in beta testing of Slide Ace 2.3. This new version of Slide Ace, which we hope to release widely by the end of year, features ReadyGo, a library of sophisticated slide templates created by design professionals. Other major changes include dashboard reporting of helpful statistics on your team's use of stored slides and a brand management tool that enables easy updating of your logo and preferred color schemes and fonts across all of your presentations.

Slide Ace 2.3 can be downloaded here. We hope you will agree to be part of this exciting step forward for the platform.

Sincerely,

Slide Ace

---

User: Roy Thornton

This is the final page of the survey. Please add any comments here that could help explain your answers to previous questions.

I gave the dashboard a "2" because it feels too cluttered. Perhaps you could make it possible to customize the types of data that are shown on the dashboard.
The new brand management tool is a great idea that will be really helpful for our company as a quickly-evolving startup. The only reason I didn't give it a perfect score is that Slide Ace crashed the first time I tried it.

Thank you for your participation!

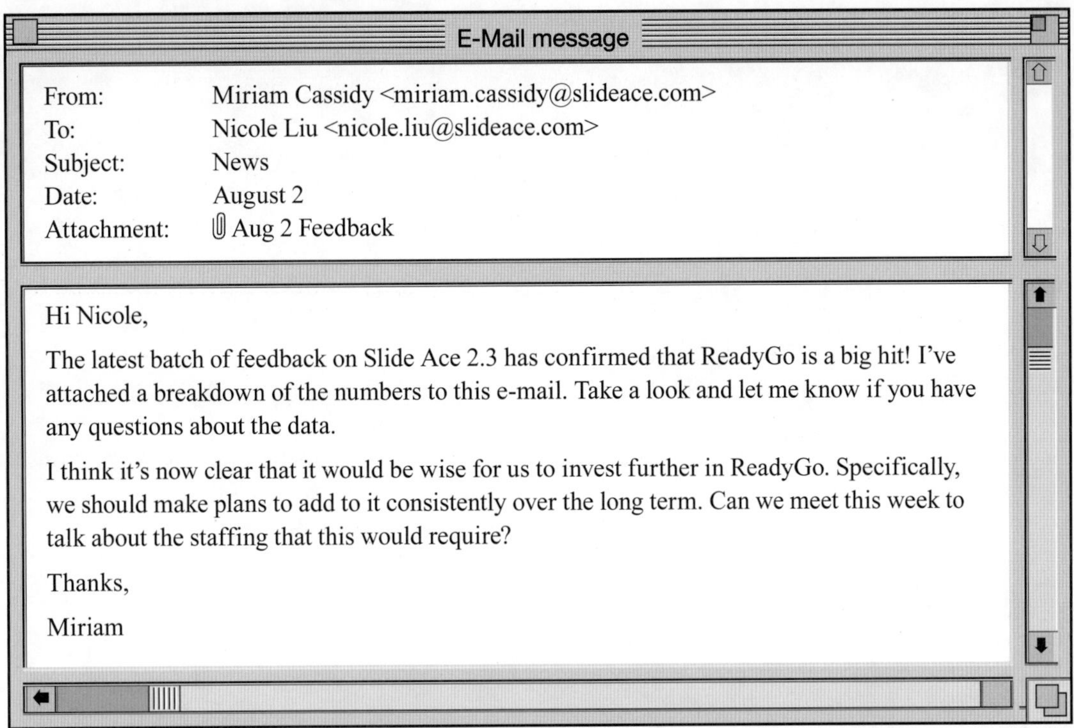
E-Mail message

From: Miriam Cassidy <miriam.cassidy@slideace.com>
To: Nicole Liu <nicole.liu@slideace.com>
Subject: News
Date: August 2
Attachment: Aug 2 Feedback

Hi Nicole,

The latest batch of feedback on Slide Ace 2.3 has confirmed that ReadyGo is a big hit! I've attached a breakdown of the numbers to this e-mail. Take a look and let me know if you have any questions about the data.

I think it's now clear that it would be wise for us to invest further in ReadyGo. Specifically, we should make plans to add to it consistently over the long term. Can we meet this week to talk about the staffing that this would require?

Thanks,

Miriam

**196.** What is the purpose of the first e-mail?
(A) To issue invitations to a demonstration
(B) To explain the reasons for planned updates
(C) To solicit suggestions for potential services
(D) To recruit a group of product testers

**197.** What is suggested about the survey?
(A) It is available in more than one format.
(B) Mr. Thornton will be paid for completing it.
(C) Slide Ace hired a company to administer it.
(D) It asks participants to give numerical ratings.

**198.** What is implied about Mr. Thornton's company?
(A) It assists its clients with data analysis.
(B) It does not store many slides in Slide Ace.
(C) It sometimes changes elements of its preferred corporate style.
(D) It frequently communicates with the public through social media.

**199.** What does Ms. Cassidy recommend doing?
(A) Expanding a collection of slide templates
(B) Increasing options for customizing some graphics
(C) Simplifying the design of an information screen
(D) Releasing a software version to more people

**200.** What does Ms. Cassidy want to discuss with Ms. Liu?
(A) A project timeline
(B) Potential personnel needs
(C) An upcoming client meeting
(D) Some negative feedback

**Stop! This is the end of the test. If you finish before time is called, you may go back to Parts 5, 6, and 7 and check your work.**

# YBM 실전토익 RC1000

## 테스트 전 체크리스트

- 중간 휴식 없이 제한 시간을 지켜서 풀이하세요.
- 제한 시간은 답안지에 마킹하는 시간도 포함시켜야 합니다.
- 찍은 문제는 번호 옆에 꼭 체크해 주세요.
- 시간 안에 풀지 못한 문제는 틀린 것으로 채점해 주세요.

# RC TEST 2

## READING TEST

In the Reading test, you will read a variety of texts and answer several different types of reading comprehension questions. The entire Reading test will last 75 minutes. There are three parts, and directions are given for each part. You are encouraged to answer as many questions as possible within the time allowed.

You must mark your answers on the separate answer sheet. Do not write your answers in your test book.

## PART 5

**Directions:** A word or phrase is missing in each of the sentences below. Four answer choices are given below each sentence. Select the best answer to complete the sentence. Then mark the letter (A), (B), (C), or (D) on your answer sheet.

**101.** If you are not ------- with the service you receive at Luxe Salon, let our manager know.

(A) pleased
(B) pleasure
(C) pleasing
(D) please

**102.** When searching for an auto glass repair shop, make sure to choose one that has certified technicians like -------.

(A) we
(B) our
(C) ours
(D) ourselves

**103.** Ms. Chin ------- Mr. Stepp's duties while he is at a weeklong marketing seminar.

(A) assumed
(B) to assume
(C) is assumed
(D) will assume

**104.** After accepting a delivery from a frozen food supplier, ------- transfer the items to the restaurant's freezer.

(A) quickly
(B) enough
(C) closely
(D) partly

**105.** Snap Sauces handed out all of its product samples to trade show attendees ------- 11 A.M. on the first day.

(A) about
(B) by
(C) for
(D) in

**106.** The Foy County Parks Department has compiled a list of hiking trails ------- by bus.

(A) accessibility
(B) accessible
(C) accessibly
(D) access

**107.** Nia Aldridge has shown ------- for learning the skills needed to become a software engineer.

(A) enthusiast
(B) enthusiastic
(C) enthusiastically
(D) enthusiasm

**108.** In accordance with company policy, incomplete requests for reimbursement will not be -------.

(A) approved
(B) achieved
(C) decided
(D) increased

109. Sonia Ray was the lead singer of the band Indigo Mist for several years ------- becoming a solo act.

(A) before
(B) except
(C) then
(D) yet

110. The employee picnic celebrating the start of summer may need to be postponed if the rain -------.

(A) continue
(B) continues
(C) had continued
(D) continuing

111. Ever since the Dwyerton Building's construction, its architecture has been considered the most ------- in the city.

(A) beauty
(B) beauties
(C) beautiful
(D) beautifully

112. UBN Tours will offer daily walking tours of downtown Peralt ------- this week onward.

(A) among
(B) from
(C) over
(D) toward

113. The management team of Shelzan Pharmaceuticals has developed a ------- for expanding its operations into China within a few years.

(A) meeting
(B) benefit
(C) strategy
(D) recognition

114. By conducting extensive marketing -------, RIV Associates can produce crucial insights into your target consumers.

(A) research
(B) researched
(C) researching
(D) researchers

115. ------- the old lighting has been replaced with more efficient fixtures, the office's electricity bills will be lower.

(A) Unless
(B) At once
(C) Now that
(D) Although

116. For the premiere of its new film, Lofton Studios's publicity team has been instructed to reserve the largest theater -------.

(A) secure
(B) certain
(C) welcome
(D) available

117. The company encourages customers to review its products ------- on shopping Web sites.

(A) favorable
(B) favorably
(C) favorite
(D) favor

118. ------- the next few weeks, the CEO of Serna Mining will announce her successor.

(A) Until
(B) Provided
(C) Within
(D) Involving

119. Planning committee members were proud that the final cost of the project matched their initial estimate -------.

(A) occasionally
(B) briefly
(C) lately
(D) exactly

120. The catalogue should include the information that dishwashers described as "compact" are ------- 18 inches wide.

(A) normal
(B) normally
(C) normalize
(D) normalization

GO ON TO THE NEXT PAGE

**121.** After considering sites around the country, Noitech ------- built its new factory in Murin.

(A) intensely
(B) ultimately
(C) concisely
(D) already

**122.** Clury Insurance made a ------- donation to charity on its tenth anniversary in business.

(A) wide
(B) primary
(C) sizable
(D) severe

**123.** Bullard Park Hotel has ------- to upgrade its business facilities in preparation for the upcoming trade convention.

(A) since
(B) shortly
(C) whereas
(D) attempted

**124.** Throughout his career as an artist, Mr. Lipscomb has ------- in creating intricate sculptures out of recycled materials.

(A) specialized
(B) distinguished
(C) approached
(D) committed

**125.** A newspaper article on the ------- of public transportation in Laes City led to calls for fare decreases.

(A) afforded
(B) affordably
(C) affordability
(D) affordable

**126.** Poulik Enterprises' stock prices rose upon the news of its proposed ------- of a competitor.

(A) investment
(B) acquisition
(C) agenda
(D) vision

**127.** Croft Fitness Center has state-of-the-art equipment but a ------- relaxed atmosphere.

(A) remark
(B) remarks
(C) remarking
(D) remarkably

**128.** The warranty expires when five years have passed since purchase or the tractor has been driven for 5,000 hours, ------- occurs first.

(A) anything
(B) whose
(C) however
(D) whichever

**129.** ------- the feedback from the focus group, we should choose a more readable font for the product label.

(A) Because
(B) Whether
(C) Considering
(D) Alongside

**130.** Following Thursday's training, Ms. Adkins ------- the advantages of the new database software.

(A) acknowledged
(B) nominated
(C) belonged
(D) permitted

## PART 6

**Directions:** Read the texts that follow. A word, phrase, or sentence is missing in parts of each text. Four answer choices for each question are given below the text. Select the best answer to complete the text. Then mark the letter (A), (B), (C), or (D) on your answer sheet.

TEST 2

**Questions 131-134** refer to the following e-mail.

From: <customerservice@office-loft.com>

To: <jahan.soltani@iux-mail.com>

Subject: Re: Order #7823

Date: July 21

Attachment: Coupon

Dear Mr. Soltani,

We are sorry to hear that Order #7823 arrived at your business after the promised date of July 14. It appears that the order ------- **131.** later than scheduled due to a problem with our shipping provider. We will refund the shipping charge to your account. In addition, please accept the attached coupon as compensation for the ------- **132.** . It will give you a 30% discount on your next order from our Web site. ------- **133.** . You may also print out the coupon and use it at ------- **134.** of our offline stores.

Sincerely,

Scott Conrad

Office Loft Customer Service

**131.** (A) will be delivered
(B) had to deliver
(C) was delivered
(D) is delivering

**132.** (A) delay
(B) work
(C) loss
(D) risk

**133.** (A) Thank you again for the feedback.
(B) Your user account will be restored soon.
(C) We hope you found the items satisfactory.
(D) Simply enter the code at the top at checkout.

**134.** (A) each
(B) one
(C) that
(D) which

*GO ON TO THE NEXT PAGE* →

**Questions 135-138** refer to the following memo.

From: Clarence Tibbetts

To: Banuelos Financial staff

Date: March 8

Subject: Carpeting work

As you all have probably noticed, the carpet in our reception area is quite ------- (135.) . It no longer makes a good impression on visitors. So, I am happy to announce that the office ------- (136.) on Friday, March 17 as that section of carpet is replaced. I have found new carpeting of the same color but made of a more durable material and have hired a contractor to perform the removal and installation.

------- (137.) the office is closed, all Banuelos Financial employees must either work from home or use a paid vacation day. ------- (138.) . If you have any questions or concerns about this situation, you may raise them at Monday's staff meeting.

**135.** (A) thick
(B) beautiful
(C) similar
(D) worn

**136.** (A) had been closed
(B) was closing
(C) close
(D) will be closed

**137.** (A) Throughout
(B) Often
(C) While
(D) At first

**138.** (A) The reception desk must be kept neat.
(B) Please reschedule client appointments accordingly.
(C) The executive team is still considering the timeline.
(D) The contractor is a well-respected local firm.

**Questions 139-142** refer to the following e-mail.

To: Grace Vaughn

From: Sergio Fonseca

Subject: Dennis-Lindstrom wedding

Date: June 3

Hi Grace,

Here are the details of the wedding we will be photographing on Saturday. The ceremony will start at 4 P.M. at Zeller Inn. -------, please arrive a full two hours beforehand to help me with photographing the preparations. After the ceremony, you can take candid shots of the reception during the time I'm taking the composed family pictures. We are then scheduled to stay until the cake is cut, which may mean quite a long evening. ------- .
**139.** **140.**

Thank you again for agreeing to ------- me with this. It is quite a high-profile event, and it will give me ------- to be supported by an experienced photographer like you.
**141.** **142.**

—Sergio

**139.** (A) Likewise
(B) If possible
(C) Before long
(D) Rather

**140.** (A) Luckily, I have an extra camera you can use.
(B) We would get extra pay after 8 P.M., though.
(C) The venue offers some lovely backdrops.
(D) All of the guests will be dressed in formal wear.

**141.** (A) assist
(B) feature
(C) provide
(D) refer

**142.** (A) confide
(B) confided
(C) confiding
(D) confidence

GO ON TO THE NEXT PAGE

**Questions 143-146** refer to the following press release.

(October 23)—Law firm Malley Turnbull Partners is proud to announce that Soo-Yeon Ko has been promoted to the rank of senior partner. She ------- **143.** managing partner Gerald Malley and four other senior partners as a partial owner of the firm.

"This recognition is well deserved," said Mr. Malley. "Ms. Ko has made ------- **144.** contributions to our success over the past several years."

Malley Turnbull Partners hired Ms. Ko five years ago as a senior associate concentrating on environmental law. ------- **145.**, the firm has won some important cases in that area.

"Ms. Ko possesses not only a very sharp legal mind but also an inspiring dedication to helping our junior lawyers grow professionally," said Mr. Malley. "------- **146.**."

**143.** (A) joins
(B) was joining
(C) has been joined
(D) would have joined

**144.** (A) entire
(B) possible
(C) sturdy
(D) major

**145.** (A) Instead
(B) Similarly
(C) Consequently
(D) In short

**146.** (A) We expect a good outcome to the case.
(B) More workshops will be organized soon.
(C) We welcome her to the leadership team.
(D) The position will not be open for long.

## PART 7

**Directions:** In this part you will read a selection of texts, such as magazine and newspaper articles, e-mails, and instant messages. Each text or set of texts is followed by several questions. Select the best answer for each question and mark the letter (A), (B), (C), or (D) on your answer sheet.

TEST 2

**Questions 147-148** refer to the following brochure.

### Deftlee

More than a decade of helping start-ups take flight

**What we offer:**

- Convenient outsourcing of human resources tasks
- Project-based consulting on personnel issues
- Full-service HR technology platform for long-term clients

Areas of expertise include recruiting, training, payroll, and much more.
Visit www.deftlee.com to schedule a consultation.

**Client testimonials:**

"I highly recommend Deftlee. Their HR platform alone is worth the prices they charge. Our managers love how it has simplified tasks like tracking time off and performance evaluations." —Ryan Maas, Aurora Logistics

"My business has grown from four employees to more than 50, and Deftlee has been there every step of the way. I'm always impressed by their ability to adapt to our changing needs." —Kasumi Tanaka, TBR Solutions

**147.** What is most likely true about Deftlee?
(A) It offers to handle employee compensation for its clients.
(B) It advises businesses on environmental issues.
(C) It has grown rapidly in a short time.
(D) It develops project management software.

**148.** What does Ms. Tanaka appreciate about Deftlee?
(A) Its pricing
(B) Its flexibility
(C) Its technology
(D) Its confidentiality

*GO ON TO THE NEXT PAGE* →

**Questions 149-150** refer to the following notice.

**CONOVER'S**

Dear Customers:

Since our opening nearly 30 years ago, Conover's has been proud to equip Mandeville residents for a wide range of indoor and outdoor sports. However, we have recently made the difficult decision to remove fishing gear, supplies, and equipment from our inventory due to poor sales. The floor space this stock used to occupy will instead be used to display additional workout apparel. This step will help Conover's remain profitable so that we can continue supporting Mandeville's athletes for many years to come. Still, we apologize for the inconvenience this will cause for the fishing enthusiasts among our customers.

—Conover's Management

**149.** What does Conover's sell?

(A) Groceries
(B) Electronics
(C) Art supplies
(D) Sporting goods

**150.** What is the notice about?

(A) A change in inventory
(B) An anniversary celebration
(C) A temporary store closure
(D) A fund-raising event

**Questions 151-152** refer to the following e-mail.

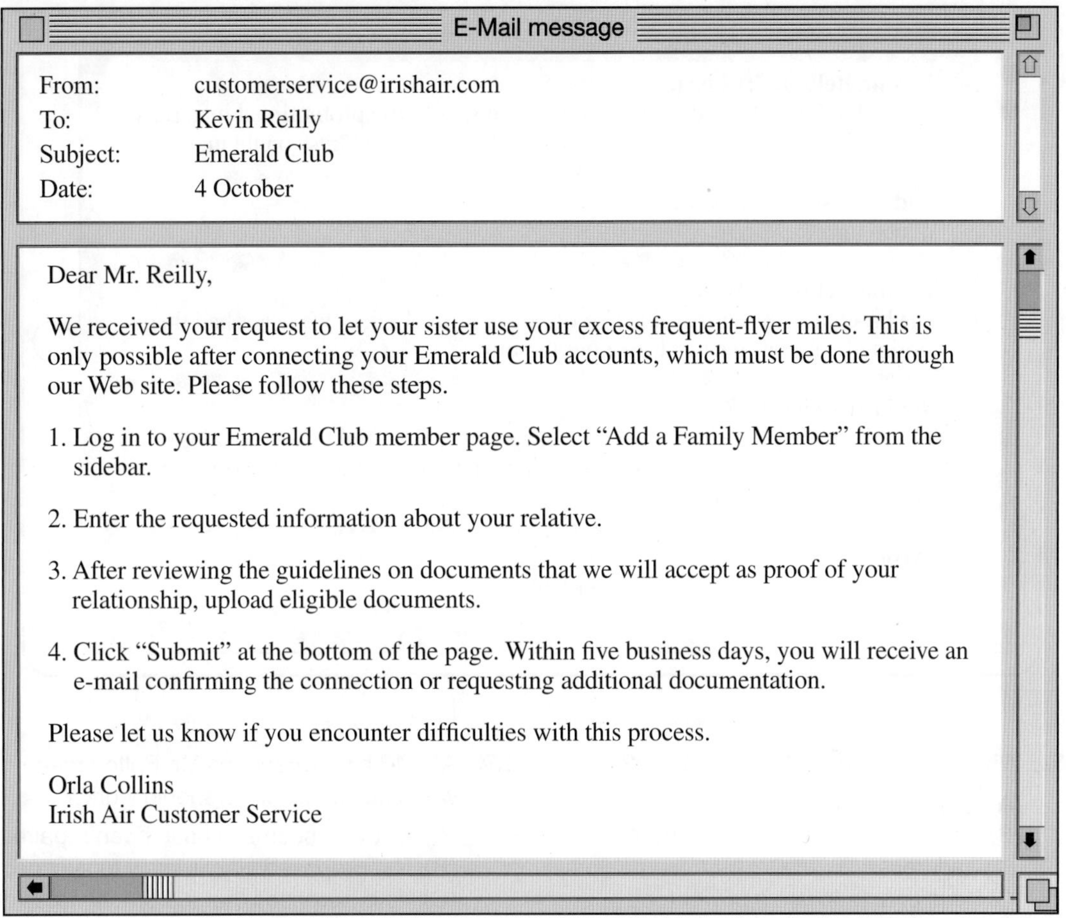
E-Mail message

From: customerservice@irishair.com
To: Kevin Reilly
Subject: Emerald Club
Date: 4 October

Dear Mr. Reilly,

We received your request to let your sister use your excess frequent-flyer miles. This is only possible after connecting your Emerald Club accounts, which must be done through our Web site. Please follow these steps.

1. Log in to your Emerald Club member page. Select "Add a Family Member" from the sidebar.

2. Enter the requested information about your relative.

3. After reviewing the guidelines on documents that we will accept as proof of your relationship, upload eligible documents.

4. Click "Submit" at the bottom of the page. Within five business days, you will receive an e-mail confirming the connection or requesting additional documentation.

Please let us know if you encounter difficulties with this process.

Orla Collins
Irish Air Customer Service

**151.** What is suggested about Mr. Reilly?
(A) He reported a security issue with his account.
(B) He is a travel agent.
(C) He often flies with Irish Air.
(D) A member of his family works for Irish Air.

**152.** What is Mr. Reilly instructed to do?
(A) Change his log-in credentials
(B) Provide some documents by mail
(C) Check his member page for updates
(D) Verify a relationship online

*GO ON TO THE NEXT PAGE*

**Questions 153-154** refer to the following text-message chain.

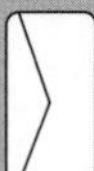

**Tyrone Belton, 7:14 P.M.**
Hi, Nadia. I just noticed we have a problem with some promotional materials I packed for the trade show. They have our Stahl Street address on them.

**Nadia Guseva, 7:15 P.M.**
Which ones?

**Tyrone Belton, 7:16 P.M.**
The brochures for our Nimble line of power tools. I guess we never had them reprinted with our new address after the move.

**Nadia Guseva, 7:17 P.M.**
Well, there are print shops near the convention center, right? You could go to one tonight or early tomorrow morning, and ask them to print correction stickers for you to put on the brochures.

**Tyrone Belton, 7:18 P.M.**
That should work! Thanks for your help.

**153.** What problem does Mr. Belton have?

(A) He misplaced some posters.
(B) He was mistaken about a venue's address.
(C) He is unable to use a power tool.
(D) He has outdated brochures.

**154.** At 7:18 P.M., what does Mr. Belton mean when he writes, "That should work"?

(A) A device seems to have been repaired.
(B) The proposed plan is likely to succeed.
(C) He is surprised that a promotional effort is unpopular.
(D) An announcement could resolve a misunderstanding.

**Questions 155-157** refer to the following job advertisement.

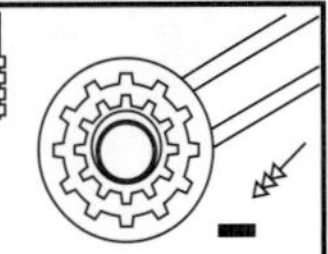

## Carder Bay Automotive Seeks Electric Auto Mechanic

To keep up with changes in consumer preferences, Carder Bay Automotive will begin providing maintenance and repair services for electric automobiles. Therefore, we are seeking an auto mechanic with knowledge of this area. Candidates must possess at least two years of work experience in maintaining, diagnosing problems with, and repairing electric vehicles.

Carder Bay Automotive requires all employees to be punctual, well-organized, and able to work well as part of a team. Mechanics must also be licensed to operate commercial vehicles. Candidates invited to interview for this position should expect to be asked a variety of questions intended to assess their technical skills. Those interested should visit www.carderbayauto.com/jobs/326 to fill out an electronic application.

**155.** Why is the mechanic position being offered?

(A) Business hours have been extended.
(B) A new type of vehicle will be serviced.
(C) An additional location is opening.
(D) New regulations will go into effect.

**156.** What is NOT a stated requirement of the position?

(A) Teamwork skills
(B) Repair experience
(C) A maintenance certification
(D) A driver's license

**157.** According to the job advertisement, what will candidates be asked to do during interviews?

(A) Discuss automotive technology
(B) Take an online proficiency test
(C) Assess the condition of an automobile
(D) Provide documents proving their qualifications

*GO ON TO THE NEXT PAGE*

**Questions 158-160** refer to the following article.

## Housing Prices on the Rise

By Yong-Joon Wang

DROSSER (May 6)—Housing prices in Drosser continue to increase, according to data from Turfle.com, the online real estate marketplace. The average home price for the area jumped 5.2% from last year to $392,500.

"Higher home values mean more revenue from property taxes," commented Ada Ferrell, chair of the Drosser Housing Authority Board. "The city will be able to generate extra funding for its social services."

However, Ms. Ferrell pointed out that the trend also poses problems for individual households.

"Some homeowners will struggle to pay their higher property tax bill," she said. "Moreover, we know that rent prices have risen correspondingly in the past year, increasing the burden on rental tenants. Rent is becoming an increasingly large share of their living costs."

Residents experiencing financial difficulties due to housing can find a variety of resources on the Drosser Housing Authority Board's Web site, www.drossercity.org/dhab.

**158.** Who most likely is Ms. Ferrell?

(A) A tax accountant
(B) The manager of a rental property
(C) A real estate agent
(D) A housing official

**159.** The word "poses" in paragraph 3, line 2, is closest in meaning to

(A) pretends
(B) models
(C) presents
(D) states

**160.** What does Ms. Ferrell mention about the rise in housing prices?

(A) It has a downside for some homeowners.
(B) A city organization is seeking ways to reverse it.
(C) It has caused more people to choose to rent housing.
(D) It is the result of the city's popular tax policies.

**Questions 161-163** refer to the following e-mail.

**E-Mail message**

| | |
|---|---|
| **To:** | Bridget Deng |
| **From:** | Candice Holt |
| **Subject:** | Information |
| **Date:** | August 27 |
| **Attachment:** | Holt_Aug27 |

Dear Bridget,

As you requested, this is your reminder that I'm starting my two-week medical leave on Monday. — [1] —. Attached you'll find the list of marketing campaigns that I'm currently working on, with details about the status of each. I've also notified the other employees involved in each campaign about my absence. — [2] —. In most cases, it will not be difficult for one of them to take over my duties for those two weeks.

The only task left is to meet with Jonathan to hand over the digital promotion plans for the launch of Yancey Cosmetic's new nail polish line. I haven't been able to do that yet because I needed to make some last-minute changes that the client requested. — [3] —. I'll make sure Jonathan is ready to update Yancey's social media accounts at the appropriate times with the posts I've created.

Finally, while I'll be unavailable during the first week of my leave, please feel free to contact me if necessary during the second. — [4] —.

Sincerely,

Candice Holt

**161.** For what type of business does Ms. Holt most likely work?

(A) An online news platform
(B) An advertising agency
(C) A cosmetics company
(D) A medical clinic

**162.** What will Ms. Holt prepare Jonathan to do?

(A) Post on social media
(B) Attend a launch event
(C) Maintain a database
(D) Meet with a client

**163.** In which of the positions marked [1], [2], [3], and [4] does the following sentence best belong?

"Now that they're finished, we've scheduled a meeting for this afternoon."

(A) [1]
(B) [2]
(C) [3]
(D) [4]

*GO ON TO THE NEXT PAGE*

**Questions 164-167** refer to the following notice.

**"The Sounds of Brilliance"**
Wednesday, May 28
4:30 P.M.–9:00 P.M.

The Rendon University Department of Music invites all members of the campus and local community to attend its yearly recital celebrating excellence among our students. Join us in Steen Music Center's Cho Recital Hall for an afternoon and evening of superb vocal, piano, cello, saxophone, and violin music.

All performers on the program are winners of the department's performance awards. Among the honorees this year is Felicia Logan, who recently reached the semifinal round of the popular singing competition TV show *Top Vocalist*. The full recital program, with details about the performers and pieces, is available at www.rendon.edu/music/soe.

The program will run from 4:30 P.M. to 6:00 P.M. and 7:30 P.M. to 9:00 P.M. There is no fee for admission, and seating is first-come, first-served. Please note that seats cannot be saved during the intermission.

Steen Music Center is located at 640 Millard Avenue. Street parking on campus is free after 4:00 P.M., and paid parking is available in the Camacho Lot directly west of the music center.

**164.** Why was the notice written?
(A) To advertise an annual concert
(B) To attract students for a music class
(C) To announce an upcoming competition
(D) To celebrate the release of an album

**165.** What is indicated about the musicians?
(A) They all play the same instrument.
(B) They are visiting from abroad.
(C) They are the recipients of awards.
(D) They will graduate from university this year.

**166.** Why most likely does the notice mention a television program?
(A) To explain the inspiration for an activity
(B) To specify that an event will be filmed
(C) To highlight the ability of a performer
(D) To indicate that a song is well-known

**167.** What is NOT suggested about the event?
(A) It will be split into two parts.
(B) It will be broadcast over the Internet.
(C) It will take place on campus.
(D) It will be free to attend.

**Questions 168-171** refer to the following online chat discussion.

| | | |
|---|---|---|
| **Ellen Chambers** | **[2:17 P.M.]** | The president wants to meet on Wednesday to talk about how we can get higher-quality job candidates for openings in our labs. Do you two have any ideas? |
| **Arjun Malhotra** | **[2:19 P.M.]** | The company could offer a referral bonus to employees. Some other biotechnology firms do that. |
| **Juana Amado** | **[2:20 P.M.]** | I like that idea. We can take advantage of employees' networks. |
| **Ellen Chambers** | **[2:21 P.M.]** | Won't that require a lot of effort from the employees? And how would we ensure that they don't refer poor candidates just to get the bonus? |
| **Arjun Malhotra** | **[2:22 P.M.]** | All the employee would have to do is provide our department with the person's contact information. |
| **Juana Amado** | **[2:23 P.M.]** | Yes, we would handle the rest, as usual. And maybe the company would only pay the full bonus if the referred person ends up both being hired and staying for a while. |
| **Arjun Malhotra** | **[2:24 P.M.]** | Precisely. We could pay half upon hiring and the other half after six months of work. |
| **Ellen Chambers** | **[2:25 P.M.]** | OK. Let's put this plan forward at the meeting. |

**168.** What is mainly being discussed?

(A) Expanding into a new industry
(B) Finding skilled workers
(C) Soliciting client referrals
(D) Increasing employee satisfaction

**169.** What is most likely true about the writers?

(A) They recently went to a networking event together.
(B) They work in different departments.
(C) They have been given a limited budget.
(D) They oversee a hiring process.

**170.** At 2:24 P.M., what does Mr. Malhotra most likely mean when he writes, "Precisely"?

(A) Ms. Amado has made a helpful suggestion.
(B) They must follow a company policy carefully.
(C) Some measurements must be accurate.
(D) A project is proceeding on schedule.

**171.** What will the writers most likely do on Wednesday?

(A) Determine the recipient of a bonus
(B) Describe an idea to an executive
(C) Participate in some job interviews
(D) Show some equipment to laboratory staff

*GO ON TO THE NEXT PAGE*

**Questions 172-175** refer to the following e-mail.

**E-Mail message**

| | |
|---|---|
| **From:** | Rosemary Wolfe |
| **To:** | Orisa Muyiwa |
| **Subject:** | RRVK care system |
| **Date:** | 16 Jul |
| **Attachment:** | RRVKcs |

Dear Ms. Muyiwa,

Thank you for writing to express your interest in the RRVK care system. As you requested, I have attached our brochure detailing the product's features, specifications, and pricing. — [1] —.

You mention that your hospital's management wants you to streamline the facility's operations. — [2] —. The RRVK care system consists of kiosks loaded with specialized software designed to do just that. Your patients can use the system to check themselves in for appointments instead of waiting in line at the hospital's front desk. This allows your staff to focus on more complex tasks. — [3] —.

If you are interested, I would be happy to give a demonstration of the system at our office. — [4] —. Simply let me know when you are available.

Sincerely,

Rosemary Wolfe

**172.** What is one purpose of the e-mail?

(A) To report on an off-site demonstration
(B) To correct some out-of-date information
(C) To share some customer testimonials
(D) To respond to a product inquiry

**173.** What is suggested about Ms. Muyiwa?

(A) She is employed in the healthcare field.
(B) She was asked to research self-service kiosks.
(C) She is usually stationed at a front desk.
(D) She uses customized scheduling software.

**174.** According to the e-mail, what can the RRVK care system do?

(A) Manage inventory
(B) Send appointment reminders
(C) Track visitors' arrivals
(D) Process payments

**175.** In which of the positions marked [1], [2], [3], and [4] does the following sentence best belong?

"Reading over it should make it very clear how the RRVK can help your organization."

(A) [1]
(B) [2]
(C) [3]
(D) [4]



*GO ON TO THE NEXT PAGE*

**Questions 176-180** refer to the following Web page and e-mail.

http://www.lockehanley.com/authors/wendell-green

Wendell Green has been represented by Locke and Hanley Literary Agents since his debut. His first full-length work, *Race Against Time*, was included in the SLP 10, the Society of Library Professionals' yearly list of the best novels aimed at teenagers. He now writes in a variety of genres. Before becoming a full-time author, Mr. Green taught history to high school students. He lives in Armenta with his wife.

**Recent Works by Wendell Green**

*In Wylie Cove*
Adventurous journalist Tony Bradley learns a startling secret while investigating strange occurrences in his small coastal town. Over two million copies sold!

*Swing Away*
The players on the Spriggs Academy baseball team have very different personalities. Can they figure out how to work together before the season ends? *Fraser's Quarterly* called this "a must-read for young baseball fans."

*Sarah Saves the World*
Middle-school student Sarah Fitch tries to keep her new superpowers a secret from her friends and family. A fun and touching graphic novel featuring illustrations by Eva Pineda.

*Nails on a Chalkboard*
Teaching may be difficult, but it is never boring! This collection of essays about the profession touches on its humorous, frustrating, and heartbreaking aspects.

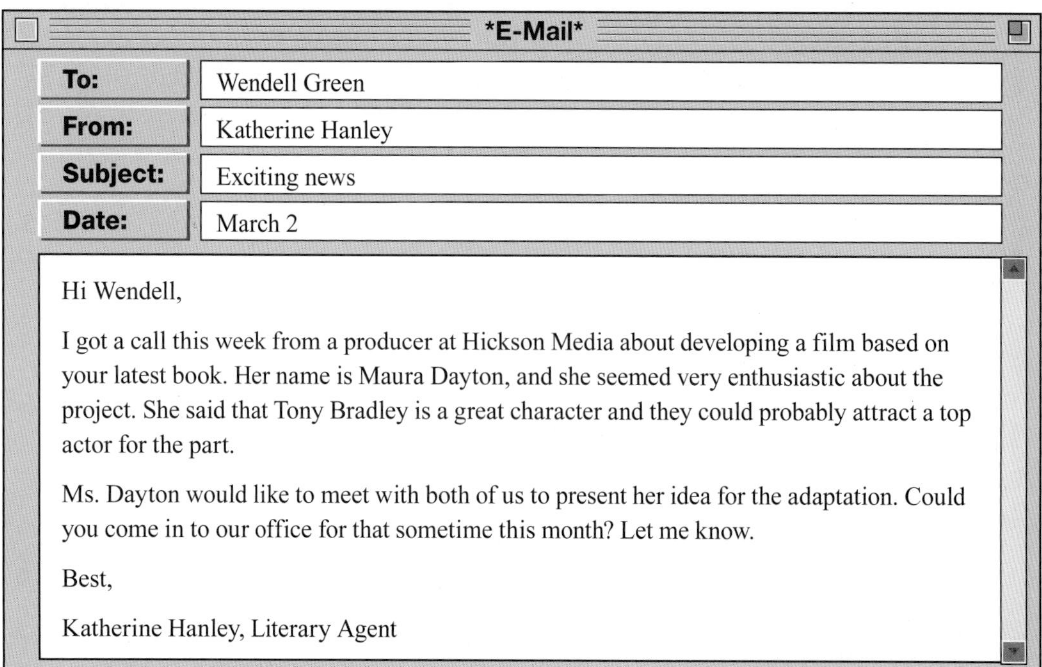

***E-Mail***

**To:** Wendell Green
**From:** Katherine Hanley
**Subject:** Exciting news
**Date:** March 2

Hi Wendell,

I got a call this week from a producer at Hickson Media about developing a film based on your latest book. Her name is Maura Dayton, and she seemed very enthusiastic about the project. She said that Tony Bradley is a great character and they could probably attract a top actor for the part.

Ms. Dayton would like to meet with both of us to present her idea for the adaptation. Could you come in to our office for that sometime this month? Let me know.

Best,

Katherine Hanley, Literary Agent

**176.** What is the SLP 10 a list of?

(A) Fictional characters
(B) First-time authors
(C) Books for youth
(D) Public libraries

**177.** What is indicated about Mr. Green?

(A) He lives near the ocean.
(B) He collaborates with a family member.
(C) He has written about his previous career.
(D) He sometimes contributes to *Fraser's Quarterly.*

**178.** In the e-mail, the word "part" in paragraph 1, line 4, is closest in meaning to

(A) component
(B) section
(C) portion
(D) role

**179.** According to the e-mail, which book may be adapted into a film?

(A) *In Wylie Cove*
(B) *Swing Away*
(C) *Sarah Saves the World*
(D) *Nails on a Chalkboard*

**180.** What does Ms. Hanley ask Mr. Green to do in March?

(A) Meet with a lawyer
(B) Listen to a proposal
(C) Make an announcement
(D) Edit some writing



GO ON TO THE NEXT PAGE

**Questions 181-185** refer to the following e-mail and form.

| | |
|---|---|
| **To:** | Member list |
| **From:** | Otis Community Center |
| **Date:** | February 3 |
| **Subject:** | Cooking classes |
| **Attachment:** | Flyer |

As part of our ongoing efforts to celebrate cultural diversity, Otis Community Center will hold a series of one-time cooking classes on Asian dishes this spring. The classes will be held on the first Wednesday evening of each month from March through June. In order, the dishes covered will be Vietnamese chicken curry, Korean kimchi stew, Thai spring rolls, and Cantonese stir-fry beef.

Guest instructors from Roark Culinary Academy will teach the classes in our dedicated cooking classroom. Advance registration and payment are required, and participants will be asked to show proof of registration to their instructor. Registration can be completed at our front desk from February 15 for all classes. Those who are not members of Otis Community Center will be required to pay a $5 registration fee.

Please see the attached flyer for details including materials fees, which vary by class. Questions about the classes may be directed to Heather Tate, our programming specialist.

Akio Hayashi, Director

## Otis Community Center

### CLASS REGISTRATION CONFIRMATION FORM

**Name:** Kayla Shull
**Membership Number:** 499560
**Class Title:** Thai Spring Rolls
**Instructor:** David Somsri
**Date & Time:** May 6, 5 P.M.
**Registration Fee:** WAIVED
**Materials Fee:** $15 Paid ☑
**Processed by:** Eric Woodard

**Note:**

Refunds of class fees are only issued for cancellations made at least one week before the class date. To cancel your registration, please visit the center or call our front desk at 555-0195.

181. Why was the e-mail written?
(A) To recruit volunteer workers
(B) To issue invitations to special dinners
(C) To ask for feedback about a program
(D) To publicize some learning opportunities

182. Where will a community activity take place?
(A) On a city street
(B) At Otis Community Center
(C) At several local restaurants
(D) At Roark Culinary Academy

183. What dish will be cooked in March?
(A) Vietnamese chicken curry
(B) Korean kimchi stew
(C) Thai spring rolls
(D) Cantonese stir-fry beef

184. Why was a fee waived for Ms. Shull?
(A) She will provide some materials herself.
(B) She is a community center member.
(C) She registered before a certain date.
(D) She attended each session of a class.

185. To whom should Ms. Shull show her confirmation form?
(A) Ms. Tate
(B) Mr. Hayashi
(C) Mr. Somsri
(D) Mr. Woodard



GO ON TO THE NEXT PAGE

**Questions 186-190** refer to the following e-mails and schedule.

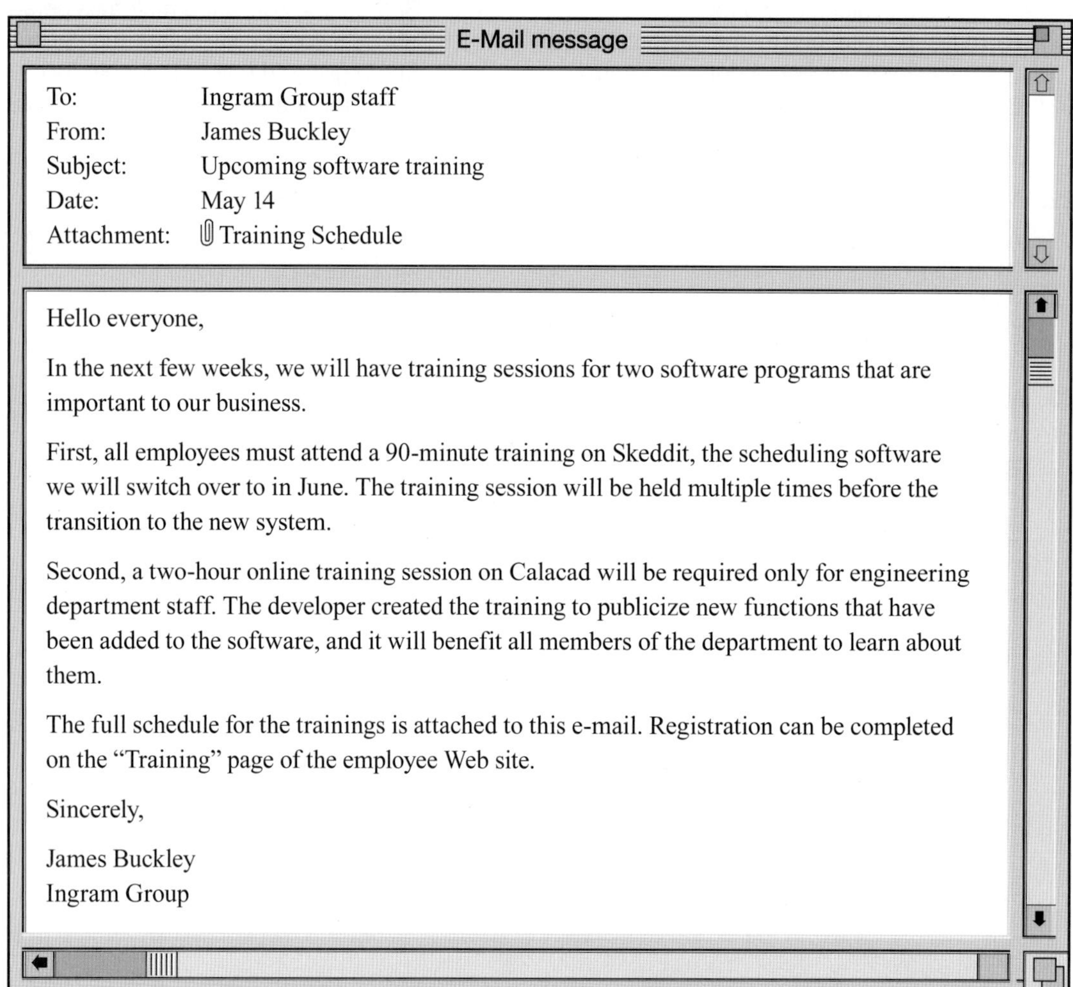

E-Mail message

To: Ingram Group staff
From: James Buckley
Subject: Upcoming software training
Date: May 14
Attachment: Training Schedule

Hello everyone,

In the next few weeks, we will have training sessions for two software programs that are important to our business.

First, all employees must attend a 90-minute training on Skeddit, the scheduling software we will switch over to in June. The training session will be held multiple times before the transition to the new system.

Second, a two-hour online training session on Calacad will be required only for engineering department staff. The developer created the training to publicize new functions that have been added to the software, and it will benefit all members of the department to learn about them.

The full schedule for the trainings is attached to this e-mail. Registration can be completed on the "Training" page of the employee Web site.

Sincerely,

James Buckley
Ingram Group

## Training Schedule

| Date | Software | Time | Location |
|---|---|---|---|
| May 26 | Calacad | 9:00 A.M.–11:00 A.M. | Online |
| May 30 | Skeddit | 9:00 A.M.–10:30 A.M. | Conference Room A |
| June 1 | Skeddit | 1:00 P.M.–2:30 P.M. | Conference Room A |
| June 5 | Calacad | 2:00 P.M.–4:00 P.M. | Online |
| June 7 | Skeddit | 10:00 A.M.–11:30 A.M. | Conference Room A |
| June 12 | Skeddit | 3:30 P.M.–5 P.M. | Conference Room A |

The Web link for the online training will be sent to participants upon registration.

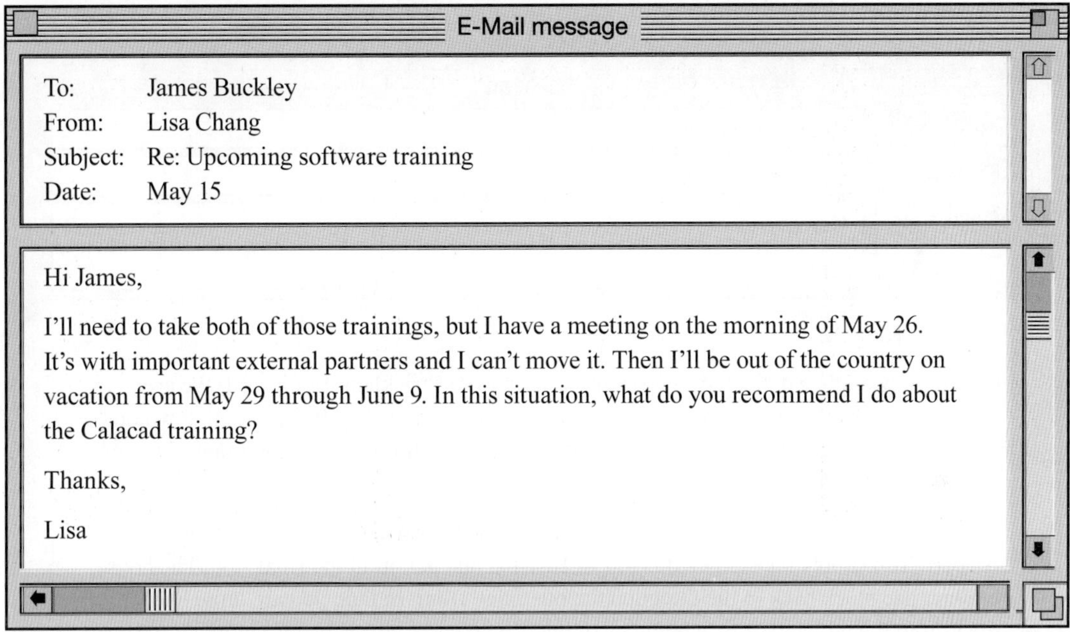
E-Mail message

To: James Buckley
From: Lisa Chang
Subject: Re: Upcoming software training
Date: May 15

Hi James,

I'll need to take both of those trainings, but I have a meeting on the morning of May 26. It's with important external partners and I can't move it. Then I'll be out of the country on vacation from May 29 through June 9. In this situation, what do you recommend I do about the Calacad training?

Thanks,

Lisa



**186.** What does the first e-mail mention about Calacad?
(A) It has acquired new capabilities.
(B) It was developed specifically for the company.
(C) It can be downloaded from the employee Web site.
(D) It is the subject of regular trainings.

**187.** What is NOT true about the schedule for Skeddit training sessions?
(A) It includes both morning and afternoon sessions.
(B) It spans a period of more than one month.
(C) All of the sessions will be held in the same location.
(D) The person who will conduct the training is not specified.

**188.** Why did Ms. Chang write to Mr. Buckley?
(A) To ask for confirmation of a registration
(B) To request advice about a scheduling difficulty
(C) To inform him of a change to her vacation plans
(D) To express concern about some technology

**189.** What is suggested about Ms. Chang?
(A) She travels frequently for work.
(B) She fulfilled a training requirement.
(C) She is a member of the engineering department.
(D) She is glad that a software program will be replaced.

**190.** On what date will Ms. Chang most likely undergo some training?
(A) May 26
(B) June 1
(C) June 7
(D) June 12

*GO ON TO THE NEXT PAGE*

**Questions 191-195** refer to the following e-mail, schedule, and notice.

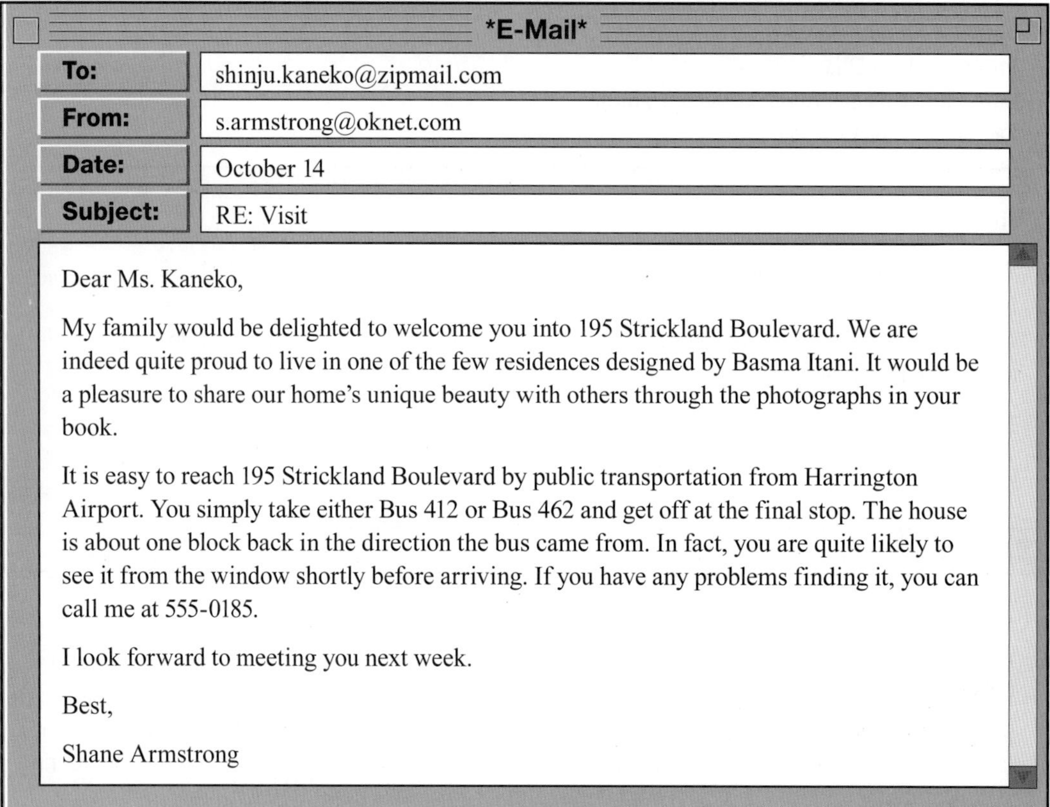

*E-Mail*

| | |
|---|---|
| **To:** | shinju.kaneko@zipmail.com |
| **From:** | s.armstrong@oknet.com |
| **Date:** | October 14 |
| **Subject:** | RE: Visit |

Dear Ms. Kaneko,

My family would be delighted to welcome you into 195 Strickland Boulevard. We are indeed quite proud to live in one of the few residences designed by Basma Itani. It would be a pleasure to share our home's unique beauty with others through the photographs in your book.

It is easy to reach 195 Strickland Boulevard by public transportation from Harrington Airport. You simply take either Bus 412 or Bus 462 and get off at the final stop. The house is about one block back in the direction the bus came from. In fact, you are quite likely to see it from the window shortly before arriving. If you have any problems finding it, you can call me at 555-0185.

I look forward to meeting you next week.

Best,

Shane Armstrong

**Harrington Airport Bus Schedule**

Seven days per week, year-round

| # | Route | First Bus | Last Bus |
|---|---|---|---|
| 410 | Airport → Downtown | 6:20 A.M. | 9:50 P.M. |
| 412 | Airport → Downtown → Belmont | 6:05 A.M. | 10:05 P.M. |
| 437 | Airport → Riverfront → Abbott Heights | 6:25 A.M. | 9:55 P.M. |
| 450 | Airport → Edgewood | 6:15 A.M. | 9:45 P.M. |
| 462 | Airport → Market District → Belmont | 6:10 A.M. | 10:10 P.M. |
| 470 | Airport → Abbott Heights | 6:30 A.M. | 10:00 P.M. |

HARRINGTON AIRPORT BUSES

Today (October 19), the airport bus to Edgewood will stop on Bishop Street instead of Yeager Avenue. This change is necessary because of road closures for the Fall Festival. For details, visit the tourism desk.

All bus passengers should be advised that, as always, your baggage cannot be placed on a seat unless you have bought the ticket for that specific seat. Otherwise, the baggage must be stored underneath the bus. The bus driver will help you load and unload it safely.



**191.** Why most likely is Ms. Kaneko traveling to Mr. Armstrong's area?

(A) To attend a design exhibition
(B) To take pictures of a property
(C) To conduct an interview for a publication
(D) To advise him on a renovation project

**192.** In his e-mail, what information does Mr. Armstrong indicate that Ms. Kaneko is already aware of?

(A) The composition of his family
(B) The architect of his house
(C) The location of his workplace
(D) The results of a building inspection

**193.** In what neighborhood is 195 Strickland Boulevard located?

(A) Downtown
(B) Belmont
(C) Abbott Heights
(D) Edgewood

**194.** Which bus's route has temporarily changed?

(A) 410
(B) 437
(C) 450
(D) 470

**195.** What does the notice indicate about Harrington Airport buses?

(A) They have assigned seating.
(B) Tickets can be bought from their drivers.
(C) They have overhead baggage compartments.
(D) Their passengers may have to stand during the ride.

GO ON TO THE NEXT PAGE

**Questions 196-200** refer to the following article, e-mail, and plan.

## Clemente Street Lot

HAYWARD (March 2)—The Hayward City Council is exploring various options for the future of a 5-acre city-owned lot located on Clemente Street. Bids and proposals are being accepted at this time, with the Greenway Collaborative, a local environmental group, advocating for leaving the lot empty and in the city's possession. Hillview Property Development is interested in purchasing the lot. It intends to build Marshall Plaza, a small building with space for retail business, and establish a courtyard and a small green area with trees, benches, and flower gardens that would be designated for public use.

"Our planned combination of retail units and green space is a viable solution for this neighborhood, which is in critical need of revitalization," said Luoyang Meng, a Hillview Property Development representative. "Our company has the resources to create an attractive and thriving retail center as well as the expertise to minimize disruptions to wildlife habitats. We hope to have the opportunity to showcase our skills."

**E-Mail message**

**From:** Clifford Mullen <clifford@busybbakery.com>

**To:** Racquel Shaw <r_shaw@hillviewprop.com>

**Date:** November 18

**Subject:** Rental inquiry

Dear Ms. Shaw,

I own the Busy Bee Bakery downtown, and I am interested in renting a second location to sell my baked goods. Marshall Plaza would be ideal for my business because of the anticipated foot traffic. I am also drawn to the convenience of the easy access to public transportation and the unloading area in the back. I need at least three hundred square meters of space, but I do not want cooking facilities, as our staff will bake at our main site and just deliver the goods to the secondary site. I'm also wondering if you could tell me the average rates for water, electricity, and gas. I know that these are not included in the monthly rental fee.

Thanks for the information,

Clifford Mullen

## Marshall Plaza Retail Units

| Unit 102<br>320 $m^2$<br>Available | Unit 103<br>270 $m^2$<br>Available | Unit 104<br>350 $m^2$<br>Benny's Sweet Shop |
|---|---|---|
| | | |
| **Unit 101**<br>225 $m^2$<br>Available | **Courtyard** | **Unit 105**<br>315 $m^2$<br>Available<br>Includes kitchen |



**196.** What is the purpose of the article?

(A) To give an update about public land
(B) To notify local residents of a closure
(C) To promote the sale of an unused lot
(D) To elicit aid for a park upgrade

**197.** What beneficial aspect of Hillview Property Development does Mr. Meng mention?

(A) Its intention to create more jobs in the city of Hayward
(B) Its experience with keeping building expenditures under control
(C) Its use of environmentally friendly construction materials
(D) Its ability to preserve spaces where animals live

**198.** What is suggested about Hillview Property Development in Mr. Mullen's e-mail?

(A) It constructed the building where his bakery is.
(B) It is awaiting the final building permits.
(C) Its proposal was accepted by city officials.
(D) Its staff usually uses public transportation.

**199.** What information about Marshall Plaza does Mr. Mullen request?

(A) The security measures for the building
(B) The cost of utilities at a site
(C) The due date for monthly fees
(D) The size of an unloading area

**200.** Which unit would Mr. Mullen most likely be interested in?

(A) Unit 101
(B) Unit 102
(C) Unit 103
(D) Unit 105

**Stop! This is the end of the test. If you finish before time is called, you may go back to Parts 5, 6, and 7 and check your work.**

# YBM 실전토익 RC 1000

### 테스트 전 체크리스트

- 중간 휴식 없이 제한 시간을 지켜서 풀이하세요.
- 제한 시간은 답안지에 마킹하는 시간도 포함시켜야 합니다.
- 찍은 문제는 번호 옆에 꼭 체크해 주세요.
- 시간 안에 풀지 못한 문제는 틀린 것으로 채점해 주세요.

# RC TEST 3

## READING TEST

In the Reading test, you will read a variety of texts and answer several different types of reading comprehension questions. The entire Reading test will last 75 minutes. There are three parts, and directions are given for each part. You are encouraged to answer as many questions as possible within the time allowed.

You must mark your answers on the separate answer sheet. Do not write your answers in your test book.

## PART 5

**Directions:** A word or phrase is missing in each of the sentences below. Four answer choices are given below each sentence. Select the best answer to complete the sentence. Then mark the letter (A), (B), (C), or (D) on your answer sheet.

**101.** Mr. Johnston is taking online classes that will assist ------- in getting promoted.

(A) his
(B) he
(C) him
(D) himself

**102.** Attendees to the event can have their book ------- signed by the author.

(A) personal
(B) personally
(C) personalize
(D) personalizes

**103.** Readers of Ms. Alcorn's column on money management appreciate her ------- financial advice.

(A) thought
(B) thoughts
(C) thoughtfully
(D) thoughtful

**104.** Prospective students are invited to learn more about the university's programs by viewing its ------- course schedule.

(A) detailed
(B) detail
(C) detailing
(D) details

**105.** At Hartway Terrace, all dishes are prepared under the ------- of master chef Yoo-Jeong Jin.

(A) style
(B) opinion
(C) attempt
(D) supervision

**106.** It is ------- that passengers be shown the safety briefing prior to the flight.

(A) abundant
(B) sudden
(C) distinctive
(D) imperative

**107.** Contract negotiations with Murphy Supplies should be conducted ------- consideration for the lack of alternative suppliers.

(A) by
(B) with
(C) so that
(D) while

**108.** Peggy Amos was ------- by the director for creating the library's popular "Future Entrepreneurs" lecture series.

(A) intended
(B) influenced
(C) commended
(D) allowed

**109.** Residential furnaces and boilers should undergo inspection ------- for safety reasons.

(A) annually
(B) overly
(C) certainly
(D) readily

**110.** To maintain client -------, the destruction of old files must be carried out carefully.

(A) confiding
(B) confidential
(C) confidentiality
(D) confidentially

**111.** The new ------- of the Home Health smartphone application features a list of exercise tips for beginners.

(A) version
(B) aspect
(C) route
(D) term

**112.** Ms. Webster's retirement party was attended by many coworkers and even several former students of -------.

(A) she
(B) her
(C) hers
(D) herself

**113.** Several canopies were set up at the outdoor concert site at Radner Park in ------- of the rain.

(A) atmosphere
(B) proportion
(C) anticipation
(D) limitation

**114.** Employees who are ------- for exceeding their output goals are more likely to maintain a high level of productivity.

(A) rewarded
(B) reward
(C) rewarding
(D) rewards

**115.** The user manual warns customers to keep the phone away from radiators and ovens because its components are ------- to heat.

(A) sensitive
(B) familiar
(C) released
(D) considerable

**116.** The prescription must be collected tomorrow because the pharmacy has ------- closed for the day.

(A) yet
(B) too
(C) already
(D) hardly

**117.** The volume of disposable items is ------- despite concerns about the impact on the environment.

(A) grows
(B) growing
(C) grow
(D) grown

**118.** The opening of the community center was only possible through the public's ------- support.

(A) generous
(B) identical
(C) bright
(D) spacious

**119.** The new yoga mat manufactured by Elita, Inc., maintains its shape even ------- many years of use.

(A) against
(B) up
(C) after
(D) without

**120.** The manufacturer offers a standard warranty on the dryer ------- three years.

(A) upon
(B) toward
(C) about
(D) for

*GO ON TO THE NEXT PAGE* →

**121.** Mr. Otis has the right ------- of people skills and career experience to succeed in the role.

(A) remedy
(B) sequence
(C) improvement
(D) combination

**122.** The focus of the board members is ------- investors react to the news of the CEO's retirement.

(A) among
(B) who
(C) where
(D) how

**123.** The program coordinator asked staff to circulate the volunteer recruitment post ------- using their personal social media accounts.

(A) widest
(B) widen
(C) wider
(D) widely

**124.** For the safety of everyone in the building, the area around the fire exit must remain ------- clear at all times.

(A) perfect
(B) perfectly
(C) perfection
(D) perfected

**125.** The architect's drawings for the structure differ greatly from the building that -------.

(A) is constructing
(B) constructed
(C) was constructed
(D) has constructed

**126.** Benjamin has chosen new videoconferencing software for the training he will ------- remotely.

(A) appear
(B) conduct
(C) participate
(D) instruct

**127.** ------- audience members arrive at the theater, an usher will direct them to the correct seats.

(A) Since
(B) Until
(C) Next
(D) Once

**128.** Performers ------- from the competition are encouraged to stay and watch the remainder of the show.

(A) eliminating
(B) are eliminated
(C) eliminated
(D) that eliminate

**129.** Many commuters are enjoying shorter driving times ------- the expansion of Highway 5 is completed.

(A) together with
(B) now that
(C) because of
(D) in case

**130.** At the Rockford Apartment Complex, tenants may have to pay a fee if they ------- their lease agreement without sufficient notice.

(A) prohibit
(B) obstruct
(C) enclose
(D) terminate

## PART 6

**Directions:** Read the texts that follow. A word, phrase, or sentence is missing in parts of each text. Four answer choices for each question are given below the text. Select the best answer to complete the text. Then mark the letter (A), (B), (C), or (D) on your answer sheet.

**Questions 131-134** refer to the following e-mail.

To: All Urias Data Staff

From: Gabriella Shaw

Subject: Staff appreciation

Date: April 15

For Urias Data's annual staff appreciation event, we will take a group hike at Walpole National Park during business hours on Friday, April 25. We hope everyone will come out to enjoy a fun day of ------- **131.** and getting to know each other better. Veronica Erikson is organizing a carpool so that employees ------- **132.** rides to the site. If you are one of the drivers, you will be reimbursed for the fuel that you use.

We know that some of you have heavy workloads right now. ------- **133.**, you should not assume that this means you will be unable to attend the event. ------- **134.**. If you have concerns in this area, please bring them to your supervisor.

**131.** (A) exercise
(B) music
(C) education
(D) volunteering

**132.** (A) who shared
(B) sharing
(C) shares
(D) can share

**133.** (A) Furthermore
(B) Likewise
(C) However
(D) Otherwise

**134.** (A) One day will be subtracted from your allowance of paid leave.
(B) It is likely that a make-up session will be scheduled soon.
(C) The deadlines of non-urgent projects can be extended.
(D) A variety of convenience facilities are available at the park.

*GO ON TO THE NEXT PAGE*

**Questions 135-138** refer to the following review.

My first impression of McVay Accountants was positive. A representative responded quickly after I filled out a contact form requesting help with my small business's taxes. Nevertheless, I ------- (135.) an appointment with the firm again. My experience was that they do not show enough concern for ------- (136.). I found no fewer than three errors in the tax return my accountant prepared for me. ------- (137.) . What is more, it took several rounds of discussion and resending of documents before he figured out the sources of the issues and fixed them. In the future, I plan to ------- (138.) a firm based on a recommendation from a friend or associate.

**135.** (A) will not be booked
(B) was not booked
(C) will not be booking
(D) might not have booked

**136.** (A) accuracy
(B) privacy
(C) communication
(D) diversity

**137.** (A) This kind of delay is unacceptable.
(B) It turned out that he had misplaced them.
(C) There must be a more secure way to share files.
(D) One could have cost me thousands of dollars.

**138.** (A) develop
(B) launch
(C) select
(D) expand

**Questions 139-142** refer to the following e-mail.

To: Samantha Vanetten <samantha@vanettenconsulting.com>

From: Phillip Lee <plee@monroe-solutions.com>

Subject: Inquiry

Date: March 2

Attachment: Monroe_Solutions

Dear, Ms. Vanetten,

I recently received a ------- (139.) from my company for your seminar on establishing relationships with clients. I was initially hesitant about the event. This is because the content of other seminars I've attended has been either too basic or too technical. ------- (140.), your talk was perfect for someone of my experience level. Our firm is interested in hiring you for a private session at our company. ------- (141.). Please let me know if you are available. I have attached a brochure ------- (142.) our company's services.

Warmest regards,

Phillip Lee

**139.** (A) deposit
(B) subscription
(C) ticket
(D) venture

**140.** (A) In other words
(B) For instance
(C) In contrast
(D) To that end

**141.** (A) I hope that you found my suggestions helpful.
(B) All thirty of our salespeople would be in attendance.
(C) The auditorium's sound system was also impressive.
(D) We have received fewer client complaints since then.

**142.** (A) being outlined
(B) outlined these
(C) is outlining
(D) that outlines

TEST 3

*GO ON TO THE NEXT PAGE*

**Questions 143-146** refer to the following notice.

The DC Analytics management team is aware that some files were permanently erased due to the recent system malfunction. We ask that you back up your work to external hard drives regularly. This will help us avoid a similar ------- (143.) in the future.

Unfortunately, we are unable to use automatic cloud storage due to security issues. ------- (144.). You can sign up by contacting the IT office on extension 14. Each day at 4:45 P.M., the IT team ------- (145.) an e-mail with a reminder about file backups. If this is too frequent for you, you can arrange ------- (146.) the messages on a weekly basis instead.

**143.** (A) delay
(B) loss
(C) expense
(D) importance

**144.** (A) Therefore, we are offering an alert system to help you remember.
(B) Do not share these files with unauthorized personnel.
(C) We will give a demonstration on how to use it next week.
(D) Of course, your home computer uses the same software.

**145.** (A) sent
(B) had been sending
(C) will send
(D) has sent

**146.** (A) receivable
(B) receipt
(C) receiving
(D) to receive

## PART 7

**Directions:** In this part you will read a selection of texts, such as magazine and newspaper articles, e-mails, and instant messages. Each text or set of texts is followed by several questions. Select the best answer for each question and mark the letter (A), (B), (C), or (D) on your answer sheet.



**Questions 147-148** refer to the following product description.

### Try our new product!

**A Great Way to Save Time**

With its stainless-steel finish and hidden control panel, the Kemper 25 is an elegant addition to any household. It can wash a full load in as little as one hour—no more waiting for clean dishes! In addition to this speedy "One-Hour" setting, the Kemper 25 offers a "Normal" setting with high water efficiency, and a "Heavy" setting useful for items like greasy pots and pans. No matter which setting you choose, the heated drying system ensures your dishes will be table-ready at the end of the cycle. Even large dishes such as serving platters can be cleaned with ease thanks to the Kemper 25's removable top rack. Visit your local Kemper dealership to learn more!

**147.** What is the product description about?

(A) An item of clothing
(B) A kitchen appliance
(C) A vacuum cleaner
(D) A fitness machine

**148.** What is indicated about the product?

(A) It is easy to keep clean.
(B) It uses energy efficiently.
(C) It has multiple noise settings.
(D) It has an adjustable structure.

*GO ON TO THE NEXT PAGE*

**Questions 149-150** refer to the following instructions.

**Bennett Mobile: Reimbursement Request Form Instructions**

1. Write your name and employee number at the top of the form.
2. For each listed item, write a brief note about the reason for the spending.
3. Staple the relevant receipts to the form.
4. Have your manager sign the form and sign it yourself as well. Unsigned requests will not be processed.
5. To have the payment appear on your monthly paycheck on the 25th, submit the form by the 15th of the month.

If you make frequent purchases, you may be eligible to receive a credit card under Bennett Mobile's account. Speak to the finance team to request approval.

**149.** According to the instructions, what must be included on the form?

(A) The employee's phone number
(B) The signature of a supervisor
(C) A department number
(D) A copy of an ID card

**150.** What is indicated about the finance team members?

(A) They can issue company credit cards.
(B) They need the form by the 25th of every month.
(C) They must approve all purchases in advance.
(D) They have recently changed a policy.

**Questions 151-152** refer to the following receipt.

## Receipt of Cash

No: 013394 Date: December 6

**Recipient Details**

**Name:** Thea Lemke
**Department:** Engineering
**Extension:** 345

**Amount Dispensed:** $150

**Description:** Meal allowance for a business trip to Atlanta (December 8-10) to perform the inspection of the Cayce Building and surrounding grounds.

**Approved by:** Steven Rivera

I agree that the above details are correct and that I have received the specified amount. I understand that I must provide records showing how it is spent and return any unused portions to the company.

**Signature:** Thea Lemke

**151.** What does Ms. Lemke plan to do in Atlanta?
(A) Inspect a building
(B) Negotiate a contract
(C) Apply for a loan
(D) Demonstrate a product

**152.** What does the receipt confirm?
(A) Ms. Lemke's enrollment in an association
(B) Issuance of funds to Ms. Lemke
(C) Ms. Lemke's purchase of travel tickets
(D) The loaning of equipment to Ms. Lemke

TEST 3

*GO ON TO THE NEXT PAGE* →

**Questions 153-154** refer to the following text-message chain.

**Nina Simpson [9:37 A.M.]**
Hi, Anthony. Do we know what's going on with the brand strategist position yet? I've had a few follow-up inquiries from the candidates we screened.

**Anthony Winslow [9:38 A.M.]**
I just spoke with Florence Gracey, the head of the marketing department. She doesn't have time to sit down with everyone who passed the phone screen because she'll be away on a business trip next week. So she wants to meet with them all at once.

**Nina Simpson [9:39 A.M.]**
Really? I don't think that's a good idea. It would be difficult to compare their answers to our questions, because some candidates would have extra time to come up with good responses. It would be better to put the process on hold for that week.

**Anthony Winslow [9:40 A.M.]**
That's true. I'll talk to Florence again and see how strongly she feels about her idea.

**153.** What does Ms. Gracey want to do?

(A) Hold a group interview
(B) Postpone her business trip
(C) Hire a temporary worker
(D) Take a marketing course

**154.** At 9:40 A.M., what does Mr. Winslow most likely mean when he writes, "That's true"?

(A) He knows that a decision is not up to him.
(B) He agrees that Ms. Gracey has a busy schedule.
(C) He shares Ms. Simpson's opinion of a job candidate.
(D) He thinks a hiring process should be paused.

**Questions 155-157** refer to the following brochure.

# VANDIVIA

## Your gateway to freshness

New owner-operator Ernesto Stewart welcomes you to Vandivia!

**Fresh Food**

We grow delicious, organic produce for fine-dining restaurants, high-end supermarkets, and more. A new batch of free samples is offered every hour. At the end of your visit, don't forget to take some more goodies home to cook with!

**Fresh Air**

Visitors are encouraged to join the bicycle tour of our grounds led by one of our employees. Take in our rustic architecture and the enticing scents of our vegetable patches and fruit orchards. The tour lasts about two hours and bicycles are provided.

**Fresh Ideas**

Vandivia holds daily workshops on growing herbs and organic gardening in our big red barn. Visitors may also be able to arrange a workshop on vegetarian cooking with Mr. Stewart, an award-winning chef, depending on his schedule.

The entrance fee is $20 per person and covers all the activities listed above. Our location is rather remote, so we recommend that drivers use a satellite navigation system to find us. Alternatively, we offer a $5 round-trip shuttle service from Wadena Station.

Visit www.vandivia.com for more information.

**155.** What most likely is Vandivia?

(A) A farm
(B) A restaurant
(C) A beach resort
(D) A national park

**156.** What is indicated about Vandivia?

(A) It has increased the charge for entry.
(B) It has been nominated for an award.
(C) It rents satellite navigation systems.
(D) It is under new management.

**157.** What is available for an additional fee?

(A) Transportation to a site
(B) Product samples
(C) Bicycle tours
(D) Educational workshops

*GO ON TO THE NEXT PAGE*

**Questions 158-160** refer to the following memo.

## MEMO

To: Coffee Max Staff
From: Adriana Clawson
Date: October 20
Subject: Special drinks

Dear Staff,

The holiday season is approaching! To get into the spirit and hopefully boost sales, I want to offer a temporary menu of holiday-themed drinks to Coffee Max customers. Please help with this project by using the café's slow periods to try to come up with a delicious and unique coffee drink. If you succeed, send me an e-mail outlining the ingredients and how to make it.

I will choose three drinks for our special menu. If yours is chosen, you will receive a $50 gift certificate to Eva Department Store, so you can shop right across the street before or after work.

The deadline for submissions is the end of the day on Sunday, October 30, and there are a few extra considerations to keep in mind. The drinks should not use too many costly ingredients, and if there are any ingredients that might be dangerous for customers with food allergies, include suggestions for substitutions. In addition, our staff must be able to make each drink quickly.

Thank you!

Adriana

**158.** Why was the memo written?

(A) To describe changes to a drinks menu
(B) To request recipe ideas from staff
(C) To ask for referrals for temporary workers
(D) To announce a holiday party

**159.** What is indicated about Eva Department Store?

(A) It is within walking distance of Coffee Max.
(B) It is holding a sales event.
(C) It gives discounts to Coffee Max employees.
(D) It will open its own coffee shop.

**160.** What is NOT mentioned as a characteristic of some drinks?

(A) They can be prepared in a short time.
(B) They are inexpensive to make.
(C) They do not include allergens.
(D) They share a seasonal theme.

**Questions 161-163** refer to the following memo.

From: Krista Nocera
To: All Staff
Date: February 11
Re: Flooring

Dear Staff,

A crew from Trevino Contractors will visit our office this weekend to renovate the main hallway. — [1] —. Because of the location of the work, it won't be necessary to move furniture or personal belongings in your office or other shared rooms. — [2] —.

However, if you need to work over the weekend, we ask that you do so remotely. We understand that some of you need specialized software to complete your tasks, so please see David Rogowski in the IT department to request the use of a company laptop. — [3] —. If you plan to work late on Friday, please let the security team know if your car is by the Boyd Street entrance. — [4] —. The crew needs the first row of the lot clear to unload their materials on Saturday morning.

Thank you for your cooperation!

Krista Nocera



**161.** What should employees speak to Mr. Rogowski about?

(A) Storing some personal items
(B) Getting a software upgrade
(C) Moving to a new office
(D) Borrowing some equipment

**162.** What is suggested about the Boyd Street entrance?

(A) It will be locked by the security team.
(B) It faces heavy traffic.
(C) It is near a parking area.
(D) It has the building's largest doors.

**163.** In which of the positions marked [1], [2], [3], and [4] does the following sentence best belong?

"The flooring will be replaced, and the walls will be repainted."

(A) [1]
(B) [2]
(C) [3]
(D) [4]

*GO ON TO THE NEXT PAGE*

**Questions 164-167** refer to the following notice.

## Springdale Connects

Are you a fashion designer? Use your talent to support your local community! Springdale Connects, a locally based nonprofit organization, is holding a fashion show at the historic Medlin Theater to raise project funds. You can help by designing and sewing a special outfit for the event using the theme "Timeless Classics".

Tickets to the fashion show will be sold on our Web site and at various businesses throughout Springdale. The proceeds from the event will be used to purchase guitars, keyboards, trumpets, and more to be given to elderly people living in Springdale to form the town's first-ever senior citizen band. This can help participants to learn a new skill and meet new people.

If you'd like to participate, please visit our Web site at www.springdaleconnects.org to find out the required submission date, the suggested clothing size, and a list of the accessories we can provide. There you can also submit a brief biography including your work and experience. This will be printed on the flyer that will be distributed to audience members when they arrive.

**164.** What does the notice ask people to do?

(A) Provide items for a fundraising event
(B) Become a member of a charity
(C) Volunteer to set up a venue
(D) Donate money to an organization

**165.** What does Springdale Connects aim to do?

(A) Host free fashion design courses
(B) Help to restore a historic theater
(C) Prepare and serve meals to elderly residents
(D) Provide musical instruments to community members

**166.** What is NOT indicated as information provided on the Web site?

(A) A photo gallery
(B) A deadline
(C) Details on available accessories
(D) Sizing recommendations

**167.** According to the notice, where will participants' biographies be seen?

(A) In an online newsletter
(B) On a handout
(C) On a Web site
(D) On a notice in the lobby

**Questions 168-171** refer to the following online chat discussion.

| | |
|---|---|
| **Charles Vaughn [1:22 P.M.]** | Good afternoon, everyone. I wanted to let you know that I still don't have any news on the Hogan Tech event. |
| **Heather Dengler [1:23 P.M.]** | Nico Apparel wants to hire us for that same day. |
| **Charles Vaughn [1:25 P.M.]** | Then we'll need to find out whether Hogan Tech has plans. We don't have enough cooks and servers to do both. Hogan Tech is a bigger order, but I'd hate to turn down another client until we know for certain what's going on. |
| **Heather Dengler [1:26 P.M.]** | I promised Nico Apparel that we would confirm either way by the end of the day. |
| **Charles Vaughn [1:27 P.M.]** | I see. I tried to get in touch with Daniel Garrett at Hogan Tech, but there was no answer at his office. Do we have another phone number for him? |
| **Natasha Kopp [1:28 P.M.]** | I've never needed one before. I'll look into that. |
| **Charles Vaughn [1:31 P.M.]** | If we end up accepting the job from Nico Apparel, we'll have to get the pricing estimate ready right away. We don't want to seem disorganized. Heather, I'd like you to do that. |
| **Natasha Kopp [1:34 P.M.]** | Got it. I've forwarded that to you, Charles. |
| **Charles Vaughn [1:42 P.M.]** | Mr. Garrett said they've decided to use a different company instead. While he liked our menu suggestions, they wanted to use a company that specializes in vegetarian dishes. So, Heather, can you send me a finished file by 3 P.M.? |
| **Heather Dengler [1:43 P.M.]** | Yes, that'll be enough time if I start now. |

**168.** Where most likely do the writers work?
(A) At a catering company
(B) At a graphic design firm
(C) At a technology firm
(D) At a clothing manufacturer

**169.** At 1:28 P.M., what does Ms. Kopp mean when she writes, "I'll look into that"?
(A) She will try to schedule a client visit.
(B) She will check a meeting space's availability.
(C) She will search for some contact information.
(D) She will inquire about a fee.

**170.** What does Mr. Vaughn tell the other writers about?
(A) When to arrive for an event
(B) Why a decision was made
(C) Who is representing Nico Apparel
(D) Where to file a report

**171.** What will Ms. Dengler most likely do next?
(A) Update a Web site
(B) Prepare an estimate
(C) Find a new supplier
(D) Speak to Mr. Garrett

TEST 3

GO ON TO THE NEXT PAGE

**Questions 172-175** refer to the following article.

## Bulk of Difficult Sewer Improvement Project Finished

STENDHAM (September 25)—Yesterday, the city of Stendham announced the conclusion of the first phase of the Lundgate Shore project. Located on the west bank of the Garmine River, the shore is named for nearby Lundgate Bridge. The covered waterways that now sit there will stop excess sewage from spilling into the river by redirecting it into Clearway, Stendham's enormous "sewage highway". — [1] —. The smooth completion of the phase is remarkable given the complex feats of engineering that were involved.

The most challenging part was the installation of the 3,700-tonne main channel. The Lundgate Shore is in a tidal area, and the river covers it completely at high tide. Bauright Group, the company responsible for Phase 1, decided to make use of this feature and float the pre-built channel into place. — [2] —. "We had successfully used tidewater to move structures in other Clearway projects," Bauright chief engineer Nancy Majors explained. Still, the method required precise timing. The channel had to pass under Lundgate Bridge, so it could not be moved during high tide. — [3] —. On the other hand, if the move was done when the water level was too low, the channel might not float all the way to its correct position. Ms. Majors said her team completed the difficult task without incident thanks to "extremely careful planning."

Yesterday's announcement also revealed that the simpler second phase of the project, which will be handled by Perriott, LLC, will end in November. — [4] —. Perriott will add a walking path, benches, and greenery to the public land above the new sewer structures.

**172.** What problem is the Lundgate Shore project most likely intended to address?

(A) Pollution of a river by wastewater
(B) Excessive traffic on a highway
(C) The deterioration of an old bridge
(D) A lack of sewer service to some homes

**173.** What is suggested by Ms. Majors?

(A) She often works on oceanfront structures.
(B) She was promoted due to her contributions to Clearway's construction.
(C) The Lundgate Shore is the largest project she has overseen.
(D) She based a decision about the Lundgate Shore on past experiences.

**174.** What is indicated about Perriot, LLC?

(A) It is owned by Bauright Group.
(B) It will create a public leisure area.
(C) It is running behind schedule.
(D) It submitted a bid to carry out Phase 1.

**175.** In which of the positions marked [1], [2], [3], and [4] does the following sentence best belong?

"Phase 1 finished on time and within budget."

(A) [1]
(B) [2]
(C) [3]
(D) [4]

TEST 3

*GO ON TO THE NEXT PAGE*

**Questions 176-180** refer to the following brochure and e-mail.

## ALPHA LANDSCAPING SERVICES

www.alpha-landscaping.net

Alpha Landscaping Services can help you make the most of your outdoor space as well as add value to your property. Make a great outdoor space your family can enjoy or update the appearance of your commercial site. Our services are outlined below. All of our staff members must pass a rigorous safety course, much stricter than the industry standards, so you can be confident about working with us. Contact us at info@alpha-landscaping.net for a price quote.

### MAINTENANCE

We can keep your garden looking its best with regular visits throughout the entire year. This includes mowing, trimming bushes and trees, and weeding. We are busiest from April to September, so book ahead to avoid disappointment. You can select from weekly, bi-weekly, or monthly visits.

### RESET

Book a one-time visit to tackle a neglected garden and get it back into shape for you to care for easily. If your outdoor space is getting out of control, we can help you return it to its original condition.

### DESIGN

Let one of our landscape artists design the garden of your dreams, no matter what your budget is. We'll keep adjusting the plan until it's just right. From lights and fountains to simple flower beds, we can make it happen. No garden is too big or too small for us to handle.

### RENTAL

Unlike other businesses, we allow customers to rent our garden equipment without having one of our employees hired to use it. That means you can do the work yourself and save money. Each piece of machinery comes with a clear user manual.

**E-Mail message**

To: info@alpha-landscaping.net
From: loriroth@thehomeinbox.com
Date: April 19
Subject: Services

To Whom It May Concern:

I've recently purchased a home in the Longmont neighborhood. Although I really enjoy gardening, this garden is too much for me to deal with initially. It hasn't had any care in several years, so I'd like to have your crew visit once to help get everything in order. I already have the standard tools and equipment that you would need. The sooner you can visit, the better. My colleague at Seltice Enterprises, Alex Brooks, used your services at his home and recommended you highly.

Sincerely,

Lori Roth

**176.** In the brochure, the word "update" in paragraph 1, line 2, is closest in meaning to
(A) modernize
(B) inform
(C) highlight
(D) invest

**177.** What is NOT indicated about Alpha Landscaping Services?
(A) It operates year-round.
(B) It works on gardens of any size.
(C) It is committed to safety.
(D) It is a family-owned business.

**178.** According to the brochure, what is unique about the equipment in the Rental service?
(A) It can be delivered for no additional fee.
(B) It does not require a company employee to use it.
(C) It is discounted for longer rental periods.
(D) It includes a training session on how to operate it.

**179.** What service will Ms. Roth probably use?
(A) Maintenance
(B) Reset
(C) Design
(D) Rental

**180.** What is suggested about Mr. Brooks?
(A) He currently lives in the Longmont neighborhood.
(B) He is the former owner of Ms. Roth's property.
(C) He is satisfied with Alpha Landscaping Services' work.
(D) He used to work as a professional gardener.



*GO ON TO THE NEXT PAGE*

**Questions 181-185** refer to the following article and letter.

## Medical World Magazine

**July Issue**

**Creating a Calming Waiting Room**

Attending a medical appointment provokes anxiety in many people. Follow the tips below to combat this issue by creating a relaxing space for your patients. This can foster a positive mindset in patients, easing built-up tension and making the appointment go more smoothly.

**Color Choices and Wall Décor**

➢ Use shades of blue or green to create a calming atmosphere.
➢ Decorate the walls with paintings in complementary colors, especially those with nature scenes.
➢ Restrict posters with medical information to those that are absolutely necessary.

**Layout and Furniture**

➢ Make sure the chairs and sofas have a soft covering to create a cozy and home-like feeling.
➢ Taller chairs are easy to get in and out of, which is useful for people with mobility issues.
➢ Use modular seating that can be moved into different configurations, as some people may visit alone and want privacy while others may come with family members and want to sit together.

**Sounds**

➢ Background music or nature sounds should be played at a low volume.
➢ Thick curtains can help to absorb sound and reduce echoes in a room.

Valued readers, we hope you have found these tips helpful. What would you like to learn about in future issues?

---

Medical World Magazine

Letters to the Editor

I would like to offer a correction to some information you provided about creating calming waiting rooms. While it is important for the furniture in a waiting room to be inviting and comfortable, this goal must not take precedence over health and safety considerations. Upholstery that is soft and cloth-like can absorb fluids into the underlying cushion, making it difficult to disinfect.

A better option is furniture that is covered in vinyl. It is robust, lasting over ten years with heavy use, and can be wiped down quickly and easily to remove dirt and germs. The stylish and practical furniture made by my company, Free-Form Inc., uses vinyl with an antimicrobial surface, effectively reducing the spread of disease in medical settings.

Dominic McAlister

**181.** What is NOT a suggestion made in the article?

(A) Keeping audio levels low
(B) Improving mobility through chairs with wheels
(C) Minimizing the use of medical posters
(D) Including colors that have a relaxing effect

**182.** Why is movable furniture mentioned?

(A) Because more empty floor space may be needed on some days
(B) Because the floor under the furniture should be cleaned daily
(C) Because changing the layout periodically gives a fresh appearance
(D) Because visitors may be in groups of different sizes

**183.** What is indicated about *Medical World Magazine*?

(A) It is provided to hospitals at no charge.
(B) Its editors want topic suggestions from readers.
(C) It sells some of the products mentioned in its publications.
(D) Its owner is seeking new freelance writers.

**184.** What is most likely true about Mr. McAlister?

(A) He previously worked at a medical clinic.
(B) He read the July edition of *Medical World Magazine.*
(C) He invented a new kind of textile.
(D) He spends a lot of time in waiting rooms.

**185.** What is suggested about products from Free-Form Inc.?

(A) They can be delivered quickly.
(B) They are made from recycled materials.
(C) They come with a ten-year warranty.
(D) They are easy to clean.



*GO ON TO THE NEXT PAGE*

**Questions 186-190** refer to the following e-mails and article.

| | |
|---|---|
| **To:** | Chloe Willis |
| **From:** | Steven Emery |
| **Date:** | August 19 |
| **Subject:** | Wonder Luggage |

Dear Ms. Willis,

It was a pleasure meeting you when I stopped in earlier today. As we discussed, I am looking for a new location for my luggage store. We are currently operating from a small retail unit in the Sandway Mall, but I would like to move to a larger space in its own building. A spacious display area is required, and on-site parking for customers would be a bonus. The maximum I prefer to spend on rent per month is $5,500.

I would like to have the business open at the new location by November 20, as that would allow our store to participate in the launch of Mizara's new Eco-Max luggage line. Please let me know if you find anything that would suit my needs. I am available any day next week to view possible sites.

Warmest regards,

Steven Emery
Owner, Wonder Luggage

| | |
|---|---|
| **To:** | Steven Emery |
| **From:** | Chloe Willis |
| **Date:** | August 20 |
| **Subject:** | Re: Wonder Luggage |

Dear Mr. Emery,

I have done some research on retail units that would be appropriate for your business. Please see the list below and let me know if there are any that you would like to visit in person.

1. Address: 1258 Tolliver Street
Square Footage: 7,512 / Monthly Rent: $5,500
Notes: This unit was previously owned by a clothing store, and the display area has been recently renovated.

2. Address: 908 Braxton Avenue
Square Footage: 8,940 / Monthly Rent: $5,000
Notes: The building owner requires the rental of the adjoining parking lot in a separate lease at $450 per month.

3. Address: 446 Cabell Street
Square Footage: 9,650 / Monthly Rent: $6,000
Notes: The foot traffic in this area is very high. There is a public parking area across the street.

Sincerely,

Chloe Willis
487-555-0149

## Wonder Luggage Finds New Home

by Katheryn Clark

STRAFFORD (November 10)—Wonder Luggage—an independently owned business selling a range of suitcases, roller bags, carry-on luggage, and more—held its grand re-opening yesterday at its new location. Previously operating from the Sandway Mall, the store has found a new home at 908 Braxton Avenue. It is open daily from 9 A.M. to 8 P.M.

Most of the staff members remain the same, and they can advise customers on what sort of bag to purchase. Owner Steven Emery says that he is excited about the new location and that the store will continue to sell high-quality luggage that can endure rough handling.

Shoppers will love not only the products but also the atmosphere, as the new location has large windows, so it isn't as dark as the mall unit. If you are looking for a long-lasting bag and excellent customer service, I highly recommend stopping by Wonder Luggage.

TEST 3

**186.** Where most likely does Ms. Willis work?
(A) At a luggage store
(B) At a manufacturing facility
(C) At a financial institution
(D) At a real estate firm

**187.** What is indicated about Wonder Luggage?
(A) It pays a monthly rental fee of six thousand dollars.
(B) It has a one-year lease at its new site.
(C) It is the largest luggage store in the area.
(D) It reopened in time for a product launch.

**188.** What is suggested about Mr. Emery?
(A) He is also renting a parking area.
(B) He plans to open another branch.
(C) He did not renovate a display area.
(D) He is benefitting from heavy foot traffic.

**189.** In the article, the word "endure" in paragraph 2, line 5, is closest in meaning to
(A) withstand
(B) meet
(C) permit
(D) continue

**190.** How is the new store different from the old store?
(A) It has a more convenient location.
(B) It has a brighter interior.
(C) It has longer opening hours.
(D) It has a larger display space.

*GO ON TO THE NEXT PAGE* →

**Questions 191-195** refer to the following announcement, Web page, and receipt.

## Foundation of Canadian Artists

The Foundation of Canadian Artists (FCA) is delighted to announce filmmaker Sunder Chadda as the winner of this year's FCA Achievement Award. You are invited to attend a banquet celebrating Mr. Chadda's work on Friday, 19 July, at 6:30 P.M., at the Irving Hotel in Toronto.

Mr. Chadda's documentaries have entertained and educated audiences for the past decade. The award-winning documentary *Flight* follows the migration of Canadian geese, with footage gathered near Mr. Chadda's hometown of Edmonton all the way to Santa Fe, New Mexico in the U.S. *Pushed Out* explores the effect of urbanization on the habitats of wolves. Mr. Chadda said that he made this film to emphasize how tough it is for these creatures to adapt to changes in their environment. *Two Little Cubs* centers on a polar bear raising her cubs. The film includes an interview with Helen Ortiz, a professor at Damon University.

Tickets for the event can be purchased online at www.fcartists.ca/events on or before 16 July. Admission includes a four-course dinner followed by entertainment featuring Josefina Adams. We have negotiated a special price on rooms at Irving Hotel for attendees (whether members or non-members) who plan to stay overnight in Toronto. In addition, those who sign up for the FCA newsletter can get a voucher for a free breakfast at the hotel.

http://www.irvinghotel.ca 

## Special Rate for Event Attendees: FCA Achievement Award Ceremony

Reserve a room at the Irving Hotel for the FCA Achievement Award Ceremony that will be held on July 19. Attendees to this event who stay for two nights or more can get 30% off the rate for any of our rooms! This gives you plenty of time to enjoy the event, which includes an after-dinner performance from a live band, and to spend some extra time in the beautiful city of Toronto. Our standard checkout time is 11 A.M., and guests can get an extended checkout time of noon for an additional $8.99. This fee is waived for members of the Irving Rewards Program. Make your booking no later than July 6 to take advantage of this offer.

**Irving Hotel, Toronto**
Customer Receipt

**Date:** 22 July
**Guest Name:** Raymond Frazer
**Payment:** Credit Card XXXX-XXXX-XXXX-8509

**Room:** 327
**Room Type:** Deluxe

**Check-in:** 19 July, 2:43 P.M.
**Check-out:** 22 July, 11:55 A.M.

| | | | |
|---|---|---|---|
| **Room Fee:** | $220.00 | x 3 | $660.00 |
| **Extended checkout:** | $0.00 | | $0.00 |
| **Discount:** | 30% (FCA) | | -$198.00 |
| | | **TOTAL:** | $462.00 |

++++++++++++++++++++++++++++++++++

Thank you for your patronage!

**191.** What do all of Mr. Chadda's listed films have in common?
(A) They were filmed only in Canada.
(B) They have a wildlife theme.
(C) They received funding from the FCA.
(D) They feature interviews with professors.

**192.** In the announcement, the word "tough" in paragraph 2, line 6, is closest in meaning to
(A) powerful
(B) stern
(C) challenging
(D) determined

**193.** What is indicated about customers receiving Irving Hotel's special rate?
(A) They will be offered a free breakfast.
(B) They must check in on July 16.
(C) They will occupy rooms on a certain floor.
(D) They must stay for a minimum of two nights.

**194.** Who most likely is Josefina Adams?
(A) An event planner
(B) A comedian
(C) A musician
(D) The FCA President

**195.** What is suggested about Mr. Frazer?
(A) He is a member of a rewards program.
(B) He signed up for a newsletter.
(C) He received a free room upgrade.
(D) He attended the event last year.

GO ON TO THE NEXT PAGE

**Questions 196-200** refer to the following Web page, e-mail, and survey.

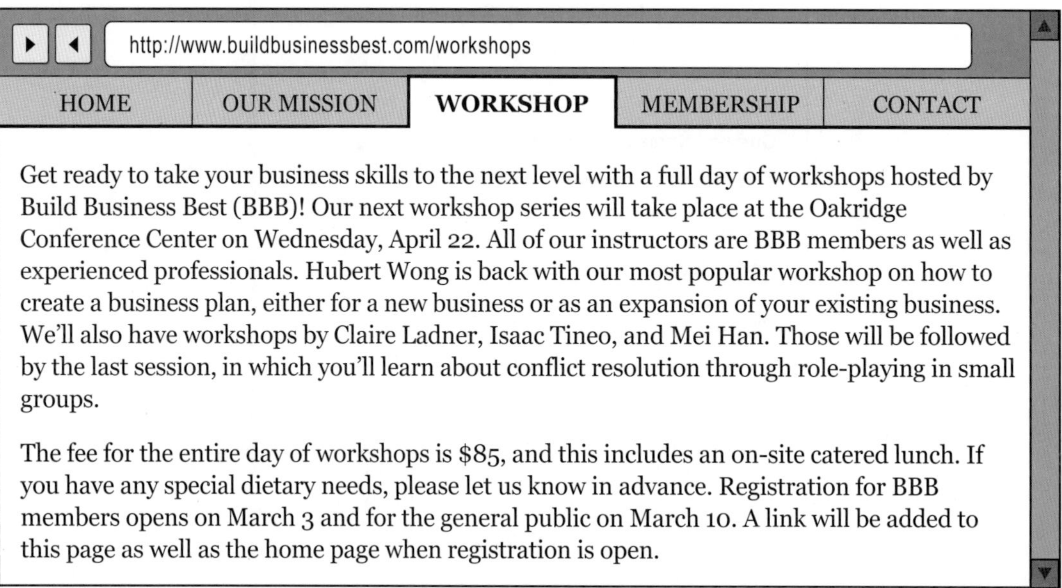

http://www.buildbusinessbest.com/workshops

HOME | OUR MISSION | **WORKSHOP** | MEMBERSHIP | CONTACT

Get ready to take your business skills to the next level with a full day of workshops hosted by Build Business Best (BBB)! Our next workshop series will take place at the Oakridge Conference Center on Wednesday, April 22. All of our instructors are BBB members as well as experienced professionals. Hubert Wong is back with our most popular workshop on how to create a business plan, either for a new business or as an expansion of your existing business. We'll also have workshops by Claire Ladner, Isaac Tineo, and Mei Han. Those will be followed by the last session, in which you'll learn about conflict resolution through role-playing in small groups.

The fee for the entire day of workshops is $85, and this includes an on-site catered lunch. If you have any special dietary needs, please let us know in advance. Registration for BBB members opens on March 3 and for the general public on March 10. A link will be added to this page as well as the home page when registration is open.

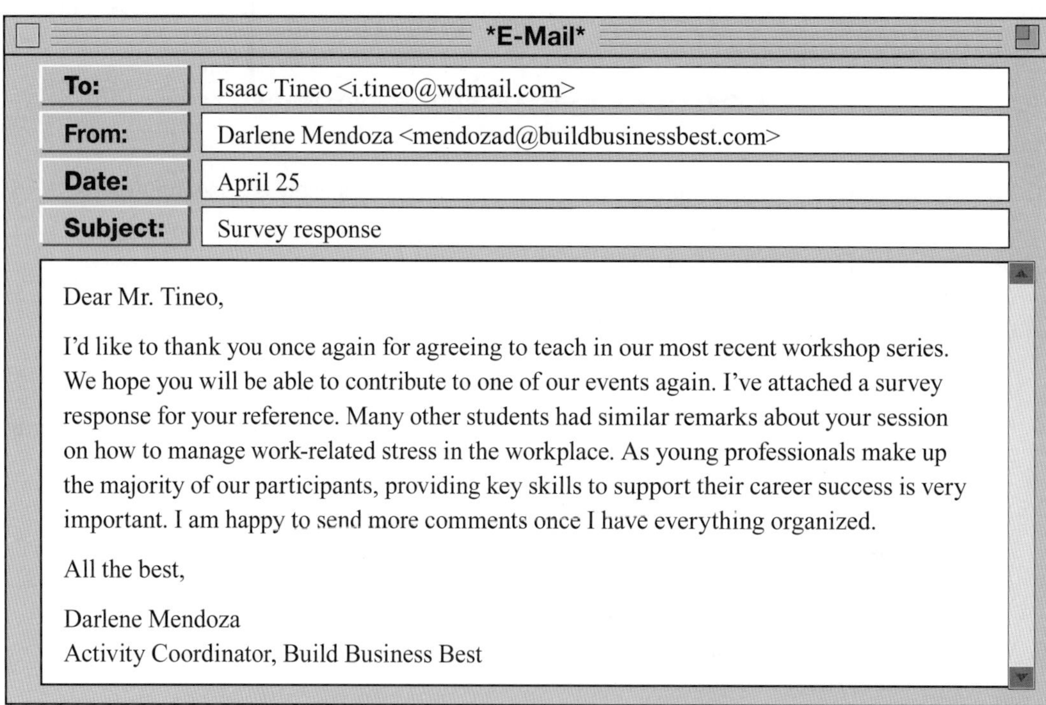

***E-Mail***

| | |
|---|---|
| **To:** | Isaac Tineo <i.tineo@wdmail.com> |
| **From:** | Darlene Mendoza <mendozad@buildbusinessbest.com> |
| **Date:** | April 25 |
| **Subject:** | Survey response |

Dear Mr. Tineo,

I'd like to thank you once again for agreeing to teach in our most recent workshop series. We hope you will be able to contribute to one of our events again. I've attached a survey response for your reference. Many other students had similar remarks about your session on how to manage work-related stress in the workplace. As young professionals make up the majority of our participants, providing key skills to support their career success is very important. I am happy to send more comments once I have everything organized.

All the best,

Darlene Mendoza
Activity Coordinator, Build Business Best

## BBB Workshop Series Feedback Survey

**Name:** Felix Roland
**Attendance Date:** April 22

**How likely are you to recommend BBB Workshops to others?**

☒ Very Likely ☐ Somewhat Likely ☐ Not Likely

**On a scale of 1 (Not Satisfied) to 5 (Very Satisfied), how would you rate the following categories?**

| | |
|---|---|
| Sign-Up Process: | 4 |
| Handouts: | 4 |
| Classroom Atmosphere: | 2 |
| Instructors' Knowledge: | 5 |
| Workshop Timing: | 5 |
| Lunch: | 5 |

**Comments:**

Overall, I believe I learned a lot from these sessions, though I had to miss the last session due to being called away on an urgent work matter. I thought the workshop on managing stress related to work was the most helpful one. My only complaint was that the classroom was very hot. This was somewhat distracting at times.

**196.** What is indicated about the workshop series?
(A) Some people can register earlier than others.
(B) BBB members are eligible for a discount.
(C) It will take place over several days.
(D) Its fee includes the cost of two meals.

**197.** Why did Ms. Mendoza send the e-mail?
(A) To ask for a survey to be completed
(B) To provide an instructor with feedback
(C) To confirm the date of the next session
(D) To suggest a new topic for instruction

**198.** In the e-mail, the phrase "make up" in paragraph 1, line 4, is closest in meaning to
(A) fill
(B) prepare
(C) invent
(D) comprise

**199.** What is suggested about Mr. Roland?
(A) He thought some noise was distracting.
(B) He has recommended the workshops to others.
(C) He did not participate in a role-play activity.
(D) He gave the handouts the top rating.

**200.** Which instructor's session did Mr. Roland find most helpful?
(A) Hubert Wong
(B) Claire Ladner
(C) Isaac Tineo
(D) Mei Han

**Stop! This is the end of the test. If you finish before time is called, you may go back to Parts 5, 6, and 7 and check your work.**

# YBM
# 실전토익
# RC 1000

**테스트 전 체크리스트**

- 중간 휴식 없이 제한 시간을 지켜서 풀이하세요.
- 제한 시간은 답안지에 마킹하는 시간도 포함시켜야 합니다.
- 찍은 문제는 번호 옆에 꼭 체크해 주세요.
- 시간 안에 풀지 못한 문제는 틀린 것으로 채점해 주세요.

# RC TEST 4

## READING TEST

In the Reading test, you will read a variety of texts and answer several different types of reading comprehension questions. The entire Reading test will last 75 minutes. There are three parts, and directions are given for each part. You are encouraged to answer as many questions as possible within the time allowed.

You must mark your answers on the separate answer sheet. Do not write your answers in your test book.

## PART 5

**Directions:** A word or phrase is missing in each of the sentences below. Four answer choices are given below each sentence. Select the best answer to complete the sentence. Then mark the letter (A), (B), (C), or (D) on your answer sheet.

**101.** Each participant in the debate will have an ------- amount of speaking time.

(A) equality
(B) equally
(C) equals
(D) equal

**102.** A recent study by Melbourne University researchers ------- that blue-light glasses may not actually prevent eye strain.

(A) suggestively
(B) suggestive
(C) suggests
(D) suggestion

**103.** New employees at Mathias Incorporated are allowed just one week of vacation time ------- their first year of work.

(A) as
(B) under
(C) during
(D) between

**104.** Next summer, all guests at Ankville-area hotels ------- a booklet of coupons for local attractions.

(A) offered
(B) will be offered
(C) were offered
(D) have been offering

**105.** Glintech's flagship mobile ------- has been downloaded by over 10 million people.

(A) application
(B) device
(C) data
(D) user

**106.** ------- to luggage sold by luxury fashion brands, the Naviga suitcase is remarkably elegant and well made.

(A) Comparable
(B) Comparably
(C) Compares
(D) Comparison

**107.** ------- its neighboring cities, where housing is now fairly expensive, Finley has not seen a rise in its real estate prices.

(A) Unlike
(B) Given
(C) Except
(D) Throughout

**108.** Yowton City's plans to build a wind farm were canceled in ------- to opposition from residents.

(A) responding
(B) responded
(C) response
(D) responses

109. Please postpone personal phone calls and text messaging until ------- scheduled break time.

(A) you
(B) your
(C) yours
(D) yourself

110. Lighthouse Pizza servers are instructed to notify a manager ------- a customer complains about the quality of the food.

(A) if
(B) since
(C) unless
(D) now that

111. Ms. Waggoner has directed the billing department to keep any ------- with clients regarding payment.

(A) correspondent
(B) correspondence
(C) corresponded
(D) corresponds

112. The mentorship program connects new hires with senior employees to the ------- benefit of both parties.

(A) central
(B) mutual
(C) inclusive
(D) expert

113. Candidates for marketing positions must demonstrate knowledge ------- our company's products.

(A) toward
(B) by
(C) of
(D) within

114. Though the amusement park remains open year-round, its hours are reduced ------- for the winter season.

(A) slight
(B) slightly
(C) slightest
(D) slighter

115. In spite of the high temperatures outdoors on the day of our appointment, Ms. Delvay ------- inspected the exterior of the property.

(A) considerably
(B) highly
(C) wholly
(D) thoroughly

116. The marble flooring in Nomura Tower's lobby is waxed ------- six months.

(A) all
(B) many
(C) another
(D) every

117. Demand for public transportation has grown ------- the capacity of the city's current infrastructure.

(A) into
(B) up
(C) plus
(D) beyond

118. To arrange a special tour of the museum ------- our normal opening hours, please call 555-0149.

(A) or
(B) while
(C) outside
(D) without

119. Because of staffing difficulties, the grand opening of our second store location must be ------- by a few days.

(A) constructed
(B) determined
(C) situated
(D) postponed

120. All component parts of Lowry automatic doors are ------- for easy replacement.

(A) standardizing
(B) standardized
(C) standardizes
(D) standardization

TEST 4

*GO ON TO THE NEXT PAGE* →

**121.** ------- placing a large order on our Web site, call the customer service line regarding bulk discounts and current stock levels.

(A) Although
(B) Anytime
(C) Before
(D) Rather

**122.** To accommodate students with limited -------, the Ault Language Institute permits flexible scheduling of its individual classes.

(A) proficiency
(B) budgets
(C) materials
(D) availability

**123.** We always ask participants beforehand about their particular interests and adjust the workshop's focus -------.

(A) consequently
(B) accordingly
(C) popularly
(D) tightly

**124.** Due to safety concerns, the Ladner Corporation has made a ------- decision to recall some models of its bicycle tires.

(A) volunteer
(B) volunteered
(C) volunteering
(D) voluntary

**125.** The Gimdan Company supplies ------- industries, including packaging, automotive, and construction, with made-to-order plastics.

(A) numerous
(B) instant
(C) usual
(D) utmost

**126.** Marcum Limited's distribution ------- is currently advertising multiple openings for experienced truck drivers.

(A) division
(B) policy
(C) network
(D) strategy

**127.** Staff at Haney Supermarket may ------- their uniform shirt for one in a different size at no charge once per year.

(A) alter
(B) request
(C) exchange
(D) purchase

**128.** If anyone ------- will be accompanying you to the party, please tell one of the organizers in advance.

(A) over
(B) other
(C) as well
(D) else

**129.** Repairs to the electrical system at Perron Hospital must be ------- by a licensed electrician.

(A) performed
(B) signed
(C) committed
(D) established

**130.** ------- caused the blockage in the breakroom sink was dissolved by the drain cleaning solution.

(A) Whatever
(B) Which
(C) Anything
(D) Who

## PART 6

**Directions:** Read the texts that follow. A word, phrase, or sentence is missing in parts of each text. Four answer choices for each question are given below the text. Select the best answer to complete the text. Then mark the letter (A), (B), (C), or (D) on your answer sheet.

**Questions 131-134** refer to the following notice.

Let's Use our Fitness Center Properly!

In order to keep enjoying the perk of having an onsite company fitness center, ------- **131.** must agree to use it neatly and respectfully. ------- **132.** . While exercising, kindly ------- **133.** your gym bag in the locker room. Do not bring in any food or drinks other than bottled water, and wear headphones to listen to audio content. Use the provided paper towels and cleaning spray to wipe down ------ **134.** immediately after use. Finally, if you are the last one to use the fitness room in the evening, please turn off the lights afterward. Thank you.

**131.** (A) each other
(B) somebody
(C) everybody
(D) they

**132.** (A) Please make an effort to do all of the following.
(B) Choose healthy meal options in the cafeteria.
(C) You may take an aerobics or weightlifting class.
(D) Tidy your desk at the end of each workday.

**133.** (A) left
(B) leave
(C) leaves
(D) leaving

**134.** (A) tools
(B) counters
(C) equipment
(D) vehicles

TEST 4

*GO ON TO THE NEXT PAGE*

**Questions 135-138** refer to the following advertisement.

Do You Want to Perfect Your Garden?

This spring, let Rutherford Garden Center help you create the garden of your dreams! Choose from among our ample collection of flowers, vegetables, herbs, shrubs, and more. ------- **135.** , pick up the appropriate supplies, from rich fertilizer to gardening implements. We even have unique decorative items! ------- **136.** . Our friendly, knowledgeable employees are happy to advise you ------- **137.** what to buy and how to tend your new plants.

All seedlings and starter plants at Rutherford Garden Center have received all ------- **138.** care and nourishment. We will not sell you a plant that is less than 100% healthy. Visit us today to see for yourself!

**135.** (A) Then
(B) At last
(C) Instead
(D) In that case

**136.** (A) Are you concerned about transporting your purchases?
(B) What other local nursery offers such great deals?
(C) Are you searching for a particular exotic plant?
(D) Will this be your first time planting a garden?

**137.** (A) from
(B) in
(C) on
(D) to

**138.** (A) recommending
(B) recommends
(C) recommended
(D) recommendation

**Questions 139-142** refer to the following announcement.

Valued Guests of Adler Hotel:

Please be advised that we will begin refurbishing the hotel swimming pool from 27 November. After being ------- (139.) drained, it will be resurfaced and repainted. ------- (140.). Any activities that may cause loud noise will be confined to the hours between 10 A.M. and 5 P.M. However, the pool and poolside areas will be completely off-limits to guests at all times during this project. The reopening of these facilities ------- (141.) for 8 December. ------- (142.), guests may use the swimming pool at Adler Plaza, our sister property at Logsdon Point. Please visit the concierge desk for details.

**139.** (A) quite
(B) fully
(C) further
(D) regularly

**140.** (A) Luckily, our hotel has other family-friendly facilities.
(B) We have not yet set a start date for the project.
(C) We do not expect this work to disturb your stay.
(D) The pool's new color will be an attractive light blue.

**141.** (A) schedule
(B) scheduled
(C) was scheduled
(D) is scheduled

**142.** (A) In the meantime
(B) On the contrary
(C) Specifically
(D) Besides



*GO ON TO THE NEXT PAGE*

**Questions 143-146** refer to the following article.

SANDLIN (January 25)—The Sandlin Main Street Association (SMSA) has been accepted into the Downtown Oregon Program. A statewide initiative, the program ------- **143.** efforts to revitalize the traditional centers of small- and mid-sized towns. Participating groups represent downtown areas ------- **144.** there is a cluster of historic commercial and public buildings. Through the program, they are given access to ------- **145.** grants, as well as training on subjects like development and advertising.

------ **146.** . With assistance from the program, the association will continue working to attract businesses and visitors to downtown Sandlin through projects including building renovations and community events.

**143.** (A) supports
(B) supported
(C) would support
(D) was supporting

**144.** (A) near
(B) so
(C) that
(D) where

**145.** (A) noticeable
(B) exclusive
(C) vacant
(D) fortunate

**146.** (A) The SMSA does not yet have the capacity to employ full-time staff.
(B) The SMSA has already brought new life to Main Street in recent years.
(C) Sandlin's Main Street is more walkable than those in neighboring towns.
(D) The Downtown Oregon Program has a rigorous application process.

## PART 7

**Directions:** In this part you will read a selection of texts, such as magazine and newspaper articles, e-mails, and instant messages. Each text or set of texts is followed by several questions. Select the best answer for each question and mark the letter (A), (B), (C), or (D) on your answer sheet.

**Questions 147-148** refer to the following e-mail.

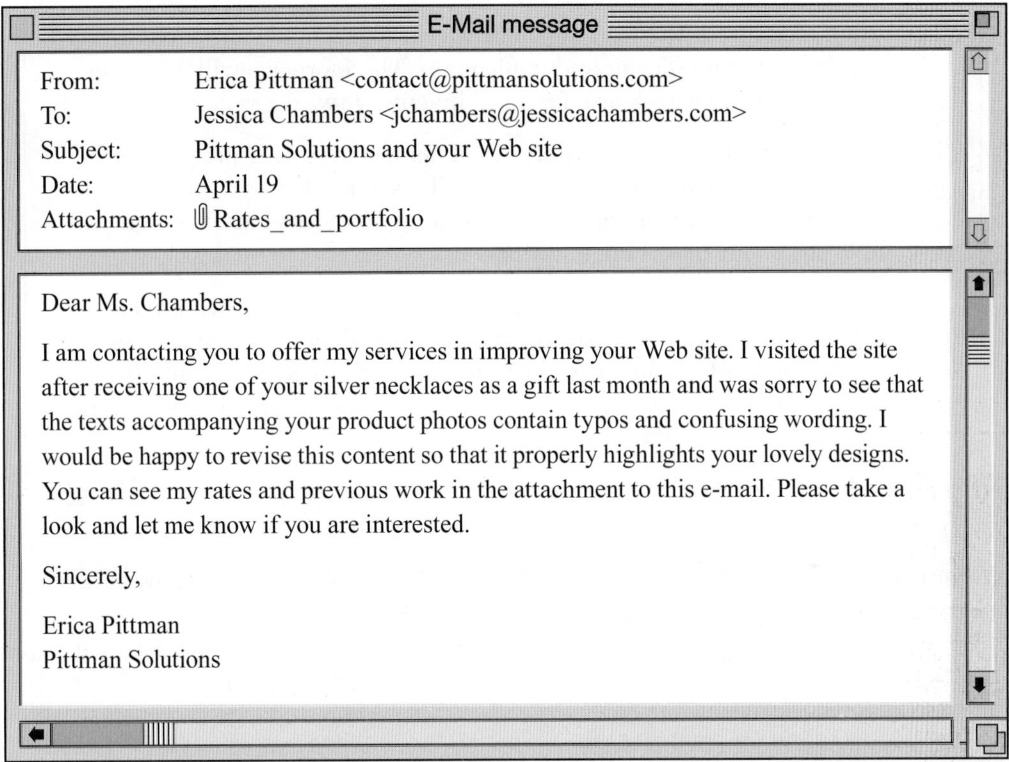

E-Mail message

From: Erica Pittman <contact@pittmansolutions.com>
To: Jessica Chambers <jchambers@jessicachambers.com>
Subject: Pittman Solutions and your Web site
Date: April 19
Attachments: Rates_and_portfolio

Dear Ms. Chambers,

I am contacting you to offer my services in improving your Web site. I visited the site after receiving one of your silver necklaces as a gift last month and was sorry to see that the texts accompanying your product photos contain typos and confusing wording. I would be happy to revise this content so that it properly highlights your lovely designs. You can see my rates and previous work in the attachment to this e-mail. Please take a look and let me know if you are interested.

Sincerely,

Erica Pittman
Pittman Solutions

**147.** Who most likely is Ms. Chambers?

(A) A clothing designer
(B) A picture framer
(C) A cake decorator
(D) A jewelry maker

**148.** What is Ms. Pittman offering to do for Ms. Chambers?

(A) Advertise a business in a publication
(B) Retouch some digital photographs
(C) Edit some product descriptions
(D) Add special features to a Web site

GO ON TO THE NEXT PAGE

**Questions 149-150** refer to the following memo.

## MEMO

To: Greegan Electronics warehouse staff
From: Kiriko Ishii, Warehouse Manager
Date: September 24, 2:30 P.M.
Subject: Warehouse inventory process

The recent increase in the range of stock we carry has made our current way of taking inventory inefficient and inadequate. Therefore, we will no longer shut down the entire warehouse for a full inventory twice a year.

Instead, we will begin taking inventories of defined groups of products either once a quarter, twice a year, or once a year. This will allow the warehouse to remain at least partially operational year-round and focus our attention on keeping track of our most valuable stock.

A project team is currently determining the classifications of each product. Group A will comprise the top 20% of products based on a combination of cost per unit and order frequency, with the next 40% in Group B and the final 40% in Group C. Once the classifications have been assigned, the first inventory of Group A will begin.

**149.** What is the purpose of the memo?

(A) To give details about the temporary shutdown of a warehouse
(B) To report a recommendation made by an external consultant
(C) To announce a more efficient system for inventorying goods
(D) To describe inaccuracies found in some stock records

**150.** According to the memo, what is being decided now?

(A) Which products are the most valuable to the company
(B) When a change to a process will be implemented
(C) Where some new merchandise will be stored
(D) Who will be assigned to lead a project team

**Questions 151-152** refer to the following text-message chain.

**Reggie Norris [11:06 A.M.]**
Hi, Sarah. I finally got an appointment to see a very busy doctor this Friday, so I'm looking for someone to take my shift at the store that day. Could you come in that afternoon?

**Sarah Klein [11:07 A.M.]**
I'll have to check my calendar. Hold on.

**Sarah Klein [11:09 A.M.]**
OK, I thought I was supposed to meet a friend for coffee then, but it turns out that's next Friday. But I've never worked hours that aren't on my schedule before—do we need to get Ms. Evans's approval?

**Reggie Norris [11:10 A.M.]**
I'll call her now. Thank you so much, Sarah!

**Sarah Klein [11:11 A.M.]**
No problem!

**151.** At 11:07 A.M., what does Ms. Klein imply when she writes, "I'll have to check my calendar"?

(A) She thinks she has been scheduled for too many shifts.
(B) She may not have time to attend a doctor's appointment.
(C) She forgot where she is supposed to have a coffee meeting.
(D) She cannot agree right away to work additional hours.

**152.** Who most likely will Mr. Norris call?

(A) A store manager
(B) A friend of Ms. Klein's
(C) A scheduler at a medical office
(D) A café worker

TEST 4

*GO ON TO THE NEXT PAGE* →

**Questions 153-154** refer to the following advertisement.

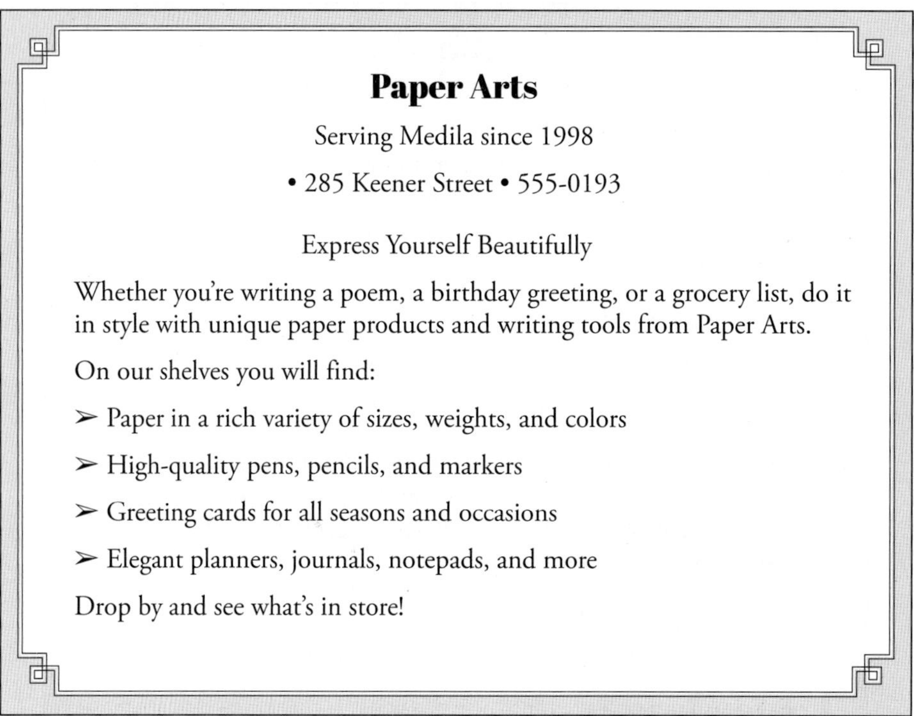

Paper Arts
Serving Medila since 1998
• 285 Keener Street • 555-0193
Express Yourself Beautifully
Whether you're writing a poem, a birthday greeting, or a grocery list, do it in style with unique paper products and writing tools from Paper Arts.
On our shelves you will find:
➢ Paper in a rich variety of sizes, weights, and colors
➢ High-quality pens, pencils, and markers
➢ Greeting cards for all seasons and occasions
➢ Elegant planners, journals, notepads, and more
Drop by and see what's in store!



**153.** What type of business is Paper Arts?

(A) A print shop
(B) A publishing agency
(C) A stationery store
(D) An art school

**154.** What information about Paper Arts is included in the advertisement?

(A) The name of its owner
(B) The year it opened
(C) The address of its Web site
(D) The number of branches it has

**Questions 155-157** refer to the following information.

## Save Money with Zipply Split

Millions of people across the country have come to depend on the Zipply app to quickly find rides for trips within their city. Now, Zipply is proud to begin offering similar convenience at even more affordable rates through Zipply Split. Zipply Split lets you receive up to 20% off your trip by simply sharing your ride with another Zipply user heading in a similar direction.

**Details:**

- Use Zipply Split by selecting it from among the ride options that appear once you input your destination.
- The discount percentage is calculated based on the time and distance traveled with your co-rider.
- Any required changes to your route will add no more than ten minutes to your trip.
- This service is not yet available in all cities in which Zipply is active.

Try Zipply Split for your next ride and see how much you save!

**155.** What is the Zipply app intended to help users do?

(A) Have food delivered
(B) Travel short distances
(C) Send money to others
(D) Communicate with their neighbors

**156.** The word "active" in paragraph 2, line 7, is closest in meaning to

(A) operating
(B) successful
(C) energetic
(D) participating

**157.** What is mentioned about the Zipply Split option?

(A) It is offered in cities throughout the country.
(B) It can be used after adjusting a display setting.
(C) The maximum delay it will cause is ten minutes.
(D) The discount amount varies by the number of people.

TEST 4

*GO ON TO THE NEXT PAGE*

**Questions 158-160** refer to the following e-mail.

***E-Mail***

| | |
|---|---|
| **From:** | <amelia.jackson@atmosrecords.com> |
| **To:** | <marcus.hawkins@mhawkinsartist.com> |
| **Subject:** | Album artwork opportunity |
| **Date:** | August 14 |

Dear Mr. Hawkins,

I am the art director for Atmos Records, and I am writing to ask whether you would consider creating the cover art for an album we are producing. It is Chris Embry's follow-up to *Rain Tomorrow*, which you may be aware was one of the top-selling albums of last year. The new album does not yet have a title, but it deals with themes of youth and friendship. — [1] —. I remembered that your photographs also explore these subjects, so I showed Chris the gallery page on your Web site. He loved your work and was very excited about the idea of collaborating. — [2] —. We are particularly interested in the possibility of recreating your *Dawn Fields* series of photos. — [3] —.

If you would like to become involved in this project or just want to know more, please get in touch. — [4] —. We hope to hear from you.

Sincerely,

Amelia Jackson
Atmos Records
(310) 555-0174

**158.** What is true about *Rain Tomorrow*?

(A) It is Mr. Embry's previous album.
(B) Its cover art is famous.
(C) It is currently in production.
(D) It features a guest performance by Mr. Hawkins.

**159.** What does the e-mail indicate about Ms. Jackson?

(A) She wants to improve Mr. Embry's Web site.
(B) She used to be a photographer.
(C) She attended an exhibition at an art gallery.
(D) She introduced Mr. Embry to Mr. Hawkins's work.

**160.** In which of the positions marked [1], [2], [3], and [4] does the following sentence best belong?

"However, we are also open to alternative ideas you might have."

(A) [1]
(B) [2]
(C) [3]
(D) [4]

**Questions 161-163** refer to the following Web page.

https://www.lmm.org.uk/exhibitions/structures_ancient_greece

***Structures of Ancient Greece***

On 2 June, the London Metropolitan Museum (LMM) will unveil *Structures of Ancient Greece*, an exhibition on the civilization's houses, temples, theatres, stadiums, and more. Scheduled to last through the end of the year, the exhibition will include large-scale replicas of famous buildings as well as archaeological artefacts drawn from the museum's own collection or generously loaned by the Greek Cultural Institute of England.

After an invitation-only launch party on its opening night, *Structures of Ancient Greece* will be accessible to all museumgoers for no extra fee from 3 June. The LMM has also engaged local experts for related lectures and a special tour on Wednesdays of the exhibition's first three weeks. On 9 June, Dr. Lorna Stewart will describe the theory behind the design of Greek temples. The following week, Dr. Shahara Bakir will explain how building materials such as marble were extracted from the earth, while Mr. David Wiley will introduce the techniques and tools used in construction on 23 June. Professor Yiorgos Galanis will lead a tour of the exhibition immediately after each lecture.

**161.** The word "drawn" in paragraph 1, line 5, is closest in meaning to
(A) attracted
(B) depicted
(C) concluded
(D) gathered

**162.** What is NOT indicated about the exhibition?
(A) It will be included in the cost of a museum ticket.
(B) It will run at the LMM for more than six months.
(C) It was previously mounted in another country.
(D) It will feature reproductions of well-known buildings.

**163.** Who will most likely discuss mining?
(A) Dr. Stewart
(B) Dr. Bakir
(C) Mr. Wiley
(D) Professor Galanis

*GO ON TO THE NEXT PAGE*

**Questions 164-167** refer to the following article.

## Streamer Looks to the Past

LOS ANGELES (July 30)—In recent months, subscription streaming service Cinematix has released or announced plans for several series based on previous films and television series. The trend is believed to be an attempt by new CEO Irina Zaitseva to attract new subscribers from among fans of the original content.

One successful example has been *Happier Home*, the continuation of *Happy Home*, a family comedy that aired its final episode 30 years ago. Many stars of the original show, including Joyce Schott, agreed to reprise their characters for *Happier Home*. Ms. Zaitseva claimed that the series was Cinematix's most watched in June, the month of its premiere.

However, the controversy over Cinematix's planned remake of *Star Seekers* demonstrates a downside of this programming approach. Mark Simmons, the new series' producer, declared in a recent interview that his version of this story of a spaceship exploring other planets would outdo the original show by featuring state-of-the-art special effects. Outraged fans have responded that Mr. Simmons is misunderstanding what made the original so beloved.

"The 1980s *Star Seekers* was special because of its optimistic worldview, not fancy technology," says Lily Colwell, moderator of the Web forum Star Seeker Alliance. "A lot of our members will cancel their Cinematix subscriptions if it harms that legacy."

**164.** What is the purpose of the article?

(A) To discuss a market strategy of a media company
(B) To provide an overview of a streaming service's catalogue
(C) To examine the career history of a business's new leader
(D) To compare past and present forms of entertainment

**165.** What is true about both Ms. Schott and Mr. Simmons?

(A) They have been hired to act in Cinematix productions.
(B) They have recently given interviews about their work.
(C) Some of their output is now available for streaming on Cinematix.
(D) They are involved in series based on relatively old content.

**166.** What is the genre of Mr. Simmons's series?

(A) Family drama
(B) Science fiction
(C) Talent competition
(D) Travel documentary

**167.** What is implied about some customers of Ms. Zaitseva's company?

(A) They complained about a show's poor special effects.
(B) They suggested remaking *Star Seekers*.
(C) They use their subscriptions to watch classic films.
(D) They belong to Ms. Colwell's online group.

**Questions 168-171** refer to the following e-mail.

**E-Mail message**

| | |
|---|---|
| **From:** | Jane Hughes <jhughes@keating-cs.com> |
| **To:** | Santosh Prasad <sprasad@who-mail.com> |
| **Date:** | March 1 |
| **Subject:** | Reply from Keating Capital Solutions |

Dear Mr. Prasad,

We are pleased that you have agreed to join Keating Capital Solutions as a network security engineer. — [1] —. It is clear from your interviews, skills test results, and references that you will make a valuable addition to the information technology team. As such, I am happy to accommodate your request to postpone your start date so that you can go on your previously planned vacation. — [2] —.

We will therefore plan to see you at our office at 9 A.M. on Monday, March 27. — [3] —. Please bring photo identification and information about your bank account so that you can fill out the necessary tax and payroll forms. Kelly Moss, one of our human resources generalists, will walk you through this paperwork in the morning. — [4] —. Ms. Moss will also familiarize you with our workplace policies and resources for employees. When she is done, I will begin your position-specific training.

Please reply to confirm that you have received this message. I am also happy to answer any questions you may have.

Sincerely,

Jane Hughes, Director of Information Technology

**168.** Why did Ms. Hughs send the e-mail?

(A) To set a deadline for the submission of some documents
(B) To explain the results of some hiring interviews
(C) To respond to a question about a staff policy
(D) To give information about a first workday

**169.** What is suggested about Mr. Prasad?

(A) He will visit his bank on March 27.
(B) He was praised by his job references.
(C) He has just returned from a vacation.
(D) He requested a flexible work schedule.

**170.** What is mentioned about Ms. Moss?

(A) She will issue an identification badge.
(B) She is revising an employee handbook.
(C) She will oversee the completion of some forms.
(D) She is in charge of evaluating job applications.

**171.** In which of the positions marked [1], [2], [3], and [4] does the following sentence best belong?

"I hope you have a nice time."

(A) [1]
(B) [2]
(C) [3]
(D) [4]

*GO ON TO THE NEXT PAGE*

**Questions 172-175** refer to the following online chat discussion.

**Camille Bordelon [10:13 A.M.]**
Ready to make our pitch to Espino?

**Jiro Furukawa [10:14 A.M.]**
Yes! And I'll go get the company credit card from Brian now so that we can leave for lunch immediately after the meeting.

**Camille Bordelon [10:15 A.M.]**
Good idea.

**Brian McCoy [10:17 A.M.]**
Hi, Camille. I'm here with Jiro. I'm sorry, but Audra has already signed out the company card, so you two won't be able to use it for your lunch.

**Camille Bordelon [10:18 A.M.]**
Oh no! I told the Espino representatives that we would take them out.

**Brian McCoy [10:19 A.M.]**
Well, Earling Kitchen has our card on file for delivery orders. You'd have to eat in the conference room, but at least the food would be very good.

**Camille Bordelon [10:20 A.M.]**
I guess there's no choice.

**Brian McCoy [10:21 A.M.]**
I'm giving Jiro a copy of their delivery menu. Let me know what you would like, and I'll call when they open.

**Camille Bordelon [10:21 A.M.]**
Thanks, Brian.

**172.** What is probably true about Ms. Bordelon and Mr. Furukawa?

(A) They are preparing a financial report.
(B) They are about to host some potential clients.
(C) They are celebrating the conclusion of a sales agreement.
(D) They are making arrangements for an office party.

**173.** Why are Ms. Bordelon and Mr. Furukawa unable to use the company credit card?

(A) They did not obtain permission in advance.
(B) Its spending limit has been exceeded.
(C) Only executives may make purchases with it.
(D) A coworker has already borrowed it.

**174.** At 10:20 A.M., what does Ms. Bordelon most likely mean when she writes, "I guess there's no choice"?

(A) She will accept a change of plan for a meal.
(B) She knows that Earling Kitchen is the best nearby eatery.
(C) She thinks the neighborhood lacks attractive dining options.
(D) She will set up a conference room by herself.

**175.** Why does Mr. McCoy want the others to look at a menu?

(A) To see images of a restaurant's interior
(B) To check a pricing range
(C) To determine a food order
(D) To verify some opening hours



GO ON TO THE NEXT PAGE

**Questions 176-180** refer to the following e-mail and schedule.

| | |
|---|---|
| **To:** | Laura Gonzales <lauragonzales@fig-mail.com> |
| **From:** | Roy Chastain <rchastain@burgess.edu> |
| **Date:** | March 18 |
| **Subject:** | Re: Invitation |

Dear Ms. Gonzales,

The Diversity, Equity & Inclusion Committee is delighted that you have accepted our invitation to join other Burgess alumni next month to discuss your career experiences as a first-generation university graduate. As many of Burgess University's current first-generation students are education majors, we expect that they will be eager to hear your perspective as someone already working in the classroom. We hope you will be able to stay for the catered reception after the discussion, as well, so that you have a chance to mingle with the students.

Regarding your question, we will not be able to reimburse you for transportation, unfortunately. The free campus shuttle bus to and from Burgess University Subway Station runs quite frequently now, so I recommend using that. As you can see from the attachment, the Sikes Building, our venue, is just across the street from the Central Library. Please arrive there by 4:30 P.M. to allow ample time for preparations before the event begins at 5:00 P.M.

Sincerely,

Roy Chastain

## Burgess University Campus Shuttle Bus

**Direction:** Burgess University Subway Station → Campus

**Stops and Departure Times**

| Burgess University Subway Station | North Gate | Central Library | College of Medicine | Shaw Dormitory |
|---|---|---|---|---|
| 4:00 P.M. | 4:15 P.M. | 4:21 P.M. | 4:25 P.M. | 4:28 P.M. |
| 4:15 P.M. | 4:30 P.M. | 4:36 P.M. | 4:40 P.M. | 4:43 P.M. |
| 4:30 P.M. | 4:45 P.M. | 4:51 P.M. | 4:55 P.M. | 4:58 P.M. |
| 4:45 P.M. | 5:00 P.M. | 5:06 P.M. | 5:10 P.M. | 5:13 P.M. |

*Shuttle buses run less frequently during the summer and winter. Visit www.burgess.edu/campus/shuttle or download the iBurgess app for up-to-date schedules as well as information about service disruptions.

**176.** What event will Ms. Gonzales participate in next month?

(A) A career fair
(B) A class reunion
(C) A panel discussion
(D) An academic conference

**177.** Who most likely is Ms. Gonzales?

(A) A university student
(B) A job recruiter
(C) A researcher
(D) An educator

**178.** What most likely is in the e-mail attachment?

(A) A campus map
(B) A catering menu
(C) A list of participants
(D) A registration form

**179.** What time will Ms. Gonzales most likely board a shuttle bus?

(A) 4:00 P.M.
(B) 4:15 P.M.
(C) 4:30 P.M.
(D) 4:45 P.M.

**180.** What does the schedule indicate about the shuttle buses?

(A) Some of them skip certain stops.
(B) Their frequency changes seasonally.
(C) One is out of service at the moment.
(D) Their locations are viewable in real time on an app.



*GO ON TO THE NEXT PAGE* →

**Questions 181-185** refer to the following Web page and e-mail.

## Albrecht Palace

**Information for Visitors**

An elegant example of seventeenth-century Saxony architecture surrounded by beautiful gardens, Albrecht Palace is open from 10 A.M. to 5 P.M. every day except Mondays and holidays. It is roughly twenty minutes from the city of Dresden by intercity bus. Drivers should leave their cars in the nearby town of Possendorf and take the shuttle bus that leaves from Hotel Oelsa.

| Ticket Types | Price | Provides |
|---|---|---|
| Saver | €5.00 | Provides access to the palace grounds |
| Standard | €12.00 | Provides Saver access AND audio tour of select first-floor rooms |
| Plus | €20.00 | Provides Standard access AND admission to the special exhibitions hall |
| Premium | €27.00 | Provides Plus access AND guided tour of select rooms on upper floors |

**Upcoming Special Exhibitions:**

Saxon Style: Local Clothing over Time (1 April – 31 May)
Royal Faces: Oil Portraits of Albrecht's Rulers (1 June – 31 July)
On the Table: 17th-Century Saxon Cuisine (1 August – 30 September)
Hooved Friends: Horses at Albrecht (1 October – 30 November)

**To:** visitor.info@albrechtpalace.de
**From:** n.romero@etn.eu
**Date:** 4 January
**Subject:** Inquiry

Hello,

My name is Naomi Romero, and I work for the European Textile Network (ETN). The ETN aims to advance the expertise of Europe's textile industry professionals by providing them with education and networking opportunities.

This year, our annual conference will take place in Dresden on 21–24 May, and we hope to offer attendees an excursion to Albrecht Palace. They would enjoy the special exhibition that will be running then. But—do you allow large groups to join the guided tours? We would really like participants to be able to see the famous tapestries and bed coverings in the rooms on the upper floors. We will limit the number of excursion participants, if necessary, to make this possible.

I hope to hear from you soon.

Sincerely,

Naomi Romero
Coordinator, ETN

**181.** What is suggested about Albrecht Palace?

(A) Its gift shop is popular.
(B) Its hours change seasonally.
(C) It is located in the middle of a city.
(D) It does not provide parking for tourists.

**182.** What is NOT the subject of an upcoming special exhibition?

(A) A style of furniture
(B) A type of animal
(C) Paintings of people
(D) An area's fashion trends

**183.** What is the purpose of the e-mail?

(A) To ask about a restriction on visitors
(B) To propose a documentary project
(C) To inquire about borrowing historic items
(D) To offer assistance with a special exhibition

**184.** According to the e-mail, what is the ETN?

(A) A history club
(B) A manufacturing company
(C) A professional association
(D) A media outlet

**185.** What type of ticket will members of the ETN group most likely need?

(A) Saver
(B) Standard
(C) Plus
(D) Premium



*GO ON TO THE NEXT PAGE*

**Questions 186-190** refer to the following conference schedule and e-mails.

**National Digital Marketing Association (NDMA)**
Fall Conference
Schedule for October 7, afternoon block

<table>
<tr><td>Location</td><td>1:00 P.M.</td><td>2:00 P.M.</td><td>3:00 P.M.</td><td>4:00 P.M.</td></tr>
<tr><td>Main Hall</td><td colspan="2">Content Creation With AI Tools (Presentation)</td><td colspan="2">Climb the Search Rankings (Presentation)</td></tr>
<tr><td>Seminar Room A</td><td colspan="3">Marketing Experimentation: Three Case Studies (Presentation)</td><td>Building Strong Client Relationships (Panel discussion)</td></tr>
<tr><td>Seminar Room B</td><td>Harnessing Big Data (Seminar)</td><td>Uses of Short-form Video (Seminar)</td><td>Effective E-mail Campaigns (Seminar)</td><td>Finding the Right Influencers (Seminar)</td></tr>
<tr><td>Terrace</td><td>Red Rabbit Marketing Solutions (Sponsored demonstration)</td><td>Networking break</td><td colspan="2">Interactive Display Technology (Exhibition)</td></tr>
</table>

**E-Mail message**

| | |
|---|---|
| **From:** | Julianne Franks |
| **To:** | Jong-Jin Ahn |
| **Date:** | October 7 |
| **Subject:** | Great job! |
| **Attachment:** | Participant_Paperwork |

Hi Jong-Jin,

Thank you again for agreeing to moderate the afternoon panel after Vince became ill. I just got a chance to see the video of the event, and I was so impressed. Glen Stanley can be a difficult panelist because of his talkativeness, but you handled him very skillfully. I could tell by their applause that the audience really enjoyed the discussion, and that was largely thanks to you.

Also, in our hurry to get you on stage, we forgot to have you complete the participant paperwork, which includes a consent form allowing the NDMA to use recordings of your participation. I've attached it to this e-mail. Could you fill it out and return it so that we can post the event video online?

Thanks,

Julianne

| | |
|---|---|
| **From:** | Annika Lindstrom |
| **To:** | Jong-Jin Ahn |
| **Date:** | November 23 |
| **Subject:** | Reaching out |

Dear Mr. Ahn,

I am a reporter for the online business magazine *DeepBiz* and am currently working on an article about how to be an effective panel moderator. Your work at the NDMA's fall conference last month, which I saw in a video on the organization's Web site, was exemplary, and I feel certain you have some tips that would be helpful for our readers. Would you be willing to let me ask you a few questions about your techniques for my article? If so, please respond to this e-mail with your phone number and availability over the next few days.

Sincerely,

Annika Lindstrom, Reporter
*DeepBiz*

**186.** Which two events are scheduled for the same time period?

(A) "Harnessing Big Data" and the networking break
(B) "Climb the Search Rankings" and "Interactive Display Technology"
(C) "Finding the Right Influencers" and "Harnessing Big Data"
(D) "Content Creation With AI Tools" and "Interactive Display Technology"

**187.** What most likely is Mr. Stanley's area of expertise?

(A) Video editing
(B) E-mail advertising
(C) Client management
(D) Marketing experimentation

**188.** What does the first e-mail suggest about Mr. Stanley?

(A) He assisted in preparing a speaker.
(B) He was in the audience at the conference.
(C) He participated in an event that was well received.
(D) He filled in for a presenter who felt unwell.

**189.** What is the main purpose of the second e-mail?

(A) To extend an interview request
(B) To suggest a revision to an article
(C) To ask for feedback on a conference
(D) To confirm some information on a Web site

**190.** What can be concluded about Mr. Ahn?

(A) He holds a leadership role in the NDMA.
(B) He gave consent for a video to be shared publicly.
(C) He was recently mentioned in an online magazine.
(D) He took part in two conferences in October.

GO ON TO THE NEXT PAGE

**Questions 191-195** refer to the following Web pages and e-mail.

https://www.larosetours.com/msat

## Mount Slagle Aerial Tour

Let Larose Tours take you on a helicopter adventure! This one-hour flight first passes over historic downtown Larose on its way to the main attraction: a stunning overhead view of Mount Slagle, an active volcano. Returning over the surrounding rainforest, passengers will also spot waterfalls so remote that they can only be observed from the air. A guide is on hand throughout to provide interesting commentary and answer questions.

The Mount Slagle Aerial Tour begins and ends at Larose Airport. It departs at 10 A.M., 1 P.M., and 3 P.M., Monday through Friday. We are also available for custom individual and group helicopter tours of the mountain; for more information, visit this page.

https://www.larosetours.com/confirmation

## Larose Tours

Thank you for reserving the following tours. In addition to the reservation details, please ensure that your contact information below is correct so that Larose will be able to provide you with instructions or updates about your tours.

Reservation Confirmation No.: 984533

**Customer Information**
Name: Devin Rice
Phone: (707) 555-0149
E-mail: devin.rice@obymail.com

**Reservation Details**

| | |
|---|---|
| Mount Slagle Aerial Tour, April 27 at 10 A.M.<br>2 adults, 2 children | $1,540.00 |
| Myrick Cave Tour, April 28 at 9 A.M.<br>2 adults, 2 children | $192.00 |
| Total | $1,732.00 |

Payment Completed (Credit card ending in 4308)

| | |
|---|---|
| **From:** | customerservice@larosetours.com |
| **To:** | devin.rice@obymail.com |
| **Subject:** | Tour cancellation |
| **Date:** | April 26 |

Dear Mr. Rice,

Larose Tours is sorry to inform you that the Mount Slagle Aerial Tour scheduled for 10 A.M. tomorrow has been canceled. The weather forecast is predicting strong winds and rain through the afternoon, and helicopter flight is unsafe in those conditions.

Since the inclement weather is not expected to last long, though, we encourage you to rebook the tour. We just had a customer cancellation that left an opening large enough for your party at 1 P.M. on April 29. Please call us at (808) 555-0173 if you would like to claim those spots.

Otherwise, we are happy to provide you with a full refund via your original payment method. You can initiate the process by responding to this e-mail or dropping in our office when you come for your cave tour.

Sincerely,

Hana Inoue, Customer Service Specialist
Larose Tours

**191.** What is indicated on the first Web page about Larose Tours?

(A) It is seeking to hire guides.
(B) It is open on the weekends.
(C) It operates personalized tours.
(D) It is headquartered in an airport.

**192.** What does the second Web page indicate about Mr. Rice?

(A) He chose activities that take place in the morning.
(B) He is organizing outings for a corporate retreat.
(C) He plans to attend a cultural performance.
(D) He made the reservations over a month in advance.

**193.** What is NOT an action suggested in the e-mail?

(A) Sending a reply e-mail
(B) Filling out an online form
(C) Visiting an office in person
(D) Making a telephone call

**194.** What is most likely true about the tour that has been canceled?

(A) It involves a helicopter landing on a mountainside.
(B) It is the company's most popular excursion.
(C) It offers the only way to see some waterfalls.
(D) It flies exclusively over nature areas.

**195.** What can be concluded about Mr. Rice?

(A) He recently changed some of his contact details.
(B) He will be unable to join the suggested alternative tour.
(C) He did not follow the instructions on the second Web page.
(D) He is eligible for a refund to his credit card.

*GO ON TO THE NEXT PAGE*

**Questions 196-200** refer to the following Web page, e-mail, and customer review.

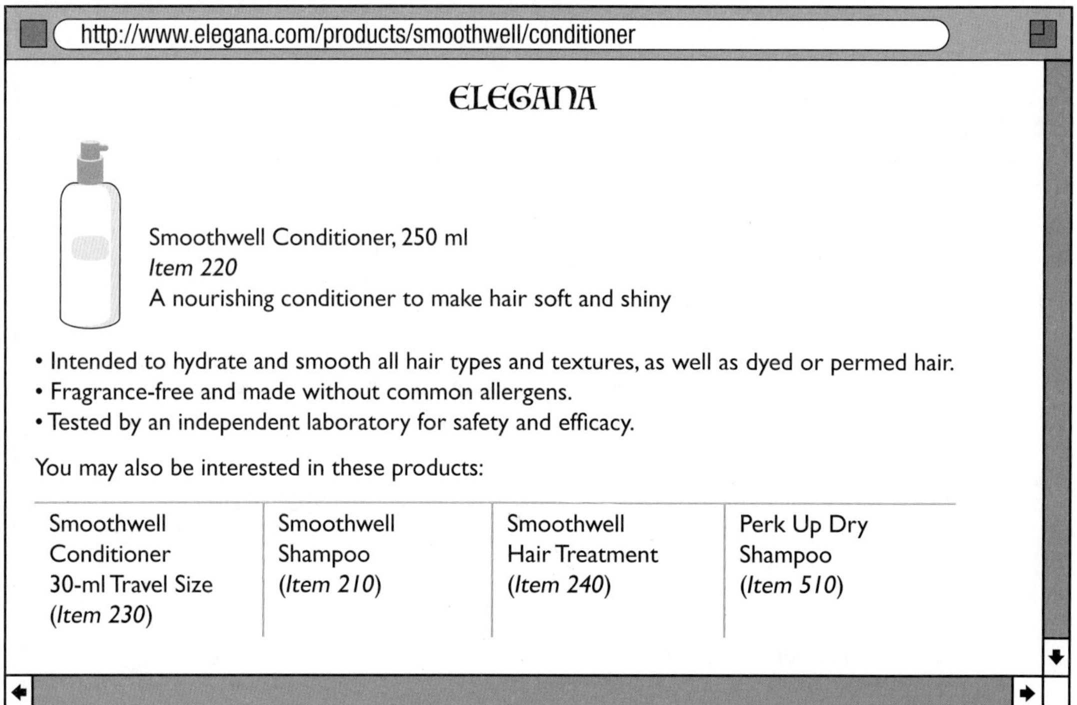

http://www.elegana.com/products/smoothwell/conditioner

ELEGANA

Smoothwell Conditioner, 250 ml
*Item 220*
A nourishing conditioner to make hair soft and shiny

- Intended to hydrate and smooth all hair types and textures, as well as dyed or permed hair.
- Fragrance-free and made without common allergens.
- Tested by an independent laboratory for safety and efficacy.

You may also be interested in these products:

| Smoothwell Conditioner 30-ml Travel Size (*Item 230*) | Smoothwell Shampoo (*Item 210*) | Smoothwell Hair Treatment (*Item 240*) | Perk Up Dry Shampoo (*Item 510*) |
|---|---|---|---|

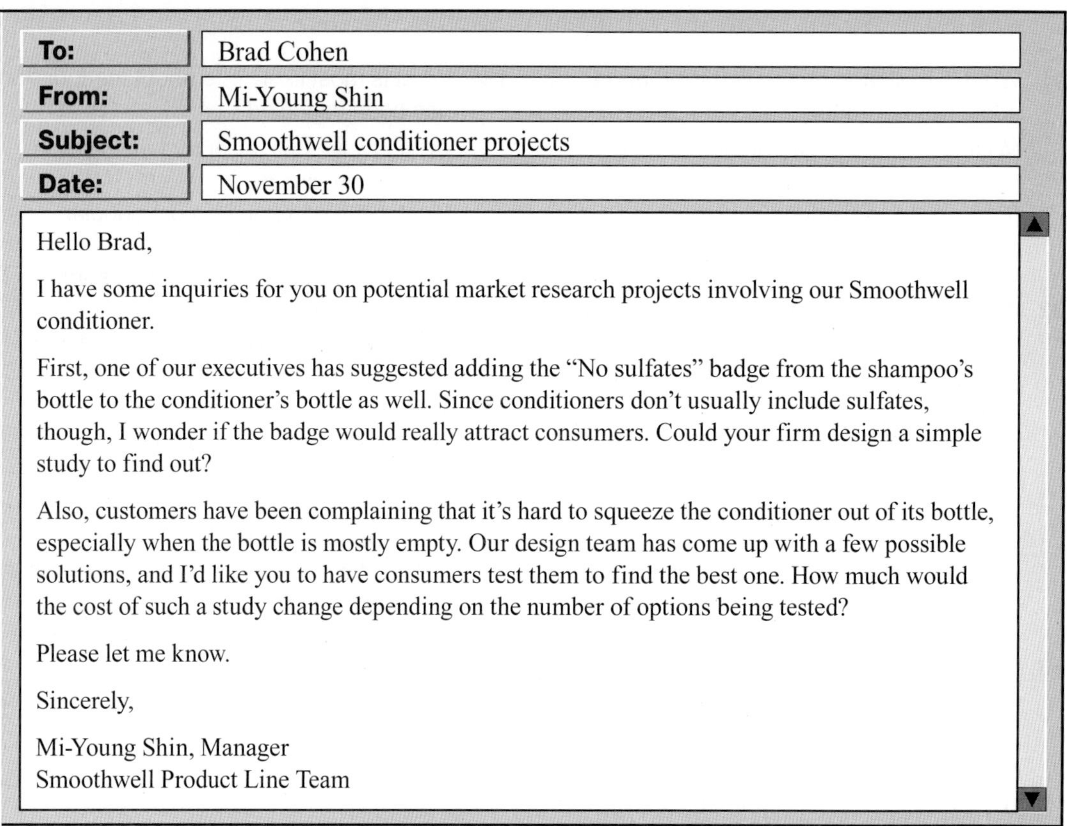

**To:** Brad Cohen
**From:** Mi-Young Shin
**Subject:** Smoothwell conditioner projects
**Date:** November 30

Hello Brad,

I have some inquiries for you on potential market research projects involving our Smoothwell conditioner.

First, one of our executives has suggested adding the "No sulfates" badge from the shampoo's bottle to the conditioner's bottle as well. Since conditioners don't usually include sulfates, though, I wonder if the badge would really attract consumers. Could your firm design a simple study to find out?

Also, customers have been complaining that it's hard to squeeze the conditioner out of its bottle, especially when the bottle is mostly empty. Our design team has come up with a few possible solutions, and I'd like you to have consumers test them to find the best one. How much would the cost of such a study change depending on the number of options being tested?

Please let me know.

Sincerely,

Mi-Young Shin, Manager
Smoothwell Product Line Team

http://www.elegana.com/products/smoothwell/conditioner/reviews

ELEGANA

**Smoothwell Conditioner, 250 ml**

Rating: ★★★★★

I'm so glad that I found this product! A few years ago, I moved to a very rainy area, and all the moisture was making my hair a frizzy mess. Luckily, a beauty store clerk recommended the Smoothwell line to me. I found the shampoo to be fine but not worth the price, so now I just use the conditioner. I love how shiny and smooth it leaves my hair. Also, I like the redesigned bottle. The larger print is easy to read, and the cap being at the bottom means it takes much less effort to get the conditioner out.

—Sandy M.

TEST 4

**196.** What is indicated about Smoothwell Conditioner?

(A) It does not have a scent.
(B) It is sold in one size only.
(C) It is widely used in salons.
(D) It is meant to be applied daily.

**197.** What is one thing Ms. Shin asks for Mr. Cohen's help with?

(A) Presenting a marketing plan to some executives
(B) Researching whether competing products include a type of ingredient
(C) Determining whether a promotional claim would be effective
(D) Designing more attractive packaging for some goods

**198.** According to the customer review, what is true about Sandy M.?

(A) She now lives in a humid climate.
(B) She works in a beauty supply store.
(C) She was dissatisfied with her most recent haircut.
(D) She thinks Smoothwell Conditioner is overpriced.

**199.** What is the item code of the other Elegana product that Sandy M. has used?

(A) 230
(B) 210
(C) 240
(D) 510

**200.** How did Elegana resolve a problem that Ms. Shin mentioned?

(A) By making a bottle's cap easier to remove
(B) By adjusting a product's formula
(C) By enlarging some printed instructions
(D) By changing the location of a bottle's opening

**Stop! This is the end of the test. If you finish before time is called, you may go back to Parts 5, 6, and 7 and check your work.**

# YBM 실전토익 RC1000

## 테스트 전 체크리스트

- 중간 휴식 없이 제한 시간을 지켜서 풀이하세요.
- 제한 시간은 답안지에 마킹하는 시간도 포함시켜야 합니다.
- 찍은 문제는 번호 옆에 꼭 체크해 주세요.
- 시간 안에 풀지 못한 문제는 틀린 것으로 채점해 주세요.

RC

# TEST 5

## READING TEST

In the Reading test, you will read a variety of texts and answer several different types of reading comprehension questions. The entire Reading test will last 75 minutes. There are three parts, and directions are given for each part. You are encouraged to answer as many questions as possible within the time allowed.

You must mark your answers on the separate answer sheet. Do not write your answers in your test book.

## PART 5

**Directions:** A word or phrase is missing in each of the sentences below. Four answer choices are given below each sentence. Select the best answer to complete the sentence. Then mark the letter (A), (B), (C), or (D) on your answer sheet.

**101.** The lunch special includes one sandwich along with a salad, fries, ------- a bowl of soup.

(A) thus
(B) or
(C) for
(D) nor

**102.** Mr. Fletcher was transferred to another branch after ------- department was eliminated in the corporate restructuring.

(A) he
(B) him
(C) his
(D) himself

**103.** The tech team's most ------- solution for the software issue will be used in the updated version of the program.

(A) innovatively
(B) innovates
(C) innovative
(D) innovation

**104.** Attendees of the writing conference can ------- participate in workshops on a number of relevant topics.

(A) activate
(B) actively
(C) activity
(D) active

**105.** If an insured vehicle is involved in an accident, we will assess the ------- quickly, within three business days.

(A) signal
(B) claim
(C) inventory
(D) conflict

**106.** Problems with the air purifier may ------- either by incorrect storage or the use of the wrong filters.

(A) realize
(B) select
(C) arise
(D) indicate

**107.** The university's new ------- coordinator has streamlined the steps to reduce processing times.

(A) admissions
(B) admitted
(C) admits
(D) to admit

**108.** Ms. Burke will encourage the staff to donate canned goods ------- she did during the holidays last year.

(A) likewise
(B) regarding
(C) as
(D) so

**109.** The pharmacy's medications and supplements must be ------- labeled.

(A) clear
(B) clarity
(C) clearer
(D) clearly

**110.** Bayside Financial has expanded its customer base by an impressive ninety percent ------- the past five years.

(A) by
(B) from
(C) between
(D) over

**111.** You must assess all aspects of the properties before ------- which best suits your personal circumstances.

(A) determines
(B) to determine
(C) determining
(D) must determine

**112.** FT Supplies' headquarters building was ------- used as a ceramics factory because the surrounding area is rich in clay deposits.

(A) to originate
(B) originally
(C) original
(D) origins

**113.** Every semester, Laurel Technical Institute offers online and in-person courses in an impressive ------- of fields.

(A) effort
(B) version
(C) array
(D) degree

**114.** Many airline employees found learning the luggage tracking system difficult, but explaining it to passengers was an even ------- challenge.

(A) hard
(B) hardly
(C) harder
(D) hardest

**115.** Once the interns have completed their probation period, a manager at Camco will evaluate ------- one of them.

(A) whole
(B) each
(C) full
(D) total

**116.** The automated system allows us to respond ------- to basic customer inquiries and requests.

(A) instantly
(B) fondly
(C) abundantly
(D) curiously

**117.** Morrison Automotive has confirmed the ------- of its accounting and finance departments due to extensive corporate growth.

(A) separated
(B) separate
(C) separates
(D) separation

**118.** The shopping mall kept the majority of its shops open ------- the renovation process because of working in phases.

(A) while
(B) prior to
(C) throughout
(D) along

**119.** The café, ------- caters to vegan and vegetarian diners, has received positive reviews so far.

(A) whether
(B) which
(C) neither
(D) it

**120.** Angela Cruz, editor of the *Newport Daily Herald*, includes nothing but ------- facts in the newspaper's articles.

(A) intensive
(B) competent
(C) verifiable
(D) economical



GO ON TO THE NEXT PAGE

**121.** The judging panel can only consider art entries received ------- the designated period of June 28 to July 5.

(A) above
(B) except
(C) among
(D) within

**122.** Ms. Kirby is ------- filling out paperwork for a small business loan for her bakery.

(A) how
(B) lately
(C) anywhere
(D) currently

**123.** Dr. Charlotte Collins requires further funding to remain at the forefront of medical ------- in the field.

(A) advanced
(B) is advancing
(C) advances
(D) advancing

**124.** Please take down the patio umbrellas today, as they are designed to ------- winds of up to twenty-five miles per hour only.

(A) forbid
(B) expose
(C) occur
(D) withstand

**125.** The temporary workers that have been hired to assemble the trade fair booth will be ------- helpful to us.

(A) enough
(B) shortly
(C) quite
(D) than

**126.** Book a room at Parkview Hotel to be looked after by our ------- staff during your stay.

(A) optimal
(B) former
(C) attentive
(D) potential

**127.** Hospital Director Owen Abbott expressed a desire to move ------- a more patient-centered approach to care.

(A) toward
(B) since
(C) alongside
(D) through

**128.** Pinewell Supermarket's customer loyalty program will continue ------- the target demographic is still participating in it.

(A) as long as
(B) in spite of
(C) rather than
(D) in order to

**129.** ------- of prevention methods over cutting-edge treatments may lead to better health outcomes.

(A) Consumption
(B) Prioritization
(C) Destination
(D) Intention

**130.** All standard orders for banner printing will ------- until the express requests have been completed and shipped.

(A) suspend
(B) be suspended
(C) have suspended
(D) be suspending

## PART 6

**Directions:** Read the texts that follow. A word, phrase, or sentence is missing in parts of each text. Four answer choices for each question are given below the text. Select the best answer to complete the text. Then mark the letter (A), (B), (C), or (D) on your answer sheet.

**Questions 131-134** refer to the following e-mail.

From: hemrich@midlandmail.com
To: ltoscani@napoliballetschool.com
Date: September 26
Subject: Job opening
Attachment: Résumé_emrich

Dear Ms. Toscani,

I am contacting you with regard to the job advertisement you posted in the most recent issue of the Napoli Ballet School newsletter. I have a great deal of respect for your ------- **131.**, and many of my friends and acquaintances have taken lessons there. I would be ------- **132.** to contribute to the site as a dance instructor.

I have worked with dancers of a wide range of ages and ability levels. ------- **133.**, I would be able to adjust my teaching style to perfectly suit students' individual needs. Please find attached a copy of my résumé, which outlines my training and work history. ------- **134.**. Should you have any questions, you can reach me at this address or at 555-3966. I hope to hear from you soon.

All the best,
Heather Emrich

**131.** (A) exhibition
(B) institute
(C) theater
(D) store

**132.** (A) delighting
(B) delight
(C) delights
(D) delighted

**133.** (A) Otherwise
(B) In addition
(C) Consequently
(D) However

**134.** (A) I am happy to teach you how to prevent injuries when dancing.
(B) To sign up for one of my classes, please download the app.
(C) I learned a great deal from your dance class last month.
(D) You can also view videos of my dancing at www.danceshowcase.com/emrich1.

GO ON TO THE NEXT PAGE

**Questions 135-138** refer to the following Web page.

Rosen Hotel is offering a 30% discount on all deluxe rooms throughout March. This special ------- **135.** is available to all guests who want to experience the luxury of our new rooms. ------- **136.** with calming colors, our deluxe rooms are the perfect place to relax after a long day. ------- **137.** come with a king-sized bed, kitchenette, spacious bathroom, and more. To make a reservation, visit www.rosen-hotel.com. Please note that a credit card is required for all bookings. ------- **138.**. We look forward to welcoming you!

**135.** (A) tour
(B) performance
(C) edition
(D) rate

**136.** (A) Decorating
(B) To decorate
(C) They decorated
(D) Decorated

**137.** (A) They
(B) Either
(C) Whichever
(D) Fewer

**138.** (A) Otherwise, a breakfast buffet is served daily from 6 A.M.
(B) The charge will not be made until twenty-four hours before check-in.
(C) Our staff aims to accommodate this request, if possible.
(D) Many hotels in the city center have vacant rooms.

**Questions 139-142** refer to the following e-mail.

To: Chloe Boyce <cboyce@merigoldcomm.com>

From: Arlington Sanitation Services <sanitation@arlington.gov>

Date: January 2

Subject: Missed collection

Dear Ms. Boyce,

Thank you for informing us ------- (139.) the missed recycling collection at your property. We have a special team for short-notice pickups, which I have dispatched. ------- (140.), you can rest assured that your recycling will be collected by 4 P.M. ------- (141.). Therefore, some crew members are not familiar with the routes. We are dedicated to providing efficient collection services of household waste and recyclables in Arlington, and your feedback helps us to ------- (142.) this responsibility.

Sincerely,

Devin Sinha

Arlington Sanitation Services

**139.** (A) with
(B) until
(C) about
(D) into

**140.** (A) For instance
(B) On the other hand
(C) Apart from that
(D) For this reason

**141.** (A) Unfortunately, we cannot take items that have not been thoroughly cleaned.
(B) You can also leave feedback on the city's Web site.
(C) Please find attached a schedule of recycling collection days.
(D) Due to the holiday, we have replacement crews working most of this week.

**142.** (A) fulfillment
(B) fulfill
(C) fulfilling
(D) fulfilled

TEST 5

*GO ON TO THE NEXT PAGE*

**Questions 143-146** refer to the following memo.

To: All employees

From: Keith Voigt, Product Development Manager

Date: March 22

Subject: Luxe-7 handbag

Due to disappointing sales of our Luxe-7 leather handbag, we have decided to discontinue this item, effective immediately. Unfortunately, consumers found our ad campaign less ------- (**143.**) than we expected. Additionally, the design did not stand out against its competitors. Moving forward, the design team will be given several ------- (**144.**) outlined by our research team to help them create prototypes of new bags. ------- (**145.**). We believe the additional work that is being requested will be difficult ------- (**146.**) beneficial.

**143.** (A) gradual
(B) compelling
(C) repetitive
(D) doubtful

**144.** (A) specifying
(B) specification
(C) specifications
(D) specifies

**145.** (A) However, less expensive materials are available.
(B) The commercial features examples of modern employees.
(C) Following that, we will gather feedback from potential customers.
(D) Your efforts helped to truly make a difference.

**146.** (A) for
(B) as
(C) yet
(D) if

## PART 7

**Directions:** In this part you will read a selection of texts, such as magazine and newspaper articles, e-mails, and instant messages. Each text or set of texts is followed by several questions. Select the best answer for each question and mark the letter (A), (B), (C), or (D) on your answer sheet.

**Questions 147-148** refer to the following e-mail.

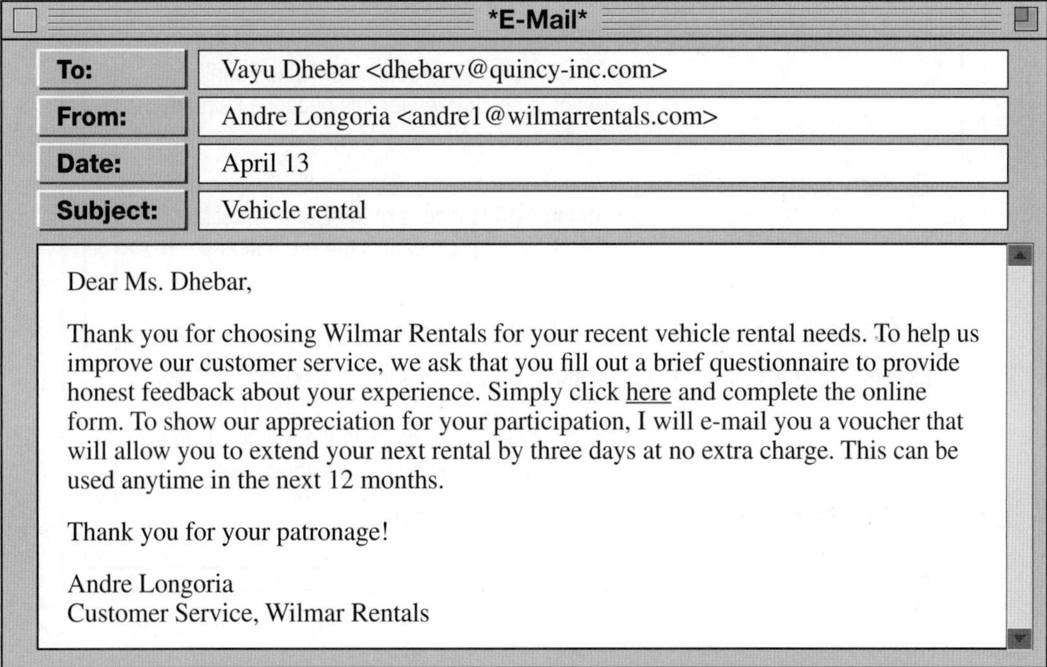

*E-Mail*

**To:** Vayu Dhebar <dhebarv@quincy-inc.com>

**From:** Andre Longoria <andre1@wilmarrentals.com>

**Date:** April 13

**Subject:** Vehicle rental

Dear Ms. Dhebar,

Thank you for choosing Wilmar Rentals for your recent vehicle rental needs. To help us improve our customer service, we ask that you fill out a brief questionnaire to provide honest feedback about your experience. Simply click here and complete the online form. To show our appreciation for your participation, I will e-mail you a voucher that will allow you to extend your next rental by three days at no extra charge. This can be used anytime in the next 12 months.

Thank you for your patronage!

Andre Longoria
Customer Service, Wilmar Rentals

**147.** What does Mr. Longoria ask Ms. Dhebar to do?

(A) Confirm her preferred vehicle size
(B) Pay the remaining balance of a bill
(C) Share her opinions about a service
(D) Participate in a free workshop

**148.** What does Mr. Longoria plan to do for Ms. Dhebar?

(A) Meet her at a customer feedback session
(B) Upgrade her vehicle to a larger size
(C) Extend a one-year subscription at no cost
(D) Provide a voucher for free rental days

*GO ON TO THE NEXT PAGE*

**Questions 149-150** refer to the following online chat discussion.

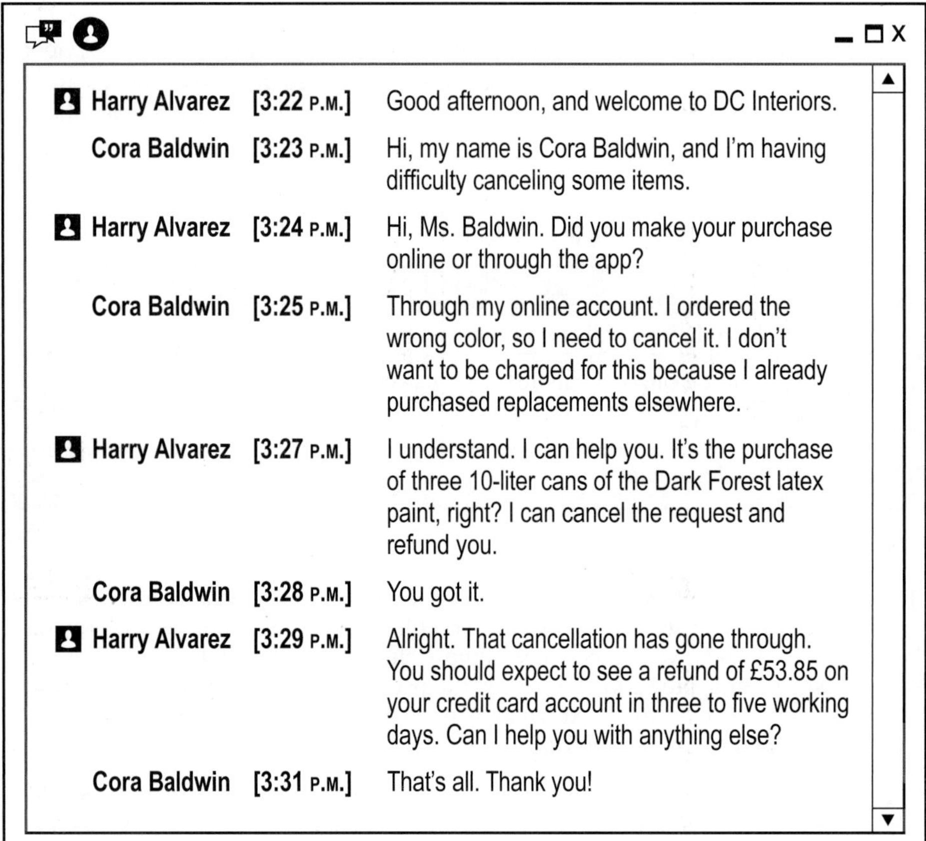

| | | |
|---|---|---|
| Harry Alvarez | [3:22 P.M.] | Good afternoon, and welcome to DC Interiors. |
| Cora Baldwin | [3:23 P.M.] | Hi, my name is Cora Baldwin, and I'm having difficulty canceling some items. |
| Harry Alvarez | [3:24 P.M.] | Hi, Ms. Baldwin. Did you make your purchase online or through the app? |
| Cora Baldwin | [3:25 P.M.] | Through my online account. I ordered the wrong color, so I need to cancel it. I don't want to be charged for this because I already purchased replacements elsewhere. |
| Harry Alvarez | [3:27 P.M.] | I understand. I can help you. It's the purchase of three 10-liter cans of the Dark Forest latex paint, right? I can cancel the request and refund you. |
| Cora Baldwin | [3:28 P.M.] | You got it. |
| Harry Alvarez | [3:29 P.M.] | Alright. That cancellation has gone through. You should expect to see a refund of £53.85 on your credit card account in three to five working days. Can I help you with anything else? |
| Cora Baldwin | [3:31 P.M.] | That's all. Thank you! |

**149.** What most likely is Mr. Alvarez's job?

(A) Customer service agent
(B) Interior designer
(C) Bank representative
(D) Smartphone application developer

**150.** At 3:28 P.M., what does Ms. Baldwin most likely mean when she writes, "You got it"?

(A) The business has an item in stock.
(B) She has already received a refund.
(C) Mr. Alvarez is referring to the correct order.
(D) She will contact the business within five days.

**Questions 151-152** refer to the following advertisement.

## Freshtime Cleaning Services

**Serving Aurora, Huntington, and Durham for the past five years!**
**Available Monday to Saturday, 8 A.M. to 8 P.M., excluding national holidays.**

Freshtime Cleaning Services provides top-notch cleaning to commercial properties. Our founder, Terry Nolan, is passionate about making your space clean and relaxing, and our dedicated team of cleaners is always thorough and careful. Whether you need a one-time deep clean, a weekly routine clean, or something else, we can help you. We use environmentally friendly cleaning products, and we are fully insured.

We are especially looking for new clients in need of cleaning between tenants. Call Jana Rogova at 555-8716 to discuss rates.

TEST 5

**151.** What is true about Freshtime Cleaning Services?

(A) It has been in business for more than a decade.
(B) It serves both homes and businesses.
(C) It operates in three different locations.
(D) It must be booked for multiple cleaning sessions.

**152.** According to the advertisement, who should call Ms. Rogova?

(A) Hotel guests
(B) Cleaning supply wholesalers
(C) Property owners
(D) Part-time cleaners

*GO ON TO THE NEXT PAGE* →

**Questions 153-154** refer to the following sign.

**TEMPORARY CLOSURE FOR INSTALLATION**

**Summary:** Installation of playground equipment
**Estimated re-opening date:** May 17

| **Department in Charge:** | **Contractor:** |
|---|---|
| New Haven Recreational Facilities | Pierson Services |
| 1756 Alvarez Street, Suite #32 | 305 Gordon Road |
| New Haven, CT 06506 | Woodbridge, CT 06525 |

Further information about the project can be found on the city's Web site. Should you experience noise disturbances or other issues, please call 203-555-1771.

**153.** Where would this sign most likely be posted?

(A) Outside a private gym
(B) In a commercial warehouse
(C) At a public park
(D) Above a department store shelf

**154.** Why should people call the phone number on the sign?

(A) To report missing items
(B) To make a complaint
(C) To donate some equipment
(D) To inquire about a schedule

**Questions 155-157** refer to the following information.

On February 8, the Centennial Community Center will host an event for local job seekers. We are looking for people to donate their time to assist with one-on-one practice interviews. A background in human resources or management is preferred. The sessions will be audio recorded, and participants will be given a printout of the conversation so they can refer to it later. This event will greatly help participants who are seeking steady employment. Please contact Lara Harvey at 555-2904 for more information.

**155.** What is the purpose of the information?

(A) To raise money for a community center
(B) To announce a policy change
(C) To publicize a volunteer opportunity
(D) To provide job interview tips

**156.** According to the information, what will participants be able to do?

(A) Apply for a management position
(B) Record a welcome video
(C) Meet local business owners
(D) Receive a transcript

**157.** The word "steady", in paragraph 1, line 6, is closest in meaning to

(A) customary
(B) durable
(C) stable
(D) persistent

TEST 5

*GO ON TO THE NEXT PAGE*

**Questions 158-160** refer to the following advertisement.

## MEDINA VIRTUAL MAILBOXES

834 Stroude Road, Beamhurst
Phone: 070 5517 3713

**Your mail is safe in our hands!**

- You can keep the same virtual address even after you move.
- With our Standard Service, we will store your mail, including envelopes and packages requiring a signature. You will be notified by text whenever your mail is dropped off to us.
- With our Gold Service, we can also forward the mail daily, open and scan it, or shred it. Simply log in from any device with your secure customer code to view an initial scan of the front of each piece of mail. Then choose what further action we should take with it.

For this month only, enroll in our Gold Service to receive 25% off the first six months of your annual contract.

**158.** When does Medina Virtual Mailboxes send a notification to customers?

(A) When it has forwarded some mail
(B) When an item arrives at the site
(C) When the subscription is about to expire
(D) When a storage area is nearly full

**159.** What should customers do to choose what happens to their mail?

(A) Log in with a secure code
(B) Set the instructions in their contract
(C) Call the company's office
(D) Send a text message to the business

**160.** How can customers be eligible for a discount?

(A) By signing up for a premium service
(B) By committing to a half-year contract
(C) By downloading a voucher from the system
(D) By paying for the service six months in advance

**Questions 161-163** refer to the following notice.

## Riverdale Bike Safety Day

Do you want to make sure your bicycle is safe to ride on the roads and trails? Then don't miss Riverdale Bike Safety Day at Sunrise Park on July 20 from 10 A.M. to 4 P.M.

Certified bicycle repair technicians will be on site to check your bicycle at no cost to you. — [1] —. They can perform basic maintenance and repairs such as fixing or replacing chains, adjusting seat heights, patching and filling flat tires, and checking brake cables. — [2] —. To save time, you can book a time slot in advance at Tony's Bike Shop. — [3] —.

Riverdale Bike Safety Day is made possible by the Meadowland Grant and sponsorship from Tony's Bike Shop. — [4] —.

For more information, visit www.riverdalecommunity.org/bikesafety.

**161.** What is the purpose of the notice?

(A) To announce the launch of a business
(B) To explain some safety regulations
(C) To promote a bike race
(D) To advertise a free service

**162.** What is expected to happen on July 20?

(A) A new public bike trail will be opened.
(B) Air will be added to some bike tires.
(C) Participants will receive a certificate.
(D) Bicycles will be sold at a discount.

**163.** In which of the positions marked [1], [2], [3], and [4] does the following sentence best belong?

"Alternatively, simply stop by and wait in line."

(A) [1]
(B) [2]
(C) [3]
(D) [4]

TEST 5

GO ON TO THE NEXT PAGE

**Questions 164-167** refer to the following online chat discussion.

| | | |
|---|---|---|
| **Aira Kasslin** | **[1:23 P.M.]** | Good afternoon, Kengo and Tammy. I wanted to check how the testing of our new allergy medicine is going. It would be best to have this round completed by Wednesday because an inspector will be checking our equipment on Thursday. |
| **Kengo Yoneda** | **[1:24 P.M.]** | We have one more analysis to run, which should be finished today. |
| **Aira Kasslin** | **[1:25 P.M.]** | That's a relief. That means we'll be able to start recruiting for the clinical trials next Monday as scheduled. Do either of you have time to compile a list of local healthcare providers from the database? |
| **Tammy Garza** | **[1:27 P.M.]** | Sorry, Aira. I'm leaving tomorrow to attend the regional conference. I wouldn't be able to start any new projects until next Tuesday. |
| **Kengo Yoneda** | **[1:28 P.M.]** | I haven't used that program, but I'm willing to try. |
| **Aira Kasslin** | **[1:31 P.M.]** | Thanks, Kengo! The software is a bit confusing to use at first, but there are clear instructions in the manual. I'll ask the IT team for a copy. |
| **Kengo Yoneda** | **[1:32 P.M.]** | That would be really helpful. |
| **Tammy Garza** | **[1:33 P.M.]** | Actually, that's not necessary. I have a printout in my desk. I'll bring it to you after lunch. |
| **Kengo Yoneda** | **[1:36 P.M.]** | Alright. Thanks, Tammy. |
| **Aira Kasslin** | **[1:37 P.M.]** | Then everything is set. Thank you both for your hard work, and I look forward to reading your reports. |

**164.** For what type of business do the writers most likely work?
(A) A supermarket chain
(B) A software testing center
(C) A dental clinic
(D) A research laboratory

**165.** When will an inspection be carried out?
(A) This Wednesday
(B) This Thursday
(C) Next Monday
(D) Next Tuesday

**166.** What is indicated about Mr. Yoneda?
(A) He is interested in attending a conference.
(B) He is not familiar with a software program.
(C) He had trouble accessing the database.
(D) He cannot take on any new projects.

**167.** At 1:33 P.M., what does Ms. Garza most likely mean when she writes, "that's not necessary"?
(A) An assignment can be given to a different employee.
(B) Mr. Kasslin does not need to contact the IT team.
(C) She can attend a conference remotely this time.
(D) A manual's instructions will be updated soon.

**Questions 168-171** refer to the following article.

## Royal Indigo to Give Brae Airlines a New Look

SYDNEY (17 February)—Brae Airlines has hired fashion house Royal Indigo to create new uniforms for the airline's cabin crew. The designs are expected to be approved in March, and from that point, it will take about three months before passengers see the new style on board.

Senior brand manager Teija Raita said the uniforms have remained the same for a decade and the change is part of the company's brand redesign.

"We're certain that Royal Indigo's creativity will produce an iconic uniform that makes our brand memorable and gives us a fresh look," said Ms. Raita. "Until now, we have not had high-end brands supply our uniforms, so we are excited about this collaboration."

Ms. Raita has been with the company for less than a year, taking over from Ava Holloway last November and immediately seeing to renovating and improving Brae's airport lounges in Sydney and Singapore. She has also streamlined the company's social media posts and commissioned a new logo, and she is now looking into working with nonprofit organizations related to travel.

TEST 5

**168.** When will the new uniforms most likely first be used?

(A) In February
(B) In March
(C) In June
(D) In November

**169.** What does the article indicate about Brae Airlines' partnership with Royal Indigo?

(A) It is Brae Airlines' first time working with a luxury brand.
(B) It is expected to last for at least ten years.
(C) It will only affect customers traveling in first class.
(D) It was finalized after three months of negotiation.

**170.** According to the article, who is Ms. Holloway?

(A) A Brae Airlines senior analyst
(B) The lead designer at Royal Indigo
(C) A former Brae Airlines brand manager
(D) The founder of Brae Airlines

**171.** What task did Ms. Raita complete first at Brae Airlines?

(A) She had the airline's logo updated.
(B) She improved the company's social media presence.
(C) She moved the main office to Singapore.
(D) She had some airport lounges upgraded.

GO ON TO THE NEXT PAGE

**Questions 172-175** refer to the following letter.

16 October

Daniel McGill
Page by Page Bookshop
477 Armory Street
Rochester, NY 14604

Dear Mr. McGill,

Grantham Publishing is seeking independent retailers to carry our latest work, *Beneath the Surface*. Having received rave reviews from literary critics, the novel brings its readers a unique combination of drama and science. — [1] —.

*Beneath the Surface* examines what happens to broken and outdated computers and smartphones once they are no longer in use. — [2] —. Although it is a fictional account of a small town negatively affected by soil contamination at its local landfill, it contains factual information based on the latest research.

The two authors of *Beneath the Surface* are Nathaniel Lee, an environmental scientist, and Dr. Cecelia Sandoval, an ecology professor at Wilford University. — [3] —. Mr. Lee has been awarded the prestigious Caldwell Prize, and Dr. Sandoval is acclaimed for consulting for an online educational program. They are making their publishing debut with *Beneath the Surface* and would be happy to sign some of the copies being sent to your store.

I can provide you with further details about *Beneath the Surface* anytime. — [4] —. I look forward to hearing from you.

All the best,

Zachary Wesley

**172.** What does Mr. Wesley want to do?

(A) Recruit judges for a writing contest
(B) Improve the availability of a book for sale
(C) Promote the grand opening of a bookshop
(D) Hire a designer to create a book cover

**173.** What is mentioned about *Beneath the Surface*?

(A) It is available as a digital file for computers.
(B) It explores the disposal of old electronics.
(C) It has been nominated for an award.
(D) It is based on a critically acclaimed drama.

**174.** What is indicated about Mr. Lee and Dr. Sandoval?

(A) They have collected soil samples.
(B) They will visit Mr. McGill's store.
(C) They are first-time authors.
(D) They founded an online education platform.

**175.** In which of the positions marked [1], [2], [3], and [4] does the following sentence best belong?

"Both are highly esteemed in their respective fields."

(A) [1]
(B) [2]
(C) [3]
(D) [4]



GO ON TO THE NEXT PAGE

**Questions 176-180** refer to the following notice and e-mail.

www.gipomcon.com

## GHI Production & Operations Management Conference

### Call for Seminar Proposals

Goh Heavy Industries (GHI) will convene the first-ever GHI Production & Operations Management Conference on 21–22 June at the Singapore Convention Centre. We are calling for proposals from production and operations experts to lead seminars on their organizations' successful actions in response to business challenges. The ideal seminar topic will relate to the conference theme of "Advances in the Age of Analytics," but other topics will also be accepted.

Proposals must be between 100 and 200 words long and accompanied by a summary of the submitter's qualifications. Roughly 30 proposals will be chosen for presentation in seminar form; if many more submissions are received, additional submitters may be invited to participate in themed 90-minute panel discussions instead. Submitters should be aware that proposals chosen for seminars must then be submitted to the Production & Operations Management Society (POMS) for approval so that each seminar will count as an hour of professional development for POMS members in attendance.

Please use this online form to submit your proposal to the conference's organizing committee by 15 November.

**E-Mail message**

| | |
|---|---|
| **From:** | Wei Chua |
| **To:** | Leslie Briggs |
| **Subject:** | Conference submission |
| **Date:** | 11 December |

Dear Ms. Briggs,

On behalf of the GHI Production & Operations Management Conference organizing committee, it is my pleasure to invite you to lead a seminar on your proposed topic, "Using Machine Learning to Optimize Backup Crew Scheduling in Airlines."

Please respond to this e-mail by 20 December to confirm your intention to participate in the conference. Once you do, I will send you information about how to begin the process of POMS accreditation.

Best,

Wei Chua
Organizing Committee
GHI Production & Operations Management Conference

**176.** What type of organization is holding the conference?

(A) A professional association
(B) A national government agency
(C) A university department
(D) A manufacturing company

**177.** What is NOT a requirement for seminar proposals?

(A) They must describe actions taken by an organization.
(B) They must be of a certain length.
(C) They must be submitted by e-mail.
(D) They must come with information about the submitter.

**178.** According to the notice, what will some submitters be asked to do?

(A) Join an alternative type of event
(B) Contribute an article to a publication
(C) Allow their presentation to be recorded
(D) Arrive at the venue especially early

**179.** For how long will Ms. Briggs most likely appear in front of an audience at the conference?

(A) 15 minutes
(B) 30 minutes
(C) One hour
(D) 90 minutes

**180.** What is suggested about Ms. Briggs?

(A) She submitted more than one seminar proposal.
(B) She is responsible for managing an aircraft design process.
(C) She works for a company that is based in Singapore.
(D) She has used technology to address a staffing issue.



*GO ON TO THE NEXT PAGE*

**Questions 181-185** refer to the following Web page and e-mail.

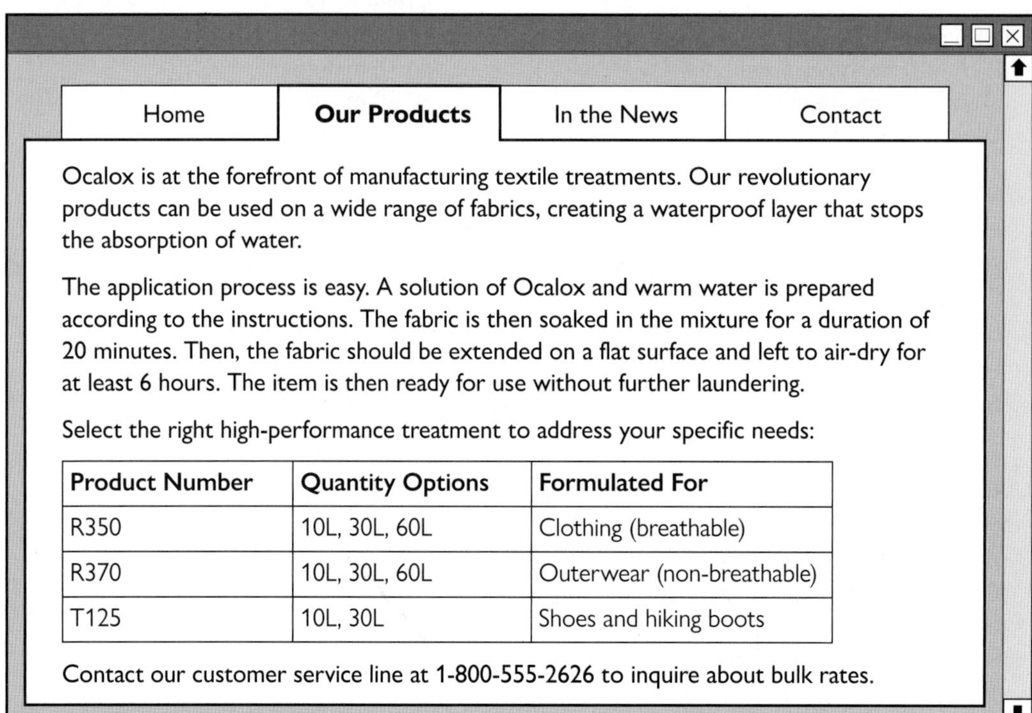

Home | **Our Products** | In the News | Contact

Ocalox is at the forefront of manufacturing textile treatments. Our revolutionary products can be used on a wide range of fabrics, creating a waterproof layer that stops the absorption of water.

The application process is easy. A solution of Ocalox and warm water is prepared according to the instructions. The fabric is then soaked in the mixture for a duration of 20 minutes. Then, the fabric should be extended on a flat surface and left to air-dry for at least 6 hours. The item is then ready for use without further laundering.

Select the right high-performance treatment to address your specific needs:

| Product Number | Quantity Options | Formulated For |
|---|---|---|
| R350 | 10L, 30L, 60L | Clothing (breathable) |
| R370 | 10L, 30L, 60L | Outerwear (non-breathable) |
| T125 | 10L, 30L | Shoes and hiking boots |

Contact our customer service line at 1-800-555-2626 to inquire about bulk rates.

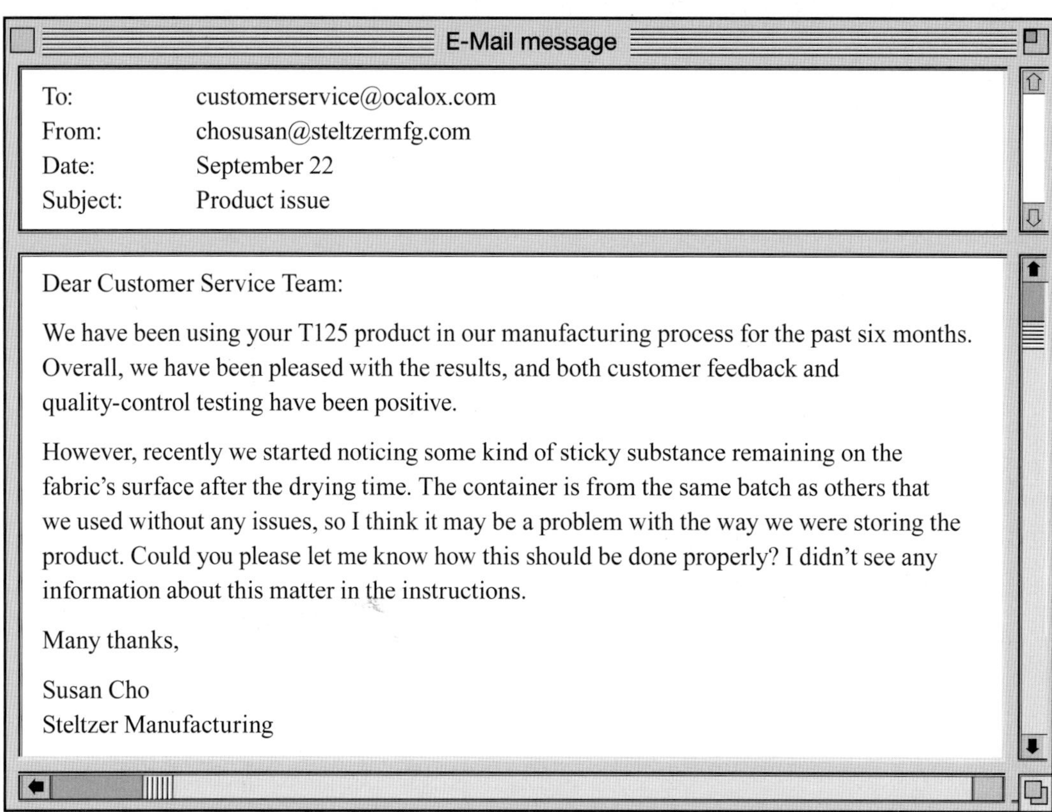

E-Mail message

To: customerservice@ocalox.com
From: chosusan@steltzermfg.com
Date: September 22
Subject: Product issue

Dear Customer Service Team:

We have been using your T125 product in our manufacturing process for the past six months. Overall, we have been pleased with the results, and both customer feedback and quality-control testing have been positive.

However, recently we started noticing some kind of sticky substance remaining on the fabric's surface after the drying time. The container is from the same batch as others that we used without any issues, so I think it may be a problem with the way we were storing the product. Could you please let me know how this should be done properly? I didn't see any information about this matter in the instructions.

Many thanks,

Susan Cho
Steltzer Manufacturing

**181.** What are Ocalox's products designed to do?

(A) Make surface colors last longer
(B) Improve the durability of fabric
(C) Provide a barrier against moisture
(D) Clean textiles gently and effectively

**182.** On the Web page, the word "extended" in paragraph 2, line 3, is closest in meaning to

(A) spread out
(B) continued
(C) put off
(D) prolonged

**183.** What is suggested about Steltzer Manufacturing?

(A) Its products failed a safety test.
(B) It was founded six months ago.
(C) It strives to use eco-friendly goods.
(D) It produces footwear commercially.

**184.** What is the purpose of Ms. Cho's e-mail?

(A) To request a copy of some instructions
(B) To get information about storage
(C) To cancel a supply contract
(D) To request a replacement product

**185.** What problem does Ms. Cho mention about her company's manufacturing process?

(A) A product has a strong odor.
(B) A residue is left behind.
(C) The drying time has increased.
(D) The fabric's surface tears easily.



*GO ON TO THE NEXT PAGE*

**Questions 186-190** refer to the following article, chart, and e-mail.

SALINAS(3 March)—Atwell Power has finalized the sites for a large-scale renewable energy project in the region that would provide electricity to thousands of homes and businesses. The project will involve the installation of wind turbines at four locations. These sites have already been inspected for environmental considerations and have received the necessary permits from the state and federal governments. Atwell Power will construct the turbines and substations themselves, but construction of the transmission lines linking the electricity output to the distribution grid will be handled by a third party. A spokesperson said that Atwell Power's project will create numerous jobs for highly skilled workers in the area, and it will begin advertising for these positions from early next month.

| Site | Number of Turbines | Annual Generation (per turbine) |
|---|---|---|
| Brunswick | 80 | 5.8 million kilowatt-hours |
| Crafton | 60 | 5.6 million kilowatt-hours |
| Ruckman Valley | 45 | 5.9 million kilowatt-hours |
| Valdosta | 75 | 6.1 million kilowatt-hours |

| | |
|---|---|
| **To:** | Alison Huber <a.huber@atwellpower.com> |
| **From:** | Guillermo Miranda <g.miranda@atwellpower.com> |
| **Date:** | May 7 |
| **Subject:** | Wind turbine project |

Dear Ms. Huber,

I'd like to follow up on the issue we discussed at last week's meeting regarding the Crafton site. As the public roadways are not suitable for the transportation of our equipment, we will need to construct a temporary access road off of Highway 162. Please note that due to the ground composition there, stability checks will need to be carried out once every three months rather than twice a year.

As for the outside contractor portion of the project, we have accepted a bid from Bassell Inc., and I will work on the contract this week.

I will update you again soon,

Guillermo Miranda

TEST 5

**186.** What is indicated about Atwell Power?
(A) It had several delays in its project plans.
(B) It has designed a new type of wind turbine.
(C) It will begin recruiting new employees in April.
(D) It had contested a decision by the federal government.

**187.** What site is expected to produce the most energy per turbine?
(A) Brunswick
(B) Crafton
(C) Ruckman Valley
(D) Valdosta

**188.** Why did Mr. Miranda write the e-mail?
(A) To request new equipment
(B) To negotiate a contract
(C) To propose a solution
(D) To apologize for an error

**189.** What task will Bassel Inc. most likely be responsible for?
(A) Building lines to connect to the power grid
(B) Inspecting proposed sites for environmental issues
(C) Constructing a roadway linked to the highway
(D) Assessing the safety of the project's substations

**190.** How many turbines will have quarterly stability checks?
(A) 45
(B) 60
(C) 75
(D) 80

GO ON TO THE NEXT PAGE

**Questions 191-195** refer to the following e-mails and press release.

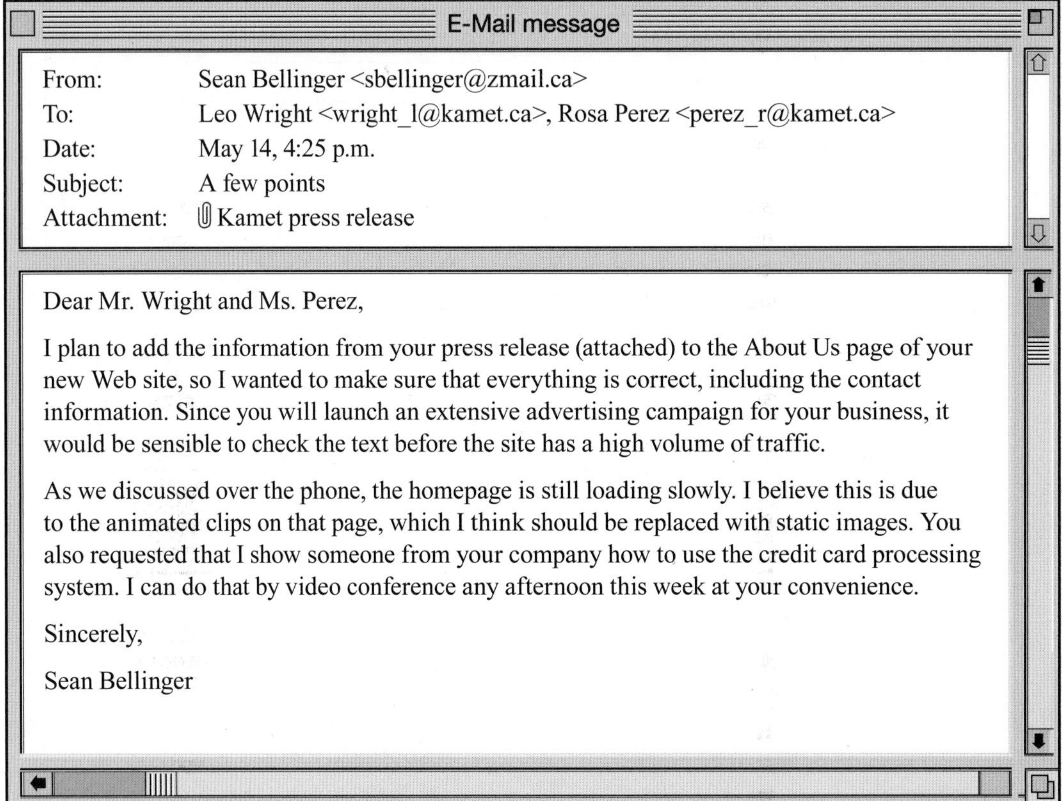

E-Mail message

From: Sean Bellinger <sbellinger@zmail.ca>
To: Leo Wright <wright_l@kamet.ca>, Rosa Perez <perez_r@kamet.ca>
Date: May 14, 4:25 p.m.
Subject: A few points
Attachment: Kamet press release

Dear Mr. Wright and Ms. Perez,

I plan to add the information from your press release (attached) to the About Us page of your new Web site, so I wanted to make sure that everything is correct, including the contact information. Since you will launch an extensive advertising campaign for your business, it would be sensible to check the text before the site has a high volume of traffic.

As we discussed over the phone, the homepage is still loading slowly. I believe this is due to the animated clips on that page, which I think should be replaced with static images. You also requested that I show someone from your company how to use the credit card processing system. I can do that by video conference any afternoon this week at your convenience.

Sincerely,

Sean Bellinger

**Press Release**

Contact: Nancy Rollins, 555-9275

Kamet, located on Cambridge Street opposite the Middleville Mall, is pleased to announce its grand opening on June 1. Kamet was founded by Lawrence Holt, who used to work in accounting but spent all of his free time outdoors, especially going on nature tours and climbing the world's tallest peaks. He wanted to provide people like him with the best tents, backpacks, sleeping bags, and more, all at affordable prices. Kamet brings you modern styles from designer Kenny Becerra, a law school graduate and former practicing attorney who had a career change later in life.

The opening day will feature complimentary refreshments, prize drawings, and product demonstrations. Summer is here, so stop in and stock up to make your time in the great outdoors comfortable and safe!

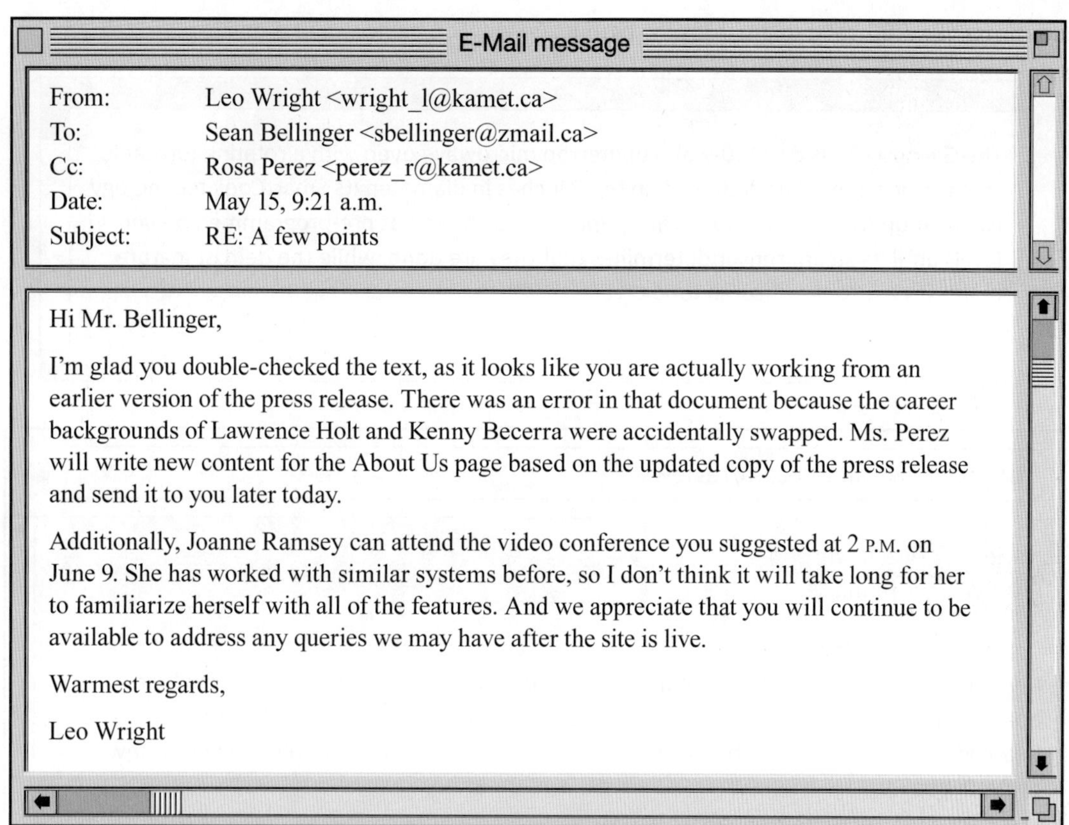
E-Mail message

From: Leo Wright <wright_l@kamet.ca>
To: Sean Bellinger <sbellinger@zmail.ca>
Cc: Rosa Perez <perez_r@kamet.ca>
Date: May 15, 9:21 a.m.
Subject: RE: A few points

Hi Mr. Bellinger,

I'm glad you double-checked the text, as it looks like you are actually working from an earlier version of the press release. There was an error in that document because the career backgrounds of Lawrence Holt and Kenny Becerra were accidentally swapped. Ms. Perez will write new content for the About Us page based on the updated copy of the press release and send it to you later today.

Additionally, Joanne Ramsey can attend the video conference you suggested at 2 P.M. on June 9. She has worked with similar systems before, so I don't think it will take long for her to familiarize herself with all of the features. And we appreciate that you will continue to be available to address any queries we may have after the site is live.

Warmest regards,

Leo Wright



**191.** Who most likely is Mr. Bellinger?
(A) A professional photographer
(B) An advertising executive
(C) A freelance journalist
(D) A Web designer

**192.** According to the first e-mail, what should be removed?
(A) Blurry images
(B) Some animation
(C) A company logo
(D) Contact information

**193.** What type of business is Kamet?
(A) A camping supplies store
(B) A tour company
(C) An outdoor performance facility
(D) A landscaping service

**194.** What will Ms. Ramsey do on June 9?
(A) Open a credit card account
(B) Learn about a payment system
(C) Select some feature artwork
(D) Visit Mr. Bellinger's office

**195.** What is true about Lawrence Holt?
(A) He used to work as a lawyer.
(B) He has recently promoted Ms. Ramsey.
(C) He has a background in accounting.
(D) He will write some text for Mr. Bellinger.

GO ON TO THE NEXT PAGE

**Questions 196-200** refer to the following product description, review, and e-mail.

The Galindo CT7 is an 1150-watt countertop microwave oven with a rotating turntable that can accommodate dishes of up to 13 inches in diameter. Its SmartCook technology can heat up five common foods like popcorn and chicken at pre-programmed power levels until its steam sensor determines that they are done, while the defrost feature makes it easy to thaw frozen foods.

http://www.galindo.com/reviews

Reviewer: Kyla Townsend
Date posted: January 9

My parents gave me their four-year-old CT7 microwave when I moved into my first apartment a few months ago. I have been using it a lot, because I eat Hansen ReadyMeals—those plastic bowls of food you put straight into the microwave—a few times a week.

Then, last week, the turntable stopped rotating. The microwave has a five-year warranty, so I called the closest certified Galindo repair service and set up an appointment. The technician said the drive motor will need to be replaced and asked to see my warranty. He then looked at the name on it and said the agreement is no longer valid because it can't be transferred between owners. Instead of being free, my repair will cost about $200, which is disappointing. I am posting this review to warn others who might not be aware of this condition of the warranty agreement.

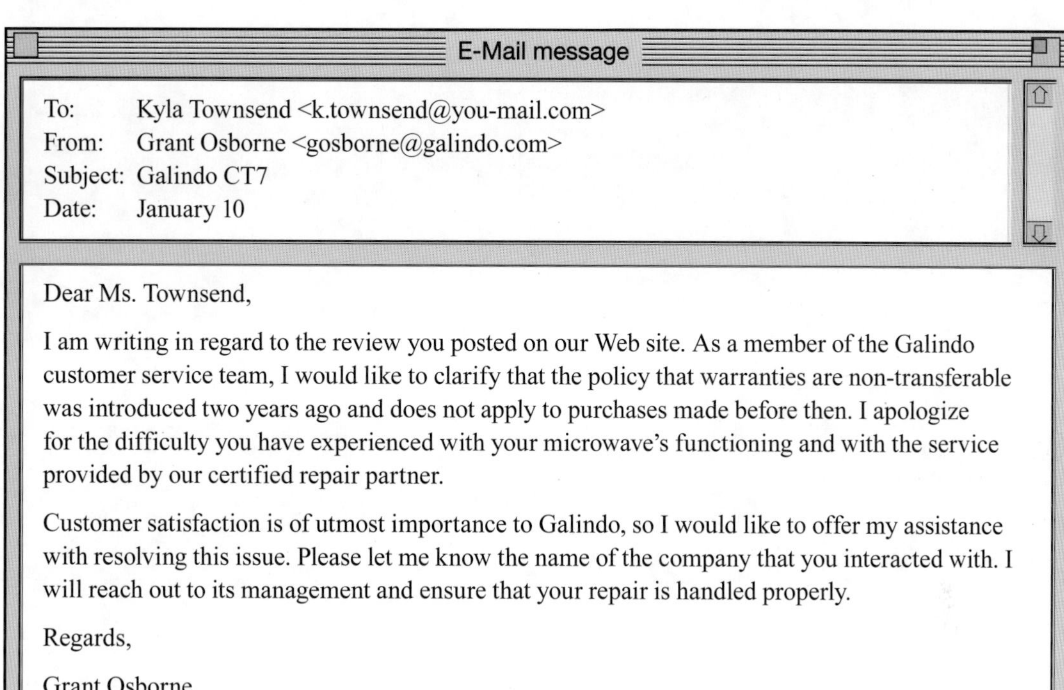
E-Mail message

To: Kyla Townsend <k.townsend@you-mail.com>
From: Grant Osborne <gosborne@galindo.com>
Subject: Galindo CT7
Date: January 10

Dear Ms. Townsend,

I am writing in regard to the review you posted on our Web site. As a member of the Galindo customer service team, I would like to clarify that the policy that warranties are non-transferable was introduced two years ago and does not apply to purchases made before then. I apologize for the difficulty you have experienced with your microwave's functioning and with the service provided by our certified repair partner.

Customer satisfaction is of utmost importance to Galindo, so I would like to offer my assistance with resolving this issue. Please let me know the name of the company that you interacted with. I will reach out to its management and ensure that your repair is handled properly.

Regards,

Grant Osborne
Customer Service Representative



**196.** According to the product description, what is true about the Galindo CT7 ?

(A) It features an interior light.
(B) It has the ability to sense steam.
(C) It is meant to be suspended over a cooktop.
(D) It comes in multiple color finishes.

**197.** What does Ms. Townsend indicate in her review about the CT7 in her apartment?

(A) She received it as a gift.
(B) It belongs to her landlord.
(C) She has owned it for four years.
(D) She bought it from a used goods store.

**198.** What is suggested about Hansen ReadyMeals?

(A) They are sold frozen.
(B) They include a chicken dish.
(C) They should be heated for five minutes.
(D) They are no larger than 13 inches across.

**199.** What incorrect information did Ms. Townsend receive from a technician?

(A) That the price of a certain replacement part is $200
(B) That Galindo introduced a new company policy within the past year
(C) That a malfunctioning drive motor is the most likely reason for her problem
(D) That the warranty on her microwave had been invalidated

**200.** What is one piece of information Mr. Osborne asks Ms. Townsend for?

(A) The name of a repair business
(B) The model number of her product
(C) The wording of a part of her warranty
(D) The address of an appliance store

**Stop! This is the end of the test. If you finish before time is called, you may go back to Parts 5, 6, and 7 and check your work.**

# YBM
# 실전토익
# RC1000

**테스트 전 체크리스트**

- 중간 휴식 없이 제한 시간을 지켜서 풀이하세요.
- 제한 시간은 답안지에 마킹하는 시간도 포함시켜야 합니다.
- 찍은 문제는 번호 옆에 꼭 체크해 주세요.
- 시간 안에 풀지 못한 문제는 틀린 것으로 채점해 주세요.

# RC TEST 6

## READING TEST

In the Reading test, you will read a variety of texts and answer several different types of reading comprehension questions. The entire Reading test will last 75 minutes. There are three parts, and directions are given for each part. You are encouraged to answer as many questions as possible within the time allowed.

You must mark your answers on the separate answer sheet. Do not write your answers in your test book.

## PART 5

**Directions:** A word or phrase is missing in each of the sentences below. Four answer choices are given below each sentence. Select the best answer to complete the sentence. Then mark the letter (A), (B), (C), or (D) on your answer sheet.

**101.** Testers report that the video game's final level is somewhat -------.

(A) frustrate
(B) frustrating
(C) frustration
(D) frustrated

**102.** Marcus Siegler is attempting to develop a new ------- for predicting solar activity.

(A) recognition
(B) direction
(C) method
(D) opinion

**103.** The university's largest dormitory, Lugo Residence Hall, accommodates ------- 600 students.

(A) enough
(B) nearly
(C) totally
(D) more

**104.** Ms. Chaney says her upcoming cookbook will feature only dishes made with ------- obtainable ingredients.

(A) easily
(B) easy
(C) ease
(D) easier

**105.** Emi Tanaka is supposed to start work on Monday, ------- Human Resources has not finished drafting her contract.

(A) once
(B) with
(C) still
(D) but

**106.** ------- the maintenance department immediately of any spills in the laboratory.

(A) Notify
(B) Notified
(C) Notifying
(D) Notification

**107.** The interior designer used certain colors ------- to create a warm atmosphere in the café's seating area.

(A) strategy
(B) strategic
(C) strategically
(D) more strategic

**108.** ------- can be done to recover your files, since they were deleted over one year ago.

(A) Either
(B) Nothing
(C) Nobody
(D) Another

109. Your meals with clients will be reimbursed by the company ------- you submit the original receipts.

(A) as long as
(B) whether
(C) afterward
(D) in case

110. After some -------, the board of directors decided to declare a dividend.

(A) deliberates
(B) deliberated
(C) deliberately
(D) deliberation

111. Although the workshop's participants were ------- from Busan, there were a few people from other areas as well.

(A) entirely
(B) repeatedly
(C) primarily
(D) overly

112. Weller Tower is a popular destination for tourists, mainly ------- the stunning view from its observation deck.

(A) now that
(B) just as
(C) together with
(D) because of

113. Renting construction machinery from a local supplier would be more ------- than having ours shipped to and from the site.

(A) efficiencies
(B) efficiency
(C) efficient
(D) efficiently

114. To preserve the artwork, museums often keep pieces from their permanent collections in storage ------- putting them on display.

(A) aside from
(B) rather than
(C) even if
(D) not only

115. According to the Cordell Pottery Exhibition's Web site, the entry fee will be ------- for Cordell residents.

(A) waives
(B) waiving
(C) waived
(D) waivers

116. Government ------- in science and technology research have been important drivers of innovation in recent decades.

(A) invests
(B) investments
(C) investor
(D) invested

117. Proceeds from the fund-raiser will go ------- resurfacing the running track in Brant Park.

(A) toward
(B) through
(C) about
(D) over

118. While it was -------, many fans were still saddened by Liam Kuhn's announcement of his retirement from professional tennis.

(A) allowed
(B) expected
(C) reduced
(D) answered

119. Due to unusually low attendance at the festival, the organizers were left with an ------- of 200 promotional T-shirts.

(A) excessive
(B) exceeding
(C) excess
(D) exceeds

120. Under the new time-off policy, employees may ------- to receive pay in exchange for their unused vacation days.

(A) opt
(B) promise
(C) afford
(D) bother

*GO ON TO THE NEXT PAGE* →

**121.** *Wipeout*, a new comedy series, will be released on the network's streaming platform 24 hours ------- its broadcast TV premiere.

(A) in front
(B) by then
(C) close to
(D) ahead of

**122.** The hiring committee believes that Ms. Ahmed's skills would nicely complement ------- of the existing members of the team.

(A) those
(B) theirs
(C) them
(D) which

**123.** With each purchase, our customers earn points that can be used to receive discounts on ------- orders.

(A) approximate
(B) subsequent
(C) inevitable
(D) gradual

**124.** Among the strawberries available at the farmer's market, the ones sold by Calkin Farms are the -------.

(A) flavors
(B) flavorful
(C) most flavorful
(D) most flavorfully

**125.** After paying the licensing fee, you will be ------- the right to use this image for commercial purposes.

(A) enforced
(B) advised
(C) renewed
(D) granted

**126.** Mr. Song ------- the market research study even before sales of our products began their recent decline.

(A) was commissioned
(B) is commissioning
(C) to be commissioning
(D) had commissioned

**127.** Kenyon XN-30 sport sunglasses come with four ------- sets of lenses to suit a variety of lighting conditions.

(A) instant
(B) interchangeable
(C) concentrated
(D) relative

**128.** With proper care, the shrubs planted along your walkway will ------- reach a height of three feet.

(A) patiently
(B) considerably
(C) exactly
(D) eventually

**129.** Although there is no maximum word limit for articles in our journal, we recommend that authors keep their manuscripts as ------- as possible.

(A) accurate
(B) orderly
(C) distinctive
(D) succinct

**130.** The ability to pay close attention to detail is an important ------- that all medical translators must have.

(A) trait
(B) outcome
(C) record
(D) practice

## PART 6

**Directions:** Read the texts that follow. A word, phrase, or sentence is missing in parts of each text. Four answer choices for each question are given below the text. Select the best answer to complete the text. Then mark the letter (A), (B), (C), or (D) on your answer sheet.

**Questions 131-134** refer to the following Web page.

http://www.ncgovparks.org/ufc

Urban Family Camping

The Nieves City Parks Department organizes urban family camping events so that local children can experience the fun of camping ------- (**131.**) in their own city. At each campout, park rangers host a limited number of families for an overnight stay in one of Nieves's beautiful parks. There is also usually an extra activity, such as a barbecue dinner, a ranger-led evening hike, or a session of storytelling around the campfire. To make participation widely accessible, the Parks Department even provides the tents and most other necessary items. ------- (**132.**).

The urban family camping ------- (**133.**) is extremely popular. ------- (**134.**) families are advised to sign up for their desired campout as soon as registration opens each spring.

**131.** (A) there
(B) like
(C) just
(D) right

**132.** (A) All that each camper needs to bring is a sleeping bag and toiletries.
(B) It also holds many daytime events for families at its parks.
(C) Camping is a great way to foster a lifelong love of nature in children.
(D) See the calendar below for the dates of all upcoming campouts.

**133.** (A) facility
(B) leader
(C) program
(D) equipment

**134.** (A) Interested
(B) Interesting
(C) Interestingly
(D) To interest

TEST 6

GO ON TO THE NEXT PAGE

**Questions 135-138** refer to the following article.

BURENNA (February 5)—Today, TCN Hospitality Group withdrew its proposal to build a combined conference center and hotel on Worth Street. The complex ------- **135.** over 200 guest rooms and 70,000 square feet of conference space.

Burenna citizens voiced ------- **136.** to the plan at an informational meeting last Thursday. Several residents expressed concern that the chosen site would be unable to handle a large increase in traffic. ------- **137.** . The day after the meeting, three city council members also indicated that they would vote against the proposal.

According to its withdrawal statement, TCN has not given up on the idea of building a conference center and hotel complex in Burenna. ------- **138.** , the scale of the complex is likely to be more modest in any future proposals.

**135.** (A) includes
(B) will include
(C) would have included
(D) would include

**136.** (A) difficulty
(B) opposition
(C) disapproval
(D) obstruction

**137.** (A) The location is the former home of Ellis Department Store.
(B) Others objected to the city's planned financial role in the project.
(C) To accommodate it, Worth Street will be widened to six lanes.
(D) TCN has opened major complexes in two other cities in recent years.

**138.** (A) However
(B) Similarly
(C) In fact
(D) Instead

**Questions 139-142** refer to the following notice.

Attention, Penny's Grill staff:

The restaurant will be getting a new point-of-sale and order management system next week. Technicians will come on our weekly day off, Monday, to do the installation and ------- (139.) our managers how to use the system. Dana and Ivan will then lead simultaneous training sessions for all dining room and kitchen staff on Tuesday morning. ------- (140.) . We need to get started that early in order to ensure that employees working normal shifts on Tuesday are fully prepared by the time lunch service ------- (141.) at 11.

Please let Dana know promptly if you are unavailable on Tuesday morning. We may arrange ------- (142.) training sessions if necessary.

**139.** (A) support
(B) teach
(C) explain
(D) introduce

**140.** (A) Fortunately, the system is largely similar to our current one.
(B) Likewise, the servers must learn to input orders on tablets.
(C) They will update the relevant sections of our handbook as well.
(D) Everyone has been scheduled for a special shift at 8 A.M.

**141.** (A) begins
(B) to begin
(C) beginning
(D) that begins

**142.** (A) regular
(B) internal
(C) additional
(D) advanced

TEST 6

**Questions 143-146** refer to the following e-mail.

From: <enewsletter@pattersonlibrary.org>

To: Noel Higgins <n.higgins@yow-mail.com>

Subject: Patterson Public Library

Date: September 19

Dear Patron,

Thank you for joining the mailing list for the Patterson Public Library's electronic newsletter. We are excited to begin updating you about important changes, upcoming events, and services on offer at the library.

As the newsletter is published twice per month, you should receive your first issue within three weeks. ------- **143.** . If you do not begin receiving the newsletter as expected, please contact our help desk staff at 555-0166. Requests to change your preferred receiving address or be removed from the mailing list can also be directed to ------- **144.** .

Would you like to hear more from the library? We also publish *Patterson's Picks*, a monthly e-mail that features book ------- **145.** from our librarians. Visit www.pattersonlibrary.org/pp to ------- **146.** .

Patterson Public Library

**143.** (A) We put a lot of care into crafting the contents.
(B) Our readership ranges from teenagers to retirees.
(C) Each issue will be sent via e-mail to this address.
(D) Previous issues are available on our Web site.

**144.** (A) me
(B) him
(C) one
(D) them

**145.** (A) recommends
(B) recommended
(C) recommendation
(D) recommendations

**146.** (A) donate
(B) subscribe
(C) volunteer
(D) enter

## PART 7

**Directions:** In this part you will read a selection of texts, such as magazine and newspaper articles, e-mails, and instant messages. Each text or set of texts is followed by several questions. Select the best answer for each question and mark the letter (A), (B), (C), or (D) on your answer sheet.

**Questions 147-148** refer to the following information.

The Dominica Advanced Steam Iron includes an auto-clean system to keep the water tank and steam vents free of mineral buildup.

To use this feature, begin by filling the water tank. Plug in the iron, and turn the steam dial to the highest setting. After allowing the iron to heat up for two minutes, unplug it. Hold the iron face down over a sink and press the "Auto-Clean" button. Hot water and steam will be released through the steam vents. Continue holding down the button until the tank has been completely emptied.

**147.** Where would the information most likely be found?

(A) In a print advertisement
(B) In an online customer review
(C) In a notice on a company's Web site
(D) On a page of a product manual

**148.** What is indicated about the auto-cleaning process?

(A) It takes approximately two minutes.
(B) It involves a particular cleaning fluid.
(C) It requires the use of an electrical outlet.
(D) The iron should not be touched while it is taking place.

TEST 6

GO ON TO THE NEXT PAGE

**Questions 149-151** refer to the following announcement.

**Cape Town Entrepreneurship Hall of Fame**

The Rondebosch University Centre for Innovation (RUCI) is seeking nominations of local business leaders for induction into the Cape Town Entrepreneurship Hall of Fame. The honour is meant to recognise the achievements of the city's business community and inspire the next generation of entrepreneurs. Past inductees include Willem Van Rooyen, Imka Kabera, and Grant Twigg. This year, the RUCI will choose ten nominees for induction at a ceremony planned for 14 June.

To be considered, nominees must:

- Be the CEO of a private or public company headquartered in the City of Cape Town
- Have held that position at the time of the company's founding and for no fewer than three years in total
- Have shown outstanding abilities in one or more of the following areas: innovation, profitability, employment generation, other positive community impact

Visit www.ronu.ac.za/ruci/ctehf to download the nomination form. Submissions must be made by 5 P.M. on 1 May.

**149.** What information is included in the announcement?

(A) What benefits Hall of Fame members receive
(B) What the purpose of the Hall of Fame is
(C) Where nominations should be submitted
(D) Who is allowed to submit a nomination

**150.** What can be concluded about Ms. Kabera?

(A) She was a CEO for at least three years.
(B) She graduated from Rondebosch University.
(C) She will attend a special event in June.
(D) She is a past employee of the RUCI.

**151.** What is most likely NOT an accomplishment that would qualify a nominee for consideration?

(A) Creating a large number of new jobs
(B) Increasing a company's net profits
(C) Achieving high rates of customer satisfaction
(D) Developing an original type of product

**Questions 152-153** refer to the following coupon.

## Titanium Gym

450 Third Street, Creville
555-0177

**25% Off a 3-month Membership**

Present this coupon upon sign-up to receive three months of membership at Titanium Gym for just $135! Members are entitled to a monthly session with a certified personal trainer and unlimited access to classes including kickboxing, aerobics, and Pilates.

Offer available only to new members. Sign-up fee not included. Membership period must begin by March 31.

**152.** According to the coupon, what is a benefit of Titanium Gym membership?

(A) A yearly health evaluation
(B) Access to special fitness equipment
(C) The ability to take a variety of classes
(D) Unlimited personal training sessions

**153.** What is true about the coupon?

(A) Its user will be required to pay a sign-up fee.
(B) It is targeted toward people whose membership ends in April.
(C) It is valid for three months from the date of issue.
(D) Its user will receive a discount of $135.

TEST 6

*GO ON TO THE NEXT PAGE*

**Questions 154-155** refer to the following text-message chain.

**Curtis Dawson** **[11:31 A.M.]**

Misako, our van has broken down in Kloss, and the mechanic says the repairs will take at least four hours.

**Misako Endo** **[11:33 A.M.]**

Oh no! Well, we need to make sure our customers still get the experience they've paid for. You're taking six people to Galvin Falls for the afternoon, right?

**Curtis Dawson** **[11:34 A.M.]**

That's right. And we're supposed to have lunch in Medford.

**Misako Endo** **[11:35 A.M.]**

OK. Do you think you could find a place to eat in Kloss instead? While you were doing that, I could rent another van from a local agency and have it driven over to you.

**Curtis Dawson** **[11:36 A.M.]**

Oh, we're right near Kloss Shopping Center. Thanks, Misako! I'll text you the exact address once we get settled.

**154.** What kind of business do the writers most likely work for?

(A) A tour operator
(B) A car rental agency
(C) A food delivery business
(D) An auto repair shop

**155.** At 11:36 A.M., what does Mr. Dawson most likely mean when he writes, "we're right near Kloss Shopping Center"?

(A) It will not be difficult to find parking for a van.
(B) There are many dining options nearby.
(C) Ms. Endo is not far from his location.
(D) He is only slightly behind schedule.

**Questions 156-157** refer to the following agenda.

## Nature Monthly 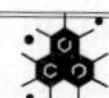

One-Day Workshop on Scientific Writing for Aspiring Contributors

**9:00 A.M. – Welcome and Introductions**

**9:30 A.M. – What Makes a Great Paper?**
Introduction of three well-written papers accepted for publication in the journal and breakdown of their characteristics

**10:15 A.M. – Break**

**10:30 A.M. – Mastering the Basics**
Overview of the ideal structure of *Nature Monthly* papers and tips on what to include in each section to impress our editors

**11:30 A.M. – The "Face" of Your Paper**
Explanation of how to write a title and abstract that are compelling, brief, and informative

**12:30 P.M. – Lunch**

**1:30 P.M. – Effective Display Items**
Guide to determining when a table, figure, or other visual aid is needed and ensuring it is clear and impactful

**2:30 P.M. – Live Edit Session**
One-on-one meeting with an editor who will review a paper submitted in advance by the participant

**3:15 P.M. – Q&A and Feedback**

**156.** What is most likely true about participants in the workshop?

(A) They will give editorial advice on each other's papers.
(B) They hope to have their writing published in *Nature Monthly*.
(C) They submitted information on their backgrounds beforehand.
(D) They are currently attending university to study science.

**157.** When would participants most likely learn how to design a chart?

(A) Between 9:30 A.M. and 10:15 A.M.
(B) Between 10:30 A.M. and 11:30 A.M.
(C) Between 11:30 A.M. and 12:30 P.M.
(D) Between 1:30 P.M. and 2:30 P.M.

GO ON TO THE NEXT PAGE

**Questions 158-160** refer to the following Web page.

http://www.alcornphotographers.com/news 

Alcorn Photographers is proud to announce that we now offer aerial photography via drone. — [1] —. This technology is an excellent way to showcase your client's home, apartment complex, or commercial space. Shooting the front, side, or rear of the building from a few dozen feet above the ground gives potential buyers a better sense of its scale and surroundings. — [2] —.

As with our other outdoor services, Alcorn Photographers will not charge for aerial photography shoots that must be canceled due to poor weather. — [3] —. We are also happy to schedule sessions at twilight to take advantage of the flattering lighting created by the setting sun.

Prices for aerial photography start at $200 for five images and increase with the number of photos desired. — [4] —. For more information or to book a shoot, please call us at 555-0162.

**158.** For whom is the information most likely intended?

(A) Property owners
(B) Drone operators
(C) Aspiring photographers
(D) Real estate agents

**159.** According to the Web page, what are customers charged more for?

(A) Having photographs taken via drone
(B) Canceling a photo shoot on short notice
(C) Holding a photo shoot in the evening
(D) Requesting additional photographs

**160.** In which of the positions marked [1], [2], [3], and [4] does the following sentence best belong?

"In addition, photographs taken from a hundred feet directly overhead can be used to show a property's full layout."

(A) [1]
(B) [2]
(C) [3]
(D) [4]

**Questions 161-163** refer to the following e-mail.

**E-Mail message**

| | |
|---|---|
| **From:** | Patricia Chilton |
| **To:** | All staff |
| **Subject:** | Overtime policy |
| **Date:** | December 2 |

Dear staff,

I really appreciate the hard work you're doing to prepare for our upcoming symposium. I know that it can be a struggle to keep up with the extra workload it involves.

That said, I'd like to remind you that our employee handbook strictly prohibits working more than 40 hours per week without getting approval from a supervisor beforehand. We're legally required to pay you at a higher rate for any overtime hours, and as a nonprofit organization, we don't have the resources to cover extra expenses in this area.

If you're unable to complete an assignment within your regular hours, you must leave it to your supervisor to decide whether to allow overtime work or to push the deadline back. Going forward, failure to follow this policy will be reflected in your performance evaluation.

Thank you.

Patricia Chilton
Executive Director
Proactive Network for Women in Engineering

**161.** What most likely caused Ms. Chilton to send the e-mail?

(A) Preparations for an event have fallen behind schedule.
(B) There has been a change in laws regarding compensation.
(C) Employees have been working overtime without permission.
(D) Some staff members missed an information session.

**162.** What is indicated about the Proactive Network for Women in Engineering?

(A) It has a limited budget for payroll.
(B) It organizes an annual symposium.
(C) Its workers regularly receive pay raises.
(D) Its legal department is very busy.

**163.** According to the e-mail, what consequence will staff face for breaking a rule?

(A) Losing the perk of flexible working hours
(B) Becoming ineligible for promotion to supervisor
(C) Receiving assignments that are less desirable
(D) Earning a worse performance review

*GO ON TO THE NEXT PAGE*

**Questions 164-167** refer to the following letter.

10 March

Kwang-Hoon Choi
233 Conner Street
Edinburgh EH3 8DN

Dear Mr. Choi,

On behalf of the Polwarth Community Garden Committee, I am excited to invite you back for another year of tending greenery together. This year's growing season begins on 3 April, and there are some changes to the garden's rules that you should be aware of. — [1] —.

First, to ensure the fair distribution of labour, it is now mandatory for all members to spend at least 10 hours annually doing the volunteer work necessary to keep the garden running. — [2] —. Fulfillment of this requirement will be tracked through a system on the garden's Web site. I will provide more information about this shortly.

Second, due to the long waiting list for our garden, this will be the final year that any household is allowed to have more than one plot. If your household has multiple plots, please notify the committee of which one you wish to keep and make certain the others are in suitable shape for reassignment at the end of the season. — [3] —.

Also, as usual, I ask that you check the bulletin board in the tool shed frequently for news and updates. — [4] —. Thank you, and I look forward to seeing you in the garden!

Sincerely,

Irvin Townsend, Chair
Polwarth Community Garden Committee

**164.** What is one purpose of the letter?

(A) To describe a new benefit of membership
(B) To announce a change to a start date
(C) To seek volunteers for an event
(D) To welcome a returning member

**165.** According to the letter, what will an online system be used for?

(A) Reporting news about the garden
(B) Keeping track of some tools
(C) Redistributing some pieces of land
(D) Recording some work hours

**166.** What is implied about Polwarth Community Garden?

(A) It does not have enough plots to meet demand.
(B) There is a diagram of its plots on display in a storage shed.
(C) Its plots must be assigned to a different household each year.
(D) The borders of its plots will be redrawn next year.

**167.** In which of the positions marked [1], [2], [3], and [4] does the following sentence best belong?

"Typical tasks include weed removal and cleaning the tool shed."

(A) [1]
(B) [2]
(C) [3]
(D) [4]

**Questions 168-171** refer to the following article.

## HRTA Project On Track for Summer

Hitchert Regional Transit Agency (HRTA) has reached another milestone in the process of adding enhanced-accessibility trains to its light-rail fleet. On January 7, HRTA staff began trial operation of the trains on the Gold and Green lines in order to discover and eliminate any issues before their deployment at the start of summer. To minimize inconvenience to transport users, the trains are being run only between the hours of 8 P.M. and 4 A.M. and are marked with large "Test Train" stickers to prevent people from boarding. Spreading rapidly to metropolitan areas across the country following their debut in Fonseca, the trains boast low, stair-free entrances, automatically-controlled ramps, and other features that make them more accessible to passengers with disabilities.



**168.** What is HRTA preparing to do?

(A) Introduce a new type of train
(B) Expand nighttime service
(C) Connect two railway lines
(D) Increase the accessibility of its stations

**169.** According to the article, what will continue to happen until summer begins?

(A) Some trains will be tested.
(B) Some staff will receive training.
(C) Transport users will be surveyed.
(D) Construction will be carried out.

**170.** What is suggested about trains with stickers on them?

(A) They only stop at two stations.
(B) They do not carry passengers yet.
(C) They have completed an inspection.
(D) They will be taken out of service soon.

**171.** Why does the writer mention Fonseca?

(A) HRTA staff visited it for research.
(B) It is the site of a production plant.
(C) It was the first place to adopt a technology.
(D) The size of its population is similar to Hitchert's.

*GO ON TO THE NEXT PAGE*

**Questions 172-175** refer to the following online chat discussion.

| | | |
|---|---|---|
| Michelle Garnier | [10:04 A.M.] | Hi, all. I just finished looking over the exit surveys from the summer interns. |
| Dominick Perkins | [10:05 A.M.] | Any surprising results? |
| Michelle Garnier | [10:07 A.M.] | Yes—they felt that we gave them too many low-level duties. They wanted to spend more time researching investment opportunities and helping us pitch them to clients. |
| Tina Osborne | [10:08 A.M.] | Really? We made such an effort to involve them in that kind of work. Maybe we need to be clearer during the application process about the scope of the internships. |
| Michelle Garnier | [10:09 A.M.] | That's a good idea. Anyway, the feedback on our mentoring and the networking opportunities was quite good, at least. |
| Dominick Perkins | [10:10 A.M.] | Michelle, I'd be interested in seeing more of the results. When would be a good time to drop by your office? |
| Michelle Garnier | [10:11 A.M.] | Oh, we'll have a review meeting in a few days. I'll put it on your calendars this afternoon. |
| Dominick Perkins | [10:12 A.M.] | Great. |
| Michelle Garnier | [10:13 A.M.] | That reminds me—before the meeting, please decide whether you'd recommend recruiting your interns after their graduations. Human Resources wants to make a note in their personnel files for easy reference. |
| Tina Osborne | [10:14 A.M.] | Do they really just want a "yes" or "no"? I think future hiring managers would prefer an overview of each person's strengths and weaknesses. |
| Michelle Garnier | [10:14 A.M.] | Good point. I'll try to find out more. |

**172.** In what field do the writers most likely work?

(A) Insurance sales
(B) Staff recruitment
(C) Wealth management
(D) Healthcare research

**173.** What is NOT mentioned as a topic covered in the survey given to the interns?

(A) The internship application process
(B) The tasks they were assigned
(C) The mentorship provided by the writers
(D) Their opportunities to make professional connections

**174.** At 10:11 A.M., what does Ms. Garnier most likely mean when she writes, "we'll have a review meeting in a few days"?

(A) Mr. Perkins will be introduced to some staff members.
(B) There is no need for Mr. Perkins to bring a document to her.
(C) Mr. Perkins should wait to learn some information.
(D) Mr. Perkins will have time to prepare for a discussion.

**175.** What most likely is Ms. Osborne's concern about the information requested by Human Resources?

(A) It will take considerable effort to gather.
(B) It is not detailed enough to be useful.
(C) It should not be accessible to other employees.
(D) It may no longer be accurate in the future.

TEST 6

*GO ON TO THE NEXT PAGE*

**Questions 176-180** refer to the following job advertisement and e-mail.

## DISTRICT SALES MANAGER

Eason Technologies, a premier provider of energy-efficient air-conditioning systems for offices and retail facilities, is seeking a sales manager for our southwest district. The position is based in Barrow.

**Responsibilities:**

- overseeing the activities of the district sales team
- identifying potential customers and acquiring their business
- forecasting and tracking sales accurately
- monitoring customer satisfaction to ensure retention

**Required qualifications:**

- a degree in business or a technical field
- five years of experience in a sales leadership role
- excellent public speaking skills
- willingness to travel frequently

To apply, send your résumé and a cover letter to hiring@easontech.com.

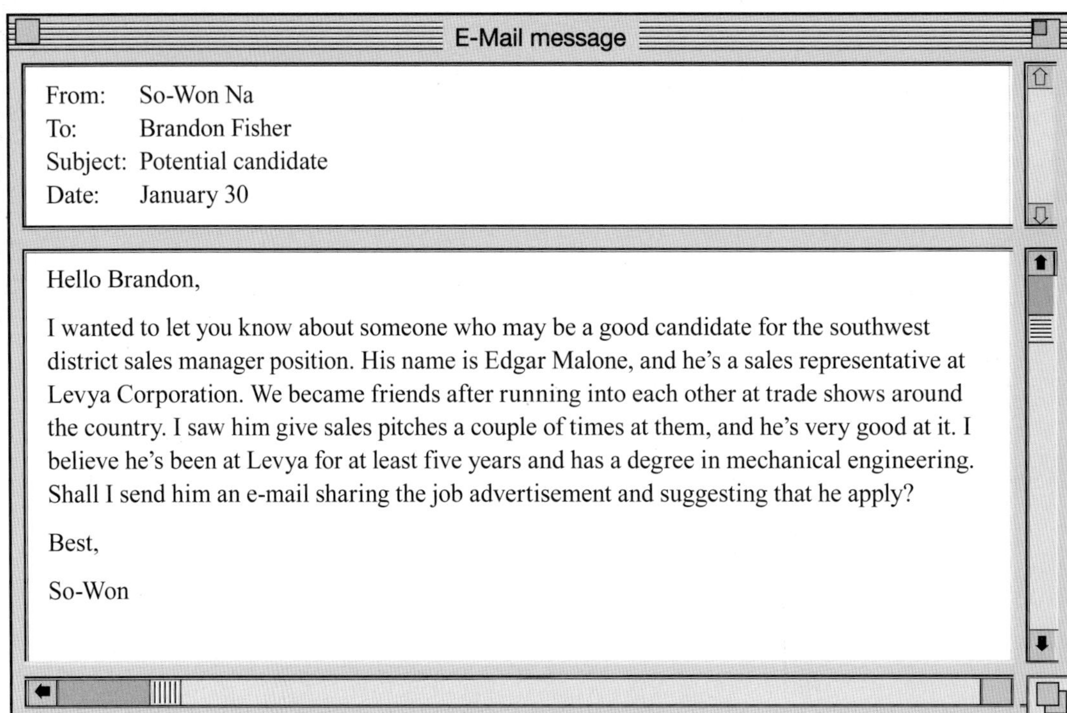

E-Mail message

From: So-Won Na
To: Brandon Fisher
Subject: Potential candidate
Date: January 30

Hello Brandon,

I wanted to let you know about someone who may be a good candidate for the southwest district sales manager position. His name is Edgar Malone, and he's a sales representative at Levya Corporation. We became friends after running into each other at trade shows around the country. I saw him give sales pitches a couple of times at them, and he's very good at it. I believe he's been at Levya for at least five years and has a degree in mechanical engineering. Shall I send him an e-mail sharing the job advertisement and suggesting that he apply?

Best,

So-Won

**176.** What is suggested about Eason Technologies?

(A) It sells its products to other businesses.
(B) It designs technology that produces renewable energy.
(C) It recently created a new sales district.
(D) It is headquartered in Barrow.

**177.** What is one responsibility of the position?

(A) Monitoring competitors' pricing
(B) Cooperating with marketing staff
(C) Correctly predicting sales revenues
(D) Proposing potential new products

**178.** What does Ms. Na explain in the e-mail?

(A) How long she has known Mr. Malone
(B) Where she saw the job advertisement
(C) How she became acquainted with Mr. Malone
(D) Why Mr. Malone might be interested in changing jobs

**179.** From Ms. Na's description, what position requirement might Mr. Malone NOT possess?

(A) A degree in a suitable field
(B) The necessary work experience
(C) Excellent public speaking ability
(D) A tolerance for frequent travel

**180.** In the e-mail, the word "sharing" in paragraph 1, line 6, is closest in meaning to

(A) dividing
(B) informing
(C) expressing
(D) delivering



*GO ON TO THE NEXT PAGE*

**Questions 181-185** refer to the following advertisement and e-mail.

## *Scrap Saver*

Tired of dealing with your business's food waste? Whether you run a restaurant or a café, a hotel or a catering company, Scrap Saver has the solution to your problem.

Since the separate disposal of commercial food waste became mandated by law last year, a growing number of businesses have turned to us for disposal of their cooking scraps and leftover food products. We provide cheap, convenient pickup and transport of these materials to our facilities, where they are converted into alternative fuels and organic fertilizer. Clients simply collect the food waste in one of our free storage bins or their own until the designated pickup time, which can be scheduled as frequently as needed.

Scrap Saver offers removal of all types of food packaging for reasonable handling fees, and we can even provide bulk transportation services for business that create more than three tons of waste per week.

Visit www.scrapsaver.com to learn more!

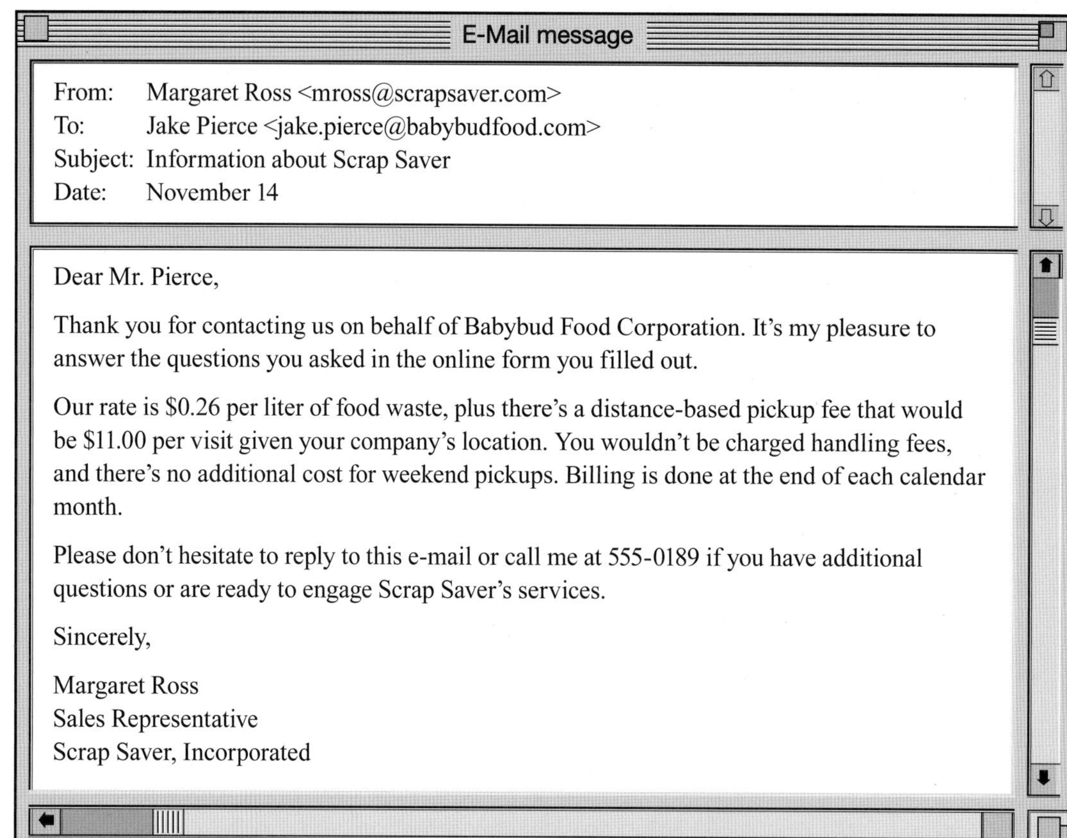

E-Mail message

From: Margaret Ross <mross@scrapsaver.com>
To: Jake Pierce <jake.pierce@babybudfood.com>
Subject: Information about Scrap Saver
Date: November 14

Dear Mr. Pierce,

Thank you for contacting us on behalf of Babybud Food Corporation. It's my pleasure to answer the questions you asked in the online form you filled out.

Our rate is $0.26 per liter of food waste, plus there's a distance-based pickup fee that would be $11.00 per visit given your company's location. You wouldn't be charged handling fees, and there's no additional cost for weekend pickups. Billing is done at the end of each calendar month.

Please don't hesitate to reply to this e-mail or call me at 555-0189 if you have additional questions or are ready to engage Scrap Saver's services.

Sincerely,

Margaret Ross
Sales Representative
Scrap Saver, Incorporated

181. What is mentioned about commercial food waste?

(A) It is growing in volume each year.
(B) It can be harmful to the environment.
(C) It is generated mostly by restaurants.
(D) It was the subject of a recent regulation.

182. What does the advertisement suggest about Scrap Saver?

(A) It operates waste processing facilities.
(B) It plans to expand the variety of materials it transports.
(C) It gives clients advice on reducing waste.
(D) Its delivery trucks run on alternative fuels.

183. In the e-mail, the word "given" in paragraph 2, line 2, is closest in meaning to

(A) regarding
(B) considering
(C) specified
(D) assigned

184. According to the e-mail, what does Scrap Saver most likely do once per month?

(A) Adjust a service rate
(B) Replace a storage container
(C) Calculate a total number of liters
(D) Confirm the desired pickup frequency

185. What can be concluded about Babybud Food Corporation?

(A) It has more than one manufacturing location.
(B) It does not plan to send packaged food to Scrap Saver.
(C) It produces multiple tons of food waste per week.
(D) It has not used a food waste disposal service previously.

TEST 6

*GO ON TO THE NEXT PAGE*

**Questions 186-190** refer to the following Web page, notice, and review.

hhttp://www.creativekates.com

## *Creative Kate's*

Creative Kate's is an arts and crafts supplies store run by creative people for our fellow makers. We have everything you need to create beautiful and unique paintings, quilts, jewelry, scrapbooks, and more. Looking for inspiration? Check out this page to see what our staff and patrons have made with materials sold at our store!

Our store is organized into the following four sections for customer convenience:

**Section A (Aisles 1–3)**
supplies for dressmaking, other sewing projects, and knitting

**Section B (Aisles 4–5)**
general crafting products such as beads, stamps, glue, and colored paper

**Section C (Aisle 6)**
painting and drawing supplies

**Section D (Aisles 7-8)**
organization and storage solutions, home and seasonal décor

## NOTICE

Attention, Customers!

Creative Kate's will soon begin offering in-store classes on various arts and crafts! Please excuse any dust or noise created as we replace part of our fabric aisles with the class space. And don't forget to look for more information on our classes in the weeks to come!

Also, please be aware that our self-service checkout machines do not accept cash. If you wish to make a cash purchase, visit a staffed register. Thank you.

http://www.shoppingcritic.com/reviews/creativekates

**Reviewer:** Etsuji Chiba

**Posted:** June 4

I had a very positive experience at Creative Kate's. I was putting together a private party at a hotel when my clients decided at the last minute that the staff there hadn't made the venue look festive enough. I ran over to Creative Kate's and explained the situation to the first employee I saw. She led me to the holiday decorations and quickly suggested a few suitable products. The prices were very reasonable, and after I'd put the items up in the venue, the atmosphere really did become much warmer and more cheerful. Thanks for your help, Creative Kate's!

**186.** What does the Web page indicate about the store's Web site?

(A) It lists the major brands that the store carries.
(B) It displays images of works created by customers.
(C) It provides instructions for independent craft projects.
(D) It includes profiles of some staff members.

**187.** What does the notice suggest about Creative Kate's?

(A) It will begin selling a new type of product.
(B) It has automated part of the shopping process.
(C) It is seeking replacement instructors for some classes.
(D) It no longer allows customers to pay with cash.

**188.** Which area of Creative Kate's will be reduced in size?

(A) Section A
(B) Section B
(C) Section C
(D) Section D

**189.** What most likely is Mr. Chiba's job?

(A) Hotel manager
(B) Art instructor
(C) Interior designer
(D) Event planner

**190.** What is implied about Mr. Chiba?

(A) He watched a demonstration led by an employee.
(B) He took advantage of a seasonal discount offer.
(C) He purchased goods from an aisle in Section D.
(D) He first visited the store to attend a celebration.

*GO ON TO THE NEXT PAGE* →

**Questions 191-195** refer to the following e-mails and form.

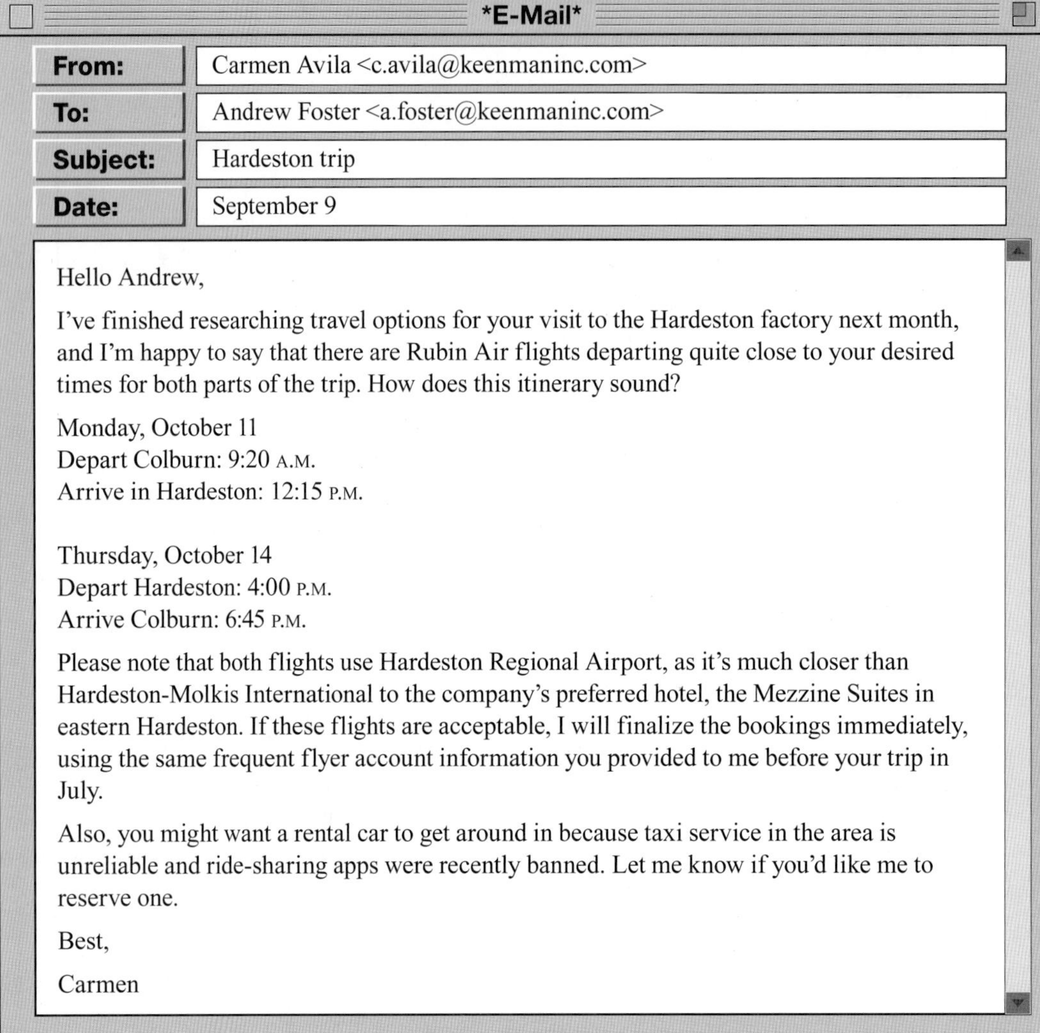

*E-Mail*

**From:** Carmen Avila <c.avila@keenmaninc.com>

**To:** Andrew Foster <a.foster@keenmaninc.com>

**Subject:** Hardeston trip

**Date:** September 9

Hello Andrew,

I've finished researching travel options for your visit to the Hardeston factory next month, and I'm happy to say that there are Rubin Air flights departing quite close to your desired times for both parts of the trip. How does this itinerary sound?

Monday, October 11
Depart Colburn: 9:20 A.M.
Arrive in Hardeston: 12:15 P.M.

Thursday, October 14
Depart Hardeston: 4:00 P.M.
Arrive Colburn: 6:45 P.M.

Please note that both flights use Hardeston Regional Airport, as it's much closer than Hardeston-Molkis International to the company's preferred hotel, the Mezzine Suites in eastern Hardeston. If these flights are acceptable, I will finalize the bookings immediately, using the same frequent flyer account information you provided to me before your trip in July.

Also, you might want a rental car to get around in because taxi service in the area is unreliable and ride-sharing apps were recently banned. Let me know if you'd like me to reserve one.

Best,

Carmen

**From:** Andrew Foster <a.foster@keenmaninc.com>

**To:** Carmen Avila <c.avila@keenmaninc.com>

**Subject:** Re: Hardeston trip

**Date:** September 10

Hi Carmen,

Thank you for the information and advice, but can you hold off on making any bookings for a few days? I'm considering whether to invite a colleague along on the trip. He's the new product manager for our handheld vacuum cleaner, and it may be helpful to show him where it's made and introduce the manufacturing team. I'll update you once the matter has been settled.

—Andrew

**MATTOX**

| **Reservation Number:** | 2023944 |
|---|---|
| **Booking Details** | |
| Vehicle: | Mireles Lyrica Sedan |
| Pickup: | Monday, October 11, 12:45 P.M.<br>Hardeston Regional Airport Branch |
| Return: | Thursday, October 14, 3:00 P.M.<br>Hardeston Regional Airport Branch |
| **Driver Information** | |
| Name: | Andrew Foster |
| Contact: | 555-0184 (mobile) |
| Additional Authorized Driver: | Rajesh Banik |
| **Additional Information** | |
| Corporate Account Number: | 45587 (Keenman Incorporated) |

TEST 6

**191.** What is indicated about Hardeston Regional Airport?

(A) It is not the only airport near the city.
(B) It has a reputation for punctual departures.
(C) It is currently undergoing renovations.
(D) It is not served frequently by Rubin Air.

**192.** What is suggested about Mr. Foster?

(A) He was recently promoted to a managerial position.
(B) He visited Hardeston in July.
(C) He has taken a trip planned by Ms. Avila before.
(D) He stated a preference for a certain hotel.

**193.** Where most likely does Mr. Foster work?

(A) At an automobile manufacturer
(B) At an appliance company
(C) At an aircraft design firm
(D) At a home furnishings business

**194.** What did Mr. Foster most likely do in response to advice?

(A) He chose different lodgings.
(B) He joined an airline loyalty program.
(C) He downloaded a mobile app.
(D) He requested a rental vehicle.

**195.** Based on the form, what can be concluded about Mr. Foster?

(A) He will be picked up at a transportation hub.
(B) He asked a coworker to accompany him.
(C) He decided to extend the length of his stay.
(D) He will pay an expense with his personal credit card.

*GO ON TO THE NEXT PAGE*

**Questions 196-200** refer to the following Web page and e-mails.

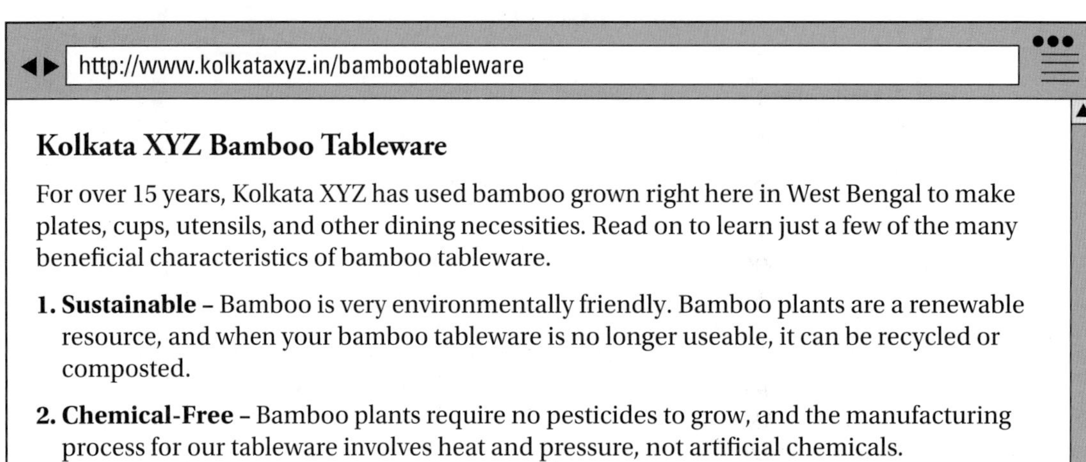
http://www.kolkataxyz.in/bambootableware

## Kolkata XYZ Bamboo Tableware

For over 15 years, Kolkata XYZ has used bamboo grown right here in West Bengal to make plates, cups, utensils, and other dining necessities. Read on to learn just a few of the many beneficial characteristics of bamboo tableware.

1. **Sustainable** – Bamboo is very environmentally friendly. Bamboo plants are a renewable resource, and when your bamboo tableware is no longer useable, it can be recycled or composted.
2. **Chemical-Free** – Bamboo plants require no pesticides to grow, and the manufacturing process for our tableware involves heat and pressure, not artificial chemicals.
3. **Durable** – Bamboo tableware is difficult to break and, though some care must be taken, it can be heated in the microwave, stored in the freezer, and washed in the dishwasher without damage.
4. **Lightweight** – Bamboo is lighter than most tableware materials, making it an excellent choice for families with young children. This also means that our products are very affordable to ship.
5. **Versatile Style** – Bamboo's neutral wood tones, which we highlight in simple, clean shapes, serve as an elegant complement to a wide range of color and design schemes.

| | |
|---|---|
| **To:** | Deepa Sanyal |
| **From:** | Sikha Lahiri |
| **Date:** | 7 October |
| **Subject:** | Bamboo utensils |

Dear Ms. Sanyal,

It was a pleasure to speak with you at last week's trade show. I found your points about the environmental advantages of your company's bamboo tableware very persuasive. So, I have decided that your travel utensil set will make an excellent thank-you gift for the Gir Society's donors, who care deeply about the Earth.

You mentioned that there are several options for the set's carrying case. Could you provide me with details about them? I am particularly interested in comparing their prices (as I prefer an affordable option) and finding the one that causes the least damage to our planet.

Sincerely,

Sikha Lahiri
The Gir Society

| To: | Sikha Lahiri |
|---|---|
| From: | Deepa Sanyal |
| Date: | 8 October |
| Subject: | Re: Bamboo utensils |

Dear Ms. Lahiri,

Thank you for your e-mail. Below is a comparison of the available types of carrying cases for the travel utensil set.

| Case | Unit price | Environmental harm |
|---|---|---|
| Hard plastic case with snap-lock closure | $1.45 | High |
| Cotton pouch with snap buttons | $1.70 | Low |
| Nylon zippered case | $2.10 | Medium |
| Canvas roll-up bag with tie straps | $2.95 | Low |

Please note that a minimum order of 50 units is required. Also, whichever type of case you choose, we would be happy to add your organization's logo and some lettering, such as a thank-you message to your donors, though this will involve an additional fee.

I hope to hear from you again soon.

Sincerely,

Deepa Sanyal
Kolkata XYZ



**196.** What is indicated about Kolkata XYZ?
(A) It also sells children's toys.
(B) It imports bamboo from abroad.
(C) Its primary customers are frequent travelers.
(D) Its tableware can be used in kitchen appliances.

**197.** What is the purpose of the first e-mail?
(A) To revise an order
(B) To solicit a corporate donor
(C) To request information
(D) To make a complaint

**198.** Which characteristic of bamboo tableware had the most influence on Ms. Lahiri?
(A) Characteristic 1
(B) Characteristic 2
(C) Characteristic 3
(D) Characteristic 4

**199.** According to the second e-mail, what is available for all of the carrying cases?
(A) Customization service
(B) A discount on a bulk purchase
(C) Care instructions
(D) A free product sample

**200.** What carrying case will Gir Society donors most likely receive?
(A) The hard plastic case
(B) The cotton pouch
(C) The nylon zippered case
(D) The canvas roll-up bag

**Stop! This is the end of the test. If you finish before time is called, you may go back to Parts 5, 6, and 7 and check your work.**

# YBM 실전토익 RC1000

## 테스트 전 체크리스트

- 중간 휴식 없이 제한 시간을 지켜서 풀이하세요.
- 제한 시간은 답안지에 마킹하는 시간도 포함시켜야 합니다.
- 찍은 문제는 번호 옆에 꼭 체크해 주세요.
- 시간 안에 풀지 못한 문제는 틀린 것으로 채점해 주세요.

RC

# TEST 7

## READING TEST

In the Reading test, you will read a variety of texts and answer several different types of reading comprehension questions. The entire Reading test will last 75 minutes. There are three parts, and directions are given for each part. You are encouraged to answer as many questions as possible within the time allowed.

You must mark your answers on the separate answer sheet. Do not write your answers in your test book.

## PART 5

**Directions:** A word or phrase is missing in each of the sentences below. Four answer choices are given below each sentence. Select the best answer to complete the sentence. Then mark the letter (A), (B), (C), or (D) on your answer sheet.

**101.** Since the weather has been unusually cold, expect ------- heating system to be used more often.

(A) us
(B) our
(C) ours
(D) ourselves

**102.** Austin Inc. strictly prohibits the sharing of ------- memos and other company correspondence.

(A) internalization
(B) internalize
(C) internally
(D) internal

**103.** Segal Bay visitors enjoy using the path ------- the coast to take in the sea air.

(A) regarding
(B) along
(C) except
(D) under

**104.** The firm has reduced its waste ------- various recycling programs and strict policies.

(A) through
(B) onto
(C) as
(D) to

**105.** The medications are ------- tested to ensure compliance with safety regulations.

(A) conveniently
(B) tightly
(C) rigorously
(D) approximately

**106.** Ms. Bracken would like ------- the diligent efforts of her team at the upcoming staff get-together.

(A) recognizing
(B) recognition
(C) to recognize
(D) having recognized

**107.** After ------- several major market fluctuations accurately, Ms. Kimball gained popularity as a financial adviser.

(A) prediction
(B) predict
(C) predicted
(D) predicting

**108.** Any international bank transfers requested ------- 3 P.M. will be made before closing time.

(A) just
(B) later
(C) by
(D) than

**109.** When working on a crucial assignment, it may be better to ------- the deadline rather than rush the work.

(A) approve
(B) expire
(C) adjust
(D) observe

**110.** Any apparel that includes custom images provided by the customer cannot be returned ------- it has been printed.

(A) although
(B) after
(C) as a result
(D) despite

**111.** Thanks to sales ------- in our newest region, we have surpassed targets by fifty percent.

(A) had gained
(B) are gained
(C) to gain
(D) gains

**112.** The highly encrypted storage system at Grendale Inc. is ideal for a ------- document or file.

(A) sensitive
(B) sensation
(C) sense
(D) sensitivity

**113.** There was severe weather over the weekend, ------- attendance at the conference was still high.

(A) nor
(B) so
(C) but
(D) for

**114.** The posters in the movie theater's display windows are ------- changed.

(A) regular
(B) regularly
(C) regularizing
(D) more regular

**115.** The office staff at Warwick International are encouraged to avoid sitting for ------- periods of time.

(A) fierce
(B) adjusted
(C) aware
(D) extended

**116.** To minimize -------, please refrain from asking questions while the presentation is still underway.

(A) to interrupt
(B) interruptions
(C) interrupt
(D) interrupted

**117.** Applicants for the position will not proceed in the screening process ------- their credentials have been confirmed.

(A) also
(B) even
(C) besides
(D) until

**118.** Due to an unexpected malfunction with the aircraft's warning lights, passengers were not able to ------- until 8 P.M.

(A) accommodate
(B) appear
(C) facilitate
(D) board

**119.** The Wilson Technical Institute is recruiting faculty members who feel ------- about their subjects.

(A) careful
(B) passionate
(C) responsible
(D) welcome

**120.** Mr. Santiago will ------- the various options for updating the layout of the office.

(A) be assessing
(B) assessed
(C) assessment
(D) to assess



*GO ON TO THE NEXT PAGE*

**121.** The noise levels inside the office complex are surprisingly low for being located on ------- a busy road.

(A) still
(B) such
(C) soon
(D) nearby

**122.** Mechanics at the Harper Garage must ------- operate the necessary equipment without assistance.

(A) influentially
(B) significantly
(C) enormously
(D) proficiently

**123.** On account of the installation of advanced laser equipment, the plant has tripled in ------- for its output.

(A) quantity
(B) economy
(C) portion
(D) permission

**124.** Mr. Huntley explained that it is difficult to ------- cohesive teams in today's job climate owing to labor shortages.

(A) assemble
(B) surpass
(C) distribute
(D) succeed

**125.** Flint Vehicle Rentals charges an additional fee for insurance ------- drivers are fully covered by their own policy.

(A) rather
(B) if
(C) unless
(D) yet

**126.** The state's legislation does not allow businesses to make cash ------- to candidates.

(A) contribute
(B) contributions
(C) contributes
(D) contributed

**127.** Even though Lakeland Bank's branches have expanded across the country, most of ------- administrative offices are in the northwest.

(A) this
(B) whose
(C) her
(D) its

**128.** ------- temporarily closing the highway for repairs, planners decided to use partial closures and work in phases.

(A) Wherever
(B) Instead of
(C) Promptly
(D) Now that

**129.** Ivy Restaurant has special ingredients to replace meat ------- dairy products in its dishes to make them vegan-friendly.

(A) in addition
(B) yet
(C) when
(D) as well as

**130.** Ms. Baek has focused ------- on digital art for commercial campaigns for multinational corporations.

(A) surprisingly
(B) frankly
(C) presently
(D) primarily

## PART 6

**Directions:** Read the texts that follow. A word, phrase, or sentence is missing in parts of each text. Four answer choices for each question are given below the text. Select the best answer to complete the text. Then mark the letter (A), (B), (C), or (D) on your answer sheet.

**Questions 131-134** refer to the following letter.

Dear Ms. Rogers,

Thank you for your interest in booking a private tour of our chocolate factory for your work colleagues. Please note that certain sections of the production line are not available to the public. -------. **131.** However, there is still a lot to see. We show all tour participants an ------- **132.** video. It will teach you about the history of our company. This ------- **133.** lasts approximately twenty minutes and can be at the beginning or the end of the tour.

Please let ------- **134.** know what date you plan to attend and how many people will be in your group. We hope you will have an enjoyable time!

Warmest regards,

Clayton Pemberton, Administrator

Bylee Chocolate Factory

**131.** (A) The ticket is valid only for the date specified.
(B) In the event of a cancellation, we will send your items back.
(C) We cannot change this due to food regulations.
(D) Each one is led by a knowledgeable member of staff.

**132.** (A) eager
(B) artistic
(C) informative
(D) abundant

**133.** (A) treatment
(B) provision
(C) trip
(D) viewing

**134.** (A) each
(B) him
(C) they
(D) us

TEST 7

*GO ON TO THE NEXT PAGE*

**Questions 135-138** refer to the following notice.

NOTICE TO TENANTS

In -------  to numerous requests from tenants, Gresham Apartments will be renovating its on-site
**135.**
fitness center from March 6 to 27. ------- we are carrying out the work, the exercise equipment
**136.**
and the room itself will be off limits to all tenants, so you will need to make other arrangements to maintain your fitness routine.

We ------- any inconvenience the project may cause, and we appreciate your patience. -------.
**137.** **138.**

The Gresham Apartments Management Team

**135.** (A) responded
(B) responder
(C) response
(D) respond

**136.** (A) Whereas
(B) However
(C) During
(D) While

**137.** (A) tolerate
(B) apologize
(C) regret
(D) encounter

**138.** (A) Please show your ID or apartment key at the door.
(B) If you are interested in viewing a two-bedroom unit, call us anytime.
(C) We are confident that the finished result will be worth the hassle.
(D) Thank you for dealing with this problem promptly.

**Questions 139-142** refer to the following e-mail.

To: Kahoda Naidu

From: info@vistapharmacy.com

Date: April 24

Subject: New Vista Pharmacy branch!

Dear Mr. Naidu,

The staff at Vista Pharmacy is ------- (139.) to announce that we will open a second branch to better serve our customers. The branch will be located at 905 Victoria Street. As with our original site, the new branch will offer a comprehensive list of services beyond filling prescriptions. ------- (140.). The Victoria Street branch also has a drive-up window.

At the window or inside, you can stop by anytime during our business hours ------- (141.) your medicine. As always, we can answer any questions you may have about what your ------- (142.) prescribed to you. We look forward to serving you!

Warmest regards,

The Vista Pharmacy Team

**139.** (A) delightful
(B) delighted
(C) delightfully
(D) delights

**140.** (A) Many of them have symptoms that may be uncomfortable.
(B) These include collecting unwanted medication for safe disposal.
(C) We can hold it for you for up to ten business days.
(D) The renovations will make the counter more accessible.

**141.** (A) to collect
(B) being collected
(C) collected
(D) collecting

**142.** (A) supervisor
(B) patient
(C) colleague
(D) physician

TEST 7

*GO ON TO THE NEXT PAGE*

**Questions 143-146** refer to the following customer review.

I recently found some old photographs that belonged to my grandmother, and I wanted to get them restored as ------- (143.) as possible to the original shots. A colleague of mine suggested Clover Photos in the Greenwood neighborhood. Carlene, the shop's owner, was helpful in explaining my options and assisting me with choosing the level of service that was right for me. She completed the restoration and framing in just three days ------- (144.) it is the busy season. The pictures look fantastic. ------- (145.).

Carlene is highly experienced. She is a ------- (146.) photo editor. I cannot recommend her highly enough.

Ida Briggs, Bristol

**143.** (A) closest
(B) closely
(C) closer
(D) closeness

**144.** (A) not only
(B) such as
(C) so that
(D) even though

**145.** (A) At least the delivery times are reliable.
(B) I am an amateur photographer myself.
(C) She used to own a gallery.
(D) The frame's quality is amazing too.

**146.** (A) talented
(B) best
(C) fortunate
(D) voluntary

## PART 7

**Directions:** In this part you will read a selection of texts, such as magazine and newspaper articles, e-mails, and instant messages. Each text or set of texts is followed by several questions. Select the best answer for each question and mark the letter (A), (B), (C), or (D) on your answer sheet.

**Questions 147-148** refer to the following job advertisement.

### English Tutors Needed

Shine Education is seeking friendly and enthusiastic instructors to teach multilingual students aged 5 to 11 on our platform. We have developed a fun and interesting curriculum, so all of the lesson planning has been done for you. And as you will be exclusively using English, communicating in a foreign language is unnecessary. All you need is a positive attitude, a laptop, and a sound and stable Internet connection.

Position highlights:

- No work on holidays, and bonus pay on weekends.
- Ultimate flexibility—open classes only when you want to.
- Fast payment—get paid by bank transfer every week.

Find out more at shineeduwow.com/apply.

**147.** What requirement is expected of all applicants?

(A) A reliable method for getting online
(B) Graduation from a four-year university
(C) Previous experience in education
(D) Samples of lesson plans they have developed

**148.** What is true about the position?

(A) It includes working with children and adults.
(B) It is only suitable for multilingual people.
(C) It allows workers to set their schedule.
(D) It involves teaching on weekends and holidays.

GO ON TO THE NEXT PAGE

**Questions 149-150** refer to the following Web page.

http://www.kennonhotel.co.uk

**An Announcement from Rosalie Willis, CEO of Kennon Hotel**

Helpline: 1-800-555-9056

Many of our valued customers have been affected by the computer glitch that caused rooms at our hotel to be double-booked. We assure you that we are doing everything we can to minimize the negative effects of the situation. Customers whom we are not able to accommodate at our site will be booked at nearby hotels in rooms of equivalent or greater size and quality, still paying only the originally quoted rate. In addition, customers usually must cancel at least 48 hours before their scheduled check-in time to avoid being charged for the first night's stay. For the next three weeks, this will be changed to 24 hours.

**149.** What is the purpose of the announcement?

(A) To explain measures to resolve a problem
(B) To introduce a newly opened hotel
(C) To promote discounted rates to loyal customers
(D) To encourage customers to use a reservation system

**150.** According to Ms. Willis, what has the hotel changed temporarily?

(A) The fee for staying more than one night
(B) The deadline for canceling at no charge
(C) The hours of operation for a helpline
(D) The wait time for checking in to the hotel

**Questions 151-152** refer to the following report.

April 5

**SOIL CONTAMINATION REPORT**

Client: Gould Manufacturing
Testing Performed By: Soil-Check Solutions
Testing Dates: March 3, May 5, July 2, September 5

Process: Samples were collected from various points at Site 1 (Lancaster), Site 2 (Canton), and Site 3 (Brockway) at a depth of 6 cm and 10 cm. The soil was tested for contaminants, and the levels were compared to assess changes over time. Following the initial test, micro-organisms were introduced at all sites.

Preliminary Findings and Recommended Actions: Contamination levels at Site 1 dropped significantly. No further action is needed. At Site 2, a soil stabilization formula should be injected into the ground. This will dry into a hardened solid, which can then be removed by specialized equipment. Micro-organisms should be reapplied. At Site 3, the grass and shrubs should be pulled from the soil, and micro-organisms should be reapplied.

**151.** What is true about the soil testing?
(A) It fulfilled a requirement set by the government.
(B) It was carried out by full-time Gould Manufacturing staff.
(C) It mainly focused on the Canton site.
(D) It had gaps between the collection days.

**152.** What action is recommended for Gould Manufacturing?
(A) Taking soil from a depth of more than ten centimeters
(B) Injecting a formula into the soil at Lancaster
(C) Ceasing micro-organism treatment at Canton
(D) Removing plants at Brockway

TEST 7

*GO ON TO THE NEXT PAGE*

**Questions 153-154** refer to the following text-message chain.

**Mason Nguyen** **[10:27 A.M.]**
Hi, Eva. I've just e-mailed you the presentation slides for our meeting with Lyndon Enterprises. It outlines how we can help them manage regulations when selling their goods abroad. Did you receive it?

**Eva Salazar** **[10:28 A.M.]**
I'm just opening it now. Is this the finished version?

**Mason Nguyen** **[10:29 A.M.]**
No. I was wondering if you could put in some statistics on slides 4 through 6.

**Eva Salazar** **[10:30 A.M.]**
Sure thing. Do you need me to prepare anything else for it?

**Mason Nguyen** **[10:31 A.M.]**
Maybe we should include information about the steps for port registration, as Lyndon Enterprises plans to bring goods into the country as well.

**Eva Salazar** **[10:33 A.M.]**
That might be a good idea. Let me check what you have and get back to you.

**153.** At 10:30 A.M., what does Ms. Salazar most likely mean when she writes, "Sure thing"?

(A) She is willing to contact Lyndon Enterprises' staff members.
(B) She can add numerical information to a presentation file.
(C) She is happy to attend a meeting in Mr. Nguyen's place.
(D) She plans to stay at work later than usual today.

**154.** What kind of work do the writers most likely do?

(A) Computer programming
(B) Safety inspections
(C) Market analysis
(D) Import-export services

**Questions 155-157** refer to the following e-mail.

**E-Mail message**

| | |
|---|---|
| **To:** | ztaheri@larabeemail.com |
| **From:** | parksoomin@civilengconf.com |
| **Date:** | August 3 |
| **Subject:** | Civil Engineering Conference |

Dear Mr. Taheri,

It was wonderful to speak with you today, and I am pleased that you have accepted our invitation to attend the 50th Annual Civil Engineering Conference, which takes place from November 5 to 8 in Atlanta. We were greatly disappointed that you were unable to share your expertise in your presentation last year, as the events on the final day of the conference were called off due to severe weather. Our attendance is up by nearly 100 compared to last year, so we are using the largest room, Navarro Hall. It has a capacity of 250, and we expect it to be full. We have you booked for the morning of the second day. As you make your preparations, please keep in mind that the talk should be a maximum of 120 minutes. You will have standard presentation equipment at your disposal, but if you require anything else, please let me know.

Best,

Soomin Park
Event Coordinator, Civil Engineering Conference

**155.** What is suggested about Mr. Taheri's previous presentation for the conference?
(A) It suffered from some technical malfunctions.
(B) It was canceled by the event organizers.
(C) It was given in Navarro Hall.
(D) It received good reviews from participants.

**156.** Approximately how many participants are expected at the event?
(A) 50
(B) 100
(C) 120
(D) 250

**157.** For when has a time slot been reserved for Mr. Taheri's talk?
(A) November 5
(B) November 6
(C) November 7
(D) November 8

TEST 7

GO ON TO THE NEXT PAGE

**Questions 158-160** refer to the following article.

## New Chapter for City Hall

(Jan. 20)—ETB has won the bid for the expansion project at City Hall, which will add 90,000 square feet of space. — [1] —. The work will be covered partially by the general budget, with the remaining funding coming from federal grants. — [2] —. ETB has invited a local community club, the Hampton Historic Society, to advise on the project due to the historical significance of City Hall. — [3] —. The additional wing will house a much-needed larger conference room and twelve offices. — [4] —. Visit the ETB Web site for further details.

**158.** What kind of business most likely is ETB?

(A) A financial institution
(B) A community club
(C) A construction company
(D) A real estate firm

**159.** What is suggested about City Hall?

(A) Scheduled changes to it will probably be postponed.
(B) It currently cannot accommodate large meetings.
(C) An individual has made a financial donation to it.
(D) It has ninety thousand square feet of space in total.

**160.** In which of the positions marked [1], [2], [3], and [4] does the following sentence best belong?

"Some will be used by the newly formed Consumer Affairs Division."

(A) [1]
(B) [2]
(C) [3]
(D) [4]

**Questions 161-163** refer to the following information.

## UTICA INC.

### Thank you for your patronage!

We hope you will enjoy all the amazing features that Utica's TX-8 model has to offer. This is one of the most fuel-efficient vehicles on the market, and it comes equipped with the latest technological advances. The automatic emergency braking system helps to improve safety for both you and your passengers, and the adaptive cruise control function monitors your distance from other objects and makes adjustments accordingly.

For further assistance from the Utica Inc. team, why not download our new smartphone application? You can chat with customer service staff or technicians 24 hours a day, 7 days a week. The app has a map that shows the nearest gas stations along with up-to-the-minute pricing information. It even allows you to check your fuel level and get an estimate of its range.

At Utica Inc., we don't just follow the trend; we lead with our own style and approach.

**161.** In what field does Utica Inc. operate?

(A) Building security
(B) Automotive manufacturing
(C) Software distribution
(D) Fuel production

**162.** What does the new Utica Inc. smartphone application allow users to do?

(A) Check for recalls and safety-related reports
(B) Learn about special offers before other customers
(C) Track product shipments in real time
(D) Compare prices at different businesses

**163.** The word "follow" in paragraph 3, line 1, is closest in meaning to

(A) stick to
(B) accompany
(C) guide
(D) replace

TEST 7

*GO ON TO THE NEXT PAGE*

**Questions 164-167** refer to the following letter.

May 14

Matthias Holtzmann
Augsburger Strasse 15
57580 Elben

Dear Mr. Holtzmann,

On behalf of the Youth Music Program (YMP), I would like to express our appreciation for your volunteering for our organization. Without the dedication and hard work of people like you, we could not achieve our common goals and have such a profound positive effect on communities throughout Germany. YMP helps young people cultivate a lifelong love of music, and share the joy of music with others, enhancing well-being and social cohesion. In just two years, we have expanded the number of program centers to twenty-three. Guided by our new executive director, Wayne Kastner, we expect this trend to continue.

Among the many exciting changes on the horizon, we are delighted to partner with Himmel Music, the country's largest supplier of musical instruments. Himmel Music will donate instruments to our organization as well as assist in our quarterly fundraising events.

To celebrate working with Himmel Music, we are holding a contest to create a slogan to represent the joint efforts of this new relationship. All YMP participants, staff, and volunteers are urged to share their ideas. The best one will be selected by a committee, and the winner will receive a $250 Himmel Music gift certificate. More information about the contest will be included in our monthly newsletter, so be sure to watch for it.

Warmest regards,

*Gabriele Reinhardt*

Gabriele Reinhardt
Development Coordinator
Youth Music Program

**164.** What is one purpose of the letter?

(A) To make a request for donations
(B) To announce a new partnership
(C) To explain an organization's name change
(D) To extend an invitation to a musical performance

**165.** The word "common" in paragraph 1, line 3, is closest in meaning to

(A) mutual
(B) popular
(C) intended
(D) ordinary

**166.** What is suggested about Mr. Holtzmann?

(A) He is encouraged to submit a slogan.
(B) He has been nominated for an award.
(C) He will be given a music store gift card.
(D) He was a founding member of YMP.

**167.** What is NOT indicated about the YMP?

(A) It holds fundraising events four times a year.
(B) It has experienced rapid growth.
(C) It is the country's largest youth organization.
(D) It has recently changed its leadership.

**Questions 168-171** refer to the following online chat discussion.

**Yurino Saiki** **1:54 P.M.**
What did you think of the applicant Ruby Fleming?

**Aziz Miri** **1:55 P.M.**
She really impressed me in the interview. I think her artwork would be a great addition to our children's series.

**Yurino Saiki** **1:56 P.M.**
If we hire her, I thought Levi could teach her how to use our on-site file-sharing program. It wouldn't be software she's worked with before. Levi, would that be an issue for you?

**Aziz Miri** **1:57 P.M.**
Of everyone we've interviewed, I think she would be the best fit for the team.

**Levi Weiler** **1:58 P.M.**
Of course not.

**Yurino Saiki** **2:00 P.M.**
Thanks a lot! I also see from her cover letter that she has built up a following on social media.

**Levi Weiler** **2:01 P.M.**
That would help to boost sales. So, are we ready to make her a job offer?

**Aziz Miri** **2:02 P.M.**
Mr. Gilliam wants to have a follow-up interview by teleconference first to talk about how she might handle the role. He says it's essential that the person can cope with being assigned numerous tasks.

**Yurino Saiki** **2:04 P.M.**
Aziz, are you setting up that meeting?

**Aziz Miri** **2:05 P.M.**
Yes, I'll take care of everything.

**168.** Where do the writers most likely work?

(A) At an employment recruitment firm
(B) At a children's clothing store
(C) At a book publisher
(D) At a movie theater

**169.** At 1:58 P.M., what does Mr. Weiler most likely mean when he writes, "Of course not"?

(A) He is willing to provide some training.
(B) He can accommodate an interview schedule.
(C) He will not miss an important deadline.
(D) He is not ready to make a decision yet.

**170.** What is indicated about Ms. Fleming?

(A) She already has her own fan base.
(B) She currently works for a social media company.
(C) She will cover shifts while Mr. Weiler is on leave.
(D) She prefers to discuss matters by teleconference.

**171.** According to the discussion, what does Mr. Gilliam think is critical to the open position?

(A) The ability to deal with several assignments efficiently
(B) A collaborative approach to work projects
(C) Dedication to improving customer service
(D) Experience working with many software programs

*GO ON TO THE NEXT PAGE*

**Questions 172-175** refer to the following e-mail.

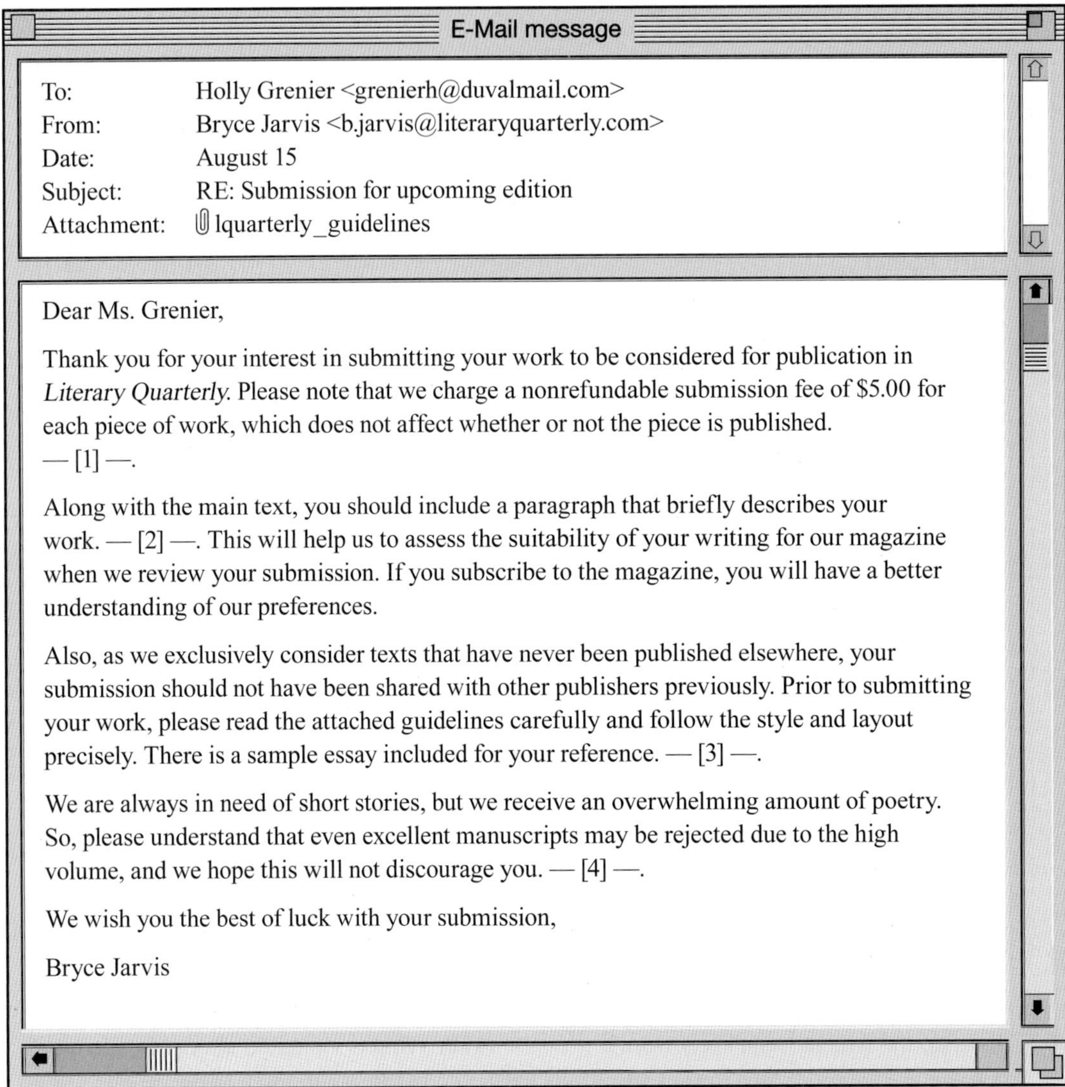

E-Mail message

To: Holly Grenier <grenierh@duvalmail.com>
From: Bryce Jarvis <b.jarvis@literaryquarterly.com>
Date: August 15
Subject: RE: Submission for upcoming edition
Attachment: lquarterly_guidelines

Dear Ms. Grenier,

Thank you for your interest in submitting your work to be considered for publication in *Literary Quarterly*. Please note that we charge a nonrefundable submission fee of $5.00 for each piece of work, which does not affect whether or not the piece is published. — [1] —.

Along with the main text, you should include a paragraph that briefly describes your work. — [2] —. This will help us to assess the suitability of your writing for our magazine when we review your submission. If you subscribe to the magazine, you will have a better understanding of our preferences.

Also, as we exclusively consider texts that have never been published elsewhere, your submission should not have been shared with other publishers previously. Prior to submitting your work, please read the attached guidelines carefully and follow the style and layout precisely. There is a sample essay included for your reference. — [3] —.

We are always in need of short stories, but we receive an overwhelming amount of poetry. So, please understand that even excellent manuscripts may be rejected due to the high volume, and we hope this will not discourage you. — [4] —.

We wish you the best of luck with your submission,

Bryce Jarvis

**172.** What is suggested about *Literary Quarterly*?

(A) Its main texts are usually produced by in-house writers.
(B) It solely publishes work being made public for the first time.
(C) Its management is considering publishing editions more frequently.
(D) It only contacts writers whose submissions have been accepted.

**173.** What is NOT mentioned as a requirement for making a submission?

(A) Paying a one-time fee
(B) Providing a short description
(C) Subscribing to the magazine
(D) Formatting the work in a specific way

**174.** What is Ms. Grenier most likely interested in writing?

(A) Poetry
(B) Short stories
(C) Essays
(D) Book reviews

**175.** In which of the positions marked [1], [2], [3], and [4] does the following sentence best belong?

"Be sure to include relevant information that will be important in the initial screening process."

(A) [1]
(B) [2]
(C) [3]
(D) [4]

TEST 7

GO ON TO THE NEXT PAGE

**Questions 176-180** refer to the following Web page and review.

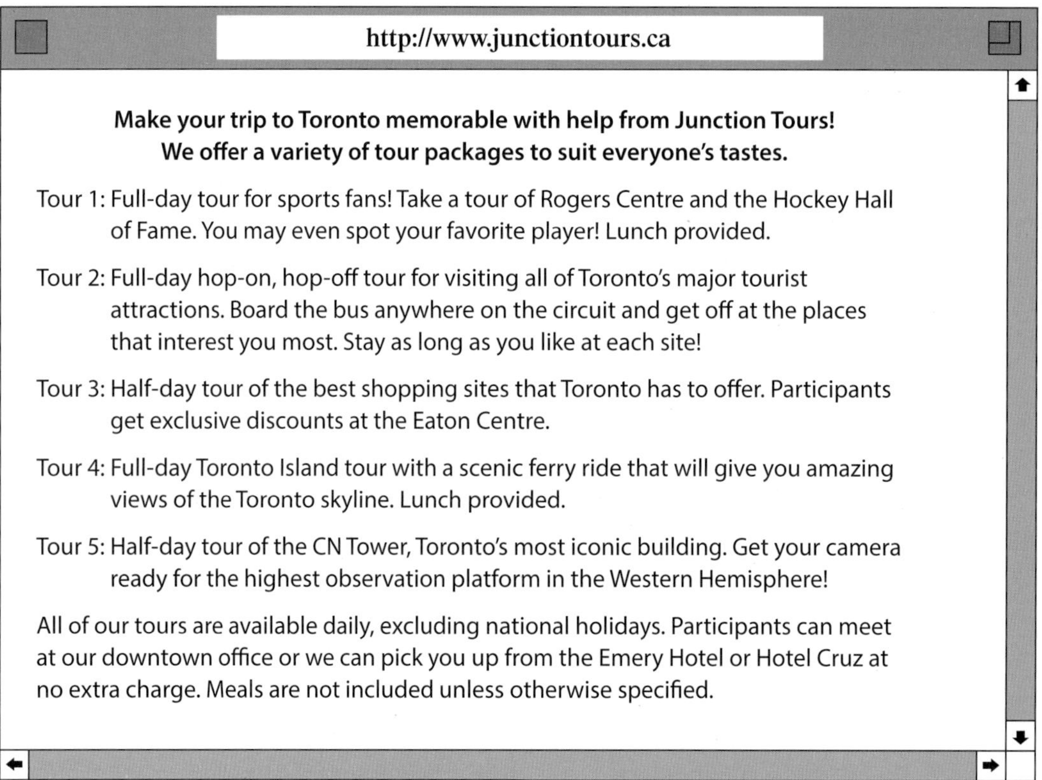

http://www.junctiontours.ca

**Make your trip to Toronto memorable with help from Junction Tours!**
**We offer a variety of tour packages to suit everyone's tastes.**

Tour 1: Full-day tour for sports fans! Take a tour of Rogers Centre and the Hockey Hall of Fame. You may even spot your favorite player! Lunch provided.

Tour 2: Full-day hop-on, hop-off tour for visiting all of Toronto's major tourist attractions. Board the bus anywhere on the circuit and get off at the places that interest you most. Stay as long as you like at each site!

Tour 3: Half-day tour of the best shopping sites that Toronto has to offer. Participants get exclusive discounts at the Eaton Centre.

Tour 4: Full-day Toronto Island tour with a scenic ferry ride that will give you amazing views of the Toronto skyline. Lunch provided.

Tour 5: Half-day tour of the CN Tower, Toronto's most iconic building. Get your camera ready for the highest observation platform in the Western Hemisphere!

All of our tours are available daily, excluding national holidays. Participants can meet at our downtown office or we can pick you up from the Emery Hotel or Hotel Cruz at no extra charge. Meals are not included unless otherwise specified.

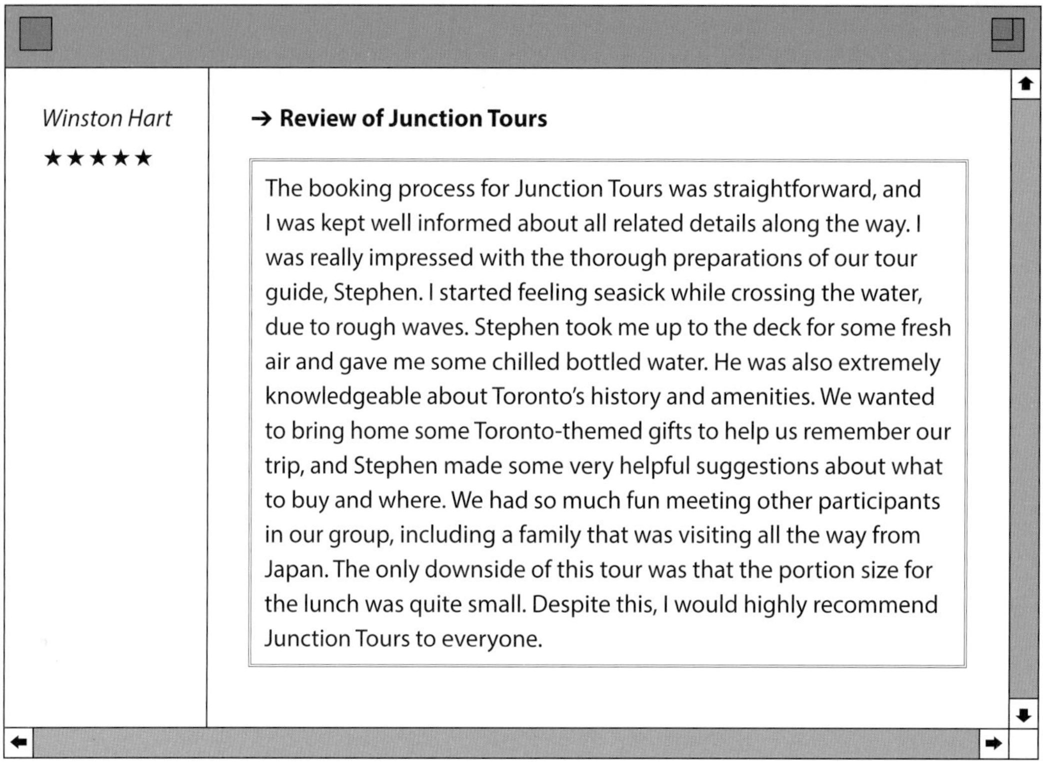

*Winston Hart*
★★★★★

**→ Review of Junction Tours**

The booking process for Junction Tours was straightforward, and I was kept well informed about all related details along the way. I was really impressed with the thorough preparations of our tour guide, Stephen. I started feeling seasick while crossing the water, due to rough waves. Stephen took me up to the deck for some fresh air and gave me some chilled bottled water. He was also extremely knowledgeable about Toronto's history and amenities. We wanted to bring home some Toronto-themed gifts to help us remember our trip, and Stephen made some very helpful suggestions about what to buy and where. We had so much fun meeting other participants in our group, including a family that was visiting all the way from Japan. The only downside of this tour was that the portion size for the lunch was quite small. Despite this, I would highly recommend Junction Tours to everyone.

**176.** How is Tour 2 different from the rest of the tours?

(A) Its participants can go at their own pace.
(B) Its attractions are famous in Toronto.
(C) It lasts for a full day.
(D) It includes help from a tour guide.

**177.** What is included in all tour packages?

(A) Lunch on the tour day
(B) Storage of participants' luggage
(C) Transportation from certain hotels
(D) A visit to the CN Tower

**178.** Which tour did Mr. Hart most likely take?

(A) Tour 1
(B) Tour 3
(C) Tour 4
(D) Tour 5

**179.** What does the review suggest about Stephen?

(A) He can speak Japanese.
(B) He has a history degree.
(C) He was born in Toronto.
(D) He gave advice on souvenirs.

**180.** Why was Mr. Hart dissatisfied with part of the tour?

(A) The guide was disorganized.
(B) A meal was small.
(C) The area was crowded.
(D) A schedule was not followed.

TEST 7

GO ON TO THE NEXT PAGE

**Questions 181-185** refer to the following e-mails.

**To:** Bradely Jackson <bjackson@cambridgestar.com>
**From:** promotions@moonlight-bedding.com
**Date:** February 10
**Subject:** Grab a bedding bargain!

Dear Customer:

Don't miss Moonlight Bedding's Annual Clearance Sale, which starts tomorrow! It's the perfect time to stock up on sheets, pillowcases, and mattress covers. Normally we hold our sale for just one week, but we're running it for two weeks this year, from February 11 to 24. A wide range of patterns, colors, and fabric types is available. And whether you have a small twin bed, a king-sized bed, or anything in between, we're sure you'll find something you love. Anyone who places an order on the first day of the sale will receive a free 50 ml. bottle of our new Lavender Sleep Spray, so be sure to shop tomorrow and use code THX05. In addition, customers who spend $50 or more will receive free shipping. The inventory in our online catalog is available only while supplies last.

We hope to serve you soon!

Billy Elwood
Promotions Team, Moonlight Bedding

Please note: This e-mail has been sent to customers who have made frequent purchases in the past year. You can unsubscribe at any time.

**To:** bjackson@cambridgestar.com
**From:** orders@moonlight-bedding.com
**Date:** February 11
**Subject:** Order confirmation

Dear Mr. Jackson,

Thank you for participating in Moonlight Bedding's Annual Clearance Sale! Your items will be shipped within three business days.

| Item# | Description | Quantity | Total |
|---|---|---|---|
| 3950 | Blue checkered sheet set (queen) | 1 | $15.99 |
| 3210 | Blue checkered pillowcase (set of 2) | 1 | $3.75 |
| 9442 | Beige flat sheet (queen) | 2 | $13.98 |
| 8674 | Blue flat sheet (twin) | 1 | $4.95 |
| 1041 | Lavender sleep spray (promo: THX05) | 1 | $0.00 |
| | | | Subtotal: $38.67 |
| | | | Shipping fee: $5.00 |
| | | | Total: $43.67 |

*Please note that the items in this order are subject to a stricter return policy than regular purchases.*

Be sure to visit our Web site again soon, as we release new patterns frequently!

**181.** Why does Mr. Elwood recommend placing an order on February 11 ?

(A) To be sent a product catalog
(B) To avoid long shipping times
(C) To receive a bonus gift
(D) To try a new bedding pattern

**182.** What is suggested about Mr. Jackson?

(A) He is a regular Moonlight Bedding customer.
(B) He owns a king-sized bed.
(C) He only purchases bedding in a certain color.
(D) He will receive his goods on February 12.

**183.** What is indicated about the items in Mr. Jackson's order?

(A) They can be exchanged for any reason.
(B) They all have a checkered pattern.
(C) They may arrive in separate boxes.
(D) They follow different return policy guidelines.

**184.** How could Mr. Jackson have taken advantage of a special promotion?

(A) By writing a product review
(B) By spending more on his order
(C) By ordering on a different day
(D) By trying some newly released merchandise

**185.** What is NOT true about Moonlight Bedding?

(A) It provides bedding in different sizes.
(B) It changes its inventory regularly.
(C) It sells curtains to match its bedding.
(D) Its clearance sale is longer this year.

TEST 7

*GO ON TO THE NEXT PAGE*

**Questions 186-190** refer to the following e-mail, product information, and invoice.

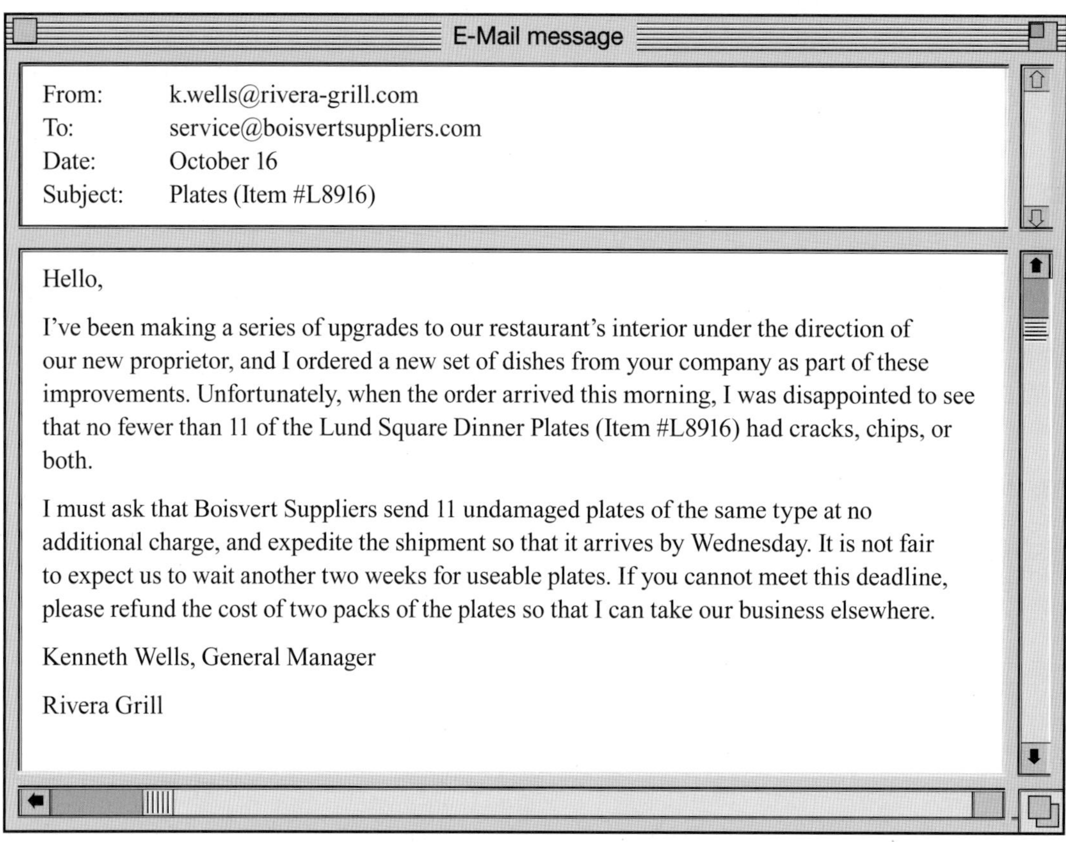

E-Mail message

From: k.wells@rivera-grill.com
To: service@boisvertsuppliers.com
Date: October 16
Subject: Plates (Item #L8916)

Hello,

I've been making a series of upgrades to our restaurant's interior under the direction of our new proprietor, and I ordered a new set of dishes from your company as part of these improvements. Unfortunately, when the order arrived this morning, I was disappointed to see that no fewer than 11 of the Lund Square Dinner Plates (Item #L8916) had cracks, chips, or both.

I must ask that Boisvert Suppliers send 11 undamaged plates of the same type at no additional charge, and expedite the shipment so that it arrives by Wednesday. It is not fair to expect us to wait another two weeks for useable plates. If you cannot meet this deadline, please refund the cost of two packs of the plates so that I can take our business elsewhere.

Kenneth Wells, General Manager

Rivera Grill

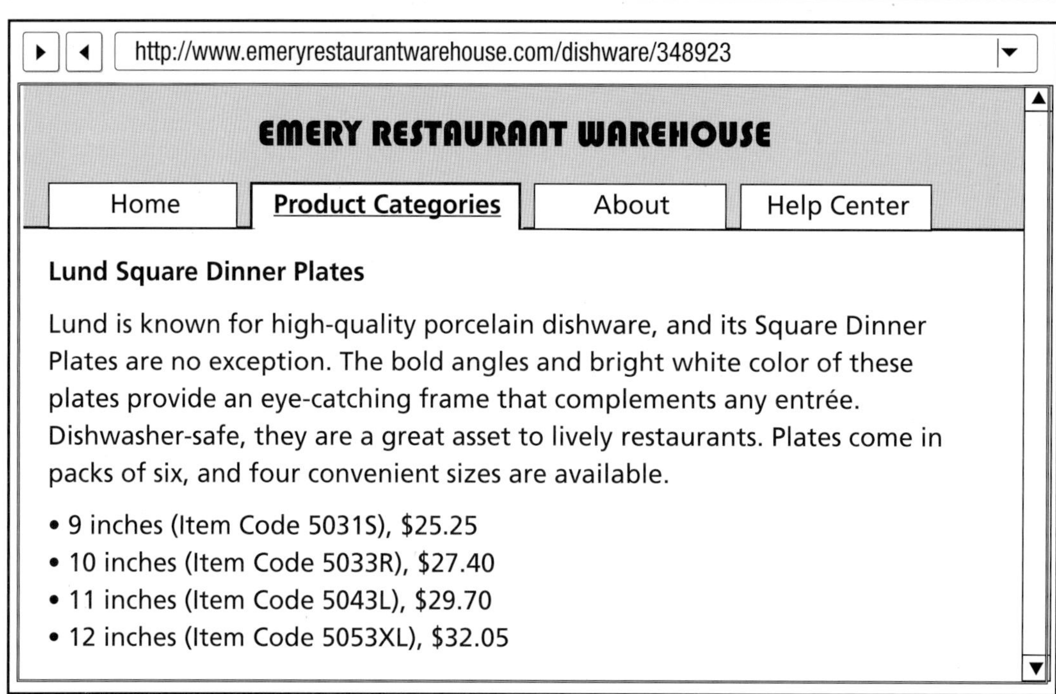

http://www.emeryrestaurantwarehouse.com/dishware/348923

EMERY RESTAURANT WAREHOUSE

Home | Product Categories | About | Help Center

**Lund Square Dinner Plates**

Lund is known for high-quality porcelain dishware, and its Square Dinner Plates are no exception. The bold angles and bright white color of these plates provide an eye-catching frame that complements any entrée. Dishwasher-safe, they are a great asset to lively restaurants. Plates come in packs of six, and four convenient sizes are available.

- 9 inches (Item Code 5031S), $25.25
- 10 inches (Item Code 5033R), $27.40
- 11 inches (Item Code 5043L), $29.70
- 12 inches (Item Code 5053XL), $32.05

## EMERY RESTAURANT WAREHOUSE

### INVOICE

**Order Date:** October 17
**Order #:** 45731

**Ship to/Bill to:** Kenneth Wells
Rivera Grill
280 Switzer Drive
Bernier, TX 78046

| Item Code | Item Name | Quantity | Unit Price | Total |
|---|---|---|---|---|
| 5033R | Lund Square Dinner Plates | 2 | $27.40 | $54.80 |
| | | | | Express Shipping: $20.00<br>Subtotal: $74.80<br>Tax (8%): $5.98<br>Total: $80.78 |

**186.** According to the e-mail, what did Rivera Grill recently do?

(A) It opened a second location.
(B) It added some items to its menu.
(C) It came under new ownership.
(D) It expanded its dining area.

**187.** What is a purpose of the e-mail?

(A) To obtain replacement pieces of tableware
(B) To request suggestions of similar products
(C) To ask about repairing some damaged plates
(D) To receive advice on choosing a shipping service

**188.** In the product information, what is stated about Lund Square Dinner Plates?

(A) They come in several colors.
(B) They are the brand's bestselling item.
(C) They are safe for use in microwave ovens.
(D) They enhance the appearance of food.

**189.** What is implied about Boisvert Suppliers?

(A) It was acquired by another company.
(B) It requires a fee of $20 for expedited shipping.
(C) It raised the prices it charges for Lund dishware.
(D) It returned some of Mr. Wells's payment.

**190.** What size are the plates Mr. Wells ordered from Emery Restaurant Warehouse?

(A) 9 inches
(B) 10 inches
(C) 11 inches
(D) 12 inches

TEST 7

GO ON TO THE NEXT PAGE

**Questions 191-195** refer to the following e-mails and notice.

| | |
|---|---|
| **To:** | Veronica Hale <vhale@castillosouthwest.com> |
| **From:** | Natalie Lewin <natalie@biz-builder.com> |
| **Date:** | August 12 |
| **Subject:** | Workshop and books |

Dear Ms. Hale,

Your registration for Ganesh Kamal's workshop on September 3 has been confirmed. As you have registered for the in-person workshop, rather than the online workshop, please let us know if you have any dietary restrictions. This will help us prepare the refreshments for the breaks. We have also processed your payment for Mr. Kamal's books below, which are eligible for a 20% discount, as they are relevant to the workshop's sessions.

| Title | Price | Discounted Price | Subtotal |
|---|---|---|---|
| *Corporate and Social Responsibility* x 1 | $16.00 | $12.80 | $12.80 |
| *Writing Effective Press Releases* x 1 | $25.00 | $20.00 | $20.00 |
| *Crisis Management in Public Relations* x 1 | $26.00 | $20.80 | $20.80 |
| *Clarifying Communications Objectives* x 1 | $21.00 | $16.80 | $16.80 |
| Total charge of $70.40 to credit card ending in -8405. | | | |

We look forward to seeing you at the event!

Natalie Lewin
Administrator, Biz-Builder

**Notice to Workshop Participants:**

Unfortunately, our question-and-answer page is not working, and it may not be fixed by September 3. Online participants can still submit questions to natalie@biz-builder.com during the event, and we will pass them along to Ganesh Kamal in a timely manner. Please also note that online participants will receive their books by express shipping, no later than September 1, and everyone else can collect their orders from the registration table.

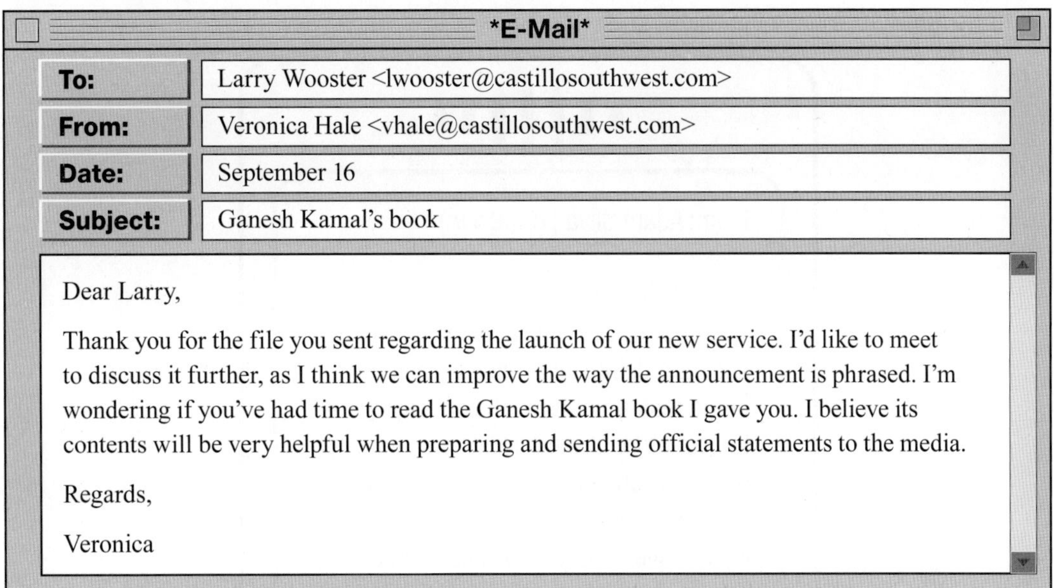

*E-Mail*

**To:** Larry Wooster <lwooster@castillosouthwest.com>

**From:** Veronica Hale <vhale@castillosouthwest.com>

**Date:** September 16

**Subject:** Ganesh Kamal's book

Dear Larry,

Thank you for the file you sent regarding the launch of our new service. I'd like to meet to discuss it further, as I think we can improve the way the announcement is phrased. I'm wondering if you've had time to read the Ganesh Kamal book I gave you. I believe its contents will be very helpful when preparing and sending official statements to the media.

Regards,

Veronica

**191.** What most likely is the workshop topic on September 3 ?

(A) Graphic design
(B) Retirement planning
(C) Public relations
(D) Software development

**192.** What is suggested about Ms. Hale?

(A) She noticed a problem on a Web page.
(B) She will receive a partial refund.
(C) She paid extra for express shipping.
(D) She picked up her books herself.

**193.** What is the purpose of the notice?

(A) To gather feedback about a workshop
(B) To promote the sale of Mr. Kamal's books
(C) To offer a solution to a problem
(D) To explain a change in location

**194.** In the second e-mail, what does Ms. Hale suggest changing?

(A) The wording of a document
(B) The date of a service launch
(C) The content of an employee manual
(D) The folder for a saved file

**195.** How much was Ms. Hale charged for the book she gave to Mr. Wooster?

(A) $12.80
(B) $20.00
(C) $20.80
(D) $16.80



*GO ON TO THE NEXT PAGE*

**Questions 196-200** refer to the following text message, article, and review.

From: Adam Silva [10:49 A.M.]

To: Frida Landvik

Good morning! The ventilation consultants and I are doing our on-site walk-through of the restaurant now. They're saying that the structure of the building will actually make it pretty easy to set up a kitchen that complies with city regulations. We won't have to route the exhaust duct all the way to the roof as we feared. So, the $10,000 we set aside for this part of the project will be more than enough to cover the work. I wanted to tell you right away since I know you were concerned about that. I'll call you with details once we're finished.

## New Restaurant to Take Over Sherman Street Landmark

GLADNEY (7 August)—Reeves House, the 130-year-old home located at 560 Sherman Street, is being converted into a restaurant set to open later this month.

The restaurant's co-owners, Frida Landvik and Adam Silva, purchased the property from Marian Reeves, the last descendant of the family that built the home. Their eatery will be named "The Oak Bistro" after the large tree that stands on the front lawn.

The graceful gray house and its grounds have been well-maintained during their long history. Mr. Silva says the structure has needed some upgrades to satisfy restaurant regulations but few repairs.

When it opens, The Oak Bistro will serve lunch and dinner dishes inspired by Ms. Landvik's childhood in Norway. Indoor seating for 25 people will be available year-round, with additional seating on the front lawn offered from June through September.

More information can be found at www.theoakbistro.com.

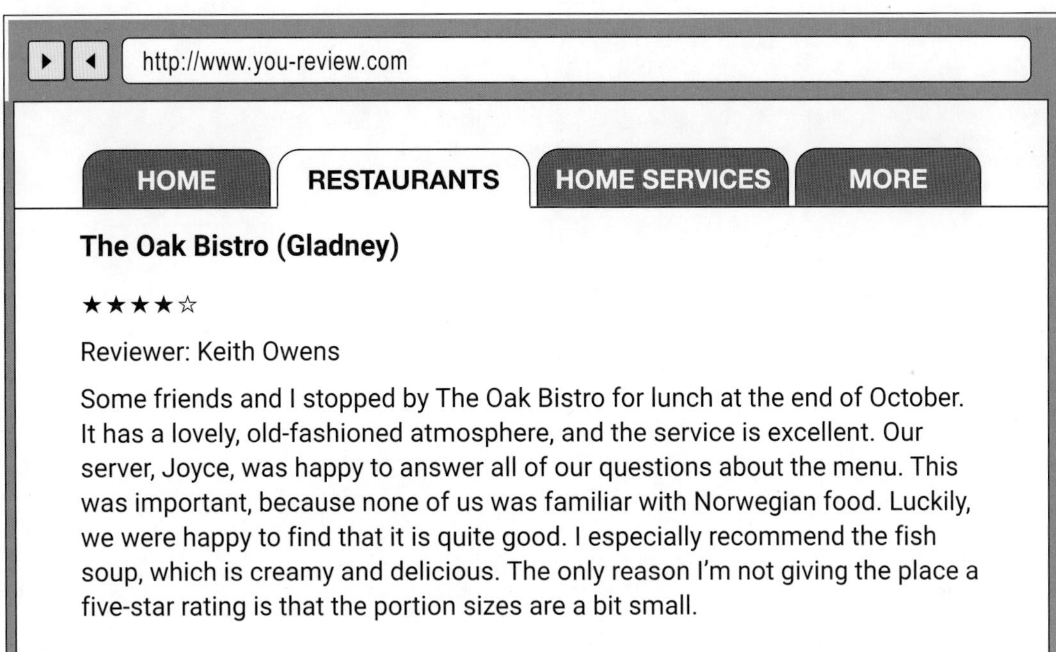
http://www.you-review.com

HOME | RESTAURANTS | HOME SERVICES | MORE

**The Oak Bistro (Gladney)**

★★★★☆

Reviewer: Keith Owens

Some friends and I stopped by The Oak Bistro for lunch at the end of October. It has a lovely, old-fashioned atmosphere, and the service is excellent. Our server, Joyce, was happy to answer all of our questions about the menu. This was important, because none of us was familiar with Norwegian food. Luckily, we were happy to find that it is quite good. I especially recommend the fish soup, which is creamy and delicious. The only reason I'm not giving the place a five-star rating is that the portion sizes are a bit small.

**196.** What is the purpose of the text message?
- (A) To suggest amending a project timeline
- (B) To provide reassurance about an allocated budget
- (C) To point out a violation of a safety regulation
- (D) To arrange a meeting at a renovation site

**197.** From where did Mr. Silva send the text message?
- (A) A historic house
- (B) An old school building
- (C) A consulting firm's office
- (D) A city government agency

**198.** In the article, what is suggested about Ms. Reeves?
- (A) She grew up in Norway.
- (B) She designed some landscaping.
- (C) She is the former owner of some real estate.
- (D) She is a Gladney city official.

**199.** What does the article mention about the property at 560 Sherman Street?
- (A) It has been kept in good condition.
- (B) It has been sold several times.
- (C) It is located near a forest.
- (D) It has a large parking area.

**200.** What can be inferred from the review?
- (A) The restaurant's menu has changed.
- (B) The restaurant's prices are reasonable.
- (C) Mr. Owens waited a long time for his food.
- (D) Mr. Owens was seated indoors at the restaurant.

**Stop! This is the end of the test. If you finish before time is called, you may go back to Parts 5, 6, and 7 and check your work.**

YBM
실전토익
RC1000

테스트 전 체크리스트

- 중간 휴식 없이 제한 시간을 지켜서 풀이하세요.
- 제한 시간은 답안지에 마킹하는 시간도 포함시켜야 합니다.
- 찍은 문제는 번호 옆에 꼭 체크해 주세요.
- 시간 안에 풀지 못한 문제는 틀린 것으로 채점해 주세요.

RC

# TEST 8

## READING TEST

In the Reading test, you will read a variety of texts and answer several different types of reading comprehension questions. The entire Reading test will last 75 minutes. There are three parts, and directions are given for each part. You are encouraged to answer as many questions as possible within the time allowed.

You must mark your answers on the separate answer sheet. Do not write your answers in your test book.

## PART 5

**Directions:** A word or phrase is missing in each of the sentences below. Four answer choices are given below each sentence. Select the best answer to complete the sentence. Then mark the letter (A), (B), (C), or (D) on your answer sheet.

**101.** Mount Teide is Spain's only peak that ------- above 3,500 meters.

(A) rise
(B) rises
(C) to rise
(D) rising

**102.** Aspiring chefs should equip ------- with a high-quality set of kitchen knives.

(A) they
(B) themselves
(C) their own
(D) their

**103.** Mr. Hayashi has the ------- career history out of the entire advisory committee.

(A) long
(B) length
(C) longer
(D) longest

**104.** All of Wester Apartments' amenities, ------- the fitness center, are available to tenants at no extra charge.

(A) sometimes
(B) including
(C) just as
(D) also

**105.** Clients appreciate that Ms. Caro is ------- incorrect about market trends.

(A) rarely
(B) yet
(C) apart
(D) far

**106.** Our library is an affiliate of Fowler Science Online, ------- library patrons can access its interactive lessons for free.

(A) once
(B) how
(C) then
(D) so

**107.** The CEO's speech presented a comprehensive ------- for the company's future.

(A) measure
(B) collection
(C) vision
(D) deadline

**108.** Only authorized staff are allowed inside the Council Chamber, ------- when there is a public meeting.

(A) during
(B) given
(C) between
(D) except

**109.** Organizations supported by the Alba Foundation must submit annual grant reports for -------.

(A) evaluate
(B) evaluates
(C) evaluation
(D) evaluative

**110.** Employees occupying shared offices are expected to be ------- of coworkers' needs for privacy.

(A) mindful
(B) willing
(C) reasonable
(D) independent

**111.** Graduates of our certification program usually ------- quickly to the working world.

(A) adapt
(B) adapts
(C) adapting
(D) is adapted

**112.** Internships are of ------- interest to students hoping to improve their résumés.

(A) relevant
(B) great
(C) farthest
(D) minimal

**113.** To communicate traffic conditions in a simple way, our app assigns colors to roads ------- their levels of congestion.

(A) adjacent to
(B) such as
(C) based on
(D) instead of

**114.** ------- of the two dessert options suggested by the caterer require refrigeration.

(A) Every
(B) Those
(C) Nothing
(D) Neither

**115.** ------- the end of the tour, participants will have the opportunity to purchase photos taken by our photographer.

(A) Without
(B) Since
(C) At
(D) About

**116.** Construction work on Snead Tower will soon -------, since new funding has been secured.

(A) ensure
(B) resume
(C) resolve
(D) maintain

**117.** A pay statement must be issued ------- the employee has not worked during the pay period in question.

(A) even if
(B) other than
(C) promptly
(D) still

**118.** Training participants will be asked to take a quiz online ------- after watching the final video.

(A) directly
(B) direct
(C) directed
(D) direction

**119.** Focus group leaders should ------- from expressing their personal opinions to the group.

(A) refuse
(B) refrain
(C) escape
(D) prevent

**120.** Dr. Jeong's award-winning research has enhanced the ------- of her department.

(A) arrangement
(B) permission
(C) reputation
(D) belief

*GO ON TO THE NEXT PAGE* →

**121.** Because the quartz countertops are its most popular -------, Earlstone features them on its home page.

(A) productively
(B) productive
(C) produces
(D) products

**122.** ------ Byrd Industries lowers its project bid, we will most likely hire Newlane Contractors for the renovation.

(A) Further
(B) Unless
(C) Hopefully
(D) Meanwhile

**123.** Once the passengers -------, the cabin crew will close the aircraft's doors.

(A) boarded
(B) are boarding
(C) have boarded
(D) to board

**124.** Carden Motors is seeking a technician who is ------- at repairing faulty transmissions.

(A) expert
(B) experts
(C) expertly
(D) expertise

**125.** In a recent interview, Sarah Fusco admitted she now regrets her ------- decision to leave the music industry.

(A) impulsive
(B) boldest
(C) unexpectedly
(D) occasional

**126.** Mr. Lin was ------- to circulating memos electronically until his colleagues pointed out it would save money.

(A) accustomed
(B) receptive
(C) limited
(D) opposed

**127.** Strunk Group's top-selling fertilizer, Ultra Green, ------- increases the amount of nutrients in poor soil.

(A) considers
(B) considerable
(C) consideration
(D) considerably

**128.** Amateurs and professionals ------- are using Illustria for graphic design projects.

(A) almost
(B) rather
(C) alike
(D) most

**129.** The paintings have been arranged ------- in order to show how Mr. Guerra's style changed over the course of his career.

(A) rightfully
(B) prominently
(C) increasingly
(D) chronologically

**130.** The travel ------- is allocated to assist with meals, taxi fares, and any other expenses incurred during your trip.

(A) documentation
(B) allowance
(C) itinerary
(D) insurance

## PART 6

**Directions:** Read the texts that follow. A word, phrase, or sentence is missing in parts of each text. Four answer choices for each question are given below the text. Select the best answer to complete the text. Then mark the letter (A), (B), (C), or (D) on your answer sheet.

**Questions 131-134** refer to the following invitation.

To Whom It May Concern:

We at the Villiers Entrepreneurs Network would like to invite your company to participate in the Villiers Venture Capital Conference (VVCC) to be held at Torres Mill on Thursday, April 7 at 2 P.M.

The first, private half of the conference will introduce participants to ------- **131.** opportunities in the Villiers region. Representatives from six promising area start-ups will give short presentations on their companies' funding needs. ------- **132.** . You are also welcome to ------- **133.** the public half of the VVCC, which will run from 4 P.M. to 6 P.M. However, this section is targeted more ------- **134.** local businesses and entrepreneurs.

Please respond to this invitation to reserve your place at the VVCC.

Sincerely,

Elias Barlow, Chair
Villiers Entrepreneurs Network

**131.** (A) education
(B) investment
(C) employment
(D) marketing

**132.** (A) These will be followed by a networking break.
(B) The VVCC first took place in April of last year.
(C) Executives from local banks will be in the audience.
(D) The city's economic climate has been unfavorable lately.

**133.** (A) record
(B) promote
(C) continue
(D) attend

**134.** (A) of
(B) than
(C) towards
(D) involved

*GO ON TO THE NEXT PAGE*

**Questions 135-138** refer to the following e-mail.

From: Anton Grier

To: Lindsay Pickard

Subject: Thank you note

Date: March 29

Hello Lindsay,

I just wanted to reach out and express my appreciation for your department's help with the search for my executive assistant. While everyone I interacted with did fine work, I especially want to single out Karl Schmidt for making an invaluable contribution to the process. -------, he discovered a specialized job board for administrative professionals. Without that -------, I wouldn't have had so many great candidates to choose from.
**135.** **136.**

As this was my first time hiring someone here at Carylon Health, I wasn't sure what ------- from the process, but I certainly couldn't have imagined that it would be so simple and collaborative. You have put together an excellent team. ------- . I hope you will pass on my thanks to everyone.
**137.** **138.**

Sincerely,

Anton Grier

Vice President of Digital Healthcare Innovations

Carylon Health

**135.** (A) Specifically
(B) Nonetheless
(C) To that end
(D) Accordingly

**136.** (A) event
(B) perk
(C) design
(D) resource

**137.** (A) expected
(B) expects
(C) to expect
(D) the expectations

**138.** (A) The orientation is certain to go quickly and smoothly.
(B) It would not be wise to expand it further at this time.
(C) I would welcome the chance to work with you all again.
(D) They will be very effective once they are fully trained.

**Questions 139-142** refer to the following memo.

To: Laboratory staff

From: Amal Khoury, Safety Director

Subject: Safety reminder

Date: January 11

I am sending this memo to remind you all of some important safety ------- **139.** . First, no employee may handle hazardous chemicals while alone in the laboratory. At least one other staff member who could provide aid in the event of a problem has to remain ------- **140.** sight or hearing at all times.

Employees may perform other types of laboratory tasks alone with prior permission from a director or manager. ------- **141.** . The SAFEX compliance management system makes this process simple.

Finally, the SAFEX mobile app's "Check-In" feature ------- **142.** whenever an employee is working alone in the lab. The offsite colleague designated as the emergency contact for the feature should also be informed of that fact beforehand.

Thank you for your compliance.

**139.** (A) trainings
(B) personnel
(C) equipment
(D) policies

**140.** (A) through
(B) within
(C) to
(D) upon

**141.** (A) Moreover, employees are encouraged to sanitize workstations frequently.
(B) However, the superior should complete a risk assessment beforehand.
(C) In fact, the layout of our lab has been designed to minimize these issues.
(D) Of course, certain kinds of work may be too complex for one technician.

**142.** (A) must be used
(B) to be used
(C) is being used
(D) would have been used

TEST 8

*GO ON TO THE NEXT PAGE*

**Questions 143-146** refer to the following e-mail.

To: Undisclosed Recipients

From: TicketWiz

Date: October 8

Subject: Blue Streak concert

Dear Blue Streak Fan,

The continuing playoff success of the Hoyle Tigers baseball team has led to several games being added to the schedule at Hoyle Stadium. For this reason, the venue ------- **143.** unavailable to host Blue Streak's October 13 concert as planned. That show has been ------- **144.** . A full refund for your ticket or tickets has been issued via your chosen payment method. Luckily, the band was able to book the nearby Peacock Resort Amphitheater for the same date and time. As a ticketholder for the stadium concert, you are ------- **145.** to purchase tickets for the amphitheater show through a special online presale that begins tomorrow at 10 A.M. ------- **146.** .

TicketWiz and Blue Streak apologize for any inconvenience caused by this change.

Sincerely,

The TicketWiz Tea

**143.** (A) was
(B) being
(C) will be
(D) has been

**144.** (A) postponed
(B) performed
(C) organized
(D) canceled

**145.** (A) eligible
(B) applied
(C) fortunate
(D) proposed

**146.** (A) The amphitheater has a capacity of just 20,000.
(B) You can expect to receive a reply within 24 hours.
(C) The two shows feature the same lineup of musicians.
(D) An e-mail with the access link will be sent later today.

## PART 7

**Directions:** In this part you will read a selection of texts, such as magazine and newspaper articles, e-mails, and instant messages. Each text or set of texts is followed by several questions. Select the best answer for each question and mark the letter (A), (B), (C), or (D) on your answer sheet.

**Questions 147-148** refer to the following memo.

**MEMO**

To: Wanda Morton and 9 others
From: Clifford Sanders, External Communications Specialist
Date: October 18
Subject: Bauer Mountain wind farm

In advance of Thursday's press conference on the project's status, I would like to issue the following reminder to members of the Renewable Energy Team and Media Relations Department. Since Ms. Trevino has designated me as our organizational spokesperson on the Bauer Mountain wind farm, I must be the one to handle media inquiries on the subject. Please pass this information on to any reporters who contact you. As you all know, the project continues to face some amount of opposition from members of the community for its possible impact on tourism. For that reason, it is crucial that our organization avoid making any remarks that are not informed by both expertise on the project and sensitivity to public opinion.

**147.** According to the memo, who can answer media inquiries about the wind farm?
(A) The Renewable Energy Team
(B) Mr. Sanders
(C) Ms. Trevino
(D) The Media Relations Department

**148.** What is mentioned about the wind farm?
(A) Its completion will be announced on Thursday.
(B) It was proposed by an environmental group.
(C) It will soon be toured by a group of reporters.
(D) It is controversial among local residents.



GO ON TO THE NEXT PAGE

**Questions 149-150** refer to the following advertisement.

Now that spring has arrived, many people are giving their houses or apartments a deep cleaning. But what if you don't have time to get rid of winter dust and grime yourself? Aspire Cleaners' dedicated staff will scrub every corner of your home from floor to ceiling—or, just the areas you ask us to handle. Call us at 555-0164 today.

**149.** What does the advertisement suggest about spring?

(A) It is a popular time for cleaning a home thoroughly.
(B) It is the best time to list a property for sale.
(C) It is the dustiest season of the year.
(D) It is the season in which Aspire Cleaners was founded.

**150.** What is indicated about Aspire Cleaners?

(A) It is offering a limited-time discount.
(B) Its staff work both indoors and outdoors.
(C) Its services can be customized.
(D) It specializes in cleaning flooring.

**Questions 151-152** refer to the following announcement.

http://www.gleason.com

## *GLEASON INTERNATIONAL AIRPORT (GIA)*

**NEWS & NOTICES**

**Announcement Regarding Misplaced Baggage**

Following the recent delay or cancellation of many flights due to winter weather, GIA has accumulated several hundred pieces of misplaced baggage. The baggage is currently being kept securely in a temporary enclosure on our second floor, near the Domestic Departures Information Desk.

As the location and delivery of misplaced baggage is ultimately the airline's responsibility, owners of lost bags should begin by filing a report with their airline. However, in order to ensure that the baggage is dispersed in a timely fashion, we are also allowing people to search for their bags themselves. To do so, bring your airline ticket and luggage tag, along with a valid form of identification, to the entrance of the enclosure. A staff member will check your documentation and then escort you inside to search. If you have questions about this process, please call our Customer Support Team at 555-0176.

**151.** What does the announcement indicate about GIA?

(A) It is assisting airline employees with a search process.
(B) It has set up a temporary holding area for some baggage.
(C) It is currently upgrading its baggage handling procedures.
(D) It recently experienced difficulties because of a staffing shortage.

**152.** What are owners of misplaced baggage asked to do?

(A) Prepare proof of their identity
(B) Keep a copy of a report
(C) Visit an information desk
(D) Describe the items over the phone



*GO ON TO THE NEXT PAGE*

**Questions 153-154** refer to the following text-message chain.

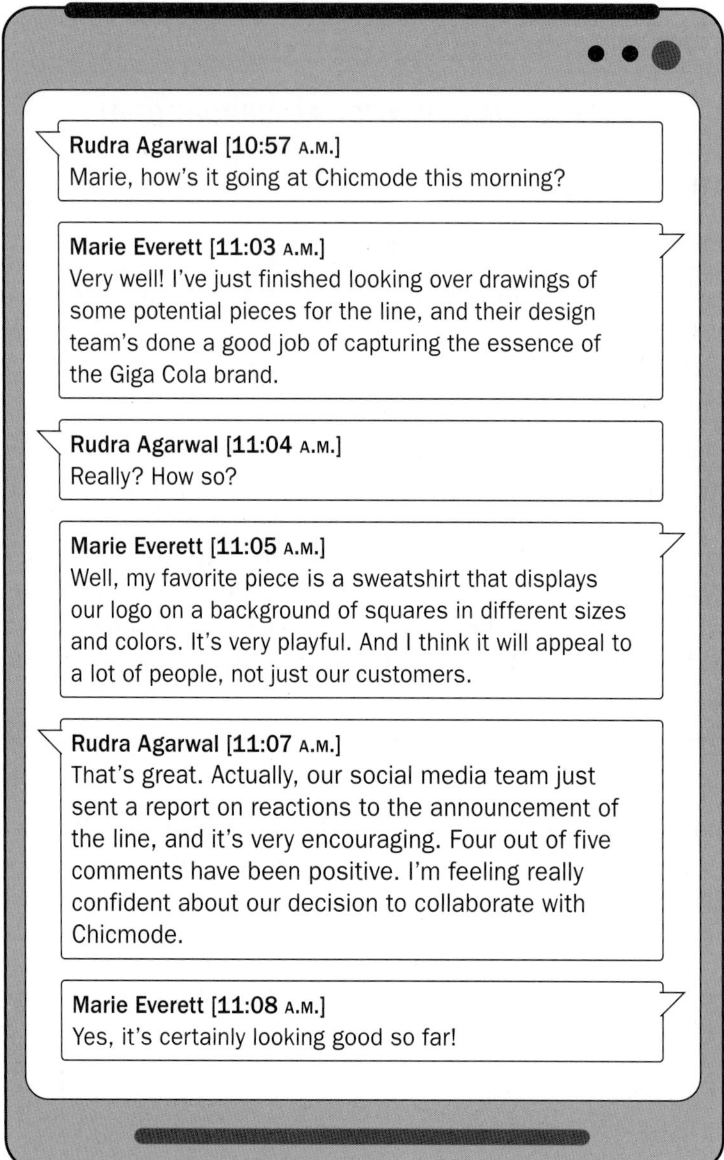

**Rudra Agarwal [10:57 A.M.]**
Marie, how's it going at Chicmode this morning?

**Marie Everett [11:03 A.M.]**
Very well! I've just finished looking over drawings of some potential pieces for the line, and their design team's done a good job of capturing the essence of the Giga Cola brand.

**Rudra Agarwal [11:04 A.M.]**
Really? How so?

**Marie Everett [11:05 A.M.]**
Well, my favorite piece is a sweatshirt that displays our logo on a background of squares in different sizes and colors. It's very playful. And I think it will appeal to a lot of people, not just our customers.

**Rudra Agarwal [11:07 A.M.]**
That's great. Actually, our social media team just sent a report on reactions to the announcement of the line, and it's very encouraging. Four out of five comments have been positive. I'm feeling really confident about our decision to collaborate with Chicmode.

**Marie Everett [11:08 A.M.]**
Yes, it's certainly looking good so far!

**153.** What is Chicmode?

(A) A fashion show
(B) A news organization
(C) A clothing company
(D) A department store

**154.** At 11:08 A.M., what does Ms. Everett most likely mean when she writes, "Yes, it's certainly looking good so far"?

(A) A team is doing extensive research.
(B) A business partnership seems promising.
(C) A social media page is appealing.
(D) Some apparel has remained in fine condition.

**Questions 155-157** refer to the following e-mail.

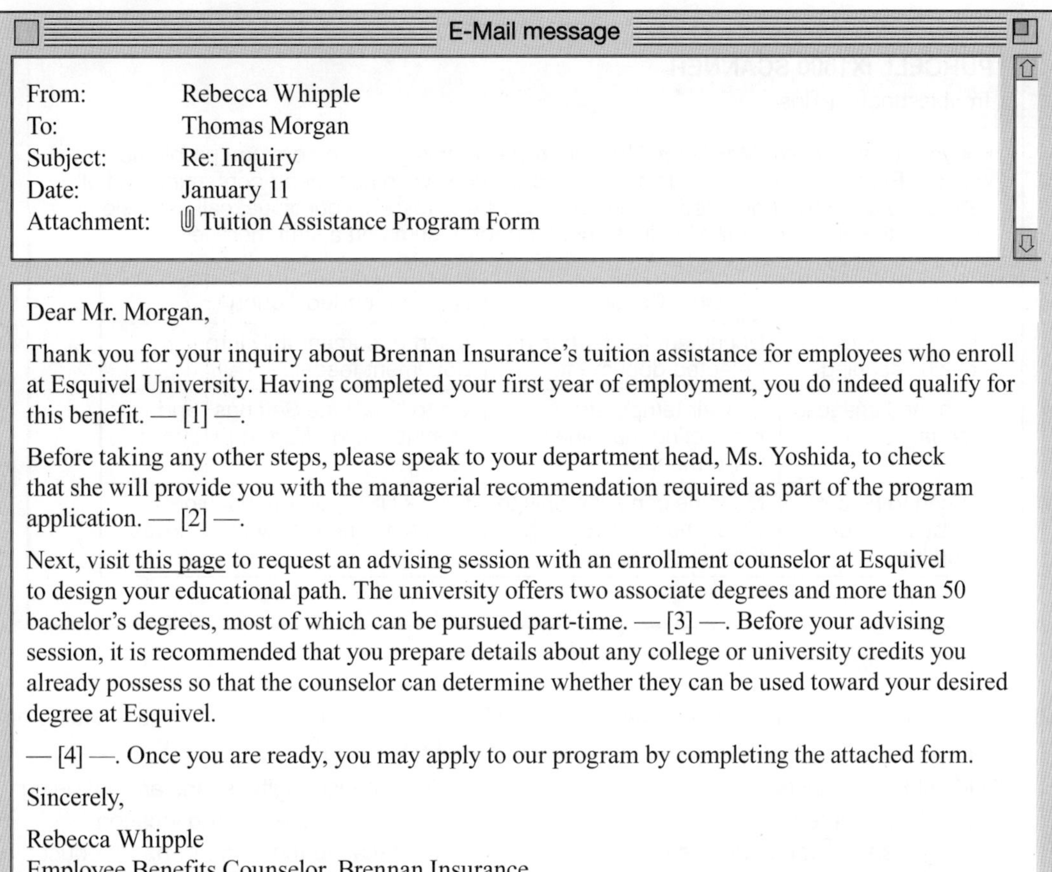

E-Mail message

From: Rebecca Whipple
To: Thomas Morgan
Subject: Re: Inquiry
Date: January 11
Attachment: Tuition Assistance Program Form

Dear Mr. Morgan,

Thank you for your inquiry about Brennan Insurance's tuition assistance for employees who enroll at Esquivel University. Having completed your first year of employment, you do indeed qualify for this benefit. — [1] —.

Before taking any other steps, please speak to your department head, Ms. Yoshida, to check that she will provide you with the managerial recommendation required as part of the program application. — [2] —.

Next, visit this page to request an advising session with an enrollment counselor at Esquivel to design your educational path. The university offers two associate degrees and more than 50 bachelor's degrees, most of which can be pursued part-time. — [3] —. Before your advising session, it is recommended that you prepare details about any college or university credits you already possess so that the counselor can determine whether they can be used toward your desired degree at Esquivel.

— [4] —. Once you are ready, you may apply to our program by completing the attached form.

Sincerely,

Rebecca Whipple
Employee Benefits Counselor, Brennan Insurance

**155.** Why is Mr. Morgan advised to speak with Ms. Yoshida?

(A) To seek advice about which field to study
(B) To remind her of a change in his employment status
(C) To confirm her approval of his participation in the program
(D) To learn about the steps of the application process

**156.** What does the e-mail suggest about Esquivel University?

(A) It conducts some of its courses online.
(B) It sometimes accepts credits earned at other institutions.
(C) It gives a tuition discount to employees of Brennan Insurance.
(D) It recently increased the number of degrees it offers.

**157.** In which of the positions marked [1], [2], [3], and [4] does the following sentence best belong?

"Graduate degrees are outside of the scope of our program."

(A) [1]
(B) [2]
(C) [3]
(D) [4]

TEST 8

*GO ON TO THE NEXT PAGE*

**Questions 158-160** refer to the following information.

**PURCELL iX1600 SCANNER**

Troubleshooting Tips

For your convenience, Maist Hotel has put together this guide to common problems with our Purcell scanner. In addition to the tips below, we recommend confirming that all cables are securely connected. If none of these steps resolve your issue, call extension 200 from the phone near the business center door to summon a staff member.

| Issue | Possible Cause | Recommended Action |
|---|---|---|
| Machine does not begin scanning. | Document feeder has not detected document. | Insert document fully into document feeder. |
| Scanned image is too faint. | Low air temperature is affecting machine's performance. | Go to "Machine Settings" and change "Scan Warm-up Time" to "Longer." |
| "Scan to Folder" function is not working. | Machine can scan only to USB when a USB flash drive is connected. | Check USB port on machine's right side and remove any drives. |

**158.** For whom is the information intended?

(A) Maist Hotel employees
(B) Maist Hotel guests
(C) Purcell repair technicians
(D) Purcell sales representatives

**159.** What is mentioned as a reason to call the provided phone number?

(A) To arrange in-person assistance
(B) To order some connector cables
(C) To have an ink cartridge replaced
(D) To check a warranty's validity

**160.** Why should the user change a setting on the scanner?

(A) Because digital scans are not being sent to the desired location
(B) Because the scanner has produced an image that is not sharp
(C) Because a document cannot be inserted into the document feeder
(D) Because the scanner is unable to detect a USB drive

**Questions 161-163** refer to the following report.

## Themeification Service Center

**Status Report**

**Issue:**

Clients using our e-commerce Web site design themes have reported a problem with the shopping cart feature. The shopping cart icon is displaying a "1" to their site's visitors even when the visitor's cart is actually empty. This is only happening to visitors using the Champona Web browser.

**Ticket filed with Themeification Service Center:**

August 20, 5:48 P.M.

**Current status:**

We determined that the issue is caused by Realtail, a necessary software plugin used in the affected design themes. We notified the maker of Realtail on August 21 at 9:12 A.M. and asked to be updated when the issue was resolved.

**Recommendation to affected Themeification clients:**

Advise dissatisfied visitors to use a different browser when accessing your Web site.

**161.** Why was the report written?

(A) To update clients about a data security risk
(B) To clarify the purpose of a product's new feature
(C) To announce the discontinuation of a design theme
(D) To explain an issue with some retail Web sites

**162.** What is Themeification Service Center staff most likely doing currently?

(A) Waiting to be contacted by another company
(B) Running further tests on some software
(C) Examining reports sent in by clients
(D) Preparing to issue a document

**163.** What does the Themeification Service Center recommend that some clients do?

(A) Select a different design theme
(B) Upgrade to the latest version of Realtail
(C) Discourage their customers from using Champona
(D) Limit visitors' access to their Web site



*GO ON TO THE NEXT PAGE*

**Questions 164-167** refer to the following e-mail.

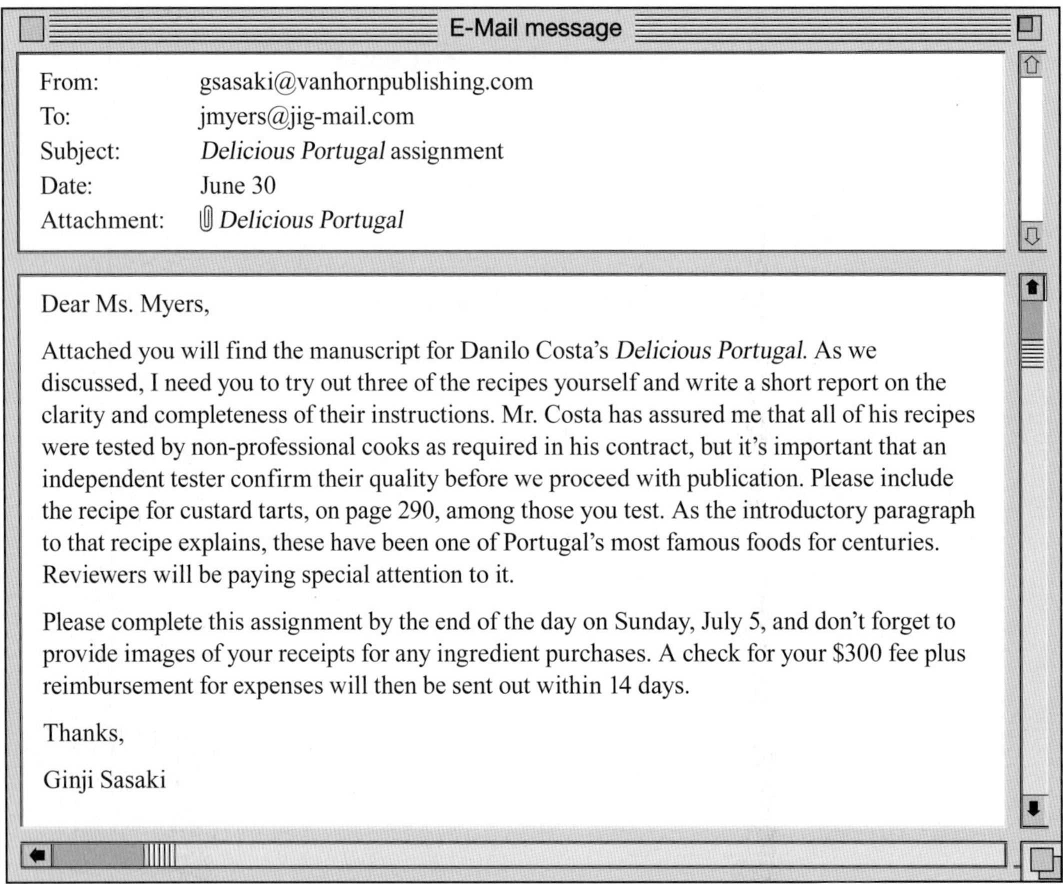

E-Mail message

From: gsasaki@vanhornpublishing.com
To: jmyers@jig-mail.com
Subject: *Delicious Portugal* assignment
Date: June 30
Attachment: *Delicious Portugal*

Dear Ms. Myers,

Attached you will find the manuscript for Danilo Costa's *Delicious Portugal.* As we discussed, I need you to try out three of the recipes yourself and write a short report on the clarity and completeness of their instructions. Mr. Costa has assured me that all of his recipes were tested by non-professional cooks as required in his contract, but it's important that an independent tester confirm their quality before we proceed with publication. Please include the recipe for custard tarts, on page 290, among those you test. As the introductory paragraph to that recipe explains, these have been one of Portugal's most famous foods for centuries. Reviewers will be paying special attention to it.

Please complete this assignment by the end of the day on Sunday, July 5, and don't forget to provide images of your receipts for any ingredient purchases. A check for your $300 fee plus reimbursement for expenses will then be sent out within 14 days.

Thanks,

Ginji Sasaki

**164.** Who most likely is Mr. Costa?

(A) A chef
(B) A food critic
(C) A travel writer
(D) A translator

**165.** What is Ms. Myers asked to do?

(A) Produce some illustrations
(B) Evaluate some instructions
(C) Check some historical claims
(D) Visit a Portuguese restaurant

**166.** According to Mr. Sasaki, what is included in the attachment?

(A) An explanation of the regions of a country
(B) Biographical details about a person
(C) A copy of a business agreement
(D) A description of a dish's significance

**167.** What will happen in July?

(A) Images will be added to a manuscript.
(B) Some writing tasks will be delegated.
(C) An order of ingredients will be shipped.
(D) A payment will be issued to a freelancer.

**Questions 168-171** refer to the following letter.

Dear Valued Customer,

— [1] —. I am pleased to announce that Lakeside Pharmacy will be changing its name to Reviva Pharmacy as of May 1. The locations and contact numbers of our branches will remain the same. However, our Web address will now be www.reviva-pharm.com.

Lakeside Pharmacy was founded 14 years ago as a single storefront in Lakeside. Thanks to your support, it now comprises eight busy branches in three cities. — [2] —. Our new name reflects our plans to continue growing into a national chain with locations throughout the country. — [3] —. You can rest assured, however, that our customers will always remain our priority. We will continue striving to meet your pharmaceutical needs with care and professionalism around the clock, 365 days per year.

— [4] —.

Sincerely,

Kyung-Taek Park, CEO

**168.** Why is the company changing its name?

(A) It will begin offering a new service.
(B) Its current one is similar to another business's name.
(C) It has merged with another company.
(D) It is expanding into more regions.

**169.** The word "busy" in paragraph 2, line 2, is closest in meaning to

(A) distant
(B) occupied
(C) bustling
(D) diligent

**170.** What is indicated about the company?

(A) It serves customers at any time of the day.
(B) It is no longer headquartered in Lakeside.
(C) It has changed its name before.
(D) It was founded by Mr. Park.

**171.** In which of the positions marked [1], [2], [3], and [4] does the following sentence best belong?

"We look forward to assisting you at your local branch of Reviva Pharmacy soon."

(A) [1]
(B) [2]
(C) [3]
(D) [4]

TEST 8

*GO ON TO THE NEXT PAGE*

**Questions 172-175** refer to the following text-message chain.

**Stanley Bowman** **[9:36 A.M.]**
Eleanor, Dazzle Home Goods wants to know if our warehouse can store 18 extra pallets of furniture parts from this afternoon until Thursday morning. They need time to resolve a distribution issue.

**Eleanor Soto** **[9:37 A.M.]**
We're pretty close to capacity right now. I'll have to check.

**Stanley Bowman** **[9:39 A.M.]**
Thanks. You know, this could help make up for that pallet of Dazzle lamps we misplaced last month.

**Eleanor Soto** **[9:40 A.M.]**
That's true, but taking on more inventory than we can hold could also lead to more mistakes. OK, I'm back in my office now. Let me open up the warehouse management software.

**Stanley Bowman** **[9:44 A.M.]**
And? Can we do it?

**Eleanor Soto** **[9:45 A.M.]**
You're in luck. A big shipment for Varney Paints is set to go out at noon, which leaves the north end of Stack 7B empty for a few days.

**Stanley Bowman** **[9:46 A.M.]**
Excellent! What loading docks should I have Dazzle send its trucks to?

**Eleanor Soto** **[9:47 A.M.]**
How many trucks will there be, and what time will they arrive?

**Stanley Bowman** **[9:48 A.M.]**
Two trucks, sometime between 3 and 3:30.

**Eleanor Soto** **[9:49 A.M.]**
OK, I'll enter the information into the system and let you know about the loading docks in a few minutes.

**Stanley Bowman** **[9:50 A.M.]**
Sounds great. Thanks again, Eleanor.

**172.** What are the writers discussing?

(A) Simplifying a distribution process
(B) Taking advantage of a sale
(C) Fulfilling a customer request
(D) Postponing an expansion project

**173.** What is suggested about Ms. Soto?

(A) Her office overlooks a warehouse floor.
(B) She did not know a mistake had been made.
(C) She spoke with a representative from Varney Paints.
(D) She changed locations during the conversation.

**174.** At 9:45 A.M., what does Ms. Soto mean when she writes, "You're in luck"?

(A) Some missing items have been recovered.
(B) A software program has a special feature.
(C) There will be space to store some goods.
(D) There is still time to cancel a shipment.

**175.** What will most likely happen next?

(A) Delivery spots will be assigned.
(B) Some trucks will be loaded.
(C) Mr. Bowman will return a call.
(D) Ms. Soto will turn on a computer.

TEST 8

*GO ON TO THE NEXT PAGE*

**Questions 176-180** refer to the following article and e-mail.

LOS ANGELES (May 3)—Connection Studios has hired Australian Lucas Pearce to direct its upcoming film *Black Door*. Mr. Pearce gained widespread attention this spring with his debut feature, *The Farm*, a terrifying ghost tale that received glowing reviews. *Black Door*, which will star Tamara Burns, is a psychological thriller set in a hospital. With a budget of $8 million, it represents a significant increase in scale for Mr. Pearce, as *The Farm* reportedly cost just $700,000 to make.

According to the press release issued by Connection, *Black Door* will begin shooting in November and is scheduled to arrive in theaters in October of next year. The studio also indicated plans to screen the film a few months earlier at the Fleming Film Festival that summer, presumably hoping that positive reviews from attendees will build anticipation among audiences.

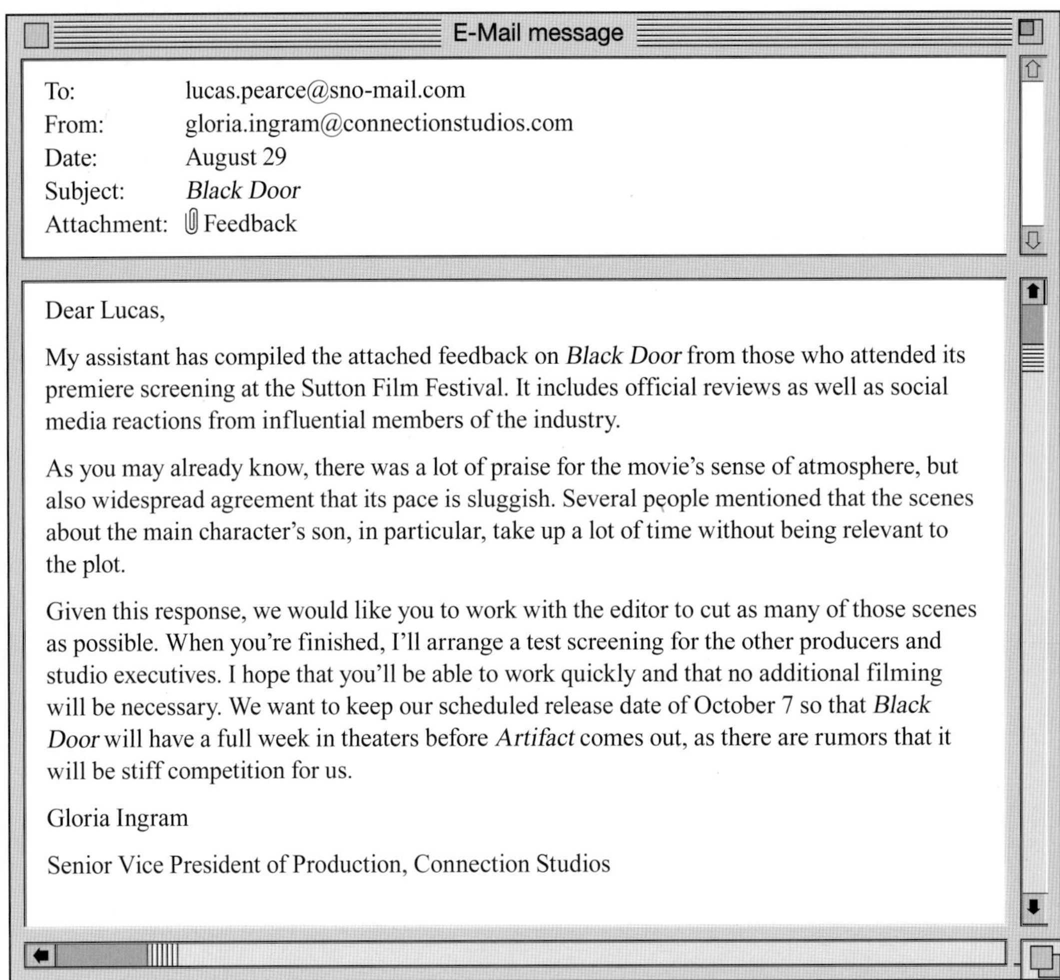

E-Mail message

To: lucas.pearce@sno-mail.com
From: gloria.ingram@connectionstudios.com
Date: August 29
Subject: *Black Door*
Attachment: Feedback

Dear Lucas,

My assistant has compiled the attached feedback on *Black Door* from those who attended its premiere screening at the Sutton Film Festival. It includes official reviews as well as social media reactions from influential members of the industry.

As you may already know, there was a lot of praise for the movie's sense of atmosphere, but also widespread agreement that its pace is sluggish. Several people mentioned that the scenes about the main character's son, in particular, take up a lot of time without being relevant to the plot.

Given this response, we would like you to work with the editor to cut as many of those scenes as possible. When you're finished, I'll arrange a test screening for the other producers and studio executives. I hope that you'll be able to work quickly and that no additional filming will be necessary. We want to keep our scheduled release date of October 7 so that *Black Door* will have a full week in theaters before *Artifact* comes out, as there are rumors that it will be stiff competition for us.

Gloria Ingram

Senior Vice President of Production, Connection Studios

**176.** What is NOT mentioned in the article about *The Farm*?

(A) It is a horror film.
(B) It had a relatively low budget.
(C) It is set during the springtime.
(D) It was praised by critics.

**177.** What does the article suggest about *Black Door*?

(A) It will take over two years to make.
(B) It will be Mr. Pearce's second film as a director.
(C) The casting process for it has not yet begun.
(D) It will be filmed in Australia.

**178.** What is the main purpose of the e-mail?

(A) To request some edits
(B) To announce a postponement
(C) To congratulate a collaborator
(D) To discuss some advertising

**179.** What is implied about the first screening of *Black Door*?

(A) Its audience was asked to take a survey.
(B) It was attended only by people who worked on the film.
(C) It took place at a different event than planned.
(D) It was conducted over the Internet.

**180.** In the e-mail, what is indicated about *Artifact*?

(A) It is also a Connection Studios film.
(B) It was shown at a film festival.
(C) It is undergoing additional filming.
(D) It will be released in October.

TEST 8

*GO ON TO THE NEXT PAGE*

**Questions 181-185** refer to the following e-mails.

**E-Mail message**

**From:** osullivan@nortech.com
**To:** inquiries@haywoodhub.com
**Subject:** Office space inquiry
**Date:** Thursday, February 2, 10:08 A.M.

Hello,

I am contacting your business by e-mail because I cannot seem to reach you via phone; each time I call the number listed on your Web site, a message says it is "unavailable."

I am seeking a coworking business in Haywood from which I can work remotely for a few weeks while dealing with a family matter. I would need a private office and the use of two large computer monitors, and my budget limit is $100 per week. Does Haywood Hub have what I am looking for?

Also, I see from your Web site that you offer parking. Could you let me know how much you charge for it, and also whether the parking area is enclosed?

I hope to hear from you very soon.

Olive Sullivan

**E-Mail message**

**From:** edchisholm@haywoodhub.com
**To:** osullivan@nortech.com
**Subject:** Re: Office space inquiry
**Date:** Thursday, February 2, 11:42 A.M.

Dear Ms. Sullivan,

I apologize for the difficulty you experienced while calling us. There was a phone service outage across our area this morning due to a tree branch having fallen on a phone line. Luckily, the issue was handled quickly.

As for your inquiries, I am pleased to tell you that we currently have suitable spaces open on our second floor for $96 per week, inclusive of the charge for the computer accessories you require. The parking fee will be waived if you pay by the week or month, and though our parking area is not enclosed, most of the spaces are covered by shade canopies.

While we do allow walk-ins, it is best to book a space ahead of time to ensure that one will be available. You can respond to this e-mail or call me directly at extension 3 from our main line in order to do this. I am also happy to answer any further questions you might have.

Sincerely,

Ed Chisholm, Service Manager
Haywood Hub

181. In the first e-mail, what does Ms. Sullivan mention about herself?

(A) She has patronized a coworking business before.
(B) She plans to use a company car on her trip.
(C) She works for a family-owned business.
(D) She is traveling to Haywood for a personal reason.

182. What is true about the spaces on Haywood Hub's second floor?

(A) Some of them are offices for individual use.
(B) They are its only spaces that cost less than $100 per week.
(C) Some of them overlook a parking area.
(D) They must be rented for at least one week at a time.

183. What does Mr. Chisholm offer Ms. Sullivan?

(A) A free loan of two computer monitors
(B) A discount on a monthlong office rental
(C) Complimentary access to the parking area
(D) An upgrade to a space with better amenities

184. In the second e-mail, the word "covered" in paragraph 2, line 4, is closest in meaning to

(A) paid for
(B) protected
(C) addressed
(D) divided

185. What does the second e-mail indicate about Haywood Hub?

(A) Its building has just been damaged in an accident.
(B) It does not require customers to make reservations.
(C) Its employee extension numbers have changed.
(D) It is having routine maintenance performed on its phone line.

TEST 8

GO ON TO THE NEXT PAGE

**Questions 186-190** refer to the following e-mails and price list.

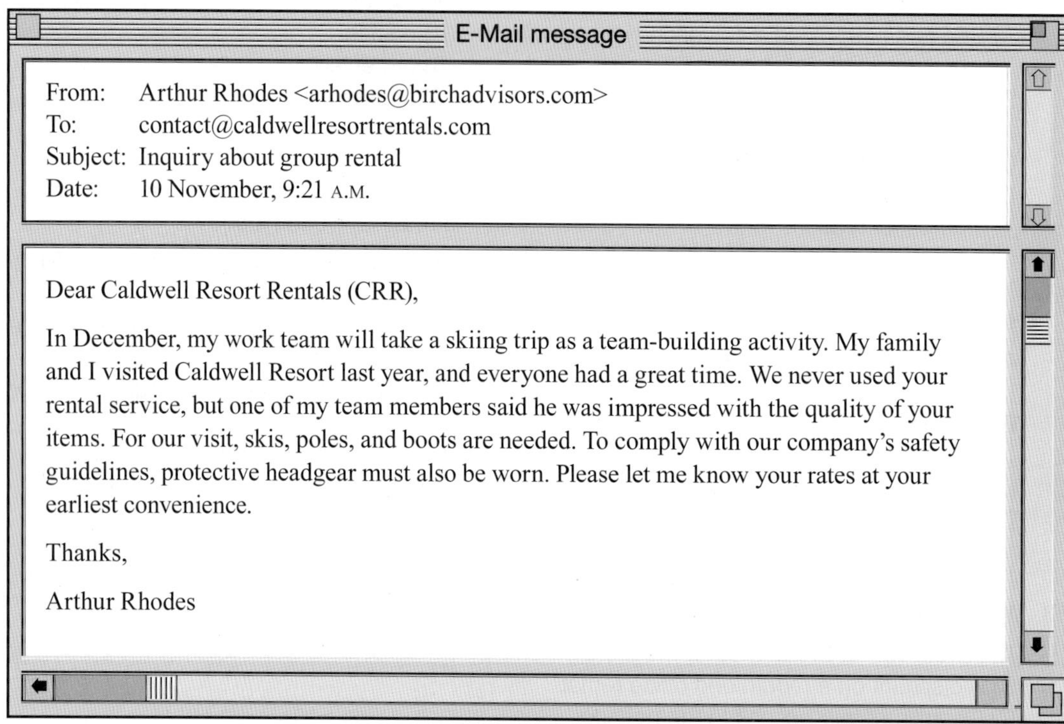

E-Mail message

From: Arthur Rhodes <arhodes@birchadvisors.com>
To: contact@caldwellresortrentals.com
Subject: Inquiry about group rental
Date: 10 November, 9:21 A.M.

Dear Caldwell Resort Rentals (CRR),

In December, my work team will take a skiing trip as a team-building activity. My family and I visited Caldwell Resort last year, and everyone had a great time. We never used your rental service, but one of my team members said he was impressed with the quality of your items. For our visit, skis, poles, and boots are needed. To comply with our company's safety guidelines, protective headgear must also be worn. Please let me know your rates at your earliest convenience.

Thanks,

Arthur Rhodes

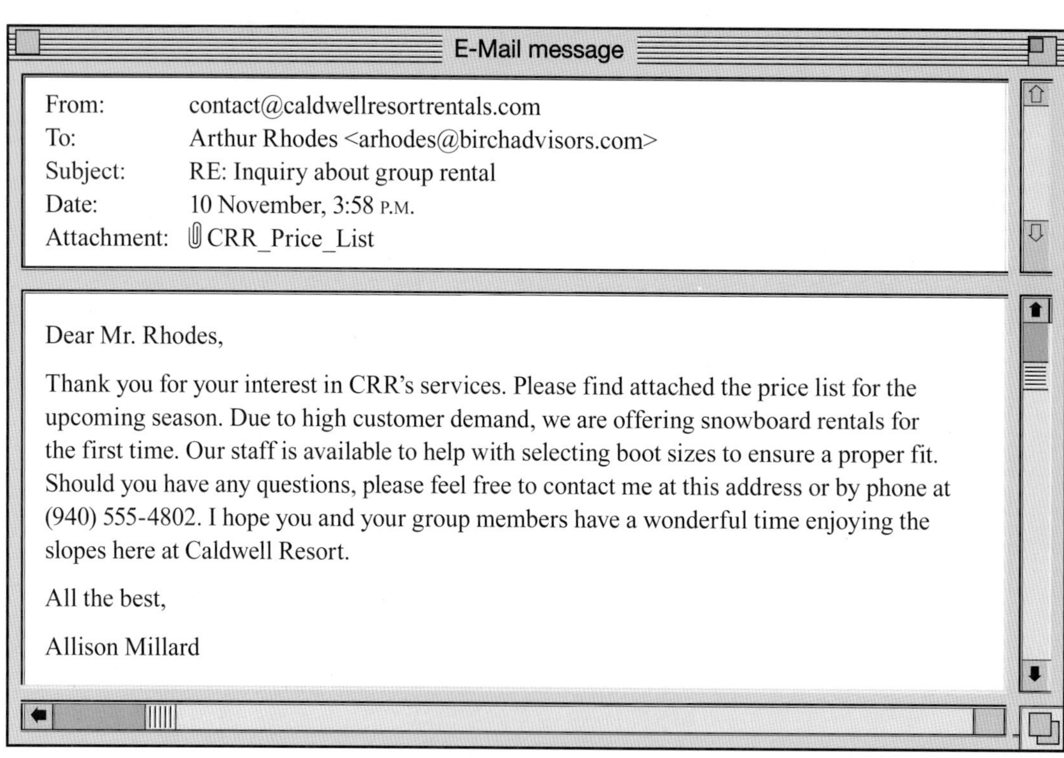

E-Mail message

From: contact@caldwellresortrentals.com
To: Arthur Rhodes <arhodes@birchadvisors.com>
Subject: RE: Inquiry about group rental
Date: 10 November, 3:58 P.M.
Attachment: CRR_Price_List

Dear Mr. Rhodes,

Thank you for your interest in CRR's services. Please find attached the price list for the upcoming season. Due to high customer demand, we are offering snowboard rentals for the first time. Our staff is available to help with selecting boot sizes to ensure a proper fit. Should you have any questions, please feel free to contact me at this address or by phone at (940) 555-4802. I hope you and your group members have a wonderful time enjoying the slopes here at Caldwell Resort.

All the best,

Allison Millard

## Caldwell Resort Rentals Price List

| Package | One-Day Rate | Two-Day Rate |
|---|---|---|
| Package 1: Skis only | £22.00 | £35.00 |
| Package 2: Skis, poles, & boots | £30.00 | £48.00 |
| Package 3: Skis, poles, boots, & helmet | £32.00 | £50.00 |
| Package 4: Snowboard only | £25.00 | £40.00 |
| Package 5: Ski jacket, ski pants, & gloves | £22.00 | £35.00 |

- We are open from mid-November to mid-February, depending on the weather.
- Items must be returned by 4:30 P.M. or you will be charged for another day.
- Items are offered on a first-come, first-served basis, so reserving items in advance is strongly advised.
- All rental charges include insurance against breakage but not against loss.
- We can accommodate nearly every size, from children aged 5+ up to XL adults.

**186.** What does Mr. Rhodes indicate in the first e-mail?

(A) His team visited Caldwell Resort last year.
(B) His coworker has used CRR before.
(C) He is interested in booking skiing lessons.
(D) He will pay for the rentals with a company credit card.

**187.** Which rental package would be best for Mr. Rhodes's group?

(A) Package 2
(B) Package 3
(C) Package 4
(D) Package 5

**188.** How much does CRR charge for using its newest rental package for one day?

(A) £22.00
(B) £25.00
(C) £30.00
(D) £32.00

**189.** What is indicated in the price list?

(A) The business is open for nine months each year.
(B) Children are not allowed to use the equipment.
(C) Discounts are offered for certain group sizes.
(D) Items are not guaranteed to be available.

**190.** According to the price list, what is suggested about all rental items?

(A) They can be returned by mail.
(B) They will incur a fee if lost.
(C) They can be insured for an additional charge.
(D) They require a deposit for possible damage.

TEST 8

*GO ON TO THE NEXT PAGE*

**Questions 191-195** refer to the following Web page, chart, and e-mail.

http://www.green-run.com/volunteering

### *VOLUNTEERING AT A GREEN RUN*

One reason for the growing popularity of Green Runs all over the world is that participation in this weekly outdoor running event isn't limited to joggers.

People able to walk a Green Run course can volunteer to set out the course markers beforehand, take them down afterwards, or help by "tail-walking"—walking after the last runner to ensure that no one is left behind on the course. Those who can only sit may act as course marshals, directing the runners at some of the course's major turns. And people handy with technology are needed to stand at the finish line and, with the help of the Green Run smartphone app, record finish times or scan runners' participation barcodes.

To get started as a volunteer, send an e-mail to your local event coordinator. All volunteers will be required to create a Green Run membership here before assisting with their first event and must be reachable by mobile phone on the day of the event.

**Wingfield Green Run Volunteer Assignments for June 7**

| Role | Number of People Needed | Volunteers |
|---|---|---|
| Course set-up/take-down | 3–5 | Stuart White, Guillermo Ramos, Donna Goldman* |
| Tail-walking | 2+ | Reuben Linney, Nicolette Picardo |
| Course marshaling | 4+ | Alexis Vu*, Patrick Scanlan, Maria Serrano, Blair Wilson |
| Timekeeping | 1 | Peter Pospisil |
| Barcode scanning | 2–4 | Travis Neisewander, Carolyn Shelby*, Svetlana Tesnes |

*New volunteer

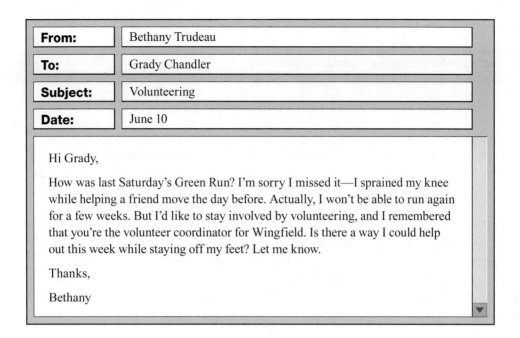

| From: | Bethany Trudeau |
|---|---|
| To: | Grady Chandler |
| Subject: | Volunteering |
| Date: | June 10 |

Hi Grady,

How was last Saturday's Green Run? I'm sorry I missed it—I sprained my knee while helping a friend move the day before. Actually, I won't be able to run again for a few weeks. But I'd like to stay involved by volunteering, and I remembered that you're the volunteer coordinator for Wingfield. Is there a way I could help out this week while staying off my feet? Let me know.

Thanks,

Bethany

**191.** What does the Web page suggest about Green Runs?

(A) They are fund-raising events.
(B) They are held in multiple countries.
(C) Their courses must exceed a minimum length.
(D) They take place seasonally.

**192.** What is NOT listed as something that volunteers must do?

(A) Sign up for a Green Run member account
(B) Read an online list of rules
(C) Carry a mobile phone
(D) Contact a Green Run official

**193.** Based on the information in the chart, what can be concluded about Mr. Neisewander?

(A) He has never volunteered before.
(B) He will be stationed at a turn along the route.
(C) He will be asked to use a special mobile app.
(D) He will need to arrive before the event begins.

**194.** What is one reason Ms. Trudeau wrote the e-mail?

(A) To change her volunteer assignment
(B) To ask about the timeline of some training
(C) To introduce herself to an organizer
(D) To explain her absence from an event

**195.** What will Mr. Chandler most likely encourage Ms. Trudeau to do?

(A) Help runners stay on course
(B) Greet participants upon their arrival
(C) Sit behind a refreshments table
(D) Inventory some equipment

GO ON TO THE NEXT PAGE

**Questions 196-200** refer to the following Web page, advertisement, and delivery confirmation.

https://www.heredia.com/appliances/cooktops/ec7030a 

**Heredia Bright 30-inch Electric Cooktop (EC7030A)**

This cooktop offers cutting-edge convenience and precision. Its four burners can be monitored and adjusted from your smartphone with the Heredia Bright app. Each burner can also be set to an exact degree temperature, making it easy to cook delicate dishes like sauces and candy.

Features:

- Completely smooth glass surface enables easy cleaning
- Includes one extra-powerful 3100-watt burner for quick boiling
- Syncs wirelessly with Bright kitchen hoods; hood fan and lights automatically turn on when cooktop does
- Hot surface indicator light and locking function ensure safety

Model EC7030A is eligible for financing through the Tally payment platform. Click here to sign up for Tally before making your purchase.

## Heredia

**SPRING INTO INNOVATION SPECIAL**

Let innovation bloom in your kitchen! This spring, earn a generous rebate by purchasing at least three kitchen appliances from among Heredia's Bright line of smart home electronics. The more you buy, the more you get back!

◇ Three appliances: $300

◇ Four appliances: $550

◇ Five appliances: $800

◇ Six or more appliances: $1,050

All purchases must be made between April 1 and May 31 from our online store or an authorized retailer of Heredia appliances. Visit www.heredia.com/promotions/siis to apply for the rebate online or print out a claim form that can be mailed in.

Heredia
www.heredia.com
1-800-555-0164

**DELIVERY CONFIRMATION**

Order No.: 56403
Order Date: April 9
Customer: Clark Eubanks, 710 Henry Drive, Shannett, RI 02809
Delivery Date: April 18

| Items | Quantity | Installation Required? |
|---|---|---|
| Bright Ultra Fresh Dishwasher (DW7550S) | 1 | ✔ |
| Bright 30-inch Electric Cooktop (EC7030A) | 1 | ✔ |
| Bright 28-cubic-feet Four-door Refrigerator (RF78233H) | 1 | ✔ |
| Bright 1.1-cubic-feet Countertop Microwave Oven (MO74403M) | 1 | |

The above items were delivered in good condition, and any required installations were performed satisfactorily.

Clark Eubanks
(Signature of Customer or Designated Recipient)

**196.** What does the Web page indicate about model EC7030A?
(A) It can be connected virtually to another appliance.
(B) It is the most powerful cooktop on the market.
(C) It is safe to use with glass cookware.
(D) It comes with access to a recipe-sharing app.

**197.** In the advertisement, what is suggested about the Spring into Innovation Special?
(A) It is available only to visitors to Heredia's online store.
(B) The rebate amount continues to increase after six purchases.
(C) Not all of the products in the Bright line qualify for it.
(D) It is automatically applied to eligible purchases.

**198.** What is indicated on the delivery confirmation?
(A) Another person accepted delivery for the customer.
(B) One appliance was not in satisfactory condition.
(C) A separate fee was paid to the delivery personnel.
(D) Installation service was provided for most of the items.

**199.** What is implied about Mr. Eubanks?
(A) He bought a cooktop with precise temperature controls.
(B) He signed up for a special payment platform.
(C) He tracked a shipment's progress with his smartphone.
(D) He disposed of some old appliances himself.

**200.** What is the highest rebate Mr. Eubanks can receive?
(A) $300
(B) $550
(C) $800
(D) $1,050



**Stop! This is the end of the test. If you finish before time is called, you may go back to Parts 5, 6, and 7 and check your work.**

# YBM 실전토익 RC1000

## 테스트 전 체크리스트

- 중간 휴식 없이 제한 시간을 지켜서 풀이하세요.
- 제한 시간은 답안지에 마킹하는 시간도 포함시켜야 합니다.
- 찍은 문제는 번호 옆에 꼭 체크해 주세요.
- 시간 안에 풀지 못한 문제는 틀린 것으로 채점해 주세요.

# RC TEST 9

## READING TEST

In the Reading test, you will read a variety of texts and answer several different types of reading comprehension questions. The entire Reading test will last 75 minutes. There are three parts, and directions are given for each part. You are encouraged to answer as many questions as possible within the time allowed.

You must mark your answers on the separate answer sheet. Do not write your answers in your test book.

## PART 5

**Directions:** A word or phrase is missing in each of the sentences below. Four answer choices are given below each sentence. Select the best answer to complete the sentence. Then mark the letter (A), (B), (C), or (D) on your answer sheet.

**101.** One purpose of the Librarian Association's blog is to bring new and ------- ideas to members' attention.

(A) diversify
(B) diversely
(C) diverse
(D) diversity

**102.** Our restaurant has served over 70,000 hamburgers ------- opening in March.

(A) within
(B) besides
(C) since
(D) past

**103.** The new customer service staff are finally knowledgeable ------- about our appliances to give troubleshooting advice to customers.

(A) even
(B) enough
(C) much
(D) already

**104.** IT department workers must respond promptly to colleagues' technical support -------.

(A) requesting
(B) will request
(C) requested
(D) requests

**105.** The intern will work ------- the direction of the senior communications officer.

(A) on
(B) under
(C) for
(D) as

**106.** Ms. Velling instructed ------- who need additional office supplies to send her a list of items by e-mail.

(A) these
(B) they
(C) those
(D) them

**107.** Because of new city ordinances, operating a business in Sanderton has become ------- difficult.

(A) increasingly
(B) increased
(C) increase
(D) increasing

**108.** The botanical gardens have played an ------- part in the recent rise in tourism to Moriva.

(A) extending
(B) extensive
(C) extension
(D) extensively

**109.** Each Ainsville Fire Department inspector will no longer ------- in a single area of fire prevention.

(A) special
(B) specialize
(C) specialization
(D) specially

**110.** Ms. Lewis has been tasked with ------- the results of our recently completed survey.

(A) summarizing
(B) performing
(C) improving
(D) achieving

**111.** Gatewood Corporation currently ------- employees from discussing their work or the company on social media.

(A) forbid
(B) forbids
(C) forbidding
(D) forbidden

**112.** The latest version of the Flamio headphones is identical to the previous one ------- some decorative elements.

(A) added
(B) prior to
(C) regardless
(D) aside from

**113.** A copy of the meeting notes should be sent to Mr. Won, ------- is currently visiting the Hong Kong office.

(A) who
(B) his
(C) that
(D) another

**114.** The noise issue with the Traction G20 truck was ------- once the cross bars on the roof rack were adjusted.

(A) resolve
(B) resolving
(C) resolution
(D) resolved

**115.** The goal of the negotiations is to find a solution that will be ------- to both parties.

(A) agreeing
(B) agreeable
(C) agreeably
(D) to agree

**116.** ------- buying computer hardware, companies with changeable needs should use technology rental services.

(A) Whenever
(B) Depending on
(C) Instead of
(D) However

**117.** The drop in our average product rating is ------- a temporary consequence of the packaging redesign.

(A) simple
(B) simpler
(C) simplest
(D) simply

**118.** An airline representative will contact you ------- your luggage has been located by a member of our staff.

(A) at first
(B) in case
(C) rather than
(D) as soon as

**119.** The space adjacent to Leland Florist is available to be ------- by a new tenant.

(A) enclosed
(B) leased
(C) permitted
(D) preoccupied

**120.** Each year, the ------- of the Barnes Engineering Conference pose for a commemorative group photo.

(A) organizing
(B) organizational
(C) organization
(D) organizers



GO ON TO THE NEXT PAGE

121. For offices, we recommend plants that grow well in ------- conditions such as low lighting and inconsistent watering.

(A) dense
(B) adverse
(C) skeptical
(D) durable

122. For its next performance, on December 11, the Peltier Symphony will be led by acclaimed ------- Misaki Ogawa.

(A) conduct
(B) conducts
(C) conductor
(D) conducting

123. Desirable parking spaces ------- the city are being converted to electric vehicle charging stations.

(A) out of
(B) next to
(C) throughout
(D) along

124. TGN Bank has received industry ------- for its Vista Credit Card, which offers its holders excellent rewards for a low annual fee.

(A) regulation
(B) demand
(C) reputation
(D) recognition

125. If your store is poorly stocked or disorganized when prospective customers visit, they may choose to shop -------.

(A) apart
(B) seldom
(C) otherwise
(D) elsewhere

126. The company returned to ------- after raising prices for its services.

(A) profitability
(B) advantage
(C) performance
(D) priority

127. The dress code should be posted in a prominent spot in the employee lounge so that ------- can see it.

(A) everyone
(B) either
(C) few
(D) whomever

128. Maxwell Publishing's textbooks include a list of ------- materials teachers can use to broaden students' understanding of each topic.

(A) deliberate
(B) superfluous
(C) supplemental
(D) approximate

129. The two films opening this week are both so highly anticipated that it is unclear ------- one will sell the most tickets.

(A) which
(B) other
(C) because
(D) about

130. Current ------- suggest that clothing will overtake footwear as our top revenue-generating category sometime this year.

(A) trends
(B) designs
(C) guidelines
(D) advertisements

## PART 6

**Directions:** Read the texts that follow. A word, phrase, or sentence is missing in parts of each text. Four answer choices for each question are given below the text. Select the best answer to complete the text. Then mark the letter (A), (B), (C), or (D) on your answer sheet.

**Questions 131-134** refer to the following notice.

The redesign of Wheeler Corporation's headquarters resulted in the removal of over 40 paintings from our hallways and offices. Management ------- **131.** to allow employees to purchase this surplus artwork at reasonable prices through a private online auction. Visit the link at the bottom of this notice to view the available items. ------- **132.** may be submitted through the same site between 9 A.M. on May 5 and 7 P.M. on May 9. Once the auction ends, the winning employees will receive an e-mail with instructions ------- **133.** payment and pick-up. ------- **134.** . All proceeds from the auction will go to a local children's charity.

www.auctionhelper.com/49321

**131.** (A) decision
(B) to decide
(C) has decided
(D) deciding

**132.** (A) Pieces
(B) Donations
(C) Nominations
(D) Bids

**133.** (A) given
(B) concerning
(C) during
(D) plus

**134.** (A) If you have not received one yet, check your spam filter.
(B) Paintings must then be collected by 5 P.M. on May 16.
(C) Wheeler Corporation is located at 390 Cranford Street.
(D) Three winners will be chosen from among the submissions.



GO ON TO THE NEXT PAGE

**Questions 135-138** refer to the following e-mail.

To: Klein Print Shop Staff

From: Leslie Klein

Subject: Document shredding

Date: January 18

Dear Staff:

I'm proud to announce that Neil and I have obtained a professional ------- (135.) in secure document destruction from the National Data Management Association. We're ------- (136.) authorized to shred documents classified by the government as containing sensitive information. In the past, you were told to refer government customers ------- (137.) other businesses for this service. ------- (138.).

Finally, if we consistently receive high volumes of work, I may consider paying for some of you to receive this qualification as well.

Leslie Klein

Owner & Operator

Klein Print Shop

**135.** (A) certifies
(B) certifiable
(C) certification
(D) is certified

**136.** (A) still
(B) now
(C) almost
(D) just

**137.** (A) to
(B) of
(C) with
(D) among

**138.** (A) This will no longer be our policy.
(B) This work is not especially profitable.
(C) Pricing information will be posted on the wall.
(D) Customers may also shred their own documents.

**Questions 139-142** refer to the following e-mail.

To: Eun-Sook Yoo

From: Earl Fowler

Subject: Notice

Date: August 23

Dear Dr. Yoo,

I am writing to give you official notice that I am resigning from my position as Hillside Clinic's office manager. My final day will be Friday, September 21. I hope this will allow you plenty of time to find my ------- (139.) . If you are able to hire him or her before I go, I would be happy to handle the training. ------- (140.), I will create detailed documentation about my work processes and make it available to everyone on the shared network. ------- (141.) . Finally, I would like to express my gratitude to you for providing such ------- (142.) support and leadership over the last five years. It was a pleasure to act as your office manager. I wish you and Hillside Clinic the best in the future.

Sincerely,

Earl Fowler

**139.** (A) funding
(B) records
(C) belongings
(D) replacement

**140.** (A) In any case
(B) On the contrary
(C) For example
(D) As always

**141.** (A) It is important to me to ease the transition for our staff and patients.
(B) This is also the fastest way for you to share documents with me.
(C) Most of my time is spent sourcing our medical and office supplies.
(D) I usually start trainings for new hires by introducing the clinic's history.

**142.** (A) exception
(B) exceptions
(C) exceptional
(D) exceptionally

TEST 9

*GO ON TO THE NEXT PAGE* →

**Questions 143-146** refer to the following article.

BERLIN (16 March)—Harbinger Studios has held HarCon, a convention centered on its online games, each November in Berlin for the past 16 years. ------- **143.** the event's continued popularity, the company has canceled this year's HarCon in favor of several smaller events in various cities. A post on Harbinger's Web site explains that this format is better ------- **144.** to this momentous year for the company. Two of its game franchises will mark major anniversaries of their initial releases, while a third is launching a widely anticipated expansion pack. ------- **145.** . However, the post also emphasizes that HarCon will return next year, reassuring readers that "Harbinger is well aware of how much this ------- **146.** means to our fans."

**143.** (A) Due to
(B) Despite
(C) Although
(D) Along with

**144.** (A) suitability
(B) suitable
(C) suited
(D) suitably

**145.** (A) Harbinger even makes several popular mobile applications.
(B) Development of entirely new games is no longer its focus.
(C) The company plans to celebrate these milestones separately.
(D) Large events are often exponentially more costly to organize.

**146.** (A) award
(B) product
(C) character
(D) gathering

## PART 7

**Directions:** In this part you will read a selection of texts, such as magazine and newspaper articles, e-mails, and instant messages. Each text or set of texts is followed by several questions. Select the best answer for each question and mark the letter (A), (B), (C), or (D) on your answer sheet.

**Questions 147-148** refer to the following Web page.

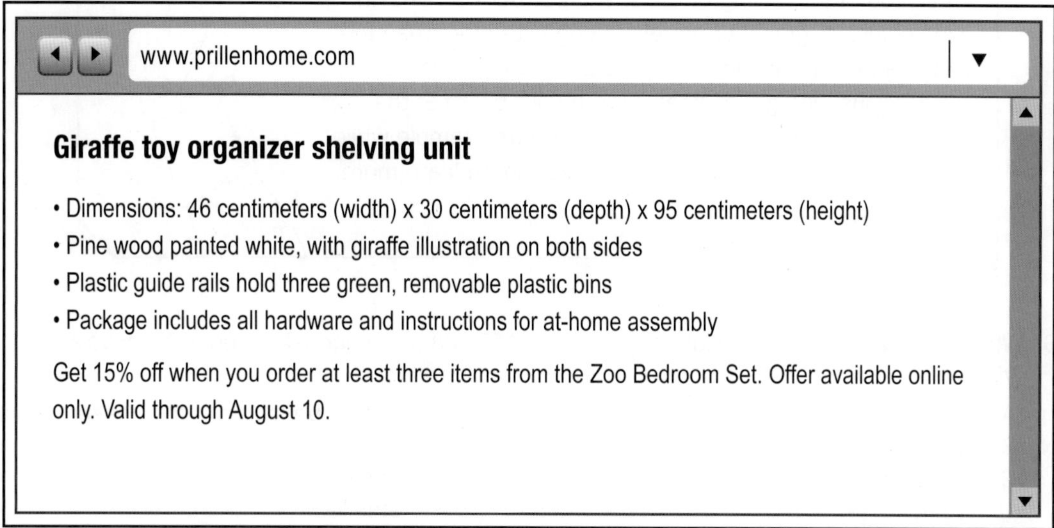

www.prillenhome.com

**Giraffe toy organizer shelving unit**

- Dimensions: 46 centimeters (width) x 30 centimeters (depth) x 95 centimeters (height)
- Pine wood painted white, with giraffe illustration on both sides
- Plastic guide rails hold three green, removable plastic bins
- Package includes all hardware and instructions for at-home assembly

Get 15% off when you order at least three items from the Zoo Bedroom Set. Offer available online only. Valid through August 10.

**147.** What is mentioned about the shelving unit?

(A) It is shaped like an animal.
(B) It has removable rails.
(C) Its bins have been printed with images.
(D) It must be put together after delivery.

**148.** What is indicated about the sale?

(A) It begins earlier for online shoppers.
(B) It requires the purchase of several items.
(C) It entitles the customer to a discount of $15.
(D) It is only available to members of a loyalty program.



GO ON TO THE NEXT PAGE

**Questions 149-150** refer to the following advertisement.

## Pocheva

Official partner of the Mahoney Triathlon

Drinking Pocheva nutritional shakes during training helps many Mahoney Triathlon participants build the muscle they need to conquer the slopes of the course's infamous peaks. Each 60-gram serving of the shake powder contains an incredible 25 grams of protein, along with more than 85 nutrients. Once blended with ice and water, it makes a delicious, energizing treat. Stop by our booth at the triathlon expo in Mahoney Square for a free sample while supplies last, or visit www.gopocheva.com to learn more.

POCHEVA

**149.** What is indicated about the Mahoney Triathlon?

(A) It takes place in a mountainous area.
(B) Its course has been made longer.
(C) It is held during a warm time of the year.
(D) Its finish line is located in Mahoney Square.

**150.** What is suggested about Pocheva's product?

(A) It should be stored in the freezer before opening.
(B) It has been endorsed by a famous athlete.
(C) It is given away at a triathlon-related event.
(D) It is sold to consumers in liquid form.

**Questions 151-152** refer to the following text-message chain.

**Benjamin Raley [1:10 P.M.]**
Greta, thanks again for letting me interview you for my article on artificial intelligence. I ended up quoting you several times.

**Greta Oleson [1:13 P.M.]**
Yes, I saw that. I'm glad I could share my research with your readers.

**Benjamin Raley [1:14 P.M.]**
Now my editor has asked me to write another article that goes into more detail about AI's effects on the workplace. Could we jump on the phone so I can get your thoughts on that?

**Greta Oleson [1:21 P.M.]**
Sure, but can you wait until five? I'm participating in a conference today.

**Benjamin Raley [1:22 P.M.]**
That would be difficult. This article is for tomorrow's edition.

**Greta Oleson [1:24 P.M.]**
OK, then the best I can do is a short chat between sessions.

**Benjamin Raley [1:25 P.M.]**
I'll take that offer! Call me when you're free.



**151.** Why is Mr. Raley contacting Ms. Oleson?
(A) To inform her about a helpful resource
(B) To obtain her expert opinion on a topic
(C) To find out the status of her research project
(D) To thank her for submitting an article

**152.** At 1:22 P.M., what does Mr. Raley most likely mean when he writes, "That would be difficult"?
(A) He is concerned about Ms. Oleson's workload.
(B) He is too busy to attend a conference.
(C) He thinks some writing is hard to understand.
(D) He prefers to have a phone call at an earlier time.

GO ON TO THE NEXT PAGE

**Questions 153-155** refer to the following e-mail.

| | |
|---|---|
| **From** | Chae-Won Yoo |
| **To** | Karen Adkins |
| **Subject** | News |
| **Date** | November 28 |
| **Attachment** | Lee |

Dear Ms. Adkins,

I have found someone who is a promising match for your company's Business Development Representative opening. His name is Conrad Lee, and he has been working in sales for Dawson Health for the past three years. As with your opening at Azora Science, this is Seoul-based work that involves selling American products to Korean companies, and Conrad has been successful at it. He was promoted from associate to junior manager last year. I also confirmed myself in a phone call that he speaks both English and Korean with native-level fluency.

Conrad has a bachelor's degree in biology and is scheduled to earn his MBA degree from Larson University's online program in December. He even has the passion for science education you are looking for, as he volunteers at a local science museum on the weekends.

Conrad's résumé is attached to this e-mail. Please respond to this e-mail if you would like me to connect you with him.

Sincerely,

Chae-Won Yoo
Hermann Korea, Inc.

**153.** What is the purpose of the e-mail?

(A) To suggest an event speaker
(B) To announce a promotion
(C) To introduce a job candidate
(D) To publicize a mentorship program

**154.** What is true about Mr. Lee?

(A) He is bilingual.
(B) He is currently unemployed.
(C) He travels to Seoul frequently.
(D) He used to work with Ms. Yoo.

**155.** What does Mr. Lee plan to do by the end of the year?

(A) Move to a different country
(B) Mount a museum exhibit
(C) Finish a volunteer project
(D) Complete a second degree

**Questions 156-158** refer to the following e-mail.

**E-Mail message**

| | |
|---|---|
| **To:** | All Residents of Tisdale Apartments |
| **From:** | Elsa Reynolds, Property Manager |
| **Date:** | May 3 |
| **Subject:** | Plumbing Repair Work |

Dear Resident,

Water service to the Tisdale Apartments building will be shut off on Tuesday, May 18. — [1] —. All units will be without access to hot or cold water from 9:00 A.M. until as late as 6:00 P.M. on that day. The shut-off is necessary so that plumbers can inspect the building's main water supply and pressure regulators to identify the cause of the water pressure issues that residents have reported. Future shut-offs may be necessary in order to facilitate repairs. — [2] —.

Please keep the following in mind before and on the day in question. The sinks, showers, baths, and toilets in all apartments will be out of operation. If you anticipate needing water for drinking or cooking, fill up containers beforehand. — [3] —. Your heater or air conditioner may be connected to the water lines. — [4] —. Avoid turning them on in order to prevent any issues.

Please contact me at e.reynolds@tisdaleapt.com if you have any questions. Thank you.

**156.** Why was the e-mail sent to residents?
(A) To explain why their water pressure is low
(B) To share tips for reducing some expenses
(C) To remind them about an upcoming community event
(D) To warn them about a disruption to a utility service

**157.** What does Ms. Reynolds recommend doing?
(A) Buying special storage containers
(B) Checking a plumbing connection
(C) Avoiding using certain appliances
(D) Reporting ongoing issues to her

**158.** In which of the positions marked [1], [2], [3], and [4] does the following sentence best belong?

"Portable toilets will also be stationed in the back alley for residents' use."

(A) [1]
(B) [2]
(C) [3]
(D) [4]



GO ON TO THE NEXT PAGE

**Questions 159-160** refer to the following letter.

National Drivers Association of Australia (NDAA)

16 September
Darren Houser
160 Frye Street
Canberra ACT 2601

Dear Mr. Houser,

Your current year of membership in the NDAA will come to an end on 31 October. Renew now to enjoy another 12 months of benefits. Remember, our members receive access to the NDAA's incredible roadside assistance—which includes emergency fuel delivery, battery charging, tyre changes, and towing—all for no extra charge. You are also eligible for discounts on auto repairs at hundreds of partner garages nationwide, as well as roadside assistance for your rental car in dozens of other countries thanks to our reciprocal agreements with automotive clubs around the globe.

Additionally, the NDAA has just entered a partnership with GoAsia Travel to offer our members exclusive tours of several top destinations in Southeast Asia. To take advantage of this benefit, return the attached form with your annual membership fee of $99.99 AUD, or go to our Web site, www.ndaa.com.au, to renew using your credit or debit card.

Thank you for being part of the NDAA family.

Sincerely,

Florence Hartley
Membership Coordinator
Encl.

**159.** What is NOT listed as something members can do?

(A) Save money on car rentals
(B) Have a vehicle towed for free
(C) Receive help while driving abroad
(D) Go on special tours overseas

**160.** What is Mr. Houser asked to do?

(A) Visit an NDAA location
(B) Make a yearly payment
(C) Fill out a feedback form
(D) Carry a membership card

**Questions 161-163** refer to the following report.

## Executive Summary

Purpose

This report has been created at the direction of the executive board of Funfair, Inc., in order to illuminate the potential advantages and disadvantages of purchasing Sutton Candle Corporation (hereafter, "Sutton").

Initial Conclusion

Sutton would likely be an overall asset to Funfair's brand portfolio. Its candles and scent diffusers are of high quality and would be a complementary addition to our décor aisles and living room displays. Keeping the Sutton name on the products could also increase foot traffic in our locations, as it enjoys strong customer loyalty.

Financial Overview of Target

Sutton currently manufactures 36 products in three categories and sells them directly to consumers through its Web site. The sales revenues for each category over the most recent year are displayed in the table below.

| | **Fiscal Quarter** | | | |
|---|---|---|---|---|
| **Product Type** | **First** | **Second** | **Third** | **Fourth** |
| Candles | $80,713 | $85,029 | $87,172 | $93,541 |
| Plug-in Diffusers | $12,453 | $16,510 | $15,384 | $14,693 |
| Diffuser Refill Packs | $16,450 | $14,478 | $15,624 | $15,722 |

**161.** What does the report discuss?

(A) The purpose of some budget revisions
(B) The need for strategies to increase sales
(C) The effects of an advertising campaign
(D) The possibility of a corporate acquisition

**162.** What kind of business is Funfair, Inc.?

(A) A home goods store
(B) A brand consulting firm
(C) An interior design company
(D) A manufacturer of fragrance products

**163.** When was over $16,000 worth of electronic products sold?

(A) The first quarter
(B) The second quarter
(C) The third quarter
(D) The fourth quarter

TEST 9

*GO ON TO THE NEXT PAGE*

**Questions 164-167** refer to the following press release.

MANCHESTER (14 August)—Local firm Centrality Partners announced today that it will begin providing its services to non-profit organisations at a discounted rate. — [1] —.

Centrality possesses one of the city's largest collections of audiovisual equipment, ranging from sound systems to large digital displays and programmable lighting fixtures. — [2] —. All of this is put at clients' disposal in service of staging polished, impressive conferences, fund-raisers, awards banquets, and much more.

No matter the occasion or audience, Centrality ensures that presenters' messages are conveyed clearly. A technical expert is present at every step of the process to minimise the possibility of distracting problems like distorted sound, incompatible presentation materials, and even unflattering lighting. — [3] —. Recent Centrality successes include the annual conference of the UK's largest insurers' association and the Manchester Book Festival.

The discount that Centrality is offering non-profit clients will vary between 10% and 20% depending on the size of the organisation. — [4] —. To be eligible, organisations must be based within Greater Manchester. Details and contact information can be found on Centrality's Web site, www.centrality.co.uk.

**164.** What does Centrality assist its clients with?
(A) Maintaining equipment
(B) Holding live events
(C) Purchasing insurance
(D) Producing video advertisements

**165.** What is stated as an advantage companies get from Centrality's service?
(A) A unique brand identity
(B) Higher employee satisfaction
(C) More effective communication
(D) Reduced operating costs

**166.** What information about the special offer is included in the press release?
(A) The region it is available in
(B) The method for obtaining it
(C) The period for which it is valid
(D) The reason for its introduction

**167.** In which of the positions marked [1], [2], [3], and [4] does the following sentence best belong?

"Its resources also include a dedicated staff of 30 with various technical specialties."

(A) [1]
(B) [2]
(C) [3]
(D) [4]

**Questions 168-171** refer to the following article.

ATLANTA (May 2)—Local crew members of the television comedy *Elena* were informed this week that the show will no longer be filmed in Atlanta, Georgia. Shooting for the third season will instead take place across the country in Los Angeles, California, where production company ASR Entertainment is based. In addition to this logistical advantage, the change will also make the production of *Elena* more economical. ASR Entertainment confirmed it will earn a large tax credit from California as part of a state program aimed at invigorating its film and television industries.

*Elena* is the fourth TV production to make this shift in the past two years. Members of the Atlanta entertainment community are said to be considering appealing to Georgia's state legislators to increase the scale of its own incentive program.

**168.** What is the article mainly about?

(A) New storylines on a television show
(B) The relocation of a television production
(C) The management of an entertainment company
(D) Difficulties experienced by a production crew

**169.** How many seasons of *Elena* have been filmed?

(A) One
(B) Two
(C) Three
(D) Four

**170.** How will ASR Entertainment save money while making *Elena*?

(A) By filming fewer episodes
(B) By making casting changes
(C) By outsourcing some work
(D) By accepting a tax benefit

**171.** The phrase "appealing to" in paragraph 2, line 4, is closest in meaning to

(A) attracting
(B) agreeing to
(C) calling upon
(D) selecting

TEST 9

GO ON TO THE NEXT PAGE

**Questions 172-175** refer to the following online chat discussion.

| | | |
|---|---|---|
| Yuvraj Bedi | 5:10 P.M. | Thanks for doing this check-in over chat, everyone. My duties at the Abbotsford site made it impossible to get to the office today. Miriam, how's the Web site upgrade coming along? |
| Miriam Thornton | 5:14 P.M. | Very well. Today I called all of our clients from the past year to ask if they'd be willing to write testimonials for the site. Five of them agreed, including Norman Limited. |
| Yuvraj Bedi | 5:15 P.M. | That's great. Cody, is there any news about prospective new projects? |
| Cody Haynes | 5:17 P.M. | Yes, there is. The owner of a clothing store just called about building a set of dressing rooms in one of its back corners. I'm putting together a quote for her. Also, do you remember Glen Webster, who designed the Griffin family's house? He recommended us to another residential client. Marvin is going to meet with both of them tomorrow. Oh, and Asami noticed a government project that we might be a good fit for. Asami? |
| Asami Yoshida | 5:20 P.M. | Thanks, Cody. The Vancouver Parks Department announced that it's accepting bids for a new storage facility at Hastings Park. I'm looking into the requirements for city contractors now, and I think we can meet them with a little effort. |
| Yuvraj Bedi | 5:21 P.M. | OK, keep me updated on that. I'll wrap up here since we all need to head home soon. Have a good evening, everyone. |

**172.** For what type of business do the chat participants most likely work?

(A) A cleaning agency
(B) A landscape design company
(C) A groundskeeping service
(D) A construction firm

**173.** What is implied about Norman Limited?

(A) It is a satisfied client of the writers' company.
(B) It filled out an online contact form.
(C) It is a new competitor of the writers' company.
(D) It participated in a survey about a Web site.

**174.** Who most likely is Mr. Webster?

(A) A store manager
(B) An architect
(C) A property owner
(D) A government official

**175.** At 5:20 P.M., what does Ms. Yoshida most likely mean when she writes, "Thanks, Cody"?

(A) She accepts Mr. Haynes's praise for her work.
(B) She is pleased to be put in charge of a new project.
(C) She has received some information from Mr. Haynes.
(D) She is glad to have a chance to discuss her idea.

TEST 9

*GO ON TO THE NEXT PAGE*

**Questions 176-180** refer to the following Web page and review.

www.momentum-program.com/home

## Momentum

The Momentum app assists freelancers and small businesses in keeping track of their working hours. Its superb flexibility means it can be adapted for almost any industry. Users have control over a wide range of elements, from the categories into which timekeeping entries can be organized to the data that is included in summary reports. And the Momentum team always welcomes suggestions about how to make our product helpful to even more people.

Three versions of Momentum are available:

**Individual**, $0. Designed for freelancers. Users can record their activities manually or automatically, create templates for fast entry of common tasks, and generate reports of their activities by date or by project.

**Enterprise**, $5 per user monthly. Designed for businesses. All users enjoy the same benefits as Individual users, plus users designated as managers can access others' records in order to monitor their productivity and calculate payroll.

*For a one-week free trial of Enterprise, click here.

**Enterprise Pro**, $8 per user monthly. This premium tier entitles businesses to enjoy all Enterprise subscription benefits, plus the ability to create client invoices based on staff timesheets and to request, permit, and track time off.

## Customer Review

Momentum has been a great choice for my small consulting firm. The nature of our work means that we all have to switch between tasks for different clients several times per workday, and it used to be very time-consuming to total these small units of time at the end of each billing period. Now, Momentum generates all of our invoices in just seconds, and I feel more confident in their accuracy. I have also found the summary reports quite useful, as they showed that certain types of projects consistently required more hours than I expected. I am now able to give more reliable time and budget estimates, which I am sure my clients appreciate.

My only complaint about Momentum is that the automatic time-tracking feature seems to use up a lot of processing power. Anytime I have tried it, I began to experience lags in all of my other programs. And they are not small ones—it took a full five seconds just to switch between tabs in my Web browser. Fortunately, it is easy to simply input timekeeping entries manually instead.

Overall, I am quite pleased with Momentum and would recommend it to other companies and individuals with time-tracking needs.

—Dwayne Jacobs

**176.** What benefit of Momentum does the Web page emphasize?

(A) Fast customer support
(B) Compatibility with mobile devices
(C) Numerous customization options
(D) Secure data storage

**177.** In the testimonial, what does Mr. Jacobs indicate about staff members at his company?

(A) They are involved in multiple projects each day.
(B) They sometimes need to work offsite.
(C) They are required to use automatic time-tracking.
(D) They often do tasks outside of regular business hours.

**178.** What is implied about Mr. Jacobs?

(A) He signed up for an Enterprise Pro account.
(B) He has become able to take on additional clients.
(C) He is using a trial version of Momentum.
(D) He is not confident in his technological skills.

**179.** In the review, the word "appreciate" in paragraph 1, line 7, is closest in meaning to

(A) increase
(B) understand
(C) enjoy
(D) value

**180.** What does Mr. Jacobs mention about his Web browser?

(A) He had to update it in order to download Momentum.
(B) Its operating speed is affected by a Momentum feature.
(C) It was recommended to him by a Momentum employee.
(D) It closes unexpectedly when he opens Momentum.

TEST 9

*GO ON TO THE NEXT PAGE*

**Questions 181-185** refer to the following article and e-mail.

## Local News

GALWAY (24 June)—Thornbriar Business Park has taken another step on the path towards its planned opening next February. Yesterday, city officials and local business leaders gathered in East Galway for the development's groundbreaking ceremony.

Thornbriar is being developed and will be owned by Thornbriar Partners, a group comprising a property developer and several business owners who plan to move their companies into the complex. Adrian Horgan, one of the latter, has explained that the group bonded over its dissatisfaction with the area's existing commercial real estate options. Thornbriar Business Park, he said, was their "solution to the issue," as it will feature "airy spaces with modern facilities."

While much of the business park's space is already reserved, several units remain available. KV Real Estate, which is handling leasing for the site, will hold an information session for potential tenants at its office on 8 July. Those interested should visit www.kvrealestate.ie/thornbriar for details.

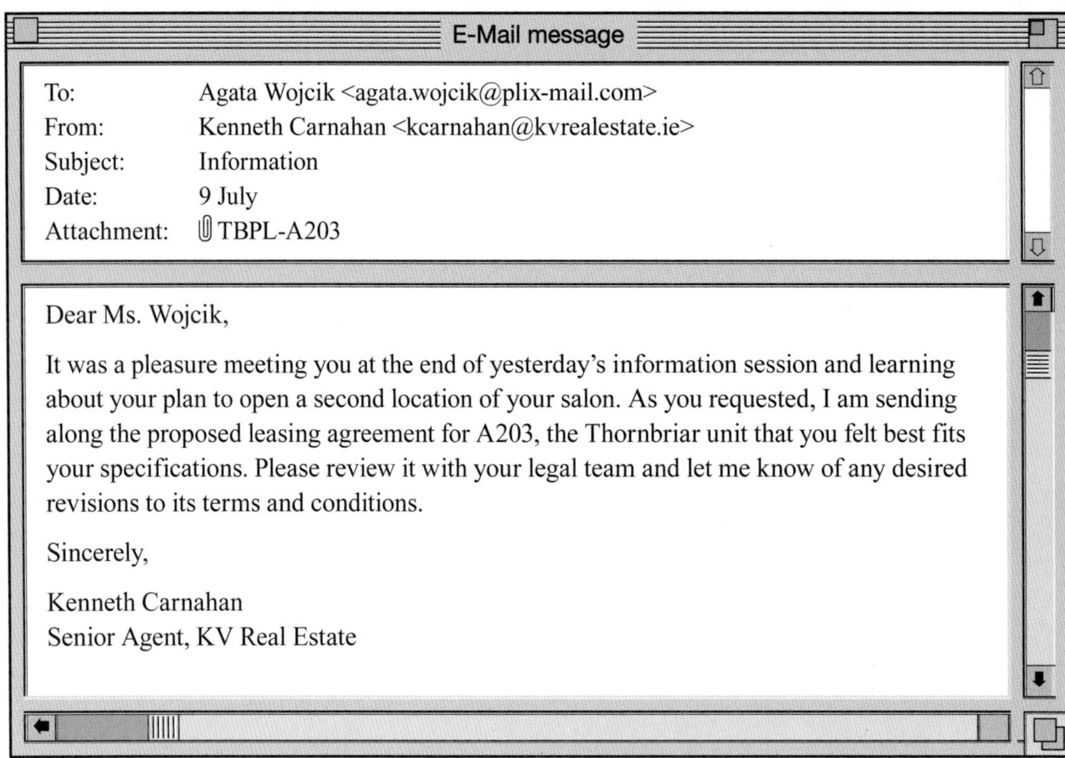

E-Mail message

To: Agata Wojcik <agata.wojcik@plix-mail.com>
From: Kenneth Carnahan <kcarnahan@kvrealestate.ie>
Subject: Information
Date: 9 July
Attachment: TBPL-A203

Dear Ms. Wojcik,

It was a pleasure meeting you at the end of yesterday's information session and learning about your plan to open a second location of your salon. As you requested, I am sending along the proposed leasing agreement for A203, the Thornbriar unit that you felt best fits your specifications. Please review it with your legal team and let me know of any desired revisions to its terms and conditions.

Sincerely,

Kenneth Carnahan
Senior Agent, KV Real Estate

**181.** According to the article, what took place yesterday?
- (A) A planning meeting for a new public park
- (B) The opening of a city government building
- (C) The start of construction on a business complex
- (D) The award ceremony of a professional association

**182.** What is most likely true about Thornbriar Partners?
- (A) It was created to carry out a single project.
- (B) It is a partnership of two people.
- (C) It has purchased a real estate agency.
- (D) It won a bid from the city of Galway.

**183.** What does the article indicate about Mr. Horgan?
- (A) He is an experienced property developer.
- (B) He intends to relocate his business.
- (C) He was unhappy about a local regulation.
- (D) He is a member of a homeowners' group.

**184.** What is the purpose of the e-mail?
- (A) To begin a tenancy negotiation
- (B) To propose touring a property
- (C) To inquire about a legal representative
- (D) To give an update on a building process

**185.** What can be concluded about Ms. Wojcik?
- (A) She runs an organization in East Galway.
- (B) She asked her lawyer to draft a contract.
- (C) She gave a presentation at an information session.
- (D) She met Mr. Carnahan at his workplace.

TEST 9

*GO ON TO THE NEXT PAGE*

**Questions 186-190** refer to the following product information and e-mails.

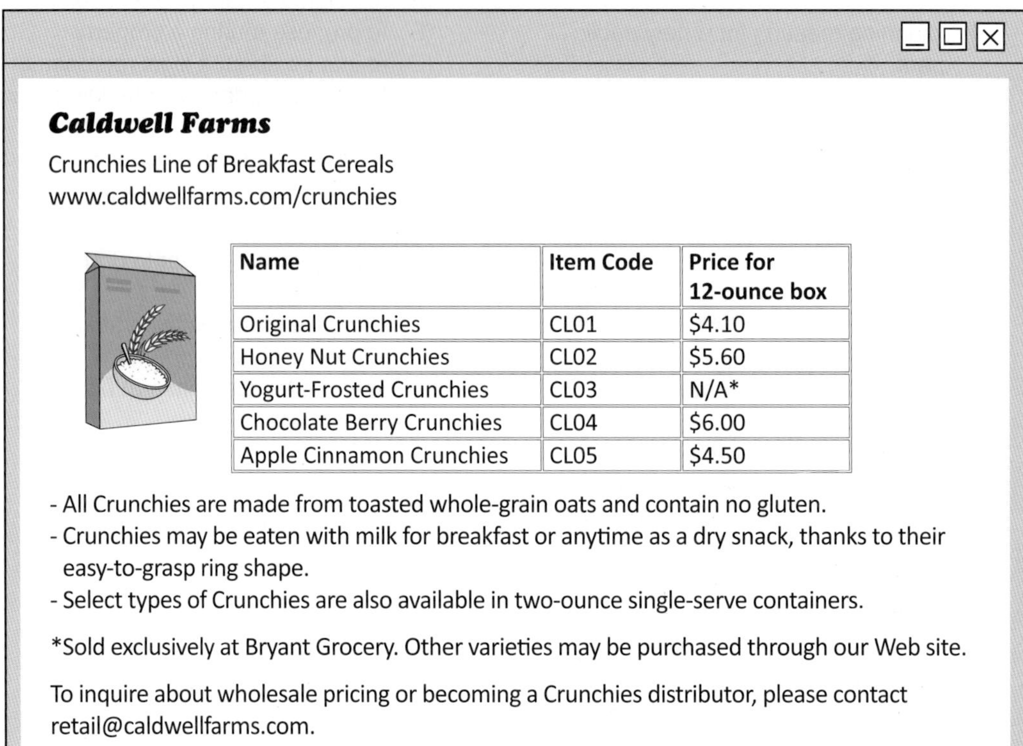

***Caldwell Farms***

Crunchies Line of Breakfast Cereals
www.caldwellfarms.com/crunchies

| Name | Item Code | Price for 12-ounce box |
|---|---|---|
| Original Crunchies | CL01 | $4.10 |
| Honey Nut Crunchies | CL02 | $5.60 |
| Yogurt-Frosted Crunchies | CL03 | N/A* |
| Chocolate Berry Crunchies | CL04 | $6.00 |
| Apple Cinnamon Crunchies | CL05 | $4.50 |

- All Crunchies are made from toasted whole-grain oats and contain no gluten.
- Crunchies may be eaten with milk for breakfast or anytime as a dry snack, thanks to their easy-to-grasp ring shape.
- Select types of Crunchies are also available in two-ounce single-serve containers.

*Sold exclusively at Bryant Grocery. Other varieties may be purchased through our Web site.

To inquire about wholesale pricing or becoming a Crunchies distributor, please contact retail@caldwellfarms.com.

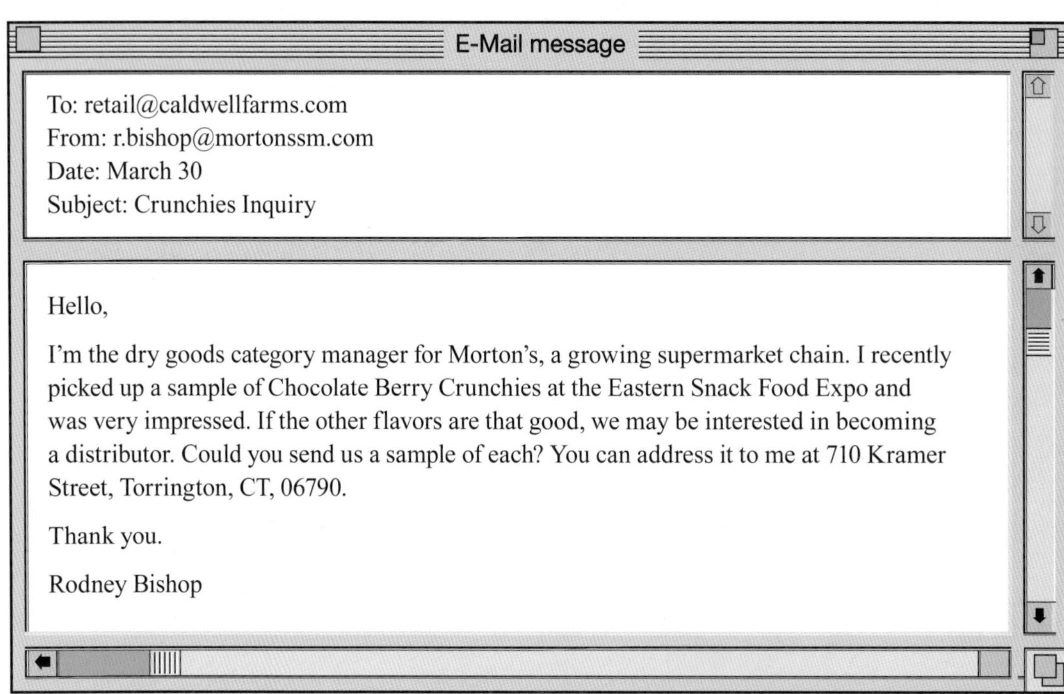

E-Mail message

To: retail@caldwellfarms.com
From: r.bishop@mortonssm.com
Date: March 30
Subject: Crunchies Inquiry

Hello,

I'm the dry goods category manager for Morton's, a growing supermarket chain. I recently picked up a sample of Chocolate Berry Crunchies at the Eastern Snack Food Expo and was very impressed. If the other flavors are that good, we may be interested in becoming a distributor. Could you send us a sample of each? You can address it to me at 710 Kramer Street, Torrington, CT, 06790.

Thank you.

Rodney Bishop

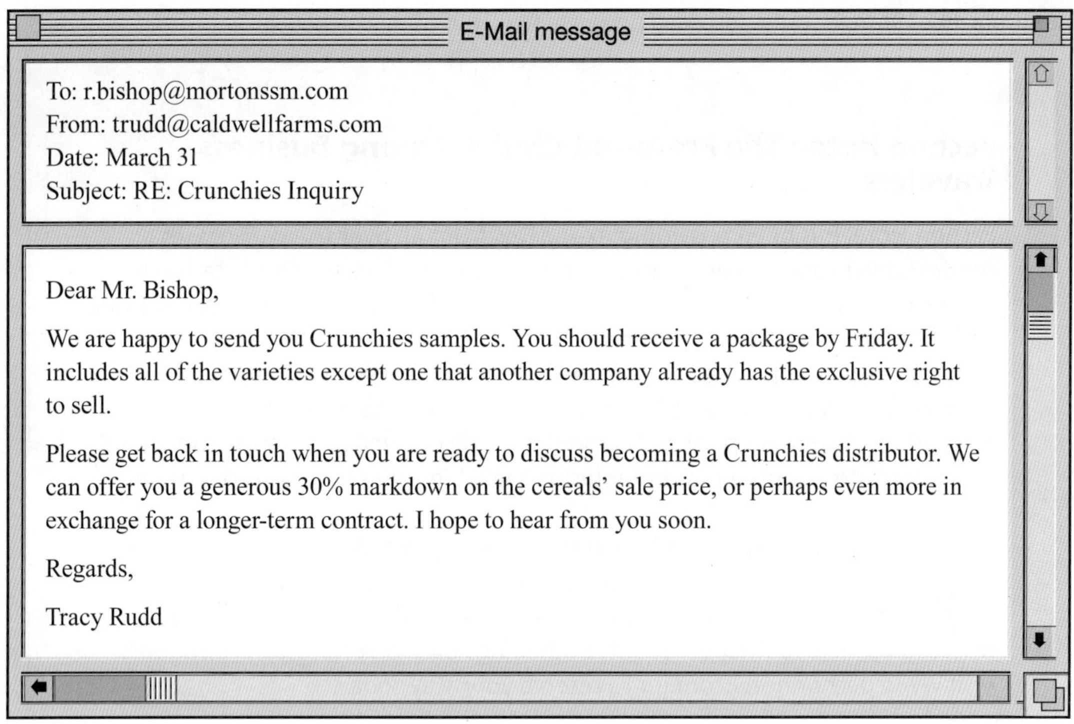

E-Mail message

To: r.bishop@mortonssm.com
From: trudd@caldwellfarms.com
Date: March 31
Subject: RE: Crunchies Inquiry

Dear Mr. Bishop,

We are happy to send you Crunchies samples. You should receive a package by Friday. It includes all of the varieties except one that another company already has the exclusive right to sell.

Please get back in touch when you are ready to discuss becoming a Crunchies distributor. We can offer you a generous 30% markdown on the cereals' sale price, or perhaps even more in exchange for a longer-term contract. I hope to hear from you soon.

Regards,

Tracy Rudd

**186.** What does the product information indicate about Crunchies?

(A) They are often included in homemade snack bars.
(B) Some of them are sold in small packs of two containers.
(C) More than one type of them features fruit flavoring.
(D) They are all currently available for online purchase only.

**187.** In what field does Mr. Bishop most likely work?

(A) Warehouse management
(B) Store merchandising
(C) Trade show organizing
(D) Cafeteria administration

**188.** What is the price of a regular box of the cereal Mr. Bishop tried?

(A) $4.10
(B) $4.50
(C) $5.60
(D) $6.00

**189.** Which type of Crunchies is NOT in the package Mr. Bishop will receive?

(A) Original Crunchies
(B) Honey Nut Crunchies
(C) Yogurt-Frosted Crunchies
(D) Chocolate Berry Crunchies

**190.** In the second e-mail, what is stated about a price discount?

(A) Its size can be negotiated.
(B) It is being offered until Friday.
(C) It will apply only to a single order.
(D) It is available for purchases of over 30 boxes.

*GO ON TO THE NEXT PAGE*

**Questions 191-195** refer to the following advertisement, e-mail, and schedule.

## Pechon Hotel: The Preferred Choice Among Business Travelers

Pechon Hotel has been providing executives from all over the world with a comfortable place to stay in Jamaica for more than 25 years. Our location in downtown Kingston is within walking distance of the Ministry of Foreign Trade and the Harbour Conference Centre.

All of the rooms and suites at Pechon Hotel feature air-conditioning, cable television, a mini-fridge, a coffeemaker, a safe, and free Wi-Fi. We also have an outdoor swimming pool with a poolside café, as well as a fitness room and business centre. Continental breakfast is available every morning for a small fee.

The single rooms with a double bed that make up our West Wing are available for 26,000 JMD per night. The suites in our East Wing, which additionally include a living room with a writing desk and a furnished balcony, can be reserved for 40,000 JMD per night. Both wings overlook Kingston Harbour.

Visit www.pechonhotel.com.jm to reserve your stay today.

**E-Mail message**

To: Glenda Douglas <g.douglas@jenkinsassociates.com>
From: Emiliano Andres <e.andres@jenkinsassociates.com>
Subject: RE: Upcoming trip
Date: 8 November

Dear Glenda,

Thank you for asking before making plans to bring your husband and child on your trip to Kingston next month for the Caribbean Travel Forum. Jenkins Associates does indeed allow employees to bring family along on work trips at their own expense. We will still pay for your airfare, the cost of a single room for two nights, and three days' meal allowance, but you must cover any other expenses. You should contact Pechon Hotel directly to arrange your upgrade to a suite and the extension of your stay through Saturday night.

Please also keep in mind that you will be expected to attend all conference events as usual, including evening ones.

Let me know if you have any other questions.

Best,

Emiliano Andres, Human Resources Specialist

| **Caribbean Travel Forum**<br>Friday, 4 December<br>Harbour Conference Center<br>Kingston, Jamaica | |
|---|---|
| 9–9:30 A.M. | Registration |
| 9:30–10 A.M. | Opening Remarks (Jalissa Vargas, President of the Caribbean Tourism Association) |
| 10 A.M.–12 P.M. | Keynote Address: Integrating Technology into Caribbean Tourism (Irene Summers, CEO of TravelZap) |
| 12–1 P.M. | Lunch |
| 1:30–3 P.M. | Seminar: Public Policy Challenges (Eric Perry, Professor at Bridgetown College) |
| 3:30–5 P.M. | Panel: Achieving Environmentally Sustainable Tourism (Various experts) |
| 6:30 P.M. | Networking Dinner |

**191.** What is an exclusive feature of the lodgings in the hotel's East Wing?

(A) Some kitchen appliances
(B) A view of a waterfront
(C) A private outdoor space
(D) Free Internet service

**192.** What is the purpose of Mr. Andres's e-mail?

(A) To confirm a company policy
(B) To question changes to an itinerary
(C) To give a work assignment
(D) To respond to a recommendation

**193.** What can be inferred about Ms. Douglas's hotel stay during the Caribbean Travel Forum?

(A) Her company will spend 26,000 JMD per night on it.
(B) She can receive a discount by extending it.
(C) Her lodgings will be located in the hotel's West Wing.
(D) She plans to use 40,000 JMD of her own money on it each night.

**194.** What is NOT one of the topics that will be addressed at the forum?

(A) Difficulties caused by government policies
(B) Marketing approaches for various target audiences
(C) Lessening negative environmental impacts of tourism
(D) Incorporating technology into tourism services

**195.** On which date will Ms. Douglas most likely leave Kingston?

(A) December 3
(B) December 4
(C) December 5
(D) December 6

*GO ON TO THE NEXT PAGE* →

**Questions 196-200** refer to the following brochure, card, and schedule.

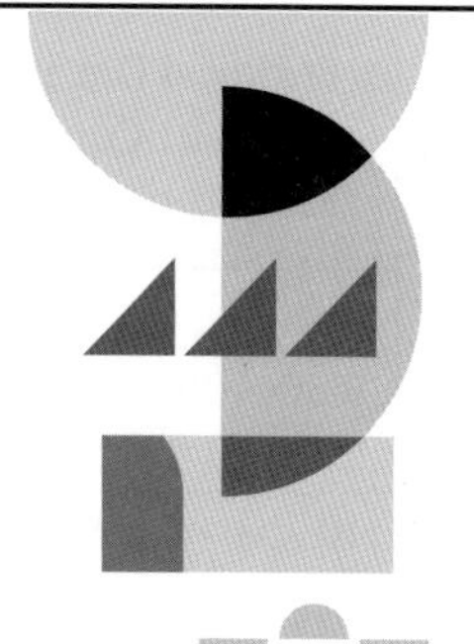

## Gossett Art Museum

1200 State Street, Gossett
555-0193

**September Membership Drive**

- Friend level - $72
- Enthusiast level - $112

Gossett Art Museum has a 25,000-piece permanent collection that would be at home in a city several times larger. It includes a wide assortment of sculptures by Celine Dupont and one of the few surviving murals by Rafael Rubio. We also frequently host world-renowned touring exhibitions.

What also sets the museum apart is our commitment to art education. We offer regular informative lectures, as well as seasonal classes for all ages in a variety of fine arts. All of the adult classes are taught by professional artists from our community.

Holders of our Friend-level memberships receive unlimited general admission to the museum, as well as priority access to tickets for special exhibitions. When registering for classes or lectures, they are entitled to a 10% discount on fees.

Enthusiast-level members have the additional perk of half-price general admission for any accompanying guests. They are also invited to visit the museum during special "Enthusiasts-only" days and hours.

To purchase a membership to Gossett Art Museum, visit the information desk in our first-floor lobby. Photo identification is required.

## Gossett Museum of Art
### Membership Card

**Member Information**

**Name:** Terrence Allen

**Identification Number:** 54830

**Membership Level:** Enthusiast

**Membership Expiration Date:** September 23

## Gossett Museum of Art

**Adult Class Schedule for Fall**
(September 2 through November 30)

Note: Instructor permission is required to join a class in progress.

| Day and Time | Class | Instructor |
|---|---|---|
| Mondays, 5-6 P.M. | Advanced Watercolor Painting | Mila Lukina |
| Wednesdays, 7-8 P.M. | Sketching Sculptures in the Galleries | Joel Page |
| Thursdays, 5-6 P.M. | Introduction to Printmaking | Tae-Shik Sun |
| Saturdays, 10-11 A.M. | Portrait Photography | Sophie Coleman |

**196.** What does the brochure suggest about Gossett Art Museum?
(A) It is trying to gain additional supporters.
(B) It was founded by Ms. Dupont and Mr. Rubio.
(C) It recently started offering classes for adults.
(D) It is located in a city with an international airport.

**197.** What is required of museum members?
(A) They must sign a registration form.
(B) They must read a list of rules.
(C) They must fill out an annual survey.
(D) They must show proof of their identity.

**198.** What membership benefit is available to Mr. Allen?
(A) Discounts on items at the museum store
(B) Personal guided tours of special exhibitions
(C) Exclusive entry to the museum on certain days
(D) Access to a convenient parking area

**199.** What is most likely true about Mr. Sun?
(A) He is a full-time employee at the museum.
(B) He will attend an art show at the end of November.
(C) He is teaching an advanced-level class.
(D) He also sells his own artwork.

**200.** What is suggested on the schedule?
(A) All of the classes take place on weekdays.
(B) Two of the classes teach students how to paint.
(C) One of the classes is held in an exhibition space.
(D) There is a limit to the number of students per class.

TEST 9

**Stop! This is the end of the test. If you finish before time is called, you may go back to Parts 5, 6, and 7 and check your work.**

YBM
실전토익
RC1000

**테스트 전 체크리스트**

- 중간 휴식 없이 제한 시간을 지켜서 풀이하세요.
- 제한 시간은 답안지에 마킹하는 시간도 포함시켜야 합니다.
- 찍은 문제는 번호 옆에 꼭 체크해 주세요.
- 시간 안에 풀지 못한 문제는 틀린 것으로 채점해 주세요.

# RC TEST 10

## READING TEST

In the Reading test, you will read a variety of texts and answer several different types of reading comprehension questions. The entire Reading test will last 75 minutes. There are three parts, and directions are given for each part. You are encouraged to answer as many questions as possible within the time allowed.

You must mark your answers on the separate answer sheet. Do not write your answers in your test book.

## PART 5

**Directions:** A word or phrase is missing in each of the sentences below. Four answer choices are given below each sentence. Select the best answer to complete the sentence. Then mark the letter (A), (B), (C), or (D) on your answer sheet.

**101.** The Palumbo Tulip Garden has become a major ------- for tourists.

(A) attracted
(B) attractive
(C) attractively
(D) attraction

**102.** Employees who work on the fourth floor may use the third-floor break room while ------- is being renovated.

(A) their
(B) theirs
(C) them
(D) they

**103.** The rock band Symbolix announced that tickets for its Sorrell Arena concert are ------- sold out.

(A) enough
(B) ever
(C) almost
(D) evenly

**104.** Parts of the air show will be extremely loud, so organizers ------- bringing hearing protection.

(A) to advise
(B) advice
(C) advise
(D) advising

**105.** The caterers will serve an array of ------- snacks when guests first arrive at the reception.

(A) lightly
(B) light
(C) lighten
(D) lightness

**106.** Elin Apparel purchases the fabric for its ------- from local textile companies.

(A) garments
(B) studios
(C) models
(D) remainders

**107.** Educator Sandy Guillen believes that ------- students have fun during a lesson, they are more likely to retain its contents.

(A) when
(B) yet
(C) so
(D) given

**108.** A *Stanton Business Journal* study found a clear connection ------- employee pay and business performance.

(A) of
(B) between
(C) around
(D) in

109. On particularly busy evenings, the restaurant's owner ------- helps prepare ingredients and serve diners.

(A) her
(B) she
(C) hers
(D) herself

110. The shuttle ------- at 8 A.M., so please pack your baggage promptly in the morning.

(A) leaving
(B) have left
(C) will be leaving
(D) having left

111. The newest Rhodes Convenience Store location will be completely unstaffed, ------- its existing stores merely offer a self-checkout option.

(A) despite
(B) whereas
(C) apart from
(D) depending on

112. Bright coloring can be used to make Web links stand out from the ------- text.

(A) surround
(B) surrounded
(C) surrounding
(D) surrounds

113. Burnett's recently ------- City Council member Joon-Ha Min is making headlines with his controversial proposal to close First Street to cars.

(A) elected
(B) formed
(C) enacted
(D) broadened

114. Saito Mobility has sold its bicycle subsidiary in order to ------- on the production of e-bikes and motorcycles.

(A) maintain
(B) insist
(C) embrace
(D) concentrate

115. Montoyo Medical Center is equipped to handle ------- surgical procedures.

(A) complex
(B) distant
(C) cautious
(D) accurate

116. Photographs taken before the wall was damaged show how the mural ------- appeared.

(A) original
(B) originally
(C) originate
(D) originating

117. Typically, organic produce is ------- more expensive than its conventional counterparts.

(A) significant
(B) significantly
(C) significance
(D) signifying

118. ------- each meeting of the audit committee, the chairperson should prepare a report on its activities for the rest of the board.

(A) Except
(B) Across
(C) Following
(D) Beside

119. Once its new terminal becomes operational, the maximum ------- of Devore Airport will increase by 30%.

(A) allowance
(B) function
(C) proportion
(D) capacity

120. Any ------- items in your shipment should be wrapped securely with a cushioning material.

(A) fragile
(B) adequate
(C) pending
(D) delectable



*GO ON TO THE NEXT PAGE*

121. A full list of program ------- can be found on our organization's Web site.

(A) sponsor
(B) sponsorship
(C) sponsoring
(D) sponsors

122. We must remind ------- at this year's conference to allow sufficient time for audience questions.

(A) presenting
(B) presented
(C) presenters
(D) presentation

123. Our analysts have been unable to determine precisely ------- is causing the drop in sales.

(A) nor
(B) what
(C) that
(D) whether

124. Few customers were ------- to fill out the entire feedback survey.

(A) willing
(B) capable
(C) fortunate
(D) detailed

125. Our busy season is in early spring, so staff should schedule their vacation time -------.

(A) formerly
(B) considerably
(C) consecutively
(D) accordingly

126. ------- of several excellent reviews in major publications, the book debuted at the top of the bestseller list.

(A) In place
(B) In the event
(C) Regardless
(D) Because

127. Any employee who has worked at Boone, Inc., for more than six months may be ------- for this recognition.

(A) nominee
(B) nominated
(C) nomination
(D) nominate

128. With the recent growth of its cattle industry, Pell County is now in ------- need of more large animal veterinarians.

(A) critically
(B) critic
(C) critical
(D) criticizing

129. Streaming service Vizzia is struggling to keep ------- with viewer demands for new content.

(A) pace
(B) output
(C) balance
(D) continuity

130. The company requires high-level employees to ------- their work processes so that others can take over their roles in their absence.

(A) access
(B) impact
(C) document
(D) permit

## PART 6

**Directions:** Read the texts that follow. A word, phrase, or sentence is missing in parts of each text. Four answer choices for each question are given below the text. Select the best answer to complete the text. Then mark the letter (A), (B), (C), or (D) on your answer sheet.

**Questions 131-134** refer to the following e-mail.

From: Chatter Customer Service
To: Melissa Ramsey
Subject: Password reset
Date: December 19

Dear Ms. Ramsey,

We have become aware of a security issue with the log-in credentials for your Chatter account. ------- **131.** identical to an e-mail address and password recently exposed by a data breach of another online service. We have no reason at present to believe that your Chatter account has ------- **132.** been accessed by anyone else. However, reusing log-in credentials like this makes a future account breach more likely.

In a proactive effort to protect the security of your Chatter account, we have blocked access to it by resetting your password. We apologize for the ------- **133.**. Please click on the link below to set a new password. ------- **134.**. We also recommend enabling two-factor authentication for all of your online accounts.

—The Chatter Team

**131.** (A) Yours is
(B) There is
(C) They are
(D) There are

**132.** (A) seriously
(B) besides
(C) later
(D) actually

**133.** (A) shortage
(B) error
(C) outcome
(D) disruption

**134.** (A) Choosing a unique password will prevent this issue from reoccurring.
(B) If you have any questions about this information, please let us know.
(C) This is a routine process required of all business users of Chatter.
(D) An unfamiliar device recently attempted to log in to your account.

**Questions 135-138** refer to the following advertisement.

Budget Builder App

Are you trying to get ahead financially? Budget Builder makes money management ------- (135.) simple, no matter the size of your income. Our app ------- (136.) you in spending your money carefully. After collecting information on current assets and expenses, we ask users to set savings goals. ------- (137.) . The app tells you how to reach your goals and tracks your progress along the way. Try Budget Builder for free for 30 days to see if it is right for you. After that period, there is a reasonable ------- (138.) fee of $12.99 per month.

**135.** (A) surprised
(B) surprisingly
(C) surprising
(D) surprise

**136.** (A) supporting
(B) will support
(C) to support
(D) supported

**137.** (A) You might want to buy a new car or pay for a vacation.
(B) It is important to keep your savings at a trustworthy bank.
(C) They can even add other users to their account.
(D) We offer helpful tutorials on each feature.

**138.** (A) cancellation
(B) transaction
(C) reservation
(D) subscription

**Questions 139-142** refer to the following article.

HALVERTON (June 8)—The National Postal Service (NPS) unveiled a set of 42 electric delivery trucks today. The vehicles ------- (139.) the first step in the organization's plan to electrify part of its fleet. They will enable mail ------- (140.) to make their deliveries with a smaller carbon footprint. The NPS has also begun outfitting some of its branches with electric vehicle charging stations. Unfortunately, many small local post offices do not have the electrical infrastructure to support the stations. ------- (141.), the organization will mainly employ electric trucks at its larger regional hubs. ------- (142.).

**139.** (A) represent
(B) representation
(C) having represented
(D) representing

**140.** (A) carried
(B) carrying
(C) carriers
(D) carries

**141.** (A) For instance
(B) After all
(C) For that reason
(D) Even so

**142.** (A) The change is also intended to reduce air pollution.
(B) There are currently 30 such facilities around the country.
(C) The vehicles boast several features that NPS's existing trucks lack.
(D) The largest centers already handle thousands of parcels per day.

TEST 10

*GO ON TO THE NEXT PAGE*

**Questions 143-146** refer to the following memo.

To: All Melnyk Corporation employees

From: Ivan Melnyk

Re: Important visit

Date: September 25

Next Tuesday, a *Parham Monthly* correspondent will visit Melnyk Corporation in preparation for writing a profile of me for the magazine. In addition to ------- **143.** me, she will take a tour of our office to learn about our operations. A flattering article could really help the business, so I hope ------- **144.** will make an effort to ensure she comes away with a good impression of us. ------- **145.** . If you end up speaking with the ------- **146.**, try to avoid making negative comments about anything—even our competitors. You should also politely refuse to answer any questions about subjects outside of your area. Thank you in advance for your cooperation in making this visit a success.

**143.** (A) training
(B) replacing
(C) introducing
(D) interviewing

**144.** (A) everyone
(B) another
(C) those
(D) someone

**145.** (A) All of our work must be thorough and completed on time.
(B) This is the public relations department's responsibility.
(C) Please keep your workspace tidy throughout the day.
(D) Our company is about to celebrate its tenth anniversary.

**146.** (A) client
(B) reporter
(C) candidate
(D) executive

## PART 7

**Directions:** In this part you will read a selection of texts, such as magazine and newspaper articles, e-mails, and instant messages. Each text or set of texts is followed by several questions. Select the best answer for each question and mark the letter (A), (B), (C), or (D) on your answer sheet.

**Questions 147-148** refer to the following product description.

**BROUWER MARINE**

eLogbook Digital Logbook

Brouwer Marine's eLogbook software program offers a convenient way to store required information about a ship's activities. It replaces traditional paper logbooks for recording details of crew actions, oil discharges, compass observations, and more. eLogbook does not require Internet access to work, and it can be run on a single computer or made available at multiple user terminals connected to a server.

Each user has unique log-in credentials to ensure that the right personnel are making and approving entries. A PIN can be set to make logging in easier. Authorized users can also send digital copies of logbook records to port management.

**147.** What is mentioned about the product?

(A) It can be set up for access from multiple sites.
(B) Its intended customers are port managers.
(C) It can be downloaded over the Internet.
(D) It is used for planning efficient shipping routes.

**148.** What option is available to customers?

(A) Bulk approval of entries
(B) A simplified log-in method
(C) A real-time information display
(D) Digitization of old records

TEST 10

*GO ON TO THE NEXT PAGE*

**Questions 149-150** refer to the following online review.

https://www.summitresort.ca/reviews

Recent Guest Reviews of Summit Resort

Some friends and I visited Summit Resort for a long weekend in January, and I expect it will be the first of many trips to this lovely place. The best thing about the resort is its location right on Walker Mountain. The view from any room is stunning, and we could ski or snowboard straight out onto the slopes from the resort's back entrance. Walker Mountain has slopes for all skill levels, and the chairlifts are reliable. In the evenings, we had dinner at the resort's Highland Grill or took the shuttle to the nearby village. On the last day, some of us decided to pay the extra fee to visit the onsite spa, and it was very nice to rest our tired muscles in its sauna before going home. Overall, we had a wonderful time and heartily recommend Summit Resort to others.

—Laverne Reese, February 10

**149.** What does Ms. Reese indicate in her review?

(A) Her room was on the back side of the resort.
(B) A friend recommended Summit Resort to her.
(C) She will probably visit Summit Resort again.
(D) She received a group discount on her stay.

**150.** What is NOT an activity mentioned by Ms. Reese?

(A) Relaxing in a sauna
(B) Shopping for souvenirs
(C) Engaging in winter sports
(D) Eating in a restaurant

**Questions 151-152** refer to the following invitation.

Pearson Theater cordially invites you and one guest to the premiere of *A Bright Line*, the latest original play by Ella Neal.

Thursday, March 2, 7:00 P.M.

Set in 1950s New York, *A Bright Line* tells the story of an art professor who inspires her students by sharing her unusual outlook on art and life.

As a Platinum-tier Pearson Theater supporter, you are also encouraged to stay for a post-show meet-and-greet with the cast and creative team. Refreshments will be provided.

Please call 555-0148 to RSVP for both events by February 24.

**151.** What is suggested about *A Bright Line*?

(A) It is being put on by students.
(B) It is on tour from New York.
(C) It is based on Ms. Neal's experiences.
(D) It has not been staged before.

**152.** What will the recipient of the invitation be able to do?

(A) Attend a lecture given by a professor
(B) View some original artwork
(C) Speak with some performers
(D) Take a feedback survey on the show

TEST 10

*GO ON TO THE NEXT PAGE*

**Questions 153-154** refer to the following online chat discussion.

**Cindy Berry (11:24 A.M.)**
Hi, Jonathan. I'm processing your latest expense report, and I noticed that you entered the wrong amount for your lunch on August 7. The restaurant receipt says $25.67, not $25.76. Could you fix that and the total amount and resubmit your report?

**Jonathan Parks (11:26 A.M.)**
Ah, sorry for the mistake. Sure, I'll get that to you first thing tomorrow.

**Cindy Berry (11:27 A.M.)**
The deadline is today. Otherwise, you'll have to wait an extra month for reimbursement.

**Jonathan Parks (11:28 A.M.)**
Well, I'm working from home today. And you don't accept reports over e-mail, right?

**Cindy Berry (11:29 A.M.)**
Right—we need a signed paper copy. OK, I'll see you tomorrow, then.

**153.** Why did Ms. Berry contact Mr. Parks?
(A) To request revisions to a report
(B) To suggest planning a business lunch
(C) To remind him to submit a receipt
(D) To warn him about a spending limit

**154.** At 11:28 A.M., what does Mr. Parks most likely mean when he writes, "I'm working from home today"?
(A) He has concluded a business trip.
(B) He will be unable to attend an event.
(C) He is making an effort to meet a deadline.
(D) He cannot bring a document to Ms. Berry.

**Questions 155-157** refer to the following information.

## Workforce Boost Programme

Is your organization having trouble finding qualified candidates for certain roles? The Workforce Boost Programme assists employers in creating apprenticeships to solve their skills shortages. — [1] —. Participant organisations are matched with a training advisor with expertise in their particular field. The advisor helps define the organization's workforce needs and design a tailored apprenticeship. — [2] —. It typically combines on-the-job training with any external education necessary for the apprentice to receive licensing or certification in the field. The programme pays directly for up to $12,000 of the cost of external instruction. — [3] —. Once the apprentice is hired or chosen from among existing employees and the apprenticeship begins, ongoing support is made available to the employer and the apprentice. — [4] —.

**155.** What is the purpose of the program?

(A) To help employers train workers for positions
(B) To connect employers with skilled job candidates
(C) To advise employers about new labor regulations
(D) To reward employers that treat their staff well

**156.** Who most likely receives money directly from the program?

(A) Companies offering certain employment benefits
(B) Organizations providing education for job qualifications
(C) Jobseekers who agree to work in unpopular fields
(D) Employees who obtain an extra certification

**157.** In which of the positions marked [1], [2], [3], and [4] does the following sentence best belong?

"The advisor meets regularly with both parties until the successful completion of the programme."

(A) [1]
(B) [2]
(C) [3]
(D) [4]

TEST 10

*GO ON TO THE NEXT PAGE*

**Questions 158-160** refer to the following notice.

## Spring Swap

**Brooksville Park**
**Saturday, May 20, 1 P.M. to 4 P.M.**

BYO Brooksville is proud to present the fourth Spring Swap! This annual event is a chance for people to give away housewares, clothing, books, and other possessions they no longer want and to take items given away by others. There is no fee for participation and no requirement to bring something. However, those who do give away items must bring them to the "drop-off table" so that organizers can ensure they are clean, complete, and in good condition before they are put on display.

BYO Brooksville is a retailer of eco-friendly goods and refill station for cleaning products, cosmetics, and foods. "BYO" stands for "Bring Your Own," as customers are required to bring their own containers and bags to carry their purchases. In addition to events like the Spring Swap, it offers regular classes on eco-friendly skills such as mending worn-out clothing.

**158.** What is suggested about the table mentioned in the notice?
(A) It will be removed before the event ends.
(B) It is located inside BYO Brooksville.
(C) It will be staffed by event personnel.
(D) It will display items that may no longer work properly.

**159.** The word "carry" in paragraph 2, line 4, is closest in meaning to
(A) sell
(B) wear
(C) transport
(D) present

**160.** According to the notice, what does BYO Brooksville provide education on?
(A) How to cook vegetarian food
(B) How to repair damaged clothing
(C) How to make your own cleaning products
(D) How to reuse plastic containers

**Questions 161-163** refer to the following e-mail.

**E-Mail message**

| | |
|---|---|
| **From:** | daiju.hasegawa@dhasegawa.com |
| **To:** | r.alvarado@shermanderm.com |
| **Subject:** | Notice |
| **Date:** | August 1 |

Dear Ms. Alvarado,

Effective September 1, I will be charging $45 per hour for my graphic design services instead of my current fee of $40 per hour. This change is necessary to cover the recent rise in the cost of living in our area. I hope that it will not be prohibitive to your medical clinic continuing to send projects my way, given your satisfaction with the template I created for your new e-mail newsletters and other work I have done. If you do have any concerns about this change, please let me know.

Sincerely,

Daiju Hasegawa

**161.** Why did Mr. Hasegawa send the e-mail?

(A) To advertise his business
(B) To inquire about a service
(C) To reschedule an appointment
(D) To announce a rate increase

**162.** The phrase "my way" in line 4 is closest in meaning to

(A) at my expense
(B) for me to do
(C) as I instructed
(D) similar to mine

**163.** What has the medical clinic recently done?

(A) It relocated to a different area.
(B) It hired a doctor with a unique specialty.
(C) It launched a new communication channel.
(D) It requested bids for a graphic design project.

TEST 10

*GO ON TO THE NEXT PAGE*

**Questions 164-167** refer to the following memo.

## MEMO

Date: February 19
To: All employees
From: Corporate headquarters
Subject: Information

As part of Employee Appreciation Week, Seaside Coffee management would like to remind employees of the variety of perks available to them year-round. — [1] —. Employees may have one free food item and one free drink from the café per shift. — [2] —. When not working, employees may receive a 25% discount on any product at all Seaside locations by giving their employee number at checkout. This is the number that you clock in and out with. — [3] —. Finally, we offer benefits at partner businesses ranging from grocery stores to music streaming services through the "Work Plus" platform. — [4] —. If you have not already done so, visit www.workplus.com/seaside to sign up and begin taking advantage of those.

As always, thank you for being a part of the Seaside family.

Reid Walden
Vice President of Human Resources

**164.** What is the purpose of the memo?
(A) To describe a change in store policies
(B) To share some complaints from customers
(C) To invite feedback on a sales promotion
(D) To give an overview of staff incentives

**165.** What is indicated about a discount on Seaside Coffee items?
(A) It can only be used once per day.
(B) It is available only for a weeklong period.
(C) It requires the provision of a numerical code.
(D) It is offered at a manager's discretion.

**166.** What are recipients of the memo encouraged to do?
(A) Take their scheduled breaks
(B) Complete an online registration process
(C) Inform customers about partner businesses
(D) Post on a social media platform

**167.** In which of the positions marked [1], [2], [3], and [4] does the following sentence best belong?

"All beverage types except pre-bottled ones are included in this offer."

(A) [1]
(B) [2]
(C) [3]
(D) [4]

**Questions 168-171** refer to the following e-mail.

E-Mail message

| | |
|---|---|
| **From:** | Beatrix Meijer |
| **To:** | Andrew Dunham |
| **Subject:** | RE: Kitchen membership |
| **Date:** | March 30 |

Dear Mr. Dunham,

Thank you for your inquiry about restarting your membership in Kelso Kitchen. Yes, I remember that you used to use our kitchen space to prepare ingredients for your food truck. I am glad to hear that you have opened a restaurant and it is doing well. Kelso Kitchen can certainly provide you with space to develop new recipes.

The monthly membership fee is now $400. This entitles you to use one of our fully equipped shared kitchens for up to 30 hours. Reservations are required and must be made through our online system. Members are allotted two lockable cages for storing their ingredients in, one of which can be kept in our walk-in refrigerator. Remember that you will be expected to clean up your space and wash any cooking implements you have used before your scheduled time ends.

Since the food you prepare in our facility will not be sold to customers, the only documentation we need from you is proof of liability insurance. You can bring that to our office anytime from 9 A.M. to 5 P.M., Tuesday through Saturday, to begin the process of restarting your membership.

Sincerely,

Beatrix Meijer

**168.** What is indicated about Mr. Dunham?
(A) He is planning to publish a book of recipes.
(B) He has operated two types of establishments.
(C) He hopes to expand his restaurant into a chain.
(D) He used to be an employee of Kelso Kitchen.

**169.** The word "develop" in paragraph 1, line 4, is closest in meaning to
(A) pick up
(B) extend
(C) work on
(D) demonstrate

**170.** What does Kelso Kitchen offer to its members?
(A) Secure storage space for food
(B) Discounts on long-term memberships
(C) Optional use of a cleaning service
(D) Monthly classes on cooking techniques

**171.** What is suggested about Kelso Kitchen?
(A) It encourages collaboration between its members.
(B) Its facility is busier on weekends than on weekdays.
(C) It requires reservations to be made more than one day in advance.
(D) It requests extra paperwork from members who sell their food.

*GO ON TO THE NEXT PAGE*

**Questions 172-175** refer to the following online chat discussion.

| | | |
|---|---|---|
| **Seul-Gi Ma** | **[9:08 A.M.]** | Good morning, Devin. Have you seen the e-mail that the museum's main account received yesterday evening? |
| **Devin Stewart** | **[9:09 A.M.]** | I'll check. |
| **Seul-Gi Ma** | **[9:10 A.M.]** | The sender's name is Veronica Gunn. She says she took one of Pramrod's tours yesterday. |
| **Devin Stewart** | **[9:12 A.M.]** | And she believes that the plaid dress in the nineteenth-century American fashion exhibition is probably from a later decade than what our label says? |
| **Seul-Gi Ma** | **[9:13 A.M.]** | Yes, because of the design of the sleeves. I think we should look into it. She seems quite knowledgeable. |
| **Devin Stewart** | **[9:13 A.M.]** | I agree. I'll bring Celia into the chat. |
| **Devin Stewart** | **[9:14 A.M.]** | Celia, I'm forwarding you an e-mail we've received about our new exhibition. Can you look over it and then get an opinion from the fashion history professor you met at Hemphill University? |
| **Celia Ball** | **[9:16 A.M.]** | Sure. How pressing is this issue? Sometimes he takes a few days to respond to e-mails. |
| **Devin Stewart** | **[9:17 A.M.]** | I'd like to get it figured out by the end of the day. |
| **Celia Ball** | **[9:18 A.M.]** | Got it. I'll call him and let you know what I find out. |

**172.** Who wrote the e-mail that Ms. Ma mentions?

(A) A tour guide
(B) A new curator
(C) A museum visitor
(D) A donor to an exhibition

**173.** What problem are the writers discussing?

(A) An item in the museum may be dated incorrectly.
(B) An old piece of clothing is fragile.
(C) The labels on some exhibits are difficult to read.
(D) Some restoration work changed the design of a dress.

**174.** What is Ms. Ball asked to do?

(A) Draft a notice for posting
(B) Remove a page from a Web site
(C) Return an item to its owner
(D) Consult an external expert

**175.** At 9:18 A.M, what does Ms. Ball most likely mean when she writes, "Got it"?

(A) She now has access to an exhibition space.
(B) She has received the e-mail forwarded by Mr. Stewart.
(C) She understands the urgency of the situation.
(D) She does not need assistance with an assignment.

TEST 10

*GO ON TO THE NEXT PAGE*

**Questions 176-180** refer to the following lease agreement and e-mail.

**Commercial Lease Agreement**

This agreement is made on March 7 between Henrietta Gibbs (landlord) and Nathan Hoffman (tenant). The landlord agrees to lease commercial space to the tenant from April 1 to December 31 for the purpose of operating Hoffman Art Gallery. Both parties agree to the following terms and conditions:

Section 1: Leased Premises
The property to be leased is located at 249 Bates Street in Bates Plaza. It consists of a 1,361-square-foot storefront plus the use of the two parking spaces directly in front of the storefront's entrance.

Section 2: Rent & Fees
The tenant agrees to pay a base rent of $1,500 on the first day of every month. The tenant will also pay a percentage rent fee of 7% of the business's net profits on a quarterly basis. The tenant will be charged $25 per month and $30 per month, respectively, for maintenance of the sidewalk and restrooms of Bates Plaza.

Section 3: Obligations of Tenant
The tenant must keep the premises clean and in good condition. All waste must be removed three times per week. Damage caused by the tenant must be reported and repaired at the tenant's expense.

Section 4: Renewal or Extension of Agreement
The tenant has the option to renew or extend this agreement. The request to do so must be made at least two months before the end of the lease period.

Landlord: Henrietta Gibbs
Henrietta Gibbs

Tenant: Nathan Hoffman
Nathan Hoffman

Date: March 7

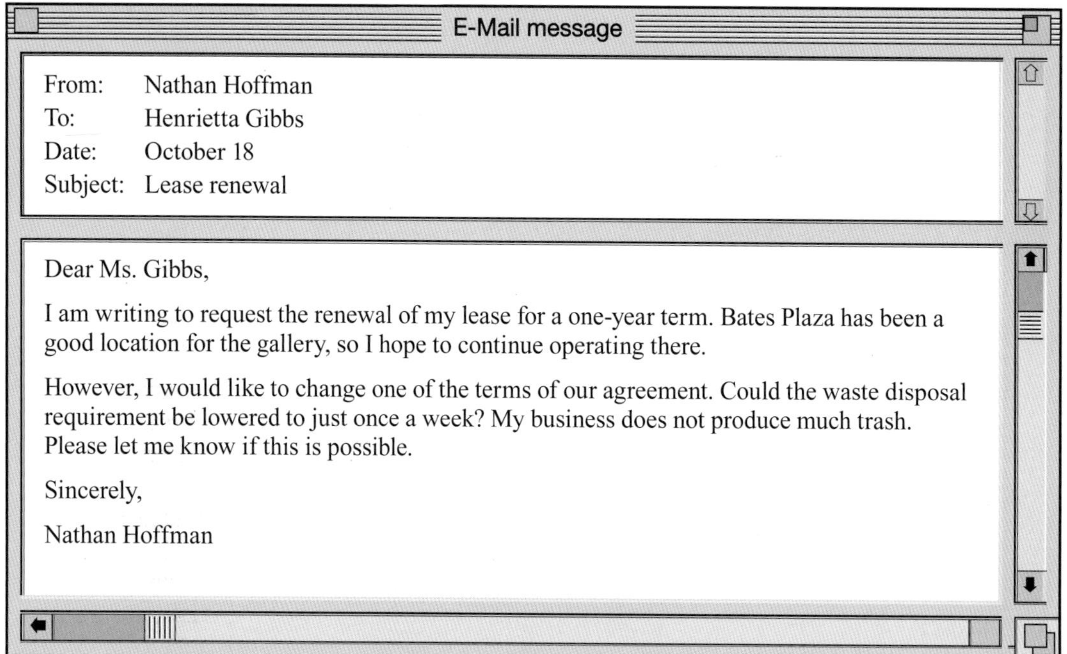

E-Mail message

From: Nathan Hoffman
To: Henrietta Gibbs
Date: October 18
Subject: Lease renewal

Dear Ms. Gibbs,

I am writing to request the renewal of my lease for a one-year term. Bates Plaza has been a good location for the gallery, so I hope to continue operating there.

However, I would like to change one of the terms of our agreement. Could the waste disposal requirement be lowered to just once a week? My business does not produce much trash. Please let me know if this is possible.

Sincerely,

Nathan Hoffman

**176.** What is true about the lease agreement?

(A) It encompasses indoor and outdoor property.
(B) It is between two businesses.
(C) It was prepared by a legal representative.
(D) It can be terminated early if both parties agree.

**177.** What is stated about the rent?

(A) It will increase incrementally every quarter.
(B) It should be sent via a particular payment method.
(C) Its total amount varies depending on the gallery's profits.
(D) There is a penalty fee for paying it late.

**178.** What does the lease agreement state that the tenant must pay for?

(A) Improvements to the leased premises
(B) Insurance to cover property damage
(C) Changing the provider of a utility service
(D) Maintenance of some common areas

**179.** What part of the lease agreement does Mr. Hoffman request a revision to?

(A) Section 1
(B) Section 2
(C) Section 3
(D) Section 4

**180.** What is implied about the renewed lease agreement proposed by Mr. Hoffman?

(A) It will include an additional condition.
(B) It spans a longer term than the original contract.
(C) He has already discussed it with Ms. Gibbs.
(D) He requested it after a specified deadline.

*GO ON TO THE NEXT PAGE* →

**Questions 181-185** refer to the following article and e-mail.

# Artist Spotlight: Lavanya Gulati

EDMONTON, Canada (5 February)—Painter Lavanya Gulati is grabbing the attention of the art world through her beautiful murals. These large-scale works of art, most of which depict the natural world, can be seen from public streets throughout Edmonton and a few other cities across Canada.

"I love the process of turning something artificial, like a concrete wall, into an entirely new creation," says Ms. Gulati. "Despite living in urban areas, we can still find ways to stay connected to the environment. I hope that my work reminds people about this."

Customer input is an essential part of the planning process, and Ms. Gulati requires a minimum of three weeks to finalize any design plan. She says that her painting can be completed quickly once she has a clear vision of the final result.

Surprisingly, Ms. Gulati's customers are expected to clean and treat the area where the mural is to be painted. Ms. Gulati says this not only cuts down on costs but also allows customers to be a part of the work. She advises on supplies for this task and has a video with comprehensive step-by-step instructions on her Web site, www.gulatiart.ca.

**E-Mail message**

| | |
|---|---|
| **To:** | contact@gulatiart.ca |
| **From:** | a_rankin@omail.ca |
| **Date:** | 8 February |
| **Subject:** | Inquiry |

Dear Ms. Gulati,

I read the recently published article about your work, and I was impressed with the photos of your murals that I found online. My coffee shop is relocating, and we need two murals:

1. On one side of the two-story building (852 Stockert Street, exterior wall), I would like a dramatic and eye-catching mural that potential customers will notice.

2. In the main indoor seating area, I'm trying to create a relaxing atmosphere with a forest scene. I will save pieces of the wooden floor of our current site, which is to be torn down, and I would like those to be included somehow.

Would it be possible to meet this week to discuss the work and get sketches of your proposed designs by 18 February? I can provide a deposit by bank transfer as soon as we sign a contract.

Albert Rankin

181. What does the article mention about Ms. Gulati's murals?

(A) They can be found throughout the world.
(B) They usually feature a nature theme.
(C) They are expected to increase in value.
(D) They are mainly funded by the public.

182. What are Ms. Gulati's clients asked to do?

(A) Prepare the painting surface
(B) Select the type of paint
(C) Take photographs of the process
(D) Clean the finished murals regularly

183. According to the article, what can visitors to Ms. Gulati's Web site do?

(A) Watch a detailed instructional video
(B) Get an estimate of a project's costs
(C) Browse reviews from previous customers
(D) Learn more about Ms. Gulati's background

184. What does Mr. Rankin want to do?

(A) Prevent an old building from being torn down
(B) Include a mural on the floor of his new coffee shop
(C) Have an artist give a talk at his business
(D) Incorporate used materials into a piece of artwork

185. What suggestion by Mr. Rankin will Ms. Gulati most likely be unable to accommodate?

(A) The payment schedule for the deposit
(B) The total fee for producing the work
(C) The timeline for creating the design
(D) The location of one of the murals

TEST 10

*GO ON TO THE NEXT PAGE*

**Questions 186-190** refer to the following Web page, e-mail, and meeting summary.

http://www.twinklemedia.com/ps

## Twinkle Media - Production Services

In addition to recording live events, Twinkle Media can assist with the production of scripted commercial and corporate videos. We offer four service packages:

Bronze – We film content that you plan and perform, and we provide the basic post-production services of editing and, if needed, adding titles and licensed or royalty-free music.

Silver – In addition to the bronze package services, we create simple animations to add visual interest to your video or illustrate difficult concepts.

Gold – Adding some of the pre-production tasks to our plate, we provide advice on structuring your video and animations and write the script.

Platinum – For an especially professional presentation, we cast actors to appear in your video to complement our top-notch videography, post-production, animation, and scriptwriting.

Fill out our contact form to get started!

| | |
|---|---|
| **From** | Jeong-Ho Woo <jeonghow@twinklemedia.com> |
| **To** | Savannah Braswell <s.braswell@accounti.com> |
| **Subject** | RE: Update |
| **Date** | September 15 |

Dear Ms. Braswell,

Thank you for the update on the budget limit for your product tutorial videos. In accordance with your wishes, we will reduce the scope of our services to be provided. Since your project is still in its early stages, we have not begun the casting process, so you can rest assured that this change will not inconvenience anyone.

I was also glad to learn that you have finished mapping out the basic points you want each video to cover. Please send us that information and give us access to Accounti. To produce the scripts, our team will need to try out the software's features ourselves and then meet with you or another Accounti employee who can answer any questions we have about it. We have availability on the morning of Thursday, September 18 or the afternoon of Monday, September 22. Please let us know which period would work best for you.

Regards,

Jeong-Ho Woo
Account Manager
Twinkle Media

## Meeting Summary

**Twinkle Media**

**Project:** Accounti Product Tutorial Videos

September 22, 1:30–4:00 P.M.
**Attendees:** Jeong-Ho Woo; Yvette Rodriguez; Shaun Freeman (client representative)

Mr. Freeman answered questions about Accounti's features (see attached notes).

**We promised to submit video scripts for client approval on the following schedule:**

"Getting Started" – September 24
"Important Settings" – September 26
"Sales and Invoices" – September 30
"Expenses" – October 2

It was decided that animations and voice-over are more suitable than an on-camera presenter for "Important Settings," so its production can begin as soon as the script is approved. Mr. Freeman will call us by Friday regarding the filming schedule for the other videos.

**186.** What does the Web page indicate about Twinkle Media?

(A) It has a large filming studio.
(B) It specializes in product advertisements.
(C) Its staff composes original music for videos.
(D) Its services include event videography.

**187.** What is one purpose of the e-mail?

(A) To confirm a modification to a project plan
(B) To request more information about a budget
(C) To introduce some of Mr. Woo's previous work
(D) To explain the steps of a filming process

**188.** What service package will Ms. Braswell most likely receive?

(A) Bronze
(B) Silver
(C) Gold
(D) Platinum

**189.** What is implied about Ms. Braswell?

(A) She is a colleague of Mr. Freeman.
(B) She failed to fulfill one of Mr. Woo's requests.
(C) She increased the number of planned videos.
(D) She chose the earliest possible meeting date.

**190.** According to the meeting summary, which video will not include footage of a person?

(A) "Getting Started"
(B) "Important Settings"
(C) "Sales and Invoices"
(D) "Expenses"



*GO ON TO THE NEXT PAGE*

**Questions 191-195** refer to the following proposal forms and e-mail.

## PROPOSAL

| Customer Information: | Contractor Information: |
|---|---|
| Greenway Accounting<br>689 Robinette Drive, Unit 1<br>Bankstown, NSW 2200 | Windham Movers<br>1150 Worthy Street<br>Bankstown, NSW 2200 |

**Project:**

Loading/Unloading of all items in customer's office space into/from truck by two-person crew, plus transport of this cargo approximately 5.2 kilometres. Furniture disassembly/assembly service included. Moving boxes and bubble wrap provided, but packing of small items must be done by client in advance.

**Contractor Proposal:**

Contractor will carry out the above project for the amount of $1,850 plus tax.
Customer will pay full amount immediately upon completion of project.
Price expires 30 days after proposal submission.

**Acceptance of Proposal**

Contractor Representative: Ah-Young Hahm

Date: 13 September

Customer Representative: ______________________

Date: __________

## NIELSON RELOCATIONS: PROPOSAL

560 Puckett Street
Yagoona, NSW 2199

| | |
|---|---|
| **Proposal for:** | Greenway Accounting<br>689 Robinette Drive, Unit 1<br>Bankstown, NSW 2200 |
| **Issued:** | 15 September |
| **Valid through:** | 14 October<br>Nielson Relocations proposes to move the entire contents of customer's current office to 77 Earls Drive, Revesby via truck. Customer must disassemble furniture and complete necessary packing before date of move. Loan of cardboard boxes and protective padding included. |
| **Cost:** | $1,490 (tax not included)<br>Customer must submit deposit of 50% ($745) at acceptance of proposal, with remainder to be paid once move is completed. |
| **Proposal prepared by:** | William Bernier |
| **Customer signature:** | ______________________ |
| **Date:** | ______________________ |

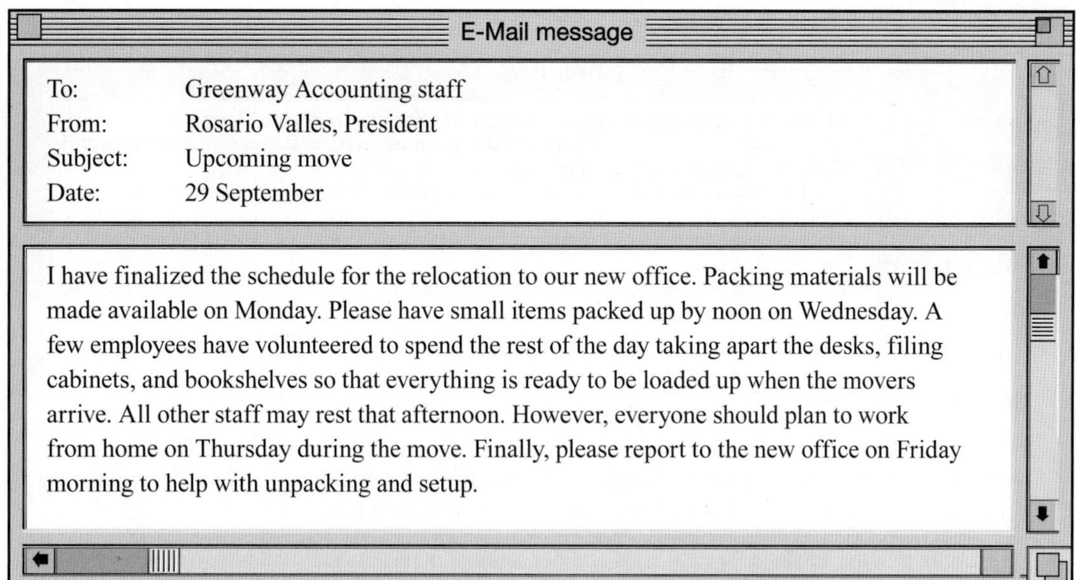

E-Mail message

To: Greenway Accounting staff
From: Rosario Valles, President
Subject: Upcoming move
Date: 29 September

I have finalized the schedule for the relocation to our new office. Packing materials will be made available on Monday. Please have small items packed up by noon on Wednesday. A few employees have volunteered to spend the rest of the day taking apart the desks, filing cabinets, and bookshelves so that everything is ready to be loaded up when the movers arrive. All other staff may rest that afternoon. However, everyone should plan to work from home on Thursday during the move. Finally, please report to the new office on Friday morning to help with unpacking and setup.

**191.** Who most likely is Ms. Hahm?
(A) A building inspector
(B) Ms. Valles's assistant
(C) A Windham Movers employee
(D) The head of Greenway Accounting

**192.** What must customers of Nielson Relocations do?
(A) Pay half of a fee in advance
(B) Drive their own moving vehicle
(C) Supply a list of their belongings
(D) Obtain necessary parking permits

**193.** What do both companies offer to customers?
(A) Insurance coverage
(B) Overnight storage of goods
(C) A discount on short-distance moves
(D) Use of packing materials

**194.** According to the e-mail, when should Greenway Accounting staff work remotely?
(A) During a moving consultant's visit
(B) On the afternoon after clearing their workstations
(C) Throughout the day of the relocation
(D) While the new office is being set up

**195.** What is implied about Greenway Accounting?
(A) It purchased extra furniture for its new location.
(B) Nielson Relocations will carry out its move.
(C) It used Windham Movers in the past.
(D) It will resume normal business activities on Friday morning.

TEST 10

*GO ON TO THE NEXT PAGE*

**Questions 196-200** refer to the following e-mails and agenda.

E-Mail message

**To:** All Farrington Integrated Logistics Staff <staff@farringtonil.com>

**From:** Venkata Nayar <v.nayar@farringtonil.com>

**Date:** February 13

**Subject:** Upcoming Plans

**Attachment:** Confirmed schedule

Dear Staff,

Throughout the month of March, Farrington Integrated Logistics (FIL) will begin offering several sessions to help our employees enhance their skills and network with people from other departments. We hope you will find them informative and worthwhile.

Please note that the sessions for new hires and department managers are mandatory. If you expect to be absent, please let me know, and I will assess the situation on a case-by-case basis. For the sessions open to all staff, there is no need to sign up for those held on site at lunchtime, but you do need to register in advance for the evening one.

Sincerely,

Venkata Nayar
Operations Manager, Farrington Integrated Logistics

**Farrington Integrated Logistics March Sessions**

| Date | Time | Details | Participants |
|---|---|---|---|
| Mon., March 3 | 12:30 P.M. | Company cafeteria, Lunch | New Hires |
| Thurs., March 13 | 12:30 P.M. | Company cafeteria, Lunch | FIL |
| Tues., March 18 | 7:00 P.M. | Sunshine Café, Dinner | Department Managers |
| Fri., March 21 | 6:30 P.M. | Victoria's Bistro, Dinner | FIL |
| Mon., March 24 | 11:30 A.M. | Company cafeteria, Lunch | FIL |

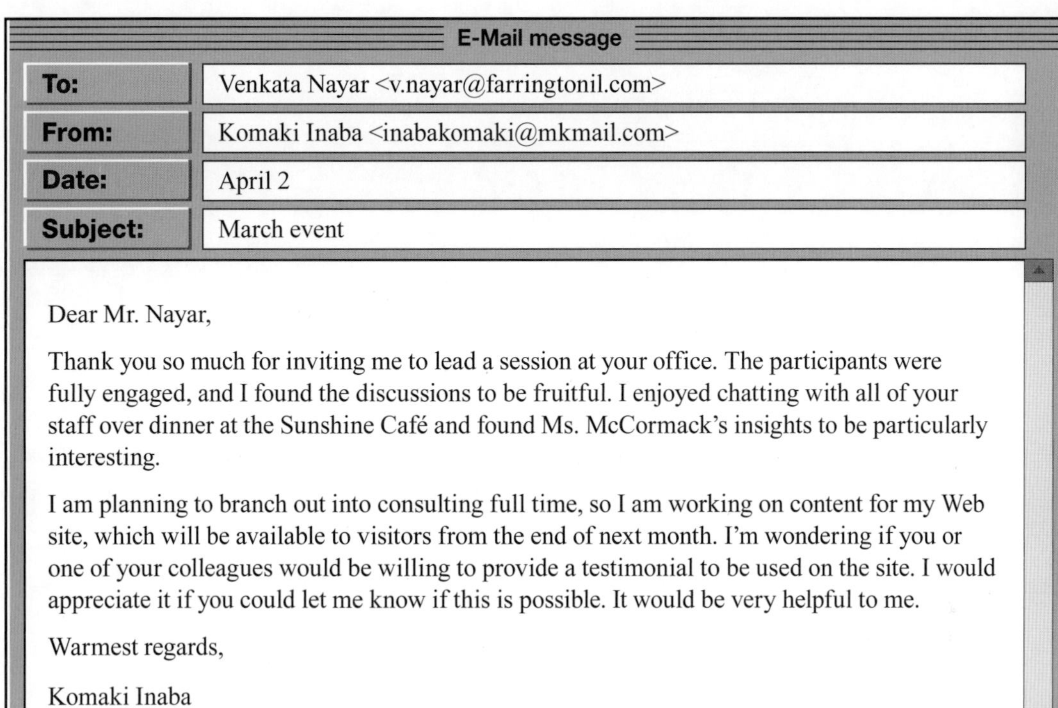

E-Mail message

To: Venkata Nayar <v.nayar@farringtonil.com>

From: Komaki Inaba <inabakomaki@mkmail.com>

Date: April 2

Subject: March event

Dear Mr. Nayar,

Thank you so much for inviting me to lead a session at your office. The participants were fully engaged, and I found the discussions to be fruitful. I enjoyed chatting with all of your staff over dinner at the Sunshine Café and found Ms. McCormack's insights to be particularly interesting.

I am planning to branch out into consulting full time, so I am working on content for my Web site, which will be available to visitors from the end of next month. I'm wondering if you or one of your colleagues would be willing to provide a testimonial to be used on the site. I would appreciate it if you could let me know if this is possible. It would be very helpful to me.

Warmest regards,

Komaki Inaba

**196.** What is a purpose of the first e-mail?

(A) To elicit suggestions for an upcoming training event
(B) To introduce a new member of the management team
(C) To notify staff of a professional development opportunity
(D) To explain a newly implemented policy on absences

**197.** What event must employees register for in advance?

(A) Lunch on March 3
(B) Lunch on March 13
(C) Dinner on March 18
(D) Dinner on March 21

**198.** What is one reason Ms. Inaba e-mails Mr. Nayar?

(A) To ask for assistance
(B) To postpone a company event
(C) To accept a job offer
(D) To inquire about a start date

**199.** Who most likely is Ms. McCormack?

(A) The manager of a department
(B) A newly hired FIL employee
(C) The owner of Sunshine Café
(D) Mr. Nayar's administrative assistant

**200.** What does the second e-mail suggest about the Web site?

(A) It is likely to generate business for FIL.
(B) It contains some incorrect information.
(C) It will be launched at the end of May.
(D) It was designed by Mr. Nayar's colleague.

**Stop! This is the end of the test. If you finish before time is called, you may go back to Parts 5, 6, and 7 and check your work.**

# ANSWERS

## TEST 1

| | | | | |
|---|---|---|---|---|
| 101 (A) | 102 (C) | 103 (A) | 104 (B) | 105 (D) |
| 106 (C) | 107 (C) | 108 (B) | 109 (D) | 110 (A) |
| 111 (B) | 112 (B) | 113 (D) | 114 (B) | 115 (C) |
| 116 (A) | 117 (D) | 118 (A) | 119 (D) | 120 (C) |
| 121 (B) | 122 (A) | 123 (B) | 124 (C) | 125 (B) |
| 126 (C) | 127 (D) | 128 (A) | 129 (D) | 130 (C) |
| 131 (B) | 132 (D) | 133 (A) | 134 (D) | 135 (C) |
| 136 (B) | 137 (C) | 138 (A) | 139 (D) | 140 (C) |
| 141 (B) | 142 (A) | 143 (A) | 144 (D) | 145 (A) |
| 146 (B) | 147 (C) | 148 (D) | 149 (D) | 150 (B) |
| 151 (A) | 152 (C) | 153 (B) | 154 (A) | 155 (B) |
| 156 (B) | 157 (A) | 158 (C) | 159 (B) | 160 (B) |
| 161 (A) | 162 (C) | 163 (D) | 164 (C) | 165 (B) |
| 166 (D) | 167 (C) | 168 (B) | 169 (A) | 170 (A) |
| 171 (D) | 172 (D) | 173 (D) | 174 (C) | 175 (C) |
| 176 (A) | 177 (B) | 178 (D) | 179 (C) | 180 (D) |
| 181 (C) | 182 (B) | 183 (D) | 184 (B) | 185 (A) |
| 186 (C) | 187 (A) | 188 (B) | 189 (C) | 190 (D) |
| 191 (B) | 192 (D) | 193 (B) | 194 (B) | 195 (C) |
| 196 (D) | 197 (D) | 198 (C) | 199 (A) | 200 (B) |

## TEST 2

| | | | | |
|---|---|---|---|---|
| 101 (A) | 102 (C) | 103 (D) | 104 (A) | 105 (B) |
| 106 (B) | 107 (D) | 108 (A) | 109 (A) | 110 (B) |
| 111 (C) | 112 (B) | 113 (C) | 114 (A) | 115 (C) |
| 116 (D) | 117 (B) | 118 (C) | 119 (D) | 120 (B) |
| 121 (B) | 122 (C) | 123 (D) | 124 (A) | 125 (C) |
| 126 (B) | 127 (D) | 128 (D) | 129 (C) | 130 (A) |
| 131 (C) | 132 (A) | 133 (D) | 134 (B) | 135 (D) |
| 136 (D) | 137 (C) | 138 (B) | 139 (B) | 140 (B) |
| 141 (A) | 142 (D) | 143 (A) | 144 (D) | 145 (C) |
| 146 (C) | 147 (A) | 148 (B) | 149 (D) | 150 (A) |
| 151 (C) | 152 (D) | 153 (D) | 154 (B) | 155 (B) |
| 156 (C) | 157 (A) | 158 (D) | 159 (C) | 160 (A) |
| 161 (B) | 162 (A) | 163 (C) | 164 (A) | 165 (C) |
| 166 (C) | 167 (B) | 168 (B) | 169 (D) | 170 (A) |
| 171 (B) | 172 (D) | 173 (A) | 174 (C) | 175 (A) |
| 176 (C) | 177 (C) | 178 (D) | 179 (A) | 180 (B) |
| 181 (D) | 182 (B) | 183 (A) | 184 (B) | 185 (C) |
| 186 (A) | 187 (B) | 188 (B) | 189 (C) | 190 (D) |
| 191 (B) | 192 (B) | 193 (B) | 194 (C) | 195 (A) |
| 196 (A) | 197 (D) | 198 (C) | 199 (B) | 200 (B) |

## TEST 3

| | | | | |
|---|---|---|---|---|
| 101 (C) | 102 (B) | 103 (D) | 104 (A) | 105 (D) |
| 106 (D) | 107 (B) | 108 (C) | 109 (A) | 110 (C) |
| 111 (A) | 112 (C) | 113 (C) | 114 (A) | 115 (A) |
| 116 (C) | 117 (B) | 118 (A) | 119 (C) | 120 (D) |
| 121 (D) | 122 (D) | 123 (D) | 124 (B) | 125 (C) |
| 126 (B) | 127 (D) | 128 (C) | 129 (B) | 130 (D) |
| 131 (A) | 132 (D) | 133 (C) | 134 (C) | 135 (C) |
| 136 (A) | 137 (D) | 138 (C) | 139 (C) | 140 (C) |
| 141 (B) | 142 (D) | 143 (B) | 144 (A) | 145 (C) |
| 146 (D) | 147 (B) | 148 (D) | 149 (B) | 150 (A) |
| 151 (A) | 152 (B) | 153 (A) | 154 (D) | 155 (A) |
| 156 (D) | 157 (A) | 158 (B) | 159 (A) | 160 (C) |
| 161 (D) | 162 (C) | 163 (A) | 164 (A) | 165 (D) |
| 166 (A) | 167 (B) | 168 (A) | 169 (C) | 170 (B) |
| 171 (B) | 172 (A) | 173 (D) | 174 (B) | 175 (A) |
| 176 (A) | 177 (D) | 178 (B) | 179 (B) | 180 (C) |
| 181 (B) | 182 (D) | 183 (B) | 184 (B) | 185 (D) |
| 186 (D) | 187 (D) | 188 (A) | 189 (A) | 190 (B) |
| 191 (B) | 192 (C) | 193 (D) | 194 (C) | 195 (A) |
| 196 (A) | 197 (B) | 198 (D) | 199 (C) | 200 (C) |

## TEST 4

| | | | | |
|---|---|---|---|---|
| 101 (D) | 102 (C) | 103 (C) | 104 (B) | 105 (A) |
| 106 (A) | 107 (A) | 108 (C) | 109 (B) | 110 (A) |
| 111 (B) | 112 (B) | 113 (C) | 114 (B) | 115 (D) |
| 116 (D) | 117 (D) | 118 (C) | 119 (D) | 120 (B) |
| 121 (C) | 122 (D) | 123 (B) | 124 (D) | 125 (A) |
| 126 (A) | 127 (C) | 128 (D) | 129 (A) | 130 (A) |
| 131 (C) | 132 (A) | 133 (B) | 134 (C) | 135 (A) |
| 136 (D) | 137 (C) | 138 (C) | 139 (B) | 140 (C) |
| 141 (D) | 142 (A) | 143 (A) | 144 (D) | 145 (B) |
| 146 (B) | 147 (D) | 148 (C) | 149 (C) | 150 (A) |
| 151 (D) | 152 (A) | 153 (C) | 154 (B) | 155 (B) |
| 156 (A) | 157 (C) | 158 (A) | 159 (D) | 160 (C) |
| 161 (D) | 162 (C) | 163 (B) | 164 (A) | 165 (D) |
| 166 (B) | 167 (D) | 168 (D) | 169 (B) | 170 (C) |
| 171 (B) | 172 (B) | 173 (D) | 174 (A) | 175 (C) |
| 176 (C) | 177 (D) | 178 (A) | 179 (A) | 180 (B) |
| 181 (D) | 182 (A) | 183 (A) | 184 (C) | 185 (D) |
| 186 (B) | 187 (C) | 188 (C) | 189 (A) | 190 (B) |
| 191 (C) | 192 (A) | 193 (B) | 194 (C) | 195 (D) |
| 196 (A) | 197 (C) | 198 (A) | 199 (B) | 200 (D) |

## TEST 5

101 (B) 102 (C) 103 (C) 104 (B) 105 (B)
106 (C) 107 (A) 108 (C) 109 (D) 110 (D)
111 (C) 112 (B) 113 (C) 114 (C) 115 (B)
116 (A) 117 (D) 118 (C) 119 (B) 120 (C)
121 (D) 122 (D) 123 (C) 124 (D) 125 (C)
126 (C) 127 (A) 128 (A) 129 (B) 130 (B)
131 (B) 132 (D) 133 (C) 134 (D) 135 (D)
136 (D) 137 (A) 138 (B) 139 (C) 140 (D)
141 (D) 142 (B) 143 (B) 144 (C) 145 (C)
146 (C) 147 (C) 148 (D) 149 (A) 150 (C)
151 (C) 152 (C) 153 (C) 154 (B) 155 (C)
156 (D) 157 (C) 158 (B) 159 (A) 160 (A)
161 (D) 162 (B) 163 (C) 164 (D) 165 (B)
166 (B) 167 (B) 168 (C) 169 (A) 170 (C)
171 (D) 172 (B) 173 (B) 174 (C) 175 (C)
176 (D) 177 (C) 178 (A) 179 (C) 180 (D)
181 (C) 182 (A) 183 (D) 184 (B) 185 (B)
186 (C) 187 (D) 188 (C) 189 (A) 190 (B)
191 (D) 192 (B) 193 (A) 194 (B) 195 (A)
196 (B) 197 (A) 198 (D) 199 (D) 200 (A)

## TEST 6

101 (B) 102 (C) 103 (B) 104 (A) 105 (D)
106 (A) 107 (C) 108 (B) 109 (A) 110 (D)
111 (C) 112 (D) 113 (C) 114 (B) 115 (C)
116 (B) 117 (A) 118 (B) 119 (C) 120 (A)
121 (D) 122 (A) 123 (B) 124 (C) 125 (D)
126 (D) 127 (B) 128 (D) 129 (D) 130 (A)
131 (D) 132 (A) 133 (C) 134 (A) 135 (C)
136 (B) 137 (B) 138 (A) 139 (B) 140 (D)
141 (A) 142 (C) 143 (C) 144 (D) 145 (D)
146 (B) 147 (D) 148 (C) 149 (B) 150 (A)
151 (C) 152 (C) 153 (A) 154 (A) 155 (B)
156 (B) 157 (D) 158 (D) 159 (D) 160 (B)
161 (C) 162 (A) 163 (D) 164 (D) 165 (D)
166 (A) 167 (B) 168 (A) 169 (A) 170 (B)
171 (C) 172 (C) 173 (A) 174 (C) 175 (B)
176 (A) 177 (C) 178 (C) 179 (B) 180 (D)
181 (D) 182 (A) 183 (B) 184 (C) 185 (B)
186 (B) 187 (B) 188 (A) 189 (D) 190 (C)
191 (A) 192 (C) 193 (B) 194 (D) 195 (B)
196 (D) 197 (C) 198 (A) 199 (A) 200 (B)

## TEST 7

101 (B) 102 (D) 103 (B) 104 (A) 105 (C)
106 (C) 107 (D) 108 (C) 109 (C) 110 (B)
111 (D) 112 (A) 113 (C) 114 (B) 115 (D)
116 (B) 117 (D) 118 (D) 119 (B) 120 (A)
121 (B) 122 (D) 123 (A) 124 (A) 125 (C)
126 (B) 127 (D) 128 (B) 129 (D) 130 (D)
131 (C) 132 (C) 133 (D) 134 (D) 135 (C)
136 (D) 137 (C) 138 (C) 139 (B) 140 (B)
141 (A) 142 (D) 143 (B) 144 (D) 145 (D)
146 (A) 147 (A) 148 (C) 149 (A) 150 (B)
151 (D) 152 (D) 153 (B) 154 (D) 155 (B)
156 (D) 157 (B) 158 (C) 159 (B) 160 (D)
161 (B) 162 (D) 163 (A) 164 (B) 165 (A)
166 (A) 167 (C) 168 (C) 169 (A) 170 (A)
171 (A) 172 (B) 173 (C) 174 (A) 175 (B)
176 (A) 177 (C) 178 (C) 179 (D) 180 (B)
181 (C) 182 (A) 183 (D) 184 (B) 185 (C)
186 (C) 187 (A) 188 (D) 189 (D) 190 (B)
191 (C) 192 (D) 193 (C) 194 (A) 195 (B)
196 (B) 197 (A) 198 (C) 199 (A) 200 (D)

## TEST 8

101 (B) 102 (B) 103 (D) 104 (B) 105 (A)
106 (D) 107 (C) 108 (D) 109 (C) 110 (A)
111 (A) 112 (B) 113 (C) 114 (D) 115 (C)
116 (B) 117 (A) 118 (A) 119 (B) 120 (C)
121 (D) 122 (B) 123 (C) 124 (A) 125 (A)
126 (D) 127 (D) 128 (C) 129 (D) 130 (B)
131 (B) 132 (A) 133 (D) 134 (C) 135 (A)
136 (D) 137 (C) 138 (C) 139 (D) 140 (B)
141 (B) 142 (A) 143 (C) 144 (D) 145 (A)
146 (D) 147 (B) 148 (D) 149 (A) 150 (C)
151 (B) 152 (A) 153 (C) 154 (B) 155 (C)
156 (B) 157 (C) 158 (B) 159 (A) 160 (B)
161 (D) 162 (A) 163 (C) 164 (A) 165 (B)
166 (D) 167 (D) 168 (D) 169 (C) 170 (A)
171 (D) 172 (C) 173 (D) 174 (C) 175 (A)
176 (C) 177 (B) 178 (A) 179 (C) 180 (D)
181 (D) 182 (A) 183 (C) 184 (B) 185 (B)
186 (B) 187 (B) 188 (B) 189 (D) 190 (B)
191 (B) 192 (B) 193 (C) 194 (D) 195 (A)
196 (A) 197 (C) 198 (D) 199 (A) 200 (B)

## TEST 9

| | | | | |
|---|---|---|---|---|
| **101** (C) | **102** (C) | **103** (B) | **104** (D) | **105** (B) |
| **106** (C) | **107** (A) | **108** (B) | **109** (B) | **110** (A) |
| **111** (B) | **112** (D) | **113** (A) | **114** (D) | **115** (B) |
| **116** (C) | **117** (D) | **118** (D) | **119** (B) | **120** (D) |
| **121** (B) | **122** (C) | **123** (C) | **124** (D) | **125** (D) |
| **126** (A) | **127** (A) | **128** (C) | **129** (A) | **130** (A) |
| **131** (C) | **132** (D) | **133** (B) | **134** (B) | **135** (C) |
| **136** (B) | **137** (A) | **138** (A) | **139** (D) | **140** (A) |
| **141** (A) | **142** (C) | **143** (B) | **144** (C) | **145** (C) |
| **146** (D) | **147** (D) | **148** (B) | **149** (A) | **150** (C) |
| **151** (B) | **152** (D) | **153** (C) | **154** (A) | **155** (D) |
| **156** (D) | **157** (C) | **158** (C) | **159** (A) | **160** (B) |
| **161** (D) | **162** (A) | **163** (B) | **164** (B) | **165** (C) |
| **166** (A) | **167** (B) | **168** (B) | **169** (B) | **170** (D) |
| **171** (C) | **172** (D) | **173** (A) | **174** (B) | **175** (D) |
| **176** (C) | **177** (A) | **178** (A) | **179** (D) | **180** (B) |
| **181** (C) | **182** (A) | **183** (B) | **184** (A) | **185** (D) |
| **186** (C) | **187** (B) | **188** (D) | **189** (C) | **190** (A) |
| **191** (C) | **192** (A) | **193** (A) | **194** (B) | **195** (D) |
| **196** (A) | **197** (D) | **198** (C) | **199** (D) | **200** (C) |

## TEST 10

| | | | | |
|---|---|---|---|---|
| **101** (D) | **102** (B) | **103** (C) | **104** (C) | **105** (B) |
| **106** (A) | **107** (A) | **108** (B) | **109** (D) | **110** (C) |
| **111** (B) | **112** (C) | **113** (A) | **114** (D) | **115** (A) |
| **116** (B) | **117** (B) | **118** (C) | **119** (D) | **120** (A) |
| **121** (D) | **122** (C) | **123** (B) | **124** (A) | **125** (D) |
| **126** (D) | **127** (B) | **128** (C) | **129** (A) | **130** (C) |
| **131** (C) | **132** (D) | **133** (D) | **134** (A) | **135** (B) |
| **136** (B) | **137** (A) | **138** (D) | **139** (A) | **140** (C) |
| **141** (C) | **142** (B) | **143** (D) | **144** (A) | **145** (C) |
| **146** (B) | **147** (A) | **148** (B) | **149** (C) | **150** (B) |
| **151** (D) | **152** (C) | **153** (A) | **154** (D) | **155** (A) |
| **156** (B) | **157** (D) | **158** (C) | **159** (C) | **160** (B) |
| **161** (D) | **162** (B) | **163** (C) | **164** (D) | **165** (C) |
| **166** (B) | **167** (B) | **168** (B) | **169** (C) | **170** (A) |
| **171** (D) | **172** (C) | **173** (A) | **174** (D) | **175** (C) |
| **176** (A) | **177** (C) | **178** (D) | **179** (C) | **180** (B) |
| **181** (B) | **182** (A) | **183** (A) | **184** (D) | **185** (C) |
| **186** (D) | **187** (A) | **188** (C) | **189** (A) | **190** (B) |
| **191** (C) | **192** (A) | **193** (D) | **194** (C) | **195** (B) |
| **196** (C) | **197** (D) | **198** (A) | **199** (A) | **200** (C) |

# ANSWER SHEET

## YBM 실전토익 RC 1000

| 수험번호 | | | | | | |
|---|---|---|---|---|---|---|

응시일자 : 20 년 월 일

| 성명 | 한 글 | |
|---|---|---|
| | 한 자 | |
| | 영 자 | |

### Test 01 (Part 5~7)

| 101 | ⓐ | ⓑ | ⓒ | ⓓ | 121 | ⓐ | ⓑ | ⓒ | ⓓ | 141 | ⓐ | ⓑ | ⓒ | ⓓ | 161 | ⓐ | ⓑ | ⓒ | ⓓ | 181 | ⓐ | ⓑ | ⓒ | ⓓ |
|---|---|---|---|---|---|---|---|---|---|---|---|---|---|---|---|---|---|---|---|---|---|---|---|---|
| 102 | ⓐ | ⓑ | ⓒ | ⓓ | 122 | ⓐ | ⓑ | ⓒ | ⓓ | 142 | ⓐ | ⓑ | ⓒ | ⓓ | 162 | ⓐ | ⓑ | ⓒ | ⓓ | 182 | ⓐ | ⓑ | ⓒ | ⓓ |
| 103 | ⓐ | ⓑ | ⓒ | ⓓ | 123 | ⓐ | ⓑ | ⓒ | ⓓ | 143 | ⓐ | ⓑ | ⓒ | ⓓ | 163 | ⓐ | ⓑ | ⓒ | ⓓ | 183 | ⓐ | ⓑ | ⓒ | ⓓ |
| 104 | ⓐ | ⓑ | ⓒ | ⓓ | 124 | ⓐ | ⓑ | ⓒ | ⓓ | 144 | ⓐ | ⓑ | ⓒ | ⓓ | 164 | ⓐ | ⓑ | ⓒ | ⓓ | 184 | ⓐ | ⓑ | ⓒ | ⓓ |
| 105 | ⓐ | ⓑ | ⓒ | ⓓ | 125 | ⓐ | ⓑ | ⓒ | ⓓ | 145 | ⓐ | ⓑ | ⓒ | ⓓ | 165 | ⓐ | ⓑ | ⓒ | ⓓ | 185 | ⓐ | ⓑ | ⓒ | ⓓ |
| 106 | ⓐ | ⓑ | ⓒ | ⓓ | 126 | ⓐ | ⓑ | ⓒ | ⓓ | 146 | ⓐ | ⓑ | ⓒ | ⓓ | 166 | ⓐ | ⓑ | ⓒ | ⓓ | 186 | ⓐ | ⓑ | ⓒ | ⓓ |
| 107 | ⓐ | ⓑ | ⓒ | ⓓ | 127 | ⓐ | ⓑ | ⓒ | ⓓ | 147 | ⓐ | ⓑ | ⓒ | ⓓ | 167 | ⓐ | ⓑ | ⓒ | ⓓ | 187 | ⓐ | ⓑ | ⓒ | ⓓ |
| 108 | ⓐ | ⓑ | ⓒ | ⓓ | 128 | ⓐ | ⓑ | ⓒ | ⓓ | 148 | ⓐ | ⓑ | ⓒ | ⓓ | 168 | ⓐ | ⓑ | ⓒ | ⓓ | 188 | ⓐ | ⓑ | ⓒ | ⓓ |
| 109 | ⓐ | ⓑ | ⓒ | ⓓ | 129 | ⓐ | ⓑ | ⓒ | ⓓ | 149 | ⓐ | ⓑ | ⓒ | ⓓ | 169 | ⓐ | ⓑ | ⓒ | ⓓ | 189 | ⓐ | ⓑ | ⓒ | ⓓ |
| 110 | ⓐ | ⓑ | ⓒ | ⓓ | 130 | ⓐ | ⓑ | ⓒ | ⓓ | 150 | ⓐ | ⓑ | ⓒ | ⓓ | 170 | ⓐ | ⓑ | ⓒ | ⓓ | 190 | ⓐ | ⓑ | ⓒ | ⓓ |
| 111 | ⓐ | ⓑ | ⓒ | ⓓ | 131 | ⓐ | ⓑ | ⓒ | ⓓ | 151 | ⓐ | ⓑ | ⓒ | ⓓ | 171 | ⓐ | ⓑ | ⓒ | ⓓ | 191 | ⓐ | ⓑ | ⓒ | ⓓ |
| 112 | ⓐ | ⓑ | ⓒ | ⓓ | 132 | ⓐ | ⓑ | ⓒ | ⓓ | 152 | ⓐ | ⓑ | ⓒ | ⓓ | 172 | ⓐ | ⓑ | ⓒ | ⓓ | 192 | ⓐ | ⓑ | ⓒ | ⓓ |
| 113 | ⓐ | ⓑ | ⓒ | ⓓ | 133 | ⓐ | ⓑ | ⓒ | ⓓ | 153 | ⓐ | ⓑ | ⓒ | ⓓ | 173 | ⓐ | ⓑ | ⓒ | ⓓ | 193 | ⓐ | ⓑ | ⓒ | ⓓ |
| 114 | ⓐ | ⓑ | ⓒ | ⓓ | 134 | ⓐ | ⓑ | ⓒ | ⓓ | 154 | ⓐ | ⓑ | ⓒ | ⓓ | 174 | ⓐ | ⓑ | ⓒ | ⓓ | 194 | ⓐ | ⓑ | ⓒ | ⓓ |
| 115 | ⓐ | ⓑ | ⓒ | ⓓ | 135 | ⓐ | ⓑ | ⓒ | ⓓ | 155 | ⓐ | ⓑ | ⓒ | ⓓ | 175 | ⓐ | ⓑ | ⓒ | ⓓ | 195 | ⓐ | ⓑ | ⓒ | ⓓ |
| 116 | ⓐ | ⓑ | ⓒ | ⓓ | 136 | ⓐ | ⓑ | ⓒ | ⓓ | 156 | ⓐ | ⓑ | ⓒ | ⓓ | 176 | ⓐ | ⓑ | ⓒ | ⓓ | 196 | ⓐ | ⓑ | ⓒ | ⓓ |
| 117 | ⓐ | ⓑ | ⓒ | ⓓ | 137 | ⓐ | ⓑ | ⓒ | ⓓ | 157 | ⓐ | ⓑ | ⓒ | ⓓ | 177 | ⓐ | ⓑ | ⓒ | ⓓ | 197 | ⓐ | ⓑ | ⓒ | ⓓ |
| 118 | ⓐ | ⓑ | ⓒ | ⓓ | 138 | ⓐ | ⓑ | ⓒ | ⓓ | 158 | ⓐ | ⓑ | ⓒ | ⓓ | 178 | ⓐ | ⓑ | ⓒ | ⓓ | 198 | ⓐ | ⓑ | ⓒ | ⓓ |
| 119 | ⓐ | ⓑ | ⓒ | ⓓ | 139 | ⓐ | ⓑ | ⓒ | ⓓ | 159 | ⓐ | ⓑ | ⓒ | ⓓ | 179 | ⓐ | ⓑ | ⓒ | ⓓ | 199 | ⓐ | ⓑ | ⓒ | ⓓ |
| 120 | ⓐ | ⓑ | ⓒ | ⓓ | 140 | ⓐ | ⓑ | ⓒ | ⓓ | 160 | ⓐ | ⓑ | ⓒ | ⓓ | 180 | ⓐ | ⓑ | ⓒ | ⓓ | 200 | ⓐ | ⓑ | ⓒ | ⓓ |

### Test 02 (Part 5~7)

| 101 | ⓐ | ⓑ | ⓒ | ⓓ | 121 | ⓐ | ⓑ | ⓒ | ⓓ | 141 | ⓐ | ⓑ | ⓒ | ⓓ | 161 | ⓐ | ⓑ | ⓒ | ⓓ | 181 | ⓐ | ⓑ | ⓒ | ⓓ |
|---|---|---|---|---|---|---|---|---|---|---|---|---|---|---|---|---|---|---|---|---|---|---|---|---|
| 102 | ⓐ | ⓑ | ⓒ | ⓓ | 122 | ⓐ | ⓑ | ⓒ | ⓓ | 142 | ⓐ | ⓑ | ⓒ | ⓓ | 162 | ⓐ | ⓑ | ⓒ | ⓓ | 182 | ⓐ | ⓑ | ⓒ | ⓓ |
| 103 | ⓐ | ⓑ | ⓒ | ⓓ | 123 | ⓐ | ⓑ | ⓒ | ⓓ | 143 | ⓐ | ⓑ | ⓒ | ⓓ | 163 | ⓐ | ⓑ | ⓒ | ⓓ | 183 | ⓐ | ⓑ | ⓒ | ⓓ |
| 104 | ⓐ | ⓑ | ⓒ | ⓓ | 124 | ⓐ | ⓑ | ⓒ | ⓓ | 144 | ⓐ | ⓑ | ⓒ | ⓓ | 164 | ⓐ | ⓑ | ⓒ | ⓓ | 184 | ⓐ | ⓑ | ⓒ | ⓓ |
| 105 | ⓐ | ⓑ | ⓒ | ⓓ | 125 | ⓐ | ⓑ | ⓒ | ⓓ | 145 | ⓐ | ⓑ | ⓒ | ⓓ | 165 | ⓐ | ⓑ | ⓒ | ⓓ | 185 | ⓐ | ⓑ | ⓒ | ⓓ |
| 106 | ⓐ | ⓑ | ⓒ | ⓓ | 126 | ⓐ | ⓑ | ⓒ | ⓓ | 146 | ⓐ | ⓑ | ⓒ | ⓓ | 166 | ⓐ | ⓑ | ⓒ | ⓓ | 186 | ⓐ | ⓑ | ⓒ | ⓓ |
| 107 | ⓐ | ⓑ | ⓒ | ⓓ | 127 | ⓐ | ⓑ | ⓒ | ⓓ | 147 | ⓐ | ⓑ | ⓒ | ⓓ | 167 | ⓐ | ⓑ | ⓒ | ⓓ | 187 | ⓐ | ⓑ | ⓒ | ⓓ |
| 108 | ⓐ | ⓑ | ⓒ | ⓓ | 128 | ⓐ | ⓑ | ⓒ | ⓓ | 148 | ⓐ | ⓑ | ⓒ | ⓓ | 168 | ⓐ | ⓑ | ⓒ | ⓓ | 188 | ⓐ | ⓑ | ⓒ | ⓓ |
| 109 | ⓐ | ⓑ | ⓒ | ⓓ | 129 | ⓐ | ⓑ | ⓒ | ⓓ | 149 | ⓐ | ⓑ | ⓒ | ⓓ | 169 | ⓐ | ⓑ | ⓒ | ⓓ | 189 | ⓐ | ⓑ | ⓒ | ⓓ |
| 110 | ⓐ | ⓑ | ⓒ | ⓓ | 130 | ⓐ | ⓑ | ⓒ | ⓓ | 150 | ⓐ | ⓑ | ⓒ | ⓓ | 170 | ⓐ | ⓑ | ⓒ | ⓓ | 190 | ⓐ | ⓑ | ⓒ | ⓓ |
| 111 | ⓐ | ⓑ | ⓒ | ⓓ | 131 | ⓐ | ⓑ | ⓒ | ⓓ | 151 | ⓐ | ⓑ | ⓒ | ⓓ | 171 | ⓐ | ⓑ | ⓒ | ⓓ | 191 | ⓐ | ⓑ | ⓒ | ⓓ |
| 112 | ⓐ | ⓑ | ⓒ | ⓓ | 132 | ⓐ | ⓑ | ⓒ | ⓓ | 152 | ⓐ | ⓑ | ⓒ | ⓓ | 172 | ⓐ | ⓑ | ⓒ | ⓓ | 192 | ⓐ | ⓑ | ⓒ | ⓓ |
| 113 | ⓐ | ⓑ | ⓒ | ⓓ | 133 | ⓐ | ⓑ | ⓒ | ⓓ | 153 | ⓐ | ⓑ | ⓒ | ⓓ | 173 | ⓐ | ⓑ | ⓒ | ⓓ | 193 | ⓐ | ⓑ | ⓒ | ⓓ |
| 114 | ⓐ | ⓑ | ⓒ | ⓓ | 134 | ⓐ | ⓑ | ⓒ | ⓓ | 154 | ⓐ | ⓑ | ⓒ | ⓓ | 174 | ⓐ | ⓑ | ⓒ | ⓓ | 194 | ⓐ | ⓑ | ⓒ | ⓓ |
| 115 | ⓐ | ⓑ | ⓒ | ⓓ | 135 | ⓐ | ⓑ | ⓒ | ⓓ | 155 | ⓐ | ⓑ | ⓒ | ⓓ | 175 | ⓐ | ⓑ | ⓒ | ⓓ | 195 | ⓐ | ⓑ | ⓒ | ⓓ |
| 116 | ⓐ | ⓑ | ⓒ | ⓓ | 136 | ⓐ | ⓑ | ⓒ | ⓓ | 156 | ⓐ | ⓑ | ⓒ | ⓓ | 176 | ⓐ | ⓑ | ⓒ | ⓓ | 196 | ⓐ | ⓑ | ⓒ | ⓓ |
| 117 | ⓐ | ⓑ | ⓒ | ⓓ | 137 | ⓐ | ⓑ | ⓒ | ⓓ | 157 | ⓐ | ⓑ | ⓒ | ⓓ | 177 | ⓐ | ⓑ | ⓒ | ⓓ | 197 | ⓐ | ⓑ | ⓒ | ⓓ |
| 118 | ⓐ | ⓑ | ⓒ | ⓓ | 138 | ⓐ | ⓑ | ⓒ | ⓓ | 158 | ⓐ | ⓑ | ⓒ | ⓓ | 178 | ⓐ | ⓑ | ⓒ | ⓓ | 198 | ⓐ | ⓑ | ⓒ | ⓓ |
| 119 | ⓐ | ⓑ | ⓒ | ⓓ | 139 | ⓐ | ⓑ | ⓒ | ⓓ | 159 | ⓐ | ⓑ | ⓒ | ⓓ | 179 | ⓐ | ⓑ | ⓒ | ⓓ | 199 | ⓐ | ⓑ | ⓒ | ⓓ |
| 120 | ⓐ | ⓑ | ⓒ | ⓓ | 140 | ⓐ | ⓑ | ⓒ | ⓓ | 160 | ⓐ | ⓑ | ⓒ | ⓓ | 180 | ⓐ | ⓑ | ⓒ | ⓓ | 200 | ⓐ | ⓑ | ⓒ | ⓓ |

# ANSWER SHEET

## YBM 실전토익 RC 1000

| 수험번호 | | | | | | |
|---|---|---|---|---|---|---|

응시일자 : 20 년 월 일

| 성명 | 한 글 | |
|---|---|---|
| | 한 자 | |
| | 영 자 | |

### Test 03 (Part 5~7)

| | | | | | | | | | |
|---|---|---|---|---|---|---|---|---|---|
| 101 | ⓐ ⓑ ⓒ ⓓ | 121 | ⓐ ⓑ ⓒ ⓓ | 141 | ⓐ ⓑ ⓒ ⓓ | 161 | ⓐ ⓑ ⓒ ⓓ | 181 | ⓐ ⓑ ⓒ ⓓ |
| 102 | ⓐ ⓑ ⓒ ⓓ | 122 | ⓐ ⓑ ⓒ ⓓ | 142 | ⓐ ⓑ ⓒ ⓓ | 162 | ⓐ ⓑ ⓒ ⓓ | 182 | ⓐ ⓑ ⓒ ⓓ |
| 103 | ⓐ ⓑ ⓒ ⓓ | 123 | ⓐ ⓑ ⓒ ⓓ | 143 | ⓐ ⓑ ⓒ ⓓ | 163 | ⓐ ⓑ ⓒ ⓓ | 183 | ⓐ ⓑ ⓒ ⓓ |
| 104 | ⓐ ⓑ ⓒ ⓓ | 124 | ⓐ ⓑ ⓒ ⓓ | 144 | ⓐ ⓑ ⓒ ⓓ | 164 | ⓐ ⓑ ⓒ ⓓ | 184 | ⓐ ⓑ ⓒ ⓓ |
| 105 | ⓐ ⓑ ⓒ ⓓ | 125 | ⓐ ⓑ ⓒ ⓓ | 145 | ⓐ ⓑ ⓒ ⓓ | 165 | ⓐ ⓑ ⓒ ⓓ | 185 | ⓐ ⓑ ⓒ ⓓ |
| 106 | ⓐ ⓑ ⓒ ⓓ | 126 | ⓐ ⓑ ⓒ ⓓ | 146 | ⓐ ⓑ ⓒ ⓓ | 166 | ⓐ ⓑ ⓒ ⓓ | 186 | ⓐ ⓑ ⓒ ⓓ |
| 107 | ⓐ ⓑ ⓒ ⓓ | 127 | ⓐ ⓑ ⓒ ⓓ | 147 | ⓐ ⓑ ⓒ ⓓ | 167 | ⓐ ⓑ ⓒ ⓓ | 187 | ⓐ ⓑ ⓒ ⓓ |
| 108 | ⓐ ⓑ ⓒ ⓓ | 128 | ⓐ ⓑ ⓒ ⓓ | 148 | ⓐ ⓑ ⓒ ⓓ | 168 | ⓐ ⓑ ⓒ ⓓ | 188 | ⓐ ⓑ ⓒ ⓓ |
| 109 | ⓐ ⓑ ⓒ ⓓ | 129 | ⓐ ⓑ ⓒ ⓓ | 149 | ⓐ ⓑ ⓒ ⓓ | 169 | ⓐ ⓑ ⓒ ⓓ | 189 | ⓐ ⓑ ⓒ ⓓ |
| 110 | ⓐ ⓑ ⓒ ⓓ | 130 | ⓐ ⓑ ⓒ ⓓ | 150 | ⓐ ⓑ ⓒ ⓓ | 170 | ⓐ ⓑ ⓒ ⓓ | 190 | ⓐ ⓑ ⓒ ⓓ |
| 111 | ⓐ ⓑ ⓒ ⓓ | 131 | ⓐ ⓑ ⓒ ⓓ | 151 | ⓐ ⓑ ⓒ ⓓ | 171 | ⓐ ⓑ ⓒ ⓓ | 191 | ⓐ ⓑ ⓒ ⓓ |
| 112 | ⓐ ⓑ ⓒ ⓓ | 132 | ⓐ ⓑ ⓒ ⓓ | 152 | ⓐ ⓑ ⓒ ⓓ | 172 | ⓐ ⓑ ⓒ ⓓ | 192 | ⓐ ⓑ ⓒ ⓓ |
| 113 | ⓐ ⓑ ⓒ ⓓ | 133 | ⓐ ⓑ ⓒ ⓓ | 153 | ⓐ ⓑ ⓒ ⓓ | 173 | ⓐ ⓑ ⓒ ⓓ | 193 | ⓐ ⓑ ⓒ ⓓ |
| 114 | ⓐ ⓑ ⓒ ⓓ | 134 | ⓐ ⓑ ⓒ ⓓ | 154 | ⓐ ⓑ ⓒ ⓓ | 174 | ⓐ ⓑ ⓒ ⓓ | 194 | ⓐ ⓑ ⓒ ⓓ |
| 115 | ⓐ ⓑ ⓒ ⓓ | 135 | ⓐ ⓑ ⓒ ⓓ | 155 | ⓐ ⓑ ⓒ ⓓ | 175 | ⓐ ⓑ ⓒ ⓓ | 195 | ⓐ ⓑ ⓒ ⓓ |
| 116 | ⓐ ⓑ ⓒ ⓓ | 136 | ⓐ ⓑ ⓒ ⓓ | 156 | ⓐ ⓑ ⓒ ⓓ | 176 | ⓐ ⓑ ⓒ ⓓ | 196 | ⓐ ⓑ ⓒ ⓓ |
| 117 | ⓐ ⓑ ⓒ ⓓ | 137 | ⓐ ⓑ ⓒ ⓓ | 157 | ⓐ ⓑ ⓒ ⓓ | 177 | ⓐ ⓑ ⓒ ⓓ | 197 | ⓐ ⓑ ⓒ ⓓ |
| 118 | ⓐ ⓑ ⓒ ⓓ | 138 | ⓐ ⓑ ⓒ ⓓ | 158 | ⓐ ⓑ ⓒ ⓓ | 178 | ⓐ ⓑ ⓒ ⓓ | 198 | ⓐ ⓑ ⓒ ⓓ |
| 119 | ⓐ ⓑ ⓒ ⓓ | 139 | ⓐ ⓑ ⓒ ⓓ | 159 | ⓐ ⓑ ⓒ ⓓ | 179 | ⓐ ⓑ ⓒ ⓓ | 199 | ⓐ ⓑ ⓒ ⓓ |
| 120 | ⓐ ⓑ ⓒ ⓓ | 140 | ⓐ ⓑ ⓒ ⓓ | 160 | ⓐ ⓑ ⓒ ⓓ | 180 | ⓐ ⓑ ⓒ ⓓ | 200 | ⓐ ⓑ ⓒ ⓓ |

### Test 04 (Part 5~7)

| | | | | | | | | | |
|---|---|---|---|---|---|---|---|---|---|
| 101 | ⓐ ⓑ ⓒ ⓓ | 121 | ⓐ ⓑ ⓒ ⓓ | 141 | ⓐ ⓑ ⓒ ⓓ | 161 | ⓐ ⓑ ⓒ ⓓ | 181 | ⓐ ⓑ ⓒ ⓓ |
| 102 | ⓐ ⓑ ⓒ ⓓ | 122 | ⓐ ⓑ ⓒ ⓓ | 142 | ⓐ ⓑ ⓒ ⓓ | 162 | ⓐ ⓑ ⓒ ⓓ | 182 | ⓐ ⓑ ⓒ ⓓ |
| 103 | ⓐ ⓑ ⓒ ⓓ | 123 | ⓐ ⓑ ⓒ ⓓ | 143 | ⓐ ⓑ ⓒ ⓓ | 163 | ⓐ ⓑ ⓒ ⓓ | 183 | ⓐ ⓑ ⓒ ⓓ |
| 104 | ⓐ ⓑ ⓒ ⓓ | 124 | ⓐ ⓑ ⓒ ⓓ | 144 | ⓐ ⓑ ⓒ ⓓ | 164 | ⓐ ⓑ ⓒ ⓓ | 184 | ⓐ ⓑ ⓒ ⓓ |
| 105 | ⓐ ⓑ ⓒ ⓓ | 125 | ⓐ ⓑ ⓒ ⓓ | 145 | ⓐ ⓑ ⓒ ⓓ | 165 | ⓐ ⓑ ⓒ ⓓ | 185 | ⓐ ⓑ ⓒ ⓓ |
| 106 | ⓐ ⓑ ⓒ ⓓ | 126 | ⓐ ⓑ ⓒ ⓓ | 146 | ⓐ ⓑ ⓒ ⓓ | 166 | ⓐ ⓑ ⓒ ⓓ | 186 | ⓐ ⓑ ⓒ ⓓ |
| 107 | ⓐ ⓑ ⓒ ⓓ | 127 | ⓐ ⓑ ⓒ ⓓ | 147 | ⓐ ⓑ ⓒ ⓓ | 167 | ⓐ ⓑ ⓒ ⓓ | 187 | ⓐ ⓑ ⓒ ⓓ |
| 108 | ⓐ ⓑ ⓒ ⓓ | 128 | ⓐ ⓑ ⓒ ⓓ | 148 | ⓐ ⓑ ⓒ ⓓ | 168 | ⓐ ⓑ ⓒ ⓓ | 188 | ⓐ ⓑ ⓒ ⓓ |
| 109 | ⓐ ⓑ ⓒ ⓓ | 129 | ⓐ ⓑ ⓒ ⓓ | 149 | ⓐ ⓑ ⓒ ⓓ | 169 | ⓐ ⓑ ⓒ ⓓ | 189 | ⓐ ⓑ ⓒ ⓓ |
| 110 | ⓐ ⓑ ⓒ ⓓ | 130 | ⓐ ⓑ ⓒ ⓓ | 150 | ⓐ ⓑ ⓒ ⓓ | 170 | ⓐ ⓑ ⓒ ⓓ | 190 | ⓐ ⓑ ⓒ ⓓ |
| 111 | ⓐ ⓑ ⓒ ⓓ | 131 | ⓐ ⓑ ⓒ ⓓ | 151 | ⓐ ⓑ ⓒ ⓓ | 171 | ⓐ ⓑ ⓒ ⓓ | 191 | ⓐ ⓑ ⓒ ⓓ |
| 112 | ⓐ ⓑ ⓒ ⓓ | 132 | ⓐ ⓑ ⓒ ⓓ | 152 | ⓐ ⓑ ⓒ ⓓ | 172 | ⓐ ⓑ ⓒ ⓓ | 192 | ⓐ ⓑ ⓒ ⓓ |
| 113 | ⓐ ⓑ ⓒ ⓓ | 133 | ⓐ ⓑ ⓒ ⓓ | 153 | ⓐ ⓑ ⓒ ⓓ | 173 | ⓐ ⓑ ⓒ ⓓ | 193 | ⓐ ⓑ ⓒ ⓓ |
| 114 | ⓐ ⓑ ⓒ ⓓ | 134 | ⓐ ⓑ ⓒ ⓓ | 154 | ⓐ ⓑ ⓒ ⓓ | 174 | ⓐ ⓑ ⓒ ⓓ | 194 | ⓐ ⓑ ⓒ ⓓ |
| 115 | ⓐ ⓑ ⓒ ⓓ | 135 | ⓐ ⓑ ⓒ ⓓ | 155 | ⓐ ⓑ ⓒ ⓓ | 175 | ⓐ ⓑ ⓒ ⓓ | 195 | ⓐ ⓑ ⓒ ⓓ |
| 116 | ⓐ ⓑ ⓒ ⓓ | 136 | ⓐ ⓑ ⓒ ⓓ | 156 | ⓐ ⓑ ⓒ ⓓ | 176 | ⓐ ⓑ ⓒ ⓓ | 196 | ⓐ ⓑ ⓒ ⓓ |
| 117 | ⓐ ⓑ ⓒ ⓓ | 137 | ⓐ ⓑ ⓒ ⓓ | 157 | ⓐ ⓑ ⓒ ⓓ | 177 | ⓐ ⓑ ⓒ ⓓ | 197 | ⓐ ⓑ ⓒ ⓓ |
| 118 | ⓐ ⓑ ⓒ ⓓ | 138 | ⓐ ⓑ ⓒ ⓓ | 158 | ⓐ ⓑ ⓒ ⓓ | 178 | ⓐ ⓑ ⓒ ⓓ | 198 | ⓐ ⓑ ⓒ ⓓ |
| 119 | ⓐ ⓑ ⓒ ⓓ | 139 | ⓐ ⓑ ⓒ ⓓ | 159 | ⓐ ⓑ ⓒ ⓓ | 179 | ⓐ ⓑ ⓒ ⓓ | 199 | ⓐ ⓑ ⓒ ⓓ |
| 120 | ⓐ ⓑ ⓒ ⓓ | 140 | ⓐ ⓑ ⓒ ⓓ | 160 | ⓐ ⓑ ⓒ ⓓ | 180 | ⓐ ⓑ ⓒ ⓓ | 200 | ⓐ ⓑ ⓒ ⓓ |

# ANSWER SHEET

## YBM 실전토익 RC 1000

| 수험번호 | | | | | | |
|---|---|---|---|---|---|---|

응시일자 : 20 년 월 일

| 성명 | 한 글 | |
|---|---|---|
| | 한 자 | |
| | 영 자 | |

### Test 05 (Part 5~7)

| | | | | | | | | | |
|---|---|---|---|---|---|---|---|---|---|
| 101 | ⓐ ⓑ ⓒ ⓓ | 121 | ⓐ ⓑ ⓒ ⓓ | 141 | ⓐ ⓑ ⓒ ⓓ | 161 | ⓐ ⓑ ⓒ ⓓ | 181 | ⓐ ⓑ ⓒ ⓓ |
| 102 | ⓐ ⓑ ⓒ ⓓ | 122 | ⓐ ⓑ ⓒ ⓓ | 142 | ⓐ ⓑ ⓒ ⓓ | 162 | ⓐ ⓑ ⓒ ⓓ | 182 | ⓐ ⓑ ⓒ ⓓ |
| 103 | ⓐ ⓑ ⓒ ⓓ | 123 | ⓐ ⓑ ⓒ ⓓ | 143 | ⓐ ⓑ ⓒ ⓓ | 163 | ⓐ ⓑ ⓒ ⓓ | 183 | ⓐ ⓑ ⓒ ⓓ |
| 104 | ⓐ ⓑ ⓒ ⓓ | 124 | ⓐ ⓑ ⓒ ⓓ | 144 | ⓐ ⓑ ⓒ ⓓ | 164 | ⓐ ⓑ ⓒ ⓓ | 184 | ⓐ ⓑ ⓒ ⓓ |
| 105 | ⓐ ⓑ ⓒ ⓓ | 125 | ⓐ ⓑ ⓒ ⓓ | 145 | ⓐ ⓑ ⓒ ⓓ | 165 | ⓐ ⓑ ⓒ ⓓ | 185 | ⓐ ⓑ ⓒ ⓓ |
| 106 | ⓐ ⓑ ⓒ ⓓ | 126 | ⓐ ⓑ ⓒ ⓓ | 146 | ⓐ ⓑ ⓒ ⓓ | 166 | ⓐ ⓑ ⓒ ⓓ | 186 | ⓐ ⓑ ⓒ ⓓ |
| 107 | ⓐ ⓑ ⓒ ⓓ | 127 | ⓐ ⓑ ⓒ ⓓ | 147 | ⓐ ⓑ ⓒ ⓓ | 167 | ⓐ ⓑ ⓒ ⓓ | 187 | ⓐ ⓑ ⓒ ⓓ |
| 108 | ⓐ ⓑ ⓒ ⓓ | 128 | ⓐ ⓑ ⓒ ⓓ | 148 | ⓐ ⓑ ⓒ ⓓ | 168 | ⓐ ⓑ ⓒ ⓓ | 188 | ⓐ ⓑ ⓒ ⓓ |
| 109 | ⓐ ⓑ ⓒ ⓓ | 129 | ⓐ ⓑ ⓒ ⓓ | 149 | ⓐ ⓑ ⓒ ⓓ | 169 | ⓐ ⓑ ⓒ ⓓ | 189 | ⓐ ⓑ ⓒ ⓓ |
| 110 | ⓐ ⓑ ⓒ ⓓ | 130 | ⓐ ⓑ ⓒ ⓓ | 150 | ⓐ ⓑ ⓒ ⓓ | 170 | ⓐ ⓑ ⓒ ⓓ | 190 | ⓐ ⓑ ⓒ ⓓ |
| 111 | ⓐ ⓑ ⓒ ⓓ | 131 | ⓐ ⓑ ⓒ ⓓ | 151 | ⓐ ⓑ ⓒ ⓓ | 171 | ⓐ ⓑ ⓒ ⓓ | 191 | ⓐ ⓑ ⓒ ⓓ |
| 112 | ⓐ ⓑ ⓒ ⓓ | 132 | ⓐ ⓑ ⓒ ⓓ | 152 | ⓐ ⓑ ⓒ ⓓ | 172 | ⓐ ⓑ ⓒ ⓓ | 192 | ⓐ ⓑ ⓒ ⓓ |
| 113 | ⓐ ⓑ ⓒ ⓓ | 133 | ⓐ ⓑ ⓒ ⓓ | 153 | ⓐ ⓑ ⓒ ⓓ | 173 | ⓐ ⓑ ⓒ ⓓ | 193 | ⓐ ⓑ ⓒ ⓓ |
| 114 | ⓐ ⓑ ⓒ ⓓ | 134 | ⓐ ⓑ ⓒ ⓓ | 154 | ⓐ ⓑ ⓒ ⓓ | 174 | ⓐ ⓑ ⓒ ⓓ | 194 | ⓐ ⓑ ⓒ ⓓ |
| 115 | ⓐ ⓑ ⓒ ⓓ | 135 | ⓐ ⓑ ⓒ ⓓ | 155 | ⓐ ⓑ ⓒ ⓓ | 175 | ⓐ ⓑ ⓒ ⓓ | 195 | ⓐ ⓑ ⓒ ⓓ |
| 116 | ⓐ ⓑ ⓒ ⓓ | 136 | ⓐ ⓑ ⓒ ⓓ | 156 | ⓐ ⓑ ⓒ ⓓ | 176 | ⓐ ⓑ ⓒ ⓓ | 196 | ⓐ ⓑ ⓒ ⓓ |
| 117 | ⓐ ⓑ ⓒ ⓓ | 137 | ⓐ ⓑ ⓒ ⓓ | 157 | ⓐ ⓑ ⓒ ⓓ | 177 | ⓐ ⓑ ⓒ ⓓ | 197 | ⓐ ⓑ ⓒ ⓓ |
| 118 | ⓐ ⓑ ⓒ ⓓ | 138 | ⓐ ⓑ ⓒ ⓓ | 158 | ⓐ ⓑ ⓒ ⓓ | 178 | ⓐ ⓑ ⓒ ⓓ | 198 | ⓐ ⓑ ⓒ ⓓ |
| 119 | ⓐ ⓑ ⓒ ⓓ | 139 | ⓐ ⓑ ⓒ ⓓ | 159 | ⓐ ⓑ ⓒ ⓓ | 179 | ⓐ ⓑ ⓒ ⓓ | 199 | ⓐ ⓑ ⓒ ⓓ |
| 120 | ⓐ ⓑ ⓒ ⓓ | 140 | ⓐ ⓑ ⓒ ⓓ | 160 | ⓐ ⓑ ⓒ ⓓ | 180 | ⓐ ⓑ ⓒ ⓓ | 200 | ⓐ ⓑ ⓒ ⓓ |

### Test 06 (Part 5~7)

| | | | | | | | | | |
|---|---|---|---|---|---|---|---|---|---|
| 101 | ⓐ ⓑ ⓒ ⓓ | 121 | ⓐ ⓑ ⓒ ⓓ | 141 | ⓐ ⓑ ⓒ ⓓ | 161 | ⓐ ⓑ ⓒ ⓓ | 181 | ⓐ ⓑ ⓒ ⓓ |
| 102 | ⓐ ⓑ ⓒ ⓓ | 122 | ⓐ ⓑ ⓒ ⓓ | 142 | ⓐ ⓑ ⓒ ⓓ | 162 | ⓐ ⓑ ⓒ ⓓ | 182 | ⓐ ⓑ ⓒ ⓓ |
| 103 | ⓐ ⓑ ⓒ ⓓ | 123 | ⓐ ⓑ ⓒ ⓓ | 143 | ⓐ ⓑ ⓒ ⓓ | 163 | ⓐ ⓑ ⓒ ⓓ | 183 | ⓐ ⓑ ⓒ ⓓ |
| 104 | ⓐ ⓑ ⓒ ⓓ | 124 | ⓐ ⓑ ⓒ ⓓ | 144 | ⓐ ⓑ ⓒ ⓓ | 164 | ⓐ ⓑ ⓒ ⓓ | 184 | ⓐ ⓑ ⓒ ⓓ |
| 105 | ⓐ ⓑ ⓒ ⓓ | 125 | ⓐ ⓑ ⓒ ⓓ | 145 | ⓐ ⓑ ⓒ ⓓ | 165 | ⓐ ⓑ ⓒ ⓓ | 185 | ⓐ ⓑ ⓒ ⓓ |
| 106 | ⓐ ⓑ ⓒ ⓓ | 126 | ⓐ ⓑ ⓒ ⓓ | 146 | ⓐ ⓑ ⓒ ⓓ | 166 | ⓐ ⓑ ⓒ ⓓ | 186 | ⓐ ⓑ ⓒ ⓓ |
| 107 | ⓐ ⓑ ⓒ ⓓ | 127 | ⓐ ⓑ ⓒ ⓓ | 147 | ⓐ ⓑ ⓒ ⓓ | 167 | ⓐ ⓑ ⓒ ⓓ | 187 | ⓐ ⓑ ⓒ ⓓ |
| 108 | ⓐ ⓑ ⓒ ⓓ | 128 | ⓐ ⓑ ⓒ ⓓ | 148 | ⓐ ⓑ ⓒ ⓓ | 168 | ⓐ ⓑ ⓒ ⓓ | 188 | ⓐ ⓑ ⓒ ⓓ |
| 109 | ⓐ ⓑ ⓒ ⓓ | 129 | ⓐ ⓑ ⓒ ⓓ | 149 | ⓐ ⓑ ⓒ ⓓ | 169 | ⓐ ⓑ ⓒ ⓓ | 189 | ⓐ ⓑ ⓒ ⓓ |
| 110 | ⓐ ⓑ ⓒ ⓓ | 130 | ⓐ ⓑ ⓒ ⓓ | 150 | ⓐ ⓑ ⓒ ⓓ | 170 | ⓐ ⓑ ⓒ ⓓ | 190 | ⓐ ⓑ ⓒ ⓓ |
| 111 | ⓐ ⓑ ⓒ ⓓ | 131 | ⓐ ⓑ ⓒ ⓓ | 151 | ⓐ ⓑ ⓒ ⓓ | 171 | ⓐ ⓑ ⓒ ⓓ | 191 | ⓐ ⓑ ⓒ ⓓ |
| 112 | ⓐ ⓑ ⓒ ⓓ | 132 | ⓐ ⓑ ⓒ ⓓ | 152 | ⓐ ⓑ ⓒ ⓓ | 172 | ⓐ ⓑ ⓒ ⓓ | 192 | ⓐ ⓑ ⓒ ⓓ |
| 113 | ⓐ ⓑ ⓒ ⓓ | 133 | ⓐ ⓑ ⓒ ⓓ | 153 | ⓐ ⓑ ⓒ ⓓ | 173 | ⓐ ⓑ ⓒ ⓓ | 193 | ⓐ ⓑ ⓒ ⓓ |
| 114 | ⓐ ⓑ ⓒ ⓓ | 134 | ⓐ ⓑ ⓒ ⓓ | 154 | ⓐ ⓑ ⓒ ⓓ | 174 | ⓐ ⓑ ⓒ ⓓ | 194 | ⓐ ⓑ ⓒ ⓓ |
| 115 | ⓐ ⓑ ⓒ ⓓ | 135 | ⓐ ⓑ ⓒ ⓓ | 155 | ⓐ ⓑ ⓒ ⓓ | 175 | ⓐ ⓑ ⓒ ⓓ | 195 | ⓐ ⓑ ⓒ ⓓ |
| 116 | ⓐ ⓑ ⓒ ⓓ | 136 | ⓐ ⓑ ⓒ ⓓ | 156 | ⓐ ⓑ ⓒ ⓓ | 176 | ⓐ ⓑ ⓒ ⓓ | 196 | ⓐ ⓑ ⓒ ⓓ |
| 117 | ⓐ ⓑ ⓒ ⓓ | 137 | ⓐ ⓑ ⓒ ⓓ | 157 | ⓐ ⓑ ⓒ ⓓ | 177 | ⓐ ⓑ ⓒ ⓓ | 197 | ⓐ ⓑ ⓒ ⓓ |
| 118 | ⓐ ⓑ ⓒ ⓓ | 138 | ⓐ ⓑ ⓒ ⓓ | 158 | ⓐ ⓑ ⓒ ⓓ | 178 | ⓐ ⓑ ⓒ ⓓ | 198 | ⓐ ⓑ ⓒ ⓓ |
| 119 | ⓐ ⓑ ⓒ ⓓ | 139 | ⓐ ⓑ ⓒ ⓓ | 159 | ⓐ ⓑ ⓒ ⓓ | 179 | ⓐ ⓑ ⓒ ⓓ | 199 | ⓐ ⓑ ⓒ ⓓ |
| 120 | ⓐ ⓑ ⓒ ⓓ | 140 | ⓐ ⓑ ⓒ ⓓ | 160 | ⓐ ⓑ ⓒ ⓓ | 180 | ⓐ ⓑ ⓒ ⓓ | 200 | ⓐ ⓑ ⓒ ⓓ |

# ANSWER SHEET

## YBM 실전토익 RC 1000

| 수험번호 | | | | | | |
|---|---|---|---|---|---|---|

응시일자 : 20 년 월 일

| 성명 | 한 글 | |
|---|---|---|
| | 한 자 | |
| | 영 자 | |

### Test 07 (Part 5~7)

| 101 | ⓐ ⓑ ⓒ ⓓ | 121 | ⓐ ⓑ ⓒ ⓓ | 141 | ⓐ ⓑ ⓒ ⓓ | 161 | ⓐ ⓑ ⓒ ⓓ | 181 | ⓐ ⓑ ⓒ ⓓ |
|---|---|---|---|---|---|---|---|---|---|
| 102 | ⓐ ⓑ ⓒ ⓓ | 122 | ⓐ ⓑ ⓒ ⓓ | 142 | ⓐ ⓑ ⓒ ⓓ | 162 | ⓐ ⓑ ⓒ ⓓ | 182 | ⓐ ⓑ ⓒ ⓓ |
| 103 | ⓐ ⓑ ⓒ ⓓ | 123 | ⓐ ⓑ ⓒ ⓓ | 143 | ⓐ ⓑ ⓒ ⓓ | 163 | ⓐ ⓑ ⓒ ⓓ | 183 | ⓐ ⓑ ⓒ ⓓ |
| 104 | ⓐ ⓑ ⓒ ⓓ | 124 | ⓐ ⓑ ⓒ ⓓ | 144 | ⓐ ⓑ ⓒ ⓓ | 164 | ⓐ ⓑ ⓒ ⓓ | 184 | ⓐ ⓑ ⓒ ⓓ |
| 105 | ⓐ ⓑ ⓒ ⓓ | 125 | ⓐ ⓑ ⓒ ⓓ | 145 | ⓐ ⓑ ⓒ ⓓ | 165 | ⓐ ⓑ ⓒ ⓓ | 185 | ⓐ ⓑ ⓒ ⓓ |
| 106 | ⓐ ⓑ ⓒ ⓓ | 126 | ⓐ ⓑ ⓒ ⓓ | 146 | ⓐ ⓑ ⓒ ⓓ | 166 | ⓐ ⓑ ⓒ ⓓ | 186 | ⓐ ⓑ ⓒ ⓓ |
| 107 | ⓐ ⓑ ⓒ ⓓ | 127 | ⓐ ⓑ ⓒ ⓓ | 147 | ⓐ ⓑ ⓒ ⓓ | 167 | ⓐ ⓑ ⓒ ⓓ | 187 | ⓐ ⓑ ⓒ ⓓ |
| 108 | ⓐ ⓑ ⓒ ⓓ | 128 | ⓐ ⓑ ⓒ ⓓ | 148 | ⓐ ⓑ ⓒ ⓓ | 168 | ⓐ ⓑ ⓒ ⓓ | 188 | ⓐ ⓑ ⓒ ⓓ |
| 109 | ⓐ ⓑ ⓒ ⓓ | 129 | ⓐ ⓑ ⓒ ⓓ | 149 | ⓐ ⓑ ⓒ ⓓ | 169 | ⓐ ⓑ ⓒ ⓓ | 189 | ⓐ ⓑ ⓒ ⓓ |
| 110 | ⓐ ⓑ ⓒ ⓓ | 130 | ⓐ ⓑ ⓒ ⓓ | 150 | ⓐ ⓑ ⓒ ⓓ | 170 | ⓐ ⓑ ⓒ ⓓ | 190 | ⓐ ⓑ ⓒ ⓓ |
| 111 | ⓐ ⓑ ⓒ ⓓ | 131 | ⓐ ⓑ ⓒ ⓓ | 151 | ⓐ ⓑ ⓒ ⓓ | 171 | ⓐ ⓑ ⓒ ⓓ | 191 | ⓐ ⓑ ⓒ ⓓ |
| 112 | ⓐ ⓑ ⓒ ⓓ | 132 | ⓐ ⓑ ⓒ ⓓ | 152 | ⓐ ⓑ ⓒ ⓓ | 172 | ⓐ ⓑ ⓒ ⓓ | 192 | ⓐ ⓑ ⓒ ⓓ |
| 113 | ⓐ ⓑ ⓒ ⓓ | 133 | ⓐ ⓑ ⓒ ⓓ | 153 | ⓐ ⓑ ⓒ ⓓ | 173 | ⓐ ⓑ ⓒ ⓓ | 193 | ⓐ ⓑ ⓒ ⓓ |
| 114 | ⓐ ⓑ ⓒ ⓓ | 134 | ⓐ ⓑ ⓒ ⓓ | 154 | ⓐ ⓑ ⓒ ⓓ | 174 | ⓐ ⓑ ⓒ ⓓ | 194 | ⓐ ⓑ ⓒ ⓓ |
| 115 | ⓐ ⓑ ⓒ ⓓ | 135 | ⓐ ⓑ ⓒ ⓓ | 155 | ⓐ ⓑ ⓒ ⓓ | 175 | ⓐ ⓑ ⓒ ⓓ | 195 | ⓐ ⓑ ⓒ ⓓ |
| 116 | ⓐ ⓑ ⓒ ⓓ | 136 | ⓐ ⓑ ⓒ ⓓ | 156 | ⓐ ⓑ ⓒ ⓓ | 176 | ⓐ ⓑ ⓒ ⓓ | 196 | ⓐ ⓑ ⓒ ⓓ |
| 117 | ⓐ ⓑ ⓒ ⓓ | 137 | ⓐ ⓑ ⓒ ⓓ | 157 | ⓐ ⓑ ⓒ ⓓ | 177 | ⓐ ⓑ ⓒ ⓓ | 197 | ⓐ ⓑ ⓒ ⓓ |
| 118 | ⓐ ⓑ ⓒ ⓓ | 138 | ⓐ ⓑ ⓒ ⓓ | 158 | ⓐ ⓑ ⓒ ⓓ | 178 | ⓐ ⓑ ⓒ ⓓ | 198 | ⓐ ⓑ ⓒ ⓓ |
| 119 | ⓐ ⓑ ⓒ ⓓ | 139 | ⓐ ⓑ ⓒ ⓓ | 159 | ⓐ ⓑ ⓒ ⓓ | 179 | ⓐ ⓑ ⓒ ⓓ | 199 | ⓐ ⓑ ⓒ ⓓ |
| 120 | ⓐ ⓑ ⓒ ⓓ | 140 | ⓐ ⓑ ⓒ ⓓ | 160 | ⓐ ⓑ ⓒ ⓓ | 180 | ⓐ ⓑ ⓒ ⓓ | 200 | ⓐ ⓑ ⓒ ⓓ |

### Test 08 (Part 5~7)

| 101 | ⓐ ⓑ ⓒ ⓓ | 121 | ⓐ ⓑ ⓒ ⓓ | 141 | ⓐ ⓑ ⓒ ⓓ | 161 | ⓐ ⓑ ⓒ ⓓ | 181 | ⓐ ⓑ ⓒ ⓓ |
|---|---|---|---|---|---|---|---|---|---|
| 102 | ⓐ ⓑ ⓒ ⓓ | 122 | ⓐ ⓑ ⓒ ⓓ | 142 | ⓐ ⓑ ⓒ ⓓ | 162 | ⓐ ⓑ ⓒ ⓓ | 182 | ⓐ ⓑ ⓒ ⓓ |
| 103 | ⓐ ⓑ ⓒ ⓓ | 123 | ⓐ ⓑ ⓒ ⓓ | 143 | ⓐ ⓑ ⓒ ⓓ | 163 | ⓐ ⓑ ⓒ ⓓ | 183 | ⓐ ⓑ ⓒ ⓓ |
| 104 | ⓐ ⓑ ⓒ ⓓ | 124 | ⓐ ⓑ ⓒ ⓓ | 144 | ⓐ ⓑ ⓒ ⓓ | 164 | ⓐ ⓑ ⓒ ⓓ | 184 | ⓐ ⓑ ⓒ ⓓ |
| 105 | ⓐ ⓑ ⓒ ⓓ | 125 | ⓐ ⓑ ⓒ ⓓ | 145 | ⓐ ⓑ ⓒ ⓓ | 165 | ⓐ ⓑ ⓒ ⓓ | 185 | ⓐ ⓑ ⓒ ⓓ |
| 106 | ⓐ ⓑ ⓒ ⓓ | 126 | ⓐ ⓑ ⓒ ⓓ | 146 | ⓐ ⓑ ⓒ ⓓ | 166 | ⓐ ⓑ ⓒ ⓓ | 186 | ⓐ ⓑ ⓒ ⓓ |
| 107 | ⓐ ⓑ ⓒ ⓓ | 127 | ⓐ ⓑ ⓒ ⓓ | 147 | ⓐ ⓑ ⓒ ⓓ | 167 | ⓐ ⓑ ⓒ ⓓ | 187 | ⓐ ⓑ ⓒ ⓓ |
| 108 | ⓐ ⓑ ⓒ ⓓ | 128 | ⓐ ⓑ ⓒ ⓓ | 148 | ⓐ ⓑ ⓒ ⓓ | 168 | ⓐ ⓑ ⓒ ⓓ | 188 | ⓐ ⓑ ⓒ ⓓ |
| 109 | ⓐ ⓑ ⓒ ⓓ | 129 | ⓐ ⓑ ⓒ ⓓ | 149 | ⓐ ⓑ ⓒ ⓓ | 169 | ⓐ ⓑ ⓒ ⓓ | 189 | ⓐ ⓑ ⓒ ⓓ |
| 110 | ⓐ ⓑ ⓒ ⓓ | 130 | ⓐ ⓑ ⓒ ⓓ | 150 | ⓐ ⓑ ⓒ ⓓ | 170 | ⓐ ⓑ ⓒ ⓓ | 190 | ⓐ ⓑ ⓒ ⓓ |
| 111 | ⓐ ⓑ ⓒ ⓓ | 131 | ⓐ ⓑ ⓒ ⓓ | 151 | ⓐ ⓑ ⓒ ⓓ | 171 | ⓐ ⓑ ⓒ ⓓ | 191 | ⓐ ⓑ ⓒ ⓓ |
| 112 | ⓐ ⓑ ⓒ ⓓ | 132 | ⓐ ⓑ ⓒ ⓓ | 152 | ⓐ ⓑ ⓒ ⓓ | 172 | ⓐ ⓑ ⓒ ⓓ | 192 | ⓐ ⓑ ⓒ ⓓ |
| 113 | ⓐ ⓑ ⓒ ⓓ | 133 | ⓐ ⓑ ⓒ ⓓ | 153 | ⓐ ⓑ ⓒ ⓓ | 173 | ⓐ ⓑ ⓒ ⓓ | 193 | ⓐ ⓑ ⓒ ⓓ |
| 114 | ⓐ ⓑ ⓒ ⓓ | 134 | ⓐ ⓑ ⓒ ⓓ | 154 | ⓐ ⓑ ⓒ ⓓ | 174 | ⓐ ⓑ ⓒ ⓓ | 194 | ⓐ ⓑ ⓒ ⓓ |
| 115 | ⓐ ⓑ ⓒ ⓓ | 135 | ⓐ ⓑ ⓒ ⓓ | 155 | ⓐ ⓑ ⓒ ⓓ | 175 | ⓐ ⓑ ⓒ ⓓ | 195 | ⓐ ⓑ ⓒ ⓓ |
| 116 | ⓐ ⓑ ⓒ ⓓ | 136 | ⓐ ⓑ ⓒ ⓓ | 156 | ⓐ ⓑ ⓒ ⓓ | 176 | ⓐ ⓑ ⓒ ⓓ | 196 | ⓐ ⓑ ⓒ ⓓ |
| 117 | ⓐ ⓑ ⓒ ⓓ | 137 | ⓐ ⓑ ⓒ ⓓ | 157 | ⓐ ⓑ ⓒ ⓓ | 177 | ⓐ ⓑ ⓒ ⓓ | 197 | ⓐ ⓑ ⓒ ⓓ |
| 118 | ⓐ ⓑ ⓒ ⓓ | 138 | ⓐ ⓑ ⓒ ⓓ | 158 | ⓐ ⓑ ⓒ ⓓ | 178 | ⓐ ⓑ ⓒ ⓓ | 198 | ⓐ ⓑ ⓒ ⓓ |
| 119 | ⓐ ⓑ ⓒ ⓓ | 139 | ⓐ ⓑ ⓒ ⓓ | 159 | ⓐ ⓑ ⓒ ⓓ | 179 | ⓐ ⓑ ⓒ ⓓ | 199 | ⓐ ⓑ ⓒ ⓓ |
| 120 | ⓐ ⓑ ⓒ ⓓ | 140 | ⓐ ⓑ ⓒ ⓓ | 160 | ⓐ ⓑ ⓒ ⓓ | 180 | ⓐ ⓑ ⓒ ⓓ | 200 | ⓐ ⓑ ⓒ ⓓ |

# ANSWER SHEET

## YBM 실전토익 RC 1000

| 수험번호 | | | | | | |
|---|---|---|---|---|---|---|

응시일자 : 20 년 월 일

| 성명 | 한 글 | |
|---|---|---|
| | 한 자 | |
| | 영 자 | |

### Test 09 (Part 5~7)

| No. | Answer | No. | Answer | No. | Answer | No. | Answer | No. | Answer |
|---|---|---|---|---|---|---|---|---|---|
| 101 | ⓐ ⓑ ⓒ ⓓ | 121 | ⓐ ⓑ ⓒ ⓓ | 141 | ⓐ ⓑ ⓒ ⓓ | 161 | ⓐ ⓑ ⓒ ⓓ | 181 | ⓐ ⓑ ⓒ ⓓ |
| 102 | ⓐ ⓑ ⓒ ⓓ | 122 | ⓐ ⓑ ⓒ ⓓ | 142 | ⓐ ⓑ ⓒ ⓓ | 162 | ⓐ ⓑ ⓒ ⓓ | 182 | ⓐ ⓑ ⓒ ⓓ |
| 103 | ⓐ ⓑ ⓒ ⓓ | 123 | ⓐ ⓑ ⓒ ⓓ | 143 | ⓐ ⓑ ⓒ ⓓ | 163 | ⓐ ⓑ ⓒ ⓓ | 183 | ⓐ ⓑ ⓒ ⓓ |
| 104 | ⓐ ⓑ ⓒ ⓓ | 124 | ⓐ ⓑ ⓒ ⓓ | 144 | ⓐ ⓑ ⓒ ⓓ | 164 | ⓐ ⓑ ⓒ ⓓ | 184 | ⓐ ⓑ ⓒ ⓓ |
| 105 | ⓐ ⓑ ⓒ ⓓ | 125 | ⓐ ⓑ ⓒ ⓓ | 145 | ⓐ ⓑ ⓒ ⓓ | 165 | ⓐ ⓑ ⓒ ⓓ | 185 | ⓐ ⓑ ⓒ ⓓ |
| 106 | ⓐ ⓑ ⓒ ⓓ | 126 | ⓐ ⓑ ⓒ ⓓ | 146 | ⓐ ⓑ ⓒ ⓓ | 166 | ⓐ ⓑ ⓒ ⓓ | 186 | ⓐ ⓑ ⓒ ⓓ |
| 107 | ⓐ ⓑ ⓒ ⓓ | 127 | ⓐ ⓑ ⓒ ⓓ | 147 | ⓐ ⓑ ⓒ ⓓ | 167 | ⓐ ⓑ ⓒ ⓓ | 187 | ⓐ ⓑ ⓒ ⓓ |
| 108 | ⓐ ⓑ ⓒ ⓓ | 128 | ⓐ ⓑ ⓒ ⓓ | 148 | ⓐ ⓑ ⓒ ⓓ | 168 | ⓐ ⓑ ⓒ ⓓ | 188 | ⓐ ⓑ ⓒ ⓓ |
| 109 | ⓐ ⓑ ⓒ ⓓ | 129 | ⓐ ⓑ ⓒ ⓓ | 149 | ⓐ ⓑ ⓒ ⓓ | 169 | ⓐ ⓑ ⓒ ⓓ | 189 | ⓐ ⓑ ⓒ ⓓ |
| 110 | ⓐ ⓑ ⓒ ⓓ | 130 | ⓐ ⓑ ⓒ ⓓ | 150 | ⓐ ⓑ ⓒ ⓓ | 170 | ⓐ ⓑ ⓒ ⓓ | 190 | ⓐ ⓑ ⓒ ⓓ |
| 111 | ⓐ ⓑ ⓒ ⓓ | 131 | ⓐ ⓑ ⓒ ⓓ | 151 | ⓐ ⓑ ⓒ ⓓ | 171 | ⓐ ⓑ ⓒ ⓓ | 191 | ⓐ ⓑ ⓒ ⓓ |
| 112 | ⓐ ⓑ ⓒ ⓓ | 132 | ⓐ ⓑ ⓒ ⓓ | 152 | ⓐ ⓑ ⓒ ⓓ | 172 | ⓐ ⓑ ⓒ ⓓ | 192 | ⓐ ⓑ ⓒ ⓓ |
| 113 | ⓐ ⓑ ⓒ ⓓ | 133 | ⓐ ⓑ ⓒ ⓓ | 153 | ⓐ ⓑ ⓒ ⓓ | 173 | ⓐ ⓑ ⓒ ⓓ | 193 | ⓐ ⓑ ⓒ ⓓ |
| 114 | ⓐ ⓑ ⓒ ⓓ | 134 | ⓐ ⓑ ⓒ ⓓ | 154 | ⓐ ⓑ ⓒ ⓓ | 174 | ⓐ ⓑ ⓒ ⓓ | 194 | ⓐ ⓑ ⓒ ⓓ |
| 115 | ⓐ ⓑ ⓒ ⓓ | 135 | ⓐ ⓑ ⓒ ⓓ | 155 | ⓐ ⓑ ⓒ ⓓ | 175 | ⓐ ⓑ ⓒ ⓓ | 195 | ⓐ ⓑ ⓒ ⓓ |
| 116 | ⓐ ⓑ ⓒ ⓓ | 136 | ⓐ ⓑ ⓒ ⓓ | 156 | ⓐ ⓑ ⓒ ⓓ | 176 | ⓐ ⓑ ⓒ ⓓ | 196 | ⓐ ⓑ ⓒ ⓓ |
| 117 | ⓐ ⓑ ⓒ ⓓ | 137 | ⓐ ⓑ ⓒ ⓓ | 157 | ⓐ ⓑ ⓒ ⓓ | 177 | ⓐ ⓑ ⓒ ⓓ | 197 | ⓐ ⓑ ⓒ ⓓ |
| 118 | ⓐ ⓑ ⓒ ⓓ | 138 | ⓐ ⓑ ⓒ ⓓ | 158 | ⓐ ⓑ ⓒ ⓓ | 178 | ⓐ ⓑ ⓒ ⓓ | 198 | ⓐ ⓑ ⓒ ⓓ |
| 119 | ⓐ ⓑ ⓒ ⓓ | 139 | ⓐ ⓑ ⓒ ⓓ | 159 | ⓐ ⓑ ⓒ ⓓ | 179 | ⓐ ⓑ ⓒ ⓓ | 199 | ⓐ ⓑ ⓒ ⓓ |
| 120 | ⓐ ⓑ ⓒ ⓓ | 140 | ⓐ ⓑ ⓒ ⓓ | 160 | ⓐ ⓑ ⓒ ⓓ | 180 | ⓐ ⓑ ⓒ ⓓ | 200 | ⓐ ⓑ ⓒ ⓓ |

### Test 10 (Part 5~7)

| No. | Answer | No. | Answer | No. | Answer | No. | Answer | No. | Answer |
|---|---|---|---|---|---|---|---|---|---|
| 101 | ⓐ ⓑ ⓒ ⓓ | 121 | ⓐ ⓑ ⓒ ⓓ | 141 | ⓐ ⓑ ⓒ ⓓ | 161 | ⓐ ⓑ ⓒ ⓓ | 181 | ⓐ ⓑ ⓒ ⓓ |
| 102 | ⓐ ⓑ ⓒ ⓓ | 122 | ⓐ ⓑ ⓒ ⓓ | 142 | ⓐ ⓑ ⓒ ⓓ | 162 | ⓐ ⓑ ⓒ ⓓ | 182 | ⓐ ⓑ ⓒ ⓓ |
| 103 | ⓐ ⓑ ⓒ ⓓ | 123 | ⓐ ⓑ ⓒ ⓓ | 143 | ⓐ ⓑ ⓒ ⓓ | 163 | ⓐ ⓑ ⓒ ⓓ | 183 | ⓐ ⓑ ⓒ ⓓ |
| 104 | ⓐ ⓑ ⓒ ⓓ | 124 | ⓐ ⓑ ⓒ ⓓ | 144 | ⓐ ⓑ ⓒ ⓓ | 164 | ⓐ ⓑ ⓒ ⓓ | 184 | ⓐ ⓑ ⓒ ⓓ |
| 105 | ⓐ ⓑ ⓒ ⓓ | 125 | ⓐ ⓑ ⓒ ⓓ | 145 | ⓐ ⓑ ⓒ ⓓ | 165 | ⓐ ⓑ ⓒ ⓓ | 185 | ⓐ ⓑ ⓒ ⓓ |
| 106 | ⓐ ⓑ ⓒ ⓓ | 126 | ⓐ ⓑ ⓒ ⓓ | 146 | ⓐ ⓑ ⓒ ⓓ | 166 | ⓐ ⓑ ⓒ ⓓ | 186 | ⓐ ⓑ ⓒ ⓓ |
| 107 | ⓐ ⓑ ⓒ ⓓ | 127 | ⓐ ⓑ ⓒ ⓓ | 147 | ⓐ ⓑ ⓒ ⓓ | 167 | ⓐ ⓑ ⓒ ⓓ | 187 | ⓐ ⓑ ⓒ ⓓ |
| 108 | ⓐ ⓑ ⓒ ⓓ | 128 | ⓐ ⓑ ⓒ ⓓ | 148 | ⓐ ⓑ ⓒ ⓓ | 168 | ⓐ ⓑ ⓒ ⓓ | 188 | ⓐ ⓑ ⓒ ⓓ |
| 109 | ⓐ ⓑ ⓒ ⓓ | 129 | ⓐ ⓑ ⓒ ⓓ | 149 | ⓐ ⓑ ⓒ ⓓ | 169 | ⓐ ⓑ ⓒ ⓓ | 189 | ⓐ ⓑ ⓒ ⓓ |
| 110 | ⓐ ⓑ ⓒ ⓓ | 130 | ⓐ ⓑ ⓒ ⓓ | 150 | ⓐ ⓑ ⓒ ⓓ | 170 | ⓐ ⓑ ⓒ ⓓ | 190 | ⓐ ⓑ ⓒ ⓓ |
| 111 | ⓐ ⓑ ⓒ ⓓ | 131 | ⓐ ⓑ ⓒ ⓓ | 151 | ⓐ ⓑ ⓒ ⓓ | 171 | ⓐ ⓑ ⓒ ⓓ | 191 | ⓐ ⓑ ⓒ ⓓ |
| 112 | ⓐ ⓑ ⓒ ⓓ | 132 | ⓐ ⓑ ⓒ ⓓ | 152 | ⓐ ⓑ ⓒ ⓓ | 172 | ⓐ ⓑ ⓒ ⓓ | 192 | ⓐ ⓑ ⓒ ⓓ |
| 113 | ⓐ ⓑ ⓒ ⓓ | 133 | ⓐ ⓑ ⓒ ⓓ | 153 | ⓐ ⓑ ⓒ ⓓ | 173 | ⓐ ⓑ ⓒ ⓓ | 193 | ⓐ ⓑ ⓒ ⓓ |
| 114 | ⓐ ⓑ ⓒ ⓓ | 134 | ⓐ ⓑ ⓒ ⓓ | 154 | ⓐ ⓑ ⓒ ⓓ | 174 | ⓐ ⓑ ⓒ ⓓ | 194 | ⓐ ⓑ ⓒ ⓓ |
| 115 | ⓐ ⓑ ⓒ ⓓ | 135 | ⓐ ⓑ ⓒ ⓓ | 155 | ⓐ ⓑ ⓒ ⓓ | 175 | ⓐ ⓑ ⓒ ⓓ | 195 | ⓐ ⓑ ⓒ ⓓ |
| 116 | ⓐ ⓑ ⓒ ⓓ | 136 | ⓐ ⓑ ⓒ ⓓ | 156 | ⓐ ⓑ ⓒ ⓓ | 176 | ⓐ ⓑ ⓒ ⓓ | 196 | ⓐ ⓑ ⓒ ⓓ |
| 117 | ⓐ ⓑ ⓒ ⓓ | 137 | ⓐ ⓑ ⓒ ⓓ | 157 | ⓐ ⓑ ⓒ ⓓ | 177 | ⓐ ⓑ ⓒ ⓓ | 197 | ⓐ ⓑ ⓒ ⓓ |
| 118 | ⓐ ⓑ ⓒ ⓓ | 138 | ⓐ ⓑ ⓒ ⓓ | 158 | ⓐ ⓑ ⓒ ⓓ | 178 | ⓐ ⓑ ⓒ ⓓ | 198 | ⓐ ⓑ ⓒ ⓓ |
| 119 | ⓐ ⓑ ⓒ ⓓ | 139 | ⓐ ⓑ ⓒ ⓓ | 159 | ⓐ ⓑ ⓒ ⓓ | 179 | ⓐ ⓑ ⓒ ⓓ | 199 | ⓐ ⓑ ⓒ ⓓ |
| 120 | ⓐ ⓑ ⓒ ⓓ | 140 | ⓐ ⓑ ⓒ ⓓ | 160 | ⓐ ⓑ ⓒ ⓓ | 180 | ⓐ ⓑ ⓒ ⓓ | 200 | ⓐ ⓑ ⓒ ⓓ |

# ANSWER SHEET

## YBM 실전토익 RC 1000

| 수험번호 | | | | | | |
|---|---|---|---|---|---|---|

응시일자 : 20 년 월 일

| 성명 | 한 글 | |
|---|---|---|
| | 한 자 | |
| | 영 자 | |

### Test (Part 5~7)

| | | | | | | | | | |
|---|---|---|---|---|---|---|---|---|---|
| 101 | ⓐ ⓑ ⓒ ⓓ | 121 | ⓐ ⓑ ⓒ ⓓ | 141 | ⓐ ⓑ ⓒ ⓓ | 161 | ⓐ ⓑ ⓒ ⓓ | 181 | ⓐ ⓑ ⓒ ⓓ |
| 102 | ⓐ ⓑ ⓒ ⓓ | 122 | ⓐ ⓑ ⓒ ⓓ | 142 | ⓐ ⓑ ⓒ ⓓ | 162 | ⓐ ⓑ ⓒ ⓓ | 182 | ⓐ ⓑ ⓒ ⓓ |
| 103 | ⓐ ⓑ ⓒ ⓓ | 123 | ⓐ ⓑ ⓒ ⓓ | 143 | ⓐ ⓑ ⓒ ⓓ | 163 | ⓐ ⓑ ⓒ ⓓ | 183 | ⓐ ⓑ ⓒ ⓓ |
| 104 | ⓐ ⓑ ⓒ ⓓ | 124 | ⓐ ⓑ ⓒ ⓓ | 144 | ⓐ ⓑ ⓒ ⓓ | 164 | ⓐ ⓑ ⓒ ⓓ | 184 | ⓐ ⓑ ⓒ ⓓ |
| 105 | ⓐ ⓑ ⓒ ⓓ | 125 | ⓐ ⓑ ⓒ ⓓ | 145 | ⓐ ⓑ ⓒ ⓓ | 165 | ⓐ ⓑ ⓒ ⓓ | 185 | ⓐ ⓑ ⓒ ⓓ |
| 106 | ⓐ ⓑ ⓒ ⓓ | 126 | ⓐ ⓑ ⓒ ⓓ | 146 | ⓐ ⓑ ⓒ ⓓ | 166 | ⓐ ⓑ ⓒ ⓓ | 186 | ⓐ ⓑ ⓒ ⓓ |
| 107 | ⓐ ⓑ ⓒ ⓓ | 127 | ⓐ ⓑ ⓒ ⓓ | 147 | ⓐ ⓑ ⓒ ⓓ | 167 | ⓐ ⓑ ⓒ ⓓ | 187 | ⓐ ⓑ ⓒ ⓓ |
| 108 | ⓐ ⓑ ⓒ ⓓ | 128 | ⓐ ⓑ ⓒ ⓓ | 148 | ⓐ ⓑ ⓒ ⓓ | 168 | ⓐ ⓑ ⓒ ⓓ | 188 | ⓐ ⓑ ⓒ ⓓ |
| 109 | ⓐ ⓑ ⓒ ⓓ | 129 | ⓐ ⓑ ⓒ ⓓ | 149 | ⓐ ⓑ ⓒ ⓓ | 169 | ⓐ ⓑ ⓒ ⓓ | 189 | ⓐ ⓑ ⓒ ⓓ |
| 110 | ⓐ ⓑ ⓒ ⓓ | 130 | ⓐ ⓑ ⓒ ⓓ | 150 | ⓐ ⓑ ⓒ ⓓ | 170 | ⓐ ⓑ ⓒ ⓓ | 190 | ⓐ ⓑ ⓒ ⓓ |
| 111 | ⓐ ⓑ ⓒ ⓓ | 131 | ⓐ ⓑ ⓒ ⓓ | 151 | ⓐ ⓑ ⓒ ⓓ | 171 | ⓐ ⓑ ⓒ ⓓ | 191 | ⓐ ⓑ ⓒ ⓓ |
| 112 | ⓐ ⓑ ⓒ ⓓ | 132 | ⓐ ⓑ ⓒ ⓓ | 152 | ⓐ ⓑ ⓒ ⓓ | 172 | ⓐ ⓑ ⓒ ⓓ | 192 | ⓐ ⓑ ⓒ ⓓ |
| 113 | ⓐ ⓑ ⓒ ⓓ | 133 | ⓐ ⓑ ⓒ ⓓ | 153 | ⓐ ⓑ ⓒ ⓓ | 173 | ⓐ ⓑ ⓒ ⓓ | 193 | ⓐ ⓑ ⓒ ⓓ |
| 114 | ⓐ ⓑ ⓒ ⓓ | 134 | ⓐ ⓑ ⓒ ⓓ | 154 | ⓐ ⓑ ⓒ ⓓ | 174 | ⓐ ⓑ ⓒ ⓓ | 194 | ⓐ ⓑ ⓒ ⓓ |
| 115 | ⓐ ⓑ ⓒ ⓓ | 135 | ⓐ ⓑ ⓒ ⓓ | 155 | ⓐ ⓑ ⓒ ⓓ | 175 | ⓐ ⓑ ⓒ ⓓ | 195 | ⓐ ⓑ ⓒ ⓓ |
| 116 | ⓐ ⓑ ⓒ ⓓ | 136 | ⓐ ⓑ ⓒ ⓓ | 156 | ⓐ ⓑ ⓒ ⓓ | 176 | ⓐ ⓑ ⓒ ⓓ | 196 | ⓐ ⓑ ⓒ ⓓ |
| 117 | ⓐ ⓑ ⓒ ⓓ | 137 | ⓐ ⓑ ⓒ ⓓ | 157 | ⓐ ⓑ ⓒ ⓓ | 177 | ⓐ ⓑ ⓒ ⓓ | 197 | ⓐ ⓑ ⓒ ⓓ |
| 118 | ⓐ ⓑ ⓒ ⓓ | 138 | ⓐ ⓑ ⓒ ⓓ | 158 | ⓐ ⓑ ⓒ ⓓ | 178 | ⓐ ⓑ ⓒ ⓓ | 198 | ⓐ ⓑ ⓒ ⓓ |
| 119 | ⓐ ⓑ ⓒ ⓓ | 139 | ⓐ ⓑ ⓒ ⓓ | 159 | ⓐ ⓑ ⓒ ⓓ | 179 | ⓐ ⓑ ⓒ ⓓ | 199 | ⓐ ⓑ ⓒ ⓓ |
| 120 | ⓐ ⓑ ⓒ ⓓ | 140 | ⓐ ⓑ ⓒ ⓓ | 160 | ⓐ ⓑ ⓒ ⓓ | 180 | ⓐ ⓑ ⓒ ⓓ | 200 | ⓐ ⓑ ⓒ ⓓ |

### Test (Part 5~7)

| | | | | | | | | | |
|---|---|---|---|---|---|---|---|---|---|
| 101 | ⓐ ⓑ ⓒ ⓓ | 121 | ⓐ ⓑ ⓒ ⓓ | 141 | ⓐ ⓑ ⓒ ⓓ | 161 | ⓐ ⓑ ⓒ ⓓ | 181 | ⓐ ⓑ ⓒ ⓓ |
| 102 | ⓐ ⓑ ⓒ ⓓ | 122 | ⓐ ⓑ ⓒ ⓓ | 142 | ⓐ ⓑ ⓒ ⓓ | 162 | ⓐ ⓑ ⓒ ⓓ | 182 | ⓐ ⓑ ⓒ ⓓ |
| 103 | ⓐ ⓑ ⓒ ⓓ | 123 | ⓐ ⓑ ⓒ ⓓ | 143 | ⓐ ⓑ ⓒ ⓓ | 163 | ⓐ ⓑ ⓒ ⓓ | 183 | ⓐ ⓑ ⓒ ⓓ |
| 104 | ⓐ ⓑ ⓒ ⓓ | 124 | ⓐ ⓑ ⓒ ⓓ | 144 | ⓐ ⓑ ⓒ ⓓ | 164 | ⓐ ⓑ ⓒ ⓓ | 184 | ⓐ ⓑ ⓒ ⓓ |
| 105 | ⓐ ⓑ ⓒ ⓓ | 125 | ⓐ ⓑ ⓒ ⓓ | 145 | ⓐ ⓑ ⓒ ⓓ | 165 | ⓐ ⓑ ⓒ ⓓ | 185 | ⓐ ⓑ ⓒ ⓓ |
| 106 | ⓐ ⓑ ⓒ ⓓ | 126 | ⓐ ⓑ ⓒ ⓓ | 146 | ⓐ ⓑ ⓒ ⓓ | 166 | ⓐ ⓑ ⓒ ⓓ | 186 | ⓐ ⓑ ⓒ ⓓ |
| 107 | ⓐ ⓑ ⓒ ⓓ | 127 | ⓐ ⓑ ⓒ ⓓ | 147 | ⓐ ⓑ ⓒ ⓓ | 167 | ⓐ ⓑ ⓒ ⓓ | 187 | ⓐ ⓑ ⓒ ⓓ |
| 108 | ⓐ ⓑ ⓒ ⓓ | 128 | ⓐ ⓑ ⓒ ⓓ | 148 | ⓐ ⓑ ⓒ ⓓ | 168 | ⓐ ⓑ ⓒ ⓓ | 188 | ⓐ ⓑ ⓒ ⓓ |
| 109 | ⓐ ⓑ ⓒ ⓓ | 129 | ⓐ ⓑ ⓒ ⓓ | 149 | ⓐ ⓑ ⓒ ⓓ | 169 | ⓐ ⓑ ⓒ ⓓ | 189 | ⓐ ⓑ ⓒ ⓓ |
| 110 | ⓐ ⓑ ⓒ ⓓ | 130 | ⓐ ⓑ ⓒ ⓓ | 150 | ⓐ ⓑ ⓒ ⓓ | 170 | ⓐ ⓑ ⓒ ⓓ | 190 | ⓐ ⓑ ⓒ ⓓ |
| 111 | ⓐ ⓑ ⓒ ⓓ | 131 | ⓐ ⓑ ⓒ ⓓ | 151 | ⓐ ⓑ ⓒ ⓓ | 171 | ⓐ ⓑ ⓒ ⓓ | 191 | ⓐ ⓑ ⓒ ⓓ |
| 112 | ⓐ ⓑ ⓒ ⓓ | 132 | ⓐ ⓑ ⓒ ⓓ | 152 | ⓐ ⓑ ⓒ ⓓ | 172 | ⓐ ⓑ ⓒ ⓓ | 192 | ⓐ ⓑ ⓒ ⓓ |
| 113 | ⓐ ⓑ ⓒ ⓓ | 133 | ⓐ ⓑ ⓒ ⓓ | 153 | ⓐ ⓑ ⓒ ⓓ | 173 | ⓐ ⓑ ⓒ ⓓ | 193 | ⓐ ⓑ ⓒ ⓓ |
| 114 | ⓐ ⓑ ⓒ ⓓ | 134 | ⓐ ⓑ ⓒ ⓓ | 154 | ⓐ ⓑ ⓒ ⓓ | 174 | ⓐ ⓑ ⓒ ⓓ | 194 | ⓐ ⓑ ⓒ ⓓ |
| 115 | ⓐ ⓑ ⓒ ⓓ | 135 | ⓐ ⓑ ⓒ ⓓ | 155 | ⓐ ⓑ ⓒ ⓓ | 175 | ⓐ ⓑ ⓒ ⓓ | 195 | ⓐ ⓑ ⓒ ⓓ |
| 116 | ⓐ ⓑ ⓒ ⓓ | 136 | ⓐ ⓑ ⓒ ⓓ | 156 | ⓐ ⓑ ⓒ ⓓ | 176 | ⓐ ⓑ ⓒ ⓓ | 196 | ⓐ ⓑ ⓒ ⓓ |
| 117 | ⓐ ⓑ ⓒ ⓓ | 137 | ⓐ ⓑ ⓒ ⓓ | 157 | ⓐ ⓑ ⓒ ⓓ | 177 | ⓐ ⓑ ⓒ ⓓ | 197 | ⓐ ⓑ ⓒ ⓓ |
| 118 | ⓐ ⓑ ⓒ ⓓ | 138 | ⓐ ⓑ ⓒ ⓓ | 158 | ⓐ ⓑ ⓒ ⓓ | 178 | ⓐ ⓑ ⓒ ⓓ | 198 | ⓐ ⓑ ⓒ ⓓ |
| 119 | ⓐ ⓑ ⓒ ⓓ | 139 | ⓐ ⓑ ⓒ ⓓ | 159 | ⓐ ⓑ ⓒ ⓓ | 179 | ⓐ ⓑ ⓒ ⓓ | 199 | ⓐ ⓑ ⓒ ⓓ |
| 120 | ⓐ ⓑ ⓒ ⓓ | 140 | ⓐ ⓑ ⓒ ⓓ | 160 | ⓐ ⓑ ⓒ ⓓ | 180 | ⓐ ⓑ ⓒ ⓓ | 200 | ⓐ ⓑ ⓒ ⓓ |

# ANSWER SHEET

## YBM 실전토익 RC 1000

| 수험번호 | | | | | | |
|---|---|---|---|---|---|---|

응시일자 : 20 년 월 일

| 성명 | 한 글 | |
|---|---|---|
| | 한 자 | |
| | 영 자 | |

### Test (Part 5~7)

| No. | | No. | | No. | | No. | | No. | |
|---|---|---|---|---|---|---|---|---|---|
| 101 | ⓐ ⓑ ⓒ ⓓ | 121 | ⓐ ⓑ ⓒ ⓓ | 141 | ⓐ ⓑ ⓒ ⓓ | 161 | ⓐ ⓑ ⓒ ⓓ | 181 | ⓐ ⓑ ⓒ ⓓ |
| 102 | ⓐ ⓑ ⓒ ⓓ | 122 | ⓐ ⓑ ⓒ ⓓ | 142 | ⓐ ⓑ ⓒ ⓓ | 162 | ⓐ ⓑ ⓒ ⓓ | 182 | ⓐ ⓑ ⓒ ⓓ |
| 103 | ⓐ ⓑ ⓒ ⓓ | 123 | ⓐ ⓑ ⓒ ⓓ | 143 | ⓐ ⓑ ⓒ ⓓ | 163 | ⓐ ⓑ ⓒ ⓓ | 183 | ⓐ ⓑ ⓒ ⓓ |
| 104 | ⓐ ⓑ ⓒ ⓓ | 124 | ⓐ ⓑ ⓒ ⓓ | 144 | ⓐ ⓑ ⓒ ⓓ | 164 | ⓐ ⓑ ⓒ ⓓ | 184 | ⓐ ⓑ ⓒ ⓓ |
| 105 | ⓐ ⓑ ⓒ ⓓ | 125 | ⓐ ⓑ ⓒ ⓓ | 145 | ⓐ ⓑ ⓒ ⓓ | 165 | ⓐ ⓑ ⓒ ⓓ | 185 | ⓐ ⓑ ⓒ ⓓ |
| 106 | ⓐ ⓑ ⓒ ⓓ | 126 | ⓐ ⓑ ⓒ ⓓ | 146 | ⓐ ⓑ ⓒ ⓓ | 166 | ⓐ ⓑ ⓒ ⓓ | 186 | ⓐ ⓑ ⓒ ⓓ |
| 107 | ⓐ ⓑ ⓒ ⓓ | 127 | ⓐ ⓑ ⓒ ⓓ | 147 | ⓐ ⓑ ⓒ ⓓ | 167 | ⓐ ⓑ ⓒ ⓓ | 187 | ⓐ ⓑ ⓒ ⓓ |
| 108 | ⓐ ⓑ ⓒ ⓓ | 128 | ⓐ ⓑ ⓒ ⓓ | 148 | ⓐ ⓑ ⓒ ⓓ | 168 | ⓐ ⓑ ⓒ ⓓ | 188 | ⓐ ⓑ ⓒ ⓓ |
| 109 | ⓐ ⓑ ⓒ ⓓ | 129 | ⓐ ⓑ ⓒ ⓓ | 149 | ⓐ ⓑ ⓒ ⓓ | 169 | ⓐ ⓑ ⓒ ⓓ | 189 | ⓐ ⓑ ⓒ ⓓ |
| 110 | ⓐ ⓑ ⓒ ⓓ | 130 | ⓐ ⓑ ⓒ ⓓ | 150 | ⓐ ⓑ ⓒ ⓓ | 170 | ⓐ ⓑ ⓒ ⓓ | 190 | ⓐ ⓑ ⓒ ⓓ |
| 111 | ⓐ ⓑ ⓒ ⓓ | 131 | ⓐ ⓑ ⓒ ⓓ | 151 | ⓐ ⓑ ⓒ ⓓ | 171 | ⓐ ⓑ ⓒ ⓓ | 191 | ⓐ ⓑ ⓒ ⓓ |
| 112 | ⓐ ⓑ ⓒ ⓓ | 132 | ⓐ ⓑ ⓒ ⓓ | 152 | ⓐ ⓑ ⓒ ⓓ | 172 | ⓐ ⓑ ⓒ ⓓ | 192 | ⓐ ⓑ ⓒ ⓓ |
| 113 | ⓐ ⓑ ⓒ ⓓ | 133 | ⓐ ⓑ ⓒ ⓓ | 153 | ⓐ ⓑ ⓒ ⓓ | 173 | ⓐ ⓑ ⓒ ⓓ | 193 | ⓐ ⓑ ⓒ ⓓ |
| 114 | ⓐ ⓑ ⓒ ⓓ | 134 | ⓐ ⓑ ⓒ ⓓ | 154 | ⓐ ⓑ ⓒ ⓓ | 174 | ⓐ ⓑ ⓒ ⓓ | 194 | ⓐ ⓑ ⓒ ⓓ |
| 115 | ⓐ ⓑ ⓒ ⓓ | 135 | ⓐ ⓑ ⓒ ⓓ | 155 | ⓐ ⓑ ⓒ ⓓ | 175 | ⓐ ⓑ ⓒ ⓓ | 195 | ⓐ ⓑ ⓒ ⓓ |
| 116 | ⓐ ⓑ ⓒ ⓓ | 136 | ⓐ ⓑ ⓒ ⓓ | 156 | ⓐ ⓑ ⓒ ⓓ | 176 | ⓐ ⓑ ⓒ ⓓ | 196 | ⓐ ⓑ ⓒ ⓓ |
| 117 | ⓐ ⓑ ⓒ ⓓ | 137 | ⓐ ⓑ ⓒ ⓓ | 157 | ⓐ ⓑ ⓒ ⓓ | 177 | ⓐ ⓑ ⓒ ⓓ | 197 | ⓐ ⓑ ⓒ ⓓ |
| 118 | ⓐ ⓑ ⓒ ⓓ | 138 | ⓐ ⓑ ⓒ ⓓ | 158 | ⓐ ⓑ ⓒ ⓓ | 178 | ⓐ ⓑ ⓒ ⓓ | 198 | ⓐ ⓑ ⓒ ⓓ |
| 119 | ⓐ ⓑ ⓒ ⓓ | 139 | ⓐ ⓑ ⓒ ⓓ | 159 | ⓐ ⓑ ⓒ ⓓ | 179 | ⓐ ⓑ ⓒ ⓓ | 199 | ⓐ ⓑ ⓒ ⓓ |
| 120 | ⓐ ⓑ ⓒ ⓓ | 140 | ⓐ ⓑ ⓒ ⓓ | 160 | ⓐ ⓑ ⓒ ⓓ | 180 | ⓐ ⓑ ⓒ ⓓ | 200 | ⓐ ⓑ ⓒ ⓓ |


### Test (Part 5~7)

| No. | | No. | | No. | | No. | | No. | |
|---|---|---|---|---|---|---|---|---|---|
| 101 | ⓐ ⓑ ⓒ ⓓ | 121 | ⓐ ⓑ ⓒ ⓓ | 141 | ⓐ ⓑ ⓒ ⓓ | 161 | ⓐ ⓑ ⓒ ⓓ | 181 | ⓐ ⓑ ⓒ ⓓ |
| 102 | ⓐ ⓑ ⓒ ⓓ | 122 | ⓐ ⓑ ⓒ ⓓ | 142 | ⓐ ⓑ ⓒ ⓓ | 162 | ⓐ ⓑ ⓒ ⓓ | 182 | ⓐ ⓑ ⓒ ⓓ |
| 103 | ⓐ ⓑ ⓒ ⓓ | 123 | ⓐ ⓑ ⓒ ⓓ | 143 | ⓐ ⓑ ⓒ ⓓ | 163 | ⓐ ⓑ ⓒ ⓓ | 183 | ⓐ ⓑ ⓒ ⓓ |
| 104 | ⓐ ⓑ ⓒ ⓓ | 124 | ⓐ ⓑ ⓒ ⓓ | 144 | ⓐ ⓑ ⓒ ⓓ | 164 | ⓐ ⓑ ⓒ ⓓ | 184 | ⓐ ⓑ ⓒ ⓓ |
| 105 | ⓐ ⓑ ⓒ ⓓ | 125 | ⓐ ⓑ ⓒ ⓓ | 145 | ⓐ ⓑ ⓒ ⓓ | 165 | ⓐ ⓑ ⓒ ⓓ | 185 | ⓐ ⓑ ⓒ ⓓ |
| 106 | ⓐ ⓑ ⓒ ⓓ | 126 | ⓐ ⓑ ⓒ ⓓ | 146 | ⓐ ⓑ ⓒ ⓓ | 166 | ⓐ ⓑ ⓒ ⓓ | 186 | ⓐ ⓑ ⓒ ⓓ |
| 107 | ⓐ ⓑ ⓒ ⓓ | 127 | ⓐ ⓑ ⓒ ⓓ | 147 | ⓐ ⓑ ⓒ ⓓ | 167 | ⓐ ⓑ ⓒ ⓓ | 187 | ⓐ ⓑ ⓒ ⓓ |
| 108 | ⓐ ⓑ ⓒ ⓓ | 128 | ⓐ ⓑ ⓒ ⓓ | 148 | ⓐ ⓑ ⓒ ⓓ | 168 | ⓐ ⓑ ⓒ ⓓ | 188 | ⓐ ⓑ ⓒ ⓓ |
| 109 | ⓐ ⓑ ⓒ ⓓ | 129 | ⓐ ⓑ ⓒ ⓓ | 149 | ⓐ ⓑ ⓒ ⓓ | 169 | ⓐ ⓑ ⓒ ⓓ | 189 | ⓐ ⓑ ⓒ ⓓ |
| 110 | ⓐ ⓑ ⓒ ⓓ | 130 | ⓐ ⓑ ⓒ ⓓ | 150 | ⓐ ⓑ ⓒ ⓓ | 170 | ⓐ ⓑ ⓒ ⓓ | 190 | ⓐ ⓑ ⓒ ⓓ |
| 111 | ⓐ ⓑ ⓒ ⓓ | 131 | ⓐ ⓑ ⓒ ⓓ | 151 | ⓐ ⓑ ⓒ ⓓ | 171 | ⓐ ⓑ ⓒ ⓓ | 191 | ⓐ ⓑ ⓒ ⓓ |
| 112 | ⓐ ⓑ ⓒ ⓓ | 132 | ⓐ ⓑ ⓒ ⓓ | 152 | ⓐ ⓑ ⓒ ⓓ | 172 | ⓐ ⓑ ⓒ ⓓ | 192 | ⓐ ⓑ ⓒ ⓓ |
| 113 | ⓐ ⓑ ⓒ ⓓ | 133 | ⓐ ⓑ ⓒ ⓓ | 153 | ⓐ ⓑ ⓒ ⓓ | 173 | ⓐ ⓑ ⓒ ⓓ | 193 | ⓐ ⓑ ⓒ ⓓ |
| 114 | ⓐ ⓑ ⓒ ⓓ | 134 | ⓐ ⓑ ⓒ ⓓ | 154 | ⓐ ⓑ ⓒ ⓓ | 174 | ⓐ ⓑ ⓒ ⓓ | 194 | ⓐ ⓑ ⓒ ⓓ |
| 115 | ⓐ ⓑ ⓒ ⓓ | 135 | ⓐ ⓑ ⓒ ⓓ | 155 | ⓐ ⓑ ⓒ ⓓ | 175 | ⓐ ⓑ ⓒ ⓓ | 195 | ⓐ ⓑ ⓒ ⓓ |
| 116 | ⓐ ⓑ ⓒ ⓓ | 136 | ⓐ ⓑ ⓒ ⓓ | 156 | ⓐ ⓑ ⓒ ⓓ | 176 | ⓐ ⓑ ⓒ ⓓ | 196 | ⓐ ⓑ ⓒ ⓓ |
| 117 | ⓐ ⓑ ⓒ ⓓ | 137 | ⓐ ⓑ ⓒ ⓓ | 157 | ⓐ ⓑ ⓒ ⓓ | 177 | ⓐ ⓑ ⓒ ⓓ | 197 | ⓐ ⓑ ⓒ ⓓ |
| 118 | ⓐ ⓑ ⓒ ⓓ | 138 | ⓐ ⓑ ⓒ ⓓ | 158 | ⓐ ⓑ ⓒ ⓓ | 178 | ⓐ ⓑ ⓒ ⓓ | 198 | ⓐ ⓑ ⓒ ⓓ |
| 119 | ⓐ ⓑ ⓒ ⓓ | 139 | ⓐ ⓑ ⓒ ⓓ | 159 | ⓐ ⓑ ⓒ ⓓ | 179 | ⓐ ⓑ ⓒ ⓓ | 199 | ⓐ ⓑ ⓒ ⓓ |
| 120 | ⓐ ⓑ ⓒ ⓓ | 140 | ⓐ ⓑ ⓒ ⓓ | 160 | ⓐ ⓑ ⓒ ⓓ | 180 | ⓐ ⓑ ⓒ ⓓ | 200 | ⓐ ⓑ ⓒ ⓓ |

토익주관사

YBM

# YBM 실전토익 RC1000

전면 개정판

1

정답 및 해설

# YBM 실전토익 RC1000

# 1

## 정답 및 해설

# TEST 1

| | | | | |
|---|---|---|---|---|
| 101 (A) | 102 (C) | 103 (A) | 104 (B) | 105 (D) |
| 106 (C) | 107 (C) | 108 (B) | 109 (D) | 110 (A) |
| 111 (B) | 112 (B) | 113 (D) | 114 (B) | 115 (C) |
| 116 (A) | 117 (D) | 118 (A) | 119 (D) | 120 (C) |
| 121 (B) | 122 (A) | 123 (B) | 124 (C) | 125 (B) |
| 126 (C) | 127 (D) | 128 (A) | 129 (D) | 130 (C) |
| 131 (B) | 132 (D) | 133 (A) | 134 (D) | 135 (C) |
| 136 (B) | 137 (C) | 138 (A) | 139 (D) | 140 (C) |
| 141 (B) | 142 (A) | 143 (A) | 144 (D) | 145 (A) |
| 146 (B) | 147 (C) | 148 (D) | 149 (D) | 150 (B) |
| 151 (A) | 152 (C) | 153 (B) | 154 (A) | 155 (B) |
| 156 (B) | 157 (A) | 158 (C) | 159 (B) | 160 (B) |
| 161 (A) | 162 (C) | 163 (D) | 164 (C) | 165 (B) |
| 166 (D) | 167 (C) | 168 (B) | 169 (A) | 170 (A) |
| 171 (D) | 172 (D) | 173 (D) | 174 (C) | 175 (C) |
| 176 (A) | 177 (B) | 178 (D) | 179 (C) | 180 (D) |
| 181 (C) | 182 (B) | 183 (D) | 184 (B) | 185 (A) |
| 186 (C) | 187 (A) | 188 (B) | 189 (C) | 190 (D) |
| 191 (B) | 192 (D) | 193 (B) | 194 (B) | 195 (C) |
| 196 (D) | 197 (D) | 198 (C) | 199 (A) | 200 (B) |

## PART 5

### 101 명사 자리 _ 전치사의 목적어

번역 공식 역사 건축물의 변경 작업은 반드시 시 의회에 사전 공지가 되어야 한다.

해설 빈칸은 전치사 of의 목적어 역할을 할 명사가 필요한 자리이므로 (A) modifications가 정답이다. (B) modifying은 동명사로 쓰이면 전치사 of 뒤에 올 수 있지만 modify가 타동사이기 때문에 목적어가 필요한데 목적어 없이 전치사구가 이어지고 있으므로 오답이다. (C) modified와 (D) modifies는 동사 형태이므로 전치사 뒤에 올 수 없다.

어휘 advance 사전의 notice 공지 official 공식의 structure 건축물 modification 변경 modify 변경하다

### 102 인칭대명사 _ 소유격

번역 설립자가 은퇴하자마자, 그 잡지는 그의 업적에 관한 특별 기사를 냈다.

해설 명사 achievements를 수식할 수 있는 소유격 대명사 (C) his가 정답이다. (A) he는 주격 대명사, (B) him은 목적격 대명사, (D) himself는 재귀대명사로 모두 명사를 수식할 수 없다.

어휘 founder 설립자 retirement 은퇴 achievement 업적, 성과

### 103 부사 자리 _ 동사 수식

번역 많은 레스토랑들이 모바일 앱을 이용하여 직원 근무 일정을 성공적으로 관리하고 있다.

해설 현재완료 진행형 동사인 have been using 사이에 빈칸이 있으므로 동사를 수식할 수 있는 부사 (A) successfully가 정답이다. have been using이 완전한 형태의 동사구이므로 (B) succeeding, (C) succeeded, (D) successes가 사이에 들어갈 수 없다.

어휘 successfully 성공적으로 succeed 성공하다, 뒤를 잇다 success 성공

### 104 의문사+to부정사

번역 메나 호텔은 경영진이 고객들을 위한 편안한 공간을 만들어 내는 방법을 이해하고 있기 때문에 번성해 왔다.

해설 동사 understands의 목적어 자리에 빈칸과 to부정사구가 이어지고 있으므로 to부정사와 함께 명사구를 구성할 수 있는 게 필요하다. 의문사는 「의문사+to부정사」 형태로 명사구를 구성할 수 있으므로 의문사 (B) how가 정답이다. 「how+to부정사」는 '~하는 방법'이라는 의미이다. (A) yet은 부사, (C) about은 전치사, (D) that은 대명사 혹은 접속사로 to부정사와 함께 명사구를 구성하지 않는다.

어휘 prosper 번성하다 management 경영진, 경영 create 만들어 내다 comfortable 편안한

### 105 부사 어휘

번역 콕스 씨의 컴퓨터는 너무 낡아서 새 화상 회의 소프트웨어를 작동시킬 수 없다.

해설 빈칸 뒤에 위치한 old that과 함께 '너무 ~해서 …하다'를 의미하는 「so+형용사+that절」을 구성해야 알맞으므로 (D) so가 정답이다. (A) too는 to부정사와 함께 「too+형용사+to부정사」 형태로 '너무 ~해서 …할 수 없다'라는 의미로 사용된다.

어휘 run 작동시키다 teleconferencing 화상 회의

### 106 to부정사 _ 목적격 보어

번역 포커스 그룹 참가자들은 그 그룹의 논의 사항들을 기밀로 유지하도록 지시받는다.

해설 동사 instruct는 to부정사를 목적격 보어로 취하는 동사로, 「instruct+목적어+to부정사」의 형태로 쓰인다. 따라서 이를 수동태로 나타낼 경우, 「be동사+instructed+to부정사」의 형태가 되므로 to부정사 (C) to keep이 정답이다. 「be동사+instructed+to부정사(~하도록 지시받다)」를 묶어서 기억하자.

어휘 participant 참가자 instruct 지시하다 confidential 기밀의

## 107 전치사 어휘

번역 저희 웹사이트를 방문하여 저희 제품에 사용된 재료의 출처를 알아보세요.

해설 과거분사 used가 이끄는 분사구가 명사 ingredients를 수식하는 구조이므로 재료(ingredients)와 제품(products) 사이의 관계를 나타낼 전치사가 필요하다. 재료는 제품 안에 들어가는 것이므로 '~ 안에'를 뜻하는 (C) in이 정답이다.

어휘 source 출처, 원천 ingredient 재료, 성분

## 108 형용사 어휘

번역 비영리 단체에 기부하는 사람들은 주의 새로운 세금 정책에 따라 넉넉한 세금 혜택을 받는다.

해설 복합명사 tax benefits를 수식해 어느 정도의 세금 혜택을 받는지를 나타낼 형용사가 필요하므로 '넉넉한, 후한' 등을 뜻하는 (B) generous가 정답이다.

어휘 donor 기부자 nonprofit 비영리의 organization 단체, 기관 benefit 혜택, 이득 policy 정책, 방침 dominant 지배적인 enthusiastic 열정적인 respective 각각의

## 109 접속사 자리 _ 부사절 접속사

번역 사무실 개조 공사가 완료될 때까지, 대부분의 몬테스 주식회사 직원들은 원격 근무를 할 것이다.

해설 빈칸 뒤에 완전한 절이 두 개 있으므로 빈칸부터 콤마(,)까지를 부사절로 만들어 주는 부사절 접속사가 필요하다. 따라서 부사절 접속사 (D) Until이 정답이다. (A) Finally는 부사, (B) During과 (C) Around는 전치사이다.

어휘 renovation 개조, 보수 complete 완료하다 remotely 원격으로

## 110 형용사 자리 _ 명사 수식

번역 스텝빌 스타 상은 지역 사회에 의미 있는 공헌을 해 온 시민들을 기린다.

해설 빈칸이 동사 have made와 목적어인 명사 contributions 사이에 있으므로 명사 contributions를 수식할 형용사 자리이다. 따라서 형용사 (A) meaningful이 정답이다.

어휘 honor 기리다, 영예를 주다 contribution 공헌, 기여 meaningful 의미 있는 mean 의미하다 meaningfully 의미 있게

## 111 명사 어휘

번역 드레이턴 슈퍼마켓 체인은 자사의 냉동식품 운송이 최신식 냉동 트럭을 통해 이루어진다고 주장한다.

해설 빈칸에는 냉동 트럭으로 할 수 있는 일을 나타내는 명사가 들어가야 하는데, '냉동 트럭으로 냉동식품을 운송한다'는 내용이 되어야 자연스러우므로 '운송, 수송'을 뜻하는 (B) transport가 정답이다.

어휘 claim 주장하다 carry out 실시하다, 수행하다 via ~을 통해 state-of-the-art 최신식의 variety 다양성 appraisal 평가 freshness 신선함

## 112 명사 자리 _ 어휘

번역 리틀턴 역사 기록 보관소는 방문객들이 소장품을 복사하는 것을 금지하고 있다.

해설 빈칸이 정관사 the와 전치사 of 사이에 있으므로 명사 자리인데, 동사 prohibits의 목적어로 금지되는 행위를 의미해야 알맞으므로 '복사'를 뜻하는 명사 (B) photocopying이 정답이다. (A) photocopier(복사기)와 (D) photocopy(복사본)도 명사이지만 의미상 적합하지 않다.

어휘 prohibit 금지하다 collection 소장품, 수집품 photocopy 복사하다; 복사본

## 113 형용사 자리 _ 주격 보어

번역 비록 그 회사가 최근 몇 년 동안 경쟁사들보다 뒤처진 성과를 내긴 했지만, 여전히 수익성이 좋다.

해설 be동사 is 뒤에 있는 빈칸은 주어 it(= the company)을 보충 설명하는 주격 보어 자리이다. '그 회사는 여전히 수익성이 좋다'라는 의미가 되어야 자연스러우므로 '수익성이 좋은'을 뜻하는 형용사 (D) profitable이 정답이다. (A) profit은 명사로 쓰이면 보어 자리에 올 수 있지만 의미가 어색하므로 오답이며, (B) profited가 빈칸에 들어가면 수동태가 되는데, profit을 '이득을 얻다'라는 의미로 쓸 때 수동태로 쓰지 않고 자동사로 사용하므로 오답이다.

어휘 outperform ~보다 나은 성과를 내다 competitor 경쟁사 profit 수익; 이득을 얻다 profitably 수익을 내어, 유익하게

## 114 동사 어휘

번역 시장 조사에 따르면 대부분의 사람들은 하드우드 짐의 회원권 가격 책정이 매우 합리적이라고 여긴다.

해설 빈칸은 「동사+목적어(Hardwood Gym's membership fee pricing)+목적격 보어(reasonable)」 구조에서 동사에 해당하는 자리이므로 형용사(reasonable)를 목적격 보어로 받을 수 있는 (B) consider가 정답이다. 「consider+목적어+목적격 보어」는 '~을 … 하다고 여기다'라는 의미이다.

어휘 pricing 가격 책정 reasonable 합리적인 appreciate 감사하다, 진가를 알아보다 agree 동의하다

## 115 접속사 자리 _ 명사절 접속사

번역 상품이 현재 그곳에 보관되고 있는지와 상관없이, 그 창고는 반드시 야간에 안전하게 지켜져야 한다.

해설 빈칸 뒤에 있는 절 goods are being stored there at the moment를 이끌어 전치사 Regardless of의 목적어 역할을 하는 명사절로 만들어 주는 명사절 접속사가 필요하다. 따라서 명사절 접속사인 (C) whether가 정답이다.

TEST 1

어휘 regardless of ~와 상관없이 store 보관하다 secure 안전하게 지키다 following ~ 후에

### 116 형용사 어휘

번역 소셜 미디어 플랫폼 커넥트라는 휴면 사용자 계정과 관련된 모든 데이터를 1년 후에 삭제한다.

해설 1년 후에 삭제되는 사용자 계정의 특징을 나타낼 형용사가 필요하므로 '휴면의, 사용되지 않는' 등을 뜻하는 (A) inactive가 정답이다.

어휘 associated with ~와 관련된 account 계정 indirect 간접적인 unlikely 있을 법하지 않은 unmistakable 오해의 여지가 없는

### 117 부사 어휘

번역 쇼비아를 통해 라이브 영상을 방송하는 기능은 그 플랫폼에서 가장 많이 요청된 기능이다.

해설 형용사 requested를 수식해 요구되는 정도와 관련된 의미를 나타낼 부사가 필요하므로 '(양 정도가) 심하게, 아주 많이' 등을 뜻하는 (D) heavily가 정답이다.

어휘 broadcast 방송하다 feature 기능, 특징 potentially 잠재적으로 sharply 날카롭게, 급격히

### 118 동사 어휘

번역 효율성 컨설턴트는 우리 생산 과정에서 간소화되어야 하는 부분들을 확인하는 데 도움을 줄 수 있다.

해설 효율성 컨설턴트가 도움을 줄 수 있는 일을 나타낼 동사가 필요하며, '간소화되어야 하는 부분들을 확인하는 데 도움을 줄 수 있다'는 내용이 되어야 자연스러우므로 '확인하다'를 뜻하는 (A) identify가 정답이다.

어휘 efficiency 효율성 process 과정 simplify 간소화하다 prevent 방지하다, 예방하다 ensure 보장하다, 확실히 하다 excel 뛰어나다, 능가하다

### 119 명사/대명사 자리 _ There is+단수 대명사

번역 우리 신임 홍보부장보다 언론의 긍정적인 관심을 끄는 데 더 능숙한 사람은 없다.

해설 빈칸에는 more skilled 이하의 수식을 받는 명사나 대명사가 필요한 자리이며, 뒤에 비교를 나타내는 than이 있으므로 than과 함께 'There is no one … than ~(~보다 더 …한 사람은 없다)' 구문을 구성하는 (D) no one이 정답이다. (A) other는 형용사, (C) whoever는 복합관계대명사로 more skilled 이하의 수식을 받을 수 없으며, (B) anyone은 대명사이지만 위와 같은 구조로 than과 쓰지 않는다.

어휘 skilled 능숙한, 숙련된 positive 긍정적인 attention 관심, 주의 public relations 홍보 whoever ~하는 사람은 누구든

### 120 접속사 자리 _ 부사절 접속사

번역 회의실에 있는 프로젝터가 고장 났었지만, 예정된 회의가 시작되기 전에 IT팀이 수리할 수 있었다.

해설 빈칸 뒤에 완전한 절이 두 개 있으므로 빈칸부터 콤마(,)까지를 부사절로 만들어 주는 부사절 접속사가 필요하며, '비록 회의실에 있는 프로젝터가 고장 났었지만'이라는 의미를 나타내야 알맞으므로 '(비록) ~일지라도'를 뜻하는 부사절 접속사 (C) Although가 정답이다. (A) Unless(~하지 않으면)는 부사절 접속사이지만 의미가 맞지 않고, (B) Besides(~ 외에)와 (D) Amid(~ 가운데, ~ 중에)는 전치사이다.

어휘 break down 고장 나다 fix 수리하다

### 121 명사 어휘

번역 카르데나스 씨는 추가 자격증을 취득함으로써 자신의 진로 전망을 개선하려고 노력하고 있다.

해설 명사 career와 복합명사를 구성해 추가 자격증을 취득함으로써 진로에 대해 개선할 수 있는 것을 나타낼 명사가 필요하므로 '전망, 가망' 등을 뜻하는 (B) prospects가 정답이다.

어휘 improve 개선하다 earn 획득하다, 얻다 additional 추가적인 qualification 자격(증) intention 의도, 목적 selection 선택, 선택 대상 obstacle 장애물

### 122 전치사 어휘

번역 <실버 스워드>의 많은 후기에서 그 영화의 끝 무렵에 나오는 짜릿한 액션 장면에 대해 감독에게 찬사를 보낸다.

해설 the end of the film과 어울려 짜릿한 액션 장면이 나오는 시점과 관련된 의미를 나타낼 전치사가 필요하므로 '~와 가까이'를 뜻하는 (A) near가 정답이다.

어휘 review 후기 give special praise to+명사 ~을 특별히 칭찬하다 thrilling 짜릿한

### 123 부사 어휘

번역 그 인테리어 전문가는 로비 면적을 정확히 측정하는 것이 자신의 설계 과정에서 중요한 부분이었다고 설명했다.

해설 앞에 있는 동명사 measuring을 수식해 로비 면적을 측정하는 방식을 나타낼 부사가 필요하므로 '정확히'를 뜻하는 (B) precisely가 정답이다.

어휘 measure 측정하다 dimensions 면적 planning 설계, 계획 process 과정 extremely 극도로, 대단히 identically 동일하게

### 124 전치사 어휘

번역 소장 미술품이 많지 않음에도 불구하고, 지엘린스키 박물관은 놀라울 정도로 많은 방문객을 지속적으로 끌어들이고 있다.

해설 '소장 미술품이 많지 않은 것'과 '놀라울 정도로 많은 방문객을 지속적으로 끌어들이는 것'은 상반되는 내용이므로 '소장 미술품이 많지 않음

에도 불구하고'와 같은 의미를 나타내야 알맞다. 따라서 '~에도 불구하고'를 뜻하는 전치사 (C) In spite of가 정답이다.

어휘 limited 제한된, 많지 않은 collection 소장(품) consistently 지속적으로 attract 끌어들이다 remarkable 놀라운, 주목할 만한 numbers of 많은 among ~ 사이에서 along with ~와 함께 rather than ~이 아니라, ~ 대신

## 125 동사 자리 _ 수 일치

번역 조 씨가 그 회사를 떠났기 때문에, 사우스 베이 법률 그룹의 또 다른 변호사가 우리의 법률 업무를 총괄하고 있다.

해설 접속사 Now that이 이끄는 절의 주어 Mr. Jo 뒤에 위치한 빈칸은 동사 자리이며, 3인칭 단수 주어 Mr. Jo와 수가 일치되는 동사의 형태인 (B) has departed가 정답이다. (A) departing과 (C) to depart는 동사의 형태가 아니므로 오답이며, (D) depart는 동사이지만 주어와 수가 일치되지 않으므로 오답이다.

어휘 now that (이제) ~이기 때문에 firm 회사 attorney 변호사 oversee 총괄하다, 감독하다 affair 업무, 일

## 126 형용사 자리 _ 명사 수식

번역 주 환경청은 대기 오염을 감소시키는 데 있어 인상적인 진전을 이루었다.

해설 빈칸은 명사 progress를 수식하는 형용사 자리이므로 '인상적인'을 뜻하는 형용사 (C) impressive가 정답이다. (B) impressed도 형용사이지만 '인상을 받은'이라는 의미로 사람에 대해 사용하므로 오답이다.

어휘 agency (정부의) 기관 progress 진척, 진행 reduce 감소시키다 pollution 오염 impressively 인상적으로 impress 인상을 남기다 impression 인상, 감명

## 127 접속사 자리 _ 부사절 접속사

번역 고객들이 이탈리아 레스토랑에 가고 싶어 하지 않을 경우에 대비해 대체 만찬 장소 목록을 작성하십시오.

해설 빈칸 앞뒤에 각각 완전한 절이 있으므로 완전한 두 절을 연결해 줄 접속사가 필요하다. 따라서 '~할 경우에 (대비해)'를 뜻하는 부사절 접속사 (D) in case가 정답이다. (A) after all(결국에는)은 부사, (B) apart from(~ 외에, ~을 제외하고)은 전치사이고, (C) which는 관계대명사로 두 절을 연결할 수 있으나 뒤에 불완전한 절이 온다.

어휘 draw up a list 목록을 작성하다 alternative 대체의 venue (행사) 장소

## 128 전치사 자리 _ 어휘

번역 이력서 작성 워크숍의 인기에 따라, 그 도서관은 구직자들을 위한 다른 행사들의 개최 여부를 결정할 것이다.

해설 빈칸 뒤에 위치한 명사구 the popularity of the résumé writing workshop을 목적어로 취할 전치사가 필요하며, '이력서 작성 워크숍의 인기에 따라'와 같은 조건을 의미해야 알맞으므로 '~에 따라'를 뜻하는 전치사 (A) Depending on이 정답이다. (B) Just as(꼭 ~처럼)는 전치사로 쓰일 수 있지만 의미가 맞지 않으며, (C) Not only는 but also와 함께 '~뿐만 아니라 …도'를 뜻하는 상관접속사를 구성한다. (D) Provided that(만약 ~라면)은 접속사이다.

어휘 popularity 인기 résumé 이력서

## 129 부사 자리 _ 동사 수식 _ 비교급

번역 진광 연구소의 다른 어떤 영업사원도 자사 의료 기기의 장점에 관해 빈센트 콥보다 더 설득력 있게 말하지 못한다.

해설 자동사 speak 뒤에 위치한 빈칸은 speak를 뒤에서 수식하는 부사 자리이며, 비교 대상을 나타내는 than이 있으므로 비교급 부사인 (D) more persuasively가 정답이다.

어휘 advantage 장점 device 기기, 장치 persuasive 설득력 있는 persuasively 설득력 있게

## 130 동사 자리 _ 시제

번역 위틀로우 엔지니어링 사는 지난 5년 동안 대학생들을 대상으로 여름 인턴 근무 프로그램을 실시해 오고 있다.

해설 '지난 5년 동안'을 뜻하는 for the past five years와 같은 전치사구는 '(계속) ~해 오고 있다'를 뜻하는 현재완료 또는 현재완료 진행형 동사와 어울리므로 현재완료 진행형인 (C) has been conducting이 정답이다.

어휘 conduct 실시하다

# PART 6

### 131-134 기사

(5월 19일)—육류 대체품, 즉 고기 같은 맛과 식감을 가진 식물성 식품이 현재 전국적으로 호황을 누리고 있다. 이러한 제품의 시장이 지난 한 해 50% 가까이 성장했으며, 이 제품들은 현재 슈퍼마켓 선반에서 패스트푸드 레스토랑에 이르기까지 131 **아주** 다양한 환경에서 찾아볼 수 있다.

이러한 경향의 주된 이유는 축산업의 환경적 영향에 대한 우려에 영향을 받은 소비자 132 **선호도** 변화이다. 식물성 식품 협회의 대변인 이반 오르테가의 말에 따르면, 새로운 육류 대체품의 가격이 저렴하고 맛이 더 좋아진 것도 133 **또한** 기여했다. 오르테가 씨는 업계의 이 분야가 앞으로 계속 성장할 것이라고 생각한다. 134 **실제로, 그는 대체품이 15년 내에 인기 면에서 육류와 동등해질 것으로 예측하고 있다.**

어휘 substitute 대체품 -based ~ 기반의 texture 질감, 식감 currently 현재 boom 호황 nationwide 전국적으로 setting 환경 consumer 소비자 affect 영향을 미치다 concern 우려 impact 영향 livestock 가축 spokesperson 대변인 contribute 원인이 되다

## 131 형용사 어휘

해설 '다양한'을 뜻하는 a range of의 range를 수식해 '아주 다양한'이라는 의미를 나타낼 때 사용하는 형용사 (B) broad가 정답이다.

어휘 total 전체의 broad 넓은 constant 지속적인 numerous 다수의, 수많은

## 132 명사 자리 _ 복합명사

해설 changing의 수식을 받아 변화하는 것을 나타내야 하므로 명사 consumer와 함께 '소비자 선호도'라는 의미의 복합명사를 구성하는 또 다른 명사 (D) preferences(선호(도))가 정답이다. consumer는 가산 명사이기 때문에 관사 없이 단수형으로 쓰일 수 없다. 따라서 복합명사를 이루지 못하는 (A) to prefer, (B) preferably, (C) preferring은 모두 오답이다.

어휘 prefer 선호하다 preferably 선호하여

## 133 부사 어휘

해설 빈칸이 속한 문장은 앞 문장에서 주된 이유로 언급한 '소비자 선호도 변화' 외의 또 다른 이유를 알리는 내용이다. 따라서 '또한, ~도'라는 의미로 추가적인 정보를 제시할 때 사용하는 (A) as well이 정답이다.

어휘 so far 지금까지 mainly 주로

## 134 문장 고르기

번역 (A) 더욱이, 그의 건강은 식단에서 육류를 뺀 뒤로 개선되어 왔다.
(B) 그의 협회에는 두유와 같은 대체 유제품 제조사들도 포함되어 있다.
(C) 따라서 그는 육류 대체품 제조 과정이 너무 복잡하다고 느낀다.
(D) 실제로, 그는 대체품이 15년 내에 인기 면에서 육류와 동등해질 것으로 예측하고 있다.

해설 빈칸 앞 문장에 지속적인 성장 전망을 언급하는 말이 쓰여 있으므로 이러한 전망과 관련된 문장인 (D)가 정답이다.

어휘 improve 개선되다 removal 없앰, 제거 include 포함하다 dairy 유제품의 alternative 대체(품), 대안 process 과정 complex 복잡한 predict 예측하다 equal 동등하다, 같다 popularity 인기

### 135-138 편지

2월 5일

루 스펠먼
선임 프로젝트 관리자
노스 퍼스 디벨로퍼스 사
도일 가 349
노스 퍼스 WA 6006

스펠먼 씨께,

스톤필드 아파트 계약 입찰에 초대해 주셔서 감사합니다. 입찰서를 동봉했으며, 여기에는 원하시는 배관을 설치해 드릴 수 있는 가격과 예상 일정이 [135] **명시되어 있습니다**. 귀하께서 이것을 매우 매력적인 [136] **제안**이라고 생각하시리라 믿습니다.

[137] **또한 저희가 최근 비슷한 프로젝트들을 작업한 것을 강조하고 싶습니다.** 저희는 현재 4층짜리 노울린 호텔의 모든 배관 설치 작업을 일정에 맞춰, 예산 내에서 마무리하고 있습니다. [138] **그에 앞서**, 저희는 리쉴리 센터의 화장실 32곳에 신뢰할 수 있는 비접촉식 세면대와 변기를 설치했습니다.

저희 입찰 내용 또는 패커드 & 바워스 직원들에 대해 귀하와 이야기 나눌 수 있다면 기쁠 것입니다. 저에게 9291 4998번으로 연락하시면 됩니다.

벨라 패커드
패커드 & 바워스 배관
동봉물

어휘 bid 입찰하다; 입찰(액) contract 계약(서) enclosed 동봉된 install 설치하다 desired 원하는 plumbing 배관 (시설) prospective 예상되는, 장래의 attractive 매력적인 currently 현재 finish up 마무리하다 under budget 예산 내에서 equip 설치하다, 장착하다 reliable 신뢰할 수 있는, 믿을 수 있는 reach 연락하다

## 135 동사 시제+수 일치

해설 주격 관계대명사 which 뒤에 있는 빈칸은 관계사절의 동사 자리로, 이때 동사의 수는 선행사에 일치시켜야 한다. 선행사가 our bid로 3인칭 단수이고, 문서가 명시하는 내용은 현재 시제로 나타내므로 (C) specifies가 정답이다.

어휘 specify 명시하다

## 136 명사 어휘

해설 빈칸에 쓰일 명사는 find의 목적어인 it(= our bid)을 설명하는 것이어야 한다. 자신들의 입찰이 매우 매력적인 제안이라고 말하는 것이 자연스러우므로 '제안'을 뜻하는 (B) proposal이 정답이다.

어휘 appliance (가전) 기기

## 137 문장 고르기

번역 (A) 입찰 초대장에 제출 마감 시한이 2월 6일이라고 쓰여 있었습니다.
(B) 귀사의 웹사이트에 있는 컴퓨터로 만든 그 복합 건물 이미지는 아주 놀랍습니다.
(C) 또한 저희가 최근 비슷한 프로젝트들을 작업한 것을 강조하고 싶습니다.
(D) 제 사업 파트너가 귀하의 회사를 잘 알고 있습니다.

해설 빈칸 뒤에 이어지는 문장들을 보면, 현재 마무리 중인 작업과 그 전에 했던 작업을 설명하고 있다. 따라서 이러한 작업을 가리킬 수 있는 our recent work(최근 작업)와 함께 유사한 프로젝트에 대한 경험이 있음을 언급하는 의미로 쓰인 (C)가 정답이다.

어휘 deadline 마감 기한 submission 제출 generate 만들어 내다 complex 복합 건물, 건물 단지 stunning 아주 놀라운 highlight 강조하다 similar 유사한 familiar 잘 아는, 익숙한

## 138 전치사 어휘

해설 빈칸 앞 문장은 현재진행형 동사(are finishing up)로 현재 진행 중인 작업을, 빈칸이 속한 문장은 과거 시제 동사(equipped)로 과거에 했던 작업을 각각 설명하고 있다. 따라서 that과 함께 '그에 앞서'라는 의미로 순서상 이전의 일을 가리켜야 알맞으므로 '~에 앞서'를 뜻하는 전치사 (A) Prior to가 정답이다.

어휘 instead of ~ 대신 concerning ~에 관해

### 139-142 이메일

수신: 네이트 홉킨스 <nate.hopkins@genmail.com>
발신: 아카리 카네코 <a.kaneko@flurry.com>
날짜: 7월 27일
제목: 알림

홉킨스 씨께,

플러리 앱이 9월 1일에 [139] **운영**을 중단할 것임을 알려 드리게 되어 유감입니다. 그날 이후로, 플러리를 통한 팟캐스트의 온라인 재생 및 다운로드와 청취가 불가능할 것입니다. 또한, 다운받은 에피소드, 선호 프로그램 목록, 그리고 청취 즐겨찾기 같은 [140] **귀하의** 플러리 계정과 관련된 데이터도 더 이상 이용하실 수 없을 것입니다. 이 정보를 저장해 다른 팟캐스트 앱으로 내보내길 원하시면, www.flurry.com/help/394에 있는 안내를 [141] **참조하시기** 바랍니다. [142] **그렇지 않다면, 귀하는 어떤 조치도 하실 필요가 없습니다.** 플러리 고객 서비스 센터에 문의하실 수 있으며, 이곳은 9월 1일까지 운영될 것입니다. 다시 한번 사과드리며, 지금까지 플러리를 이용해 주셔서 감사드립니다.

아카리 카네코
대표, 플러리 주식회사

어휘 cease 중단하다 stream (온라인으로) 재생하다 have access to+명사 ~을 이용할 수 있다 associated with ~와 관련된 account 계정 preferences 선호(하는 것) export 내보내다 instruction 안내, 설명 direct a question to+명사 ~에게 질문하다 remain ~한 채로 유지되다

## 139 명사 자리_목적어

해설 동사 cease 뒤에 빈칸이 있으므로 빈칸에는 목적어가 들어가야 한다. 따라서 명사 (D) operations가 정답이다.

어휘 operate 운영하다, 가동하다 operative 운영되는, 가동되는 operation 운영, 가동

## 140 대명사 어휘

해설 빈칸이 속한 문장의 주어 you와 마찬가지로 상대방인 고객의 플러리 계정을 가리켜야 알맞으므로 (C) your가 정답이다.

## 141 동사 어휘

해설 명사구 the instructions를 목적어로 취할 타동사가 들어갈 자리로, '안내를 참조하시기 바랍니다'라는 의미가 되어야 자연스러우므로 '참조하다'라는 뜻의 타동사 (B) consult가 정답이다. (C) refer는 '참조하다'라는 의미로 쓸 때 자동사로 쓰므로 refer to 형태가 되어야 한다.

어휘 unveil 공개하다, 발표하다 refer 참조하다, 참조하게 하다 contact 연락하다

## 142 문장 고르기

번역 (A) 그렇지 않다면, 귀하는 어떤 조치도 하실 필요가 없습니다.
(B) 그 후에, 플러리가 더욱 순조롭게 작동될 것입니다.
(C) 새로운 저희 모회사에서 자체 팟캐스트 앱을 제공합니다.
(D) 저희는 귀하께서 최신 업데이트를 다운로드하지 않으신 것으로 알고 있습니다.

해설 빈칸 앞 문장에 다른 팟캐스트 앱으로 내보내고 싶을 경우에 필요한 조치를 설명하는 내용이 쓰여 있으므로 '그렇지 않으면'을 뜻하는 Otherwise와 함께 그 반대의 경우와 관련된 조치를 언급하는 (A)가 정답이다.

어휘 action 조치 on one's part ~의 측에서 run 작동되다, 운영되다 parent company 모회사 recent 최신의

### 143-146 기사

오크리지 (11월 22일)—오크리지 당국은 어제 시외 고속버스 운영업체 스위프트버스가 그 도시의 정류장에 대한 서비스를 [143] **중단할 것**이라는 통보를 받았다. 이 회사는 12월 1일을 그 변화의 효력 발생일로 명시했다. 오크리지 플라자 앞에 위치한 곧 [144] **중단되는** 정류장은 올해 초에 빌렛과 냅턴 사이를 운행하는 노선에 추가되었다. [145] **그 노선은 요일에 따라 하루에 최대 2회 서비스되어 왔다.** 공지에서, 스위프트버스는 그러한 결정에 대한 이유로 낮은 승객 이용률을 언급했다. [146] **그곳은** 또한 나중에 수요가 증가되면 그 도시에 대한 서비스를 회복시키겠다는 의향도 표명했다.

어휘 authorities 당국 notify 통보하다 intercity 도시 간의 operator 회사, 운영자 specify 명시하다 run 운행하다 cite (이유 등을) 언급하다 ridership 승객 이용률 express 표명하다, 표현하다 willingness 의향 reestablish 회복시키다, 재정립하다 increase in ~의 증가 demand 수요

## 143 동사 시제

해설 동사의 시제를 묻는 문제로 다음 문장에 변화의 효력 발생일로 언급된 12월 1일(December 1)은 이 기사의 작성일로 표기된 11월 22일(November 22)보다 미래 시점이므로 미래진행형 동사인 (A) will be halting이 정답이다.

어휘 halt 중단하다

## 144 동사 어휘

해설 빈칸은 앞에 있는 soon-to-be의 수식을 받으며 뒤에 있는 stop을 수식하는 말이 들어갈 자리인데, 첫 문장에 그 도시의 정류장(its stop in the city)에 대한 서비스를 중단한다는 말이 쓰여 있으므로 '곧 중

단되는 정류장'이라는 의미가 되어야 자연스럽다. 따라서 '중단하다'를 뜻하는 discontinue의 과거분사 (D) discontinued가 정답이다.

어휘 grant 승인하다, 허용하다 inspect 점검하다 expand 확대하다

## 145 문장 고르기

번역 (A) 그 노선은 요일에 따라 하루에 최대 2회 서비스되어 왔다.
(B) 오크리지 관계자들은 교통 서비스를 개선할 더 많은 방법을 찾고 있다.
(C) 그 플라자는 그 이후로 오크리지의 문화 중심지가 되어 왔다.
(D) 두 곳에 모두 탄탄한 제조업체들이 있다.

해설 빈칸 앞 문장에 중단될 정류장이 올해 초에 빌렛과 냅턴 사이를 운행하는 노선에 추가되었다는 사실이 쓰여 있으므로 이 노선을 뜻하는 The route와 함께 서비스가 제공되어 온 주기를 언급하는 (A)가 정답이다.

어휘 serve 서비스를 제공하다 up to 최대 ~의 depending on ~에 따라 official 관계자 seek 찾다 improve 개선하다 transit 교통 destination 목적지 manufacturing 제조(업)

## 146 대명사 어휘

해설 빈칸 뒤에 특정 조건에 따라 서비스를 회복시키겠다는 의향을 표명했다는 말이 쓰여 있는데, 이는 앞 문장에 언급된 버스 회사 Swiftbus의 입장을 나타낸다. 따라서 Swiftbus를 대신할 수 있는 단수 대명사 (B) It이 정답이다.

# PART 7

### 147-148 공지

> 스태턴 그릴 기업 본사
> 다가오는 인터넷 세미나
>
> 주제: 고객 만족
> 강연자: 마누엘 리오스, 리오스 레스토랑 컨설팅 설립자이자 <프런트 오브 하우스: 레스토랑 내 접대의 중요성>의 저자
> 날짜: 9월 19일, [148] **오전 10시**
> [148] **장소: www.v-meet.co.uk** (행사 ID: 093 657 893)
>
> [147] **이 인터넷 세미나는 고객들과 직접 소통하는 스태턴 그릴 직원들은 의무적으로 참석해야 합니다.** 컴퓨터 접속이 필요합니다. [148] **지연을 방지하기 위해 9시 55분까지 참여하시기 바랍니다.**
>
> 어휘 headquarters 본사 upcoming 다가오는 webinar 인터넷상의 세미나 satisfaction 만족 hospitality 접대, 환대 venue (행사) 장소 mandatory 의무적인 interact 소통하다, 교류하다 patron 고객 access 접속, 접근 required 필수인 prevent 방지하다

## 147 추론

번역 누가 인터넷 세미나에 참석할 것 같은가?
(A) 주방 직원들
(B) 메뉴 개발 담당자들
(C) 종업원 및 계산 담당자들
(D) 잠재적인 체인점 소유주들

해설 마지막 단락에 고객들과 직접 소통하는 스태턴 그릴 직원들은 의무적으로 참석해야 한다(This Webinar is mandatory for Staton Grill employees who interact directly with patrons)는 말이 쓰여 있으므로 고객들과 직접 소통하는 일을 하는 종업원과 계산 담당자들을 뜻하는 (C)가 정답이다.

## 148 세부 사항

번역 참석자들은 무엇을 하도록 요청받는가?
(A) 회사 컴퓨터 이용하기
(B) 책 미리 읽기
(C) 개인 ID 코드 제공하기
(D) 웹 행사장에 일찍 입장하기

해설 마지막 단락에 지연을 방지하기 위해 9시 55분까지 참여하길 바란다(Please join by 9:55 to prevent delays)는 말이 쓰여 있는데, 이는 앞서 언급된 시간인 오전 10시(10:00 A.M.)보다 일찍 웹사이트 행사장(Venue: www.v-meet.co.uk)에 입장하라는 뜻이므로 (D)가 정답이다.

어휘 attendee 참석자 beforehand 미리

> **Paraphrasing**
> 지문의 join by 9:55 → 정답의 Enter the Web venue early

### 149-150 이메일

> 발신: 나이란 차이야
> 수신: 레베카 브릭스
> 제목: 정보
> 날짜: 1월 25일
> 첨부: 목록
>
> 브릭스 씨께,
>
> 전화 통화에서 약속해 드린 바와 같이, [149] **방콕의 입주 가능한 주택 및 아파트 목록을 첨부했습니다.** 모든 집이 귀하께서 제공해 주신 기준에 부합하며, 이주하는 임원들을 위해 귀사에서 할당한 임대료 범위 내로 가격이 책정되어 있습니다. 실내 사진과 인근 지도뿐만 아니라 평형과 편의 시설 같은 세부 정보도 포함해 드렸습니다. [150] **목록을 살펴보시고 어느 집을 선호하시는지 알려 주셔야** 제가 필요한 서류 준비를 시작할 수 있습니다. 이곳들 중 일부는 꽤 매력적이므로, 서두르실 것을 권해 드립니다.
>
> 궁금한 점이 생기면 전화 주시기 바랍니다.
>
> 나이란 차이야
> 기업 이주 전문가
> 차오 프라야 서비스 사

어휘 attached 첨부된 available 이용 가능한 property 건물, 부동산 fit 적합하다, 맞다 criteria 기준 priced 가격이 책정된 rental 임대 allowance 할당액, 비용, 수당 relocate 이주시키다 executive 임원 include 포함하다 details 세부 정보 amenities 편의 시설 desirable 매력적인, 탐나는

## 149 주제 / 목적

번역 이메일의 한 가지 목적은 무엇인가?
(A) 이주의 어려움들을 설명하는 것
(B) 임원들을 위한 새로운 혜택을 홍보하는 것
(C) 수당 지급을 준비하는 것
(D) 주택 선택에 관한 정보를 제공하는 것

해설 지문 초반부에 방콕의 입주 가능한 주택 및 아파트 목록을 첨부했다(attached you will find a list of available houses and apartments in Bangkok)며, 주택 선택과 관련된 정보를 제공하고 있으므로 (D)가 정답이다.

어휘 describe 설명하다 promote 홍보하다 benefit 혜택 arrange 준비하다, 마련하다 supply 제공하다

> **Paraphrasing**
> 지문의 a list of available houses and apartments
> → 정답의 information on housing options

## 150 세부 사항

번역 브릭스 씨는 무엇을 하도록 요청받는가?
(A) 일정표 확인하기
(B) 선호 사항 전달하기
(C) 집들 방문하기
(D) 서류들 취합하기

해설 지문 중반부에 목록을 살펴보고 어느 집을 선호하는지 알려 달라(Please review the list and tell me which property you prefer)고 요청하고 있으므로 (B)가 정답이다.

어휘 confirm 확인하다 communicate (정보 등을) 전달하다 preference 선호(하는 것) collect 취합하다, 모으다

> **Paraphrasing**
> 지문의 tell me which property you prefer
> → 정답의 Communicate a preference

### 151-152 안내문

[151] **경미한 의료 문제로 지역 내 송민 클리닉에 가실 시간이 없으신가요? 온라인 방문은 어디에 계시든 도움을 받으실 수 있는 편리한 방법입니다.** 다음 단계를 따르세요.

1. [152] **저희 웹사이트(www.songminhealth.com)로 가서** 로그인하십시오.

2. "온라인 방문" 탭에 마우스를 올리신 다음, 드롭 다운 메뉴에서 "온라인 방문 시작하기"를 선택하십시오.

3. [152] **나온 양식의 질문에 증상 및 우려 사항에 대해 답변하십시오.** 가급적 명확하고 구체적으로 하시기 바랍니다. 양식을 제출하십시오.

4. 송민 클리닉 의사가 보낸 답변을 보실 수 있도록 이메일 수신함을 확인하십시오. 이는 권고, 검사 위탁, 또는 약품 처방전을 포함할 수 있습니다.

5. 영업시간 기준으로 2시간 내에 답변을 받지 못하시는 경우, 또는 증상에 변화가 생기신 경우, 저희 지원 전화 1-800-555-0138번으로 전화 주시기 바랍니다.

송민 의료원

어휘 convenient 편리한 follow 따르다 sign in 로그인하다 hover 위를 맴돌다 select 선택하다 drop-down menu (아래로 펼쳐지는) 드롭 다운 메뉴 resulting 결과로 나타나는 symptom 증상 concern 우려 specific 구체적인 referral 위탁, 소개 prescription 처방전

## 151 추론

번역 안내문은 누구를 대상으로 하겠는가?
(A) 환자들
(B) 병원 의사들
(C) 의료 기록 담당 직원들
(D) 기술 지원 서비스 제공자들

해설 첫 번째 단락에 의료 문제를 위해 송민 클리닉을 방문하는 것에 대해 질문하면서 온라인 방문이 도움을 받을 수 있는 편리한 방법임(Don't have time to go to your local Songmin clinic for a minor medical issue? E-visits are a convenient way to get help wherever you are)을 알리고 있다. 이는 해당 병원을 찾는 사람들, 즉 환자들을 대상으로 전하는 말이므로 (A)가 정답이다.

## 152 세부 사항

번역 안내문을 읽는 사람은 무엇을 하도록 요청받는가?
(A) 명확한 권고 사항 제공하기
(B) 이메일 메시지에 답장하기
(C) 온라인에서 서류 작성하기
(D) 미리 예약하기

해설 1번 항목에서 웹사이트로 가라(Go to our Web site)고 알린 후, 3번 항목에 그 사이트에서 해야 하는 것으로 양식의 질문에 증상 및 우려 사항에 대해 답변하라(Answer the questions on the resulting form about your symptoms and concerns)는 요청 사항이 쓰여 있으므로 (C)가 정답이다.

어휘 recommendation 권고, 추천(서) fill out 작성하다 make an appointment 예약하다 in advance 미리, 사전에

> **Paraphrasing**
> 지문의 our Web site → 정답의 online
> 지문의 Answer the questions on the resulting form
> → 정답의 Fill out a document

## 153-154 문자 메시지

곽이슬 [오후 1시 16분]
스테이시, 점심 식사 마치고 돌아오셨나요?

스테이시 울리히 [오후 1시 17분]
네, 제 책상이에요. 무슨 일이시죠?

곽이슬 [오후 1시 18분]
사무실에 필요한 용품을 구입하려고 매장에 와 있는데, 부탁이 하나 있어요. [153] **변호사들이 즐겨 쓰는 그 노란색 메모지 아시죠? 그게 얼마나 남았는지 모르겠어요.**

스테이시 울리히 [오후 1시 19분]
알겠어요, 제가 알아볼게요. 어디를 봐야 하죠?

곽이슬 [오후 1시 20분]
비품실에 있는 상자에 있어요.

스테이시 울리히 [오후 1시 22분]
비품실이 상자로 가득해요.

곽이슬 [오후 1시 23분]
[154] **아, 그렇죠. 문 근처의 아래쪽 선반에 있는데, "바이넘 주식회사"가 옆면에 인쇄되어 있어요.**

스테이시 울리히 [오후 1시 24분]
찾았어요. 여기 있는 메모지는 하나뿐이에요.

곽이슬 [오후 1시 25분]
그러면 분명 충분하지 않아요! 확인해 보길 잘했네요. 고마워요, 스테이시!

어휘 pick up 사다, 가져오다 supplies 용품 favor 부탁 realize 알게 되다 find out 알아보다 be full of ~로 가득하다 bottom 아래쪽의 definitely 분명히

## 153 세부 사항

번역 곽 씨에게 어떤 문제가 있는가?
(A) 배송 물품을 받을 수 없을 것이다.
(B) 재고량을 확실히 알지 못한다.
(C) 일부 용품의 위치를 찾을 수 없다.
(D) 자신의 책상을 사용할 수 없다.

해설 곽 씨가 1시 18분에 작성한 메시지에, 변호사들이 즐겨 쓰는 노란색 메모지가 얼마나 남았는지 모른다(You know those yellow notepads that the lawyers like to use? I just realized I'm not sure how many of them we have left)는 문제가 언급되어 있다. 이는 해당 물품의 재고량을 확실히 알지 못한다는 뜻이므로 (B)가 정답이다.

어휘 unavailable 시간이 나지 않는 uncertain 확실하지 않은 inventory 재고(품) level 수준, 양 locate 위치를 찾다

**Paraphrasing**
지문의 not sure how many of them we have left
→ 정답의 uncertain about an inventory level

## 154 의도 파악

번역 오후 1시 22분에 울리히 씨가 "비품실이 상자로 가득해요"라고 쓸 때, 의미하는 것은 무엇인가?
(A) 더 자세한 설명이 필요하다.
(B) 곽 씨가 제품을 구입하지 말아야 한다.
(C) 일부 물품을 넣을 공간을 찾을 수 없다.
(D) 곽 씨가 그 방을 정리해야 할 것이다.

해설 울리히 씨가 "비품실이 상자로 가득해요"라고 쓰자, 곧바로 곽 씨가 문 근처의 아래쪽 선반에 있다는 말과 함께 "바이넘 주식회사"가 옆면에 인쇄되어 있다(It's on a bottom shelf near the door, and "Bynum, Inc." is printed on the sides)고 구체적으로 설명하고 있다. 따라서 물품을 찾기 위해 더 자세한 설명이 필요하다는 것을 알 수 있으므로 (A)가 정답이다.

어휘 detailed 자세한 description 설명 organize 정리하다

## 155-157 구인 공고

산책로 승마 담당 직원 모집

모리스 폴즈 게스트 랜치에서는 고객들에게 인기 있는 산책로 승마 프로그램에 도움을 주실 승마 애호가를 찾고 있습니다. 이 정규직 직책의 업무에는 고객들에게 말을 타기 위해 준비하는 방법을 가르치는 것과 주변 산책로를 따라 소규모 승마 참가자들을 인솔하는 것, 그리고 저희 마구간에서 전반적인 말 관리 업무를 [155] **처리하는 것**을 포함합니다.

[156(A)] **지원자는 반드시 높은 수준의 승마 기술을 발휘할 수 있어야 합니다.** 기타 자격 요건에는 [156(C)] **최소 6개월 이상 유급 또는 자원봉사로 마구간에서 근무한 경험이 있어야 하며** [156(D)] **밝고 친근한 성격을 지녀야 합니다.** 주말 근무가 가능해야 하며, 합격한 지원자는 일주일에 최소 한 차례 주말 교대 근무가 있을 것으로 예상해야 합니다.

지원하시려면, "산책로 승마 담당 직원 지원서 - (이름)"이라는 제목으로 이력서 및 간단한 자기 소개서를 첨부해 contact@morrisfalls.com으로 이메일을 보내시기 바랍니다.

[157] **저희 마구간 및 승마용 산책로의 세부 정보 및 사진을 보시려면, www.morrisfalls.com/riding을 방문하시기 바랍니다.**

어휘 associate 직원, 동료 ranch 목장 seek 찾다, 구하다 horseback riding 승마 enthusiast 애호가 assist with ~에 도움을 주다 trail 산책로, 오솔길 include 포함하다 handle 처리하다 task 업무, 일 barn 마구간 applicant 지원자 (= candidate) demonstrate 발휘하다, 보여주다 qualification 자격(증) volunteer 자원봉사의 possession 소유 cheerful 쾌활한 availability (이용) 가능성 must 필수(인 것) apply 지원하다 entitled ~라는 제목의 résumé 이력서 cover letter 자기 소개서 details 세부 정보

## 155 동의어

번역 첫 번째 단락, 네 번째 줄에 쓰인 "handling"과 의미가 가장 가까운 것은?
(A) 만지는 것
(B) 수행하는 것
(C) 교육하는 것
(D) 판매하는 것

해설 동명사구 handling general horse-care tasks in our barn은 '마구간에서 전반적인 말 관리 업무를 처리하는 것'을 의미한다. 여기서 업무를 처리한다는 말은 그러한 업무를 수행한다는 의미이므로 '수행하다'를 뜻하는 동사 perform의 동명사 (B) performing이 정답이다.

## 156 Not / True

번역 해당 일자리에 대한 요건으로 언급되지 않은 것은?
(A) 특별한 신체 능력
(B) 특정 지역에 대한 익숙함
(C) 업무 경험
(D) 특정한 성격적 특성

해설 두 번째 단락 초반부에 지원자는 반드시 높은 수준의 승마 기술을 발휘할 수 있어야 한다(Applicants must be able to demonstrate high-level horseback riding skills)고 언급한 부분에서 특별한 신체 능력을 뜻하는 (A)를, 같은 단락 중반부에 최소 6개월 이상 유급 또는 자원봉사로 마구간에서 근무한 경험이 있어야 한다(having done at least six months of paid or volunteer work in a horse barn)고 언급한 부분에서 업무 경력을 의미하는 (C)를, 밝고 친근한 성격을 지녀야 한다(possession of a cheerful, friendly personality)고 언급된 부분에서 특정한 성격적 특성을 뜻하는 (D)를 확인할 수 있다. 하지만, 특정 지역에 대한 익숙함과 관련된 정보는 제시되어 있지 않으므로 (B)가 정답이다.

어휘 familiarity 익숙함 region 지역 specific 특정한, 구체적인 trait 특성

> Paraphrasing
> 지문의 high-level horseback riding skills
> → 보기 (A)의 A special physical ability
> 지문의 at least six months of paid or volunteer work in a horse barn
> → 보기 (C)의 Experience with some of its duties
> 지문의 a cheerful, friendly personality
> → 보기 (D)의 Specific character traits

## 157 세부 사항

번역 구인 공고에 따르면, 공고를 읽은 사람이 왜 해당 목장의 웹사이트를 방문해야 하는가?
(A) 그곳의 시설에 관해 알기 위해
(B) 지원서를 제출하기 위해
(C) 다른 구인 공고 목록을 보기 위해
(D) 그곳의 역사에 관해 읽어 보기 위해

해설 마지막 단락에 마구간 및 승마용 산책로의 세부 정보 및 사진을 보려면 www.morrisfalls.com/riding을 방문하라(For details and photographs of our horse barn and horseback-riding trails, visit www.morrisfalls.com/riding)고 알리고 있다. 웹사이트에서 목장의 시설물에 대해 알 수 있는 것이므로 (A)가 정답이다.

어휘 facility 시설 application 지원(서) listing 목록

> Paraphrasing
> 지문의 our horse barn and horseback-riding trails
> → 정답의 its facilities

## 158-160 양식

예약 확인서

오트리 자동차 대여
위버 가 1200, 스털턴
www.autrycarrental.com
고객 서비스 전화: 1-800-555-0176

| | |
|---|---|
| 고객: | 러셀 램 |
| 핸드폰 | 1-314-555-0141 |
| 159 **주소:** | **스프링 길 450, 헌틀리** |

대여 세부 정보

| | |
|---|---|
| 차량: | 클라빈스 C70 승용차 |
| 대여 지점 / 날짜: | 브래넘 / 12월 8일 |
| 160 **반납 지점 / 날짜:** | **루카스빌 / 12월 10일** |
| 158 **주행 거리 상한:** | **450마일**(150마일/일) |
| 운전자: | 러셀 램 |

**청구 요금**

| 설명 | 금액 |
|---|---|
| 차량 대여: | 168.72달러 (56.24달러/일 x 3일) |
| 159 **고객 자택으로 차량 탁송:** | 30달러 |
| **총:** | 198.72달러 |
| 예약 시 지불한 선금: | 59.62달러 |
| 160 **차량 반납 시 지불할 잔액:** | **139.1달러** |

어휘 reservation 예약 confirmation 확인(서) rental 대여 details 세부 정보 branch 지점 cap 상한 charge 청구 요금 description 설명 deposit 선금, 보증금 balance due 잔금

## 158 Not / True

번역 대여 조항에 대해 언급된 것은?
(A) 일일 요금이 다르다.
(B) 두 명의 고객이 운전하도록 허용된다.
(C) 주행 거리에 제한이 있다.
(D) 막판 예약 시에는 수수료가 부과된다.

해설 지문 중반부에 주행 거리 상한(Mileage Cap)이 450마일(450 miles)로 제시되어 있으므로 (C)가 정답이다.

어휘 term 조항, 조건 vary 다르다 allow 허용하다 limit 제한, 한계 last-minute 마지막 순간의

> Paraphrasing
> 지문의 Mileage Cap
> → 정답의 a limit on the driving distance

## 159 세부 사항

번역 고객은 어디에서 차량을 운전하기 시작할 것인가?
(A) 스털턴에서
(B) 헌틀리에서
(C) 브래넘에서
(D) 루카스빌에서

해설 지문 후반부에 고객 자택으로 차량 탁송(Delivery of vehicle to customer's home) 항목이 쓰여 있어 고객이 집에서 차량을 받아 운전을 시작한다는 것을 알 수 있으며, 초반부에 고객 주소가 헌틀리(450 Spring Drive, Huntley)로 쓰여 있으므로 (B)가 정답이다.

## 160 세부 사항

번역 오트리 자동차 대여회사가 12월 10일에 얼마의 금액을 받을 것인가?
(A) 59.62달러
(B) 139.1 달러
(C) 168.72달러
(D) 198.72달러

해설 12월 10일이라는 날짜는 지문 중반부에 차량 반납 날짜(Return Branch / Date, Lucasville / December 10)로 제시되어 있고, 지문 후반부에 반납 시 지불해야 하는 금액이 139.1달러(Balance Due Upon Vehicle Return: $139.10)로 표기되어 있으므로 (B)가 정답이다.

### 161-163 보도 자료

즉시 보도용

연락 담당자: 알베르토 구티에레즈, a.gutierrez@viga.com

밴쿠버 (7월 13일)—[161] **VIGA는 8대의 누넌 N250 항공기 구입을 발표하게 되어 자랑스럽습니다. 약 2년 후에 이 항공기들이 배송되면 회사의 총 보유 항공기 수는 156대가 될 것이며, 이는 캐나다의 항공사 중에서 세 번째로 큰 규모입니다.**

이 계약은 VIGA와 누넌 사 사이의 오랜 성공적인 관계에서 가장 최근의 계약입니다. 동시에, 이는 지속 가능성이라는 목표를 향한 발걸음일 뿐만 아니라 항공사의 보유 항공기에 새롭고 흥미로운 모델을 추가하는 것을 의미하는 것이기도 합니다.

누넌 N250 항공기는 정교한 TF8 터보팬 엔진을 특징으로 하며, 이는 훌륭한 연료 효율성을 제공하면서 이산화탄소는 거의 배출하지 않습니다. [162] **TF8은 또한 다른 엔진들보다 더 적은 소음 범위를 지니고 있어, 여행객들께 평화로운 객실 이용 경험을 제공해 드립니다.** 단일 통로 항공기로, 각각의 N250은 총 130명의 탑승객을 운송할 수 있습니다.

[163] **VIGA는 밴쿠버의 허브 공항과 미국의 여러 공항들 사이를 오가는 새로운 국제 서비스 노선을 추가하는 데 이 항공기들을 이용할 계획입니다.** 관련된 구체적인 목적지는 아직 결정되지 않았습니다. 수요에 따라, 기존 항공편의 빈도도 늘릴 수 있습니다.

어휘 approximately 약, 대략 fleet (한 업체가 소유한) 전체 항공기[차량] relationship 관계 mark 의미하다, 나타내다 addition 추가 sustainability 지속 가능성 feature 특징으로 하다 sophisticated 정교한, 세련된 efficiency 효율(성) emit 배출하다 carbon dioxide 이산화탄소 noise footprint 소음 범위 afford 제공하다 intend 계획하다, 의도하다 hub 중심(지) depending on ~에 따라 demand 수요 frequency 빈도 existing 기존의

## 161 추론

번역 VIGA는 무엇일 것 같은가?
(A) 상업 항공사
(B) 항공기 제조사
(C) 공항 관리 회사
(D) 조종사 교육 시설

해설 첫 번째 단락에 VIGA가 8대의 누넌 N250 항공기를 구입한 사실을 알리며, 총 보유 항공기 수가 156대가 될 것이고, 이는 캐나다의 항공사 중에서 세 번째로 큰 규모(VIGA is proud to announce the purchase of eight Noonan N250 airplanes. ~ will bring the company's total fleet size to 156 aircraft, the third largest among Canadian carriers)라고 했으므로 VIGA가 항공사임을 알 수 있다. 따라서 (A)가 정답이다.

## 162 Not / True

번역 해당 항공기에 대해 언급된 것은?
(A) 해외 공장에서 만들어진다.
(B) 최근 구매 업체에 전달되었다.
(C) 기내에서 비교적 조용하다.
(D) 특정 유형의 연료를 사용한다.

해설 세 번째 단락에 TF8이 다른 엔진들보다 더 적은 소음 범위를 지니고 있어 여행객들에게 평화로운 객실 이용 경험을 제공한다(The TF8 also has a lower noise footprint than other engines, affording travelers a peaceful in-cabin experience)고 쓰여 있어 기내가 조용하다는 사실을 알 수 있으므로 (C)가 정답이다.

어휘 overseas 해외의 relatively 비교적 particular 특정한

**Paraphrasing**
지문의 has a lower noise footprint
→ 정답의 relatively quiet
지문의 in-cabin → 정답의 in flight

## 163 문장 삽입

번역 [1], [2], [3], [4]로 표시된 곳 중에서 다음 문장이 가장 적합한 곳은 어디인가?
"관련된 구체적인 목적지는 아직 결정되지 않았습니다."
(A) [1]
(B) [2]
(C) [3]
(D) [4]

해설 제시된 문장은 구체적인 목적지가 아직 결정되지 않았다는 의미이므로 앞에 목적지와 관련된 내용이 있어야 한다. [4] 앞에 밴쿠버와 미국의 여러 공항들 사이를 오가는 새로운 국제 서비스 노선을 추가하는 데 이 항공기들을 이용할 계획(VIGA intends to use the planes to add new international service routes between its hub in Vancouver and airports in the United States)이라고 새로운 노선에 대해 언급하고 있으므로 이 뒤에 주어진 문장이 들어가야 자연스럽다. 따라서 (D)가 정답이다.

어휘 specific 구체적인 destination 목적지 involved 관련된 determine 결정하다

### 164-167 기사

태양열 지붕의 힘
레슬리 로저스 작성

태양열 지붕은 사람과 차량이 그 아래를 지날 수 있을 만큼 충분히 높게 태양열 전지판을 배열한 것이다. 가장 흔히 주차 공간 위에 설치되며, 대학교에서부터 쇼핑몰에 이르기까지 그러한 시설이 있는 어떤 종류의 장소에도 적합하다. 태양열 지붕을 설치하면 165(C) **전기 요금 절감** 및 165(D) **환경친화적이라는 평판** 등의 이점이 있을 뿐만 아니라 165(A) **비와 눈을 피할 수 있는 쉼터와 그늘을 제공함으로써** 운전자에게 주차 공간을 더 쾌적하게 만들어 준다.

164 **주차 공간에 태양열 지붕을 설치하는 데 관심이 있는 사람들은 먼저 몇 가지 조건을 결정하는 것부터 시작해야 한다.** 여기에는 프로젝트 예산, 지붕이 가리게 될 이상적인 면적, 그리고 그것을 설치해야 하는 높이가 포함된다.

다음으로, 166, 167 **사용할 특정 태양열 기술과 관련된 결정을 해야 한다.** 예를 들어, 현재 구매자들은 수집된 에너지를 저장하기 위해 세 가지 유형의 배터리 중에서 선택할 수 있다. 166 **태양열 에너지 컨설턴트가 이용 가능한 옵션들의 장점과 단점을 설명해 줄 수 있다.** 추가로, 태양열 지붕에 투자하는 것을 고려하는 사람은 판매세 면제 또는 설치 지원금 같은 유익한 공공 정책에 대해 재생 가능 에너지 보상책 데이터베이스를 확인해 보는 것이 좋다.

어휘 canopy 지붕, 덮개 array 배열(된 것) allow 할 수 있게 해 주다, 허용하다 suitable 적합한 facility 시설(물) advantage 장점 reputation 평판, 명성 conscious 의식적인 determine 결정하다 condition 조건 include 포함하다 budget 예산 ideal 이상적인 particular 특정한 available 이용 가능한 consider 고려하다 invest in ~에 투자하다 renewable 재생 가능한 incentive 보상책 exemption 면제 subsidy 보조금

### 164 세부 사항

번역 기사는 주로 누구를 대상으로 하는가?
(A) 장차 기업가가 되려는 사람
(B) 공공 정책 입안자
(C) 부동산 소유주
(D) 조경 건축가

해설 두 번째 단락에 주차 공간에 태양열 지붕을 설치하는 데 관심이 있는 사람들은 먼저 몇 가지 조건을 결정하는 것부터 시작해야 한다(Those who are interested in adding a solar canopy to their parking area will need to start by determining a few conditions)고 언급하는 것에서 주차 공간이 있는 부동산을 소유한 사람들이 주요 대상임을 알 수 있다. 따라서 (C)가 정답이다.

어휘 aspiring 장차 ~이 되려는 property 건물, 부동산

### 165 Not / True

번역 태양열 지붕의 이점으로 언급되지 않은 것은?
(A) 기상 상황으로부터 보호해 준다.
(B) 화석 연료의 소비를 줄인다.
(C) 에너지 지출을 줄인다.
(D) 시설의 평판에 긍정적으로 영향을 미친다.

해설 첫 번째 단락 중반부에 전기 요금 절감(lower electricity bills)을 언급한 것에서 (C)를, 환경을 생각한다는 평판(a reputation for being environmentally conscious)을 언급한 것에서 (D)를, 같은 단락 마지막 부분에 비와 눈을 피할 수 있는 쉼터와 그늘을 제공한다(providing shade and shelter from rain and snow)고 언급한 것에서 (A)를 확인할 수 있다. 하지만 화석 연료의 소비 감소와 관련된 정보는 제시되어 있지 않으므로 (B)가 정답이다.

어휘 benefit 이점, 혜택 reduce 줄이다 consumption 소비 fossil fuel 화석 연료 decrease 줄이다 expense 지출 positively 긍정적으로 affect 영향을 미치다 establishment 시설, 기관

**Paraphrasing**
지문의 lower electricity bills → 보기 (C)의 decrease energy expenses
지문의 a reputation for being environmentally conscious → 보기 (D)의 positively affect an establishment's repuTation
지문의 providing shade and shelter from rain and snow → 보기 (A)의 offer protection from weather conditions

### 166 세부 사항

번역 기사에 따르면, 컨설턴트가 무엇을 이야기할 수 있는가?
(A) 설치 과정의 단계들
(B) 데이터베이스를 이용하는 최고의 방법
(C) 태양열 지붕 설치 가능 장소
(D) 일부 기술의 특징

해설 마지막 단락에 태양열 기술과 관련된 결정을 해야 한다(decisions must be made about the particular solar technologies that will be used)며, 태양열 에너지 컨설턴트가 이용 가능한 옵션들의 장점과 단점을 설명해 줄 수 있다(A solar energy consultant can explain the advantages and disadvantages of the options available)고 알리고 있다. 컨설턴트가 각 기술들의 특징을 설명해 줄 수 있다는 말이므로 (D)가 정답이다.

어휘 characteristic 특징

**Paraphrasing**
지문의 the advantages and disadvantages → 정답의 Characteristics

TEST 1

## 167 문장 삽입

번역 [1], [2], [3], [4]로 표시된 곳 중에서 다음 문장이 가장 적합한 곳은 어디인가?

"예를 들어, 현재 구매자들은 수집된 에너지를 저장하기 위해 세 가지 유형의 배터리 중에서 선택할 수 있다."

(A) [1]
(B) [2]
(C) [3]
(D) [4]

해설 제시된 문장은 예시를 말할 때 사용하는 For example과 함께 구매자들이 세 가지 유형의 배터리 중에서 선택할 수 있다는 의미를 나타낸다. 따라서 특정 태양열 기술과 관련된 결정을 해야 한다(decisions must be made about the particular solar technologies that will be used)고 알리는 문장 뒤에 위치한 [3]에 들어가 결정해야 하는 기술의 예시를 나타내는 흐름이 되어야 자연스러우므로 (C)가 정답이다.

어휘 have a choice of ~에 대한 선택권이 있다 store 저장하다 captured 수집된, 얻은

### 168-171 이메일

수신: 전 직원
발신: 셰리 코헨
제목: 대표이사님 방문
날짜: 4월 21일 월요일
첨부: Doc_1

안녕하세요, 여러분,

168, 169 **이번 주에 있을 사이토 대표이사님의 지점 방문이 수요일 단 하루로 줄었다는 사실을 알려 드리게 되어 유감입니다.** 168 **내일 본사에 머물러 계셔야 하는 긴급한 일이 생긴 듯합니다.**

분명, 170 **이것은 제가 방문 일정을 조정해야 했음을 의미합니다. 첨부 파일의 강조 표시된 부분들을 확인하시기 바랍니다.** 가장 주목할 만한 부분은, 169 **사이토 대표이사님을 위한 환영 행사가 근무 시간 중이 아니라 오후 5시에 열릴 것입니다. 설사 이것이 퇴근 후의 약속 일정을 재조정하는 것을 의미한다 하더라도, 참석하도록 노력해 주시기 바랍니다.** 추가로, 계획된 여러 가지 발표들을 축소해야 할 것이며, 171 **접객업 인력 공급 서비스 시장에 관한 것은 완전히 취소되었습니다.**

갑작스러운 변경으로 인해 불편을 드려 죄송합니다. 그럼에도 불구하고, 전문성과 유연성을 갖고 받아들여서 사이토 대표이사님께 좋은 인상을 남겨 드리도록 해 봅시다.

셰리 코헨
에이버턴 지점장
던스태드

어휘 branch 지점 shorten 줄이다 urgent 긴급한 come up 생겨나다 headquarters 본사 obviously 분명히 make an adjustment 조정하다 itinerary 일정(표) highlight 강조하다 attachment 첨부(한 것) notably 주목할 만하게 on-site 구내의, 현장의 reception (환영) 연회 make an effort 노력하다 commitment 약속 condensed 간결한, 축약된 staffing 인력 (공급) hospitality 접객(업) altogether 완전히 arise 생기다, 일어나다 make a good impression 좋은 인상을 남기다 accept 받아들이다 flexibility 유연성

## 168 추론

번역 대표이사의 방문에 대해 암시된 것은?

(A) 이 지점에서는 처음일 것이다.
(B) 내일 시작하기로 되어 있었다.
(C) 거기에는 긴급한 이유가 있다.
(D) 갑자기 공지되었다.

해설 첫 번째 단락에 대표이사의 방문이 수요일 하루로 줄었다(this week's branch visit from our CEO, Mr. Saito, has been shortened to just one day, Wednesday)고 언급하면서 내일 본사에 있어야 하는 급한 일이 생겼다(an urgent matter has come up that will require him to stay at headquarters tomorrow)고 알리고 있다. 따라서 내일부터 방문하려던 일정이 축소되었다는 것을 알 수 있으므로 (B)가 정답이다.

어휘 be supposed to ~하기로 되어 있다 suddenly 갑자기

## 169 세부 사항

번역 코헨 씨는 수요일에 무엇을 하도록 직원들에게 요청하는가?

(A) 평소 업무 종료 시간보다 늦게까지 있기
(B) 준비를 위한 회의에 참석하기
(C) 행사장 준비하는 일 돕기
(D) 시장 조사 내용 발표하기

해설 첫 번째 단락에 대표이사가 수요일에 방문한다고 하였고, 두 번째 단락에 근무 시간 중이 아니라 오후 5시에 대표이사를 위한 연회가 열린다(the on-site reception for Mr. Saito will be held at 5 P.M. instead of during working hours)고 알리면서 퇴근 후의 약속 일정을 재조정하더라도 꼭 참석할 것(Please make an effort to attend, even if it means rescheduling an after-work commitment)을 당부하고 있다. 따라서 업무 종료 시간보다 늦게까지 있을 것을 요청하고 있는 것이므로 (A)가 정답이다.

어휘 usual 평소의 preparatory 준비를 위한 set up 준비하다 present 발표하다

## 170 추론

번역 이메일에 무엇이 포함되어 있을 것 같은가?

(A) 업데이트된 일정표
(B) 임원 프로필
(C) 편집된 슬라이드 쇼
(D) 선택 가능한 음식 목록

해설 두 번째 단락 초반부에 방문 일정을 조정해야 했다며 첨부 파일의 강조 표시된 부분들을 확인하라(I've had to make adjustments to the itinerary for the visit; see the highlighted sections of the attachment)고 요청하고 있으므로 수정된 방문 일정표가 이메일에 첨부되어 있다고 추론할 수 있다. 따라서 (A)가 정답이다.

어휘 executive 임원, 이사 edit 편집하다

> Paraphrasing
> 지문의 make adjustments to the itinerary
> → 정답의 An updated schedule

## 171 추론

번역 던스태드는 어떤 종류의 업체일 것 같은가?
(A) 호텔 체인
(B) 병원
(C) 보험 회사
(D) 직업 소개 서비스 업체

해설 던스태드는 이메일 작성자가 속한 회사인데 두 번째 단락 후반부에 발표 변경에 대해서 언급하면서 접객업 인력 공급 서비스 시장에 관한 것은 완전히 취소되었다(the one on the market for staffing services in the hospitality industry has been cancelled altogether)고 한 것에서 인력 공급 서비스를 제공하는 업체인 것을 추론할 수 있으므로 (D)가 정답이다.

## 172-175 온라인 채팅

말릭 하산 [오전 10시]
안녕하세요, 여러분! 우리가 3월호에 대한 계획을 세우기 위해 이따가 모인다는 사실을 알긴 하지만, 지금 여러분께 좋은 소식을 공유하고 싶었어요. [172] **릴라 버나디가 잡지의 웹사이트를 위해 "스타를 향한 10가지 질문" 영상을 촬영하기로 동의했어요.**

아만다 추 [오전 10시 1분]
와우, 잘됐네요! 그분께서 하셨던 다른 인터뷰들로 판단할 때, 분명 질문들에 대해 재미있는 답변을 하실 거예요.

브라이언 쿡 [오전 10시 1분]
아주 좋습니다! [173] **그렇게 하면 정말 웹사이트의 인지도가 높아질 거예요.**

아만다 추 [오전 10시 2분]
분명합니다. 그분은 전 세계 여러 국가들에 팬이 있잖아요.

말릭 하산 [오전 10시 3분]
이번 일을 계기로 그분의 음반사도 잡지의 특집 기사 협업을 고려하게 되길 바랍니다.

브라이언 쿡 [오전 10시 4분]
[174] **리게일먼트 사에는 훌륭한 공연자들이 아주 많이 소속되어 있죠.**

말릭 하산 [오전 10시 6분]
있잖아요, 하이 타이드 밴드가 여름에 앨범을 하나 내는데, 그걸 홍보하고 싶을 거예요. 버나디의 영상이 잘되면, 하이 타이드의 멤버들과 서면 인터뷰를 하게 해 달라고 제가 리게일먼트 사를 설득해 볼 수 있을 겁니다.

**아만다 추 [오전 10시 7분]**
아주 좋은 생각이에요, 말릭.

**말릭 하산 [오전 10시 7분]**
좋습니다, 두 분 모두 다시 업무를 보시도록 해 드려야겠네요. [175] **하지만, 오늘 오후에 흥미진진한 기사 제안을 좀 들어 볼 수 있기를 고대합니다.**

브라이언 쿡 [오전 10시 8분]
분명 그러실 거예요! [175] **우리가 작년에 두어 차례 함께 일했던 프리랜서 기자인 소냐 아길라에게서 아주 흥미로운 것을 막 받았습니다.**

어휘 agree to ~하는 데 동의하다 judge from ~로 판단하다 awareness 인식, 알고 있음 consider 고려하다 collaborate on ~에 대해 협업하다 feature 특집 기사 roster (직원) 명단 promote 홍보하다 go well 잘되다 convince 설득하다 look forward to+명사 ~하기를 고대하다 proposal 제안(서)

## 172 세부 사항

번역 하산 씨가 다른 메시지 작성자들에게 공지하는 것은?
(A) 잡지 주제
(B) 회의 안건 변경
(C) 최근 프로젝트에 관한 의견
(D) 업무의 긍정적인 진전

해설 하산 씨가 처음으로 쓴 메시지에 좋은 소식이 있다는 말과 함께 릴라 버나디가 잡지의 웹사이트를 위해 "스타를 향한 10가지 질문" 영상을 촬영하기로 동의했다(Lila Bernardi has agreed to film a "10 Questions for a Star" video for the magazine's Web site)고 알리고 있다. 이는 업무에 긍정적인 진전이 있었던 것이므로 (D)가 정답이다.

어휘 theme 주제 agenda 안건, 의제 positive 긍정적인 development 진전, 전개

## 173 의도 파악

번역 오전 10시 2분에 추 씨가 "분명합니다"라고 쓸 때, 의미하는 것은 무엇인가?
(A) 일부 내용이 다른 언어들로 번역되어야 한다.
(B) 웹사이트가 잡지의 소중한 마케팅 도구이다.
(C) 유명 인사의 과거 인터뷰가 즐거웠다.
(D) 웹사이트가 더 유명해질 것이다.

해설 Definitely는 '분명하다, 틀림없다' 등의 의미로 강한 긍정을 나타낼 때 사용하므로 앞서 쿡 씨가 그렇게 하면 웹사이트의 인지도가 높아질 것(That should really increase awareness of the Web site)이라고 언급한 것에 대한 긍정의 답변임을 알 수 있다. 따라서 (D)가 정답이다.

어휘 content 내용(물) translate 번역하다 valuable 소중한 celebrity 유명 인사 achieve fame 유명해지다, 명성을 얻다

> Paraphrasing
> 지문의 increase awareness of the Web site
> → 정답의 The Web site will achieve greater fame.

## 174 세부 사항

번역 리게일먼트 사는 어떤 업계에 속해 있는가?
(A) 출판
(B) 웹 디자인
(C) 음반 제작
(D) 패션

해설 리게일먼트 사가 언급되는 10시 4분 메시지에 훌륭한 공연자들이 아주 많이 소속되어 있다(Regalement has so many great performers on its roster)고 하였고, 뒤이어 앨범을 내는 밴드에 대해서 언급되므로 음반과 관련된 업계에 속한 회사라는 것을 알 수 있다. 따라서 (C)가 정답이다.

## 175 추론

번역 쿡 씨는 오후에 무엇을 할 것 같은가?
(A) 이전 공동 작업자에게 이메일 보내기
(B) 홍보 영상 촬영 감독하기
(C) 프리랜서 기자가 제안한 아이디어 공유하기
(D) 아길라 씨가 작성한 기사 교정하기

해설 '오후'라는 시점이 언급되는 10시 7분 메시지에, 하산 씨가 오늘 오후에 흥미진진한 기사 제안을 들어 볼 수 있기를 고대한다(I'm looking forward to hearing some exciting article proposals this afternoon)고 언급하자, 쿡 씨가 프리랜서 기자인 소냐 아길라에게서 아주 흥미로운 것을 하나 받았다(I just received a very interesting one from Sonya Aguilar, the freelance journalist)고 알리고 있다. 이는 프리랜서 기자가 제안한 기사 아이디어에 대해 오후에 이야기하겠다는 뜻이므로 (C)가 정답이다.

어휘 previous 이전의 collaborator 공동 작업자 oversee 감독하다 promotional 홍보의 proofread 교정하다

## 176-180 정보+이메일

AIM

스테일리 재단

[176] **스테일리 재단은 소기업 소유주들을 위한 멘토 프로그램인 AIM을 통해 소기업들의 성장을 지원하는 것을 자랑스럽게 생각합니다.** 이 프로그램에서 멘토의 상담을 받으시는 분들은 자원봉사 멘토와 짝을 이루게 되며, 그 멘토가 이후에 무료로 계속 전문적인 조언을 해 드립니다. 기술이든 또는 음식 서비스든 상관없이, 멘토의 상담을 받는 분의 특정 분야에 대한 식견을 지닌 멘토를 찾기 위한 노력을 기울이고 있지만, 이 조언은 사업 계획과 인적 자원 같은 일반적인 사안에 초점을 맞추고 있습니다. 멘토의 상담을 받는 분은 또한 빈번하게 열리는 AIM 교육 행사에 참가할 수 있는 자격과 자료 보관실을 이용할 수 있는 자격을 얻게 됩니다. AIM을 통한 멘토 서비스를 받기 위한 신청서는 수시로 접수하고 있습니다. [176] **신청자는 반드시 햄릭 시 대도시권에 거주하며,** [179] **지난 12개월 안에 사업을 시작했어야 합니다.** www.staleyfoundation.org/aim을 방문하셔서 지원 방법을 알아보시기 바랍니다.

스테일리 재단에 관해

[177] **스테일리 재단은 로잘린 스테일리를 기리기 위해 그분의 따님이신 에밀리 바렛에 의해 설립되었습니다.** 스테일리는 획기적인 경제 전문가이자 현재도 여전히 여러 대학 강의실에서 흔히 읽는 작품을 쓴 저자였습니다. 재단의 사명은 경제적 자율권을 통해 햄릭 시민들의 삶의 질을 개선하는 것입니다.

어휘 mentorship program 멘토 프로그램(전문가 등이 상담과 조언을 제공) mentee 멘토의 상담을 받는 사람 be matched with ~와 짝을 이루다 volunteer 자원봉사의 focus on ~에 초점을 맞추다 insight 식견 specific 특정한 eligible 자격이 있는 participate in ~에 참가하다 access 이용하다, 접근하다 application 신청(서) on a rolling basis 수시로 applicant 신청자 reside 거주하다 metropolitan 대도시의 launch 시작하다 apply 신청하다 establish 설립하다 in honor of ~을 기리기 위해 groundbreaking 획기적인 improve 개선하다 empowerment 자율권, 권한 이양

수신: 알리야 윌리엄스
발신: 마민우
제목: 회신: 문제
날짜: 4월 4일

윌리엄스 씨께,

[179] **귀하의 AIM 멘토**와 처음 만나는 약속을 잡는 데 문제를 겪고 있다니 유감입니다. 봄철은 조경 전문가들에게 바쁜 시기라는 것을 염두에 두세요. 그럼에도 불구하고 저희 직원들 중 한 명이 이 문제에 대해 핀 씨와 이야기할 것이며, 필요할 경우, 답변을 더 잘 해 드리는 다른 멘토로 배정해 드리겠습니다.

무슨 일이 있어도, [178] **저희가 5월 1일로 막 일정을 잡은 브랜드 구축에 관한 워크숍에 참석하시기 바랍니다.** [180] **진행자이신 몰리 테이트는 수년 동안 성공적인 실내 디자인 업체를 운영하셨습니다.** 물론, 이 워크숍 자체는 일반 청중을 대상으로 하지만, [180] **이후에 테이트 씨께 귀하의 분야에 특정된 조언을 추가로 요청할 수 있습니다.** 관심이 있으신지 제게 알려 주시기 바랍니다.

마민우
스테일리 재단

어휘 arrange 마련하다, 주선하다 keep in mind 명심하다, 염두에 두다 landscaper 조경 전문가 assign 배정하다, 할당하다 responsive 대답을 잘 하는, 즉각 반응하는 be intended for ~을 대상으로 하다 audience 청중, 관객 approach (부탁·제안 등을 하기 위해) 접촉하다 specific to+명사 ~에 특정된

## 176 주제 / 목적

번역 정보의 목적은 무엇인가?
(A) 지역 내 멘토 프로그램에 대한 기회를 알리는 것
(B) 자선 목적의 기부를 요청하는 것
(C) 경제 계획의 성공에 관해 알리는 것
(D) 단체에 필요한 자원봉사자를 모집하는 것

해설 정보의 첫 번째 단락에 스테일리 재단의 멘토 프로그램을 소개하면서 (The Staley Foundation is proud to support the growth of small businesses through AIM, its mentorship program ~) 같은 단락 후반부에 신청자는 반드시 햄릭 시 대도시

권에 거주하고 있어야 한다(Applicants must reside in the Hamrick City metropolitan area)는 참가 자격을 알리고 있다. 따라서 지역 내에서 진행되는 멘토 프로그램에 참가할 수 있는 기회를 알리는 글임을 알 수 있으므로 (A)가 정답이다.

어휘 publicize 알리다 local 지역의 opportunity 기회 seek 요청하다, 구하다 donation 기부 charitable 자선의 cause 목적, 대의 initiative 계획 recruit 모집하다 organization 단체, 기관

## 177 세부 사항

번역 바렛 씨는 누구인가?
(A) 교재 집필자
(B) 단체 설립자
(C) 프로그램의 이전 참가자
(D) 경제학 교수

해설 정보의 두 번째 단락에 스테일리 재단이 로잘린 스테일리를 기리기 위해 그 사람의 딸인 에밀리 바렛에 의해 설립되었다(The Staley Foundation was established in honor of Rosaline Staley by her daughter, Emily Barrett)는 말이 쓰여 있으므로 (B)가 정답이다.

> **Paraphrasing**
> 지문의 The Staley Foundation was established ~ by her daughter, Emily Barrett
> → 정답의 The founder of an organization

## 178 주제 / 목적

번역 마 씨가 이메일을 보낸 한 가지 이유는 무엇인가?
(A) 문제에 관한 세부 정보를 요청하는 것
(B) 브랜딩에 관해 의견을 제공하는 것
(C) 재배정 요청을 거절하는 것
(D) 행사에 초대하는 것

해설 이메일의 두 번째 단락에 5월 1일로 막 일정을 잡은 브랜드 구축에 관한 워크숍에 참석하길 바란다(I hope you will attend a workshop on brand-building that we just scheduled for May 1)는 말이 쓰여 있어 이 행사에 초대하는 것이 한 가지 목적임을 알 수 있으므로 (D)가 정답이다.

어휘 details 세부 정보 refuse 거절하다 reassignment 재배정, 재할당 issue an invitation to + 명사 ~에 초대하다

> **Paraphrasing**
> 지문의 I hope you will attend a workshop
> → 정답의 issue an invitation to an event

## 179 연계

번역 윌리엄스 씨에 대해 어떤 결론을 내릴 수 있는가?
(A) 테이트 씨의 자격에 관해 문의했다.
(B) 마 씨에게 전화로 연락할 수 없었다.
(C) 사업을 시작한 지 1년이 되지 않았다.
(D) 다음 달에 여유 시간이 더 많을 것이다.

해설 수신자가 윌리엄스 씨인 이메일의 첫 번째 단락에 귀하의 AIM 멘토(your AIM mentor)가 언급된 것에서 윌리엄스 씨가 멘토 프로그램 참가자임을 알 수 있다. 정보의 첫 번째 단락 후반부에 이 멘토 프로그램의 신청 조건이 언급되는데 신청하려면 지난 12개월 안에 사업을 시작했어야 한다(have launched their business within the past 12 months)고 했으므로 이 프로그램 참가자인 윌리엄스 씨는 사업을 시작한 지 1년이 되지 않았다는 사실을 알 수 있다. 따라서 (C)가 정답이다.

어휘 conclude 결론을 내리다 inquire 문의하다 qualification 자격 (요건)

> **Paraphrasing**
> 지문의 have launched their business within the past 12 months
> → 정답의 started a business less than a year ago

## 180 추론

번역 윌리엄스 씨는 어떤 업계에서 일하고 있을 것 같은가?
(A) 기술
(B) 음식 서비스
(C) 조경
(D) 실내 디자인

해설 이메일의 두 번째 단락에 워크숍 진행자인 몰리 테이트는 수년 동안 실내 디자인 업체를 운영했다(The leader, Molly Tate, ran a successful interior design firm for years)며, 워크숍 후에 테이트 씨에게 윌리엄스 씨의 분야에 특정된 조언을 요청할 수 있다(~ but you could approach Ms. Tate afterwards about providing some extra guidance specific to your field)는 말이 쓰여 있다. 이를 통해 실내 디자인 전문가에게 자신의 분야에 관한 조언을 요청하는 윌리엄스 씨도 같은 업계에 속해 있다고 추론할 수 있으므로 (D)가 정답이다.

## 181-185 웹페이지 + 후기

https://www.crowdview.com/search

사용자: 귀네스 림

내 주변 최고의 세탁 서비스 업체
내 위치: 센트럴 가 680, 래넘 (변경)
거리 제한: 10마일

| | |
|---|---|
| 그린월드 클리너스<br>[181] ★★★★☆ 4.5 (18개의 후기)<br>특별 서비스: 드라이 클리닝; 수거/배달 | 프루이트 가 180<br>엠브리빌, OK<br>거리: 4.5마일 |
| 챔피언 클리닝<br>[181] ★★★★☆ 4.5 (23개의 후기)<br>특별 서비스: 드라이 클리닝; 의류 변형/수선 | 1번 가 455<br>래넘, OK<br>[184] **거리: 1.4마일** |
| 바거 패밀리 클리너스<br>★★★★☆ 4.0 (16개의 후기)<br>특별 서비스: 드라이 클리닝; [182] **가정용 리넨 제품** | 오크 가 2400<br>치스홀트, OK<br>거리: 5.2마일 |

| 그린월드 클리너스 래넘 | 펄 로 48 |
|---|---|
| ★★★☆☆ 3.5 (27개의 후기) | 래넘, OK |
| 특별 서비스: 드라이 클리닝; 수거/배달 | 거리: 0.8마일 |
| 밀번 런드리 서비스 | 체스터 가 364 |
| ★★★☆☆ 3 (9개의 후기) | 엠브리빌, OK |
| 특별 서비스: 드라이 클리닝; 익일 처리 완료; 의류 변형/수선 | 거리: 3.9마일 |

어휘 pickup 수거, 가져가기 alteration 변형, 변경 household 가정의 linen 리넨 제품(식탁보나 침대 시트 등) turnaround (처리) 소요 시간

사용자: 귀네스 림

내 최신 후기

항목: 세탁 서비스

게시일: 1월 14일

183 **제가 최근에 할머니에게서 아름다운 아이보리 실크 드레스를 물려받았는데,** 오래되어서 몇 군데가 누렇게 변하고 치마 부분에 작게 찢어진 곳이 있었습니다. 184 **다른 크라우드뷰 사용자의 상세 후기를 보니 챔피언 클리닝에서 그 사람의 실크 제품들 중 하나에 생긴 비슷한 문제를 해결해 주었다고 해서, 제 드레스를 그곳으로 가져갔습니다.** 그렇게 해서 다행입니다! 그들은 변색 자국을 없애고 찢어진 부분을 너무나 세심하게 수선할 수 있어서 몇 인치 떨어져서 보면 겨우 바느질 자국만 보일 정도였습니다. 카운터에 계시는 직원 분도 시간을 내서 앞으로 드레스를 올바르게 보관하는 방법을 설명해 주셨습니다. 185 **챔피언 클리닝에 대한 제 유일한 불만은 그 훌륭한 작업이 높은 가격에 제공된다는 점입니다.** 저에게 덜 귀중한 제품의 관리를 위해서는 그렇게 많은 돈을 지불할 것 같지 않습니다.

어휘 inherit 물려받다 yellowed 누렇게 변한 with age 오래된 tear 찢긴 부분 detailed 상세한 fix 바로잡다, 고치다 similar 비슷한 issue 문제, 사안 remove 없애다, 제거하다 discoloration 변색 mend 수선하다 delicately 세심하게 notice 알아차리다 stitch 바느질 자국, 바늘땀 take the time to ~하기 위해 시간을 내다 store 보관하다 properly 적절히, 제대로 complaint 불만 be willing to 기꺼이 ~하다 care 관리, 주의 precious 귀중한

## 181 세부 사항

번역 목록의 첫 두 업체는 어떻게 유사한가?
(A) 같은 기업 체인의 일부이다.
(B) 같은 도시에 위치해 있다.
(C) 평점이 같다.
(D) 받은 후기의 수가 같다.

해설 첫 지문에 제시된 목록의 첫 두 업체인 그린월드 클리너스와 챔피언 클리닝은 동일하게 4.5점의 평점을 받은 것으로 표기되어 있으므로 (C)가 정답이다.

어휘 corporate 기업의 be located in ~에 위치해 있다 rating 등급, 평점

## 182 세부 사항

번역 웹페이지에 따르면, 바거 패밀리 클리너스는 무엇을 할 수 있겠는가?
(A) 24시간 내에 드라이 클리닝하기
(B) 창문 커튼 세트 세탁하기
(C) 세탁된 제품을 고객의 집으로 갖다주기
(D) 셔츠 소매 줄이기

해설 목록에 세 번째 업체로 기재된 바거 패밀리 클리너스가 제공하는 특별 서비스에 가정용 리넨 제품(household linens)이라는 말이 쓰여 있는데, 이는 식탁보나 침대 시트, 커튼, 베갯잇 등의 제품을 가리키므로 (B)가 정답이다.

어휘 transport 옮기다, 운송하다 shorten 줄이다, 짧게 하다

## 183 세부 사항

번역 림 씨는 자신의 드레스에 대해 무슨 말을 하는가?
(A) 색상이 특수 염색 기법의 결과물이다.
(B) 오랫동안 자신의 장롱에 보관되어 왔다.
(C) 원래의 바느질 일부가 수작업으로 이뤄졌다.
(D) 전에 자신의 가족 중 한 사람이 소유했다.

해설 후기 시작 부분에 최근에 할머니에게서 아름다운 아이보리 실크 드레스를 물려받았다(I recently inherited a beautiful ivory silk dress from my grandmother)고 했으므로 (D)가 정답이다.

어휘 dyeing 염색 belong to+명사 ~의 소유이다 relative 친척

> Paraphrasing
> 지문의 inherited ~ from my grandmother
> → 정답의 used to belong to one of her relatives

## 184 연계

번역 림 씨가 선택한 업체는 집에서 얼마나 멀리 떨어져 있는가?
(A) 0.8마일
(B) 1.4마일
(C) 3.9마일
(D) 4.5마일

해설 후기 초반부에 림 씨가 다른 사람의 후기를 보고 챔피언 클리닝에 드레스를 가져갔다(Another Crowdview user's detailed review said that Champion Cleaning had fixed similar issues with one of her silk items, so I brought my dress there)고 했다. 웹페이지 목록에서 챔피언 클리닝의 거리가 1.4마일(Distance: 1.4 mines)로 표기되어 있으므로 (B)가 정답이다.

## 185 세부 사항

번역 후기에 따르면, 무엇 때문에 림 씨가 실망했는가?
(A) 서비스에 청구된 가격
(B) 직원이 제공한 조언
(C) 크라우드뷰에 올라온 후기의 정확성
(D) 세탁 후에도 남아 있는 문제

해설 두 번째 지문 후반부에 챔피언 클리닝에 대한 유일한 불만이 높은 가

격(My only complaint about Champion Cleaning is that their excellent work comes at a high price)이라고 했으므로 (A)가 정답이다.

어휘 charge 청구하다 accuracy 정확(성) persistence 지속(성)

### 186-190 기사+일정표+이메일

벨라미 공원 도로에 예정된 개선 작업

(3월 10일)—앞으로 몇 주에 걸쳐, 그로버트 교통국이 콜웰 가와 하인즈 크릭 길 사이에 있는 벨라미 공원 도로의 주요 교차로 중 일부에 대한 개선 작업을 감독할 것이다. 각 교차로 주변의 공원 도로를 넓혀 좌회전과 우회전을 위한 회전 차선을 만들고, 좌회전 차선을 통제하는 전용 신호등을 추가할 것이다.

186 **"별도의 회전 차선 덕분에 회전 대기 중인 차량 뒤에 차가 쌓이지 않고 교통 흐름이 원활해질 것입니다."라고 로드 손턴 교통국장이 설명했다.** "시의 인구가 늘어나면서, 이는 특히 교통 혼잡 시간대와 록 힐즈 초등학교 근처에서 문제가 되어 왔습니다." 187 **불만스러운 그로버트 유권자들은 이 180만 달러 규모의 프로젝트 비용을 지불할 수 있도록 시의 재산세 단기 인상에 찬성했다.**

188 **각 교차로 개선 작업이 진행되는 동안에는 작업 인력과 장비를 위한 공간을 확보하기 위해 해당 지역의 공원 도로는 4개 차선 중 2개 차선의 교통이 통제될 예정이다.** 벨라미 공원 도로를 자주 이용하는 차량 운전자들은 교통국 웹사이트를 방문해 도로 작업 일정을 확인하기 바란다.

어휘 improvement 개선, 향상 oversee 감독하다 widen 확장하다 create 만들다 dedicated 전용의 control 통제하다 allow 할 수 있게 해 주다 flow 흐르다 smoothly 순조롭게 build up 늘어나다, 누적되다 make a turn 회전하다 population 인구 frustrated 불만스러운 voter 유권자 approve 찬성하다 short-term 단기의 property tax 재산세 relevant 관련된 equipment 장비

벨라미 공원 도로 개선 작업 일정

188 **3월 14일 - 3월 25일: 콜웰 가 교차로**
3월 28일 - 4월 8일: 하인즈 크릭 길 교차로
190 **4월 11일 - 4월 22일: 뉴턴 가 교차로**
4월 25일 - 5월 6일: 실바 대로 교차로

이 일정의 지연 또는 기타 변동 사항들은 교통국 웹사이트 홈페이지에 공지될 것입니다.

어휘 delay 지연, 지체

수신: 릴리안 마가노
발신: 유리코 후지타
날짜: 190 **4월 7일**
제목: 도로 작업 알림 메시지

안녕하세요, 릴리안.

제가 학교 일정표를 막 훑어보고 있었는데, 190 **다음 주 월요일인 11일부터 우리 학교로 이어지는 갈림길에서 도로 보수 작업이 시작된다는 것을 알았습니다.** 오늘 퇴근하시기 전에, 189 **이에 관한 추가 알림 메시지를 학부모님들께 전송해 주시겠습니까?** 워낙 가까이에서 진행될 것이기 때문에, 이 공원 도로의 다른 구간 개선 공사보다 학교에 더 많은 불편함을 초래할 것으로 생각합니다. 오후에 스쿨버스가 예정보다 약간 늦어질 수 있다는 점과 직접 차를 운전하시는 경우 픽업 및 하차 시간이 지연될 수 있다는 점을 학부모들에게 알려야 합니다.

감사합니다.

유리코 후지타
교감

어휘 reminder (상기시키기 위한) 알림 메시지 look over ~을 훑어보다 turnoff 지선도로, 분기점 additional 추가적인 close by 가까이에서 inconvenience 불편함 warn 통지하다 behind schedule 일정보다 뒤처진 pick-up (차에) 태워 가기 drop-off (차에서) 내려 주기

### 186 Not / True

번역 기사에 따르면, 계획된 개선 작업에 대해 무엇이 사실인가?
(A) 시범 프로그램의 일부이다.
(B) 손상된 부분의 수리를 포함한다.
(C) 교통 혼잡을 완화해 줄 것이다.
(D) 새 안전 법규에 의해 요구되는 것이다.

해설 기사의 두 번째 단락에 개선 작업으로 인한 효과로 별도의 회전 차선 덕분에 회전 대기 중인 차량 뒤에 차가 쌓이지 않고 교통 흐름이 원활해질 것(Separate turn lanes will allow traffic to flow smoothly instead of building up behind cars that are waiting to make a turn)이라는 말이 쓰여 있다. 이는 교통 혼잡이 완화되는 것을 의미하므로 (C)가 정답이다.

어휘 pilot program 시범 프로그램 include 포함하다 relieve 완화하다 congestion 혼잡

Paraphrasing
지문의 allow traffic to flow smoothly
→ 정답의 relieve traffic congestion

### 187 Not / True

번역 기사에서 프로젝트 비용에 대해 무엇을 언급하는가?
(A) 세수로 충당될 것이다.
(B) 처음에 예상된 것보다 더 높을 것이다.
(C) 공표되지 않았다.
(D) 합리적이다.

해설 기사의 두 번째 단락에 그로버트 유권자들은 이 180만 달러 규모의 프로젝트 비용을 지불할 수 있도록 시의 재산세 단기 인상에 찬성했다(Frustrated Grovert voters approved a short-term increase in the city's property taxes to pay for the $1.8 million project)고 알리고 있다. 세금 인상을 통해 프로젝트 비용을 지불하는 것은 세수로 그 비용을 충당한다는 뜻이므로 (A)가 정답이다.

어휘 cover (비용 등을) 충당하다 revenue 수익, 수입 initially 처음에 make public 공표하다 reasonable 합리적인

## 188 연계

번역 3월 14일에 무슨 일이 있을 것인가?
(A) 시민들이 제안에 대해 투표할 것이다.
(B) 도로의 일부 차선이 폐쇄될 것이다.
(C) 일정 변경이 공지될 것이다.
(D) 시 부서에서 설명회를 주최할 것이다.

해설 벨라미 공원 도로 개선 작업 일정에서 3월 14일에 콜웰 가 교차로 개선 작업(March 14-March 25: Colwell Street intersection)이 있음을 알 수 있다. 이 개선 작업에 대해, 기사의 마지막 단락에 각 교차로 개선 작업이 진행되는 동안에는 해당 지역의 공원 도로는 4개 차선 중 2개 차선의 교통이 통제될 예정(During the improvements to each intersection, two of the parkway's four lanes will be closed to traffic in the relevant area ~)이라고 알리고 있으므로 도로의 일부 차선이 폐쇄될 것이라는 의미로 쓰인 (B)가 정답이다.

어휘 vote 투표하다 proposal 제안(서) revision 변경, 수정 host 주최하다 information session 설명회

> Paraphrasing
> 지문의 two of the parkway's four lanes will be closed to traffic
> → 정답의 Some lanes of a street will be closed

## 189 주제 / 목적

번역 후지타 씨가 왜 이메일을 썼는가?
(A) 일정표 항목의 의미를 설명하기 위해
(B) 대체 교통편을 나열하기 위해
(C) 연락하는 업무를 배정하기 위해
(D) 픽업 시간 늦추는 것을 제안하기 위해

해설 이메일의 초반부에 추가 알림 메시지를 학부모님들께 전송해 줄 것(could you send out an additional reminder to parents about it?)을 요청하고 있다. 이는 학부모들에게 연락하는 업무를 배정하는 것이므로 (C)가 정답이다.

어휘 entry 항목 alternative 대체, 대안 assign 배정하다, 할당하다 task 업무, 일

> Paraphrasing
> 지문의 send out an additional reminder to parents
> → 정답의 a communication task

## 190 연계

번역 마가노 씨에 대해 암시된 것은?
(A) 우편물 수신을 신청했다.
(B) 다음 주에 후지타 씨를 만날 것이다.
(C) 아이가 초등학교에 다닌다.
(D) 직장이 뉴턴 가에 있다.

해설 마가노 씨가 수신인인 이메일에 자신들이 있는 곳의 도로 작업이 다음 주 월요일인 11일에 시작된다(the roadwork on the turnoff to our street starts next Monday, the eleventh)고 하였고, 상단의 이메일 작성일이 4월 7일(April 7)이므로 4월 11일에 마가노 씨의 직장이 있는 곳에서 도로 작업이 시작된다는 것을 알 수 있다. 또한, 일정표에 4월 11일이 뉴턴 가 교차로 작업 시작일(April 11-April 22: Newton Street intersection)로 쓰여 있으므로 직장이 뉴턴 가에 있다는 것을 알 수 있다. 따라서 (D)가 정답이다.

어휘 subscribe to+명사 ~에 대한 가입을 신청하다 mailing list 우편물 수신 명단

## 191-195 안내 책자+이메일+이메일

에그먼트

웰링턴의 중심 상업 지구에 자리잡고 있는, 에그먼트는 개인 축하 행사와 기업 회의, 모금 행사 등을 열 수 있는 시에서 가장 인기 있는 행사장들 중 하나입니다. 수많은 호텔과 여러 버스 정류장, 그리고 기차역에서 도보로 얼마 되지 않는 편리한 위치에 있습니다.

에그먼트에는 두 개의 넓은 다목적 행사 공간이 있습니다. 마누카 룸은 100에서 200명 사이의 단체에 가장 적합하며, 가장 큰 공간인 [193] **카우리 룸은 최대 300명에 달하는 손님들을 편안하게 수용할 수 있습니다.** 저희는 또한 두 개의 전용 컨퍼런스 룸인 레이타 룸과 피카오 룸을 보유하고 있으며, 이곳의 최대 수용 인원은 각각 35명과 70명입니다.

[191] **저희 모든 공간에서 최신식 프로젝터와 스피커, 그리고 기타 멀티미디어 장비가 이용 가능하며, 편리한 내부 기술 지원 서비스가 지원됩니다.** 추가로, 저희 에그먼트의 음식 제공 서비스는 가벼운 다과에서부터 여러 코스의 만찬에 이르기까지 다양한 상황에 맞는 맛있는 맞춤형 음식을 만들 수 있습니다.

특정 요일 및 시간대에 공간을 예약하시는 첫 방문 고객들께서는 10% 할인을 받으실 수 있습니다. 상세 정보를 보시려면 www.theegmont.co.nz를 방문하시기 바랍니다.

어휘 situated in ~에 자리잡은 venue 행사장 celebration 기념 행사 fund-raiser 모금 행사 numerous 다수의 spacious 널찍한 multi-purpose 다목적의 comfortably 편안하게 dedicated 전용의 maximum capacity 최대 수용 인원 respectively 각각 state-of-the-art 최신식의 equipment 장비 available 이용 가능한 in-house (조직) 내부의 catering 출장 요리 제공 custom 주문 제공되는 fare 음식, 식사 refreshments 다과 reserve 예약하다 eligible for ~을 할 수 있는, ~에 대한 자격이 있는

수신: 애런 존스
발신: 루스 헤나레
날짜: 10월 12일
제목: 시상식 만찬 장소

안녕하세요, 애런.

오늘 아침에 제가 우리 연례 시상식 만찬 주최에 대해 에그먼트에 전화했습니다. [193] **이곳은 200명 이상으로 늘어난 우리 전체 손님을 수용**

**할 수 있는 공간과 음식 제공 능력을 분명 갖추고 있습니다.** 하지만, 우리가 필요한 공간은 11월의 모든 토요일 저녁에 이미 예약이 되어 있기 때문에, 11월 11일은 더 이상 선택 대상이 아닙니다. 하지만, 그 주 일요일인 11월 12일은 비어 있으며, 11월 17일 금요일도 마찬가지입니다. 또한, [195] **11월 16일 목요일은 할인된 요금으로 이용 가능합니다.**

저는 우리가 이곳을 이용해야 한다고 생각합니다. [192] **원래 행사장이 예기치 못하게 문을 닫았다고 설명하면 참석자들이 날짜 변경을 이해할 겁니다.** [194] **이 모든 날짜들이 빠르게 다가오고 있으며 여전히 준비할 것이 많이 남아 있기 때문에 조만간 제게 결정 사항을 알려 주셨으면 합니다.**

감사합니다.

루스

어휘 annual 연례적인 capacity 능력, 수용력 accommodate 수용하다 entire 전체의 available 이용 가능한 rate 요금 attendee 참석자 shut down 문을 닫다 unexpectedly 예기치 못하게 decision 결정 approach 다가오다 preparation 준비

수신: 루스 헤나레
발신: 애런 존스
날짜: 10월 12일
제목: 시상식 만찬 장소

안녕하세요, 루스.

에그먼트가 좋은 선택이라는 말씀에 동의합니다. 우리 예산을 고려해서, [195] **할인이 되는 날짜로 예약해 주셨으면 합니다. 감사합니다.**

애런 존스
회장, 웰링턴 상공 협의회

어휘 agree 동의하다 with ~ in mind ~을 고려해, ~을 염두에 두고 budget 예산

## 191 추론

번역 안내 책자가 에그먼트에 대해 암시하는 것은?
(A) 웰링턴에서 기차로 짧은 거리에 있다.
(B) 직원 중에 시청각 기술자가 포함되어 있다.
(C) 최근 두 번째 레스토랑을 추가했다.
(D) 대규모 연례 모금 행사 장소이다.

해설 안내 책자의 세 번째 단락에 모든 공간에서 최신식 프로젝터와 스피커, 그리고 기타 멀티미디어 장비가 이용 가능하며, 편리한 내부 기술 지원 서비스가 지원된다(State-of-the-art projectors, speakers, and other multimedia equipment are available ~ supported by convenient in-house technical assistance)고 하였다. 따라서 프로젝터와 스피커에 대한 기술 지원 서비스를 제공하는 직원, 즉 시청각 기술자가 있다는 사실을 알 수 있으므로 (B)가 정답이다.

어휘 include 포함하다 audiovisual 시청각의 fund-raiser 모금 행사

## 192 Not / True

번역 헤나레 씨가 시상식 만찬에 대해 언급하는 것은?
(A) 뷔페 식사를 특징으로 할 것이다.
(B) 호텔 매니저를 기릴 것이다.
(C) 참석할 수 없을 것이다.
(D) 그것을 위한 새 장소를 찾고 있다.

해설 헤나레 씨가 작성한 이메일은 에그먼트를 행사장으로 추천하는 내용이며, 두 번째 단락에 원래 행사장이 예기치 못하게 문을 닫았다(~ our original venue shut down unexpectedly)는 말이 있는데, 이를 통해 원래 계획했던 행사장이 문을 닫아서 새로운 행사장을 찾고 있는 것임을 알 수 있으므로 (D)가 정답이다.

어휘 feature 특징으로 하다 honor 기리다, 영예를 주다 seek 찾다

## 193 연계

번역 해당 단체가 어디에서 시상식 만찬을 개최할 것 같은가?
(A) 마누카 룸
(B) 카우리 룸
(C) 레이타 룸
(D) 피카오 룸

해설 첫 번째 이메일 첫 번째 단락에서 손님이 200명 이상으로 늘어났다(~ our entire guest list, which has grown beyond 200 people)는 말이 언급되었는데, 안내 책자의 두 번째 단락에 카우리 룸이 최대 300명에 달하는 손님들을 편안하게 수용할 수 있다(the Kauri Room, can hold up to 300 guests comfortably)는 정보가 제시되어 있으므로 (B)가 정답이다.

## 194 세부 사항

번역 헤나레 씨는 왜 우려하는가?
(A) 많은 사람들이 초대를 거절해서
(B) 행사를 준비하는 데 시간이 많지 않아서
(C) 음식 제공 서비스가 예상보다 더 비싸서
(D) 행사장을 한번도 직접 보지 못해서

해설 헤나레 씨가 작성한 이메일의 두 번째 단락에 결정 사항을 곧 알려 달라는 말과 함께 날짜들이 빠르게 다가오고 있고 여전히 준비할 것이 많이 남아 있다(I hope you'll let me know your decision soon, as all of these dates are approaching quickly and there are many preparations still to be made)고 했다. 따라서 행사를 준비할 시간이 많지 않은 상황임을 알 수 있으므로 (B)가 정답이다.

어휘 decline 거절하다 in person 직접 (가서)

> **Paraphrasing**
> 지문의 all of these dates are approaching quickly and there are many preparations still to be made
> → 정답의 There is not much time to prepare for an event

## 195 연계

번역 웰링턴 상공 협의회의 시상식 만찬이 어느 날짜에 개최될 것 같은가?
(A) 11월 11일
(B) 11월 12일
(C) 11월 16일
(D) 11월 17일

해설 두 번째 이메일에 할인이 되는 날짜로 예약해 주길 바란다(I'd like you to make the reservation for the discounted date)는 말이 있는데, 첫 번째 이메일 첫 번째 단락에 11월 16일 목요일은 할인된 요금으로 이용 가능하다(Thursday, 16 November is available at a discounted rate)고 쓰여 있으므로 (C)가 정답이다.

어휘 take place 개최되다, 진행되다

## 196-200 이메일+설문 발췌+이메일

발신: 슬라이드 에이스 <contact@slideace.com>
수신: 로이 손턴 <roy.thornton@gannitt.com>
제목: 기회
날짜: 7월 10일

손턴 씨께,

슬라이드 에이스 2.2의 소중한 이용자이신, [196] **귀하와 귀하의 직원들께 슬라이드 에이스 2.3 베타 테스트 참여를 요청드립니다.** 이 새로운 버전의 슬라이드 에이스는 연말쯤 대대적으로 출시하기를 바라고 있는데, [199] **디자인 전문가들이 만든 세련된 슬라이드 템플릿 라이브러리인 '레디고'를** 특징으로 합니다. 다른 주요 변경 사항으로는 귀하의 팀에서 저장된 슬라이드를 이용하는 것에 대한 유익한 통계 자료를 대시보드에 보고하는 기능과 [198] **모든 발표 자료에서 귀사의 로고와 선호하는 색상 조합 및 서체를 쉽게 업데이트할 수 있는 브랜드 관리 툴이 있습니다.**

슬라이드 에이스 2.3은 여기에서 다운로드하실 수 있습니다. 플랫폼의 흥미로운 발전에 동참해 주시길 바랍니다.

슬라이드 에이스

어휘 opportunity 기회 valued 소중한 participate in ~에 참여하다 release 출시하다, 공개하다 feature 특징으로 하다 sophisticated 세련된 include 포함하다 statistics 통계 (자료) store 저장하다 enable 가능하게 하다 preferred 선호하는 scheme 조합, 체계 agree 동의하다

사용자: 로이 손턴

이제 설문의 마지막 페이지입니다. 앞선 질문들에 대한 귀하의 답변을 설명하는 데 도움이 될 수 있는 의견을 이곳에 추가해 주시기 바랍니다.

[197] **저는 대시보드에 "2점"을 주었는데,** 너무 어수선한 느낌이기 때문입니다. 아마 대시보드에 보여지는 데이터의 유형을 사용자가 지정하도록 할 수 있을 것 같습니다.
[198] **새로운 브랜드 관리 툴은 빠르게 발전하는 신생 기업인 저희 회사에 정말로 유익할 좋은 아이디어입니다.** 제가 만점을 주지 않은 유일한 이유는 슬라이드 에이스를 처음 시도했을 때 갑자기 작동을 멈췄기 때문입니다.
참여해 주셔서 감사합니다!

어휘 comment 의견, 발언 previous 앞선, 이전의 cluttered 어수선한 customize 맞춤 제공하다, 맞춤 제작하다 evolving 발전하는, 진화하는 startup 신생 기업 crash (프로그램 등이) 갑자기 작동을 멈추다 participation 참여, 참가

발신: 미리엄 캐시디 <miriam.cassidy@slideace.com>
수신: 니콜 리우 <nicole.liu@slideace.com>
제목: 소식
날짜: 8월 2일
첨부: 8월 2일 피드백

안녕하세요, 니콜,

슬라이드 에이스 2.3에 대한 최신 피드백을 통해 레디고가 큰 인기를 끌고 있음을 확인했습니다! 이 이메일에 그 수치들에 대한 분석 자료를 첨부했습니다. 살펴보시고 데이터에 대해 궁금한 점이 있으면 알려 주세요.

[199] **이제 우리가 레디고에 더 투자하는 게 현명하다는 것이 분명해진 것 같습니다. 특히, 장기간에 걸쳐 지속적으로 추가할 수 있는 계획을 세워야 합니다.** [200] **이번 주에 만나서 이 일에 필요할 직원 구성에 대해 이야기 나눌 수 있을까요?**

감사합니다.

미리엄

어휘 batch (일괄 처리되는) 분량, 한 회분, 한 묶음 confirm 확실하게 해 주다, 확정하다 attach 첨부하다 breakdown 분석, 분해, 명세 invest 투자하다 further 추가로, 한층 더 specifically 특히, 구체적으로 consistently 지속적으로, 일관되게 over the long term 장기간에 걸쳐 staffing 직원 구성, 인력 충원

## 196 주제 / 목적

번역 첫 번째 이메일의 목적은 무엇인가?
(A) 시연회 초대장을 보내는 것
(B) 계획된 업데이트의 이유를 설명하는 것
(C) 잠재적인 서비스에 대한 제안을 요청하는 것
(D) 제품 테스터 그룹을 모집하는 것

해설 첫 번째 이메일 시작 부분에 상대방과 상대방 직원들에게 슬라이드 에이스 2.3 베타 테스트 참여를 요청한다(you and your staff are invited to participate in beta testing of Slide Ace 2.3)는 말이 쓰여 있어 제품 테스트를 위해 사람들을 모집하는 것을 알 수 있으므로 (D)가 정답이다.

어휘 issue an invitation 초대장을 보내다 demonstration 시연(회) solicit 요청하다 potential 잠재적인 recruit 모집하다

> **Paraphrasing**
> 지문의 you and your staff are invited to participate in beta testing of Slide Ace 2.3
> → 정답의 recruit a group of product testers

## 197 추론

번역 설문조사에 대해 암시된 것은?
(A) 두 가지 이상의 형식으로 이용할 수 있다.
(B) 완료하는 경우에 손턴 씨가 비용을 지급받을 것이다.
(C) 슬라이드 에이스는 이를 운영해줄 회사를 고용했다.
(D) 참여자들에게 숫자 평점을 줄 것을 요청한다.

해설 설문 발췌 지문 두 번째 단락에 대시보드에 2점을 주었다(I gave the dashboard a "2")고 언급하고 있으므로 (D)가 정답이다.

어휘 available 이용 가능한 format 형식, 구성 administer 실시하다, 집행하다 participant 참여자 numerical 숫자의, 숫자와 관련된 rating 평점, 등급

> **Paraphrasing**
> 지문의 gave the dashboard a "2"
> → 정답의 to give numerical ratings

## 198 연계

번역 손턴 씨의 회사에 대해 암시된 것은?
(A) 고객들의 데이터 분석을 돕는다.
(B) 슬라이드 에이스에 많은 슬라이드를 저장하지 않는다.
(C) 때때로 선호하는 기업 스타일 요소들을 변경한다.
(D) 소셜 미디어를 통해 일반인들과 자주 소통한다.

해설 손턴 씨의 의견이 제시된 설문 발췌 지문 세 번째 단락에, 새로운 브랜드 관리 툴은 빠르게 발전하는 신생 기업인 본인의 회사에 정말로 유익할 좋은 아이디어(The new brand management tool is a great idea that will be really helpful for our company as a quickly-evolving startup)라는 말이 쓰여 있다. 이 툴에 대해 첫 번째 이메일 첫 단락에 모든 발표 자료에서 귀사의 로고와 선호하는 색상 조합 및 서체를 쉽게 업데이트할 수 있는 브랜드 관리 툴(a brand management tool that enables easy updating of your logo and preferred color schemes and fonts across all of your presentations)이라고 써 있는데, 이 툴을 사용한다는 것은 로고나 색상 조합, 서체 등의 스타일을 종종 변경한다는 것으로 볼 수 있으므로 (C)가 정답이다.

어휘 assist 지원하다, 돕다 analysis 분석 store 저장하다, 보관하다 element 요소 preferred 선호하는 corporate 기업의

## 199 연계

번역 캐시디 씨는 무엇을 하도록 권하는가?
(A) 슬라이드 템플릿 모음 확장하기
(B) 시각 자료를 사용자가 지정할 수 있는 옵션 늘리기
(C) 정보 화면의 디자인 단순화하기
(D) 더 많은 사람들에게 소프트웨어 버전 공개하기

해설 캐시디 씨가 작성한 이메일 두 번째 단락에, 레디고에 더 투자하는 게 현명하다는 것이 분명해진 것 같다는 말과 함께 장기간에 걸쳐 지속적으로 그것을 늘릴 수 있는 계획을 세우는 것이 좋겠다(I think it's now clear that it would be wise for us to invest further in ReadyGo. Specifically, we should make plans to add to it consistently over the long term)고 했다. 여기서 말하는 레디고에 대해 첫 번째 이메일 첫 단락에 세련된 슬라이드 템플릿 라이브러리(ReadyGo, a library of sophisticated slide templates)라고 쓰여 있어 그 슬라이드 템플릿 규모를 확대하도록 권하고 있는 것임을 알 수 있다. 따라서 (A)가 정답이다.

어휘 expand 확대하다, 확장하다 simplify 단순화하다, 간소화하다 release 공개하다, 출시하다

## 200 세부 사항

번역 캐시디 씨는 리우 씨와 무엇을 논의하고 싶어 하는가?
(A) 프로젝트 진행 일정
(B) 잠재적인 인력 수요
(C) 다가오는 고객 회의
(D) 일부 부정적인 의견

해설 두 번째 이메일 두 번째 단락에 레디고에 대한 추가 투자 및 장기적인 확대 계획을 이야기하면서 이번 주에 만나서 이 일에 필요할 직원 구성에 대해 이야기 나눌 수 있을지(Can we meet this week to talk about the staffing that this would require?) 묻고 있으므로 (B)가 정답이다.

어휘 personnel 인력, 인사(부) upcoming 다가오는, 곧 있을 negative 부정적인

> **Paraphrasing**
> 지문의 staffing that this would require
> → 정답의 Potential personnel needs

# TEST 2

| | | | | |
|---|---|---|---|---|
| 101 (A) | 102 (C) | 103 (D) | 104 (A) | 105 (B) |
| 106 (B) | 107 (D) | 108 (A) | 109 (A) | 110 (B) |
| 111 (C) | 112 (B) | 113 (C) | 114 (A) | 115 (C) |
| 116 (D) | 117 (B) | 118 (C) | 119 (D) | 120 (B) |
| 121 (B) | 122 (C) | 123 (D) | 124 (A) | 125 (C) |
| 126 (B) | 127 (D) | 128 (D) | 129 (C) | 130 (A) |
| 131 (C) | 132 (A) | 133 (D) | 134 (B) | 135 (D) |
| 136 (D) | 137 (C) | 138 (B) | 139 (B) | 140 (B) |
| 141 (A) | 142 (D) | 143 (A) | 144 (D) | 145 (C) |
| 146 (C) | 147 (A) | 148 (B) | 149 (D) | 150 (A) |
| 151 (C) | 152 (D) | 153 (D) | 154 (B) | 155 (B) |
| 156 (C) | 157 (A) | 158 (D) | 159 (C) | 160 (A) |
| 161 (B) | 162 (A) | 163 (C) | 164 (A) | 165 (C) |
| 166 (C) | 167 (B) | 168 (B) | 169 (D) | 170 (A) |
| 171 (B) | 172 (D) | 173 (A) | 174 (C) | 175 (A) |
| 176 (C) | 177 (C) | 178 (D) | 179 (A) | 180 (B) |
| 181 (D) | 182 (B) | 183 (A) | 184 (B) | 185 (C) |
| 186 (A) | 187 (B) | 188 (B) | 189 (C) | 190 (D) |
| 191 (B) | 192 (B) | 193 (B) | 194 (C) | 195 (A) |
| 196 (A) | 197 (D) | 198 (C) | 199 (B) | 200 (B) |

## PART 5

### 101 감정 분사 _ 과거분사 vs. 현재분사

번역 룩스 미용실에서 받는 서비스에 만족하지 못하면, 저희 매니저에게 알려 주시기 바랍니다.

해설 주어 you를 보충 설명하는 주격 보어 자리로, you가 기쁨을 느끼는 것이므로 과거분사인 (A) pleased가 정답이다. be pleased with는 '~에 만족하다, ~에 기뻐하다'라는 의미로 자주 쓰이는 표현이니 알아 두자.

### 102 인칭 대명사 _ 소유대명사

번역 자동차 유리 수리점을 찾으실 때, 반드시 저희 기술자들처럼 공인된 기술자가 있는 곳을 선택하세요.

해설 전치사 like의 목적어 자리이므로 목적어 자리에 올 수 있는 대명사 (C)와 (D) 중, our technicians(저희 기술자들)를 받을 수 있는 (C) ours가 정답이다. (D) ourselves는 '우리 자신'이라는 의미의 재귀대명사로 주어와 동일한 대상을 가리킬 때 사용하므로 적합하지 않다.

어휘 choose 선택하다 certified 공인된

### 103 동사 자리 _ 태+시제

번역 스텝 씨가 일주일간 마케팅 세미나에 가 있는 동안 친 씨가 그의 업무를 맡을 것이다.

해설 while 이하는 부사절이고 주절에 동사가 없으므로 빈칸은 주절의 동사 자리이며, 빈칸 뒤에 Mr. Stepp's duties가 목적어로 있으므로 능동태가 되어야 한다. 또한, while절의 동사가 현재 시제(is)일 때 주절에는 현재 시제 또는 미래 시제 동사를 사용할 수 있으므로 미래 시제 능동태인 (D) will assume이 정답이다.

어휘 assume 맡다

### 104 부사 어휘

번역 냉동식품 공급업체로부터 배송품을 받은 후에는, 신속히 제품을 식당 냉동고로 옮기시기 바랍니다.

해설 냉동식품 공급업체로부터 받은 물품을 냉동고로 옮기는 방식을 나타낼 부사가 필요하므로 '신속히'를 뜻하는 (A) quickly가 정답이다.

어휘 accept 받다 supplier 공급업체 transfer 옮기다 closely 자세히, 면밀히 partly 부분적으로

### 105 전치사 어휘

번역 스냅 소스 사는 무역 박람회 참석자들에게 첫날 오전 11시까지 자사의 제품 샘플을 모두 나눠 주었다.

해설 빈칸 뒤에 시점을 나타내는 11 A.M.이 쓰여 있으므로 시점 명사와 함께 '~까지'라는 의미로 기한을 나타내는 (B) by가 정답이다.

어휘 hand out 나눠 주다 attendee 참석자

### 106 형용사 자리 _ 명사 수식

번역 포이 카운티 공원 관리국은 버스로 접근 가능한 등산로 목록을 정리했다.

해설 by bus는 등산로로 가는 방법이므로 빈칸과 by bus가 명사구 hiking trails를 뒤에서 수식하는 구조여야 한다. 따라서 명사구를 뒤에서 수식할 수 있는 형용사 (B) accessible(접근 가능한)이 정답이다.

어휘 compile (자료 등을 모아) 정리하다, 편집하다 accessibility 접근성 accessibly 접근 가능하게 access 접근; 접근하다

### 107 명사 자리 _ 동사의 목적어

번역 니아 앨드리지는 소프트웨어 엔지니어가 되기 위해 필요한 기술을 배우는 데 열정을 보였다.

해설 현재완료 시제 동사 has shown 뒤에 위치한 빈칸은 목적어 역할을 할 명사 자리이며, '열정을 보였다'가 알맞은 의미이므로 '열정'을 뜻하는 명사 (D) enthusiasm이 정답이다. (A) enthusiast(애호가)도 명사이기는 하지만 의미가 적합하지 않다.

어휘 enthusiastic 열정적인 enthusiastically 열정적으로

### 108 동사 어휘

번역 회사 정책에 따라, 미비한 환급 요청서는 승인되지 않을 것입니다.

해설 미비한 요청서에 대해 취할 수 있는 부정적인 조치를 나타내야 하므로 not be와 함께 '승인되지 않다'를 의미하는 (A) approved가 정답이다.

어휘 in accordance with ~에 따라 policy 정책 incomplete 미비한, 불완전한 reimbursement (비용) 환급 approve 승인하다 achieve 달성하다, 성취하다 increase 증가시키다, 증가하다

### 109 전치사 자리 _ 어휘

번역 소냐 레이는 솔로 공연자가 되기 전에 수년 동안 밴드 인디고 미스트의 리드 싱어였다.

해설 빈칸 앞에 완전한 문장이 있고, 빈칸 뒤에 동명사구 becoming a solo act가 있으므로, 동명사구를 목적어로 취할 전치사가 필요하며, '공연자가 되기 전에'를 의미해야 알맞으므로 '~ 전에'를 뜻하는 전치사 (A) before가 정답이다. (B) except(~을 제외하고)도 전치사이지만 의미상 적합하지 않으며, (C) then(그 다음에)과 (D) yet(아직)은 부사이므로 동명사구를 목적어로 취할 수 없다.

어휘 act 공연자, 그룹

### 110 동사 자리 _ 수 일치 + 시제

번역 비가 지속된다면 여름의 시작을 기념하는 직원 야유회가 미뤄져야 할 수도 있다.

해설 빈칸은 if절의 동사 자리이며, 주어가 the rain으로 3인칭 단수이다. 또한 주절의 동사가 may need처럼 미래(가능성)를 나타낼 때 if절에는 현재 시제 동사를 사용하므로 3인칭 단수 현재 시제 동사인 (B) continues가 정답이다.

어휘 celebrate 기념하다, 축하하다 postpone 연기하다, 미루다

### 111 형용사 자리 _ 목적격 보어

번역 드워턴 빌딩이 건설된 이래로, 그 건축물은 도시에서 가장 아름다운 것으로 여겨져 왔다.

해설 빈칸 앞에 수동태로 쓰인 consider 동사와 최상급을 만드는 the most가 있고, '가장 아름다운 것으로 여겨진다'라는 의미가 되어야 자연스러우므로 '아름다운'이란 의미의 형용사 (C) beautiful이 정답이다. 「consider + 목적어 + 목적격 보어」 구조의 5형식 문장이 수동태가 된 것이다.

어휘 architecture 건축(물) consider 여기다, 고려하다

### 112 전치사 어휘

번역 UBN 여행사는 이번 주부터 계속 퍼랠트 시내 일일 도보 투어를 제공할 것이다.

해설 this week onward와 함께 '이번 주부터 계속'이라는 의미로 도보 여행을 제공하기 시작하는 시점을 나타내야 알맞으므로 '~부터'를 뜻하는 전치사 (B) from이 정답이다.

어휘 onward 계속, 앞으로

### 113 명사 어휘

번역 셀잔 제약회사의 경영팀은 몇 년 내에 중국으로 사업을 확장하기 위한 전략을 개발했다.

해설 사업을 확장하기 위해 회사가 개발하는 것을 나타낼 명사가 필요하므로 '전략'을 의미하는 (C) strategy가 정답이다.

어휘 develop 개발하다, 발전시키다 expand 확장하다, 확대하다 operation 사업, 운영 benefit 혜택 recognition 인정, 인식

### 114 명사 자리 _ 복합명사

번역 광범위한 마케팅 조사를 실시함으로써, RIV 어소시에이츠 사는 여러 분의 타깃 소비자들에 대한 중요한 통찰력을 얻을 수 있습니다.

해설 marketing과 복합명사를 이루어 동명사 conducting의 목적어 역할을 하는 명사 자리이다. (A)와 (D)가 명사인데 '마케팅 조사를 실시함으로써'라는 의미가 되어야 자연스러우므로 '조사'를 뜻하는 명사 (A) research가 정답이다.

어휘 conduct 실시하다 extensive 광범위한 crucial 중대한 insight 통찰력, 이해 consumer 소비자 researcher 조사자

### 115 접속사 자리 _ 부사절 접속사

번역 오래된 전등이 더 효율적인 조명으로 교체되었으므로, 사무실의 전기료가 더 낮아질 것이다.

해설 빈칸 뒤에 완전한 절 두 개가 콤마로 이어져 있으므로 빈칸은 부사절 접속사 자리이다. 또한, '오래된 전등이 더 효율적인 조명으로 교체되었으므로 전기료가 낮아질 것이다'가 알맞은 의미이므로 '(이제) ~이므로'를 뜻하는 접속사 (C) Now that이 정답이다. (A) Unless(~이 아니라면)와 (D) Although(비록 ~이기는 하지만)도 접속사이지만 의미상 적합하지 않으며, (B) At once(즉시, 한 번에)는 부사구이다.

어휘 replace 교체하다 efficient 효율적인 fixture 고정물, 설비

### 116 형용사 어휘

번역 자사의 신작 영화 개봉을 위해, 로프턴 스튜디오스의 홍보팀은 이용 가능한 가장 큰 영화관을 예약하라는 지시를 받았다.

해설 명사구 the largest theater를 수식해 '이용 가능한 가장 큰 영화관'이라는 의미를 구성해야 자연스러우므로 '이용 가능한'을 뜻하는 형용사 (D) available이 정답이다. 최상급과 결합된 명사인 경우 -able로 끝나는 형용사가 뒤에서 수식한다.

어휘 premiere 개봉, 초연 publicity 홍보 instruct 지시하다 reserve 예약하다 secure 안전한, 확실한 certain 특정한, 확실한

## 117 부사 자리 _ to부정사구 수식

번역 그 회사는 고객에게 쇼핑 웹사이트에 자사 제품에 대해 호의적으로 후기를 작성하도록 권한다.

해설 빈칸 앞에 주어(The company)와 동사(encourages), 목적어(customers), 그리고 to부정사구(to review its products)가 쓰여 있어 이미 문장 구성이 완전한 상태이다. 따라서 부가적인 요소로 to부정사 to review를 수식할 부사가 쓰여야 알맞으므로 (B) favorably(호의적으로)가 정답이다.

어휘 encourage 권하다 review 평가하다, 후기를 작성하다 favorable 호의적인 favorite 좋아하는; 좋아하는 것 favor 호의, 친절

## 118 전치사 자리 _ 명사구 목적어

번역 앞으로 몇 주 이내에, 세르나 마이닝 사의 CEO가 후임자를 발표할 것이다.

해설 빈칸 뒤에 기간을 나타내는 명사구인 the next few weeks가 있고, '앞으로 몇 주 이내에'라는 의미가 자연스러우므로 '~ 이내에'라는 의미의 전치사 (C) Within이 정답이다.

어휘 successor 후임자, 후계자

## 119 부사 어휘

번역 기획 위원회 위원들은 프로젝트의 최종 비용이 자신들의 최초 견적과 정확히 일치한 것을 자랑스러워했다.

해설 동사 matched를 수식해 최종 비용과 최초 견적이 어떻게 일치했는지를 나타낼 부사가 필요하므로 '정확히'를 뜻하는 (D) exactly가 정답이다.

어휘 committee 위원회 proud 자랑스러워하는 match 일치하다 initial 최초의, 처음의 estimate 추정(치), 견적 occasionally 가끔, 때때로 briefly 간단히, 잠시 lately 최근

## 120 부사 자리 _ 형용사구 수식

번역 카탈로그는 "소형"으로 설명된 식기세척기가 일반적으로 폭이 18인치라는 정보를 포함해야 한다.

해설 be동사 are와 형용사구 보어 18 inches wide 사이에 위치할 수 있는 것은 형용사구를 수식하는 부사이므로 (B) normally(일반적으로, 보통)가 정답이다.

어휘 include 포함하다 describe 설명하다 compact 소형의 normalize 정상화하다 normalization 정상화

## 121 부사 어휘

번역 전국의 부지들을 고려한 끝에, 노이테크 사는 최종적으로 무린에 새 공장을 지었다.

해설 여러 부지를 고려한 후에 무린이란 곳이 선택된 것이므로 '최종적으로'라는 의미의 부사 (B) ultimately가 정답이다.

어휘 consider 고려하다 site 부지, 현장 intensely 격하게, 열심히 concisely 간결하게

## 122 형용사 어휘

번역 클러리 보험회사는 창립 10주년 기념일에 자선 단체에 상당한 액수를 기부했다.

해설 명사 donation을 수식해 기부금의 크기와 관련된 의미를 나타낼 형용사가 필요하므로 '상당한, 꽤 많은'을 뜻하는 (C) sizable이 정답이다.

어휘 make a donation 기부하다 charity 자선 활동, 자선 단체 anniversary (해마다 돌아오는) 기념일 primary 주된, 초기의 severe 극심한, 가혹한

## 123 동사 자리 _ have p.p.

번역 불러드 파크 호텔은 다가오는 무역 컨벤션에 대비해 비즈니스 시설을 업그레이드하려 했다.

해설 빈칸 앞에 has가 있고 뒤에 to부정사가 있으므로 to부정사를 목적어로 받는 동사 자리이다. 따라서 has와 함께 현재완료 시제를 구성하는 (D) attempted가 정답이다.

어휘 facility 시설(물) in preparation for ~에 대비해 upcoming 다가오는, 곧 있을

## 124 동사 어휘

번역 예술가로서의 경력 전반에 걸쳐, 립스컴 씨는 재활용 재료로 복잡한 조각품을 만드는 것을 전문으로 해 왔다.

해설 빈칸 뒤에 위치한 전치사 in과 어울리는 자동사로서 경력 전반에 걸쳐 주로 해 온 일을 의미해야 알맞으므로 '전문으로 하다'를 뜻하는 (A) specialized가 정답이다.

어휘 create 만들다 intricate 복잡한 sculpture 조각품 out of (재료 등) ~로 recycled 재활용의 material 재료, 자재 distinguish 구별하다 approach 다가가다 commit 전념하다

## 125 명사 자리 _ 정관사와 전치사구의 수식

번역 라에스 시 대중교통의 가격 적정성에 대한 신문 기사가 요금 인하 요구로 이어졌다.

해설 관사 the와 전치사 of 사이에 빈칸이 있으므로 빈칸은 명사 자리이다. 따라서 (C) affordability(가격 적정성)가 정답이다.

어휘 public transportation 대중교통 lead to ~로 이어지다 call for ~에 대한 요구 fare (교통) 요금 decrease 하락, 감소 afford 여유가 되다 affordably 저렴하게, 감당할 수 있게 affordable 저렴한, 가격이 적정한

## 126 명사 어휘

번역 경쟁사 인수 제안 소식에 포울릭 엔터프라이즈 사의 주가가 상승했다.

해설 빈칸이 포함된 부분이 주가 상승의 원인이 되어야 하고, 경쟁사와 관련된 것이므로 '경쟁사 인수 제안 소식'이 되는 게 가장 자연스럽다. 따라서 '인수'를 뜻하는 (B) acquisition이 정답이다.

어휘 stock 주식 propose 제안하다 competitor 경쟁사, 경쟁자 investment 투자(금) agenda 의제 vision 시력, 비전

## 127 부사 자리 _ 형용사 수식

번역 크로프트 피트니스 센터에는 최신식 장비가 있지만 놀라울 정도로 편안한 분위기이다.

해설 부정관사 a와 형용사 relaxed 사이에 위치한 빈칸은 형용사를 수식할 부사가 들어갈 수 있는 자리이므로 (D) remarkably(놀라울 정도로)가 정답이다.

어휘 state-of-the-art 최신식의 equipment 장비 relaxed 편안한, 느긋한 atmosphere 분위기 remark 말; 말하다

## 128 접속사 자리 _ 복합관계대명사

번역 품질 보증은 구입 후 5년이 경과하거나 트랙터를 5,000시간 동안 운행하는 것 중 어느 쪽이든 먼저 발생하는 시점에 만료됩니다.

해설 빈칸 뒤에 주어 없이 동사 occurs와 부사 first만 쓰여 있으므로 주어 역할과 동시에 빈칸 앞 절과 연결하는 접속사 역할까지 할 수 있는 복합관계대명사 (D) whichever(어느 쪽이 ~하든)가 정답이다. 대명사 (A) anything은 주어 역할은 가능하지만 접속사 역할은 하지 못한다. 소유격관계대명사 (B) whose와 복합관계부사 (C) however는 접속사 역할은 가능하지만 주어 역할은 하지 못한다.

어휘 warranty 품질 보증(서) expire 만료되다 occur 발생하다

## 129 전치사 자리 _ 명사구 목적어

번역 포커스 그룹의 의견을 고려해, 우리는 제품 라벨에 더 가독성 있는 서체를 선택해야 합니다.

해설 빈칸 뒤에 위치한 명사구 the feedback from the focus group을 목적어로 취하는 전치사가 필요한 자리이며, '포커스 그룹의 의견을 고려해'라는 의미가 되는 것이 적절하므로 '~을 고려해'라는 뜻의 (C) Considering이 정답이다.

어휘 feedback 의견 readable 읽기 쉬운, 가독성 있는 font 서체

## 130 동사 어휘

번역 목요일에 있었던 교육 후에, 앳킨스 씨는 새 데이터베이스 소프트웨어의 장점들을 인정했다.

해설 교육을 받은 후에 새 소프트웨어의 장점에 대해 보일 수 있는 태도나 행위 등을 나타낼 동사가 필요하므로 '인정하다'를 뜻하는 (A) acknowledged가 정답이다.

어휘 following ~ 후에 advantage 장점 nominate (후보로) 지명하다, 임명하다 belong 속하다 permit 허락하다

# PART 6

### 131-134 이메일

발신: <customerservice@office-loft.com>
수신: <jahan.soltani@iux-mail.com>
제목: 회신: 주문 번호 7823
날짜: 7월 21일
첨부: 쿠폰

솔타니 씨께,

주문 번호 7823 제품이 약속된 날짜인 7월 14일 이후에 귀하의 업체에 도착했다는 말씀을 듣게 되어 유감스럽습니다. 이 주문품이 저희 배송 업체의 문제로 인해 예정보다 더 늦게 131 **배송된** 것으로 보입니다. 귀하의 계좌로 배송 요금을 환불해 드리겠습니다. 추가로, 132 **지연** 문제에 대한 보상으로 첨부해 드린 쿠폰을 받아 주시기 바랍니다. 이는 저희 웹사이트에서 다음 주문 시 30% 할인해 드릴 것입니다. 133 **계산 페이지 상단에 코드를 입력하기만 하면 됩니다**. 이 쿠폰을 출력하셔서 저희 오프라인 매장들 중 134 **한 곳**에서 사용하셔도 됩니다.

스캇 콘래드
오피스 로프트 고객 서비스

어휘 than scheduled 예정보다 due to ~로 인해 provider 공급업체 refund 환불해 주다 charge (청구) 요금 account 계좌 in addition 추가로 accept 받아들이다 attached 첨부된 compensation 보상

## 131 동사 시제+태

해설 deliver는 타동사인데 뒤에 목적어가 없으며, 주어 the order가 배송되는 대상이므로 수동태가 되어야 한다. 또한 앞 문장의 동사 arrived에서 주문품 도착 시점이 과거인 것을 알 수 있으므로 시제는 과거 시제가 되어야 한다. 따라서 과거 시제이자 수동태인 (C) was delivered가 정답이다.

## 132 명사 어휘

해설 전치사 for의 목적어 자리인 빈칸은 보상(compensation)의 이유를 나타내야 하므로 앞선 문장에서 말하는 '예정보다 더 늦게(later than scheduled)' 물품이 배송된 것에 대한 보상을 의미해야 한다. 따라서 '지연, 지체'를 뜻하는 (A) delay가 정답이다.

어휘 loss 분실, 손실 risk 위험

## 133 문장 고르기

번역 (A) 의견에 대해 다시 한번 감사드립니다.
(B) 귀하의 사용자 계정이 곧 복구될 것입니다.
(C) 제품이 만족스러우셨길 바랍니다.
(D) 계산 페이지 상단에 코드를 입력하기만 하면 됩니다.

해설 빈칸 앞뒤 문장이 모두 보상으로 지급하는 쿠폰과 관련된 내용이므로 빈칸에도 쿠폰과 관련된 문장이 와야 한다. 따라서 웹사이트에서 쿠폰을 사용하는 방법을 알리는 (D)가 정답이다.

어휘 account 계정 restore 복구하다, 회복시키다 satisfactory 만족스러운 checkout 계산 페이지, 계산대

## 134 대명사 어휘

해설 쿠폰을 사용할 수 있는 장소로서 전치사구 of our offline stores와 함께 '저희 오프라인 매장들 중 한 곳'을 의미해야 알맞으므로 '한 곳, 하나'를 뜻하는 (B) one이 정답이다. (A) each(각각)와 (C) that(저곳, 저것), 그리고 (D) which(어느 것)는 의미상 적합하지 않다.

### 135-138 회람

발신: 클래런스 티베츠
수신: 바누엘로스 파이낸셜 직원들
날짜: 3월 8일
제목: 카펫 작업

여러분 모두가 아마 알아차리셨겠지만, 우리 접수 공간의 카펫이 상당히 [135] **낡은** 상태입니다. 더 이상 방문객들께 좋은 인상을 주지 못합니다. 따라서 그 구역의 카펫이 교체되기 때문에 사무실이 3월 17일 금요일에 [136] **문을 닫을** 것이라는 사실을 알려 드리게 되어 기쁩니다. 제가 동일 색상이지만 더 내구성이 좋은 재료로 만들어진 새 카펫을 찾았으며, 제거 및 설치 작업을 실시할 업체를 고용했습니다.

사무실이 문을 닫는 [137] **동안**, 바누엘로스 파이낸셜 전 직원은 반드시 재택 근무를 하거나 유급 휴가를 사용해야 합니다. [138] **그에 따라 고객 예약 일정을 재조정하시기 바랍니다.** 이 상황에 대해 어떤 질문이나 우려 사항이 있으시면, 월요일 직원 회의 시간에 제기하시면 됩니다.

어휘 notice 알아차리다 reception 안내, 접수 make a good impression 좋은 인상을 남기다 replace 교체하다 durable 내구성이 좋은 material 재료, 자재 contractor 계약업체, 계약업자 perform 실시하다 removal 제거 installation 설치 paid vacation 유급 휴가 concern 우려 raise (문제 등을) 제기하다

## 135 형용사 어휘

해설 빈칸 뒤에 더 이상 좋은 인상을 주지 못한다는 말과 카펫이 교체된다는 말이 쓰여 있어 접수 공간의 카펫 상태가 좋지 않다는 것을 알 수 있다. 따라서 '낡은, 닳아 해진'을 뜻하는 (D) worn이 정답이다.

어휘 thick 두꺼운

## 136 동사 시제

해설 빈칸 뒤에 쓰인 날짜 3월 17일(March 17)이 지문 상단의 회람 작성 날짜 3월 8일(March 8)보다 미래이므로 미래 시제 동사인 (D) will be closed가 정답이다.

## 137 접속사 자리

해설 빈칸 뒤에 완전한 절 두 개가 콤마로 이어져 있으므로 빈칸은 부사절 접속사이다. 따라서 '~ 동안'이라는 의미의 부사절 접속사 (C) While이 정답이다.

어휘 throughout ~ 전체에 걸쳐, ~ 동안 내내

## 138 문장 고르기

번역 (A) 접수처는 반드시 말끔한 상태로 유지되어야 합니다.
(B) 그에 따라 고객 예약 일정을 재조정하시기 바랍니다.
(C) 임원진이 여전히 진행 일정을 고려하고 있습니다.
(D) 그 업체는 좋은 평가를 받는 지역 회사입니다.

해설 빈칸 앞 문장에 사무실이 문을 닫는 기간에 전 직원이 재택 근무를 하거나 유급 휴가일을 사용해야 한다고 알리고 있으므로 이에 관련된 업무 조치로 고객 예약 일정을 재조정하도록 당부하는 (B)가 정답이다.

어휘 neat 말끔한, 정돈된 reschedule 일정을 재조정하다 appointment 예약, 약속 accordingly 그에 따라 executive 임원, 이사 consider 고려하다 well-respected 높이 평가받는 local 지역의 firm 회사, 업체

### 139-142 이메일

수신: 그레이스 본
발신: 세르지오 폰세카
제목: 데니스-린드스트롬 결혼식
날짜: 6월 3일

안녕하세요, 그레이스,

여기 우리가 토요일에 촬영할 결혼식 세부 정보입니다. 식은 오후 4시에 젤러 인에서 시작할 것입니다. [139] **가능하다면**, 두 시간 전에 도착하셔서 준비 과정을 촬영하는 것을 도와주시기 바랍니다. 식 후에는, 제가 가족 사진을 촬영하는 시간 동안 피로연의 자연스러운 모습을 촬영하시면 되겠습니다. 우리는 그 후 케이크를 자를 때까지 머물러 있을 예정이므로, 저녁 시간이 꽤 길어질 수도 있습니다. [140] **하지만 우리는 오후 8시 이후에는 추가 수당을 받을 것입니다.**

이 일을 [141] **도와주시는 데** 동의해 주셔서 다시 한번 감사합니다. 이는 상당히 주목받는 행사인데, 귀하와 같은 경험 많은 사진작가의 지원을 받는 것은 제게 [142] **자신감**을 제공해 줄 것입니다.

세르지오

어휘 details 세부 정보 photograph 사진 촬영하다 ceremony 행사, 의식 beforehand 미리 preparation 준비 take a candid shot 자연스러운 모습을 촬영하다 reception 연회 composed 구성된 agree 동의하다 high-profile 사람들의 이목을 끄는 support 지원하다 experienced 경험 많은

## 139 접속부사

해설 빈칸 앞 문장에는 식이 오후 4시에 시작한다는 말이, 빈칸 뒤에는 2시간 전에 미리 도착해 달라고 요청하는 말이 쓰여 있다. 따라서 빈칸에는 '가능하다면'이라는 말이 들어가서 '식은 4시에 시작하지만 가능하면 2시간 일찍 와 달라'는 내용이 되어야 자연스럽다. 따라서 '가능하다면'이라는 의미로 쓰이는 (B) If possible이 정답이다.

어휘 likewise 마찬가지로 before long 머지 않아 rather 오히려, 다소

## 140 문장 고르기

번역 (A) 다행히 당신이 사용하실 수 있는 여분의 카메라가 제게 있습니다.
(B) 하지만 우리는 오후 8시 이후에는 추가 수당을 받을 것입니다.
(C) 행사장에 아름다운 배경이 있습니다.
(D) 모든 손님들께서 정장을 입으실 것입니다.

해설 빈칸 앞 문장에 케이크를 자를 때까지 머물러 있을 예정이므로, 저녁 시간이 꽤 길어질 수도 있다고 쓰여 있다. 따라서 저녁 시간에 일하는 것과 관련된 보상으로 8시 이후에는 추가 수당을 받는다는 사실을 알리는 (B)가 정답이다.

어휘 extra 여분의, 추가의 venue 행사장 backdrop 배경

## 141 동사 어휘

해설 빈칸 뒤에 위치한 「사람 목적어+with 전치사구」와 어울리는 동사가 필요하며, 첫 단락에서 상대방이 글쓴이를 돕는 사람임을 알 수 있으므로 도와주기로 동의한 것에 대한 감사의 뜻을 나타내는 문장이어야 한다. 따라서 '돕다'를 뜻하는 (A) assist가 정답이다.

어휘 feature 특징으로 하다 refer 참조하다, 언급하다

## 142 명사 자리 _ 직접 목적어

해설 동사 give는 두 개의 목적어를 취해 「give+간접 목적어+직접 목적어」의 구조로 쓰인다. 따라서 간접 목적어 me 뒤에 직접 목적어 역할을 할 명사가 쓰여야 알맞으므로 (D) confidence(자신감)가 정답이다.

어휘 confide (비밀을) 털어놓다

### 143-146 보도 자료

(10월 23일)—법률회사 맬리 턴불 파트너스는 고수연 씨가 선임 파트너의 지위로 승진되었음을 발표하게 되어 자랑스럽습니다. 고 씨는 회사의 부분 소유주로 제럴드 맬리 전무 이사 및 네 명의 다른 선임 파트너와 [143] **함께합니다**.

"이러한 인정은 충분히 받을 만한 것입니다"라고 맬리 씨가 밝혔습니다. "고 씨는 지난 수년간 우리의 성공에 [144] **주요한** 공헌을 해 왔습니다."

맬리 턴불 파트너스는 5년 전에 환경법을 전문으로 하는 선임 변호사로 고 씨를 고용했습니다. [145] **그 결과**, 회사는 그 분야의 몇몇 중요한 소송에서 승소했습니다.

"고 씨는 아주 날카로운 법적 사고력을 가지고 있을 뿐 아니라 후배 변호사들이 전문적으로 성장할 수 있도록 돕는 일에도 헌신적입니다"라고 맬리 씨가 밝혔습니다. [146] **"우리는 운영진에 합류한 그녀를 환영합니다."**

어휘 promote 승진시키다 rank 지위 partial 부분적인 owner 소유주 recognition 인정 well deserved 충분히 받을 만한 contribution 공헌 success 성공 associate 동료 concentrate on ~에 집중하다 firm 회사 case 소송 사건 possess 소유하다 legal 법률의 inspiring 고무적인 dedication 헌신(성)

## 143 동사 시제+태

해설 빈칸 뒤에 위치한 명사구 managing partner Gerald Malley and four other senior partners를 목적어로 취할 수 있는 능동태여야 하며, 앞선 문장에서 현재완료 시제 동사 has been promoted로 현재 승진된 상태임을 알리고 있으므로 현재 시제 능동태인 (A) joins가 정답이다. (D) would have joined는 '함께했을 것이다'라는 의미로 과거의 일에 대한 가정을 나타내므로 어울리지 않는다.

어휘 join 함께하다, 합류하다

## 144 형용사 어휘

해설 '공헌, 기여'를 뜻하는 명사 contributions를 수식해 그 정도나 중요성과 관련된 의미를 나타낼 형용사가 필요하므로 '주요한'을 뜻하는 (D) major가 정답이다.

어휘 entire 전체의 sturdy 견고한, 튼튼한

## 145 접속부사

해설 빈칸 앞에는 5년 전에 환경법을 전문으로 하는 선임 변호사로 고 씨를 고용했다는 말이, 빈칸 뒤에는 해당 분야의 몇몇 중요한 소송에서 승소했다는 말이 쓰여 있다. 이는 고 씨를 고용한 것에 따른 긍정적인 결과를 말하는 흐름이므로 '그 결과'를 뜻하는 (C) Consequently가 정답이다.

어휘 instead 대신 similarly 유사하게 in short 간단히 말해서

## 146 문장 고르기

번역 (A) 우리는 그 사건에 대해 좋은 결과를 기대합니다.
(B) 더 많은 워크숍이 곧 마련될 것입니다.
(C) 우리는 경영진에 합류한 그녀를 환영합니다.
(D) 그 직책은 오랫동안 공석으로 있지 않을 것입니다.

해설 지문 전체 내용이 고 씨의 승진을 알리는 글이며, 빈칸 앞 문장에서 제시된 맬리 씨의 말이 고 씨의 장점을 말하는 내용이므로, 빈칸에도 고 씨의 승진과 관련된 내용이 와야 적합하다. 따라서 고 씨의 경영진 합류를 축하한다는 의미의 (C)가 정답이다.

어휘 outcome 결과 organize 마련하다, 조직하다 position 직책, 일자리

# PART 7

## 147-148 안내 책자

데프틀리
10년 이상 스타트업의 도약을 지원해왔습니다

제공하는 것:
- [147] **편리한 인사 업무 위탁**
- 인사 문제에 대한 프로젝트 기반 컨설팅
- 장기 고객사를 위한 풀서비스 인사 기술 플랫폼

[147] **전문 분야에는 채용, 교육, 급여 등이 포함됩니다.**
www.deftlee.com을 방문하셔서 상담 일정을 잡으세요.

고객 추천 후기:

"저는 데프틀리를 적극 추천합니다. 인사 플랫폼 하나만으로도 이곳에서 청구하는 비용의 가치가 있습니다. 우리 회사 관리자들이 휴가 파악 및 성과 평가 같은 업무가 간소화된 것을 아주 마음에 들어 하십니다." - 라이언 마스, 오로라 로지스틱스

"제 회사는 4명의 직원에서 50명 이상으로 성장했으며, 데프틀리가 그 과정의 모든 단계에서 함께해 왔습니다. [148] **변화하는 저희 요구에 맞추는 그곳의 능력에 항상 깊은 인상을 받고 있습니다."**
**- 카스미 타나카,** TBR 솔루션즈

어휘 decade 10년 start-up 신생 기업 take flight 비상하다 convenient 편리한 outsourcing 위탁 human resources 인적 자원, 인사부 based ~ 기반의 personnel 인사(부) long-term 장기적인 expertise 전문 지식 include 포함하다 recruiting 채용 payroll 급여 (명단) testimonial 추천 후기 worth ~의 가치가 있는 simplify 간소화하다 track 파악하다, 추적하다 time off 휴무, 휴가 evaluation 평가 impressed 깊은 인상을 받는 ability to ~할 수 있는 능력 adapt to+명사 ~에 적응하다

### 147 추론

번역 데프틀리에 대해 무엇이 사실이겠는가?
(A) 고객사의 직원 급여를 처리하는 일을 제공한다.
(B) 업체들에 환경 문제에 관해 조언한다.
(C) 단기간에 빠르게 성장해 왔다.
(D) 프로젝트 관리 소프트웨어를 개발한다.

해설 데프틀리의 제공 서비스가 제시되는 첫 단락에 편리한 인사 업무 위탁(Convenient outsourcing of human resources tasks)이라는 말과 함께 전문 분야에 급여가 포함된다(Areas of expertise include recruiting, training, payroll ~)고 써 있으므로 급여 관리 서비스를 제공하는 것을 알 수 있다. 따라서 (A)가 정답이다.

어휘 handle 처리하다, 다루다 compensation 급여 advise 조언하다

### 148 세부 사항

번역 타나카 씨는 데프틀리에 대해 무엇을 높이 평가하는가?
(A) 가격 책정
(B) 유연성
(C) 기술력
(D) 기밀 유지

해설 타나카 씨의 의견이 제시된 마지막 단락에 변화하는 자신들의 요구에 맞추는 능력에 항상 깊은 인상을 받고 있다(I'm always impressed by their ability to adapt to our changing needs)고 쓰여 있다. 이는 데프틀리의 유연성을 높이 평가하는 것이므로 (B)가 정답이다.

어휘 appreciate 높이 평가하다, 진가를 인정하다 flexibility 유연성 confidentiality 비밀

> **Paraphrasing**
> 지문의 their ability to adapt to our changing needs
> → 정답의 flexibility

## 149-150 공지

커노버스

고객 여러분,

거의 30년 전에 문을 연 이후로, [149] **커노버스는 맨더빌 주민들께 아주 다양한 실내외 스포츠용 장비를 제공해 온 것을 자랑스럽게 여겨 왔습니다.** 하지만, [150] **최근 저희는 저조한 판매량으로 인해 재고 목록에서 낚시용 도구와 용품과 장비를 제외하는 힘든 결정을 내렸습니다.** 이 재고품이 차지하고 있던 매장 공간은 대신 추가 운동복을 진열하는 데 이용될 것입니다. 이 조치는 커노버스가 앞으로 오랫동안 맨더빌의 체육인들을 지속적으로 지원할 수 있도록 수익성을 유지하는 데 도움을 줄 것입니다. 그럼에도 불구하고 이것이 저희 고객들 중 낚시 애호가들께 초래할 불편함에 대해 사과드립니다.

커노버스 경영진

어휘 equip (장비를) 갖춰 주다 resident 주민 a wide range of 아주 다양한 decision 결정 remove 없애다, 제거하다 supplies 용품 equipment 장비 inventory 재고 (목록) stock 재고(품) occupy 차지하다 display 진열하다 workout apparel 운동복 profitable 수익성 있는 support 지원하다 athlete 체육인, 운동선수 apologize 사과하다 inconvenience 불편함 enthusiast 애호가

### 149 세부 사항

번역 커노버스는 무엇을 판매하는가?
(A) 식료품
(B) 전자제품
(C) 미술용품
(D) 운동용품

해설 지문 초반부에 커노버스는 맨더빌 주민들께 아주 다양한 실내외 스포츠용 장비를 제공해 온 것을 자랑스럽게 여겨 왔다(Conover's has been proud to equip Mandeville residents for a wide range of indoor and outdoor sports)고 했으므로 (D)가 정답이다.

## 150 주제 / 목적

번역 공지는 무엇에 관한 것인가?
(A) 재고 목록의 변화
(B) 기념일 축하 행사
(C) 매장 임시 폐점
(D) 모금 행사

해설 지문 중반부에 저조한 판매량으로 인해 재고 목록에서 낚시용 도구와 용품과 장비를 제외하기로 결정했다(we have recently made the difficult decision to remove fishing gear, supplies, and equipment from our inventory)고 했으므로 (A)가 정답이다.

어휘 anniversary 기념일 celebration 축하 행사 temporary 임시의 fund-raising 모금, 자금 마련

> **Paraphrasing**
> 지문의 remove fishing gear, supplies, and equipment from our inventory → 정답의 A change in inventory

### 151-152 이메일

발신: customerservice@irishair.com
수신: 케빈 라일리
제목: 에메랄드 클럽
날짜: 10월 4일

라일리 씨께,

151 **상용고객 마일리지 초과분**을 고객님의 여동생이 사용하도록 해 달라는 요청을 받았습니다. 이는 귀하의 에메랄드 클럽 계정에 연결한 후에만 가능하며, 반드시 저희 웹사이트를 통해 이뤄져야 합니다. 다음 단계를 따르시기 바랍니다.

1. 고객님의 에메랄드 클럽 회원 페이지에 로그인하십시오. 사이드바에서 "가족 추가하기"를 선택하십시오.

2. 요청된 가족 정보를 입력하십시오.

3. 152 **저희가 관계 증명으로 인정할 서류에 관한 가이드라인을 검토하신 후, 적합한 서류를 업로드하십시오.**

4. 페이지 하단에 있는 "제출하기"를 클릭하십시오. 영업일 기준 5일 이내에, 연결되었음을 확인하는 이메일이나 추가 서류를 요청하는 이메일을 받으실 것입니다.

이 처리 과정에서 어려움을 겪으시는 경우, 저희에게 알려 주시기 바랍니다.

올라 콜린스

아일랜드 항공 고객 서비스부

어휘 excess 여분의, 초과의 frequent-flyer miles (항공편) 단골 고객 마일리지 connect 연결하다, 접속하다 follow 따르다 relative 인척, 친척 accept 받다, 수락하다 proof 증명(서) relationship 관계 eligible 적합한, 적격인 confirm 확인해 주다 connection 연결 additional 추가의 documentation 서류, 문서 encounter 마주치다, 맞닥뜨리다

## 151 추론

번역 라일리 씨에 대해 암시된 것은?
(A) 자신의 계정 관련 보안 문제를 보고했다.
(B) 여행사 직원이다.
(C) 아일랜드 항공을 자주 이용한다.
(D) 가족 한 명이 아일랜드 항공에서 근무한다.

해설 첫 단락에 라일리 씨의 상용고객 마일리지 초과분(your excess frequent-flyer miles)을 언급하고 있어 라일리 씨가 비행기를 자주 이용하는 고객임을 알 수 있으므로 (C)가 정답이다.

어휘 security 보안 account 계정 fly 비행기를 타고 가다

> **Paraphrasing**
> 지문의 frequent-flyer → 정답의 often flies

## 152 세부 사항

번역 라일리 씨는 무엇을 하라는 안내를 받는가?
(A) 로그인 개인 식별 정보 변경하기
(B) 우편으로 일부 서류 제공하기
(C) 회원 페이지에서 업데이트 확인하기
(D) 온라인으로 관계 인증하기

해설 지문 중반부의 3번 항목에 항공사가 관계 증명으로 인정할 서류에 관한 가이드라인을 검토한 후에 적합한 서류를 업로드하라(After reviewing the guidelines on documents that we will accept as proof of your relationship, upload eligible documents)는 말이 나온다. 따라서 온라인상에서 관계를 인증해야 한다는 것을 알 수 있으므로 (D)가 정답이다.

어휘 instruct 안내하다, 지시하다 credentials (로그인 시의) 개인 식별 정보 verify 인증하다, 입증하다

> **Paraphrasing**
> 지문의 proof of your relationship, upload eligible documents → 정답의 Verify a relationship

### 153-154 문자 메시지

> 타이론 벨턴, 오후 7시 14분
> 안녕하세요, 나디아. 제가 무역 박람회를 위해 꾸려 놨던 홍보 자료에 문제가 있다는 것을 방금 알았습니다. 거기에 우리 스탈 가 주소가 적혀 있어요.
>
> 나디아 구세바, 오후 7시 15분
> 어느 것에요?
>
> 타이론 벨턴, 오후 7시 16분
> [153] **우리 님블 제품 라인 전동 공구들에 대한 안내 책자요. 회사 이전 후에 새 주소로 다시 인쇄하지 않은 것 같아요.**
>
> 나디아 구세바, 오후 7시 17분
> 음, [154] **컨벤션 센터 근처에 인쇄소들이 있잖아요, 그렇죠? 오늘 밤이나 내일 아침 일찍 한 군데 가셔서 안내 책자에 붙일 수정용 스티커를 인쇄해 달라고 요청해 보실 수 있을 거예요.**
>
> 타이론 벨턴, 오후 7시 18분
> 그렇게 하면 되겠네요! 도와주셔서 감사합니다.
>
> 어휘 promotional 홍보의 material 자료, 물품 pack (짐을) 꾸리다 brochure 안내 책자 correction 수정, 정정

## 153 세부 사항

번역 벨턴 씨에게 무슨 문제가 있는가?
(A) 포스터를 분실했다.
(B) 행사장 주소를 잘못 알고 있었다.
(C) 전동 공구를 사용할 수 없다.
(D) 최신 상태가 아닌 안내 책자를 갖고 있다.

해설 오후 7시 16분에 벨턴 씨가 님블 제품 라인 전동 공구들에 대한 안내 책자를 언급하면서 회사 이전 후에 새 주소로 다시 인쇄하지 않았다(The brochures for our Nimble line of power tools. I guess we never had them reprinted with our new address after the move)고 알리고 있다. 따라서 과거의 정보가 담긴 안내 책자를 갖고 있다는 사실을 알 수 있으므로 (D)가 정답이다.

어휘 misplace 분실하다 mistaken 잘못 알고 있는 venue 행사장 outdated 구식의, 최신 상태가 아닌

## 154 의도 파악

번역 오후 7시 18분에 벨턴 씨가 "그렇게 하면 되겠네요"라고 쓸 때, 의미하는 것은 무엇인가?
(A) 기기가 수리된 것 같다.
(B) 제안된 계획이 성공할 것 같다.
(C) 홍보를 위한 노력이 인기가 없어서 놀라워하고 있다.
(D) 공지를 통해 오해를 해결할 수 있을 것이다.

해설 구세바 씨가 오후 7시 17분에 근처 인쇄소에 안내 책자에 붙일 수정용 스티커 인쇄를 요청할 수 있을 것(there are print shops near the convention center, right? ~ ask them to print correction stickers)이라고 해결 방법을 제안했는데, 그 제안에 동의하는 말이다. 따라서 (B)가 정답이다.

어휘 proposed 제안된 effort 노력 unpopular 인기 없는 resolve 해결하다 misunderstanding 오해

### 155-157 구인 광고

> 카더 베이 오토모티브 사에서 전기차 정비사를 찾습니다.
>
> 소비자 선호 변화에 발맞추기 위해, [155] **카더 베이 오토모티브 사는 전기차에 대한 유지 관리 및 수리 서비스를 제공하기 시작할 것입니다.** [157] **따라서 저희는 이 분야 지식을 지닌 자동차 정비사를 찾고 있습니다.** 지원자는 반드시 최소 2년간 전기차를 유지 관리하고, 문제를 진단하고, [156 (B)] **수리한 경력을 보유하고 있어야 합니다.**
>
> 카더 베이 오토모티브 사는 모든 직원에게 시간을 엄수하고, 아주 체계적이며, [156 (A)] **팀의 일원으로 잘 근무할 수 있는 능력을 요구합니다.** [156 (D)] **정비사는 또한 반드시 상업용 차량을 운전할 수 있는 면허가 있어야 합니다.** [157] **이 직책의 면접을 요청받은 지원자는 기술 능력 평가를 목적으로 하는 다양한 질문을 받을 것으로 예상해야 합니다.** 관심 있는 분들께서는 www.carderbayauto.com/jobs/326을 방문해 온라인 지원서를 작성하시기 바랍니다.
>
> 어휘 seek 찾다, 구하다 mechanic 정비사 keep up with ~에 발맞추다, ~에 뒤처지지 않다 preference 선호(도) maintenance 유지 관리 candidate 지원자, 후보자 possess 소유하다 diagnose 진단하다 vehicle 차량 punctual 시간을 엄수하는 well-organized 아주 체계적인 license 면허를 주다 operate 운행하다, 작동하다 commercial 상업의 a variety of 다양한 intend 목적으로 하다, 의도하다 assess 평가하다 fill out 작성하다 application 지원(서)

## 155 세부 사항

번역 정비사 직책이 왜 제안되고 있는가?
(A) 영업시간이 연장되었다.
(B) 새로운 종류의 차량이 서비스될 것이다.
(C) 추가 지점이 문을 연다.
(D) 새로운 규정이 시행될 것이다.

해설 첫 단락 시작 부분에 전기차에 대한 유지 관리 및 수리 서비스를 제공하기 시작한다(Carder Bay Automotive will begin providing maintenance and repair services for electric automobiles)고 알리는 말이 쓰여 있으므로 (B)가 정답이다.

어휘 extend 연장하다 regulation 규정, 규제 go into effect 시행되다

> **Paraphrasing**
> 지문의 begin providing maintenance and repair services for electric automobiles
> → 정답의 A new type of vehicle will be serviced

## 156 Not / True

번역 해당 직책에 대해 언급된 자격 요건이 아닌 것은?
(A) 팀워크 능력
(B) 수리 경력
(C) 유지 관리 자격증
(D) 운전 면허증

해설 첫 번째 단락에 언급된 전기차 수리 경력(work experience in ~ repairing electric vehicles)에서 (B)를, 두 번째 단락에 팀의 일원으로 잘 근무할 수 있는 능력(able to work well as part of a team)이 언급된 부분에서 팀워크 능력을 뜻하는 (A)를, 그리고 바로 뒤이어 상업용 차량을 운전할 수 있는 면허(be licensed to operate commercial vehicles)를 말하는 부분에서 운전 면허증을 의미하는 (D)를 각각 확인할 수 있다. 하지만 유지 관리 자격증과 관련된 정보는 제시되어 있지 않으므로 (C)가 정답이다.

> **Paraphrasing**
> 지문의 work experience in ~ repairing electric vehicles
> → 보기 (B)의 Repair experience
> 지문의 able to work well as part of a team
> → 보기 (A)의 Teamwork skills
> 지문의 be licensed to operate commercial vehicles
> → 보기 (D)의 A driver's license

## 157 세부 사항

번역 구인 공고에 따르면, 지원자는 면접 중에 무엇을 요청받을 것인가?
(A) 자동차 기술 관련 이야기하기
(B) 온라인 능력 시험 치르기
(C) 자동차의 상태 평가하기
(D) 자격을 증명하는 문서 제공하기

해설 첫 번째 단락에 전기차 분야 지식을 갖춘 정비사를 찾는다(we are seeking an auto mechanic with knowledge of this area)고 했고, 두 번째 단락에 지원자는 기술 능력 평가를 목적으로 하는 다양한 질문을 받을 것을 예상해야 한다(Candidates invited to interview for this position should expect to be asked a variety of questions intended to assess their technical skills)고 했으므로, 지원자들이 면접 중에 자동차 기술 관련 질문을 받아서 답변해야 할 것임을 알 수 있다. 따라서 (A)가 정답이다.

어휘 proficiency 능숙(도), 숙달 prove 증명하다 qualification 자격(증)

### 158-160 기사

> 상승세에 있는 주택 가격
>
> 왕용준 작성
>
> 드로서 (5월 6일)—온라인 부동산 시장인 Turfle.com의 데이터에 따르면, 드로서 지역의 주택 가격이 지속적으로 오르고 있다. 그 지역의 평균 주택 가격이 작년보다 5.2% 뛰어올라 392,500달러에 이르렀다.
>
> "주택 가치 상승은 재산세를 통한 세입 증가를 의미합니다."라고 158 **드로서 주택 사업 관리국의 에이다 페럴 관리국장**이 언급했다. "시에서 사회 복지 사업에 필요한 추가 자금을 만들어 낼 수 있을 것입니다."
>
> 하지만 페럴 씨는 이 추세는 개별 가정에 문제를 159 **일으키기도** 한다는 점을 지적했다.
>
> 160 **"일부 주택 소유주들은 높아진 재산세를 지불하기 힘겨울 것입니다."**라고 페럴 씨가 밝혔다. "더욱이 지난 한 해 그에 맞춰 임대료가 상승하여, 임대 세입자들의 부담을 증가시킨 것을 알고 있습니다. 임대료가 그 사람들의 생활비에서 점점 더 큰 비중을 차지하고 있습니다."
>
> 주택으로 인해 금전적 어려움을 겪고 있는 주민들은 드로서 주택 사업 관리국의 웹사이트 www.drossercity.org/dhab에서 다양한 방편을 찾을 수 있다.
>
> 어휘 on the rise 상승세에 있는 increase 증가하다 real estate 부동산 value 가치 revenue 세입, 수입 property tax 재산세 generate 만들어 내다 funding 자금 (제공) point out 지적하다 trend 경향, 추세 pose (문제 등을) 일으키다, 제기하다 struggle to ~하는 데 힘겨워하다 rent 임대(료) correspondingly 그에 상응하여 burden 부담(감) tenant 세입자 increasingly 점점 더 share 지분, 몫 resident 주민 financial 금전적인, 재정의 resource 방편, 수단

## 158 추론

번역 페럴 씨는 누구이겠는가?
(A) 세무사
(B) 임대용 건물 관리자
(C) 부동산 중개업자
(D) 주택 담당 공무원

해설 두 번째 단락에 드로서 주택 사업 관리국의 에이다 페럴 관리국장(Ada Ferrell, chair of the Drosser Housing Authority Board)이라고 쓰여 있으므로 (D)가 정답이다.

> **Paraphrasing**
> 지문의 chair of the Drosser Housing Authority Board
> → 정답의 A housing official

## 159 동의어

번역 세 번째 단락, 두 번째 줄에 쓰인 "poses"와 의미가 가장 가까운 것은?
(A) ~인 척하다
(B) 모형을 만들다
(C) 야기하다
(D) 말하다

해설 동사 poses 뒤에 '문제'를 의미하는 목적어 problems가 쓰여 있어 문제를 일으킨다는 의미로 판단할 수 있으며, 이는 문제를 야기하는 것과 같으므로 '야기하다, 제시하다' 등을 뜻하는 (C) presents가 정답이다.

## 160 Not / True

번역 페럴 씨가 주택 가격의 상승에 대해 언급하는 것은?
(A) 일부 주택 소유주들에게 불리한 면이 있다.
(B) 시 기관이 역전시킬 방법을 찾고 있다.
(C) 더 많은 사람들이 임대 주택을 선택하게끔 야기시켰다.
(D) 시의 인기 있는 세금 정책의 결과이다.

해설 네 번째 단락에 페럴 씨의 인터뷰 내용 중에 일부 주택 소유주들은 높아진 재산세를 지불하기 힘겨울 것(Some homeowners will struggle to pay their higher property tax bill)이라고 언급한 부분이 있다. 이는 일부 주택 소유주들에게 불리한 면이 있다는 뜻이므로 (A)가 정답이다.

어휘 downside 불리한 면 organization 기관, 단체 seek 찾다 reverse 역전시키다, 뒤집다 policy 정책, 방침

### 161-163 이메일

수신: 브리짓 뎅
발신: 캔디스 홀트
제목: 정보
날짜: 8월 27일
첨부: 홀트_8월27일

브리짓 씨께,

요청하신 바와 같이, 이 이메일은 제가 월요일에 2주간의 병가를 시작한다고 알려 드리는 메시지입니다. [161] **제가 현재 진행 중인 마케팅 캠페인의 목록과 각 캠페인의 상황에 대한 자세한 내용을 첨부해 드립니다.** 각각의 캠페인에 관여하고 있는 다른 직원들께도 제 부재에 대해 알려 드렸습니다. 대부분의 경우, 그들 중 한 명이 그 2주 동안 제 업무를 대신하시는 게 어렵진 않을 것입니다.

유일하게 남은 업무는 조나단을 만나 얀시 코즈메틱 사의 새 매니큐어 제품 라인의 출시를 위한 디지털 홍보 계획을 넘겨주는 것입니다. [163] **아직 그렇게 할 수 없었던 이유는 고객사에서 요청한 막판 수정 작업을 해야 했기 때문입니다.** 이제 그것들이 완료되어서, 오늘 오후로 회의 일정을 잡아 두었습니다. [162] **조나단이 제가 만들어 둔 게시물을 적절한 시점에 얀시 사의 소셜 미디어 계정에 업데이트할 준비가 되도록 해 놓겠습니다.**

마지막으로 제 병가 중 첫 번째 주에는 시간이 되지 않겠지만, 두 번째 주에는 필요 시에 제게 편히 연락하시기 바랍니다.

캔디스 홀트

어휘 reminder (상기시키는) 알림 메시지 attached 첨부된 currently 현재 details 세부 사항 status (진행) 상황 involved 관여된 absence 부재 take over 대신하다, 이어받다 task 업무 hand over 넘겨주다 promotion 홍보 launch 출시, 발표 last-minute 마지막 순간의 make sure (that) 반드시 ~하도록 하다 account 계정 appropriate 적절한 post 게시물 unavailable 시간이 나지 않는

### 161 추론

번역 홀트 씨는 어떤 종류의 업체에서 근무하겠는가?
(A) 온라인 뉴스 플랫폼
(B) 광고 대행사
(C) 화장품 회사
(D) 병원

해설 첫 번째 단락에 홀트 씨가 현재 작업 중인 마케팅 캠페인 목록을 첨부했다(Attached you'll find the list of marketing campaigns that I'm currently working on ~)고 했으므로 마케팅 캠페인 업무를 수행할 수 있는 업체인 (B)가 정답이다.

### 162 세부 사항

번역 홀트 씨가 조나단에게 무엇을 하도록 준비시킬 것인가?
(A) 소셜 미디어에 게시물 올리기
(B) 출시 행사에 참석하기
(C) 데이터베이스 유지 관리하기
(D) 고객 만나기

해설 두 번째 단락에 조나단이 홀트 씨가 만들어 둔 게시물을 적절한 시점에 얀시 사의 소셜 미디어 계정에 업데이트할 준비가 되도록 하겠다(I'll make sure Jonathan is ready to update Yancey's social media accounts at the appropriate times with the posts I've created)고 알리고 있다. 이는 소셜 미디어에 게시물을 올리는 것을 의미하므로 (A)가 정답이다.

어휘 post 게시물을 올리다 maintain 유지 관리하다

> **Paraphrasing**
> 지문의 update Yancey's social media accounts ~ with the posts → 정답의 Post on social media

### 163 문장 삽입

번역 [1], [2], [3], [4]로 표시된 곳 중에서 다음 문장이 가장 적합한 곳은 어디인가?
"이제 그것들이 완료되어서, 오늘 오후로 회의 일정을 잡아 두었습니다."
(A) [1]
(B) [2]
(C) [3]
(D) [4]

해설 제시된 문장의 they가 받을 수 있는 것을 찾아보면, 고객사에서 요청한 막판 수정 작업을 해야 했다(~ I needed to make some last-minute changes that the client requested)는 문장 뒤 [3]에 들어가는 것이 가장 자연스럽다. 여기서 they는 changes를 받아 수정 사항들이 완료된 것으로 볼 수 있다. 따라서 정답은 (C)이다.

어휘 now that (이제) ~이므로

### 164-167 공지

"더 사운즈 오브 브릴리언스"
5월 28일 수요일
오후 4시 30분 - 오후 9시

[164] **렌든 대학교 음악학과는 캠퍼스 및 지역 사회의 모든 구성원들을 저희 학생들의 우수성을 축하하는 연례 연주회 자리에 초대합니다.** 스틴 뮤직 센터의 조 연주홀에서 멋진 보컬과 피아노, 첼로, 색소폰, 그리고 바이올린 음악이 있는 오후 및 저녁 시간을 저희와 함께 하시기 바랍니다.

[165] **이 프로그램의 모든 공연자들은 우리 학과의 우수 연주상 수상자들입니다.** 올해 수상자 중에는 [166] **인기 있는 노래 경연 TV 프로그램인**

**<탑 보컬리스트>에서 최근 준결승에 오른 펠리샤 로건도 있습니다.** 전체 연주회 일정표와 공연자 및 작품에 관한 상세 정보는 www.rendon.edu/music/soe에서 확인하실 수 있습니다.

167 (A) **이 프로그램은 오후 4시 30분부터 오후 6시까지, 그리고 오후 7시 30분부터 오후 9시까지 진행될 것입니다.** 167 (D) **입장료는 없으며,** 좌석은 선착순입니다. 중간 휴식 시간에 자리를 맡아 두실 수 없다는 점에 유의하시기 바랍니다.

167 (C) **스틴 뮤직 센터는 밀라드 가 640번지에 위치해 있습니다. 캠퍼스 내의 도로 주차는 오후 4시 이후에 무료이며,** 유료 주차는 뮤직 센터의 바로 서쪽 편에 있는 카마초 주차장을 이용하실 수 있습니다.

어휘 community 지역 사회 yearly 연례의 recital 연주회 celebrate 축하하다, 기념하다 excellence 우수함, 훌륭함 performance 공연, 연주(회) honoree 수상자 reach 도달하다 semifinal 준결승 competition 경연, 대회 details 상세 정보 piece 작품 available 이용 가능한 run 진행되다 admission 입장 first-come, first-served 선착순의 save 맡아 두다 intermission 중간 휴식 시간 located 위치한 paid 유료의

## 164 주제 / 목적

번역 공지는 왜 쓰였는가?
(A) 연례 콘서트를 광고하기 위해
(B) 음악 수업에 학생을 유치하기 위해
(C) 다가오는 경연을 알리기 위해
(D) 앨범 발매를 축하하기 위해

해설 첫 단락 시작 부분에 렌든 대학교 음악학과는 캠퍼스 및 지역 사회의 모든 구성원들을 연례 연주회 자리에 초대한다(The Rendon University Department of Music invites all members of the campus and local community to attend its yearly recital ~)고 쓰여 있으므로 (A)가 정답이다.

어휘 annual 연례적인 attract 유치하다, 끌어들이다 upcoming 다가오는 release 발매, 출시

> **Paraphrasing**
> 지문의 yearly recital → 정답의 annual concert

## 165 Not / True

번역 해당 음악가들에 대해 언급된 것은?
(A) 모두 같은 악기를 연주한다.
(B) 해외에서 방문한다.
(C) 수상자들이다.
(D) 올해 대학교를 졸업할 것이다.

해설 두 번째 단락 시작 부분에 프로그램의 모든 공연자들은 학과의 우수 연주상 수상자들(All performers on the program are winners of the department's performance awards)이라고 하므로 (C)가 정답이다.

어휘 instrument 악기 from abroad 해외에서, 해외로부터 recipient 받는 사람, 수령인 graduate 졸업하다

> **Paraphrasing**
> 지문의 winners of the department's performance awards → 정답의 recipients of awards

## 166 추론

번역 공지에서 왜 텔레비전 프로그램을 언급하는 것 같은가?
(A) 활동에 영감을 준 것을 설명하기 위해
(B) 행사가 촬영될 것임을 명시하기 위해
(C) 공연자의 능력을 강조하기 위해
(D) 곡이 잘 알려진 것임을 나타내기 위해

해설 텔레비전 프로그램이 언급되는 두 번째 단락에 인기 있는 노래 경연 TV 프로그램인 <탑 보컬리스트>에서 펠리샤 로건이 준결승에 올랐다(Felicia Logan, who recently reached the semifinal round of the popular singing competition TV show *Top Vocalist*)는 말이 쓰여 있다. 이는 펠리샤 로건이라는 공연자가 뛰어난 능력을 지닌 사람임을 강조하기 위한 말이므로 (C)가 정답이다.

어휘 inspiration 영감 specify 명시하다 highlight 강조하다 ability 능력 indicate 나타내다 well-known 잘 알려진

## 167 Not / True

번역 행사에 대해 암시되지 않은 것은?
(A) 두 파트로 나뉠 것이다.
(B) 인터넷으로 방송될 것이다.
(C) 캠퍼스 내에서 개최될 것이다.
(D) 참석은 무료일 것이다.

해설 세 번째 단락에 프로그램은 오후 4시 30분부터 오후 6시까지, 그리고 오후 7시 30분부터 오후 9시까지 진행된다(The program will run from 4:30 P.M. to 6:00 P.M. and 7:30 P.M. to 9:00 P.M.)고 쓰여 있어 (A)를 확인할 수 있으며, 바로 뒤이어 입장료가 없다(There is no fee for admission)는 말을 통해 (D)도 확인할 수 있다. 또한, 마지막 단락에서 스틴 뮤직 센터는 밀라드 가 640번지에 위치해 있는데 캠퍼스 내의 도로 주차가 오후 4시 이후에 무료(Steen Music Center is located at 640 Millard Avenue. Street parking on campus is free after 4:00 P.M.)라고 언급하고 있어 (C)도 추론이 가능하다. 하지만 인터넷 방송과 관련된 정보는 제시되어 있지 않으므로 (B)가 정답이다.

어휘 split 나누다 broadcast 방송하다

> **Paraphrasing**
> 지문의 There is no fee for admission
> → 보기 (D)의 It will be free to attend.

### 168-171 온라인 채팅

엘렌 체임버스 [오후 2시 17분] 168, 171 **대표님께서 수요일에 만나서 우리 연구소 공석을 위해 더 우수한 지원자를 받을 수 있는 방법에 대해 이야기하고 싶어 하세요. 두 분 아이디어 있으세요?**

아르준 말호트라 [오후 2시 19분] 169 **회사에서 직원들에게 추천**

**보너스를 제공할 수 있을 거예요.** 다른 몇몇 생명 공학 회사들이 그렇게 하고 있거든요.

후아나 아마도 [오후 2시 20분] 저는 그 아이디어가 마음에 들어요. 우리가 직원들의 인맥을 활용할 수 있잖아요.

엘렌 체임버스 [오후 2시 21분] 직원들의 노력이 많이 필요하지 않을까요? 그리고 직원들이 단지 보너스를 받기 위해 좋지 못한 지원자를 추천하지 않도록 어떻게 해야 할까요?

아르준 말호트라 [오후 2시 22분] 169 **직원들은 우리 부서에 그 사람의 연락처만 제공하면 될 거예요.**

후아나 아마도 [오후 2시 23분] 169 **네, 우리가 나머지를 처리할 거예요, 평소처럼요.** 그리고 170 **추천된 사람이 고용되어 한동안 근속하는 경우에만 회사에서 보너스 전액을 지급하는 거예요.**

아르준 말호트라 [오후 2시 24분] 바로 그거예요. 우리가 고용 시에 절반, 그리고 근무 6개월 후에 나머지 절반을 지급할 수 있을 거예요.

엘렌 체임버스 [오후 2시 25분] 좋아요. 171 **회의 시간에 이 계획을 제안해 봅시다.**

어휘 high-quality 수준 높은, 질 좋은 candidate 지원자, 후보자 lab 실험실, 연구소 referral 추천, 소개 biotechnology 생명 공학 take advantage of ~을 활용하다 ensure that 반드시 ~하도록 하다, ~임을 보장하다 refer 추천하다, 소개하다 handle 처리하다 the rest 나머지 end up 결국 ~하게 되다 put forward 제안하다

## 168 주제 / 목적

번역 무엇이 주로 이야기되고 있는가?
(A) 새로운 업계로 사업 확장하기
(B) 숙련된 직원 찾기
(C) 고객 추천 요청하기
(D) 직원 만족도 높이기

해설 체임버스 씨의 첫 번째 메시지에서 회사 대표가 연구소 공석을 위해 더 우수한 지원자를 받을 수 있는 방법에 대해 이야기하고 싶어 한다(~ how we can get higher-quality job candidates for openings in our labs)고 알리면서 아이디어가 있는지(Do you two have any ideas?) 물은 뒤로 그 방법을 논의하고 있다. 따라서 숙련된 직원을 찾는 일이 주제임을 알 수 있으므로 (B)가 정답이다.

어휘 expand 확장하다, 확대하다 industry 업계 skilled 숙련된 solicit 요청하다, 간청하다 satisfaction 만족(도)

> **Paraphrasing**
> 지문의 get higher-quality job candidates
> → 정답의 Finding skilled workers

## 169 추론

번역 메시지 작성자들에 대해 무엇이 사실이겠는가?
(A) 최근 함께 인적 교류 행사에 갔다.
(B) 서로 다른 부서에 근무한다.
(C) 제한된 예산이 주어졌다.
(D) 고용 과정을 감독한다.

해설 말호트라 씨가 각각 2시 19분 메시지와 2시 22분 메시지에서 회사가 직원들에게 추천 보너스를 제공할 수 있을 것(The company could offer a referral bonus to employees)이라며 직원들은 자신들의 부서에 추천하는 사람의 연락처만 제공하면 된다(All the employee would have to do is provide our department with the person's contact information)고 알리자, 2시 23분에 아마도 씨가 자신들이 평소처럼 나머지를 처리할 것(Yes, we would handle the rest, as usual)이라고 언급하고 있다. 이는 메시지 작성자들이 고용 과정을 감독하는 사람들임을 의미하므로 (D)가 정답이다.

어휘 networking 인적 교류 limited 제한된 budget 예산 oversee 감독하다 hiring 고용

## 170 의도 파악

번역 오후 2시 24분에 말호트라 씨가 "바로 그거예요"라고 쓸 때, 의미하는 것은 무엇인가?
(A) 아마도 씨가 유익한 제안을 했다.
(B) 회사 정책을 주의 깊게 따라야 한다.
(C) 치수가 정확해야 한다.
(D) 프로젝트가 일정대로 진행되고 있다.

해설 Precisely는 '바로 그거예요'라는 의미로 강한 긍정을 나타낸다. 앞선 메시지에서 아마도 씨가 추천된 사람이 고용되어 한동안 근속하는 경우에만 회사에서 보너스 전액 지급하면 된다(maybe the company would only pay the full bonus if the referred person ends up both being hired and staying for a while)는 제안에 대해 '바로 그거예요'라고 대답한 것이므로 이는 보너스 지급에 관한 아마도 씨의 제안에 찬성하는 말임을 알 수 있다. 따라서 (A)가 정답이다.

어휘 follow 따르다 policy 정책, 방침 measurements 치수, 크기 accurate 정확한 proceed 진행되다

## 171 추론

번역 메시지 작성자들은 수요일에 무엇을 하겠는가?
(A) 보너스 수령인 결정하기
(B) 임원에게 아이디어 설명하기
(C) 구인 면접에 참가하기
(D) 연구소 직원들에게 장비 보여 주기

해설 2시 17분에 체임버스 씨가 회사 대표가 수요일에 만나 연구소 공석을 위해 더 우수한 지원자를 받을 수 있는 방법에 대해 이야기하고 싶어 한다(The president wants to meet on Wednesday to talk about ~)고 언급했고, 2시 25분 체임버스 씨의 마지막 메시지에서 서로 얘기한 계획을 회의 시간에 제안해 보자(Let's put this plan forward at the meeting)고 알리고 있으므로 수요일에 회사 대표에게 아이디어를 설명할 것임을 알 수 있다. 따라서 (B)가 정답이다.

어휘 determine 결정하다, 알아내다 recipient 수령인, 받는 사람 describe 설명하다 executive 임원, 이사 participate in ~에 참가하다 equipment 장비 laboratory 실험실, 연구소

> **Paraphrasing**
> 지문의 The president → 정답의 an executive
> 지문의 put this plan forward at the meeting
> → 정답의 Describe an idea

## 172-175 이메일

발신: 로즈메리 울프
수신: 오리사 무이와
제목: RRVK 케어 시스템
날짜: 7월 16일
첨부: @RRVKcs

무이와 씨께,

[172] **RRVK 케어 시스템에 관심을 표하는 이메일을 보내 주셔서 감사합니다.** [175] **요청하신 대로, 제품의 특징과 사양, 그리고 가격을 상세히 설명하는 저희 안내 책자를 첨부해 드렸습니다.** 그것을 읽어 보시면 RRVK가 어떻게 귀하의 단체를 도울 수 있는지 아주 명확히 알 수 있을 것입니다.

[173] **귀하의 병원 경영진이 귀하께 병원 시설의 운영을 간소화하길 원한다고 언급하셨습니다.** RRVK 케어 시스템은 바로 그런 일을 하도록 고안된 전문 소프트웨어가 장착된 키오스크들로 구성됩니다. [174] **환자들은 이 시스템을 이용해 병원 프런트 데스크에서 줄을 서서 기다리지 않고 직접 진료 접수를 할 수 있습니다.** 이를 통해 직원들이 더욱 복잡한 업무에 집중할 수 있습니다.

관심이 있으시면, 저희 사무실에서 이 시스템을 시연해 드리겠습니다. 시간이 언제 되시는지 알려 주세요.

로즈메리 울프

어휘 interest in ~에 대한 관심 attach 첨부하다 brochure 안내 책자 detail 상세히 설명하다 feature 특징, 기능 specifications 사양 pricing 가격 (책정) streamline 간소화하다 operation 운영, 영업 consist of ~로 구성되다 kiosk 키오스크 loaded with ~이 장착된, ~이 실려 있는 specialized 전문적인 patient 환자 check in 체크인하다, 접수하다 appointment (진료) 예약, 약속 allow 할 수 있게 해 주다 focus on ~에 집중하다 complex 복잡한 demonstration 시연(회) available 시간이 되는

## 172 주제 / 목적

번역 이메일의 한 가지 목적은?
(A) 외부 시연회에 관해 알리는 것
(B) 오래된 정보를 바로잡는 것
(C) 고객 추천 후기를 공유하는 것
(D) 제품 문의에 답변하는 것

해설 첫 단락에서 RRVK 케어 시스템에 관심을 표하는 이메일을 보내줘서 감사하다(Thank you for writing to express your interest in the RRVK care system)고 한 것과 요청한 대로 안내 책자를 첨부했다(As you requested, I have attached our brochure ~)는 것에서 문의에 대한 답변임을 알 수 있다. 따라서 (D)가 정답이다.

어휘 off-site 외부에서 하는 correct 바로잡다 out-of-date 오래된, 구식의 testimonial 추천 후기 inquiry 문의

## 173 추론

번역 무이와 씨에 대해 암시된 것은?
(A) 의료 서비스 분야에 고용되어 있다.
(B) 셀프 서비스 키오스크를 조사하라는 요청을 받았다.
(C) 보통 프런트 데스크에서 근무한다.
(D) 주문 제작된 일정 관리 소프트웨어를 이용한다.

해설 두 번째 단락에서 무이와 씨의 병원 경영진이 무이와 씨에게 병원 시설의 운영을 간소화하길 원한다고 언급했다(You mention that your hospital's management wants you to streamline the facility's operations)고 쓰여 있어 병원에 근무하는 사람임을 알 수 있으므로 (A)가 정답이다.

어휘 employ 고용하다 field 분야 station 배치하다 customized 주문 제작된

> **Paraphrasing**
> 지문의 your hospital
> → 정답의 is employed in the healthcare field

## 174 세부 사항

번역 이메일에 따르면, RRVK 케어 시스템은 무엇을 할 수 있는가?
(A) 재고 목록 관리하기
(B) 예약 알림 메시지 전송하기
(C) 방문객 도착 정보 파악하기
(D) 결제 처리하기

해설 두 번째 단락에 환자들은 RRVK 케어 시스템을 이용해 병원 프런트 데스크에서 줄을 서서 기다리지 않고 직접 진료 접수를 할 수 있다(Your patients can use the system to check themselves in for appointments)고 알리고 있다. 이는 방문객인 환자의 도착 정보를 파악할 수 있다는 뜻이므로 (C)가 정답이다.

어휘 inventory 재고 (목록) reminder (상기시키는) 알림 메시지 track 파악하다, 추적하다 arrival 도착 process 처리하다

## 175 문장 삽입

번역 [1], [2], [3], [4]로 표시된 곳 중에서 다음 문장이 가장 적합한 곳은 어디인가?
"그것을 읽어 보시면 RRVK가 어떻게 귀하의 단체를 도울 수 있는지 아주 명확히 알 수 있을 것입니다."
(A) [1]
(B) [2]
(C) [3]
(D) [4]

해설 주어진 문장의 it이 가리키는 대상, 즉 읽어보면 RRVK가 어떻게 도울 수 있는지 알 수 있을 만한 것이 앞에 언급되어야 한다. 따라서 제품의 특징과 사양, 그리고 가격을 상세히 설명하는 안내 책자를 첨부했다(I have attached our brochure detailing the product's features, specifications, and pricing)고 안내 책자를 언급한 문장 뒤인 [1]에 들어가 안내 책자를 부연 설명하는 흐름이 되어야 알맞으므로 (A)가 정답이다.

어휘 organization 단체, 기관

## 176-180 웹페이지+이메일

http://www.lockehanley.com/authors/wendell-green

웬델 그린은 데뷔 이후로 로크 앤 핸리 저작권 대행사에 소속되어 있습니다. 그의 첫 장편 작품인 <시간과의 싸움>은 176 **도서관 전문가 협회가 매년 선정하는 10대 대상 베스트 소설 목록인 SLP 10**에 포함되었습니다. 그는 현재 아주 다양한 장르를 집필하고 있습니다. 전업 작가가 되기 전에, 177 **그린 씨는 고등학생들에게 역사를 가르쳤습니다**. 그린 씨는 아내와 함께 아르멘타에 거주하고 있습니다.

웬델 그린의 최근 작품

<와일리 코브에서>
179 **모험심 강한 저널리스트 토니 브래들리가 자신의 작은 해변 마을에서 발생한 수상한 사건을 조사하면서 깜짝 놀랄 만한 비밀을 알게 됩니다**. 200만부 이상 판매!

<스윙 어웨이>
스프릭스 아카데미 야구팀 선수들은 아주 다른 개성을 지니고 있습니다. 이들은 시즌이 끝나기 전에 협력하는 방법을 알아낼 수 있을까요? <프레이저스 계간지>는 이 작품을 "젊은 야구 팬들의 필독서"라고 불렀습니다.

<사라, 세상을 구하다>
중학생인 사라 피치는 자신의 새로운 초능력을 친구와 가족에게 비밀로 하려 합니다. 에바 피네다의 삽화를 특징으로 하는 재미있고 감동적인 만화 소설.

<칠판을 손톱으로 긁는 소리>
177 **가르치는 일은 어려울 순 있지만, 절대 지루하지 않습니다! 그 직업에 관한 이 에세이 모음집**은 유쾌하고 좌절감도 주면서, 가슴 아프게 만드는 측면들에 관해 다룹니다.

어휘 represent 대리하다, 대표하다 full-length 장편의 include 포함하다 aimed at ~을 대상으로 하는, ~을 목표로 하는 a variety of 다양한 adventurous 모험심 강한 startling 깜짝 놀랄 investigate 조사하다, 수사하다 occurrence 사건, 발생한 일 personality 개성, 특성 figure out 알아내다, 파악하다 keep ~ a secret ~을 비밀로 하다 touching 감동적인 feature 특징으로 하다 illustration 삽화 nail 손톱 chalkboard 칠판 profession 직업 touch on ~에 관해 다루다, ~에 관해 언급하다 frustrating 좌절감을 주는 aspect 측면, 양상

수신: 웬델 그린
발신: 캐서린 핸리
제목: 흥미로운 소식
180 **날짜: 3월 2일**

안녕하세요, 웬델,

179 **제가 이번 주에 힉슨 미디어의 프로듀서에게서 귀하의 최신작을 바탕으로 한 영화 제작에 관한 전화를 받았습니다**. 그녀의 이름은 모라 데이턴이며, 이 프로젝트에 대해 매우 열정적으로 보였습니다. 179 **이분은 토니 브래들리가 훌륭한 캐릭터이며, 아마도 그 178 배역에 최고의 배우를 섭외할 수 있을 것이라고 말했습니다**.

180 **데이턴 씨는 우리 두 사람과 만나 각색에 대한 자신의 생각을 알리고 싶어 합니다**. 이를 위해 **이번 달 중으로 저희 사무실에 와 주실 수 있나요?** 제게 알려 주시기 바랍니다.

캐서린 핸리, 저작권 대리인

어휘 develop 만들다, 개발하다 based on ~을 바탕으로 enthusiastic 열정적인 attract 끌어들이다 present 제시하다 adaptation 각색

### 176 세부 사항

번역 SLP 10은 무엇에 대한 목록인가?
(A) 소설의 캐릭터
(B) 처음 글을 쓰는 작가
(C) 청소년을 위한 도서
(D) 공공 도서관

해설 SLP 10이 언급되는 웹페이지 첫 번째 단락에서 도서관 전문가 협회가 매년 선정하는 10대 대상 베스트 소설 목록인 SLP 10(SLP 10, the Society of Library Professionals' yearly list of the best novels aimed at teenagers)이라고 했으므로 (C)가 정답이다.

어휘 fictional 소설의, 허구적인

> **Paraphrasing**
> 지문의 the best novels aimed at teenagers
> → 정답의 Books for youth

### 177 Not / True

번역 그린 씨에 대해 언급된 것은?
(A) 바다 근처에 살고 있다.
(B) 가족과 함께 작업한다.
(C) 자신의 과거 경력에 관해 집필했다.
(D) 때때로 <프레이저스 계간지>에 기고한다.

해설 웹페이지 첫 번째 단락에서 그린 씨가 고등학생들에게 역사를 가르쳤다(~ Mr. Green taught history to high school students)고 했고, 마지막 문단에 있는 그린 씨 도서 설명에 가르치는 일을 언급하면서 그 직업에 관한 에세이 모음집(Teaching may be difficult ~ This collection of essays about the profession)이라고 알리고 있다. 따라서 학생들을 가르친 경험을 바탕으로 에세이를 집필한 것으로 볼 수 있으므로 (C)가 정답이다.

어휘 collaborate 공동 작업하다, 협업하다 previous 과거의, 이전의 contribute 기고하다

### 178 동의어

번역 이메일의 첫 번째 단락, 네 번째 줄에 쓰인 "part"와 의미가 가장 가까운 것은?
(A) 요소, 부품
(B) 부분, 구획
(C) 부분, 일부
(D) 배역, 역할

해설 part 앞에 '최고의 배우'를 뜻하는 a top actor가 쓰여 있어 part가 영화의 배역을 뜻한다는 것을 알 수 있으므로 동일한 의미로 쓰이는 (D) role이 정답이다.

## 179 연계

번역 이메일에 따르면, 어느 도서가 영화로 각색될 수 있는가?
(A) <와일리 코브에서>
(B) <스윙 어웨이>
(C) <사라, 세상을 구하다>
(D) <칠판을 손톱으로 긁는 소리>

해설 이메일의 첫 번째 단락에서 영화 제작에 대해 언급하며, 토니 브래들리는 훌륭한 캐릭터이고 그 배역에 최고의 배우를 섭외할 수 있을 것(She said that Tony Bradley is a great character and they could probably attract a top actor for the part)이라고 했고 웹페이지의 작품 소개 중 첫 번째에 있는 <와일리 코브에서>에서 모험심 강한 저널리스트 토니 브래들리(Adventurous journalist Tony Bradley)라며 등장 인물로 소개하고 있으므로 해당 작품이 영화로 각색될 것임을 알 수 있다. 따라서 (A)가 정답이다.

어휘 adapt 각색하다, 개작하다

## 180 세부 사항

번역 핸리 씨가 그린 씨에게 3월에 무엇을 하도록 요청하는가?
(A) 변호사와 만나기
(B) 제안 들어 보기
(C) 공지하기
(D) 일부 글 편집하기

해설 3월이라는 시점은 이메일의 작성 날짜(Date: March 2)에서 확인할 수 있다. 이메일 두 번째 단락에 데이턴 씨가 만나 각색에 대한 자신의 생각을 알리고 싶어 한다(Ms. Dayton would like to meet with both of us to present her idea for the adaptation)고 알리면서 3월을 가리키는 this month와 함께 이번 달 중으로 사무실에 와 달라(Could you come in to our office for that sometime this month?)고 요청하고 있다. 따라서 3월 중에 데이턴 씨와 만나 제안 사항을 들어 볼 것을 요청하는 것이므로 (B)가 정답이다.

> Paraphrasing
> 지문의 her idea for the adaptation → 정답의 a proposal

### 181-185 이메일+양식

수신: 회원 목록
182 **발신: 오티스 지역 문화 센터**
날짜: 2월 3일
제목: 요리 강좌
첨부: 전단

문화적 다양성을 기념하기 위한 지속적인 노력의 일환으로, 181 **오티스 지역 문화 센터는 올봄에 일련의 일회성 아시아 요리 강좌들을 개설할 것입니다.** 183 **이 강좌는 3월부터 6월까지 매달 첫 번째 수요일 저녁에 열릴 것입니다. 순차적으로, 다뤄질 요리는 베트남 치킨 카레,** 한국 김치찌개, 태국 스프링 롤, 그리고 광둥 쇠고기 볶음입니다.

182 **로크 요리 학원의 초청 강사들께서 저희 전용 요리 교실에서 이 강좌를 진행할 것입니다.** 사전 등록 및 결제는 필수이며, 185 **참가자들께서는 각자의 강사에게 등록증을 제시하도록 요청받을 것입니다.** 2월 15일부터 저희 프런트 데스크에서 모든 강좌를 등록하실 수 있습니다. 184 **오티스 지역 문화 센터의 회원이 아닌 사람들은 5달러의 등록비를 지불해야 합니다.**

강좌에 따라 달라지는 재료비를 포함한 자세한 정보는 첨부된 전단을 확인하시기 바랍니다. 강좌에 관한 질문은 저희 프로그램 편성 전문가인 헤더 테이트에게 하시면 됩니다.

아키오 하야시, 센터장

어휘 flyer 전단 as part of ~의 일환으로 ongoing 계속되는 effort 노력 celebrate 기념하다, 축하하다 diversity 다양성 in order 순차적으로 cover (주제 등을) 다루다 dedicated 전용의 advance 사전의 registration 등록 required 필수인 participant 참가자 proof 증명(서) complete 완료하다 attached 첨부된 details 상세 정보 including ~을 포함해 material 재료, 물품 direct 전달하다, 보내다

오티스 지역 문화 센터
강좌 등록 확인서

성명: 카일라 셜
184 **회원 번호: 499560**
강좌 제목: 태국 스프링 롤
185 **강사: 데이빗 솜스리**
날짜 & 시간: 5월 6일, 오후 5시
184 **등록비: 면제**
재료비: 15달러 결제 ☑
처리 담당자: 에릭 우더드

참고:
수강료 환불은 강좌 날짜보다 최소 일주일 전에 취소한 경우에만 가능합니다. 등록을 취소하시려면, 센터를 방문하시거나 555-0195번으로 저희 프런트 데스크에 전화 주십시오.

어휘 confirmation 확인, 확정 form 양식, 서식 waive 면제하다, 철회하다 refund 환불(액) issue 지급하다, 발급하다 cancellation 취소 at least 최소한, 적어도

## 181 주제 / 목적

번역 이메일은 왜 쓰였는가?
(A) 자원봉사자들을 모집하기 위해
(B) 특별 만찬에 초대하기 위해
(C) 프로그램에 관한 의견을 요청하기 위해
(D) 배움의 기회를 홍보하기 위해

해설 이메일의 첫 단락에서 오티스 지역 문화 센터가 요리 강좌를 개설한다(Otis Community Center will hold a series of one-time cooking classes ~)고 알리면서 강좌 관련 정보를 제공하고 있다. 이는 배움의 기회를 알리는 것이므로 (D)가 정답이다.

어휘 recruit 모집하다 volunteer 자원봉사의 issue an invitation 초대하다 feedback 의견 publicize 홍보하다, 알리다 opportunity 기회

> **Paraphrasing**
> 지문의 a series of one-time cooking classes
> → 정답의 learning opportunities

## 182 세부 사항

번역 지역 문화 활동은 어디에서 진행될 것인가?
(A) 도시 거리에서
(B) 오티스 지역 문화 센터에서
(C) 여러 지역 레스토랑에서
(D) 로크 요리 학원에서

해설 이메일의 두 번째 단락에서 글쓴이가 있는 시설의 전용 요리 교실에서 강좌가 진행된다(~ will teach the classes in our dedicated cooking classroom)고 했는데 이메일을 발신처가 오티스 지역 문화 센터(From: Otis Community Center)이므로 (B)가 정답이다.

어휘 take place 진행되다, 개최되다 local 지역의

> **Paraphrasing**
> 지문의 the classes → 질문의 a community activity

## 183 세부 사항

번역 3월에 어떤 음식이 요리될 것인가?
(A) 베트남 치킨 카레
(B) 한국 김치찌개
(C) 태국 스프링 롤
(D) 광동 쇠고기 볶음

해설 이메일의 첫 번째 단락에서 강좌는 3월부터 6월까지 매달 첫 번째 수요일 저녁에 열릴 것(The classes will be held on the first Wednesday evening of each month from March through June)이라고 한 것에서 매월 하나의 요리 강좌가 열린다는 것을 알 수 있다. 그리고 다뤄질 요리가 순차적으로 언급되는데 그중 베트남 치킨 카레(In order, the dishes covered will be Vietnamese chicken curry ~)가 첫 번째로 언급되므로 3월에 요리될 것임을 알 수 있다. 따라서 (A)가 정답이다.

## 184 연계

번역 셜 씨는 왜 비용이 면제되었는가?
(A) 직접 일부 재료를 제공할 것이다.
(B) 지역 문화 센터 회원이다.
(C) 특정 날짜 이전에 등록했다.
(D) 강좌의 모든 세션에 참석했다.

해설 이메일의 두 번째 단락 끝부분에 오티스 지역 문화 센터의 회원이 아닌 사람들은 5달러의 등록비를 지불해야 한다(Those who are not members of Otis Community Center will be required to pay a $5 registration fee)고 했으므로 회원은 면제임을 알 수 있다. 또한, 셜 씨의 등록 확인서에 회원 번호(Membership Number: 499560)가 쓰여 있고 등록비가 면제(Registration Fee: WAIVED)된 것으로 보아 회원이라 등록비가 면제된 것을 알 수 있다. 따라서 (B)가 정답이다.

어휘 register 등록하다 certain 특정한 session (특정 활동을 하는) 시간

## 185 연계

번역 셜 씨는 누구에게 자신의 확인서를 제시해야 하는가?
(A) 테이트 씨
(B) 하야시 씨
(C) 솜스리 씨
(D) 우더드 씨

해설 이메일의 두 번째 단락에서 참가자들은 각자의 강사에게 등록증을 제시하도록 요청받을 것(participants will be asked to show proof of registration to their instructor)이라는 말이 쓰여 있다. 셜 씨의 등록 확인서에서 강사가 솜스리(Instructor: David Somsri)로 표기되어 있으므로 (C)가 정답이다.

### 186-190 이메일 + 일정표 + 이메일

수신: 인그램 그룹 직원
발신: 제임스 버클리
제목: 다가오는 소프트웨어 교육
날짜: 5월 14일
첨부: 교육 일정표

여러분, 안녕하세요.

앞으로 몇 주 동안, 우리는 회사에 중요한 두 가지 소프트웨어 프로그램에 대한 교육을 진행할 것입니다.

첫 번째로, 전 직원은 반드시 스케디트에 관한 90분 길이의 교육에 참석해야 하며, 이는 우리가 6월에 변경할 일정 관리 소프트웨어입니다. 이 교육은 새로운 시스템으로 전환되기 전에 여러 차례 개최될 것입니다.

두 번째로, [189] **캘러캐드에 관한 2시간 길이의 온라인 교육은 오직 기술부 직원들만 필요한 것입니다.** 개발업체가 [186] **이 소프트웨어에 추가된 새로운 기능들을 알리기 위해 교육 시간을 만들었으며,** 그 부서의 모든 구성원은 이 기능을 배우면 도움이 될 것입니다.

이번 교육의 전체 일정표는 이 이메일에 첨부되어 있습니다. 등록은 직원 웹사이트의 "교육" 페이지에서 완료하실 수 있습니다.

제임스 버클리
인그램 그룹

어휘 upcoming 다가오는 switch over 변경하다 transition 전환 required 필수인 create 만들다 publicize 알리다 function 기능 benefit ~에게 도움이 되다 attach 첨부하다 registration 등록 complete 완료하다

교육 일정표

| 날짜 | 소프트웨어 | 시간 | 장소 |
|---|---|---|---|
| 5월 26일 | 캘러캐드 | 오전 9시 - 오전 11시 | 온라인 |
| 187(B) **5월 30일** | 스케디트 | 187(A) **오전 9시 - 오전 10시 30분** | 187(C) **회의실 A** |
| 6월 1일 | 스케디트 | 187(A) **오후 1시 - 오후 2시 30분** | 187(C) **회의실 A** |
| 6월 5일 | 캘러캐드 | 오후 2시 - 오후 4시 | 온라인 |
| 6월 7일 | 스케디트 | 오전 10시 - 오전 11시 30분 | 187(C) **회의실 A** |
| 187(B),190 **6월 12일** | 스케디트 | 오후 3시 30분 - 오후 5시 | 187(C) **회의실 A** |

온라인 교육을 위한 웹 링크는 등록 시 참가자들에게 전송될 것입니다.

어휘 participant 참가자

수신: 제임스 버클리
발신: 리사 창
제목: 회신: 다가오는 소프트웨어 교육
날짜: 5월 15일

안녕하세요, 제임스,

189 **저는 두 가지 교육을 모두 들어야 하는데,** 190 **5월 26일 아침에 회의가 있습니다.** 중요한 외부 협력업체와 함께 하는 것이라서 옮길 수 없습니다. 그 후에는, 190 **제가 휴가 때문에 5월 29일부터 6월 9일까지 외국에 가 있을 것입니다.** 이런 상황에서, 188 **캘러캐드 교육에 대해 제가 어떻게 하길 추천하시나요?**

감사합니다.

리사

어휘 external 외부의 on vacation 휴가로

## 186 Not / True

번역 첫 번째 이메일에서 캘러캐드에 대해 언급하는 것은?
(A) 새로운 기능이 추가됐다.
(B) 해당 회사를 위해 특별히 개발되었다.
(C) 직원 웹사이트에서 다운로드할 수 있다.
(D) 정기 교육의 주제이다.

해설 세 번째 단락에 캘러캐드에 대해 언급하며, 이 소프트웨어에 추가된 새로운 기능들을 알리기 위해 교육 시간을 만들었다(The developer created the training to publicize new functions that have been added to the software)고 했으므로 (A)가 정답이다.

어휘 acquire 얻다, 획득하다 capability 기능, 성능 subject 주제 regular 정기적인, 정규의

> **Paraphrasing**
> 지문의 new functions that have been added to the software → 정답의 has acquired new capabilities

## 187 Not / True

번역 스케디트 교육 일정에 대해 사실이 아닌 것은?
(A) 오전 및 오후 시간을 모두 포함한다.
(B) 한 달이 넘는 기간에 걸쳐 진행된다.
(C) 모든 교육이 같은 장소에서 열릴 것이다.
(D) 교육을 진행할 사람이 명시되지 않았다.

해설 교육 일정표의 스케디트 항목을 보면, 오전 시간(9:00 A.M.-10:30 A.M.)과 오후 시간(1:00 P.M.-2:30 P.M.)이 모두 포함되어 있으므로 (A)를 확인할 수 있고, 장소가 모두 회의실 A(Conference Room A)로 쓰여 있어 (C)도 확인 가능하다. 또한, 일정표에 교육 진행 담당자가 표기되어 있지 않으므로 (D)도 확인할 수 있다. 하지만 가장 빠른 날짜는 5월 30일(May 30)이고, 가장 늦은 날짜는 6월 12일(June 12)이므로 한 달 동안 진행되지 않는다는 것을 알 수 있다. 따라서 (B)가 정답이다.

어휘 span (기간에) 걸쳐 이어지다 conduct 진행하다, 실시하다 specify 명시하다

## 188 주제 / 목적

번역 창 씨는 왜 버클리 씨에게 이메일을 썼는가?
(A) 등록 확인을 요청하기 위해
(B) 일정상의 어려움에 관해 조언을 요청하기 위해
(C) 휴가 계획 변동을 알리기 위해
(D) 일부 기술에 대한 우려를 표하기 위해

해설 두 번째 이메일에서 창 씨가 회의 및 휴가 일정이 교육과 겹치는 것을 말하면서 캘러캐드 교육에 대해 자신이 어떻게 하길 추천하는지(what do you recommend I do about the Calacad training?) 묻고 있다. 이는 일정 문제에 대해 조언해 달라는 뜻이므로 (B)가 정답이다.

어휘 confirmation 확인 concern 우려

> **Paraphrasing**
> 지문의 what do you recommend I do
> → 정답의 request advice

## 189 연계

번역 창 씨에 대해 암시된 것은?
(A) 일 때문에 자주 여행한다.
(B) 교육 요건을 충족했다.
(C) 기술부의 일원이다.
(D) 소프트웨어 프로그램이 교체되는 것을 기뻐한다.

해설 창 씨가 쓴 이메일에서 자신은 두 가지 교육을 모두 들어야 한다(I'll need to take both of those trainings)고 했는데, 첫 번째 이메일 세 번째 단락에 캘러캐드에 관한 2시간 길이의 온라인 교육은 오직 기술부 직원들만 필요한 것(a two-hour online training session on Calacad will be required only for engineering department staff)이라고 쓰여 있어 창 씨가 기술부 직원임을 알 수 있다. 따라서 (C)가 정답이다.

어휘 frequently 자주 fulfill 충족하다, 이행하다 requirement 요건, 필수 조건 replace 교체하다

## 190 연계

번역 창 씨가 어느 날짜에 일부 교육을 받을 것 같은가?
(A) 5월 26일
(B) 6월 1일
(C) 6월 7일
(D) 6월 12일

해설 창 씨가 이메일에서 5월 26일 아침에 회의가 있다(I have a meeting on the morning of May 26)고 했고, 5월 29일부터 6월 9일까지는 휴가로 외국에 가 있을 것(I'll be out of the country on vacation from May 29 through June 9)이라고 했다. 일정표에서 이 기간을 제외한 교육 날짜는 6월 12일(June 12)이므로 (D)가 정답이다.

어휘 undergo 받다, 겪다

### 191-195 이메일+일정표+공지

수신: shinju.kaneko@zipmail.com
발신: s.armstrong@oknet.com
날짜: 10월 14일
제목: 회신: 방문

가네코 씨께,

저희 가족에게 스트릭랜드 대로 195번지에서 귀하를 맞이하는 건 기분 좋은 일일 것입니다. [192] **저희는 바스마 이타니가 디자인한 몇 군데 되지 않는 주택들 중 한 곳에 살고 있어서 사실 꽤 자랑스럽습니다.** [191] **귀하의 책에 실리는 사진을 통해 저희 집의 독특한 아름다움을 다른 분들과 공유한다면 기쁠 것입니다.**

[193] **해링턴 공항에서 대중교통을 이용하면 스트릭랜드 대로 195번지에 쉽게 올 수 있습니다. 그저 412번이나 462번 버스를 타고 종점에서 내리면 됩니다.** 집은 버스가 온 방향으로 약 한 블록 뒤쪽에 있습니다. 사실, 도착하시기 직전에 창문을 통해 보일 가능성이 꽤 높습니다. 찾는 데 문제가 있으시면, 555-0185번으로 제게 전화 주세요.

다음 주에 뵙기를 고대합니다.

셰인 암스트롱

어휘 indeed 사실, 실제로 residence 주택 unique 독특한

해링턴 공항 버스 운행 일정표
연중, 일주일에 7일

| 번호 | 경로 | 첫차 | 막차 |
|---|---|---|---|
| 410 | 공항 → 시내 | 오전 6시 20분 | 오후 9시 50분 |
| [193] **412** | **공항 → 시내 → 벨먼트** | 오전 6시 5분 | 오후 10시 5분 |
| 437 | 공항 → 리버프런트 → 애벗 하이츠 | 오전 6시 25분 | 오후 9시 55분 |
| [194] **450** | **공항 → 에지우드** | 오전 6시 15분 | 오후 9시 45분 |
| [193] **462** | **공항 → 시장 구역 → 벨먼트** | 오전 6시 10분 | 오후 10시 10분 |
| 470 | 공항 → 애벗 하이츠 | 오전 6시 30분 | 오후 10시 |

해링턴 공항 버스

[194] **오늘(10월 19일), 에지우드행 공항 버스가 예거 대로 대신 비숍 가에서 정차할 것입니다.** 이 변동은 폴 페스티벌을 위한 도로 폐쇄 때문에 필수적입니다. 상세 정보는, 관광 안내 데스크를 방문하십시오.

모든 버스 승객들께서는, 늘 그렇듯이, [195] **해당 좌석 승차권을 구입하지 않았다면 짐을 좌석에 놓아 두실 수 없다는 점에 유의하시기 바랍니다.** 그 외에는, 짐을 버스 아래쪽 공간에 보관하셔야 합니다. 버스 기사가 안전하게 싣고 내리도록 도와 드릴 것입니다.

어휘 necessary 필수적인, 필요한 details 상세 정보, 세부 사항 specific 특정한, 구체적인 otherwise 그 외에는, 그렇지 않으면 store 보관하다, 저장하다

## 191 추론

번역 가네코 씨는 왜 암스트롱 씨가 있는 지역으로 가는 것 같은가?
(A) 디자인 전시회에 참석하기 위해
(B) 건물 사진을 촬영하기 위해
(C) 출판물에 필요한 인터뷰를 하기 위해
(D) 개조 프로젝트에 관해 조언해 주기 위해

해설 이메일 첫 번째 단락에 가네코 씨의 책에 실리는 사진을 통해 집의 독특한 아름다움을 다른 사람들과 공유한다면 기쁠 것(It would be a pleasure to share our home's unique beauty with others through the photographs in your book)이라는 말이 쓰여 있어 책에 실을 사진을 찍으러 가는 것임을 알 수 있다. 따라서 (B)가 정답이다.

어휘 exhibition 전시회 property 건물, 부동산 conduct 실시하다 publication 출판(물) renovation 개조, 보수

## 192 세부 사항

번역 이메일에서, 암스트롱 씨는 가네코 씨가 어떤 정보를 이미 알고 있음을 나타내는가?
(A) 자신의 가족 구성
(B) 자신의 집을 지은 건축가
(C) 자신의 직장 위치
(D) 건물 점검 결과

해설 이메일 첫 단락에 바스마 이타니가 디자인한 몇 군데 되지 않는 주택들 중 한 곳에 살고 있어서 꽤 자랑스럽다(We are indeed quite proud to live in one of the few residences designed by Basma Itani)고 했는데 이것은 이미 상대방이 그 집의 건축가를 알고 있다는 전제하에 하는 말이므로 (B)가 정답이다.

어휘 be aware of ~을 알고 있다 composition 구성(원) architect 건축가 inspection 점검, 조사

> Paraphrasing
> 지문의 residences designed by Basma Itani
> → 정답의 The architect of his house

## 193 연계

번역 스트릭랜드 대로 195번지는 어느 지역에 위치해 있는가?
(A) 시내
(B) 벨먼트
(C) 애벗 하이츠
(D) 에지우드

해설 이메일 두 번째 단락에 해링턴 공항에서 대중교통을 이용하면 스트릭랜드 대로 195번지에 쉽게 올 수 있다며, 그저 412번이나 462번 버스를 타고 종점에서 내리면 된다(It is easy to reach 195 Strickland Boulevard ~ You simply take either Bus 412 or Bus 462 and get off at the final stop)고 쓰여 있다. 버스 운행 일정표에 412번 버스와 462번 버스의 종점이 모두 Belmont로 표기되어 있으므로 (B)가 정답이다.

## 194 연계

번역 어느 버스의 경로가 일시적으로 변경되었는가?
(A) 410
(B) 437
(C) 450
(D) 470

해설 공지 첫 단락에 에지우드행 공항 버스가 예거 대로 대신 비숍 가에서 정차할 것(Today (October 19), the airport bus to Edgewood will stop on Bishop Street instead of Yeager Avenue)이라고 했다. 버스 운행 일정표에 에지우드행 버스 번호가 450으로 표기되어 있으므로 (C)가 정답이다.

어휘 temporarily 일시적으로, 임시로

> Paraphrasing
> 지문의 will stop on Bishop Street instead of Yeager Avenue → 질문의 has temporarily changed

## 195 Not / True

번역 공지에서 해링턴 공항 버스에 대해 언급하는 것은?
(A) 배정된 좌석이 있다.
(B) 기사를 통해 승차권을 구입할 수 있다.
(C) 머리 위쪽에 짐 보관용 칸이 있다.
(D) 승객들이 운행 중에 서 있어야 할 수도 있다.

해설 공지 두 번째 단락에 해당 좌석 승차권을 구입하지 않으면 짐을 좌석에 놓아둘 수 없다(your baggage cannot be placed on a seat unless you have bought the ticket for that specific seat)고 알리고 있다. 이는 배정된 좌석을 이용해야 한다는 뜻이므로 (A)가 정답이다.

어휘 assign 배정하다, 할당하다 compartment 짐 보관용 칸

## 196-200 기사+이메일+도면

클레멘테 가 부지

헤이워드 (3월 2일) - 196 **헤이워드 시 의회가 클레멘테 가에 위치한 시 소유의 5에이커 부지의 미래에 대해 다양한 선택지를 살펴보고 있다.** 현재 입찰과 제안을 받고 있으며, 지역 환경 단체인 그린웨이 컬래버러티브는 이 부지를 비워 놓고 시 소유로 남겨 두는 것을 지지하고 있다. 198 **힐뷰 부동산 개발회사에서 이 부지를 매입하는 데 관심을 갖고 있다. 이 회사는 소매업을 위한 공간이 있는 작은 건물인 마샬 플라자를 짓고,** 나무, 벤치, 꽃밭이 있는 작은 녹지와 정원을 조성해 공공용으로 사용할 계획이다.

"저희가 계획한 소매 점포들과 녹지 공간의 조화는, 활성화가 절실히 필요한 이 지역을 위해 실행 가능한 해결책입니다"라고 힐뷰 부동산 개발회사의 대변인 루오양 멩이 밝혔다. "저희 회사는 197 **야생 동물 서식지에 대한 방해를 최소화할 수 있는 전문 지식**뿐만 아니라 매력적이고 번창하는 소매점을 만들 자원을 보유하고 있습니다. 저희 능력을 선보일 기회가 있기를 바랍니다."

어휘 lot 부지, 용지 council 의회 explore 살펴보다, 탐구하다 various 다양한 -owned ~이 소유한 located on ~에 위치한 bid 입찰 proposal 제안(서) local 지역의 advocate for ~을 지지하다, 옹호하다 possession 소유(물) intend to ~할 계획이다, 작정이다 retail 소매(업) establish 확립하다 designate 지정하다 combination 조화, 조합 unit (상가 등의) 점포 viable 실행 가능한 solution 해결책 neighborhood 인근, 이웃 critical 중대한 revitalization 재활성화 representative 대변인 resources 자원 attractive 매력적인 thriving 번창하는 expertise 전문 지식 disruption 방해, 지장 habitat 서식지 opportunity 기회 showcase 선보이다

발신: 클리퍼드 뮬렌 <clifford@busybbakery.com>
수신: 래켈 쇼 <r_shaw@hillviewprop.com>
날짜: 11월 18일
제목: 임대 문의

쇼 씨께,

저는 시내에 비지 비 베이커리를 소유하고 있는데, 제 제과 상품을 판매할 두 번째 지점을 임대하는 데 관심이 있습니다. 기대 유동 인구 때문에 198 **마샬 플라자가 제 사업에 이상적일 것입니다.** 대중교통을 쉽게 이용할 수 있는 편리함과 뒤쪽에 있는 화물 하차 구역에도 마음이 끌립니다. 200 **최소한 300제곱미터의 공간이 필요하긴 하지만, 조리 시설은 원하지 않습니다.** 직원들이 본점에서 구워 두 번째 지점으로 상품을 전달할 것이기 때문입니다. 199 **평균적인 수도, 전기, 가스 요금을 제게 알려 주실 수 있는지도 궁금합니다.** 이것들이 월 임대료에 포함되지 않는 것으로 알고 있습니다.

감사합니다.

클리퍼드 뮬렌

어휘 rental 임대, 대여 inquiry 문의 own 소유하다 rent 임대하다, 대여하다 location 지점, 위치 goods 상품 ideal 이상적인 anticipated 기대되는 foot traffic 유동 인구 be drawn to+명사 ~에 마음이 끌리다 convenience 편의(성) access 접근, 이용 public transportation 대중교통 unloading 화물 하차, 하역 site 장소, 현장 average 평균의 rate 요금 include 포함하다

마샬 플라자 소매 점포

| 200 **102호**<br>**320제곱미터**<br>**임대 가능** | 103호<br>270제곱미터<br>임대 가능 | 104호<br>350제곱미터<br>베니스 과자점 |
|---|---|---|
| | | |
| 101호<br>225제곱미터<br>임대 가능 | 정원 | 105호<br>315제곱미터<br>임대 가능<br>주방 포함 |

어휘 available 이용 가능한

## 196 주제 / 목적

번역 기사의 목적은 무엇인가?
(A) 공공 부지에 관한 최신 정보를 제공하는 것
(B) 지역 주민들에게 폐쇄를 알리는 것
(C) 이용하지 않는 부지의 매각을 홍보하는 것
(D) 공원 업그레이드를 위한 지원을 이끌어 내는 것

해설 기사 첫 단락에 헤이워드 시 의회가 클레멘테 가에 위치한 시 소유의 5에이커 부지의 미래에 대해 다양한 선택지를 살펴보고 있다(The Hayward City Council is exploring various options for the future of a 5-acre city-owned lot located on Clemente Street)고 언급한 뒤로 그 활용 방법에 대해 이야기하고 있다. 이는 시 소유의 공공 부지에 관한 최신 정보를 제공하는 것이므로 (A)가 정답이다.

어휘 resident 주민 promote 홍보하다 unused 이용하지 않는 elicit 이끌어 내다 aid 지원, 도움

## 197 세부 사항

번역 멩 씨가 힐뷰 부동산 개발회사의 어떤 유익한 측면을 언급하는가?
(A) 헤이워드 시에 더 많은 일자리를 창출하려는 의도
(B) 건축 비용을 통제한 경험
(C) 환경친화적인 건축 자재 이용
(D) 동물이 서식하는 공간을 보존하는 능력

해설 멩 씨의 이름이 언급되는 기사 두 번째 단락에 힐뷰 부동산 개발회사가 야생 동물 서식지에 대한 방해를 최소화할 수 있는 전문 지식(the expertise to minimize disruptions to wildlife habitats)을 보유하고 있다고 했으므로 (D)가 정답이다.

어휘 beneficial 유익한 aspect 측면, 양상 intention 의도, 목적 keep ~ under control ~을 조절하다, ~을 통제하다 expenditure 지출 (비용) environmentally friendly 환경친화적인 material 자재, 재료 ability 능력 preserve 보존하다

> **Paraphrasing**
> 지문의 minimize disruptions to wildlife habitats
> → 정답의 preserve spaces where animals live

## 198 연계

번역 뮬렌 씨의 이메일에서 힐뷰 부동산 개발회사에 대해 암시된 것은?
(A) 그의 제과점이 있는 건물을 지었다.
(B) 최종 건축 허가를 기다리고 있다.
(C) 그곳의 제안서를 시 관계자들이 받아들였다.
(D) 그곳의 직원들은 평소에 대중교통을 이용한다.

해설 뮬렌 씨의 이메일 초반부에 마샬 플라자가 자신의 업체에 이상적일 것(Marshall Plaza would be ideal for my business)이라고 언급했는데 마샬 플라자는 기사 첫 단락에 힐뷰 부동산 개발회사가 부지를 매입해 지으려 했던 건물의 명칭(Hillview Property Development is interested in purchasing the lot. It intends to build Marshall Plaza, ~)으로 제시되어 있다. 따라서 시에서 힐뷰 부동산 개발회사의 제안을 받아들여 마샬 플라자가 지어진 것으로 볼 수 있으므로 (C)가 정답이다.

어휘 await 기다리다 permit 허가(증) official 관계자, 당국자 usually 평소에, 일반적으로

## 199 세부 사항

번역 뮬렌 씨가 마샬 플라자에 대한 어떤 정보를 요청하는가?
(A) 건물의 보안 조치
(B) 건물의 공과금
(C) 월 사용료 납기일
(D) 하차 구역의 크기

해설 뮬렌 씨의 이메일 후반부에 평균적인 수도, 전기, 가스 요금을 알려 줄 수 있는지 궁금하다(I'm also wondering if you could tell me the average rates for water, electricity, and gas)고 쓰여 있다. 이는 공과금 관련 정보를 요청하는 것이므로 (B)가 정답이다.

어휘 measures 조치 cost of utilities 공과금 due date 납기일, 만기일

> **Paraphrasing**
> 지문의 the average rates for water, electricity, and gas
> → 정답의 cost of utilities

## 200 연계

번역 뮬렌 씨는 어느 점포에 관심이 있을 것 같은가?
(A) 101호
(B) 102호
(C) 103호
(D) 105호

해설 뮬렌 씨의 이메일 중반부에 최소한 300제곱미터의 공간이 필요하며 조리 시설은 원하지 않는다(I need at least three hundred square meters of space, but I do not want cooking facilities)는 조건이 언급되어 있다. 도면에서 300제곱미터보다 넓고 조리 시설은 없으면서 임대 가능한 점포는 왼쪽 상단에 있는 Unit 102이므로 (B)가 정답이다.

# TEST 3

| | | | | |
|---|---|---|---|---|
| 101 (C) | 102 (B) | 103 (D) | 104 (A) | 105 (D) |
| 106 (D) | 107 (B) | 108 (C) | 109 (A) | 110 (C) |
| 111 (A) | 112 (C) | 113 (C) | 114 (A) | 115 (A) |
| 116 (C) | 117 (B) | 118 (A) | 119 (C) | 120 (D) |
| 121 (D) | 122 (D) | 123 (D) | 124 (B) | 125 (C) |
| 126 (B) | 127 (D) | 128 (C) | 129 (B) | 130 (D) |
| 131 (A) | 132 (D) | 133 (C) | 134 (C) | 135 (C) |
| 136 (A) | 137 (D) | 138 (C) | 139 (C) | 140 (C) |
| 141 (B) | 142 (D) | 143 (B) | 144 (A) | 145 (C) |
| 146 (D) | 147 (B) | 148 (D) | 149 (B) | 150 (A) |
| 151 (A) | 152 (B) | 153 (A) | 154 (D) | 155 (A) |
| 156 (D) | 157 (A) | 158 (B) | 159 (A) | 160 (C) |
| 161 (D) | 162 (C) | 163 (A) | 164 (A) | 165 (D) |
| 166 (A) | 167 (B) | 168 (A) | 169 (C) | 170 (B) |
| 171 (B) | 172 (A) | 173 (D) | 174 (B) | 175 (A) |
| 176 (A) | 177 (D) | 178 (B) | 179 (B) | 180 (C) |
| 181 (B) | 182 (D) | 183 (B) | 184 (B) | 185 (D) |
| 186 (D) | 187 (D) | 188 (A) | 189 (A) | 190 (B) |
| 191 (B) | 192 (C) | 193 (D) | 194 (C) | 195 (A) |
| 196 (A) | 197 (B) | 198 (D) | 199 (C) | 200 (C) |

## PART 5

### 101 인칭대명사 _ 목적격 대명사

번역 존스턴 씨는 승진에 도움이 될 온라인 강좌들을 수강하고 있다.

해설 동사 assist의 목적어 자리이며, 온라인 강의가 존스턴 씨에게 도움이 되는 것이므로 목적격 대명사 (C) him이 정답이다. (A) his가 소유대명사(그의 것)로 쓰이면 목적어 자리에 올 수 있지만 의미상 적절하지 않고, (D) himself는 재귀대명사로 목적어 자리에 올 수 있지만 주어와 목적어가 동일할 때 사용한다.

어휘 assist 돕다, 지원하다 get promoted 승진되다

### 102 부사 자리 _ 과거분사 수식

번역 행사 참석자들은 자신의 책에 저자의 사인을 직접 받을 수 있다.

해설 「have+목적어+과거분사」 구조에서 목적어 their book과 과거분사 signed 사이에 위치한 빈칸은 과거분사를 수식할 부사가 들어갈 수 있는 자리이므로 (B) personally(직접)가 정답이다.

어휘 attendee 참석자 author 저자, 작가 personal 개인의 personalize (개인의 필요에) 맞추다

### 103 형용사 자리 _ 명사 수식

번역 자산 관리에 관한 알콘 씨의 칼럼을 읽는 독자들은 그녀의 사려 깊은 재정적 조언을 높이 평가한다.

해설 소유격 대명사 her와 financial advice 사이에 있는 빈칸에는 형용사 financial을 수식하는 부사나 financial과 함께 명사 advice를 수식하는 형용사가 들어갈 수 있다. (C) thoughtfully(사려 깊게)가 부사인데 financial(재무의)을 수식하는 것은 의미상 어색하므로 오답이고, 명사 advice를 자연스럽게 수식하는 형용사 (D) thoughtful(사려 깊은)이 정답이다.

어휘 column (신문 등의) 칼럼 appreciate 높이 평가하다, 감사하다 financial 재무의, 금융의

### 104 형용사 자리 _ 복합명사 수식

번역 예비 학생들은 상세한 학사 일정을 확인하여 대학 프로그램에 대해 더 알아보도록 요청받는다.

해설 소유격 대명사 its와 복합명사 course schedule 사이에 위치한 빈칸은 복합명사를 수식할 형용사가 들어갈 수 있는 자리이므로 (A) detailed(상세한)가 정답이다.

어휘 prospective 장래의, 장차 ~이 될 invite 요청하다

### 105 명사 어휘

번역 하트웨이 테라스에서는 모든 요리가 진유정 최고 주방장의 감독하에 준비된다.

해설 요리 준비와 관련해 최고 주방장이 하는 일을 나타낼 명사가 필요하므로 '감독, 지휘'를 뜻하는 (D) supervision이 정답이다. under the supervision of는 '~의 감독하에'를 뜻하는 표현이니 알아 두자.

어휘 opinion 의견 attempt 시도

### 106 형용사 어휘

번역 비행 전에 승객들에게 반드시 안전 교육이 제공되어야 한다.

해설 「It is ~ that절」로 구성된 가주어/진주어 문장에서 is와 that절 사이에 들어갈 올바른 형용사를 찾아야 한다. that절의 동사가 be로 동사원형이 왔으므로 동사 앞에 should가 생략된 것을 알 수 있다. 따라서 빈칸에는 당위성을 나타내는 형용사가 와야 하므로 '필수인, 반드시 해야 하는'을 뜻하는 (D) imperative가 정답이다. imperative나 necessary처럼 당위성을 나타내는 형용사나 주장/제안/요청의 동사 뒤 that절에는 (should+) 동사 원형이 온다.

어휘 passenger 승객 safety briefing 안전 교육 abundant 풍부한 sudden 갑작스러운 distinctive 독특한, 특색 있는

### 107 전치사 자리

번역 머피 서플라이 사와의 계약 협상은 대체 공급업체의 부족을 고려하여 실시되어야 합니다.

TEST 3

해설 빈칸 뒤에 명사 consideration과 전치사구만 쓰여 있으므로 consideration을 목적어로 취할 전치사가 필요하며, '~을 고려하여'를 뜻하는 전치사구 with consideration for를 구성해야 알맞으므로 (B) with가 정답이다. (A) by(~에 의해)도 전치사이지만 consideration for와 어울리지 않으며, (C) so that(~할 수 있도록)과 (D) while(~ 동안)은 접속사이다.

어휘 contract 계약(서) negotiation 협상 conduct 실시하다 consideration 고려 lack 부족 alternative 대체의, 대안의 supplier 공급업체

## 108 동사 어휘

번역 페기 에이머스는 도서관의 인기 강연 시리즈인 "미래의 기업가들"을 제작한 것에 대해 관장의 칭찬을 받았다.

해설 인기 있는 강연 시리즈를 제작한 것에 대해 관장으로부터 '칭찬 받았다'라는 의미를 나타내야 자연스러우므로 '칭찬하다'를 뜻하는 commend의 과거분사 (C) commended가 정답이다.

어휘 create 만들어 내다 entrepreneur 기업가 intend 의도하다 influence 영향을 미치다 allow 허용하다

## 109 부사 어휘

번역 주거용 난로 및 보일러는 안전상의 이유로 해마다 점검을 받아야 한다.

해설 주거용 난로 및 보일러가 안전상의 이유로 점검을 받는 방식을 나타낼 부사가 필요하므로 '해마다, 연례적으로'를 뜻하는 (A) annually가 정답이다. (C) certainly는 '(의심할 여지없이) 확실히, 틀림없이'라는 의미인데 화자가 무엇을 강력히 믿고 있음을 나타내거나 사실임을 강조하기 위해 쓰이는 표현이므로 빈칸에는 적절하지 않다.

어휘 residential 주거의, 주택지의 furnace 난로, 화로 undergo (검사, 변화 등을) 받다, 겪다 inspection 점검 overly 지나치게, 너무 certainly 확실히, 틀림없이 readily 즉시, 손쉽게

## 110 명사 자리 _ 복합명사

번역 고객 기밀을 유지하기 위해, 오래된 파일의 파기는 조심스럽게 실시되어야 한다.

해설 가산명사 client 앞에 한정사가 없으므로, 빈칸에는 client와 함께 복합명사를 이루어 To maintain의 목적어 역할을 하는 명사가 들어가야 한다. 따라서 '기밀'을 뜻하는 (C) confidentiality가 정답이다.

어휘 maintain 유지하다 destruction 파기, 파괴 carry out 실시하다, 수행하다 carefully 조심스럽게 confiding 신뢰하는 confidential 기밀의 confidentially 은밀하게

## 111 명사 어휘

번역 홈 헬스 스마트폰 애플리케이션의 새 버전에는 초보자들을 위한 운동 팁 목록이 포함되어 있다.

해설 형용사 new와 of the Home Health smartphone application의 수식을 받는 명사가 들어갈 자리로, '홈 헬스 스마트폰 애플리케이션의 새 버전'이라는 의미가 되어야 자연스러우므로 '버전, 판'을 의미하는 (A) version이 정답이다.

어휘 feature 특징으로 하다, 특별히 포함하다 aspect 측면, 양상 route 경로, 노선 term 기간, 용어

## 112 인칭 대명사 _ 소유대명사

번역 웹스터 씨의 은퇴 파티에 많은 동료 직원을 비롯해 심지어 과거의 여러 제자들도 참석했다.

해설 웹스터 씨의 여러 제자들이 참석했다는 내용으로 빈칸 앞의 소유의 의미인 of가 있으므로 her students(그녀의 제자들)를 대신하는 소유대명사 (C) hers(그녀의 것)가 정답이다. '그녀의 제자들 중 여러 제자가 참석했다'는 의미이다.

어휘 retirement 은퇴 coworker 동료 (직원) former 과거의, 전 ~의

## 113 명사 어휘

번역 비가 올 것이 예상되어 래드너 공원의 야외 콘서트장에 여러 개의 천막이 설치되었다.

해설 in ____ of 구조에 어울리는 명사로서 비가 올 가능성과 관련된 명사가 필요하므로 '예상, 예측'을 뜻하는 (C) anticipation이 정답이다. in anticipation of는 '~이 예상되어, ~을 예상하고'를 뜻하는 표현이니 알아 두자.

어휘 canopy 지붕 모양의 시설물, 천막 atmosphere 분위기 proportion 비율, 부분 limitation 한계, 제약

## 114 분사 자리 _ 과거분사

번역 자신의 생산 목표를 초과하는 것에 대해 보상을 받는 직원이 높은 수준의 생산성을 유지할 가능성이 더 크다.

해설 빈칸 앞에 be동사 are가 있으므로 명사나 형용사 혹은 분사가 들어갈 수 있다. 주어가 Employees이므로 명사가 들어가면 의미가 어색하고, 분사 (A) rewarded와 (C) rewarding 중 현재분사 rewarding은 뒤에 목적어가 필요하므로 정답은 과거분사 (A) rewarded이다.

어휘 exceed 초과하다 output 생산, 산출 maintain 유지하다 productivity 생산성 reward 보상; 보상하다

## 115 형용사 어휘

번역 전화기 부품은 열에 민감하기 때문에 사용 설명서는 고객들에게 전화기를 라디에이터와 오븐에서 멀리 하도록 경고한다.

해설 열에 민감하기 때문에 라디에이터와 오븐에서 멀리 하도록 경고한다는 내용이 되어야 자연스러우므로 '민감한'을 뜻하는 (A) sensitive가 정답이다.

어휘 warn 경고하다, 주의를 주다 component 부품, 구성 요소 familiar 익숙한, 잘 아는 released 발표된, 출시된 considerable 상당한, 많은

## 116 부사 어휘

번역 약국이 이미 문을 닫았기 때문에 처방약은 내일 받아 와야 한다.

해설 현재완료 시제 동사를 구성하는 has와 과거분사 closed 사이에 빈칸이 있으며, 약국이 이미 문을 닫았다는 내용이 되어야 자연스러우므로 '이미'라는 의미의 부사 (C) already가 정답이다.

어휘 prescription 처방약, 처방전 collect 받아 오다, 수집하다 pharmacy 약국 hardly 거의 ~ 않다

## 117 분사 자리 _ 현재분사

번역 환경에 미치는 영향에 대한 우려에도 불구하고 일회용 제품의 양이 증가하고 있다.

해설 be동사 is 뒤에 빈칸이 있으므로 grow는 분사 형태가 되어야 한다. grow가 '증가하다'의 의미일 때는 자동사로 사용되므로 현재분사 (B) growing이 정답이다. 자동사는 수동태가 될 수 없기 때문에 과거분사인 (D) grown은 오답이다.

어휘 volume 양, 용량 disposable 일회용의 concern 우려 impact 영향

## 118 형용사 어휘

번역 지역 문화 센터의 개장은 오직 대중의 아낌없는 후원으로 가능했다.

해설 '후원, 지원'을 뜻하는 명사 support를 수식해 그 정도를 나타낼 형용사가 쓰여야 알맞으므로 '아낌없는, 넉넉한' 등을 의미하는 (A) generous가 정답이다.

어휘 the public 일반인들, 일반 대중 identical 동일한 bright 밝은 spacious 널찍한

## 119 전치사 어휘

번역 엘리타 주식회사가 제조하는 새 요가 매트는 심지어 수년 동안 사용한 후에도 그 모양을 유지한다.

해설 빈칸 뒤에 있는 many years of use를 목적어로 받는 전치사 자리로, 여러 해 동안 사용한 후에도 모양이 유지된다는 내용이 되어야 자연스러우므로 '~ 후에'를 뜻하는 전치사 (C) after가 정답이다.

어휘 manufacture 제조하다 maintain 유지하다

## 120 전치사 어휘

번역 그 제조사는 드라이기에 대해 3년 동안 표준 보증을 제공한다.

해설 기간을 나타내는 명사구 three years와 어울려 '3년 동안'이라는 의미를 구성해야 알맞으므로 '~ 동안'을 뜻하는 전치사 (D) for가 정답이다.

어휘 manufacturer 제조사 warranty 보증(서)

## 121 명사 어휘

번역 오티스 씨는 그 역할에서 성공하기 위해 필요한 대인 관계 능력 및 경력을 조화롭게 지니고 있다.

해설 어떤 역할에서 성공하기 위해 필요한 두 가지 요소가 알맞게 어우러진 상태를 나타낼 명사가 필요하므로 '조화, 조합'을 뜻하는 (D) combination이 정답이다.

어휘 succeed in ~에서 성공하다 remedy 치료(약), 해결책 sequence 연속(성), 순서 improvement 개선, 향상

## 122 명사절 접속사 _ how

번역 이사진이 집중하는 것은 투자자들이 CEO의 은퇴 소식에 어떻게 반응하는가이다.

해설 is 뒤에 빈칸이 있고, 빈칸 뒤에 주어(investors)와 동사(react)를 포함한 완전한 절이 있으므로 이 절을 이끌어 명사절로 만들어 주는 명사절 접속사가 필요하다. 또한, 의미상 'CEO의 은퇴 소식에 어떻게 반응하는가'가 되어야 자연스러우므로 '어떻게'를 뜻하는 (D) how가 정답이다. (A) among(~ 중에)은 전치사이며, (B) who는 주어나 목적어가 빠진 불완전한 명사절을 이끌어야 하므로 오답이다. (C) where는 의미가 어울리지 않는다.

어휘 focus 초점, 중점 board member 이사 investor 투자자 react 반응하다 retirement 은퇴

## 123 부사 자리 _ to부정사 수식

번역 프로그램 책임자는 직원들에게 각자의 개인 소셜 미디어 계정을 이용해 자원봉사자 모집 게시물을 널리 유포할 것을 요청했다.

해설 to부정사(to circulate)와 to부정사의 목적어(the volunteer recruitment post) 뒤에 빈칸이 있으므로 빈칸은 to부정사를 수식하는 부사 자리이다. 또한, 빈칸이 없이도 완전한 문장이 되는 것으로 보아 빈칸이 부사 자리임을 알 수 있다. 따라서 부사 (D) widely(널리, 대단히)가 정답이다.

어휘 coordinator 책임자 circulate 유포하다 volunteer 자원봉사자 recruitment 모집 post 게시물 account 계정, 계좌 widen 넓히다

## 124 부사 자리 _ 형용사 수식

번역 건물 내 모든 사람의 안전을 위해, 비상구 주변 구역은 항상 완전히 비워져 있어야 한다.

해설 동사 remain과 형용사 보어 clear 사이에 빈칸이 있으므로 빈칸에는 형용사를 수식하는 부사가 들어가야 한다. 따라서 (B) perfectly(완전히, 완벽하게)가 정답이다.

어휘 fire exit 비상구 perfect 완벽한; 완벽하게 하다 perfection 완벽

## 125 동사의 태

번역 건축가가 그린 그 구조물의 도면과 지어진 건물은 많이 다르다.

해설 빈칸이 속한 that절이 수식하는 the building은 사람에 의해 지어지는 것이고, 빈칸 뒤에 목적어가 없으므로 동사는 수동태가 되어야 한다. 따라서 (C) was constructed가 정답이다.

어휘 architect 건축가 drawing 도면, 도안 structure 구조(물) differ 다르다 greatly 크게, 대단히 construct 짓다, 건설하다

## 126 동사 어휘

번역 벤자민은 자신이 원격으로 실시할 교육을 위해 새 화상 회의 소프트웨어를 선택했다.

해설 he will ~ remotely는 관계대명사가 생략된 채로 앞에 있는 the training을 수식하는 관계대명사절이다. 따라서 교육을 수식하는 말이 들어가야 하는데, '원격으로 실시할 교육'이라는 의미가 되어야 자연스러우므로 '실시하다, 수행하다'를 뜻하는 (B) conduct가 정답이다. (C) participate는 '참가하다, 참여하다'라는 뜻으로 의미상 가능해 보이지만 빈칸은 목적어를 갖는 타동사 자리이다. participate는 자동사여서 뒤에 목적어를 쓰려면 전치사 in이 와야 하므로 오답이다.

어휘 videoconferencing 화상 회의 remotely 원격으로 appear 나타나다, ~인 것 같다 participate 참가하다 instruct 지시하다, 설명하다

## 127 접속사 어휘

번역 관람객들이 극장에 도착하는 대로, 안내원이 정확한 좌석으로 안내할 것이다.

해설 빈칸 뒤에 완전한 절 두 개가 콤마로 이어져 있으므로 빈칸은 부사절 접속사 자리이다. 또한 '관람객들이 극장에 도착하는 대로, 안내원이 정확한 좌석으로 안내할 것'이라는 말이 자연스러우므로 '(일단) ~하는 대로, ~하자마자'를 뜻하는 접속사 (D) Once가 정답이다.

어휘 audience members 관객, 청중 usher (좌석) 안내원 direct 안내하다, 길을 알려 주다

## 128 과거분사 _ 명사 후치 수식

번역 경연에서 탈락된 공연자들은 남아서 나머지 공연을 관람하시기 바랍니다.

해설 문장에 동사 are encouraged가 있으므로 빈칸은 동사 자리가 아니며, 빈칸에서 from the competition까지가 명사 Performers를 뒤에서 수식하는 구조가 되어야 한다. 빈칸 뒤에 목적어가 아닌 전치사구가 이어지고 있으며, '탈락된 공연자들'을 의미해야 알맞으므로 수동의 의미를 나타내는 과거분사 (C) eliminated가 정답이다.

어휘 competition 경연, 대회 encourage 권장하다, 장려하다 remainder 나머지 eliminate 탈락시키다, 없애다

## 129 접속사 자리 _ 부사절 접속사

번역 5번 고속도로의 확장 공사가 완료되어 많은 통근자들이 운전 시간이 줄어든 것을 즐거워하고 있다.

해설 빈칸 앞뒤에 각각 완전한 절이 있으므로 빈칸에는 접속사가 필요하며, 5번 고속도로의 확장 공사가 완료된 것은 통근자들이 즐거워하는 원인에 해당하므로 '(이제) ~이므로'를 뜻하는 부사절 접속사 (B) now that이 정답이다.

어휘 commuter 통근자 expansion 확장, 확대

## 130 동사 어휘

번역 록퍼드 아파트 단지에서는 세입자들이 충분히 시간을 둔 통지 없이 임대 계약을 종료하면 수수료를 지불해야 할 수도 있다.

해설 빈칸이 포함된 if절은 세입자들이 요금을 지불해야 할 수도 있는 상황을 나타내야 하므로 '충분히 시간을 둔 통지 없이 계약을 종료하면'이라는 내용이 되어야 자연스럽다. 따라서 '종료하다'를 뜻하는 (D) terminate가 정답이다.

어휘 tenant 세입자 pay a fee 요금을 지불하다 lease 임대 (계약) agreement 계약(서), 합의(서) sufficient 충분한 notice 통지(서), 알림 prohibit 금지하다 obstruct 막다, 방해하다 enclose 동봉하다

# PART 6

### 131-134 이메일

수신: 유리아스 데이터 사 전 직원
발신: 가브리엘라 쇼
제목: 직원 감사 행사
날짜: 4월 15일

유리아스 데이터 사의 연례 직원 감사 행사로, 4월 25일 금요일 업무 시간에 월폴 국립공원에서 단체 하이킹을 할 것입니다. 모두 나와서 [131] **운동**과 함께 서로 더 잘 알게 되는 즐거운 하루를 즐기시기 바랍니다. 직원들이 행사 장소까지 차량을 [132] **공유할 수** 있도록 베로니카 에릭슨이 카풀을 구성하고 있습니다. 운전자인 경우, 사용한 연료의 비용을 환급받으실 것입니다.

여러분 중 일부는 지금 업무량이 많은 것으로 알고 있습니다. [133] **하지만**, 그렇다고 해서 행사에 참석할 수 없다고 생각하지 마시기 바랍니다. [134] **긴급하지 않은 프로젝트의 마감 기한은 연장될 수 있습니다.** 이 부분에 있어 우려 사항이 있으신 경우, 여러분의 상사에게 말씀해보세요.

어휘 appreciation 감사(의 마음) annual 연례적인, 해마다의 get to ~하게 되다 organize 구성하다, 마련하다 carpool 카풀, 승용차 함께 타기 ride (자동차 등을) 타고 가기 reimburse 비용을 환급해 주다 workload 업무량 assume 생각하다, 추정하다 supervisor 부서장, 상관

## 131 명사 어휘

해설 무엇을 하면서 즐거운 하루를 즐길 것인지를 나타낼 명사가 필요하며, 앞 문장에 단체 하이킹을 한다는 말이 쓰여 있으므로 '운동'을 의미하는 (A) exercise가 정답이다.

어휘 education 교육 volunteering 자원봉사

## 132 동사 자리_수 일치

해설 부사절 접속사 so that 뒤에 주어(employees)만 있고 동사가 없으므로 빈칸은 동사 자리이다. (C)와 (D)가 동사인데, 주어가 복수이므로 조동사 can을 포함한 (D) can share가 정답이다. (C) shares는 단수 동사로 주어와 수 일치가 되지 않는다.

어휘 share 공유하다, 함께 이용하다

## 133 접속부사

해설 빈칸 앞에는 현재 업무량이 많은 걸 알고 있다는 내용이 있는데, 빈칸 뒤에는 그게 참석할 수 없음을 의미하는 건 아니라는 내용이 쓰여 있다. 이 둘은 대조적인 내용이므로 '하지만'이라는 의미의 (C) However가 정답이다.

어휘 furthermore 더욱이, 게다가 likewise 마찬가지로 otherwise 그렇지 않으면, 그 외에는

## 134 문장 고르기

번역 (A) 여러분의 유급 휴가 일수에서 하루가 차감될 것입니다.
(B) 보충 시간 일정이 곧 잡히게 될 가능성이 높습니다.
(C) 긴급하지 않은 프로젝트의 마감 기한은 연장될 수 있습니다.
(D) 공원에 있는 다양한 편의 시설을 이용할 수 있습니다.

해설 앞에 업무량이 많다고 해서 행사에 참석할 수 없다고 생각하지 말라는 말이 쓰여 있다. 이는 업무량이 많은 사람도 행사에 참석하길 바란다는 의미이므로 행사 참석을 독려하기 위한 조치에 해당하는 (C)가 정답이다.

어휘 subtract 빼다 allowance 할당량, 수당 paid leave 유급 휴가 make-up 보충 deadline 마감 기한 non-urgent 긴급하지 않은 extend 연장하다, 확장하다 a variety of 다양한 convenience 편의 available 이용 가능한

**135-138 후기**

맥베이 회계 법인에 대한 제 첫인상은 긍정적이었습니다. 제 작은 사업체의 세금에 관해 도움을 요청하는 양식을 작성하자 담당자가 신속하게 응답해 주었습니다. 그럼에도 불구하고, 저는 다시는 이 업체를 135 **예약하지 않을 예정입니다**. 제 경험에 따르면 이곳은 136 **정확성**에 충분한 관심을 보이지 않았습니다. 담당 회계사가 저를 위해 준비해 준 세금 신고서에서 오류를 무려 세 개나 발견했습니다. 137 **하나는 제가 수천 달러를 낼 수도 있었던 것이었습니다**. 더욱이, 그는 문제의 근원을 파악해 바로잡기 전까지 여러 차례 논의와 문서 재전송이 필요했습니다. 앞으로는, 친구나 동료의 추천을 바탕으로 업체를 138 **선택할** 계획입니다.

어휘 impression 인상, 느낌 positive 긍정적인 representative 직원 respond 응답하다, 답변하다 fill out 작성하다 nevertheless 그럼에도 불구하고 appointment 예약, 약속 concern 관심(사), 우려 no fewer than 무려 ~나 되는 tax return 세금 신고서 accountant 회계사 what is more 더욱이 discussion 논의 resending 재발송 figure out 파악하다, 알아내다 source 근원 issue 문제, 사안 fix 바로잡다 based on ~을 바탕으로 recommendation 추천 associate 동료

## 135 동사 시제+태

해설 빈칸 뒤에 명사 an appointment가 목적어로 있으므로 보기의 동사 book은 능동태로 써야 한다. 또한, 앞에 첫인상은 긍정적이었다는 말이 있고, 대조의 의미의 Nevertheless(그럼에도 불구하고)로 문장이 시작되므로 미래에는 다시는 예약하지 않겠다는 의미가 되어야 자연스럽다. 따라서 미래진행 시제 능동태인 (C) will not be booking이 정답이다.

어휘 might have p.p. ~했을지도 모른다

## 136 명사 어휘

해설 뒤 문장에 세금 신고서에 오류가 세 개나 있었음을 언급하고 있으므로 빈칸의 문장은 그 업체가 정확성에 충분한 관심을 보이지 않았다는 의미를 나타내야 알맞다. 따라서 '정확성'을 뜻하는 (A) accuracy가 정답이다.

어휘 privacy 사생활 diversity 다양성

## 137 문장 고르기

번역 (A) 이런 종류의 지연은 용납될 수 없습니다.
(B) 그가 그것들을 분실한 것으로 드러났습니다.
(C) 파일들을 공유할 더 안전한 방법이 틀림없이 있습니다.
(D) 하나는 제가 수천 달러를 낼 수도 있었던 것이었습니다.

해설 앞 문장에 담당 회계사가 준비한 세금 신고서에서 오류를 세 개나 발견했다는 말이 쓰여 있으므로 그중 하나를 One으로 지칭해 그 오류의 심각성을 말하는 의미를 지닌 (D)가 정답이다.

어휘 unacceptable 용납할 수 없는, 수용할 수 없는 misplace 분실하다 secure 안전한 share 공유하다 could have p.p. ~할 수도 있었다

## 138 동사 어휘

해설 앞서 글쓴이가 겪은 좋지 못한 경험이 쓰여 있으므로 앞으로는 친구나 동료의 추천을 바탕으로 업체를 선택할 계획이라는 의미를 나타내야 알맞다. 따라서 '선택하다'를 뜻하는 (C) select가 정답이다.

어휘 develop 개발하다 launch 시작하다 expand 확장하다

**139-142 이메일**

수신: 사만다 배네튼 <samantha@vanettenconsulting.com>
발신: 필립 리 <plee@monroe-solutions.com>
제목: 문의
날짜: 3월 2일
첨부: 먼로_솔루션즈

배네튼 씨께,

TEST 3

최근 회사에서 고객과의 관계 확립에 관한 귀하의 세미나 [139] **입장권**을 받았습니다. 처음에는 이 행사에 가는 것이 망설여졌습니다. 전에 참석했던 다른 세미나들의 내용이 너무 기초적이거나 너무 전문적이었기 때문입니다. [140] **그에 반해서,** 귀하의 강연은 제 경력 수준에 해당하는 사람에게 완벽했습니다. 저희 회사는 사내 강연을 위해 귀하를 고용하고 싶습니다. [141] **30명의 저희 영업사원들 모두 참석할 것입니다.** 가능하신지 제게 알려 주시기 바랍니다. 저희 회사의 서비스를 [142] **개괄적으로 설명하는** 안내 책자를 첨부해 드렸습니다.

필립 리

어휘 inquiry 문의 establish 확립하다 relationship 관계 initially 처음에 hesitant 망설이는, 주저하는 content 내용(물) be interested in ~에 관심이 있다 private 비공개의, 사적인 available 시간이 있는 attach 첨부하다 brochure 안내 책자

## 139 명사 어휘

해설 세미나와 관련해 회사에서 받은 것을 나타낼 명사가 필요하므로 '입장권'을 뜻하는 (C) ticket이 정답이다.

어휘 deposit 선금, 보증금 subscription 구독 venture 모험적 사업

## 140 접속부사

해설 앞 문장에는 다른 세미나들이 너무 기초적이거나 너무 전문적이었다는 부정적인 말이, 뒤에는 상대방의 강연이 자신과 같은 사람에게 완벽했다는 긍정적인 말이 쓰여 있다. 빈칸 앞뒤로 대조적인 내용이 있으므로 '그에 반해서'라는 의미의 (C) In contrast가 정답이다.

어휘 in other words 다시 말해서 for instance 예를 들어 to that end 그러기 위해서, 그 목적을 위해서

## 141 문장 고르기

번역 (A) 저의 제안이 유익하다고 생각하셨기를 바랍니다.
(B) 30명의 저희 영업사원들 모두 참석할 것입니다.
(C) 그 강당의 음향 시스템도 인상적이었습니다.
(D) 그 이후로 저희는 고객 불만을 더 적게 받습니다.

해설 앞 문장에 사내 강연을 해 주길 원한다는 내용이 있고, 뒤 문장에는 가능한지 알려 달라는 말이 있다. 따라서 사내 강연과 관련된 문장이 빈칸에 쓰여야 알맞으므로 예상 참석 인원을 알리는 (B)가 정답이다.

어휘 suggestion 의견, 제안 in attendance 참석한 impressive 인상적인 complaint 불만

## 142 관계대명사절 _ 관계대명사 + 동사

해설 빈칸 앞에 주어, 동사, 목적어가 있는 완전한 문장이므로 빈칸 이하는 a brochure를 설명하는 말이 와야 한다. 따라서 빈칸 뒤에 위치한 명사구 our company's services를 목적어로 취할 수 있는 능동태 동사를 포함한 관계대명사절을 구성하는 (D) that outlines가 정답이다.

어휘 outline 개괄적으로 설명하다

**143-146 공지**

DC 애널리틱스 사 경영진은 최근 시스템 오작동으로 일부 파일이 영구적으로 삭제된 것을 알고 있습니다. 여러분께 주기적으로 작업물을 외장 하드 드라이브에 백업하실 것을 요청드립니다. 이는 앞으로 우리가 유사한 [143] **손실**을 피하는 데 도움이 될 것입니다.

안타깝게도, 우리는 보안 문제로 인해 클라우드 자동 저장을 이용할 수 없습니다. [144] **따라서 기억하는 데 도움이 되는 알림 시스템을 제공하고 있습니다.** 내선번호 14번으로 IT팀에 연락하여 신청하실 수 있습니다. 매일 오후 4시 45분에, IT팀이 파일 백업과 관련된 알림 메시지를 담은 이메일을 [145] **보낼 것입니다.** 이것이 너무 잦다면, 대신 일주일 단위로 메시지를 [146] **받도록** 조치할 수 있습니다.

어휘 aware 알고 있는 permanently 영구적으로 erase 삭제하다, 지우다 malfunction 오작동, 작동 불량 regularly 주기적으로 avoid 피하다 unfortunately 안타깝게도 storage 저장 (공간) issue 문제, 사안 sign up 등록하다, 신청하다 extension 내선전화 reminder (상기시키는) 알림 메시지 frequent 잦은, 빈번한 arrange 조치하다, 조정하다 on a weekly basis 일주일 단위로

## 143 명사 어휘

해설 앞에서 파일이 영구적으로 삭제된 것과 관련된 요청 사항을 알리는 말이 쓰여 있다. 따라서 빈칸에는 파일이 삭제되는 것을 의미할 수 있는 '손실, 손해'를 뜻하는 (B) loss가 정답이다.

어휘 delay 지연, 지체 expense 지출, 경비 importance 중요성

## 144 문장 고르기

번역 (A) 따라서 기억하는 데 도움이 되는 알림 시스템을 제공하고 있습니다.
(B) 권한이 없는 직원들과 이 파일들을 공유하지 마십시오.
(C) 다음 주에 그것의 사용 방법에 대해 시연해 드릴 것입니다.
(D) 물론, 여러분의 집 컴퓨터는 같은 소프트웨어를 이용합니다.

해설 앞 문장에 보안 문제로 인해 클라우드 자동 저장을 이용할 수 없다는 내용이 언급되어 있으므로 결과를 말할 때 사용하는 Therefore(따라서)를 포함해 대안을 제시하는 (A)가 정답이다.

어휘 alert 알림, 경보 unauthorized 권한이 없는, 승인되지 않은 personnel 직원들 give a demonstration 시연하다

## 145 동사 시제

해설 앞 문장에 조동사 can과 함께 IT팀에 연락해 신청할 수 있다는 말이 있으므로 빈칸이 속한 문장에 제시된 Each day at 4:45 P.M.은 신청 이후의 시점인 미래를 가리키는 것임을 알 수 있다. 따라서 미래 시제 동사인 (C) will send가 정답이다.

## 146 to부정사 _ 명사적 용법

해설 빈칸 앞에 위치한 동사 arrange와 어울리면서 명사구 the messages를 목적어로 취할 수 있는 것이 필요한데 arrange는 to

부정사와 쓰므로 to부정사 (D) to receive가 정답이다.

어휘 receivable 받아야 할, 믿을 만한 receipt 영수증, 수취

# PART 7

**147-148 제품 설명**

저희 신제품을 한번 이용해 보세요!
시간을 절약할 수 있는 뛰어난 방법

스테인리스 스틸로 마감되어 있고 조작판이 숨겨져 있는 켐퍼 25는 어느 가정이든 우아함을 더해 주는 제품입니다. [147] **1시간 만에가득 채운 양을 세척할 수 있으므로, 더 이상 깨끗한 접시를 기다리실 필요가 없습니다!** 이 신속한 "1시간" 설정뿐만 아니라, 켐퍼 25는 물 효율이 높은 "보통" 설정과 기름기 많은 냄비와 팬 같은 품목에 유용한 "강력" 설정도 제공합니다. 어느 설정을 선택하시든, 가열 건조 시스템이 작동 종료 시에 여러분의 그릇을 식탁에 바로 올릴 수 있는 상태가 되도록 만들어 드립니다. [148] **심지어 서빙용 접시 같은 큰 그릇도 켐퍼 25의 분리 가능한 상단 거치대 덕분에 손쉽게 세척하실 수 있습니다.** 여러분의 지역 켐퍼 대리점을 방문하셔서 더 많은 것을 알아보시기 바랍니다!

어휘 finish 마감 (작업) hidden 숨겨진 control panel 조작판, 제어판 elegant 우아한 addition 추가(되는 것) household 가정 setting (기기 등의) 설정 efficiency 효율(성) greasy 기름기 많은 no matter which 어느 ~을 …하든 ensure 반드시 ~하도록 하다 table-ready 식탁에 바로 올릴 수 있는 상태인 cycle 1회의 작동 platter 큰 접시 with ease 손쉽게 removable 분리 가능한 rack 거치대, 받침대 dealership 대리점

## 147 주제 / 목적

번역 무엇에 관한 제품 설명인가?
(A) 의류
(B) 주방 기기
(C) 진공청소기
(D) 운동 기계

해설 초반부에 1시간 만에 가득 채운 양을 세척할 수 있어서 더 이상 깨끗한 접시를 기다릴 필요가 없다(It can wash a full load in as little as one hour—no more waiting for clean dishes)고 쓰여 있으므로 (B)가 정답이다.

## 148 Not / True

번역 제품에 대해 언급된 것은?
(A) 깨끗하게 유지하기 쉽다.
(B) 에너지를 효율적으로 이용한다.
(C) 소음 관련 설정이 다양하다.
(D) 조절 가능한 구조로 되어 있다.

해설 후반부에 큰 그릇도 분리 가능한 상단 거치대 덕분에 손쉽게 세척할 수 있다(Even large dishes such as serving platters can be cleaned with ease thanks to the Kemper 25's removable top rack)며 분리 가능한 상단 거치대를 언급하고 있으므로 (D)가 정답이다.

어휘 efficiently 효율적으로 multiple 다양한, 다수의 adjustable 조절 가능한 structure 구조(물)

> Paraphrasing
> 지문의 removable top rack
> → 정답의 adjustable structure

**149-150 안내문**

베넷 모바일: 비용 환급 신청서 안내

1. 성명과 직원 번호를 양식 상단에 기재하십시오.
2. 나열된 각 항목에 대해, 지출 사유를 간략히 작성하십시오.
3. 관련 영수증을 양식에 스테이플러로 고정하십시오.
4. [149] **양식에 소속 부서장님의 서명을 받으신 다음, 여러분도 직접 서명하십시오. 서명되지 않은 신청서는 처리되지 않을 것입니다.**
5. 25일에 여러분의 급여에서 지급액을 확인하시려면, 당월 15일까지 양식을 제출하십시오.

[150] **자주 구매하시는 경우, 베넷 모바일 사 계정의 신용 카드를 받을 자격이 될 수도 있습니다. 재무팀에 말해 승인을 요청하세요.**

어휘 reimbursement 비용 환급 instructions 안내, 설명 brief 간략한, 짧은 staple 스테이플러로 고정하다 relevant 관련된 receipt 영수증 process 처리하다 payment 지급(액) paycheck 급여 frequent 잦은, 빈번한 be eligible to ~할 자격이 있다 approval 승인

## 149 세부 사항

번역 안내문에 따르면, 무엇이 양식에 반드시 포함되어야 하는가?
(A) 직원 전화번호
(B) 부서장 서명
(C) 부서 번호
(D) 신분증 사본

해설 4번 항목에 소속 부서장에게 서명을 받으라는 말과 함께 서명되지 않은 신청서는 처리되지 않는다(Have your manager sign the form ~ Unsigned requests will not be processed)고 언급되어 있으므로 (B)가 정답이다.

어휘 signature 서명 supervisor 부서장, 감독자 department 부서 ID card 신분증

> Paraphrasing
> 지문의 Have your manager sign
> → 정답의 signature of a supervisor

### 150 Not / True

번역 재무팀 직원에 대해 언급된 것은?
(A) 회사 신용 카드를 발급해 줄 수 있다.
(B) 매달 25일까지 양식을 필요로 한다.
(C) 반드시 모든 구매를 미리 승인해야 한다.
(D) 최근 정책을 변경했다.

해설 재무팀이 언급되는 마지막 단락에 자주 구매하는 사람은 회사 계정의 신용 카드를 받을 수도 있으니 재무팀에 승인을 요청하라(If you make frequent purchases, you may be eligible to receive a credit card under Bennett Mobile's account. Speak to the finance team to request approval)는 말이 쓰여 있다. 따라서 재무팀 직원이 회사 신용 카드를 발급해 줄 수 있다는 것을 알 수 있으므로 (A)가 정답이다.

어휘 issue 발급하다 approve 승인하다 in advance 미리, 사전에

> **Paraphrasing**
> 지문의 a credit card under Bennett Mobile's account
> → 정답의 company credit cards

**151-152 수령증**

현금 수령증 번호: 013394 날짜: 12월 6일

**수령인 상세 정보**
성명: 테아 렘케
부서: 기술부
내선번호: 345

지급액: 150달러
설명: 151 **케이스 빌딩 및 주변 부지 점검을 실시하기 위한 애틀랜타 출장(12월 8일~10일)** 식대.

승인자: 스티브 리베라

152 **상기 상세 정보가 틀림없으며 명시된 액수를 지급받았음을 인정합니다.** 어떻게 지출되었는지 보여 주는 기록을 제공하고 미사용분은 회사에 반환해야 한다는 사실을 이해하고 있습니다.

서명: 테아 렘케

어휘 receipt 수령, 영수증 recipient 수령인, 수취인 extension 내선전화(번호) dispense 제공하다 description 설명 allowance 비용, 수당 perform 실시하다, 수행하다 inspection 점검 surrounding 주변의 grounds 부지, 구내 approve 승인하다 agree 인정하다, 동의하다 above 상기의, 위의 specified 명시된 unused 미사용된 portion 부분, 일부

### 151 세부 사항

번역 렘케 씨는 애틀랜타에서 무엇을 할 계획인가?
(A) 건물 점검
(B) 계약 협상
(C) 대출 신청
(D) 제품 시연

해설 애틀랜타가 언급되는 중반부에 케이스 빌딩 및 주변 부지 점검을 실시하기 위한 애틀랜타 출장(a business trip to Atlanta (December 8-10) to perform the inspection of the Cayce Building and surrounding grounds)이라는 정보가 제시되어 있으므로 (A)가 정답이다.

> **Paraphrasing**
> 지문의 perform the inspection of the Cayce Building
> → 정답의 Inspect a building

### 152 세부 사항

번역 수령증이 무엇을 확인해 주는가?
(A) 렘케 씨의 협회 등록
(B) 렘케 씨에게 비용 지급
(C) 렘케 씨의 여행 티켓 구입
(D) 렘케 씨에게 장비 대여

해설 마지막 단락에 상기 상세 정보가 틀림없고 명시된 액수를 지급받았음을 인정한다(I agree that the above details are correct and that I have received the specified amount)는 말이 쓰여 있고, 아래 렘케 씨가 서명한 것이 있으므로 렘케 씨에게 비용이 지급되었음을 알 수 있다. 따라서 (B)가 정답이다.

어휘 enrollment 등록 association 협회 issuance 지급, 발급 fund 비용, 자금 loaning 대여 equipment 장비

> **Paraphrasing**
> 지문의 have received the specified amount
> → 정답의 Issuance of funds

**153-154 문자 메시지**

니나 심슨 [오전 9시 37분]
안녕하세요, 앤서니. 브랜드 전략 담당자 자리는 어떻게 되고 있는지 아시나요? 우리가 심사한 지원자들로부터 후속 문의를 좀 받았거든요.

앤서니 윈슬로우 [오전 9시 38분]
제가 방금 플로렌스 그레이시 마케팅 부장님과 이야기 나눴습니다. 부장님이 다음 주에 출장으로 자리를 비우시기 때문에 전화 심사를 통과한 모든 사람들을 만나 차분히 얘기할 시간은 없어요. 153 **그래서 모두 한꺼번에 만나기를 원하세요.**

니나 심슨 [오전 9시 39분]
정말로요? 좋은 생각 같지 않은데요. 일부 지원자들은 좋은 답변을 생각해 낼 시간을 추가로 갖게 될 테니 우리 질문에 대한 지원자들의 대답을 비교하기 어려울 거예요. 154 **그 주에는 진행을 보류하는 게 더 나을 겁니다.**

앤서니 윈슬로우 [오전 9시 40분]
맞습니다. 제가 플로렌스 부장님께 다시 말씀을 드려서 부장님의 생각이 얼마나 확고한지 알아볼게요.

어휘 strategist 전략가 follow-up 후속적인 inquiry 문의 candidate 지원자, 후보자 screen 심사하다; 심사 pass 통과하다

compare 비교하다 extra 별도의, 추가의 come up with ~을 제시하다 response 답변 put ~ on hold ~을 보류하다 process (진행) 과정

## 153 세부 사항

번역 그레이시 씨는 무엇을 하고 싶어 하는가?
(A) 단체 면접
(B) 출장 연기
(C) 임시 직원 고용
(D) 마케팅 강의 수강

해설 그레이시 씨의 이름이 언급되는 9시 38분 메시지에 그레이시 씨를 she로 지칭해 전화 심사를 통과한 사람들을 모두 한꺼번에 만나기를 원한다(she wants to meet with them all at once)는 말이 쓰여 있으므로 (A)가 정답이다.

어휘 postpone 연기하다 temporary 임시의, 일시적인

> **Paraphrasing**
> 지문의 meet with them all at once
> → 정답의 Hold a group interview

## 154 의도 파악

번역 오전 9시 40분에 윈슬로우 씨가 "맞습니다"라고 쓸 때, 의미하는 것은 무엇인가?
(A) 결정이 자신에게 달려 있지 않다는 것을 안다.
(B) 그레이시 씨 일정이 바쁘다는 데 동의한다.
(C) 한 지원자에 대해 심슨 씨와 의견이 같다.
(D) 채용 진행을 잠시 멈춰야 한다고 생각한다.

해설 앞선 메시지에서 심슨 씨가 그 주에는 진행을 보류하는 게 더 나을 것(It would be better to put the process on hold for that week)이라고 말한 것에 대해 윈슬로우 씨가 맞다고 동의하는 것이므로 (D)가 정답이다.

어휘 decision 결정 up to ~에게 달려 있는 opinion 의견 pause 잠시 멈추다

> **Paraphrasing**
> 지문의 It would be better to put the process on hold
> → 정답의 a hiring process should be paused

### 155-157 안내 책자

밴디비아
신선함에 이르는 길

**[156] 새로운 소유주 겸 운영자 어네스토 스튜어트가 밴디비아를 찾으시는 여러분을 환영합니다!**

신선한 식품
**[155] 저희는 고급 레스토랑과 고급 슈퍼마켓 등 여러 곳에 공급하는 맛있는 유기농 농산물을 재배합니다.** 매시간 새로운 무료 샘플이 제공됩니다. 방문이 끝나면, 집에 가서 요리하실 맛있는 먹거리도 추가로 챙겨 가시는 걸 잊지 마시기 바랍니다!

신선한 공기
방문객들은 저희 직원이 진행하는 저희 부지 자전거 투어에 참여해 보시기 바랍니다. 저희 시골풍 건축 양식 및 채소밭과 과수원의 매력적인 향을 느껴 보시기 바랍니다. 이 투어는 약 2시간 동안 지속되며, 자전거는 제공됩니다.

신선한 아이디어
밴디비아는 붉은색 대형 헛간에서 허브 재배 및 유기농 원예에 관한 일일 워크숍을 개최합니다. 방문객들께는 수상 경력을 지닌 요리사인 스튜어트 씨와 함께 하는 채식 요리에 관한 워크숍이 이분의 일정에 따라 마련될 수도 있습니다.

입장료는 1인당 20달러이며, 위에 기재된 모든 활동을 포함합니다. 위치가 다소 멀리 떨어져 있으므로, 운전자들은 위성 내비게이션 시스템을 이용하여 찾아오시기를 추천 드립니다. **[157] 또는, 와데나 역에서 왕복 셔틀버스 서비스를 5달러에 제공해 드리고 있습니다.**

추가 정보는 www.vandivia.com을 방문하시기 바랍니다.

어휘 gateway to+명사 ~로 이르는 길 owner-operator 자영업자 organic 유기농의 produce 농산물 fine-dining 고급 식당 high-end 고급의 a batch of 한 차례의, 한 묶음의 goodies 맛있는 먹거리 grounds 부지, 구내 rustic 시골풍의 architecture 건축 (양식) enticing 매력적인 patch 밭 orchard 과수원 last 지속되다 barn 헛간 arrange 마련하다 award-winning 수상 경력이 있는 depending on ~에 따라 cover 포함하다 remote 멀리 떨어진 alternatively 또는 round-trip 왕복의

## 155 추론

번역 밴디비아는 무엇일 것 같은가?
(A) 농장
(B) 식당
(C) 해변 리조트
(D) 국립공원

해설 밴디비아를 소개하는 안내 책자인데 신선한 식품을 소개하는 단락에 고급 레스토랑과 고급 슈퍼마켓 등 여러 곳에 공급하는 맛있는 유기농 농산물을 재배한다(We grow delicious, organic produce for fine-dining restaurants, high-end supermarkets, and more)고 쓰여 있으므로 (A)가 정답이다.

## 156 Not / True

번역 밴디비아에 대해 언급된 것은?
(A) 입장료를 인상했다.
(B) 수상 후보로 지명되었다.
(C) 위성 내비게이션 시스템을 대여해 준다.
(D) 새로운 경영진 아래에 있다.

해설 첫 문장에 새로운 소유주 겸 운영자가 밴디비아에 오는 사람들을 환영한다(New owner-operator Ernesto Stewart welcomes you to Vandivia)고 했으므로 경영진이 새로 바뀐 것을 알 수 있다. 따라서 (D)가 정답이다.

TEST 3

어휘 increase 인상하다, 증가시키다 charge (청구) 요금 nominate 후보로 지명하다 rent 대여해 주다 management 경영진, 운영진

> Paraphrasing
> 지문의 New owner-operator
> → 정답의 new management

## 157 세부 사항

번역 추가 요금으로 이용 가능한 것은?
(A) 어떤 장소로 가는 교통편
(B) 제품 샘플
(C) 자전거 투어
(D) 교육 워크숍

해설 마지막 단락에 왕복 셔틀버스 서비스를 5달러에 제공한다 (Alternatively, we offer a $5 round-trip shuttle service from Wadena Station)고 했으므로 (A)가 정답이다.

> Paraphrasing
> 지문의 round-trip shuttle service
> → 정답의 Transportation

## 158-160 회람

수신: 커피 맥스 직원
발신: 애드리아나 클로슨
날짜: 10월 20일
제목: 특별 음료

직원 여러분,

연휴 시즌이 다가오고 있습니다! 그 분위기에 동참하고 매출 증대를 바라는 마음으로, 커피 맥스 고객들께 160(D) **연휴를 주제로 한 음료를 일시적인 메뉴로 제공하고 싶습니다.** 158 **카페가 한가한 시간을 이용해 맛있고 독특한 커피를 개발하기 위해 노력을 기울여 이 프로젝트를 도와주세요. 성공하실 경우, 재료 및 그 제조 방법을 간략히 설명하는 이메일을 제게 보내 주십시오.**

제가 세 가지 음료를 특별 메뉴로 선정할 것입니다. 159 **선정되시면, 50달러어치 에바 백화점 상품권을 받게 될 것이므로, 근무 전후로 바로 길 건너편에서 쇼핑하실 수 있습니다.**

제출 마감 기한은 10월 30일, 일요일 영업 종료 시점이며, 명심하셔야 하는 몇 가지 추가 고려 사항이 있습니다. 160(B) **이 음료는 비싼 재료를 너무 많이 사용하지 말아야 하며,** 음식 알레르기가 있는 고객들께 위험할 수 있는 재료가 들어가는 경우, 대체품을 제안해 주셔야 합니다. 추가로, 160(A) **우리 직원들이 음료를 신속히 만들 수 있어야 합니다.**

감사합니다!

애드리아나

어휘 approach 다가오다 get into the spirit 분위기에 동참하다 hopefully 바라는 마음으로, 희망하여 boost 증대하다 temporary 임시의, 일시적인 -themed ~을 주제로 한 slow periods 바쁘지 않은 시간대 come up with ~을 생산하다, 제시하다 unique 독특한 succeed 성공하다 outline 간략히 설명하다 ingredient 재료, 성분 gift certificate 상품권 deadline 마감 기한 submission 제출 extra 추가의, 별도의 consideration 고려 (사항) keep in mind 명심하다 costly 비싼 suggestion 제안 substitution 대체(품)

## 158 주제 / 목적

번역 회람이 왜 쓰였는가?
(A) 음료 메뉴의 변화를 설명하기 위해
(B) 직원들에게 조리법 아이디어를 요청하기 위해
(C) 임시 직원 추천을 요청하기 위해
(D) 연휴 파티를 공지하기 위해

해설 첫 단락에 맛있고 독특한 커피를 개발하여 재료 및 제조 방법을 간략히 설명하는 이메일을 보내 달라(~ to try to come up with a delicious and unique coffee drink. If you succeed, send me an e-mail outlining the ingredients and how to make it)고 요청하고 있다. 이는 직원들에게 새 음료를 만드는 아이디어를 제공해 달라고 요청하는 것이므로 (B)가 정답이다.

어휘 describe 설명하다 recipe 조리법 referral 추천, 소개

> Paraphrasing
> 지문의 come up with a delicious and unique coffee drink / send me an e-mail outlining the ingredients and how to make it → 정답의 request recipe ideas

## 159 Not / True

번역 에바 백화점에 대해 언급된 것은?
(A) 커피 맥스에서 걸어서 갈 수 있는 거리에 있다.
(B) 할인 행사를 개최하고 있다.
(C) 커피 맥스 직원들에게 할인을 제공한다.
(D) 자체 커피 매장을 열 것이다.

해설 에바 백화점이 언급되는 두 번째 단락에 선정되면 50달러어치 에바 백화점 상품권을 받을 것이니 바로 길 건너편에서 쇼핑할 수 있다(If yours is chosen, you will receive a $50 gift certificate to Eva Department Store, so you can shop right across the street ~)고 했으므로 (A)가 정답이다.

어휘 within walking distance 걸어서 갈 수 있는 거리에 있는

> Paraphrasing
> 지문의 right across the street
> → 정답의 within walking distance

## 160 Not / True

번역 음료의 특징으로 언급되지 않은 것은?
(A) 짧은 시간에 준비될 수 있다.
(B) 만드는 데 비싸지 않다.
(C) 알레르기 유발 물질을 포함하지 않는다.
(D) 시즌 특유의 주제를 담고 있다.

해설 첫 단락에 연휴를 주제로 한 음료를 제공하고 싶다(I want to offer a temporary menu of holiday-themed drinks)고 한 부분에서 (D)를, 마지막 단락에 비용이 많이 드는 재료를 많이 사용하지 말아야 한다(The drinks should not use too many costly ingredients)고 언급한 부분에서 (B)를, 직원들이 신속히 만들 수 있어야 한다(our staff must be able to make each drink quickly)고 말한 부분에서 (A)를 확인할 수 있다. 하지만 음식 알레르기가 있는 고객에게 위험할 수 있는 재료는 대체품을 제안하라고 했으므로 (C)가 정답이다.

어휘 characteristic 특징 inexpensive 비싸지 않은 allergen 알레르기 유발 물질

> **Paraphrasing**
> 지문의 holiday-themed drinks
> → 보기 (D)의 share a seasonal theme
> 지문의 not use too many costly ingredients
> → 보기 (B)의 are inexpensive to make
> 지문의 be able to make each drink quickly
> → 보기 (A)의 can be prepared in a short time

**161-163 회람**

발신: 크리스타 노세라
수신: 전 직원
날짜: 2월 11일
제목: 바닥 공사

직원 여러분,

**[163] 트레비노 시공사의 작업팀이 중앙 복도를 개조하기 위해 이번 주말에 우리 사무실을 방문할 것입니다.** 바닥재가 교체되고, 벽이 다시 페인트칠될 것입니다. **[163] 작업 위치 때문에, 사무실이나 다른 공용 공간에 있는 가구나 개인 물품을 옮길 필요는 없을 것입니다.**

하지만 주말 동안 근무하셔야 하는 경우, 원격으로 하시기를 요청드립니다. 여러분 중 일부는 업무를 완료하기 위해 전문 소프트웨어가 필요한 것을 알고 있으니, **[161] IT부서의 데이빗 로고우스키를 만나 회사 노트북 컴퓨터 사용을 요청하시기 바랍니다. [162] 금요일에 늦게까지 근무할 계획인데 차량이 보이드 가 입구 옆에 있다면 보안팀에 알리시기 바랍니다. 작업팀이 토요일 아침에 자재를 내릴 수 있도록 주차장 첫 번째 줄이 비워져 있어야 합니다.**

여러분의 협조에 감사드립니다!

크리스타 노세라

어휘 flooring 바닥 공사, 바닥재 renovate 개조하다, 보수하다 necessary 필요한, 필수적인 belongings 소유물, 소지품 shared 공용의 remotely 원격으로 specialized 전문적인 task 업무, 일 row 줄, 열 lot 주차장 unload (짐 등을) 내리다 material 자재, 물품 cooperation 협조, 협력

## 161 세부 사항

번역 직원들이 로고우스키 씨에게 무엇과 관련해 이야기해야 하는가?
(A) 개인 물품 보관하기
(B) 소프트웨어 업그레이드 받기
(C) 새 사무실로 이전하기
(D) 장비 빌리기

해설 로고우스키 씨의 이름이 언급되는 두 번째 단락에 IT부서의 데이빗 로고우스키에게 회사 노트북 컴퓨터 사용을 요청하라(please see David Rogowski in the IT department to request the use of a company laptop)는 말이 나오고 있다. 이는 장비를 빌리는 일을 의미하므로 (D)가 정답이다.

어휘 store 보관하다 borrow 빌리다 equipment 장비

> **Paraphrasing**
> 지문의 request the use of a company laptop
> → 정답의 Borrowing some equipment

## 162 추론

번역 보이드 가 입구에 대해 암시된 것은?
(A) 보안팀에 의해 잠길 것이다.
(B) 교통량이 많은 곳이다.
(C) 주차 구역 근처에 있다.
(D) 건물에서 가장 큰 출입문들이 있다.

해설 두 번째 단락에 금요일에 늦게까지 근무할 계획인데 차량이 보이드 가 입구 옆에 있다면 보안팀에 알리라(~ please let the security team know if your car is by the Boyd Street entrance)는 말과 함께 그 이유로 작업팀이 토요일 아침에 자재를 내릴 수 있도록 주차장 첫 번째 줄이 비워져 있어야 한다(The crew needs the first row of the lot clear to unload their materials on Saturday morning)고 쓰여 있다. 따라서 보이드 가 입구가 주차장과 가깝다는 것을 알 수 있으므로 (C)가 정답이다.

어휘 face 마주하다, 직면하다 traffic 교통량, 차량들

## 163 문장 삽입

번역 [1], [2], [3], [4]로 표시된 곳 중에서 다음 문장이 가장 적합한 곳은 어디인가?
"바닥재가 교체되고, 벽이 다시 페인트칠될 것입니다."
(A) [1]
(B) [2]
(C) [3]
(D) [4]

해설 제시된 문장은 구체적인 작업 내용을 알리는 문장이다. 따라서 개조 일정을 알리는 첫 번째 문장과 해당 작업을 가리키는 the work를 포함한 문장 사이에 있는 [1]에 들어가 중앙 복도 개조의 구체적인 작업 내용을 알리는 흐름이 되어야 알맞으므로 (A)가 정답이다.

어휘 replace 교체하다

TEST 3

## 164-167 공지

스프링데일 커넥츠

패션 디자이너이신가요? 여러분의 재능을 활용해 지역 사회를 후원하십시오! 스프링데일 커넥츠는 지역에 기반을 둔 비영리 단체로서, [164] **프로젝트 기금을 마련하기 위해 역사적인 메들린 극장에서 패션쇼를 개최합니다. 여러분께서는 "시대를 초월한 클래식"이라는 주제로 이 행사를 위한 특별 의상을 디자인하고 제작함으로써 도움을 주실 수 있습니다.**

이 패션쇼 입장권은 저희 웹사이트와 스프링데일 전역의 다양한 업체에서 판매될 것입니다. [165] **행사를 통해 얻은 수익금은 도시 최초의 노년 밴드를 결성할 수 있도록 스프링데일에 거주 중이신 나이 드신 분들께 제공될 기타와 키보드, 트럼펫 등 여러 가지를 구입하는 데 쓰일 것입니다.** 이는 참가자들이 새로운 기술을 익히고 새로운 사람들을 만나는 데 도움을 줄 것입니다.

참가를 원하시면, 저희 웹사이트 www.springdaleconnects.org를 방문하셔서 [166(B)] **제출 요구일**과 [166(D)] **추천 의류 사이즈**, 그리고 [166(C)] **저희가 제공해 드릴 수 있는 액세서리 목록**을 확인해 보시기 바랍니다. [167] **그 사이트에서 여러분의 작품 및 경력을 포함한 간단한 약력을 제출하실 수도 있습니다. 이는 관람객들께서 도착하실 때 배부될 전단에 인쇄될 것입니다.**

어휘 local 지역의 community (지역) 사회, 공동체 locally based 지역에 기반을 둔 nonprofit 비영리의 organization 단체, 기관 raise funds 기금을 마련하다, 모금하다 sew (바느질로) 만들다 outfit 의상, 옷 proceeds 수익금 form 결성하다, 형성하다 first-ever 사상 최초의 participant 참가자 participate 참가하다 submission 제출 brief 간략한 biography 전기, 일대기 including ~을 포함해 flyer 전단 distribute 배부하다 audience members 관람객들, 청중

### 164 세부 사항

번역 공지에서 사람들에게 하도록 요청하는 것은?
(A) 기금 마련 행사에 물품 제공하기
(B) 자선 단체의 회원 되기
(C) 행사장 설치 자원하기
(D) 단체에 돈 기부하기

해설 첫 단락에 프로젝트 기금 마련을 위한 패션쇼 개최 사실을 언급하면서 그 행사를 위한 특별 의상을 디자인하고 제작함으로써 도움을 줄 수 있다(~ holding a fashion show at the historic Medlin Theater to raise project funds. You can help by designing and sewing a special outfit for the event ~)고 알리고 있다. 이는 기금 마련 행사에 의상 제공을 요청하는 것이므로 (A)가 정답이다.

어휘 fundraising 기금 마련, 모금 charity 자선 단체 volunteer 자원하다 set up 설치하다, 마련하다 venue 행사장 donate 기부하다

> **Paraphrasing**
> 지문의 to raise project funds / designing and sewing a special outfit for the event
> → 정답의 Provide items for a fundraising event

### 165 세부 사항

번역 스프링데일 커넥츠는 무엇을 목표로 하는가?
(A) 무료 패션 디자인 강좌 주최하기
(B) 역사적인 극장의 복원 돕기
(C) 식사를 준비해 노년층 주민들에게 제공하기
(D) 지역 사회 구성원들에게 악기 제공하기

해설 두 번째 단락에 행사를 통해 얻은 수익금은 노년 밴드를 결성할 수 있도록 나이 드신 분들께 제공될 기타와 키보드, 트럼펫 등 여러 가지를 구입하는 데 쓰인다(The proceeds from the event will be used to purchase guitars, keyboards, trumpets, and more to be given to elderly people living in Springdale ~)고 했으므로 (D)가 정답이다.

어휘 aim 목표로 하다 host 주최하다 restore 복원하다, 회복시키다

> **Paraphrasing**
> 지문의 guitars, keyboards, trumpets
> → 정답의 musical instruments
> 지문의 people living in Springdale
> → 정답의 community members

### 166 Not / True

번역 웹사이트에서 제공되는 정보로 언급되지 않은 것은?
(A) 사진 갤러리
(B) 마감 기한
(C) 이용 가능한 액세서리에 관한 상세 정보
(D) 사이즈 권장 사항

해설 세 번째 단락에 웹사이트에 방문해서 제출 요구일(required submission date)과 추천 의류 사이즈(the suggested clothing size), 제공하는 액세서리 목록(a list of the accessories we can provide)을 확인하라고 한 것에서 (B), (C), (D)를 확인할 수 있다. 하지만 사진 갤러리와 관련된 정보는 제시되어 있지 않으므로 (A)가 정답이다.

어휘 details 상세 정보 available 이용 가능한 sizing 사이즈 (측정)

> **Paraphrasing**
> 지문의 required submission date
> → 보기 (B)의 A deadline
> 지문의 the accessories we can provide
> → 보기 (C)의 Details on available accessories
> 지문의 the suggested clothing size
> → 보기 (D)의 Sizing recommendations

### 167 세부 사항

번역 공지에 따르면, 참가자들의 약력은 어디서 보게 될 것인가?
(A) 온라인 소식지
(B) 유인물
(C) 웹사이트
(D) 로비에 있는 공지

해설 마지막 단락에 작품 및 경력을 포함한 간단한 약력도 제출할 수 있는

데 이는 관람객들에게 배부될 전단에 인쇄될 것(There you can also submit a brief biography including your work and experience. This will be printed on the flyer that will be distributed to audience members ~)이라고 했으므로 (B)가 정답이다.

> **Paraphrasing**
> 지문의 the flyer that will be distributed
> → 정답의 a handout

### 168-171 온라인 채팅

찰스 본 (오후 1시 22분)
안녕하세요, 여러분. 호건 테크 사의 행사와 관련해 아직 어떤 소식도 없다는 사실을 알려 드리고 싶었어요.

헤더 뎅글러 (오후 1시 23분)
니코 어패럴 사도 같은 날에 우리를 고용하고 싶어 해요.

찰스 본 (오후 1시 25분)
그럼 우리는 호건 테크 사가 계획이 있는 건지 파악해 봐야 할 거예요. **168 우리는 두 곳을 모두 맡을 만큼 요리사와 서빙 직원이 충분하지 않습니다.** 호건 테크 사의 주문 규모가 더 크긴 하지만, 어떻게 되는지 확실히 알기 전까진 다른 고객사를 거절하고 싶지 않습니다.

헤더 뎅글러 (오후 1시 26분)
제가 니코 어패럴 사에 우리가 오늘 업무 종료 시점까지 어느 쪽이든 확인해 주겠다고 약속했어요.

찰스 본 (오후 1시 27분)
알겠습니다. 제가 호건 테크 사의 대니얼 가렛에게 연락해 보려 했지만, 그분 사무실에서 아무런 응답이 없었어요. **169 우리가 그분의 다른 전화번호를 갖고 있나요?**

나타샤 코프 (오후 1시 28분)
전에는 필요했던 적이 없었어요. 제가 그걸 알아볼게요.

찰스 본 (오후 1시 31분)
우리가 결과적으로 니코 어패럴 사의 일을 수락하게 된다면, **171 즉시 가격 견적서를 준비해 둬야 할 겁니다.** 체계적이지 못한 것처럼 보이고 싶지 않거든요. **171 헤더, 당신이 이걸 해 주었으면 합니다.**

나타샤 코프 (오후 1시 34분)
찾았습니다. 전송해 드렸습니다, 찰스.

찰스 본 (오후 1시 42분)
가렛 씨가 회사 측에서 다른 회사를 대신 이용하기로 결정했다고 말씀하셨어요. **170 그분은 우리가 제안한 메뉴를 마음에 들어 하셨지만, 그 회사 측에서 채식 요리를 전문으로 하는 회사를 이용하고 싶어 했습니다.** 그럼, **171 헤더, 오후 3시까지 완료된 파일을 제게 보내 주시겠어요?**

헤더 뎅글러 (오후 1시 43분)
**171 네, 지금 시작하면 시간이 충분할 거예요.**

어휘 turn down 거절하다 get in touch with ~에게 연락하다 look into 알아보다, 살펴보다 end up -ing 결국 ~하게 되다 accept 수락하다 pricing 가격 (책정) estimate 견적(서) disorganized 체계적이지 못한 forward 전송하다 specialize in ~을 전문으로 하다

## 168 추론

번역 메시지 작성자들은 어디에서 근무하고 있겠는가?
(A) 출장 요리 제공 회사
(B) 그래픽 디자인 회사
(C) 기술 회사
(D) 의류 제조사

해설 본이 1시 25분에 작성한 메시지에 두 곳을 모두 맡을 만큼 요리사와 서빙 직원이 충분하지 않다(We don't have enough cooks and servers to do both)고 했으므로 음식과 관련된 서비스를 제공하는 회사인 (A)가 정답이다.

## 169 의도 파악

번역 오후 1시 28분에 코프 씨가 "제가 그걸 알아볼게요"라고 쓸 때, 의미하는 것은 무엇인가?
(A) 고객 방문 일정을 잡으려 할 것이다.
(B) 회의 공간을 이용할 수 있는지 확인할 것이다.
(C) 연락처를 찾아볼 것이다.
(D) 요금에 관해 문의할 것이다.

해설 앞선 메시지에서 본이 대니얼 가렛 씨의 다른 전화번호를 갖고 있는지(Do we have another phone number for him?) 묻는 것에 대해 코프가 '제가 그걸 알아볼게요'라고 대답하는 흐름이다. 이는 가렛의 연락처 정보를 알아보겠다는 의미이므로 (C)가 정답이다.

어휘 availability 이용 가능성 inquire about ~에 관해 문의하다

> **Paraphrasing**
> 지문의 another phone number
> → 정답의 some contact information

## 170 세부 사항

번역 본 씨가 나머지 메시지 작성자들에게 무엇에 관해 말하는가?
(A) 행사장 도착 시간
(B) 결정을 내린 이유
(C) 니코 어패럴 사를 대표하는 사람
(D) 보고서를 제출할 곳

해설 본이 1시 42분에 작성한 메시지를 보면, 가렛은 우리가 제안한 메뉴를 마음에 들어 했지만, 회사 측에서 채식 요리를 전문으로 하는 회사를 이용하고 싶어 했다(While he liked our menu suggestions, they wanted to use a company that specializes in vegetarian dishes)고 알리고 있다. 이는 가렛의 회사에서 다른 업체를 이용하기로 결정한 이유를 설명하는 것이므로 (B)가 정답이다.

어휘 decision 결정 represent 대표하다 file a report 보고서를 제출하다

TEST 3

## 171 추론

번역 뎅글러 씨는 다음에 무엇을 하겠는가?
(A) 웹사이트 업데이트하기
(B) 견적서 준비하기
(C) 새 공급 업체 찾기
(D) 가렛 씨와 이야기하기

해설 본이 오후 1시 31분에 가격 견적서를 준비해 둬야 할 것(we'll have to get the pricing estimate ready right away)이라며, 헤더에게 그것을 해 주면 좋겠다(Heather, I'd like you to do that)고 요청했고, 1시 42분에 헤더에게 오후 3시까지 완료된 파일을 보내 줄 수 있는지(Heather, can you send me a finished file by 3 P.M.?) 묻자, 헤더 뎅글러가 알겠다며 지금 시작하면 시간이 충분할 것(Yes, that'll be enough time if I start now)이라고 했다. 이는 뎅글러가 견적서를 준비하겠다고 한 것이므로 (B)가 정답이다.

> **Paraphrasing**
> 지문의 get the pricing estimate ready
> → 정답의 Prepare an estimate

### 172-175 기사

어려운 하수관 개선 프로젝트 대부분 완료

스텐덤 (9월 25일) - 어제, 스텐덤 시는 런드게이트 강변 프로젝트의 1단계 종료를 발표했다. 가민 강의 서쪽 제방에 위치한 이 강변은 근처의 런드게이트 다리의 이름을 딴 것이다. [172] **현재 그곳에 자리잡고 있는 복개 수로가 넘치는 하수를 스텐덤의 거대한 "하수 고속도로"인 클리어웨이로 방향을 돌려 놓음으로써 강으로 흘러 들어가지 못하게 막을 것이다.** 1단계는 기한에 맞춰 예산 범위 내에서 완료되었다. [175] **복잡한 엔지니어링 작업이 수반된 것을 고려하면 이 단계가 순조롭게 마무리된 것은 놀라운 일이다.**

가장 어려웠던 부분은 3,700톤에 달하는 주요 수로의 설치 작업이었다. 런드게이트 강변이 조수 지역에 있어서 만조 시에는 강물이 그곳을 완전히 뒤덮는다. [173] **1단계를 책임진 회사인 바우라이트 그룹은 이러한 특징을 활용해 미리 만들어 놓은 수로를 띄워 옮기기로 결정했다. "다른 클리어웨이 프로젝트에서 조수를 이용해 구조물들을 성공적으로 옮긴 적이 있습니다."라고 바우라이트 책임 엔지니어 낸시 메이저스가 설명했다.** 그럼에도 이 방식은 정확한 타이밍을 필요로 했다. 이 수로가 런드게이트 다리 밑을 지나가야 했기 때문에, 만조 시에는 옮겨질 수 없었다. 반면에, 수위가 너무 낮을 때 이동이 이뤄진다면, 수로가 그 정확한 위치까지 쭉 떠가지 못할지도 모른다. 메이저스 씨는 "대단히 신중한 계획" 덕분에 본인의 팀이 사고 없이 어려운 일을 완수했다고 말했다.

어제 발표에서는 또 이 프로젝트의 더 간단한 2단계가 페리엇 LLC 사에 의해 진행될 것이고, 11월에 종료될 것이라고 밝혔다. [174] **페리엇 사는 새로운 하수관 구조물 위에 있는 공공 부지에 산책로와 벤치, 그리고 녹지 공간을 추가할 것이다.**

어휘 bulk of 대부분의, 대량의 improvement 개선, 향상 conclusion 종료, 종결 phase 단계 shore 강변, 해안 be named for ~의 이름을 따다 covered 복개된 excess 초과된, 과도한 sewage 하수 spill into ~로 흘러 들어가다 redirect 방향을 돌려 놓다 enormous 거대한, 엄청난 smooth 순조로운 completion 완료 remarkable 놀라운, 주목할 만한 complex 복잡한 feat 기술, 솜씨 involve 수반하다, 관련되다 installation 설치 channel 수로 tidal 조수의 at high tide 만조 시에 responsible for ~을 책임지는 make use of ~을 이용하다 feature 특징 float 띄우다, 떠오르다 pre-built 미리 만들어 놓은 structure 구조(물) method 방식 precise 정확한 all the way to+명사 ~까지 쭉 (이어서) incident 사고 reveal 드러내다 handle 처리하다 greenery 녹지 (공간)

## 172 추론

번역 런드게이트 강변 프로젝트는 어떤 문제를 처리할 목적이겠는가?
(A) 하수로 의한 강물 오염
(B) 과도한 고속도로 교통량
(C) 오래된 다리의 노후화
(D) 일부 주택에 하수 처리 서비스 부족

해설 첫 단락에 복개 수로가 넘치는 하수가 강으로 흘러 들어가지 못하게 막을 것(The covered waterways that now sit there will stop excess sewage from spilling into the river ~)이라고 했다. 하수가 강으로 흘러 들어가지 못하게 막는 것은 하수로 의한 강물 오염을 막는 것이므로 (A)가 정답이다.

어휘 pollution 오염 excessive 과도한 traffic 교통량 deterioration 악화, 저하 lack 부족

## 173 추론

번역 메이저스 씨가 암시하는 것은?
(A) 종종 해안가 구조물 관련 일을 한다.
(B) 클리어웨이 건설에 기여한 공로로 승진되었다.
(C) 런드게이트 강변이 그녀가 감독한 것 중 가장 큰 프로젝트이다.
(D) 과거의 경험을 바탕으로 런드게이트 강변에 대한 결정을 내렸다.

해설 두 번째 단락에 바우라이트 그룹이 미리 만들어 놓은 수로를 띄워 옮기기로 결정했다(Bauright Group ~ decided to make use of this feature and float the pre-built channel into place)고 언급한 뒤, 다른 클리어웨이 프로젝트에서 조수를 이용해 구조물들을 성공적으로 옮긴 적이 있다(We had successfully used tidewater to move structures in other Clearway projects)는 메이저스의 설명이 인용되어 있다. 이는 과거의 성공 경험으로 내린 결정에 대해 설명하는 것이므로 (D)가 정답이다.

어휘 oceanfront 바다 가까이에 있는 contribution 공헌, 기여 oversee 감독하다 base 바탕을 두다

## 174 Not / True

번역 페리엇 LLC 사와 관련해 언급된 것은?
(A) 바우라이트 그룹이 소유하고 있다.
(B) 공공 여가 구역을 만들 것이다.
(C) 일정보다 뒤처져 있다.
(D) 1단계를 수행하기 위해 입찰했다.

해설 세 번째 단락에 페리엇 사는 새로운 하수관 구조물 위에 있는 공공 부지에 산책로와 벤치, 그리고 녹지 공간을 추가할 것(Perriott will add a walking path, benches, and greenery to the public land above the new sewer structures)이라고 했으므로 (B)가 정답이다.

어휘 run behind schedule 일정보다 뒤처져 있다 submit a bid 입찰하다 carry out 수행하다

> Paraphrasing
> 지문의 add a walking path, benches, and greenery to the public land → 정답의 create a public leisure area

## 175 문장 삽입

번역 [1], [2], [3], [4]로 표시된 곳 중에서 다음 문장이 가장 적합한 곳은 어디인가?

"1단계는 기한에 맞춰 예산 범위 내에서 완료되었다."

(A) [1]
(B) [2]
(C) [3]
(D) [4]

해설 주어진 문장에서 기한과 예산에 맞춰 완료되었다는 말은 순조롭게 완료되었다는 뜻이므로 이 단계가 순조롭게 마무리된 것은 놀라운 일(The smooth completion of the phase is remarkable ~)이라고 말하는 문장 앞인 [1]에 들어가는 게 자연스럽다. 따라서 (A)가 정답이다.

어휘 on time 제때 budget 예산

### 176-180 안내 책자+이메일

알파 조경 서비스

www.alpha-landscaping.net

알파 조경 서비스는 여러분의 건물에 가치를 더할 뿐 아니라 옥외 공간을 최대한 활용하도록 도와 드릴 수 있습니다. 가족이 즐길 수 있는 훌륭한 옥외 공간을 만드시거나 상업용 부지의 외관을 176 **업데이트해 보세요.** 저희 서비스는 아래에 간략히 설명되어 있습니다. 177(C) **저희 모든 직원은 반드시 철저한 안전 교육 과정을 통과해야 하며,** 이는 업계 기준보다 훨씬 더 엄격하므로, 저희와 함께 작업하는 데 확신을 가지셔도 됩니다. 가격 견적을 알아보시려면 저희에게 info@alpha-landscaping.net으로 연락하시기 바랍니다.

유지 관리

177(A) **저희는 일 년 내내 정기적인 방문을 통해 여러분의 정원이 최상의 상태로 보이도록 유지해 드릴 수 있습니다.** 이는 잔디 깎기, 관목과 나무 손질, 그리고 잡초 제거를 포함합니다. 저희가 4월부터 9월까지 가장 분주하므로, 실망하지 않으려면 미리 예약하시기 바랍니다. 매주, 격주, 매월 방문 중에서 선택하실 수 있습니다.

179 **재단장**

**방치된 정원을 손봐서 손쉽게 관리할 수 있는 원래의 모습으로 되돌리는 일회성 방문을 예약하세요.** 옥외 공간이 통제할 수 없는 상태가 되고 있다면, 저희가 원래의 상태로 되돌리는 걸 도와 드릴 수 있습니다.

디자인

예산의 규모에 상관없이 저희 조경 예술 전문가에게 꿈에 그리는 정원을 설계하도록 맡겨 보세요. 딱 원하는 모습이 될 때까지 지속적으로 계획을 조정할 것입니다. 조명과 분수대에서부터 간단한 화단에 이르기까지, 저희가 실현해 드릴 수 있습니다. 177(B) **너무 크든 너무 작든 상관없이 어떤 정원도 저희가 작업해 드립니다.**

대여

178 **다른 업체들과 달리, 저희는 장비를 다룰 직원을 고용하지 않고도 고객들이 정원용 장비를 대여할 수 있게 해 드리고 있습니다.** 직접 작업하여 비용을 절약하실 수 있다는 의미입니다. 각각의 기계에 명확한 사용자 설명서가 딸려 있습니다.

어휘 landscaping 조경 make the most of ~을 최대한 활용하다 value 가치 property 건물, 부동산 appearance 외관 commercial 상업의 outline 간략히 설명하다 rigorous 철저한, 엄격한 strict 엄격한 confident 확신하는 quote 견적서 maintenance 유지 관리 mowing 잔디 깎기 trim 손질하다 weeding 잡초 제거 avoid 피하다 disappointment 실망(감) bi-weekly 격주로 reset 재단장하다, 다시 설정하다 tackle (문제 등을) 다루다 neglected 방치된 get ~ back into shape ~을 원래 모습으로 되돌리다 care for ~을 관리하다 out of control 통제할 수 없는 adjust 조정하다 make it happen 실현하다 handle 처리하다 rental 대여 rent 대여하다 equipment 장비 come with ~이 딸려 있다 user manual 사용자 설명서

수신: info@alpha-landscaping.net
발신: loriroth@thehomeinbox.com
날짜: 4월 19일
제목: 서비스

관계자께,

저는 최근 롱몬트 지역에 주택을 구입했습니다. 정원 가꾸기를 정말 즐거워하긴 하지만, 이 정원은 제가 처음에 처리할 일이 너무 많습니다. 179 **수년 동안 아무런 관리도 받지 않았기 때문에, 귀사의 팀이 한 번 방문해서 모든 것을 정리하는 데 도움을 주셨으면 합니다.** 필요하실 만한 기본적인 도구와 장비는 이미 갖고 있습니다. 빨리 방문해 주실수록 좋습니다. 셀타이스 엔터프라이즈 사의 제 동료 180 **알렉스 브룩스가 집에서 귀사의 서비스를 이용해 보고 적극 추천해 주었습니다.**

로리 로스

어휘 neighborhood 지역, 인근 deal with ~을 처리하다 initially 처음에 care 관리, 보살핌 get ~ in order ~을 정리하다 colleague 동료 (직원)

## 176 동의어

번역 안내 책자의 첫 번째 단락, 두 번째 줄에 쓰인 "update"와 의미가 가장 가까운 것은?

(A) 현대화하다
(B) 알리다
(C) 강조하다
(D) 투자하다

해설 update the appearance of your commercial site는 상업용 부지의 외관을 업데이트하라는 의미인데, 이는 그 외관을 더 새로운 방식으로 바꾸라는 말과 같으므로 '현대화하다'를 뜻하는 (A) modernize가 정답이다.

## 177 Not / True

번역 알파 조경 서비스에 대해 언급되지 않은 것은?
(A) 일년 내내 운영된다.
(B) 어떤 크기의 정원도 작업한다.
(C) 안전에 전념하고 있다.
(D) 가족 경영 업체이다.

해설 안내 책자의 첫 단락에 모든 직원이 반드시 철저한 안전 교육 과정을 통과해야 한다(All of our staff members must pass a rigorous safety course, ~)고 말하는 부분에서 (C)를, 두 번째 단락에 일 년 내내 정기적인 방문을 통해 정원이 최상의 상태로 보이도록 유지해 줄 수 있다(We can keep your garden looking its best with regular visits throughout the entire year)는 부분에서 (A)를, 그리고 네 번째 단락에 너무 크든 너무 작든 상관없이 어떤 정원도 작업한다(No garden is too big or too small for us to handle)고 언급하는 부분에서 (B)를 각각 확인할 수 있다. 하지만 가족 경영과 관련된 정보는 찾아볼 수 없으므로 (D)가 정답이다.

어휘 year-round 일년 내내, 연중 be committed to ~에 전념하다
family-owned 가족이 경영하는

> **Paraphrasing**
> 지문의 must pass a rigorous safety course
> → 보기 (C)의 is committed to safety
> 지문의 throughout the entire year
> → 보기 (A)의 year-round
> 지문의 No garden is too big or too small for us to handle → 보기 (B)의 works on gardens of any size

## 178 세부 사항

번역 안내 책자에 따르면, 장비 대여 서비스의 특별한 점은?
(A) 추가 요금 없이 배달될 수 있다.
(B) 회사 직원이 그것을 사용할 필요가 없다.
(C) 대여 기간이 길면 할인된다.
(D) 작동하는 방법에 관한 교육 시간을 포함한다.

해설 안내 책자의 마지막 단락에 다른 업체들과 달리, 장비를 다룰 직원을 고용하지 않고도 정원용 장비를 대여할 수 있게 해 준다(Unlike other businesses, we allow customers to rent our garden equipment without having one of our employees hired to use it)고 알리는 말이 쓰여 있다. 따라서 (B)가 정답이다.

어휘 additional 추가적인 include 포함하다 operate 작동하다

> **Paraphrasing**
> 지문의 Unlike other businesses → 질문의 unique
> 지문의 without having one of our employees hired to use it
> → 정답의 does not require a company employee to use it

## 179 연계

번역 로스 씨는 아마 어떤 서비스를 이용하겠는가?
(A) 유지 관리
(B) 재단장
(C) 설계
(D) 대여

해설 로스 씨가 작성한 이메일에 수년 동안 아무런 관리도 받지 않았기 때문에, 귀사의 팀이 한 번 방문해서 모든 것을 정리하는 데 도움을 주면 좋겠다(It hasn't had any care in several years, so I'd like to have your crew visit once to help get everything in order)고 요청하는 말이 쓰여 있다. 이는 안내 책자의 '재단장' 항목에서 설명하는, 방치된 정원을 손봐서 손쉽게 관리할 수 있는 원래의 모습으로 되돌리는 일회성 방문(~ a one-time visit to tackle a neglected garden and get it back into shape for you to care for easily) 서비스에 해당하므로 (B)가 정답이다.

## 180 추론

번역 브룩스 씨에 대해 암시된 것은?
(A) 현재 롱몬트 지역에 살고 있다.
(B) 로스 씨 건물의 전 소유주이다.
(C) 알파 조경 서비스의 작업에 만족하고 있다.
(D) 전에 전문 원예사로 일했다.

해설 이메일의 마지막 문장에 동료인 알렉스 브룩스가 집에서 서비스를 이용해 보고 적극 추천했다(Alex Brooks, used your services at his home and recommended you highly)고 했으므로 (C)가 정답이다.

어휘 former 전 ~의, 과거의 be satisfied with ~에 만족하다

### 181-185 기사+편지

<메디컬 월드 매거진>

[184] **7월호**

**차분한 대기실 만들기**

진료를 보러 가는 것은 많은 사람에게 불안감을 불러일으킵니다. 아래 팁에 따라 환자들에게 편안한 공간을 조성하여 이 문제를 해결하세요. 이렇게 하면 환자들에게 긍정적인 마음가짐을 조성해, 쌓인 긴장을 완화시키고 진료를 보다 원활하게 진행할 수 있습니다.

색상 선택 및 벽 장식

- [181(D)] **푸른색 또는 초록색 색조를 활용해 차분한 분위기를 만드십시오.**
- 보색으로 이루어진 그림, 특히 자연 풍경을 담은 그림들로 벽을 장식하십시오.
- [181(C)] **의료 정보가 담긴 포스터는 꼭 필요한 것들로 제한하십시오.**

공간 배치 및 가구

- [184] **의자 및 소파는 아늑하면서 집에 있는 듯한 느낌을 만들어 낼 수 있도록 반드시 커버가 부드러운 것으로 놓으십시오.**
- 높은 의자는 앉았다 일어나기 쉬우며, 거동이 불편한 분들께 유용합니다.
- [182] **혼자 방문하여 프라이버시를 원하는 사람이 있는 반면, 가족과 함께 와서 함께 앉고 싶어 하는 사람도 있을 수 있으므로 다양한 구성으로 배열할 수 있는 모듈식 좌석을 사용하세요.**

소리
- **181 (A) 배경 음악 또는 자연의 소리를 낮은 음량으로 틀어 두셔야 합니다.**
- 두꺼운 커튼은 공간 내의 소리를 흡수하고 울림을 줄이는 데 도움이 될 수 있습니다.

소중한 독자 여러분, 이 팁들이 유익하셨기를 바랍니다. **183 앞으로 나올 호에서는 무엇에 대해 알고 싶으신가요?**

어휘 issue (출판물의) 호 calming 차분한 appointment 예약, 약속 provoke 자아내다 anxiety 불안(감) follow 따르다, 준수하다 combat (문제 등에) 대처하다, 맞서다 relaxing 편안한, 느긋하게 해 주는 foster 촉진하다, 조성하다 positive 긍정적인 mindset 마음가짐 ease 완화하다 built-up 쌓여 있는 tension 긴장(감) décor 장식(물) shade 색조 atmosphere 분위기 decorate 장식하다 complementary color 보색 restrict 제한하다 absolutely 전적으로, 완전히 layout 공간 배치, 구획 covering 덮개 cozy 아늑한 mobility 이동성 modular 개별 단위로 된 configuration 배열 privacy 프라이버시, 사생활 thick 두꺼운 absorb 흡수하다 echo 울림, 반향 valued 소중한

<메디컬 월드 매거진>

편집자께 보내는 편지

**184 차분한 대기실 만들기와 관련하여 제공하신 정보 중 일부를 바로잡아 드리고자 합니다.** 대기실 내의 가구가 좋은 느낌을 주고 편해야 한다는 점이 중요하기는 하지만, 그 목적이 건강과 안전 관련 사항들보다 우선시되지 말아야 합니다. 부드럽고 천 같은 덮개 장식은 아래에 있는 쿠션 부분으로 액체가 흡수될 수 있고, 살균하기 어렵습니다.

**185 더 나은 선택지는 비닐로 덮여 있는 가구입니다. 이것은 튼튼하면서, 많이 사용해도 10년 넘게 유지되며, 신속하고 쉽게 닦여 먼지와 세균을 제거할 수 있습니다. 저희 프리-폼 주식회사에서 제조하는 세련되고 실용적인 가구는 항균성 표면으로 된 비닐을 사용해,** 의료 현장에서 질병의 확산을 효과적으로 줄여 줍니다.

도미닉 맥앨리스터

어휘 correction 바로잡음, 정정 inviting 좋은 느낌을 주는 comfortable 편한 take precedence over ~보다 우선시되다 consideration 고려 (사항) upholstery (가구 등의) 덮개 장식 absorb 흡수하다 fluid 액체 underlying 아래에 있는 disinfect 살균하다, 소독하다 robust 튼튼한 last 지속되다 heavy (양, 정도 등이) 많은, 심한 wipe down 닦아내다 remove 제거하다, 없애다 germ 세균 practical 실용적인 antimicrobial 항균성의 surface 표면 effectively 효과적으로 spread 확산 disease 질병 setting 환경

## 181 Not / True

번역 기사에서 제안하는 사항이 아닌 것은?
(A) 오디오 음량을 낮게 유지하기
(B) 바퀴 달린 의자로 이동성 개선하기
(C) 의료 관련 포스터 사용 최소화하기
(D) 편안한 효과를 주는 색상 포함하기

해설 중반부의 색상 선택 및 벽 장식(Color Choices and Wall Décor) 항목에 언급된 푸른색 또는 초록색 색조를 활용해 차분한 분위기를 만드는 것(Use shades of blue or green to create a calming atmosphere)과 의료 정보를 담은 포스터를 제한하는 것(Restrict posters with medical information to those that are absolutely necessary)에서 (D)와 (C)를, 기사 후반부의 소리(Sounds) 항목에 제시된 배경 음악 또는 자연 의 소리를 낮은 음량으로 틀어 놓는 것(Background music or nature sounds should be played at a low volume)에서 (A)를 각각 확인할 수 있다. 하지만 바퀴 달린 의자와 관련된 정보는 제시되어 있지 않으므로 (B)가 정답이다.

어휘 improve 개선하다, 향상시키다 minimize 최소화하다 include 포함하다 effect 효과, 영향

TEST 3

## 182 세부 사항

번역 이동 가능한 가구가 왜 언급되는가?
(A) 어떤 날에는 빈 바닥 공간이 더 많이 필요할 수 있기 때문에
(B) 가구 아래 바닥을 매일 청소해야 하기 때문에
(C) 공간 배치를 주기적으로 변경하는 것이 새로운 모습을 제공하기 때문에
(D) 방문객들이 다른 규모로 그룹을 이룰 수 있기 때문에

해설 기사 중반부의 공간 배치 및 가구(Layout and Furniture) 항목의 세 번째에 모듈식 좌석, 즉 이동 가능한 좌석(Use modular seating that can be moved into different configurations)이 언급되어 있는데, 이는 혼자 방문하여 프라이버시를 원하는 사람이 있는 반면, 가족과 함께 와서 함께 앉고 싶어 하는 사람도 있을 수 있기 때문(as some people may visit alone and want privacy while others may come with family members and want to sit together)이라는 이유가 제시되어 있으므로 (D)가 정답이다.

어휘 periodically 주기적으로 appearance 모습, 외관

**Paraphrasing**
지문의 modular seating that can be moved
→ 질문의 movable furniture
지문의 some people may visit alone / others may come with family members
→ 정답의 visitors may be in groups of different sizes

## 183 Not / True

번역 <메디컬 월드 매거진>에 대해 언급된 것은?
(A) 병원에 무료로 제공된다.
(B) 편집자들이 독자들의 주제 제안을 원한다.
(C) 출판물에 언급된 일부 제품을 판매한다.
(D) 소유주가 새로운 프리랜서 저자를 찾고 있다.

해설 기사 마지막 문장에 앞으로 나올 호에서는 무엇에 대해 알고 싶은지(What would you like to learn about in future issues?) 묻고 있어 독자들에게 기사 주제를 제안하도록 요청하고 있다는 것을 알 수 있다. 따라서 (B)가 정답이다.

어휘 at no charge 무료로 publication 출판(물) seek 찾다

> Paraphrasing
> 지문의 What would you like to learn about
> → 정답의 topic

## 184 연계

번역 맥앨리스터 씨에 대해 사실일 것 같은 것은?
(A) 과거에 병원에서 근무했다.
(B) <메디컬 월드 매거진> 7월호를 읽었다.
(C) 새로운 종류의 직물을 발명했다.
(D) 대기실에서 많은 시간을 보낸다.

해설 맥앨리스터 씨가 쓴 편지인 두 번째 지문 첫 단락에 차분한 대기실 만들기와 관련하여 제공한 정보 중 일부를 바로잡고 싶다(I would like to offer a correction to some information you provided about creating calming waiting rooms)는 말이 쓰여 있다. <메디컬 월드 매거진> 기사에서 차분한 대기실 만들기(Creating a Calming Waiting Room)를 확인할 수 있고, 그 위에 7월호(July Issue)라고 표기되어 있어 맥앨리스터 씨가 <메디컬 월드 매거진> 7월호를 읽고 편지를 썼다는 것을 알 수 있으므로 (B)가 정답이다.

어휘 previously 과거에, 이전에 medical clinic 진료소 invent 발명하다 textile 직물

## 185 추론

번역 프리-폼 주식회사의 제품에 대해 암시된 것은?
(A) 신속하게 배송될 수 있다.
(B) 재활용품으로 만들어진다.
(C) 10년 품질 보증 서비스가 포함된다.
(D) 청소하기 쉽다.

해설 편지 두 번째 단락에 비닐로 덮여 있는 가구를 언급하면서 신속하고 쉽게 닦여 먼지와 세균을 제거할 수 있다(A better option is furniture that is covered in vinyl. ~ and can be wiped down quickly and easily to remove dirt and germs)고 했고, 프리-폼 주식회사에서 제조하는 가구가 항균성 표면으로 된 비닐을 사용한다(The stylish and practical furniture made by my company, Free-Form Inc., uses vinyl ~)고 했다. 이를 통해 프리-폼 주식회사의 제품이 청소하기 쉽다는 것을 알 수 있으므로 (D)가 정답이다.

어휘 recycled materials 재활용품 come with ~을 포함하다 warranty 품질 보증(서)

> Paraphrasing
> 지문의 can be wiped down quickly and easily to remove dirt and germs → 정답의 easy to clean

### 186-190 이메일+이메일+기사

[186] **수신: 클로이 윌리스**
발신: 스티븐 에메리
날짜: 8월 19일
제목: 원더 러기지

윌리스 씨께,

아까 제가 잠시 들렀을 때 만나 뵙게 되어 기뻤습니다. 논의한 것처럼, [186] **제 가방 매장을 위한 새 장소를 찾고 있습니다.** 저희는 현재 샌드웨이 쇼핑몰의 작은 소매 점포에서 영업하고 있지만, 자체 건물 내의 더 넓은 공간으로 이전하고자 합니다. 널찍한 진열 공간은 필수이며, 고객들을 위한 주차 공간이 있으면 더 좋겠습니다. 한 달에 임대료로 지출하고 싶은 최대 금액은 5,500달러입니다.

[187] **11월 20일까지는 새로운 곳에서 저희 매장 문을 열었으면 하는데, 그래야 저희 매장이 미자라의 새 에코 맥스 가방 제품 라인의 출시에 맞출 수 있을 것이기 때문입니다.** 제 요구에 맞는 곳을 찾으시면 알려 주시기 바랍니다. 저는 다음 주 어느 요일이든 가능한 장소들을 둘러볼 시간이 있습니다.

스티븐 에메리
소유주, 원더 러기지

어휘 stop in 잠시 들르다 luggage (여행용) 가방 operate 영업하다, 운영하다 retail unit 소매 점포 spacious 널찍한 on-site 구내의, 현장의 maximum 최고, 최대 rent 임대료, 월세 allow 할 수 있게 해 주다, 허용하다 participate in ~에 참가하다 launch 출시 (행사) suit 적합하다 available 시간이 나는

수신: 스티븐 에메리
발신: 클로이 윌리스
날짜: 8월 20일
제목: 회신: 원더 러기지

에메리 씨께,

귀하의 업체에 어울릴 만한 소매 점포들을 좀 조사해 봤습니다. 아래의 목록을 확인해 보시고 어디든 직접 방문해 보고 싶은 곳이 있으면 제게 알려 주십시오.

1. 주소: 톨리버 가 1258
평방 피트: 7,512 / 월 임대료: 5,500달러
메모: 이 점포는 이전에 의류 매장이 소유하고 있었으며, 진열 공간이 최근 개조되었습니다.

[188] **2. 주소: 브랙스턴 대로 908**
평방 피트: 8,940 / 월 임대료: 5,000달러
[188] **메모: 건물 소유주가 매달 450달러의 별도 임대 계약을 통해 인접한 주차장의 임대를 요구하고 있습니다.**

3. 주소: 커벨 가 446
평방 피트: 9,650 / 월 임대료: 6,000달러
메모: 이 지역의 유동 인구가 매우 많습니다. 길 건너편에 공용 주차 공간이 있습니다.

클로이 윌리스
487-555-0149

어휘 appropriate 어울리는, 적절한 in person 직접 (가서) square footage 평방 피트 previously 이전에 own 소유하다 renovate 개조하다 adjoining 인접한 separate 별도의, 분리된 lease 임대 (계약) foot traffic 유동 인구(수)

원더 러기지, 새 보금자리를 찾다
캐서린 클락 작성

스트래퍼드 [187] **(11월 10일)—다양한 여행 가방과 롤러백, 기내 휴대용 가방을 비롯한 많은 제품을 판매하는 독립적으로 운영되는 업체인 원더 러기지가 어제 새로운 곳에서 성대한 재개장식을 개최했다.** 이전에 샌드웨이 쇼핑몰에서 영업했던, [188] **이 매장은 브랙스턴 대로 908에 새 보금자리를 찾았다.** 이곳은 매일 오전 9시부터 오후 8시까지 영업한다.
대부분의 직원들이 그대로 있어, 이들은 고객들에게 어떤 종류의 가방을 구매할 것인지에 관해 조언해 줄 수 있다. 소유주인 스티븐 에메리는 새로운 매장에 대한 기대가 크며 이 매장에서 험하게 사용해도 [189] **견딜** 수 있는 고품질 가방을 계속 판매할 것이라고 말한다.
[190] **새로운 매장은 큰 창문이 있어 쇼핑몰 점포만큼 어둡지 않기 때문에**, 쇼핑객들이 제품뿐 아니라 그 분위기도 아주 좋아할 것이다. 오래 사용할 수 있는 가방과 훌륭한 고객 서비스를 찾고 있다면, 원더 러기지에 들러 볼 것을 적극 추천한다.

어휘 independently 독립적으로 a range of 다양한 carry-on 기내 휴대용의 previously 이전에 endure 견디다 rough 거친; 거칠게 handling 취급 atmosphere 분위기 long-lasting 오래 지속되는

## 186 추론

번역 윌리스 씨는 어디에서 일하겠는가?
(A) 가방 매장
(B) 제조 시설
(C) 금융 기관
(D) 부동산 업체

해설 첫 번째 이메일의 수신인이 윌리스(To: Chloe Willis)로 표기되어 있으며, 첫 단락에 에메리가 자신의 가방 매장을 위한 새 장소를 찾고 있다(I am looking for a new location for my luggage store)는 말이 쓰여 있다. 이는 부동산 업체 직원에게 할 수 있는 말이므로 (D)가 정답이다.

## 187 연계

번역 원더 러기지에 대해 언급된 것은?
(A) 월 임대료로 6천 달러를 지불한다.
(B) 새로운 곳에 1년 임대 계약이 되어 있다.
(C) 지역에서 가장 큰 가방 매장이다.
(D) 제품 출시에 늦지 않게 재개장했다.

해설 첫 번째 이메일의 두 번째 단락에 11월 20일까지는 새로운 곳에서 매장 문을 열었으면 하는데, 그래야 미자라의 새 에코 맥스 가방 제품 라인의 출시에 맞출 수 있을 것(I would like to have the business open at the new location by November 20, ~ the launch of Mizara's new Eco-Max luggage line)이라고 했다. 이와 관련해, 11월 10일에 작성된 기사의 지문 첫 단락에 원더 러기지가 어제 새로운 곳에서 재개장식을 개최했다((November 10) — Wonder Luggage ~ held its grand re-opening yesterday at its new location)고 쓰여 있어 새 제품 라인의 출시 전에 재개장한 것을 알 수 있다. 따라서 (D)가 정답이다.

어휘 lease 임대 (계약) in time 늦지 않게, 시간 맞춰

## 188 연계

번역 에메리 씨에 대해 암시된 것은?
(A) 주차 공간도 임대하고 있다.
(B) 또 다른 지점을 열 계획이다.
(C) 진열 공간을 개조하지 않았다.
(D) 많은 유동 인구로 이득을 보고 있다.

해설 기사의 첫 단락에 에메리의 업체인 원더 러기지가 브랙스턴 대로 908에 새 보금자리를 찾았다(the store has found a new home at 908 Braxton Avenue)고 알리고 있다. 이 주소가 제시된 두 번째 이메일의 2번 항목 메모에 건물 소유주가 매달 450달러의 별도 임대 계약을 통해 인접한 주차장의 임대를 요구하고 있다(The building owner requires the rental of the adjoining parking lot in a separate lease at $450 per month)는 정보가 쓰여 있어 주차 공간도 임대하고 있다는 사실을 유추할 수 있다. 따라서 (A)가 정답이다.

어휘 branch 지점, 지사 renovate 개조하다, 보수하다 benefit from ~로부터 이득을 보다

## 189 동의어

번역 기사의 두 번째 단락, 다섯 번째 줄에 쓰인 "endure"와 의미가 가장 가까운 것은?
(A) 견디다
(B) 만나다, 충족하다
(C) 허가하다
(D) 지속하다

해설 endure가 포함된 부분은 '험하게 사용해도 견딜 수 있는 고품질 가방'이라는 의미로 해석된다. 여기서 endure는 '견디다'라는 의미로 쓰인 것이므로 동일한 의미로 쓰이는 동사 (A) withstand가 정답이다.

## 190 세부 사항

번역 새 매장은 이전 매장과 어떻게 다른가?
(A) 더 편리한 위치에 있다.
(B) 실내가 더 밝다.
(C) 영업시간이 더 길다.
(D) 진열 공간이 더 넓다.

해설 기사의 세 번째 단락에 새로운 매장은 큰 창문이 있어 그 쇼핑몰 점포만큼 어둡지 않다(the new location has large windows, so it isn't as dark as the mall unit)고 했으므로 (B)가 정답이다.

> **Paraphrasing**
> 지문의 isn't as dark as the mall unit
> → 정답의 a brighter interior

### 191-195 공고+웹페이지+영수증

캐나다 예술가 재단

캐나다 예술가 재단(FCA)은 영화 감독 선더 차다를 올해의 FCA 공로상 수상자로 발표하게 되어 기쁩니다. 7월 19일 금요일 오후 6시 30분에

TEST 3

토론토의 어빙 호텔에서 열리는 차다 씨의 업적을 기념하는 연회에 여러분을 초대합니다.

차다 씨의 다큐멘터리는 지난 10년 동안 시청자들에게 즐거움을 선사하고 교육을 제공해 왔습니다. 수상작 다큐멘터리 191 **<플라이트>는 차다 씨의 고향인 에드먼턴 근처에서 미국 뉴멕시코주의 샌타페이까지 가는 길에서 수집한 영상들로 캐나다 기러기의 이주 과정을 따라갑니다.** 191 **<푸쉬드 아웃>은 도시화가 늑대 서식지에 미치는 영향을 탐구합니다.** 차다 씨는 이 생물체가 환경 변화에 적응하는 것이 얼마나 192 **힘든** 일인지 강조하기 위해 이 영화를 제작했다고 밝혔습니다. 191 **<투 리틀 컵스>는 새끼를 기르는 북극곰 한 마리를 중심으로 합니다.** 이 영화는 데이먼 대학의 헬렌 오티즈 교수와의 인터뷰를 포함하고 있습니다.

이 행사 입장권은 7월 16일까지 www.fcartists.ca/events에서 온라인으로 구입하실 수 있습니다. 194 **입장료에는 네 가지 코스의 저녁 식사와 그 후에 이어지는 조세피나 애덤스 특별 공연이 포함됩니다.** 저희가 (회원 또는 비회원이든 상관없이) 토론토에서 하룻밤 머무르실 계획이신 참석자 분들을 위해 어빙 호텔과 객실 특별가를 협의해 두었습니다. 추가로 FCA 소식지를 신청하는 분들은 이 호텔 무료 조식 쿠폰을 받을 수 있습니다.

어휘 achievement 공로, 업적 banquet 연회 celebrate 기념하다, 축하하다 entertain 즐겁게 해 주다 audience 시청자 decade 10년 award-winning 수상한 migration 이주 footage 영상 gather 수집하다 explore 탐구하다 urbanization 도시화 habitat 서식지 emphasize 강조하다 creature 생물체 adapt to+명사 ~에 적응하다 center on ~을 중심으로 하다 raise 기르다 include 포함하다 feature 특별히 출연하다, 특징으로 하다 negotiate 협의하다 attendee 참석자 sign up for ~을 신청하다, 등록하다 voucher 쿠폰, 상품권

http://www.irvinghotel.ca

행사 참석자 특별 요금:
FCA 공로상 기념식

7월 19일에 열리는 FCA 공로상 시상식을 위해 어빙 호텔의 객실을 예약하세요. 193 **2박 이상 숙박하시는 이 행사 참석자들은 저희 모든 객실 요금을 30% 할인받으실 수 있습니다.** 194 **이렇게 하시면 저녁 식사 후의 라이브 밴드 공연을 포함하는 행사를 즐기시는 것은 물론,** 아름다운 도시 토론토에서 추가로 시간을 보내실 수 있는 충분한 시간을 갖게 됩니다. 195 **저희 체크아웃 시간은 오전 11시이며, 고객들은 8.99달러의 추가 요금을 내시면 체크아웃 시간을 정오로 늦추실 수 있습니다. 어빙 고객 보상 프로그램 회원들은 이 요금이 면제됩니다.** 이 할인 혜택을 이용하시려면 늦어도 7월 6일까지 예약하시기 바랍니다.

어휘 rate 요금 reserve 예약하다 performance 공연, 연주 extra 추가의, 여분의 extended 연장된 additional 추가의 waive 면제해 주다, 철회하다 take advantage of ~을 이용하다

어빙 호텔, 토론토
고객 영수증

| | | |
|---|---|---|
| 날짜: | 7월 22일 | |
| 195 **고객 성명:** | **레이먼드 프레이저** | |
| 지불: | 신용카드 XXXX-XXXX-XXXX-8509 | |
| 객실: | 327 | |
| 객실 종류: | 디럭스 | |
| 체크인: | 7월 19일, 오후 2시 43분 | |
| 195 **체크아웃:** | **7월 22일, 오전 11시 55분** | |
| 객실 요금: | 220달러 x 3 | 660달러 |
| 195 **체크아웃 연장:** | **0달러** | **0달러** |
| 할인: | 30% (FCA) | -198달러 |
| | 총액: | 462달러 |

이용해 주셔서 감사합니다!

어휘 receipt 영수증 patronage 애용, 성원

## 191 세부 사항

번역 기재된 차다 씨의 모든 영화의 공통점은?
(A) 오직 캐나다에서만 촬영되었다.
(B) 야생 동물을 주제로 한다.
(C) FCA에서 자금을 받았다.
(D) 교수들의 인터뷰를 특징으로 한다.

해설 차다 씨의 작품이 제시된 공고의 두 번째 단락에 <플라이트>는 캐나다 기러기(*Flight* follows the migration of Canadian geese)를, <푸쉬드 아웃>은 늑대(*Pushed Out* explores the effect of urbanization on the habitats of wolves)를, <투 리틀 컵스>는 북극곰(*Two Little Cubs* centers on a polar bear)을 각각 주제로 한다고 설명하고 있으므로 (B)가 정답이다.

어휘 have ~ in common ~이 공통점이다 funding 자금 (제공)

> **Paraphrasing**
> 지문의 geese / wolves / a polar bear → 정답의 wildlife

## 192 동의어

번역 공고의 두 번째 단락, 여섯 번째 줄에 쓰인 "tough"와 의미가 가장 가까운 것은?
(A) 강력한
(B) 엄격한
(C) 힘든, 어려운
(D) 단호한

해설 tough가 속한 부분은 '환경 변화에 적응하는 것이 얼마나 힘든 일인지'로 해석된다. 여기서 tough는 '힘든'이라는 의미로 쓰인 것이므로 '힘든, 어려운'을 뜻하는 (C) challenging이 정답이다.

## 193 Not / True

번역 어빙 호텔의 특별 요금 혜택을 받는 고객에 대해 언급된 것은?
(A) 무료 조식이 제공될 것이다.
(B) 반드시 7월 16일에 체크인해야 한다.
(C) 특정 층에 있는 객실을 사용할 것이다.
(D) 최소 2박 이상 숙박해야 한다.

해설 어빙 호텔의 요금과 관련된 정보가 제시된 웹페이지의 초반부에 2박 이상 숙박하는 이 행사 참석자들은 모든 객실 요금을 30% 할인받는다(Attendees to this event who stay for two nights or more can get 30% off the rate for any of our rooms!)고 쓰여 있으므로 (D)가 정답이다.

어휘 occupy 차지하다, 점유하다 a minimum of 최소 ~의

> **Paraphrasing**
> 지문의 two nights or more
> → 정답의 a minimum of two nights

## 194 연계

번역 조세피나 애덤스는 누구일 것 같은가?
(A) 행사 기획자
(B) 코미디언
(C) 음악가
(D) FCA 대표

해설 공고의 세 번째 단락에 입장료에는 네 가지 코스의 저녁 식사와 그 후에 이어지는 조세피나 애덤스 특별 공연이 포함된다(a four-course dinner followed by entertainment featuring Josefina Adams)고 언급되어 있다. 이 공연과 관련해, 웹페이지 중반부에 저녁 식사 후의 라이브 밴드 공연(an after-dinner performance from a live band)이 쓰여 있어 조세피나 애덤스가 라이브 밴드 공연을 하는 음악가인 것을 알 수 있다. 따라서 (C)가 정답이다.

## 195 연계

번역 프레이저 씨와 관련해 암시된 것은?
(A) 보상 프로그램 회원이다.
(B) 소식지를 신청했다.
(C) 무료 객실 업그레이드를 받았다.
(D) 작년 행사에 참석했다.

해설 웹페이지 후반부에 체크아웃 시간은 오전 11시이며, 8.99달러의 추가 요금을 내면 정오로 체크아웃 시간을 늦출 수 있는데, 어빙 고객 보상 프로그램 회원은 요금이 면제된다(Our standard checkout time is 11 A.M., and guests can get an extended checkout time of noon for an additional $8.99. This fee is waived for members of the Irving Rewards Program)고 쓰여 있다. 이와 관련해, 프레이저 씨의 영수증에 체크아웃 시간이 오전 11시 55분(Check-out: 22 July, 11:55 A.M.)인데, 체크아웃 연장 요금이 0달러(Extended checkout: $0.00 / $0.00)로 표기되어 있어 프레지어 씨가 보상 프로그램 회원임을 알 수 있다. 따라서 (A)가 정답이다.

## 196-200 웹페이지+이메일+설문지

http://www.buildbusinessbest.com/workshops

| 홈 | 회사의 사명 | 워크숍 | 회원 | 연락처 |
|---|---|---|---|---|

빌드 비즈니스 베스트(BBB)가 주최하는 하루 동안 진행되는 워크숍으로 여러분의 비즈니스 기술을 한 단계 업그레이드할 준비를 하세요! 다음 저희 워크숍 시리즈는 4월 22일 수요일에 오크리지 컨퍼런스 센터에서 개최될 것입니다. 저희 모든 강사들은 경험 많은 전문가일 뿐 아니라 BBB 회원이기도 합니다. 허버트 웡이 새로운 사업이나 기존 사업 확장을 위해 사업 계획을 만드는 방법에 관한 가장 인기 있는 워크숍으로 다시 돌아옵니다. 또한 클레어 래드너, 아이작 티네오, 그리고 메이 한이 진행하는 워크숍들도 있습니다. 199 **이어지는 마지막 세션에서는 소그룹 역할극을 통해 갈등 해결에 관해 배우실 것입니다.**

워크숍들이 열리는 하루 전체 참가비는 85달러이며, 이는 구내에서 출장 요리로 제공되는 점심 식사를 포함합니다. 특별한 식단 관련 요구 사항이 있으실 경우, 저희에게 미리 알려 주시기 바랍니다. 196 **BBB 회원 등록은 3월 3일에, 일반인 등록은 3월 10일에 시작됩니다.** 등록이 시작되면 홈페이지뿐만 아니라 이 페이지에도 링크가 추가될 것입니다.

어휘 host 주최하다 create 만들다 expansion 확장 existing 기존의 session (특정 활동을 위한) 시간 conflict 갈등, 충돌 resolution 해결 role-playing 역할극 entire 전체의 include 포함하다 on-site 구내의, 현장의 catered 출장 요리로 제공되는 dietary 식사의, 음식물의 in advance 미리, 사전에 registration 등록

200 **수신: 아이작 티네오** <i.tineo@wdmail.com>
발신: 달린 멘도자 <mendozad@buildbusinessbest.com>
날짜: 4월 25일
제목: 설문 조사 응답

티네오 씨께,

저희 가장 최근 워크숍 시리즈에서 강연하시는 데 동의해 주셔서 다시 한번 감사드립니다. 저희 행사에 또 기여해 주실 수 있기를 바랍니다. 197 **참고하실 수 있도록 설문 응답지를 첨부해 드렸습니다.** 200 **많은 다른 수강생들도 직장 내 업무 관련 스트레스를 관리하는 방법에 관한 귀하의 강연에 대해 비슷한 말을 남겼습니다.** 젊은 전문가들이 우리 참가자들의 대부분을 198 **구성하기** 때문에, 그분들의 직업적 성공을 뒷받침할 수 있는 핵심 기술을 제공하는 것은 매우 중요합니다. 모든 것이 정리되는 대로 더 많은 의견을 보내 드리겠습니다.

달린 멘도자
활동 기획자, 빌드 비즈니스 베스트

어휘 contribute 기여하다 attach 첨부하다 reference 참고 remark 말, 발언 -related ~와 관련된 make up 구성하다 the majority of 대부분의 participant 참가자 support 뒷받침하다 career 직업 경력, 직장 생활 comment 의견 organize 정리하다, 체계화하다

BBB 워크숍 시리즈 피드백 설문지

성명: 펠릭스 롤랜드
참석 날짜: 4월 22일

BBB 워크숍을 다른 사람들에게 추천하실 의향이 얼마나 되십니까?
☒ 매우 높음 ☐ 보통 ☐ 없음

1점(불만족)에서 5점(매우 만족)까지, 다음 항목들에 대해 어떻게 평가하시겠습니까?
신청 과정: 4
유인물: 4
강의실 분위기: 2
강사의 지식: 5
워크숍 시기: 5
점심 식사: 5

의견:
전반적으로, [199] **긴급한 업무로 불려 나가서 마지막 시간은 빠져야 했지만,** 저는 이 시간들을 통해 많은 것을 배웠다고 생각합니다. [200] **저는 업무 관련 스트레스 관리에 관한 워크숍이 가장 유익하다고 생각했습니다.** 제 유일한 불만은 강의실이 너무 더웠다는 것입니다. 이것이 때때로 다소 방해가 됐습니다.

어휘 scale 등급 rate 평가하다 category 항목, 범주 sign-up 신청, 등록 handout 유인물 atmosphere 분위기 overall 전반적으로 urgent 긴급한 complaint 불만, 불평 distracting (집중에) 방해가 되는

## 196 Not / True

번역 워크숍 시리즈에 대해 언급된 것은?
(A) 일부 사람들은 다른 사람들보다 더 일찍 등록할 수 있다.
(B) BBB 회원들은 할인을 받을 자격이 있다.
(C) 며칠에 걸쳐 개최된다.
(D) 참가비에 두 끼 식사 비용이 포함된다.

해설 웹페이지의 두 번째 단락에 BBB 회원 등록은 3월 3일에, 일반인 등록은 3월 10일에 시작된다(Registration for BBB members opens on March 3 and for the general public on March 10)고 했으므로 (A)가 정답이다.

어휘 be eligible for ~에 대한 자격이 있다

> **Paraphrasing**
> 지문의 Registration for BBB members opens on March 3 and for the general public on March 10
> → 정답의 Some people can register earlier than others.

## 197 주제 / 목적

번역 멘도자 씨는 왜 이메일을 보냈는가?
(A) 설문 조사 작성을 요청하기 위해
(B) 강사에게 피드백을 제공하기 위해
(C) 다음 강연의 날짜를 확정하기 위해
(D) 강연용 새 주제를 제안하기 위해

해설 이메일의 초반부에 참고할 수 있도록 설문 응답지를 첨부했다(I've attached a survey response for your reference)고 했으므로 (B)가 정답이다.

어휘 confirm 확정하다, 확인해 주다 instruction 강연, 가르침

## 198 동의어

번역 이메일의 첫 번째 단락, 네 번째 줄에 쓰인 "make up"과 의미가 가장 가까운 것은?
(A) 채우다
(B) 준비하다
(C) 발명하다
(D) 구성하다

해설 make up이 포함된 부분은 '젊은 전문가들이 우리 참가자들의 대부분을 구성한다'로 해석된다. 따라서 '구성하다'를 뜻하는 (D) comprise가 정답이다.

## 199 연계

번역 롤랜드 씨에 대해 암시된 것은?
(A) 소음이 방해가 됐다고 생각했다.
(B) 워크숍을 다른 사람들에게 추천했다.
(C) 역할극 활동에 참가하지 않았다.
(D) 유인물에 최고 평점을 주었다.

해설 롤랜드 씨가 작성한 설문지 하단에 긴급한 업무로 불려 나가서 마지막 시간은 빠져야 했다(I had to miss the last session due to being called away on an urgent work matter)고 했는데, 웹페이지의 첫 단락에 마지막 시간에 소그룹 역할극을 통해 갈등 해결에 관해 배울 것(Those will be followed by the last session, in which you'll learn about conflict resolution through role-playing in small groups)이라고 써 있다. 따라서 롤랜드 씨가 역할극 활동을 하지 못했음을 알 수 있으므로 (C)가 정답이다.

어휘 participate in ~에 참가하다 rating 평점, 등급

## 200 연계

번역 롤랜드 씨는 어느 강사의 시간이 가장 유익하다고 생각했는가?
(A) 허버트 웡
(B) 클레어 래드너
(C) 아이작 티네오
(D) 메이 한

해설 롤랜드 씨가 설문지 하단에 업무 관련 스트레스 관리에 관한 워크숍이 가장 유익하다고 생각했다(I thought the workshop on managing stress related to work was the most helpful one)고 작성했는데, 이메일 중반부에 보면 많은 다른 수강생들도 직장 내 업무 관련 스트레스를 관리하는 방법에 관한 귀하의 강연에 대해 비슷한 말을 남겼다(Many other students had similar remarks about your session on how to manage work-related stress in the workplace)는 말이 나온다. 이메일 수신자가 진행한 워크숍이라는 것을 알 수 있고, 이 이메일의 수신자는 아이작 티네오이므로 (C)가 정답이다.

# TEST 4

| | | | | |
|---|---|---|---|---|
| 101 (D) | 102 (C) | 103 (C) | 104 (B) | 105 (A) |
| 106 (A) | 107 (A) | 108 (C) | 109 (B) | 110 (A) |
| 111 (B) | 112 (B) | 113 (C) | 114 (B) | 115 (D) |
| 116 (D) | 117 (D) | 118 (C) | 119 (D) | 120 (B) |
| 121 (C) | 122 (D) | 123 (B) | 124 (D) | 125 (A) |
| 126 (A) | 127 (C) | 128 (D) | 129 (A) | 130 (A) |
| 131 (C) | 132 (A) | 133 (B) | 134 (C) | 135 (A) |
| 136 (D) | 137 (C) | 138 (C) | 139 (B) | 140 (C) |
| 141 (D) | 142 (A) | 143 (A) | 144 (D) | 145 (B) |
| 146 (B) | 147 (D) | 148 (C) | 149 (C) | 150 (A) |
| 151 (D) | 152 (A) | 153 (C) | 154 (B) | 155 (B) |
| 156 (A) | 157 (C) | 158 (A) | 159 (D) | 160 (C) |
| 161 (D) | 162 (C) | 163 (B) | 164 (A) | 165 (D) |
| 166 (B) | 167 (D) | 168 (D) | 169 (B) | 170 (C) |
| 171 (B) | 172 (B) | 173 (D) | 174 (A) | 175 (C) |
| 176 (C) | 177 (D) | 178 (A) | 179 (A) | 180 (B) |
| 181 (D) | 182 (A) | 183 (A) | 184 (C) | 185 (D) |
| 186 (B) | 187 (C) | 188 (C) | 189 (A) | 190 (B) |
| 191 (C) | 192 (A) | 193 (B) | 194 (C) | 195 (D) |
| 196 (A) | 197 (C) | 198 (A) | 199 (B) | 200 (D) |

## PART 5

### 101 형용사 자리 _ 명사 수식

번역 토론회의 각 참가자는 동일한 발언 시간을 갖게 될 것이다.

해설 부정관사 an과 명사 amount 사이에 위치한 빈칸은 명사를 수식할 형용사가 들어갈 수 있는 자리이므로 (D) equal(동일한)이 정답이다.

어휘 participant 참가자 debate 토론(회) equality 평등, 균등 equally 동일하게 equal 동일한; 동일하다, 같다

### 102 동사 자리

번역 멜버른 대학교 연구진의 최근 연구는 블루 라이트 안경이 실제로 눈의 피로를 예방하지 못할 수도 있다고 암시한다.

해설 주어 A recent study by Melbourne University researchers와 that절 사이에 위치한 빈칸은 that절을 목적어로 취할 동사가 들어갈 자리이므로 (C) suggests(암시하다)가 정답이다. by Melbourne University researchers는 주어 A recent study를 수식하는 전치사구이다.

어휘 recent 최근의 prevent 방지하다, 막다 eye strain 눈의 피로 suggestively 암시하는 듯이 suggestive 암시적인 suggestion 암시, 제안

### 103 전치사 어휘

번역 마티아스 주식회사의 신입 사원들은 입사 첫해에 단 일주일의 휴가만 허용된다.

해설 빈칸 뒤에 위치한 명사구 their first year of work가 기간을 나타내므로 기간 명사구를 목적어로 취할 수 있는 전치사 (C) during(~ 중에, ~ 동안)이 정답이다.

어휘 allow 허용하다 as ~처럼, ~로서 under ~ 아래에, ~하에 between ~ 사이에

### 104 동사 시제

번역 내년 여름에 앵크빌 지역 호텔의 모든 투숙객은 지역 명소 쿠폰 책자를 제공받을 것이다.

해설 미래 시점 표현인 Next summer가 있으므로 이와 어울리는 미래 시제 동사 (B) will be offered가 정답이다.

어휘 booklet (작은) 책자 local 지역의, 현지의 attraction 명소

### 105 명사 어휘

번역 글린테크 사의 대표 모바일 애플리케이션이 1천만 명이 넘는 사람들에 의해 다운로드되었다.

해설 빈칸 앞에 있는 mobile과 의미가 어울리면서 사람들에 의해 다운로드될 수 있는 것을 나타낼 명사가 필요하므로 '애플리케이션'을 뜻하는 (A) application이 정답이다.

어휘 flagship 대표 상품, 주력 상품 device 기기, 장치

### 106 형용사 자리 _ 주어 수식

번역 고급 패션 브랜드에서 판매하는 가방과 비교해도 손색이 없는 내비가 여행 가방은 놀라울 정도로 우아하고 잘 만들어졌다.

해설 콤마(,) 뒤로 문장의 주어 the Naviga suitcase와 동사 is가 있으므로 빈칸부터 콤마까지는 수식어가 되어야 한다. 따라서 빈칸 뒤의 전치사 to와 어울려 '~에 필적하는, 비길 만한'이라는 수식어구를 만들 수 있는 형용사 (A) Comparable(필적하는, 비길 만한)이 정답이다. (B) Comparably(비교할 수 있을 만큼, 동등하게)는 빈칸 뒤의 to와 함께 쓰이지 않고, (C) Compares(비교하다)는 3인칭 단수 현재형 동사인데, 3인칭 단수형 동사로 문장이 시작할 수 없으므로 오답이며, 이미 문장의 주어가 콤마 뒤에 있으므로 또 다른 명사 (D) Comparison(비교)을 쓸 수 없다.

어휘 luggage (여행) 가방, 수하물 remarkably 놀라울 정도로 elegant 우아한

### 107 전치사 어휘

번역 현재 주택 가격이 상당히 비싼 인접 도시들과 달리, 핀리는 부동산 가격이 상승하지 않았다.

해설 주택 가격이 비싼 도시들과 부동산 가격이 상승하지 않은 핀리 사이의 차이를 나타내야 알맞으므로 '~와 달리'를 뜻하는 (A) Unlike가 정답이다.

TEST 4

어휘 neighboring 인접한 housing 주택 fairly 꽤, 상당히 rise in ~의 상승 real estate 부동산 given ~을 고려해 볼 때 except ~을 제외하고 throughout ~ 전역에 걸쳐, ~ 동안 내내

## 108 명사 자리 _ 전치사의 목적어

번역 요우턴 시의 풍력 발전 단지 건설 계획이 주민들의 반대로 취소되었다.

해설 빈칸 앞에 전치사 in이 있으므로 빈칸에는 명사나 동명사가 와야 하고, 빈칸 뒤에 전치사 to가 있으므로 빈칸 앞뒤에 있는 in, to와 함께 '~에 대응해, ~에 응하여'라는 의미의 전치사구를 구성하는 명사 (C) response(대응, 반응)가 정답이다.

어휘 wind farm 풍력 발전 단지 opposition 반대 respond 대응하다, 반응하다

## 109 인칭 대명사 _ 소유격 대명사

번역 개인 전화와 문자 메시지 전송은 예정된 휴식 시간까지 미뤄 주시기 바랍니다.

해설 전치사 until과 명사구 scheduled break time 사이에 위치한 빈칸은 명사구를 수식할 대명사가 들어갈 수 있는 자리이므로 소유격 대명사 (B) your가 정답이다. until을 접속사로, scheduled를 동사로 보면 주격 대명사인 (A) you도 구조적으로는 가능하지만, 의미상 어색하기 때문에 오답이다.

어휘 postpone 미루다, 연기하다 text messaging 문자 메시지 전송 scheduled 예정된

## 110 접속사 어휘

번역 라이트하우스 피자의 종업원들은 고객이 음식 품질에 대해 불만을 제기하는 경우에 매니저에게 알리도록 지시를 받는다.

해설 빈칸 이하 부분이 '고객이 음식 품질에 대해 불만을 제기하는 경우에'라는 의미로 종업원들이 매니저에게 알리게 되는 조건을 나타내야 알맞으므로 '~하는 경우에, ~한다면'을 뜻하는 (A) if가 정답이다.

어휘 instruct 지시하다, 안내하다 notify 알리다, 통보하다 complain 불만을 제기하다 quality 질, 품질 since ~한 이후로, ~하기 때문에 unless ~하지 않는다면 now that (이제) ~이므로

## 111 명사 자리 _ 동사의 목적어

번역 웨고너 씨는 비용 청구 담당 부서에 결제와 관련하여 고객에게 보내는 모든 통신문을 보관하도록 지시했다.

해설 any의 수식을 받을 수 있으면서 keep의 목적어 역할을 할 명사가 필요하며, 보관이 가능한 사물을 나타내야 하므로 '통신문, 편지'를 뜻하는 (B) correspondence가 정답이다. (A) correspondent(특파원, 편지 쓰는 사람)는 사람 명사이므로 의미가 어색하다.

어휘 direct 지시하다 billing 비용 청구, 청구서 발부 regarding ~에 대해 correspond 편지를 주고받다, 일치하다

## 112 형용사 어휘

번역 멘토십 프로그램은 신입 사원을 선배 직원과 연결시켜 양측 모두의 상호 이익을 가져다준다.

해설 '양측 모두의 이익'을 뜻하는 명사구 benefit of both parties와 의미가 어울리는 형용사가 필요하므로 '상호 간의, 서로의'를 뜻하는 (B) mutual이 정답이다.

어휘 mentorship 멘토십(경력자나 선배 등이 제공하는 조언, 또는 그 기간) connect 연결시키다, 관련시키다 new hire 신입 사원 benefit 이익, 혜택 party 당사자 central 중앙의, 중심의 inclusive 포함된 expert 전문가의

## 113 전치사 어휘

번역 마케팅직 지원자들은 반드시 저희 회사 제품에 관한 지식을 보여 주어야 합니다.

해설 빈칸 앞에 있는 명사 knowledge와 어울려 '~에 관한 지식'을 의미할 때 사용하는 전치사가 필요하므로 (C) of가 정답이다.

어휘 candidate 지원자, 후보자 demonstrate 보여 주다, 시연하다 toward ~을 향해 by ~ 옆에, ~에 의해 within ~ 이내에

## 114 부사 자리 _ 동사 수식

번역 그 놀이공원은 일 년 내내 운영하지만, 겨울철에는 운영 시간이 약간 단축된다.

해설 수동태 동사 are reduced와 전치사 for 사이에 위치한 빈칸은 동사를 뒤에서 수식할 부사가 들어갈 수 있는 자리이므로 (B) slightly(약간, 조금)가 정답이다.

어휘 remain ~한 상태로 남아 있다 year-round 일 년 내내, 연중 reduce 줄이다, 감소시키다 slight 약간의, 조금의

## 115 부사 어휘

번역 예약 당일 야외 온도가 높았음에도 불구하고, 뎀베이 씨는 건물 외부를 철저히 점검했다.

해설 동사 inspected를 수식해 건물 외부를 점검한 방식을 나타낼 부사가 필요하므로 '철저히'를 뜻하는 (D) thoroughly가 정답이다.

어휘 appointment 예약, 약속 inspect 점검하다 exterior 외부 property 건물, 부동산 considerably 상당히, 많이 highly 매우, 대단히 wholly 완전히, 전적으로

## 116 형용사 어휘

번역 노무라 타워 로비의 대리석 바닥은 6개월마다 왁스칠을 한다.

해설 six months 앞에 빈칸이 있으며 '6개월마다'라는 의미가 되어야 자연스러우므로, 기간을 나타내는 명사구를 수식해 '~마다, ~에 한 번씩'을 의미하는 (D) every가 정답이다.

어휘 marble 대리석 flooring 바닥재

## 117 전치사 어휘

번역 대중교통에 대한 수요가 도시의 현 기반 시설이 지닌 수용력 이상으로 증가했다.

해설 빈칸 앞에 수요가 증가했다는 말이 쓰여 있어 수용력을 넘어선 상태임을 나타내야 의미가 자연스러우므로 '~ 이상, ~을 넘어서'를 뜻하는 (D) beyond가 정답이다.

어휘 demand 수요, 요구 public transportation 대중교통 capacity 수용력, 능력 current 현재의 infrastructure (사회) 기반 시설

## 118 전치사 자리

번역 저희 정규 운영 시간 외에 박물관 특별 투어 일정을 잡으시려면, 555-0149번으로 전화 주십시오.

해설 빈칸 뒤에 위치한 명사구 our normal opening hours를 목적어로 취할 전치사가 필요하며, 특별 투어는 정규 운영 시간 외의 행사로 볼 수 있으므로 '~ 외에'를 뜻하는 전치사 (C) outside가 정답이다. (A) or(또는)와 (B) while(~인 반면, ~하는 동안)은 접속사이며, (D) without(~ 없이, ~이 없다면)은 전치사이지만 의미가 맞지 않는다.

어휘 arrange 일정을 잡다, 마련하다

## 119 동사 어휘

번역 직원 채용의 어려움 때문에, 우리 두 번째 지점의 개장을 며칠 연기해야 합니다.

해설 직원 채용의 어려움으로 인한 지점 개장과 관련된 문제를 나타낼 수 있는 동사가 필요하므로 빈칸 앞의 be동사와 함께 '연기되다'의 의미를 나타내는 (D) postponed가 정답이다.

어휘 staffing 직원 채용 location 지점, 위치 construct 건설하다 determine 결정하다 situate 위치시키다

## 120 수동태

번역 로우리 자동문의 모든 구성품은 간편한 교체를 위해 표준화되어 있다.

해설 be동사 are 뒤에 빈칸이 있으므로 명사인 (D), 분사인 (A), (B)가 들어갈 수 있는데, '간편한 교체를 위해 표준화되어 있다'라는 의미가 되어야 자연스러우므로 be동사 are와 함께 수동태 동사를 이루는 과거분사 (B) standardized가 정답이다. 명사가 be동사 뒤에 보어로 쓰일 수 있지만 의미가 어색하므로 (D)는 오답이다.

어휘 component part 구성 부품 replacement 교체(품) standardize 표준화하다 standardization 표준화

## 121 접속사 자리 _ 접속사를 포함한 분사구문

번역 저희 웹사이트에서 대량 주문을 하시기 전에, 대량 주문 할인 및 현 재고 수준에 대해 고객 서비스 센터로 전화하시기 바랍니다.

해설 빈칸 뒤에 분사구와 콤마(,)가 있고 그 뒤에 주절이 이어지고 있으므로 빈칸에는 분사를 수식하는 부사가 오거나 접속사가 와서 「접속사+분사구」 분사구문 구조를 만들어야 한다. 또한 '대량 주문을 하기 전에 전화하라'는 의미가 되어야 알맞으므로 '~하기 전에'를 뜻하는 접속사 (C) Before가 정답이다. (A) Although(비록 ~이지만)도 접속사이지만 의미가 맞지 않으며, (B) Anytime(언제든지)은 문장 전체를 수식하고, (D) Rather(다소, 오히려)는 분사를 수식할 수 있지만 의미가 맞지 않다.

어휘 line 전화 regarding ~에 대해 bulk 대량 주문의 current 현재의 stock 재고(품)

## 122 명사 어휘

번역 시간이 제한적인 학생들을 수용하기 위해, 올트 어학원은 개별 수업 일정을 유연하게 짜는 것을 허용한다.

해설 빈칸이 포함된 to부정사구는 유연한 수업 일정을 허용하는 목적을 나타낸다. 따라서 '시간이 제한적인 학생들을 수용하기 위해'라는 의미가 되어야 자연스러우므로 '시간 가능 여부'를 의미하는 (D) availability가 정답이다.

어휘 accommodate 수용하다 limited 제한된 permit 허용하다 flexible 탄력적인, 유연한 scheduling 일정 (조정) proficiency 능숙함, 숙련(도) budget 예산 material 자료, 재료

## 123 부사 어휘

번역 저희는 항상 참가자들에게 사전에 특정 관심사에 관해 물어보고 그에 따라 워크숍의 초점을 조정합니다.

해설 참가자들에게 특정 관심사를 미리 물어보는 것은 그 내용에 따라 워크숍의 초점을 조정하려는 것이므로 '그에 따라, 그에 알맞게'를 의미하는 (B) accordingly가 정답이다.

어휘 participant 참가자 beforehand 사전에 particular 특정한 interests 관심사 adjust 조정하다, 조절하다 focus 초점 consequently 그 결과 popularly 일반적으로 tightly 빽빽하게, 꽉

## 124 형용사 자리 _ 명사 수식

번역 안전과 관련된 우려 때문에, 래드너 주식회사는 자사의 일부 자전거 타이어 모델을 회수하겠다는 자발적인 결정을 내렸다.

해설 부정관사 a와 명사 decision 사이에 위치한 빈칸은 명사를 수식하는 형용사가 들어갈 수 있는 자리이므로 (D) voluntary(자발적인)가 정답이다. (A) volunteer는 decision과 복합명사를 이루지 않고, (B) volunteered와 (C) volunteering은 분사형 형용사로 쓰이지 않는다.

어휘 concern 우려 recall (결함 제품을) 회수하다 volunteer 자원하다; 자원봉사자

## 125 형용사 어휘

번역 짐던 사는 포장, 자동차, 건설을 포함한 많은 산업에 주문 제작 플라스틱을 공급한다.

TEST 4

해설 빈칸은 industries(산업)를 수식하는 형용사가 들어갈 자리인데, 포장, 자동차, 건설을 포함한다는 말이 있으므로 '많은'을 뜻하는 (A) numerous가 정답이다.

어휘 supply 공급하다 including ~을 포함해 automotive 자동차의 made-to-order 주문 제작의 instant 즉각적인 usual 평소의, 보통의 utmost 최고의

## 126 명사 어휘

번역 마컴 주식회사의 유통 관리부는 현재 경험 많은 트럭 기사들을 찾기 위해 다수의 채용 공고를 내고 있다.

해설 명사 distribution과 복합명사를 구성해 채용 공고를 내는 주체를 나타낼 명사가 필요하므로 '(회사 등의) 부, 과'를 뜻하는 (A) division이 정답이다.

어휘 distribution 유통, 분배 currently 현재 advertise 광고하다 multiple 다수의 opening 공석 experienced 경험 많은 policy 정책, 방침 strategy 전략

## 127 동사 어휘

번역 헤이니 슈퍼마켓의 직원들은 일 년에 한 번 무료로 유니폼 셔츠를 사이즈가 다른 것으로 교환할 수 있다.

해설 빈칸 뒤에 「목적어+for+명사구」 구조로 되어 있고, '유니폼 셔츠를 다른 사이즈로 교환할 수 있다'는 의미가 되어야 자연스러우므로 「exchange A for B」의 구조로 쓰여 'A를 B로 교환하다'를 나타내는 (C) exchange가 정답이다. (A) alter는 교환의 의미가 아니라 '(크기·성질·형상 따위를) 바꾸다'라는 의미이다.

어휘 at no charge 무료로 alter 바꾸다, 고치다

## 128 형용사 자리 _ 대명사 후치 수식

번역 다른 사람이 파티에 동행할 예정이시면, 미리 주최자에게 알려 주시기 바랍니다.

해설 대명사 anyone을 뒤에서 수식하여 '다른 사람'이라는 의미를 나타내는 말이 들어가야 하므로 형용사 (D) else(다른, 그 밖의)가 정답이다.

어휘 accompany 동행하다 organizer 준비 위원, 주최자 in advance 미리, 사전에

## 129 동사 어휘

번역 페런 병원의 전기 시스템 수리 작업은 반드시 자격증이 있는 전기 기사에 의해 실시되어야 한다.

해설 빈칸 뒤에 있는 by a licensed electrician(자격증이 있는 전기 기사에 의해)이 수리 작업을 하는 사람을 나타내므로 '실시하다, 수행하다'를 뜻하는 (A) performed가 정답이다.

어휘 licensed 자격증이 있는 electrician 전기 기사 sign 서명하다 commit 전념하다, 헌신하다 establish 확립하다, 설립하다

## 130 복합관계대명사

번역 휴게실 싱크대를 막히게 한 것이 무엇이었든지 배수관 세정액으로 분해되었다.

해설 빈칸 뒤에 주어 없이 동사로 시작하는 불완전한 절 caused the blockage in the breakroom sink가 있고 그 뒤에 또 다른 동사 was dissolved가 쓰여 있다. 따라서 빈칸부터 sink까지가 문장 전체의 주어 역할을 하는 명사절이 되어야 하며, '막히게 한 것이 무엇이었든지 분해되었다'가 알맞은 의미이므로 '~하는 무엇이든'이라는 뜻으로 명사절을 이끄는 복합관계대명사 (A) Whatever가 정답이다.

어휘 blockage 막힘 breakroom 휴게실 dissolve 분해하다, 녹이다 drain 배수관 solution 용액

# PART 6

### 131-134 공지

> 우리 피트니스 센터를 올바르게 이용합시다!
>
> 회사 구내 피트니스 센터의 특혜를 계속 누리기 위해서는, 131 **모두가** 이곳을 깨끗하고 점잖게 이용하는 데 동의해야 합니다. 132 **다음 사항을 모두 이행하도록 노력해 주시기 바랍니다.** 운동 중에는 운동 가방을 탈의실에 133 **두시기** 바랍니다. 물 외에는 어떤 음식이나 음료도 가져오지 마시고, 오디오를 들으시려면 헤드폰을 착용하십시오. 이용 직후에는 제공된 종이 타월과 세정용 스프레이를 사용해 134 **장비**를 말끔히 닦아 주십시오. 마지막으로, 저녁에 피트니스 룸을 마지막으로 이용하시는 분들은 이용 후 불을 꺼 주시기 바랍니다. 감사합니다.
>
> 어휘 properly 올바르게, 적절히 perk 혜택, 특전 onsite 구내의 agree 동의하다 neatly 깨끗하게 respectfully 공손히, 정중하게 exercise 운동하다 wipe down 말끔히 닦다 immediately after ~ 직후에 turn off 끄다 afterward 그 후에, 나중에

## 131 대명사 어휘

해설 피트니스를 깨끗하고 점잖게 이용해야 하는 사람은 피트니스를 이용하는 모든 사람이므로 '모든 사람'을 뜻하는 (C) everybody가 정답이다.

## 132 문장 고르기

번역 (A) 다음 사항을 모두 이행하도록 노력해 주시기 바랍니다.
(B) 구내식당에서 건강에 좋은 식사를 선택하십시오.
(C) 에어로빅 또는 웨이트 운동 강좌를 수강하실 수 있습니다.
(D) 매 근무일 업무 종료 시에 책상을 말끔히 정리하십시오.

해설 빈칸 앞 문장에는 구내 피트니스 센터 이용과 관련된 공지임을 알리는 말이, 빈칸 뒤에는 세부적인 주의 사항들이 제시되어 있다. 따라서 이러한 주의 사항들을 the following으로 가리켜 그것들을 모두 이행하도록 당부하는 의미로 쓰인 (A)가 정답이다.

어휘 make an effort to ~하도록 노력하다 following 다음의 것 choose 선택하다 option 옵션, 선택 (가능한 것) cafeteria 구내식당 tidy 말끔히 정리하다

## 133 동사 자리 _ 명령문

해설 문장에 동사가 없으므로 빈칸은 동사 자리이며, 주어 없이 동사로 시작하는 명령문에서는 동사 원형을 쓰므로 (B) leave가 정답이다.

## 134 명사 어휘

해설 구내 피트니스 센터에서 이용 직후에 종이 타월 및 세정용 스프레이로 닦아야 하는 대상을 나타낼 명사가 필요하므로 '장비'를 뜻하는 (C) equipment가 정답이다.

어휘 tool 도구, 공구 counter 계산대, 조리대 vehicle 차량

### 135-138 광고

완벽한 정원을 원하시나요?

올봄, 러더퍼드 가든 센터에서 여러분이 꿈꾸는 정원을 만드는 것을 도와 드리겠습니다! 저희가 소장하고 있는 풍부한 꽃과 채소, 허브, 관목을 비롯한 그 외의 많은 제품 중에서 선택해 보세요. 135 **그런 다음**, 영양분이 많은 비료에서부터 정원용 도구까지, 적절한 용품을 구입하십시오. 저희는 심지어 독특한 장식용 제품도 갖추고 있습니다! 136 **이번에 처음으로 정원에 식물을 심으시나요?** 친절하고 지식이 풍부한 저희 직원들이 무엇을 구매할지와 새 식물을 관리하는 137 방법**에 관해** 기꺼이 조언해 드릴 것입니다.

러더퍼드 가든 센터의 모든 묘목과 초보자용 식물은 138 **권장되는** 모든 관리 및 영양 공급을 받습니다. 저희는 100%의 건강 상태에 미치지 못하는 식물은 판매하지 않습니다. 오늘 저희를 방문하셔서 직접 확인해 보세요!

어휘 ample 풍부한, 충분한 collection 소장(품), 수집(품) pick up 구입하다 appropriate 적절한, 알맞은 supplies 용품, 물품 fertilizer 비료 implement 도구, 용구 unique 독특한, 특별한 decorative 장식의 knowledgeable 지식이 풍부한, 많이 아는 tend 돌보다 seedling 묘목 care 관리, 관심 nourishment 영양(분) for oneself 직접, 혼자 힘으로

## 135 접속부사

해설 빈칸 앞 문장에는 꿈꾸는 정원을 만들기 위해 많은 식물들 중에서 선택하라는 말이, 빈칸 뒤에는 비료와 도구 등의 용품을 구입하라는 말이 쓰여 있다. 이는 물품 구입과 관련된 정보를 차례로 나열하는 흐름이므로 '그런 다음'이라는 의미로 다음 순서를 언급할 때 사용하는 (A) Then이 정답이다.

어휘 at last 마침내 instead 대신 in that case 그런 경우에

## 136 문장 고르기

번역 (A) 구매 물품을 운송하는 것이 걱정인가요?
(B) 지역 내에 어느 묘목장이 이렇게 좋은 조건을 제공하나요?
(C) 이국적인 특정 식물을 찾고 있나요?
(D) 이번에 처음으로 정원에 식물을 심으시나요?

해설 빈칸 뒤에 구입해야 하는 것과 새 식물을 관리하는 방법에 관해 직원들이 조언해 준다는 말이 쓰여 있다. 이는 처음 식물을 구입하는 사람에게 하는 조언으로 볼 수 있으므로 처음으로 식물을 심는 것인지 묻는 (D)가 정답이다.

어휘 concerned 걱정하는, 우려하는 transport 운송하다 local 지역의, 현지의 nursery 묘목장 deal 거래 조건, 거래 제품 particular 특정한, 특별한 exotic 이국적인

## 137 전치사 어휘

해설 빈칸 앞뒤에 각각 위치한 advise you와 what to buy and how to tend your new plants가 '무엇을 구매할지와 새 식물을 관리하는 방법에 관해 조언하다'라는 의미를 구성해야 자연스러우므로 '~에 관해'를 뜻하는 (C) on이 정답이다.

## 138 형용사/분사 자리 _ 명사 수식

해설 형용사 all과 명사 care 사이에 있는 빈칸은 all과 함께 명사 care를 수식할 또 다른 형용사가 들어갈 수 있는 자리인데, 선택지에 형용사가 없으므로 이를 대신할 수 있는 분사 중에서 하나를 골라야 한다. care는 사람에 의해 '권장되는' 것이므로 수동의 의미를 나타내는 과거분사 (C) recommended가 정답이다. 명사 (D) recommendation은 care와 복합명사를 구성하지 않으므로 오답이다.

### 139-142 공고

애들러 호텔의 소중한 고객님들께,

저희가 11월 27일부터 호텔 수영장을 재단장하기 시작할 것임을 알려 드립니다. 139 **완전히** 물을 빼낸 후, 표면 처리를 새로 하고 페인트칠도 다시 할 것입니다. 140 **이 작업이 숙박에 방해가 되지는 않을 것으로 예상합니다.** 큰 소음을 유발할 수 있는 모든 작업은 오전 10시에서 오후 5시 사이로 제한될 것입니다. 하지만, 이 프로젝트가 진행되는 동안 수영장과 수영장 주변 공간은 고객 출입이 전면 통제될 것입니다. 이 시설들의 재개장은 12월 8일로 141 **예정되어 있습니다.** 142 **그 사이에**, 고객들께서는 록스던 포인트에 있는 저희 자매 호텔인 애들러 플라자의 수영장을 이용하실 수 있습니다. 자세한 내용은 안내 데스크를 방문하시기 바랍니다.

어휘 valued 소중한 refurbish 재단장하다 drain 물을 빼다 resurface 표면 처리를 새로 하다, 재포장하다 confine 국한하다 completely 완전히 off-limits 출입 금지의 property 건물, 부동산 concierge (호텔의) 안내원 details 상세 정보

## 139 부사 어휘

해설 수영장 재단장 공사를 위해 물을 빼내는 방식을 나타낼 부사가 필요하며, 물을 전부 빼내야 공사를 진행할 수 있으므로 '완전히, 전적으로' 등을 뜻하는 (B) fully가 정답이다.

어휘 quite 꽤, 상당히 further 더 깊이, 한층 더 regularly 주기적으로, 규칙적으로

## 140 문장 고르기

번역 (A) 다행히, 저희 호텔에 다른 가족 친화적인 시설들이 있습니다.
(B) 저희는 이 프로젝트 시작 날짜를 아직 정하지 않았습니다.
(C) 이 작업이 숙박에 방해가 되지는 않을 것으로 예상합니다.
(D) 이 수영장의 새 색상은 매력적인 하늘색이 될 것입니다.

해설 빈칸 앞에는 수영장 재단장 공사 시작일과 작업 내용을 알리는 말이, 빈칸 다음 문장에는 큰 소음이 나는 작업이 오전 10시에서 오후 5시 사이로 제한된다는 말이 각각 쓰여 있다. 따라서 해당 공사를 this work로 지칭해 공사 소음이 숙박에 방해가 되지는 않을 것이라는 의미로 쓰인 (C)가 정답이다.

어휘 -friendly ~ 친화적인 disturb 지장을 주다 attractive 매력적인

## 141 동사 시제+태

해설 문장의 주어 reopening(재개장)은 사람에 의해 '예정되는' 것이므로 수동태 동사가 필요하다. 또한, 현재 시점 기준으로 예정된 재개장 날짜를 알리는 것이므로 현재 시제가 되어야 한다. 따라서 현재 예정되어 있는 상태임을 나타내는 현재 시제 수동태 (D) is scheduled가 정답이다.

## 142 접속부사

해설 빈칸 앞에는 공사 중인 시설들이 전면 통제되어 12월 8일에 재개장한다는 말이, 빈칸 뒤에는 애들러 플라자의 수영장을 이용할 수 있다는 말이 각각 쓰여 있다. 이는 12월 8일에 재개장하기 전까지 이용 가능한 대체 시설을 알리는 흐름임을 알 수 있으므로 '그 사이에'라는 의미의 (A) In the meantime이 정답이다.

어휘 on the contrary 그와 반대로 specifically 특히, 분명히 besides 게다가, 그뿐만 아니라

## 143-146 기사

샌들린 (1월 25일)—샌들린 메인 가 협회(SMSA)가 오리건 도심 프로그램에 참여하게 되었다. 주 전역에서 시행되는 이 프로그램은 중소 규모 도시의 전통적인 중심지를 다시 활성화하기 위한 노력을 [143] **지원한다**. 역사적인 상업 및 공공 건물들이 무리를 이루고 [144] **있는** 도심 구역을 대표하는 단체들이 참여한다. 이 프로그램을 통해, 그들은 개발과 광고 같은 주제에 관한 교육뿐 아니라 [145] **전용** 보조금도 받게 된다.

[146] **SMSA는 이미 최근 몇 년 동안 메인 가에 새로운 활력을 불어넣어 왔다.** 이 프로그램의 지원을 받아, 이 협회는 건물 개조와 지역 사회 행사를 포함한 프로젝트들을 통해 샌들린 도심으로 여러 업체 및 방문객들을 끌어들이기 위한 노력을 지속할 것이다.

어휘 accept 받아들이다 statewide 주 전역의 initiative 계획 effort 노력 revitalize 부활시키다, 다시 활성화하다 traditional 전통적인 participating 참여하는 represent 대표하다 cluster 무리, 집단 be given access to+명사 ~을 이용할 수 있게 되다 grant 보조금 development 개발, 발전 advertising 광고 (활동) assistance 지원, 도움 attract 끌어들이다 including ~을 포함해 renovation 개조, 보수 community 지역 사회

## 143 동사 시제

해설 보기의 단어들이 모두 시제만 다른 능동태 동사이므로 시제와 관련된 단서를 찾아야 한다. 빈칸이 속한 문장은 프로그램의 목적을 설명하는 문장이므로 일반적인 사실을 설명할 때 사용하는 현재 시제 (A) supports가 정답이다.

어휘 support 지원하다, 지지하다

## 144 접속사 자리 _ 관계부사

해설 빈칸 앞뒤로 각각 주어와 동사를 포함한 절이 있으므로 빈칸에는 접속사가 와야 하며, 빈칸 이하 부분이 명사구 downtown areas를 설명하는 내용이므로 명사구를 수식하는 관계사절을 구성해야 한다. 또한, 빈칸 뒤에 있는 절이 빠진 요소 없이 구성이 완전하므로 완전한 절을 이끄는 관계부사 (D) where가 정답이다. (A) near는 전치사, (B) so는 등위 접속사이며, (C) that은 주어나 목적어가 빠진 불완전한 절을 이끄는 관계대명사이다.

## 145 형용사 어휘

해설 빈칸이 속한 문장의 주어 they가 가리키는 참여 그룹들(Participating groups)이 어떤 보조금(grants)을 받게 되는지 나타낼 형용사가 필요하므로 '전용의, 독점적인'을 뜻하는 (B) exclusive가 정답이다.

어휘 noticeable 주목할 만한, 현저한 vacant 비어 있는 fortunate 다행인, 운이 좋은

## 146 문장 고르기

번역 (A) SMSA는 정규직 직원을 고용할 여력이 아직 없다.
(B) SMSA는 이미 최근 몇 년 동안 메인 가에 새로운 활력을 불어넣어 왔다.
(C) 샌들린의 메인 가는 인근 도시들의 거리보다 걷기에 더욱 적합하다.
(D) 오리건 도심 프로그램은 신청 과정이 엄격하다.

해설 빈칸 다음 문장에 the program(오리건 도심 프로그램)의 지원과 함께 the association(SMSA)이 샌들린 도심으로 여러 업체와 방문객들을 끌어들이기 위한 노력을 지속할 것이라는 말이 쓰여 있다. 따라서 이러한 노력에 해당하는 것으로서 SMSA가 최근에 이미 해 온 일을 의미하는 (B)가 정답이다.

어휘 capacity 능력, 수용력 employ 고용하다 walkable 걷기에 적합한 neighboring 인근의 rigorous 엄격한, 철저한 application 신청(서), 지원(서) process 과정

## PART 7

### 147-148 이메일

발신: 에리카 피트먼 <contact@pittmansolutions.com>
수신: 제시카 체임버스 <jchambers@jessicachambers.com>
제목: 피트먼 솔루션즈 사와 귀사의 웹사이트
날짜: 4월 19일
첨부: @요금과_포트폴리오

체임버스 씨께,

귀사의 웹사이트를 개선하는 데 있어 제 서비스를 제공해 드리고자 연락 드립니다. 147 **지난달에 선물로 귀사의 은 목걸이 하나를 받은 후에 사이트를 방문했는데,** 유감스럽게도 148 **귀사의 제품 사진에 딸려 있는 글에 오타와 헷갈리는 문구가 포함되어 있는 것**을 보게 되었습니다. 귀사의 사랑스러운 디자인을 적절히 강조하도록 148 **제가 이 내용을 수정해 드릴 수 있다면 기쁠 것입니다.** 이 이메일의 첨부 파일에서 요금 및 이전의 작업물을 확인해 보실 수 있습니다. 한번 살펴보시고 관심 있으시면 제게 알려 주시기 바랍니다.

에리카 피트먼
피트먼 솔루션즈

어휘 rate 요금, 비율 portfolio 포트폴리오(작업물 모음집) improve 개선하다 text 글, 문자 accompany 딸려 있다, 동반하다 contain 포함하다 typo 오타 confusing 헷갈리게 하는, 혼란스럽게 만드는 wording 문구, 글귀 revise 수정하다 content 내용(물) properly 적절히, 제대로 highlight 강조하다 previous 이전의, 과거의 attachment 첨부(된 것)

### 147 추론

번역 체임버스 씨는 누구일 것 같은가?
(A) 의류 디자이너
(B) 액자 세공사
(C) 케이크 장식 전문가
**(D) 장신구 제조가**

해설 초반부에 체임버스 씨를 your로 지칭해 상대방 회사의 은 목걸이 하나를 받았음(~ receiving one of your silver necklaces as a gift)을 언급하는 말이 있으므로 (D)가 정답이다.

### 148 세부 사항

번역 피트먼 씨는 체임버스 씨를 위해 무엇을 하겠다고 하는가?
(A) 출판물에서 업체 광고하기
(B) 디지털 사진 수정하기
**(C) 제품 설명 수정하기**
(D) 웹사이트에 특별 기능 추가하기

해설 중반부에 제품 사진에 딸려 있는 글에 오타와 헷갈리는 문구가 포함되어 있어 그 내용을 수정해 주고 싶다(~ the texts accompanying your product photos contain typos and confusing wording. I would be happy to revise this content ~)는 말이 있으므로 (C)가 정답이다.

어휘 publication 출판(물) retouch 수정하다, 손보다 description 설명 feature 기능, 특징

**Paraphrasing**
지문의 the texts accompanying your product photos / revise this content
→ 정답의 Edit some product descriptions

### 149-150 회람

수신: 그리건 일렉트로닉스 사 창고 직원
발신: 키리코 이시이, 창고 관리자
날짜: 9월 24일, 오후 2시 30분
제목: 창고 재고 조사 과정

149 **우리가 취급하는 재고 물품의 종류가 최근에 증가하면서 현재 재고 조사를 하는 방식이 비효율적이고 부적절해졌습니다. 따라서 더 이상 일 년에 두 번씩 전체 재고 조사를 위해 창고 전체를 닫지 않을 것입니다.**

149 **대신, 분기에 한 번이나 일 년에 두 번, 또는 일 년에 한 번씩 지정된 제품 그룹에 대한 재고 조사를 시작할 것입니다.** 이렇게 하면 최소한 부분적으로라도 창고를 일 년 내내 운영할 수 있고, 150 **가장 가치 있는 재고를 파악하는 데 주의를 집중할 수 있습니다.**

150 **프로젝트 팀이 현재 각 제품에 대한 분류를 결정하고 있습니다. 그룹 A는 개당 가격 및 주문 빈도의 조합을 바탕으로 상위 20% 제품으로 구성할 것이며,** 다음 40%는 그룹 B가, 마지막 40%는 그룹 C가 될 것입니다. 이 분류가 지정되는 대로, 그룹 A에 대한 첫 번째 재고 조사가 시작될 것입니다.

어휘 inventory 재고 (조사), 재고 목록 process 과정 increase 증가; 증가시키다 range 종류, 범위 stock 재고 (물품) carry 취급하다 current 현재의 inefficient 비효율적인 inadequate 부적절한 shut down 닫다, 폐쇄하다 entire 전체의 defined 지정된 quarter 분기 allow 할 수 있게 해 주다, 허용하다 partially 부분적으로 operational 운영 중인, 가동 중인 year-round 연중, 일 년 내내 focus 집중하다, 초점을 맞추다 attention 주의(력), 관심 keep track of ~을 파악하다 valuable 소중한 determine 결정하다 classification 분류 comprise 구성하다 based on ~을 바탕으로 combination 조합, 결합 unit (제품의) 한 개 frequency 빈도 assign 배정하다, 할당하다

### 149 주제 / 목적

번역 회람의 목적은?
(A) 창고 임시 폐쇄에 관한 세부 정보를 제공하는 것
(B) 외부 컨설턴트가 권고한 사항을 알리는 것
**(C) 더욱 효율적인 상품 재고 조사 시스템을 알리는 것**
(D) 일부 재고 기록에서 발견한 부정확성을 설명하는 것

해설 첫 단락과 두 번째 단락에, 현재의 재고 조사 방식이 비효율적이고 부적절해졌다(~ has made our current way of taking inventory inefficient and inadequate)는 말과 새로운 방식으로 재고 조사를 시작한다(Instead, we will begin taking inventories ~)는 내용이 쓰여 있다. 따라서 더 효율적인 재고 조사 방식을 알리는 것이 목적임을 알 수 있으므로 (C)가 정답이다.

어휘 details 세부 정보 temporary 임시의 external 외부의 describe 설명하다 inaccuracy 부정확함

## 150 세부 사항

번역 회람에 따르면, 무엇이 지금 결정되고 있는가?
(A) 어느 제품이 회사에 가장 소중한지
(B) 언제 과정상의 변경을 시행할지
(C) 어디에 새 상품을 보관할지
(D) 누가 프로젝트 팀을 이끌도록 배정될지

해설 두 번째 단락에 재고 조사 방식을 바꾸면, 가장 가치 있는 재고를 파악하는 데 주의를 집중할 수 있다(~ focus our attention on keeping track of our most valuable stock)고 했고, 세 번째 단락에서 프로젝트 팀이 현재 각 제품에 대한 분류를 결정하고 있다(A project team is currently determining the classifications of each product)는 말과 함께, 그룹 A는 개당 가격 및 주문 빈도의 조합을 바탕으로 상위 20% 제품으로 구성할 것(Group A will comprise the top 20% of products based on a combination of cost per unit and order frequency)이라고 알리고 있다. 이는 어느 제품이 회사에 가장 소중한지 파악하는 과정이므로 (A)가 정답이다.

어휘 implement 시행하다 merchandise 상품 store 보관하다 lead 이끌다

> Paraphrasing
> 지문의 is currently determining
> → 질문의 is being decided now

### 151-152 문자 메시지

레지 노리스 [오전 11시 6분]
안녕하세요, 사라. 제가 드디어 이번 주 금요일에 아주 바쁜 의사 선생님의 진료 예약을 해서, 151 **그날 매장에서 제 교대 근무를 대신해 줄 사람을 찾고 있어요. 그날 오후에 와 주실 수 있나요?**

사라 클라인 [오전 11시 7분]
제 일정표를 확인해 봐야 할 거예요. 잠시만요.

사라 클라인 [오전 11시 9분]
괜찮아요, 그때 친구를 만나 커피를 마시기로 한 줄 알았는데, 알고 보니 다음 주 금요일이네요. 152 **하지만 제가 전에는 제 근무 일정이 아닌 시간에 근무해 본 적이 없는데, 우리가 에반스 씨의 승인을 받아야 하나요?**

레지 노리스 [오전 11시 10분]
152 **제가 지금 그분께 전화 드릴게요.** 정말 고마워요, 사라!

사라 클라인 [오전 11시 11분]
별말씀을요.

어휘 appointment 예약, 약속 shift 교대 근무(조) be supposed to ~하기로 되어 있다, ~해야 하다 it turns out 알고 보니 ~이다, ~인 것으로 드러나다 approval 승인

## 151 의도 파악

번역 오전 11시 7분에 클라인 씨가 "제 일정표를 확인해 봐야 할 거예요"라고 쓸 때, 의미하는 것은 무엇인가?
(A) 너무 많은 교대 근무 일정이 잡혀 있다고 생각한다.
(B) 의사 진료 예약에 갈 시간이 없을지도 모른다.
(C) 어디서 커피 모임을 하기로 했는지 잊었다.
(D) 추가 근무에 바로 동의할 수 없다.

해설 앞선 메시지에서 노리스가 자신의 교대 근무를 대신할 사람을 찾는다(I'm looking for someone to take my shift at the store that day)고 알리면서 클라인에게 와 줄 수 있는지(Could you come in that afternoon?) 묻는 것에 대해 '제 일정표를 확인해 봐야 할 거예요'라고 대답하는 흐름이다. 이는 노리스를 대신하여 근무하는 것에 대해 곧바로 대답해 줄 수 없다는 뜻이므로 (D)가 정답이다.

어휘 agree 동의하다 additional 추가의

## 152 추론

번역 노리스 씨는 누구에게 전화할 것 같은가?
(A) 매장 관리자
(B) 클라인 씨의 친구
(C) 병원 일정 관리 담당자
(D) 카페 직원

해설 11시 9분 메시지에 클라인이 근무 시간 변경에 대해 에반스 씨의 승인을 받아야 하는지(do we need to get Ms. Evans's approval?) 묻자, 노리스가 곧바로 그 사람에게 전화하겠다(I'll call her now)고 대답하고 있다. 따라서 근무 시간 변경을 승인해 줄 수 있는 위치에 있는 사람, 즉 매장 관리자에게 전화한다는 것을 알 수 있으므로 (A)가 정답이다.

### 153-154 광고

페이퍼 아츠
154 **1998년부터 메딜라에서 영업**
• 키너 가 285 • 555-0193

여러분 자신을 아름답게 표현해 보세요

시를 쓰시든 아니면 생일 축하 인사나 식료품 목록을 작성하시든, 153 **페이퍼 아츠의 특별한 종이 제품과 필기구로 멋지게 작성하세요.**

저희 선반에서 찾아보실 수 있습니다.
➢ 아주 다양한 크기, 무게, 색상의 종이
➢ 고품질 펜, 연필, 마커
➢ 모든 계절과 상황에 맞는 인사 카드
➢ 고급스러운 플래너와 일지, 메모장을 비롯한 다수의 제품
잠깐 들르셔서 매장에 있는 것을 확인해 보세요!

어휘 express 표현하다 poem 시 greeting 인사(글) grocery 식료품 in style 세련되게, 멋지게 unique 특별한, 독특한 a rich variety of 아주 다양한 occasion 행사, 경우 elegant 고급스러운, 우아한 drop by 잠깐 들르다

## 153 세부 사항

번역 페이퍼 아츠는 어떤 종류의 업체인가?
(A) 인쇄소
(B) 출판사
(C) 문구점
(D) 미술 학원

해설 중반부에 페이퍼 아츠의 종이 제품과 필기구(unique paper products and writing tools from Paper Arts)가 언급되어 있으므로 (C)가 정답이다.

> Paraphrasing
> 지문의 paper products and writing tools
> → 정답의 stationery

## 154 세부 사항

번역 페이퍼 아츠에 관한 어떤 정보가 광고에 포함되어 있는가?
(A) 소유주 이름
(B) 개업한 연도
(C) 웹사이트 주소
(D) 보유하고 있는 지점 수

해설 초반부에 1998년부터 메딜라에서 영업해 왔다(Serving Medila since 1998)고 했으므로 (B)가 정답이다.

### 155-157 정보

지플리 스플릿으로 돈을 절약하세요

[155] **전국에 있는 수백만 명의 사람들이 각자의 도시 내에서 이동을 위한 교통수단을 신속히 찾기 위해 지플리 앱에 의존하게 되었습니다.** 현재, 지플리 사는 지플리 스플릿을 통해 유사한 편의를 훨씬 더 저렴한 요금으로 제공해 드리기 시작하는 것을 자랑스럽게 생각합니다. 지플리 스플릿은 비슷한 방향으로 향하는 다른 지플리 사용자와 단지 교통수단을 공유함으로써 최대 20% 할인을 받을 수 있게 해 드립니다.

상세 정보:
- 목적지를 입력하면 나타나는 교통수단 선택 사항 중에서 지플리 스플릿을 선택하여 이용하십시오.
- 할인 비율은 동승자와 함께 이동하신 시간과 거리를 바탕으로 계산됩니다.
- [157] **경로 변경이 필요한 경우 10분 이상 추가되지 않을 것입니다.**
- 이 서비스는 아직 지플리가 [156] **활성화되어 있는** 모든 도시에서 이용할 수 있는 것은 아닙니다.

다음 번 교통수단을 이용하실 때 지플리 스플릿을 이용해 보고, 얼마나 많이 절약되는지 확인해 보세요!

어휘 come to ~하게 되다 depend on ~에 의존하다 ride 교통수단, 탈 것 similar 유사한, 비슷한 convenience 편의 affordable 저렴한 rate 요금, 등급 up to 최대 ~의 share 공유하다 head 향하다 appear 나타나다 input 입력하다 destination 목적지 calculate 계산하다 based on ~을 바탕으로 available 이용 가능한 active 활성화된

## 155 세부 사항

번역 지플리 앱은 사용자들이 무엇을 하는 데 도움을 주기 위한 것인가?
(A) 음식 배달
(B) 짧은 거리 이동
(C) 다른 사람에게 송금
(D) 이웃과 소통

해설 지플리 앱이 언급되는 첫 단락에 사람들이 각자의 도시 내에서 이동을 위한 교통수단을 신속히 찾기 위해 지플리 앱에 의존하게 되었다(Millions of people across the country have come to depend on the Zipply app to quickly find rides for trips within their city)고 했으므로 (B)가 정답이다.

어휘 be intended to ~하기 위한 것이다 communicate 의사소통하다

> Paraphrasing
> 지문의 trips within their city
> → 정답의 Travel short distances

## 156 동의어

번역 두 번째 단락, 일곱 번째 줄에 쓰인 "active"와 의미가 가장 가까운 것은?
(A) 작동하는
(B) 성공적인
(C) 활력적인
(D) 참여하는

해설 프로그램 등에 대해 active는 '활성화된, 운영되는' 등을 의미하며, 이는 작동 중인 상태와 같으므로 '작동하는'을 뜻하는 (A) operating이 정답이다.

## 157 Not / True

번역 지플리 스플릿 선택 사항에 대해 언급된 것은?
(A) 전국의 도시에서 제공된다.
(B) 디스플레이 설정을 조정한 후에 사용할 수 있다.
(C) 발생할 수 있는 최대 지연 시간은 10분이다.
(D) 할인액은 사람 수에 따라 다르다.

해설 상세 정보의 세 번째 항목에 경로 변경이 필요한 경우 10분 이상 추가되지 않을 것(Any required changes to your route will add no more than ten minutes to your trip)이라는 말이 쓰여 있다. 이는 최대로 지연되는 시간이 10분이라는 의미이므로 (C)가 정답이다.

어휘 adjust 조정하다 setting (기기 등의) 설정 maximum 최대의 delay 지연, 지체 vary 다르다

> Paraphrasing
> 지문의 will add no more than ten minutes
> → 정답의 The maximum delay it will cause is ten minutes.

## 158-160 이메일

발신: <amelia.jackson@atmosrecords.com>
수신: <marcus.hawkins@mhawkinsartist.com>
제목: 앨범 표지 작업 기회
날짜: 8월 14일

호킨스 씨께,

저는 애트머스 레코드의 미술 감독이며, 저희가 제작 중인 앨범의 표지 제작을 고려해 보시면 어떨지 여쭤 보고자 이메일을 씁니다. [158] **이 앨범은 크리스 엠브리의 <레인 투모로우> 후속작이며, 이는 아실지 모르겠지만 작년에 최고의 판매량을 기록한 앨범들 중 하나였습니다.** 새 앨범이 아직 타이틀은 없지만, 청춘과 우정을 주제로 다룹니다. 귀하의 사진들도 이 주제들을 탐구하는 것으로 기억하고 있어서, [159] **귀하의 웹사이트에 있는 갤러리 페이지를 크리스에게 보여 주었습니다.** 크리스는 귀하의 작품을 아주 좋아했으며, 공동 작업 아이디어에 대해 대단히 기뻐했습니다. [160] **저희는 특히 귀하의 <던 필즈> 사진 시리즈를 재창작하는 가능성에 관심이 있습니다.** 하지만 저희는 귀하의 다른 아이디어에도 열려 있습니다.

이 프로젝트에 참여하기를 원하시거나 더 알아보고 싶으시면, 연락 주시기 바랍니다. 귀하의 답변을 들을 수 있기를 바랍니다.

아멜리아 잭슨
애트머스 레코드
(310) 555-0174

어휘 opportunity 기회 consider 고려하다 cover art 표지 follow-up 후속작 aware 알고 있는 deal with ~을 다루다 theme 주제 explore 탐구하다 subject 주제 collaborate 공동 작업하다, 협업하다 particularly 특히 be interested in ~에 관심이 있다 possibility 가능성 recreate 재창작하다 involved in ~에 참여하는, ~에 관여하는 get in touch 연락하다

## 158 Not / True

번역 <레인 투모로우>에 대해 사실인 것은?
(A) 엠브리 씨의 이전 앨범이다.
(B) 표지가 유명하다.
(C) 현재 제작 중이다.
(D) 호킨스 씨의 객원 연주를 특징으로 한다.

해설 초반부에 제작 중인 앨범이 크리스 엠브리의 <레인 투모로우> 후속작(It is Chris Embry's follow-up to *Rain Tomorrow* ~)이라는 말이 쓰여 있어 <레인 투모로우>는 엠브리의 이전 앨범임을 알 수 있다. 따라서 (A)가 정답이다.

어휘 previous 이전의 currently 현재 in production 제작 중인 feature 특징으로 하다

## 159 Not / True

번역 이메일에서 잭슨 씨에 대해 언급하는 것은?
(A) 엠브리 씨의 웹사이트를 개선하고 싶어 한다.
(B) 전에 사진 작가였다.
(C) 미술관에서 열린 전시회에 참석했다.
(D) 엠브리 씨에게 호킨스 씨의 작품을 소개했다.

해설 중반부에 상대방인 호킨스의 사진을 언급하면서 그의 웹사이트에 있는 갤러리 페이지를 크리스에게 보여 주었다(I showed Chris the gallery page on your Web site)고 하므로 (D)가 정답이다.

어휘 improve 개선하다, 향상시키다 exhibition 전시(회) introduce 소개하다

> **Paraphrasing**
> 지문의 showed Chris the gallery page on your Web site
> → 정답의 introduced Mr. Embry to Mr. Hawkins's work

## 160 문장 삽입

번역 [1], [2], [3], [4]로 표시된 곳 중에서 다음 문장이 가장 적합한 곳은 어디인가?
"하지만 저희는 귀하의 다른 아이디어에도 열려 있습니다."
(A) [1]
(B) [2]
(C) [3]
(D) [4]

해설 제시된 문장은 대조나 반대를 나타낼 때 사용하는 However(하지만)로 시작하고, 상대방의 다른 아이디어에도 열려 있다는 의미를 지니고 있다. 따라서 상대방의 <던 필즈> 사진 시리즈를 재창작하는 것에 관심이 있다(We are particularly interested in the possibility of recreating your *Dawn Fields* series of photos)고 언급하는 문장 뒤인 [3]에 들어가 다른 아이디어도 고려해 볼 의향이 있음을 알리는 흐름이 되어야 자연스럽다. 따라서 (C)가 정답이다.

어휘 alternative 대체하는, 대안의

## 161-163 웹페이지

https://www.lmm.org.uk/exhibitions/structures_ancient_greece

<고대 그리스의 건축물>

[162(B)] **6월 2일 런던 메트로폴리탄 박물관(LMM)에서는 <고대 그리스의 건축물>을 선보일 것이며,** 이는 그 문명 사회의 주택과 신전, 극장, 경기장 등에 관한 전시회입니다. [162(B)] **연말까지 지속될 예정인** 이번 전시회에는 박물관 소장품에서 [161] **선별되거나** 잉글랜드 그리스 문화원에서 너그러이 대여해 준 고고학적 인공 유물뿐 아니라 [162(D)] **유명한 건물들의 대규모 모형도 포함될 것입니다.**

초대 손님만 참석할 수 있는 첫날 밤 개최 기념 파티 후, [162(A)] **6월 3일부터는 모든 박물관 관람객들이 추가 요금 없이 <고대 그리스의 건축물>을 관람할 수 있습니다.** LMM은 이 전시회의 첫 3주 동안 수요일마다 있을 관련 강연과 특별 투어를 위해 현지 전문가들도 모셔 두었습니다. 6월 9일에는 로나 스튜어트 박사님이 그리스 신전의 설계 이면에 있는 이론을 설명해 주실 것입니다. 그 다음 주에는 [163] **샤하라 바키르 박사님이 대리석 같은 건축 자재를 땅에서 어떻게 추출했는지 설명해 줄 것이며,** 데이빗 와일리 씨는 6월 23일에 건축 과정에 이용된 공법과 도구를 소개해 줄 것입니다. 이오르고스 갈라니스 교수님은 각 강연 직후에 있을 전시회 투어를 진행하실 것입니다.

어휘 structure 건축물, 구조(물) ancient 고대의 unveil 선보이다, 공개하다 exhibition 전시(회) civilization 문명 (사회) temple 신전 last 지속되다 include 포함하다 large-scale 대규모의 replica 모형, 복제물 archaeological 고고학의 artefact 인공 유물 draw 뽑다, 끌어내다 collection 소장(품) generously 너그러이 loan 대여해 주다 launch 개최, 출시 accessible 출입할 수 있는, 이용할 수 있는 museumgoer 박물관 관람객 for no extra fee 추가 요금 없이 engage 고용하다, 관여시키다 describe 설명하다 theory 이론 following 다음의 material 자재, 재료 marble 대리석 extract 추출하다 earth 지면, 땅 immediately after ~ 직후에

## 161 동의어

번역 첫 번째 단락, 다섯 번째 줄에 쓰인 "drawn"과 의미가 가장 가까운 것은?
(A) 끌린
(B) 묘사된
(C) 결론지어진
(D) 모아진

해설 drawn 앞뒤에 각각 쓰여 있는 archaeological artefacts와 from the museum's own collection으로 볼 때, '박물관의 자체 소장품에서 선별된 고고학적 인공 유물'과 같은 의미를 나타내야 자연스럽다. 이는 소장품 중에서 골라 모으는 방식으로 생각할 수 있으므로 '모아진'을 뜻하는 (D) gathered가 정답이다.

## 162 Not / True

번역 전시회에 대해 언급되지 않은 것은?
(A) 박물관 입장권 요금에 포함될 것이다.
(B) LMM에서 6개월 넘게 진행될 것이다.
(C) 앞서 다른 나라에서 시작되었다.
(D) 잘 알려진 건물들의 모형을 특별히 포함할 것이다.

해설 첫 단락에서 6월 2일에 선보인다(On 2 June, ~ will unveil *Structures of Ancient Greece*)고 한 것과 연말까지 지속될 예정(Scheduled to last through the end of the year)이라고 한 것에서 (B)를, 뒤이어 유명 건물들의 대규모 모형도 포함될 것(the exhibition will include large-scale replicas of famous buildings)이라고 한 부분에서 (D)도 확인할 수 있다. 두 번째 단락에서 6월 3일부터 추가 요금 없이 관람할 수 있을 것(Structures of Ancient Greece will be accessible to all museumgoers for no extra fee)이라고 한 것에서 (A)를 확인할 수 있다. 따라서 (C)가 정답이다.

어휘 run 진행되다 previously 앞서, 전에 mount 시작하다 feature 특징으로 하다, 특별히 포함하다 reproduction 복제(물) well-known 잘 알려진

> **Paraphrasing**
> 지문의 On 2 June, ~ will unveil / Scheduled to last through the end of the year → 보기 (B)의 will run at the LMM for more than six months
> 지문의 include large-scale replicas of famous buildings → 보기 (D)의 feature reproductions of well-known buildings
> 지문의 accessible to all museumgoers for no extra fee → 보기 (A)의 included in the cost of a museum ticket

## 163 추론

번역 누가 채굴 작업을 이야기할 것 같은가?
(A) 스튜어트 박사
**(B) 바키르 박사**
(C) 와일리 씨
(D) 갈라니스 교수

해설 두 번째 단락 중반부에 샤하라 바키르 박사가 대리석 같은 건축 자재를 땅에서 어떻게 추출했는지 설명해 줄 것(Dr. Shahara Bakir will explain how building materials such as marble were extracted from the earth)이라고 말한 부분이 채굴 작업에 관한 이야기에 해당하므로 (B)가 정답이다.

어휘 mining 채굴, 광업

> **Paraphrasing**
> 지문의 extracted from the earth → 질문의 mining

TEST 4

## 164-167 기사

과거를 돌아보는 스트리밍 업체

로스앤젤레스 (7월 30일)—최근 몇 달 사이에, [164] **구독형 스트리밍 서비스인 시네마틱스가 예전 영화와 텔레비전 시리즈를 기반으로 한 여러 시리즈를 공개하거나 계획을 발표했다. 이러한 경향은 오리지널 콘텐츠의 팬들 중에서 신규 구독자를 유치하려는** [167] **이리나 자이체바 신임 CEO의 시도로 여겨진다.**

[165] **한 가지 성공 사례는 30년 전에 최종화가 방영됐던 가족 코미디 <해피 홈>의 속편 <해피어 홈>이다. 조이스 쇼트를 포함해 원작에 출연했던 많은 스타들이 <해피어 홈>에서 자신의 캐릭터를 다시 연기하는 데 동의했다.** 자이체바 씨는 이 시리즈의 첫 방송이 있었던 6월에 시네마틱스에서 시청률이 가장 높았다고 주장했다.

[165] **하지만 시네마틱스가 기획한 <스타 시커스> 리메이크에 대한 논란은 이러한 프로그램 제작 방식의 부정적인 측면을 보여 준다. 이 신규 시리즈의 프로듀서인 마크 시먼스는** 최근의 한 인터뷰에서 [166] **다른 행성들을 탐험하는 우주선에 대한 이야기를** 담은 자신의 버전이 최신 특수 효과를 특징으로 하여 원작을 능가할 것이라고 단언했다. 격분한 팬들은 시먼스 씨가 무엇 때문에 원작이 그렇게 사랑받았는지 오해하고 있다는 반응을 보였다.

[165] **"1980년대의 <스타 시커스>는** 낙관적인 세계관 때문에 특별했죠, 화려한 기술 때문이 아니고요"라고 [167] **웹 포럼 스타 시커 연합의 운영자 릴리 콜웰은 말한다. "그러한 유산에 해를 끼친다면 많은 저희 회원들이 시네마틱스 구독을 취소할 겁니다."**

어휘 streamer 스트리밍 업체 subscription 구독 (가입) streaming 스트리밍(영상 또는 음성 등의 다중매체 파일을 전송 및 재생하는 방식) release 공개하다, 출시하다 based on ~을 바탕으로 previous 과거의, 이전의 trend 경향, 추세 attempt 시도 attract 유치하다, 끌어들이다 subscriber 구독자, 가입자 continuation 속편 air 방송하다 episode (방송의) 1회분 including ~을 포함해 reprise 반복하다 claim 주장하다 premiere 첫 방송 controversy 논란 demonstrate 보여 주다 downside 부정적인 측면 approach (접근) 방식 declare 단언하다, 공표하다 explore 탐험하다 outdo 능가하다

feature 특징으로 하다 state-of-the-art 최신의, 첨단의 outraged 격분한 respond 반응하다 optimistic 낙관적인 worldview 세계관 fancy 화려한, 고급의 moderator 조정자, 사회자 harm 해를 끼치다 legacy 유산

## 164 주제 / 목적

번역 기사의 목적은?
(A) 미디어 회사의 시장 전략에 대해 논의하는 것
(B) 스트리밍 서비스 업체의 상품 목록 개요를 제공하는 것
(C) 업체 신임 대표의 경력을 살펴보는 것
(D) 과거와 현재의 오락 형태를 비교하는 것

해설 첫 단락에 구독형 스트리밍 서비스인 시네마틱스가 과거의 영화와 텔레비전 시리즈를 기반으로 한 여러 시리즈를 공개하거나 계획을 발표했다(subscription streaming service Cinematix has released or announced plans for several series based on previous films and television series)는 말과 함께 그것이 신규 구독자를 끌어들이기 위한 신임 CEO의 시도로 여겨진다(The trend is believed to be an attempt by new CEO Irina Zaitseva to attract new subscribers ~)고 언급하고 있다. 이는 시장 전략에 해당하므로 (A)가 정답이다.

어휘 strategy 전략 overview 개요 catalogue (상품, 자료) 목록 examine 살펴보다 compare 비교하다

> **Paraphrasing**
> 지문의 subscription streaming service
> → 정답의 media company

## 165 Not / True

번역 쇼트 씨와 시먼스 씨 둘 다에 대해 사실인 것은?
(A) 시네마틱스 제작 작품에서 연기하도록 고용되었다.
(B) 최근에 작품에 관한 인터뷰에 응했다.
(C) 현재 일부 작품을 시네마틱스에서 스트리밍으로 볼 수 있다.
(D) 비교적 오래된 콘텐츠를 바탕으로 하는 시리즈에 관련되어 있다.

해설 두 번째 단락에 조이스 쇼트는 30년 전에 종영한 프로그램에 출연한 배우로서 후속작에서 동일 캐릭터를 다시 연기한다(Many stars of the original show, including Joyce Schott, agreed to reprise their characters for *Happier Home*)고 쓰여 있다. 세 번째 단락에는 마크 시먼스가 <스타 시커스> 리메이크 작품의 프로듀서(~ remake of *Star Seekers* ~ Mark Simmons, the new series' producer ~)라고 쓰여 있는데, 네 번째 단락에 <스타 시커스>가 1980년대 작품(The 1980s *Star Seekers*)으로 언급되어 있다. 따라서 두 사람 모두 오래된 과거의 프로그램을 바탕으로 제작하는 시리즈에 관련되어 있음을 알 수 있으므로 (D)가 정답이다.

어휘 production 제작 작품 output 작품 available 이용 가능한 be involved in ~에 관련되다, ~에 참여하다 relatively 비교적, 상대적으로

## 166 세부 사항

번역 시먼스 씨의 시리즈는 어떤 장르인가?
(A) 가족 드라마
(B) 공상 과학
(C) 재능 경연
(D) 여행 다큐멘터리

해설 시먼스의 이름이 언급되는 세 번째 단락에 그가 프로듀서를 맡은 프로그램이 다른 행성들을 탐험하는 우주선에 대한 이야기(this story of a spaceship exploring other planets)라고 쓰여 있으므로 (B)가 정답이다.

## 167 추론

번역 자이체바 씨 회사의 일부 고객에 대해 암시된 것은?
(A) 한 프로그램의 형편없는 특수 효과에 불만을 제기했다.
(B) <스타 시커스> 리메이크를 제안했다.
(C) 고전 영화를 보기 위해 구독 서비스를 이용한다.
(D) 콜웰 씨의 온라인 단체에 속해 있다.

해설 자이체바는 시네마틱스의 계획을 알리는 첫 단락에 이 업체의 신임 CEO(new CEO Irina Zaitseva)로 쓰여 있고, 마지막 단락에는 웹 포럼 스타 시커 연합의 관리자 릴리 콜웰이 이 연합의 많은 회원들이 시네마틱스 구독을 취소할 가능성이 있음(~ Lily Colwell, moderator of the Web forum Star Seeker Alliance. "A lot of our members will cancel their Cinematix subscriptions ~)을 암시하는 말이 쓰여 있다. 따라서 자이체바의 회사인 시네마틱스를 이용하는 일부 고객이 콜웰의 온라인 단체 소속임을 알 수 있으므로 (D)가 정답이다.

어휘 complain 불만을 제기하다 belong to+명사 ~에 속하다

## 168-171 이메일

> 발신: 제인 휴즈 <jhughes@keating-cs.com>
> 수신: 산토시 프라사드 <sprasad@who-mail.com>
> 날짜: 3월 1일
> 제목: 키팅 캐피탈 솔루션즈 사의 답변
>
> 프라사드 씨께,
>
> [168] **네트워크 보안 엔지니어로 키팅 캐피탈 솔루션즈 사에 입사하시는 데 동의해 주셔서 기쁩니다.** [169] **면접, 능력 테스트 결과, 추천서로 볼 때 귀하께서 정보 기술팀에 소중한 보탬이 되실 것이 분명합니다.** 따라서 [171] **귀하께서 앞서 계획하신 휴가를 떠날 수 있도록 근무 시작일을 미뤄 달라는 요청을 기꺼이 수용하고자 합니다.** 즐거운 시간 보내시기 바랍니다.
>
> [168] **따라서 저희는 3월 27일, 월요일, 오전 9시에 저희 사무실에서 귀하를 만나 뵙도록 하겠습니다.** 사진이 부착된 신분증과 은행 계좌 정보를 갖고 와주십시오. 그래야 [170] **세금 및 급여 관련하여 필요한 양식을 작성하실 수 있습니다. 저희 인사팀 직원 중 한 명인 켈리 모스가 오전에 이 서류 작업을 차근차근 설명해 줄 것입니다.** 모스 씨가 회사 정책과 직원들을 위한 자원도 자세히 안내해 줄 것입니다. 그것이 끝나면, 제가 귀하의 직책에 특화된 교육을 시작할 것입니다.

이 메시지를 받았다는 확인 답장 부탁드립니다. 궁금한 점 있으시면 무엇이든지 기꺼이 답변해 드리겠습니다.

제인 휴즈, 정보 기술 이사

어휘 reference 추천(서), 추천인 valuable 소중한 addition 보탬(이 되는 것) as such 따라서 accommodate 수용하다 postpone 미루다, 연기하다 previously 앞서, 이전에 identification 신분증 account 계좌, 계정 fill out 작성하다 necessary 필수의 payroll 급여 대상자 명단 human resources 인사(부) generalist (관청, 회사의) 일반인 직원 walk ~ through … ~에게 …을 차근차근 설명하다 familiarize 익숙하게 하다 policy 정책, 방침 resource 자원 -specific ~에 특화된 confirm 확인해 주다

## 168 주제 / 목적

번역 휴즈 씨는 왜 이메일을 보냈는가?
(A) 서류 제출 마감 기한을 정하기 위해
(B) 고용 면접 결과를 설명하기 위해
(C) 직원 정책에 관한 질문에 답변하기 위해
(D) 첫 출근일에 관한 정보를 제공하기 위해

해설 첫 단락에서 회사 입사에 동의해서 기쁘다(We are pleased that you have agreed to join Keating Capital Solutions ~)고 했고, 두 번째 단락에서는 3월 27일, 월요일, 오전 9시에 사무실에서 만나기(We will therefore plan to see you at our office at 9 A.M. on Monday, March 27)로 하면서 첫 출근 시간과 장소를 알리고 있다. 따라서 프라사드의 첫 출근일에 대해 알리기 위해 이메일을 보냈다는 것을 알 수 있으므로 (D)가 정답이다.

어휘 deadline 마감 기한 submission 제출 hiring 고용

## 169 추론

번역 프라사드 씨에 대해 암시된 것은?
(A) 3월 27일에 은행을 방문할 것이다.
(B) 직장 추천인들로부터 칭찬받았다.
(C) 막 휴가에서 복귀했다.
(D) 탄력적인 근무 일정을 요청했다.

해설 첫 단락에 면접, 능력 테스트 결과, 추천서를 볼 때 프라사드가 정보 기술팀에 소중한 보탬이 될 것이 분명하다(It is clear from your interviews, skills test results, and references that you will make a valuable addition to the information technology team)고 했다. 이를 통해 추천서에 프라사드를 칭찬하는 내용이 포함되어 있다는 사실을 알 수 있으므로 (B)가 정답이다.

어휘 praise 칭찬하다 flexible 탄력적인, 유연한

## 170 Not / True

번역 모스 씨에 대해 언급된 것은?
(A) 사원증을 발급해 줄 것이다.
(B) 직무 안내 책자를 수정할 것이다.
(C) 몇몇 양식 작성을 감독할 것이다.
(D) 입사 지원서 평가를 책임지고 있다.

해설 모스 씨의 이름이 언급되는 두 번째 단락에 세금 및 급여 관련하여 필요한 양식을 작성할 것(you can fill out the necessary tax and payroll forms)이라는 말과 함께 켈리 모스가 그 서류 작업을 차근차근 설명해 줄 것(Kelly Moss, ~ will walk you through this paperwork ~)이라고 알리고 있다. 이는 모스가 해당 서류의 작성을 감독한다는 뜻이므로 (C)가 정답이다.

어휘 issue 발급하다, 지급하다 revise 수정하다 oversee 감독하다 completion 완료 in charge of ~을 책임지고 있는 evaluate 평가하다 application 지원(서), 신청(서)

> **Paraphrasing**
> 지문의 fill out the necessary tax and payroll forms / walk you through this paperwork
> → 정답의 oversee the completion of some forms

## 171 문장 삽입

번역 [1], [2], [3], [4]로 표시된 곳 중에서 다음 문장이 가장 적합한 곳은 어디인가?
"즐거운 시간 보내시기 바랍니다."
(A) [1]
(B) [2]
(C) [3]
(D) [4]

해설 제시된 문장이 즐거운 시간을 보내기 바란다는 의미이므로 프라사드가 미리 계획한 휴가가 언급되는 문장 뒤인 [2]에 들어가는 것이 가장 자연스럽다. 따라서 (B)가 정답이다.

### 172-175 온라인 채팅

까미유 보들런 [오전 10시 13분]
[172] **에스피노 사에 프레젠테이션을 할 준비가 되셨나요?**

지로 후루카와 [오전 10시 14분]
네! 그리고 우리가 회의 직후에 점심 식사하러 나갈 수 있도록 지금 브라이언에게 회사 법인 카드를 받으러 갈 거예요.

까미유 보들런 [오전 10시 15분]
좋은 생각입니다.

브라이언 맥코이 [오전 10시 17분]
안녕하세요, 까미유. 여기 지로와 함께 있는데요. 죄송하지만, [173] **오드라가 이미 회사 법인 카드를 서명하고 가져가셔서, 두 분께서는 점심 식사를 위해 사용하실 수 없을 겁니다.**

까미유 보들런 [오전 10시 18분]
아, 이런! [172, 174] **제가 에스피노 사 직원들께 모시고 나갈 거라고 말씀드렸거든요.**

브라이언 맥코이 [오전 10시 19분]
음, [174] **얼링 키친에 배달 주문을 위해 우리 회사 카드가 등록되어 있어요. 회의실에서 식사하셔야 하겠지만,** 적어도 음식은 아주 맛있을 겁니다.

TEST 4

까미유 보들런 [오전 10시 20분]
선택의 여지가 없는 것 같네요.

브라이언 맥코이 [오전 10시 21분]
**[175] 제가 지로에게 그곳 배달 메뉴를 한 부 드릴게요. 원하시는 것을 제게 알려 주시면, 그곳이 문을 열 때 전화하겠습니다.**

까미유 보들런 [오전 10시 21분]
감사합니다, 브라이언.

어휘 pitch 홍보, 구입 권유 sign out 서명하고 사용하다 representative 직원, 대표자 take ~ out ~을 데리고 나가다 choice 선택(권)

## 172 추론

번역 보들런 씨와 후루카와 씨에 관해 무엇이 사실일 것 같은가?
(A) 재무 보고서를 준비하고 있다.
(B) 잠재 고객을 맞이하려는 참이다.
(C) 판매 계약 체결을 축하하고 있다.
(D) 사무실 파티를 준비하고 있다.

해설 첫 메시지에 보들런이 후루카와에게 에스피노 사에 프레젠테이션을 할 준비가 되었는지(Ready to make our pitch to Espino?) 물었고, 10시 18분 메시지에는 에스피노 사 직원들을 모시고 나갈 것(I told the Espino representatives that we would take them out)이라고 했다. 이를 통해 에스피노 사에 프레젠테이션을 하고 접대를 하려는 것으로 보아 잠재 고객을 맞는 상황이라고 판단할 수 있으므로 (B)가 정답이다.

어휘 financial 재무의, 재정의 be about to 막 ~하려는 참이다 host 맞이하다 potential 잠재적인 celebrate 축하하다 conclusion 체결, 종결 agreement 계약(서), 합의(서) make arrangements 준비하다, 마련하다

## 173 세부 사항

번역 보들런 씨와 후루카와 씨는 왜 회사 법인 카드를 사용할 수 없는가?
(A) 미리 승인을 받지 못했다.
(B) 한도액이 초과되었다.
(C) 오직 임원만 그것으로 구매할 수 있다.
(D) 동료 직원이 이미 빌려 갔다.

해설 맥코이가 10시 17분 메시지에 오드라가 이미 회사 법인 카드를 서명하고 가져가서 사용할 수 없을 것(Audra has already signed out the company card, so you two won't be able to use it for your lunch)이라고 말하므로 (D)가 정답이다.

어휘 obtain 받다 permission 승인 in advance 미리, 사전에 exceed 초과하다 executive 임원 coworker 동료 직원 borrow 빌리다

> **Paraphrasing**
> 지문의 Audra has already signed out the company card → 정답의 A coworker has already borrowed it.

## 174 의도 파악

번역 오전 10시 20분에, 보들런 씨가 "선택의 여지가 없는 것 같네요"라고 쓸 때, 의미하는 것은 무엇인가?
(A) 식사 계획 변경을 받아들일 것이다.
(B) 얼링 키친이 인근에서 가장 좋은 음식점임을 알고 있다.
(C) 그 동네에 매력적인 식당이 부족하다고 생각한다.
(D) 혼자 회의실을 준비할 것이다.

해설 10시 18분에 보들런이 에스피노 사 직원들에게 모시고 나갈 거라고 말했다(I told the Espino representatives that we would take them out)고 하자, 곧바로 맥코이가 얼링 키친에서 주문해서 대회의실에서 식사해야 한다(Earling Kitchen has our card on file for delivery orders. You'd have to eat in the conference room ~)고 말하고 있다. 이에 대해 보들런이 '선택의 여지가 없는 것 같다'고 대답한 것은 어쩔 수 없이 기존의 계획과 다르게 식사해야 한다는 사실을 수용한다는 뜻이므로 (A)가 정답이다.

어휘 accept 받아들이다 eatery 음식점 neighborhood 지역, 인근 lack 부족하다 attractive 매력적인 dining 식사 set up 준비하다, 설치하다 by oneself 혼자

## 175 세부 사항

번역 맥코이 씨는 왜 다른 사람들이 메뉴를 보기를 원하는가?
(A) 레스토랑의 실내 이미지를 보기 위해
(B) 가격대를 확인하기 위해
(C) 주문할 음식을 결정하기 위해
(D) 영업시간을 확인하기 위해

해설 10시 21분 메시지에 맥코이가 지로에게 배달 메뉴를 한 부 주겠다(I'm giving Jiro a copy of their delivery menu)는 말과 함께 원하는 것을 자신에게 알려 주면 전화하겠다(Let me know what you would like, and I'll call when they open)고 말하고 있다. 이는 원하는 음식을 결정해 알려 주면 주문해주겠다는 뜻이므로 (C)가 정답이다.

어휘 pricing range 가격대 determine 결정하다 verify 확인하다

### 176-180 이메일+일정표

수신: 로라 곤잘레스 <lauragonzales@fig-mail.com>
발신: 로이 채스테인 <rchastain@burgess.edu>
날짜: 3월 18일
제목: 회신: 초청

곤잘레스 씨께,

다양성, 형평성 및 포괄성 위원회는 **[176] 다음 달에 다른 버제스 동문들과 함께 1세대 대학 졸업생으로서 귀하의 경력에 대해 이야기해 달라는 요청을 수락해 주셔서** 기쁘게 생각합니다. **[177] 버제스 대학교의 현 1세대 학생 중 많은 사람들이 교육 전공자이므로, 이미 강의실에서 일하고 있는 귀하의 관점을 듣고 싶어 할 것으로 예상합니다.** 학생들과 어울릴 수 있도록 **[176] 토론이 끝난 후** 출장 요리 연회 시간에도 머무를 수 있으시길 바랍니다.

귀하의 질문에 대해서는, 유감스럽게도, 저희가 교통편 비용을 환급해 드릴 수 없을 것입니다. **[179] 버제스 대학 지하철역을 오가는 무료 셔틀**

버스가 현재 꽤 자주 운행되고 있으므로, 이것을 이용하실 것을 권해 드립니다. [178, 179] **첨부 파일에서 확인하실 수 있는 것처럼, 저희 행사장인 사익스 빌딩은 중앙 도서관 바로 건너편에 있습니다. 오후 5시에 행사가 시작되기 전에 준비하는 데 필요한 시간을 충분히 가질 수 있도록 오후 4시 30분까지 도착해 주시기 바랍니다.**

로이 채스테인

**어휘** diversity 다양성 equity 형평성, 공평 inclusion 포괄, 포함 alumni 동문, 동창 first-generation 1세대의 graduate 졸업생 major 전공자 be eager to ~하기를 간절히 바라다 perspective 관점, 시각 catered 출장 요리가 제공되는 reception 연회 mingle with ~와 어울리다 reimburse 비용을 환급해 주다 transportation 교통(편) unfortunately 유감스럽게도 attachment 첨부 파일 ample 충분한 preparation 준비

버제스 대학 캠퍼스 셔틀버스

운행 방향: 버제스 대학 지하철역 → 캠퍼스
정류장 및 출발 시각

| 버제스 대학 지하철역 | 북문 | 중앙 도서관 | 의대 | 쇼 기숙사 |
|---|---|---|---|---|
| [179]**오후 4시** | 오후 4시 15분 | [179]**오후 4시 21분** | 오후 4시 25분 | 오후 4시 28분 |
| 오후 4시 15분 | 오후 4시 30분 | 오후 4시 36분 | 오후 4시 40분 | 오후 4시 43분 |
| 오후 4시 30분 | 오후 4시 45분 | 오후 4시 51분 | 오후 4시 55분 | 오후 4시 58분 |
| 오후 4시 45분 | 오후 5시 | 오후 5시 6분 | 오후 5시 10분 | 오후 5시 13분 |

• [180] **여름철과 겨울철에는 셔틀버스가 덜 빈번하게 운행합니다.** 서비스 중단 관련 정보뿐 아니라 최신 일정표를 보려면 www.burgess.edu/campus/shuttle을 방문하시거나 i버제스 앱을 다운로드하시기 바랍니다.

**어휘** direction 방향, 길 안내 dormitory 기숙사 up-to-date 최신의 disruption 중단, 지장

## 176 세부 사항

**번역** 곤잘레스 씨는 다음 달에 어떤 행사에 참가할 것인가?
(A) 취업 박람회
(B) 동창회
(C) 패널 토론회
(D) 학술 컨퍼런스

**해설** 이메일 첫 단락에 곤잘레스 씨가 다음 달에 다른 버제스 동문들과 함께 1세대 대학 졸업자로서 자신의 경력을 이야기해 달라는 요청을 수락했다(you have accepted our invitation to join other Burgess alumni next month to discuss your career experiences ~)는 말이 쓰여 있다. 또한, 토론 후(after the discussion)에는 연회가 있다는 말도 있으므로 대학 졸업생 동기들이 패널로 나와 자신의 경력에 대해 토론하는 행사임을 알 수 있다. 따라서 (C)가 정답이다.

## 177 추론

**번역** 곤잘레스 씨는 누구일 것 같은가?
(A) 대학생
(B) 인력 채용 담당자
(C) 연구가
(D) 교육자

**해설** 이메일 첫 단락에 많은 사람들이 교육 전공자이므로 강의실에서 일하고 있는 곤잘레스 씨의 관점을 듣고 싶어 할 것으로 예상한다(~ they will be eager to hear your perspective as someone already working in the classroom)고 했으므로 (D)가 정답이다.

> **Paraphrasing**
> 지문의 someone already working in the classroom
> → 정답의 An educator

## 178 추론

**번역** 이메일 첨부 파일에 무엇이 있을 것 같은가?
(A) 캠퍼스 지도
(B) 출장 요리 메뉴
(C) 참가자 명단
(D) 등록 양식

**해설** 이메일 두 번째 단락에 첨부 파일에서 확인할 수 있는 것처럼 행사장인 사익스 빌딩이 중앙 도서관 바로 건너편에 있다(As you can see from the attachment, the Sikes Building, our venue, is just across the street from the Central Library)고 한 것에서 캠퍼스 지도가 있음을 유추할 수 있다. 따라서 (A)가 정답이다.

## 179 연계

**번역** 곤잘레스 씨가 몇 시에 셔틀버스에 탑승할 것 같은가?
(A) 오후 4시
(B) 오후 4시 15분
(C) 오후 4시 30분
(D) 오후 4시 45분

**해설** 이메일 두 번째 단락에 버제스 대학 지하철역을 오가는 무료 셔틀버스(The free campus shuttle bus to and from Burgess University Subway Station)를 이용하도록 권하면서 행사장이 있는 중앙 도서관 건너편 건물에 4시 30분까지 도착해 달라(the Sikes Building, our venue, is just across the street from the Central Library. Please arrive there by 4:30 P.M.)고 당부하는 말이 쓰여 있다. 일정표에서 4시 30분까지 중앙 도서관에 도착하려면 버제스 대학 지하철역에서 4시에 출발하는 버스를 타야 함을 알 수 있다. 따라서 (A)가 정답이다.

## 180 Not / True

**번역** 일정표에서 셔틀버스에 대해 언급하는 것은?
(A) 일부는 특정 정류장을 건너뛴다.
(B) 운행 빈도가 계절에 따라 다르다.
(C) 현재 한 대는 운행하고 있지 않다.
(D) 앱에서 실시간으로 위치를 볼 수 있다.

해설 일정표 하단에 셔틀버스가 여름철과 겨울철에는 덜 빈번하게 운행한다(Shuttle buses run less frequently during the summer and winter)는 내용이 있으므로 (B)가 정답이다.

어휘 skip 건너뛰다 frequency 빈도 at the moment 현재, 지금 viewable 볼 수 있는 in real time 실시간으로

> Paraphrasing
> 지문의 run less frequently during the summer and winter → 정답의 frequency changes seasonally

## 181-185 웹페이지+이메일

알브레히트 궁전

방문객용 정보

아름다운 정원들로 둘러싸인 17세기 색스니 건축 양식의 우아한 표본인, 알브레히트 궁전이 월요일과 공휴일을 제외하고 매일 오전 10시부터 오후 5시까지 개방됩니다. 이곳은 드레스덴 시에서 시외 버스로 약 20분 거리에 있습니다. [181] **차량 운전자들께서는 인근의 포센도르프 마을에 자동차를 세워 두신 다음, 오엘사 호텔에서 출발하는 셔틀버스를 이용하셔야 합니다.**

| 입장권 종류 | 가격 | 제공 서비스 |
|---|---|---|
| 세이버 | 5유로 | 궁전 구내 입장권 제공 |
| 스탠다드 | 12유로 | 세이버 서비스 이용 및 선별된 1층 방들에 대한 오디오 투어 제공 |
| 플러스 | 20유로 | 스탠다드 서비스 이용 및 특별 전시홀 입장권 제공 |
| [185] **프리미엄** | 27유로 | **플러스 서비스 이용 및 위층의 선별된 방들에 대한 가이드 투어 제공** |

다가오는 특별 전시회:

[182(D)] **색슨 스타일: 시간의 흐름에 따른 지역 의류** (4월 1일-5월 31일)

[182(C)] **왕의 얼굴: 알브레히트 통치자들의 유화 초상화** (6월 1일-7월 31일)

식탁 위의 모습: 17세기 색슨 요리 (8월 1일-9월 30일)

[182(B)] **발굽을 지닌 친구들: 알브레히트의 말들** (10월 1일-11월 30일)

어휘 architecture 건축 (양식) surrounded by ~로 둘러싸인 roughly 약, 대략 grounds 구내 access 이용(권) select 선별된 admission 입장 exhibition 전시(회) upcoming 다가오는 local 지역의 portrait 초상화 cuisine 요리 hooved(= hoofed) 발굽이 있는

수신: visitor.info@albrechtpalace.de
발신: n.romero@etn.eu
날짜: 1월 4일
제목: 문의

안녕하세요,

제 이름은 나오미 로메로이며, 유럽 섬유 협회(ETN)에서 근무하고 있습니다. [184] **ETN은 유럽의 섬유 업계 전문가들에게 교육과 교류 기회를 제공함으로써 이분들의 전문 지식을 발전시키는 것을 목표로 하고 있습니다.**

올해, 저희 연례 컨퍼런스가 5월 21일부터 24일까지 드레스덴에서 개최될 것이며, 참석자들께 알브레히트 궁전 관람을 제공해 드리기를 바라고 있습니다. 이분들께서는 그때 운영되는 특별 전시회를 즐거워하실 것입니다. 그런데 [183, 185] **대규모 단체 관람객이 가이드 투어에 참가할 수 있나요?** 저희는 참가자들께서 위층 방에 있는 그 유명한 태피스트리와 침대 커버를 보실 수 있기를 정말로 원합니다. 이를 가능하게 하기 위해, 필요할 경우, 저희는 이 관람의 참가자 수를 제한할 것입니다.

곧 소식 들을 수 있기를 바랍니다.

나오미 로메로
담당자, ETN

어휘 textile 섬유 aim 목표로 하다 advance 발전시키다 expertise 전문 지식 professional 전문가 opportunity 기회 annual 연례적인 take place 개최되다, 진행되다 attendee 참석자 excursion (짧은) 여행 participant 참가자 tapestry 태피스트리(여러 색실로 그림을 짜 넣은 직물)

### 181 추론

번역 알브레히트 궁전에 관해 암시된 것은?
(A) 기념품 매장이 인기 있다.
(B) 운영 시간이 계절마다 다르다.
(C) 도시 중심에 위치해 있다.
(D) 관광객들에게 주차 공간을 제공하지 않는다.

해설 웹페이지 첫 번째 단락에 차량 운전자들은 인근의 포센도르프 마을에 자동차를 세워 두고 오엘사 호텔에서 출발하는 셔틀버스를 이용해야 한다(Drivers should leave their cars in the nearby town of Possendorf and take the shuttle bus that leaves from Hotel Oelsa)고 쓰여 있어 알브레히트 궁전 내에 주차할 수 없다는 것을 알 수 있으므로 (D)가 정답이다.

어휘 be located in ~에 위치해 있다

### 182 Not / True

번역 다가오는 특별 전시회의 주제가 아닌 것은?
(A) 가구 양식
(B) 한 종류의 동물
(C) 인물화
(D) 한 지역의 패션 경향

해설 다가오는 특별 전시회 관련 정보가 제시되는 웹페이지 마지막 단락에 색슨 스타일: 시간의 흐름에 따른 지역 의류(Saxon Style: Local Clothing over Time)에서 (D), 왕의 얼굴: 알브레히트 통치자들의 유화 초상화(Royal Faces: Oil Portraits of Albrecht's Rulers)에서 (C), 그리고 발굽을 지닌 친구들: 알브레히트의 말들(Hooved Friends: Horses at Albrecht)에서 (B)를 각각 확인할 수 있다. 하지만, 가구 양식과 관련된 정보는 언급되어 있지 않으므로 (A)가 정답이다.

> **Paraphrasing**
> 지문의 Local Clothing over Time
> → 보기 (D)의 An area's fashion trends
> 지문의 Oil Portraits of Albrecht's Rulers
> → 보기 (C)의 Paintings of people
> 지문의 Horses at Albrecht
> → 보기 (B)의 A type of animal

## 183 주제 / 목적

번역 이메일의 목적은 무엇인가?
(A) 방문객 제한에 관해 묻는 것
(B) 다큐멘터리 프로젝트를 제안하는 것
(C) 역사적인 물품을 빌리는 일에 관해 문의하는 것
(D) 특별 전시회에 지원을 제공하는 것

해설 이메일의 두 번째 단락에 컨퍼런스 참석자들에게 관람을 제공하고 싶다고 말하며 대규모 단체 관람객이 가이드 투어에 참가할 수 있는지(do you allow large groups to join the guided tours?) 묻고 있으므로 (A)가 정답이다.

어휘 restriction 제한 inquire 문의하다 borrow 빌리다 assistance 지원, 도움

> **Paraphrasing**
> 지문의 do you allow large groups to join the guided tours? → 정답의 ask about a restriction on visitors

## 184 세부 사항

번역 이메일에 따르면, ETN은 무엇인가?
(A) 역사 동호회
(B) 제조 회사
(C) 전문가 협회
(D) 언론 매체

해설 이메일의 첫 번째 단락에 나오미 로메로가 자신은 유럽 섬유 협회(ETN)에서 근무하고 있고, ETN은 유럽의 섬유 업계 전문가들에게 교육과 교류 기회를 제공함으로써 그들의 전문 지식을 발전시키는 것을 목표로 한다(The ETN aims to advance the expertise of Europe's textile industry professionals by providing them with education and networking opportunities)고 쓰여 있어 전문가들을 위한 협회임을 알 수 있으므로 (C)가 정답이다.

## 185 연계

번역 ETN 단체 입장객들은 어떤 종류의 입장권이 필요할 것 같은가?
(A) 세이버
(B) 스탠다드
(C) 플러스
(D) 프리미엄

해설 이메일의 두 번째 단락에 대규모 단체 관람객이 가이드 투어에 참가하도록 허용하는지(do you allow large groups to join the guided tours?) 묻고 있어 가이드 투어가 필요하다는 것을 알 수 있다. 웹 도표의 마지막 항목에 프리미엄 입장권이 가이드 투어를 제공한다(Premium / Provides Plus access AND guided tour of select rooms on upper floors)고 쓰여 있으므로 (D)가 정답이다.

## 186-190 컨퍼런스 일정표 + 이메일 + 이메일

전국 디지털 마케팅 협회 (NDMA)
가을 컨퍼런스
10월 7일, 오후 일정표

| 장소 | 오후 1시 | 오후 2시 | 오후 3시 | 오후 4시 |
|---|---|---|---|---|
| 중앙 홀 | AI 툴을 이용한 콘텐츠 창작 (발표) | | [186] **검색 순위 상승시키기** (발표) | |
| 세미나실 A | 마케팅 실험: 세 가지 사례 연구 (발표) | | | [187] **강력한 고객 관계 구축 (패널 토론)** |
| 세미나실 B | 빅 데이터 활용 (세미나) | 숏폼 영상 이용 (세미나) | 효과적인 이메일 캠페인 (세미나) | 적절한 인플루언서 찾기(세미나) |
| 테라스 | 레드 래빗 마케팅 솔루션즈 (후원을 받은 시연회) | 친목을 위한 휴식 | [186] **대화형 디스플레이 기술** (전시) | |

어휘 creation 창작, 창조 climb 상승시키다, 오르다 ranking 순위 experimentation 실험 case study 사례 연구 relationship 관계 harness 이용하다 effective 효과적인 sponsored 후원을 받은 demonstration 시연(회) break 휴식 시간 interactive 대화형의, 상호 작용의 exhibition 전시(회)

발신: 줄리앤 프랭크스
수신: 안종진
날짜: 10월 7일
제목: 수고 많으셨습니다!
첨부: 참가자_서류

안녕하세요, 종진.

빈스의 몸이 안 좋아진 뒤에 오후 패널 시간을 진행하는 것에 동의해 주셔서 다시 한번 감사드립니다. 제가 그 행사 동영상을 볼 기회가 있었는데, 정말 깊은 인상을 받았습니다. [187, 188] **글렌 스탠리가 말씀이 많아서 힘든 토론 참가자일 수 있는데, 아주 능숙하게 대해 주셨습니다. 청중의 박수 소리로 볼 때 정말로 토론을 즐거워했다는 것을 알 수 있었으며, 이는 대부분 귀하 덕분이었습니다.**

그리고 서둘러 무대로 모시느라, [190] **귀하께 참가자 서류를 작성하도록 하는 것을 잊었는데, 거기에는 NDMA가 귀하의 참가 녹화 영상을 사용할 수 있도록 허락하는 동의서가 포함되어 있습니다.** 제가 이것을 이 이메일에 첨부해 드렸습니다. [190] **저희가 행사 동영상을 온라인에 게시할 수 있도록 이것을 작성해서 다시 보내 주시겠습니까?**

감사합니다.

줄리앤

TEST 4

어휘 participant 참가자 agree 동의하다 moderate 진행하다, 사회를 보다 ill 아픈 impressed 깊은 인상을 받은 talkativeness 수다스러움 handle 대하다, 다루다 skillfully 능숙하게 applause 박수 audience 청중, 관객 largely 대부분, 대체로 in one's hurry 서두른 나머지 include 포함하다 consent 동의, 합의 allow 허용하다 participation 참가 attach 첨부하다 fill out 작성하다 post 게시하다

발신: 애니카 린드스트롬
수신: 안종진
날짜: 11월 23일
제목: 연락 드립니다

안 씨께,

저는 온라인 비즈니스 잡지 <딥비즈>의 기자이며, 현재 유능한 패널 진행자가 되는 법에 관한 기사를 작성하고 있습니다. **[190] 지난달 귀하가 NDMA 가을 컨퍼런스에서 보여 주신 모습을, 제가 그 단체의 웹사이트에 올라온 동영상으로 보았는데,** 본보기가 될 만한 것이었으며, 저희 독자들에게 유용할 팁이 있으실 거라는 확신이 들었습니다. **[189] 제 기사를 위해 귀하의 기법과 관련해 몇 가지 질문을 드려도 될까요?** 괜찮으시면, 귀하의 전화번호와 향후 며칠간 언제 시간이 되시는지를 이 이메일에 회신해 알려 주시기 바랍니다.

애니카 린드스트롬, 기자
<딥비즈>

어휘 effective 유능한, 효과적인 moderator 진행자, 사회자 organization 단체, 기관 exemplary 본보기가 될 만한, 모범적인 be willing to ~할 의향이 있다 availability 시간이 되는지 여부

## 186 세부 사항

번역 어느 두 행사가 같은 시간대에 예정되어 있는가?
(A) "빅 데이터 활용"과 친목을 위한 휴식
(B) "검색 순위 상승시키기"와 "대화형 디스플레이 기술"
(C) "적절한 인플루언서 찾기"와 "빅 데이터 활용"
(D) "AI 툴을 이용한 콘텐츠 창작"과 "대화형 디스플레이 기술"

해설 일정표에 '검색 순위 상승시키기(Climb the Search Rankings)'와 '대화형 디스플레이 기술(Interactive Display Technology)'이 각각 중앙홀과 테라스에서 3시부터 진행되는 것으로 나와 있으므로 (B)가 정답이다.

## 187 연계

번역 스탠리 씨의 전문 영역은 무엇이겠는가?
(A) 영상 편집
(B) 이메일 광고
(C) 고객 관리
(D) 마케팅 실험

해설 첫 번째 이메일의 첫 단락에 글렌 스탠리가 말이 많아서 힘든 토론 참가자일 수 있다(Glen Stanley can be a difficult panelist because of his talkativeness)고 했으므로 스탠리가 토론 참가자였음을 알 수 있다. 그리고 일정표에서 '강력한 고객 관계 구축'(Building Strong Client Relationships)이 패널 토론(Panel discussion)으로 진행되는 것을 알 수 있으므로 (C)가 정답이다.

## 188 추론

번역 첫 번째 이메일이 스탠리 씨에 대해 암시하는 것은?
(A) 연사의 준비를 도왔다.
(B) 컨퍼런스 청중으로 있었다.
(C) 호평을 받은 행사에 참가했다.
(D) 몸이 안 좋았던 발표자를 대신했다.

해설 첫 번째 이메일의 첫 단락에 스탠리가 토론 참가자(Glen Stanley can be a difficult panelist ~)라는 말이 있고, 청중의 박수 소리로 볼 때 정말로 토론을 즐거워했다는 것을 알 수 있었다(I could tell by their applause that the audience really enjoyed the discussion ~)고 했다. 따라서 스탠리가 사람들로부터 좋은 평가를 받은 행사에 참가했음을 알 수 있으므로 (C)가 정답이다.

어휘 participate in ~에 참가하다 fill in for ~을 대신하다 unwell 몸이 편찮은

**Paraphrasing**
지문의 the audience really enjoyed the discussion
→ 정답의 an event that was well received

## 189 주제 / 목적

번역 두 번째 이메일의 주 목적은?
(A) 인터뷰를 요청하는 것
(B) 기사 수정을 제안하는 것
(C) 컨퍼런스에 관한 피드백을 요청하는 것
(D) 웹사이트상의 정보를 확인해 주는 것

해설 두 번째 이메일 후반부에 자신의 기사를 위해 몇 가지 질문을 해도 될지(Would you be willing to let me ask you a few questions about your techniques for my article?) 묻고 있다. 이는 기사 작성을 위한 인터뷰를 요청하는 것이므로 (A)가 정답이다.

어휘 extend a request 요청하다 revision 수정 confirm 확인해 주다

**Paraphrasing**
지문의 let me ask you a few questions
→ 정답의 interview request

## 190 연계

번역 안 씨에 대해 어떤 결론을 내릴 수 있는가?
(A) NDMA에서 리더 역할을 맡고 있다.
(B) 동영상이 공개적으로 공유되는 데 동의했다.
(C) 최근 온라인 잡지에서 언급되었다.
(D) 10월에 두 곳의 컨퍼런스에 참가했다.

해설 첫 번째 이메일 두 번째 단락에 참가 녹화 영상을 사용할 수 있도록 허락하는 동의서가 있다(~ which includes a consent form allowing the NDMA to use recordings of your participation)며, 동영상을 온라인에 게시할 수 있도록 그것을 작성해서 보내 줄 수 있는지(Could you fill it out and return it so that we can post the event video online?) 안 씨에게 물었는데, 두 번째 이메일 초반부에 NDMA 가을 컨퍼런스에 참석한 안 씨의 모습을 그 단체의 웹사이트에 올라온 동영상으로 봤다(~ which I saw in a video on the organization's Web site ~)고 했다. 이를 통해 안 씨가 동영상 게시를 동의했음을 알 수 있으므로 (B)가 정답이다.

어휘 hold 맡다, 유지하다 publicly 공개적으로 take part in ~에 참가하다

**191-195 웹페이지+웹페이지+이메일**

https://www.larosetours.com/msat

슬래글 산 항공 투어

라로즈 투어에서 헬리콥터 모험을 즐겨보세요! 한 시간 길이의 이 비행은 먼저 역사적인 라로즈 시내 상공을 지나 주요 명소인 활화산인 슬래글 산의 멋진 경관이 내려다보이는 곳을 향해 날아갑니다. 주변의 우림 지역 상공을 지나 복귀하는 동안, 194 **탑승객들은 너무 멀리 떨어져 있어서 오직 공중에서만 볼 수 있는 폭포도 발견하게 됩니다.** 가이드가 내내 함께하면서 흥미로운 설명을 제공하고 질문에 답변해 드립니다.

슬래글 산 항공 투어는 라로즈 공항에서 출발하고 종료됩니다. 월요일부터 금요일까지 오전 10시, 오후 1시, 오후 3시에 출발합니다. 191 **이 산에 대한 개인 및 그룹 맞춤형 헬리콥터 투어도 이용 가능합니다.** 추가 정보는 이 페이지를 방문하십시오.

어휘 aerial 하늘의, 공중의 historic 역사적인 attraction 명소, 인기 장소 stunning 굉장히 멋진 overhead 머리 위의 active volcano 활화산 surrounding 주변의 rainforest 우림 spot 발견하다 remote 멀리 떨어진 observe 관찰하다 on hand 함께하는, 대기하는 throughout 내내 commentary 설명, 해설 available 이용 가능한 custom 맞춤의, 주문 제작의

https://www.larosetours.com/confirmation

라로즈 투어

다음 투어를 예약해 주셔서 감사합니다. 예약 세부 내역뿐 아니라, 라로즈가 귀하의 투어와 관련된 안내 또는 최신 정보를 제공해 드릴 수 있도록 아래에 있는 귀하의 연락처가 정확한지도 확인해 주시기 바랍니다.

예약 확인 번호: 984533

고객 정보
성명: 데빈 라이스
전화번호: (707) 555-0149
이메일: devin.rice@obymail.com

예약 세부 내역

| | |
|---|---|
| 슬래글 산 항공 투어, 4월 27일 192 **오전 10시**<br>성인 2인, 어린이 2인 | 1,540달러 |
| 미릭 동굴 투어, 4월 28일 192 **오전 9시**<br>성인 2인, 어린이 2인 | 192달러 |
| 총액 | 1,732달러 |

195 **결제 완료 (신용카드 마지막 숫자 4308)**

어휘 reserve 예약하다 following 다음의, 아래의 details 상세 정보 ensure 확실히 하다, 보장하다 correct 정확한 instructions 안내, 설명 confirmation 확인, 확정 cave 동굴 complete 완료하다

발신: customerservice@larosetours.com
수신: devin.rice@obymail.com
제목: 투어 취소
날짜: 4월 26일

라이스 씨께,

라로즈 투어에서는 194 **내일 오전 10시로 예정되었던 슬래글 산 항공 투어가 취소되었음**을 알려 드리게 되어 유감스럽게 생각합니다. 일기 예보에서 오후까지 강한 비바람을 예측하고 있으며, 이러한 상황에서 헬리콥터 비행은 안전하지 않습니다.

하지만 악천후가 오래 지속될 것으로 예상되지는 않기 때문에, 투어를 다시 예약하시는 걸 권해 드립니다. 방금 취소하신 고객이 있어서 4월 29일 오후 1시에 귀하의 일행 분들께서 예약할 수 있는 빈자리가 생겼습니다. 이 자리를 원하시면 193(D) **저희에게 (808) 555-0173번으로 전화 주시기 바랍니다.**

그렇게 하지 않으면 195 **귀하께서 원래 결제하신 방법으로 전액 환불해 드립니다.** 193(A) **이 이메일에 답장하시거나** 동굴 투어를 위해 오실 때 193(C) **저희 사무실에 들르셔서** 이 절차를 시작하실 수 있습니다.

하나 이노우에, 고객 서비스 담당자
라로즈 투어

어휘 cancellation 취소 predict 예측하다 condition 조건, 상태 inclement weather 악천후 last 지속되다 encourage 권하다 rebook 다시 예약하다 opening 빈자리, 공석 party 일행 claim 차지하다, 요청하다 spot 자리, 장소 otherwise 그렇지 않으면 refund 환불 via ~을 통해 method 방식 initiate 시작하다 process 과정 drop in ~에 들르다

**191 Not / True**

번역 첫 번째 웹페이지에서 라로즈 투어에 대해 언급된 것은?
(A) 가이드를 고용하려 하고 있다.
(B) 주말에 영업한다.
(C) 개인 맞춤형 투어를 운영한다.
(D) 공항에 본사를 두고 있다.

해설 첫 번째 웹페이지 두 번째 단락에 개인 및 그룹 맞춤형 헬리콥터 투어도 이용 가능하다(We are also available for custom individual and group helicopter tours of the mountain)고 했으므로 (C)가 정답이다.

어휘 seek to ~하려 하다 operate 운영하다 personalized 개인에게 맞춘 be headquartered in ~에 본사를 두다

> Paraphrasing
> 지문의 available for custom individual ~ tours
> → 정답의 operates personalized tours

## 192 Not / True

번역 두 번째 웹페이지에서 라이스 씨에 대해 언급된 것은?
(A) 오전에 하는 활동을 선택했다.
(B) 회사 야유회를 준비하고 있다.
(C) 문화 공연에 참석할 계획이다.
(D) 한 달도 더 전에 미리 예약했다.

해설 두 번째 웹페이지 예약 세부 내역에 두 차례의 투어가 모두 오전 시간(10 A.M., 9 A.M.)으로 표기되어 있으므로 (A)가 정답이다.

어휘 activity 활동 organize 준비하다, 조직하다 outing 나들이, 짧은 여행 corporate 기업의 retreat 야유회 in advance 미리, 사전에

## 193 Not / True

번역 이메일에서 제안된 조치가 아닌 것은?
(A) 이메일 답장 보내기
(B) 온라인 양식 작성하기
(C) 직접 사무실 방문하기
(D) 전화하기

해설 이메일 두 번째 단락에 다른 고객이 취소한 자리를 원하면 전화하라(Please call us at (808) 555-0173 ~)고 한 부분에서 (D)를, 세 번째 단락에 이메일에 답장하거나(responding to this e-mail) 사무실에 들러(dropping in our office) 환불을 할 수 있다고 알리는 부분에서 (A)와 (C)를 확인할 수 있다. 하지만 온라인 양식 작성과 관련된 정보는 제시되어 있지 않으므로 (B)가 정답이다.

어휘 fill out 작성하다 form 양식, 서식 in person 직접 (가서)

> Paraphrasing
> 지문의 Please call us at ~
> → 보기 (D)의 Making a telephone call
> 지문의 responding to this e-mail
> → 보기 (A)의 Sending a reply e-mail
> 지문의 dropping in our office
> → 보기 (C)의 Visiting an office in person

## 194 연계

번역 취소된 투어에 대해 무엇이 사실일 것 같은가?
(A) 산비탈에 착륙하는 헬리콥터를 포함한다.
(B) 그 회사에서 가장 인기 있는 여행이다.
(C) 몇몇 폭포를 볼 수 있는 유일한 방법을 제공한다.
(D) 자연 지역 위로만 비행한다.

해설 이메일 첫 단락에 내일 오전 10시로 예정되었던 슬래글 산 항공 투어가 취소되었다(the Mount Slagle Aerial Tour scheduled for 10 A.M. tomorrow has been canceled)는 말이 쓰여 있는데, 슬래글 산 항공 투어를 설명하는 첫 번째 웹페이지 첫 단락에 너무 멀리 떨어져 있어서 오직 공중에서만 볼 수 있는 폭포도 발견할 것(passengers will also spot waterfalls so remote that they can only be observed from the air)이라는 정보가 제시되어 있으므로 (C)가 정답이다.

어휘 involve 포함하다 land 착륙하다 mountainside 산등성이 excursion (짧은) 여행, 야유회 exclusively 독점적으로

> Paraphrasing
> 지문의 they(waterfalls) can only be observed from the air → 정답의 the only way to see some waterfalls

## 195 연계

번역 라이스 씨에 대해 어떤 결론을 내릴 수 있는가?
(A) 최근에 일부 연락처가 변경됐다.
(B) 제안된 대체 투어에 참가할 수 없을 것이다.
(C) 두 번째 웹페이지에 있는 안내를 따르지 않았다.
(D) 신용카드로 환불을 받을 자격이 있다.

해설 이메일 세 번째 단락에 라이스 씨에게 원래 결제한 방법으로 전액 환불해 준다(we are happy to provide you with a full refund via your original payment method)고 했는데, 두 번째 웹페이지 마지막 부분에 라이스 씨가 신용카드로 결제(Payment Completed (Credit card ending in 4308))한 것을 확인할 수 있다. 따라서 (D)가 정답이다.

어휘 alternative 대체의, 대안의 follow 따르다 instructions 안내, 설명 be eligible for ~에 대한 자격이 있다

## 196-200 웹페이지 + 이메일 + 고객 후기

http://www.elegana.com/products/smoothwell/conditioner

엘레가나
스무스웰 컨디셔너, 250ml
제품 번호 220
모발을 부드럽고 윤기 있게 하는 영양 컨디셔너

* 염색이나 파마한 모발뿐만 아니라 모든 유형과 질감의 모발에 수분을 공급하고 부드럽게 하기 위한 용도
* 196 **무향이며**, 일반적인 알레르기 유발 물질 없이 제조
* 독립 연구소에서 안전성 및 효능 테스트

이 제품들도 확인해보세요.

| 스무스웰 컨디셔너 30ml 여행용 사이즈 (제품 번호 230) | [199] **스무스웰 샴푸 (제품 번호 210)** | 스무스웰 헤어 트리트먼트 (제품 번호 240) | 생기를 더해 주는 드라이 샴푸 (제품 번호 510) |
|---|---|---|---|

어휘 nourishing 영양분이 많은 intended to ~하기 위한 hydrate 수분을 공급하다 smooth 매끄럽게 만들다 texture 질감 dyed 염색한 permed 파마한 fragrance 향, 향기 allergen 알레르기 유발 물질 independent 독립적인 laboratory 연구소, 실험실 efficacy 효능, 효험 perk up 생기를 더해 주다 dry shampoo 물 없이 사용하는 샴푸

수신: 브래드 코헨
발신: 신미영
제목: 스무스웰 컨디셔너 프로젝트
날짜: 11월 30일

안녕하세요, 브래드.

저희 스무스웰 컨디셔너와 관련된 잠재 시장 조사 프로젝트에 관해 질문이 있습니다.

[197] **첫 번째는, 저희 임원 중 한 분께서 샴푸 병에 있는 "황산 무첨가" 표시를 컨디셔너 병에도 추가하자고 제안해 주셨습니다. 하지만 컨디셔너에는 일반적으로 황산이 포함되지 않기 때문에, 이 표시가 정말로 소비자들을 끌어들일지 궁금합니다. 이를 알아보기 위해 간단한 조사를 기획해 주실 수 있을까요?**

또한, [200] **고객들은 컨디셔너를 병에서 짜기 힘들다는 불만을 계속 제기하고 있습니다. 특히 병이 거의 비어 있을 때요.** 저희 디자인팀에서 몇 가지 가능성 있는 해결책을 제시해 주었는데, 가장 좋은 것을 알아낼 수 있도록 소비자들이 테스트하게 해 주셨으면 합니다. 테스트하는 옵션의 수에 따라 이러한 조사 비용은 얼마나 달라지나요?

알려 주시기 바랍니다.

신미영, 부장
스무스웰 제품 라인팀

어휘 inquiry 질문, 문의 potential 잠재적인 involve 관련되다, 수반하다 executive 임원, 이사 sulfate 황산(염) include 포함하다 attract 끌어들이다 consumer 소비자 firm 회사, 업체 design 고안하다, 만들다 complain 불만을 제기하다 squeeze 짜내다 especially 특히, 특별히 come up with ~을 제시하다, ~을 생각해 내다 solution 해결책 depending on ~에 따라, ~에 달려 있는

http://www.elegana.com/products/smoothwell/conditioner/reviews

엘레가나

스무스웰 컨디셔너, 250ml

평점: ★★★★★

이 제품을 발견해서 너무 기뻐요! [198] **몇 년 전에, 비가 많이 오는 지역으로 이사했는데,** 습기 때문에 제 머리가 부스스하게 엉망이 되었거든요. 다행히, [199] **미용 제품 매장 점원이 스무스웰 라인을 추천해 주었어요. 샴푸가 괜찮긴 하지만** 가격만큼의 가치가 있다는 생각은 들지 않아서, 지금은 컨디셔너만 사용하고 있습니다. 제 머리를 얼마나 윤기 있고 부드럽게 만들어 주는지 아주 마음에 들어요. 그리고 새로 디자인된 병도 마음에 듭니다. 글씨가 더 커져서 읽기 쉽고, [200] **뚜껑이 하단에 있어 컨디셔너를 짜는 데 훨씬 힘이 덜 들어요.**

- 샌디 M.

어휘 rating 평점, 등급 moisture 습기 frizzy 부스스한, 곱슬곱슬한 mess 엉망(인 상태) worth 가치가 있는 cap 뚜껑 take less effort to ~하는 데 힘이 덜 들다

TEST 4

## 196 Not / True

번역 스무스웰 컨디셔너에 대해 언급된 것은?
(A) 향이 없다.
(B) 한 가지 사이즈로만 판매된다.
(C) 미용실에서 폭넓게 쓰인다.
(D) 매일 사용해야 한다.

해설 웹페이지 초반부에 쓰여 있는 스무스웰 컨디셔너의 특징 세 가지 중 두 번째 항목에 무향(Fragrance-free)이라는 정보가 언급되어 있으므로 (A)가 정답이다.

어휘 scent 향, 냄새 be meant to ~해야 하다, ~하기 위한 것이다 apply 사용하다, 바르다

> Paraphrasing
> 지문의 Fragrance-free → 정답의 does not have a scent

## 197 세부 사항

번역 신 씨가 코헨 씨에게 도움을 요청하는 한 가지는 무엇인가?
(A) 임원들에게 마케팅 계획 발표하기
(B) 경쟁 제품에 특정 성분이 포함되어 있는지 조사하기
(C) 홍보 문구가 효과적일지 결정하기
(D) 상품을 위해 더 매력적인 포장지 디자인하기

해설 신 씨가 작성한 이메일의 두 번째 단락에, "황산 무첨가" 표시를 컨디셔너 병에도 추가하자는 임원의 제안과 관련해, 컨디셔너에는 일반적으로 황산이 포함되지 않기 때문에 그 표시가 정말로 소비자들을 끌어들일지 궁금하다면서 알리면서 이를 파악할 수 있는 조사를 기획해 달라(~ I wonder if the badge would really attract consumers. Could your firm design a simple study to find out?)고 요청하고 있다. 이는 고객을 끌어들이기 위한 홍부 문구가 효과가 있을지 확인해 달라고 하는 것이므로 (C)가 정답이다.

어휘 present 발표하다 competing 경쟁하는 include 포함하다
ingredient 성분, 재료 determine 밝혀 내다, 결정하다
promotional 홍보의 claim 주장 effective 효과적인
attractive 매력적인 packaging 포장(지) goods 상품

## 198 Not / True

번역 고객 후기에 따르면, 샌디 M.에 대해 사실인 것은?
(A) 현재 기후가 습한 곳에 살고 있다.
(B) 미용 제품 매장에서 근무한다.
(C) 최근에 자른 머리 모양이 불만스러웠다.
(D) 스무스웰 컨디셔너가 너무 비싸다고 생각한다.

해설 샌디 M.은 고객 후기를 작성한 사람이며, 초반부에 몇 년 전에 비가 많이 오는 지역으로 이사했다(A few years ago, I moved to a very rainy area)고 했으므로 (A)가 정답이다.

어휘 humid 습한 be dissatisfied with ~에 불만스러워하다
overpriced 너무 비싼

> Paraphrasing
> 지문의 a very rainy area → 정답의 in a humid climate

## 199 연계

번역 샌디 M.이 사용했던 나머지 엘레가나 제품의 제품 코드는 무엇인가?
(A) 230
(B) 210
(C) 240
(D) 510

해설 고객 후기 중반부에 미용 제품 매장 점원이 스무스웰 라인을 추천했다는 말과 함께 샴푸가 괜찮았다(a beauty store clerk recommended the Smoothwell line to me. I found the shampoo to be fine)는 말이 있다. 웹페이지에 스무스웰 샴푸 코드가 210(Smoothwell Shampoo (Item 210))으로 표기되어 있으므로 (B)가 정답이다.

## 200 연계

번역 엘레가나는 신 씨가 언급한 문제를 어떻게 해결했는가?
(A) 병 뚜껑을 제거하기 더 쉽게 만듦으로써
(B) 제품의 제조법을 조정함으로써
(C) 인쇄된 설명을 확대함으로써
(D) 병 입구의 위치를 변경함으로써

해설 이메일 세 번째 단락에 고객들이 컨디셔너를 병에서 짜기 힘들다는 불만을 제기하고 있다(customers have been complaining that it's hard to squeeze the conditioner out of its bottle)고 문제가 언급되어 있다. 이와 관련해, 고객 후기 후반부에 뚜껑이 하단에 있어 컨디셔너를 짜는 데 훨씬 힘이 덜 든다(the cap being at the bottom means it takes much less effort to get the conditioner out)고 쓰여 있으므로 (D)가 정답이다.

어휘 remove 제거하다, 없애다 adjust 조정하다, 조절하다 formula 제조법 enlarge 확대하다 instructions 설명, 안내

# TEST 5

| | | | | |
|---|---|---|---|---|
| 101 (B) | 102 (C) | 103 (C) | 104 (B) | 105 (B) |
| 106 (C) | 107 (A) | 108 (C) | 109 (D) | 110 (D) |
| 111 (C) | 112 (B) | 113 (C) | 114 (C) | 115 (B) |
| 116 (A) | 117 (D) | 118 (C) | 119 (B) | 120 (C) |
| 121 (D) | 122 (D) | 123 (C) | 124 (D) | 125 (C) |
| 126 (C) | 127 (A) | 128 (A) | 129 (B) | 130 (B) |
| 131 (B) | 132 (D) | 133 (C) | 134 (D) | 135 (D) |
| 136 (D) | 137 (A) | 138 (B) | 139 (C) | 140 (D) |
| 141 (D) | 142 (B) | 143 (B) | 144 (C) | 145 (C) |
| 146 (C) | 147 (C) | 148 (D) | 149 (A) | 150 (C) |
| 151 (C) | 152 (C) | 153 (C) | 154 (B) | 155 (C) |
| 156 (D) | 157 (C) | 158 (B) | 159 (A) | 160 (A) |
| 161 (D) | 162 (B) | 163 (C) | 164 (D) | 165 (B) |
| 166 (B) | 167 (B) | 168 (C) | 169 (A) | 170 (C) |
| 171 (D) | 172 (B) | 173 (B) | 174 (C) | 175 (C) |
| 176 (D) | 177 (C) | 178 (A) | 179 (C) | 180 (D) |
| 181 (C) | 182 (A) | 183 (D) | 184 (B) | 185 (B) |
| 186 (C) | 187 (D) | 188 (C) | 189 (A) | 190 (B) |
| 191 (D) | 192 (B) | 193 (A) | 194 (B) | 195 (A) |
| 196 (B) | 197 (A) | 198 (D) | 199 (D) | 200 (A) |

## PART 5

### 101 접속사 자리 _ 등위 접속사

번역 그 점심 특선에는 샌드위치 한 개와 샐러드나 감자 튀김, 또는 수프 한 그릇이 포함된다.

해설 빈칸 앞뒤에 세 가지 명사(구)가 쓰여 있으므로 문법적으로 동일한 요소를 연결할 때 사용하는 등위 접속사가 필요하다. 따라서 (B) or가 정답이다. (A) thus(따라서, 그러므로)는 부사, (C) for는 전치사 또는 이유를 나타내는 등위 접속사이지만 절과 절만 연결할 수 있으며, (D) nor(~도 아니다)는 neither나 not과 짝을 이루는 상관 접속사이다.

어휘 include 포함하다 along with ~와 함께

### 102 인칭 대명사 _ 소유격 대명사

번역 플레처 씨는 소속 부서가 기업 구조 조정 과정에서 없어진 후 다른 지사로 전근되었다.

해설 after절의 주어인 명사 department를 앞에서 수식할 수 있는 대명사가 필요하므로 소유격 대명사 (C) his가 정답이다.

어휘 transfer 전근시키다 branch 지사, 지점 department 부서 eliminate 없애다, 제거하다 corporate 기업의 restructuring 구조 조정

### 103 형용사 자리 _ 명사 수식

번역 그 소프트웨어 문제에 대한 기술팀의 가장 혁신적인 해결책은 프로그램의 업데이트된 버전에서 사용될 것이다.

해설 most와 명사 solution 사이에 빈칸이 있으므로 빈칸은 most와 함께 최상급 형용사를 구성해 명사를 수식할 형용사가 필요한 자리이다. 따라서 형용사 (C) innovative(혁신적인)가 정답이다.

어휘 solution 해결책 issue 문제, 사안 innovatively 혁신적으로 innovate 혁신하다 innovation 혁신

### 104 부사 자리 _ 동사 수식

번역 글쓰기 컨퍼런스 참석자들은 다수의 관련 주제를 다루는 워크숍에 적극적으로 참가할 수 있다.

해설 조동사 can과 동사 participate 사이에 있는 빈칸은 동사를 수식하는 부사가 들어갈 자리이므로 (B) actively(적극적으로)가 정답이다.

어휘 attendee 참석자 participate in ~에 참가하다 a number of 다수의, 많은 relevant 관련된 activate 활성화하다, 작동시키다 activity 활동 active 적극적인, 활동적인

### 105 명사 어휘

번역 보험에 가입한 차량이 사고에 연루되면, 저희는 영업일 기준 3일 이내에 신속히 청구를 심사할 것입니다.

해설 보험에 가입한 차량의 사고와 관련해서 평가 대상이 될 수 있는 것을 나타낼 명사가 필요하므로 '(보상금 등의) 청구'를 의미하는 (B) claim이 정답이다.

어휘 insured 보험에 가입한 vehicle 차량 be involved in ~와 관련되다 assess 평가하다 signal 신호 inventory 재고(품), 재고 목록 conflict 충돌, 갈등

### 106 동사 어휘

번역 공기 청정기의 문제는 잘못된 보관이나 잘못된 필터 사용으로 인해 발생할 수 있다.

해설 '문제'를 뜻하는 Problems가 주어이고, 뒤에는 문제를 일으키는 원인을 나타내는 by 전치사구가 쓰여 있으므로 '발생하다, 유발되다'를 뜻하는 (C) arise가 정답이다. 참고로, (A) realize와 (B) select, (D) indicate는 모두 목적어가 필요한 타동사이므로 목적어 없이 전치사구가 뒤에 이어지는 빈칸에 쓰일 수 없다.

어휘 air purifier 공기 청정기 incorrect 부정확한 storage 보관, 저장 realize 알아차리다 select 선택하다 indicate 나타내다

### 107 명사 자리 _ 복합명사

번역 그 대학의 신임 입학 사정관은 처리 시간을 줄이기 위해 단계를 간소화했다.

해설 빈칸 앞에 소유격 The university's와 형용사 new가 있고, 뒤에 명사 coordinator가 있으므로 빈칸에는 명사 coordinator를

TEST 5

수식하는 형용사나 복합명사를 이루는 명사가 들어갈 수 있다. (B) admitted는 과거분사로 쓰이면 명사 앞에 올 수 있으나 의미가 어색하며, coordinator와 복합명사를 이뤄 '입학 사정관'이라는 뜻으로 쓰이는 명사 (A) admissions가 정답이다. (C) admits는 동사, (D) to admit은 to부정사이므로 빈칸에 올 수 없다.

어휘 coordinator 조정 담당자, 진행 담당자 streamline 간소화하다 reduce 줄이다, 감소시키다 processing 처리 admission 입학, 입장 admit 인정하다, 입학을 허락하다

## 108 접속사 자리 _ 부사절 접속사

번역 버크 씨는 자신이 작년 연휴 기간에 그랬던 것처럼 통조림 제품을 기부하도록 직원들에게 독려할 것이다.

해설 빈칸 앞뒤에 각각 완전한 절이 있으므로 두 절을 연결해 줄 접속사가 필요하다. 또한 '자신이 작년 연휴 기간에 그랬던 것처럼'이라는 의미가 되어야 자연스러우므로 '~하는 것처럼, ~하는 대로'를 뜻하는 접속사 (C) as가 정답이다. (D) so(그래서)는 등위 접속사로 두 절을 연결할 수 있지만 의미가 맞지 않고, (A) likewise(마찬가지로)는 부사, (B) regarding(~에 대해)은 전치사이므로 오답이다.

어휘 encourage 권하다, 장려하다 donate 기부하다 canned goods 통조림 제품

## 109 부사 자리 _ 수동태 동사 수식

번역 그 약국의 약품과 보충제는 반드시 명확히 라벨 표기가 되어야 한다.

해설 수동태 동사를 구성하는 be동사 be와 과거분사 labeled 사이에 위치한 빈칸은 수동태 동사를 수식할 부사가 들어갈 자리이므로 (D) clearly(명확히)가 정답이다.

어휘 pharmacy 약국 medication 약(품) supplement 보충(물) label 라벨로 표기하다 clarity 명확성, 선명도

## 110 전치사 어휘

번역 베이사이드 파이낸셜은 지난 5년 동안 고객층을 무려 90퍼센트나 확대했다.

해설 빈칸 뒤에 위치한 명사구 the past five years가 기간을 나타내므로 '~ 동안'이라는 의미로 기간 명사(구)와 함께 사용하는 전치사 (D) over가 정답이다.

어휘 expand 확대하다, 확장하다 customer base 고객층 impressive 인상적인

## 111 동명사 자리 _ 전치사의 목적어

번역 어느 것이 귀하의 개인 상황에 가장 적합한지 결정하시기 전에 반드시 그 건물들의 모든 측면을 평가해 보셔야 합니다.

해설 전치사 before 뒤에 빈칸이 있으므로 전치사의 목적어 역할을 할 수 있는 동명사 (C) determining이 정답이다. (A) determines(결정하다)는 동사, (B) to determine은 to부정사, 그리고 (D) must determine은 「조동사+동사 원형」이므로 모두 전치사 뒤에 쓸 수 없다.

어휘 assess 평가하다 aspect 측면, 양상 property 건물, 부동산 suit 적합하다, 어울리다 circumstance 상황

## 112 부사 자리 _ 수동태 동사 수식

번역 주변 지역의 점토 매장량이 풍부하기 때문에 FT 서플라이즈 사의 본사 건물은 원래 도자기 공장으로 쓰였었다.

해설 수동태 동사를 구성하는 be동사 was와 과거분사 used 사이에 빈칸이 있으므로 빈칸은 수동태 동사를 수식하는 부사 자리이다. 따라서 (B) originally(원래, 처음에)가 정답이다.

어휘 headquarters 본사 ceramics 도자기 clay 점토 deposit 매장량, 매장물 originate 유래하다, 비롯되다 original 원래의, 독창적인 origin 기원, 출신

## 113 명사 어휘

번역 매 학기 로렐 공과 대학은 인상적일 정도로 다양한 분야의 온라인 및 대면 수업을 제공한다.

해설 수업을 제공하는 분야의 다양성과 관련된 의미를 나타내야 알맞으므로 빈칸 앞뒤에 위치한 an 및 of와 함께 '다양한, 다수의'를 뜻하는 표현 an array of를 구성하는 (C) array가 정답이다.

어휘 semester 학기 in-person 대면의, 직접 가서 하는 impressive 인상적인 degree 정도, 학위

## 114 형용사 자리 _ 비교급 형용사

번역 많은 항공사 직원들은 수하물 추적 시스템을 배우는 것이 어렵다고 생각했는데, 그것을 탑승객들에게 설명하는 것은 훨씬 더 힘든 일이었다.

해설 부사 even과 명사 challenge 사이에 빈칸이 있으므로 빈칸은 명사를 수식하는 형용사가 들어갈 자리이며, 비교급을 수식하는 부사 even(훨씬)과 어울려야 하므로 비교급 형용사 (C) harder가 정답이다.

어휘 luggage tracking 수하물 추적 challenge (어려운) 일, 도전

## 115 형용사 어휘

번역 인턴 사원들이 수습 기간을 완료하는 대로, 캠코 사의 책임자가 그들 각각을 평가할 것이다.

해설 빈칸은 one을 수식하는 자리이므로, one을 수식할 수 있는 형용사가 필요하며, '각각의 인턴 사원들'이라는 의미가 되어야 자연스러우므로 (B) each(각각의)가 정답이다.

어휘 once (일단) ~하는 대로, ~하자마자 complete 완료하다 probation period 수습 기간 evaluate 평가하다 whole 전체의 full 가득한 total 총 ~의, 전체의

## 116 부사 어휘

번역 자동화된 시스템으로 인해 저희는 기본적인 고객 문의와 요청에 즉각적으로 대응할 수 있습니다.

해설 빈칸 앞에 있는 to respond를 수식해 고객 문의와 요청에 대응하는 방식을 나타낼 부사가 빈칸에 쓰여야 알맞으므로 '즉각적으로'를 뜻하는 (A) instantly가 정답이다.

어휘 automated 자동화된 allow 할 수 있게 하다 respond 대응하다, 반응하다 inquiry 문의 fondly 좋게, 애정을 갖고 abundantly 풍부하게 curiously 궁금한 듯이, 신기하게

## 117 명사 자리 _ 동사의 목적어

번역 모리슨 자동차는 기업의 광범위한 성장으로 인해 회계부와 재무부를 분리하기로 확정했다.

해설 빈칸은 동사 has confirmed의 목적어 자리이며, 정관사 the와 전치사 of 사이에 빈칸이 있으므로 명사가 들어갈 자리이다. 따라서 명사 (D) separation(분리)이 정답이다.

어휘 confirm 확정하다, 확인해 주다 accounting 회계(부) finance 재무, 재정 extensive 광범위한 corporate 기업의 separate 분리된; 분리하다

## 118 전치사 자리 _ 어휘

번역 그 쇼핑몰은 단계적으로 작업하고 있기 때문에 보수 공사 과정 내내 대부분의 매장을 영업 중인 상태로 유지했다.

해설 빈칸 뒤에 위치한 명사구 the renovation process를 목적어로 취하는 전치사 자리이다. the renovation process(보수 공사 과정)는 하나의 기간에 해당하므로 기간을 나타내는 명사(구)와 함께 사용하는 '~ 전반에 걸쳐, ~ 동안 내내'를 의미하는 전치사 (C) throughout이 정답이다.

어휘 the majority of 대부분의 renovation 보수, 개조 process 과정 in phases 단계적으로 prior to ~에 앞서, ~ 전에 along (거리 등) ~을 따라

## 119 관계대명사 _ 주격

번역 완전 채식주의 및 일반 채식주의 식사 손님들의 기호를 충족하는 그 카페는 지금까지 긍정적인 평가를 받는다.

해설 빈칸에서부터 diners까지가 문장의 주어 The café와 동사 has received 사이에 삽입되어 주어를 수식하는 형태이므로 빈칸에는 관계대명사가 들어가야 한다. 또한, 빈칸 뒤에 주어 없이 동사로 바로 이어지므로 주격 관계대명사 (B) which가 정답이다. (A) whether(~인지, ~와 상관없이)는 부사절 또는 명사절을 이끄는 접속사이며, (C) neither(둘 중 어느 것도 ~ 아니다)는 nor와 짝을 이루는 상관 접속사이고, (D) it은 대명사이므로 오답이다.

어휘 cater to ~의 기호를 충족하다 vegan 완전 채식주의의 vegetarian 일반 채식주의의 diner 식사하는 손님 positive 긍정적인 so far 지금까지

## 120 형용사 어휘

번역 <뉴포트 데일리 헤럴드>의 앤젤라 크루즈 편집장은 신문 기사에 오직 확인 가능한 사실만 포함한다.

해설 빈칸에 쓰일 형용사는 명사 facts를 수식해 어떤 사실이 신문 기사로 실리는지 나타내야 하므로 '확인 가능한, 증명할 수 있는'이라는 의미의 (C) verifiable이 정답이다.

어휘 include 포함하다 nothing but 오직 fact 사실 intensive 집중적인 competent 유능한 economical 경제적인

## 121 전치사 어휘

번역 심사 위원단은 오직 6월 28일부터 7월 5일까지 지정된 기간 내에 접수되는 미술 출품작들만 심사할 수 있다.

해설 빈칸 뒤에 위치한 명사구 the designated period가 '지정된 기간'을 의미하므로 기간을 나타내는 명사(구)와 함께 사용하는 '~ 내에'를 뜻하는 전치사 (D) within이 정답이다.

어휘 judging panel 심사 위원단 consider 검토하다, 고려하다 entry 출품작 designated 지정된 above ~ 위에, ~을 넘어서는 except ~을 제외하고 among ~ 중에서

## 122 부사 어휘

번역 커비 씨는 현재 자신의 제과점에 필요한 소상공인 대출을 위한 서류를 작성하고 있다.

해설 현재진행형 동사 is filling out을 수식하는 부사 자리이며, '현재 작성하고 있다'라는 의미가 되어야 자연스러우므로 '현재'라는 의미의 (D) currently가 정답이다. currently는 현재진행 시제와 자주 쓰이는 부사이다.

어휘 fill out 작성하다 paperwork 서류 (작업) loan 대출 lately 최근에 anywhere 어디든, 어디에서도

## 123 명사 자리 _ 전치사의 목적어

번역 샬럿 콜린스 박사는 해당 분야의 의학 발전에서 선두 자리를 유지하기 위해 추가 자금을 필요로 한다.

해설 빈칸은 형용사 medical의 수식을 받는 자리이자 전치사 of의 목적어 자리이므로 명사가 들어가야 한다. 따라서 (C) advances(발전, 진보)가 정답이다.

어휘 further 추가의 funding 자금 (제공) at the forefront of ~에 앞장서는, ~의 선두에 서 있는 advance 발전, 진보; 나아가다

## 124 동사 어휘

번역 그 파라솔은 최대 시속 25마일까지의 바람만 견딜 수 있도록 설계되었으므로, 오늘은 걷어 주시기 바랍니다.

해설 빈칸 뒤에 바람의 최대 시속을 나타내는 말(winds of up to twenty-five miles per hour)이 쓰여 있어 파라솔이 견딜 수 있는 바람의 속도임을 알 수 있다. 따라서 '견디다'를 뜻하는 (D) withstand가 정답이다.

어휘 take down (구조물을) 치우다, 걷어 내다 patio umbrella 파라솔 design 설계하다, 고안하다 up to 최대 ~까지 forbid 금지하다 expose 노출시키다, 드러내다 occur 발생하다, 일어나다

## 125 부사 자리 _ 어휘

번역 무역 박람회 부스를 조립하기 위해 고용된 임시 작업자들이 우리에게 꽤 도움이 될 겁니다.

해설 be동사와 보어 역할을 하는 형용사 helpful 사이에 빈칸이 있으므로 빈칸에는 형용사를 수식하는 부사가 와야 한다. 따라서 형용사 helpful을 앞에서 수식해 강조할 수 있는 부사 (C) quite(꽤, 상당히)이 정답이다. (A) enough(충분히, 충분한)는 부사 또는 형용사로 쓰이며, 부사일 경우에 형용사나 다른 부사를 뒤에서 수식하므로 오답이다. (B) shortly(곧)는 형용사를 수식하지 않는 부사이며, (D) than(~보다)은 접속사 또는 전치사로 쓰인다.

어휘 temporary 임시의, 일시적인 assemble 조립하다 trade fair 무역 박람회

## 126 형용사 어휘

번역 파크뷰 호텔의 객실을 예약하고 머무는 동안 세심한 직원들의 보살핌을 받으세요.

해설 빈칸에 쓰일 형용사는 명사 staff를 수식해 호텔 직원들의 특성과 관련된 의미를 나타내야 하므로 '세심한, 배려하는' 등을 뜻하는 (C) attentive가 정답이다.

어휘 book 예약하다 look after ~을 보살피다, 돌보다 optimal 최적의 former 이전의, 전직 ~의 potential 잠재적인

## 127 전치사 어휘

번역 오웬 애벗 병원장은 더욱 환자 중심적인 치료 방식을 지향하고자 하는 열망을 표명했다.

해설 변화나 진행 또는 이동을 나타내는 동사 move와 어울리는 전치사로서 '~을 지향하다, ~으로 향하다' 등을 의미할 때 사용하는 (A) toward가 정답이다.

어휘 express 표현하다, 나타내다 desire 소망, 바람 patient 환자 centered ~ 중심적인 approach (접근) 방식 care 돌봄, 치료 alongside ~ 옆에, ~와 함께 through ~을 통해, ~ 내내

## 128 접속사 자리 _ 부사절 접속사

번역 파인웰 슈퍼마켓의 충성 고객 프로그램은 대상 고객층이 여전히 참여하고 있는 한 계속될 것이다.

해설 빈칸 앞뒤로 두 개의 완전한 절이 있으므로 두 절을 연결해 줄 접속사가 필요하다. 따라서 부사절 접속사 (A) as long as(~하는 한)가 정답이다. (B) in spite of(~에도 불구하고)와 (C) rather than(~이 아니라, ~ 대신)은 전치사이며, (D) in order to(~하기 위해) 뒤에는 동사 원형이 쓰여야 한다.

어휘 customer loyalty program 충성 고객 프로그램 target demographic 대상이 되는 인구층 participate in ~에 참여하다

## 129 명사 어휘

번역 최첨단 치료보다 예방법을 우선시하는 것이 더 나은 건강 결과로 이어질 수 있다.

해설 prevention methods(예방법)와 cutting-edge treatments (최첨단 치료) 사이의 비교 우위를 나타내는 명사가 빈칸에 쓰여야 알맞으므로 '우선시, 우선화'를 뜻하는 (B) Prioritization이 정답이다.

어휘 prevention 예방 method 방법 cutting-edge 최첨단의 treatment 치료(법) lead to+명사 ~로 이어지다 outcome 결과 consumption 소비 destination 목적지, 도착지 intention 의도, 목적

## 130 수동태

번역 모든 일반 현수막 인쇄 주문 건은 긴급 요청 건이 완료되어 배송될 때까지 보류될 것이다.

해설 '중단하다, 보류하다'를 의미하는 동사 suspend는 목적어를 필요로 하는 타동사인데, 빈칸 뒤에 목적어 없이 접속사 until이 있으므로 수동태로 쓰여야 한다. 따라서 수동태인 (B) be suspended가 정답이다. (A) suspend와 (C) have suspended, 그리고 (D) be suspending은 모두 능동태이다.

어휘 standard 일반의, 표준의 banner 현수막 express 긴급의, 급행의

# PART 6

### 131-134 이메일

발신: hemrich@midlandmail.com
수신: ltoscani@napoliballetschool.com
날짜: 9월 26일
제목: 공석
첨부: 이력서_엠리치

토스카니 씨께,

나폴리 발레 학교 소식지의 최신 호에 게시하신 구인 공고와 관련하여 연락을 드립니다. 저는 귀하의 131 **기관**에 대해 아주 큰 경의를 지니고 있으며, 많은 제 친구와 지인들이 그곳에서 수강한 바 있습니다. 제가 그곳에서 댄스 강사로서 기여할 수 있다면 132 **기쁠** 것입니다.

저는 연령 및 수준이 아주 다양한 여러 댄서들과 함께 일해 왔습니다. 133 **따라서** 수강생들 개인의 요구에 완벽히 맞도록 강의 방식을 조정할 수 있습니다. 제가 받은 교육 및 근무 경력을 개괄적으로 보여 드리는 이력서를 첨부해 드렸으니 확인해 보시기 바랍니다. 134 **www.danceshowcase.com/emrich1에서 제가 춤추는 동영상을 보실 수도 있습니다.** 질문이 있으시면, 이 주소 또는 555-3966번으로 제게 연락하시면 됩니다. 곧 소식 들을 수 있기를 바랍니다.

헤더 엠리치

어휘 job opening 공석 résumé 이력서 with regard to+명사 ~에 대해 advertisement 광고 post 게시하다 a great deal of 아주 많은 respect 경의, 존경 acquaintance 지인 contribute 기여하다 site 현장, 장소 a wide range of 아주 다양한 ability 능력 adjust 조정하다 suit 어울리다, 적합하다 individual 개별의, 개인의 outline 개괄적으로 설명하다

### 131 명사 어휘

해설 your 뒤에 있는 빈칸에는 앞 문장에 언급된 상대방의 단체인 Napoli Ballet School을 가리킬 명사가 들어가야 하므로 '기관, 협회' 등의 의미로 쓰이는 (B) institute가 정답이다.

어휘 exhibition 전시(회)

### 132 형용사 자리 _ 과거분사

해설 주어인 I를 보충 설명하는 주격 보어 자리로, 문맥상 I가 감정을 느끼는 것이므로 과거분사 (D) delighted(기쁜)가 정답이다. (A) delighting은 감정을 유발하는 대상을 묘사할 때 쓴다.

### 133 접속부사

해설 빈칸 앞에는 연령 및 수준이 아주 다양한 여러 댄서들과 함께 일해 왔다는 사실이, 빈칸 뒤에는 수강생들 개인의 필요에 완벽히 맞게 강의 방식을 조정할 수 있다는 말이 쓰여 있다. 이는 '이유(경험이 많은 것)+결과(수강생에 따른 강의 방식 조정)'의 흐름에 해당하므로 '따라서, 그 결과'라는 의미로 결과를 말할 때 사용하는 (C) Consequently가 정답이다.

어휘 otherwise 그렇지 않으면, 그 외에는 in addition 게다가, 더욱이

### 134 문장 고르기

번역 (A) 춤출 때 부상을 방지하는 방법을 기꺼이 가르쳐 드리겠습니다.
(B) 제 강좌들 중 하나를 신청하시려면, 해당 앱을 다운로드하시기 바랍니다.
(C) 지난달에 귀하의 댄스 강좌에서 아주 많이 배웠습니다.
(D) www.danceshowcase.com/emrich1에서 제가 춤추는 동영상을 보실 수도 있습니다.

해설 앞서 자신의 능력을 어필하며, 교육 및 근무 경력을 보여주는 이력서를 첨부했다는 말이 쓰여 있으므로 이와 관련된 내용이 오는 것이 적절하다. 따라서 자신의 능력을 보여줄 수 있는 춤추는 동영상을 볼 수 있는 방법을 언급하는 (D)가 정답이다.

어휘 prevent 방지하다, 막다 injury 부상 sign up for ~을 신청하다, ~에 등록하다 a great deal 많은 것

**135-138 웹페이지**

로젠 호텔은 3월 한 달 내내 모든 디럭스 객실을 30% 할인합니다. 이 특별 [135] **요금**은 저희 새 객실의 고급스러움을 경험해 보기를 원하시는 모든 고객께서 이용하실 수 있습니다. 차분한 색상으로 [136] **장식된**, 저희 디럭스 객실은 긴 하루를 보내신 후에 느긋하게 휴식하기에 안성맞춤인 곳입니다. [137] **이 객실에는** 킹 사이즈 침대와 작은 주방, 널찍한 욕실을 비롯한 여러 시설이 포함되어 있습니다. 예약하시려면, www.rosen-hotel.com을 방문하십시오. 신용카드가 모든 예약에 필수라는 점에 유의하시기 바랍니다. [138] **요금 청구는 체크인 24시간 전까지 이뤄지지 않을 것입니다.** 여러분을 맞이할 수 있기를 고대합니다!

어휘 available 이용 가능한 luxury 고급스러움, 호화로움 calming 차분한 relax 휴식하다 come with ~을 포함하다 kitchenette 작은 주방 spacious 널찍한 note 유의하다, 주목하다 booking 예약 look forward to -ing ~하기를 고대하다

### 135 명사 어휘

해설 앞 문장에 디럭스 객실을 30% 할인한다는 말이 쓰여 있어 This special과 함께 '30% 할인'을 대신할 수 있는 명사가 빈칸에 쓰여야 알맞다. 이는 결국 요금 할인을 의미하는 것이므로 '요금'을 뜻하는 (D) rate가 정답이다.

어휘 performance 공연, 성과 edition (출판물 등의) 판, 호

### 136 분사구문

해설 문장의 주어 our deluxe rooms 앞에 접속사와 주어 없이 쓰일 수 있는 분사가 빈칸에 들어가 전치사구 with calming colors와 함께 주어를 설명하는 분사구문을 구성해야 알맞다. 또한, 주어 our deluxe rooms는 사람에 의해 장식되는 것이므로 '장식된'이라는 수동의 의미를 나타내는 과거분사 (D) Decorated가 정답이다. 사물 주어인 our deluxe rooms가 장식하는 일을 할 수 없으므로 현재분사 (A) Decorating은 오답이며, 목적을 나타내는 (B) To decorate는 의미가 맞지 않는다. 주어와 동사인 (C) They decorated는 문장에 접속사가 없으므로 쓰일 수 없다.

### 137 인칭 대명사 _ 주격 대명사

해설 빈칸 뒤에 침대와 작은 주방, 그리고 욕실을 포함한다는 말이 쓰여 있어 앞 문장에 쓰여 있는 our deluxe rooms의 특징임을 알 수 있다. 따라서 앞서 언급된 복수 명사를 대신할 수 있는 복수 주격 대명사 (A) They가 정답이다. 대명사 (B) Either(둘 중 하나)와 복합관계대명사 (C) Whichever(~하는 어느 것이든)는 모두 복수 명사 our deluxe rooms를 대신할 수 없으며 대명사 (D) Fewer(더 적은 사람들/것들)는 의미가 적절하지 않다.

### 138 문장 고르기

번역 (A) 그렇지 않으면, 조식 뷔페가 매일 오전 6시부터 제공됩니다.
(B) 요금 청구는 체크인 24시간 전까지 이뤄지지 않을 것입니다.
(C) 저희 직원들은 가급적이면 이 요청을 수용하는 것을 목표로 합니다.
(D) 도심에 위치한 많은 호텔에 빈 객실이 있습니다.

해설 앞 문장에 신용카드가 예약에 필수라는 말이 쓰여 있으므로 신용카드를 통한 요금 청구와 관련된 내용이 언급된 (B)가 정답이다.

어휘 charge (청구) 요금 aim 목표로 하다 accommodate 수용하다 vacant 비어 있는

## 139-142 이메일

수신: 클로에 보이스 <cboyce@merigoldcomm.com>
발신: 알링턴 위생 관리국 <sanitation@arlington.gov>
날짜: 1월 2일
제목: 놓친 수거 작업

보이스 씨께,

귀하 건물의 재활용품 수거를 누락한 [139] **것에 관해** 알려 주셔서 감사합니다. 저희는 긴급 수거 작업을 위한 전문 팀이 있어서, 그들을 보내 드렸습니다. [140] **이런 이유로**, 귀하의 재활용품은 오후 4시까지 수거될 것이니 안심하셔도 됩니다. [141] **휴일로 인해, 이번 주는 대부분 대체 작업조가 근무하고 있습니다.** 따라서 일부 작업원들이 경로에 익숙하지 않습니다. 저희는 알링턴에서 가정 쓰레기 및 재활용품을 효율적으로 수거하는 서비스를 제공하기 위해 최선을 다하고 있으며, 귀하의 의견은 저희가 이러한 책임을 [142] **다하는 데** 도움이 됩니다.

데븐 시나
알링턴 위생 관리국

어휘 missed 놓친, 빠트린 collection 수거 recycling 재활용(품) property 건물, 부동산 short-notice 촉박한, 갑작스럽게 통보하는 pickup 수거, 가져감 dispatch 보내다, 파견하다 (you can) rest assured that ~라는 점에 안심하셔도 됩니다 collect 수거하다 crew 작업조 be familiar with ~에 익숙하다, ~을 잘 알다 dedicated to+명사 ~에 전념하는 efficient 효율적인 household 가정의 recyclables 재활용품 feedback 의견 responsibility 책임

### 139 전치사 어휘

해설 빈칸 앞에 알려 줘서 감사하다고 쓰여 있고, 뒤에는 알려준 내용이 제시되어 있으므로, 재활용품 수거를 누락한 것에 관해 알려 줘서 감사하다는 의미가 되어야 자연스럽다. 따라서 '~에 관해'를 뜻하는 전치사 (C) about이 정답이다.

### 140 접속부사

해설 빈칸 앞 문장에 긴급 수거 작업을 위한 전문 팀이 있어서 그 팀을 보냈다는 말이 쓰여 있는데, 이는 빈칸 뒤에 있는 안심해도 된다는 말에 대한 이유로 볼 수 있다. 따라서 '이런 이유로'라는 의미의 (D) For this reason이 정답이다.

어휘 for instance 예를 들어 on the other hand 다른 한편으로는 apart from that 그 외에도, 그 외에

### 141 문장 고르기

번역 (A) 유감스럽게도, 저희는 완전히 세척되지 않은 물품은 가져갈 수 없습니다.
(B) 시의 웹사이트에도 의견을 남기실 수 있습니다.
(C) 재활용품 수거 일정표를 첨부해 드렸습니다.
(D) 휴일로 인해, 이번 주는 대부분 대체 작업조가 근무하고 있습니다.

해설 빈칸 뒤에 '따라서, 그러므로'라는 의미로 결과를 말할 때 사용하는 Therefore와 함께 일부 작업원들이 경로에 익숙하지 않다는 말이 쓰여 있다. 따라서 그러한 상황이 발생한 이유로서 대체 작업조가 근무하고 있다는 사실을 밝히는 (D)가 정답이다.

어휘 unfortunately 유감스럽게도, 안타깝게도 thoroughly 철저히 replacement 대체(자)

### 142 to부정사 _ 목적격 보어

해설 동사 help는 「help+목적어+(to)부정사」의 구조로 '~가 …하는 데 도움이 되다'라는 뜻으로 쓰인다. 따라서 빈칸 앞에 있는 to와 함께 to 부정사를 구성하는 동사 원형 (B) fulfill이 정답이다.

어휘 fulfillment 이행, 완수 fulfill 완수하다, 이행하다

## 143-146 회람

수신: 전 직원
발신: 키스 보이트, 제품 개발부장
날짜: 3월 22일
제목: 럭스-7 핸드백

럭스-7 가죽 핸드백의 실망스러운 판매량으로 인해, 우리는 즉시 이 제품의 생산을 중단하기로 결정했습니다. 유감스럽게도, 소비자들은 광고 캠페인이 우리 예상보다 덜 [143] **매력적이라고** 생각했습니다. 게다가, 디자인이 경쟁 제품들에 비해 돋보이지 않았습니다. 앞으로, 디자인팀은 새 가방의 시제품 제작을 돕기 위해 연구팀에서 윤곽을 그린 몇 가지 [144] **사양**을 받게 됩니다. [145] **그 후에, 우리는 잠재 고객들로부터 의견을 수집할 것입니다.** 우리는 요구되는 추가 작업이 [146] 어렵**지만** 유익할 것으로 생각합니다.

어휘 disappointing 실망시키는 discontinue (생산을) 중단하다 effective immediately 즉시 (시행되는) unfortunately 유감스럽게도, 안타깝게도 consumer 소비자 ad 광고 additionally 게다가, 추가로 stand out 돋보이다, 눈에 띄다 competitor 경쟁자 moving forward 앞으로 outline 개요를 서술하다, 윤곽을 그리다 prototype 시제품 additional 추가적인 beneficial 유익한

### 143 형용사 어휘

해설 동사 found의 목적어인 our ad campaign의 특징을 나타낼 형용사가 빈칸에 쓰여야 한다. 앞 문장에서 제품의 생산을 중단하기로 결정했다고 알리는 것에 대해, less와 함께 광고 캠페인의 부정적인 면을 의미해야 하므로 '마음을 끄는, 눈을 뗄 수 없는' 등을 뜻하는 (B) compelling이 정답이다.

어휘 gradual 점진적인 repetitive 반복적인 doubtful 의심스러운, 불확실한

### 144 명사 자리 _ 수 일치

해설 형용사 several의 수식을 받는 자리이므로 명사 자리이고, several은 복수 명사를 수식하므로 (C) specifications가 정답이다. (B)

specification(사양, 설명서)은 단수 명사이므로 오답이다.

어휘 specify 명시하다 specification 사양, 설명서

### 145 문장 고르기

번역 (A) 하지만, 덜 비싼 재료를 이용할 수 있습니다.
(B) 그 광고에는 현대 직장인들의 사례가 등장합니다.
(C) 그 후에, 우리는 잠재 고객들로부터 의견을 수집할 것입니다.
(D) 여러분의 노력이 진정으로 차이를 만들어 내는 데 도움이 되었습니다.

해설 빈칸 앞 문장에 디자인팀이 시제품 제작을 위한 사양을 받게 된다는 말이 있으므로 다음 순서의 일을 나타낼 때 사용하는 Following that(그 후에)과 함께 시제품을 만든 후에 할 일을 언급하는 (C)가 정답이다.

어휘 material 재료, 자재 available 이용 가능한 commercial 광고 방송 feature 특징으로 하다 following ~ 후에 gather 수집하다, 모으다 feedback 의견 potential 잠재적인 effort 노력 make a difference 차이를 만들어 내다

### 146 접속사 자리 _ 등위 접속사

해설 빈칸 앞뒤에 형용사 difficult와 beneficial이 각각 쓰여 있으므로 문법적으로 동일한 요소를 연결할 때 사용하는 등위 접속사 (C) yet이 정답이다. (A) for도 등위 접속사로 쓰일 수 있지만 절과 절을 연결할 때에만 쓰이므로 오답이다. (B) as와 (D) if는 모두 부사절 접속사로 쓰이므로 빈칸에 맞지 않는다.

## PART 7

### 147-148 이메일

수신: 바유 데바르 <dhebarv@quincy-inc.com>
발신: 안드레 롱고리아 <andre1@wilmarrentals.com>
날짜: 4월 13일
제목: 차량 대여

데바르 씨께,

최근 차량 대여를 위해 윌마 렌탈을 선택해 주셔서 감사합니다. 저희가 고객 서비스를 개선하는 데 도움이 될 수 있도록, [147] **간단한 설문지를 작성하셔서 귀하의 경험에 관해 솔직한 의견을 제공해 주시기를 요청드립니다.** 여기를 클릭하셔서 온라인 양식을 작성해 주시기 바랍니다. [148] **참여에 대한 감사의 표시로, 다음 대여 시 추가 비용 없이 3일 연장할 수 있는 바우처를 이메일로 보내 드릴 것입니다.** 이것은 향후 12개월 동안 언제든지 사용할 수 있습니다.

귀하의 성원에 감사드립니다!

안드레 롱고리아
고객 서비스부, 윌마 렌탈

어휘 vehicle 차량 rental 대여 improve 개선하다 fill out 작성하다 brief 간략한, 짧은 questionnaire 설문지 appreciation 감사(하는 마음) participation 참여 voucher 바우처, 상품권 allow ~할 수 있게 해 주다 extend 연장하다 at no extra charge 추가 비용 없이 patronage 성원, 후원, 애용

### 147 세부 사항

번역 롱고리아 씨는 데바르 씨에게 무엇을 하도록 요청하는가?
(A) 선호하는 차량 크기 확정하기
(B) 청구서의 남은 잔금 지불하기
(C) 서비스에 관한 의견 공유하기
(D) 무료 워크숍에 참여하기

해설 지문 중반부에 간단한 설문지를 작성해 경험에 관해 솔직한 의견을 제공하기를 요청한다(we ask that you fill out a brief questionnaire to provide honest feedback about your experience)고 했으므로 (C)가 정답이다.

어휘 confirm 확정하다, 확인해 주다 preferred 선호하는 remaining 나머지의, 남아 있는 balance 잔금, 잔액 participate in ~에 참여하다

> Paraphrasing
> 지문의 provide honest feedback about your experience
> → 정답의 Share her opinions about a service

### 148 세부 사항

번역 롱고리아 씨는 데바르 씨를 위해 무엇을 할 계획인가?
(A) 고객 의견 제공 시간에 만나기
(B) 더 큰 차량으로 업그레이드하기
(C) 무료로 1년 구독 연장하기
(D) 무료 대여 바우처 제공하기

해설 지문 후반부에 감사의 표시로, 다음 대여 시 추가 비용 없이 3일 연장할 수 있는 바우처를 이메일로 보내겠다(I will e-mail you a voucher that will allow you to extend your next rental by three days at no extra charge)고 했으므로 (D)가 정답이다.

어휘 session (특정 활동을 위한) 시간 subscription 가입, 구독 at no cost 무료로

> Paraphrasing
> 지문의 e-mail you a voucher ~ extend your next rental by three days at no extra charge
> → 정답의 Provide a voucher for free rental days

### 149-150 온라인 채팅

해리 알바레즈 [오후 3시 22분]
안녕하세요, DC 인테리어에 연락 주신 것을 환영합니다.

코라 볼드윈 [오후 3시 23분]
안녕하세요, 제 이름은 코라 볼드윈이고, [149] **제품을 취소하는 데 어려움을 겪고 있습니다.**

해리 알바레즈 [오후 3시 24분]
안녕하세요, 볼드윈 씨. 온라인에서 구입하셨나요, 아니면 앱을 통해 하셨나요?

코라 볼드윈 [오후 3시 25분]
제 온라인 계정을 통해서요. 제가 색상을 잘못 주문해서, 취소해야 합니다. 이 제품에 대해 비용이 청구되지 않았으면 하는데, 제가 이미 다른 곳에서 대체품을 구입했기 때문입니다.

해리 알바레즈 [오후 3시 27분]
알겠습니다. 제가 도와드리겠습니다. 150 **다크 포레스트 라텍스 페인트 10리터짜리 3캔을 구입하신 것이 맞으시죠?** 이 요청을 취소하고 환불해 드리겠습니다.

코라 볼드윈 [오후 3시 28분]
맞습니다.

해리 알바레즈 [오후 3시 29분]
좋습니다. 취소가 됐습니다. 영업일 기준 3~5일 후에 신용카드 계정으로 53.85파운드가 환불될 예정입니다. 다른 도움이 필요하신가요?

코라 볼드윈 [오후 3시 31분]
그게 전부입니다. 감사합니다!

어휘 have difficulty -ing ~하는 데 어려움을 겪다 account 계정, 계좌 be charged for ~에 대한 비용이 청구되다 replacement 대체(품) elsewhere 다른 곳에서 refund 환불해 주다; 환불(액) cancellation 취소 go through 이뤄지다, 성사되다

## 149 추론

번역 알바레즈 씨의 직업은 무엇일 것 같은가?
(A) 고객 서비스 담당 직원
(B) 실내 디자이너
(C) 은행 직원
(D) 스마트폰 애플리케이션 개발자

해설 오후 3시 23분 메시지에 볼드윈 씨가 알바레즈 씨에게 제품을 취소하는 데 어려움을 겪고 있다(I'm having difficulty canceling some items)는 말로 도움을 요청하고 있다. 이는 고객 서비스를 담당하는 직원에게 할 수 있는 말이므로 (A)가 정답이다.

## 150 의도 파악

번역 오후 3시 28분에, 볼드윈 씨가 "맞습니다"라고 쓸 때, 의미하는 것은 무엇인가?
(A) 업체가 제품을 재고로 보유하고 있다.
(B) 이미 환불을 받았다.
(C) 알바레즈 씨가 정확한 주문 사항을 언급하고 있다.
(D) 5일 내로 업체에 연락할 것이다.

해설 You got it은 '맞습니다, 알겠습니다'와 같이 확인이나 수용의 의미를 나타낼 때 사용한다. 오후 3시 27분에 알바레즈 씨가 '다크 포레스트 라텍스 페인트 10리터짜리 3캔을 구입하신 것이 맞으시죠?(It's the purchase of three 10-liter cans of the Dark Forest latex paint, right?)'라고 묻는 것에 대해 맞다고 확인해 주는 것이므로 (C)가 정답이다.

어휘 have ~ in stock ~을 재고로 보유하다 refer to+명사 ~을 언급하다 correct 정확한, 맞는

## 151-152 광고

프레시타임 청소 서비스

151 **지난 5년 동안 오로라와 헌팅턴, 그리고 더럼 지역에 서비스 제공!**
월요일에서 토요일까지, 오전 8시부터 오후 8시까지 가능, 국경일 제외.

프레시타임 청소 서비스는 상업용 건물에 최고의 청소 서비스를 제공합니다. 설립자인 테리 놀란은 여러분의 공간을 깔끔하고 편안한 곳으로 만드는 일에 열정적이며, 헌신적인 저희 청소 팀은 언제나 철저하고 신중합니다. 일회성 대청소든, 일주일 단위 정기 청소든, 그 외의 어떤 청소가 필요하시든 저희가 도와드릴 수 있습니다. 저희는 환경친화적인 청소용 제품을 사용하며, 종합 보험에 가입되어 있습니다.

152 **저희는 특히 세입자가 바뀌는 시점에 청소 서비스가 필요하신 신규 고객들을 찾고 있습니다. 555-8716번으로 제이나 로고바에게 전화하셔서 요금을 논의하시기 바랍니다.**

어휘 available 이용 가능한 excluding ~을 제외하고 top-notch 최고의 commercial 상업의 property 건물, 부동산 be passionate about ~하는 데 열정적이다 relaxing 편안한, 느긋한 dedicated 헌신적인 thorough 철저한 environmentally friendly 환경친화적인 insured 보험에 가입한 tenant 세입자 rate 요금, 등급

## 151 Not / True

번역 프레시타임 청소 서비스에 대해 사실인 것은?
(A) 10년 넘게 영업해 왔다.
(B) 주택과 사업체 모두에 서비스를 제공한다.
(C) 세 곳의 다른 장소에서 운영한다.
(D) 여러 번의 청소 시간을 예약해야 한다.

해설 지문 상단에 지난 5년 동안 오로라와 헌팅턴, 그리고 더럼 지역에 서비스를 제공해 왔다(Serving Aurora, Huntington, and Durham for the past five years!)는 말이 쓰여 있으므로 (C)가 정답이다.

어휘 in business 영업하는 decade 10년 operate 운영하다 multiple 다양한, 다수의

**Paraphrasing**
지문의 Serving Aurora, Huntington, and Durham
→ 정답의 operates in three different locations

## 152 세부 사항

번역 광고에 따르면, 누가 로고바 씨에게 전화해야 하는가?
(A) 호텔 손님들
(B) 청소용품 도매업자
(C) 건물 소유주
(D) 시간제 청소 직원

해설 로고바 씨의 이름이 언급되는 마지막 단락에, 세입자가 바뀌는 시점에 청소 서비스가 필요한 고객들을 찾고 있다는 말과 함께 로고바 씨에게 전화하라(We are especially looking for new clients in need of cleaning between tenants. Call Jana Rogova ~)고 알리고 있다. 기존 세입자가 나가고 신규 세입자가 들어오는 사이에 청소 서비스를 필요로 할 사람은 해당 건물 소유주이므로 (C)가 정답이다.

## 153-154 안내판

설치 공사를 위한 임시 폐쇄

[153] **요약: 놀이터 장비 설치**

예상 재개장일: 5월 17일

| [153] **책임 부서:** | 계약업체: |
|---|---|
| **뉴 헤이븐 여가 시설 관리팀** | 피어슨 서비스 사 |
| 알바레즈 가 1756, 스위트 #32 | 고든 로 305 |
| 뉴 헤이븐, CT 06506 | 우드브리지, CT 06525 |

이 프로젝트와 관련된 추가 정보는 시 웹사이트에서 찾아보실 수 있습니다. [154] **소음으로 인한 피해나 기타 문제를 겪으시면, 203-555-1771번으로 전화 주시기 바랍니다.**

어휘 temporary 임시의, 일시적인 installation 설치 (공사) summary 요약 equipment 장비 estimated 추정되는, 예상되는 in charge 책임지고 있는 contractor 계약업체 disturbance 지장, 방해 issue 문제, 사안

### 153 추론

번역 이 안내판은 어디에 게시되어 있을 것 같은가?

(A) 사설 체육관 바깥에
(B) 상업용 창고에
(C) 공원에
(D) 백화점 선반 위에

해설 지문 상단의 요약(Summary) 항목에 놀이터 장비 설치(Installation of playground equipment)라고 쓰여 있고, 그 아래 책임 부서(Department in Charge)에 뉴 헤이븐 여가 시설 관리팀(New Haven Recreational Facilities)이라고 쓰여 있으므로 정답은 (C)이다.

### 154 세부 사항

번역 사람들이 왜 안내판에 있는 전화번호로 전화해야 하는가?

(A) 분실한 물품을 신고하기 위해
(B) 항의를 하기 위해
(C) 장비를 기증하기 위해
(D) 일정에 관해 문의하기 위해

해설 지문 하단에 소음으로 인한 피해나 기타 문제를 겪으면 전화하라(Should you experience noise disturbances or other issues, please call 203-555-1771)고 알리고 있다. 따라서 (B)가 정답이다.

어휘 missing 분실한, 사라진 make a complaint 항의하다 donate 기증하다, 기부하다 inquire 문의하다

> **Paraphrasing**
> 지문의 Should you experience noise disturbances or other issues, please call → 정답의 make a complaint

## 155-157 정보

2월 8일에, 센테니얼 지역 문화 센터에서 지역 구직자들을 위한 행사를 개최할 것입니다. [155] **저희는 일대일 면접 연습을 돕기 위해 시간을 할애해 주실 분들을 찾고 있습니다.** 인사 또는 관리 분야의 경력이 있으신 분을 선호합니다. 이 시간은 녹음될 것이며, [156] **나중에 참고할 수 있도록 참가자들에게 대화 인쇄물이 제공될 것입니다.** 이 행사는 [157] **안정적인** 일자리를 찾고 있는 참가자들에게 크게 도움이 될 것입니다. 추가 정보는 555-2904번으로 라라 하비에게 연락하시기 바랍니다.

어휘 host 개최하다 local 지역의, 현지의 donate 기부하다, (시간 등) 제공하다 assist 돕다 one-on-one 일대일의 management 관리, 경영 preferred 선호하는 session (특정 활동을 위한) 시간 participant 참가자 printout 인쇄물 refer to+명사 ~을 참고하다 steady 안정적인, 고정적인 employment 일자리, 고용

### 155 주제 / 목적

번역 정보의 목적은 무엇인가?

(A) 지역 문화 센터를 위해 모금하는 것
(B) 정책 변화를 알리는 것
(C) 자원봉사 기회를 알리는 것
(D) 구직 면접 팁을 제공하는 것

해설 지문 초반부에 일대일 면접 연습을 돕기 위해 시간을 할애해 줄 수 있는 사람을 찾고 있다(We are looking for people to donate their time to assist ~)고 알리는 말이 쓰여 있다. 이는 자원봉사자를 찾는다는 뜻이므로 (C)가 정답이다.

어휘 raise money 모금하다 publicize 알리다, 홍보하다 volunteer 자원봉사 opportunity 기회

> **Paraphrasing**
> 지문의 donate their time to assist → 정답의 volunteer

### 156 세부 사항

번역 정보에 따르면, 참가자들은 무엇을 할 수 있을 것인가?

(A) 관리자 직책에 지원하기
(B) 환영 동영상 녹화하기
(C) 지역 업체 소유주들 만나기
(D) 대화 기록 받기

해설 지문 중반부에 나중에 참고할 수 있도록 참가자들에게 대화 인쇄물이 제공될 것(participants will be given a printout of the conversation so they can refer to it later)이라고 했으므로 (D)가 정답이다.

어휘 apply for ~에 지원하다, ~을 신청하다 transcript 글로 옮긴 것

TEST 5

> Paraphrasing
> 지문의 be given a printout of the conversation
> → 정답의 Receive a transcript

## 157 동의어

번역 첫 번째 단락, 여섯 번째 줄에 쓰인 "steady"와 의미가 가장 가까운 것은?
(A) 습관적인, 관례적인
(B) 내구성이 좋은
(C) 안정적인
(D) 계속되는, 고집하는

해설 employment가 '일자리, 고용' 등을 뜻하므로 steady employment는 구직자들이 찾는 안정적인 일자리를 의미하는 것으로 볼 수 있다. 따라서 '안정적인'이라는 의미의 (C) stable이 정답이다.

### 158-160 광고

메디나 가상 우편함
스트로우드 로 834, 빔허스트
전화번호: 070 5517 3713

여러분의 우편물이 저희 손에 안전하게 보관됩니다!

- 심지어 이사하신 후에도 동일한 가상 주소를 유지하실 수 있습니다.
- 저희 스탠다드 서비스를 이용하시면, 서명을 요구하는 봉투 및 소포를 포함해 여러분의 우편물을 보관해 드립니다. [158] **여러분의 우편물이 저희에게 전달될 때마다 문자 메시지로 알려 드립니다.**
- 저희 골드 서비스를 이용하시면, 매일 우편물을 전달하거나, 개봉하여 스캔하거나, 파쇄할 수 있습니다. [159] **어떤 기기에서든 고객 보안 코드를 이용해 로그인하기만 하면 각 우편물의 앞면 스캔본을 볼 수 있습니다. 그런 다음, 저희가 어떤 추가 조치를 취할지 선택하시면 됩니다.**

이번 달에 한해, [160] **저희 골드 서비스에 등록하시면 1년 계약 중 첫 6개월 동안 25% 할인을 받습니다.**

어휘 virtual 가상의 store 보관하다 including ~을 포함해 envelope 봉투 drop off 놓아 두다, 내려 주다 forward 전달하다 shred 파쇄하다 secure 안전한 initial 처음의 further 추가적인, 한층 더 한 action 조치 enroll in ~에 등록하다 annual 연간의, 해마다의

## 158 세부 사항

번역 메디나 가상 우편함은 언제 고객들에게 알림을 보내는가?
(A) 우편물을 전달했을 때
(B) 물품이 그곳에 도착할 때
(C) 가입한 서비스 기간이 만료되려 할 때
(D) 보관 구역이 거의 찼을 때

해설 지문 중반부의 두 번째 항목에 우편물이 전달될 때마다 문자 메시지로 알려 준다(You will be notified by text whenever your mail is dropped off to us)는 말이 쓰여 있으므로 (B)가 정답이다.

어휘 subscription 가입, 구독 be about to 막 ~하려 하다 expire 만료되다 storage 보관, 저장

> Paraphrasing
> 지문의 whenever your mail is dropped off to us
> → 정답의 When an item arrives at the site

## 159 세부 사항

번역 고객들이 자신의 우편물을 어떻게 할지 선택하려면 무엇을 해야 하는가?
(A) 보안 코드로 로그인하기
(B) 계약서에 지시 사항 지정하기
(C) 회사 사무실에 전화하기
(D) 업체에 문자 메시지 보내기

해설 지문 중반부의 세 번째 항목에, 어떤 기기에서든 고객 보안 코드를 이용해 로그인하기만 하면 각 우편물의 앞면 스캔본을 볼 수 있고, 그 후에 업체가 취해야 하는 추가 조치를 선택하면 된다(Simply log in from any device with your secure customer code ~ choose what further action we should take with it)고 알리고 있다. 따라서 (A)가 정답이다.

어휘 set 지정하다, 설정하다 instructions 지시, 설명 contract 계약(서)

## 160 세부 사항

번역 고객들은 어떻게 할인 자격을 얻을 수 있는가?
(A) 상위 서비스에 등록함으로써
(B) 반년 계약을 약속함으로써
(C) 시스템에서 바우처를 다운로드함으로써
(D) 6개월 전에 미리 서비스 비용을 지불함으로써

해설 마지막 단락에 골드 서비스에 등록하면 1년 계약 중 첫 6개월 동안 25% 할인을 받는다(enroll in our Gold Service to receive 25% off the first six months of your annual contract)고 언급되어 있으므로 (A)가 정답이다.

어휘 sign up for ~에 등록하다, ~을 신청하다 premium (같은 종류의 다른 것보다) 상급의, 고급의 commit to+명사 ~을 약속하다 in advance 미리, 사전에

> Paraphrasing
> 지문의 enroll in our Gold Service
> → 정답의 signing up for a premium service

### 161-163 공지

리버데일 자전거 안전의 날

[161] **여러분의 자전거가 도로와 산길에서 타기에 안전한지 확인하고 싶으신가요?** 그러면 [162] **7월 20일** 오전 10시부터 오후 4시까지 선라이즈 공원에서 열리는 리버데일 자전거 안전의 날 행사를 놓치지 마십시오.

공인 자전거 수리 기술자들이 현장에서 [161] **무료로** 여러분의 자전거를 점검해 드릴 것입니다. 이 기술자들은 체인 수리 또는 교체, 안장 높이 조절, [162] **펑크 난 타이어 패치 부착 및 공기 주입**, 그리고 브레이크 케이블 점검 같은 기본적인 관리 및 수리를 해 드릴 수 있습니다. [163] **시간을 절약하려면, 토니스 자전거 전문점에서 미리 시간대를 예약하시면 됩니다.** 또는, 그냥 들러서 줄을 서서 기다리셔도 됩니다.

리버데일 자전거 안전의 날 행사는 메도우랜드 그랜트와 토니스 자전거 전문점의 후원을 통해 개최 가능하게 되었습니다.

추가 정보를 원하시는 분은, www.riverdalecommunity.org/bikesafety를 방문하시기 바랍니다.

어휘 trail 산길 certified 공인된, 면허를 가진 on site 현장에서 at no cost 무료로 perform 실시하다 maintenance 유지 관리 adjust 조절하다 patch 패치를 부착하다 flat tire 펑크 난 타이어 time slot 시간대 in advance 미리, 사전에 sponsorship 후원

## 161 주제 / 목적

번역 공지의 목적은 무엇인가?
(A) 업체의 시작을 알리는 것
(B) 안전 규정을 설명하는 것
(C) 자전거 경주 대회를 홍보하는 것
(D) 무료 서비스를 광고하는 것

해설 첫 단락에서 자전거가 타기에 안전한지 확인해 주는 행사(Do you want to make sure your bicycle is safe to ride on the roads and trails?)를 소개한 후, 두 번째 단락에 무료(at no cost)라고 알리고 있으므로 (D)가 정답이다.

어휘 launch 시작, 출시 regulation 규정, 규제 promote 홍보하다 free 무료의

> **Paraphrasing**
> 지문의 at no cost → 정답의 free

## 162 세부 사항

번역 7월 20일에 무슨 일이 있을 것으로 예상되는가?
(A) 새로운 공공 자전거 전용 도로가 개통될 것이다.
(B) 일부 자전거 타이어에 공기가 주입될 것이다.
(C) 참가자들이 인증서를 받을 것이다.
(D) 자전거가 할인된 가격에 판매될 것이다.

해설 7월 20일은 첫 단락에 행사 개최 날짜로 제시되어 있으며, 두 번째 단락에 이 행사에서 제공되는 서비스의 하나로 펑크 난 타이어 패치 부착 및 공기 주입(patching and filling flat tires)이 쓰여 있으므로 (B)가 정답이다.

어휘 participant 참가자 certificate 인증서

> **Paraphrasing**
> 지문의 filling flat tires
> → 정답의 Air will be added to some bike tires

## 163 문장 삽입

번역 [1], [2], [3], [4]로 표시된 곳 중에서 다음 문장이 가장 적합한 곳은 어디인가?

"또는, 그냥 들러서 줄을 서서 기다리셔도 됩니다."
(A) [1]
(B) [2]
(C) [3]
(D) [4]

해설 제시된 문장은 '또는, 그 대신' 등의 의미로 대안을 말할 때 사용하는 Alternatively로 시작한다. 이는 행사 참가 방법을 설명한 문장 뒤에 와서 그 외의 참가 방법을 언급하는 흐름이 되어야 자연스럽다. 따라서 미리 시간대를 예약하라(you can book a time slot in advance at Tony's Bike Shop)는 문장 뒤인 [3]에 오는 것이 가장 알맞으므로 정답은 (C)이다.

어휘 alternatively 또는, 그 대신 stop by 들르다

### 164-167 온라인 채팅

아이라 캐슬린 (오후 1시 23분)
안녕하세요, 켄고 그리고 태미. [164] **알레르기 신약 테스트**가 어떻게 되어 가고 있는지 확인하고 싶어서요. [165] **목요일에 검사관이 장비를 점검할 예정이니까** 수요일까지 완료되면 가장 좋을 것 같습니다.

켄고 요네다 (오후 1시 24분)
분석 작업을 해야 하는 게 하나 더 있는데, 오늘 끝날 겁니다.

아이라 캐슬린 (오후 1시 25분)
다행입니다. 그 말은 우리가 예정대로 다음 주 월요일에 [164] **임상 실험을 위한 인원 모집**을 시작할 수 있을 것이란 뜻이네요. 두 분 중 아무나 데이터베이스에서 지역 의료 서비스 제공자 목록을 정리할 시간이 있으신가요?

태미 가르자 (오후 1시 27분)
죄송해요, 아이라. 저는 지역 컨퍼런스에 참석하기 위해 내일 출발해요. 다음 주 화요일이나 되어야 어떤 새로운 프로젝트든 시작할 수 있을 겁니다.

켄고 요네다 (오후 1시 28분)
[166] **저는 그 프로그램을 이용해 본 적은 없지만, 한번 시도해보겠습니다.**

아이라 캐슬린 (오후 1시 31분)
고마워요, 켄고! 그 소프트웨어가 처음엔 사용하기가 조금 헷갈리긴 하지만, [167] **설명서에 명확한 설명이 있습니다. 제가 IT팀에 한 부 요청할게요.**

켄고 요네다 (오후 1시 32분)
그럼 정말 도움이 될 거예요.

태미 가르자 (오후 1시 33분)
실은, 그러실 필요 없습니다. [167] **제 책상에 출력해 둔 게 있거든요.** 제가 점심 식사 후에 갖다 드릴게요.

켄고 요네다 (오후 1시 36분)
좋습니다. 고마워요, 태미.

아이라 캐슬린 (오후 1시 37분)
그럼 모든 게 준비됐네요. 두 분 모두의 수고에 감사드리고, 보고서 읽는 걸 기대합니다.

어휘 round 한 차례, 한 회 inspector 점검자, 조사자 equipment 장비 analysis 분석 run 진행하다 relief 다행인 것, 안심 recruit 인원을 모집하다 clinical trial 임상 실험 compile (자료 등을 모아) 정리하다 regional 지역의 a bit 조금, 약간 confusing 헷갈리게 하는 instructions 설명, 안내 necessary 필요한, 필수의 set 준비된, 마련된 look forward to -ing ~하기를 기대하다

## 164 추론

번역 메시지 작성자들은 어떤 종류의 업체에서 근무하고 있을 것 같은가?
(A) 슈퍼마켓 체인
(B) 소프트웨어 테스트 센터
(C) 치과
(D) 연구소

해설 1시 23분과 1시 25분에 작성된 메시지에, 알레르기 신약 테스트(the testing of our new allergy medicine)와 임상 실험을 위한 인원 모집(recruiting for the clinical trials)이라는 말이 쓰여 있어 약품과 관련된 실험을 하는 연구소에 근무하는 사람들인 것으로 볼 수 있다. 따라서 (D)가 정답이다.

## 165 세부 사항

번역 점검이 언제 실시될 것인가?
(A) 이번 주 수요일
(B) 이번 주 목요일
(C) 다음 주 월요일
(D) 다음 주 화요일

해설 1시 23분 메시지에 검사관이 목요일에 장비를 점검할 예정(an inspector will be checking our equipment on Thursday)이라고 제시되어 있으므로 (B)가 정답이다.

## 166 Not / True

번역 요네다 씨에 대해 언급된 것은?
(A) 컨퍼런스에 참석하는 데 관심이 있다.
(B) 한 소프트웨어 프로그램에 익숙하지 않다.
(C) 데이터베이스에 접속하는 데 어려움이 있었다.
(D) 어떤 새 프로젝트도 맡을 수 없다.

해설 1시 28분 메시지에 요네다 씨가 앞서 언급된 프로그램에 대해 그것을 이용해 본 적은 없지만 한번 시도해보겠다(I haven't used that program, but I'm willing to try)고 말하고 있어 그 프로그램에 익숙하지 않다는 것을 알 수 있으므로 (B)가 정답이다.

어휘 be familiar with ~에 익숙하다, ~을 잘 알다 access 접근하다, 이용하다 take on ~을 맡다

> **Paraphrasing**
> 지문의 haven't used that program
> → 정답의 is not familiar with a software program

## 167 의도 파악

번역 오후 1시 33분에, 가르자 씨가 "그러실 필요 없습니다"라고 쓸 때, 의미하는 것은 무엇인가?
(A) 배정되는 업무가 다른 직원에게 주어질 수 있다.
(B) 캐슬린 씨가 IT팀에 연락할 필요가 없다.
(C) 이번에는 원격으로 컨퍼런스에 참석할 수 있다.
(D) 설명서의 설명이 곧 업데이트될 것이다.

해설 1시 31분 메시지에 캐슬린 씨가 설명서를 언급하면서 IT팀에 한 부 요청하겠다(~ the manual. I'll ask the IT team for a copy)고 한 것에 대해, 1시 33분에 가르자 씨가 그럴 필요 없다는 말과 함께 자신이 출력한 것을 갖고 있다(I have a printout in my desk)고 대답하는 흐름이다. 이는 캐슬린 씨가 IT팀에 설명서를 요청할 필요가 없다는 뜻이므로 (B)가 정답이다.

어휘 assignment 배정(되는 일) remotely 원격으로, 멀리서

### 168-171 기사

브래 항공사에 새로운 모습을 선사하는 로얄 인디고

시드니(2월 17일)—브래 항공사는 자사 객실 승무원들의 새 유니폼을 제작하기 위해 패션 전문업체 로얄 인디고를 고용했다. [168] **디자인은 3월에 승인될 것으로 예상되며, 그 시점부터 승객들이 기내에서 새로운 스타일을 보기까지는 약 3개월이 걸릴 것이다.**

[170] **테이자 레이타 수석 브랜드 관리 책임자**는 유니폼이 10년간 동일했고, 이 변화는 회사 브랜드를 다시 디자인하는 것의 일환이라고 말했다.

"로얄 인디고의 창의성이 저희 브랜드를 기억에 남게 하고 신선한 모습을 선사하는 상징적인 유니폼을 제작해 줄 것이라고 확신합니다"라고 레이타 씨가 말했다. "[169] **지금까지 고급 브랜드에서 유니폼을 공급받은 적이 없었기 때문에** 이번 협업에 대한 기대가 큽니다."

레이타 씨는 입사한 지 1년이 채 되지 않았으며, 작년 11월 [170] **에 이바 할로웨이의 자리를 이어받아,** [171] **곧바로 시드니와 싱가포르에 있는 브래 항공사의 공항 라운지를 개조하고 개선하는 일을 맡았다.** 레이타 씨는 또한 회사의 소셜 미디어 게시물을 간소화하고 새로운 로고를 의뢰했으며, 현재 여행과 관련된 비영리 단체들과 협업하는 것을 검토하고 있다.

어휘 create 만들어 내다 approve 승인하다 decade 10년 creativity 창의성 iconic 상징적인 memorable 기억에 남을 만한 high-end 고급의 supply 공급하다 collaboration 협업, 공동 작업 take over from ~로부터 이어받다 see to -ing ~하는 일을 맡다, 처리하다 renovate 개조하다, 보수하다 improve 향상시키다 streamline 간소화하다 commission 의뢰하다 look into ~을 검토하다, 살펴보다 nonprofit 비영리의 organization 단체, 기관 related to+명사 ~와 관련된

## 168 추론

번역 새로운 유니폼은 언제 처음 사용될 것 같은가?
(A) 2월에
(B) 3월에
(C) 6월에
(D) 11월에

해설 첫 단락에 디자인이 3월에 승인되어 승객들이 기내에서 새로운 스타일을 보기까지는 그로부터 약 3개월이 걸릴 것(The designs are expected to be approved in March, and from that point, it will take about three months before passengers see the new style on board)이라고 쓰여 있으므로 3월부터 3개월 뒤인 (C)가 정답이다.

## 169 Not / True

번역 기사에서 브래 항공사와 로얄 인디고의 제휴 관계에 관해 언급하는 것은?
(A) 브래 항공사는 고급 브랜드 회사와 처음 협업하는 것이다.
(B) 최소 10년 동안 지속될 것으로 예상된다.
(C) 오직 일등석으로 여행하는 고객들에게만 영향을 미칠 것이다.
(D) 3개월간의 협의 끝에 최종 확정되었다.

해설 세 번째 단락에 브래 항공사 직원인 레이타 씨가 지금까지 고급 브랜드에서 유니폼을 공급받은 적이 없었다(Until now, we have not had high-end brands supply our uniforms)고 인터뷰한 내용이 쓰여 있다. 이는 고급 브랜드 회사와 처음 협업한다는 뜻이므로 (A)가 정답이다.

어휘 last 지속되다 affect 영향을 미치다 negotiation 협의, 협상

> **Paraphrasing**
> 지문의 have not had high-end brands supply our uniforms → 정답의 Brae Airlines' first time working with a luxury brand

## 170 세부 사항

번역 기사에 따르면, 할로웨이 씨는 누구인가?
(A) 브래 항공사 선임 분석관
(B) 로얄 인디고의 수석 디자이너
(C) 브래 항공사의 전임 브랜드 관리 책임자
(D) 브래 항공사의 설립자

해설 네 번째 단락에 레이타 씨가 할로웨이 씨의 자리를 이어받은(taking over from Ava Holloway) 사실이 쓰여 있고, 두 번째 단락에 레이타 씨가 현재 수석 브랜드 관리 책임자(Senior brand manager Teija Raita)로 표기되어 있다. 이를 통해 할로웨이 씨가 전임 브랜드 관리 책임자임을 알 수 있으므로 (C)가 정답이다.

어휘 analyst 분석가 former 전임의, 전직 ~의

## 171 세부 사항

번역 레이타 씨는 브래 항공사에서 어떤 업무를 처음 완료했는가?
(A) 항공사의 로고를 업데이트했다.
(B) 회사 소셜 미디어의 존재감을 향상시켰다.
(C) 본사를 싱가포르로 옮겼다.
(D) 공항 라운지를 업그레이드했다.

해설 네 번째 단락에 레이타 씨는 에이바 할로웨이 씨의 자리를 이어받아, 곧바로 시드니와 싱가포르에 있는 브래 항공사의 공항 라운지를 개조하고 향상시키는 일을 맡았다(immediately seeing to renovating and improving Brae's airport lounges in Sydney and Singapore)고 했으므로 (D)가 정답이다.

어휘 task 업무, 일 presence 존재(감)

> **Paraphrasing**
> 지문의 renovating and improving Brae's airport lounges → 정답의 had some airport lounges upgraded

## 172-175 편지

10월 16일

대니얼 맥길
페이지 바이 페이지 서점
아머리 가 477
로체스터, NY 14604

맥길 씨께,

172 **그랜섬 출판사에서는 저희 최신작 <비니스 더 서피스>를 취급할 독립 소매업체를 찾고 있습니다.** 문학 평론가들로부터 극찬을 받은 이 소설은 독자들에게 드라마와 과학의 독특한 조합을 선사합니다.

173 **<비니스 더 서피스>는 고장 나고 낡은 컴퓨터와 스마트폰들이 더 이상 쓰이지 않게 되면 어떻게 되는지 살펴봅니다.** 지역 쓰레기 매립지의 토양 오염으로 인해 부정적인 영향을 받은 작은 마을에 대한 가상의 이야기이지만, 최근 연구에 기반한 실제 정보를 포함하고 있습니다.

175 **<비니스 더 서피스>의 두 저자는 환경 과학자 나다니엘 리와 월포드 대학의 생태학 교수 세실리아 샌도벌 박사입니다.** 두 분 모두 각자의 분야에서 높이 평가받고 계십니다. 175 **리 씨는 권위 있는 캘드웰 상을 수상하셨으며, 샌도벌 박사님은 온라인 교육 프로그램 컨설팅으로 찬사를 받고 계십니다.** 174 **두 분은 <비니스 더 서피스>로 출판 데뷔를 하고 있으며,** 귀하의 서점으로 보내지는 일부 책에 기꺼이 사인도 해 드릴 것입니다.

제가 언제든지 <비니스 더 서피스>와 관련된 추가 상세 정보를 제공해 드릴 수 있습니다. 귀하로부터 답변 들을 수 있기를 고대합니다.

재커리 172 **웨슬리**

어휘 seek 찾다, 구하다 independent 독립적인 retailer 소매업체 rave 극찬하는 literary 문학의 critic 평론가 unique 독특한 combination 조합 examine 살펴보다, 조사하다 outdated 낡은, 구식의 fictional 소설의 account 이야기 negatively 부정적으로 soil 토양 contamination 오염 landfill 쓰레기 매립지 contain 포함하다 factual 실제의, 사실의 based on ~을 바탕으로 environmental 환경의 ecology 생태학 award 수여하다 prestigious 권위 있는 be acclaimed for ~로 찬사를 받다 further 추가의

## 172 세부 사항

번역 웨즐리 씨는 무엇을 하고 싶어 하는가?
(A) 글쓰기 대회를 위한 심사 위원 모집하기
(B) 한 도서의 판매 가능성 향상시키기
(C) 서점의 개업식 홍보하기
(D) 책 표지를 만들 디자이너 고용하기

TEST 5

해설 웨즐리 씨는 편지를 쓴 사람이고, 첫 단락에 그랜섬 출판사가 최신작 <비니스 더 서피스>를 취급할 독립 소매업체를 찾고 있다(Grantham Publishing is seeking independent retailers to carry our latest work, *Beneath the Surface*)고 알리고 있다. 이는 해당 도서의 판매처를 늘리는 일에 해당하므로 (B)가 정답이다.

어휘 recruit 모집하다 judge 심사 위원 improve 향상시키다 availability 이용 가능성 promote 홍보하다

## 173 Not / True

번역 <비니스 더 서피스>에 대해 언급된 것은?
(A) 컴퓨터용 디지털 파일로 이용할 수 있다.
(B) 낡은 전자기기의 폐기 처분에 대해 탐구한다.
(C) 상의 후보로 지명되었다.
(D) 평론가들의 찬사를 받은 드라마를 바탕으로 한다.

해설 두 번째 단락에 <비니스 더 서피스>가 고장 나고 낡은 컴퓨터와 스마트폰들이 더 이상 쓰이지 않게 되면 어떻게 되는지 살펴본다(*Beneath the Surface* examines what happens to broken and outdated computers and smartphones once they are no longer in use)고 쓰여 있으므로 (B)가 정답이다.

어휘 explore 탐구하다 disposal 처분 electronics 전자기기 be nominate for ~에 대한 후보로 지명되다 critically acclaimed 평론가들의 찬사를 받은

> **Paraphrasing**
> 지문의 examines what happens to broken and outdated computers and smartphones
> → 정답의 explores the disposal of old electronics

## 174 Not / True

번역 리 씨와 샌도벌 박사에 대해 언급된 것은?
(A) 토양 샘플을 수집해 왔다.
(B) 맥길 씨의 매장을 방문할 것이다.
(C) 처음 책을 내는 작가이다.
(D) 온라인 교육 플랫폼을 설립했다.

해설 두 사람의 이름이 언급되는 세 번째 단락에 <비니스 더 서피스>로 출판 데뷔를 한다(They are making their publishing debut with *Beneath the Surface* ~)고 쓰여 있는 것에서 처음 책을 내는 작가임을 알 수 있다. 따라서 (C)가 정답이다.

어휘 collect 수집하다 soil 토양

> **Paraphrasing**
> 지문의 They are making their publishing debut
> → 정답의 first-time authors

## 175 문장 삽입

번역 [1], [2], [3], [4]로 표시된 곳 중에서 다음 문장이 가장 적합한 곳은 어디인가?
"두 분 모두 각자의 분야에서 높이 평가받고 계십니다."
(A) [1]
(B) [2]
(C) [3]
(D) [4]

해설 주어진 문장의 '두 사람'이 먼저 제시되어야 한다. [3] 앞에 나다니엘 리와 세실리아 샌도벌 박사가 책의 저자로 언급되므로 이 뒤에 주어진 문장이 들어가는 것이 적절하다. 또한 [3] 뒤에 두 사람이 어떤 좋은 평가를 받았는지 세부적으로 설명하는 내용이 나오므로 이어지는 내용도 자연스럽다. 따라서 (C)가 정답이다.

어휘 highly esteemed 높이 평가받는 respective 각자의, 각각의 field 분야

## 176-180 공지+이메일

www.gipomcon.com

GHI 생산 및 경영 관리 컨퍼런스
세미나 제안서 요청

176 **고 중공업(GHI)이 싱가포르 컨벤션 센터에서 6월 21일부터 22일까지 제1회 GHI 생산 및 운영 관리 컨퍼런스를 개최합니다.** 177(A), 180 **저희는 사업상 도전 과제에 대응하여 소속 단체에서 성공적으로 조치한 것에 관한 세미나를 이끌어 주실 생산 및 운영 전문가들의 제안서를 모집하고 있습니다.** 이상적인 세미나 주제는 컨퍼런스 주제인 "분석 시대의 발전"과 관련된 것이지만, 다른 주제도 허용됩니다.

177(B) **제안서는 100~200단어 분량으로,** 177(D) **제출자의 자격을 요약한 것이 첨부되어야 합니다.** 약 30개의 제안서가 세미나 방식의 발표를 위해 선정될 것이며, 178 **더 많은 제출물이 접수되는 경우, 추가 제출자들께서는 대신 주제가 있는 90분 길이의 패널 토론회에 참여하시도록 요청받으실 수도 있습니다.** 179 **각 세미나는 참석한 생산 및 운영 관리 협회(POMS) 회원들에게 한 시간의 능력 개발 시간으로 간주될 것이므로 제출자들께서는 제안서가 세미나를 위해 선정된 후 승인을 위해 POMS에 제출되어야 한다는 점에 유의하시기 바랍니다.**

이 온라인 양식을 이용하셔서 11월 15일까지 컨퍼런스 조직 위원회에 여러분의 제안서를 제출해 주시기 바랍니다.

어휘 proposal 제안(서) convene (회의 등을) 개최하다, 소집하다 call for ~을 요청하다 organization 단체, 기관 ideal 이상적인 relate to+명사 ~와 관련되다 advance 진보, 발전 analytics 분석 (자료) accompany 동반하다 summary 요약(문) submitter 제출자 qualification 자격(증) roughly 약, 대략 submission 제출(되는 것) themed 주제가 있는 approval 승인 count as ~로 여겨지다, 간주되다 in attendance 참석한 organizing committee 조직 위원회

발신: 웨이 추아
수신: 레슬리 브릭스
제목: 컨퍼런스 제출물
날짜: 12월 11일

브릭스 씨께,

GHI 생산 및 운영 관리 컨퍼런스 조직 위원회를 대표해, 179, 180 **귀하께서 제안해 주신 주제, "기계 학습을 활용한 항공사 예비 승무원 일정 관리 최적화"에 관한 세미나 진행을 요청드리게 되어 기쁩니다.**

12월 20일까지 이 이메일에 답장하셔서 귀하의 컨퍼런스 참가 의사를 확인해 주시기 바랍니다. 그렇게 하시는 대로, POMS 승인 과정을 시작하시는 방법과 관련된 정보를 보내 드리겠습니다.

웨이 추아
조직 위원회
GHI 생산 및 운영 관리 컨퍼런스

어휘 on behalf of ~을 대표해 optimize 최적화하다 backup 예비의, 보조의 respond 답장하다, 반응하다 intention 의사, 의도 process 과정 accreditation 승인, 인가

## 176 세부 사항

번역 어떤 종류의 단체가 컨퍼런스를 개최하는가?
(A) 전문적인 협회
(B) 국가 정부 기관
(C) 대학교 학과
(D) 제조회사

해설 공지 첫 단락에 고 중공업(GHI)이 싱가포르 컨벤션 센터에서 6월 21일부터 22일까지 첫 번째 GHI 생산 및 운영 관리 컨퍼런스를 개최한다(Goh Heavy Industries (GHI) will convene the first-ever GHI Production & Operations Management Conference ~)고 쓰여 있으므로 (D)가 정답이다.

> Paraphrasing
> 지문의 Goh Heavy Industries
> → 정답의 A manufacturing company

## 177 Not / True

번역 세미나 제안서에 대한 요건이 아닌 것은?
(A) 한 단체에서 취한 조치를 설명해야 한다.
(B) 특정 길이로 된 것이어야 한다.
(C) 이메일로 제출해야 한다.
(D) 제출자에 관한 정보를 포함해야 한다.

해설 공지 첫 단락에 사업상 도전 과제에 대응하여 소속 단체에서 성공적으로 조치한 것에 관한 세미나(seminars on their organizations' successful actions in response to business challenges)라고 쓰여 있는 부분을 통해 (A)를, 두 번째 단락에 100~200단어 분량이어야 한다(Proposals must be between 100 and 200 words long)고 한 것에서 (B)를, 제출자의 자격을 요약한 것이 첨부되어야 한다(accompanied by a summary of the submitter's qualifications)한 것에서 (D)를 확인할 수 있다. 하지만 이메일로 제출해야 한다는 내용은 없으므로 (C)가 정답이다.

어휘 requirement 요건, 필수 조건 come with ~을 포함하다

> Paraphrasing
> 지문의 organizations' successful actions
> → 보기 (A)의 actions taken by an organization
> 지문의 must be between 100 and 200 words long
> → 보기 (B)의 must be of a certain length
> 지문의 accompanied by a summary of the submitter's qualifications → 보기 (D)의 come with information about the submitter

## 178 세부 사항

번역 공지에 따르면, 일부 제출자들은 무엇을 하도록 요청받을 것인가?
(A) 다른 유형의 행사 참가하기
(B) 출판물에 기사 기고하기
(C) 발표 녹화 허용하기
(D) 특별히 일찍 행사장 도착하기

해설 공지 두 번째 단락에 더 많은 제출물이 접수되는 경우에 추가 제출자들이 대신 주제가 있는 90분 길이의 패널 토론회에 참여하도록 요청받을 수 있다(~ additional submitters may be invited to participate in themed 90-minute panel discussions instead)고 쓰여 있다. 세미나 진행이 아닌 다른 종류의 행사 참가를 요청받는 것을 의미하므로 (A)가 정답이다.

어휘 alternative 대체의, 대안의 contribute 기고하다 publication 출판(물) venue 행사장, 개최 장소

> Paraphrasing
> 지문의 themed 90-minute panel discussions instead
> → 정답의 an alternative type of event

## 179 연계

번역 브릭스 씨는 컨퍼런스에서 청중 앞에 얼마나 오래 모습을 보일 것 같은가?
(A) 15분
(B) 30분
(C) 1시간
(D) 90분

해설 이메일 첫 단락에 브릭스 씨에게 세미나 진행을 요청한다(it is my pleasure to invite you to lead a seminar on your proposed topic)는 말이 쓰여 있어 세미나 진행자로 선정되었음을 알 수 있다. 세미나에 대해, 공지 두 번째 단락에 각 세미나가 한 시간의 직무 능력 개발 시간으로 간주될 것(each seminar will count as an hour of professional development)이라는 내용이 제시되어 있으므로 1시간 동안 진행될 것임을 알 수 있다. 따라서 (C)가 정답이다.

## 180 연계

번역 브릭스 씨에 대해 암시된 것은?
(A) 세미나 제안서를 1개보다 많이 제출했다.
(B) 항공기 디자인 과정을 관리하는 책임을 지고 있다.
(C) 싱가포르에 본사를 두고 있는 회사에서 근무한다.
(D) 기술을 활용해 직원 구성 문제를 해결한 적이 있다.

해설 이메일 첫 단락에 브릭스 씨가 제안한 세미나 주제가 '기계 학습을 활용한 항공사 예비 승무원 일정 관리 최적화(Using Machine Learning to Optimize Backup Crew Scheduling in Airlines)'라고 쓰여 있고, 공지 첫 단락에는 사업상 도전 과제에 대응하여 소속 단체에서 성공적으로 조치한 것에 관한 세미나(~ seminars on their organizations' successful actions in response to business challenges)임을 알리는 내용이 제시되어 있다. 따라서 브릭스 씨가 기술을 활용해 직원 관련 문제에 대응한 적이 있었던 사람으로 볼 수 있으므로 (D)가 정답이다.

어휘 be responsible for ~에 대한 책임을 지고 있다 be based in ~에 본사를 두고 있다 address (문제 등을) 해결하다, 처리하다 staffing 직원 구성, 직원 채용

## 181-185 웹페이지+이메일

| 홈 | 제품 | 뉴스 보도 | 연락처 |
|---|---|---|---|

오칼록스는 섬유 처리제 제조업을 선도하고 있습니다. 혁신적인 저희 제품은 아주 다양한 직물에 사용될 수 있으며, [181] **물기 흡수를 막는 방수층을 만들어 냅니다.**

적용 과정은 간단합니다. 지침에 따라 오칼록스와 따뜻한 물을 섞은 용액을 준비합니다. 그 후 직물을 20분 동안 이 혼합액에 담가 둡니다. 그런 다음, 직물을 평평한 표면에 [182] **펼쳐 놓고** 최소 6시간 동안 자연 건조되도록 놓아 둡니다. 그러면 추가 세탁 없이 제품을 바로 사용할 준비가 됩니다.

여러분의 특정 요구 사항을 해결하기에 적합한 고성능 세제를 선택하세요.

| 제품 번호 | 용량 선택 | 적용 대상 |
|---|---|---|
| R350 | 10L, 30L, 60L | 의류 (통기성) |
| R370 | 10L, 30L, 60L | 외투 (비통기성) |
| [183] **T125** | **10L, 30L** | **신발 및 등산화** |

대량 주문 가격에 대해 문의하시려면 저희 고객 서비스 전화번호 1-800-555-2626번으로 연락 주시기 바랍니다.

어휘 at the forefront of ~을 선도하는, ~의 선두에 있는 manufacture 제조하다 textile 섬유 treatment 처리(제) revolutionary 혁신적인 a wide range of 아주 다양한 fabric 직물 waterproof 방수의 layer 층, 막 absorption 흡수 application 적용 process 과정 solution 용액 instructions 설명, 안내 soak 담그다 mixture 혼합물 duration 지속 (시간) extend 펼치다 surface 표면 air-dry 자연 건조하다 laundering 세탁 high-performance 고성능의 address (문제 등을) 해결하다, 처리하다 specific 특정한, 구체적인 quantity 용량, 수량 formulate 만들다 breathable 통기성의 inquire 문의하다 bulk 대량 판매되는 rate 요금, 등급

수신: customerservice@ocalox.com
발신: chosusan@steltzermfg.com
날짜: 9월 22일
제목: 제품 문제

고객 서비스 팀에게,

[183] **저희는 귀사의 T125 제품을 제조 과정에서 6개월째 사용해 오고 있습니다.** 전반적으로, 저희는 결과에 대해 만족해 왔으며, 고객 의견과 품질 관리 테스트도 모두 긍정적이었습니다.

하지만 최근에 [185] **건조 시간 이후 직물 표면에 일종의 끈적한 물질이 남아 있는 것을 발견하기 시작했습니다.** 해당 용기는 저희가 아무런 문제없이 사용했던 다른 제품과 같은 묶음의 제품이라서, [184] **제 생각엔 저희가 제품을 보관한 방식이 문제였을 수 있을 것 같습니다. 어떻게 보관해야 적절한지 알려 주실 수 있나요?** 설명서에서 이 문제와 관련된 어떤 정보도 찾을 수 없었습니다.

대단히 감사합니다.

수잔 조
스텔저 제조사

어휘 issue 문제, 사안 overall 전반적으로 quality-control 품질 관리 positive 긍정적인 sticky 끈적한 substance 물질 surface 표면 container 용기, 그릇 batch (작업 등의) 1회분 store 보관하다 properly 적절히, 제대로

## 181 세부 사항

번역 오칼록스 제품의 용도는 무엇인가?
(A) 표면 색상을 더 오래 지속되도록 만들기
(B) 직물의 내구성 향상시키기
(C) 수분 차단막 제공하기
(D) 섬유를 부드럽고 효과적으로 세척하기

해설 웹페이지 첫 단락에 물기 흡수를 막는 방수층을 만들어 낸다(creating a waterproof layer that stops the absorption of water)는 말이 쓰여 있으므로 이러한 특징에 해당하는 (C)가 정답이다.

어휘 last 지속되다 durability 내구성 barrier 장벽 moisture 수분 gently 부드럽게 effectively 효과적으로

> **Paraphrasing**
> 지문의 creating a waterproof layer that stops the absorption of water
> → 정답의 Provide a barrier against moisture

## 182 동의어

번역 웹페이지에서 두 번째 단락, 세 번째 줄에 쓰인 "extended"와 의미가 가장 가까운 것은?
(A) 펼쳐진
(B) 지속된
(C) 연기된
(D) 연장된

해설 extended는 혼합액에 담갔던 직물을 평평한 표면에 놓아 두는 방식과 관련된 단어로서 '펼쳐진'을 뜻하는 것으로 볼 수 있으므로 동일한 의미로 쓰이는 (A) spread out이 정답이다.

## 183 연계

번역 스텔저 제조사에 대해 암시된 것은?
(A) 제품이 안전 테스트에서 탈락했다.
(B) 6개월 전에 설립되었다.
(C) 친환경적인 제품을 이용하려 애쓴다.
(D) 신발을 상업적으로 생산한다.

해설 스텔저 제조사의 직원인 수잔 조 씨가 보낸 이메일 첫 단락에 T125 제품을 제조 과정에서 사용하고 있다(We have been using your T125 product in our manufacturing process)는 말이 쓰여 있다. 웹페이지 하단의 제품 목록에 T125 제품이 신발에 쓰이는 것(T125, Shoes and hiking boots)으로 표기되어 있으므로 (D)가 정답이다.

어휘 fail 탈락하다, 실패하다 found 설립하다 strive to ~하려 애쓰다 eco-friendly 친환경적인 commercially 상업적으로

## 184 주제 / 목적

번역 조 씨가 이메일을 쓴 목적은 무엇인가?
(A) 설명서를 한 부 요청하는 것
(B) 보관에 관한 정보를 얻는 것
(C) 공급 계약을 취소하는 것
(D) 대체 제품을 요청하는 것

해설 이메일 두 번째 단락에 문제 상황을 언급하면서 보관 방식이 문제였을 수 있을 것 같다는 말과 함께 어떻게 보관해야 적절한지 알려 줄 것(I think it may be a problem with the way we were storing the product. Could you please let me know how this should be done properly?)을 요청하고 있다. 따라서 (B)가 정답이다.

어휘 storage 보관, 저장 supply 공급 contract 계약(서) replacement 대체(품)

## 185 세부 사항

번역 조 씨는 소속 회사의 제조 과정에 대해 어떤 문제를 언급하는가?
(A) 제품에서 강한 냄새가 난다.
(B) 잔여물이 남는다.
(C) 건조 시간이 늘어났다.
(D) 직물 표면이 쉽게 찢어진다.

해설 이메일 두 번째 단락에 건조 시간 이후 직물 표면에 일종의 끈적한 물질이 남아 있는 것을 발견하기 시작했다(we started noticing some kind of sticky substance remaining on the fabric's surface)는 말이 쓰여 있으므로 (B)가 정답이다.

어휘 odor 냄새 residue 잔여물 leave behind 남기다 tear 찢어지다

> **Paraphrasing**
> 지문의 sticky substance remaining
> → 정답의 residue is left behind

## 186-190 기사+차트+이메일

살리나스 [186] **(3월 3일)**—애트웰 전력회사가 수천 개의 가정과 업체에 전기를 공급할 대규모 재생 에너지 프로젝트를 위한 부지를 확정했다. 이 프로젝트는 네 곳에 풍력 발전용 터빈을 설치하는 것을 포함할 것이다. 이 부지들은 이미 환경적 고려 사항에 대한 점검을 받았으며, 주 정부와 연방 정부로부터 필요한 허가를 받았다. 애트웰 전력회사가 직접 터빈과 변전소를 지을 것이지만, [189] **전기 출력부와 배전망을 연결하는 송전선 공사는 제3자에 의해 진행될 것이다.** 대변인은 애트웰 전력회사의 프로젝트가 지역 내의 고도로 숙련된 작업자들을 위한 많은 일자리를 창출할 것이며, [186] **다음 달 초부터 이 일자리들에 대한 공고를 시작할 것이라고 밝혔다.**

어휘 site 부지, 현장 large-scale 대규모의 renewable 재생 가능한 region 지역 involve 포함하다 wind turbine 풍력 발전용 터빈 consideration 고려 permit 허가(증) federal 연방제의 substation 변전소 transmission lines 송전선 output 출력 distribution grid 배전망 handle 처리하다 third party 제3자 spokesperson 대변인 create 창출하다 numerous 많은, 다수의

| 부지 | 터빈 개수 | 연간 발전량 (터빈당) |
|---|---|---|
| 브런즈윅 | 80 | 580만 킬로와트시 |
| [190] **크래프턴** | **60** | 560만 킬로와트시 |
| 러크먼 밸리 | 45 | 590만 킬로와트시 |
| [187] **밸도스타** | 75 | **610만 킬로와트시** |

어휘 annual 연간의, 해마다의 generation 발전(량)

수신: 앨리슨 휴버 <a.huber@atwellpower.com>
발신: 기예르모 미란다 <g.miranda@atwellpower.com>
날짜: 5월 7일
제목: 풍력 터빈 프로젝트

휴버 씨께,

[188] **지난주 회의에서 논의했던** [190] **크래프턴 부지 관련 문제에 대한 후속 조치를 말씀드리고자 합니다.** 그 공공 도로가 장비 운송에 적합하지 않기 때문에, [188] **162번 고속도로에 임시 진입로를 구축해야 할 것입니다.** [190] **그곳의 지반 구조 때문에 안정성 검사를 1년에 두 번이 아닌 3개월에 한 번씩 해야 한다는 점에 유의하시기 바랍니다.**

[189] **프로젝트의 외부 계약업체 부분에 대해서는, 바셀 주식회사로부터 입찰을 받았으며,** 제가 이번 주에 계약서 작업을 진행할 것입니다.

곧 다시 소식 전해 드리겠습니다.

기예르모 미란다

어휘 follow up on ~에 대해 후속 정보를 제공하다 suitable 적합한, 어울리는 transportation 수송 equipment 장비 temporary 임시의, 일시적인 access 출입, 접근 composition 구성 (요소) stability 안정(성) carry out 실시하다 as for ~에 대해서는 contractor 계약업체 portion 부분 bid 입찰

## 186 Not / True

번역 애트웰 전력회사에 대해 언급된 것은?
(A) 프로젝트 계획에 몇 차례 지연이 있었다.
(B) 새로운 유형의 풍력 터빈을 설계했다.
(C) 4월에 새로운 직원을 모집하기 시작할 것이다.
(D) 연방 정부의 결정에 이의를 제기했다.

해설 기사 마지막 문장에 다음 달 초부터 새 일자리에 대한 공고를 시작할 것(it will begin advertising for these positions from early next month)이라고 했는데, 기사 작성 날짜가 3월 3일(3 March)이므로 4월에 새로운 직원을 모집하기 시작한다는 것을 알 수 있다. 따라서 (C)가 정답이다.

어휘 recruit 모집하다 contest 이의를 제기하다 decision 결정

> **Paraphrasing**
> 지문의 begin advertising for these positions
> → 정답의 begin recruiting new employees

## 187 세부 사항

번역 어느 부지가 터빈당 가장 많은 에너지를 생산할 것으로 예상되는가?
(A) 브런즈윅
(B) 크래프턴
(C) 러크먼 밸리
(D) 밸도스타

해설 차트에서 가장 아래에 표기된 밸도스타가 610만 킬로와트시(6.1 million kilowatt-hours)로 가장 많은 발전량을 나타내고 있으므로 (D)가 정답이다.

## 188 주제/목적

번역 미란다 씨는 왜 이메일을 썼는가?
(A) 새로운 장비를 요청하기 위해
(B) 계약을 협상하기 위해
(C) 해결책을 제안하기 위해
(D) 오류에 대해 사과하기 위해

해설 이메일 첫 단락에 지난주 회의에서 논의했던 크래프턴 부지 관련 문제에 대한 후속 조치를 말하고자 한다(I'd like to follow up on the issue we discussed ~)며 162번 고속도로에 임시 진입로를 구축해야 한다(~ we will need to construct a temporary access road off of Highway 162)는 방안을 언급하고 있다. 이는 문제 해결책을 제안하는 것이므로 (C)가 정답이다.

어휘 negotiate 협의하다, 협상하다 propose 제안하다 solution 해결책 apologize for ~에 대해 사과하다

## 189 연계

번역 바셀 주식회사는 어떤 일을 책임지게 될 가능성이 가장 큰가?
(A) 전력망과 연결되는 전선 설치
(B) 제안된 부지에 대한 환경 문제 조사
(C) 고속도로와 연결되는 도로 건설
(D) 프로젝트 변전소의 안전성 평가

해설 이메일 두 번째 단락에 바셀 주식회사는 프로젝트의 외부 계약업체(As for the outside contractor portion of the project, we have accepted a bid from Bassell Inc.)로 언급되어 있다. 이에 대해, 기사 후반부에는 전기 출력부와 배전망을 연결하는 송전선 공사는 제3자에 의해 진행될 것(construction of the transmission lines linking the electricity output to the distribution grid will be handled by a third party)이라는 정보가 제시되어 있다. 이를 통해, 제3자에 해당하는 외부 계약업체인 바셀 주식회사가 전선 공사를 할 것으로 볼 수 있으므로 (A)가 정답이다.

어휘 power grid 전력망 inspect 점검하다 proposed 제안된 linked to+명사 ~와 연결되는 assess 평가하다

## 190 연계

번역 몇 개의 터빈이 분기마다 안정성 확인을 받을 것인가?
(A) 45
(B) 60
(C) 75
(D) 80

해설 이메일 첫 단락에 크래프턴 부지(regarding the Crafton site)에 대해 이야기하면서 그곳의 안정성 검사가 세 달에 한 번씩 실시되어야 한다(~ stability checks will need to be carried out once every three months ~)고 언급하고 있다. 두 번째 지문에 크래프턴 부지의 터빈 숫자가 60으로 쓰여 있으므로 (B)가 정답이다.

어휘 quarterly 분기의

> **Paraphrasing**
> 지문의 once every three months → 질문의 quarterly

**191-195 이메일+보도 자료+이메일**

발신: 션 벨린저 <sbellinger@zmail.ca>
수신: 레오 라이트 <wright_l@kamet.ca>, 로사 페레즈 <perez_r@kamet.ca>
날짜: 5월 14일, 오후 4시 25분
제목: 몇 가지 요점
첨부: ⓐ카메트 보도 자료

라이트 씨와 페리즈 씨께,

[191] **귀사의 새 웹사이트의 '회사 소개' 페이지에 보도 자료(첨부)의 정보를 추가할 계획이므로,** 연락 정보를 포함해, 모든 것이 정확한지 확인하고 싶었습니다. 업체를 위해 광범위한 광고 캠페인을 시작하실 것이기 때문에, 사이트에 접속량이 많아지기 전에 글을 확인해 보는 것이 현명할 것입니다.

전화로 논의한 바와 같이, [191] **홈페이지가 여전히 느리게 로딩되고 있습니다.** [192] **해당 페이지에 있는 애니메이션 동영상 때문인 것 같은데, 움직이지 않는 이미지로 교체해야 할 것 같습니다.** [194] **또한 귀사의 직원에게 신용카드 처리 시스템 사용 방법을 알려 달라고 요청하셨습니다. 이번 주 오후 아무 때나 편하신 시간에 화상 회의를 통해 알려 드릴 수 있습니다.**

션 벨린저

어휘 point 요점 press release 보도 자료 attach 첨부하다 including ~을 포함해 launch 시작하다 extensive 광범위한 advertising 광고 (활동) sensible 현명한, 합리적인 animated 애니메이션으로 만든 clip 동영상 replace 대체하다 static 정지 상태의 processing 처리 at one's convenience ~가 편리한 시간에

보도 자료
연락 담당자: 낸시 롤린스, 555-9275

캠브리지 가 미들빌 쇼핑몰 맞은편에 위치한 카메트에서 6월 1일에 있을 개장을 알려 드리게 되어 기쁩니다. 카메트는 로렌스 홀트에 의해 설립되었으며, 그는 한때 회계 분야에서 근무했지만, 특히 자연으로 여행을 떠나고 세계에서 가장 높은 산봉우리에 오르면서 모든 여유 시간을 야외에서 보냈습니다. 193 **그는 본인과 같은 사람들에게 최고의 텐트와 배낭, 침낭 등 모든 것을 저렴한 가격에 제공하고 싶었습니다.** 카메트는 195 **로스쿨을 졸업하고 개업 변호사로 일하다가 나중에 경력을 바꾼 디자이너 케니 베세라**의 현대적인 스타일을 선보입니다.

개장일에는 무료 다과와 경품 추첨, 제품 시연이 특별히 준비되어 있습니다. 여름이 왔으니, 들러서 편안하고 안전한 야외 활동을 위해 필요한 물품을 구입하세요!

어휘 located on ~에 위치한 opposite ~ 맞은편에 found 설립하다 accounting 회계 climb 오르다 peak 산봉우리 affordable 저렴한, 가격이 알맞은 graduate 졸업생 former 전직 ~의, 이전의 practicing 개업한 attorney 변호사 feature 특별히 포함하다 complimentary 무료의 refreshments 다과, 간식 drawing 추첨 demonstration 시연(회) stop in 들르다 stock up 갖춰 놓다, 비축하다 comfortable 편한

발신: 레오 라이트 <wright_l@kamet.ca>
수신: 션 벨린저 <sbellinger@zmail.ca>
참조: 로사 페레즈 <perez_r@kamet.ca>
날짜: 5월 15일, 오전 9시 21분
제목: 회신: 몇 가지 요점

안녕하세요, 벨린저 씨.

글을 다시 확인해 주셔서 다행입니다. 이전 버전의 보도 자료로 작업을 하고 계신 것 같아요. 그 문서에는 오류가 있어요. 195 **로렌스 홀트와 케니 베세라의 경력이 바뀌어 잘못 들어가 있기 때문입니다.** 페레즈 씨가 업데이트된 보도 자료를 바탕으로 '회사 소개' 페이지에 들어갈 내용을 새로 작성해서 오늘 중으로 보내 드릴 것입니다.

추가로, 194 **조앤 램지가 6월 9일 오후 2시에 귀하께서 제안하신 화상 회의에 참석하실 수 있습니다.** 그분이 이전에 비슷한 시스템으로 일한 경험이 있으므로 모든 기능을 숙지하는 데 오래 걸리지 않을 것으로 생각합니다. 그리고 사이트가 오픈된 후에 생길 수 있는 문의도 계속 처리해 주실 수 있음에 감사드립니다.

레오 라이트

어휘 accidentally 실수로, 우연히 swap 바꾸다 content 내용(물) based on ~을 바탕으로 familiarize oneself with ~에 익숙해지다, ~을 숙지하다 feature 기능, 특징 available 시간이 있는 address (문제 등을) 처리하다 query 문의

## 191 추론

번역 벨린저 씨는 누구일 것 같은가?
(A) 전문 사진가
(B) 광고 책임자
(C) 프리랜서 기자
(D) 웹 디자이너

해설 벨린저 씨가 쓴 이메일 첫 단락과 두 번째 단락에, 상대방 회사의 웹사이트에 보도 자료 정보를 추가하는 일(I plan to add the information from your press release (attached) to the About Us page of your new Web site)을 언급했고, 홈페이지가 느리게 로딩되고 있다(the homepage is still loading slowly)며 원인과 해결 방안을 제시하는 말이 쓰여 있다. 이는 웹 디자이너가 할 수 있는 일에 해당하므로 (D)가 정답이다.

## 192 세부 사항

번역 첫 번째 이메일에 따르면, 무엇이 제거되어야 하는가?
(A) 흐릿한 이미지
(B) 일부 애니메이션
(C) 회사 로고
(D) 연락 정보

해설 첫 번째 이메일 두 번째 단락에 애니메이션 동영상 문제를 언급하면서 움직이지 않는 이미지로 교체해야 할 것 같다(I believe this is due to the animated clips on that page, which I think should be replaced with static images)고 알리고 있으므로 (B)가 정답이다.

어휘 remove 제거하다, 없애다 blurry 흐릿한, 뿌연

> Paraphrasing
> 지문의 animated clips → 정답의 animation

## 193 세부 사항

번역 카메트는 어떤 종류의 업체인가?
(A) 캠핑용품 매장
(B) 여행사
(C) 야외 공연 시설
(D) 조경 서비스 회사

해설 카메트의 설립 배경이 소개되는 보도 자료 첫 단락에 설립자인 홀트가 최고의 텐트와 배낭, 침낭 등을 저렴한 가격에 제공하고 싶어 했다(He wanted to provide people like him with the best tents, backpacks, sleeping bags, and more, all at affordable prices)는 내용이 제시되어 있으므로 (A)가 정답이다.

> Paraphrasing
> 지문의 tents, backpacks, sleeping bags
> → 정답의 camping supplies

TEST 5

## 194 연계

번역 램지 씨는 6월 9일에 무엇을 할 것인가?
(A) 신용카드 계좌 개설하기
(B) 지불 시스템에 관해 배우기
(C) 특색을 이룰 예술품 선택하기
(D) 벨린저 씨의 사무실 방문하기

해설 두 번째 이메일 두 번째 단락에 6월 9일 오후 2시에 벨린저 씨가 제안한 화상 회의에 램지 씨가 참석할 수 있다(Joanne Ramsey can attend the video conference you suggested at 2 P.M. on June)는 내용이 있다. 이에 대해, 첫 번째 이메일 두 번째 단락에 벨린저 씨가 신용카드 처리 시스템 사용 방법을 화상 회의를 통해 알려 주겠다(~ how to use the credit card processing system. I can do that by video conference ~)고 하므로 (B)가 정답이다.

어휘 account 계좌, 계정

> Paraphrasing
> 지문의 the credit card processing system
> → 정답의 a payment system

## 195 연계

번역 로렌스 홀트에 대해 사실인 것은?
(A) 전에 변호사로 일했다.
(B) 최근에 램지 씨를 승진시켰다.
(C) 회계 분야의 경력을 지니고 있다.
(D) 벨린저 씨를 위해 글을 작성할 것이다.

해설 두 번째 이메일 첫 단락에 이전 보도 자료에 로렌스 홀트와 케니 베세라의 경력이 바뀌어 잘못 들어가 있다(~ the career backgrounds of Lawrence Holt and Kenny Becerra were accidentally swapped)는 말이 있는데, 보도 자료 첫 단락에 케니 베세라가 로스쿨을 졸업하고 개업 변호사로 일했다(Kenny Becerra, a law school graduate and former practicing attorney)는 말이 있으므로 실제로는 이것이 홀트의 경력임을 알 수 있다. 따라서 (A)가 정답이다.

어휘 recently 최근에 promote 승진시키다

### 196-200 제품 설명+후기+이메일

**[198] 갤린도 CT7은 최대 지름이 13인치인 접시까지 담을 수 있는 회전식 턴테이블이 있는 1150와트짜리 조리대용 전자레인지입니다.** 스마트쿡 기술은 **[196] 스팀 센서가 다 익었다고 판단할 때까지** 미리 프로그래밍된 출력으로 팝콘, 치킨 등 5가지 일반적인 음식을 데울 수 있으며, 해동 기능으로 냉동식품을 쉽게 해동할 수 있습니다.

어휘 countertop 조리대 rotating 회전하는 accommodate 수용하다 diameter 지름 preprogrammed 사전에 프로그램된 determine 결정하다 defrost 해동 feature 기능, 특징 thaw 해동하다

http://www.galindo.com/reviews

후기 작성자: 카일라 타운센드
게시 날짜: 1월 9일

**[197,199] 몇 달 전에 첫 아파트로 이사했을 때 부모님께서 사용하시던 4년 된 CT7 전자레인지를 주셨습니다. [198] 저는 전자레인지에 곧바로 넣는 플라스틱 공기에 담긴 음식인 한센 레디밀즈를 일주일에 몇 번씩 먹기 때문에 이걸 계속 많이 사용하고 있습니다.**

그러다 지난주에 턴테이블이 회전을 멈췄습니다. 이 전자레인지는 품질 보증 기간이 5년이기 때문에, 가장 가까운 공인 갤린도 수리 서비스 매장에 전화해 예약 일정을 잡았습니다. 기사님께서는 드라이브 모터가 교체되어야 할 거라고 말씀하시면서 제 품질 보증서를 보여 달라고 요청하셨습니다. 그 후 거기 써 있는 이름을 보시더니 **[199] 소유주들 사이에서 이전될 수 없기 때문에 그 계약서가 더 이상 유효하지 않다고 말씀하셨습니다.** 무료가 아니라 수리를 받는 데 약 200달러의 비용이 들텐데, 이는 실망스러운 부분입니다. 품질 보증 계약서의 이런 조항을 알고 계시지 못할 수도 있는 다른 분들께 경고해 드리기 위해 이 후기를 게시합니다.

어휘 reviewer 후기 작성자, 평가자 post 게시하다 warranty 품질 보증(서) certified 공인된, 인증된 appointment 예약, 약속 replace 교체하다 agreement 계약(서), 합의(서) valid 유효한 transfer 이전하다, 옮기다 warn 경고하다, 주의를 주다 be aware of ~을 알고 있다 condition 조건, 조항

수신: 카일라 타운센드 <k.townsend@you-mail.com>
발신: 그랜트 오스본 <gosborne@galindo.com>
제목: 갤린도 CT7
날짜: 1월 10일

타운센드 씨께,

저희 웹사이트에 게시하신 후기와 관련해 이메일을 씁니다. 갤린도 고객 서비스팀의 일원으로서, **[199] 품질 보증 서비스가 이전될 수 없다는 정책은 2년 전에 도입되었으며, 그 전에 이뤄진 구매에 대해서는 적용되지 않는다는 점**을 분명히 밝혀 드리고자 합니다. 귀하께서 전자레인지의 기능에 대해, 그리고 저희 공인 수리 제휴업체가 제공해 드린 서비스에 대해 겪으셨던 어려움에 대해 사과드립니다.

고객 만족이 갤린도에게는 가장 중요하므로, 이 문제를 해결하는 데 있어 도움을 제공해 드리고자 합니다. **[200] 귀하께서 소통하셨던 회사의 명칭을 제게 알려 주시기 바랍니다.** 제가 그곳 관리자에게 연락해서 귀하의 수리 서비스가 제대로 처리되도록 하겠습니다.

그랜트 오스본
고객 서비스 담당

어휘 in regard to+명사 ~에 대해 clarify 분명히 밝히다 introduce 도입하다, 소개하다 apply 적용되다 functioning 기능 utmost 최고의 assistance 도움, 지원 resolve 해결하다 interact 소통하다 ensure 보장하다, 반드시 ~하도록 하다 handle 처리하다, 다루다 properly 제대로, 적절히

## 196 Not / True

번역 제품 설명에 따르면, 갤린도 CT7에 대해 사실인 것은?
(A) 내부 전등이 특징이다.
(B) 스팀을 감지하는 기능이 있다.
(C) 쿡탑 위에 걸어 놓아야 한다.
(D) 마감 색상이 다양하게 출시된다.

해설 제품 설명 후반부에 스팀 센서가 다 익었다고 판단한다(its steam sensor determines that they are done)고 언급되어 있는 것에서 스팀 감지 기능이 있음을 알 수 있다. 따라서 (B)가 정답이다.

어휘 feature 특징으로 하다 sense 감지하다 be meant to ~해야 하다, ~하기로 되어 있다 suspend 걸다, 매달다 come in ~로 출시되다

> Paraphrasing
> 지문의 steam sensor determines that they are done
> → 정답의 has the ability to sense steam

## 197 Not / True

번역 타운센드 씨가 후기에서 자신의 아파트에 있는 CT7에 대해 언급하는 것은?
(A) 선물로 받았다.
(B) 건물주 소유이다.
(C) 4년 동안 소유해 왔다.
(D) 중고 상품 매장에서 구입했다.

해설 후기 첫 단락에 타운센드 씨가 첫 아파트로 이사했을 때 부모님께서 4년 된 CT7 전자레인지를 주셨다(My parents gave me their four-year-old CT7 microwave when I moved into my first apartment ~)고 쓰여 있으므로 (A)가 정답이다.

어휘 belong to+명사 ~의 소유이다 landlord 건물주 own 소유하다

> Paraphrasing
> 지문의 My parents gave me their four-year-old CT7 microwave when I moved into my first apartment
> → 정답의 received it as a gift

## 198 연계

번역 한센 레디밀즈에 대해 암시된 것은?
(A) 냉동 상태로 판매된다.
(B) 치킨 요리를 포함한다.
(C) 5분 동안 가열되어야 한다.
(D) 지름이 13인치보다 더 크지 않다.

해설 후기 첫 단락에 타운센드 씨가 한센 레디밀즈를 CT7 전자레인지에 넣어 먹는다(I eat Hansen ReadyMeals—those plastic bowls of food you put straight into the microwave)고 언급하는 부분이 있는데, 제품 설명 시작 부분에 CT7 전자레인지가 최대 지름이 13인치인 접시까지 담을 수 있다(can accommodate dishes of up to 13 inches in diameter)고 쓰여 있으므로 (D)가 정답이다.

어휘 include 포함하다

## 199 연계

번역 타운센드 씨가 기사로부터 어떤 부정확한 정보를 받았는가?
(A) 특정 교체 부품의 가격이 200달러라고
(B) 갤린도가 지난 1년 내에 새로운 회사 정책을 도입했다고
(C) 오작동되는 드라이브 모터가 문제의 원인일 가능성이 가장 크다고
(D) 전자레인지 품질 보증 서비스가 무효화되었다고

해설 후기 두 번째 단락에 타운센드 씨가 수리 기사로부터 품질 보증 서비스가 더 이상 유효하지 않다(the agreement is no longer valid ~)는 말을 들었다고 쓰여 있다. 이에 대해, 이메일 첫 단락에 해당 정책이 2년 전에 도입되었고 그 이전에 이뤄진 구매에 대해서는 적용되지 않는다(the policy that warranties are non-transferable was introduced two years ago and does not apply to purchases made before then)는 정보가 제시되어 있고, 후기 첫 단락에는 타운센드 씨의 전자레인지가 4년 된 제품(four-year-old CT7 microwave)이라고 쓰여 있으므로 (D)가 정답이다.

어휘 replacement 교체(품) malfunctioning 오작동되는 invalidate 무효화하다

## 200 세부 사항

번역 오스본 씨가 타운센드 씨에게 요청한 한 가지 정보는 무엇인가?
(A) 수리 업체의 명칭
(B) 제품 모델 번호
(C) 품질 보증서의 한 곳에 쓰인 표현
(D) 가전 기기 매장 주소

해설 오스본 씨가 작성한 이메일 두 번째 단락에 타운센드 씨가 수리를 위해 소통했던 회사의 명칭을 알려 달라(Please let me know the name of the company that you interacted with)고 요청하는 말이 쓰여 있으므로 (A)가 정답이다.

어휘 wording 표현, 단어 선택 appliance 가전 기기

> Paraphrasing
> 지문의 the name of the company
> → 정답의 The name of a repair business

# TEST 6

| | | | | |
|---|---|---|---|---|
| 101 (B) | 102 (C) | 103 (B) | 104 (A) | 105 (D) |
| 106 (A) | 107 (C) | 108 (B) | 109 (A) | 110 (D) |
| 111 (C) | 112 (D) | 113 (C) | 114 (B) | 115 (C) |
| 116 (B) | 117 (A) | 118 (B) | 119 (C) | 120 (A) |
| 121 (D) | 122 (A) | 123 (B) | 124 (C) | 125 (D) |
| 126 (D) | 127 (B) | 128 (D) | 129 (D) | 130 (A) |
| 131 (D) | 132 (A) | 133 (C) | 134 (A) | 135 (C) |
| 136 (B) | 137 (B) | 138 (A) | 139 (B) | 140 (D) |
| 141 (A) | 142 (C) | 143 (C) | 144 (D) | 145 (D) |
| 146 (B) | 147 (D) | 148 (C) | 149 (B) | 150 (A) |
| 151 (C) | 152 (C) | 153 (A) | 154 (A) | 155 (B) |
| 156 (B) | 157 (D) | 158 (D) | 159 (D) | 160 (B) |
| 161 (C) | 162 (A) | 163 (D) | 164 (D) | 165 (D) |
| 166 (A) | 167 (B) | 168 (A) | 169 (A) | 170 (B) |
| 171 (C) | 172 (C) | 173 (A) | 174 (C) | 175 (B) |
| 176 (A) | 177 (C) | 178 (C) | 179 (B) | 180 (D) |
| 181 (D) | 182 (A) | 183 (B) | 184 (C) | 185 (B) |
| 186 (B) | 187 (B) | 188 (A) | 189 (D) | 190 (C) |
| 191 (A) | 192 (C) | 193 (B) | 194 (D) | 195 (B) |
| 196 (D) | 197 (C) | 198 (A) | 199 (A) | 200 (B) |

## PART 5

### 101 형용사 자리 _ 현재분사

번역 테스터들은 그 비디오 게임의 마지막 단계가 다소 불만스럽다고 전한다.

해설 빈칸은 부사 somewhat의 수식을 받으면서 be동사 is 뒤에 있으므로 형용사가 올 자리인데, the video game's final level이 사람을 불만스럽게 만드는 것이므로 '불만스럽게 만드는(불만스러운)'을 뜻하는 현재분사 (B) frustrating이 정답이다. (A) frustrate(불만스럽게 만들다)는 동사, (C) frustration(불만, 좌절)은 명사이므로 오답이다. (D) frustrated(불만을 느낀, 좌절감을 느낀)는 사람의 감정을 나타내므로 사물 주어와 어울리지 않는다.

어휘 somewhat 다소, 어느 정도

### 102 명사 어휘

번역 마커스 시글러는 태양의 활동을 예측하는 새로운 방법을 개발하려 시도하고 있다.

해설 태양의 활동을 예측하기 위해 개발할 수 있는 것을 나타낼 명사가 필요하므로 '방법'을 뜻하는 (C) method가 정답이다.

어휘 attempt 시도하다 predict 예측하다 solar 태양의 recognition 인식, 인정 direction 방향, 지시 opinion 의견

### 103 부사 어휘

번역 그 대학교의 가장 큰 기숙사인 루고 레지던스 홀은 거의 600명의 학생을 수용한다.

해설 빈칸은 뒤에 있는 600을 수식하는 자리이므로 숫자 표현 앞에 위치할 수 있는 부사로서 '거의'를 뜻하는 (B) nearly가 정답이다.

어휘 dormitory 기숙사 accommodate 수용하다 totally 완전히

### 104 부사 자리 _ 형용사 수식

번역 체이니 씨는 곧 출시될 자신의 요리책이 쉽게 구할 수 있는 재료로 만들어지는 요리들만 다룰 것이라고 말한다.

해설 전치사 with와 형용사 obtainable 사이에 있는 빈칸은 형용사를 수식하는 부사가 필요한 자리이므로 (A) easily(쉽게)가 정답이다.

어휘 upcoming 곧 있을, 다가오는 feature 특별히 포함하다 obtainable 구할 수 있는, 얻을 수 있는 ingredient 재료, 성분 ease 쉬움, 용이함; 완화하다

### 105 접속사 자리 _ 등위 접속사

번역 에미 타나카는 월요일에 근무를 시작하기로 되어 있지만, 인사부에서 그녀의 계약서 초안 작성을 끝마치지 못했다.

해설 빈칸 앞뒤에 각각 완전한 절이 있으므로 두 절을 연결할 수 있는 접속사가 필요하다. '월요일에 근무를 시작하기로 되어 있지만, 인사부에서 계약서 초안 작성을 끝마치지 못했다'가 알맞은 의미이므로 '하지만'을 뜻하는 접속사 (D) but이 정답이다. (A) once는 접속사로 쓰이지만 '~하자마자, ~하는 대로'라는 뜻으로 의미가 맞지 않는다. (B) with는 전치사, (C) still은 부사이다.

어휘 be supposed to ~하기로 되어 있다, ~할 예정이다 Human Resources 인사(부) draft 초안을 작성하다

### 106 동사 자리 _ 명령문

번역 실험실에서 유출이 발생하면 즉시 시설 관리부에 알리시기 바랍니다.

해설 빈칸 뒤에 명사구와 전치사구들만 있고 동사가 없으므로 동사 원형으로 시작하는 명령문임을 알 수 있다. 따라서 동사 원형인 (A) Notify(알리다, 통지하다)가 정답이다.

어휘 maintenance 시설 관리 immediately 즉시 spill 유출(물) laboratory 실험실 notification 알림, 통지

### 107 부사 자리 _ 동사 수식

번역 실내 디자이너는 카페의 좌석 공간에 따뜻한 분위기를 만들어 내기 위해 특정 색상들을 전략적으로 사용했다.

해설 주어(The interior designer)와 동사(used), 그리고 목적어(certain colors)로 구성된 완전한 절 뒤에 빈칸과 to부정사가 이어지는 구조이므로 빈칸에는 동사를 수식하는 부사가 쓰여야 한다. 따라서 (C) strategically(전략적으로)가 정답이다.

어휘 atmosphere 분위기 strategy 전략 strategic 전략적인

### 108 대명사 어휘

번역 삭제된 지 1년 이상 지났기 때문에 귀하의 파일을 복구하기 위해 할 수 있는 게 아무것도 없습니다.

해설 콤마 뒤에 '삭제된 지 1년 이상 지났기 때문에'라는 이유가 있으므로 '복구하기 위해 할 수 있는 게 없다'는 의미가 되어야 자연스럽다. 따라서 '아무것도 (~ 않다)'를 뜻하는 (B) Nothing이 정답이다.

어휘 recover 복구하다, 회복시키다

### 109 접속사 자리_부사절 접속사

번역 고객과의 식사 비용은 영수증 원본을 제출하면 회사에서 환급해 드립니다.

해설 빈칸 앞뒤에 각각 완전한 절이 있으므로 두 절을 연결할 수 있는 접속사가 필요하다. '영수증 원본을 제출하면 회사에서 환급해 준다'는 의미가 되는 것이 가장 알맞으므로 '~하는 한, ~하기만 하면'을 뜻하는 접속사 (A) as long as가 정답이다. (B) whether(~인지, ~와 상관없이)와 (D) in case(~하는 경우를 대비해)도 접속사이지만 의미가 맞지 않으며, (C) afterward(그 후에, 나중에)는 부사이다.

어휘 reimburse (비용을) 환급해 주다 original 원본의, 원래의 receipt 영수증

### 110 명사 자리_전치사의 목적어

번역 약간의 심사숙고 끝에, 이사회는 배당금을 공표하기로 결정했다.

해설 빈칸은 형용사 some의 수식을 받음과 동시에 전치사 After의 목적어 역할을 하는 자리이므로 명사가 들어가야 한다. 따라서 명사 (D) deliberation(심사숙고)이 정답이다.

어휘 board of directors 이사회, 이사진 declare 공표하다, 선언하다 dividend 배당(금) deliberate 심사숙고하다 deliberately 신중히, 고의로

### 111 부사 어휘

번역 워크숍 참가자들은 주로 부산에서 온 사람들이긴 했지만, 다른 지역에서 온 사람들도 몇몇 있었다.

해설 다른 지역에서 온 사람들이 몇몇 있었다는 말이 있으므로 부산에서 온 사람들이 많았다는 의미가 되어야 자연스럽다. 따라서 '주로'를 뜻하는 (C) primarily가 정답이다.

어휘 participant 참가자 entirely 전적으로, 완전히 repeatedly 반복해서, 거듭 overly 지나치게, 과도하게

### 112 전치사 자리_어휘

번역 웰러 타워는 전망대에서 보이는 아주 멋진 경관 때문에 여행객들에게 인기 있는 목적지이다.

해설 빈칸 뒤에 있는 명사구를 목적어로 취할 전치사가 필요하며, '전망대에서 보이는 아주 멋진 경관'은 인기의 이유에 해당하므로 '~ 때문에'를 뜻하는 전치사 (D) because of가 정답이다. (A) now that(이제 ~이므로)은 접속사이며, (B) just as(꼭 ~처럼)와 (C) together with(~와 함께)는 의미가 맞지 않는다.

어휘 destination 목적지, 도착지 stunning 아주 멋진 observation deck 전망대

### 113 형용사 자리_비교급

번역 지역 공급업체에서 건설 장비를 임대하는 것이 우리 장비를 현장으로 운송하는 것보다 더 효율적일 것입니다.

해설 be동사 뒤에 빈칸이 있으므로 보어 자리이고, 빈칸 앞뒤에 비교급을 나타내는 more와 than이 있으므로 형용사가 들어갈 자리이다. 따라서 (C) efficient(효율적인)가 정답이다.

어휘 rent 임대하다, 대여하다 construction 건설 machinery 장비, 기계 local 지역의, 현지의 supplier 공급업체 site 현장, 부지 efficiency 효율 efficiently 효율적으로

### 114 전치사 자리_어휘

번역 미술품을 보존하기 위해, 박물관들은 종종 영구 소장품을 전시하지 않고 창고에 보관한다.

해설 빈칸 뒤에 있는 동명사구를 목적어로 취할 전치사가 필요하며, '전시하지 않고 창고에 보관한다'는 의미가 되어야 자연스러우므로 '~하기 보다, ~하는 대신'을 뜻하는 전치사 (B) rather than이 정답이다. (A) aside from(~을 제외하고, ~뿐만 아니라)은 의미가 맞지 않는 전치사이며, (C) even if(설사 ~한다 하더라도)는 접속사이다. (D) not only(~뿐만 아니라)는 but also(~도 역시)와 짝을 이루는 상관 접속사이다.

어휘 preserve 보존하다 keep ~ in storage ~을 (창고에) 보관하다 piece 작품 permanent 영구적인 collection 소장(품) put ~ on display ~을 전시하다

### 115 수동태

번역 코델 도자기 전시회 웹사이트에 따르면, 코델 주민들은 입장료가 면제될 것이다.

해설 주어 the entry fee(입장료)는 사람에 의해 면제되는 것이므로 be동사와 함께 수동태 동사를 구성하는 과거분사 (C) waived가 정답이다. (A) waives는 동사이므로 be동사 뒤에 쓸 수 없으며, (B) waiving은 현재분사로서 will be와 함께 능동태 미래 진행 시제를 구성하는데, waive는 타동사이므로 빈칸 뒤에 목적어가 없어 오답이다. (D) waivers는 명사로 주격 보어 역할을 할 수는 있지만 이 문장에서는 어색하다.

어휘 entry fee 입장료 resident 주민 waive 면제하다 waiver 포기 (증서)

TEST 6

## 116 명사 자리 _ 복합명사

번역 과학 기술 연구에 대한 정부 투자가 최근 수십 년 동안 혁신의 중요한 원동력이었다.

해설 문장에 동사 have been이 있으므로 빈칸은 Government와 함께 문장의 주어 역할을 할 복합명사를 구성하는 또 다른 명사가 필요한 자리임을 알 수 있다. 또한, 동사 have been이 복수 동사이므로 이와 수가 일치되는 복수 명사 (B) investments가 정답이다.

어휘 driver 원동력 innovation 혁신 decade 10년 invest 투자하다 investment 투자 investor 투자자

## 117 전치사 어휘

번역 모금 행사의 수익금은 브랜트 공원의 육상 트랙을 재포장하는 데 쓰일 것이다.

해설 빈칸 뒤에 위치한 동명사구의 의미(브랜트 공원의 육상 트랙 재포장)로 볼 때, 행사 수익금이 쓰이는 목적임을 알 수 있다. 따라서 '~하는 데, ~을 위해' 등의 의미로 목적을 나타낼 때 사용하는 전치사 (A) toward가 정답이다. go toward는 '(돈이) ~에 쓰이다'라는 의미로 수익금, 기부금 등 돈을 나타내는 주어와 함께 자주 쓰이니 알아두자.

어휘 proceeds 수익금 fund-raiser 모금 행사 resurface (길 등을) 재포장하다

## 118 동사 어휘

번역 예상된 일이었지만, 리암 쿤의 프로 테니스 선수 생활 은퇴 발표에 많은 팬들이 여전히 슬퍼했다.

해설 '예상된 일이었지만, 많은 팬들이 여전히 슬퍼했다'는 의미가 되어야 자연스러우므로 '예상하다'를 뜻하는 expect의 과거분사 (B) expected가 정답이다.

어휘 sadden 슬프게 하다 announcement 발표, 공지 retirement 은퇴, 퇴직 allow 허락하다 reduce 감소시키다

## 119 명사 자리 _ 전치사의 목적어

번역 이례적일 정도로 저조한 축제 참석자 수로 인해, 주최측에 200장이 넘는 홍보용 티셔츠가 남았다.

해설 빈칸은 전치사 with의 목적어 자리이고, 부정관사 an의 수식을 받으므로 단수 명사 (C) excess(초과, 과도함)가 정답이다.

어휘 unusually 이례적으로, 평소와 달리 attendance 참석, 참석자 수 organizer 주최자, 조직자 promotional 홍보의 excessive 과도한, 지나친 exceed 초과하다

## 120 동사 어휘

번역 새로운 휴가 정책에 따라 직원들은 사용하지 않은 휴가에 대한 대가로 급여를 받는 것을 선택할 수 있다.

해설 '휴가 대신 급여 받는 것을 선택한다'는 의미가 되어야 자연스러우므로 '선택하다'를 뜻하는 (A) opt가 정답이다.

어휘 time-off 휴가, 휴무 pay 보수, 급여 in exchange for ~에 대한 대가로, ~ 대신 unused 미사용의 afford (금전적, 시간적) 여유가 되다 bother 귀찮게 하다, 애써 ~하다

## 121 전치사 자리 _ 어휘

번역 새 코미디 시리즈인 <와이프아웃>은 TV 첫 방송보다 24시간 앞서 그 방송국 스트리밍 플랫폼에서 공개될 것이다.

해설 빈칸 뒤에 위치한 명사구를 목적어로 취할 수 있는 전치사가 필요하며, 빈칸 앞에 쓰인 24 hours와 어울려야 하므로 '(시간, 순서상) ~보다 앞서'를 뜻하는 (D) ahead of가 정답이다. (A) in front(앞쪽에)와 (B) by then(그때까지는)은 이미 하나의 전치사구를 이뤄 부사 역할을 하므로 명사구를 목적어로 취할 수 없으며, (C) close to(~와 가까운; ~와 가까이에)는 의미가 맞지 않는다.

어휘 release 공개하다, 개봉하다 premiere 첫 방송, 초연

## 122 지시대명사 _ those

번역 고용위원회는 아메드 씨의 능력이 기존 팀원들의 능력을 훌륭히 보완해 줄 것으로 생각한다.

해설 빈칸은 같은 명사를 반복하지 않기 위해 사용되는 지시대명사 that이나 those가 들어가야 할 자리이다. 원래는 the skills of the existing members of the team이 맞지만, 앞의 skills를 다시 쓰지 않기 위해 복수형 지시대명사인 those를 사용하는 것이 좋다. 따라서 (A) those가 정답이다.

어휘 hiring committee 고용위원회 complement 보완하다 existing 기존의

## 123 형용사 어휘

번역 구매할 때마다, 고객들은 이후 주문 시 할인을 받는 데 사용할 수 있는 포인트를 받습니다.

해설 빈칸은 orders(주문)를 수식하는 자리로, 포인트를 쓸 수 있는 시점을 나타내야 자연스러우므로 '이후의, 나중의'를 뜻하는 형용사 (B) subsequent가 정답이다.

어휘 earn 얻다, 받다 approximate 대략적인 inevitable 불가피한 gradual 점차적인

## 124 형용사 자리 _ 최상급

번역 농산물 직판장에서 구입할 수 있는 딸기들 중에서, 캘킨 농장에서 판매하는 것들이 가장 맛이 좋다.

해설 빈칸은 be동사 are 뒤에 있으므로 보어 자리이고, 앞에 정관사 the가 있으므로 명사나 최상급 형용사가 들어갈 수 있다. 명사 (A) flavors(맛, 풍미)는 주격 보어 역할을 할 수는 있지만 이 문장에서는 어색하고, 최상급 형용사 (C) most flavorful(가장 맛이 좋은)이 정답이다.

어휘 available 구입 가능한, 이용 가능한 flavorful 맛이 좋은 flavorfully 풍미 있게

## 125 동사 어휘

번역 사용료를 지불하면 이 이미지를 상업적 목적으로 사용할 수 있는 권리를 얻게 될 것입니다.

해설 사용료를 지불하면 사용할 수 있는 권리가 주어지는 것이므로 '주다, 승인하다'를 뜻하는 동사 grant의 과거분사 (D) granted가 정답이다.

어휘 licensing (사용 등을) 허가하는 fee 요금 right 권리 commercial 상업적인 enforce 시행하다, 집행하다 advise 조언하다 renew 갱신하다

## 126 동사 자리 _ 시제+태

번역 송 씨는 심지어 최근 우리 제품의 매출 하락이 시작되기 전부터 시장 조사를 의뢰했다.

해설 접속사 before 앞에 있는 주절에 주어 Mr. Song과 명사구 the market research study만 있어 빈칸이 주절의 동사 자리임을 알 수 있다. 또한, 명사구 the market research study를 목적어로 취할 능동태 동사가 필요하며, before절에 과거 시제 동사가 쓰였으니 과거나 과거완료 시제 동사가 쓰여야 함을 알 수 있다. 따라서 능동태 과거완료 시제 동사인 (D) had commissioned가 정답이다.

어휘 decline 감소 commission 의뢰하다

## 127 형용사 어휘

번역 케년 XN-30 스포츠 선글라스는 다양한 조명 환경에 맞출 수 있게 교체 가능한 렌즈 4세트를 포함한다.

해설 렌즈 4세트의 특성을 적절히 묘사하는 형용사를 선택해야 한다. '다양한 조명 환경에 맞출 수 있게 교체 가능한 렌즈 4세트를 포함한다'라는 의미가 되는 것이 자연스러우므로 '교체 가능한'이란 의미의 (B) interchangeable이 정답이다.

어휘 come with ~을 포함하다, ~이 딸려 있다 suit 맞다, 어울리다 a variety of 다양한 instant 즉각적인 concentrated 집중적인, 농축된 relative 비교상의, 상대적인

## 128 부사 어휘

번역 적절히 관리하면, 통로를 따라 심은 관목이 마침내는 3피트 높이까지 자랄 것입니다.

해설 동사 reach를 수식하는 부사 자리로, '적절히 관리하면 3피트 높이까지 자란다'는 내용이 되어야 자연스러우므로 '결국, 마침내'를 뜻하는 (D) eventually가 정답이다.

어휘 proper 적절한, 제대로 된 care 관리, 보살핌 shrub 관목 plant 심다 reach 이르다, 도달하다 patiently 참을성 있게 considerably 상당히 (많이) exactly 정확히

## 129 형용사 어휘

번역 저희 저널 기사에 최대 단어 수 제한은 없지만, 집필자들께 원고를 가능한 한 간결하게 유지하도록 권합니다.

해설 앞에 '단어 수 제한은 없지만'이라는 전제가 있으므로 뒤에도 글자 수와 관련된 내용이 나와야 한다. 따라서 '간결한'을 뜻하는 (D) succinct가 정답이다.

어휘 maximum 최대의 limit 제한, 한도 manuscript 원고 accurate 정확한 orderly 정돈된, 질서 있는 distinctive 독특한, 뚜렷이 구별되는

## 130 명사 어휘

번역 세부 요소에 세심하게 주의를 기울이는 능력은 모든 의료 번역가들이 반드시 지니고 있어야 하는 중요한 특징이다.

해설 의료 번역가들이 반드시 지니고 있어야 하는 것으로서 '세부 요소에 세심하게 주의를 기울이는 능력'을 대신할 수 있는 명사가 필요하므로 '특징, 특색'을 뜻하는 (A) trait가 정답이다.

어휘 pay close attention to+명사 ~에 세심하게 주의를 기울이다 detail 세부 요소, 상세 사항 translator 번역가 outcome 결과 practice 연습, 실행

# PART 6

### 131-134 웹페이지

http://www.ncgovparks.org/ufc

가족을 위한 도시 캠핑

니베스 도시 공원 관리국은 지역 내 아이들이 [131] **바로** 자신이 사는 도시에서 캠핑의 즐거움을 경험할 수 있도록 가족을 위한 도시 캠핑 행사를 주최합니다. 각 야영 공간에서 공원 순찰대가 니베스의 아름다운 공원에서 1박을 할 제한된 수의 가족들을 맞이합니다. 일반적으로 바비큐 저녁 식사, 순찰대가 이끄는 저녁 하이킹, 또는 모닥불 주변에서 이뤄지는 이야기 시간 같은 추가 활동도 있습니다. 폭넓은 참여를 위해, 공원 관리국에서 심지어 텐트와 대부분의 기타 필수 물품도 제공합니다. [132] **각 캠핑 참가자께서는 침낭과 세면도구만 가지고 오시면 됩니다.**

가족을 위한 도시 캠핑 [133] **프로그램**은 대단히 인기가 높습니다. [134] **관심 있는** 가족들께서는 매년 봄 신청이 시작되는 대로 희망하시는 야영을 신청하실 것을 권장합니다.

어휘 urban 도시의 organize 주최하다, 조직하다 local 지역의, 현지의 campout 야영 host 맞이하다 a limited number of 제한된 숫자의 overnight stay 1박 usually 일반적으로, 보통 extra 추가의, 별도의 -led ~이 이끄는 session (특정 활동을 하는) 시간 participation 참여, 참가 widely 폭넓게 accessible 이용 가능한, 접근 가능한 necessary 필수의, 필요한 extremely 대단히, 매우 be advised to ~하도록 권장되다 sign up for ~을 신청하다, ~에 등록하다 registration 신청, 등록

## 131 부사 어휘

해설 장소 전치사구 앞에 위치해 그 의미를 강조하는 역할을 할 부사가 필요하므로 '바로'를 뜻하는 부사 (D) right이 정답이다. (A) there는 대명

TEST 6

사나 부사로는 쓰이지만, 강조 부사로는 쓰이지 않으며, (B) like는 전치사 또는 접속사이므로 오답이다. (C) just는 '바로 꼭, 단지' 등의 의미이다.

## 132 문장 고르기

번역 (A) 각 캠핑 참가자께서는 침낭과 세면도구만 가지고 오시면 됩니다.
(B) 또한 공원에서 가족들을 위한 많은 주간 행사도 개최합니다.
(C) 캠핑은 아이들에게 평생 동안 자연을 사랑하는 마음을 길러 줄 수 있는 아주 좋은 방법입니다.
(D) 다가오는 모든 야영 날짜를 아래 달력에서 확인해 보시기 바랍니다.

해설 빈칸 앞 문장에 공원 관리국에서 텐트와 대부분의 기타 필수 물품도 제공한다는 말이 쓰여 있어, 캠핑용 물품 이용과 관련된 추가 정보에 해당하는 (A)가 정답이다.

어휘 toiletries 세면도구 foster 기르다, 조성하다 upcoming 다가오는, 곧 있을

## 133 명사 어휘

해설 빈칸 앞에 위치한 명사구 urban family camping은 이 지문에서 전체적으로 설명하는 행사의 명칭이며, 이는 하나의 프로그램으로 볼 수 있으므로 (C) program이 정답이다.

어휘 facility 시설(물) equipment 장비

## 134 형용사 자리 _ 명사 수식

해설 빈칸 뒤에 있는 명사 families를 수식할 형용사가 필요한데, 분사가 형용사를 대신할 수 있으며, 관심이 있거나 흥미를 느낀 가족들이 행사 참가 신청을 하는 것이므로 '관심 있는, 흥미를 느낀'을 뜻하는 (A) Interested가 정답이다. (B) Interesting은 '흥미를 느끼게 만드는' 이라는 의미로 흥미를 유발하는 원인에 대해 사용한다.

### 135-138 기사

버레나 (2월 5일) - 오늘, TCN 호스피탤리티 그룹은 워스 가에 복합 컨퍼런스 센터 및 호텔을 짓겠다는 제안을 철회했다. 이 복합 건물은 200개 이상의 객실과 70,000평방 피트의 컨퍼런스 공간이 135 **포함될 예정이었다.**

버레나 시민들은 지난 목요일에 열린 설명회에서 이 계획에 대해 136 **반대**의 목소리를 냈다. 여러 주민들이 선정된 부지가 큰 폭의 교통량 증가를 감당할 수 없을 것이라는 우려를 표명했다. 137 **다른 사람들은 이 프로젝트에서 시가 계획한 재정적 역할을 반대했다.** 설명회 다음 날, 세 명의 시의회 의원들도 이 제안에 반대표를 던질 것이라는 뜻을 나타냈다.

철회 성명에 따르면, TCN은 버레나에 컨퍼런스 센터 및 호텔을 짓는 아이디어를 포기하지 않았다. 138 **하지만,** 향후의 제안에서 이 복합 건물의 규모는 더 줄어들 가능성이 높다.

어휘 withdraw 철회하다, 취소하다 proposal 제안(서) combined 결합된 complex 복합 건물 voice 목소리를 내다 resident 주민 express 표현하다 concern 우려, 걱정 handle 대처하다, 처리하다 increase in ~의 증가 traffic 교통량 council 의회 indicate 나타내다, 가리키다 vote against ~에 반대표를 던지다 statement 성명(서) give up on ~을 포기하다 scale 규모 modest 평범한, 보통의

## 135 동사 시제

해설 앞 문장에 복합 건물을 짓겠다는 제안을 철회했다는 말이 쓰여 있다. 따라서 만약 그 건물이 지어졌을 경우의 규모를 가정하는 의미를 나타내야 알맞으므로 '~했을 것이다'를 뜻하는 would have p.p. 형태인 (C) would have included가 정답이다.

## 136 명사 어휘

해설 이 다음 문장에 주민들이 교통량 증가 때문에 우려를 표명했다는 말이 쓰여 있는데, 이는 건축 계획에 반대하는 것이므로 전치사 to와 어울려 '~에 대한 반대'를 뜻하는 (B) opposition이 정답이다. 참고로, (C) disapproval은 전치사 of와 함께 사용한다.

어휘 disapproval 반감, 못마땅함 obstruction 방해, 장애물

## 137 문장 고르기

번역 (A) 위치는 과거 엘리스 백화점이 자리잡고 있던 곳이다.
(B) 다른 사람들은 이 프로젝트에서 시가 계획한 재정적 역할을 반대했다.
(C) 이를 수용하기 위해, 워스 가가 6차선으로 확장될 것이다.
(D) TCN은 최근 몇 년 사이에 두 곳의 다른 도시에 주요 복합 건물들을 개장했다.

해설 앞 문장에 시민들이 설명회에서 건축 계획에 대해 우려를 표명했다는 말이 쓰여 있어 이러한 의견과 관련된 문장으로서 시의 재정적 역할에 반대한 다른 사람들의 의견을 알리는 (B)가 정답이다.

어휘 former 과거의, 이전의 object 반대하다 financial 재정의, 재무의 role 역할 accommodate 수용하다 widen 확장하다, 넓히다 recent 최근의

## 138 접속부사

해설 빈칸 앞에는 TCN이 버레나에 컨퍼런스 센터 및 호텔을 짓는 아이디어를 포기하지 않았다는 말이, 빈칸 뒤에는 그 복합 건물의 규모가 더 줄어들 가능성이 높다는 말이 각각 쓰여 있다. 이는 TCN이 복합 건물을 지을 계획은 여전하지만 규모면에서는 차이가 생길 것이라는 대조적인 흐름으로 볼 수 있으므로 '하지만'이라는 의미로 대조 또는 반대를 나타낼 때 사용하는 (A) However가 정답이다.

어휘 similarly 유사하게, 마찬가지로 in fact 실제로 instead 대신

### 139-142 공지

페니스 그릴 직원 여러분에게 알립니다.

우리 식당에 다음 주에 새로운 판매 및 주문 관리 시스템을 도입할 예정입니다. 우리 주간 휴무일인 월요일에 기사들이 와서 설치하고 우리

매니저들에게 이 시스템 사용법을 [139] **가르쳐** 줄 것입니다. 그런 다음 화요일 오전에 다나와 이반이 모든 식사 공간 및 주방 직원들을 대상으로 동시에 교육을 진행할 것입니다. [140] **모든 사람이 오전 8시에 특별 근무 일정이 잡혀 있습니다.** 화요일에 정상 근무를 하는 직원들이 점심 서비스가 [141] **시작되는** 11시까지는 완전히 준비될 수 있도록 그만큼 일찍 시작해야 합니다.

화요일 오전에 시간이 안 되실 경우 다나에게 즉시 알리시기 바랍니다. 필요하다면 [142] **추가** 교육을 잡을 수 있습니다.

어휘 point-of-sale 판매 관리 시스템(POS) day off 휴무 installation 설치 lead 진행하다, 이끌다 simultaneous 동시의 session (특정 활동을 하는) 시간 ensure 보장하다, 반드시 ~하도록 하다 shift 교대 근무(조) fully 완전히, 모두 promptly 즉시, 지체 없이 unavailable 시간이 나지 않는 arrange 마련하다, 주선하다

## 139 동사 어휘

해설 기사들이 새로운 시스템을 설치한 후에 그 사용법에 대해 사람들에게 무엇을 할 것인지를 나타낼 동사가 필요하다. 또한, 빈칸 뒤가 '간접 목적어(our managers)+직접 목적어(how to use the system)' 구조이므로 이러한 구조로 '~에게 …을 가르치다'를 의미하는 (B) teach가 정답이다. (C) explain과 (D) introduce는 간접 목적어를 취하지 않는 타동사이다.

어휘 support 지원하다, 지지하다 explain 설명하다 introduce 소개하다, 도입하다

## 140 문장 고르기

번역 (A) 다행히, 이 시스템은 우리가 현재 이용하는 것과 대체로 유사합니다.
(B) 마찬가지로, 종업원들은 반드시 태블릿에서 주문을 입력하는 방법을 배워야 합니다.
(C) 그들이 우리 직무 안내서의 관련 영역들도 업데이트할 것입니다.
(D) 모든 사람이 오전 8시에 특별 근무 일정이 잡혀 있습니다.

해설 빈칸 앞 문장에 화요일 오전에 다나와 이반이 모든 직원들을 대상으로 교육을 진행한다는 말이 있고, 빈칸 뒤에는 그만큼 일찍(that early) 시작해야 한다는 말이 있으므로 오전 8시 특별 근무 일정을 알리는 (D)가 정답이다.

어휘 fortunately 다행히 largely 대체로 current 현재의 likewise 마찬가지로 input 입력하다 relevant 관련된 handbook 직무 안내서

## 141 동사 자리

해설 접속사처럼 쓰이는 by the time 뒤에 주어 lunch service와 빈칸, 그리고 at 전치사구만 쓰여 있어 빈칸이 이 절의 동사 자리임을 알 수 있다. 따라서 동사인 (A) begins가 정답이다.

## 142 형용사 어휘

해설 앞 문장에서 시간이 안 되는 사람은 알리라고 했으므로 빈칸이 포함된 문장은 그에 대한 대안으로 추가 교육을 잡을 수 있다는 의미가 되어야 자연스럽다. 따라서 '추가적인'을 뜻하는 (C) additional이 정답이다.

어휘 regular 주기적인, 보통의 internal 내부의 advanced 선진의, 고급의

## 143-146 이메일

발신: <enewsletter@pattersonlibrary.org>
수신: 노엘 히긴스 <n.higgins@yow-mail.com>
제목: 패터슨 공공 도서관
날짜: 9월 19일

고객님께,

패터슨 공공 도서관 온라인 소식지 수신 서비스에 가입해 주셔서 감사합니다. 중요한 변동 사항과 다가오는 행사, 그리고 도서관에서 제공하는 서비스에 대해 귀하께 소식을 전해 드리기 시작하게 되어 기쁩니다.

소식지는 한 달에 두 번 발간되기 때문에, 3주 내에 첫 번째 호를 받으시게 될 것입니다. [143] **각 호는 이메일을 통해 이 주소로 발송될 것입니다.** 소식지 수신이 예상대로 시작되지 않으면, 555-0166번으로 저희 고객 지원 센터 직원에게 연락 주시기 바랍니다. 선호하시는 수신 주소 변경 또는 수신 명단 삭제 요청도 [144] **그들**에게 전달하시면 됩니다.

도서관으로부터 더 많은 소식을 듣고 싶으신가요? 저희 사서들의 도서 [145] **추천**이 실리는 월간 이메일 <패터슨스 픽스>도 발행하고 있습니다. [146] **구독하시려면** www.pattersonlibrary.org/pp를 방문하시기 바랍니다.

패터슨 공공 도서관

어휘 mailing list (우편물 등의) 수신자 명단 upcoming 다가오는, 곧 있을 on offer 제공되는 issue (출판물 등의) 호 preferred 선호하는 remove 삭제하다, 없애다 direct 전달하다, 보내다 feature 특별히 포함하다, 특징을 이루다 librarian 사서

## 143 문장 고르기

번역 (A) 콘텐츠를 만드는 데 많은 정성을 들이고 있습니다.
(B) 저희 독자층은 십대에서 은퇴자까지 다양합니다.
(C) 각 호는 이메일을 통해 이 주소로 발송될 것입니다.
(D) 이전 호들은 저희 웹사이트에서 볼 수 있습니다.

해설 앞 문장에 3주 내에 첫 번째 호를 받게 된다는 말이 쓰여 있으므로 이와 관련하여 어떻게 전달될 것인지를 알리는 (C)가 정답이다.

어휘 put a lot of care into ~에 많은 정성을 들이다 craft 공들여 만들다 readership 독자층 range from ~ to ... 범위가 ~에서 …에 이르다 retiree 은퇴자, 퇴직자 via ~을 통해 previous 이전의, 과거의 available 이용 가능한

## 144 대명사 어휘

해설 빈칸에 쓰일 대명사는 고객인 상대방의 요청을 전달받는 사람을 나타내야 하며, 앞선 문장에 언급된 help desk staff(고객 지원 센터 직원들)를 가리켜야 알맞으므로 (D) them이 정답이다.

TEST 6

## 145 명사 자리_복합명사

해설 가산명사 book 앞에 한정사가 없으므로, 빈칸에는 book과 함께 복합 명사를 이루어 features의 목적어 역할을 하는 복수 명사 또는 불가산명사가 들어가야 한다. 명사 recommendation은 추천 항목 등을 나타낼 때 가산명사로 쓰이므로 단수 명사인 (C) recommendation은 오답이고, 복수 명사인 (D) recommendations가 정답이다.

## 146 동사 어휘

해설 빈칸에는 앞 문장에서 소개하는 이메일 소식지 <패터슨스 픽스>에 대해 웹사이트에 방문해서 할 수 있는 일을 나타내야 하므로 '구독하다, 서비스에 가입하다'를 뜻하는 (B) subscribe가 정답이다.

어휘 donate 기부하다 volunteer 자원하다 enter 참가하다, 입력하다

## 148 Not / True

번역 자동 세척 과정에 대해 언급된 것은?
(A) 약 2분의 시간이 소요된다.
(B) 특정 세척 용액을 필요로 한다.
(C) 전기 콘센트 이용이 필요하다.
(D) 진행되는 동안 다리미를 건드리지 말아야 한다.

해설 지문 중반부에 다리미의 전원 코드를 꽂는(Plug in the iron) 과정이 언급되어 있으므로 (C)가 정답이다.

어휘 approximately 약, 대략 involve 필요로 하다, 포함하다 particular 특정한 fluid 용액, 액체 electrical outlet 전기 콘센트 take place 진행되다, 발생되다

> **Paraphrasing**
> 지문의 Plug in the iron
> → 정답의 use of an electrical outlet

# PART 7

### 147-148 정보

**[147] 도미니카 고급 스팀 다리미에는 자동 청소 시스템이 있어 물탱크와 스팀 배출구에 미네랄이 쌓이지 않도록 유지합니다. 이 기능을 이용하시려면, 먼저 물탱크를 채워주세요. [148] 다리미의 전원 코드를 꽂은 다음,** 스팀 다이얼을 가장 높은 설정으로 맞춥니다. 2분간 다리미가 가열되도록 놓아 둔 다음, 전원 코드를 뽑습니다. 다림면을 싱크대 아래로 향하게 들고 "자동 세척" 버튼을 누르세요. 뜨거운 물과 증기가 스팀 배출구를 통해 나올 것입니다. 물탱크가 완전히 비워질 때까지 계속 버튼을 누르고 계십시오.

어휘 include 포함하다 vent 배출구, 통풍구 free of ~이 없는 mineral 무기물 buildup 축적, 누적 feature 기능, 특징 fill 채우다 plug in 전원 코드를 꽂다 setting (기기 등의) 설정 heat up 가열되다 release 내보내다, 배출하다 completely 완전히 empty 비우다

## 147 추론

번역 어디에서 정보를 찾아볼 수 있을 것 같은가?
(A) 인쇄 광고에서
(B) 온라인 고객 후기에서
(C) 회사 웹사이트의 공지에서
(D) 제품 사용 설명서 페이지에서

해설 지문 초반부에 도미니카 고급 스팀 다리미의 자동 세척 시스템을 소개하면서 그 기능을 이용하는 방법(The Dominica Advanced Steam Iron includes an auto-clean system ~ To use this feature, begin by filling the water tank)을 설명하고 있다. 이는 제품을 처음 구매한 고객이 사용 시 알아야 하는 정보에 해당하므로 (D)가 정답이다.

어휘 advertisement 광고 notice 공지 manual 사용 설명서

### 149-151 공고

케이프타운 기업가 명예의 전당

론데보쉬 대학 혁신 센터(RUCI)에서 케이프타운 기업가 명예의 전당에 헌액될 지역 기업 리더를 추천받고 있습니다. **[149] 그 영예는 케이프타운의 기업계가 이룬 업적을 인정하고 차세대 기업가들에게 영감을 불어넣기 위한 것입니다. [150] 과거에 헌액되신 분들 중에는 빌럼 판 루옌, 임카 카베라,** 그리고 그랜트 트웍이 포함되어 있습니다. 올해, RUCI는 6월 14일로 예정된 기념식에서 헌액 후보자 10명을 선정할 것입니다.

심사 대상이 되시려면, 후보자는 반드시 다음에 해당되어야 합니다.
- 케이프타운 시에 본사를 둔 사기업 또는 공기업의 **[150] CEO**
- **[150] 회사 설립 당시에 그 직책을 맡아 총 3년 이상 유지**
- 다음 중 한 가지 이상의 부문에서 뛰어난 능력을 보임: **[151 (D)] 혁신, [151 (B)] 수익성, [151 (A)] 고용 창출**, 기타 지역 사회에 긍정적인 영향

www.ronu.ac.za/ruci/ctehf를 방문하셔서 후보 추천 양식을 다운로드하세요. 5월 1일 오후 5시까지 제출해야 합니다.

어휘 entrepreneurship 기업가 정신 innovation 혁신 seek 찾다, 추구하다 nomination 후보 추천, 지명 induction 헌액, 입회 honour 영예, 명예 be meant to ~하기 위한 것이다, ~하기로 되어 있다 recognise 인정하다 achievement 공로, 업적 community ~계, 공동체 inspire 영감을 주다 generation 세대, 창출 entrepreneur 기업가 past 과거의, 지나간 inductee 헌액된 사람 nominee (상 등의) 후보, 지명된 사람 ceremony 기념식 headquartered in ~에 본사를 둔 founding 설립 outstanding 뛰어난, 우수한 ability 능력 profitability 수익성 employment 고용, 일자리 positive 긍정적인 submission 제출

## 149 세부 사항

번역 공고에 어떤 정보가 포함되어 있는가?
(A) 명예의 전당 회원들이 받는 혜택
(B) 명예의 전당의 목적
(C) 추천서를 제출하는 곳
(D) 후보자 추천서를 제출할 수 있는 사람

해설 첫 단락에 명예의 전당 헌액이라는 영예가 케이프타운의 기업계가 이룬 업적을 인정하고 차세대 기업가들에게 영감을 불어넣기 위한 것(The honour is meant to recognise the achievements of the city's business community and inspire the next generation of entrepreneurs)이라고 쓰여 있는데, 이는 명예의 전당의 목적에 해당하므로 (B)가 정답이다.

어휘 benefit 혜택, 이득 be allowed to ~하도록 허용되다

## 150 추론

번역 카베라 씨에 대해 어떤 결론을 내릴 수 있는가?
(A) 최소 3년 동안 CEO였다.
(B) 론데보쉬 대학교를 졸업했다.
(C) 6월에 있을 특별 행사에 참석할 것이다.
(D) RUCI의 과거 직원이다.

해설 카베라 씨의 이름은 첫 단락에 과거 명예의 전당에 헌액된 사람(Past inductees include Willem Van Rooyen, Imka Kabera, ~)으로 언급되어 있다. 또한, 두 번째 단락에 명예의 전당 헌액 요건으로 CEO여야(Be the CEO) 한다는 점과 이 직책을 최소 3년 동안 유지해야(Have held that position ~ for no fewer than three years in total) 한다는 점이 쓰여 있어, 카베라 씨도 최소 3년 동안 CEO로 재직했음을 알 수 있다. 따라서 (A)가 정답이다.

어휘 graduate from ~을 졸업하다

## 151 Not / True

번역 심사 대상 후보의 자격이 될 만한 업적이 아닌 것은?
(A) 많은 수의 신규 일자리 창출
(B) 회사의 순이익 증대
(C) 높은 고객 만족도 달성
(D) 독창적인 유형의 제품 개발

해설 많은 수의 신규 일자리 창출을 뜻하는 (A)는 두 번째 단락 세 번째 항목의 employment generation(고용 창출)에서, 회사의 순이익 증대를 의미하는 (B)는 같은 항목의 profitability(수익성)에서, 그리고 독창적인 제품 개발을 나타내는 (D)도 같은 항목의 innovation(혁신)에서 각각 확인할 수 있다. 하지만 고객 만족도와 관련된 정보는 제시되어 있지 않으므로 (C)가 정답이다.

어휘 qualify ~의 자격을 갖추게 해 주다 create 창출하다, 만들어 내다 net profit 순이익 achieve 달성하다, 이루다 rate 비율, 등급 satisfaction 만족 original 독창적인

## 152-153 쿠폰

티타늄 체육관
3번 가 450, 크레빌
555-0177

3개월 회원권 25% 할인

등록 시에 이 쿠폰을 제시하면 단 135달러에 티타늄 체육관 3개월 회원권을 받을 수 있습니다! 회원은 월 1회 전문 개인 트레이너와의 수업 기회가 주어지며, [152] **킥복싱과 에어로빅, 그리고 필라테스를 포함한 여러 강좌를 무제한으로 이용하실 수 있습니다.**

오직 신규 회원에게만 제공되는 혜택입니다. [153] **등록비는 포함되어 있지 않습니다.** 회원권 기간은 반드시 3월 31일 전에 시작되어야 합니다.

어휘 present 제시하다 sign-up 등록, 신청 be entitled to+명사 ~에 대한 자격이 있다 session (특정 활동을 하는) 시간 certified 공인된, 자격증이 있는 unlimited 무제한의 access 이용, 접근 including ~을 포함해 offer 할인 혜택, 할인 제품 available 이용 가능한

## 152 세부 사항

번역 쿠폰에 따르면, 티타늄 체육관 회원권의 혜택은 무엇인가?
(A) 연 1회 건강 상태 평가
(B) 특수 피트니스 장비 이용
(C) 다양한 강좌 수강 가능
(D) 무제한 개인 트레이닝 시간

해설 첫 단락에 킥복싱과 에어로빅, 그리고 필라테스를 포함한 여러 강좌를 무제한으로 이용(access to classes including kickboxing, aerobics, and Pilates)할 수 있다는 말이 제시되어 있으므로 (C)가 정답이다.

어휘 benefit 이점, 혜택 evaluation 평가 equipment 장비 ability 가능, 능력 a variety of 다양한

> **Paraphrasing**
> 지문의 access to classes including kickboxing, aerobics, and Pilates
> → 정답의 The ability to take a variety of classes

## 153 Not / True

번역 쿠폰에 대해 사실인 것은?
(A) 사용자는 등록비를 지불해야 할 것이다.
(B) 4월에 회원권이 종료되는 사람들을 대상으로 한다.
(C) 발급일로부터 3개월 동안 유효하다.
(D) 사용자는 135달러를 할인받을 것이다.

해설 두 번째 단락에 등록비가 포함되어 있지 않다(Sign-up fee not included)는 말이 쓰여 있어 쿠폰을 사용하는 사람이 등록비를 내야 한다는 것을 알 수 있으므로 (A)가 정답이다.

어휘 be targeted toward ~을 대상으로 하다 valid 유효한 issue 발급, 지급

TEST 6

> **Paraphrasing**
> 지문의 Sign-up fee not included
> → 정답의 will be required to pay a sign-up fee

### 154-155 문자 메시지

커티스 도슨 [오전 11시 31분]
미사코, 우리 승합차가 클로스에서 고장 났는데, 정비사 말로는 수리 작업이 최소 4시간이 걸릴 거랍니다.

미사코 엔도 [오전 11시 33분]
아, 이런! [154] **음, 그래도 고객이 비용을 지불한 체험을 할 수 있도록 해야 해요. 오후에 6명을 갤빈 폭포로 모시고 가는 것이 맞죠?**

커티스 도슨 [오전 11시 34분]
그렇습니다. 그리고 메드퍼드에서 점심 식사를 하기로 되어 있습니다.

미사코 엔도 [오전 11시 35분]
알겠어요. [155] **대신 클로스에서 식사할 곳을 찾을 수 있을까요?** 그렇게 하시는 동안, 제가 지역 대리점에서 다른 승합차를 빌려서 계신 곳으로 보내 드릴 수 있을 거예요.

커티스 도슨 [오전 11시 36분]
아, 저희는 클로스 쇼핑센터 바로 근처에 있습니다. [155] **감사해요, 미사코!** 자리잡는 대로 정확한 주소를 문자 메시지로 보내 드릴게요.

어휘 break down 고장 나다 be supposed to ~하기로 되어 있다 rent 빌리다 local 지역의, 현지의 agency 대리점, 업체 get settled 자리잡다

## 154 추론

번역 메시지 작성자들은 어떤 종류의 업체에서 근무하고 있을 것 같은가?
(A) 여행사
(B) 렌터카 대리점
(C) 음식 배송 업체
(D) 자동차 정비소

해설 11시 33분 메시지에 고객이 비용을 지불한 체험을 언급하면서 오후에 6명을 갤빈 폭포로 데리고 가는 일정(Well, we need to make sure our customers still get the experience they've paid for. You're taking six people to Galvin Falls for the afternoon, right?)에 대해 묻는 말이 쓰여 있다. 사람들을 데리고 폭포를 보러 가는 일을 할 수 있는 회사는 여행사이므로 (A)가 정답이다.

## 155 의도 파악

번역 오전 11시 36분에, 도슨 씨가 "저희는 클로스 쇼핑센터 바로 근처에 있습니다"라고 쓸 때, 의미하는 것은?
(A) 승합차용 주차 공간을 찾기 어렵지 않을 것이다.
(B) 근처에 다양한 식당이 있다.
(C) 엔도 씨가 자신의 위치에서 멀리 있지 않다.
(D) 예정보다 약간 늦어지고 있을 뿐이다.

해설 엔도 씨가 11시 35분에 클로스에서 식사할 곳을 찾을 수 있는지(Do you think you could find a place to eat in Kloss instead?) 물으며, 식사하는 동안 다른 차를 구해 보내준다고 한 것에 대해 '클로스 쇼핑센터 근처에 있다'는 말과 함께 감사의 인사를 전하고 있다. 이는 쇼핑센터 근처라 식사할 곳이 많다는 의미이므로 (B)가 정답이다.

어휘 dining 식사 slightly 약간, 조금

### 156-157 의제 목록

<월간 네이처>

[156] **기고자 지망생을 위한 과학적 글쓰기 일일 워크숍**

오전 9시 - 환영 인사 및 소개

오전 9시 30분 - 무엇이 뛰어난 논문을 만드는가?
저널 게재가 승인된 세 편의 잘 작성된 논문 소개 및 그 특성 분석

오전 10시 15분 - 휴식

오전 10시 30분 - 기초 터득하기
[156] **이상적인 <월간 네이처>에 실리는 논문의 이상적인 구조에 대한 개요 및 편집자들에게 깊은 인상을 남기기 위해 각 섹션에 포함해야 하는 것에 관한 팁**

오전 11시 30분 - 논문의 "얼굴"
설득력 있고, 간결하면서, 유익한 정보를 담은 제목과 초록 작성 방법 설명

오후 12시 30분 - 점심 식사

오후 1시 30분 - 효과적인 정보 표시 항목
[157] **도표나 그림, 또는 기타 시각 자료가 언제 필요할지 결정하고 명확하면서 강렬한 인상을 남기도록 만드는 법에 대한 가이드**

오후 2시 30분 - 라이브 편집 시간
참가자가 미리 제출한 논문을 검토할 편집자와 일대일 회의

오후 3시 15분 - 질의응답 및 피드백

어휘 aspiring 지망하는, 장차 ~가 되려는 contributor 기고자 introduction 소개 paper 논문 publication 게재, 발간 breakdown 분석, 분해 characteristic 특징 master 터득하다, 숙달하다 overview 개요 ideal 이상적인 structure 구조, 구성 impress 깊은 인상을 남기다 editor 편집자 explanation 설명 abstract 초록, 개요 compelling 설득력 있는 brief 간결한 informative 유익한 정보를 주는 effective 효과적인 determine 결정하다 table 도표 figure 그림, 도해 visual aid 시각 자료 impactful 강렬한 인상을 주는 in advance 미리, 사전에 participant 참가자

## 156 추론

번역 워크숍 참가자들에 대해 사실일 것 같은 것은?
(A) 서로의 논문에 대해 편집과 관련된 조언을 제공할 것이다.
(B) 자신의 글이 <월간 네이처>에 게재되기를 바란다.
(C) 자신의 배경에 관한 정보를 미리 제출했다.
(D) 현재 과학을 공부하기 위해 대학교에 다니고 있다.

해설 지문 시작 부분에 기고자 지망생을 위한 글쓰기 워크숍(One-Day Workshop on Scientific Writing for Aspiring Contributors)이라는 제목이 쓰여 있고, 오전 10시 30분에는 <월간 네이처>에 실리는 논문의 이상적인 구조에 대한 개요와 편집자들에게 깊은 인상을 남기기 위해 각 섹션에 포함해야 하는 것에 관한 팁(Overview of the ideal structure of *Nature Monthly* papers and tips on what to include in each section to impress our editors)을 이야기하는 순서가 언급되어 있다. 따라서 <월간 네이처>에 글이 게재되기를 바라는 사람들을 위한 워크숍이라는 것을 알 수 있으므로 (B)가 정답이다.

어휘 editorial 편집과 관련된 beforehand 미리 currently 현재

## 157 추론

번역 참가자들이 언제 차트를 디자인하는 방법을 배울 것 같은가?
(A) 오전 9시 30분과 오전 10시 15분 사이
(B) 오전 10시 30분과 오전 11시 30분 사이
(C) 오전 11시 30분과 오후 12시 30분 사이
(D) 오후 1시 30분과 오후 2시 30분 사이

해설 오후 1시 30분에 시작하는 시간에 도표나 그림, 또는 기타 시각 자료와 관련된 가이드(Guide to determining when a table, figure, or other visual aid is needed and ensuring it is clear and impactful)를 제공한다는 정보가 제시되어 있어 차트를 디자인하는 방법을 배울 것으로 볼 수 있으므로 (D)가 정답이다.

### 158-160 웹페이지

http://www.alcornphotographers.com/news

앨콘 포토그래퍼스는 현재 드론을 이용한 공중 촬영을 제공해 드린다는 사실을 알려 드리게 되어 자랑스럽게 생각합니다. [158] **이 기술은 여러분 고객의 주택과 아파트 단지, 그리고 상업용 공간을 보여줄 수 있는 훌륭한 방법입니다.** [160] **건물의 정면이나 측면, 또는 후면을 지상에서 몇 십 피트 높은 곳에서 촬영하면 잠재 구매자들이 건물의 규모와 주변 환경을 더 잘 파악할 수 있습니다.** 게다가, 바로 위 100피트 상공에서 촬영한 사진은 건물의 전체 배치를 보여 주는 데 이용될 수 있습니다.

다른 야외 서비스들과 마찬가지로, 앨콘 포토그래퍼스는 날씨가 좋지 않아서 취소해야 하는 공중 사진 촬영에 대해서는 요금을 부과하지 않습니다. 저희는 또한 석양이 만들어내는 아름다운 빛을 활용하기 위해 해질녘에도 촬영 일정을 잡아 드립니다.

[159] **공중 촬영의 가격은 이미지 5장에 200달러이며, 원하시는 사진 숫자에 따라 인상됩니다.** 추가 정보가 필요하시거나 촬영을 예약하시려면, 555-0162번으로 저희에게 전화 주시기 바랍니다.

어휘 aerial 공중의 photography 사진 촬영(술) via ~을 통해 showcase 선보이다 complex (건물) 단지, 복합 건물 commercial 상업의 shoot 촬영하다; 촬영 potential 잠재적인 sense 이해, 감 scale 규모 surroundings 주변(부) charge 청구하다 twilight 해질녘 take advantage of ~을 이용하다 flattering 돋보이게 하는 setting sun 석양 desired 원하는

## 158 추론

번역 정보는 누구를 대상으로 할 것 같은가?
(A) 건물 소유주들
(B) 드론 조종사들
(C) 사진가 지망생들
(D) 부동산 중개업자들

해설 첫 단락에 드론을 이용해 촬영한 사진이 이 글을 읽는 사람들의 고객들이 소유한 주택과 아파트 단지, 그리고 상업용 공간을 보여줄 수 있는 훌륭한 방법(This technology is an excellent way to showcase your client's home, apartment complex, or commercial space)이라고 알리는 내용이 제시되어 있다. 건물 소유주의 의뢰를 받아 건물을 보여 주는 일을 하는 사람들은 부동산 중개업자일 것이므로 (D)가 정답이다.

어휘 property 건물, 부동산 aspiring 지망하는, 장차 ~가 되려는

## 159 세부 사항

번역 웹페이지에 따르면, 무엇에 대해 고객들에게 추가 요금이 청구되는가?
(A) 드론으로 사진 촬영하기
(B) 촉박하게 통보해 사진 촬영 취소하기
(C) 저녁 시간에 사진 촬영하기
(D) 추가 사진 요청하기

해설 마지막 단락에 공중 촬영의 가격이 이미지 5장에 200달러이며, 원하는 사진 숫자에 따라 인상된다(Prices for aerial photography start at $200 for five images and increase with the number of photos desired)는 말이 언급되어 있다. 따라서 5장을 초과해 사진을 요청하는 경우에 추가 요금이 청구된다는 것을 알 수 있으므로 (D)가 정답이다.

어휘 on short notice 촉박하게 통보해

> **Paraphrasing**
> 지문의 Prices ~ increase → 질문의 are charged more

## 160 문장 삽입

번역 [1], [2], [3], [4]로 표시된 곳 중에서 다음 문장이 가장 적합한 곳은 어디인가?

"게다가, 바로 위 100피트 상공에서 촬영한 사진은 건물의 전체 배치를 보여 주는 데 이용될 수 있습니다."
(A) [1]
(B) [2]
(C) [3]
(D) [4]

TEST 6

해설 제시된 문장은 '게다가, 더욱이'라는 의미로 유사한 정보를 추가할 때 사용하는 In addition과 함께 100피트 상공에서 촬영한 사진이 건물의 전체 배치를 보여 주는 데 이용될 수 있다는 의미를 나타낸다. 이는 촬영한 사진의 용도를 설명하는 내용이므로 비슷한 용도가 언급된 문장 뒤인 [2]에 들어가 유사 정보를 추가하는 흐름이 되는 게 자연스럽다. 따라서 (B)가 정답이다.

어휘 in addition 게다가, 더욱이 overhead 머리 위로, 머리 위의 layout 배치, 구획

### 161-163 이메일

발신: 파트리샤 칠턴
수신: 전 직원
제목: 초과 근무 정책
날짜: 12월 2일

직원 여러분께,

다가오는 심포지엄을 준비하느라 고생하시는 여러분께 진심으로 감사드립니다. 심포지엄에 수반되는 추가 업무들을 감당하는 것이 쉽지 않다는 것을 잘 알고 있습니다.

그렇긴 하지만, **161 우리 직원 안내서는 사전에 책임자로부터 승인을 받지 않고 주당 40시간 넘게 근무하는 것을 엄격히 금하고 있다는 것을 여러분께 상기시켜 드리고자 합니다. 162 법적으로 모든 초과 근무 시간에 대해 더 높은 급료를 지불해야 하며, 우리 회사는 비영리 단체로서 이 부분에 추가 비용을 감당할 자원이 없습니다.**

할당된 업무를 정규 근무 시간 내에 완료할 수 없는 경우, 초과 근무를 허용할 것인지 아니면 마감 기한을 미룰 것인지 여러분의 부서장님께서 결정하시도록 맡기셔야 합니다. 앞으로, **163 이 정책을 준수하지 못하는 경우에는 여러분의 인사 고과에 반영될 것입니다.**

감사합니다.

파트리샤 칠턴
이사
엔지니어링 분야의 여성들을 위한 선제적 네트워크

어휘 overtime 초과 근무 upcoming 다가오는, 곧 있을 struggle 힘겨운 일 keep up with (진행 등) ~을 따라잡다 workload 업무량 involve 관련되다, 수반하다 employee handbook 직원 안내서 strictly 엄격히 prohibit 금지하다 approval 승인 supervisor 책임자, 부서장, 상사 beforehand 사전에, 미리 legally 법적으로 rate 급료, 요금 nonprofit 비영리의 organization 단체, 기관 resource 자산, 자원 cover (비용 등을) 감당하다, 충당하다 expense 지출 (비용) assignment 할당(된 일) push back 미루다 deadline 마감 기한 failure 하지 못함, 불이행 follow 준수하다 reflect 반영하다 performance (수행) 능력, 성과 evaluation 평가(서) proactive 사전 대책을 강구하는

### 161 추론

번역 칠턴 씨가 이메일을 보낸 이유는 무엇이겠는가?
(A) 행사 준비가 일정보다 뒤처졌다.
(B) 보상 관련 법률에 변화가 있다.
(C) 직원들이 승인 없이 추가 근무를 하고 있다.
(D) 일부 직원들이 설명회에 빠졌다.

해설 두 번째 단락에 사전에 책임자로부터 승인을 받지 않고 주당 40시간 넘게 근무하는 것을 엄격히 금하고 있다는 것을 상기시켜 주려 한다(I'd like to remind you that our employee handbook strictly prohibits working ~ without getting approval from a supervisor beforehand)는 말이 쓰여 있다. 따라서 승인 없이 추가 근무를 하고 있는 직원들에게 해당 내용을 상기시키기 위한 이메일로 볼 수 있으므로 (C)가 정답이다.

어휘 fall behind ~에 뒤처지다 compensation 보상 permission 승인, 허락 miss 빠지다, 놓치다 information session 설명회

### 162 Not / True

번역 엔지니어링 분야의 여성들을 위한 선제적 네트워크에 대해 언급된 것은?
(A) 급여 총액을 위한 예산이 제한되어 있다.
(B) 연례 심포지엄을 주최한다.
(C) 소속 직원들은 정기적으로 급여 인상을 받는다.
(D) 소속 법률 관련 부서는 매우 바쁘다.

해설 두 번째 단락에 법적으로 초과 근무 시간에 대해 더 높은 급료를 지불해야 하지만, 비영리 단체로서 그러한 추가 비용을 감당할 자원이 없다(We're legally required to pay you at a higher rate for any overtime hours ~ we don't have the resources to cover extra expenses in this area)는 내용이 있다. 이를 통해 직원 급여를 지급할 수 있는 회사 재정이 한정적이라는 사실을 알 수 있으므로 (A)가 정답이다.

어휘 limited 제한된 budget 예산 payroll 급여 총액, 전체 급여 대상자 명단 organize 주최하다, 조직하다 annual 연례적인, 해마다의 regularly 주기적으로, 규칙적으로

> **Paraphrasing**
> 지문의 don't have the resources to cover extra expenses → 정답의 has a limited budget

### 163 세부 사항

번역 이메일에 따르면, 규칙을 위반한 직원은 어떤 결과에 직면할 것인가?
(A) 탄력 근무제 혜택을 잃을 것이다.
(B) 책임자 승진 자격을 얻지 못할 것이다.
(C) 덜 선호되는 업무를 할당받을 것이다.
(D) 더 나쁜 인사 고과를 받을 것이다.

해설 세 번째 단락에 지문 전체적으로 언급한 정책을 준수하지 못하는 경우에는 인사 고과에 반영될 것(failure to follow this policy will be reflected in your performance evaluation)이라는 말이 쓰여 있다. 이는 좋지 못한 평가를 받게 될 것임을 의미하므로 (D)가 정답이다.

어휘 consequence 결과 face 직면하다 break 위반하다, 어기다 perk 혜택, 특혜 flexible 탄력적인, 유연한 ineligible 자격이 없는 promotion 승진 desirable 매력적인, (사람들이) 원하는

**Paraphrasing**
지문의 failure to follow this policy
→ 질문의 breaking a rule
지문의 be reflected in your performance evaluation
→ 정답의 Earning a worse performance review

### 164-167 편지

3월 10일

최광훈
코너 가 233
에든버러 EH3 8DN

최 씨께,

폴워스 커뮤니티 가든 위원회를 대표해, [164] **또 한 해 동안 함께 녹지를 가꾸기 위해 귀하를 다시 초대하게 되어 기쁩니다.** 올해의 재배 시즌은 4월 3일에 시작되며, 여러분이 알아 두셔야 할 몇 가지 변경된 정원 규칙이 있습니다.

[165,167] **첫 번째로, 노동을 공정하게 분배하기 위해, 이제 모든 회원들은 연간 최소 10시간 이상 정원을 운영하는 데 필요한 자원봉사 일을 해야 합니다.** 잡초 제거 및 도구 창고 청소가 대표적인 일에 포함됩니다. [165] **이 필수 요건의 이행 여부는 정원 웹사이트의 시스템을 통해 파악될 것입니다.** 곧 이와 관련된 추가 정보를 제공해 드리겠습니다.

두 번째로, [166] **우리 정원의 대기자 명단이 길기 때문에,** 올해는 한 가구가 두 개 이상의 텃밭을 보유할 수 있는 마지막 해가 될 것입니다. 귀하의 가정이 여러 개의 밭을 보유하고 있으면, 어느 것을 유지하기 원하는지 위원회에 알려 주시기 바라며, 나머지는 시즌이 끝날 때 재배정하기 적절한 상태가 되도록 해 주십시오.

또한, 평소와 마찬가지로, 새로운 소식과 업데이트 확인을 위해 도구 창고 내의 게시판을 자주 확인하실 것을 요청 드립니다. 감사드리며, 정원에서 뵐 수 있기를 고대합니다!

어빈 타운센드, 회장
폴워스 커뮤니티 가든 위원회

어휘 on behalf of ~을 대표해 tend 관리하다, 돌보다 greenery 녹지 (공간) growing 재배 be aware of ~을 알고 있다 ensure 보장하다 fair 공정한 distribution 분배, 배포 labour 노동, 노동력 mandatory 의무적인 annually 연간, 해마다 volunteer 자원봉사 fulfillment 이행, 완수 requirement 요건, 필수 조건 track 파악하다, 추적하다 be allowed to ~하도록 허용되다 plot 밭, 작은 땅 multiple 다수의 make certain 반드시 ~하도록 하다, ~임을 확실히 하다 suitable 적절한, 알맞은 shape 상태, 형태 reassignment 재배정, 재할당 tool shed 공구 창고 look forward to -ing ~하기를 고대하다

### 164 주제 / 목적

번역 편지의 한 가지 목적은?
(A) 회원권의 새로운 혜택을 설명하는 것
(B) 시작 날짜의 변경을 공지하는 것
(C) 행사에 필요한 자원봉사자를 찾는 것
(D) 다시 돌아오는 회원을 환영하는 것

해설 첫 단락에 또 한 해 동안 함께 녹지를 가꾸기 위해 다시 초대하게 되어 기쁘다(I am excited to invite you back for another year of tending greenery together)는 말에서 다시 돌아오는 회원을 맞이하기 위한 편지인 것을 알 수 있으므로 (D)가 정답이다.

어휘 describe 설명하다 benefit 혜택, 이점 seek 찾다, 구하다

### 165 세부 사항

번역 편지에 따르면, 온라인 시스템은 무엇에 이용될 것인가?
(A) 정원에 관한 뉴스 전하기
(B) 도구 사용 현황 파악하기
(C) 토지 구획 재분배하기
(D) 작업 시간 기록하기

해설 두 번째 단락에 연간 최소 10시간 이상 자원봉사 일을 해야 한다고 알리면서 그 이행 여부가 웹사이트의 시스템을 통해 파악될 것(it is now mandatory for all members to spend at least 10 hours annually doing the volunteer work necessary to keep the garden running. Fulfillment of this requirement will be tracked through a system on the garden's Web site)이라고 알리고 있다. 따라서 자원봉사 활동 시간이 온라인 시스템에 기록된다는 것을 알 수 있으므로 (D)가 정답이다.

어휘 keep track of ~을 파악하다, ~을 추적하다 redistribute 재분배하다, 재배포하다

**Paraphrasing**
지문의 a system on the garden's Web site
→ 질문의 an online system
지문의 Fulfillment of this requirement will be tracked
→ 정답의 Recording some work hours

### 166 추론

번역 폴워스 커뮤니티 가든에 대해 암시된 것은?
(A) 수요를 충족할 만큼 밭이 충분하지 않다.
(B) 보관용 창고에 밭 구획도가 게시되어 있다.
(C) 밭이 매년 다른 가정에 배정되어야 한다.
(D) 내년에 밭들의 경계가 다시 그려질 것이다.

해설 세 번째 단락에 정원의 대기자 명단이 길다(due to the long waiting list for our garden)는 말이 언급되어 있는데, 대기자가 많다는 말은 이용 가능한 밭이 충분히 많지 않다는 의미이므로 (A)가 정답이다.

어휘 demand 수요, 요구 diagram 도표 storage 보관, 저장 assign 배정하다, 할당하다 border 경계(선) redraw 다시 그리다

## 167 문장 삽입

번역 [1], [2], [3], [4]로 표시된 곳 중에서 다음 문장이 가장 적합한 곳은 어디인가?

"잡초 제거 및 도구 창고 청소가 대표적인 일에 포함됩니다."

(A) [1]
(B) [2]
(C) [3]
(D) [4]

해설 잡초 제거와 도구 창고 청소를 대표적인 예로 제시하는 문장이다. 따라서 의무적으로 자원봉사를 해야 한다고 말한 문장 뒤인 [2]에 들어가서 그 자원봉사 일의 구체적인 예를 언급한 흐름이 되어야 가장 자연스러우므로 (B)가 정답이다.

어휘 typical 일반적인, 전형적인 task 일, 업무 weed 잡초 removal 제거, 없앰

## 168-171 기사

여름을 향해 순조롭게 진행 중인 HRTA 프로젝트

[168] **히처트 지역 교통국(HRTA)은 경전철에 접근성이 향상된 열차를 추가하는 과정에서 또 한 번 중요한 단계에 이르렀다.** 1월 7일에 [169] **HRTA 직원들은 초여름 운행에 앞서 문제를 발견해 제거하기 위해 골드 노선과 그린 노선 열차의 시범 운행을 시작했다.** 이용객들을 수송하는 데 있어 불편을 최소화하기 위해, 이 열차들은 오직 오후 8시에서 오전 4시 사이에만 운행되며, [170] **사람들이 탑승하지 않도록 "테스트용 열차"라고 적힌 대형 스티커가 부착된다.** [171] **폰세카에서 첫선을 보인 이후로 전국 각지의 대도시권으로 빠르게 확산되고 있는** 이 열차는 장애를 지닌 탑승객들이 이용하기 더 쉽게 만들어 주는 낮고 계단 없는 출입문, 자동으로 제어되는 진입로를 비롯한 기타 여러 특징들을 자랑한다.

어휘 on track 잘 진행되고 있는 milestone 중대 시점, 중요한 단계 enhanced-accessibility 접근성을 개선한 light-rail 경전철 fleet 전체 열차, 전체 차량 trial operation 시범 운영 eliminate 없애다, 제거하다 deployment 배치 inconvenience 불편함 transport 수송하다 mark 표시하다 prevent 방지하다 spread 확산되다 metropolitan 대도시의 following ~ 후에 debut 첫선, 데뷔 boast 자랑하다 -free ~이 없는 automatically-controlled 자동으로 제어되는 ramp 진입로, 경사로 feature 특징 accessible 접근 가능한 disability 장애

## 168 세부 사항

번역 HRTA가 준비하고 있는 것은?

(A) 새로운 유형의 열차 도입
(B) 야간 서비스 확대
(C) 두 열차 노선 연결
(D) 역의 접근성 향상

해설 지문 초반부에 히처트 지역 교통국(HRTA)이 경전철에 접근성이 향상된 열차를 추가하는 과정에서 또 한 번 중요한 단계에 이르렀다(Hitchert Regional Transit Agency (HRTA) has reached another milestone in the process of adding enhanced-accessibility trains to its light-rail fleet)고 했으므로 (A)가 정답이다.

어휘 introduce 도입하다, 소개하다 expand 확대하다, 확장하다 connect 연결하다

> Paraphrasing
> 지문의 adding enhanced-accessibility trains
> → 정답의 Introduce a new type of train

## 169 세부 사항

번역 기사에 따르면, 여름이 시작될 때까지 무슨 일이 계속될 것인가?

(A) 열차가 테스트될 것이다.
(B) 직원이 교육을 받을 것이다.
(C) 교통편 이용객들에게 설문 조사를 할 것이다.
(D) 공사가 실시될 것이다.

해설 지문 초반부에 HRTA 직원들이 초여름 운행에 앞서 문제를 발견해 제거하기 위해 골드 노선과 그린 노선 열차의 시범 운행을 시작했다(HRTA staff began trial operation of the trains on the Gold and Green lines in order to discover and eliminate any issues before their deployment at the start of summer)고 언급되어 있으므로 (A)가 정답이다.

어휘 transport 교통(편) carry out 실시하다, 수행하다

> Paraphrasing
> 지문의 trial operation of the trains
> → 정답의 Some trains will be tested

## 170 추론

번역 스티커가 부착된 열차에 대해 암시된 것은?

(A) 오직 두 곳의 정류장에만 정차한다.
(B) 아직 승객을 태우지 않는다.
(C) 점검을 완료했다.
(D) 곧 운행이 중단될 것이다.

해설 지문 중반부에 사람들이 탑승하지 않도록 "테스트용 열차"라고 적힌 대형 스티커가 부착된다(are marked with large "Test Train" stickers to prevent people from boarding)고 했으므로 승객을 태우지 않는다는 것을 알 수 있다. 따라서 (B)가 정답이다.

어휘 inspection 점검, 조사 be taken out of service 운행이 중단되다, 사용하지 않게 되다

> Paraphrasing
> 지문의 prevent people from boarding
> → 정답의 do not carry passengers yet

## 171 세부 사항

번역 글쓴이는 왜 폰세카를 언급하는가?

(A) HRTA 직원들이 조사를 위해 그곳에 방문했다.
(B) 생산 공장 부지이다.
(C) 기술을 채택한 첫 번째 장소였다.
(D) 인구 규모가 히처트와 비슷하다.

해설 지문 후반부에 폰세카를 언급하면서 그곳에서 첫선을 보인 이후로 전국 각지의 대도시권으로 빠르게 확산되고 있다(Spreading rapidly to metropolitan areas across the country following their debut in Fonseca)고 설명하고 있다. 이는 지문 전체적으로 이야기하는 새로운 기술이 적용된 열차를 처음 채택해 활용한 곳이 폰세카라는 말이므로 (C)가 정답이다.

어휘 site 부지, 장소 adopt 채택하다 population 인구

### 172-175 온라인 채팅

미쉘 가니에 (오전 10시 4분)
안녕하세요, 여러분. 제가 방금 여름 인턴들에게서 받은 수료 설문 조사 내용을 살펴봤습니다.

도미닉 퍼킨스 (오전 10시 5분)
놀라운 결과가 있나요?

미쉘 가니에 (오전 10시 7분)
네, 173 (B) **인턴들은 우리가 수준 낮은 업무를 너무 많이 주었다고 느꼈어요.** 172 **투자 기회를 조사하고 우리를 도와 고객들에게 그 기회를 설명하는 데 더 많은 시간을 보내기를 원했어요.**

티나 오스본 (오전 10시 8분)
정말로요? 우리가 그런 종류의 일에 인턴들을 참여시키기 위해 꽤나 노력했잖아요. 어쩌면 지원 과정에서 인턴 프로그램의 범위에 대해 더 명확하게 설명할 필요가 있을 것 같습니다.

미쉘 가니에 (오전 10시 9분)
좋은 생각입니다. 어쨌든, 173 (C) **우리의 멘토링**과 173 (D) **인적 교류 기회**에 대한 의견은 꽤 좋았어요, 적어도요.

도미닉 퍼킨스 (오전 10시 10분)
174 **미쉘, 결과를 더 보고 싶어요. 당신 사무실에 들르기 좋은 시간이 언제일까요?**

미쉘 가니에 (오전 10시 11분)
아, 며칠 후에 평가 회의를 할 거예요. 오늘 오후에 여러분 일정표에 기재해 놓을 게요.

도미닉 퍼킨스 (오전 10시 12분)
좋습니다.

미쉘 가니에 (오전 10시 13분)
그래서 생각난 게 있는데, 회의 전에, 인턴들이 졸업한 후 직원 채용을 추천할 것인지 결정해 주세요. 인사부에서 간단히 참고할 수 있게 인사 파일에 내용을 적어 두기를 원하네요.

티나 오스본 (오전 10시 14분)
175 **그쪽에서 정말 그냥 "예"나 "아니오"라는 말만 원하는 건가요? 미래의 고용 관리자들은 각 개인의 장단점에 대한 개요를 선호할 것 같아요.**

미쉘 가니에 (오전 10시 14분)
좋은 지적입니다. 제가 더 알아 볼게요.

어휘 look over ~을 살펴보다 exit survey 출구 조사, 퇴사 조사 low-level 수준이 낮은 duty 업무, 임무 investment 투자 opportunity 기회 pitch (제품 구매 등을 위해) 설명하다, 홍보하다 involve 참여시키다, 관여하게 하다 application 지원, 신청 process 과정 scope 범위 mentoring 멘토링(경험자나 선배 등이 조언을 제공) networking 인적 교류 drop by ~에 들르다 recruit 채용하다, 모집하다 graduation 수료, 졸업 reference 참고, 참조 overview 개요 strength 장점, 강점 weakness 단점, 약점 find out 파악하다, 알아내다

### 172 추론

번역 메시지 작성자들은 어떤 분야에서 일하겠는가?
(A) 보험 영업
(B) 직원 채용
(C) 자산 관리
(D) 의료 연구

해설 가니에 씨가 10시 7분에 작성한 메시지에 투자 기회를 조사하고 고객들에게 그 기회를 설명하는(researching investment opportunities and helping us pitch them to clients) 업무가 언급되어 있는 것을 통해 자산 관리 분야에서 일하는 사람들임을 알 수 있으므로 (C)가 정답이다.

### 173 Not / True

번역 인턴들에게 제공된 설문에서 다뤄진 주제로 언급되지 않은 것은?
(A) 인턴 프로그램 지원 과정
(B) 배정받은 업무
(C) 메시지 작성자들이 제공한 멘토링
(D) 직업상 인맥을 형성할 수 있는 기회

해설 가니에 씨가 10시 7분에 작성한 메시지에 인턴들은 우리가 수준 낮은 업무를 너무 많이 주었다고 생각했다(they felt that we gave them too many low-level duties)고 한 부분에서 (B)를, 10시 9분에 작성한 메시지에 멘토링(our mentoring)과 인적 교류 기회(the networking opportunities)에 관해 언급된 부분을 통해 (C)와 (D)를 각각 확인할 수 있다. 하지만 설문에서 인턴 프로그램 지원 과정을 다뤘다는 말은 없으므로 (A)가 정답이다.

어휘 cover (주제 등을) 다루다 task 업무, 일 assign 배정하다

### 174 의도 파악

번역 오전 10시 11분에 가니에 씨가 "며칠 후에 평가 회의를 할 거예요"라고 쓸 때, 의미하는 것은 무엇인가?
(A) 퍼킨스 씨가 직원들에게 소개될 것이다.
(B) 퍼킨스 씨가 자신에게 문서를 가져다줄 필요가 없다.
(C) 퍼킨스 씨는 정보를 얻기 위해 기다려야 한다.
(D) 퍼킨스 씨가 토론을 준비할 시간이 있을 것이다.

해설 퍼킨스 씨가 10시 10분에 결과를 더 보고 싶다는 말과 함께 가니에 씨의 사무실에 들르기 좋은 시간이 언제인지(Michelle, I'd be interested in seeing more of the results. When would be a good time to drop by your office?) 묻자, 가니에 씨가 "며칠 후에 평가 회의 시간을 가질 것"이라고 대답하고 있다. 이는 사무실로 찾아오지 말고 그 회의 시간까지 기다리라는 뜻이므로 (C)가 정답이다.

## 175 추론

번역 인사부에서 요청한 정보에 관해 오스본 씨의 우려는 무엇이겠는가?
(A) 수집하는 데 상당한 노력이 들 것이다.
(B) 유용할 정도로 충분히 상세하지 않다.
(C) 다른 직원들이 접근할 수 없어야 한다.
(D) 나중에는 더 이상 정확하지 않을 수도 있다.

해설 오스본 씨가 10시 14분에 작성한 메시지에 그냥 "예"나 "아니오"라는 말만 있는 게 아니라 인턴들의 장단점에 대한 개요가 있으면 좋을 것(Do they really just want a "yes" or "no"? I think future hiring managers would prefer an overview of each person's strengths and weaknesses)이라는 의견이 제시되어 있다. 이는 조금 더 상세한 정보가 필요하다는 의미이므로 (B)가 정답이다.

어휘 considerable 상당한 gather 수집하다, 모으다 detailed 상세한 accessible 접근 가능한, 이용 가능한 accurate 정확한

### 176-180 구인 광고+이메일

영업 지부장

[176] **사무실 및 소매 시설에 에너지 효율이 높은 에어컨 시스템을 제공하는 최고의 업체인 이슨 테크놀로지**에서 남서부 지역을 담당할 영업 지부장을 찾고 있습니다. 이 직책의 근무지는 배로우에 있습니다.

책임 직무:
- 지역 영업팀의 활동 감독
- 잠재 고객 파악 및 거래 확보
- [177] **정확한 판매 예측 및 추적**
- 고객 만족도 모니터링을 통한 고객 유지율 보장

필수 자격 요건:
- [179 (A)] **경영 또는 기술 분야 학위**
- [179 (B)] **영업 책임자 역할 경력 5년**
- [179 (C)] **뛰어난 대중 연설 능력**
- [179 (D)] **잦은 출장 의향**

지원하시려면, hiring@easontech.com으로 이력서와 자기 소개서를 보내 주시기 바랍니다.

어휘 district 지역, 구역 premier 최고의 energy-efficient 에너지 효율이 높은 retail 소매 seek 찾다, 구하다 be based in ~을 기반으로 하다 responsibility 책무, 책임 oversee 총괄하다, 감독하다 identify 확인하다 potential 잠재적인 acquire 얻다, 획득하다 forecast 예측하다 track 파악하다, 추적하다 accurately 정확하게 monitor 관찰하다 satisfaction 만족(도) ensure 보장하다 retention 유지, 보유 qualification 자격 (요건) degree 학위 willingness 의지, 의향 frequently 자주, 빈번히 résumé 이력서 cover letter 자기 소개서

발신: 나소원
수신: 브랜든 피셔
제목: 잠재 후보자
날짜: 1월 30일

안녕하세요, 브랜든.

남서부 영업 지부장 직책에 좋은 후보가 될 수도 있는 분을 알려 드리고 싶었습니다. 이름은 에드가 말론이며, 레비아 주식회사의 [179 (B)] **영업사원**입니다. [178, 179 (D)] **전국 각지에서 열린 무역 박람회에서 우연히 마주친 후에 친구 사이가 되었습니다.** [179 (C)] **박람회에서 두어 차례 제품 프레젠테이션을 하는 것을 봤는데, 아주 잘 하더군요.** 레비아 사에서 최소 5년 동안 재직해 온 데다, [179 (A)] **기계 공학 학위를 보유한** 것 같습니다. 제가 이분께 구인 광고를 [180] **공유해** 드리면서 지원하도록 제안하는 이메일을 보내 드릴까요?

소원

어휘 candidate 후보자, 지원자 representative 직원, 대표자 run into ~와 우연히 마주치다 trade show 무역 박람회 pitch (제품 구매 등을 위한) 설명(회), 홍보 share 공유하다

## 176 추론

번역 이슨 테크놀로지에 대해 암시된 것은?
(A) 제품을 다른 업체에 판매한다.
(B) 재생 가능한 에너지를 만들어 내는 기술을 설계한다.
(C) 최근 새로운 영업 지역을 만들었다.
(D) 배로우에 본사가 있다.

해설 구인 광고 첫 단락에 이슨 테크놀로지가 사무실 및 소매 시설에 에너지 효율이 높은 에어컨 시스템을 제공하는 최고의 업체(Eason Technologies, a premier provider of energy-efficient air-conditioning systems for offices and retail facilities)라는 말이 쓰여 있다. 이를 통해 다른 업체들에 제품을 파는 곳임을 알 수 있으므로 (A)가 정답이다.

어휘 renewable 재생 가능한 be headquartered in ~에 본사가 있다

> **Paraphrasing**
> 지문의 provider / for offices and retail facilities
> → 정답의 sells its products to other businesses

## 177 세부 사항

번역 해당 직책의 한 가지 책임은 무엇인가?
(A) 경쟁사의 가격 책정 관찰하기
(B) 마케팅 직원들과 협력하기
(C) 영업 수익 정확하게 예측하기
(D) 잠재적 신제품 제안하기

해설 구인 광고 중반부의 직무 항목 중에 정확한 판매 예측 및 추적(forecasting and tracking sales accurately)이 있으므로 (C)가 정답이다.

어휘 cooperate 협력하다 correctly 정확하게 predict 예측하다 revenue 수익, 수입

> **Paraphrasing**
> 지문의 forecasting ~ sales accurately
> → 정답의 Correctly predicting sales revenues

## 178 세부 사항

번역 나 씨가 이메일에서 설명하는 것은 무엇인가?
(A) 얼마나 오래 말론 씨와 알고 지냈는지
(B) 어디서 해당 구인 광고를 봤는지
(C) 어떻게 말론 씨와 아는 사이가 됐는지
(D) 말론 씨가 왜 이직에 관심이 있는지

해설 이메일 중반부에 말론 씨를 소개하면서 전국 각지에서 열린 무역 박람회에서 우연히 마주친 후에 친구 사이가 되었다(We became friends after running into each other at trade shows around the country)고 쓰여 있으므로 (C)가 정답이다.

어휘 acquainted with ~와 아는 사이인

> Paraphrasing
> 지문의 became friends → 정답의 became acquainted

## 179 연계

번역 나 씨의 설명에 따르면, 말론 씨는 어떤 자격 요건을 갖추지 못했을 것인가?
(A) 적합한 분야의 학위
(B) 필수 근무 경력
(C) 뛰어난 대중 연설 능력
(D) 잦은 출장 용인

해설 구인 광고 후반부 자격 요건에 영업 책임자 역할 경력 5년(five years of experience in a sales leadership role)이 제시되어 있는데, 이메일에 말론 씨가 영업사원(a sales representative)이라고 언급되어 있다. 영업 책임자 경력이 자격 요건인데, 일반 사원급이므로 경력 요건을 갖추지 못했음을 알 수 있다. 따라서 (B)가 정답이다.

어휘 suitable 적합한, 알맞은 ability 능력 tolerance 인내(심), 용인 frequent 잦은, 빈번한

## 180 동의어

번역 이메일의 첫 번째 단락, 여섯 번째 줄에 쓰인 'sharing'과 의미가 가장 가까운 것은?
(A) 나누는
(B) 알리는
(C) 표현하는
(D) 전달하는

해설 sharing을 포함한 부분은 구인 광고를 공유하는 이메일을 보내겠다(send him an e-mail sharing the job advertisement)라고 해석되는데, 구인 광고를 공유하겠다는 것은 구인 광고를 보내겠다는 의미이므로 '전달하다'를 뜻하는 deliver의 현재분사 (D) delivering이 정답이다. inform은 뒤에 사람 목적어가 오기 때문에 (B) informing은 오답이다.

### 181-185 광고+이메일

스크랩 세이버

사업장의 음식물 쓰레기를 처리하는 데 지치셨나요? 레스토랑이나 카페를 운영하시든, 호텔이나 출장 요리 업체를 운영하시든, 스크랩 세이버에 그 문제의 해결책이 있습니다.

[181] **작년에 상업용 음식물 쓰레기의 분리 배출이 법으로 의무화된 이후로**, 점점 더 많은 사업체들이 요리 찌꺼기와 남은 음식물의 처리를 저희에게 의탁하고 있습니다. [182] **저희는 이런 음식물 쓰레기를 저렴하고 편리하게 수거하여 당사 시설로 운반하는 서비스를 제공하며, 이곳에서 그것들은 대체 연료와 유기농 비료로 전환됩니다.** 고객은 지정된 수거 시간까지 저희 무료 보관 용기나 자체 용기에 음식물 쓰레기를 모아 두시면 되며, 그 시간은 필요한 만큼 자주 예약할 수 있습니다.

[185] **스크랩 세이버는 합리적인 수준의 취급 수수료를 내면 모든 종류의 음식물 포장을 제거하는 서비스를 제공하며**, 심지어 매주 3톤 이상의 쓰레기를 배출하는 업체를 대상으로 대량 운송 서비스도 제공합니다.

www.scrapsaver.com을 방문하셔서 더 많은 정보를 알아보시기 바랍니다!

어휘 deal with ~을 처리하다 catering 출장 요리 제공(업) solution 해결책 separate 분리된, 별도의 disposal 처리, 처분 commercial 상업의 mandate 의무화하다 turn to+명사 ~에 의탁하다, 의지하다 scraps (음식) 찌꺼기, 잔여물 leftover food 남은 음식 convenient 편리한 pickup 수거, 가져 가기 transport 운송, 수송 material 물품, 물질 convert 전환하다 alternative 대체의 organic 유기농의 fertilizer 비료 collect 모으다, 수거하다 storage 보관, 저장 bin (보관용) 통 designated 지정된 frequently 자주, 빈번히 removal 제거, 없앰 packaging 포장 용기 reasonable 합리적인, 가격이 알맞은 handling 처리 fee 요금 bulk (주문 등이) 대량의

발신: 마가렛 로스 <mross@scrapsaver.com>
수신: 제이크 피어스 <jake.pierce@babybudfood.com>
제목: 스크랩 세이버 관련 정보
날짜: 11월 14일

피어스 씨께,

베이비버드 푸드 주식회사를 대표해 저희에게 연락 주셔서 감사합니다. 온라인 양식에 작성하신 질문에 대해 답변해 드리게 되어 기쁩니다.

[184] **저희 요금은 음식물 쓰레기 1리터당 0.26달러**이고, 귀사의 위치를 [183] **고려하면** 방문당 11달러의 거리 기반 수거 요금이 있습니다. [185] **취급 수수료는 청구되지 않을 것이며**, 주말 수거에 대한 추가 비용도 없습니다. [184] **청구서 발급은 매달 말일에 이뤄집니다.**

추가 질문이 있으시거나 스크랩 세이버의 서비스를 예약하실 준비가 되시면 주저 마시고 이 이메일에 답장하거나 555-0189번으로 제게 전화 주시기 바랍니다.

마가렛 로스
영업사원
스크랩 세이버 주식회사

어휘 on behalf of ~을 대표해 fill out ~을 작성하다 rate 요금, 등급 -based ~ 기반의 location 위치, 지점 charge 청구하다 billing 청구서 발급 hesitate 주저하다 engage 예약하다

## 181 Not / True

번역 상업용 음식물 쓰레기에 대해 언급된 것은?
(A) 매년 양이 증가하고 있다.
(B) 환경에 해로울 수 있다.
(C) 대부분 레스토랑에서 발생한다.
(D) 최근 규제 대상이 되었다.

해설 광고 두 번째 단락에 작년에 상업용 음식물 쓰레기의 분리 배출이 법으로 의무화되었다(the separate disposal of commercial food waste became mandated by law last year)고 한 것에서 최근에 규제 대상이 되었다는 점을 알 수 있으므로 (D)가 정답이다.

어휘 volume 양, 용량 generate 만들어 내다 subject 대상, 사안 regulation 규제, 규정

> **Paraphrasing**
> 지문의 became mandated by law last year
> → 정답의 the subject of a recent regulation

## 182 추론

번역 광고에서 스크랩 세이버에 대해 암시하는 것은?
(A) 쓰레기 처리 시설을 운영하고 있다.
(B) 운송하는 폐기물의 종류를 확대할 계획이다.
(C) 고객들에게 쓰레기 감소에 관한 조언을 제공한다.
(D) 그곳의 운송 트럭은 대체 연료로 운행된다.

해설 광고 두 번째 단락에 스크랩 세이버가 음식물 쓰레기를 자사 시설로 운송하는 서비스를 제공한다는 사실과 함께 그곳에서 대체 연료와 유기농 비료로 전환된다(We provide cheap, convenient pickup and transport of these materials to our facilities, where they are converted into alternative fuels and organic fertilizer)고 알리고 있다. 따라서 (A)가 정답이다.

어휘 operate 운영하다 variety 종류, 다양성

> **Paraphrasing**
> 지문의 our facilities, where they are converted into alternative fuels and organic fertilizer
> → 정답의 waste processing facilities

## 183 동의어

번역 이메일의 두 번째 단락, 두 번째 줄에 쓰인 'given'과 의미가 가장 가까운 것은?
(A) ~와 관련된
(B) ~을 고려해 (볼 때)
(C) 명시된
(D) 배정된, 할당된

해설 given은 명사(구)를 목적어로 취하는 전치사로서 '~을 고려해 (볼 때)'라는 의미를 나타내므로, 동일한 의미로 쓰이는 전치사 (B) considering이 정답이다.

## 184 추론

번역 이메일에 따르면, 스크랩 세이버가 한 달에 한 번씩 무엇을 할 것 같은가?
(A) 서비스 요금 조정
(B) 보관 용기 교체
(C) 총 리터 수 계산
(D) 원하는 수거 빈도 확인

해설 이메일 두 번째 단락에 스크랩 세이버의 요금이 음식물 쓰레기 1리터당 0.26달러(Our rate is $0.26 per liter of food waste)라는 말과 함께 청구서 발급이 매달 말일에 이뤄진다(Billing is done at the end of each calendar month)고 언급되어 있다. 따라서 한 달 단위로 총 리터를 계산해 청구서를 발급하는 것으로 볼 수 있으므로 (C)가 정답이다.

어휘 adjust 조정하다, 조절하다 replace 교체하다, 대체하다 container 용기, 그릇 calculate 계산하다 confirm 확인하다, 확정하다 desired 요구되는, 원하는 frequency 빈도

## 185 연계

번역 베이비버드 푸드 주식회사에 대해 어떤 결론을 내릴 수 있는가?
(A) 제조 시설이 두 군데 이상이다.
(B) 스크랩 세이버에 포장된 음식물을 보낼 계획이 없다.
(C) 매주 수 톤의 음식물 쓰레기를 배출한다.
(D) 이전에 음식물 쓰레기 처리 서비스를 이용해 본 적이 없다.

해설 이메일 두 번째 단락에 베이비버드 푸드 주식회사에 취급 수수료가 청구되지 않을 것(You wouldn't be charged handling fees)이라고 했는데, 취급 수수료 관련해서 광고 세 번째 단락에 합리적인 수준의 취급 수수료를 내면 음식물 포장을 제거하는 서비스를 제공한다(Scrap Saver offers removal of all types of food packaging for reasonable handling fees)고 언급되어 있다. 이를 통해 베이비버드 푸드 주식회사는 음식물 포장을 제거하는 서비스를 이용하지 않을 것임을 알 수 있으므로 (B)가 정답이다.

어휘 manufacturing 제조 multiple 다수의, 많은 previously 이전에, 과거에

### 186-190 웹페이지+공지+후기

http://www.creativekates.com

크리에이티브 케이츠

크리에이티브 케이츠는 창의적인 사람들이 동료 제작자를 위해 운영하는 예술 및 공예 용품점입니다. 저희는 아름답고 독특한 그림과 퀼트, 장신구, 스크랩북 등을 만들기 위해 필요한 모든 것을 보유하고 있습니다. 영감을 찾고 계신가요? [186] **저희 직원들과 고객들이 매장에서 판매되는 재료로 만든 것을 볼 수 있는 이 페이지를 확인해 보시기 바랍니다.**

저희 매장은 고객 편의를 위해 다음과 같이 네 구역으로 구성되어 있습니다.

[188] 구역 A (1~3번 통로)
**의상 제작, 기타 재봉 프로젝트 및 뜨개질용 용품**

구역 B (4~5번 통로)
구슬, 스탬프, 접착제, 색지 같은 일반 공예용 제품

구역 C (6번 통로)
그림 및 소묘 관련 용품

구역 D (7~8번 통로)
정리 및 보관 용품, 가정용 및 [190] **계절성 장식용품**

어휘 craft 공예(품) supplies 용품, 물품 run 운영하다 creative 창의적인 fellow 동료의, 같은 처지에 있는 unique 독특한, 특별한 inspiration 영감(을 주는 것) patron 고객 material 재료, 물품 be organized into ~로 구성되다, 조직되다 following 다음의, 아래의 convenience 편의(성) aisle 통로 sewing 바느질 knitting 뜨개질 bead 구슬 organization 정리, 구성 storage 보관, 저장 décor 장식(품)

공지

고객 여러분께 알립니다!

크리에이티브 케이츠가 곧 다양한 미술 및 공예에 관한 매장 내 강좌를 제공하기 시작합니다! [188] **직물 제품 통로 일부를 수업 공간으로 교체하는 과정에서** 먼지와 소음이 발생되니 양해해 주시기 바랍니다. 그리고 앞으로 몇 주 후에 진행될 저희 강좌에 관한 자세한 정보를 찾아보는 것도 잊지 마시기 바랍니다.

또한, [187] **저희 셀프 서비스 결제 기계**는 현금 사용이 안 된다는 점에 유의하시기 바랍니다. 현금 결제를 원하시면, 직원이 있는 계산대로 가시기 바랍니다. 감사합니다.

어휘 in-store 매장 내의 various 다양한 excuse 양해하다 dust 먼지 replace 교체하다, 대체하다 fabric 직물 aware 알고 있는 checkout 계산대 staffed 직원이 있는 register 계산대, 금전 등록기

http://www.shoppingcritic.com/reviews/creativekates

후기 작성자: 에츠지 치바
게시일: 6월 4일

저는 크리에이티브 케이츠에서 매우 긍정적인 경험을 했습니다. [189] **제가 한 호텔에서 프라이빗 파티를 준비하고 있었는데, 제 고객이 마지막 순간에 그곳 직원들이 행사장을 충분히 축제 분위기로 꾸미지 못했다고 판단했습니다.** 저는 크리에이티브 케이츠로 달려가 제가 만난 첫 번째 직원에게 상황을 설명했습니다. [190] **그분은 저를 연말 축제용 장식용품 코너로 안내하고 신속히 몇 가지 적합한 제품을 권해 주셨습니다. 가격은 매우 합리적이었고, 제가 그 제품들을 행사장에 설치하자,** 분위기가 정말 훨씬 더 따뜻해지고 밝아졌습니다. 도와주셔서 감사합니다, 크리에이티브 케이츠!

어휘 positive 긍정적인 put together 준비하다, 마련하다 private 개인의, 사적인 venue 행사장 festive 축제 같은 situation 상황 decoration 장식(품) suitable 적절한, 알맞은 reasonable 합리적인, 가격이 알맞은 put up 설치하다, 내걸다 atmosphere 분위기 cheerful 밝은, 기분 좋은

## 186 Not / True

번역 웹페이지에서 매장 웹사이트에 대해 언급하는 것은?
(A) 매장에서 취급하는 주요 브랜드가 나열되어 있다.
(B) 고객들이 만든 작품 이미지를 보여 준다.
(C) 독립 공예 프로젝트를 위한 설명을 제공한다.
(D) 일부 직원들의 프로필을 포함하고 있다.

해설 웹페이지 첫 단락에 직원들과 고객들이 매장에서 판매되는 재료로 만든 것을 볼 수 있는 페이지를 확인해 보라(Check out this page to see what our staff and patrons have made with materials sold at our store)는 말이 쓰여 있다. 따라서 고객들이 만든 것을 이미지로 확인할 수 있는 페이지가 있다는 것을 알 수 있으므로 (B)가 정답이다.

어휘 instructions 설명, 지시 independent 독립적인 include 포함하다

> Paraphrasing
> 지문의 what our patrons have made
> → 정답의 works created by customers

## 187 추론

번역 공지에서 크리에이티브 케이츠에 대해 암시하는 것은?
(A) 새로운 종류의 제품을 판매하기 시작할 것이다.
(B) 쇼핑 과정에서 자동화된 부분이 있다.
(C) 일부 강좌의 대체 강사를 찾고 있다.
(D) 더 이상 고객이 현금으로 결제하는 것을 허용하지 않는다.

해설 공지 두 번째 단락에 셀프 서비스 결제 기계(our self-service checkout machines)가 있다고 언급된 것에서 자동화된 부분이 있음을 알 수 있으므로 (B)가 정답이다.

어휘 automated 자동화된 process 과정 seek 찾다, 구하다 replacement 대체(자)

> Paraphrasing
> 지문의 self-service checkout machines
> → 정답의 automated part of the shopping process

## 188 연계

번역 크리에이티브 케이츠의 어느 구역이 규모가 줄어들 것인가?
(A) 구역 A
(B) 구역 B
(C) 구역 C
(D) 구역 D

TEST 6

해설 공지 첫 단락에 직물 제품 통로 일부를 수업 공간으로 바꾼다(we replace part of our fabric aisles with the class space)는 정보가 제시되어 있어 이 구역의 규모가 줄어든다는 것을 알 수 있다. 직물 제품은 웹페이지 중반부 구역 A에 쓰여 있는 의상 제작, 기타 재봉 프로젝트 및 뜨개질(dressmaking, other sewing projects, and knitting)과 관련된 제품으로 볼 수 있으므로 (A)가 정답이다.

## 189 추론

번역 치바 씨의 직업은 무엇일 것 같은가?
(A) 호텔 매니저
(B) 미술 강사
(C) 실내 디자이너
(D) 행사 기획자

해설 치바 씨가 작성한 후기 초반부에 한 호텔에서 프라이빗 파티를 준비하고 있었다(I was putting together a private party at a hotel)는 점과 고객들이 해당 행사장 분위기에 대해 의견을 제시(my clients decided at the last minute ~)한 부분이 있다는 점을 통해 행사 기획자인 것으로 볼 수 있으므로 (D)가 정답이다.

## 190 연계

번역 치바 씨에 대해 암시된 것은?
(A) 한 직원이 진행하는 시연 행사를 봤다.
(B) 계절 할인 혜택을 이용했다.
(C) 구역 D에 있는 통로에서 상품을 구입했다.
(D) 기념 행사에 참석하기 위해 해당 매장을 처음 방문했다.

해설 후기 후반부에 치바 씨가 연말 축제용 장식용품 코너로 안내를 받았고, 그 제품들을 행사장에 설치했다(She led me to the holiday decorations ~ I'd put the items up in the venue)는 내용이 언급되어 있다. 또한, 웹페이지의 구역 안내에서 장식용품이 언급된 곳은 계절성 장식용품(seasonal décor)을 판매하는 곳으로 표기된 구역 D이므로 구역 D에서 제품을 구매한 것을 알 수 있다. 따라서 (C)가 정답이다.

어휘 demonstration 시연, 설명 take advantage of ~을 이용하다 celebration 기념 행사

## 191-195 이메일+이메일+양식

발신: 카르멘 아빌라 <c.avila@keenmaninc.com>
수신: 앤드류 포스터 <a.foster@keenmaninc.com>
제목: 하데스턴 출장
날짜: 9월 9일

안녕하세요, 앤드류.

다음 달 당신의 하데스턴 공장 방문을 위한 출장 항공편 조사를 마쳤는데, 출장을 떠날 때와 올 때 모두 원하시는 시간과 꽤 가깝게 출발하는 루빈 에어 항공편이 있다는 사실을 말씀드리게 되어 기쁩니다. 이 일정이 어떠신가요?

10월 11일, 월요일
콜번 출발: 오전 9시 20분
하데스턴 도착: 오후 12시 15분

10월 14일, 목요일
하데스턴 출발: 오후 4시
콜번 도착: 오후 6시 45분

191 **두 항공편 모두 하데스턴 지역 공항을 이용한다는 점에 유의하시기 바랍니다. 이는 하데스턴-몰키스 국제 공항보다 회사에서 선호하는 호텔인, 하데스턴 동부 지역의 메진 스위츠와 훨씬 더 가깝기 때문입니다.** 이 항공편들이 괜찮으시면, 192 **7월 출장 전에 제게 제공해 주셨던 것과 동일한 상용 고객 계정 정보를 이용해, 즉시 예약을 확정하겠습니다.**

그리고 그 지역 택시 서비스는 신뢰할 수 없고 차량 공유 앱은 최근에 금지되었기 때문에 194 **타고 다니실 렌터카가 좋으실 수도 있습니다. 예약해 드리길 원하시는지 알려 주세요.**

카르멘

어휘 depart 출발하다 desired 희망하는, 바라는 itinerary 여행 일정(표) note 유의하다, 주목하다 preferred 선호하는 acceptable 수용 가능한, 괜찮은 booking 예약 immediately 즉시 frequent flyer (항공사의) 상용 고객 account 계정, 계좌 rental 대여, 임대 get around 이리저리 돌아다니다 unreliable 신뢰할 수 없는 ride-sharing 탑승 공유 ban 금지하다

발신: 앤드류 포스터 <a.foster@keenmaninc.com>
수신: 카르멘 아빌라 <c.avila@keenmaninc.com>
제목: 회신: 하데스턴 출장
날짜: 9월 10일

안녕하세요, 카르멘.

정보와 조언은 감사하지만, 며칠 동안 예약은 보류해 주시겠어요? 195 **동료에게 출장 동행을 요청할지 고려 중입니다.** 193 **우리 소형 진공 청소기를 담당하는 신임 제품 관리자인데,** 제품이 어디서 만들어지는지 보여 드리고 제조팀을 소개해 드리는 것이 도움이 될지도 몰라서요. 이 문제가 결정되는 대로 알려 드리겠습니다.

— 앤드류

어휘 hold off 보류하다, 미루다 colleague 동료 (직원) handheld 소형의, 손에 들고 사용하는 manufacturing 제조 matter 문제, 사안 settle 결정하다

매텍스

예약 번호: 2023944

예약 상세 정보:

| | |
|---|---|
| 194 **차량:** | **미렐레스 리리카 승용차** |
| 수령: | 10월 11일, 월요일, 오후 12시 45분<br>하데스턴 지역 공항 지점 |
| 반납: | 10월 14일, 목요일, 오후 3시<br>하데스턴 지역 공항 지점 |

194 **운전자 정보:**

| | |
|---|---|
| **성명:** | **앤드류 포스터** |
| 연락처: | 555-0184 (휴대전화) |
| 195 **허가받은 추가 운전자:** | **라예시 바닉** |

추가 정보:

| | |
|---|---|
| 기업 계정 번호: | 45587 (킨먼 주식회사) |

어휘 vehicle 차량 pickup 수령, 가져감 authorized 권한이 부여된, 승인된 corporate 기업의 account 계정, 계좌

## 191 Not / True

번역 하데스턴 지역 공항에 대해 언급된 것은?
(A) 도시 근처에 있는 유일한 공항이 아니다.
(B) 정시 출발로 정평이 나 있다.
(C) 현재 개조 공사 중이다.
(D) 루빈 에어는 자주 운항하지 않는다.

해설 첫 번째 이메일 후반부에 하데스턴 지역 공항이 하데스턴-몰키스 국제 공항보다 회사에서 선호하는 호텔과 훨씬 더 가깝다(~ Hardeston Regional Airport, as it's much closer than Hardeston-Molkis International to the company's preferred hotel ~)는 말이 쓰여 있다. 따라서 하데스턴에서 이용 가능한 공항이 한 곳이 아니라는 사실을 알 수 있으므로 (A)가 정답이다.

어휘 reputation 명성, 평판 punctual 시간을 엄수하는 undergo 거치다, 겪다 renovation 개조, 보수 frequently 자주, 빈번히

## 192 추론

번역 포스터 씨에 대해 암시된 것은?
(A) 최근 관리자 직책으로 승진되었다.
(B) 7월에 하데스턴을 방문했다.
(C) 전에 아빌라 씨가 계획한 출장을 떠난 적이 있다.
(D) 특정 호텔에 대한 선호를 말했다.

해설 첫 번째 이메일 후반부에 카르멘 아빌라 씨가 앤드류 포스터 씨에게 7월 출장 전에 자신에게 제공했던 것과 동일한 상용 고객 계정 정보를 이용해 즉시 예약을 확정할 것(I will finalize the bookings immediately, using the same frequent flyer account information you provided to me before your trip in July)이라는 말이 쓰여 있다. 이를 통해 아빌라 씨가 과거에도 포스터 씨의 출장 준비를 해준 적이 있다는 것을 알 수 있으므로 (C)가 정답이다.

어휘 managerial 관리의, 운영의 state 말하다 preference 선호(도)

## 193 추론

번역 포스터 씨는 어디에서 근무하고 있을 것 같은가?
(A) 자동차 제조사
(B) 가전 제품 회사
(C) 항공기 디자인 업체
(D) 가정용 가구 업체

해설 두 번째 이메일 중반부에 포스터 씨가 동료 직원에 관해 이야기하면서 소형 진공청소기를 담당하는 신임 제품 관리자(He's the new product manager for our handheld vacuum cleaner ~)라고 했으므로 (B)가 정답이다.

> **Paraphrasing**
> 지문의 handheld vacuum cleaner → 정답의 appliance

## 194 연계

번역 포스터 씨는 조언에 대한 반응으로 무엇을 했을 것 같은가?
(A) 다른 숙소를 선택했다.
(B) 항공사 충성 고객 프로그램에 가입했다.
(C) 모바일 앱을 다운로드했다.
(D) 차량 대여를 요청했다.

해설 첫 번째 이메일 마지막 단락에 타고 다닐 렌터카가 있으면 좋을 것(you might want a rental car to get around in)이라고 하며 예약하길 원하면 알려 달라(Let me know if you'd like me to reserve one)고 했는데, 양식에 차량 종류(Vehicle: Mireles Lyrica Sedan), 운전자(Driver Information / Name: Andrew Foster)를 나타내는 정보가 제시되어 있어 렌터카를 요청했음을 알 수 있다. 따라서 (D)가 정답이다.

어휘 in response to + 명사 ~에 대한 반응으로, ~에 대응해 lodging 숙소 loyalty program 충성 고객 프로그램

## 195 연계

번역 양식에 따르면, 포스터 씨에 대해 어떤 결론을 내릴 수 있는가?
(A) 교통 중심지에서 차에 탈 것이다.
(B) 동료에게 동행할 것을 요청했다.
(C) 체류 기간을 연장하기로 결정했다.
(D) 개인 신용카드로 경비를 지불할 것이다.

해설 두 번째 이메일 중반부에 동료에게 출장 동행을 요청할지 고려 중(I'm considering whether to invite a colleague along on the trip)이라는 말이 쓰여 있는데, 양식 후반부에 추가 운전자로 한 사람이 더 표기되어 있어(Additional Authorized Driver: Rajesh Banik) 포스터 씨가 동료에게 함께 가자고 요청했다는 것을 알 수 있다. 따라서 (B)가 정답이다.

어휘 pick up 차로 데려 가다 transportation 교통(편) hub 중심지 coworker 동료 (직원) accompany 동행하다, 동반하다 extend 연장하다 expense 경비, 지출 (비용)

## 196-200 웹페이지 + 이메일 + 이메일

http://www.kolkataxyz.in/bambootableware

콜카타 XYZ 대나무 식기

15년 넘게, 콜카타 XYZ는 바로 이곳 서벵골에서 재배되는 대나무를 이용해 접시와 컵, 조리 기구, 그리고 기타 식사용 필수품을 만들어 왔습니다. 대나무 식기의 여러 가지 유익한 특징 중 몇 가지를 확인해 보세요.

TEST 6

198 **1. 지속 가능성 - 대나무는 대단히 환경친화적입니다.** 대나무 초목은 재생 가능한 자원이며, 여러분의 대나무 식기를 더 이상 사용할 수 없을 경우, 재활용하거나 퇴비로 만들 수 있습니다.

2. 화학 성분 없음 - 대나무 초목은 재배하는 데 살충제가 필요치 않으며, 저희 식기 제조 과정은 인공 화학 물질이 아닌, 열과 압력을 수반합니다.

3. 뛰어난 내구성 - 대나무 식기는 잘 깨지지 않으며, 약간의 관리는 해야 하지만, 196 **전자레인지에 넣고 가열하거나 냉장고에 보관할 수 있으며, 손상 없이 식기 세척기로 세척할 수 있습니다.**

4. 경량 - 대나무는 대부분의 식기 재료들보다 더 가벼워서, 어린아이들이 있는 가정에 탁월한 선택입니다. 이는 또한 저희 제품의 배송비가 아주 저렴하다는 것을 의미합니다.

5. 다용도 스타일 - 단순하고 깔끔한 형태로 강조되는 대나무의 중성적인 나무 색조는 매우 다양한 색상과 디자인을 우아하게 보완하는 역할을 합니다.

어휘 necessities 필수품 beneficial 유익한 characteristic 특징 sustainable 지속 가능한 environmentally friendly 환경친화적인 renewable 재생 가능한 resource 자원 compost 퇴비로 만들다 chemical-free 화학 성분이 없는 pesticide 살충제 involve 수반하다, 포함하다 artificial 인공의 durable 내구성이 좋은 lightweight 경량의 material 재료 affordable 저렴한, 가격이 알맞은 versatile 다용도의, 다재다능한 serve as ~의 역할을 하다 complement 보완(하는 것) scheme 계획

수신: 디파 사냘
발신: 시카 라히리
날짜: 10월 7일
제목: 대나무 조리 기구

사냘 씨께,

지난주에 무역 박람회에서 귀하와 이야기를 나눌 수 있어서 기뻤습니다. 198 **저는 귀사의 대나무 식기가 지닌 환경적인 장점에 관한 귀하의 주장이 매우 설득력 있다고 생각했습니다.** 따라서 저는 귀사의 여행용 조리 기구 세트가 지구를 대단히 소중히 여기는 기르 협회의 기부자들에게 훌륭한 감사 선물이 될 것이라고 생각했습니다.

귀하께서 이 세트의 휴대용 케이스에 대해 여러 가지 선택지가 있다고 하셨는데요. 197 **이것들과 관련된 상세 정보를 제공해 주시겠습니까?** 200 **저는 특히 가격을 비교해 보고 (저렴한 선택지를 선호하기 때문에) 지구에 가장 적은 피해를 초래하는 것을 찾는 데 관심이 있습니다.**

시카 라히리
기르 협회

어휘 point 주장, 요점 advantage 장점 persuasive 설득력 있는 donor 기부자 care deeply about ~을 대단히 소중히 여기다 details 상세 정보 particularly 특히 be interested in ~에 관심이 있다 compare 비교하다

수신: 시카 라히리
발신: 디파 사냘
날짜: 10월 8일
제목: 회신: 대나무 조리 기구

라히리 씨께,

이메일 감사합니다. 아래는 여행용 식기 세트의 현재 이용 가능한 휴대용 케이스 종류를 비교한 것입니다.

| 케이스 | 개당 가격 | 환경적 유해성 |
|---|---|---|
| 스냅록으로 닫는 딱딱한 플라스틱 케이스 | 1.45달러 | 높음 |
| 200 **스냅 단추가 달린 면 파우치** | **1.7달러** | **낮음** |
| 지퍼가 달린 나일론 케이스 | 2.1달러 | 중간 |
| 묶음용 끈이 달린 캔버스 롤업 가방 | 2.95달러 | 낮음 |

최소 50개 이상 주문해야 한다는 점에 유의하시기 바랍니다. 또한, 199 **어느 종류의 케이스를 선택하시든, 귀하의 단체 로고와 기부자들께 전하는 감사 메시지 같은 약간의 글자를 기꺼이 추가해 드릴 수 있지만,** 이는 요금이 추가될 것입니다.

곧 다시 연락 주시기를 바랍니다.

디파 사냘
콜카타 XYZ

어휘 comparison 비교 available 이용 가능한 harm 해로움 note 유의하다 organization 단체, 기관 involve 포함하다, 수반하다 additional 추가적인 fee 요금

## 196 Not / True

번역 콜카타 XYZ에 대해 언급된 것은?
(A) 아동용 장난감도 판매한다.
(B) 해외에서 대나무를 수입한다.
(C) 주 고객은 자주 여행하는 사람들이다.
(D) 그곳의 식기는 주방 가전제품에서 사용될 수 있다.

해설 웹페이지 3번 항목에 전자레인지에 넣고 가열하거나 냉장고에 보관할 수 있으며, 손상 없이 식기 세척기로 세척할 수 있다(it can be heated in the microwave, stored in the freezer, and washed in the dishwasher without damage)는 특징이 언급되어 있다. 따라서 (D)가 정답이다.

어휘 import 수입하다 primary 주된 frequent 잦은, 빈번한 appliance 기구, 기기

> **Paraphrasing**
> 지문의 can be heated in the microwave, stored in the freezer, and washed in the dishwasher
> → 정답의 can be used in kitchen appliances

## 197 주제 / 목적

번역 첫 번째 이메일의 목적은 무엇인가?
(A) 주문 변경
(B) 기업의 기부자에게 간청
(C) 정보 요청
(D) 불만 제기

해설 첫 번째 이메일의 두 번째 단락에 휴대용 케이스를 언급하면서 이것들과 관련된 상세 정보를 제공해 줄 것(Could you provide me with details about them?)을 요청하고 있으므로 (C)가 정답이다.

어휘 revise 변경하다, 수정하다 solicit ~에게 간청하다

> Paraphrasing
> 지문의 Could you provide me with details
> → 정답의 request information

## 198 연계

번역 대나무 식기의 어떤 특징이 라히리 씨에게 가장 큰 영향을 미쳤는가?
(A) 특징 1
(B) 특징 2
(C) 특징 3
(D) 특징 4

해설 라히리 씨가 쓴 이메일의 첫 번째 단락에 대나무 식기가 지닌 환경적인 장점에 관한 주장이 매우 설득력 있다고 생각했다(I found your points about the environmental advantages of your company's bamboo tableware very persuasive)고 언급되어 있다. 이러한 환경적 장점과 관련된 것이 웹페이지 1번 항목에 언급된 지속 가능하고 환경친화적(1. Sustainable - Bamboo is very environmentally friendly)이라는 특징이므로 (A)가 정답이다.

어휘 influence 영향(력)

## 199 세부 사항

번역 두 번째 이메일에 따르면, 모든 휴대용 케이스에 이용 가능한 것은?
(A) 주문 제작 서비스
(B) 대량 구매 할인
(C) 취급 설명서
(D) 무료 제품 샘플

해설 두 번째 이메일의 마지막 단락에 어느 종류의 케이스를 선택하든 단체 로고와 기부자들에게 전하는 감사 메시지 같은 약간의 글자를 추가할 수 있다(whichever type of case you choose, we would be happy to add your organization's logo and some lettering)고 알리고 있다. 이는 주문 제작이 가능하다는 말이므로 (A)가 정답이다.

> Paraphrasing
> 지문의 add your organization's logo and some lettering
> → 정답의 Customization service

## 200 연계

번역 기르 협회 기부자들이 어떤 휴대용 케이스를 받을 것 같은가?
(A) 하드 플라스틱 케이스
(B) 면 파우치
(C) 지퍼가 달린 나일론 케이스
(D) 캔버스 롤업 가방

해설 첫 번째 이메일의 두 번째 단락에 저렴한 선택지를 선호하고 지구에 가장 적은 피해를 초래하는 것을 찾는다((as I prefer an affordable option) and finding the one that causes the least damage to our planet)고 쓰여 있다. 두 번째 이메일의 도표에서 가장 저렴하면서 환경적 유해성이 가장 낮은 제품이 두 번째 줄에 $1.70와 Low로 표기된 스냅 단추가 달린 면 파우치(Cotton pouch with snap buttons)이므로 (B)가 정답이다.

# TEST 7

| | | | | |
|---|---|---|---|---|
| 101 (B) | 102 (D) | 103 (B) | 104 (A) | 105 (C) |
| 106 (C) | 107 (D) | 108 (C) | 109 (C) | 110 (B) |
| 111 (D) | 112 (A) | 113 (C) | 114 (B) | 115 (D) |
| 116 (B) | 117 (D) | 118 (D) | 119 (B) | 120 (A) |
| 121 (B) | 122 (D) | 123 (A) | 124 (A) | 125 (C) |
| 126 (B) | 127 (D) | 128 (B) | 129 (D) | 130 (D) |
| 131 (C) | 132 (C) | 133 (D) | 134 (D) | 135 (C) |
| 136 (D) | 137 (C) | 138 (C) | 139 (B) | 140 (B) |
| 141 (A) | 142 (D) | 143 (B) | 144 (D) | 145 (D) |
| 146 (A) | 147 (A) | 148 (C) | 149 (A) | 150 (B) |
| 151 (D) | 152 (D) | 153 (B) | 154 (D) | 155 (B) |
| 156 (D) | 157 (B) | 158 (C) | 159 (B) | 160 (D) |
| 161 (B) | 162 (D) | 163 (A) | 164 (B) | 165 (A) |
| 166 (A) | 167 (C) | 168 (C) | 169 (A) | 170 (A) |
| 171 (A) | 172 (B) | 173 (C) | 174 (A) | 175 (B) |
| 176 (A) | 177 (C) | 178 (C) | 179 (D) | 180 (B) |
| 181 (C) | 182 (A) | 183 (D) | 184 (B) | 185 (C) |
| 186 (C) | 187 (A) | 188 (D) | 189 (D) | 190 (B) |
| 191 (C) | 192 (D) | 193 (C) | 194 (A) | 195 (B) |
| 196 (B) | 197 (A) | 198 (C) | 199 (A) | 200 (D) |

## PART 5

### 101 인칭 대명사 _ 소유격 대명사

번역 날씨가 이례적으로 춥기 때문에, 우리 난방 시스템이 더 자주 가동될 것으로 예상하시기 바랍니다.

해설 동사 expect와 명사구 목적어 heating system 사이에 있는 빈칸에 올 수 있는 대명사는 명사구를 수식할 수 있는 소유격 대명사이므로 (B) our가 정답이다.

어휘 unusually 이례적으로, 유난히

### 102 형용사 자리 _ 명사 수식

번역 오스틴 주식회사는 내부 회람과 다른 회사 서신의 공유를 엄격히 금지한다.

해설 전치사 of와 명사 목적어 memos 사이에 있는 빈칸은 명사를 수식할 형용사가 필요한 자리이므로 (D) internal(내부의)이 정답이다. 복합명사를 구성할 때는 명사 앞에 명사가 올 수 있지만, (A) internalization(내면화, 내재화)은 memos와 복합명사를 구성하지 않는 명사이다.

어휘 strictly 엄격히 prohibit 금지하다 sharing 공유 correspondence 서신 internalize 내면화하다 internally 내부적으로

### 103 전치사 어휘

번역 세갈 베이 방문객들은 해안을 따라 이어진 길을 이용하여 바닷바람을 쐬는 것을 즐긴다.

해설 빈칸 앞뒤에 있는 명사 path와 coast 사이에서 위치 관계를 나타낼 전치사가 필요하므로 '~을 따라'라는 의미로 쓰이는 (B) along이 정답이다.

어휘 path 길 take in ~을 들이마시다, 섭취하다 regarding ~에 대해 except ~을 제외하고

### 104 전치사 어휘

번역 그 회사는 다양한 재활용 프로그램과 엄격한 정책을 통해 폐기물을 줄였다.

해설 빈칸 뒤에 있는 다양한 재활용 프로그램과 엄격한 정책은 폐기물을 줄이기 위해 사용한 방법으로 볼 수 있으므로 '~을 통해'라는 의미로 방법을 나타낼 때 사용하는 전치사 (A) through가 정답이다.

어휘 firm 회사, 업체 reduce 줄이다, 감소시키다 various 다양한 recycling 재활용 strict 엄격한 policy 정책, 방침

### 105 부사 어휘

번역 그 약품들은 안전 규정을 준수하기 위해 엄격히 테스트된다.

해설 빈칸에 쓰일 부사는 수동태 동사 are tested를 수식해 약품이 테스트되는 방식을 나타내야 하므로 '엄격히'를 뜻하는 (C) rigorously가 정답이다.

어휘 medication 약(품) ensure 보장하다 compliance with ~에 대한 준수 regulation 규정, 규제 conveniently 편리하게 tightly 단단히, 꽉 approximately 약, 대략

### 106 to부정사 _ 명사적 용법

번역 브래큰 씨는 다가오는 직원 회식 자리에서 소속 팀이 근면하게 노력한 것을 치하해 주고 싶어 한다.

해설 '~하고 싶다'를 뜻하는 would like는 to부정사 또는 명사(구)를 목적어로 취하는데, 빈칸 뒤에 명사구 the diligent efforts가 있으므로 이를 목적어로 취하려면 to부정사가 쓰여야 한다. 따라서 (C) to recognize가 정답이다.

어휘 diligent 근면한 effort 노력 upcoming 다가오는, 곧 있을 get-together 회식, 모임 recognize 인정하다, 표창하다 recognition 인정, 표창

### 107 동명사 자리 _ 전치사의 목적어

번역 몇 차례 주요 시장 변동을 정확히 예측한 후, 킴볼 씨는 재정 자문으로 인기를 얻었다.

해설 빈칸은 전치사 After의 목적어 자리이며, 빈칸 뒤에 있는 명사구 several major market fluctuations를 목적어로 취해야 하므로 동명사 자리이다. 따라서 (D) predicting이 정답이다.

어휘 fluctuation 변동, 등락 accurately 정확히 popularity 인기 financial 재정의, 재무의 adviser 자문, 조언자 prediction 예측 predict 예측하다

## 108 전치사 자리 _ 어휘

번역 오후 3시까지 요청된 해외 은행 송금은 마감 시간 전에 처리될 것이다.

해설 3 P.M. 같은 시점 명사를 목적어로 취할 수 있는 전치사가 필요하며, 기한을 나타내야 알맞으므로 '~까지'를 뜻하는 전치사 (C) by가 정답이다. (A) just(바로, 단지)와 (B) later(나중에)는 부사이며, (D) than(~보다)은 전치사이지만 의미가 맞지 않는다.

어휘 bank transfer 은행 송금, 계좌 이체

## 109 동사 어휘

번역 중요한 업무를 할 때는 서두르기보다는 마감일을 조정하는 것이 더 나을지도 모른다.

해설 마감일(the deadline)을 목적어로 취하는 자리로, 일을 서두르는 것보다 더 나을 수 있는 방법을 나타내야 하므로 '마감일을 미루다, 조정하다' 등이 되는 것이 자연스럽다. 따라서 '조정하다, 조절하다'를 뜻하는 (C) adjust가 정답이다.

어휘 crucial 아주 중요한, 중대한 assignment 배정(된 일) deadline 마감 rush 성급하게 하다, 서두르다 approve 승인하다 expire 만료되다 observe 관찰하다, 살펴보다

## 110 접속사 자리 _ 부사절 접속사

번역 고객이 제공한 맞춤 제작 이미지를 포함한 의류는 인쇄된 후에는 반품될 수 없습니다.

해설 빈칸 앞뒤에 각각 완전한 절이 있으므로 두 절을 연결할 수 있는 접속사가 필요하며, '인쇄된 후에는 반품될 수 없다'는 의미가 자연스러우므로 '~한 후에'를 뜻하는 접속사 (B) after가 정답이다. (A) although(비록 ~이기는 하지만)는 의미가 맞지 않는 접속사이고, (C) as a result(결과적으로)는 부사와 같은 역할을 하는 전치사구이며, (D) despite(~에도 불구하고)는 전치사이므로 오답이다.

어휘 apparel 의류 include 포함하다 custom 맞춤 제작의

## 111 명사 자리 _ 복합명사

번역 신규 지역에서의 매출 증가 덕분에, 우리는 목표를 50퍼센트 초과했습니다.

해설 빈칸 앞에 위치한 명사 sales와 함께 전치사 Thanks to의 목적어 역할을 할 복합명사를 구성해야 알맞으므로 명사 (D) gains(증가, 이익)가 정답이다. (A) had gained와 (B) are gained는 동사의 형태이며, (C) to gain은 to부정사이므로 명사가 필요한 빈칸에 맞지 않는다.

어휘 region 지역 surpass 초과하다, 능가하다 gain 증가, 이익; 얻다

## 112 형용사 자리 _ 명사 수식

번역 그렌데일 주식회사의 고도로 암호화된 저장 시스템은 민감한 문서나 파일에 이상적이다.

해설 부정관사 a와 명사 document 사이에 위치한 빈칸은 명사를 수식하는 형용사가 들어갈 자리이므로 (A) sensitive(민감한)가 정답이다. 명사인 (B) sensation(큰 화제, 감각)과 (D) sensitivity(세심함, 감성)는 document와 복합명사를 구성하지 않으므로 오답이다. (C) sense(감각; 감지하다)는 명사 또는 동사로 쓰이는데, 명사일 때 마찬가지로 document와 복합명사를 구성하지 않으므로 오답이다.

어휘 highly 대단히, 매우 encrypted 암호화된 storage 저장, 보관 ideal 이상적인

## 113 접속사 어휘

번역 주말 동안 궂은 날씨가 이어졌지만 컨퍼런스 참석률은 여전히 높았다.

해설 선택지가 모두 접속사이므로 의미가 알맞은 것을 찾아야 한다. '궂은 날씨가 이어졌지만, 참석률은 높았다'는 의미가 문맥상 자연스러우므로 '하지만'을 뜻하는 (C) but이 정답이다.

어휘 severe weather 궂은 날씨 attendance 참석률, 참석자 수

## 114 부사 자리 _ 동사 수식

번역 그 영화관 진열창에 있는 포스터들은 주기적으로 바뀐다.

해설 수동태 동사를 구성하는 are와 과거분사 changed 사이에 있는 빈칸은 동사를 수식하는 부사가 들어갈 자리이므로 부사 (B) regularly(주기적으로, 규칙적으로)가 정답이다.

어휘 display 진열(품), 전시(품) regular 주기적인, 규칙적인 regularize 규칙화하다

## 115 형용사 어휘

번역 워릭 인터내셔널 사의 사무직 직원들은 장시간 앉아 있는 것을 피하도록 권장된다.

해설 빈칸에 쓰일 형용사는 명사구 periods of time을 수식해 앉아 있는 시간 길이와 관련된 의미를 나타내야 하므로 '장시간에 걸친, 연장된'을 뜻하는 형용사 (D) extended가 정답이다.

어휘 avoid 피하다 fierce 극심한, 격렬한 adjusted 조정된, 조절된 aware 알고 있는

## 116 명사 자리 _ 동사의 목적어

번역 방해를 최소화하기 위해, 발표가 진행되는 동안에는 질문하는 것을 삼가시기 바랍니다.

해설 to부정사로 쓰인 타동사 minimize의 목적어 역할을 할 명사가 들어갈 자리이므로 (B) interruptions(방해, 지장)가 정답이다.

어휘 minimize 최소화하다 refrain from -ing ~하는 것을 삼가다 underway 진행 중인 interrupt 방해하다

### 117 접속사 자리 _ 부사절 접속사

번역 그 직책의 지원자들은 자격이 확인될 때까지 심사 절차가 진행되지 않을 것입니다.

해설 빈칸 앞뒤에 각각 완전한 절이 있으므로 두 절을 연결할 수 있는 접속사가 필요하다. 따라서 (D) until(~할 때까지)이 정답이다. (A) also(또한, ~도)와 (B) even(심지어, 훨씬)은 부사이며, (C) besides(게다가; ~을 제외하고)는 부사 또는 전치사로 쓰인다.

어휘 applicant 지원자 position 직책, 일자리 proceed 계속 나아가다, 계속 진행되다 screening 선별, 심사 process 과정 credential 자격(증) confirm 확인하다

### 118 동사 어휘

번역 항공기 경고등의 예기치 못한 오작동으로 인해, 승객들이 오후 8시까지 탑승할 수 없었다.

해설 항공기의 경고등 문제로 인해 승객들이 오후 8시까지 할 수 없었던 것을 나타낼 동사가 들어가야 하므로 '탑승하다'를 뜻하는 동사 (D) board가 정답이다.

어휘 unexpected 예기치 못한 malfunction 오작동, 작동 불량 warning light 경고등 passenger 승객 accommodate 수용하다 appear 나타나다, ~처럼 보이다 facilitate 용이하게 하다, 촉진하다

### 119 형용사 어휘

번역 윌슨 공과 대학은 자신의 과목에 열정을 가진 교수진을 모집하고 있다.

해설 빈칸 뒤에 있는 전치사 about과 어울리는 형용사가 필요하며, '과목에 열정을 가진 교수진'이라는 의미를 나타내야 알맞으므로 '열정적인'을 뜻하는 (B) passionate이 정답이다.

어휘 recruit 모집하다 faculty members 교수진 subject 과목, 주제 careful 조심하는, 신중한 responsible 책임이 있는, 원인이 되는

### 120 동사 자리 _ 조동사 뒤 동사 원형

번역 산티아고 씨가 사무실 배치를 업데이트하기 위한 다양한 옵션들을 평가할 것이다.

해설 will 같은 조동사 뒤에는 동사 원형이 와야 하므로 (A) be assessing이 정답이다.

어휘 various 다양한 option 옵션, 선택 (사항) layout 배치(도), 구획 assess 평가하다

### 121 such + a(n) + 형용사 + 명사

번역 사무실 단지 내 소음 수준은 그렇게 번화한 도로에 위치한 것에 비해 놀라울 정도로 낮다.

해설 전치사 on의 목적어로 쓰인 a busy road와 같은 명사구 앞에 위치해 「such + a(n) + 형용사 + 명사(그렇게 ~한 …)」를 구성하는 (B) such가 정답이다. 부사인 (A) still(여전히, 그럼에도 불구하고)과 (C) soon(곧), 그리고 형용사 또는 부사로 쓰이는 (D) nearby(가까운; 가까이)는 모두 이 자리에 올 수 없다.

어휘 complex 복합 건물 surprisingly 놀라울 정도로, 놀랍게도 be located on ~에 위치해 있다

### 122 부사 어휘

번역 하퍼 정비소의 정비사들은 필요한 장비를 도움 없이 능숙하게 조작할 수 있어야 한다.

해설 빈칸에 쓰일 부사는 동사 operate를 앞에서 수식해 장비를 조작하는 방식을 나타내야 하므로 '능숙하게, 숙련되게'를 뜻하는 (D) proficiently가 정답이다.

어휘 mechanic 정비사 operate 조작하다, 작동시키다 necessary 필요한, 필수의 equipment 장비 assistance 도움, 지원 influentially 영향력 있게 significantly 상당히, 많이 enormously 엄청나게, 대단히

### 123 명사 어휘

번역 첨단 레이저 장비를 설치한 덕분에 공장의 생산량이 세 배로 증가했다.

해설 빈칸 앞에 위치한 동사 has tripled가 '세 배로 증가했다'를 의미하므로 생산에 대해 세 배로 늘어날 수 있는 것을 나타낼 명사가 들어가야 한다. 따라서 '양, 수량'을 뜻하는 (A) quantity가 정답이다.

어휘 on account of ~로 인해, ~ 때문에 installation 설치 advanced 고급의, 진보한 equipment 장비 triple 세 배가 되다 output 생산(량), 산출(량) economy 경제 portion 몫, (음식의) 1인분 permission 허락, 승인

### 124 동사 어휘

번역 헌틀리 씨는 인력 부족 문제로 인해 오늘날의 직업 풍조에서는 응집력 있는 팀을 구성하는 것이 어렵다고 설명했다.

해설 빈칸에 들어갈 동사는 뒤에 있는 명사구 cohesive teams를 목적어로 받으며, 빈칸이 속한 that절이 '인력 부족 문제로 인해 응집력 있는 팀을 구성하는 것이 어렵다'와 같은 의미를 나타내야 알맞으므로 '구성하다, 모으다' 등을 뜻하는 동사 (A) assemble이 정답이다.

어휘 cohesive 응집력 있는, 화합하는 climate (사회나 시대 등의) 풍조, 분위기 owing to + 명사 ~ 때문에 labor 인력, 노동력 shortage 부족 surpass 초과하다, 능가하다 distribute 나눠 주다, 배부하다 succeed 성공하다, ~의 뒤를 잇다

### 125 접속사 자리 _ 어휘

번역 플린트 렌터카 회사는 운전자들이 자신의 보험으로 완전히 보장받지 못하는 경우에 보험료를 추가로 청구한다.

해설 빈칸 앞뒤에 각각 완전한 절이 있으므로 두 절을 연결할 수 있는 접속사가 필요하며, '자신의 보험으로 완전히 보장받지 못하는 경우에'를 의미해야 알맞으므로 '~하지 않는 경우에, ~하지 않는다면'을 뜻하는 접속사 (C) unless가 정답이다. (B) if(~한다면)와 (D) yet(아직; 그렇

지만)은 접속사로 쓰이지만 의미가 어울리지 않는다. (A) rather(다소, 오히려)는 부사이다.

어휘 charge 청구하다 additional 추가적인 fee 요금, 수수료 insurance 보험 fully 완전히, 전적으로 cover (보험 등이) 보장하다 policy 보험 증서

## 126 명사 자리 _ 복합명사

번역 주 법률은 사업체들이 후보자에게 현금을 기부하는 것을 허용하지 않는다.

해설 cash와 어울리는 또 다른 명사가 빈칸에 들어가 make의 목적어 역할을 할 복합명사를 구성해야 알맞으므로 (B) contributions(기부, 공헌)가 정답이다.

어휘 state (행정 구역) 주 legislation 법률, 법령 allow 허용하다, ~할 수 있게 해 주다 candidate 후보자, 지원자 contribute 기부하다, 공헌하다

## 127 인칭 대명사 _ 소유격 대명사

번역 레이크랜드 은행의 지점들은 전국으로 확대되었지만, 은행의 행정 사무실 대부분은 북서부 지역에 있다.

해설 빈칸 뒤에 위치한 명사구 administrative offices가 Even though절에 언급된 레이크랜드 은행(Lakeland Bank)의 행정 사무실을 가리켜야 알맞으므로 Lakeland Bank를 지칭할 수 있는 소유격 대명사 (D) its가 정답이다.

어휘 branch 지점, 지사 expand 확대되다, 확장되다 administrative 행정의, 경영의

## 128 전치사 자리

번역 수리를 위해 고속도로를 일시적으로 폐쇄하는 대신, 계획 담당자들은 부분적으로 폐쇄하고 단계적으로 작업하기로 결정했다.

해설 빈칸 뒤에 있는 동명사구 temporarily closing the highway for repairs를 목적어로 취할 수 있는 전치사가 필요하므로 (B) Instead of(~하는 대신)가 정답이다. (A) Wherever(~할 때마다, ~할 때는 언제든)와 (D) Now that(이제 ~이므로)은 접속사이며, (C) Promptly(즉시, 지체 없이)는 부사이므로 오답이다.

어휘 temporarily 일시적으로, 임시로 partial 부분적인 closure 폐쇄, 닫음 in phases 단계적으로

## 129 상관접속사 _ A as well as B

번역 아이비 레스토랑은 비건 친화적인 요리를 만들기 위해 육류와 유제품을 대체할 수 있는 특별한 식재료를 보유하고 있다.

해설 빈칸 앞뒤에 있는 meat와 dairy products는 각각 명사, 명사구로서 둘 다 to부정사 to replace의 목적어로 쓰였다. 따라서 '~뿐만 아니라 …도'라는 의미로 동일 요소를 연결할 때 사용하는 상관접속사 (D) as well as가 정답이다. (A) in addition(추가로, 게다가)은 부사와 같은 역할을 하는 전치사구이며, (B) yet(아직; 하지만)은 부사나 접속사로 쓰인다. (C) when(~할 때)은 접속사이다.

어휘 ingredient (음식) 재료, 성분 replace 대체하다 dairy product 유제품 vegan 비건(엄격한 채식주의자); 비건의

## 130 부사 어휘

번역 백 씨는 주로 다국적 기업의 광고 캠페인을 위한 디지털 아트에 초점을 맞춰 왔다.

해설 자동사 focused와 전치사 on 사이에 위치할 수 있는 부사가 와야 하며, '주로 ~에 초점을 맞춰 왔다'라는 의미가 가장 자연스러우므로 '주로'라는 의미의 (D) primarily가 정답이다. (A) surprisingly(놀랍게도)는 예상 외의 일이라는 맥락이 주어지지 않아 답이 되기엔 부족하며, (B) frankly는 '솔직히 말해서'라는 의미를 담고 있기에 문장 맨 앞에 온다면 말이 될 수 있지만 위치적으로 어울리지 않는다. (C)의 presently(현재, 지금)는 현재 진행 시제와 어울리므로 답이 될 수 없다.

어휘 focus on ~에 초점을 맞추다 commercial 상업의 campaign (광고, 운동 등의) 캠페인 multinational 다국적의 corporation 기업 surprisingly 놀랍게도 frankly 솔직히 (말해서) presently 현재, 지금

# PART 6

### 131-134 편지

로저스 씨께,

귀하의 회사 동료들을 위해 저희 초콜릿 공장 개별 견학을 예약하는 것에 관심을 가져 주셔서 감사합니다. 생산 라인의 특정 구역들은 일반인에게 공개되지 않는다는 점에 유의하시기 바랍니다. 131 **식품 관련 규정 때문에 이를 변경할 수 없습니다.** 그러나 여전히 볼거리가 많습니다. 저희는 모든 견학 참가자들께 132 **유익한** 동영상을 보여 드립니다. 이것은 저희 회사의 연혁에 대해 알려 드릴 것입니다. 이 133 **영상 시청**은 약 20분 동안 지속되며, 견학 시작 또는 종료 시에 시청할 수 있습니다.

며칠에 참석하실 계획인지, 그리고 인원이 얼마나 되는지 134 **저희에게** 알려 주십시오. 즐거운 시간 되시기를 바랍니다!

클레이튼 펨버턴, 책임자
바이리 초콜릿 공장

어휘 interest in ~에 대한 관심 book 예약하다 private 개별적인, 개인의 colleague 동료 note 유의하다, 주목하다 available 이용할 수 있는 the public 일반인들 participant 참가자 last 지속되다 approximately 약, 대략

## 131 문장 고르기

번역 (A) 입장권은 오직 명시된 날짜에만 유효합니다.
(B) 취소되는 경우에, 저희가 귀하의 물품들을 반송해 드릴 것입니다.
(C) 식품 관련 규정 때문에 이를 변경할 수 없습니다.
(D) 각각의 견학은 지식이 풍부한 직원에 의해 진행됩니다.

해설 빈칸 앞 문장에 생산 라인의 특정 구역들은 일반인에게 공개되지 않는다는 말이 쓰여 있으므로 이러한 방침을 this로 지칭해 그 이유를 밝히는 (C)가 정답이다.

어휘 valid 유효한 specify 명시하다 cancellation 취소 regulation 규제, 규정 lead 진행하다, 이끌다 knowledgeable 지식이 풍부한, 아는 것이 많은

## 132 형용사 어휘

해설 빈칸 뒤에 있는 video(동영상)를 수식하는 형용사가 들어가야 하며, 다음 문장에 동영상을 It으로 지칭해 회사의 역사에 대해 알려 준다는 말이 쓰여 있으므로 '정보를 제공하는, 유익한' 등을 뜻하는 형용사 (C) informative가 정답이다.

어휘 eager 간절히 바라는, 열심인 artistic 예술의, 예술적인 abundant 풍부한, 많은

## 133 명사 어휘

해설 앞에서 동영상에 대해 서술하고 있으며, 빈칸 뒤에 약 20분 동안 지속된다는 말이 쓰여 있으므로 빈칸에는 동영상을 보는 일을 나타내는 단어가 들어가야 함을 알 수 있다. 따라서 '시청, 보기' 등을 의미하는 (D) viewing이 정답이다.

어휘 treatment 치료(법), 처리 provision 공급, 대비

## 134 인칭 대명사 _ 목적격 대명사

해설 날짜와 인원수를 알려 달라는 내용이므로 빈칸에는 편지를 쓴 사람이나 그 사람의 회사를 가리키는 대명사가 와야 한다. 따라서 글쓴이의 회사를 가리키는 (D) us가 정답이다.

### 135-138 공지

세입자 여러분께 알립니다

세입자들의 수많은 요청에 [135] **응**하여, 그리셤 아파트는 3월 6일부터 27일까지 단지 내 피트니스 센터를 개조할 예정입니다. 공사를 [136] **진행하는 동안**, 모든 세입자들에게 운동 기구 사용과 공간 출입이 제한될 것이므로, 운동 루틴을 유지하기 위해서는 다른 조치를 취해야 할 것입니다.

이 프로젝트가 초래할 수 있는 모든 불편함에 대해 [137] **유감스럽게 생각하며**, 여러분의 인내에 감사드립니다. [138] **완성된 결과물이 이러한 번거로움을 감수할 만한 가치가 있을 것이라 확신합니다.**

그리셤 아파트 관리팀

어휘 tenant 세입자 numerous 수많은 renovate 개조하다, 보수하다 on-site 부지 내의, 현장의 carry out 실시하다, 수행하다 exercise 운동 equipment 장비 off limits 출입이 제한된, 출입 금지의 make arrangements 조치하다, 준비하다 maintain 유지하다 routine 루틴, 일상(적인 것) inconvenience 불편함 appreciate 감사하다 patience 인내(심)

## 135 명사 자리 _ 전치사의 목적어

해설 빈칸 앞의 전치사 in과 빈칸 뒤의 전치사 to와 호응할 수 있는 명사 (C) response(대응, 반응)가 정답이다. in response to는 '~에 응하여, ~에 대한 반응으로'를 뜻하는 빈출 표현이니 알아 두자.

## 136 접속사 자리 _ 부사절 접속사

해설 빈칸과 접속사 so 사이에 주어와 동사를 각각 포함한 절 두 개가 콤마로 이어져 있으므로 이 두 개의 절을 연결할 접속사가 필요하다. 또한, '공사를 진행하는 동안, 운동 기구 사용과 공간 출입이 제한될 것이다'가 자연스러운 의미이므로 '~하는 동안'을 뜻하는 접속사 (D) While이 정답이다. (A) Whereas(~인 반면)도 접속사이지만 의미가 맞지 않으며, 접속사 또는 부사로 쓰이는 (B) However(아무리 ~해도; 하지만)도 접속사일 때 의미가 어울리지 않는다. (C) During(~ 중에, ~ 동안)은 전치사이다.

## 137 동사 어휘

해설 빈칸 앞에 위치한 주어 We는 이 공지를 작성한 주체, 즉 앞 단락에 언급된 피트니스 센터 개조 공사를 진행하는 아파트 관리팀을 가리킨다. 따라서 공사 프로젝트로 인한 불편함에 대해 유감이나 사과의 뜻을 나타내야 하는데, 명사구 any inconvenience를 목적어로 취해야 하므로 '유감스럽게 생각하다'를 의미하는 타동사 (C) regret이 정답이다. (B) apologize(사과하다)는 자동사이기 때문에 목적어인 명사 any inconvenience를 바로 취할 수 없고 apologize for의 형태로 써야 한다.

어휘 tolerate 용인하다, 참다 apologize (for) (~에 대해) 사과하다 encounter 마주치다, 맞닥뜨리다

## 138 문장 고르기

번역 (A) 입구에서 신분증이나 아파트 키를 보여 주시기 바랍니다.
(B) 침실 두 개짜리 세대를 둘러보시는 데 관심이 있으시면, 언제든지 전화 주십시오.
(C) 완성된 결과물이 이러한 번거로움을 감수할 만한 가치가 있을 것이라 확신합니다.
(D) 이 문제를 지체 없이 처리해 주셔서 감사합니다.

해설 앞 문장에 공사 프로젝트에 따른 불편함을 언급하면서 인내에 감사한다는 말이 쓰여 있다. 따라서 그러한 불편함을 the hassle(번거로움)로 대신해 공사 결과물이 불편함을 감수할 만한 가치가 있을 것이라는 의미로 쓰인 (C)가 정답이다.

어휘 unit (아파트 등의) 한 세대 confident 확신하는 worth ~의 가치가 있는 hassle 번거로움, 성가심 deal with ~을 처리하다 promptly 지체 없이, 즉시

### 139-142 이메일

수신: 카호다 나이두
발신: info@vistapharmacy.com
날짜: 4월 24일
제목: 비스타 약국 새 지점!

나이두 씨께,

비스타 약국 직원들은 고객들께 더 나은 서비스를 제공하기 위해 두 번째 지점을 열게 된 것을 알려 드리게 되어 [139] **기쁩니다**. 이 지점은 빅토리아 가 905번지에 위치할 것입니다. 저희 본점과 마찬가지로, 이 새 지점에서도 처방약 조제 이상의 종합적인 서비스를 제공할 것입니다. [140] **여기에는 원치 않는 약을 안전하게 폐기하기 위해 수거하는 것도 포함됩니다**. 빅토리아 가 지점에도 차를 탄 채로 서비스를 받는 창구가 있습니다.

약품 [141] **수령을 위해** 영업시간 중 언제든 창구 또는 내부에 들르셔도 됩니다. 늘 그렇듯이, 저희는 여러분의 [142] **의사**가 처방한 약과 관련해 어떤 질문이든 답변해 드릴 수 있습니다. 귀하께 서비스를 제공해 드리기를 고대합니다!

비스타 약국 팀

어휘 branch 지점, 지사 serve 서비스를 제공하다 be located at ~에 위치해 있다 as with ~와 마찬가지로, ~에서처럼 original 원래의, 애초의 site 장소, 부지 comprehensive 종합적인 fill prescriptions 처방약을 조제하다 drive-up window 차를 탄 채로 서비스를 받는 창구 stop by ~에 들르다 prescribe 처방하다, 처방전을 쓰다 look forward to -ing ~하기를 고대하다

## 139 형용사 자리 _ 주격 보어

해설 빈칸은 주어 The staff at Vista Pharmacy를 보충 설명하는 주격 보어 자리이고, '알려 드리게 되어 기쁘다'는 의미가 되어야 하므로 (B) delighted(기쁜, 즐거운)가 정답이다. be delighted to는 '~해서 기쁘다'라는 뜻의 빈출 표현이므로 알아 두자. (A) delightful(기쁨을 주는, 즐거운)은 '기쁨을 느낀다'는 의미가 아니라 '기쁨을 준다'는 의미이며, 명사 (D) delights(기쁨, 즐거움)는 보어 자리에 올 수 있지만 의미가 어색하다. (C) delightfully(기쁘게, 즐겁게)는 부사이므로 주격 보어 자리에 올 수 없다.

## 140 문장 고르기

번역 (A) 그들 중 많은 사람들이 불편할 수 있는 증상이 있습니다.
(B) 여기에는 원치 않는 약을 안전하게 폐기하기 위해 수거하는 것도 포함됩니다.
(C) 영업일 기준 최대 10일까지 귀하를 위해 보관해 드릴 수 있습니다.
(D) 이 개조 공사로 카운터를 이용하기 더 쉬워질 것입니다.

해설 빈칸 앞 문장에 처방약 조제 이상으로 종합적인 서비스를 제공한다는 말이 쓰여 있으므로 포함되는 서비스를 알리는 (B)가 정답이다.

어휘 symptom 증상 uncomfortable 불편한 include 포함하다 collect 수거하다, 모으다 unwanted 원치 않는 disposal 처리, 처분 hold 보관하다, 유지하다 up to 최대 ~의 renovation 개조, 보수 accessible 접근할 수 있는, 이용할 수 있는

## 141 to부정사 _ 부사적 용법

해설 빈칸 앞에 주어 동사를 갖춘 완전한 절이 있으므로 빈칸과 명사구 your medicine은 부가적인 요소가 되어야 한다. 따라서 your medicine을 목적어로 받으면서 부사적 용법으로 쓰일 수 있는 to부정사 (A) to collect가 정답이다.

## 142 명사 어휘

해설 빈칸 뒤에 위치한 동사 prescribed가 '처방하다, 처방전을 쓰다'를 의미하므로 그러한 일을 할 수 있는 사람을 나타내는 명사가 들어가야 한다. 따라서 '의사, 내과 의사'를 뜻하는 (D) physician이 정답이다.

어휘 supervisor 감독, 책임자 patient 환자 colleague 동료

### 143-146 고객 후기

제가 최근에 저희 할머니께서 갖고 계셨던 오래된 사진 몇 장을 찾았는데, 가능한 한 원본 사진과 [143] **가깝게** 복원하기를 원했습니다. 제 동료 한 명이 그린우드 지역에 있는 클로버 포토스를 권해 주었습니다. 이곳의 주인이신 칼린은 옵션에 대해 설명하고 저에게 적합한 서비스 수준을 선택할 수 있도록 도와주었습니다. 이분은 바쁜 [144] 시기임**에도 불구하고** 3일 만에 복원 및 액자 작업을 완료해 주셨습니다. 그 사진들은 훌륭해 보입니다. [145] **액자의 품질도 놀랍습니다**.

칼린은 대단히 경험이 많은 분입니다. 이분은 [146] **능력 있는** 사진 편집자입니다. 저는 이분을 강력 추천합니다.

아이다 브릭스, 브리스톨

어휘 recently 최근에 belong to+명사 ~의 소유이다 restore 복원하다, 복구하다 original 원본의, 원래의 shot 사진, 촬영본 colleague 동료 neighborhood 지역, 인근 assist 돕다 restoration 복원, 복구 framing 액자에 넣기 highly 대단히, 매우 experienced 경험 많은 editor 편집자

## 143 부사 자리 _ 원급 비교

해설 '가능한 한 ~하게[~한]'를 의미하는 as ~ as possible에서 두 as 사이에는 원급 부사 또는 원급 형용사를 사용하므로 원급 부사인 (B) closely(가깝게, 밀접하게)가 정답이다. (A) closest(가장 가까운, 가장 가까이)는 최상급 형용사 또는 부사, (C) closer(더 가까운, 더 가까이)는 비교급 형용사 또는 부사, (D) closeness(근접, 밀접)는 명사로 모두 두 as 사이에 쓸 수 없다.

## 144 접속사 자리 _ 부사절 접속사

해설 빈칸 앞뒤에 각각 완전한 절이 있으므로 두 절을 연결할 수 있는 접속사가 필요하며, '바쁜 시기임에도 불구하고 3일 만에 완료해 주었다'가 알맞은 의미이므로 '~에도 불구하고, ~이기는 하지만'을 뜻하는 부사절 접속사 (D) even though가 정답이다. (A) not only는 but also와 함께 '~뿐만 아니라 …도'를 뜻하는 상관접속사를 구성하며, (B) such as(~와 같이, 예를 들어)는 전치사이다. (C) so that(그래서, 그러므로)도 부사절 접속사이기는 하지만 의미가 맞지 않는다.

## 145 문장 고르기

번역 (A) 적어도 배송 시간은 신뢰할 수 있습니다.
(B) 저는 아마추어 사진가입니다.
(C) 이분은 전에 미술관을 소유했었습니다.
(D) 액자의 품질도 놀랍습니다.

TEST 7

해설 앞 문장에 사진들이 훌륭해 보인다는 말이 쓰여 있으므로 이와 같은 맥락으로 액자도 만족한다고 말하는 (D)가 정답이다.

어휘 reliable 신뢰할 수 있는 own 소유하다 quality 품질, 질 amazing 놀라운

## 146 형용사 어휘

해설 바로 앞 문장에 경험이 아주 많다는 말이 쓰여 있고, 앞 단락 마지막 부분에는 복원된 사진이 훌륭해 보인다는 문장이 쓰여 있다. 따라서 유능한 사진 편집자임을 알 수 있으므로 이러한 의미에 해당하는 형용사로서 '능력 있는, 재능 있는'을 뜻하는 (A) talented가 정답이다.

어휘 fortunate 다행인, 운이 좋은 voluntary 자발적인, 자원봉사의

# PART 7

### 147-148 구인 광고

영어 개인 지도 교사 모집

샤인 에듀케이션에서는 저희 플랫폼에서 5~11세 사이의 다국어를 사용하는 학생들을 가르칠 친절하고 열정적인 강사를 찾고 있습니다. 저희가 재미있고 흥미로운 교육 과정을 개발했기 때문에, 모든 수업 계획이 준비되어 있습니다. 그리고 오로지 영어만 사용할 것이므로, 외국어로 소통하실 필요가 없습니다. 여러분께 필요한 것은 긍정적인 태도와 노트북 컴퓨터, 그리고 [147] **이상 없이 안정적인 인터넷 접속**뿐입니다.

직책 관련 주요 사항:
- 휴일 근무는 없으며, 주말 근무 시 보너스 지급
- [148] **최고의 근무 탄력성 - 오직 원할 때만 수업 진행**
- 신속한 급여 지급 - 매주 은행 계좌 이체로 급여 지급

shineeduwow.com/apply에서 더 많은 정보를 알아보시기 바랍니다.

어휘 seek 찾다, 구하다 enthusiastic 열정적인 multilingual 다국어를 사용하는 develop 개발하다, 발전시키다 curriculum 교육 과정, 교과 과정 exclusively 오로지, 독점적으로 communicate 소통하다 unnecessary 불필요한 positive 긍정적인 attitude 태도 sound 이상 없는, 온전한 stable 안정적인 highlight 주요 사항, 중요 부분 ultimate 최고의, 최대의 flexibility 탄력성, 유연성 payment 지급(액), 지불(액) bank transfer 은행 계좌 이체 find out 알아내다, 파악하다

## 147 세부 사항

번역 어떤 필수 조건이 모든 지원자에게 요구되는가?
(A) 신뢰할 수 있는 온라인 접속 방법
(B) 4년제 대학 졸업
(C) 교육 분야 경력
(D) 자신이 개발한 수업 계획 샘플

해설 첫 단락 마지막 문장에 지원자들에게 필요한 것의 하나로 이상 없이 안정적인 인터넷 접속(a sound and stable Internet connection)이 언급되어 있으므로 (A)가 정답이다.

어휘 reliable 신뢰할 수 있는 method 방법 graduation 졸업 previous 과거의, 이전의

> **Paraphrasing**
> 지문의 a sound and stable Internet connection
> → 정답의 A reliable method for getting online

## 148 Not / True

번역 해당 직책에 대해 사실인 것은?
(A) 아이들 및 성인들과 함께 일하는 것을 포함한다.
(B) 오직 다국어를 사용하는 사람들에게만 적합하다.
(C) 근무자가 자신의 일정을 정할 수 있게 해 준다.
(D) 주말과 공휴일에도 수업을 해야 한다.

해설 두 번째 단락 두 번째 항목에 원할 때만 수업을 진행하는 근무 탄력성(Ultimate flexibility — open classes only when you want to)이 언급되어 있는데, 이는 강사가 스스로 수업 일정을 정할 수 있다는 의미이므로 (C)가 정답이다.

어휘 include 포함하다 suitable 적합한, 알맞은 allow 할 수 있게 해 주다, 허용하다 set 정하다 involve 포함하다, 관련되다

> **Paraphrasing**
> 지문의 Ultimate flexibility — open classes only when you want to
> → 정답의 allows workers to set their schedule

### 149-150 웹페이지

http://www.kennonhotel.co.uk

케넌 호텔의 CEO 로잘리 윌리스가 전하는 말씀

문의 전화: 1-800-555-9056

저희 소중한 고객들 중 많은 분이 [149] **저희 호텔 객실의 이중 예약을 초래한 컴퓨터 오류로 인해 불편을 겪으셨습니다.** 저희는 이번 사태로 인한 부정적인 영향을 최소화하기 위해 할 수 있는 모든 조치를 취하고 있다고 분명히 말씀드립니다. [149] **저희 호텔에서 수용할 수 없는 고객들께는 인근 호텔의 크기와 수준이 동등하거나 더 나은 객실로 예약해 드릴 것이며,** 원래 견적 요금만 지불하시면 됩니다. 추가로, [150] **고객들은 일반적으로 체크인 예정 시간 최소 48시간 전까지 예약을 취소해야 첫날 숙박 요금이 부과되지 않습니다. 앞으로 3주 동안은 이것이 24시간으로 변경될 것입니다.**

어휘 helpline 문의 전화, 전화 상담 valued 소중한 glitch 오류, 결함 double-book 이중 예약하다 assure 분명히 말하다, 장담하다 minimize 최소화하다 negative 부정적인 situation 상황 accommodate 수용하다 site 장소, 부지 nearby 근처의 equivalent 동등한 originally 애초에, 원래 quoted 견적된 rate 요금 avoid 피하다 charge 요금을 부과하다

## 149 주제 / 목적

번역 공지의 목적은 무엇인가?
(A) 문제를 해결하기 위한 조치를 설명하는 것
(B) 새롭게 문을 연 호텔을 소개하는 것
(C) 단골 고객들에게 할인된 요금을 홍보하는 것
(D) 고객들에게 예약 시스템을 이용하도록 권하는 것

해설 지문 초반부에 예약과 관련된 컴퓨터 오류(the computer glitch that caused rooms at our hotel to be double-booked)를 언급하면서, 그에 따른 조치로 인근 호텔의 객실을 예약해 줄 것(Customers whom we are not able to accommodate at our site will be booked at nearby hotels ~)이라고 알리고 있다. 이는 문제 해결을 위한 조치를 설명하는 것이므로 (A)가 정답이다.

어휘 measures 조치 resolve 해결하다 promote 홍보하다 reservation 예약

## 150 세부 사항

번역 윌리스 씨에 따르면, 호텔에서 일시적으로 변경한 것은?
(A) 하룻밤이 넘는 숙박에 대한 요금
(B) 무료로 취소할 수 있는 기한
(C) 문의 전화 운영 시간
(D) 호텔에 체크인하기 위한 대기 시간

해설 지문 마지막 부분에 일반적으로 체크인 예정 시간 최소 48시간 전까지 예약을 취소해야 첫날 숙박 요금이 부과되지 않지만, 앞으로 3주 동안은 24시간으로 변경된다(customers usually must cancel at least 48 hours ~ For the next three weeks, this will be changed to 24 hours)는 정보가 제시되어 있다. 이는 무료로 예약을 취소할 수 있는 기한을 변경한 것이므로 (B)가 정답이다.

어휘 temporarily 일시적으로, 임시로 deadline (마감) 기한 at no charge 무료로 hours of operation 운영 시간

> Paraphrasing
> 지문의 For the next three weeks → 질문의 temporarily

## 151-152 보고서

4월 5일

토양 오염 보고서

고객: 굴드 제조회사
테스트 수행: 소일-체크 솔루션즈
151 **테스트 날짜: 3월 3일, 5월 5일, 7월 2일, 9월 5일**

과정: 부지 1(랭커스터)과 부지 2(캔턴), 그리고 152 **부지 3(브록웨이)**의 다양한 지점으로부터 6센티미터와 10센티미터 깊이에서 151 **샘플을 수집했습니다.** 토양에 오염 물질이 있는지 테스트했으며, 그 정도를 비교하여 시간 경과에 따른 변화를 평가했습니다. 첫 테스트 후, 미생물을 모든 부지에 주입했습니다.

예비 결과 및 권장 조치: 부지 1의 오염 수준은 상당히 하락했습니다. 추가 조치는 필요하지 않습니다. 부지 2에서는, 토양 안정화 영양제를 땅에 주입해야 합니다. 이것은 굳은 고체로 건조되어 특수 장비로 제거할 수 있습니다. 미생물은 다시 주입해야 합니다. 152 **부지 3에서는, 풀과 관목을 그 토양에서 뽑아내야 하며,** 미생물을 다시 주입해야 합니다.

어휘 soil 토양, 흙 contamination 오염 perform 실시하다, 수행하다 process 과정 collect 수집하다, 모으다 site 부지, 장소 contaminant 오염원 compare 비교하다 assess 평가하다 following ~ 후에 initial 처음의 micro-organism 미생물 introduce 도입하다, 소개하다 preliminary 예비의 findings (조사 등의) 결과 drop 하락하다, 떨어지다 significantly 상당히 further 추가적인, 한층 더 한 stabilization 안정화 formula (식물) 영양제 inject 주입하다 hardened 경화된, 굳은 solid 고체 remove 제거하다, 없애다 specialized 특수한 equipment 장비 reapply 다시 사용하다, 재적용하다 shrub 관목

## 151 Not / True

번역 토양 테스트에 대해 사실인 것은?
(A) 정부에서 정한 요건을 충족했다.
(B) 굴드 제조회사 정규직 직원에 의해 실시되었다.
(C) 주로 캔턴 부지에 초점을 맞췄다.
(D) 수집 날짜들 사이에 공백이 있다.

해설 상단에 테스트 날짜가 '3월 3일, 5월 5일, 7월 2일, 9월 5일(Testing Dates: March 3, May 5, July 2, September 5)'로 표기되어 있고, 첫 번째 단락에 샘플을 수집했다(Samples were collected)고 했으므로 (D)가 정답이다.

어휘 fulfill (요구, 조건 등을) 충족하다, 준수하다 requirement 요건, 필수 조건 carry out 실시하다 focus on ~에 초점을 맞추다 gap 공백(기), 격차 collection 수집, 수거

## 152 세부 사항

번역 어떤 조치가 굴드 제조회사에 권고되는가?
(A) 10센티미터가 넘는 깊이에서 흙 채취하기
(B) 랭커스터의 토양에 영양제 주입하기
(C) 캔턴에서 미생물 처리 중단하기
(D) 브록웨이에서 식물 제거하기

해설 권고되는 조치가 언급된 두 번째 단락에, 부지 3에서 풀과 관목을 뽑아 내야 한다(At Site 3, the grass and shrubs should be pulled from the soil)는 말이 쓰여 있는데, 첫 번째 단락에 부지 3이 브록웨이(Site 3 (Brockway))로 표기되어 있으므로 (D)가 정답이다.

어휘 cease 중단하다 treatment 처리 remove 제거하다, 없애다

> Paraphrasing
> 지문의 the grass and shrubs should be pulled
> → 정답의 Removing plants

TEST 7

## 153-154 문자 메시지

메이슨 응우옌 (오전 10시 27분)
안녕하세요, 에바. 린든 엔터프라이즈 사와의 회의에 필요한 153 **발표 슬라이드**를 방금 이메일로 보내 드렸어요. 154 **그들이 상품을 해외에 판매할 때 규제에 대처하는 걸 우리가 어떻게 도울 수 있는지 간략히 설명하고 있어요.** 받으셨나요?

에바 살라자르 (오전 10시 28분)
지금 막 열어 보는 중이에요. 이게 완성된 버전인가요?

메이슨 응우옌 (오전 10시 29분)
아뇨. 153 **4번 슬라이드에서 6번 슬라이드까지 몇몇 통계 자료를 넣어 주실 수 있는지 궁금한데요.**

에바 살라자르 (오전 10시 30분)
물론이죠. 제가 준비해야 하는 게 또 있나요?

메이슨 응우옌 (오전 10시 31분)
154 **린든 엔터프라이즈 사가 국내로 물품을 반입할 계획도 있기 때문에 항만 등록 절차에 대한 정보를 포함해야 할 것 같습니다.**

에바 살라자르 (오전 10시 33분)
좋은 생각일 수 있겠네요. 말씀하신 부분을 확인해 보고 다시 알려 드릴게요.

어휘 outline 간략히 설명하다 manage 대처하다, 처리하다 regulation 규제, 규정 abroad 해외에, 해외로 put in ~을 집어넣다 statistics 통계 (자료) include 포함하다 port 항구 registration 등록 get back to+명사 ~에게 다시 연락하다

## 153 의도 파악

번역 오전 10시 30분에, 살라자르 씨가 "물론이죠"라고 쓸 때 의미하는 것은?
(A) 린든 엔터프라이즈 사의 직원들에게 기꺼이 연락할 것이다.
(B) 발표 파일에 수치 정보를 추가할 수 있다.
(C) 응우옌 씨가 있는 곳에서 기꺼이 회의에 참석할 것이다.
(D) 오늘 평소보다 늦게까지 일할 계획이다.

해설 Sure thing은 '물론이죠, 당연하죠' 등의 의미로 상대방의 요청이나 제안을 수락할 때 사용하는 표현이다. 따라서 응우옌 씨가 10시 27분에 언급한 발표 슬라이드(the presentation slides)에 대해 10시 29분에 4번 슬라이드에서 6번 슬라이드까지 통계 자료를 넣어 줄 수 있는지(I was wondering if you could put in some statistics on slides 4 through 6) 요청하는 말에 대한 수락의 답변임을 알 수 있으므로 (B)가 정답이다.

어휘 be willing to 기꺼이 ~하다, ~할 의향이 있다 numerical 수치의, 숫자의

> **Paraphrasing**
> 지문의 put in some statistics on slides 4 through 6
> → 정답의 add numerical information to a presentation file

## 154 추론

번역 메시지 작성자들은 어떤 종류의 일을 할 것 같은가?
(A) 컴퓨터 프로그래밍
(B) 안전 점검
(C) 시장 분석
(D) 수출입 서비스

해설 응우옌 씨가 10시 27분과 10시 31분에 각각 작성한 메시지에 업체가 상품을 해외에 판매할 때 규제에 대처하는 걸 우리가 어떻게 도울 수 있는지(how we can help them manage regulations when selling their goods abroad)와 그 업체가 상품을 국내로 들여올 때 항만 등록 절차에 대한 정보(information about the steps for port registration, as Lyndon Enterprises plans to bring goods into the country as well)를 언급하고 있다. 이는 수출 및 수입과 관련된 업무에 해당하므로 (D)가 정답이다.

어휘 inspection 점검, 조사 analysis 분석

> **Paraphrasing**
> 지문의 selling their goods abroad / bring goods into the country → 정답의 Import-export

## 155-157 이메일

수신: ztaheri@larabeemail.com
발신: parksoomin@civilengconf.com
날짜: 8월 3일
제목: 토목 공학 컨퍼런스

태허리 씨께,

오늘 귀하와 이야기 나눌 수 있어서 즐거웠으며, 157 **11월 5일부터 8일까지 애틀랜타에서 개최되는 제50회 연례 토목 공학 컨퍼런스**에 참석해 주십사 하는 저희의 초청을 수락해 주셔서 기쁩니다. 155 **작년에 악천후로 인해 컨퍼런스 마지막 날 행사들이 취소되어 귀하의 발표를 통해 전문 지식을 공유할 수 없어서 대단히 안타까웠습니다.** 참석자 수가 작년에 비해 거의 100명 정도 늘었으므로, 가장 큰 공간인 나바로 홀을 이용할 것입니다. 156 **이곳은 수용 인원이 250명이며, 가득 찰 것으로 예상하고 있습니다.** 157 **귀하는 두 번째 날 오전으로 예약해 드렸습니다.** 준비하시면서, 강연 시간은 최대 120분이라는 점에 유의하시기 바랍니다. 귀하께서 마음껏 이용하실 수 있는 일반적인 발표 장비는 있지만, 다른 무엇이든 필요하시면, 제게 알려 주시기 바랍니다.

박수민
행사 진행 책임자, 토목 공학 컨퍼런스

어휘 civil engineering 토목 공학 accept 수락하다, 받아들이다 invitation 초청(장) annual 연례적인, 해마다의 disappointed 실망한 expertise 전문 지식 call off ~을 취소하다 severe weather 악천후 attendance 참석자 수, 참석률 compared to+명사 ~와 비교해 capacity 수용 인원, 수용력 make one's preparation 준비하다 keep in mind that ~임에 유의하다 maximum 최대(치), 최고(치) equipment 장비 at one's disposal ~이 마음껏 이용할 수 있는

## 155 추론

번역 태허리 씨의 이전 컨퍼런스 발표에 대해 암시된 것은?
(A) 기술적인 오작동 문제에 시달렸다.
(B) 행사 주최측에 의해 취소되었다.
(C) 나바로 홀에서 진행되었다.
(D) 참가자들로부터 좋은 평가를 받았다.

해설 지문 중반부에 작년에 악천후로 인해 컨퍼런스 마지막 날 행사들이 취소되어 태허리 씨가 발표를 할 수 없어서 대단히 안타까웠다(~ you were unable to share your expertise in your presentation last year, as the events on the final day of the conference were called off due to severe weather)고 했다. 이는 날씨 때문에 주최측에서 어쩔 수 없이 취소한 것으로 볼 수 있으므로 (B)가 정답이다.

어휘 suffer from ~에 시달리다, ~로 고통받다 malfunction 오작동, 기능 불량 organizer 주최자, 조직자 participant 참가자

> **Paraphrasing**
> 지문의 your presentation last year
> → 질문의 Mr. Taheri's previous presentation
> 지문의 were called off → 정답의 was canceled

## 156 세부 사항

번역 대략 몇 명의 참가자들이 행사에 올 것으로 예상되는가?
(A) 50명
(B) 100명
(C) 120명
(D) 250명

해설 지문 중반부에 행사장인 나바로 홀의 수용 인원이 250명이라는 점과 함께 이곳이 가득 찰 것으로 예상하고 있다(It has a capacity of 250, and we expect it to be full)는 말이 쓰여 있으므로 (D)가 정답이다.

어휘 approximately 대략, 약

## 157 세부 사항

번역 태허리 씨의 강연을 위한 시간은 언제로 예약되었는가?
(A) 11월 5일
(B) 11월 6일
(C) 11월 7일
(D) 11월 8일

해설 지문 중반부에 태허리 씨를 두 번째 날 오전으로 예약해 두었다(We have you booked for the morning of the second day)고 했는데 지문 초반부에 행사 기간이 11월 5일부터 8일까지(the 50th Annual Civil Engineering Conference, which takes place from November 5 to 8)라고 쓰여 있어 11월 6일 오전으로 예약되었다는 것을 알 수 있다. 따라서 (B)가 정답이다.

어휘 time slot 시간대 reserve 예약하다

> **Paraphrasing**
> 지문의 booked → 질문의 reserved

## 158-160 기사

새로운 장을 여는 시청

(1월 20일) - [158] **ETB 사가 9만 평방 피트의 공간을 추가하는 시청 확장 공사 프로젝트 입찰을 따냈다.** 이 공사는 일반 예산으로 일부분 충당될 것이며, 나머지 자금은 연방 보조금으로 충당된다. 시청이 지니는 역사적 중요성 때문에 ETB 사는 지역 공동체 모임인 햄턴 역사 학회에 이 프로젝트에 대해 조언해 달라고 요청했다. [159, 160] **추가 부속 건물에는 절실히 필요했던 대형 회의실과 12개의 사무실이 포함될 것이다.** 일부는 새롭게 구성된 소비자 업무 지원부가 이용할 것이다. 추가 정보는 ETB 웹사이트를 방문하여 확인할 수 있다.

어휘 bid 입찰(가) expansion 확장, 확대 square feet 평방 피트 cover (비용 등을) 충당하다, 감당하다 partially 부분적으로 general 일반적인, 전반적인 budget 예산 remaining 나머지의 funding 자금 (제공) federal 연방의, 연방 정부의 grant 보조금 local 지역의 community 지역 공동체, 지역 사회 advise 조언하다 significance 중요성 additional 추가적인 wing 부속 건물 house (건물 등이) 포함하다, 공간을 제공하다 further 추가적인, 한층 더 한 details 상세 정보, 세부 사항

## 158 추론

번역 ETB 사는 어떤 종류의 업체일 것 같은가?
(A) 금융 기관
(B) 지역 동호회
(C) 건설 회사
(D) 부동산 중개업체

해설 지문 시작 부분에 ETB 사가 9만 평방 피트의 공간을 추가하는 시청 확장 공사 프로젝트 입찰을 따냈다(ETB has won the bid for the expansion project at City Hall)는 정보가 제시되어 있다. 건물 확장 공사 프로젝트는 건설 회사에서 맡을 수 있는 일이므로 (C)가 정답이다.

## 159 추론

번역 시청에 대해 암시된 것은?
(A) 예정된 변화들이 아마 미뤄질 것이다.
(B) 현재는 대규모 회의를 수용할 수 없다.
(C) 개인이 그곳에 금전적 기부를 했다.
(D) 총 9만 평방 피트의 공간이 있다.

해설 지문 후반부에 절실히 필요했던 대형 회의실이 포함될 것(The additional wing will house a much-needed larger conference room)이라는 말이 쓰여 있는데, 이를 통해 현재는 대규모 회의를 진행할 장소가 없다는 것을 알 수 있으므로 (B)가 정답이다.

어휘 postpone 미루다, 연기하다 currently 현재 accommodate 수용하다 individual 개인, 사람 make a donation 기부하다 financial 금전적인, 재정의

TEST 7

## 160 문장 삽입

번역 [1], [2], [3], [4]로 표시된 곳 중에서 다음 문장이 가장 적합한 곳은 어디인가?

"일부는 새롭게 구성된 소비자 업무 지원부가 이용할 것이다."

(A) [1]
(B) [2]
(C) [3]
(D) [4]

해설 제시된 문장은 앞서 언급된 것 중 일부를 Some으로 지칭해 그곳을 새로 만들어진 부서에서 이용할 것이라는 의미를 담고 있다. 따라서 추가 부속 건물에 포함되는 12개의 사무실이 언급된 문장 뒤에 위치해 그 사무실들 중 일부의 용도를 설명하는 흐름이 되어야 자연스러우므로 (D)가 정답이다.

어휘 form 구성하다, 형성하다

### 161-163 정보

유티카 주식회사
여러분의 성원에 감사드립니다!

유티카의 TX-8 모델이 제공하는 모든 놀라운 기능을 누리시기 바랍니다. [161] **이 제품은 시중에서 가장 연비가 뛰어난 차량 중 하나이며**, 최신 기술이 탑재되어 있습니다. 자동 긴급 제동 시스템은 여러분과 동승자 모두의 안전을 향상시키는 데 도움을 주며, 감응식 순항 제어 기능은 다른 사물들과의 거리를 감지해 그에 따라 조정됩니다.

유티카 주식회사 팀의 추가 지원을 위해, 새 스마트폰 애플리케이션을 다운로드해 보시면 어떨까요? 매일 24시간 언제든 고객 서비스 직원 또는 기술자와 채팅하실 수 있습니다. [162] **이 앱에는 가장 최신의 가격 정보와 함께 가장 가까운 주유소들을 보여주는 지도가 포함되어 있습니다**. 심지어 연료량을 확인하고 주행 가능 거리를 예상할 수 있게 해줍니다.

유티카 주식회사는 그저 유행만을 [163] **따르지** 않으며, 저희만의 스타일과 방식으로 선도합니다.

어휘 patronage 성원, 애용 feature 기능 fuel-efficient 연비가 좋은 vehicle 차량 come equipped with ~가 장착되어 출시되다, 갖춰져 나오다 advance 발전, 진보 emergency 긴급 상황, 비상 사태 improve 향상시키다, 개선하다 adaptive cruise control 감응식 순항 제어 function 기능 monitor 감지하다, 관찰하다 object 사물, 물체 make an adjustment 조절하다, 조정하다 accordingly 그에 알맞게, 그에 따라 further 추가적인, 한층 더 한 assistance 지원, 도움 up-to-the-minute 가장 최근의 pricing 가격 (책정) allow 할 수 있게 해 주다 estimate 추정 range 거리, 범위 follow 따르다, 따라 하다 trend 유행 approach (접근) 방식

## 161 세부 사항

번역 유티카 주식회사는 어떤 분야에서 사업을 운영하는가?

(A) 건물 보안
(B) 자동차 제조
(C) 소프트웨어 유통
(D) 연료 생산

해설 첫 단락 시작 부분에 TX-8 모델을 소개하면서 가장 연비가 뛰어난 차량 중 하나(This is one of the most fuel-efficient vehicles on the market)라고 알리고 있으므로 (B)가 정답이다.

어휘 operate 운영하다, 영업하다 distribution 유통, 분배

## 162 세부 사항

번역 새 유티카 주식회사 스마트폰 애플리케이션은 사용자들에게 무엇을 할 수 있게 해 주는가?

(A) 제품 회수 및 안전 관련 보고 확인하기
(B) 다른 고객들보다 먼저 특가 할인 파악하기
(C) 실시간으로 제품 배송 추적하기
(D) 여러 업체들의 가격 비교하기

해설 유티카 사의 스마트폰 애플리케이션이 언급된 두 번째 단락에 가장 최신의 가격 정보와 함께 가장 가까운 주유소들을 보여주는 지도가 포함되어 있다(The app has a map that shows the nearest gas stations along with up-to-the-minute pricing information)고 했다. 이는 사용자들이 앱을 통해 인근 주유소들의 가격을 비교할 수 있다는 말이므로 (D)가 정답이다.

어휘 recall (결함 제품의) 회수 -related ~와 관련된 track 추적하다 shipment 배송 in real time 실시간으로 compare 비교하다

> **Paraphrasing**
> 지문의 shows the nearest gas stations along with up-to-the-minute pricing information
> → 정답의 Compare prices at different businesses

## 163 동의어

번역 세 번째 단락, 첫 번째 줄의 단어 "follow"와 의미가 가장 가까운 것은?

(A) 고수하다, 준수하다
(B) 동행하다, 동반하다
(C) 안내하다, 지도하다
(D) 대체하다, 교체하다

해설 follow의 목적어인 명사 trend가 '유행, 경향'을 뜻하는데, 그 뒤에 자신들만의 스타일과 방식으로 선도한다는 말이 쓰여 있어 단순히 유행을 따르지 않는다는 의미가 자연스럽다. 따라서 '따르다'와 유사한 의미를 지닌 것으로서 '고수하다, 준수하다' 등을 뜻하는 (A) stick to가 정답이다.

### 164-167 편지

5월 14일

마티아스 홀츠먼
아우크스부르크 가 15
57580 엘벤

홀츠먼 씨께,

청년 뮤직 프로그램(YMP)을 대표해, [166] **저희 기관을 위해 자원봉사를 해 주신 것**에 감사드립니다. 귀하 같은 분들의 헌신과 노고가 없었다면,

저희가 [165] **공동의** 목표를 달성할 수 없었을 것이며 독일 전역의 지역 사회에 그렇게 큰 긍정적인 영향을 미칠 수 없었을 것입니다. YMP는 젊은이들이 음악에 대한 평생의 사랑을 키우고 음악의 즐거움을 다른 사람들과 나누도록 도와 행복과 사회적 결속력을 높입니다. [167 (B)] **불과 2년 만에, 저희는 프로그램 센터의 수를 23개로 확장했습니다.** [167 (D)] **웨인 카스트너 신임 운영 이사님의 지휘 아래** 이러한 추세가 지속될 것으로 예상합니다.

곧 있을 흥미로운 변화들 중에서, 전국 최대 악기 공급업체인 [164] **힘멜 뮤직과 제휴 관계를 맺게 되어 기쁩니다.** 힘멜 뮤직은 [167 (A)] **분기별 모금 행사**를 지원할 뿐 아니라 저희 기관에 악기를 기증할 것입니다.

힘멜 뮤직과의 협업을 기념하기 위해, 저희가 [166] **이 새로운 관계를 위한 공동의 노력을 표현할 슬로건 제작 공모전을 개최합니다. 모든 YMP 참가자와 직원, 그리고 자원봉사자들은 각자의 아이디어를 공유해 주시길 바랍니다.** 위원회에서 최우수작을 선정할 것이며, 우승자는 250달러에 상응하는 힘멜 뮤직 상품권을 받게 됩니다. 이 공모전에 관한 추가 정보는 저희 월간 소식지에 포함될 것이므로, 반드시 확인해 보시기 바랍니다.

가브리엘레 라인하르트

가브리엘레 라인하르트
개발 코디네이터
청년 뮤직 프로그램

어휘 on behalf of ~을 대표해, 대신해 appreciation 감사(의 뜻) volunteering 자원봉사 organization 단체, 기관 dedication 헌신 achieve 달성하다, 이루다 common 공동의, 일반의 profound 깊이 있는, 심오한 positive 긍정적인 community 지역 사회, 지역 공동체 cultivate (태도, 습관 등을) 고양하다, 기르다 enhance 향상시키다, 강화하다 cohesion 화합, 결속(력) guide 인도하다, 안내하다 trend 추세, 경향 on the horizon 떠오르는, 곧 있을 partner with ~와 제휴 관계를 맺다 supplier 공급업체 musical instrument 악기 donate 기증하다, 기부하다 assist 지원하다, 돕다 quarterly 분기의 fundraising 모금 celebrate 기념하다 represent 상징하다, 대표하다 joint 공동의 relationship 관계 participant 참가자 committee 위원회 gift certificate 상품권 include 포함하다

## 164 주제 / 목적

번역 편지의 한 가지 목적은 무엇인가?
(A) 기부를 요청하는 것
(B) 새로운 제휴를 알리는 것
(C) 기관 이름 변경을 설명하는 것
(D) 음악 공연에 초대하는 것

해설 첫 단락의 전반적인 상황 설명에 이어, 두 번째 단락에서 힘멜 뮤직과 제휴를 맺게 된 것(we are delighted to partner with Himmel Music)을 알린 뒤, 그에 대한 이야기가 이어지고 있으므로 (B)가 정답이다.

어휘 extend an invitation to+명사 ~에 초대하다

> **Paraphrasing**
> 지문의 partner with Himmel Music
> → 정답의 partnership

## 165 동의어

번역 첫 번째 단락, 세 번째 줄에 쓰인 "common"과 의미가 가장 가까운 것은?
(A) 공동의, 공통의
(B) 인기 있는, 대중적인
(C) 의도된, 대상이 되는
(D) 보통의, 평범한

해설 common goals는 단체 등에서 함께 나아가는 데 필요한 공동의 목표를 의미하므로 '공동의, 공통의'를 뜻하는 (A) mutual이 정답이다.

## 166 추론

번역 홀츠먼 씨에 대해 암시된 것은?
(A) 슬로건을 제출하도록 권장된다.
(B) 상의 후보로 지명되었다.
(C) 음반 매장 상품권을 받을 것이다.
(D) YMP의 창립 멤버였다.

해설 첫 단락에서 홀츠먼 씨가 YMP의 자원봉사자(your volunteering for our organization)라는 것을 알 수 있고, 세 번째 단락에 슬로건 창작 공모전에 모든 YMP 참가자와 직원, 그리고 자원봉사자들이 각자의 아이디어를 공유해 주길 바란다(~ create a slogan to represent the joint efforts of this new relationship. All YMP participants, staff, and volunteers are urged to share their ideas)는 내용이 있으므로 자원봉사자인 홀츠먼 씨도 슬로건 관련 아이디어를 내는 것이 권장된다는 것을 알 수 있다. 따라서 (A)가 정답이다.

어휘 nominate 후보로 지명하다 founding 창립, 설립

> **Paraphrasing**
> 지문의 share their ideas → 정답의 submit a slogan

## 167 Not / True

번역 YMP에 대해 언급되지 않은 것은?
(A) 일 년에 네 번 모금 행사를 개최한다.
(B) 빠른 성장을 경험했다.
(C) 전국 최대의 청년 단체이다.
(D) 최근 경영진에 변화가 있었다.

해설 첫 단락 후반부에 2년 만에 프로그램 센터를 23곳으로 확장했다(In just two years, we have expanded the number of program centers to twenty-three)는 부분에서 (B)를, 신임 운영 이사(Guided by our new executive director, Wayne Kastner)를 언급하는 부분에서 (D)를, 두 번째 단락 마지막 부분에 언급된 분기별 모금 행사(our quarterly fundraising events)를 통해 (A)를 확인할 수 있다. 하지만 전국 최대의 청년 단체라는 언급은 없으므로 (C)가 정답이다.

어휘 growth 성장 leadership 경영진, 지도부

> **Paraphrasing**
> 지문의 In just two years, we have expanded the number → 보기 (B)의 has experienced rapid growth
> 지문의 new executive director
> → 보기 (D)의 has recently changed its leadership
> 지문의 quarterly → 보기 (A)의 four times a year

**168-171 온라인 채팅**

유리노 사이키 오후 1시 54분
루비 플레밍 지원자는 어땠나요?

아지즈 미리 오후 1시 55분
면접 볼 때 정말 인상적이었어요. 168 **그녀의 삽화가 우리 아동용 시리즈에 추가되면 아주 좋을 것 같아요.**

유리노 사이키 오후 1시 56분
그녀를 고용하면, 169 **리바이가 우리 사내 파일 공유 프로그램 사용법을 가르쳐 줄 수 있을 거라 생각했어요.** 그녀가 전에 사용해 본 적 없는 소프트웨어일 테니까요. 169 **리바이 씨, 그게 문제가 될까요?**

아지즈 미리 오후 1시 57분
우리가 면접 본 모든 사람 중에서, 그녀가 팀에 가장 적합한 것 같아요.

리바이 웨일러 오후 1시 58분
물론 그렇지 않습니다.

유리노 사이키 오후 2시
정말 고마워요! 170 **그녀의 자기 소개서에 소셜 미디어에 팬층이 형성되어 있다고도 나와 있네요.**

리바이 웨일러 오후 2시 1분
그건 판매를 높이는 데 도움이 될 겁니다. 그럼, 이분에게 일자리를 제안할 준비가 된 건가요?

아지즈 미리 오후 2시 2분
길리엄 씨는 먼저 원격 회의로 후속 면접을 진행해 이 역할을 어떻게 수행할 것인지에 대해 이야기하고 싶어 해요. 171 **그는 담당자에게 수많은 업무가 주어졌을 때 대처할 수 있는 능력이 필수적이라고 말해요.**

유리노 사이키 오후 2시 4분
아지즈, 당신이 그 회의를 준비할 건가요?

아지즈 미리 오후 2시 5분
네, 제가 모든 걸 처리할 겁니다.

어휘 applicant 지원자 impress 깊은 인상을 남기다 addition 보탬(이 되는 것), 추가(되는 것) on-site 회사 내의, 구내의 file-sharing 파일 공유 issue 문제, 사안 fit 적합한 사람[것] cover letter 자기 소개서 following 팬들, 추종자들 boost 촉진하다, 증진하다 follow-up 후속적인 teleconference 화상 회의 handle 감당하다, 다루다 essential 필수적인 cope with ~에 대처하다 assign 배정하다, 할당하다 numerous 다수의 task 업무, 일 set up 준비하다, 마련하다 take care of ~을 처리하다

## 168 추론

번역 메시지 작성자들은 어디에서 근무할 것 같은가?
(A) 인력 채용 회사
(B) 아동복 매장
(C) 도서 출판사
(D) 영화관

해설 오후 1시 55분에 아지즈 미리 씨가 작성한 메시지에 지원자의 삽화가 우리 아동용 시리즈에 추가되면 아주 좋을 것 같다(I think her artwork would be a great addition to our children's series)고 언급된 것에서 도서를 출판하는 회사의 직원들임을 추론할 수 있으므로 (C)가 정답이다.

## 169 의도 파악

번역 오후 1시 58분에 웨일러 씨가 "물론 그렇지 않습니다"라고 쓸 때, 의미하는 것은 무엇이겠는가?
(A) 기꺼이 교육을 제공할 것이다.
(B) 면접 일정을 수용할 수 있다.
(C) 중요한 마감 기한을 놓치지 않을 것이다.
(D) 아직 결정을 내릴 준비가 되어 있지 않다.

해설 유리노 사이키 씨가 오후 1시 56분에 작성한 메시지에서 리바이가 사내 파일 공유 프로그램 사용법을 지원자에게 가르쳐 줄 수 있을 거라 생각했다(I thought Levi could teach her how to use our on-site file-sharing program)며, 리바이에게 그게 문제가 될지(Levi, would that be an issue for you?) 물었는데, 그에 대해 '그렇지 않다'고 대답하는 흐름이다. 이는 기꺼이 사용법을 알려 주겠다는 뜻이므로 (A)가 정답이다.

어휘 accommodate 수용하다 miss 놓치다, 빠뜨리다 deadline 마감 기한

## 170 Not / True

번역 플레밍 씨에 대해 언급된 것은?
(A) 이미 개인 팬층을 보유하고 있다.
(B) 현재 소셜 미디어 회사에서 근무한다.
(C) 웨일러 씨가 자리를 비운 동안 근무를 대신할 것이다.
(D) 화상 회의로 사안들을 논의하는 것을 선호한다.

해설 오후 2시에 유리노 사이키 씨가 작성한 메시지에 플레밍의 자기 소개서에 소셜 미디어에 팬층이 형성되어 있다고 나와 있다(I also see from her cover letter that she has built up a following on social media)는 언급이 있으므로 (A)가 정답이다.

어휘 base ~층 currently 현재 cover 대신하다 shift 교대 근무(조) matter 사안, 문제

> **Paraphrasing**
> 지문의 has built up a following
> → 정답의 has her own fan base

## 171 세부 사항

번역 채팅에 따르면, 길리엄 씨는 해당 공석에 대해 무엇이 중요하다고 생각하는가?
(A) 배정된 여러 업무를 효율적으로 처리할 수 있는 능력
(B) 업무 프로젝트에 대한 협력적 접근 방식
(C) 고객 서비스 개선에 대한 헌신
(D) 다양한 소프트웨어 프로그램 작업 경험

해설 길리엄 씨가 언급되는 2시 2분 메시지에 길리엄 씨는 담당자에게 수많은 업무가 주어졌을 때 대처할 수 있는 능력이 필수적이라고 말한다(He says it's essential that the person can cope with being assigned numerous tasks)고 쓰여 있다. 이는 여러 업무를 효율적으로 처리하는 능력을 말하는 것이므로 (A)가 정답이다.

어휘 critical 중대한, 중요한 open position 공석 deal with ~을 처리하다 assignment 배정(된 일) efficiently 효율적으로 collaborative 협력적인, 공동 작업의 approach (접근) 방식 dedication 헌신, 전념 improve 개선하다, 향상시키다

> **Paraphrasing**
> 지문의 cope with being assigned numerous tasks
> → 정답의 deal with several assignments efficiently

### 172-175 이메일

수신: 홀리 그레니어 <grenierh@duvalmail.com>
발신: 브라이스 자비스 <b.jarvis@literaryquarterly.com>
날짜: 8월 15일
제목: 회신: 다가오는 호를 위한 투고
첨부: lquarerly_guidelines

그레니어 씨께,

<문학 계간지>에 게재하는 것을 고려할 수 있도록 작품 제출에 관심을 가져주셔서 감사합니다. 173 (A) **저희는 작품 당 5달러의 환불되지 않는 제출 수수료를 부과하고 있으며**, 이것이 작품의 게재 여부에는 영향을 미치지 않는다는 것에 유의하시기 바랍니다.

본문과 함께, 173 (B), 175 **귀하의 작품을 간략히 설명하는 단락을 포함해야 합니다**. 초기 심사 과정에서 중요한 관련 정보를 반드시 포함하시기 바랍니다. 이는 저희가 귀하의 제출물을 검토할 때 귀하의 글이 저희 잡지에 적합한지 평가하는 데 도움이 될 것입니다. 잡지를 구독하시면, 저희가 선호하는 것을 더 잘 이해하시게 될 것입니다.

또한, 172 **저희는 다른 곳에 출판된 적이 없는 글만 고려하기 때문에** 귀하의 제출물은 이전에 다른 출판사에 공유된 적이 없어야 합니다. 작품을 제출하시기 전에, 173 (D) **첨부해 드린 가이드라인을 신중히 읽어 보신 다음, 양식 및 구성 방식을 정확히 따라 주시기 바랍니다**. 참고를 위한 샘플 에세이가 포함되어 있습니다.

저희는 항상 단편 소설이 부족한데, 174 **압도적으로 시가 많이 접수되고 있습니다. 따라서 훌륭한 원고라 하더라도 양이 많아서 거절될 수 있다는 점을 양해해 주시기 바라며, 이로 인해 낙담하지 않기를 바랍니다.**

귀하가 제출하신 작품에 행운이 있기를 기원합니다.

브라이스 자비스

어휘 submission 제출(물) edition (출판물, 제품 등의) 호, 판 consider 고려하다 publication 출간(물), 간행(물) note 유의하다, 주목하다 charge 부과하다, 청구하다 nonrefundable 환불되지 않는 fee 수수료, 요금 paragraph 단락 briefly 간략히, 짧게 assess 평가하다 suitability 적합성 subscribe 구독하다 preference 선호(하는 것) exclusively 오로지, 독점적으로 elsewhere 다른 곳에서 previously 과거에, 이전에 attached 첨부된 carefully 신중히 follow 따르다, 준수하다 layout (지면, 공간 등의) 구성, 구획 precisely 정확히 reference 참고 short story 단편 소설 overwhelming 압도적인 manuscript 원고 reject 거절하다 volume 양, 용량 discourage 낙담시키다

## 172 추론

번역 <문학 계간지>에 대해 암시된 것은?
(A) 주된 글들은 대체로 내부 저자들에 의해 작성된다.
(B) 오직 대중에게 처음 공개되는 작품만 게재한다.
(C) 경영진은 더 자주 출간하는 것을 고려하고 있다.
(D) 오직 제출물이 받아들여진 저자들에게만 연락한다.

해설 세 번째 단락에 다른 곳에 출판된 적이 없는 글만 고려한다(~ we exclusively consider texts that have never been published elsewhere)고 했으므로 (B)가 정답이다.

어휘 in-house (단체 등의) 내부의 solely 오로지, 단지 be made public 일반에게 공개되다 management 경영진, 운영진 frequently 자주, 빈번히

> **Paraphrasing**
> 지문의 texts that have never been published elsewhere
> → 정답의 work being made public for the first time

## 173 Not / True

번역 제출을 위한 요건으로 언급되지 않은 것은?
(A) 일회성 수수료 지불하기
(B) 간단한 설명 제공하기
(C) 잡지 구독하기
(D) 특정 방식으로 작품 형태 갖추기

해설 첫 단락에 5달러의 환불되지 않는 제출 수수료를 부과한다(we charge a nonrefundable submission fee of $5.00)고 한 부분에서 (A)를, 두 번째 단락에 작품을 간략히 설명하는 내용을 포함해야 한다(you should include a paragraph that briefly describes your work)고 한 부분에서 (B)를, 그리고 세 번째 단락에 첨부한 가이드라인을 읽고 그 양식 및 구성 양식을 정확히 따라 달라(please read the attached guidelines carefully and follow the style and layout precisely)고 한 부분에서 (D)를 각각 확인할 수 있다. 하지만 잡지 구독은 작품 제출을 위한 요건으로 언급되지 않았으므로 (C)가 정답이다.

어휘 description 설명 format 형태를 갖추다, 구성하다 specific 특정한, 구체적인

TEST 7

**Paraphrasing**
지문의 charge a nonrefundable submission fee
→ 보기 (A)의 Paying a one-time fee
지문의 include a paragraph that briefly describes your work → 보기 (B)의 Providing a short description
지문의 follow the style and layout
→ 보기 (D)의 Formatting the work in a specific way

## 174 추론

번역 그레니어 씨는 무엇을 쓰는 데 관심이 있을 것 같은가?
(A) 시
(B) 단편 소설
(C) 에세이
(D) 도서 평론

해설 네 번째 단락에 시가 압도적으로 많이 접수되고 있다는 말과 함께 양이 많아서 거절될 수 있다고 알리며 이로 인해 낙담하지 않기를 바란다(we receive an overwhelming amount of poetry. ~ we hope this will not discourage you)고 했다. 이는 그레니어 씨가 시를 제출하기 전에 사전 주의를 주는 말에 해당하므로 (A)가 정답이다.

## 175 문장 삽입

번역 [1], [2], [3], [4]로 표시된 곳 중에서 다음 문장이 가장 적합한 곳은 어디인가?
"초기 심사 과정에서 중요한 관련 정보를 반드시 포함하시기 바랍니다."
(A) [1]
(B) [2]
(C) [3]
(D) [4]

해설 제시된 문장은 초기 심사 과정에서 중요한 관련 정보를 꼭 포함하도록 당부하는 의미를 지니고 있다. 따라서 작품을 간략히 설명하는 단락을 포함하도록 알리는 문장 뒤에 위치한 [2]에 들어가 어떤 정보를 포함해야 하는지 부가적으로 설명하는 흐름이 되어야 자연스러우므로 (B)가 정답이다.

어휘 relevant 관련된 initial 초기의, 처음의 screening 선별, 선발 process 과정

## 176-180 웹페이지+후기

http://www.junctiontours.ca

정션 여행사의 도움으로 기억에 남는 토론토 여행을 만들어 보십시오!
모든 분의 취향에 맞는 다양한 패키지 투어를 제공합니다.

투어 1: 스포츠 팬들을 위한 전일 여행! 로저스 센터와 하키 명예의 전당을 견학해 보세요. 어쩌면 좋아하는 선수를 만나실지도 모릅니다. 점심 식사 제공.

투어 2: 토론토의 모든 주요 관광 명소를 방문할 수 있는 전일 도심 버스 여행. 176 **순환 노선 어디서든 버스에 탑승해 가장 흥미로운 장소에서 내리세요. 각 지점에서 원하시는 만큼 머무르세요!**

투어 3: 토론토 최고의 쇼핑 명소를 둘러보는 반나절 투어. 참가자들은 이턴 센터에서 독점 할인을 받습니다.

178 **투어 4: 멋진 경치가 보이는 여객선을 타고 토론토 스카이라인의 멋진 전망을 감상할 수 있는 토론토 아일랜드 전일 투어.** 점심 식사 제공.

투어 5: 토론토에서 가장 상징적인 건물인 CN 타워 반나절 투어. 서반구에서 가장 높은 전망대에 오르시려면 카메라를 준비하세요!

모든 투어는 국경일을 제외하고 매일 진행됩니다. 참가자는 시내 사무실에서 만나거나 177 **에머리 호텔 또는 호텔 크루즈에서 추가 비용 없이 픽업해 드립니다.** 식사는 별도로 명시되지 않는 한 포함되지 않습니다.

어휘 memorable 기억에 남는 suit 어울리다, 적합하다 taste 취향, 입맛 spot 발견하다 hop-on, hop-off tour (원하는 곳에서 타고 내리는) 도심 버스 여행 attraction 명소, 인기 장소 board 탑승하다 circuit 순환 노선 participant 참가자 exclusive 독점적인, 전용의 scenic 경치가 멋진 ferry 여객선 ride (차, 배 등) 타고 다니기 iconic 상징적인 observation platform 전망대 hemisphere 반구 available 이용 가능한 excluding ~을 제외하고 pick ~ up ~을 차로 데리러 가다 at no extra charge 추가 비용 없이 include 포함하다

윈스턴 하트
★★★★★

정션 여행사 이용 후기

정션 여행사의 예약 과정은 간단했으며, 그 과정에서 모든 관련 세부 정보를 잘 제공받았습니다. 저희 투어 가이드였던 스티븐의 철저한 준비에 정말 깊은 인상을 받았습니다. 178 **거친 파도 때문에, 물을 건너는 동안 저는 뱃멀미를 하기 시작했습니다.** 스티븐은 저를 갑판으로 데리고 올라가 신선한 공기를 쐴 수 있게 해주었고 시원한 생수를 주었습니다. 그는 또한 토론토의 역사 및 편의시설에 대해 대단히 많이 알고 있었습니다. 179 **저희는 여행을 기억하는 데 도움이 될 만한 토론토 주제의 기념품 몇 가지를 집에 사 가고 싶었는데 스티븐이 무엇을 어디서 사야 할지 아주 유용한 제안을 해 주셨습니다.** 저희는 멀리 일본에서 방문한 가족을 포함해, 그룹 내의 다른 참가자들을 만나서 아주 즐거운 시간을 보냈습니다. 180 **이 투어의 유일한 단점이라면 점심 식사의 1인분 양이 꽤 적었다는 점이었습니다.** 그럼에도 불구하고, 모든 분에게 정션 여행사를 적극 추천합니다.

어휘 booking 예약 process 과정 straightforward 간단한 be kept well informed 계속 정보를 잘 제공받다 related 관련된 details 세부 사항, 상세 정보 thorough 철저한, 꼼꼼한 preparation 준비 feel seasick 뱃멀미를 하다 deck 갑판 chilled 시원한, 냉장된 extremely 대단히, 매우 knowledgeable 아는 것이 많은 amenities 편의시설 -themed ~을 주제로 하는 suggestion 제안, 의견 participant 참가자 downside 단점, 결점 portion (음식의) 1인분

## 176 세부 사항

번역 투어 2는 나머지 투어들과 어떻게 다른가?
(A) 참가자들이 각자의 속도로 다닐 수 있다.
(B) 명소들이 토론토에서 유명하다.
(C) 하루 종일 지속된다.
(D) 투어 가이드의 도움을 포함한다.

해설 웹페이지의 Tour 2 항목에 순환 노선 어디서든 버스에 탑승해 가장 흥미로운 장소에서 내리라며, 각 지점에서 원하는 만큼 머무르라(Stay as long as you like at each site)는 말이 쓰여 있다. 이는 투어 참가자들이 자유롭게 다니면서 각자 원하는 속도로 투어를 즐길 수 있다는 의미이므로 (A)가 정답이다.

어휘 pace 속도 last 지속되다

## 177 세부 사항

번역 모든 패키지 투어에 포함되는 것은?
(A) 투어 당일의 점심 식사
(B) 참가자들의 짐 보관 서비스
(C) 특정 호텔에서 출발하는 교통편
(D) CN 타워 방문

해설 웹페이지 마지막 단락에 모든 투어에 공통적으로 해당하는 정보가 제시되어 있는데, 에머리 호텔 또는 호텔 크루즈에서 추가 비용 없이 픽업해 준다(we can pick you up from the Emery Hotel or Hotel Cruz at no extra charge)고 언급되어 있으므로 (C)가 정답이다.

어휘 storage 보관, 저장 luggage 짐, 수하물 transportation 교통(편)

> **Paraphrasing**
> 지문의 pick you up from the Emery Hotel or Hotel Cruz → 정답의 Transportation from certain hotels

## 178 연계

번역 하트 씨는 어느 투어를 떠났을 것 같은가?
(A) 투어 1
(B) 투어 3
(C) 투어 4
(D) 투어 5

해설 후기 초반부에 하트 씨가 거친 파도 때문에 물을 건너는 동안 뱃멀미를 하기 시작했다(I started feeling seasick while crossing the water, due to rough waves)고 했다. 이를 통해 웹페이지 Tour 4 항목에 언급된 여객선을 이용한 토론토 아일랜드 투어(Full-day Toronto Island tour with a scenic ferry ride)를 이용한 것으로 볼 수 있으므로 (C)가 정답이다.

## 179 추론

번역 후기에서 스티븐에 대해 암시하는 것은?
(A) 일본어를 할 수 있다.
(B) 역사학 학위가 있다.
(C) 토론토에서 태어났다.
(D) 기념품에 대해 조언했다.

해설 후기 중반부에 하트 씨가 여행을 기억하는 데 도움이 될 만한 토론토 주제의 기념품 몇 가지를 집에 사 가고 싶었는데 스티븐이 무엇을 어디서 사야 할지 아주 유용한 제안을 해 주었다(We wanted to bring home some Toronto-themed gifts ~ Stephen made some very helpful suggestions about what to buy and where)고 했으므로 (D)가 정답이다.

어휘 degree 학위 souvenir 기념품

> **Paraphrasing**
> 지문의 Toronto-themed gifts / made some very helpful suggestions
> → 정답의 gave advice on souvenirs

## 180 세부 사항

번역 하트 씨는 왜 투어의 일부분이 불만스러웠는가?
(A) 가이드가 체계적이지 못했다.
(B) 식사가 적었다.
(C) 그 구역이 붐볐다.
(D) 일정이 준수되지 않았다.

해설 후기 후반부에 하트 씨가 자신이 떠난 투어의 단점을 언급하면서 점심 식사의 1인분 양이 꽤 적었다(The only downside of this tour was that the portion size for the lunch was quite small)고 했으므로 (B)가 정답이다.

어휘 be dissatisfied with ~을 불만스러워하다 disorganized 체계적이지 못한 crowded 붐비는 follow 준수하다, 따르다

> **Paraphrasing**
> 지문의 the portion size for the lunch was quite small
> → 정답의 A meal was small.

**181-185 이메일+이메일**

수신: 브레들리 잭슨 <bjackson@cambridgestar.com>
발신: promotions@moonlight-bedding.com
날짜: 2월 10일
제목: 침구 할인 기회를 잡으세요!

고객님께,

내일부터 시작하는 저희 문라이트 침구회사의 연례 재고 정리 할인 행사를 놓치지 마십시오! 시트와 베갯잇, 그리고 매트리스 커버를 비축하기에 완벽한 시기입니다. 185(D) **보통 저희는 단 일주일 동안만 할인 행사를 개최하지만, 올해는 2월 11일부터 24일까지 2주 동안 진행합니다.** 아주 다양한 패턴과 색상, 그리고 원단이 구입 가능합니다. 185(A) **그리고 작은 트윈 침대나 킹사이즈 침대, 또는 그 중간의 어떤 침대를 소유하고 있든 상관없이, 분명 아주 마음에 드시는 제품을 찾으시게 될 것입니다.** 181 **할인 행사 첫째 날에 주문하시는 분들은 저희 새 라벤더 슬립 스프레이 50ml 병을 무료로 받으실 것이므로, 꼭 내일 쇼핑하시고 코드번호 THX05를 사용하시기 바랍니다.** 184 **게다가, 50달러 이상 소비하시는 고객들께서는 무료 배송 서비스도 받으실 것입니다.** 저희 온라인 카탈로그의 재고품은 물품이 남아 있는 동안에만 구입하실 수 있습니다.

TEST 7

곧 만나뵙길 바랍니다!

빌리 엘우드
판촉 행사 관리팀, 문라이트 침구회사

[182] **참고 바랍니다: 이 이메일은 작년에 자주 구매해 주신 고객들께 발송되었습니다.** 언제든지 수신을 해지할 수 있습니다.

어휘 clearance sale 재고 정리 할인 행사 stock up 비축해 놓다 a wide range of 아주 다양한 fabric 원단, 직물 available 구입 가능한 inventory 재고(품) supplies 물품, 용품 last 지속되다 unsubscribe (가입 등을) 해지하다

수신: bjackson@cambridgestar.com
발신: orders@moonlight-bedding.com
날짜: 2월 11일
제목: 주문 확인서

잭슨 씨께,

문라이트 침구회사의 연례 재고 정리 할인 행사에 함께해 주셔서 감사합니다! 귀하의 제품이 영업일 기준 3일 내에 배송될 것입니다.

| 제품 번호 | 설명 | 수량 | 합산 금액 |
|---|---|---|---|
| 3950 | 블루 체크무늬 시트 세트 (퀸) | 1 | 15.99달러 |
| 3210 | 블루 체크무늬 베갯잇 (2장 1세트) | 1 | 3.75달러 |
| 9442 | 베이지 플랫 시트 (퀸) | 2 | 13.98달러 |
| 8674 | 블루 플랫 시트 (트윈) | 1 | 4.95달러 |
| 1041 | 라벤더 슬립 스프레이 (판촉 코드: THX05) | 1 | 0달러 |
| | | | [184] **소계: 38.67달러** |
| | | | **배송비: 5달러** |
| | | | 총액: 43.67달러 |

[183] **이 주문서의 제품은 일반 구매 제품보다 더 엄격한 반품 정책을 적용받는다는 점에 유의하시기 바랍니다.**

[185(B)] **저희가 새로운 패턴을 자주 출시하므로,** 저희 웹사이트를 곧 다시 방문하시기 바랍니다!

어휘 confirmation 확인(서) participate in ~에 참가하다 checkered 체크무늬의 flat 평평한 be subject to+명사 ~을 적용 받다, ~의 대상이 되다 strict 엄격한 policy 정책, 방침 release 출시하다

## 181 세부 사항

번역 엘우드 씨는 왜 2월 11일에 주문하는 것을 추천하는가?
(A) 제품 카탈로그를 받기 위해
(B) 긴 배송 기간을 피하기 위해
(C) 보너스 선물을 받기 위해
(D) 새 침구 패턴을 사용해 보기 위해

해설 엘우드 씨는 첫 번째 이메일의 발신자이다. 이메일 초반부에 행사가 2월 11일부터 진행한다(from February 11 to 24)고 했고, 중반부에 할인 행사 첫째 날에 주문하는 사람들은 새 라벤더 슬립 스프레이 50ml 병을 무료로 받을 것이니 꼭 내일 쇼핑하라(Anyone who places an order on the first day of the sale will receive a free 50 ml. bottle of our new Lavender Sleep Spray, so be sure to shop tomorrow ~)고 했다. 따라서 2월 11일에 주문하면 무료 선물을 받는다는 뜻이므로 (C)가 정답이다.

어휘 avoid 피하다

> **Paraphrasing**
> 지문의 a free 50 ml. bottle ~ → 정답의 a bonus gift

## 182 추론

번역 잭슨 씨에 대해 암시된 것은?
(A) 문라이트 침구회사의 단골 고객이다.
(B) 킹사이즈 침대를 소유하고 있다.
(C) 오직 특정 색의 침구만 구매한다.
(D) 2월 12일에 물건을 받을 것이다.

해설 잭슨 씨가 받은 첫 번째 이메일의 하단에 이 이메일은 작년에 자주 구매한 고객들에게 발송되었다(This e-mail has been sent to customers who have made frequent purchases in the past year)고 했으므로 (A)가 정답이다.

어휘 regular customer 단골 고객 own 소유하다

> **Paraphrasing**
> 지문의 customers who have made frequent purchases → 정답의 a regular ~ customer

## 183 Not / True

번역 잭슨 씨가 주문한 제품에 대해 언급된 것은?
(A) 어떤 사유로든 교환될 수 있다.
(B) 모두 체크무늬로 되어 있다.
(C) 별도의 상자에 담겨 도착할 수 있다.
(D) 다른 반품 정책 가이드라인을 따른다.

해설 잭슨 씨가 받은 두 번째 이메일의 하단에 그 주문서의 제품이 일반 구매 제품보다 더 엄격한 반품 정책을 적용받는다(~ the items in this order are subject to a stricter return policy than regular purchases)고 쓰여 있으므로 다른 제품과는 반품 정책이 다름을 알 수 있다. 따라서 (D)가 정답이다.

어휘 exchange 교환하다 separate 별도의, 분리된 follow 따르다

> **Paraphrasing**
> 지문의 are subject to a stricter return policy than regular purchases
> → 정답의 follow different return policy guidelines

## 184 연계

번역 어떻게 하면 잭슨 씨는 특별 판촉 혜택을 이용할 수 있었겠는가?
(A) 제품 후기를 작성함으로써
(B) 주문에 더 많은 비용을 지출함으로써
(C) 다른 날에 주문함으로써
(D) 일부 새로 출시된 상품을 사용해 봄으로써

해설 첫 번째 이메일의 후반부에 50달러 이상 소비하는 고객들은 무료 배송 서비스를 받는다(customers who spend $50 or more will receive free shipping)고 했는데, 잭슨 씨의 주문 확인 메일인 두 번째 이메일의 도표 밑에 소계가 38.67달러(Subtotal: $38.67), 배송비가 5달러(Shipping fee: $5.00)로 표기되어 있다. 잭슨 씨가 주문을 더 했으면 무료 배송 서비스를 받을 수 있었던 것이므로 (B)가 정답이다.

어휘 take advantage of ~을 이용하다 merchandise 상품

## 185 Not / True

번역 문라이트 침구회사와 관련해 사실이 아닌 것은?
(A) 다양한 사이즈의 침구를 제공한다.
(B) 주기적으로 재고 물품을 변경한다.
(C) 침구와 어울리는 커튼을 판매한다.
(D) 올해 재고 정리 할인 행사가 더 길다.

해설 첫 번째 이메일의 초반부에 보통 할인 행사를 일주일 진행하지만 올해는 2주 동안 진행한다(Normally we hold our sale for just one week, but we're running it for two weeks this year)고 언급하는 부분에서 (D)를, 첫 번째 이메일의 중반부에 침대 사이즈와 상관없이 아주 마음에 드는 제품을 찾을 것(whether you have a small twin bed, a king-sized bed, or anything in between, we're sure you'll find something you love)이라고 알리는 부분에서 (A)를, 그리고 두 번째 이메일의 마지막 문장에 자주 새 패턴을 출시한다(we release new patterns frequently)고 말하는 부분에서 (B)를 각각 확인할 수 있다. 하지만, 커튼 판매와 관련된 정보는 제시되어 있지 않으므로 (C)가 정답이다.

어휘 regularly 주기적으로 match 어울리다, 일치하다

> **Paraphrasing**
> 지문의 Normally ~ for just one week, but ~ for two weeks this year → 보기 (D)의 is longer this year
> 지문의 a small twin bed, a king-sized bed, or anything in between → 보기 (A)의 different sizes
> 지문의 we release new patterns frequently → 보기 (B)의 changes its inventory regularly

### 186-190 이메일+제품 정보+거래 내역서

발신: k.wells@rivera-grill.com
수신: service@boisvertsuppliers.com
날짜: 10월 16일
제목: 접시 (제품 번호 L8916)

안녕하세요,

저는 [186] **새 소유주의 감독하에** 저희 레스토랑 실내에 일련의 업그레이드 작업을 계속 진행하고 있으며, 이 개선 작업의 일환으로 귀사에 새 접시 세트를 주문했습니다. 유감스럽게도, 주문한 물건이 오늘 오전에 도착했을 때, 무려 11개나 되는 런드 스퀘어 만찬용 접시(제품 번호 L8916)에 금이 가 있거나 깨져 있거나 두 가지가 다 있는 경우도 있는 것을 보고 실망했습니다.

[187, 189] **보아버트 서플라이어즈 사에서 추가 비용 없이 동일한 종류의 손상되지 않은 접시 11개를 발송하고, 수요일까지 도착하도록 배송을 신속히 처리해 주시기를 요청합니다.** 사용 가능한 접시를 받기까지 2주 더 기다리라는 것은 부당합니다. [189] **이 기한을 맞출 수 없다면, 저희가 다른 곳에서 거래할 수 있도록 접시 두 팩의 비용을 환불해 주시기 바랍니다.**

케네스 웰스, 총지배인
리베라 그릴

어휘 under the direction of ~의 감독하에, ~의 관리하에 proprietor 소유주 improvement 개선, 향상 unfortunately 유감스럽게도, 안타깝게도 be disappointed to ~해서 실망하다 crack 균열, 금 chip 깨진 부분, 이빨 빠진 부분 undamaged 손상되지 않은 expedite 더 신속히 처리하다 deadline 마감 기한 refund 환불해 주다

http://www.emeryrestaurantwarehouse.com/dishware/348923

에머리 레스토랑 웨어하우스

| 홈 | 제품 카테고리 | 회사 소개 | 고객 지원 |
|---|---|---|---|

런드 스퀘어 만찬용 접시

런드 사는 고품질 도자기 식기로 알려져 있으며, 스퀘어 만찬용 접시도 예외는 아닙니다. [188] **각이 뚜렷한 디자인과 밝은 흰색의 이 접시들은 사람들의 시선을 사로잡으며 어떤 요리든 보완해줍니다.** 식기세척기 사용이 가능한 이 제품은 활기 넘치는 레스토랑에 훌륭한 자산이 됩니다. 이 접시는 6개들이 묶음으로 출시되며, 네 가지의 편리한 크기로 구매 가능합니다.

- 9인치 (제품 코드 5031S), 25.25달러
- [190] **10인치 (제품 코드 5033R), 27.4달러**
- 11인치 (제품 코드 5043L), 29.7달러
- 12인치 (제품 코드 5053XL), 32.05달러

어휘 category 카테고리, 범주 porcelain 도자기 exception 예외 bold 대담한 angle 각도 eye-catching 시선을 사로잡는 complement 보완하다 entrée 주 요리 asset 자산, 재산 convenient 편리한 available 구매 가능한, 이용 가능한

[189] **에머리 레스토랑 웨어하우스**
거래 내역서

주문 날짜: 10월 17일
주문 번호: 45731

배송 / 비용 청구: 케네스 웰스
리베라 그릴
스위처 드라이브 280
버니어, TX 78046

| 제품 코드 | 제품명 | 수량 | 개당 가격 | 총액 |
|---|---|---|---|---|
| [189, 190] 5033R | **런드 스퀘어 만찬용 접시** | 2 | 27.4달러 | 54.8달러 |
| | | | | 특급 배송: 20달러 |
| | | | | 소계: 74.8달러 |
| | | | | 세금 (8%): 5.98달러 |
| | | | | 총계: 80.78달러 |

TEST 7

어휘 invoice 거래 내역서 quantity 수량 unit (물품 등의) 한 개

### 186 세부 사항

번역 이메일에 따르면, 리베라 그릴은 최근 무엇을 했는가?
(A) 두 번째 지점을 열었다.
(B) 메뉴에 품목을 추가했다.
(C) 새로운 소유주의 관리를 받게 되었다.
(D) 식사 공간을 확장했다.

해설 이메일 첫 단락에 새 소유주의 감독하에(under the direction of our new proprietor) 레스토랑 실내 업그레이드 작업을 하고 있다고 했으므로 (C)가 정답이다.

어휘 location 지점, 위치 ownership 소유권 expand 확장하다

Paraphrasing
지문의 under the direction of our new proprietor
→ 정답의 under new ownership

### 187 주제 / 목적

번역 이메일의 목적은 무엇인가?
(A) 교체 식기를 받는 것
(B) 유사 제품 제안을 요청하는 것
(C) 손상된 접시의 수리에 관해 묻는 것
(D) 배송 서비스 선택에 관한 조언을 받는 것

해설 이메일 두 번째 단락에 보아버트 서플라이어즈 사에서 추가 비용 없이 동일한 종류의 손상되지 않은 접시 11개를 발송하고, 수요일까지 도착하도록 배송을 신속히 처리해 주기를 요청한다(I must ask that Boisvert Suppliers send 11 undamaged plates of the same type at no additional charge, and expedite the shipment so that it arrives by Wednesday)는 말이 쓰여 있으므로 (A)가 정답이다.

어휘 obtain 얻다, 획득하다 replacement 교체(품) suggestion 제안, 의견 similar 유사한

### 188 Not / True

번역 제품 정보에서, 런드 스퀘어 만찬용 접시에 대해 언급된 것은?
(A) 여러 색상으로 출시된다.
(B) 해당 브랜드의 베스트셀러 제품이다.
(C) 전자레인지에 사용해도 안전하다.
(D) 음식의 외관을 돋보이게 해준다.

해설 제품 정보 첫 단락에 사람들의 시선을 사로잡으며 어떤 요리든 보완해 준다(provide an eye-catching frame that complements any entrée)고 했다. 이는 음식의 외관을 돋보이게 해 준다는 뜻이므로 (D)가 정답이다.

어휘 enhance 향상시키다, 강화하다 appearance 모습, 외관

Paraphrasing
지문의 complements any entrée
→ 정답의 enhance the appearance of food

### 189 연계

번역 보아버트 서플라이어즈 사에 대해 암시된 것은?
(A) 다른 회사에 인수되었다.
(B) 빠른 배송은 20달러의 요금을 부과한다.
(C) 런드 식기 가격을 인상했다.
(D) 웰스 씨의 결제 금액 일부를 환불해 주었다.

해설 이메일 두 번째 단락에 웰스 씨가 보아버트 서플라이어즈 사에 손상된 접시의 교체 제품을 수요일까지 보내 달라(I must ask that Boisvert Suppliers send 11 undamaged plates of the same type ~)고 요청하면서 그렇게 할 수 없으면 다른 곳과 거래할 수 있도록 환불해 달라(If you cannot meet this deadline, please refund the cost of two packs of the plates so that I can take our business elsewhere)고 했다. 이와 관련해, 거래 내역서에 다른 업체인 에머리 레스토랑 웨어하우스(EMERY RESTAURANT WAREHOUSE)에서 동일한 접시 제품(Lund Square Dinner Plates)을 구입한 내역이 기재되어 있어 웰스 씨가 보아버트 서플라이어즈 사에서 해당 비용을 환불받고 다른 업체에서 구입했음을 추론할 수 있으므로 (D)가 정답이다.

어휘 acquire 인수하다, 획득하다 raise 인상하다, 높이다

### 190 연계

번역 웰스 씨는 에머리 레스토랑 웨어하우스에서 어떤 사이즈의 접시를 주문했는가?
(A) 9인치
(B) 10인치
(C) 11인치
(D) 12인치

해설 거래 내역서에 구입한 제품의 코드가 5033R로 쓰여 있는데, 이는 제품 정보 하단에 10인치 제품의 코드(10 inches (Item Code 5033R))로 표기되어 있으므로 (B)가 정답이다.

### 191-195 이메일+공지+이메일

수신: 베로니카 헤일 <vhale@castillosouthwest.com>
발신: 나탈리 르윈 <natalie@biz-builder.com>
날짜: 8월 12일
제목: 워크숍과 도서

헤일 씨께,

9월 3일에 있을 가네시 카말의 워크숍 등록이 확정되었습니다. 온라인 워크숍이 아닌, [192] **대면 워크숍에 등록하셨으므로**, 음식 관련 제한이 있으면 알려 주시기 바랍니다. 그러면 휴식 시간을 위한 다과를 준비하는 데 도움이 될 것입니다. 저희가 아래와 같이 카말 씨의 도서 결제 비용도 처리해 드렸는데, 20퍼센트 할인되며, [191] **이는 도서들이 워크숍 세션과 관련이 있기 때문입니다**.

| 제목 | 가격 | 할인된 가격 | 소계 |
|---|---|---|---|
| [191] **<기업적, 사회적 책임> X 1** | 16달러 | 12.8달러 | 12.8달러 |
| [191,195] **<효과적인 보도 자료 작성> X 1** | 25달러 | 20달러 | **20달러** |

| 191 <홍보에 있어서 위기 관리> X 1 | 26달러 | 20.8달러 | 20.8달러 |
|---|---|---|---|
| 191 <소통의 목적 명확히 하기> X 1 | 21달러 | 16.8달러 | 16.8달러 |
| 총액 70.4달러가 -8405로 끝나는 신용카드로 청구됩니다. | | | |

행사장에서 뵙기를 고대합니다!

나탈리 르윈
관리 책임, 비즈-빌더

어휘 registration 등록 confirm 확정하다, 확인해 주다 register for ~에 등록하다 in-person 직접 방문하는, 직접 가는 dietary 음식물의, 식사의 restriction 제한 refreshments 간식, 다과 break 휴식 시간 process 처리하다 be eligible for ~에 대한 자격이 있다 relevant to+명사 ~와 관련된 session 세션, (특정 활동을 위한) 시간 corporate 기업의 responsibility 책임 effective 효과적인 press release 보도 자료 crisis 위기 public relations 홍보 clarify 분명히 말하다 objective 목적 charge 청구 요금

워크숍 참가자들께 전하는 공지

**193 유감스럽게도, 저희 질의응답 페이지가 작동하지 않고 있으며, 9월 3일까지 고쳐지지 않을 수 있습니다. 온라인 참가자들께서는 여전히 행사 중에 natalie@biz-builder.com으로 질문을 제출하실 수 있으며,** 저희가 적절한 시기에 가네시 카말에게 전달해 드릴 것입니다. 온라인 참가자들은 늦어도 9월 1일까지는 빠른 배송으로 도서를 받으실 것이며, **192 다른 분들은 모두 등록 테이블에서 주문한 것을 받아가실 수 있습니다.**

어휘 participant 참가자 unfortunately 유감스럽게도 fix 바로잡다, 고치다 in a timely manner 제때, 때에 맞춰 note 유의하다, 주목하다 express shipping 특급 배송 collect 가져가다, 수거하다

수신: 래리 우스터 <lwooster@castillosouthwest.com>
발신: 베로니카 헤일 <vhale@castillosouthwest.com>
날짜: 9월 16일
제목: 가네시 카말의 도서

래리 씨께,

우리 신규 서비스의 출시와 관련해 보내 주신 파일에 감사드립니다. 만나서 더 깊이 있게 논의하고 싶은데, **194 발표 내용을 표현하는 방식을 개선할 수 있다고 생각하기 때문입니다. 195 제가 드린 가네시 카말의 책을 읽어 보실 시간이 있으셨는지 궁금합니다. 그 내용이 언론에 공식 성명서를 준비해 보낼 때 아주 유익할 것이라고 생각합니다.**

베로니카

어휘 launch 출시, 시작 further 더 깊이 있게, 한층 더 improve 개선하다, 향상시키다 announcement 발표 (내용), 알림 phrase 표현하다 content 내용(물) official 공식적인, 정식의 statement 성명(서)

## 191 추론

번역 9월 3일에 있을 워크숍 주제가 무엇일 것 같은가?
(A) 그래픽 디자인
(B) 은퇴 계획
(C) 홍보
(D) 소프트웨어 개발

해설 첫 번째 이메일 첫 단락에 도서들이 워크숍 세션과 관련 있다(they are relevant to the workshop's sessions)는 말이 쓰여 있고, 그 아래에 표기된 도서들의 제목이 <기업적, 사회적 책임(*Corporate and Social Responsibility*)>, <효과적인 보도 자료 작성(*Writing Effective Press Releases*)>, <홍보에 있어서 위기 관리(*Crisis Management in Public Relations*)>, <소통의 목적 명확히 하기(*Clarifying Communications Objectives*)>라고 각각 쓰여 있다. 이 도서들은 모두 홍보와 가장 관련이 있어 보이므로 (C)가 정답이다.

## 192 연계

번역 헤일 씨에 대해 암시된 것은?
(A) 웹페이지에서 문제를 발견했다.
(B) 부분 환불을 받을 것이다.
(C) 빠른 배송을 위해 추가 비용을 지불했다.
(D) 직접 자신의 책을 받아갔다.

해설 첫 번째 이메일 첫 단락에 헤일 씨가 대면 워크숍에 등록했다(you have registered for the in-person workshop)고 쓰여 있고, 공지 마지막 부분에는 온라인 참가자 외의 다른 사람은 모두 등록 테이블에서 주문한 것을 받아갈 수 있다(everyone else can collect their orders from the registration table)고 써 있다. 따라서 방문 참가하는 워크숍에 등록한 헤일 씨는 주문한 도서를 현장에서 직접 받아갔다는 것을 알 수 있으므로 (D)가 정답이다.

어휘 notice 알아차리다, 주목하다 partial 부분적인 refund 환불(액) pay extra 추가 비용을 지불하다 pick up 가져가다, 가져오다

## 193 주제 / 목적

번역 공지의 목적은 무엇인가?
(A) 워크숍에 관한 의견을 모으는 것
(B) 카말 씨 도서의 판매를 촉진하는 것
(C) 문제에 대한 해결책을 제공하는 것
(D) 위치 변경을 설명하는 것

해설 공지 시작 부분에 질의응답 페이지가 작동하지 않고 있다는 문제점과 함께 온라인 참가자들이 여전히 행사 중에 natalie@biz-builder.com으로 질문을 제출할 수 있다(Unfortunately, our question-and-answer page is not working, ~ Online participants can still submit questions to natalie@biz-builder.com during the event ~)는 해결책을 알리고 있으므로 (C)가 정답이다.

어휘 gather 모으다 feedback 의견 promote 촉진하다, 증진하다 solution 해결책

TEST 7

## 194 세부 사항

번역 두 번째 이메일에서, 헤일 씨는 무엇을 바꾸도록 제안하는가?
(A) 문서의 표현
(B) 서비스 출시일
(C) 직무 설명서 내용
(D) 저장된 파일의 폴더

해설 두 번째 이메일 초반부에 헤일 씨가 발표 내용을 표현하는 방식을 개선할 수 있다고 생각한다(I think we can improve the way the announcement is phrased)고 했는데, 이는 발표에서 사용하는 표현을 바꾸자는 말이므로 (A)가 정답이다.

어휘 wording 표현, 단어 선택 employee manual 직무 설명서

> **Paraphrasing**
> 지문의 the way the announcement is phrased
> → 정답의 wording of a document

## 195 연계

번역 헤일 씨는 우스터 씨에게 준 책에 대해 얼마를 청구받았는가?
(A) 12.8달러
(B) 20달러
(C) 20.8달러
(D) 16.8달러

해설 헤일 씨가 우스터 씨에게 준 책이 언급되는 두 번째 이메일 마지막 부분에 그 내용이 언론에 공식 성명서를 준비해 보낼 때 아주 유익할 것이라고 생각한다(~ I believe its contents will be very helpful when preparing and sending official statements to the media)고 쓰여 있다. 첫 번째 이메일에 제시된 도서들 중에서, 이러한 내용에 해당되는 제목이 <효과적인 보도 자료 작성(*Writing Effective Press Releases*)>이며, 이 책의 소계가 20달러로 표기되어 있으므로 (B)가 정답이다.

어휘 charge 청구하다, 부과하다

### 196-200 문자 메시지+기사+후기

**[197] 발신: 애덤 실바 [오전 10시 49분]**
**[197] 수신: 프리다 랜드빅**

안녕하세요! [197] **환기 전문가들과 제가 지금 레스토랑 현장 조사를 하고 있어요.** 건물 구조상 시 규정을 준수하는 주방을 설치하는 게 매우 쉬울 거라고 말씀하시네요. 우리가 우려했던 것처럼 배기용 덕트를 지붕까지 연결하지 않아도 될 거예요. [196] **그래서 우리가 프로젝트의 이 부분을 위해 확보해 놓은 10,000달러로 작업 비용을 충분히 충당하고도 남을 겁니다. 이에 대해 우려하셨다는 걸 알고 있어서 곧장 말씀드리고 싶었습니다.** 끝마치는 대로 자세한 내용을 전화로 알려 드리겠습니다.

어휘 ventilation 통풍, 환기 on-site 현장의 walk-through 조사 structure 구조(물) set up 설치하다 comply with ~을 준수하다 regulation 규정, 규제 route 보내다, 발송하다 exhaust duct 배기 덕트 all the way to+명사 ~까지 쭉 이어서 fear 우려하다 set aside 확보하다 cover 충당하다

셔먼 가 명소를 인수하는 새 레스토랑

글래드니 (8월 7일)—[197] **셔먼 가 560에 위치한 130년 된 주택인 리브스 하우스가 이달 말 개업 예정인 레스토랑으로 개조되고 있다.** [197, 198] **이 레스토랑의 공동 소유주인 프리다 랜드빅과 애덤 실바가 이 주택을 지은 가문의 마지막 후손인 매리언 리브스로부터 건물을 매입했다.** 이 식당의 이름은 앞쪽 잔디밭에 서 있는 큰 나무를 따서 "더 오크 비스트로"가 될 것이다.

[199] **이 우아한 회색 주택과 이곳의 부지는 그 오랜 역사에 걸쳐 잘 유지 관리되어 왔다.** 실바는 이 건물이 레스토랑 규정을 충족하기 위해 약간의 업그레이드가 필요했지만 수리 작업은 거의 없었다고 말한다.

개업하면, 더 오크 비스트로는 랜드빅 씨가 노르웨이에서 보낸 어린 시절에서 영감을 받은 점심 및 저녁 식사 요리를 제공할 것이다. [200] **25명이 앉을 수 있는 실내 좌석은 연중 이용이 가능할 것이며, 6월에서 9월까지는 앞쪽 잔디밭에 추가 좌석이 제공될 것이다.**

추가 정보는 www.theoakbistro.com에서 찾아볼 수 있다.

어휘 take over 인수하다, 이어받다 landmark 명소, 주요 지형지물 located 위치한 convert 개조하다, 전환하다 set to ~할 예정인 property 건물, 부동산 descendant 후손 eatery 음식점 name 이름 짓다 grounds 부지, 구내 well-maintained 잘 유지 관리된 satisfy 충족하다 serve (음식을) 제공하다 inspire 영감을 주다 available 이용 가능한 year-round 연중, 일년 내내

http://www.you-review.com

| 홈 | 레스토랑 | 홈 서비스 | 기타 |
|---|---|---|---|

더 오크 비스트로 (글래드니)

★★★★☆
후기 작성자: 키스 오웬스

[200] **저는 몇몇 친구들과 10월 말에 점심 식사를 위해 더 오크 비스트로에 들렀습니다.** 이곳은 아름답고 고풍스러운 분위기를 지니고 있으며, 서비스는 훌륭합니다. 저희 서비스 담당자였던 조이스는 메뉴에 관한 모든 질문에 기꺼이 대답해 주셨습니다. 이는 중요한 부분이었는데, 저희들 중 누구도 노르웨이 음식에 익숙하지 않았기 때문이었습니다. 다행히, 저희는 꽤 맛있다는 걸 알게 되어 기뻤습니다. 저는 특히 생선 수프를 추천하는데, 부드럽고 맛있습니다. 제가 이곳에 별점 5개를 주지 않는 유일한 이유는 1인분 양이 좀 적기 때문입니다.

어휘 stop by ~에 들르다 old-fashioned 고풍스러운, 옛날 방식의 atmosphere 분위기 unfamiliar with ~에 익숙하지 않은 rating 평점, 등급 portion 1인분

## 196 주제 / 목적

번역 문자 메시지의 목적은?
(A) 프로젝트 일정 변경을 제안하는 것
(B) 할당된 예산에 대해 안심시키는 것
(C) 안전 규정 위반을 지적하는 것
(D) 개조 공사 현장에서의 회의를 마련하는 것

해설 문자 메시지 후반부에 프로젝트를 위해 확보해 놓은 10,000달러로 작업 비용을 충분히 충당할 수 있다(the $10,000 we set aside for ~ enough to cover the work)고 하면서 그에 대해 우려했다는 걸 알고 있어서 곧장 말하고 싶었다(I wanted to tell you ~ you were concerned about that)고 전하고 있다. 이는 예산에 대해 우려할 필요가 없다고 안심시키기 위한 말이므로 (B)가 정답이다.

어휘 amend 수정하다 reassurance 안도감, 안도시키는 말 allocate 할당하다 budget 예산 point out 지적하다 violation 위반 arrange 마련하다, 조치하다 renovation 개조, 보수

> **Paraphrasing**
> 지문의 the $10,000 we set aside for this part of the project → 정답의 an allocated budget

## 197 연계

번역 실바 씨는 어디에서 문자 메시지를 보냈는가?
(A) 역사적인 주택
(B) 오래된 학교 건물
(C) 컨설팅 회사 사무실
(D) 시 정부 기관

해설 문자 메시지 초반부에 실바가 현재 레스토랑 현장 조사를 하고 있다(~ I are doing our on-site walk-through of the restaurant now)고 알리고 있다. 이 레스토랑에 대해, 기사의 첫 단락과 두 번째 단락에 130년 된 주택을 레스토랑으로 개조한다(Reeves House, the 130-year-old home, ~ is being converted into a restaurant ~)는 말과 레스토랑 공동 소유주인 랜드빅 씨와 실바가 그 주택을 매입했다(The restaurant's co-owners, Frida Landvik and Adam Silva, purchased the property ~)고 쓰여 있다. 따라서 오래된 주택을 레스토랑으로 개조하는 현장에서 문자 메시지를 보냈다는 것을 알 수 있으므로 (A)가 정답이다.

> **Paraphrasing**
> 지문의 the 130-year-old home
> → 정답의 A historic house

## 198 추론

번역 기사에서 리브스 씨에 대해 암시된 것은?
(A) 노르웨이에서 자랐다.
(B) 일부 조경을 디자인했다.
(C) 어떤 부동산의 전 소유주였다.
(D) 글래드니 시 관계자이다.

해설 기사 두 번째 단락에 레스토랑의 공동 소유주인 프리다 랜드빅과 애덤 실바가 매리언 리브스로부터 주택을 매입했다(The restaurant's co-owners, Frida Landvik and Adam Silva, purchased the property from Marian Reeves, ~)고 했다. 따라서 리브스 씨가 해당 주택의 이전 소유주임을 알 수 있으므로 (C)가 정답이다.

어휘 landscaping 조경 former 전 ~의, 이전의 official 관계자

## 199 Not / True

번역 기사에서 셔먼 가 560의 건물에 대해 언급하는 것은?
(A) 좋은 상태로 유지되어 왔다.
(B) 여러 차례 매각되었다.
(C) 숲 근처에 있다.
(D) 넓은 주차 구역이 있다.

해설 기사의 세 번째 단락에 우아한 회색 주택과 부지가 오랜 역사에 걸쳐 잘 유지 관리되어 왔다(The graceful gray house and its grounds have been well-maintained during their long history)고 쓰여 있으므로 (A)가 정답이다.

> **Paraphrasing**
> 지문의 have been well-maintained
> → 정답의 has been kept in good condition

## 200 연계

번역 후기에서 유추할 수 있는 것은?
(A) 레스토랑 메뉴가 변경되었다.
(B) 레스토랑 가격이 합리적이다.
(C) 오웬스 씨가 음식을 오래 기다렸다.
(D) 오웬스 씨가 레스토랑 실내에 앉았다.

해설 후기 첫 번째 문장에서 작성자인 오웬스 씨는 10월 말에 더 오크 비스트로에 들렀다(Some friends and I stopped by The Oak Bistro for lunch at the end of October)고 했고, 기사 네 번째 단락에서 실내 좌석은 연중 이용 가능하지만, 6월에서 9월까지는 앞쪽 잔디밭에 추가 좌석이 제공될 것(~ with additional seating on the front lawn offered from June through September)이라고 했다. 오웬스 씨가 들른 10월에는 실내 좌석만 가능하므로 실내에 앉았다는 것을 유추할 수 있다. 따라서 (D)가 정답이다.

어휘 reasonable 합리적인, 가격이 알맞은

# TEST 8

| | | | | |
|---|---|---|---|---|
| 101 (B) | 102 (B) | 103 (D) | 104 (B) | 105 (A) |
| 106 (D) | 107 (C) | 108 (D) | 109 (C) | 110 (A) |
| 111 (A) | 112 (B) | 113 (C) | 114 (D) | 115 (C) |
| 116 (B) | 117 (A) | 118 (A) | 119 (B) | 120 (C) |
| 121 (D) | 122 (B) | 123 (C) | 124 (A) | 125 (A) |
| 126 (D) | 127 (D) | 128 (C) | 129 (D) | 130 (B) |
| 131 (B) | 132 (A) | 133 (D) | 134 (C) | 135 (A) |
| 136 (D) | 137 (C) | 138 (C) | 139 (D) | 140 (B) |
| 141 (B) | 142 (A) | 143 (C) | 144 (D) | 145 (A) |
| 146 (D) | 147 (B) | 148 (D) | 149 (A) | 150 (C) |
| 151 (B) | 152 (A) | 153 (C) | 154 (B) | 155 (C) |
| 156 (B) | 157 (C) | 158 (B) | 159 (A) | 160 (B) |
| 161 (D) | 162 (A) | 163 (C) | 164 (A) | 165 (B) |
| 166 (D) | 167 (D) | 168 (D) | 169 (C) | 170 (A) |
| 171 (D) | 172 (C) | 173 (D) | 174 (C) | 175 (A) |
| 176 (C) | 177 (B) | 178 (A) | 179 (C) | 180 (D) |
| 181 (D) | 182 (A) | 183 (C) | 184 (B) | 185 (B) |
| 186 (B) | 187 (B) | 188 (B) | 189 (D) | 190 (B) |
| 191 (B) | 192 (B) | 193 (C) | 194 (D) | 195 (A) |
| 196 (A) | 197 (C) | 198 (D) | 199 (A) | 200 (B) |

## PART 5

### 101 동사 자리 _ 관계대명사절

번역 테이드 산은 스페인에서 유일하게 3,500미터 이상 솟아 있는 산봉우리이다.

해설 관계대명사 that이 이끄는 절이 선행사인 peak를 수식하는 구조인데, that절에 동사가 없으므로 빈칸은 동사 자리이다. that절에 주어 또한 없으므로 that이 주격 관계대명사인 것을 알 수 있는데, 주격 관계대명사절의 동사의 수는 선행사와 일치시키므로 peak와 수가 일치하는 단수 동사 (B) rises가 정답이다.

어휘 peak 산봉우리, 꼭대기 rise 솟다

### 102 인칭 대명사 _ 재귀대명사

번역 요리사 지망생들은 고품질 주방용 칼 세트를 갖추고 있어야 한다.

해설 빈칸은 동사 equip의 목적어 자리이므로, 대명사의 목적격이 들어가야 한다. (A) they는 주격이고, (C) their own은 소유격의 강조형, (D) their는 소유격이므로 모두 답이 될 수 없다. 빈칸에 들어갈 대명사가 가리키는 대상이 주어인 Aspiring chefs이므로 재귀대명사인 (B) themselves가 정답이다.

어휘 aspiring 지망하는, 장차 ~이 되려는 high-quality 고품질의

### 103 형용사 자리 _ 최상급

번역 하야시 씨는 전체 자문 위원회 중 가장 긴 경력을 보유하고 있다.

해설 빈칸은 명사 career history를 수식하는 형용사가 들어갈 자리이고, 비교 범위를 나타내는 「out of 복수 명사구」와 어울려 '전체 자문 위원회 중 가장 ~한 경력'을 뜻하는 최상급 표현을 구성해야 알맞으므로 최상급 형용사의 형태인 (D) longest가 정답이다. (A) long은 원급 형용사, (B) length(길이)는 명사, (C) longer는 비교급 형용사이므로 오답이다.

어휘 career history 경력, 이력 out of ~에서, ~ 중에서 entire 전체의 advisory committee 자문 위원회

### 104 전치사 자리 _ 명사구 목적어

번역 피트니스 센터를 포함한 웨스터 아파트의 모든 편의시설은 세입자들이 추가 비용 없이 이용할 수 있다.

해설 빈칸 앞에 주어(All of Wester Apartments' amenities)가, 뒤에 동사(are)가 있으므로, 빈칸에는 명사구 the fitness center를 목적어로 취할 수 있는 전치사가 들어가 주어와 동사 사이에 전치사구가 삽입된 구조가 되어야 한다. 또한, '피트니스 센터를 포함한, 웨스터 아파트의 모든 편의시설'을 의미해야 자연스러우므로 '~을 포함한'을 뜻하는 전치사 (B) including이 정답이다. (A) sometimes(때때로)와 (D) also(또한, ~도)는 부사이며, (C) just as(꼭 ~처럼)는 접속사로 쓰이거나 「just as A as B」와 같은 형태로 동급 비교에서 쓰인다.

어휘 amenities 편의시설 available 이용 가능한
at no extra charge 추가 비용 없이

### 105 부사 어휘

번역 고객들은 카로 씨가 시장 동향에 대해 틀린 적이 거의 없다는 점을 높이 평가한다.

해설 be동사와 형용사 보어 사이에 위치할 수 있는 부사가 필요하며, '틀린 적이 거의 없다는 점을 높이 평가한다'가 가장 자연스러운 의미이므로 '좀처럼 ~ 않다'를 뜻하는 (A) rarely가 정답이다.

어휘 appreciate 진가를 알아보다 incorrect 틀린, 부정확한 trend 동향, 추세 apart 떨어져, 따로

### 106 접속사 자리 _ 등위 접속사

번역 저희 도서관은 파울러 사이언스 온라인의 제휴 기관이므로, 도서관 고객들은 그곳의 대화형 수업을 무료로 이용할 수 있습니다.

해설 빈칸 앞뒤로 두 개의 완전한 절이 있으므로 두 절을 연결해 줄 접속사가 필요하다. 그리고 앞의 절과 뒤의 절이 원인과 결과의 관계이므로 '~이므로, 그래서' 등을 뜻하는 등위 접속사 (D) so가 정답이다. (A) once(~하는 대로, ~하자마자)는 부사절 접속사이지만 의미가 어울리지 않는다.

어휘 affiliate 제휴 기관, 계열사 patron 고객, 손님 access 이용하다 interactive 대화형의, 상호 작용하는

## 107 명사 어휘

번역 CEO의 연설은 회사의 미래에 대한 종합적인 비전을 제시했다.

해설 연설을 통해 회사의 미래에 대해 종합적으로 제시할 수 있는 것을 나타낼 명사가 필요하므로 '비전, 미래상' 등을 뜻하는 (C) vision이 정답이다.

어휘 present 제시하다, 발표하다 comprehensive 종합적인 measure 측정(치), 조치 collection 수거, 수집(품) deadline 마감 기한

## 108 전치사 어휘

번역 공청회가 있는 경우를 제외하면 오직 승인된 직원만 의회 회의실 내부에 출입할 수 있다.

해설 빈칸 뒤에 있는 when이 이끄는 명사절을 목적어로 취하는 전치사 자리로, '공청회가 있는 경우를 제외하면 승인된 직원만 출입할 수 있다'는 의미가 되어야 자연스러우므로 '~을 제외하고'를 뜻하는 전치사 (D) except가 정답이다.

어휘 authorized 승인된, 인가된 be allowed inside ~ 내부에 들어가도록 허용되다 public meeting 공청회 given ~을 고려해 볼 때

## 109 명사 자리 _ 전치사의 목적어

번역 알바 재단의 지원을 받는 단체들은 평가를 위해 연간 보조금 보고서를 제출해야 한다.

해설 전치사 for 뒤에 빈칸이 있으므로 전치사의 목적어인 명사가 들어갈 자리이다. 따라서 명사 (C) evaluation(평가)이 정답이다.

어휘 organization 단체, 기관 annual 연간의 grant 보조금 evaluate 평가하다 evaluative 평가하는

## 110 형용사 어휘

번역 공유 오피스를 이용하는 직원들은 동료의 사생활 보호에 대한 요구를 염두에 두어야 한다.

해설 빈칸 앞뒤에 위치한 be동사 및 전치사 of와 어울려 쓰이는 형용사가 필요하며, '동료의 사생활 보호에 대한 요구를 염두에 두어야 한다'를 의미해야 자연스러우므로 '~을 염두에 두다, 유념하다'를 뜻하는 be mindful of를 구성하는 (A) mindful이 정답이다.

어휘 occupy (공간을) 이용하다, 점유하다 shared 공용의, 공유된 coworker 동료 privacy 사생활 willing 기꺼이 하는 reasonable 합리적인 independent 독립적인

## 111 동사 자리 _ 수 일치

번역 저희 자격증 프로그램 수료자들은 일반적으로 직장 생활에 빠르게 적응합니다.

해설 문장에 동사가 없으므로 빈칸은 동사 자리이며, 주어 Graduates가 복수이므로 복수 주어와 수가 일치되는 (A) adapt(적응하다)가 정답이다. (B) adapts와 (D) is adapted는 단수 동사이며, (C) adapting은 동명사 또는 현재분사이므로 오답이다.

어휘 graduate 수료자, 졸업생 certification 인증, 증명(서)

## 112 형용사 어휘

번역 자신의 이력서를 향상시키기를 바라는 학생들은 인턴 과정에 큰 관심을 갖는다.

해설 명사 interest(관심, 흥미)를 수식하는 자리로 관심의 정도를 나타낼 형용사가 필요하며, '큰 관심을 갖는다'를 의미해야 자연스러우므로 '큰, 대단한' 등을 뜻하는 (B) great이 정답이다. 「be of interest to 사람」은 '~에게는 흥미가 있다'는 의미이다.

어휘 improve 향상시키다, 개선하다 résumé 이력서 relevant 관련된 farthest 가장 먼; 가장 멀리 minimal 최소의

## 113 전치사 어휘

번역 교통 상황을 알기 쉽게 전달하기 위해 저희 어플은 혼잡한 정도에 따라 도로에 색상을 부여합니다.

해설 빈칸 뒤에 위치한 명사구 their levels of congestion이 '혼잡한 정도'를 의미하는데, 이는 도로에 색상을 부여하는 기준에 해당하므로 '~에 근거하여'라는 의미로 기준이나 근거를 나타낼 때 사용하는 (C) based on이 정답이다.

어휘 communicate 전달하다, 소통하다 traffic 교통(량) assign 부여하다, 배정하다 congestion 혼잡 adjacent to + 명사 ~와 인접한

## 114 부정 대명사 _ neither

번역 출장 요리업체가 제안한 두 가지 디저트 옵션 모두 냉장 보관이 필요하지 않다.

해설 빈칸 뒤에 있는 「of the two 복수 명사」의 수식을 받을 수 있는 대명사가 필요하므로, two와 어울리는 말을 찾아야 한다. '둘 다 냉장 보관이 필요하다거나, 둘 다 필요하지 않다는 의미가 되어야 자연스러운데, (A) Every는 형용사이므로 뒤에 of가 바로 올 수 없고, (B) Those와 (C) Nothing은 two와 어울리지 않는다. 따라서 정답은 '둘 다 아닌'을 뜻하는 (D) Neither이다. 「Neither of the 복수 명사」 뒤에는 단수 동사와 복수 동사가 모두 가능하다.

어휘 caterer 출장 요리업체 refrigeration 냉장 (보관)

## 115 전치사 어휘

번역 투어 종료 시에, 참가자들은 저희 사진사가 촬영한 사진을 구입할 기회가 있을 것입니다.

해설 빈칸 뒤 명사구 the end of the tour를 목적어로 취하는 전치사 자리이므로, '투어 종료 시에'라는 의미를 나타낼 수 있는 (C) At이 정답이다.

어휘 participant 참가자

TEST 8

## 116 동사 어휘

번역 새로운 자금이 확보되어서, 스니드 타워의 공사가 곧 재개될 것입니다.

해설 자금이 확보됨에 따라 공사와 관련된 변화를 나타낼 수 있는 자동사가 빈칸에 쓰여야 알맞으므로 '재개되다'를 뜻하는 자동사 (B) resume이 정답이다. 참고로, (A) ensure, (C) resolve, (D) maintain은 모두 목적어를 필요로 하는 타동사이다.

어휘 funding 자금 (제공) secure 확보하다 ensure 보장하다, 반드시 ~하도록 하다 resolve 해결하다 maintain 유지하다

## 117 접속사 자리 _ 부사절 접속사

번역 직원이 문제의 해당 급여 기간 동안 근무하지 않은 경우에도 급여 명세서를 발급해야 한다.

해설 빈칸 앞뒤에 각각 완전한 절이 있으므로 두 절을 연결할 수 있는 접속사가 필요하다. 따라서 부사절 접속사인 (A) even if(설사 ~한다 하더라도)가 정답이다. (B) other than(~ 외에, ~을 제외하고)은 전치사이며, (C) promptly(즉각, 지체 없이)와 (D) still(여전히, 그럼에도 불구하고)은 부사이다.

어휘 pay 급여 statement 명세서, 내역서 issue 발급하다 in question 문제의, 논의가 되고 있는

## 118 부사 자리

번역 교육 참가자들은 마지막 동영상을 시청한 직후에 온라인으로 퀴즈를 풀도록 요청받을 것이다.

해설 빈칸 앞에는 빠진 요소가 없는 완전한 절이 있고, 빈칸 뒤에는 after로 시작하는 전치사구가 있으므로, 빈칸에는 부사가 들어갈 수 있다. 따라서 부사인 (A) directly가 정답이다. directly after는 '직후에'라는 뜻으로 자주 쓰이는 표현이니 알아 두자.

어휘 participant 참가자 direct 감독하다, 지시하다; 직접적인 direction 지시, 방향

## 119 동사 어휘

번역 포커스 그룹 리더들은 그룹에 개인적인 의견을 표현하는 것을 삼가야 한다.

해설 빈칸 뒤에 있는 전치사 from과 어울리는 동사가 필요한데, from과 같이 다니는 동사는 (B) refrain과 (D) prevent이다. 그러나 prevent는 뒤에 목적어를 취하여 주로 「prevent+목적어+from(~가 …하는 것을 막다)」의 형태로 쓰인다. 이 문장은 목적어 없이 바로 from이 왔으므로 자동사가 들어가야 하며 문맥상 '개인적인 의견을 표현하는 것을 삼가야 한다'가 자연스러운 의미이므로 '삼가다'를 뜻하는 자동사 (B) refrain이 정답이다.

어휘 focus group 포커스 그룹(시장 조사 등을 위해 구성한 그룹) express 표현하다, 나타내다 refuse 거절하다, 거부하다 escape 벗어나다, 탈출하다 prevent 막다, 예방하다

## 120 명사 어휘

번역 상을 받은 정 박사의 연구가 소속 학과의 명성을 높여 주었다.

해설 상을 받은 연구로 높일 수 있는 것을 나타낼 단어가 필요하며, '소속 학과의 명성을 높여 주었다'라는 의미가 자연스러우므로 '명성, 평판'을 뜻하는 (C) reputation이 정답이다.

어휘 award-winning 상을 받은, 수상한 enhance 높이다, 향상시키다 department 부서 arrangement 준비, 배치 permission 허락, 승인 belief 믿음

## 121 명사 자리 _ 주격 보어

번역 석영 조리대가 회사에서 가장 인기 있는 제품이기 때문에, 얼스톤은 자사 홈페이지에서 그것들을 크게 소개한다.

해설 주어인 the quartz countertops를 보충 설명하는 주격 보어 자리이자 최상급 형용사 its most popular의 수식을 받는 명사 자리이므로 명사인 (D) products(제품들)가 정답이다.

어휘 quartz 석영 countertop 조리대 feature 특색으로 삼다, 특별히 포함하다 productively 생산적으로 productive 생산적인

## 122 접속사 자리 _ 부사절 접속사

번역 버드 인더스트리스 사가 프로젝트 입찰 금액을 낮추지 않는다면, 우리는 그 개조 공사를 위해 뉴레인 컨트랙터스 사를 고용할 가능성이 클 것입니다.

해설 빈칸 뒤로 완전한 절 두 개가 콤마(,)로 이어져 있으므로 두 절을 연결할 수 있는 접속사가 필요하다. 따라서 부사절 접속사인 (B) Unless(~하지 않는다면, ~가 아니라면)가 정답이다. (A) Further(더 멀리; 더 먼)는 부사 또는 형용사이며, (C) Hopefully(희망하여, 기대하여)와 (D) Meanwhile(그 사이에, 그러는 동안)은 부사이다.

어휘 lower 낮추다, 내리다 bid 입찰(액) renovation 개조, 보수

## 123 동사 자리 _ 시제

번역 승객들이 탑승하는 대로, 객실 승무원이 비행기 출입문을 닫을 것이다.

해설 부사절 접속사 Once와 주어 the passengers 뒤에 있는 빈칸은 Once절의 동사가 들어갈 자리이며, 주절의 동사가 미래 시제일 때 부사절에는 현재 또는 현재완료 시제 동사를 사용하므로 현재완료 시제인 (C) have boarded(탑승하다)가 정답이다.

어휘 once (접) ~하자마자 cabin 객실 crew 승무원

## 124 형용사 자리 _ 주격 보어

번역 카든 모터스는 결함이 있는 변속기 수리에 능숙한 기술자를 찾고 있다.

해설 be동사 is 뒤에 있는 빈칸은 보어 자리이므로 명사나 형용사가 올 수 있는데, 복수 명사인 (B) experts(전문가들)와 불가산명사인 (D) expertise(전문 지식)가 들어가면 의미가 어색하므로 오답이며, be expert at의 형태로 '~에 능숙하다'라는 뜻을 구성하는 형용사 (A) expert(능숙한)가 정답이다.

어휘 seek 찾다, 구하다 faulty 결함이 있는 transmission 변속기 expertly 전문적으로, 능숙하게

## 125 형용사 자리 _ 어휘

번역 최근 인터뷰에서, 새라 푸스코는 음악계를 떠나기로 했던 충동적인 결정을 지금 후회한다고 인정했다.

해설 소유격 대명사 her와 명사 decision 사이에 있는 빈칸은 명사를 수식할 형용사가 들어갈 자리이며, '음악계를 떠나기로 했던 충동적인 결정을 후회하다'를 의미해야 가장 자연스러우므로 '충동적인'을 뜻하는 (A) impulsive가 정답이다. (B) boldest(가장 대담한, 가장 용감한)와 (D) occasional(가끔 있는, 때때로의)은 의미가 맞지 않는 형용사이며, (C) unexpectedly(예기치 못하게)는 부사이다.

어휘 recent 최근의 admit 인정하다 regret 후회하다, 유감으로 생각하다 decision 결정 industry 업계

## 126 형용사 어휘

번역 린 씨는 동료 직원들이 돈을 절약하게 될 거라고 지적할 때까지는 전자 회람을 돌리는 걸 반대했다.

해설 '동료 직원들이 돈을 절약하게 될 거라고 지적할 때까지 전자 회람을 돌리는 걸 반대했다'라는 의미를 구성해야 가장 자연스러우므로 '~을 반대하다'를 뜻하는 be opposed to -ing를 구성하는 형용사 (D) opposed가 정답이다.

어휘 circulate (문서 등을) 돌리다, 배부하다 memo 회람 electronically 전자식으로 colleague 동료 직원 point out 지적하다 accustomed 익숙한 receptive 수용적인, 잘 받아들이는 limited 제한된, 한정된

## 127 부사 자리 _ 동사 수식

번역 스트렁크 그룹의 베스트셀러 비료인 울트라 그린은 좋지 못한 토양에 영양분 양을 상당히 증가시켜 준다.

해설 문장의 동사 increases 앞에 위치한 빈칸은 동사를 앞에서 수식할 부사가 들어갈 수 있는 자리이므로 (D) considerably(상당히)가 정답이다.

어휘 fertilizer 비료 increase 증가시키다 nutrient 영양(분) soil 토양, 흙 consider 고려하다, 여기다 considerable 상당한 consideration 고려, 숙고

## 128 부사 어휘

번역 아마추어와 전문가들 모두 그래픽 디자인 프로젝트를 위해 일러스트리아를 이용하고 있다.

해설 두 개의 명사가 and로 연결된 주어와 동사 are 사이에 빈칸이 위치해 있으므로 'A와 B 둘 다 (똑같이)'라는 의미를 나타내는 A and B alike를 구성하는 부사 (C) alike가 정답이다.

어휘 professional 전문가, 전문직 종사자 rather 다소, 약간

## 129 부사 어휘

번역 이 그림들은 게라 씨가 경력을 쌓는 동안 그의 스타일이 어떻게 변화했는지 보여주기 위해 연대순으로 배열되어 있다.

해설 그림 스타일이 어떻게 변화했는지 보여주기 위한 배열 방식을 나타낼 부사가 필요하므로 '연대순으로'를 뜻하는 (D) chronologically가 정답이다.

어휘 arrange 배치하다, 정렬하다 rightfully 합법적으로, 옳게 prominently 두드러지게, 눈에 잘 띄게 increasingly 점점 더

## 130 명사 어휘

번역 출장 수당은 식사, 택시 요금 및 출장 중에 발생하는 기타 경비를 지원하기 위해 할당됩니다.

해설 식사와 택시 요금, 그리고 기타 경비를 지원하기 위해 할당될 수 있는 것, 즉 비용과 관련된 명사가 빈칸에 쓰여야 알맞으므로 '수당'을 뜻하는 (B) allowance가 정답이다.

어휘 allocate 할당하다, 배정하다 assist 지원하다, 돕다 fare (교통편의) 요금 expense 경비, 지출 incur (비용을) 발생시키다 documentation 문서(화) itinerary (여행 등의) 일정표 insurance 보험

# PART 6

### 131-134 초대장

관계자께,

저희 빌리어스 기업가 네트워크는 4월 7일, 목요일 오후 2시에 토레스 밀에서 열리는 빌리어스 벤처 캐피털 컨퍼런스(VVCC)에 귀사를 초대하고자 합니다.

먼저, 비공개로 진행되는 이 컨퍼런스의 전반부에서는 참가자들께 빌리어스 지역의 131 **투자** 기회를 소개해 드릴 것입니다. 유망한 지역 신생 기업 여섯 곳의 직원들이 각자 회사의 자금 수요에 관해 간략히 발표할 것입니다. 132 **그 후에는 인맥 형성을 위한 휴식 시간이 이어집니다**. 오후 4시부터 오후 6시까지 공개적으로 진행되는 VVCC의 후반부에 133 **참석하시는 것**도 환영합니다. 하지만 이 시간은 지역 업체들과 134 기업가들**에게** 더 초점이 맞춰져 있습니다.

이 초대장에 답장하셔서 VVCC 자리를 예약하시기 바랍니다.

엘리아스 발로우, 의장
빌리어스 기업가 네트워크

어휘 participate in ~에 참가하다 private 비공개의, 전용의 introduce 소개하다 participant 참가자 opportunity 기회 representative 직원, 대표자 promising 유망한 start-up 신생 기업 funding 자금 (제공) public 공개적인, 공공의 targeted 초점이 맞춰진, 대상으로 하는 local 지역의 entrepreneur 기업가 respond 답장하다, 반응하다 reserve 예약하다

TEST 8

## 131 명사 어휘

해설 다음 문장에 신생 기업들이 각 회사의 자금 수요(funding needs)에 관해 발표한다는 내용이 있으므로 자금이 필요한 신생 기업에게 투자할 기회에 대한 내용임을 알 수 있다. 따라서 빈칸에는 자금과 관련된 단어인 (B) investment(투자)가 정답이다.

어휘 employment 고용, 취업

## 132 문장 고르기

번역 (A) 그 후에는 인맥 형성을 위한 휴식 시간이 이어집니다.
(B) VVCC는 작년 4월에 처음 개최되었습니다.
(C) 현지 은행의 임원들이 청중으로 참석할 예정입니다.
(D) 최근 그 도시의 경제 상황이 좋지 않습니다.

해설 빈칸을 기준으로 앞뒤에 각각 행사 전반부와 후반부를 소개하는 내용이 제시되어 있다. 따라서 행사 진행 순서와 관련된 문장이 빈칸에 들어가야 흐름이 자연스러우므로 전반부 이후의 중간 휴식 시간을 언급하는 (A)가 정답이다.

어휘 follow 뒤따르다, 뒤이어 일어나다 networking 인적 교류 break 휴식 executive 임원, 이사 audience 청중, 관객 climate 기류, 분위기 unfavorable 호의적이지 못한, 불리한 lately 최근에

## 133 동사 어휘

해설 명사구 the public half of the VVCC를 목적어로 취하는 타동사 자리이다. 후반부 시간에도 참석하도록 권하는 의미를 나타내야 자연스러우므로 '참석하다'를 뜻하는 (D) attend가 정답이다.

어휘 promote 홍보하다, 승진시키다

## 134 전치사 어휘

해설 빈칸 뒤에 '지역 업체들과 기업가들'을 뜻하는 명사구가 쓰여 있어 후반부 시간의 주요 대상을 알리는 문장임을 알 수 있다. 따라서 빈칸 앞에 위치한 동사 is targeted와 어울려 '~에 초점이 맞춰져 있다, ~을 대상으로 하다'를 의미할 때 사용하는 전치사 (C) towards가 정답이다.

어휘 involved 관련된, 수반된

### 135-138 이메일

발신: 앤턴 그리어
수신: 린지 피커드
제목: 감사의 글
날짜: 3월 29일

안녕하세요, 린지,

귀 부서에서 저의 행정 비서를 구하는 데 도움을 주신 것에 대해 감사의 말씀을 드리고자 연락 드렸습니다. 제가 소통했던 모든 분이 다 일을 잘 해 주셨지만, 특히 그 과정에서 값진 기여를 해 주신 칼 슈미트 씨를 특별히 언급하고 싶습니다. [135] **구체적으로 말하면**, 그가 행정 업무 전문가들을 위한 전문 구인 게시판을 발견했습니다. 그 [136] **방편**이 없었다면, 선택할 수 있는 훌륭한 후보자들이 그렇게 많지 않았을 것입니다.

제가 이곳 캐릴런 헬스 사에서 직원을 채용하는 것은 처음이라 그 과정에서 무엇을 [137] **기대해야** 할지 잘 몰랐는데, 이렇게 간단하고 협업이 잘 이루어질 줄은 상상도 못했습니다. 훌륭한 팀을 꾸리셨군요. [138] **여러분 모두와 다시 함께 일할 수 있는 기회가 주어진다면 정말 기쁠 것 같습니다.** 제 감사의 인사를 모든 분에게 전해 주시기를 바랍니다.

앤턴 그리어
디지털 헬스케어 혁신 사업 부사장
캐릴런 헬스

어휘 reach out 연락하다 express 표현하다 appreciation 감사(의 뜻) department 부서 executive assistant 비서 interact 소통하다, 교류하다 single out 특별히 언급하다, 특별히 지목하다 make a contribution 기여하다, 공헌하다 invaluable 귀중한 process 과정 discover 발견하다 specialized 전문적인, 전문화된 job board 구인 게시판 administrative 행정의, 관리의 candidate 후보자, 지원자 certainly 분명히, 확실히 collaborative 협력적인 put together 구성하다, 한데 모으다 pass on ~을 전달하다

## 135 접속부사

해설 빈칸 앞에는 슈미트 씨가 값진 기여를 했다는 말이, 빈칸 뒤에는 슈미트 씨가 전문 구인 게시판을 발견한 사실이 쓰여 있다. 슈미트 씨가 어떻게 기여했는지 구체적으로 설명하는 흐름이므로 '구체적으로 말하면'이라는 의미의 (A) Specifically가 정답이다.

어휘 nonetheless 그럼에도 불구하고 to that end 그러기 위해 accordingly 그에 따라

## 136 명사 어휘

해설 빈칸 앞에 위치한 that은 앞 문장에 언급된 단수 명사구 a specialized job board(전문 구인 게시판)를 가리킨다. 빈칸이 없었다면, 선택할 수 있는 훌륭한 후보자들이 그렇게 많지 않았을 것이라고 쓰여 있어 그 구인 게시판이 후보자 선택을 위한 방편이었음을 알 수 있으므로 '방편, 수단'을 뜻하는 (D) resource가 정답이다.

어휘 perk 특전, 특혜

## 137 to부정사 _ what+to부정사

해설 명사절 접속사 what 뒤에는 주어나 목적어가 빠진 불완전한 절이나 to부정사가 올 수 있으므로 to부정사인 (C) to expect가 정답이다. (A) expected, (B) expects, (D) the expectations는 절을 구성할 수 없다.

어휘 expect 예상하다, 기대하다 expectation 기대(치)

## 138 문장 고르기

번역 (A) 오리엔테이션은 반드시 신속하고 순조롭게 진행될 것입니다.
(B) 지금은 그것을 더 확대하는 건 현명하지 않을 것입니다.
(C) 여러분 모두와 다시 함께 일할 수 있는 기회가 주어진다면 정말 기쁠 것 같습니다.
(D) 그들은 완전히 교육받고 나면 아주 유능해질 것입니다.

해설 빈칸 앞뒤로 상대방이 훌륭한 팀을 꾸렸다는 말과 그 구성원 모두에게 감사의 뜻을 전해 달라는 말이 쓰여 있다. 이는 앞서 언급한 '비서를 찾는 과정'에서 많은 도움을 준 사람들에 대한 칭찬임을 알 수 있으며, 그 연장선상에서 앞으로도 함께 일할 수 있는 기회가 있기를 바란다는 뜻을 나타내는 (C)가 정답이다.

어휘 smoothly 순조롭게 further 추가로, 한층 더 at this time 지금, 현재 effective (사람이) 유능한 fully 완전히, 전적으로

### 139-142 회람

수신: 실험실 직원
발신: 아말 코우리, 안전 관리 책임자
제목: 안전 관련 알림
날짜: 1월 11일

여러분 모두에게 중요한 안전 관련 139 **정책**을 상기시키기 위해 이 회람을 보냅니다. 첫 번째로, 어떤 직원도 실험실 내에 혼자 있는 동안 위험한 화학 물질을 다룰 수 없습니다. 문제 발생 시에 도움을 제공해 줄 수 있는 최소 한 명의 다른 직원이 항상 시야에 들어오거나 소리가 들리는 범위 140 **내에** 있어야 합니다.

직원들은 책임자 또는 관리자의 사전 승인을 받아 혼자 다른 종류의 실험실 업무를 수행할 수 있습니다. 141 **하지만 상사가 사전에 위험도 평가를 완료해야 합니다.** SAFEX 규정 준수 관리 시스템은 이 과정을 간단하게 만들어 줍니다.

마지막으로, 직원이 실험실에서 혼자 근무할 때는 SAFEX 모바일 앱의 "체크인" 기능을 142 **이용해야 합니다.** 해당 기능의 비상 연락처로 지정된 외부에 있는 동료에게도 이 사실을 미리 알려야 합니다.

준수해 주셔서 감사합니다.

어휘 laboratory 실험실, 연구실(= lab) reminder (상기시키는) 알림, 메시지 handle 다루다, 처리하다 hazardous 위험한 chemicals 화학 물질 aid 도움 in the event of ~ 발생 시에, ~의 경우에 (대비해) perform 수행하다 task 업무, 일 prior 사전의, 앞선 permission 승인, 허락 compliance (규정 등의) 준수, 따름 process 과정 feature 기능, 특징 offsite 현장 밖의, 떨어진 곳에 있는 colleague 동료 designated 지정된 beforehand 사전에, 미리

## 139 명사 어휘

해설 뒤에 이어지는 문장들을 보면, 실험실 내에서 일하는 동안 지켜야 하는 세부 규정을 설명하고 있으므로 안전 관련 정책을 상기시키기 위한 회람인 것을 알 수 있다. 따라서 '정책, 방침'을 뜻하는 (D) policies가 정답이다.

어휘 training 교육, 훈련 personnel 인사(부) equipment 장비

## 140 전치사 어휘

해설 빈칸 앞에 문제 발생 시에 도움을 제공해 줄 수 있는 최소 한 명의 다른 직원이 있어야 한다는 말이 쓰여 있다. 도움을 제공하려면 눈에 보이거나 소리가 들리는 범위 내에 위치해 있어야 하므로 '~ 내에'를 뜻하는 (B) within이 정답이다.

어휘 through ~을 통해, ~ 내내 upon ~하자마자

## 141 문장 고르기

번역 (A) 더욱이 직원들은 업무 공간을 자주 소독하도록 권장됩니다.
(B) 하지만 상사가 사전에 위험도 평가를 완료해야 합니다.
(C) 실제로 우리 실험실의 공간 배치는 이러한 문제들을 최소화하도록 디자인되었습니다.
(D) 물론, 특정 종류의 일은 한 명의 기술자가 하기에는 너무 복잡할 수 있습니다.

해설 빈칸 앞에 책임자 또는 관리자의 사전 승인을 받아 직원 혼자 다른 종류의 실험실 업무를 수행할 수 있다고 알리는 문장이 쓰여 있다. 따라서 사전 승인을 받기 위한 과정의 하나로서 상사가 미리 얼마나 위험한지 평가해야 한다는 의미로 쓰인 (B)가 정답이다.

어휘 moreover 더욱이, 게다가 sanitize 살균하다, 위생 처리하다 frequently 자주, 빈번히 superior 상사, 상관 risk 위험(도) assessment 평가 layout 배치, 구획

## 142 동사 자리 _ 시제

해설 우선, 접속사 whenever 앞에 명사구 주어와 빈칸만 있으므로 빈칸은 주절의 동사 자리이다. 또한, 직원이 실험실에서 혼자 근무할 때는 SAFEX 모바일 앱의 "체크인" 기능을 이용해야 한다는 의미가 되어야 자연스러우므로 (A) must be used가 정답이다.

### 143-146 이메일

수신: 미공개 수신인
발신: 티켓위즈 사
날짜: 10월 8일
제목: 블루 스트릭 콘서트

블루 스트릭 팬 여러분께,

호일 타이거즈 야구팀이 플레이오프 경기에서 계속 승리함에 따라 호일 스타디움 일정에 몇 건의 경기가 추가되었습니다. 이런 이유로, 그 장소에서 블루 스트릭의 10월 13일 콘서트를 예정대로 개최할 수 143 **없게 되었습니다.** 그 공연은 144 **취소되었습니다.** 여러분의 티켓은 선택하신 결제 수단을 통해 전액 환불되었습니다. 다행히, 밴드가 같은 날 같은 시간에 근처 피콕 리조트 원형 극장을 예약할 수 있었습니다. 스타디움 콘서트 티켓 소지자로서, 여러분은 내일 오전 10시에 시작되는 특별 온라인 사전 판매를 통해 이 원형 극장 공연 티켓을 구입하실 수 있는 145 **자격이 있습니다.** 146 **접속 링크를 포함한 이메일이 오늘 중으로 발송될 것입니다.**

TEST 8

티켓위즈와 블루 스트릭은 이번 변경으로 인해 불편을 끼쳐드린 점 사과드립니다.

티켓위즈 팀

어휘 undisclosed 미공개의 recipient 수신인, 수령인 continuing 지속되는 success 성공 lead to+명사 ~로 이어지다 venue 개최 장소, 행사장 unavailable 이용할 수 없는 host 주최하다 refund 환불(액) issue 지급하다, 발급하다 via ~을 통해 method 방식, 방법 ticketholder 입장권 소지자 amphitheater 원형 극장, 원형 경기장 presale 사전 판매 apologize 사과하다 inconvenience 불편함

## 143 동사 자리 _ 시제

해설 빈칸이 있는 문장에 동사가 없으므로 빈칸이 동사 자리임을 알 수 있다. 또한, 빈칸 뒤에 행사 날짜로 언급된 10월 13일(October 13)은 상단의 이메일 작성 날짜인 10월 8일(Date: October 8)보다 미래이므로 미래 시제 동사인 (C) will be가 정답이다.

## 144 동사 어휘

해설 빈칸 뒤에 이어지는 문장에 전액 환불되었다는 말과 함께 새로운 콘서트 장소를 예약했다는 말이 쓰여 있다. 따라서 주어 That show가 가리키는 호일 스타디움 콘서트는 취소되었다는 것을 알 수 있으므로 (D) canceled가 정답이다.

어휘 postpone 연기하다, 미루다 perform 공연하다, 연주하다 organize 조직하다, 준비하다

## 145 형용사 어휘

해설 빈칸 앞의 주어 you는 그 앞에 있는 As 전치사구(As a ticketholder for the stadium concert)에 언급된 스타디움 콘서트 티켓 소지자들을 가리킨다. 앞서 스타디움 콘서트가 일정 충돌 문제로 취소되어 원형 극장을 새로 예약했다는 말이 쓰여 있어, 기존 티켓 소지자들은 사전 판매를 통해 원형 극장 공연 티켓을 구입할 자격이 있다는 의미가 되어야 자연스러우므로 '자격이 있는'을 뜻하는 (A) eligible이 정답이다.

어휘 applied 적용된 fortunate 다행인, 운 좋은 proposed 제안된

## 146 문장 고르기

번역 (A) 원형 극장은 딱 20,000명을 수용할 수 있습니다.
(B) 24시간 내로 답장을 받으실 것입니다.
(C) 두 공연은 동일한 뮤지션 라인업이 등장합니다.
(D) 접속 링크를 포함한 이메일이 오늘 중으로 발송될 것입니다.

해설 빈칸 앞에 특별 온라인 사전 판매를 통해 원형 극장 공연 티켓을 구입하는 일이 언급되어 있으므로 그 온라인 사전 판매 서비스를 이용할 수 있는 방법을 알리는 (D)가 정답이다.

어휘 capacity 수용 규모, 수용력 feature (특별히) 포함하다, 특징으로 하다 lineup 출연진 access 접속, 이용

# PART 7

## 147-148 회람

회람

수신: 완다 모턴 외 9명
147 **발신: 클리퍼드 샌더스**, 외부 커뮤니케이션 전문가
날짜: 10월 18일
제목: 바우어 산 풍력 발전소

목요일에 있을 프로젝트 현황에 관한 기자 회견에 앞서, 재생 에너지팀과 언론 홍보부 직원들께 다음과 같은 사항을 알려 드리고자 합니다. 147 **트레비노 씨께서 바우어 산 풍력 발전소 관련해서 저를 기관 대변인으로 지정하셨기 때문에, 제가 그 주제에 관한 언론의 질문을 처리해야 합니다.** 이 정보를 여러분과 연락하는 모든 기자들에게 전달해 주시기 바랍니다. 모두 아시다시피, 148 **이 프로젝트는 관광 산업에 미칠 수 있는 영향 때문에 지역 사회 구성원들의 반대에 계속 직면하고 있습니다.** 그런 이유로 우리 기관에서는 프로젝트에 대한 전문 지식과 여론에 대한 민감성을 모두 고려하지 않은 발언은 피하는 것이 중요합니다.

어휘 external 외부의 wind farm 풍력 발전소 in advance of ~에 앞서 press conference 기자 회견 status 현황, 상황 issue 발표하다, 공표하다 following 다음의, 아래의 designate 지정하다 organizational 기관의, 조직의 spokesperson 대변인 handle 처리하다, 다루다 inquiry 질문, 문의 subject 주제 pass 전달하다 opposition 반발, 반대 impact 영향 crucial 대단히 중요한 avoid 피하다 make a remark 발언하다 inform 숙지하다 expertise 전문 지식 sensitivity 민감성 public opinion 여론

## 147 세부 사항

번역 회람에 따르면, 누가 풍력 발전소에 관한 언론의 질문에 답변할 수 있는가?
(A) 재생 에너지팀
(B) 샌더스 씨
(C) 트레비노 씨
(D) 언론 홍보부

해설 지문 중반부에 트레비노 씨가 자신을 대변인으로 지정한 사실과 함께 자신이 언론의 질문을 처리해야 한다(~ I must be the one to handle media inquiries on the subject)는 내용이 제시되어 있다. 이는 상단의 발신인 항목에 기재된 클리퍼드 샌더스(From: Clifford Sanders)가 전하는 말이므로 (B)가 정답이다.

## 148 Not / True

번역 풍력 발전소에 대해 언급된 것은?
(A) 완공이 목요일에 발표될 것이다.
(B) 환경 단체가 제안했다.
(C) 곧 기자들이 견학할 것이다.
(D) 지역 주민들 사이에서 논란이 많다.

해설 지문 중반부에 프로젝트는 관광 산업에 미칠 수 있는 영향 때문에 지역 사회 구성원들의 반대에 계속 직면하고 있다(the project continues to face some amount of opposition from members of the community)는 내용이 제시되어 있어 논란이 많다는 사실을 알 수 있으므로 (D)가 정답이다.

어휘 completion 완공, 완료 controversial 논란이 많은

> Paraphrasing
> 지문의 opposition from members of the community
> → 정답의 controversial among local residents

**149-150 광고**

**[149] 이제 봄이 와서, 많은 분들이 주택이나 아파트를 대청소하고 있습니다.** 하지만 겨울에 쌓인 먼지와 때를 직접 제거하실 시간이 없다면 어쩌지요? **[150] 어스파이어 클리너스의 헌신적인 직원들이 바닥에서부터 천장까지 여러분의 집안 구석구석을, 또는 저희에게 요청하신 구역들만 청소해 드리겠습니다.** 오늘 555-0164번으로 저희에게 전화 주십시오.

어휘 now that 이제 ~이므로 get rid of ~을 제거하다, 없애다 grime 때 dedicated 헌신적인, 전념하는 scrub (문질러서) 청소하다 handle 처리하다, 다루다

## 149 추론

번역 광고에서 봄에 대해 암시하는 것은?
(A) 집을 꼼꼼히 청소하기 좋은 시기이다.
(B) 부동산 매물을 등록하기 가장 좋은 시기이다.
(C) 일년 중에서 먼지가 가장 많은 계절이다.
(D) 어스파이어 클리너스가 설립된 계절이다.

해설 첫 문장에 이제 봄이 와서, 많은 사람들이 주택이나 아파트를 대청소하고 있다(Now that spring has arrived, many people are giving their houses or apartments a deep cleaning)는 말이 쓰여 있으므로 (A)가 정답이다.

어휘 thoroughly 철저히 list 목록에 올리다 property 건물, 부동산 found 설립하다

## 150 Not / True

번역 어스파이어 클리너스에 대해 언급된 것은?
(A) 기간 한정 할인을 제공하고 있다.
(B) 직원들이 실내와 실외에서 모두 일한다.
(C) 서비스가 맞춤 제공될 수 있다.
(D) 바닥 청소를 전문으로 한다.

해설 지문 중반부에 어스파이어 클리너스가 고객들이 요청한 구역만 청소할 수도 있다(Aspire Cleaners' dedicated staff will scrub ~ or, just the areas you ask us to handle)는 내용이 제시되어 있다. 이는 맞춤 서비스를 제공할 수 있다는 뜻이므로 (C)가 정답이다.

어휘 limited-time 기간이 한정된 customize 맞춤 제공하다, 주문 제작하다 specialize 전문으로 하다 flooring 바닥(재)

> Paraphrasing
> 지문의 just the areas you ask us to handle
> → 정답의 can be customized

**151-152 공지**

http://www.gleason.com

글리슨 국제 공항 (GIA)

뉴스 & 공지

분실 수하물 관련 공지

겨울 날씨로 인해 최근 많은 항공편이 지연 또는 결항됨에 따라 GIA에는 수백 개의 분실 수하물이 쌓였습니다. **[151] 이 수하물은 현재 2층에 있는 국내선 출발 안내 데스크 근처에 위치한 임시 보관소에 안전하게 보관되고 있습니다.**

분실 수하물의 위치 추적 및 전달은 궁극적으로 항공사의 책임이므로, 분실 수하물의 소유주는 해당 항공사에 신고하는 것부터 시작하시기 바랍니다. 하지만 수하물이 제때 처리되도록 하기 위해 사람들이 직접 각자의 가방을 찾아보시는 것도 허용하고 있습니다. 그렇게 하려면, **[152] 유효 신분증과 함께 항공권과 수하물 표를 지참하셔서 보관소 입구로 오시기 바랍니다.** 직원이 서류를 확인한 다음, 찾으실 수 있도록 내부로 안내해 드릴 것입니다. 이 과정에 대해 질문이 있으시면, 555-0176번으로 저희 고객 지원팀에 전화 주시기 바랍니다.

어휘 misplace 분실하다, 둔 곳을 잊다 following ~ 후에 accumulate 모으다, 축적하다 currently 현재 securely 안전하게 temporary 임시의, 일시적인 enclosure 칸막이 공간, 울타리를 친 곳 location 위치 (추적) ultimately 궁극적으로, 본질적으로 responsibility 책임 file a report 신고하다 ensure 보장하다 disperse 분산시키다 in a timely fashion 제때, 적절한 시점에 valid 유효한 form of identification 신분증 escort 안내하다 documentation 서류 process 과정

## 151 Not / True

번역 공지에서 GIA에 대해 언급하는 것은?
(A) 항공사 직원들의 검색 과정을 돕고 있다.
(B) 일부 수하물을 위해 임시 보관 구역을 설치했다.
(C) 현재 수하물 처리 절차를 업그레이드하고 있다.
(D) 최근 직원 부족으로 인해 어려움을 겪었다.

해설 첫 번째 단락에 분실 수하물들이 현재 2층에 있는 국내선 출발 안내 데스크 근처에 있는 임시 보관소에 안전하게 보관되고 있다(The baggage is currently being kept securely in a temporary enclosure on our second floor)는 정보가 제시되어 있다. 따라서 임시 보관 구역을 설치했다는 것을 알 수 있으므로 (B)가 정답이다.

어휘 assist 돕다, 지원하다 set up 설치하다 holding area 보관 구역 handling 처리, 취급 procedure 절차 staffing 직원 배치, 직원 채용 shortage 부족

> Paraphrasing
> 지문의 temporary enclosure
> → 정답의 temporary holding area

TEST 8

## 152 세부 사항

번역 분실 수하물의 소유주들은 무엇을 하도록 요청받는가?
(A) 신분증 준비하기
(B) 신고서 사본 보관하기
(C) 안내 데스크 방문하기
(D) 전화로 물품 설명하기

해설 두 번째 단락에 직접 가방을 찾으려면 유효 신분증과 함께 항공권과 수하물 표를 지참해서 보관소 입구로 오라(bring your airline ticket and luggage tag, along with a valid form of identification, to the entrance of the enclosure)고 했으므로 (A)가 정답이다.

어휘 identity 신분, 신원 describe 설명하다

> Paraphrasing
> 지문의 form of identification
> → 정답의 proof of their identity

### 153-154 문자 메시지

루드라 아가왈 [오전 10시 57분]
마리, [153] **오늘 아침 시크모드에서의 일은 어떻게 되어 가고 있나요?**

마리 에버렛 [오전 11시 3분]
아주 잘돼 가요! [153] **방금 그 제품 라인을 위한 몇 가지 후보 도안을 살펴봤는데, 이쪽 디자인 팀에서 기가 콜라 브랜드의 본질을 잘 포착해줬어요.**

루드라 아가왈 [오전 11시 4분]
정말로요? 어떻게요?

마리 에버렛 [오전 11시 5분]
음, [153] **가장 마음에 드는 건 다양한 크기와 색상의 사각형 배경 위로 우리 로고를 보여 주는 맨투맨 티셔츠예요.** 아주 유쾌해요. 그리고 단순히 우리 고객뿐 아니라, 많은 사람들이 좋아할 것 같아요.

루드라 아가왈 [오전 11시 7분]
아주 잘됐네요. 사실, 우리 소셜 미디어팀이 이 제품 라인의 발표에 대한 반응을 담은 보고서를 막 보내 줬는데, 아주 고무적입니다. 다섯 가지 의견 중 네 가지가 긍정적이었어요. [154] **저는 시크모드와 협업하기로 한 우리의 결정에 대해 정말로 확신이 들고 있어요.**

마리 에버렛 [오전 11시 8분]
네, 지금까지 분명 좋아 보여요!

어휘 drawing 도안, 그림 potential 잠재적인 capture 담아내다, 포착하다 essence 본질, 정수 sweatshirt 맨투맨 티셔츠 square 정사각형 playful 유쾌한, 즐거운 appeal 마음에 들다, 관심을 끌다 reaction 반응 encouraging 고무적인, 격려하는 comment 의견, 발언 positive 긍정적인 confident 확신하는, 자신 있는 decision 결정 collaborate 협업하다

## 153 세부 사항

번역 시크모드는 무엇인가?
(A) 패션쇼
(B) 언론 기관
(C) 의류 회사
(D) 백화점

해설 첫 메시지에서 아가왈 씨가 시크모드에서의 일이 어떻게 되어 가고 있는지 묻는 것에 대해, 에버렛 씨가 11시 3분 메시지와 11시 5분 메시지를 통해 그곳의 디자인 팀이 그린 도안을 살펴본 일(I've just finished looking over drawings of some potential pieces for the line, and their design team's done a good job ~)과 자신이 가장 마음에 드는 것이 맨투맨 티셔츠(my favorite piece is a sweatshirt)임을 밝히고 있다. 따라서 시크모드가 의류 제작과 관련된 회사임을 알 수 있으므로 (C)가 정답이다.

## 154 의도 파악

번역 오전 11시 8분에, 에버렛 씨가 "네, 지금까지 분명 좋아 보여요"라고 쓸 때, 의미하는 것은 무엇인가?
(A) 팀이 폭넓게 조사하고 있다.
(B) 사업 제휴 전망이 좋다.
(C) 소셜 미디어 페이지가 매력적이다.
(D) 일부 의류 상태가 좋다.

해설 오전 11시 7분에 아가왈 씨가 시크모드와 협업하기로 한 결정에 대해 정말로 확신이 들고 있다(I'm feeling really confident about our decision to collaborate with Chicmode)고 말한 것에 대해 에버렛 씨가 "네, 지금까지 분명 좋아 보여요"라고 대답하는 흐름이다. 이는 협업이 잘될 거라는 확신을 나타내는 말이므로 이러한 의미에 해당하는 (B)가 정답이다.

어휘 extensive 폭넓은, 광범위한 partnership 제휴 관계 promising 유망한, 장래가 촉망되는 appealing 매력적인

### 155-157 이메일

발신: 레베카 위플
수신: 토머스 모건
제목: 회신: 문의
날짜: 1월 11일
첨부: 등록금 지원 프로그램 양식

모건 씨께,
에스퀴벨 대학교에 등록하는 직원들을 위한 브레넌 보험 회사의 등록금 지원에 대해 문의해 주셔서 감사합니다. 입사 첫해를 마치셨으므로 귀하는 실제로 이 혜택을 받을 자격이 있습니다.

다른 조치를 취하기 전에, [155] **귀하의 부서장인 요시다 씨에게 말해서 프로그램 신청에 필요한 관리자 추천서를 제공할 수 있는지 확인하시기 바랍니다.**

다음으로, 이 페이지를 방문해서 에스퀴벨 대학교의 입학 상담사와의 상담을 요청하여 교육 방향을 설계하세요. [157] **이 대학교는 2개의 준학사 학위와 50개 이상의 학사 학위를 제공하며, 대부분 시간제로 취득하실 수 있습니다.** 대학원 학위는 저희 프로그램의 범위를 벗어납니다. 상

담 시간에 앞서, [156] **이미 보유하고 계신 대학 학점과 관련된 세부 자료를 준비하여 상담사가 에스퀴벨에서 귀하가 원하는 학위에 그 학점이 사용될 수 있는지 판단할 수 있도록 하는 것이 좋습니다.**

준비되는 대로, 첨부한 양식을 작성하여 저희 프로그램을 신청하실 수 있습니다.

레베카 위플
직원 복지 담당, 브레넌 보험회사

어휘 tuition 등록금 assistance 지원, 도움 inquiry 문의 enroll 등록하다 employment 고용, 취업 qualify for ~에 대한 자격이 있다 benefit 혜택, 이점 take steps 조치를 취하다 managerial 관리의, 운영의 recommendation 추천(서) application 신청, 지원 advising 조언하는 counselor 상담 전문가 associate degree 준학사 학위 bachelor's degree 학사 학위 pursue 해 나가다, 추구하다 credit 학점 possess 보유하다, 소유하다 desired 원하는, 바라는 apply 신청하다, 지원하다 attached 첨부된

## 155 세부 사항

번역 모건 씨는 왜 요시다 씨와 이야기하도록 권장되는가?
(A) 어느 분야를 공부할지에 대해 조언을 구하기 위해
(B) 자신의 고용 상태의 변화를 상기시키기 위해
(C) 프로그램 참여에 대한 승인을 확인받기 위해
(D) 신청 과정의 단계에 대해 알아보기 위해

해설 두 번째 단락에 부서장인 요시다 씨에게 말해서 프로그램 신청에 필요한 관리자 추천서를 제공할 수 있는지 확인하기 바란다(please speak to your department head, Ms. Yoshida, to check that she will provide you with the managerial recommendation required as part of the program application)는 내용이 쓰여 있다. 이는 해당 프로그램을 신청하기 위한 일종의 승인을 받는 과정으로 볼 수 있으므로 (C)가 정답이다.

어휘 seek 찾다, 구하다 status 상태 confirm 확인하다 approval 승인 participation 참여

> Paraphrasing
> 지문의 check that she will provide you with the managerial recommendation required as part of the program application → 정답의 confirm her approval of his participation in the program

## 156 추론

번역 이메일에서 에스퀴벨 대학교에 대해 암시하는 것은?
(A) 일부 강의를 온라인으로 실시한다.
(B) 때때로 다른 기관에서 취득한 학점을 받아들인다.
(C) 브레넌 보험회사 직원들에게 등록금 할인을 제공한다.
(D) 제공하는 학위의 수를 최근에 늘렸다.

해설 세 번째 단락에 이미 보유하고 있는 대학 학점과 관련된 세부 자료를 준비하여 상담사가 에스퀴벨에서 원하는 학위에 그 학점이 사용될 수 있는지 판단할 수 있도록 하는 것이 좋다(you prepare details about any college or university credits you already possess so that the counselor can determine whether they can be used toward your desired degree at Esquivel)고 알리고 있다. 이는 에스퀴벨 대학교가 다른 교육 기관에서 취득한 학점을 인정해 줄 수도 있다는 뜻이므로 (B)가 정답이다.

어휘 conduct 실시하다, 수행하다 accept 받아들이다 earn 획득하다, 얻다 institution 기관, 협회

## 157 문장 삽입

번역 [1], [2], [3], [4]로 표시된 곳 중에서 다음 문장이 가장 적합한 곳은 어디인가?
"대학원 학위는 저희 프로그램의 범위를 벗어납니다."
(A) [1]
(B) [2]
(C) [3]
(D) [4]

해설 주어진 문장은 대학원 학위는 자사 프로그램에는 해당되지 않는다는 의미이다. 따라서 에스퀴벨 대학교에서 제공하는 학위의 종류를 언급하는 문장 뒤에 위치한 [3]에 들어가 지원되는 학위의 범위를 알리는 흐름이 되어야 자연스러우므로 (C)가 정답이다.

어휘 graduate degree 대학원 학위 scope 범위, 영역

## 158-160 정보

퍼셀 iX1600 스캐너
문제 해결 팁

[158] **여러분의 편의를 위해, 마이스트 호텔에서는 저희 퍼셀 스캐너에 흔히 나타나는 문제들을 위한 가이드를 마련했습니다.** 아래의 팁 외에도, 모든 케이블이 확실히 연결되어 있는지 확인해 보시기를 권합니다. [158, 159] **이 조치 중 어느 것도 문제를 해결하지 못하는 경우, 비즈니스 센터 출입문 근처에 있는 전화기에서 내선번호 200번으로 전화하셔서 직원을 호출하시기 바랍니다.**

| 문제 | 가능성 있는 원인 | 권고되는 조치 |
|---|---|---|
| 기계가 스캔 작업을 시작하지 않는다. | 문서 공급 장치가 문서를 인식하지 못했습니다. | 문서 공급 장치 안으로 문서를 완전히 삽입하십시오. |
| [160] **스캔된 이미지가 너무 흐리다.** | 낮은 기온이 기계 성능에 영향을 미칩니다. | [160] **"기기 설정"으로 가신 다음, "스캔 준비 시간"을 "더 길게"로 변경하십시오.** |
| "스캔 파일 폴더 저장" 기능이 작동하지 않는다. | USB 플래시 드라이브가 연결되어 있는 경우에 기계는 오직 USB로만 스캔 파일을 저장할 수 있습니다. | 기계의 오른쪽 측면에 있는 USB 포트를 확인하여 모든 드라이브를 제거하십시오. |

어휘 troubleshooting 문제 해결, 고장 수리 convenience 편의(성) put together 마련하다, 만들다 confirm 확인하다 securely 확실히, 단단히 step 조치 resolve 해결하다 extension 내선전화(번호) summon 호출하다, 소환하다 feeder (용지 등의) 공급 장치 detect 인식하다, 감지하다 insert 삽입하다 faint 희미한 affect 영향을 미치다 performance 성능 function 기능

TEST 8

## 158 세부 사항

번역 정보는 누구를 대상으로 하는가?
(A) 마이스트 호텔 직원들
(B) 마이스트 호텔 고객들
(C) 퍼셀 수리 기사들
(D) 퍼셀 영업 사원들

해설 첫 단락 초반부에 마이스트 호텔에서 퍼셀 스캐너에 흔히 나타나는 문제들을 위한 가이드를 마련했다(For your convenience, Maist Hotel has put together this guide to common problems with our Purcell scanner)고 했고, 같은 단락 후반부에는 문제가 해결되지 않을 경우에는 내선전화를 통해 직원을 호출하라(If none of these steps resolve your issue, call extension 200 ~ to summon a staff member)고 했으므로 호텔 고객들이 대상임을 알 수 있다. 따라서 (B)가 정답이다.

## 159 세부 사항

번역 제공된 전화번호로 전화해야 하는 이유로 언급된 것은?
(A) 사람이 직접 제공하는 도움을 받기 위해
(B) 연결 케이블을 주문하기 위해
(C) 잉크 카트리지를 교체하기 위해
(D) 품질 보증 서비스의 유효성을 확인하기 위해

해설 첫 단락 후반부에 문제가 해결되지 않을 경우에는 내선번호 200번으로 전화해서 직원을 호출하라(If none of these steps resolve your issue, call extension 200 ~ to summon a staff member)고 알리는 내용이 제시되어 있다. 이는 직원이 직접 와서 도와줄 수 있다는 뜻이므로 (A)가 정답이다.

어휘 arrange 주선하다, 조치하다 in-person 직접 (가서) replace 교체하다 warranty 품질 보증(서) validity 유효(성)

> Paraphrasing
> 지문의 to summon a staff member
> → 정답의 To arrange in-person assistance

## 160 세부 사항

번역 이용자가 왜 스캐너의 설정을 변경해야 하는가?
(A) 디지털 스캔 파일이 원하는 위치로 보내지지 않고 있기 때문에
(B) 스캐너가 선명하지 않은 이미지를 만들어 냈기 때문에
(C) 문서를 문서 공급 장치에 삽입할 수 없기 때문에
(D) 스캐너가 USB 드라이브를 인식할 수 없기 때문에

해설 도표에서 스캔된 이미지가 너무 흐리다(Scanned image is too faint)는 문제에 대한 조치로 기기 설정을 변경하는 방법(Go to "Machine Settings" and change "Scan Warm-up Time" to "Longer)이 언급되어 있으므로 (B)가 정답이다.

어휘 desired 원하는, 바라는 sharp 선명한, 뚜렷한

> Paraphrasing
> 지문의 Scanned image is too faint → 정답의 the scanner has produced an image that is not sharp

## 161-163 보고서

시미피케이션 서비스 센터

현황 보고

사안:
161 **우리 전자 상거래 웹사이트 디자인 테마를 이용하시는 여러 고객사에서 쇼핑 카트 기능에 발생한 문제를 알려 주셨습니다.** 이 쇼핑 카트 아이콘이 방문자의 카트가 실제로 비어 있는 경우에도 사이트 방문자들에게 "1"을 표시하고 있습니다. 163 **이는 챔포나 웹 브라우저를 이용하는 방문객들에게만 발생하고 있습니다.**

시미피케이션 서비스 센터에 접수된 고객 문의:
8월 20일, 오후 5시 48분

현재 상황:
영향을 받은 디자인 테마에서 사용하는 필수 소프트웨어 플러그인인 리얼테일에 의해 이 문제가 초래되었다는 사실을 밝혀 냈습니다. 162 **저희는 8월 21일 오전 9시 12분에 리얼테일 제조사에 통보해 이 문제가 해결되면 알려 달라고 요청했습니다.**

163 **영향을 받은 시미피케이션 고객사에 대한 권고 사항:**
**불만이 있는 방문객들에게 귀사 웹사이트 접속 시에 다른 브라우저를 이용하도록 권하십시오.**

어휘 status 현황, 상황 feature 기능, 특징 ticket (온라인 일대일 문의 등의) 고객 문의 file 신청하다, 제기하다 current 현재의 determine 밝혀 내다, 결정하다 plugin 플러그인(기능 확장 소프트웨어) resolve 해결하다 dissatisfied 불만이 있는 access 접속하다, 이용하다

## 161 주제 / 목적

번역 보고서는 왜 작성되었는가?
(A) 고객사에 데이터 보안 위험에 관해 알리기 위해
(B) 제품의 새로운 기능의 목적을 분명히 밝히기 위해
(C) 디자인 테마의 단종을 알리기 위해
(D) 몇몇 소매 웹사이트에 나타난 문제를 설명하기 위해

해설 첫 번째 단락에 전자 상거래 웹사이트 디자인 테마를 이용하는 여러 고객사에서 쇼핑 카트 기능에 발생한 문제를 알려 주었다(Clients using our e-commerce Web site design themes have reported a problem with the shopping cart feature)고 언급한 뒤로 해당 문제에 관한 구체적인 설명과 조치 등이 제시되어 있으므로 (D)가 정답이다.

어휘 risk 위험 (요소) clarify 분명히 밝히다 discontinuation 단종 retail 소매(업)

> Paraphrasing
> 지문의 Clients using our e-commerce Web site design themes have reported a problem
> → 정답의 an issue with some retail Web sites

## 162 추론

번역 시미피케이션 서비스 센터 직원들은 현재 무엇을 하고 있겠는가?
(A) 다른 회사의 연락 기다리기
(B) 일부 소프트웨어에 대해 추가 테스트 진행하기
(C) 고객사에서 발송한 보고서 살펴보기
(D) 문서 발급 준비하기

해설 현재 상황에 관한 정보가 쓰여 있는 곳에 8월 21일 오전 9시 12분에 리얼테일 제조사에 통보해 문제가 해결되면 알려 달라고 요청했다(We notified the maker of Realtail on August 21 at 9:12 A.M. and asked to be updated when the issue was resolved)는 내용이 쓰여 있어 이 제조사의 연락을 기다리고 있을 것으로 볼 수 있으므로 (A)가 정답이다.

어휘 further 추가적인, 한층 더 한 issue 발급하다, 발행하다

## 163 세부 사항

번역 시미피케이션 서비스 센터에서 일부 고객사에 무엇을 하도록 권하는가?
(A) 다른 디자인 테마 선택하기
(B) 리얼테일의 최신 버전으로 업그레이드하기
(C) 고객들이 챔포나를 이용하는 것을 막기
(D) 웹사이트 방문자 접속 제한하기

해설 권고 사항이 제시되어 있는 마지막 단락에 회사 웹사이트 접속 시에 다른 브라우저를 이용하도록 고객들에게 권하라(Advise dissatisfied visitors to use a different browser when accessing your Web site)는 말이 쓰여 있다. 첫 단락에 챔포나 웹 브라우저에 문제가 발생하는 것(This is only happening to visitors using the Champona Web browser)으로 언급되어 있어 이 브라우저를 이용하지 못하게 하라는 말이므로 (C)가 정답이다.

어휘 discourage 막다, 단념시키다 limit 제한하다

> Paraphrasing
> 지문의 Advise dissatisfied visitors to use a different browser → 정답의 Discourage their customers from using Champona

### 164-167 이메일

발신: gsasaki@vanhornpublishing.com
수신: jmyers@jig-mail.com
제목: <딜리셔스 포르투갈> 업무
날짜: 6월 30일
첨부: <딜리셔스 포르투갈>

마이어스 씨께,

[166] **다닐로 코스타의 <딜리셔스 포르투갈> 원고를 첨부했습니다.** 논의한 대로, [165] **직접 이 세 가지 조리법을 시험해 보신 다음, 그 설명의 명확성과 완성도에 관한 간단한 보고서를 작성해 주셨으면 합니다.** [164] **코스타 씨는 본인의 모든 조리법**이 계약서에서 요구하는 바와 같이 요리 비전문가에 의해 테스트되었다고 장담하시긴 했지만, 출간을 진행하기 전에 독립적인 평가자가 그 수준을 확인해 보는 것이 중요합니다. 290페이지에 있는 커스타드 타르트 조리법을 테스트에 포함해 주시기 바랍니다. [166] **그 조리법의 도입부 문단에서 설명하듯이, 수세기 동안 포르투갈에서 가장 유명한 음식 중 하나였습니다.** 평가자들이 이 부분에 특별히 관심을 기울이게 될 것입니다.

[167] **7월 5일 일요일 자정까지 이 과제를 완료해 주시기 바라며,** 재료를 구입한 영수증 이미지를 잊지 말고 제공해 주십시오. [167] **300달러의 비용 및 지출 환급액에 대한 수표가 14일 내로 발송될 것입니다.**

감사합니다.

긴지 사사키

어휘 assignment (배정된) 업무, 일 manuscript 원고 recipe 조리법 clarity 명확성 completeness 완성도, 완전성 instructions 설명, 안내 assure 장담하다, 보장하다 as required 요구된 대로 contract 계약(서) independent 독립적인 proceed with ~을 진행하다 publication 출판(물) include 포함하다 introductory 도입부의, 서두의 paragraph 문단, 단락 reviewer 평가자, 후기 작성자 pay attention to+명사 ~에 관심을 기울이다 receipt 영수증 ingredient (음식의) 재료 reimbursement 환급(액) expense 지출, 경비

## 164 추론

번역 코스타 씨는 누구일 것 같은가?
(A) 요리사
(B) 음식 평론가
(C) 여행 작가
(D) 번역가

해설 첫 단락 초반부에 코스타 씨의 이름과 함께 조리법(Mr. Costa has assured me that all of his recipes ~)을 언급하는 부분이 있으므로 (A)가 정답이다.

## 165 세부 사항

번역 마이어스 씨는 무엇을 하라는 요청을 받는가?
(A) 삽화 만들기
(B) 설명 평가하기
(C) 역사적 주장 확인하기
(D) 포르투갈 레스토랑 방문하기

해설 첫 단락 초반부에 이메일 수신인인 마이어스 씨에게 직접 세 가지 조리법을 시험해 보고 그 설명의 명확성과 완성도에 관한 간단한 보고서를 작성해 달라(I need you to try out three of the recipes yourself and write a short report on the clarity and completeness of their instructions)고 요청하는 내용이 쓰여 있다. 이는 그 조리법 설명 내용에 대해 평가하는 보고서를 작성해 달라는 뜻이므로 (B)가 정답이다.

어휘 illustration 삽화 evaluate 평가하다 claim 주장, 요구

> Paraphrasing
> 지문의 write a short report on the clarity and completeness of their instructions
> → 정답의 Evaluate some instructions

TEST 8

## 166 세부 사항

번역 사사키 씨에 따르면, 첨부 파일에 무엇이 포함되어 있는가?
(A) 한 나라의 지역들에 대한 설명
(B) 한 사람에 관한 전기적 세부 정보
(C) 업무 협약서 사본
(D) 한 요리의 의의에 대한 설명

해설 첫 단락 시작 부분에 다닐로 코스타의 <딜리셔스 포르투갈> 원고를 첨부했다(Attached you will find the manuscript for Danilo Costa's *Delicious Portugal*)고 알리고 있고, 이 단락 마지막 부분에는 조리법의 도입부 문단에서 설명하듯이, 수세기 동안 포르투갈에서 가장 유명한 음식 중 하나였다(As the introductory paragraph to that recipe explains, these have been one of Portugal's most famous foods for centuries)는 내용이 있다. 따라서 첨부 파일의 조리법 도입부에 그 요리가 지니는 의의를 설명한 내용이 포함되어 있다는 것을 알 수 있으므로 (D)가 정답이다.

어휘 explanation 설명 region 지역, 지방 biographical 전기의 agreement 계약(서), 합의(서) description 설명, 묘사 significance 의의, 중요성

> Paraphrasing
> 지문의 have been one of Portugal's most famous foods for centuries → 정답의 a dish's significance

## 167 세부 사항

번역 7월에 무슨 일이 있을 것인가?
(A) 이미지들이 원고에 추가될 것이다.
(B) 일부 집필 업무가 위임될 것이다.
(C) 재료 주문품이 배송될 것이다.
(D) 비용이 프리랜서에게 지급될 것이다.

해설 두 번째 단락에 이 과제를 7월 5일까지 완료해 달라(Please complete this assignment by the end of the day on Sunday, July 5)고 요청하면서 그 후 14일 내로 비용이 지급될 것(A check for your $300 fee plus reimbursement for expenses will then be sent out within 14 days)이라고 알리고 있으므로 (D)가 정답이다.

어휘 task 업무, 일 delegate 위임하다 issue 지급하다, 발급하다

> Paraphrasing
> 지문의 A check for your $300 fee plus reimbursement for expenses will then be sent out
> → 정답의 A payment will be issued

### 168-171 편지

소중한 고객님께,

레이크사이드 약국이 5월 1일부로 레비바 약국으로 상호를 변경할 것이라는 사실을 알려 드리게 되어 기쁩니다. 저희 지점들의 위치와 연락처는 동일하게 유지될 것입니다. 하지만 저희 웹 주소는 이제 www.reviva-pharm.com입니다.

레이크사이드 약국은 14년 전 레이크사이드에서 단 하나의 매장으로 설립되었습니다. 여러분의 성원 덕분에, 이제 세 개 도시에 여덟 개의 [169] **분주한** 지점을 갖추고 있습니다. [168] **신규 상호는 전국에 지점이 있는 전국적인 체인으로 계속 성장하려는 계획을 반영하는 것입니다.** 하지만 저희는 언제나 고객을 최우선으로 생각하므로 안심하셔도 됩니다. [170, 171] **저희는 1년 365일, 하루 24시간, 세심하고 전문적으로 여러분께 의약품에 대한 필요를 충족시켜 드리기 위해 계속 노력할 것입니다.**

곧 귀하의 지역에 있는 레비바 약국에서 도움을 드릴 수 있기를 고대합니다.

박경택, CEO

어휘 location 위치, 지점 contact number 연락처 branch 지점, 지사 found 설립하다 storefront (거리) 상점 comprise ~로 구성되다 reflect 반영하다 priority 우선 순위 strive to ~하려 애쓰다 pharmaceutical 의약품의, 약학의

## 168 세부 사항

번역 회사는 왜 상호를 변경하는가?
(A) 새로운 서비스를 제공하기 시작할 것이라서
(B) 현재의 상호가 다른 업체의 상호와 유사해서
(C) 다른 회사와 합병해서
(D) 더 많은 지역으로 사업을 확장하고 있어서

해설 두 번째 단락에 신규 상호는 전국에 지점이 있는 전국적인 체인으로 계속 성장하려는 계획을 반영하는 것(Our new name reflects our plans to continue growing into a national chain with locations throughout the country)이라는 내용이 제시되어 있다. 따라서 전국의 더 많은 지역으로 사업을 확장하고 있기 때문이라는 것을 알 수 있으므로 (D)가 정답이다.

어휘 merge with ~와 합병하다

> Paraphrasing
> 지문의 continue growing into a national chain with locations throughout the country
> → 정답의 is expanding into more regions

## 169 동의어

번역 두 번째 단락, 두 번째 줄에 쓰인 "busy"와 의미가 가장 가까운 것은?
(A) 먼, 멀리 있는
(B) (공간 등이) 이용 중인, 점유된
(C) 북적거리는, 부산한
(D) 성실한, 근면한

해설 busy가 지점을 뜻하는 branches를 수식하는 것으로 볼 때, '분주한, 바쁜'을 의미한다는 것을 알 수 있으므로 유사한 형용사로서 '북적거리는, 부산한' 등을 뜻하는 (C) bustling이 정답이다.

## 170 Not / True

번역 회사에 대해 언급된 것은?
(A) 하루 종일 언제든 고객들에게 서비스를 제공한다.
(B) 더 이상 레이크사이드에 본사를 두지 않는다.
(C) 전에 상호를 변경한 적이 있다.
(D) 박 씨에 의해 설립되었다.

해설 두 번째 단락에 1년 365일, 하루 24시간, 세심하고 전문적으로 의약품에 대한 필요를 충족시키기 위해 계속 노력할 것(We will continue striving to meet your pharmaceutical needs with care and professionalism around the clock, 365 days per year)이라고 알리는 부분을 통해 하루 24시간 서비스를 제공한다는 것을 알 수 있으므로 (A)가 정답이다.

어휘 be headquartered in ~에 본사가 있다

> Paraphrasing
> 지문의 continue striving to meet your pharmaceutical needs / around the clock
> → 정답의 serves customers at any time of the day

## 171 문장 삽입

번역 [1], [2], [3], [4]로 표시된 곳 중에서 다음 문장이 가장 적합한 곳은 어디인가?
"곧 귀하의 지역에 있는 레비바 약국에서 도움을 드릴 수 있기를 고대합니다."
(A) [1]
(B) [2]
(C) [3]
(D) [4]

해설 주어진 문장은 고객들에게 서비스를 제공할 수 있기를 고대한다는 기대와 바람을 나타낸다. 따라서 마지막 부분인 [4]에 들어가, 편지를 마무리하는 흐름이 되어야 자연스러우므로 (D)가 정답이다.

어휘 look forward to -ing ~하기를 고대하다 assist 돕다, 지원하다

### 172-175 문자 메시지

스탠리 보먼 [오전 9시 36분]
엘리노어, 172, 174, 175 **대즐 홈 굿즈 사에서 우리 창고에 오늘 오후부터 목요일 오전까지 가구 부품 팔레트 18개를 추가로 보관할 수 있는지 알고 싶어 해요.** 유통 문제를 해결할 시간이 필요하답니다.

엘리노어 소토 [오전 9시 37분]
현재 수용 가능 용량에 거의 근접했습니다. 확인해 봐야겠어요.

스탠리 보먼 [오전 9시 39분]
고마워요. 있잖아요, 이게 우리가 지난달에 분실한 대즐 램프 팔레트를 보상하는 데 도움이 될 수도 있어요.

엘리노어 소토 [오전 9시 40분]
맞아요, 하지만 우리가 수용할 수 있는 것보다 더 많은 재고를 맡는 것도 추가 실수로 이어질 수 있습니다. 173 **자, 지금 제 사무실로 돌아왔어요.** 창고 관리 소프트웨어를 열어 볼게요.

스탠리 보먼 [오전 9시 44분]
그래서요? 174 **우리가 할 수 있을까요?**

엘리노어 소토 [오전 9시 45분]
운이 좋네요. 바니 페인츠 사로 가는 대형 배송품이 정오에 출발할 예정이라서, 적치장 7B의 북쪽 끝이 며칠 동안 빕니다.

스탠리 보먼 [오전 9시 46분]
잘됐네요! 175 **대즐 사에게 어느 하역장으로 트럭을 보내라고 할까요?**

엘리노어 소토 [오전 9시 47분]
트럭이 몇 대나 될까요, 그리고 몇 시에 도착하죠?

스탠리 보먼 [오전 9시 48분]
트럭은 두 대이고, 3시에서 3시 30분 사이입니다.

엘리노어 소토 [오전 9시 49분]
좋아요, 시스템에 그 정보를 입력한 다음, 175 **몇 분 후에 하역장과 관련해서 알려 드릴게요.**

스탠리 보먼 [오전 9시 50분]
좋습니다. 다시 한번 감사합니다, 엘리노어.

어휘 warehouse 창고 store 보관하다, 저장하다 extra 추가의, 별도의 pallet (화물 운반용) 팔레트(화물을 쌓는 틀) resolve 해결하다 distribution 유통, 분배 capacity 수용력 make up for ~에 대해 보상하다, ~을 만회하다 misplace 분실하다 take on (책임 등) ~을 떠맡다 inventory 재고 (목록) hold 수용하다, 유지하다 in luck 운이 좋은 shipment 배송(품) be set to ~할 예정이다 loading dock 하역장

## 172 주제 / 목적

번역 메시지 작성자들이 이야기하고 있는 것은?
(A) 유통 과정 간소화하기
(B) 세일 행사 이용하기
(C) 고객 요청 이행하기
(D) 확장 프로젝트 연기하기

해설 9시 36분에 보먼 씨가 대즐 홈 굿즈 사에서 오늘 오후부터 목요일 오전까지 가구 부품 팔레트 18개를 추가로 보관할 수 있는지 알고 싶어 한다(Dazzle Home Goods wants to know if our warehouse can store 18 extra pallets of furniture parts from this afternoon until Thursday morning)고 알린 뒤로 그 가능성에 대해 이야기하고 있다. 이는 고객사의 서비스 요청을 이행하는 일에 해당하므로 (C)가 정답이다.

어휘 simplify 간소화하다 take advantage of ~을 이용하다 fulfill 이행하다, 완수하다 postpone 연기하다, 미루다 expansion 확장, 확대

> Paraphrasing
> 지문의 Dazzle Home Goods wants to know if ~
> → 정답의 a customer request

## 173 추론

번역 소토 씨에 대해 암시된 것은?
(A) 사무실에서 창고 작업장이 내려다보인다.
(B) 실수가 있었다는 사실을 알지 못했다.
(C) 바니 페인츠 사의 직원과 이야기했다.
(D) 대화 중에 장소를 이동했다.

해설 소토 씨가 9시 40분에 자신의 사무실로 돌아왔다(OK, I'm back in my office now)고 했으므로 대화 중간에 이동했다는 것을 알 수 있다. 따라서 (D)가 정답이다.

어휘 overlook (건물 등이) 내려다보다 representative 직원, 대표자

## 174 의도 파악

번역 오전 9시 45분에, 소토 씨가 "운이 좋네요"라고 쓸 때, 의미하는 것은 무엇인가?
(A) 분실품들을 되찾았다.
(B) 소프트웨어 프로그램에 특별한 기능이 있다.
(C) 상품을 보관할 공간이 있을 것이다.
(D) 아직 배송을 취소할 시간이 있다.

해설 바로 앞선 메시지에서 보먼 씨가 가능할지 묻자, '운이 좋네요'라는 긍정적인 대답을 하는 상황이다. 여기서 보먼 씨가 자신들이 가능할지 물은 것은 9시 36분 메시지에서 말하는 대즐 홈 굿즈 사의 가구 부품 팔레트 보관(Dazzle Home Goods wants to know if our warehouse can store 18 extra pallets of furniture parts ~)을 말하는 것이므로 (C)가 정답이다.

어휘 missing 분실된, 사라진 recover 되찾다 feature 기능, 특징 goods 상품

## 175 추론

번역 곧이어 무슨 일이 있겠는가?
(A) 인도 장소가 배정될 것이다.
(B) 트럭에 짐을 실을 것이다.
(C) 보먼 씨가 답신 전화를 할 것이다.
(D) 소토 씨가 컴퓨터를 켤 것이다.

해설 9시 46분에 보먼 씨가 대즐 사에게 어느 하역장으로 트럭을 보내라고 할지(What loading docks should I have Dazzle send its trucks to?) 묻자 9시 49분 메시지에 소토 씨가 몇 분 후에 하역장과 관련해서 알려 주겠다(let you know about the loading docks in a few minutes)고 했다. 이는 9시 36분 메시지에 언급된 가구 부품 팔레트를 내릴 장소를 배정해서 알려 주겠다는 뜻이므로 (A)가 정답이다.

어휘 spot 장소, 자리 assign 배정하다, 할당하다 load 짐을 싣다 return a call 답신 전화를 하다

### 176-180 기사+이메일

로스앤젤레스 (5월 3일) - [177] **커넥션 영화사는 개봉 예정인 영화 <블랙 도어>의 감독으로 호주 출신 루카스 피어스를 고용했다.** 피어스 씨는 [176 (D)] **극찬을 받은** [176 (A)] **섬뜩한 귀신 이야기인 데뷔작 <더 팜>으로 올봄 폭넓은 주목을 받았다.** 타마라 번즈가 주연을 맡을 <블랙 도어>는 병원을 배경으로 하는 심리 스릴러이다. [176 (B)] **<더 팜>의 제작비가 70만 달러에 불과했다고 알려진 만큼,** 예산이 800만 달러인 이 작품은 피어스 씨로서는 스케일이 엄청나게 커졌음을 시사한다.

커넥션에서 발표한 보도 자료에 따르면, <블랙 도어>는 11월에 촬영을 시작해 내년 10월에 영화관에 상영될 예정이다. [179] **또한 내년 여름 플레밍 영화제에서 이 영화를 몇 달 일찍 상영할 계획을 밝혔는데,** 아마 참석자들의 긍정적인 평가가 관객들에게 기대감을 불러일으키기를 바라는 것으로 보인다.

어휘 studio 영화사 direct 감독하다 upcoming 다가오는 gain 얻다 widespread 폭넓은, 광범위한 attention 주목, 주의 debut feature 데뷔작 terrifying 섬뜩한, 무서운 tale 이야기 glowing 극찬하는 star 주연을 맡다 psychological 심리적인, 정신적인 set in ~이 배경인 budget 예산 represent 보여 주다 significant 상당한 scale 스케일, 규모 reportedly 알려진 바에 따르면 cost 비용이 들다 press release 보도 자료 issue 발표하다 shoot 촬영하다 indicate 나타내다 screen 상영하다 presumably 아마 positive 긍정적인 attendee 참석자 anticipation 기대, 예상 audience 관객, 청중

수신: lucas.pearce@sno-mail.com
발신: gloria.ingram@connectionstudios.com
날짜: 8월 29일
제목: <블랙 도어>
첨부: 의견

루카스 씨께,

제 비서가 [179] **서튼 영화제에서 <블랙 도어> 첫 상영회**에 참석하신 분들의 피드백을 정리했습니다. 업계에서 영향력 있는 분들의 소셜 미디어 반응뿐 아니라 공식 평론도 포함하고 있습니다.

이미 알고 계실 수도 있지만, 영화 분위기에 대한 칭찬이 많았지만, 전개 속도가 느리다는 의견도 널리 퍼져 있었습니다. 몇몇 분들은 주인공의 아들 장면들이 줄거리와 관련되어 있지 않은데도 특히 많은 시간을 차지한다고 언급했습니다.

이러한 반응을 고려해 볼 때, [178] **편집 담당자와 협력해 그 장면들을 가능한 한 많이 잘라내 주셨으면 합니다.** 마무리되시면, 나머지 제작자 및 영화사 임원들을 대상으로 테스트 상영을 준비하겠습니다. 신속히 작업하실 수 있기를, 그리고 추가 촬영이 필요하지 않기를 바랍니다. [180] **저희는 <아티팩트> 개봉 전 <블랙 도어>가 극장가에서 일주일 내내 상영될 수 있도록 10월 7일로 예정된 개봉일을 지키고자 합니다.** 경쟁이 치열할 것이라는 소문이 있기 때문입니다.

글로리아 잉그램
제작 수석 부사장, 커넥션 스튜디오

어휘 compile (자료 등을 모아) 정리하다, 편집하다 attach 붙이다, 첨부하다 premiere screening 첫 상영회, 초연 include 포함하다 official 공식적인, 정식의 influential 영향력 있는 praise 칭찬 atmosphere 분위기 agreement 공감, 동의 pace 속도 sluggish 느릿느릿한 in particular 특히 take up 차지하다 relevant to+명사 ~와 관련 있는 plot 줄거리 arrange 마련하다, 조치하다 executive 임원, 이사

additional 추가적인 filming 촬영 release 개봉, 출시
stiff 팽팽한, 심한 competition 경쟁 (상대)

## 176 Not / True

번역 기사에서 <더 팜>에 대해 언급되지 않은 것은?
(A) 공포 영화이다.
(B) 상대적으로 예산이 적었다.
(C) 봄철을 배경으로 한다.
(D) 평론가들의 찬가를 받았다.

해설 기사 첫 단락에 <더 팜>이 극찬을 받은 섬뜩한 귀신 이야기(a terrifying ghost tale that received glowing reviews)라고 언급된 것에서 (A)와 (D)를, 같은 단락 마지막 부분에 제작비가 70만 달러에 불과하다(The Farm reportedly cost just $700,000 to make)는 것에서 (B)를 확인할 수 있다. 하지만 봄이 작품의 배경이라는 정보는 제시되어 있지 않으므로 (C)가 정답이다.

어휘 relatively 상대적으로, 비교적 budget 예산 praise 칭찬하다
critic 평론가

Paraphrasing
지문의 a terrifying ghost tale → 보기 (A)의 a horror film
지문의 received glowing reviews
→ 보기 (D)의 praised by critics
지문의 cost just $700,000
→ 보기 (B)의 a relatively low budget

## 177 추론

번역 기사에서 <블랙 도어>에 대해 암시하는 것은?
(A) 제작하는 데 2년 넘게 걸릴 것이다.
(B) 감독으로서 피어스 씨의 두 번째 영화가 될 것이다.
(C) 출연진 섭외 과정이 아직 시작되지 않았다.
(D) 호주에서 촬영될 것이다.

해설 기사 첫 번째 단락에 피어스 씨가 <블랙 도어>의 감독을 맡는다(Connection Studios has hired Australian Lucas Pearce to direct its upcoming film *Black Door*)는 말과 함께, 데뷔작 <더 팜>으로 올봄 많은 주목을 받았다(Mr. Pearce gained widespread attention this spring with his debut feature, The Farm)는 정보가 제시되어 있다. 따라서 <블랙 도어>가 감독으로서 작업하는 두 번째 영화임을 추론할 수 있으므로 (B)가 정답이다.

어휘 casting process 출연진 섭외 과정

## 178 주제 / 목적

번역 이메일의 주 목적은 무엇인가?
(A) 편집을 요청하는 것
(B) 연기를 알리는 것
(C) 공동 작업자를 축하해 주는 것
(D) 광고에 대해 논의하는 것

해설 이메일 초반에 상영회 반응을 먼저 언급한 다음, 세 번째 단락에서 부정적인 반응에 대한 조치로 편집 담당자와 협력해 불필요한 장면들을 가능한 한 많이 잘라내 달라(we would like you to work with the editor to cut as many of those scenes as possible)고 요청하고 있으므로 (A)가 정답이다.

어휘 postponement 연기, 뒤로 미룸 congratulate 축하하다
collaborator 공동 작업자, 협력자 advertising 광고 (활동)

Paraphrasing
지문의 would like you to work with the editor to cut as many of those scenes as possible
→ 정답의 request some edits

## 179 연계

번역 <블랙 도어>의 첫 상영에 대해 암시된 것은?
(A) 관객들은 설문 요청을 받았다.
(B) 그 영화 작업을 한 사람들만 참석했다.
(C) 계획된 것과 다른 행사에서 상영되었다.
(D) 인터넷상에서 상영되었다.

해설 기사 두 번째 단락에 플레밍 영화제에서 이 작품을 상영할 계획을 내비쳤다(The studio also indicated plans to screen the film a few months earlier at the Fleming Film Festival)고 했는데, 이메일 첫 단락에는 첫 상영회가 서튼 영화제에서 있었던 것(its premiere screening at the Sutton Film Festival)으로 언급되어 있다. 따라서 애초의 계획과 다른 영화제에서 처음 상영되었다는 것을 알 수 있으므로 (C)가 정답이다.

어휘 conduct 실시하다

## 180 Not / True

번역 이메일에서, <아티팩트>에 대해 언급된 것은?
(A) 이것 또한 커넥션 영화사의 작품이다.
(B) 영화제에서 상영되었다.
(C) 추가 촬영을 진행하고 있다.
(D) 10월에 개봉될 것이다.

해설 이메일 마지막 단락에 <아티팩트>가 나오기 전에 <블랙 도어>가 극장가에서 일주일 내내 상영될 수 있게 10월 7일로 예정된 개봉일을 지키고자 한다(We want to keep our scheduled release date of October 7 so that *Black Door* will have a full week in theaters before *Artifact* comes out)고 쓰여 있어 <아티팩트>도 10월에 개봉한다는 것을 알 수 있다. 따라서 (D)가 정답이다.

어휘 undergo 거치다, 겪다

### 181-185 이메일+이메일

발신: osullivan@nortech.com
수신: inquiries@haywoodhub.com
제목: 사무용 공간 문의
날짜: 2월 2일 목요일, 오전 10시 8분

안녕하세요,

TEST 8

전화로 연락이 되지 않아 이메일로 연락 드립니다. 귀사의 웹사이트에 기재된 번호로 전화할 때마다, "연결될 수 없다"는 메시지가 나옵니다.

[181] **저는 가족 문제를 처리하는 몇 주 동안 원격으로 일할 수 있는 헤이우드에 있는 공유 오피스 업체를 찾고 있습니다.** [182] **개인 사무실과 대형 컴퓨터 모니터 2대를 사용할 수 있어야 하며,** 예산 한도는 주당 100달러입니다. 헤이우드 허브에 제가 찾는 것이 있나요?

그리고 웹사이트에서 주차를 제공한다는 것을 보았습니다. 요금이 얼마인지, 그리고 그 주차 공간에 울타리가 설치되어 있는지 알려 주시겠습니까?

빨리 회신해 주시기 바랍니다.

올리브 설리번

어휘 inquiry 문의, 질문 unavailable 이용할 수 없는 seek 찾다, 구하다 coworking 업무 공간을 공유하는 remotely 원격으로, 멀리서 deal with ~을 처리하다, ~에 대처하다 budget 예산 charge 청구하다 enclosed 울타리가 설치된

발신: edchisholm@haywoodhub.com
수신: osullivan@nortech.com
제목: 회신: 사무용 공간 문의
날짜: 2월 2일 목요일, 오전 11시 42분

설리번 씨께,

전화 연결에 어려움을 겪으신 것에 대해 사과드립니다. 나뭇가지가 전화선에 떨어지는 바람에 오늘 아침에 지역 전체의 전화 서비스가 중단되었습니다. 다행히, 이 문제는 신속히 처리되었습니다.

문의하신 내용과 관련하여, [182] **현재 2층에 귀하께서 요청하시는 컴퓨터 용품에 대한 요금까지 포함하여 주당 96달러인 적합한 공간들이 있습니다.** [183] **주나 월 단위로 지불하시는 경우엔 주차 요금을 면제해 드리며,** 주차 공간에 울타리는 설치되어 있지는 않지만, 대부분의 공간이 그늘막으로 [184] **가려져** 있습니다.

[185] **예약하지 않고 오셔도 되지만,** 사용 가능한 공간이 있는지 확실히 하려면 미리 자리를 예약하시는 것이 가장 좋습니다. 이 이메일에 답장하시거나 대표전화 내선 3번으로 제게 바로 전화하여 예약하실 수 있습니다. 추가 질문이 있으시면 기꺼이 답변해 드리겠습니다.

에드 치스홀름, 서비스 관리자
헤이우드 허브

어휘 outage 중단, 정전 branch 나뭇가지 handle 처리하다, 다루다 currently 현재 suitable 적합한, 어울리는 inclusive of ~을 포함하는 accessories 부대용품 waive 면제하다, 철회하다 shade canopy (지붕 부분을 이루는) 그늘막 walk-in 예약 없는 방문 ahead of time 미리, 사전에 ensure 반드시 ~하도록 하다, 보장하다 available 이용 가능한 extension 내선전화(번호)

## 181 Not / True

번역 첫 번째 이메일에서 설리번 씨가 자신에 대해 언급하는 것은?
(A) 전에 공유 오피스 업체를 애용한 적이 있다.
(B) 출장에 회사 차량을 이용할 계획이다.
(C) 가족 소유 업체에서 근무한다.
(D) 개인적인 이유로 헤이우드에 간다.

해설 첫 번째 이메일 두 번째 단락에 가족 문제를 처리하는 몇 주 동안 원격으로 일할 수 있는 헤이우드에 있는 공유 오피스 업체를 찾고 있다(I am seeking a coworking business in Haywood from which I can work remotely for a few weeks while dealing with a family matter)고 했으므로 (D)가 정답이다.

어휘 patronize 애용하다 family-owned 가족 소유의

> Paraphrasing
> 지문의 a family matter → 정답의 a personal reason

## 182 연계

번역 헤이우드 허브의 2층에 있는 공간에 대해 사실인 것은?
(A) 그중 일부는 개인용 사무실이다.
(B) 주당 100달러 미만의 비용으로 이용할 수 있는 유일한 공간이다.
(C) 그중 일부는 주차 구역이 내려다보인다.
(D) 한 번에 최소 일주일 동안 임대되어야 한다.

해설 첫 번째 이메일 두 번째 단락에 개인 사무실이 필요할 것(I would need a private office)이라고 했는데, 두 번째 이메일 두 번째 단락에 2층에 적합한 공간들이 있다(we currently have suitable spaces open on our second floor)고 했다. 따라서 2층 공간에 개인용 사무실이 있다는 것을 알 수 있으므로 (A)가 정답이다.

어휘 individual 개인적인, 개별적인 overlook (건물 등이) 내려다보다 rent 임대하다

> Paraphrasing
> 지문의 a private office
> → 정답의 offices for individual use

## 183 세부 사항

번역 치스홀름 씨가 설리번 씨에게 무엇을 제안하는가?
(A) 컴퓨터 모니터 두 대 무료 대여
(B) 한 달 사무실 임대료 할인
(C) 주차장 무료 이용
(D) 더 나은 편의시설이 있는 공간으로 업그레이드

해설 두 번째 이메일 두 번째 단락에 주나 월 단위로 지불하는 경우에 주차 요금을 면제해 줄 것(The parking fee will be waived if you pay by the week or month)이라고 했으므로 (C)가 정답이다.

어휘 loan 대여 rental 임대, 대여 complimentary 무료의 access 이용, 접근 amenities 편의시설

> Paraphrasing
> 지문의 The parking fee will be waived
> → 정답의 Complimentary access to the parking area

## 184 동의어

번역 두 번째 이메일의 두 번째 단락, 네 번째 줄에 쓰인 "covered"와 의미가 가장 가까운 것은?
(A) ~에 대해 지불된
(B) 보호된
(C) 해결된, 처리된
(D) 분리된

해설 covered가 쓰인 문장은 대부분의 공간이 그늘막으로 가려져 있다는 의미이다. 이는 그늘막으로 보호되어 있다고 표현할 수 있으므로 '보호된'을 뜻하는 (B) protected가 정답이다.

## 185 Not / True

번역 두 번째 이메일에서 헤이우드 허브에 대해 언급하는 것은?
(A) 건물이 사고로 인해 막 손상되었다.
(B) 고객이 예약을 하지 않아도 된다.
(C) 직원들의 내선번호가 변경되었다.
(D) 전화선에 일상적인 유지관리 작업을 실시하고 있다.

해설 두 번째 이메일 세 번째 단락에 예약하지 않고 와도 된다(we do allow walk-ins)고 했으므로 (B)가 정답이다.

어휘 routine 일상적인 maintenance 유지관리 (작업) perform 실시하다

> Paraphrasing
> 지문의 allow walk-ins → 정답의 does not require customers to make reservations

## 186-190 이메일+이메일+가격표

발신: 아서 로즈 <arhodes@birchadvisors.com>
수신: contact@caldwellresortrentals.com
제목: 단체 대여에 관한 문의
날짜: 11월 10일, 오전 9시 21분

콜드웰 리조트 대여점 담당자께,

12월에 저희 팀이 팀워크 강화 활동으로 스키 여행을 떠날 예정입니다. 저는 가족들과 작년에 콜드웰 리조트를 방문했는데, 모두 아주 즐거운 시간을 보냈습니다. 저희는 귀사의 대여 서비스를 이용해 본 적은 없지만, [186] **저희 팀원들 중 한 명이 귀사 용품의 품질에 깊은 인상을 받았다고 얘기해 주었습니다.** [187] **이번 방문에는 스키와 스키 폴, 그리고 스키 부츠가 필요합니다. 저희 회사 안전 가이드라인을 준수하기 위해, 보호용 헬멧도 착용해야 합니다.** 가급적 빠른 시일 내에 요금을 알려 주시기 바랍니다.

감사합니다.

아서 로즈

어휘 inquiry 문의 rental 대여 be impressed with ~에 깊은 인상을 받다 quality 품질, 질 comply with ~을 준수하다 protective headgear 보호용 헬멧 rate 요금

발신: contact@caldwellresortrentals.com
수신: 아서 로즈 <arhodes@birchadvisors.com>
제목: 회신: 단체 대여에 관한 문의
날짜: 11월 10일, 오후 3시 58분
첨부: CRR_가격표

로즈 씨께,

CRR의 서비스에 관심을 가져주셔서 감사드립니다. 다가오는 시즌의 가격표를 첨부해 드립니다. 높은 고객 수요로 인해, [188] **처음으로 스노우보드 대여 서비스를 제공합니다.** 저희 직원들이 잘 맞는 부츠 사이즈를 선택할 수 있도록 도와 드릴 수 있습니다. 질문이 있으시면, 이 주소로 또는 전화번호 (940) 555-4802번으로 언제든지 연락 주시기 바랍니다. 귀하와 귀하의 일행이 여기 콜드웰 리조트에서 슬로프를 즐기며 멋진 시간을 보내시기 바랍니다.

앨리슨 밀라드

어휘 interest 관심 attached 첨부된 upcoming 다가오는, 곧 있을 demand 수요, 요구 available (사람이) 시간이 나는, (사물 등이) 이용 가능한 select 선택하다 ensure 보장하다 proper 적절한 fit 착용감

콜드웰 리조트 대여 가격표

| 패키지 | 일일 요금 | 2일 요금 |
|---|---|---|
| 패키지 1: 스키만 | 22파운드 | 35파운드 |
| 패키지 2: 스키, 폴, 부츠 | 30파운드 | 48파운드 |
| [187] **패키지 3: 스키, 폴, 부츠, 헬멧** | 32파운드 | 50파운드 |
| [188] **패키지 4: 스노우보드만** | **25파운드** | 40파운드 |
| 패키지 5: 스키 재킷, 스키 바지, 장갑 | 22파운드 | 35파운드 |

- 저희는 날씨에 따라 11월 중순부터 2월 중순까지 개장합니다.
- 용품은 오후 4시 30분까지 반납되어야 하며, 그렇지 않으면 다음 날 요금이 부과됩니다.
- [189] **용품은 선착순으로 제공되므로, 사전 예약을 적극 권합니다.**
- [190] **모든 대여 요금에는 파손에 대한 보험이 포함되어 있지만, 분실에 대해서는 적용되지 않습니다.**
- 저희는 5세 이상 아동에서부터 성인용 XL 사이즈까지 거의 모든 사이즈를 대여해 드릴 수 있습니다.

어휘 depending on ~에 따라 (다른), ~에 달려 있는 charge 요금을 청구하다; 청구 요금 on a first-come, first-served basis 선착순으로 reserve 예약하다 in advance 사전에, 미리 include 포함하다 insurance 보험 breakage 파손 loss 분실 accommodate 수용하다, 융통하다

## 186 Not / True

번역 로즈 씨가 첫 번째 이메일에서 언급하는 것은?
(A) 자신의 팀이 작년에 콜드웰 리조트를 방문했다.
(B) 자신의 동료가 전에 CRR을 이용한 적이 있다.
(C) 스키 강습을 예약하는 데 관심이 있다.
(D) 회사 법인카드로 대여 비용을 지불할 것이다.

TEST 8

해설 첫 번째 이메일 중반부에 로즈 씨가 자신의 팀원들 중 한 명이 CRR 용품의 품질에 깊은 인상을 받았다고 얘기했다(one of my team members said he was impressed with the quality of your items)고 언급되어 있으므로 (B)가 정답이다.

어휘 coworker 동료 be interested in ~에 관심이 있다 book 예약하다

## 187 연계

번역 어느 대여 패키지가 로즈 씨 그룹에 가장 알맞을 것인가?
(A) 패키지 2
(B) 패키지 3
(C) 패키지 4
(D) 패키지 5

해설 첫 번째 이메일 후반부에 필요한 용품으로 스키와 스키 폴, 스키 부츠, 그리고 보호용 헬멧(For our visit, skis, poles, and boots are needed. ~ protective headgear must also be worn)이 언급되어 있다. 가격표 중반부에 이 네 가지 용품을 포함하는 패키지가 'Package 3: Skis, poles, boots, & helmet'으로 쓰여 있으므로 (B)가 정답이다.

## 188 연계

번역 CRR은 자사의 최신 대여 패키지를 하루 이용하는 것에 얼마를 청구할 것인가?
(A) 22파운드
(B) 25파운드
(C) 30파운드
(D) 32파운드

해설 두 번째 이메일 중반부에 최신 대여 패키지에 해당하는 것으로 스노우보드 대여를 처음 제공한다(we are offering snowboard rentals for the first time)는 정보가 제시되어 있다. 가격표 중반부에 스노우보드만 대여하는 패키지인 'Package 4: Snowboard only'의 일일 요금(One-Day Rate)이 £25.00로 표기되어 있으므로 (B)가 정답이다.

> **Paraphrasing**
> 지문의 snowboard rentals for the first time
> → 질문의 newest rental package

## 189 Not / True

번역 가격표에 언급된 것은?
(A) 해당 업체는 매년 9개월 동안 문을 연다.
(B) 아이들은 장비를 사용할 수 없다.
(C) 특정 단체 규모에 대해서는 할인이 제공된다.
(D) 용품 이용이 보장되지 않는다.

해설 가격표 하단의 세 번째 항목에 용품이 선착순으로 제공되기 때문에 사전 예약을 적극 권한다(Items are offered on a first-come, first-served basis, so reserving items in advance is strongly advised)는 정보가 쓰여 있다. 이는 용품 이용이 선착순이기 때문에 늦으면 이용하지 못할 수 있다는 것을 의미한다. 따라서 (D)가 정답이다.

어휘 be allowed to ~하도록 허용되다 equipment 장비 guarantee 보장하다 available 이용 가능한

## 190 추론

번역 가격표에 따르면, 모든 대여 용품에 대해 암시된 것은?
(A) 우편으로 반납될 수 있다.
(B) 분실하면 요금이 발생될 것이다.
(C) 추가 비용을 지불하고 보험에 가입할 수 있다.
(D) 파손 가능성 때문에 보증금이 필요하다.

해설 가격표 하단의 네 번째 항목에 모든 대여 요금에는 파손에 대한 보험이 포함되어 있지만, 분실에 대해서는 적용되지 않는다(All rental charges include insurance against breakage but not against loss)고 언급되어 있다. 이를 통해 분실 시에는 보험 처리가 되지 않아 따로 보상해야 함을 유추할 수 있다. 따라서 (B)가 정답이다.

어휘 incur (비용 등을) 발생시키다 fee 요금, 수수료 insured 보험에 든 additional 추가적인 deposit 보증금, 선금

### 191-195 웹페이지+차트+이메일

http://www.green-run.com/volunteering

그린 런에서의 자원봉사

191 **그린 런의 인기가 전 세계적으로 증가하는** 이유 하나는 이 주간 야외 달리기 행사의 참여가 달리기하는 사람들로 제한되지 않는다는 점입니다.

그린 런 코스를 걸을 수 있는 사람들은 사전에 코스 표시물을 설치하고 나중에 철거하는 자원봉사를 하거나, 마지막 주자의 뒤를 따라 걷는 '꼬리 걷기'를 하면서 코스에 아무도 남지 않도록 도와줄 수 있습니다. 195 **오직 앉아만 있을 수 있는 사람들은 코스의 주요 전환 지점에서 주자들을 안내하는 코스 진행 요원 역할을 할 수 있습니다.** 그리고 기계를 잘 다루는 사람들은 결승선 앞에 서 있다가 193 **그린 런 스마트폰 앱의 도움을 받아, 결승선 통과 시간을 기록하거나 주자들의 참가 바코드를 스캔하기 위해 필요합니다.**

자원봉사자가 되려면, 192 (D) **거주 지역의 행사 진행 담당자에게 이메일을 보내시기 바랍니다.** 192 (A) **모든 자원봉사자들은 행사에서 처음으로 도움을 주시기 전에 여기에서 그린 런 회원 계정을 만들어야 하며,** 192 (C) **행사 당일에 휴대전화로 연락이 가능해야 합니다.**

어휘 volunteer 자원봉사하다; 자원봉사자 popularity 인기 participation 참여, 참가 limit 제한하다 set out 설치하다, 진열하다 beforehand 사전에, 미리 take ~ down ~을 철거하다 afterwards 나중에, 그 후에 ensure 확인하다, 보장하다 act 역할을 하다 marshal 진행 요원 direct 안내하다 turn 전환 지점 handy 잘 다루는 local 지역의 coordinator 진행 담당자 create 만들다 assist 도움을 주다 reachable 연락 가능한

6월 7일 윙필드 그린 런 자원봉사 배정

| 역할 | 필요한 인원 수 | 자원봉사자 |
|---|---|---|
| 코스 설치/철거 | 3-5 | 스튜어트 화이트, 기예르모 라모스, 도나 골드먼* |
| 꼬리 걷기 | 2+ | 루벤 리니, 니콜렛 피카도 |
| 코스 진행 요원 | 4+ | 알렉시스 부*, 패트릭 스캔런, 마리아 세라노, 블레어 윌슨 |
| 시간 기록 | 1 | 피터 포스피실 |
| [193] **바코드 스캔** | 2-4 | [193] **트래비스 나이즈완더,** 캐롤린 쉘비*, 스베틀라나 테스네스 |

* 신규 자원봉사자

어휘 assignment 배정(된 일), 배치

발신: 베서니 트루도
수신: 그래디 챈들러
제목: 자원봉사
날짜: 6월 10일

안녕하세요, 그래디,

[194] **지난주 토요일에 있었던 그린 런은 어땠나요? 못 가서 죄송합니다. 제가 그 전날에 친구 이사를 도와주다가 무릎을 삐었어요.** 사실, 몇 주 동안은 다시 달릴 수 없을 겁니다. 하지만 자원봉사를 통해 계속 참여하고 싶은데 당신이 윙필드 자원봉사 진행 담당자인 게 기억났습니다. [195] **제가 움직이지 못하는 상태에서 이번 주에 도와드릴 수 있는 방법이 있을까요?** 알려 주시기 바랍니다.

감사합니다.

베서니

어휘 miss 가지 못하다, 놓치다 sprain 삐다 involved 참여하는, 관여하는 off one's feet 움직이지 못하는

## 191 추론

번역 웹페이지에서 그린 런에 대해 암시하는 것은?
(A) 기금 마련 행사이다.
(B) 다양한 국가에서 개최된다.
(C) 코스들이 최소 길이를 초과해야 한다.
(D) 계절마다 열린다.

해설 웹페이지 첫 번째 단락에 그린 런의 인기가 전 세계적으로 증가하고 있다(the growing popularity of Green Runs all over the world)는 말이 있으므로 (B)가 정답이다.

어휘 fund-raising 기금 마련, 모금 multiple 다양한, 다수의 exceed 초과하다 take place 개최되다 seasonally 계절적으로

> Paraphrasing
> 지문의 all over the world → 정답의 in multiple countries

## 192 Not / True

번역 자원봉사자들이 해야 하는 일로 기재되지 않은 것은?
(A) 그린 런 회원 계정에 등록하기
(B) 온라인상의 규칙 목록 읽어 보기
(C) 휴대전화 휴대하기
(D) 그린 런 관계자에게 연락하기

해설 웹페이지 세 번째 단락에 거주 지역의 행사 진행 담당자에게 이메일을 보내라(send an e-mail to your local event coordinator)는 말에서 (D)를, 그린 런 회원 계정을 만들어야 한다(All volunteers will be required to create a Green Run membership here)는 말에서 (A)를, 행사 당일에 휴대전화로 연락이 가능해야 한다(must be reachable by mobile phone on the day of the event)고 언급하는 부분에서 (C)를 확인할 수 있다. 하지만 온라인에서 규칙 목록을 읽는 일과 관련된 정보는 나타나 있지 않으므로 (B)가 정답이다.

어휘 sign up for ~에 등록하다, ~을 신청하다 account 계정, 계좌 official 관계자

> Paraphrasing
> 지문의 send an e-mail to your local event coordinator
> → 보기 (D)의 Contact a Green Run official
> 지문의 create a Green Run membership
> → 보기 (A)의 Sign up for a Green Run member account
> 지문의 must be reachable by mobile phone
> → 보기 (C)의 Carry a mobile phone

## 193 연계

번역 차트의 정보를 바탕으로, 나이즈완더 씨에 대해 어떤 결론을 내릴 수 있는가?
(A) 전에 자원봉사를 해본 적이 없다.
(B) 경로를 따라 전환 지점에 배치될 것이다.
(C) 특별한 모바일 앱을 사용하도록 요청받을 것이다.
(D) 행사가 시작되기 전에 도착해야 할 것이다.

해설 나이즈완더 씨의 이름은 차트 맨 마지막 칸에서 볼 수 있으며, 해당 역할이 바코드 스캔(Barcode scanning)으로 표기되어 있다. 바코드 스캔 업무는 웹페이지 두 번째 단락에 그린 런 스마트폰 앱의 도움을 받아 주자들의 참가 바코드를 스캔하는 것(with the help of the Green Run smartphone app, record finish times or scan runners' participation barcodes)으로 언급되어 있어 이 모바일 앱을 이용하도록 요청받을 것으로 볼 수 있다. 따라서 (C)가 정답이다.

어휘 conclude 결론을 내리다 station 배치하다

## 194 주제 / 목적

번역 트루도 씨가 이메일을 쓴 한 가지 이유는?
(A) 자원봉사 배정 업무를 변경하기 위해
(B) 일부 교육 일정에 대해 묻기 위해
(C) 주최자에게 자신을 소개하기 위해
(D) 행사에 불참한 이유를 설명하기 위해

해설 이메일 초반부에 지난주 토요일에 있었던 그린 런은 어땠는지 물으면

서 그 전날에 친구가 이사하는 걸 도와주다가 무릎을 삐어서 가지 못해 미안하다(How was last Saturday's Green Run? I'm sorry I missed it — I sprained my knee while helping a friend move the day before)는 사과의 말이 쓰여 있다. 이는 지난주 토요일 행사에 참가하지 못한 이유를 설명하는 것이므로 (D)가 정답이다.

어휘 timeline 진행 일정 organizer 주최자, 조직자 absence 부재, 결근

## 195 연계

번역 챈들러 씨는 트루도 씨에게 무엇을 하도록 권할 것 같은가?
(A) 주자들이 코스를 벗어나지 않도록 돕기
(B) 참가자들이 도착할 때 맞이하기
(C) 간식 테이블 뒤에 앉기
(D) 장비 재고 조사하기

해설 이메일 후반부에 트루도 씨가 움직이지 못하는 상태에서 도와줄 수 있는 방법이 있는지(Is there a way I could help out this week while staying off my feet?) 묻고 있다. 이와 관련해, 웹페이지 두 번째 단락에 오직 앉아만 있을 수 있는 사람들은 코스의 주요 전환 지점에서 주자들을 안내하는 코스 진행 요원의 역할을 할 수 있다(Those who can only sit may act as course marshals, directing the runners at some of the course's major turns)는 내용이 제시되어 있으므로 (A)가 정답이다.

어휘 greet 맞이하다 refreshments 간식, 다과 inventory 재고 조사를 하다 equipment 장비

> Paraphrasing
> 지문의 directing the runners at some of the course's major turns → 정답의 Help runners stay on course

## 196-200 웹페이지+광고+배송 확인서

https://www.heredia.com/appliances/cooktops/ec7030a

헤레디아 브라이트 30인치 전기 쿡탑 (EC7030A)

이 쿡탑은 최첨단 편의성과 정확성을 제공합니다. 네 개의 버너가 여러분의 스마트폰에서 헤레디아 브라이트 앱을 통해 관찰되고 조절될 수 있습니다. 199 **또한 각 버너를 정확한 온도로 설정할 수 있어서**, 소스와 캔디 같이 세심한 주의가 필요한 음식을 요리하는 것이 쉬워집니다.

특징:
- 완전히 매끄러운 유리 표면으로 손쉬운 청소 가능
- 신속한 가열을 위한 3100와트 초강력 버너 한 개 포함
- 196 **브라이트 주방용 후드와 무선으로 동기화되어, 쿡탑이 켜지면 후드 팬과 전등이 자동으로 켜짐**
- 고온 표면 표시등과 잠금 기능으로 안전 보장

EC7030A 모델은 탤리 결제 플랫폼을 통한 금융 서비스 대상입니다. 여기를 클릭하셔서 구매하시기 전에 탤리에 가입하세요.

어휘 cutting-edge 최첨단의 convenience 편의(성) precision 정확(성) monitor 관찰하다 adjust 조절하다 exact 정확한 degree (온도, 각도 등의) 도 temperature 온도 delicate 세심한 주의가 필요한 feature 특징, 기능 surface 표면 enable 가능하게 하다 include 포함하다 extra 별도의, 추가의 sync 동기화하다, 동시 작동하다 turn on 켜지다 indicator 표시(기) function 기능 ensure 보장하다 be eligible for ~의 대상이 되다 sign up for ~에 가입하다

헤레디아
혁신의 봄 특별 행사

주방에서 혁신을 꽃피우세요! 올봄, 197 **헤레디아의 브라이트 라인 스마트 홈 전자 제품 중에서 최소 세 개의 주방 가전을 구입하고 두둑한 리베이트를 받으세요**. 더 많이 구입할수록, 더 많이 돌려받습니다!

◇ 가전 세 개: 300달러
◇ 200 **가전 네 개: 550달러**
◇ 가전 다섯 개: 800달러
◇ 가전 여섯 개 이상: 1,050달러

모든 구매는 4월 1일에서 5월 31일 사이에 저희 온라인 매장이나 헤레디아 가전 공식 판매점을 통해 이뤄져야 합니다. www.heredia.com/promotions/siis를 방문하셔서 온라인으로 리베이트를 신청하시거나 우편 발송될 수 있는 요청서를 출력하시기 바랍니다.

어휘 innovation 혁신 bloom 꽃을 피우다 earn 얻다 generous 넉넉한, 후한 rebate 리베이트 appliance 가전기기 electronics 전자기기 authorized 공인된 retailer 소매점 apply for ~을 신청하다 claim form 요청서

헤레디아
www.heredia.com
1-800-555-0164
배송 확인서
주문 번호: 56403
주문 날짜: 4월 9일
고객: 클락 유뱅크스, 헨리 길 710, 샤넷, RI 02809
배송 날짜: 4월 18일

| 제품 | 수량 | 설치가 필요하신가요? |
|---|---|---|
| 200 **브라이트 울트라 프레시 식기세척기 (DW7550S)** | 1 | 198 ∨ |
| 199, 200 **브라이트 30인치 전기 쿡탑 (EC7030A)** | 1 | 198 ∨ |
| 200 **브라이트 28입방피트 4도어 냉장고 (RF78233H)** | 1 | 198 ∨ |
| 200 **브라이트 1.1입방피트 조리대용 전자레인지 (MO74403M)** | 1 | |

198 **상기 제품들이 이상 없이 배송되었으며, 요청된 모든 설치 작업이 만족스럽게 실시되었습니다.**

[198] 클락 유뱅크스
(고객 또는 지정 수령인 서명)

어휘 confirmation 확인(서) quantity 수량 installation 설치 countertop 조리대 above 상기의, 위의 perform 실시하다 satisfactorily 만족스럽게 designated 지정된 recipient 수령인, 수취인

## 196 Not / True

번역 웹페이지에서 EC7030A 모델에 대해 언급하는 것은?
(A) 다른 가전과 가상으로 연결될 수 있다.
(B) 시중에서 가장 강력한 쿡탑이다.
(C) 유리 조리 도구와 함께 사용해도 안전하다.
(D) 조리법 공유 앱 이용 권한을 포함한다.

해설 웹페이지 중반부에 제시된 특징 중 세 번째 항목에 브라이트 주방용 후드와 무선으로 동기화되어, 쿡탑이 켜지면 후드 팬과 전등이 자동으로 켜진다(Syncs wirelessly with Bright kitchen hoods; hood fan and lights automatically turn on when cooktop does)고 했다. 이는 다른 가전과 디지털적으로 연결된다는 뜻이므로 (A)가 정답이다.

어휘 connect 연결하다 virtually 가상으로 cookware 조리 도구 come with ~을 포함하다, ~이 딸려 있다 access 이용 (권한) recipe 조리법

> **Paraphrasing**
> 지문의 Syncs wirelessly with Bright kitchen hoods
> → 정답의 connected virtually to another appliance

## 197 추론

번역 광고에서, 혁신의 봄 특별 행사에 대해 암시된 것은?
(A) 헤레디아 온라인 매장 방문객만 이용할 수 있다.
(B) 여섯 개 구매 후에도 리베이트 금액은 계속 늘어난다.
(C) 브라이트 라인의 모든 제품이 그 대상이 되는 것은 아니다.
(D) 대상이 되는 구매품에 자동으로 적용된다.

해설 광고 첫 단락에 헤레디아의 브라이트 라인 스마트 홈 전자 제품 중에서 최소 세 개의 주방 가전을 구입하고 두둑한 리베이트를 받으라(~ earn a generous rebate by purchasing at least three kitchen appliances from among Heredia's Bright line of smart home electronics)는 말이 쓰여 있다. 즉 브라이트 가전 제품 중 주방 가전만 행사의 대상임을 알 수 있으므로 (C)가 정답이다.

어휘 available 이용 가능한 increase 늘어나다, 증가하다 qualify for ~의 대상이 되다 apply 적용하다 eligible 대상이 되는

## 198 Not / True

번역 배송 확인서에 언급된 것은?
(A) 다른 사람이 고객을 위해 배송품을 받았다.
(B) 가전 한 개는 상태가 만족스럽지 않았다.
(C) 별도의 요금이 배송 직원에게 지불되었다.
(D) 대부분의 제품에 설치 서비스가 제공되었다.

해설 배송 확인서 중간에 있는 표에 설치가 필요한지(Installation Required?) 묻는 항목을 보면, 네 개의 제품 중 세 개에 대해 표시되어 있다. 그리고 그 아래 제품들이 이상 없이 배송되었으며, 요청된 모든 설치 작업이 만족스럽게 실시되었다(The above items were delivered in good condition, and any required installations were performed satisfactorily)는 문구와 함께 유뱅크스의 확인 서명이 있으므로 (D)가 정답이다.

어휘 accept 받아들이다 satisfactory 만족스러운 separate 별도의, 분리된 personnel 직원, 인력

## 199 연계

번역 유뱅크스 씨에 대해 암시된 것은?
(A) 정확한 온도 조절 기능이 있는 쿡탑을 구입했다.
(B) 특별 결제 플랫폼에 가입했다.
(C) 스마트폰으로 배송 진행 상황을 파악했다.
(D) 몇 개의 오래된 가전을 직접 처분했다.

해설 유뱅크스의 구입 물품이 기재된 배송 확인서에 있는 도표에 브라이트 30인치 전기 쿡탑(Bright 30-inch Electric Cooktop (EC7030A))이 포함되어 있다. 이 제품은 웹페이지에 소개된 것이며, 웹페이지 첫 단락에 각 버너를 정확한 온도로 설정할 수 있다(Each burner can also be set to an exact degree temperature ~)고 했으므로 (A)가 정답이다.

어휘 precise 정확한 control 조절, 통제 track 파악하다, 추적하다 progress 진행 상황, 진척 dispose of ~을 처분하다

> **Paraphrasing**
> 지문의 Each burner can also be set to an exact degree temperature → 정답의 a cooktop with precise temperature controls

## 200 연계

번역 유뱅크스 씨가 받을 수 있는 최대 리베이트 금액은 얼마인가?
(A) 300달러
(B) 550달러
(C) 800달러
(D) 1,050달러

해설 배송 확인서에 있는 도표에 유뱅크스가 총 네 개의 가전을 구입한 것으로 쓰여 있다. 이에 대해, 두 번째 지문 중반부에 가전 네 개를 구입하는 경우에 리베이트를 받는 금액이 550달러(Four appliances: $550)로 표기되어 있으므로 (B)가 정답이다.

TEST 8

# TEST 9

| | | | | |
|---|---|---|---|---|
| 101 (C) | 102 (C) | 103 (B) | 104 (D) | 105 (B) |
| 106 (C) | 107 (A) | 108 (B) | 109 (B) | 110 (A) |
| 111 (B) | 112 (D) | 113 (A) | 114 (D) | 115 (B) |
| 116 (C) | 117 (D) | 118 (D) | 119 (B) | 120 (D) |
| 121 (B) | 122 (C) | 123 (C) | 124 (D) | 125 (D) |
| 126 (A) | 127 (A) | 128 (C) | 129 (A) | 130 (A) |
| 131 (C) | 132 (D) | 133 (B) | 134 (B) | 135 (C) |
| 136 (B) | 137 (A) | 138 (A) | 139 (D) | 140 (A) |
| 141 (A) | 142 (C) | 143 (B) | 144 (C) | 145 (C) |
| 146 (D) | 147 (D) | 148 (B) | 149 (A) | 150 (C) |
| 151 (B) | 152 (D) | 153 (C) | 154 (A) | 155 (D) |
| 156 (D) | 157 (C) | 158 (C) | 159 (A) | 160 (B) |
| 161 (D) | 162 (A) | 163 (B) | 164 (B) | 165 (C) |
| 166 (A) | 167 (B) | 168 (B) | 169 (B) | 170 (D) |
| 171 (C) | 172 (D) | 173 (A) | 174 (B) | 175 (D) |
| 176 (C) | 177 (A) | 178 (A) | 179 (D) | 180 (B) |
| 181 (C) | 182 (A) | 183 (B) | 184 (A) | 185 (D) |
| 186 (C) | 187 (B) | 188 (D) | 189 (C) | 190 (A) |
| 191 (C) | 192 (A) | 193 (A) | 194 (B) | 195 (D) |
| 196 (A) | 197 (D) | 198 (C) | 199 (D) | 200 (C) |

## PART 5

### 101 형용사 자리 _ 명사 수식

번역 사서 협회 블로그의 목적 중 하나는 새롭고 다양한 아이디어에 회원들이 관심을 갖게 하는 것이다.

해설 new와 빈칸의 형용사가 등위 접속사 and로 연결된 구조로, 빈칸은 명사 ideas를 수식하는 형용사가 들어갈 자리이므로 (C) diverse가 정답이다.

어휘 bring ~ to one's attention ~에 …의 관심을 불러일으키다
diversify 다양화하다 diversely 다양하게 diverse 다양한
diversity 다양성

### 102 전치사 어휘

번역 저희 레스토랑은 3월에 문을 연 이후로 7만 개 이상의 햄버거를 제공해 왔습니다.

해설 현재완료 시제 동사 has served와 어울려 '3월 개장 이후로 ~해 왔습니다'라는 의미를 구성해야 알맞으므로 '~ 이후로'를 뜻하는 전치사 (C) since가 정답이다.

어휘 serve (음식 등) 제공하다 besides ~ 외에, ~을 제외하고
past (시간, 위치 등) ~을 지나, ~을 넘어

### 103 부사 어휘

번역 새 고객 서비스 직원들은 마침내 고객에게 문제 해결에 대한 조언을 제공할 수 있을 만큼 가전 제품에 대한 지식이 풍부해졌다.

해설 빈칸에는 형용사 knowledgeable을 뒤에서 수식할 수 있는 부사가 와야 하며, 뒤에 있는 to부정사구와 함께 '~할 만큼 충분히'라는 의미를 나타내야 알맞으므로 (B) enough가 정답이다.

어휘 knowledgeable 많이 아는, 박식한 appliance 가전 기기
troubleshooting 문제 해결, 고장 수리

### 104 명사 자리 _ 복합명사

번역 IT 부서 직원들은 동료들의 기술 지원 요청에 즉각적으로 대응해야 한다.

해설 IT 부서 직원들은 무엇에 즉시 대응해야 한다는 문맥이 되어야 하는데, 업무 특성상 동료들의 기술 지원 요청에 즉시 대응해야 한다는 말이 자연스러우므로, '요청'을 뜻하는 명사 (D) requests가 정답이다.

어휘 respond to+명사 ~에 대응하다 promptly 즉각, 지체 없이
colleague 동료

### 105 전치사 어휘

번역 인턴은 선임 홍보 책임자의 감독하에 근무할 것이다.

해설 빈칸 뒤에 위치한 the direction of와 어울려 '~의 감독하에'라는 의미를 구성할 때 사용하는 전치사 (B) under가 정답이다.

어휘 senior 선임의, 고위의 communications officer 홍보 책임자

### 106 인칭 대명사 _ those who(~하는 사람들)

번역 벨링 씨는 추가 사무용품이 필요한 사람들에게 이메일로 자신에게 물품 목록을 보내라고 지시했다.

해설 빈칸 뒤에 있는 who가 이끄는 관계대명사절의 수식을 받아 '~하는 사람들'이라는 의미를 나타낼 수 있는 대명사가 필요하므로 (C) those가 정답이다.

어휘 instruct 지시하다 additional 추가적인 supplies 용품, 물품

### 107 부사 자리 _ 형용사 수식

번역 도시의 새로운 법령 때문에, 샌더턴에서 사업체를 운영하는 일이 점점 더 어려워졌다.

해설 동사 has become과 형용사 보어 difficult 사이에 위치한 빈칸은 형용사를 앞에서 수식하는 부사가 들어갈 수 있는 자리이므로 (A) increasingly가 정답이다.

어휘 ordinance 법령, 조례 operate 운영하다, 가동하다
increasingly 점점 더 increase 증가하다, 증가시키다

## 108 형용사 자리 _ 명사 수식

번역 식물원은 최근 모리바를 찾는 관광객이 느는 데 큰 역할을 해 왔다.

해설 부정관사 an과 명사 part 사이에 있는 빈칸에는 명사를 수식하는 형용사나 복합명사를 이루는 명사가 들어갈 수 있다. 문맥상 '큰 역할'이라는 내용이 되어야 하므로 형용사인 (B) extensive가 정답이다. 명사 (C) extension은 part와 복합명사를 구성하지 않는다.

어휘 botanical garden 식물원 extensive 광범위한, 폭넓은 extension 연장, 확장 extensively 광범위하게, 폭넓게

## 109 동사 자리

번역 에인스빌 소방서의 각 조사관은 더 이상 한 가지 화재 예방 분야만 전문적으로 담당하지 않을 것이다.

해설 조동사 will 뒤에는 동사 원형이 필요하므로 (B) specialize가 정답이다. no longer는 부정의 의미를 나타내는 부사이다.

어휘 inspector 조사관, 점검 담당자 no longer 더 이상 ~ 않다 prevention 예방, 방지 specialize 전문으로 하다 specialization 전문화, 특수화

## 110 동사 어휘

번역 루이스 씨는 최근 완료된 설문 조사의 결과를 요약하는 일을 맡았다.

해설 '설문 조사의 결과'를 목적어로 취하는 동명사가 들어갈 자리로, '설문 조사 결과를 요약하는 일을 맡았다'라는 의미가 되는 게 가장 자연스럽다. 따라서 '요약하다'를 뜻하는 (A) summarizing이 정답이다.

어휘 be tasked with ~하는 일을 맡다 perform 수행하다, 공연하다 improve 개선하다, 향상시키다 achieve 이루다, 달성하다

## 111 동사 자리 _ 수 일치

번역 게이트우드 주식회사는 현재 직원들이 소셜 미디어에서 자신의 업무나 회사 이야기를 하는 것을 금지하고 있다.

해설 문장에 동사가 없으므로 빈칸은 동사 자리이며, 주어 Gatewood Corporation이 3인칭 단수이므로 단수 동사인 (B) forbids가 정답이다. (A) forbid도 동사이지만 3인칭 단수 주어와 수가 일치하지 않는다.

어휘 currently 현재 forbid 금지하다

## 112 전치사 자리 _ 어휘

번역 플래미오 헤드폰의 최신 버전은 몇 가지 장식적인 요소들 외에는 이전의 것과 동일하다.

해설 최신 버전이 기존의 것과 동일하다는 말이 쓰여 있어 빈칸 뒤에 위치한 명사구 some decorative elements(몇 가지 장식적인 요소들)는 동일하지 않은 요소를 나타내야 의미가 알맞다. 따라서 '~ 외에는'이라는 의미로 제외 대상을 나타낼 때 사용하는 전치사 (D) aside from이 정답이다. (A) added(추가된)는 형용사이며, (B) prior to(~ 전에, ~에 앞서)는 의미가 맞지 않는 전치사이다. (C) regardless(상관없이)는 형용사 또는 부사로 쓰인다.

어휘 identical to+명사 ~와 동일한 previous 이전의, 과거의 decorative 장식적인, 장식의 element 요소

## 113 관계대명사 _ 주격

번역 현재 홍콩 사무실을 방문하고 있는 원 씨에게 회의록을 한 부 보내야 한다.

해설 주절과 콤마 뒤에 주어 없이 동사 is visiting으로 시작하는 불완전한 절이 쓰여 있으므로 콤마 뒤에 쓰일 수 있으면서 불완전한 절을 이끄는 관계대명사 (A) who가 정답이다. (B) his와 (D) another(또 다른 하나)는 불완전한 절을 이끄는 역할을 할 수 없는 대명사이며, (C) that은 불완전한 절을 이끄는 관계대명사이기는 하지만 콤마 뒤에 쓸 수 없으므로 오답이다.

어휘 meeting notes 회의록

## 114 수동태

번역 지붕 거치대의 크로스바를 조정하자 트랙션 G20 트럭의 소음 문제가 해결되었다.

해설 빈칸 뒤는 접속사 once가 이끄는 부사절이고, 빈칸에는 be동사 was와 결합될 수 있는 단어가 들어가야 한다. 주어가 The noise issue이므로 과거분사 (D) resolved를 넣어 '소음 문제가 해결되었다'는 의미의 수동태가 되는 것이 자연스럽다. 따라서 정답은 (D)이다. (A) resolve(해결하다)는 동사 원형이므로 be동사와 결합될 수 없으며, (B) resolving은 be동사 was와 결합될 수 있는 현재분사이지만, 목적어를 필요로 하므로 빈칸 뒤에 목적어가 없는 이 문장에 맞지 않는다. (C) resolution(해결)은 명사로 주격 보어 역할을 할 수는 있지만 이 문장에서는 어색하다.

어휘 issue 문제, 사안 once ~하자마자, ~하는 대로 roof rack (자동차) 지붕 거치대, 지붕 위 짐칸 adjust 조정하다, 조절하다

## 115 형용사 자리 _ 주격 보어

번역 그 협상의 목표는 양측 당사자들이 모두 수용할 수 있는 해결책을 찾는 것이다.

해설 빈칸이 속한 that절은 선행사 solution을 수식해 어떤 해결책인지 나타내야 하므로 be동사 뒤에 위치할 수 있으면서 해결책의 특징과 관련된 의미를 나타낼 수 있는 형용사 (B) agreeable(수용할 수 있는, 알맞은)이 정답이다. (A) agreeing(동의하다)과 (D) to agree는 각각 현재분사와 to부정사로서 be동사와 결합할 수는 있지만, 빈칸에는 어울리지 않으며, (C) agreeably(기분 좋게)는 be동사 뒤에 쓰일 수 없는 부사이다.

어휘 negotiation 협의, 협상 solution 해결책 party (계약 등의) 당사자, 일행

TEST 9

## 116 전치사 자리 _ 어휘

번역 컴퓨터 하드웨어를 구입하는 대신, 필요한 것이 바뀔 수 있는 회사들은 기술 장비 대여 서비스를 이용해야 한다.

해설 동명사구 buying computer hardware를 목적어로 취하는 전치사 자리이다. 기술 장비 대여 서비스를 이용해야 한다는 말이 있어 '컴퓨터 하드웨어를 구입하는 대신'이라는 의미를 구성해야 알맞으므로 '~하는 대신'을 뜻하는 전치사 (C) Instead of가 정답이다. (B) Depending on(~에 따라, ~에 달려 있는)은 전치사이나 의미가 맞지 않는다. 접속사 뒤에 현재분사가 오기도 하지만 (A) Whenever(~할 때마다)와 (D) However(아무리 ~해도)는 의미가 적절하지 않다.

어휘 changeable 바뀔 수 있는, 변할 수 있는 rental 대여, 임대

## 117 부사 자리 _ 강조

번역 우리 제품의 평균 평점 하락은 포장 디자인 변경에 따른 일시적인 결과일 뿐이다.

해설 빈칸을 빼고 보면 is와 a temporary consequence는 「be동사+주격 보어」를 이루는 완전한 구조이다. 따라서 문장의 의미를 풍부하게 해주지만 없어도 문장이 성립하는 부사 (D) simply가 정답이다. (A) simple과 (B) simpler, (C) simplest는 각각 원급, 비교급, 최상급 형용사로, 관사 앞에 올 수 없다.

어휘 drop in ~의 하락 rating 평점, 등급 temporary 일시적인, 임시의 consequence 결과 packaging 포장(지) simply 단순히, 그저

## 118 접속사 자리 _ 부사절 접속사

번역 저희 직원이 귀하의 수하물을 찾는 대로 항공사에서 연락을 드릴 것입니다.

해설 빈칸 앞뒤에 각각 완전한 절이 있으므로 두 절을 연결해 줄 접속사가 필요하다. 또한, '수하물을 찾는 대로 연락을 줄 것이다'라는 의미가 되어야 자연스러우므로 '~하는 대로, ~하자마자'를 뜻하는 부사절 접속사 (D) as soon as가 정답이다. (A) at first(처음에는)는 부사이며, (B) in case(~할 경우에)는 의미가 맞지 않는 접속사이다. (C) rather than(~보다는, ~하지 않고)은 전치사이다.

어휘 representative 직원, 대표자 contact 연락하다 luggage 수하물, 짐 locate 위치를 찾다

## 119 동사 어휘

번역 릴랜드 플로리스트에 인접한 공간은 새로운 세입자가 임대할 수 있다.

해설 세입자가 할 수 있는 것으로 자연스러운 것은 공간을 '임대하는' 것이므로 '임대하다'를 뜻하는 (B) leased가 정답이다.

어휘 adjacent to+명사 ~에 인접한 available 이용 가능한 tenant 세입자 enclose 둘러싸다, 동봉하다 permit 허가하다, 허용하다 preoccupy 선점하다

## 120 명사 자리 _ 주어

번역 매년, 반스 엔지니어링 컨퍼런스의 주최자들은 단체 기념 사진을 위해 포즈를 취한다.

해설 빈칸은 문장의 주어 자리이고, 정관사 the와 전치사 of 사이에 있으므로 명사 자리이다. 또한, 동사 pose와 어울리는 명사가 쓰여야 알맞으므로 '주최자들'을 뜻하는 (D) organizers가 정답이다. (C) organization(조직, 단체)도 명사이지만 의미가 맞지 않고, 복수 동사인 pose와 수가 일치하지 않는다.

어휘 commemorative 기념하는 organize 주최하다, 조직하다 organizational 조직의, 구성의

## 121 형용사 어휘

번역 사무실용으로는 어두운 조명과 규칙적으로 물을 주지 못하는 불리한 조건에서도 잘 자라는 식물을 추천합니다.

해설 빈칸 뒤에 such as와 함께 예시로 언급된 low lighting(어두운 조명)과 inconsistent watering(불규칙한 물 주기)이 어떤 환경인지 나타낼 수 있는 형용사가 필요하므로 '불리한, 부정적인'을 뜻하는 (B) adverse가 정답이다.

어휘 condition 조건, 환경 inconsistent 불규칙한, 일관성 없는 watering 물 주기, 급수 dense 밀집한, 빽빽한 skeptical 회의적인 durable 내구성이 좋은

## 122 명사 자리 _ 전치사의 목적어

번역 12월 11일에 있을 다음 공연에서는 호평받는 지휘자 미사키 오가와가 펠티어 교향악단을 이끌 것이다.

해설 빈칸은 전치사 by의 목적어 자리이며, 앞에 위치한 형용사 acclaimed의 수식을 받는 자리이므로 명사 (C) conductor(지휘자)가 정답이다. 동명사 (D) conducting은 형용사의 수식을 받을 수 없다.

어휘 lead 이끌다, 진행하다 acclaimed 인정받는, 호평을 받는 conduct 실시하다, 수행하다 conductor 지휘자

## 123 전치사 어휘

번역 도시 전역에 있는 좋은 주차 공간들이 전기차 충전소로 전환되고 있다.

해설 빈칸 뒤에 있는 장소 명사 the city와 어울리는 전치사가 필요하며, '도시 전역에 있는 주차 공간들이 전기차 충전소로 전환되고 있다'가 자연스러운 의미이므로 '~ 전역에 위치한, ~ 전체에 걸친'을 뜻하는 전치사 (C) throughout이 정답이다.

어휘 desirable 바람직한, 가치 있는 convert 변환시키다, 전환하다 charging station 충전소 along (도로 등) ~을 따라

## 124 명사 어휘

번역 TGN 은행은 카드 소지자에게 낮은 연회비에 훌륭한 보상을 제공하는 비스타 신용카드로 업계의 인정을 받아 왔다.

해설 which절에 비스타 신용카드가 훌륭한 보상을 제공한다는 말이 쓰여 있어 그러한 신용카드에 대해 업계의 인정을 받았다는 의미를 나타내야 자연스러우므로 '인정, 인식' 등을 뜻하는 명사 (D) recognition이 정답이다.

어휘 industry 업계 holder 소지자, 보유자 reward 보상 annual 연간의, 연례적인 regulation 규정, 규제 demand 요구, 수요 reputation 명성, 평판

## 125 부사 어휘

번역 잠재 고객이 방문했을 때 매장이 재고가 부족하거나 정리되어 있지 않으면, 그들은 다른 곳에서 쇼핑하기로 선택할 수 있습니다.

해설 매장의 상태가 좋지 못한 경우에 '고객들이 다른 곳에서 쇼핑할 수도 있다'와 같은 의미를 구성해야 자연스러우므로 '다른 곳에서'를 뜻하는 부사 (D) elsewhere가 정답이다.

어휘 stocked (재고 등이) 갖춰진, 채워져 있는 disorganized 정리되지 않은, 체계적이지 못한 prospective 잠재적인, 장래의 apart 따로, 떨어져 seldom 좀처럼 ~ 않다 otherwise 그렇지 않으면

## 126 명사 어휘

번역 회사는 서비스 가격을 인상한 후에 수익성을 회복했다.

해설 서비스 가격을 인상하여 회사가 회복할 수 있는 것을 나타내는 명사가 들어가야 하므로 '수익성'을 뜻하는 (A) profitability가 정답이다.

어휘 raise 인상하다, 올리다 advantage 장점, 이점 performance 성과, 공연 priority 우선 순위

## 127 대명사 어휘

번역 복장 규정은 모든 사람이 볼 수 있도록 직원 휴게실 내 눈에 잘 띄는 곳에 게시되어야 한다.

해설 눈에 잘 띄는 곳에 게시하는 목적은 모든 사람이 잘 볼 수 있게 하는 것이므로 '모든 사람'을 뜻하는 대명사 (A) everyone이 정답이다.

어휘 dress code 복장 규정 post 게시하다 prominent 눈에 잘 띄는 spot 곳, 장소

## 128 형용사 어휘

번역 맥스웰 출판사의 교재들은 교사들이 각 주제에 대한 학생들의 이해를 넓히는 데 이용할 수 있는 보충 자료 목록을 포함하고 있다.

해설 명사 materials를 수식해 교사들이 학생들의 이해를 넓히기 위해 어떤 자료를 이용할 수 있는지를 나타낼 형용사가 필요하므로 '보충의, 추가의'를 뜻하는 (C) supplemental이 정답이다.

어휘 include 포함하다 material 자료, 재료 broaden 넓히다, 확장하다 deliberate 신중한, 의도적인 superfluous 과잉의, 불필요한 approximate 대략적인

## 129 접속사 자리 _ 명사절 접속사

번역 이번 주에 개봉하는 두 편의 영화가 모두 너무 많은 기대를 받고 있어서 어느 것이 가장 많은 티켓을 판매할지 알 수 없다.

해설 빈칸 앞에 있는 it은 가주어이고, 빈칸부터 문장 끝까지가 진주어인 명사절이다. 따라서 명사절을 이끄는 접속사가 필요하므로 (A) which가 정답이다. (B) other(다른)는 형용사이며, (C) because는 부사절 접속사, (D) about(~에 관해, 약)은 전치사 또는 부사이므로 모두 오답이다.

어휘 highly anticipated 많은 기대를 받는 unclear 명확하지 않은, 잘 모르는

## 130 명사 어휘

번역 현재 추세라면 올해 안에 의류가 신발을 제치고 가장 높은 수익을 창출하는 카테고리가 될 것으로 보인다.

해설 빈칸에 쓰일 명사는 의류가 수익 창출 면에서 신발을 앞지를 것임을 알 수 있게 해 주는 일종의 근거나 정보 출처에 해당해야 하므로 '추세, 경향'을 의미하는 (A) trends가 정답이다.

어휘 suggest 나타내다, 암시하다 overtake 앞지르다, 추월하다 revenue 수익, 수입 generate 창출하다, 만들어 내다 category 카테고리, 범주 guideline 지침, 기준 advertisement 광고

# PART 6

### 131-134 공지

휠러 주식회사 본사를 재설계하면서 복도와 사무실에 있던 40여 점 이상의 그림을 철거했습니다. 경영진은 이 여분의 예술품을 비공개 온라인 경매를 통해 직원들이 합리적인 가격에 구입할 수 있게 하기로 131 **결정했습니다**. 이 공지 하단의 링크를 방문해 구입 가능한 품목을 확인해 보시기 바랍니다. 132 **입찰**은 5월 5일 오전 9시에서 5월 9일 오후 7시 사이에 동일 사이트를 통해 제출할 수 있습니다. 경매가 종료되면, 낙찰된 직원은 결제 및 133 수령**에 관한** 안내가 담긴 이메일을 받을 것입니다. 134 **그런 다음 5월 16일 오후 5시까지 그림을 수령해야 합니다**. 경매의 모든 수익금은 지역 어린이 자선 단체에 기부될 것입니다.

www.auctionhelper.com/49321

어휘 headquarters 본사 removal 제거, 치움 management 경영(진), 관리 allow 허용하다 surplus 여분의 reasonable 합리적인 auction 경매 available 구입 가능한, 이용 가능한 instructions 안내, 설명 proceeds 수익금 local 지역의 charity 자선 (단체)

## 131 동사 자리

해설 문장에 동사가 없으므로 빈칸은 동사 자리이다. 따라서 선택지에서 유일하게 동사의 형태인 (C) has decided가 정답이다.

TEST 9

## 132 명사 어휘

해설 빈칸 뒤에 동일한 사이트를 통해 제출될 수 있다는 말이 있으므로 앞서 언급한 온라인 경매 사이트에 제출할 수 있는 것을 나타낼 명사가 들어가야 한다. 따라서 '입찰'을 뜻하는 (D) Bids가 정답이다.

어휘 piece 조각, 한 개 donation 기부 nomination 후보 지명

## 133 전치사 어휘

해설 빈칸 앞뒤에 위치한 명사 instructions와 명사구 payment and pick-up의 관계를 고려했을 때 '결제 및 수령에 관한 안내'라는 의미를 구성해야 가장 자연스러우므로 '~에 관한'을 뜻하는 전치사 (B) concerning이 정답이다.

어휘 given ~을 고려해 볼 때

## 134 문장 고르기

번역 (A) 아직 받지 못하셨다면, 스팸 필터를 확인해 보십시오.
(B) 그런 다음 5월 16일 오후 5시까지 그림을 수령해야 합니다.
(C) 휠러 주식회사는 크랜퍼드 가 390에 위치해 있습니다.
(D) 제출된 작품 중에서 세 명의 수상자가 선정될 것입니다.

해설 빈칸 앞 문장에 경매 행사에서 낙찰된 사람이 결제 및 수령에 관한 안내 이메일을 받는다는 내용이 쓰여 있으므로 낙찰된 사람이 이메일을 받은 후에 해야 할 일과 관련된 내용이 언급된 (B)가 정답이다.

어휘 collect 가져가다, 수령하다 be located at ~에 위치해 있다
winner 수상작, 수상자 submission 제출(물)

### 135-138 이메일

수신: 클라인 인쇄소 직원들
발신: 레슬리 클라인
제목: 문서 파쇄
날짜: 1월 18일

직원 여러분께,

닐과 제가 전국 데이터 관리 협회로부터 안전한 문서 파기 전문 [135] **자격증**을 취득했다는 사실을 알려 드리게 되어 자랑스럽습니다. 저희는 [136] **이제** 정부가 민감한 정보를 포함하고 있는 것으로 분류한 문서를 파쇄할 수 있는 자격을 갖추게 되었습니다. 과거에는 정부 고객들에게 그 서비스는 다른 [137] **업체를** 소개하라는 지시를 받았습니다. [138] **이는 더 이상 우리 정책이 아닐 것입니다.**

마지막으로, 우리에게 지속적으로 일이 많이 들어온다면, 여러분 중 몇몇 분들도 이 자격증을 취득할 수 있도록 비용을 지불하는 것을 고려할 수도 있습니다.

레슬리 클라인
소유주 및 운영 책임
클라인 인쇄소

어휘 shredding 파쇄, 분쇄 be proud to ~해서 자랑스럽다 obtain 획득하다, 얻다 secure 안전한 destruction 파기, 파괴 authorized 공인된, 인증된 classify 분류하다 contain 포함하다, 담고 있다 sensitive 민감한 refer 알아보도록 하다, 소개하다 consistently 지속적으로, 일관되게 volume 양, 용량 consider 고려하다 qualification 자격(증)

## 135 명사 자리 _ 동사의 목적어

해설 빈칸은 동사 have obtained의 목적어 자리이며 형용사 professional의 수식을 받는 자리이므로 명사 자리이다. 따라서 명사 (C) certification이 정답이다.

어휘 certify 자격증을 주다, 인증하다 certifiable 인증할 수 있는, 증명할 수 있는 certification 자격증, 증명서

## 136 부사 어휘

해설 앞 문장에 자격증을 취득한 사실을 알리는 말이 있으므로 현재는 자격을 갖춘 상태임을 알 수 있다. 따라서 '이제 자격을 갖추게 되었다'라는 의미가 되는 것이 자연스러우므로 '이제, 지금'을 뜻하는 부사 (B) now가 정답이다.

## 137 전치사 어휘

해설 to부정사로 쓰인 동사 refer와 어울려 '~에게 …을 소개하다'를 의미하는 「refer ~ to …」를 구성해야 알맞으므로 전치사 (A) to가 정답이다.

## 138 문장 고르기

번역 (A) 이는 더 이상 우리 정책이 아닐 것입니다.
(B) 이 일은 특별히 수익성이 있지는 않습니다.
(C) 가격 책정 정보가 벽에 게시될 것입니다.
(D) 고객이 직접 문서를 파쇄할 수도 있습니다.

해설 앞에 글쓴이가 문서 파쇄 관련 자격증이 없던 과거에는 정부 고객들을 다른 업체로 보냈다는 말이 있다. 따라서 자격증이 생긴 지금은 더 이상 그럴 필요가 없다는 의미로 쓰인 (A)가 정답이다.

어휘 profitable 수익성이 있는 pricing 가격 (책정) post 게시하다

### 139-142 이메일

수신: 유은숙
발신: 얼 파울러
제목: 통지
날짜: 8월 23일

유 박사님께,

힐사이드 병원의 사무 관리자직에서 사임할 것임을 공식적으로 알려 드리고자 이메일을 씁니다. 제 마지막 근무일은 9월 21일 금요일이 될 것입니다. 제 [139] **후임자**를 찾을 시간이 충분하시길 바랍니다. 제가 가기 전에 누군가 고용하실 수 있다면, 기꺼이 교육을 해 드리겠습니다. [140] **어쨌든,** 제 업무 프로세스에 관한 상세한 문서를 만들어, 공유 네트워크에서 모든 사람이 이용할 수 있게 할 것입니다. [141] **우리 직원들과**

**환자들을 위해 이 변화 과정이 순조롭게 되는 것이 제겐 중요합니다.** 마지막으로, 지난 5년간 142 **뛰어난** 지원과 리더십을 제공해 주신 것에 대해 감사의 뜻을 표하고자 합니다. 박사님 병원의 사무 관리자 역할을 할 수 있어서 기뻤습니다. 앞으로 박사님과 힐사이드 병원에 좋은 일만 가득하기를 바랍니다.

얼 파울러

어휘 resign 사임하다 handle 처리하다, 다루다 detailed 상세한 documentation 문서 (작업) available 이용 가능한 shared 공유된 gratitude 감사 act as ~의 역할을 하다

### 139 명사 어휘

해설 빈칸에 쓰일 명사는 to부정사로 쓰인 동사 find의 목적어로서 무엇을 찾는 것인지 나타내야 한다. 앞에 글쓴이가 사임할 예정이라는 말이 있어 자신을 대신할 사람을 찾는 것에 대해 이야기하는 것이 흐름상 자연스러우므로 '후임(자), 대체(자)'를 뜻하는 (D) replacement가 정답이다.

어휘 funding 자금 (제공) record 기록 belongings 소지품

### 140 접속부사

해설 빈칸 앞에는 글쓴이가 떠나기 전에 누군가 고용되면 기꺼이 그 사람을 교육하겠다는 말이, 빈칸 뒤에는 자신의 업무 프로세스에 관한 상세한 문서를 만들어 모두에게 공유하겠다는 말이 쓰여 있다. 이는 새로운 직원을 고용하는 일이 어떻게 진행되든 인수인계 문서를 만들어 놓겠다는 뜻이므로 '어쨌든 (상관없이)'을 의미하는 (A) In any case가 정답이다.

어휘 on the contrary 그에 반해, 대조적으로

### 141 문장 고르기

번역 (A) 우리 직원들과 환자들을 위해 이 인수인계가 순조롭게 되는 것이 제겐 중요합니다.
(B) 이것은 제게 문서를 공유해 주실 수 있는 가장 빠른 방법이기도 합니다.
(C) 저는 대부분의 시간을 의료 및 사무용품을 조달하는 데 보냅니다.
(D) 저는 보통 우리 병원의 연혁을 소개하는 것으로 신입 사원 교육을 시작합니다.

해설 앞에 자신의 업무 프로세스에 관한 상세한 문서를 만들어 공유 네트워크에서 모든 사람이 이용할 수 있게 하겠다는 말이 쓰여 있다. 이는 인수인계를 순조롭게 하기 위한 노력이므로 (A) 문장이 이어지는 것이 가장 자연스럽다. 따라서 (A)가 정답이다.

어휘 ease 원활하게 하다, 완화하다 transition 전환 patient 환자 source 조달하다, 공급받다 supplies 용품, 물품

### 142 형용사 자리 _ 명사 수식

해설 빈칸은 뒤에 있는 명사 support를 수식하는 자리이므로 형용사 (C) exceptional(뛰어난, 이례적인)이 정답이다. (A) exception은 support와 복합명사를 구성하지 않는다.

어휘 exception 예외, 제외 exceptional 뛰어난, 이례적인 exceptionally 뛰어나게, 이례적으로

### 143-146 기사

베를린 (3월 16일) - 하빈저 스튜디오는 지난 16년 동안 매년 11월에 베를린에서 자사의 온라인 게임들을 중심으로 하는 컨벤션인 하콘을 개최해 왔다. 행사의 지속적인 143 인기**에도 불구하고**, 회사는 다양한 도시에서 열리는 더 작은 규모의 여러 행사들을 위해 올해의 하콘을 취소했다. 하빈저의 웹사이트에 올라온 게시물은 이러한 형식이 회사에 중요한 올 한 해와 더 잘 144 **어울린다**고 설명하고 있다. 두 개의 게임 프랜차이즈가 첫 출시 기념일을 맞이하고, 세 번째 게임 프랜차이즈는 많은 기대를 받고 있는 확장팩을 출시할 예정이다. 145 **회사는 이 중요한 일들을 각각 따로 기념할 계획이다.** 하지만 이 게시물은 "하빈저는 이 146 **모임**이 팬들께 얼마나 큰 의미를 지니는지 잘 알고 있습니다"라는 말로 읽는 사람들을 안심시키면서, 하콘이 내년에 다시 돌아올 것이라는 점도 강조하고 있다.

어휘 centered on ~을 중심으로 하는 popularity 인기 in favor of ~을 위해 post 게시(물) format 구성 방식, 형식 momentous 중대한 mark 축하하다, 기념하다 anniversary (해마다 돌아오는) 기념일 initial 처음의 release 발매, 출시 launch 출시하다, 공개하다 widely anticipated 많은 기대를 받는 expansion 확장, 확대 emphasize 강조하다 reassure 안심시키다 be aware of ~을 알고 있다, 인식하고 있다

### 143 전치사 자리 _ 어휘

해설 빈칸 뒤에 명사구 the event's continued popularity가 있고, 콤마(,) 뒤로 완전한 절이 이어져 있으므로, 빈칸에는 명사구를 목적어로 취할 전치사가 필요하다. 또한, '행사의 지속적인 인기에도 불구하고, 회사가 올해의 하콘을 취소했다'가 자연스러운 의미이므로 '~에도 불구하고'를 뜻하는 전치사 (B) Despite가 정답이다. (A) Due to(~ 때문에)와 (D) Along with(~와 함께)는 의미가 맞지 않는 전치사이며, (C) Although(비록 ~하기는 하지만)는 주어와 동사를 포함한 절을 이끄는 접속사이다.

### 144 형용사 자리 _ 주격 보어

해설 빈칸 앞에 be동사 is가 있고, 빈칸 뒤에는 to 전치사구가 있으므로, 이와 어울려 '~에 어울리다, ~에 적합하다'를 뜻하는 「be suited to+명사」를 구성하는 형용사 (C) suited가 정답이다. (A) suitability는 명사로 be동사 뒤에 보어로 올 수 있지만 의미가 맞지 않으며, (B) suitable은 「be suitable for(~에 어울리다)」 또는 「be suitable to부정사(~하는 데 적합하다)」의 구조로 쓰인다. (D) suitably는 부사로 보어 자리에 올 수 없다.

어휘 suitability 어울림, 적합함 suitable 어울리는, 적합한 suitably 어울리게, 적합하게

### 145 문장 고르기

번역 (A) 하빈저는 심지어 여러 인기 모바일 애플리케이션도 제작한다.
(B) 완전히 새로운 게임의 개발은 더 이상 회사가 집중하는 것이 아니다.
(C) 회사는 이 중요한 일들을 각각 따로 기념할 계획이다.
(D) 대규모 행사들은 종종 주최하는 데 기하급수적으로 더 많은 비용이 든다.

TEST 9

해설 앞에 게임 프랜차이즈들의 기념일과 확장팩 출시가 언급되어 있으므로 이러한 일들을 these milestones로 지칭해 관련된 회사의 계획을 언급하는 (C)가 정답이다.

어휘 entirely 완전히, 전적으로 focus 초점, 중점 celebrate 기념하다, 축하하다 milestone 중요한 단계, 중요한 사건 separately 따로, 별도로 exponentially 기하급수적으로 costly 많은 비용이 드는 organize 주최하다, 조직하다

## 146 명사 어휘

해설 빈칸이 속한 how 명사절의 내용을 보면 '이것이 팬들에게 얼마나 큰 의미를 지니는지'라는 의미이므로, this는 앞에서 언급한 '하콘(Harcon)'이라는 행사를 가리킨다는 것을 알 수 있다. 따라서 이 행사를 대신할 수 있는 명사가 빈칸에 쓰여야 알맞으므로 '모임'을 뜻하는 (D) gathering이 정답이다.

어휘 award 상 character 성격, 특성

# PART 7

### 147-148 웹페이지

www.prillenhome.com

장난감 정리용 기린 선반

- 크기: 46cm (폭) x 30cm (깊이) x 95cm (높이)
- 흰색으로 칠해진 소나무, 양쪽에 기린 그림
- 세 개의 분리 가능한 녹색 플라스틱 통을 지탱하는 플라스틱 가이드 레일
- **147 가정에서 조립할 수 있도록 모든 도구와 설명서가 패키지에 포함**

**148 동물원 침실 세트에서 최소 세 가지 제품을 주문하시면 15% 할인해 드립니다.** 할인은 오직 온라인에서만 적용됩니다. 8월 10일까지 유효.

어휘 organizer 정리함 shelving unit 선반 dimensions 크기, 면적 illustration 그림, 삽화 hold 고정하다, 지탱하다 removable 분리 가능한 bin 통 include 포함하다 hardware 도구, 철물 instructions 설명(서), 안내(서) assembly 조립 available 이용 가능한 valid 유효한

## 147 Not / True

번역 선반에 대해 언급된 것은?
(A) 동물 모양이다.
(B) 분리 가능한 레일이 있다.
(C) 통에 그림이 인쇄되어 있다.
(D) 배송 후에 조립되어야 한다.

해설 첫 단락 네 번째 항목을 보면 패키지에 가정에서 조립할 수 있도록 모든 도구 및 설명서가 포함되어 있다(Package includes all hardware and instructions for at-home assembly)고 쓰여 있는데, 이는 제품을 집에서 직접 조립해야 함을 의미하므로 (D)가 정답이다.

어휘 be shaped like ~ 같은 모양으로 되어 있다 put together 조립하다

## 148 Not / True

번역 할인에 대해 언급된 것은?
(A) 온라인 쇼핑객에게는 더 일찍 시작된다.
(B) 제품을 여러 개 구입해야 한다.
(C) 고객은 15달러를 할인받을 수 있다.
(D) 충성 고객 프로그램 회원들만 이용할 수 있다.

해설 두 번째 단락에 동물원 침실 세트에서 최소 세 가지 제품을 주문하면 15% 할인을 해준다(Get 15% off when you order at least three items from the Zoo Bedroom Set)고 했으므로 (B)가 정답이다.

어휘 entitle 자격을 주다 loyalty program 충성 고객 프로그램

> Paraphrasing
> 지문의 order at least three items
> → 정답의 purchase of several items

### 149-150 광고

포체바
마호니 철인 3종 경기 공식 파트너

**149 마호니 철인 3종 경기 참가자들이 훈련 중에 포체바 영양 쉐이크를 마시면 이 경기 코스의 악명 높은 산봉우리 경사를 정복하기 위해 필요한 근육을 발달시키는 데 도움이 됩니다.** 60그램의 쉐이크 파우더 1회분에는 85가지가 넘는 영양소와 함께 25그램의 놀라운 단백질이 함유되어 있습니다. 얼음과 물을 섞으면 맛있고 활력을 주는 간식이 됩니다. **150 마호니 광장에서 열리는 철인 3종 경기 박람회의 저희 부스에 들러 재고 소진 시까지 제공되는 무료 샘플을 받아 보세요.** 또는, 더 많은 정보를 원하시면 www.gopocheva.com을 방문하시기 바랍니다.

포체바

어휘 triathlon 철인 3종 경기 nutritional 영양의 participant 참가자 conquer 정복하다 slope 경사지 infamous 악명 높은 peak 산봉우리, 정점 serving 1회 제공량, 1인분 contain 포함하다, 담고 있다 incredible 믿을 수 없는, 놀라운 protein 단백질 nutrient 영양소 blended with ~와 혼합된 treat 특별 간식, 특별 음식 stop by ~에 들르다 expo 박람회 supply 공급(량) last 유지되다, 지속되다

## 149 Not / True

번역 마호니 철인 3종 경기에 대해 언급된 것은?
(A) 산악 지역에서 열린다.
(B) 코스가 더 길어졌다.
(C) 일년 중 따뜻한 시기에 개최된다.
(D) 결승선이 마호니 광장에 있다.

해설 초반부에 마호니 철인 3종 경기 코스에 대해 이야기하면서 악명 높은 산봉우리 경사를 정복하는 것(to conquer the slopes of the course's infamous peaks)을 언급하는 부분이 있으므로 (A)가 정답이다.

어휘 mountainous 산악의, 산이 많은 be located in ~에 위치해 있다

> Paraphrasing
> 지문의 the slopes of the course's infamous peaks
> → 정답의 a mountainous area

## 150 추론

번역 포체바의 제품에 대해 암시된 것은?
(A) 개봉 전에 냉동고에 보관해야 한다.
(B) 유명 운동선수가 홍보한다.
(C) 철인 3종 경기 관련 행사에서 증정된다.
(D) 액체 형태로 소비자들에게 판매된다.

해설 후반부에 마호니 광장에서 열리는 철인 3종 경기 박람회의 부스에 들러 무료 샘플을 받아 보라(Stop by our booth at the triathlon expo in Mahoney Square for a free sample)는 정보가 제시되어 있으므로 (C)가 정답이다.

어휘 store 보관하다 freezer 냉동고 endorse (유명인이) 홍보하다 athlete 운동선수 give away 증정하다 consumer 소비자 liquid 액체의

> Paraphrasing
> 지문의 free → 정답의 is given away

## 151-152 문자 메시지

벤자민 레일리 [오후 1시 10분]
[151] **그레타, 인공지능에 관한 제 기사를 위해 인터뷰에 응해 주셔서 다시 한번 감사드립니다.** 결국 당신의 말을 여러 번 인용하게 되었어요.

그레타 올슨 [오후 1시 13분]
네, 저도 봤어요. [151] **제 연구 내용을 독자들과 공유할 수 있어서 기쁩니다.**

벤자민 레일리 [오후 1시 14분]
[151] **이제 저희 편집장께서 AI가 업무 현장에 미치는 영향에 관해 더 자세히 다룬 다른 기사를 써 달라고 요청했습니다.** [151, 152] **이에 관한 의견을 들어볼 수 있도록 전화 통화를 할 수 있을까요?**

그레타 올슨 [오후 1시 21분]
[152] **물론이죠, 하지만 5시까지 기다려 주시겠어요?** 제가 오늘 컨퍼런스에 참가하고 있거든요.

벤자민 레일리 [오후 1시 22분]
그건 어려울 것 같습니다. [152] **이 기사는 내일 발행할 예정이거든요.**

그레타 올슨 [오후 1시 24분]
좋아요, 그럼 제가 할 수 있는 최선은 세션들 사이에 짧게 대화하는 것이에요.

벤자민 레일리 [오후 1시 25분]
그 제안을 받아들이겠습니다! 시간 되실 때 전화 주세요.

어휘 artificial intelligence 인공 지능 quote 인용하다 share 공유하다 editor 편집장, 편집자 go into more detail 더 자세히 살펴보다 participate in ~에 참가하다 edition (출판물 등의) 호, 판

## 151 세부 사항

번역 레일리 씨는 왜 올슨 씨에게 연락하는가?
(A) 유용한 자료에 관해 알리기 위해
(B) 한 주제에 대한 전문가 의견을 얻기 위해
(C) 올슨 씨 연구 프로젝트의 현황을 파악하기 위해
(D) 기사를 제출해 준 것에 대해 감사하기 위해

해설 오후 1시 10분에서 1시 14분에 걸친 메시지를 통해 레일리 씨가 인공 지능에 대해 기사를 위해 올슨 씨를 인터뷰(letting me interview you for my article on artificial intelligence)한 것과 올슨 씨가 자신의 연구 내용을 공유해 준(I could share my research) 점, 그리고 AI가 업무 현장에 미치는 영향에 관해 더 자세히 다룬 다른 기사를 작성하도록(to write another article that goes into more detail about AI's effects on the workplace) 편집장이 요청한 것에 대해 올슨 씨에게 의견을 얻을 수 있는지(get your thoughts on that?) 묻는 내용이 제시되어 있다. 이는 전문가인 올슨 씨의 의견을 얻으려는 것이므로 (B)가 정답이다.

어휘 resource 자료 obtain 얻다, 획득하다 expert 전문적인

## 152 의도 파악

번역 오후 1시 22분에 레일리 씨가 "그건 어려울 것 같습니다"라고 쓸 때, 의미하는 것은 무엇인가?
(A) 올슨 씨의 업무량을 우려하고 있다.
(B) 컨퍼런스에 참석하기에는 너무 바쁘다.
(C) 일부 글이 이해하기 어렵다고 생각한다.
(D) 더 이른 시간에 통화하는 것을 선호한다.

해설 1시 14분에 레일리 씨가 올슨 씨의 의견을 들을 수 있도록 전화 통화를 할 수 있을지(Could we jump on the phone so I can get your thoughts on that?) 묻는 것에 대해 올슨 씨가 5시까지 기다릴 수 있는지(can you wait until five?) 되묻자, 레일리 씨가 '그건 어려울 것 같습니다'라는 말과 함께 기사가 내일 발행될 예정(This article is for tomorrow's edition)이라고 밝히고 있다. 이는 내일 실을 기사를 위해 올슨 씨가 언급한 5시보다 더 일찍 통화해야 한다는 뜻이므로 (D)가 정답이다.

어휘 be concerned about ~을 우려하다 workload 업무량

## 153-155 이메일

발신: 유채원
수신: 캐런 앳킨스
제목: 뉴스
날짜: 11월 28일
첨부: 리

TEST 9

앳킨스 씨께,

[153] **귀사의 사업 개발 담당자 공석에 적합해 보이는 분을 찾았습니다. 이분의 성함은 콘래드 리이며,** 지난 3년 동안 도슨 헬스 사에서 영업직으로 근무해 오신 분입니다. 귀사인 애조라 사이언스 사의 공석과 마찬가지로, 이 일도 미국 제품을 한국 회사에 판매하는 일을 포함한 서울에 기반을 둔 업무이며, 콘래드는 이 일을 성공적으로 수행해 왔습니다. 작년에는 사원에서 대리로 승진했습니다. 전화 통화를 통해 [154] **그가 영어와 한국어 둘 다 원어민 수준으로 유창하게 구사한다는 점**도 직접 확인했습니다.

[155] **콘래드는 생물학 학사 학위를 소지하고 있고, 12월에 라슨 대학교 온라인 프로그램을 통해 MBA 학위도 취득할 예정입니다.** 그는 심지어 귀하께서 찾고 있는 과학 교육에 대한 열정도 있는데, 지역 과학 박물관에서 주말마다 자원봉사를 하고 있기 때문입니다.

콘래드의 이력서는 이 이메일에 첨부되어 있습니다. 이분과 연락하길 원하시면 이 이메일에 답장해 주시기 바랍니다.

유채원
허먼 코리아 주식회사

어휘 promising 유망한, 전망이 좋은 match 어울리는 사람[것] opening 공석 -based ~을 기반으로 하는 involve 포함하다, 수반하다 promote 승진시키다 associate 사원 confirm 확인하다 fluency 유창함 bachelor's degree 학사 학위 biology 생물학 earn 얻다, 획득하다 MBA 경영학 석사 passion 열정 volunteer 자원봉사하다 local 지역의 résumé 이력서 attach 첨부하다 connect 연락하다, 연결하다

## 153 주제 / 목적

번역 이메일의 목적은 무엇인가?
(A) 행사 연설자를 제안하는 것
(B) 승진을 발표하는 것
(C) 일자리의 후보자를 소개하는 것
(D) 멘토십 프로그램을 알리는 것

해설 첫 단락에 상대방 회사의 공석에 어울리는 사람을 찾은 사실과 함께 이름이 콘래드 리(I have found someone who is a promising match for your company's Business Development Representative opening. His name is Conrad Lee)라고 밝히면서 이 사람의 경력 등에 대해 이야기하고 있다. 따라서 인력 채용 대행사 직원이 일자리의 후보자를 소개하는 내용임을 알 수 있으므로 (C)가 정답이다.

어휘 promotion 승진 candidate 지원자, 후보자 publicize 알리다, 광고하다 mentorship 멘토십(경험자 등이 조언을 해 주는 것)

## 154 Not / True

번역 리 씨에 대해 사실인 것은?
(A) 2개 국어 사용자이다.
(B) 현재 무직 상태이다.
(C) 서울로 자주 출장 간다.
(D) 전에 유 씨와 함께 일했다.

해설 첫 단락 마지막 부분에 리 씨가 영어와 한국어 둘 다 원어민 수준으로 유창하게 구사한다(he speaks both English and Korean with native-level fluency)고 제시되어 있으므로 (A)가 정답이다.

어휘 bilingual 2개 국어를 하는 unemployed 무직인

> Paraphrasing
> 지문의 speaks both English and Korean
> → 정답의 bilingual

## 155 세부 사항

번역 리 씨가 올 연말쯤 무엇을 할 계획인가?
(A) 다른 국가로 이주하기
(B) 박물관 전시물 설치하기
(C) 자원봉사 프로젝트 끝마치기
(D) 두 번째 학위 과정 이수하기

해설 두 번째 단락에 콘래드 리 씨가 생물학 학사 학위를 소지하고 있다는 사실과 함께 12월에 라슨 대학교 온라인 프로그램을 통해 MBA 학위도 취득할 예정(Conrad has a bachelor's degree in biology and is scheduled to earn his MBA degree from Larson University's online program in December)이라고 알리고 있으므로 (D)가 정답이다.

어휘 mount (특정 위치 등에) 설치하다, 탑재하다 exhibit 전시(물)

> Paraphrasing
> 지문의 in December → 질문의 by the end of the year
> 지문의 to earn his MBA degree
> → 정답의 Complete a second degree

## 156-158 이메일

수신: 티스데일 아파트 전 주민
발신: 엘사 레이놀즈, 건물 관리 책임자
날짜: 5월 3일
제목: 배관 수리 작업

주민 여러분께,

[156] **티스데일 아파트 건물의 수도 공급이 5월 18일 화요일에 차단될 것입니다.** 모든 세대가 당일 오전 9시부터 오후 6시까지 온수 또는 냉수를 이용하지 못하게 될 것입니다. 이 수도 차단은 주민 여러분께서 보고해 주신 수압 문제의 원인을 확인하기 위해 배관 작업자들이 건물의 주요 수도 공급 및 압력 조절기를 점검할 수 있도록 하기 위해 필요합니다. 수리 작업을 용이하게 하기 위해 향후에 차단이 필요할 수 있습니다.

문제가 되는 당일 및 그 전까지 다음 사항을 유념해 주시기 바랍니다. [158] **모든 아파트 건물 내의 싱크대와 샤워기, 욕조, 변기가 작동되지 않을 것입니다. 식수나 조리를 위해 물이 필요할 것으로 예상되는 경우 미리 용기에 물을 채우시기 바랍니다.** 이동식 화장실도 주민 여러분께서 이용하실 수 있도록 뒤쪽 골목에 설치될 것입니다. [157] **여러분의 난방기 또는 에어컨이 수도관과 연결되어 있을 수 있습니다. 어떤 문제든 예방할 수 있도록 이것들을 켜지 마십시오.**

질문이 있으시면 e.reynolds@tisdaleapt.com으로 제게 연락 주시기 바랍니다. 감사합니다.

어휘 resident 주민 plumbing 배관 shut off 차단하다 unit 세대 access 이용, 접근; 이용하다, 접근하다 plumber 배관 작업자 inspect 점검하다 supply 공급(량) regulator 조절기 identify 확인하다, 발견하다 facilitate 용이하게 하다 keep ~ in mind ~을 유념하다, 명심하다 in question 문제가 되는 out of operation 작동되지 않는 anticipate 예상하다, 기대하다 fill up 가득 채우다 container 용기, 그릇 beforehand 미리, 사전에 avoid 피하다 turn ~ on ~을 켜다 prevent 예방하다

## 156 주제 / 목적

번역 이메일은 왜 주민들에게 발송되었는가?
(A) 수압이 왜 낮은지 설명하기 위해
(B) 지출을 줄이기 위한 팁을 공유하기 위해
(C) 다가오는 지역 사회 행사에 관해 상기시키기 위해
(D) 공공 서비스 중단에 대해 주의를 주기 위해

해설 첫 단락 시작 부분에 아파트 건물의 수도 공급이 5월 18일 화요일에 차단될 것(Water service to the Tisdale Apartments building will be shut off on Tuesday, May 18)이라고 알리면서 그와 관련된 작업 및 주의 사항 등을 전달하고 있으므로 (D)가 정답이다.

어휘 reduce 줄이다, 감소시키다 expense 지출 (비용), 경비 upcoming 다가오는, 곧 있을 warn 주의를 주다 disruption 중단, 방해 utility service 공공 서비스

> Paraphrasing
> 지문의 Water service to the Tisdale Apartments building will be shut off
> → 정답의 a disruption to a utility service

## 157 세부 사항

번역 레이놀즈 씨가 권하는 것은?
(A) 특별한 보관 용기 구입하기
(B) 배관 연결 상태 확인하기
(C) 특정 가전 기기 사용 피하기
(D) 계속되는 문제를 자신에게 보고하기

해설 두 번째 단락 마지막 부분에 난방기 또는 에어컨이 수도관과 연결되어 있을 수 있다고 언급하면서 어떤 문제든 예방할 수 있도록 이것들을 켜지 말라(Your heater or air conditioner maybe connected to the water lines. Avoid turning them on in order to prevent any issues)고 권하고 있으므로 (C)가 정답이다.

어휘 storage 보관, 저장 appliance 가전 기기 ongoing 계속되는

> Paraphrasing
> 지문의 Avoid turning them(heater or air conditioner) on → 정답의 Avoiding using certain appliances

## 158 문장 삽입

번역 [1], [2], [3], [4]로 표시된 곳 중에서 다음 문장이 가장 적합한 곳은 어디인가?
"이동식 화장실도 주민 여러분께서 이용하실 수 있도록 뒤쪽 골목에 설치될 것입니다."
(A) [1]
(B) [2]
(C) [3]
(D) [4]

해설 제시된 문장은 추가 정보를 제공할 때 사용하는 also와 함께 이동식 화장실도 설치된다는 조치 사항을 알리는 의미를 지니고 있다. 따라서 수도가 차단되는 당일에 필요한 구체적인 조치를 설명하는 문장 뒤인 [3]에 들어가 유사 정보를 추가로 제공하는 흐름이 되어야 자연스러우므로 (C)가 정답이다.

어휘 portable 이동식의, 휴대용의 be stationed 설치되다, 배치되다 alley 골목

## 159-160 편지

호주 전국 운전자 협회 (NDAA)

9월 16일
대런 하우저
프라이 가 160
캔버라 ACT 2601

하우저 씨께,

귀하의 금년 NDAA 회원 자격이 10월 31일에 종료될 것입니다. 160 **지금 갱신하셔서 혜택을 12개월 더 누리시기 바랍니다.** 기억하세요. 159(B) **회원은 추가 비용 없이 긴급 연료 공급, 배터리 충전, 타이어 교체 및 견인을 포함한 NDAA의 놀라운 긴급 출동 서비스를 이용할 수 있습니다.** 또한 전 세계에 있는 자동차 클럽과 상호 협약을 맺은 덕분에 159(C) **수십 개 국가에서 렌터카 이용 시 긴급 출동 서비스**를 받을 수 있을 뿐 아니라 전국 수백 개의 제휴 정비소에서 자동차 수리 할인을 받을 수 있습니다.

추가로, NDAA는 저희 회원들께 159(D) **동남 아시아의 여러 인기 여행지에 대한 독점 투어**를 제공하기 위해 고아시아 여행사와 막 제휴 관계도 맺었습니다. 이 혜택을 이용하시려면, 160 **호주 달러로 99.99달러의 연간 회비와 함께 동봉해 드린 양식을 보내주시거나, 저희 웹사이트 www.ndaa.com.au를 방문하셔서 신용카드 또는 직불카드를 이용해 갱신하세요.**

NDAA 가족의 일원이 되어 주셔서 감사합니다.

플로렌스 하틀리
회원 서비스 관리 책임
동봉물

어휘 association 협회 renew 갱신하다 benefit 혜택, 이점 access 이용 (권한) incredible 믿을 수 없는 assistance 지원, 도움 towing 견인 for no extra charge 추가 비용 없이 be eligible for ~에 대한 자격이 있다 garage 정비소 nationwide 전국에; 전국적인 rental 대여, 임대 reciprocal 상호 간의

TEST 9

agreement 협약, 협의(서) automotive 자동차의 enter a partnership 제휴 관계를 맺다 exclusive 독점적인, 전용의 destination 여행지, 목적지 take advantage of ~을 이용하다 attached 동봉된, 첨부된 annual 연간의, 연례적인 debit card 직불카드 encl. 동봉된; 동봉물(= enclosed; enclosure)

## 159 Not / True

번역 회원이 할 수 있는 일로 기재되지 않은 것은?
(A) 차량 대여 비용 절약하기
(B) 무료로 차량 견인하기
(C) 해외에서 운전 중에 도움받기
(D) 해외로 특별 여행 떠나기

해설 첫 단락에 추가 비용 없이 견인 서비스(~ towing — all for no extra charge) 등을 이용할 수 있다는 것에서 (B)를, 수십 개 국가에서 긴급 출동 서비스(roadside assistance for your rental car in dozens of other countries)를 받을 수 있다는 것에서 (C)를 확인할 수 있다. 또한, 두 번째 단락에 동남 아시아의 여러 인기 여행지에 대한 독점 투어(exclusive tours of several top destinations in Southeast Asia)를 제공하기 위해 협약을 맺었다는 것에서 (D)도 확인 가능하다. 하지만 차량 대여 비용 절약에 대해서는 언급되어 있지 않으므로 (A)가 정답이다.

어휘 vehicle 차량 abroad 해외에서, 해외로(= overseas)

> Paraphrasing
> 지문의 for no extra charge → 보기 (B)의 for free
> 지문의 other countries → 보기 (C)의 abroad
> 지문의 exclusive tours of several top destinations in Southeast Asia → 보기 (D)의 special tours overseas

## 160 세부 사항

번역 하우저 씨는 무엇을 하도록 요청받는가?
(A) NDAA 지사 방문
(B) 연간 비용 결제
(C) 의견 양식 작성
(D) 회원 카드 소지

해설 첫 번째 단락 초반부에 지금 연간 회원권을 갱신하라(Renew now ~)고 했고, 두 번째 단락에 99.99달러의 연간 회비와 함께 동봉된 양식을 보내거나, 웹사이트를 방문해 신용카드 또는 직불카드를 이용해 갱신하라(~ with your annual membership fee of $99.99 AUD, ~ to renew using your credit or debit card)는 말이 있으므로 (B)가 정답이다.

어휘 location 지사, 지점 fill out 작성하다

> Paraphrasing
> 지문의 annual membership fee of $99.99 AUD
> → 정답의 a yearly payment

## 161-163 보고서

개요서

목적
**[161] 이 보고서는 서턴 캔들 주식회사(이하 "서턴 사") 인수의 잠재적 장단점들을 조명하기 위해 펀페어 주식회사 이사회의 지시에 따라 작성되었습니다.**

초기 결론
서턴 사는 펀페어 사의 브랜드 포트폴리오에 종합적인 자산이 될 가능성이 있습니다. **[162] 이 회사의 양초 및 방향용 디퓨저는 품질이 뛰어나며, 우리의 장식품 통로와 거실 진열품을 보완하는 추가 제품이 될 것입니다.** 제품에 서턴의 이름을 유지하면, 고객 충성도가 높기 때문에 매장 내 유동 인구도 증가할 수 있습니다.

목표 회사의 재무 개요
서턴 사는 현재 세 가지 카테고리에서 36개 제품을 제조하고 있으며, 자사 웹사이트를 통해 소비자들에게 직접 판매하고 있습니다. 최근 한 해 동안 카테고리별 판매 수익은 아래의 표에 제시되어 있습니다.

| | 회계 분기 | | | |
|---|---|---|---|---|
| 제품 유형 | 1분기 | 2분기 | 3분기 | 4분기 |
| 양초 | 80,713달러 | 85,029달러 | 87,172달러 | 93,541달러 |
| **[163] 플러그인 디퓨저** | 12,453달러 | **[163] 16,510달러** | 15,384달러 | 14,693달러 |
| 디퓨저 리필용 팩 | 16,450달러 | 14,478달러 | 15,624달러 | 15,722달러 |

어휘 executive summary 개요(서) direction 지시, 감독 executive board 이사회 illuminate 조명하다, 분명히 밝히다 potential 잠재적인 advantage 장점 hereafter (계약서 등에서) 이하, 이후로 initial 초기의, 처음의 conclusion 결론 overall 종합적인, 전반적인 asset 자산, 재산 portfolio 포트폴리오, 목록 scent 향 complementary 보완하는 addition 추가(되는 것) décor 장식물 aisle 통로 foot traffic 유동 인구 customer loyalty 고객 충성도 financial 재무의, 재정의 overview 개요 manufacture 제조하다 revenue 수익, 수입 table 표, 도표 fiscal 회계의, 재정의 quarter 분기

## 161 주제 / 목적

번역 보고서에서 다루는 것은?
(A) 예산 수정의 목적
(B) 판매량 증가 전략의 필요성
(C) 광고 캠페인의 효과
(D) 기업 인수 가능성

해설 '목적'에 해당하는 첫 단락에 이 보고서는 서턴 캔들 주식회사의 인수가 지니는 잠재적 장단점들을 조명하기 위해 작성되었다(This report has been created ~ in order to illuminate the potential advantages and disadvantages of purchasing Sutton Candle Corporation)고 쓰여 있으므로 (D)가 정답이다.

어휘 budget 예산 revision 수정, 변경 strategy 전략 advertising 광고 (활동) possibility 가능성 corporate 기업의 acquisition 인수, 획득

> Paraphrasing
> 지문의 purchasing Sutton Candle Corporation
> → 정답의 a corporate acquisition

### 162 세부 사항

번역 펀페어 주식회사는 어떤 종류의 업체인가?
(A) 가정용품 매장
(B) 브랜드 컨설팅 업체
(C) 인테리어 디자인 회사
(D) 방향 제품 제조사

해설 두 번째 단락에 인수 가능성이 있는 서턴 사의 양초 및 방향용 디퓨저를 이야기하면서 장식품 통로와 거실 진열품을 보완해 주는 추가 제품이 될 것(Its candles and scent diffusers ~ would be a complementary addition to our décor aisles and living room displays)이라고 했으므로 (A)가 정답이다.

> Paraphrasing
> 지문의 décor aisles and living room displays
> → 정답의 home goods

### 163 세부 사항

번역 16,000달러 이상의 전자 제품이 판매된 것은 언제인가?
(A) 1분기
(B) 2분기
(C) 3분기
(D) 4분기

해설 도표에서 전자 제품에 해당하는 플러그인 디퓨저(Plug-in Diffusers)의 2분기(Second) 수익이 16,510달러로 표기되어 있으므로 (B)가 정답이다.

어휘 worth 값어치, 가치

> Paraphrasing
> 지문의 Plug-in Diffusers → 질문의 electronic products

### 164-167 보도 자료

맨체스터 (8월 14일) - 지역 업체인 센트랠러티 파트너스는 비영리 단체에 자사 서비스를 할인된 요금으로 제공하기 시작할 것이라고 오늘 발표했다.

[167] **센트랠러티는 시에서 시청각 장비를 가장 많이 보유한 곳들 중 하나이며, 그 범위가 음향 시스템에서 대형 디지털 디스플레이 및 프로그래밍 가능한 조명 기구에까지 이른다.** 그곳의 자원에는 다양한 전문 기술을 가진 30명의 헌신적인 직원들도 포함된다. [164] **세련되고 인상적인 컨퍼런스, 모금 행사, 시상식 연회 등을 개최하기 위해 이 모든 것을 고객이 원하는 대로 사용할 수 있다.**

[165] **행사나 청중에 관계없이, 센트랠러티는 발표자의 메시지가 명확히 전달되도록 한다.** 왜곡된 소리나 호환되지 않는 발표 자료들, 심지어 어울리지 않는 조명 등과 같이 지장을 주는 문제들의 가능성을 최소화하기 위해 전문 기술자가 프로세스의 모든 단계에서 함께 한다. 최근 센트랠러티에서 성공적으로 개최한 행사에는 영국 최대 보험사 협회의 연례 컨퍼런스와 맨체스터 도서전이 포함된다.

센트랠러티가 비영리 고객들에게 제공하는 할인은 기관의 규모에 따라 10%에서 20%까지 다양하다. [166] **자격이 되려면 단체가 반드시 광역 맨체스터 권역 내에 본사를 두고 있어야 한다.** 상세 정보 및 연락처는 센트랠러티의 웹사이트 www.centrality.co.uk에서 찾아볼 수 있다.

어휘 non-profit 비영리의 organisation 단체, 기관 rate 요금 audiovisual 시청각의 equipment 장비 range from ~ to … 범위가 ~에서 …에 이르다 lighting fixture 조명 기구 at one's disposal ~이 마음대로 할 수 있는 stage 개최하다, 무대에 올리다 polished 세련된 impressive 인상적인 fundraiser 모금 행사 banquet 연회 occasion 행사 audience 청중, 관객 convey 전달하다 present 있는, 존재하는 distract 지장을 주다, 방해하다 distorted 왜곡된 incompatible 호환되지 않는 material 자료, 재료 unflattering 어울리지 않는 insurer 보험사 association 협회 vary 다양하다 depending on ~에 따라 eligible 자격이 있는

### 164 세부 사항

번역 센트랠러티는 고객들이 무엇을 하는 것을 돕는가?
(A) 장비 유지 관리
(B) 라이브 행사 개최
(C) 보험 상품 구입
(D) 영상 광고 제작

해설 두 번째 단락에 이용 가능한 장비를 소개하면서 컨퍼런스, 모금 행사, 시상식 연회 등을 개최하기 위해 이 모든 것을 고객이 원하는 대로 사용할 수 있다(All of this is put at clients' disposal in service of staging polished, impressive conferences, fund-raisers, awards banquets, and much more)는 정보가 제시되어 있으므로 (B)가 정답이다.

어휘 insurance 보험 advertisement 광고

> Paraphrasing
> 지문의 staging polished, impressive conferences, fund-raisers, awards banquets
> → 정답의 Holding live events

### 165 Not / True

번역 회사들이 센트랠러티의 서비스를 통해 얻는 장점으로 언급된 것은?
(A) 특별한 브랜드 정체성
(B) 더 높은 직원 만족도
(C) 더 효과적인 의사소통
(D) 운영 비용 절감

해설 세 번째 단락에 행사나 청중에 관계없이, 센트랠러티는 발표자의 메시지가 명확히 전달되도록 한다(No matter the occasion or audience, Centrality ensures that presenters' messages are conveyed clearly)는 내용이 쓰여 있으므로 (C)가 정답이다.

TEST 9

어휘 unique 특별한, 독특한 identity 정체성 satisfaction 만족(도) effective 효과적인 reduced 감소된

> Paraphrasing
> 지문의 presenters' messages are conveyed clearly
> → 정답의 More effective communication

## 166 세부 사항

번역 특별 할인과 관련된 어떤 정보가 보도 자료에 포함되어 있는가?
(A) 이용 가능한 지역
(B) 받는 방법
(C) 유효 기간
(D) 도입한 이유

해설 마지막 단락에 자격이 되려면 단체가 반드시 광역 맨체스터 권역 내에 본사를 두고 있어야 한다(To be eligible, organisations must be based within Greater Manchester)는 요건이 언급되어 있으므로 이용 가능한 지역을 뜻하는 (A)가 정답이다.

어휘 region 지역 available 이용 가능한 method 방법 obtain 받다, 얻다 valid 유효한 introduction 도입, 소개

## 167 문장 삽입

번역 [1], [2], [3], [4]로 표시된 곳 중에서 다음 문장이 가장 적합한 곳은 어디인가?
"그곳의 자원에는 다양한 전문 기술을 가진 30명의 헌신적인 직원들도 포함됩니다."
(A) [1]
(B) [2]
(C) [3]
(D) [4]

해설 제시된 문장은 전문 기술을 가진 직원들도 그곳의 자원(Its resources)에 포함된다는 의미이므로 자원으로 지칭할 수 있는 것이 언급된 뒤에 들어가야 한다. 따라서 '자원'으로 지칭할 수 있는 다양한 장비의 보유 사실 및 종류를 알리는 문장 뒤인 [2]에 들어가 인적 자원도 있음을 알리는 흐름이 되어야 자연스러우므로 (B)가 정답이다.

어휘 resource 자원 dedicated 헌신적인 various 다양한 specialty 전문성, 전문 분야

### 168-171 기사

> 애틀랜타 (5월 2일) - 텔레비전 코미디 <엘레나>의 지역 제작진은 [168] **이 프로그램이 더 이상 조지아주 애틀랜타에서 촬영되지 않을 것이라는 사실을 이번 주에 통보받았다.** [168, 169] **대신 세 번째 시즌의 촬영은 미국을 가로질러 캘리포니아주 로스앤젤레스에서 진행될 것이며,** 이곳은 제작사 ASR 엔터테인먼트가 있는 곳이다. 물류상의 이점 외에도 [170] **이러한 변화는 <엘레나>의 제작을 더욱 경제적으로 만들 것이다. ASR 엔터테인먼트는 영화와 텔레비전 산업의 활성화를 목적으로 하는 주 정부 프로그램의 일환으로 캘리포니아주로부터 많은 세금 공제 혜택을 받을 것이라는 사실을 확인해 주었다.**
>
> <엘레나>는 지난 2년 동안 이런 변화를 모색한 네 번째 TV 제작물이다. 애틀랜타 연예계 구성원들은 조지아주 의회 의원들에게 자체 인센티브 프로그램의 규모를 늘려 달라고 [171] **호소하는 것**을 고려하고 있는 것으로 알려졌다.
>
> 어휘 crew members (방송 프로그램 등의) 제작진 film 촬영하다 shooting 촬영 logistical 물류 수송의 advantage 장점 production 제작, 제작물 economical 경제적인 earn 받다, 얻다 tax credit 세금 공제 혜택 aimed at ~을 목적으로 하는 invigorate 활성화하다 shift 변화 consider 고려하다 appeal 호소하다 legislator 의회 의원 scale 규모 incentive 인센티브, 장려 정책

## 168 주제 / 목적

번역 기사는 주로 무엇에 관한 것인가?
(A) 텔레비전 프로그램의 새로운 줄거리
(B) 텔레비전 프로그램 제작의 장소 변경
(C) 연예 기획사의 경영
(D) 제작진이 겪은 어려움

해설 첫 단락에 <엘레나>라는 텔레비전 프로그램이 더 이상 조지아주의 애틀랜타에서 촬영되지 않을 것이고, 세 번째 시즌의 촬영은 캘리포니아주의 로스앤젤레스로 옮겨 진행될 것(the show will no longer be filmed in Atlanta, Georgia. Shooting for the third season will instead take place across the country in Los Angeles, California)이라며 관련 내용을 설명하고 있으므로 (B)가 정답이다.

어휘 relocation 위치 이전, 재배치

> Paraphrasing
> 지문의 no longer be filmed in Atlanta / will instead take place ~ in Los Angeles, California
> → 정답의 relocation

## 169 세부 사항

번역 <엘레나>는 지금까지 몇 개의 시즌이 촬영되었는가?
(A) 한 개
(B) 두 개
(C) 세 개
(D) 네 개

해설 첫 단락에 세 번째 시즌의 촬영이 캘리포니아주의 로스앤젤레스로 옮겨 진행될 것(Shooting for the third season will instead take place across the country in Los Angeles, California)이라고 했으므로 그 동안 두 개의 시즌이 촬영되었다는 사실을 알 수 있다. 따라서 (B)가 정답이다.

## 170 세부 사항

번역 ASR 엔터테인먼트는 <엘레나>를 제작하면서 어떻게 비용을 절약할 것인가?
(A) 방송 회차를 더 적게 촬영하여서
(B) 출연진에 변화를 주어서
(C) 일부 작업을 외부에 위탁하여서
(D) 세금 혜택을 받아서

해설 첫 단락에 <엘레나> 제작이 더욱 경제적으로 될 것이라는 말과 함께 캘리포니아주로부터 많은 세금 공제 혜택을 받는다(it will earn a large tax credit from California)고 했으므로 (D)가 정답이다.

어휘 episode (방송의) 회차, 1회분 casting 출연진 outsource 외부에 위탁하다 benefit 혜택, 이점

> Paraphrasing
> 지문의 a large tax credit → 정답의 a tax benefit

## 171 동의어

번역 두 번째 단락, 네 번째 줄에 쓰인 "appealing to"와 의미가 가장 가까운 것은?
(A) 끌어들이는 것
(B) 합의하는 것
(C) 요구하는 것
(D) 선택하는 것

해설 appealing to 뒤에 목적어인 조지아주 의회 의원들(Georgia's state legislators)과 함께 to부정사구 '인센티브 프로그램의 규모를 늘리는 일(to increase the scale of its own incentive program)'이 쓰여 있다. 따라서 appealing to는 인센티브 프로그램의 규모를 늘리도록 의회 의원들에게 요청하는 것을 의미하는 표현으로 볼 수 있으므로 '요구하는 것'을 뜻하는 (C) calling upon이 정답이다.

### 172-175 온라인 채팅

유브라즈 베디, 오후 5시 10분
채팅으로 이렇게 확인할 수 있게 해줘서 고마워요. 여러분. 애버츠퍼드 현장 일 때문에 오늘 사무실에 출근할 수 없었어요. 미리엄, 웹사이트 업그레이드 작업은 어떻게 되어 가고 있죠?

미리엄 손턴, 오후 5시 14분
아주 잘되고 있습니다. [173] **오늘 제가 작년의 모든 고객들에게 전화해서 웹사이트용 고객 추천 후기를 작성해 줄 의향이 있을지 물어봤습니다. 다섯 곳이 동의했는데, 노먼 주식회사도 포함되어 있습니다.**

유브라즈 베디, 오후 5시 15분
잘됐네요. 코디, 곧 있을 새 프로젝트와 관련된 소식이 있나요?

코디 헤인즈, 오후 5시 17분
네, 있습니다. [172] **한 의류 매장 소유주께서 뒤쪽 구석 공간 중 한 곳에 탈의실을 만드는 일에 관해 방금 전화 주셨습니다. 그분을 위한 견적서를 작성하고 있습니다.** 그리고, [174] **그리핀 가족의 집을 설계한 글렌 웹스터를 기억하세요?** 그가 다른 집주인 고객에게 우리를 추천해 주었습니다. 마빈이 내일 두 분을 함께 만나 볼 예정입니다. [175] **아, 그리고 우리가 적격일지도 모르는 정부 프로젝트를 아사미가 발견했어요. 아사미?**

아사미 요시다, 오후 5시 20분
고마워요, 코디. 밴쿠버 공원 관리국에서 헤이스팅스 공원의 새 저장 시설을 위한 입찰을 받을 것이라고 발표했어요. 제가 지금 시의 계약업체에 대한 자격 요건을 살펴보고 있는데, 우리가 조금만 노력하면 충족할 수 있을 것 같아요.

유브라즈 베디, 오후 5시 21분
알겠어요, 그 일에 대해서 제게 계속 알려 주세요. 우리 모두 곧 집에 가야 하니까 여기서 마무리할게요. 즐거운 저녁 시간 보내세요, 여러분.

어휘 duty 업무, 임무 testimonial 고객 추천 후기 including ~을 포함해 prospective 곧 있을, 유망한 owner 주인 put together 작성하다, 만들다 quote 가격 견적(서) residential 거주지의, 주택의 be a good fit for ~에 적격이다, ~에 적임자이다 bid 입찰 (가격) storage 저장, 보관 requirements 자격 요건, 필수 조건 contractor 계약업체, 계약업자 keep ~ updated ~에게 계속 알리다 wrap up 마무리하다 head 가다, 향하다

## 172 추론

번역 채팅 참가자들은 어떤 종류의 업체에서 근무하고 있을 것 같은가?
(A) 청소 대행 업체
(B) 조경 디자인 회사
(C) 공원 관리 서비스 업체
(D) 건축 회사

해설 헤인즈가 5시 17분에 작성한 메시지에 한 의류 매장 소유주가 매장 내에 탈의실을 만드는 일에 관해 전화했다며 그 견적서를 작성하고 있다(The owner of a clothing store just called about building a set of dressing rooms in one of its back corners. I'm putting together a quote for her)고 했으므로 건물 구조를 변경하는 일을 할 수 있는 업체인 (D)가 정답이다.

어휘 participant 참가자 landscape 조경 groundskeeping (공원, 운동장 등의) 부지 관리

> Paraphrasing
> 지문의 building a set of dressing rooms
> → 정답의 construction

## 173 추론

번역 노먼 주식회사에 대해 암시된 것은?
(A) 메시지 작성자들의 회사에 만족한 고객이다.
(B) 온라인 연락처 양식을 작성했다.
(C) 메시지 작성자들의 회사의 새로운 경쟁사이다.
(D) 웹사이트에 관한 설문 조사에 참여했다.

해설 노먼 주식회사가 언급된 5시 14분 메시지에 손턴이 작년의 모든 고객들에게 전화해서 고객 추천 후기를 작성해 줄 의향이 있을지 물었고, 다섯 곳이 동의했는데, 노먼 주식회사도 포함되어 있다(Today I called all of our clients from the past year to ask if they'd be willing to write testimonials for the site. Five of them agreed, including Norman Limited)는 내용이 있다. 이를 통해 노먼 주식회사가 추천 후기를 작성해 줄 정도로 서비스에 만족한 고객사임을 알 수 있으므로 (A)가 정답이다.

어휘 satisfied 만족한 fill out 작성하다 competitor 경쟁사, 경쟁자 participate in ~에 참여하다

TEST 9

## 174 추론

번역 웹스터 씨는 누구일 것 같은가?
(A) 매장 관리자
(B) 건축가
(C) 건물 소유주
(D) 정부 관계자

해설 웹스터 씨가 언급되는 5시 17분 메시지에 글렌 웹스터가 그리핀 가족의 집을 설계했다(Glen Webster, who designed the Griffin family's house)는 말이 쓰여 있으므로 (B)가 정답이다.

어휘 property 건물, 부동산 official 관계자, 당국자

> Paraphrasing
> 지문의 who designed the Griffin family's house
> → 정답의 architect

## 175 의도 파악

번역 오후 5시 20분에, 요시다 씨가 "고마워요, 코디"라고 쓸 때, 의미하는 것은 무엇인가?
(A) 자신의 업무에 대한 헤인즈 씨의 칭찬을 받아들이고 있다.
(B) 새 프로젝트를 책임지게 되어 기쁘다.
(C) 헤인즈 씨로부터 일부 정보를 받았다.
(D) 자신의 생각을 이야기할 기회가 생겨서 기쁘다.

해설 바로 앞선 메시지에서 헤인즈가 자신들의 회사가 적격일지 모르는 정부 프로젝트를 아사미가 알게 되었다고 언급하면서 아사미의 이름을 불렀는데(Oh, and Asami noticed a government project that we might be a good fit for. Asami?) 그 뒤에 아사미 씨가 '고마워요, 코디'라고 반응하는 흐름이다. 이는 그 정부 프로젝트에 대해 이야기할 수 있도록 발언 순서를 넘겨준 것에 대한 감사의 인사이므로 (D)가 정답이다.

어휘 praise 칭찬 be put in charge of ~을 책임지게 되다

### 176-180 웹페이지+후기

www.momentum-program.com/home

모멘텀

모멘텀 앱은 프리랜서와 소규모 업체가 근무 시간을 추적할 수 있도록 도와줍니다. 이 앱은 유연성이 뛰어나 거의 모든 산업에 적용할 수 있습니다. [176] **사용자는 근무 시간 기록을 체계화할 수 있는 카테고리부터 요약 보고서에 포함되는 데이터에 이르기까지 다양한 요소를 제어할 수 있습니다.** 그리고 모멘텀 팀은 더 많은 사람들에게 도움이 되는 제품을 만드는 방법과 관련된 제안을 언제나 환영합니다.

세 가지 버전의 모멘텀을 이용할 수 있습니다.

개인용, 0달러. 프리랜서용으로 제작. 사용자들이 수동이나 자동으로 활동을 기록하고, 흔히 있는 업무를 빠르게 입력할 수 있도록 템플릿을 만들며, 날짜나 프로젝트 단위로 활동 보고서를 만들 수 있습니다.

기업용, 사용자 1인당 월 5달러. 업체용으로 제작. 모든 사용자는 개인용 사용자와 동일한 혜택을 누리며, 그에 더해 관리자로 지정된 사용자들은 생산성을 관찰하고 급여를 계산하기 위해 다른 사용자들의 기록에 접근하실 수 있습니다.

* 기업용을 일주일 무료로 체험해 보시려면, 여기를 클릭하십시오.

[178] **기업용 프로**, 사용자 1인당 월 8달러. 이 프리미엄 등급은 모든 기업용 혜택을 비롯해, 직원 근무 시간 기록표를 바탕으로 [178] **고객 청구서를 생성하는 기능과** 휴무를 요청, 승인, 파악하는 기능을 이용할 수 있습니다.

어휘 assist 돕다 keep track of ~을 기록하다, 추적하다 superb 뛰어난, 우수한 flexibility 유연성, 탄력성 adapt 적용하다 have control over ~을 제어할 수 있다 a wide range of 아주 다양한 element 요소 timekeeping 시간 기록 entry 입력(되는 것) organize 체계화하다, 정리하다 summary 요약 manually 수동으로 task 업무, 일 generate 만들어 내다 benefit 혜택, 이점 designated 지정된 access 접근하다, 이용하다 monitor 관찰하다 productivity 생산성 calculate 계산하다 payroll 급여(명단) trial 체험, 시험 tier 등급, 단계 entitle 자격을 주다 subscription 가입, 구독 invoice 청구서 timesheet 근무 시간 기록표 permit 승인하다 time off 휴일

고객 후기

모멘텀은 제 소규모 컨설팅 회사에 아주 좋은 선택이었습니다. 저희 업무 특성상 [177] **하루에도 여러 번 여러 고객을 위해 업무를 전환해야 하는데**, 청구 기간이 끝날 때마다 작은 단위의 시간을 합산하는 데 많은 시간이 소요되곤 했었습니다. 이제는 [178] **모멘텀이 단 몇 초 만에 모든 청구서를 생성하며**, 그 청구서의 정확성에 대해 더욱 확신을 갖게 되었습니다. 요약 보고서도 꽤 유용하다고 생각하는데, 특정 유형의 프로젝트들이 제가 예상했던 것보다 지속적으로 더 많은 시간을 필요로 한다는 것을 보여 주었기 때문입니다. 저는 이제 더욱 신뢰할 수 있는 시간 및 예산 견적을 제공할 수 있으며, 고객들도 이를 [179] **높이 평가하고** 있습니다.

모멘텀에 대한 제 유일한 불만은 [180] **자동 시간 추적 기능이 많은 처리 능력을 소모하는 것 같다는 점입니다. 제가 이걸 시도했을 때마다, 다른 모든 프로그램에서 지연이 발생하기 시작했습니다. 웹 브라우저에서 탭을 전환하는 데만 5초가 걸리는 등 작은 문제가 아니었습니다.** 다행히, 대신 근무 시간을 수동으로 입력하는 것은 쉽습니다.

전반적으로, 저는 모멘텀이 상당히 만족스러우며, 시간 추적이 필요한 다른 회사 및 개인에게 추천하고 싶습니다.

- 드웨인 제이콥스

어휘 nature 특성, 본질 switch 바꾸다, 전환하다 time-consuming 시간 소모적인 unit 단위 billing 청구서 발급 confident in ~에 자신 있는 accuracy 정확성 consistently 지속적으로, 일관되게 reliable 신뢰할 수 있는 budget 예산 estimate 견적(서) appreciate 높이 평가하다, 진가를 알아보다 complaint 불만, 불평 feature 기능, 특징 use up 소모하다, 다 써버리다 processing power 처리 능력 lag 지연 fortunately 다행히 input 입력하다 overall 전반적으로 individual 개인, 사람

## 176 세부 사항

번역 웹페이지에서 모멘텀의 어떤 이점을 강조하는가?
(A) 신속한 고객 지원
(B) 모바일 기기 호환성
(C) 다양한 사용자 맞춤 설정
(D) 안전한 데이터 저장

해설 첫 단락에 사용자가 근무 시간 기록을 체계화할 수 있는 카테고리부터 요약 보고서에 포함되는 데이터에 이르기까지 다양한 요소를 제어할 수 있다(Users have control over a wide range of elements, from the categories into which timekeeping entries can be organized to the data that is included in summary reports)고 했으므로 (C)가 정답이다.

어휘 emphasize 강조하다 compatibility 호환성 numerous 다수의, 수많은 customization 사용자 맞춤 secure 안전한 storage 저장, 보관

> Paraphrasing
> 지문의 Users have control over a wide range of elements → 정답의 Numerous customization options

## 177 Not / True

번역 후기에서 제이콥스 씨가 자신의 회사 직원들에 대해 언급하는 것은?
(A) 매일 다양한 프로젝트에 관여한다.
(B) 때때로 외부에서 근무해야 한다.
(C) 자동 시간 추적 기능을 이용해야 한다.
(D) 종종 정규 근무 시간 외에도 업무를 한다.

해설 제이콥스 씨가 작성한 후기 첫 단락에 소속 회사의 직원들이 하루에도 여러 번 여러 고객을 위해 업무를 전환해야 한다(we all have to switch between tasks for different clients several times per workday)고 했는데, 이는 매일 여러 프로젝트에 관여한다는 뜻이므로 (A)가 정답이다.

어휘 be involved in ~에 관여하다 multiple 다양한, 다수의 offsite 부지 밖에서

> Paraphrasing
> 지문의 have to switch between tasks for different clients several times per workday
> → 정답의 are involved in multiple projects each day

## 178 연계

번역 제이콥스 씨에 대해 암시된 것은?
(A) 기업용 프로 계정에 등록했다.
(B) 추가 고객을 맡을 수 있게 되었다.
(C) 모멘텀의 체험 버전을 이용하고 있다.
(D) 자신의 기술력에 자신이 없다.

해설 후기 첫 단락에 모멘텀이 모든 청구서를 생성한다(Momentum generates all of our invoices ~)고 했는데, 이는 웹페이지 마지막 단락에 기업용 프로의 특징으로 언급된 고객 청구서 만드는 기능(to create client invoices)에 해당한다. 따라서 제이콥스 씨가 기업용 프로를 이용 중이라는 사실을 알 수 있으므로 (A)가 정답이다.

어휘 sign up for ~에 등록하다, ~을 신청하다 account 계정 take on ~을 맡다 additional 추가적인

## 179 동의어

번역 후기에서 첫 번째 단락, 일곱 번째 줄에 있는 "appreciate"와 의미가 가장 가까운 것은?
(A) 증가시키다
(B) 이해하다
(C) 즐기다
(D) 가치 있게 여기다

해설 appreciate를 포함한 부분은 '더욱 신뢰할 수 있는 시간 및 예산 견적을 제공할 수 있으며, 고객들도 이를 높이 평가하고 있다(I am now able to give more reliable time and budget estimates, which I am sure my clients appreciate)'라고 해석되는데 여기서 appreciate는 '높이 평가하다'라는 뜻으로 쓰였다. 따라서 '가치 있게 여기다'라는 의미의 (D) value가 정답이다.

## 180 Not / True

번역 제이콥스 씨가 자신의 웹 브라우저에 대해 언급하는 것은?
(A) 모멘텀을 다운로드하기 위해 업데이트해야 했다.
(B) 작동 속도가 모멘텀의 기능에 영향을 받는다.
(C) 모멘텀의 직원이 추천했다.
(D) 모멘텀을 열 때 예기치 않게 닫힌다.

해설 후기 두 번째 단락에 모멘텀에 대한 불만을 언급하면서 자동 시간 추적 기능이 지닌 단점과 함께 다른 모든 프로그램들이 지연 문제를 겪기 시작한 점, 그리고 웹 브라우저에서 탭을 전환하는 데만 5초가 걸리는 점(the automatic time-tracking feature ~ it took a full five seconds just to switch between tabs in my Web browser)을 이야기하고 있다. 따라서 모멘텀이 웹 브라우저의 작동에 영향을 미치고 있다는 것을 알 수 있으므로 (B)가 정답이다.

어휘 affect 영향을 미치다 unexpectedly 예기치 못하게

## 181-185 기사+이메일

지역 뉴스

골웨이 (6월 24일)—181 **손브라이어 비즈니스 파크가 내년 2월로 계획된 개장을 향해 한 걸음 더 나아갔다. 어제, 시 관계자들과 지역 기업 대표들이 이 개발 사업의 기공식을 위해 이스트 골웨이에 모였다.**

182 **손브라이어는 손브라이어 파트너스가 개발 중이고 소유할 예정인데,** 183 **그들은 부동산 개발업체와 이 복합 건물로 회사를 이전할 계획인 여러 기업 소유주들로 구성된 그룹이다. 후자 중 한 명인 애드리언 호건은** 182 **이 지역의 기존 상업용 부동산 옵션에 대한 불만으로 인해 그룹이 결속했다고 설명했다.** 그는 손브라이어 비즈니스 파크는 "그 문제에 대한 해결책"이라고 말했는데, "현대적인 시설을 갖춘 통풍이 잘 되는 공간들"을 특징으로 할 것이기 때문이다.

이 상업용 건물의 많은 공간이 이미 예약되어 있지만, 몇 개의 매장이 아직 남아 있다. 185 **이곳의 임대를 담당하고 있는 KV 부동산은 7월 8일에 자사 사무실에서 잠재 세입자들을 위한 설명회를 개최할 예정이**

TEST 9

다. 관심 있는 사람들은 www.kvrealestate.ie/thornbriar에 방문하여 자세한 내용을 확인하면 된다.

어휘 take another step 한 걸음 더 나아가다 path 과정, 길 official 관계자 local 지역의, 현지의 gather 모이다 development 개발, 발전 groundbreaking ceremony 기공식 own 소유하다 comprise 구성하다 property 부동산, 건물 complex 복합 건물, 단지 the latter (앞서 언급된 둘 중) 후자 bond 결속하다 dissatisfaction 불만 existing 기존의 real estate 부동산 solution 해결책 issue 문제, 사안 feature 특징으로 하다 airy 통풍이 잘 되는 unit (상가 등) 매장, (아파트 등) 세대 available 이용 가능한 handle 처리하다 information session 설명회 potential 잠재적인 tenant 세입자

수신: 아가타 워이치크 <agata.wojcik@plix-mail.com>
발신: 케네스 카나한 <kcarnahan@kvrealestate.ie>
제목: 정보
185 **날짜: 7월 9일**
첨부: @TBPL-A203

워이치크 씨께,

185 **어제 설명회가 끝난 후 귀하를 만나** 미용실 2호점 개장 계획에 대해 알게 되어 기뻤습니다. 요청하신 대로, 184 **귀하의 조건에 가장 적합하다고 생각하신 손브라이어 A203호 매장의 임대 계약 제안서를 보내드립니다. 귀사의 법무팀과 함께 검토해 보신 후, 조항 수정을 원하는 게 있으면 알려 주시기 바랍니다.**

케네스 카나한
선임 중개 담당, KV 부동산

어휘 location 지점, 위치 proposed 제안되는 leasing agreement 임대 계약서 fit 적합하다, 알맞다 specifications 사양, 설명서 legal 법률과 관련된 desired 원하는, 바라는 revision 수정, 변경 terms and conditions 조항, 약관

## 181 세부 사항

번역 기사에 따르면, 어제 무슨 일이 있었는가?
(A) 새로운 공원을 위한 기획 회의
(B) 시 청사 개관
(C) 비즈니스 복합 건물의 착공
(D) 전문 협회의 시상식

해설 첫 단락에 내년 2월에 개장하는 손브라이어 비즈니스 파크 개발 사업의 기공식이 어제 있었다(Thornbriar Business Park ~ Yesterday, city officials and local business leaders gathered in East Galway for the development's groundbreaking ceremony)는 말이 쓰여 있고, 두 번째 단락에 그곳이 복합 건물(the complex)이라고 알리고 있으므로 (C)가 정답이다.

> **Paraphrasing**
> 지문의 groundbreaking ceremony
> → 정답의 start of construction

## 182 추론

번역 손브라이어 파트너스에 대해 무엇이 사실일 것 같은가?
(A) 하나의 프로젝트를 실시하기 위해 만들어졌다.
(B) 두 사람 사이의 사업 제휴이다.
(C) 부동산 중개업체를 매입했다.
(D) 골웨이 시로부터 낙찰 받았다.

해설 두 번째 단락에 손브라이어는 손브라이어 파트너스에 의해 개발되고 있다(Thornbriar is being developed ~ by Thornbriar Partners)며, 그들은 부동산 개발업체와 이 복합 건물로 회사를 이전할 계획인 여러 기업 소유주들로 구성된 그룹(a group ~ owners who plan to move their companies into the complex)이라고 설명했다. 이어서 기존 상업용 부동산 옵션에 대한 불만 때문에 결속했다(the group bonded over its dissatisfaction with the area's existing commercial real estate options)고 그룹이 만들어진 이유가 나와 있으므로, 손브라이어 파트너스는 이 비즈니스 파크 프로젝트를 위해 만들어진 그룹으로 볼 수 있다. 따라서 (A)가 정답이다.

어휘 carry out 실시하다 partnership 사업 제휴 bid 입찰, 응찰

## 183 Not / True

번역 기사에서 호건 씨에 대해 언급하는 것은?
(A) 경험 많은 부동산 개발업자이다.
(B) 자신의 업체를 이전할 생각이다.
(C) 지역의 규제에 대해 불만이 있었다.
(D) 주택 보유자 단체의 회원이다.

해설 호건의 이름이 언급되는 두 번째 단락에 손브라이어 파트너스가 부동산 개발업체와 이 복합 건물로 회사를 이전할 계획인 여러 기업 소유주들로 구성된 그룹이고, 호건이 후자 중 한 명(~ a group comprising a property developer and several business owners who plan to move their companies into the complex. Adrian Horgan, one of the latter ~)이라고 했다. 따라서 호건이 업체를 이전할 계획을 갖고 있다는 것을 알 수 있으므로 (B)가 정답이다.

어휘 experienced 경험 많은 intend ~할 생각이다 relocate 이전하다 regulation 규제, 규정

> **Paraphrasing**
> 지문의 plan to move → 정답의 intends to relocate

## 184 주제 / 목적

번역 이메일의 목적은 무엇인가?
(A) 임대 협의를 시작하는 것
(B) 건물을 둘러볼 것을 제안하는 것
(C) 법무 대리인에 관해 문의하는 것
(D) 건축 과정에 관한 최신 정보를 전하는 것

해설 이메일에서 손브라이어 A203호 매장의 임대 계약 제안서를 보낸다(I am sending along the proposed leasing agreement for A203, the Thornbriar unit ~)며, 검토 후 조항 수정을 원하는 게 있으면 알려 달라(Please review it with your legal team and let me know of any desired revisions to its terms and conditions)고 요청하고 있다. 이는 임대 계약과 관련된 조건을 협의하는 과정에 해당하므로 (A)가 정답이다.

어휘 tenancy 임대 negotiation 협의, 협상 inquire 문의하다 representative 대리인

## 185 연계

번역 워이치크 씨에 관해 어떤 결론을 내릴 수 있는가?
(A) 이스트 골웨이에서 한 단체를 운영하고 있다.
(B) 자신의 변호사에게 계약서 초안 작성을 요청했다.
(C) 설명회에서 발표했다.
(D) 카나한 씨의 직장에서 카나한 씨를 만났다.

해설 KV 부동산의 카나한이 워이치크에게 보낸 이메일 시작 부분에 어제 설명회에서 만났다(~ meeting you at the end of yesterday's information session)고 했는데, 이메일 상단의 작성 날짜가 7월 9일(Date: 9 July)이므로 만난 날은 7월 8일임을 알 수 있다. 7월 8일은 기사 마지막 단락에 KV 부동산이 자사 사무실에서 잠재 세입자들을 위한 설명회를 개최하는 날(KV Real Estate, ~ will hold an information session for potential tenants at its office on 8 July)로 언급되어 있어 카나한이 자신의 사무실에서 워이치크와 만났다는 것을 알 수 있다. 따라서 (D)가 정답이다.

어휘 run 운영하다 organization 단체, 기관 draft 초안을 작성하다 contract 계약(서)

### 186-190 제품 정보+이메일+이메일

콜드웰 팜스
아침 식사용 크런치 시리얼 제품 라인
www.caldwellfarms.com/crunchies

| 제품명 | 제품 코드 | 12온스 상자 가격 |
|---|---|---|
| 오리지널 크런치 | CL01 | 4.1달러 |
| 허니 너트 크런치 | CL02 | 5.6달러 |
| 189 **요거트-프로스티드 크런치** | CL03 | **해당 없음 *** |
| 186, 188 **초콜릿 베리 크런치** | CL04 | **6달러** |
| 186 **애플 시나몬 크런치** | CL05 | 4.5달러 |

- 모든 크런치 제품은 볶은 통곡물 귀리로 만들어지며, 글루텐을 포함하지 않습니다.
- 크런치 제품은 아침 식사로 우유와 함께 먹을 수도 있고, 잡기 쉬운 링 모양 덕택에 마른 간식으로도 언제든 즐길 수 있습니다.
- 선별된 종류의 크런치는 2온스 용량의 1인분 용기로도 제공됩니다.

189 *** 브라이언트 식료품점에서 독점 판매됩니다.** 다른 종류들은 저희 웹사이트를 통해 구입하실 수 있습니다.

도매 가격 또는 크런치 유통 업체가 되시는 것에 대해 문의하시려면, retail@caldwellfarms.com으로 연락 주시기 바랍니다.

어휘 toasted 볶은, 구운 whole-grain 통곡물의 contain 포함하다, 담고 있다 gluten 글루텐(곡류에 들어 있는 단백질 성분) single-serve 1인분의 container 용기, 그릇 exclusively 독점적으로, 전용으로 variety 종류, 품종 inquire 문의하다 wholesale 도매의 distributor 유통 업체

수신: retail@caldwellfarms.com
발신: r.bishop@mortonssm.com
날짜: 3월 30일
제목: 크런치 문의

안녕하세요,

187 **저는 성장하고 있는 슈퍼마켓 체인인 모턴스의 건조 제품 부문 관리자입니다.** 188 **제가 최근 이스턴 간식 박람회에서 초콜릿 베리 크런치 샘플 제품을 받아 왔는데, 대단히 깊은 인상을 받았습니다.** 나머지 맛들도 그 정도로 좋다면, 저희가 유통 업체가 되는 데 관심이 생길 것 같습니다. 각 제품의 샘플을 저희에게 보내 주시겠습니까? '크레이머가 710, 토링턴, CT, 06790' 주소로 보내 주시면 됩니다.

감사합니다.

로드니 비숍

어휘 dry goods 건조 제품 growing 성장하는 recently 최근 pick up 가져오다, 구입하다 flavor 맛, 풍미

수신: r.bishop@mortonssm.com
발신: trudd@caldwellfarms.com
날짜: 3월 31일
제목: 회신: 크런치 문의

비숍 씨께,

크런치 샘플을 보내 드리게 되어 기쁩니다. 금요일까지 배송품을 받으실 것입니다. 189 **다른 회사가 이미 독점 판매권을 보유하고 있는 한 가지를 제외하고 모든 종류를 포함하고 있습니다.**

크런치 유통 업체가 되는 것에 관해 논의하실 준비가 되면 다시 연락 주시기 바랍니다. 190 **저희는 넉넉하게 이 시리얼 제품을 판매가에서 30% 인하해 드릴 수 있으며, 더 장기적인 계약의 경우 훨씬 더 인하해 드릴 수도 있습니다.** 곧 연락 주실 수 있기를 바랍니다.

트레이시 러드

어휘 exclusive 독점적인, 전용의 generous 넉넉한, 후한 markdown 가격 인하 in exchange for ~에 대한 대가로 long-tern 장기간의

## 186 Not / True

번역 제품 정보에서 크런치에 대해 언급하는 것은?
(A) 흔히 집에서 만드는 스낵바에 포함된다.
(B) 일부는 두 개의 용기로 구성된 작은 팩으로 판매된다.
(C) 두 가지 이상의 종류에 과일 맛이 포함되어 있다.
(D) 현재 모두 온라인에서만 구입할 수 있다.

해설 표에 초콜릿 베리 크런치(Chocolate Berry Crunchies)와 애플 시나몬 크런치(Apple Cinnamon Crunchies)가 있어 과일 맛이 두 종류 이상인 것을 알 수 있으므로 (C)가 정답이다.

## 187 추론

번역 비숍 씨는 어떤 분야에서 일하고 있을 것 같은가?
(A) 창고 관리
(B) 매장 상품 판매
(C) 무역 박람회 조직
(D) 구내식당 운영

해설 비숍 씨가 작성한 이메일 초반부에 모턴스라는 슈퍼마켓 체인의 건조 제품 부문 관리자(I'm the dry goods category manager for Morton's, a growing supermarket chain)라고 했으므로 (B)가 정답이다.

어휘 merchandising 상품 판매, 상품화 administration 운영, 관리

## 188 연계

번역 비숍 씨가 먹어 본 시리얼의 일반 상자 가격은 얼마인가?
(A) 4.1달러
(B) 4.5달러
(C) 5.6달러
(D) 6달러

해설 비숍 씨가 작성한 이메일에 이스턴 간식 박람회에서 초콜릿 베리 크런치 샘플을 받았다(I recently picked up a sample of Chocolate Berry Crunchies at the Eastern Snack Food Expo ~)는 말이 있다. 제품 정보에 있는 표에 초콜릿 베리 크런치 12온스 1상자 가격이 6달러로 표기되어 있으므로 (D)가 정답이다.

어휘 regular 보통의, 정규의

## 189 연계

번역 비숍 씨가 받을 배송품에 어느 종류의 크런치가 들어 있지 않은가?
(A) 오리지널 크런치
(B) 허니 너트 크런치
(C) 요거트-프로스티드 크런치
(D) 초콜릿 베리 크런치

해설 두 번째 이메일 첫 단락에 비숍 씨에게 보낸 제품 샘플은 다른 회사가 이미 독점 판매권을 보유하고 있는 한 가지를 제외하고 모든 종류를 포함하고 있다(It includes all of the varieties except one that another company already has the exclusive right to sell)고 했다. 독점 판매 관련해서 제품 정보 하단에 별표와 함께 브라이언트 식료품점에서 독점 판매된다(* Sold exclusively at Bryant Grocery)고 했는데, 도표에 별표가 되어 있는 것은 Yogurt-Frosted Crunchies이므로 (C)가 정답이다.

## 190 Not / True

번역 두 번째 이메일에서, 가격 할인에 대해 언급된 것은?
(A) 할인 규모는 협상될 수 있다.
(B) 금요일까지 제공된다.
(C) 단 한 번의 주문에만 적용될 것이다.
(D) 30상자 이상 구매 시 이용 가능하다.

해설 두 번째 단락에 이 시리얼 제품을 판매가에서 30% 인하해 줄 수 있으며, 더 장기적인 계약의 경우 훨씬 더 인하해 줄 수도 있다(We can offer you a generous 30% markdown on the cereals' sale price, or perhaps even more in exchange for a longer-term contract)고 했다. 이는 할인 규모를 협상할 수 있다는 뜻이므로 (A)가 정답이다.

어휘 negotiate 협의하다, 협상하다 apply 적용되다

### 191-195 광고+이메일+일정표

페천 호텔: 출장 여행객들이 선호하는 곳

페천 호텔은 25년 넘게 전 세계 각지에서 오시는 임원들께 자메이카에서 편히 머물 수 있는 공간을 제공해 오고 있습니다. 킹스턴 시내에 위치하여 대외무역부와 하버 컨퍼런스 센터에서 걸어서 오실 수 있는 거리에 있습니다.
페천 호텔의 모든 객실과 스위트룸에는 에어컨과 케이블 텔레비전, 미니 냉장고, 커피메이커, 금고, 무료 Wi-Fi가 있습니다. 또한 피트니스 룸과 비즈니스 센터뿐만 아니라 카페가 있는 야외 수영장도 있습니다. 매일 아침 적은 비용으로 유럽식 조식을 즐길 수 있습니다.
**193 서쪽 동을 구성하는 더블 침대가 있는 싱글룸은 1박당 26,000 자메이카 달러에 이용할 수 있습니다. 191 동쪽 동에 있는 스위트룸은 책상이 있는 거실과 가구가 비치된 발코니를 추가로 포함하고 있으며,** 1박당 40,000 자메이카 달러에 예약할 수 있습니다. 두 곳 모두 킹스턴 항구가 내려다보입니다.
www.pechonhotel.com.jm을 방문하셔서 오늘 여러분의 숙박을 예약하시기 바랍니다.

어휘 preferred 선호하는 executive 임원, 이사 comfortable 편한 within walking distance of ~에서 걸어서 갈 수 있는 거리에 있는 fridge 냉장고 safe 금고 continental breakfast 유럽식 아침 식사 make up 구성하다 wing (건물의) 동, 부속 건물 furnished 가구가 딸린 overlook (건물 등이) 내려다보다

수신: 글렌다 더글러스 <g.douglas@jenkinsassociates.com>
발신: 에밀리아노 안드레스 <e.andres@jenkinsassociates.com>
제목: 회신: 다가오는 출장
날짜: 11월 8일

글렌다 씨께,

다음 달 카리브해 여행 포럼을 위해 킹스턴으로 떠나시는 출장에 남편과 아이를 동반하고 가실 계획을 세우기 전에 질문해 주셔서 감사합니다. **192 젠킨스 어소시에이츠는 실제로 직원들이 자비로 출장에 가족을 동반하는 것을 허용하고 있습니다. 193 회사에서 당신의 항공료와 싱글룸 2박 비용, 그리고 3일간의 식비는 여전히 지불하겠지만,** 그 외 다른 비용은 본인이 부담해야 합니다. **193, 195 스위트룸으로 업그레이드하고 토요일 밤까지 숙박 기간을 연장하는 것은 페천 호텔에 직접 연락하시기 바랍니다.**

저녁 행사를 포함해, 평소대로 모든 컨퍼런스 행사에 참석하셔야 하는 것도 명심하시기 바랍니다.

다른 질문이 있으시면 제게 알려 주십시오.

에밀리아노 안드레스, 인사 관리 전문가

어휘 upcoming 다가오는, 곧 있을 indeed 실제로, 정말로 allowance 수당, 비용 cover (비용 등을) 충당하다 arrange 조치하다, 준비하다 extension 연장, 확장 keep in mind 명심하다, 유념하다 including ~을 포함해

카리브해 여행 포럼

[195] **12월 4일 금요일**
하버 컨퍼런스 센터
킹스턴, 자메이카

| 오전 9시 - 9시 30분 | 등록 |
|---|---|
| 오전 9시 30분 - 10시 | 개회사 (잴리사 바르가스, 카리브해 관광 산업 협회장) |
| 오전 10시 - 오후 12시 | 기조 연설: 194 (D) **카리브해 관광 산업에 기술 접목하기** (아이린 서머스, 트래블잽 CEO) |
| 오후 12시 - 1시 | 점심 식사 |
| 오후 1시 30분 - 오후 3시 | 세미나: 194 (A) **공공 정책상의 도전 과제** (에릭 페리, 브리지타운 대학 교수) |
| 오후 3시 30분 - 오후 5시 | 패널 토론: 194 (B) **환경적으로 지속 가능한 관광 산업 실현하기** (다양한 전문가들) |
| 오후 6시 30분 | 교류를 위한 만찬 |

어휘 registration 등록 opening remarks 개회사 keynote address 기조 연설 integrate 통합하다 achieve 달성하다 sustainable 지속 가능한 networking 인적 교류

## 191 세부 사항

번역 호텔의 동쪽 동에 있는 숙박 시설의 독점적인 특징은?
(A) 주방용 가전 기기
(B) 물가 전망
(C) 개별 옥외 공간
(D) 무료 인터넷 서비스

해설 광고 세 번째 단락에 동쪽 동에 위치한 스위트룸은 책상이 있는 거실과 가구가 비치된 발코니를 포함하고 있다(The suites in our East Wing, which additionally include a living room with a writing desk and a furnished balcony)는 특징이 언급되어 있으므로 (C)가 정답이다.

어휘 exclusive 독점적인, 전용의 lodging 숙박 시설, 숙소 appliance 가전 기기 waterfront 물가

Paraphrasing
지문의 a furnished balcony
→ 정답의 A private outdoor space

## 192 주제 / 목적

번역 안드레스 씨가 보낸 이메일의 목적은 무엇인가?
(A) 회사 정책 확인
(B) 일정 변경에 대한 문의
(C) 업무 배정
(D) 추천에 대한 응답

해설 이메일 첫 단락에 직원들이 자비로 출장에 가족을 동반하는 것을 허용하고 있다(Jenkins Associates does indeed allow employees to bring family along on work trips at their own expense)는 내용이 제시되어 있다. 이는 회사의 출장 관련 정책을 분명히 밝히는 말에 해당하므로 (A)가 정답이다.

어휘 itinerary 일정(표) assignment 배정, 할당

## 193 연계

번역 카리브해 여행 포럼 중의 더글러스 씨 호텔 숙박에 대해 유추할 수 있는 것은?
(A) 회사가 1박당 26,000 자메이카 달러를 낼 것이다.
(B) 기간을 연장함으로써 할인을 받을 수 있다.
(C) 이용하려는 숙소가 호텔의 서쪽 동에 위치해 있을 것이다.
(D) 매일 밤 자비로 40,000 자메이카 달러를 쓸 계획이다.

해설 이메일 첫 단락에 회사에서 항공료와 싱글룸 2박 비용, 3일간의 식비를 지불한다(We will still pay for your airfare, the cost of a single room for two nights, ~)고 말한 것으로 보아, 숙박에 대해서는 싱글룸 비용을 회사에서 지불해준다는 것을 알 수 있다. 광고 세 번째 단락에 페천 호텔의 싱글룸은 1박당 26,000 자메이카 달러(The single rooms ~ are available for 26,000 JMD per night)라고 쓰여 있으므로 (A)가 정답이다.

어휘 extend 연장하다, 확장하다 be located in ~에 위치해 있다

## 194 Not / True

번역 포럼에서 다뤄질 주제가 아닌 것은?
(A) 정부 정책으로 인한 어려움
(B) 다양한 목표 고객들을 위한 마케팅 접근 방식
(C) 관광 산업이 환경에 미치는 부정적 영향 감소
(D) 기술을 관광 산업 서비스에 접목하기

해설 일정표에서 오전 10시에 시작하는 기조 연설의 주제인 '카리브해 관광 산업에 기술 접목하기(Integrating Technology into Caribbean Tourism)'를 통해 (D)를, 오후 1시 30분에 시작하는 세미나의 주제인 '공공 정책상의 도전 과제(Public Policy Challenges)'를 통해 (A)를 확인할 수 있다. 또한, 오후 3시 30분에 시작하는 패널 토론회의 주제인 '환경적으로 지속 가능한 관광 산업 실현하기(Achieving Environmentally Sustainable Tourism)'를 통해 (C)도 확인 가능하다. 하지만 마케팅 접근법과 관련된 주제는 제시되어 있지 않으므로 (B)가 정답이다.

어휘 address 다루다 approach 접근법 target audiences 목표 고객들 lessen 줄이다 negative 부정적인 impact 영향

TEST 9

> Paraphrasing
> 지문의 Integrating Technology into Caribbean Tourism → 보기 (D)의 Incorporating technology into tourism services
> 지문의 Public Policy Challenges → 보기 (A)의 Difficulties caused by government policies
> 지문의 Achieving Environmentally Sustainable Tourism → 보기 (C)의 Lessening negative environmental impacts of tourism

## 195 연계

번역 더글러스 씨는 어느 날짜에 킹스턴을 떠날 것 같은가?
(A) 12월 3일
(B) 12월 4일
(C) 12월 5일
(D) 12월 6일

해설 이메일 첫 번째 단락에 더글러스 씨에게 토요일 밤까지 숙박 기간을 연장하는 것은 페천 호텔에 직접 연락하라(You should contact Pechon Hotel directly to arrange ~ the extension of your stay through Saturday night)고 쓰여 있다. 일정표 상단에 여행 포럼 개최 날짜가 12월 4일 금요일(Friday, 4 December)로 기재되어 있어 12월 5일 토요일 밤까지 숙박을 연장해서 12월 6일 일요일에 떠날 것으로 볼 수 있으므로 (D)가 정답이다.

## 196-200 안내 책자+카드+일정표

고셋 미술관

스테이트 가 1200, 고셋
555-0193

[196] **9월 회원 모집**
* 친구 등급 - 72달러
* 애호가 등급 - 112달러

고셋 미술관에는 몇 배는 더 큰 도시에서나 있을 법한 규모인 25,000점의 영구 소장품이 있습니다. 여기에는 셀린 듀퐁의 아주 다양한 조각품과 라파엘 루비오의 몇 안 남은 벽화 중 하나가 포함되어 있습니다. 또한 세계적으로 유명한 순회 전시회도 자주 개최합니다.

또한 미술 교육에 대한 헌신도 이 미술관을 차별화하는 요소입니다. 저희는 유익한 정기 강연과 다양한 미술 분야에서 모든 연령대의 사람들을 대상으로 계절별 강좌를 제공합니다. [199] **모든 성인 강좌는 우리 지역 사회 출신의 직업 미술가들이 수업을 합니다.**

친구 등급 회원권 소지자는 평상시 미술관 무제한 입장 권한과 특별 전시회 입장권 우선 구매 혜택을 받습니다. 강좌나 강연에 등록할 때, 요금을 10% 할인받습니다.

애호가 등급 회원에게는 동반 고객의 일반 입장료가 반값이라는 추가 혜택이 있습니다. [198] **또한 "애호가들만을 위한" 특별한 날이나 시간에 미술관에 초대됩니다.**

[197] **고셋 미술관 회원권을 구입하시려면, 1층 로비에 있는 안내 데스크를 방문하세요. 사진이 포함된 신분증이 필요합니다.**

어휘 membership drive 회원 모집 enthusiast 애호가, 열성적인 팬 permanent 영구적인 collection 소장품, 수집품 include 포함하다 a wide assortment of 아주 다양한 sculpture 조각품 surviving 남아 있는, 잔존하는 mural 벽화 world-renowned 세계적으로 유명한 exhibition 전시회 set ~ apart ~을 차별화하다, ~을 돋보이게 하다 commitment 헌신 informative 유익한 a variety of 다양한 fine arts 미술 holder 소지자, 보유자 unlimited 무제한의 admission 입장(료) priority 우선권, 우선 순위 access 이용, 접근 be entitled to +명사 ~에 대한 자격이 있다 perk 특혜, 특전 accompanying 동반하는, 동행하는 identification 신분 확인(증)

고셋 미술관
회원 카드

회원 정보

[198] **성명: 테렌스 앨런**
회원 번호: 54830
[198] **회원 등급: 애호가**
회원권 만료일: 9월 23일

어휘 expiration 만료, 만기

고셋 미술관
가을 학기 성인 강좌 일정
(9월 2일부터 11월 30일까지)

주의: 진행 중인 강좌에 참여하시려면 강사의 승인이 필요합니다.

| 요일 및 시간 | 강좌 | 강사 |
|---|---|---|
| 매주 월요일, 오후 5-6시 | 수채화 고급반 | 밀라 루키나 |
| 매주 수요일, 오후 7-8시 | [200] **미술관에 있는 조각품 스케치** | 조엘 페이지 |
| 매주 목요일, 오후 5-6시 | 판화 입문반 | [199] **선태식** |
| 매주 토요일, 오전 10-11시 | 인물 사진 촬영 | 소피 콜먼 |

어휘 permission 승인, 허락 in progress 진행 중인 advanced 고급의, 발전된 watercolor painting 수채화 introduction 입문, 소개 printmaking 판화 portrait 인물 사진, 초상화

## 196 추론

번역 안내 책자에서 고셋 미술관에 대해 암시하는 것은?
(A) 후원자들을 추가로 확보하려 하고 있다.
(B) 듀퐁 씨와 루비오 씨에 의해 설립되었다.
(C) 성인 강좌를 최근 제공하기 시작했다.
(D) 국제 공항이 있는 도시에 있다.

해설 안내 책자 상단에 '9월 회원 모집(September Membership Drive)'이라는 말이 쓰여 있으므로 (A)가 정답이다.

어휘 gain 확보하다, 얻다 supporter 지지자, 후원자 found 설립하다

> Paraphrasing
> 지문의 Membership → 정답의 supporters

## 197 세부 사항

번역 미술관 회원들에게 요구되는 것은?
(A) 등록 양식에 서명해야 한다.
(B) 규정 목록을 읽어야 한다.
(C) 연례 설문지를 작성해야 한다.
(D) 신분증을 제시해야 한다.

해설 안내 책자 마지막 단락에 고셋 미술관 회원권을 구입할 때 사진이 포함된 신분증이 필요하다(To purchase a membership to Gossett Art Museum, ~ Photo identification is required)고 제시되어 있으므로 (D)가 정답이다.

어휘 registration 등록 fill out 작성하다 annual 연례적인, 해마다의 proof 증명(서) identity 신분, 신원

> Paraphrasing
> 지문의 Photo identification is required
> → 정답의 must show proof of their identity

## 198 연계

번역 앨런 씨는 어떤 회원 혜택을 이용할 수 있는가?
(A) 미술관 매장 제품 할인
(B) 특별 전시회 개인 가이드 투어
(C) 특정한 날에 미술관 특별 입장
(D) 편리한 주차 공간 이용

해설 앨런 씨의 이름은 회원 카드에서 볼 수 있으며, 회원 등급이 '애호가(Membership Level: Enthusiast)'로 쓰여 있다. 이 등급에 대해, 안내 책자 네 번째 단락에 "애호가들만을 위한" 특별한 날이나 시간에 미술관에 초대된다(They are also invited to visit the museum during special "Enthusiasts-only" days and hours)는 정보가 언급되어 있으므로 (C)가 정답이다.

어휘 exclusive 전용의, 배타적인 convenient 편리한

> Paraphrasing
> 지문의 visit the museum during special "Enthusiasts-only" days → 정답의 Exclusive entry to the museum on certain days

## 199 연계

번역 선 씨에 대해 무엇이 사실일 것 같은가?
(A) 미술관 정규직 직원이다.
(B) 11월 말에 미술 전시회에 참석할 것이다.
(C) 고급반 강좌를 가르치고 있다.
(D) 자신의 미술품도 판매한다.

해설 선 씨의 이름(Tae-Shik Sun)은 일정표에 강사로 표기되어 있다. 강사들에 대해, 안내 책자 두 번째 단락에 모든 성인 강좌는 지역 사회 출신의 직업 미술가들이 수업을 한다(All of the adult classes are taught by professional artists from our community)고 언급되어 있어 선 씨도 직업 미술가임을 알 수 있다. 따라서 (D)가 정답이다.

> Paraphrasing
> 지문의 professional artists
> → 정답의 sells his own artwork

## 200 추론

번역 일정표에서 암시된 것은?
(A) 모든 강좌는 평일에 열린다.
(B) 두 강좌가 수강생에게 그림 그리는 법을 가르친다.
(C) 한 강좌는 전시 공간에서 열린다.
(D) 강좌마다 수강생 수 제한이 있다.

해설 일정표 두 번째 칸에 '미술관에 있는 조각품 스케치(Sketching Sculptures in the Galleries)'라는 명칭의 강좌가 기재되어 있어 전시 공간에서 진행되는 강좌임을 알 수 있으므로 (C)가 정답이다.

> Paraphrasing
> 지문의 in the Galleries → 정답의 in an exhibition space

TEST 9

# TEST 10

| | | | | |
|---|---|---|---|---|
| 101 (D) | 102 (B) | 103 (C) | 104 (C) | 105 (B) |
| 106 (A) | 107 (A) | 108 (B) | 109 (D) | 110 (C) |
| 111 (B) | 112 (C) | 113 (A) | 114 (D) | 115 (A) |
| 116 (B) | 117 (B) | 118 (C) | 119 (D) | 120 (A) |
| 121 (D) | 122 (C) | 123 (B) | 124 (A) | 125 (D) |
| 126 (D) | 127 (B) | 128 (C) | 129 (A) | 130 (C) |
| 131 (C) | 132 (D) | 133 (D) | 134 (A) | 135 (B) |
| 136 (B) | 137 (A) | 138 (D) | 139 (A) | 140 (C) |
| 141 (C) | 142 (B) | 143 (D) | 144 (A) | 145 (C) |
| 146 (B) | 147 (A) | 148 (B) | 149 (C) | 150 (B) |
| 151 (D) | 152 (C) | 153 (A) | 154 (D) | 155 (A) |
| 156 (B) | 157 (D) | 158 (C) | 159 (C) | 160 (B) |
| 161 (D) | 162 (B) | 163 (C) | 164 (D) | 165 (C) |
| 166 (B) | 167 (B) | 168 (B) | 169 (C) | 170 (A) |
| 171 (D) | 172 (C) | 173 (A) | 174 (D) | 175 (C) |
| 176 (A) | 177 (C) | 178 (D) | 179 (C) | 180 (B) |
| 181 (B) | 182 (A) | 183 (A) | 184 (D) | 185 (C) |
| 186 (D) | 187 (A) | 188 (C) | 189 (A) | 190 (B) |
| 191 (C) | 192 (A) | 193 (D) | 194 (C) | 195 (B) |
| 196 (C) | 197 (D) | 198 (A) | 199 (A) | 200 (C) |

## PART 5

### 101 명사 자리 _ 주격 보어

번역 팰럼보 튤립 가든은 관광객들의 주요 명소가 되었다.

해설 빈칸은 동사 become 뒤 주격 보어 자리이고, 부정관사 a와 형용사 major의 수식을 받는 자리이므로 명사가 들어갈 자리이다. 따라서 명사 (D) attraction이 정답이다.

어휘 attract 마음을 끌다 attractive 매력적인 attractively 매력적이게 attraction 명소

### 102 인칭 대명사 _ 소유 대명사

번역 4층에 근무하는 직원들은 그곳 휴게실이 개조되는 동안 3층 휴게실을 이용할 수 있습니다.

해설 접속사 while과 동사 is being renovated 사이에 위치한 빈칸은 while절의 주어 자리이며, 개조되는 대상이 빈칸에 들어가야 하므로 4층 직원들의 휴게실을 가리킬 수 있는 소유 대명사 (B) theirs(그들의 것)가 정답이다. 소유격 대명사 (A) their와 목적격 대명사 (C) them은 주어 역할을 하지 못하며, 주격 대명사 (D) they는 4층 직원들을 가리키게 되므로 적절치 않다.

어휘 break room 휴게실 renovate 개조하다, 보수하다

### 103 부사 어휘

번역 록밴드 심볼릭스는 자신들의 소렐 아레나 콘서트 입장권이 거의 매진되었다고 발표했다.

해설 수동태 동사를 구성하는 be동사와 과거분사 사이에 위치할 수 있으면서 입장권 매진과 관련된 의미를 나타낼 수 있는 부사가 필요하므로 '거의'를 뜻하는 (C) almost가 정답이다.

어휘 be sold out 매진되다, 품절되다 evenly 고르게, 균등하게

### 104 동사 자리

번역 에어쇼의 일부는 대단히 시끄러울 것이기 때문에, 주최 측은 청각 보호 장치를 지참할 것을 권장한다.

해설 접속사 so와 주어 organizers 뒤로 bringing이 이끄는 동명사구만 쓰여 있으므로 빈칸이 so절의 동사 자리임을 알 수 있다. 따라서 동사인 (C) advise(권장하다, 조언하다)가 정답이다.

어휘 extremely 대단히, 매우 organizer 주최자, 조직자 protection 보호 (장치) advice 조언, 충고 advise 권장하다, 조언하다

### 105 형용사 자리 _ 명사 수식

번역 손님들이 연회에 처음 도착하면 출장 요리 업체 직원들이 다양한 가벼운 간식을 제공할 것이다.

해설 전치사 of와 명사 목적어 snacks 사이에 빈칸이 있으므로 명사를 수식하는 형용사 (B) light가 정답이다. 명사 앞에 명사가 와서 복합명사를 만들 수도 있으나 (D) lightness는 snacks와 복합명사를 구성하지 않으므로 오답이다.

어휘 caterer 출장 요리 제공업자[업체] serve (음식 등을) 제공하다 an array of 다양한 reception (환영, 축하 등의) 연회 lighten 가볍게 하다, 밝게 하다 lightness 가벼움, 밝음

### 106 명사 어휘

번역 엘린 어패럴 사는 자사의 의류용 직물을 지역 섬유회사들로부터 매입한다.

해설 지역 섬유회사들로부터 매입한 직물의 용도와 관련된 명사가 빈칸에 쓰여야 알맞으므로 '의류, 옷'을 뜻하는 (A) garments가 정답이다.

어휘 fabric 직물, 천 local 지역의, 현지의 textile 섬유, 직물 remainder 나머지, 잔여(물)

### 107 접속사 어휘

번역 교육가 샌디 길렌은 학생들이 수업 중에 재미있어 할 때, 그 내용을 기억할 가능성이 더 크다고 생각한다.

해설 빈칸 뒤로 두 개의 완전한 절이 콤마(,)로 이어져 있으므로, 빈칸에는 students부터 lesson까지를 부사절로 만들어 줄 부사절 접속사가 들어가야 하며, '재미있어 할 때 기억할 가능성이 크다'는 의미가 되어야 자연스러우므로 '~할 때'를 뜻하는 (A) when이 정답이다.

어휘 retain 간직하다, 유지하다 content 내용(물) yet 그렇지만, 그럼에도 불구하고 given (that) ~임을 고려하면, ~라고 가정하면

## 108 전치사 어휘

번역 <스탠턴 비즈니스 저널>에 실린 한 연구에서 직원 급여와 기업 성과 사이의 분명한 연계성을 밝혀냈다.

해설 빈칸에 들어갈 전치사는 뒤에 있는 'A and B' 구조와 어울려야 하고, '직원 급여와 기업 성과 사이의 연계성'이라는 의미가 되어야 자연스러우므로 '~ 사이의'를 뜻하는 전치사 (B) between이 정답이다.

어휘 connection 연계(성), 연결 (관계) pay 급여, 보수 performance 성과, 실적

## 109 인칭 대명사 _ 재귀대명사

번역 특히 바쁜 저녁에 그 식당의 주인은 재료 준비와 손님에게 서빙하는 일을 직접 돕는다.

해설 주어 the restaurant's owner와 동사 helps 사이에 위치한 빈칸은 부사가 쓰일 수 있는 자리이므로 '직접'이라는 의미로 부사와 같은 역할을 할 수 있는 재귀대명사 (D) herself가 정답이다.

어휘 particularly 특히, 특별히 owner 소유주 ingredient (음식) 재료, 성분 serve 서비스를 제공하다 diner 식사 손님

## 110 동사 자리 _ 시제

번역 셔틀버스가 오전 8시에 출발할 예정이므로, 오전에 지체 없이 짐을 싸기 바랍니다.

해설 접속사 so 앞에 있는 절에 주어(The shuttle)와 전치사구(at 8 A.M.)만 있으므로 빈칸은 동사 자리이다. 또한, so절에 쓰인 명령문은 앞으로 할 일을 알리는 말이므로 이와 동일한 미래의 일을 나타내는 미래진행 시제 동사 (C) will be leaving이 정답이다.

어휘 pack (짐을) 꾸리다, 싸다 baggage 짐, 수하물 promptly 지체 없이, 즉시

## 111 접속사 자리 _ 부사절 접속사

번역 로즈 편의점의 최신 지점은 완전 무인으로 운영될 것이지만, 기존 매장들은 그저 셀프 계산대 선택권만 제공할 뿐이다.

해설 빈칸 앞뒤로 각각 완전한 절이 있으므로 두 절을 연결해 줄 접속사가 필요하다. 따라서 선택지에서 유일하게 접속사인 (B) whereas(~이지만, ~인 반면)가 정답이다. (A) despite(~에도 불구하고)와 (C) apart from(~을 제외하고, ~ 뿐만 아니라), 그리고 (D) depending on(~에 따라, ~에 달려 있는)은 모두 전치사이다.

어휘 completely 완전히, 전적으로 unstaffed 무인으로 운영되는, 직원이 없는 existing 기존의 merely 그저, 단지 self-checkout 셀프 계산대

## 112 형용사 자리 _ 명사 수식

번역 밝은 색감이 웹 링크를 주변 글자보다 돋보이게 만드는 데 이용될 수 있다.

해설 정관사 the와 명사 text 사이에 위치한 빈칸은 명사를 수식할 형용사가 들어갈 수 있는 자리이며, '웹 링크를 주변 글자보다 돋보이게 만드는 데'와 같은 의미를 나타내야 가장 자연스러우므로 '주변의, 둘러싸는'을 뜻하는 (C) surrounding이 정답이다. (A) surround와 (D) surrounds는 동사이며, (B) surrounded는 '둘러싸인'을 뜻하므로 의미가 맞지 않는다.

어휘 stand out 돋보이다, 두드러지다 surround 둘러싸다

## 113 동사 어휘 _ 과거분사

번역 버넷에서 최근 당선된 민준하 시의원은 1번 가에 차량 통행을 금지하겠다는 논란이 많은 제안으로 헤드라인을 장식하고 있다.

해설 빈칸에 들어갈 과거분사는 앞에 있는 부사 recently의 수식을 받고, 뒤에 있는 명사구 City Council member Joon-Ha Min을 수식하는데, '최근 당선된 민준하 시의원'을 의미해야 가장 자연스러우므로 '선출하다, 당선시키다'를 뜻하는 동사 elect의 과거분사 (A) elected가 정답이다.

어휘 council 의회 controversial 논란이 많은 proposal 제안(서) elect 선출하다, 당선시키다 form 형성하다, 구성하다 enact (법을) 제정하다, 규정하다 broaden 넓히다, 넓어지다

## 114 동사 어휘

번역 사이토 모빌리티 사는 전기 자전거와 오토바이 생산에 집중하기 위해 자사의 자전거 계열사를 매각했다.

해설 빈칸 뒤에 있는 전치사 on과 어울리는 자동사가 필요하며, '전기 자전거와 오토바이 생산에 집중하기 위해'라는 의미를 구성하는 것이 가장 자연스러우므로 '집중하다'를 뜻하는 자동사 (D) concentrate가 정답이다.

어휘 subsidiary 계열사, 자회사 maintain 유지하다 insist 주장하다 embrace 수용하다 concentrate 집중하다

## 115 형용사 어휘

번역 몬토요 병원은 복잡한 수술 절차를 처리할 수 있는 장비를 갖추고 있다.

해설 빈칸은 surgical procedures를 수식하는 형용사 자리로, '복잡한 수술 절차를 처리할 수 있는 시설을 갖추고 있다'와 같은 의미를 구성하는 것이 가장 자연스러우므로 '복잡한'을 뜻하는 (A) complex가 정답이다.

어휘 be equipped to ~할 수 있는 장비를 갖추고 있다 handle 처리하다 surgical 수술의, 외과의 procedure 절차 complex 복잡한 distant 먼, 멀리 떨어진 cautious 신중한, 조심스러운 accurate 정확한

### 116 부사 자리 _ 동사 수식

번역 그 벽이 손상되기 전에 촬영된 사진들은 그 벽화가 원래 어떤 모습이었는지 보여 준다.

해설 how절의 주어 the mural과 동사 appeared 사이에 위치한 빈칸은 동사를 수식할 부사가 들어갈 수 있는 자리이므로 부사 (B) originally가 정답이다.

어휘 mural 벽화 appear ~한 모습이다 original 원래의, 독창적인 originally 원래, 독창적으로 originate 비롯되다, 유래하다

### 117 부사 자리 _ 형용사 수식

번역 일반적으로, 유기농 농산물은 전통적인 농산물보다 훨씬 더 비싸다.

해설 비교급 형용사 more expensive를 수식하는 자리에 빈칸이 있으므로 부사 (B) significantly가 정답이다.

어휘 typically 일반적으로, 전형적으로 produce 농산물 conventional 전통적인 counterpart (사람, 사물 등) 상대방, 대응 관계에 있는 것 significant 상당한, 중요한 significantly 훨씬, 상당히 significance 중요성, 의의 signify 뜻하다

### 118 전치사 어휘

번역 회계 감사 위원회의 각 회의 후에, 위원장은 나머지 이사진을 위해 활동에 관한 보고서를 준비해야 한다.

해설 명사구 each meeting of the audit committee를 목적어로 취하는 전치사 자리로, '각 회의 후에, 보고서를 준비해야 한다'와 같은 의미로 일의 순서를 나타내야 가장 자연스러우므로 '~ 후에'를 뜻하는 전치사 (C) Following이 정답이다.

어휘 audit 회계 감사 committee 위원회 chairperson 위원장 the rest of ~의 나머지 board 이사진, 이사회

### 119 명사 어휘

번역 새 터미널이 운영되면, 데보레 공항의 최대 수용 인원은 30퍼센트 증가할 것이다.

해설 새 터미널이 운영되면 공항에서 증가하는 것으로 자연스러운 것은 최대 수용 인원이므로 '수용 인원, 수용력'을 뜻하는 명사 (D) capacity가 정답이다.

어휘 operational 운영되는, 영업하는 maximum 최대의 allowance 수당, 할당량 function 기능 proportion 부분, 비율

### 120 형용사 어휘

번역 배송품 중 깨지기 쉬운 물건은 완충재로 안전하게 포장되어야 합니다.

해설 items를 수식하는 형용사 자리로, 완충재로 포장해야 하는 물건의 특성을 나타낼 형용사가 필요하므로 '깨지기 쉬운, 취약한' 등을 뜻하는 (A) fragile이 정답이다.

어휘 shipment 배송(품) wrap 포장하다, 싸다 securely 안전하게 cushioning material 완충재 adequate 적절한, 충분한 pending 임박한, 미정인 delectable 아주 맛있는

### 121 명사 자리 _ 복합명사

번역 프로그램 후원 업체들을 담은 전체 목록은 저희 단체의 웹사이트에서 찾아보실 수 있습니다.

해설 빈칸 앞에 있는 program과 복합명사를 구성해 어떤 목록인지를 나타낼 명사가 필요하다. (C) sponsoring은 동명사 또는 현재분사이므로 우선 제외하고, (B) sponsorship은 명사이지만 '후원, 협찬'이라는 의미로 어색하므로 제외한다. sponsor는 가산 명사로 한정사 없이 단수 형태로 쓸 수 없는데 program 앞에 한정사가 없으므로 복수형인 (D) sponsors가 정답이다.

어휘 organization 단체, 조직, 기관

### 122 명사 자리 _ 동사의 목적어

번역 우리는 올해의 컨퍼런스 발표자들에게 청중의 질문을 위한 시간을 충분히 할애할 것을 상기시켜야 합니다.

해설 빈칸은 동사 remind의 목적어 자리이므로 명사가 올 수 있는데, remind는 사람 명사를 목적어로 취하므로 '발표자들'을 뜻하는 (C) presenters가 정답이다. (D) presentation(발표, 제공)은 사물 명사로, 의미가 맞지 않는다.

어휘 allow 허용하다 sufficient 충분한 audience 청중

### 123 명사절 접속사

번역 우리 분석가들은 매출 하락의 원인을 정확히 밝혀낼 수 없었다.

해설 동사 determine 뒤에 빈칸을 포함한 절이 이어지고 있으므로 빈칸에는 빈칸 이하를 명사절로 바꿔줄 수 있는 명사절 접속사가 들어가야 한다. 또한 빈칸 이하가 주어 없이 동사 is causing으로 시작하는 불완전한 구조이므로 불완전한 절을 이끄는 명사절 접속사 (B) what이 정답이다. (A) nor는 명사절 접속사가 아니며, (C) that과 (D) whether는 구조가 완전한 절을 이끄는 명사절 접속사이다.

어휘 analyst 분석가 determine 밝혀내다, 결정하다 precisely 정확히 cause 야기시키다, 초래하다 drop 하락, 감소

### 124 형용사 어휘

번역 전체 피드백 설문 조사지를 기꺼이 작성한 고객은 거의 없었다.

해설 빈칸 앞뒤를 보아 「be동사+형용사+to부정사」 형태로 잘 쓰이는 형용사가 필요하며, '설문 조사지를 기꺼이 작성한 고객은 거의 없었다'가 가장 자연스러운 의미이므로 '기꺼이 하는, 의향이 있는'을 뜻하는 (A) willing이 정답이다.

어휘 entire 전체의 survey 설문 조사(지) capable 할 수 있는, 유능한 fortunate 다행스러운, 운이 좋은 detailed 상세한, 세부적인

## 125 부사 어휘

번역 초봄은 우리에게 바쁜 시기이므로, 직원들은 휴가 일정을 그에 맞춰 잡아야 합니다.

해설 휴가 일정을 잡는 방식을 묘사할 부사가 필요하며, '바쁜 시기이므로 그에 맞춰 휴가를 잡아야 한다'는 의미를 구성하는 것이 가장 자연스러우므로 '그에 맞춰'를 뜻하는 (D) accordingly가 정답이다.

어휘 formerly 전에, 과거에 considerably 상당히, 많이 consecutively 연이어, 연속적으로

## 126 전치사 어휘

번역 주요 출판물에서 여러 차례 호평을 받아서 그 책은 베스트셀러 1위로 데뷔했다.

해설 '책이 베스트셀러 1위'가 될 수 있었던 이유는 '호평을 받았기 때문'이므로 빈칸 뒤에 있는 of와 함께 '~로 인해, ~ 때문에'를 뜻하는 전치사를 구성하는 (D) Because가 정답이다.

어휘 publication 출판(물) debut 첫선을 보이다, 데뷔하다 in place of ~ 대신에 in the event of ~의 경우에 regardless of ~와 상관없이

## 127 수동태

번역 분 주식회사에서 6개월 이상 근무한 직원이라면 누구나 이 상의 후보로 지명될 수 있습니다.

해설 be동사 뒤에 빈칸이 있으므로 빈칸에는 명사 (A), (C)와 과거분사 (B)가 올 수 있는데, 주어인 직원들(Any employee)은 지명되는 대상이므로 수동태가 쓰이는 게 자연스럽다. 따라서 과거분사 (B) nominated가 정답이다. (A) nominee(지명된 사람, 후보)는 가산명사이므로 관사가 필요하며, (C) nomination(후보 지명)은 의미가 어색하다. 동사 원형 (D) nominate(후보로 지명하다)는 be동사 뒤에 쓰일 수 없다.

어휘 nominee 지명된 사람, 후보 nominate 후보로 지명하다 nomination 후보 지명 recognition 상, 인정

## 128 형용사 자리 _ 명사 수식

번역 최근 축산업의 성장으로 인해, 펠 카운티는 현재 더 많은 대형 동물 수의사가 절실히 필요한 상태이다.

해설 빈칸은 명사 need를 수식하는 형용사 자리이므로, (C) critical(중대한, 비판적인)이 정답이다. 명사 앞에 명사가 올 수도 있지만, (B) critic(평론가, 비평가)은 need와 복합명사를 구성하지 않는 명사이다.

어휘 cattle (집합적으로) 소 veterinarian 수의사 critically 중대하게, 비판적으로 critic 평론가, 비평가 critical 중대한, 비판적인 criticize 비난하다, 평론하다

## 129 명사 어휘

번역 스트리밍 서비스 업체 비지아는 새로운 콘텐츠에 대한 시청자 수요를 따라잡으려고 애쓰고 있다.

해설 빈칸 앞뒤의 keep, with와 함께 어울려 쓰이는 명사가 들어가야 한다. '시청자 수요를 따라잡으려 애쓰다'의 의미를 나타내야 가장 자연스러우므로, '~을 따라잡다, ~와 보조를 맞추다'라는 의미의 keep pace with를 구성하는 (A) pace가 정답이다.

어휘 struggle 애쓰다, 고군분투하다 output 생산(량), 출력 balance 균형 continuity 연속(성), 지속(성)

## 130 동사 어휘

번역 회사는 고위급 직원이 부재 시 다른 직원이 자신의 역할을 대신할 수 있도록 업무 프로세스를 문서화하도록 요구합니다.

해설 their work processes를 목적어로 취하는 동사 어휘가 들어가야 하며, '다른 직원이 역할을 대신하기 위해' 할 수 있는 일로 가장 자연스러운 것은 '업무 프로세스를 문서화하는' 것이므로 '문서화하다, 기록하다'를 뜻하는 (C) document가 정답이다.

어휘 process 과정 take over 넘겨받다, 인수하다 absence 부재, 결근 access 이용하다, 접근하다 impact 영향을 미치다 permit 허용하다, 허락하다

# PART 6

### 131-134 이메일

발신: 채터 고객 서비스부
수신: 멜리사 램지
제목: 비밀번호 재설정
날짜: 12월 19일

램지 씨께,

귀하의 채터 계정의 로그인 개인 정보와 관련된 보안 문제를 인식하게 되었습니다. 131 **그것들은** 다른 온라인 서비스 업체의 데이터 유출로 인해 최근 노출된 이메일 주소 및 비밀번호와 동일합니다. 현재로서는 귀하의 채터 계정이 다른 사람에 의해 132 **실제로** 접속되었다고 생각할 이유가 없습니다. 하지만 이렇게 로그인 개인 정보를 재사용하면 앞으로 계정 유출 가능성이 더 높아지게 됩니다.

귀하의 채터 계정을 보호하기 위한 사전 예방적 노력의 일환으로, 귀하의 비밀번호를 재설정하여 귀하 계정으로의 접속을 차단했습니다. 계정이 133 **중단**된 것에 대해 사과드립니다. 아래의 링크를 클릭하여 새로운 비밀번호를 설정하시기 바랍니다. 134 **독특한 비밀번호를 선택하면 이런 문제가 재발하는 것을 방지할 수 있습니다.** 저희는 또한 귀하의 모든 온라인 계정에 2단계 인증을 사용하도록 설정하시길 권합니다.

- 채터 팀

어휘 reset 재설정; 재설정하다 log-in credentials 로그인 개인 정보 account 계정, 계좌 identical 동일한 expose 노출시키다 breach 유출, 위반 access 접속하다; 접속 proactive 사전 예방적인 block 차단하다 apologize 사과하다 two-factor authentication 이중 인증

TEST 10

## 131 대명사 어휘

해설 빈칸 뒤에 최근 노출된 이메일 주소 및 비밀번호와 동일하다는 말이 쓰여 있어 앞 문장에 언급된 로그인 개인 정보에 대한 설명임을 알 수 있다. 따라서 복수 명사구인 log-in credentials를 가리킬 수 있는 복수 대명사와 동사로 구성된 (C) They are가 정답이다. (A) Yours is는 단수 동사 is가 쓰여 있어 맞지 않으며, '~이 있다'를 뜻하는 (B) There is와 (D) There are 뒤에는 각각 단수 명사(구)와 복수 명사(구)가 쓰여야 한다.

## 132 부사 어휘

해설 앞에서 로그인 개인 정보와 관련된 보안 문제를 인식했고, 유출된 이메일 주소와 비밀번호가 동일하다는 말이 쓰여 있으므로 빈칸이 속한 that절이 '채터 계정이 다른 사람에 의해 실제로 접속되었다'와 같은 의미를 구성하는 것이 가장 자연스럽다. 따라서 '실제로, 사실은'을 뜻하는 부사 (D) actually가 정답이다.

어휘 seriously 심각하게, 진지하게 besides 게다가, 뿐만 아니라

## 133 명사 어휘

해설 전치사 for의 목적어인 빈칸은 사과하는 이유에 해당하며, 앞 문장에 비밀번호를 재설정해 계정 접속을 차단했다는 말이 쓰여 있어 이러한 불편함을 가리킬 수 있는 명사가 쓰여야 하므로 '중단, 지장' 등을 뜻하는 (D) disruption이 정답이다.

어휘 shortage 부족 outcome 결과(물)

## 134 문장 고르기

번역 (A) 독특한 비밀번호를 선택하면 이런 문제가 재발하는 것을 방지할 수 있습니다.
(B) 이 정보에 대해 질문이 있으실 경우, 저희에게 알려 주시기 바랍니다.
(C) 이는 채터의 모든 비즈니스 이용자들에게 요구되는 일상적인 과정입니다.
(D) 최근 낯선 기기에서 귀하의 계정에 로그인을 시도했습니다.

해설 앞 문장에 아래의 링크를 클릭하여 새로운 비밀번호를 설정하라는 말이 쓰여 있어 새로운 비밀번호를 설정하는 것과 관련된 문장이 필요하다. 따라서 어떤 비밀번호가 좋은지 조언하는 (A)가 정답이다.

어휘 unique 독특한, 특별한 prevent 방지하다, 막다 reoccur 재발생하다 routine 일상적인 process 과정 unfamiliar 낯선, 익숙하지 않은 attempt 시도하다

### 135-138 광고

버짓 빌더 앱

재정적으로 앞서 나가려고 노력 중이신가요? 버짓 빌더는 여러분의 소득 규모와 상관없이, 자금 관리를 [135] **놀라울 정도로** 단순하게 만들어 드립니다. 저희 앱은 여러분이 돈을 신중히 소비하도록 [136] **도와드릴 것입니다.** 현재 자산과 지출에 관한 정보를 수집한 후, 이용자들께 목표 저축액을 설정하도록 요청드립니다. [137] **여러분은 새 차를 구입하거나 휴가를 위해 돈을 쓰고 싶을지도 모릅니다.** 이 앱은 목표에 도달하는 방법을 알려 드리고 그 과정에서 진행 상황을 추적합니다. 여러분께 적합한지 알아볼 수 있도록 버짓 빌더를 30일간 무료로 사용해 보시기 바랍니다. 그 기간 후에는, 매달 12.99달러라는 합리적인 [138] **이용** 요금이 있습니다.

어휘 get ahead 앞서 나가다 financially 재정적으로, 금전적으로 income 소득, 수입 asset 자산, 재산 expense 지출 (비용), 경비 track 파악하다, 추적하다 progress 진행 상황, 진척 reasonable 합리적인 fee 요금

## 135 부사 자리 _ 형용사 수식

해설 동사 makes의 목적격 보어 역할을 하는 형용사 simple 앞에 빈칸이 있으므로 빈칸은 형용사를 수식하는 부사가 들어갈 자리이다. 따라서 (B) surprisingly(놀라운 정도로)가 정답이다.

## 136 동사 자리 _ 시제

해설 빈칸은 주어 Our app의 동사 자리로, you를 목적어로 취한다. 또한, '버짓 빌더'라는 자금 관리 앱을 이용하도록 광고하는 글이므로 이 앱을 이용하면 이 앱이 돈을 신중히 소비하도록 도울 것이라는 미래 의미가 되어야 자연스럽다. 따라서 미래 시제 동사인 (B) will support가 정답이다.

## 137 문장 고르기

번역 (A) 여러분은 새 차를 구입하거나 휴가를 위해 돈을 쓰고 싶을지도 모릅니다.
(B) 신뢰할 수 있는 은행에 예금액을 보관하는 것이 중요합니다.
(C) 심지어 다른 이용자들을 각자의 계정에 추가할 수도 있습니다.
(D) 각 기능에 대해 도움이 되는 사용 설명서를 제공합니다.

해설 앞 문장에 현재 자산과 지출에 관한 정보를 수집한 후에 목표 저축액을 설정하도록 요청한다는 말이 쓰여 있으므로 자산 및 지출 정보나 저축하는 목표와 관련된 문장이 이어져야 흐름이 자연스럽다. 따라서 이런 예시에 해당하는 (A)가 정답이다.

어휘 trustworthy 신뢰할 수 있는 tutorial 사용 설명서, 지침서 feature 특징, 기능

## 138 명사 어휘

해설 앞 문장에 앱을 30일 동안 무료로 사용해 볼 수 있다는 말이 쓰여 있으므로, 그 기간 후에는 이용 요금이 있다는 내용으로 이어져야 자연스럽다. 따라서 '(서비스 등의) 이용, 구독'을 뜻하는 (D) subscription이 정답이다.

어휘 cancellation 취소 transaction 거래 (업무), 처리 reservation 예약

### 139-142 기사

헬버튼 (6월 8일) - 국립 우편국(NPS)이 오늘 전기 배달 트럭 42대를 공개했다. 이 차량들은 전체 보유 차량 중 일부를 전기화하려는 기관의

계획의 첫 단계에 139 **해당한다.** 이 차량들로 인해 우편 140 **배달원들**은 더 적은 탄소 발자국으로 배달할 수 있을 것이다. NPS는 일부 지사에 전기 자동차 충전 시설도 갖춰 놓기 시작했다. 안타깝게도, 많은 소규모 지방 우체국에는 이 충전 시설들을 뒷받침할 수 있는 전기 관련 기반 시설이 없다. 141 **그러한 이유로 인해,** 이 기관은 주로 규모가 더 큰 지역 거점들에서 전기 트럭을 활용할 것이다. 142 **현재 전국에 그러한 시설이 30곳 존재한다.**

어휘 unveil 공개하다, 선보이다 organization 기관, 단체 electrify 전기화하다 fleet (한 단체가 보유한) 전체 차량[항공기] carbon footprint 탄소 발자국(개인이나 단체가 발생시키는 이산화탄소 배출량) outfit 갖춰 주다 charging station 충전 시설, 충전소 unfortunately 안타깝게도, 유감스럽게도 infrastructure (사회) 기반 시설 employ 활용하다 hub 거점, 중심지

## 139 동사 자리

해설 빈칸은 주어 The vehicles의 동사 자리로, the first step을 목적어로 취한다. 따라서 동사인 (A) represent가 정답이다.

어휘 represent 해당하다, 대표하다 representation 표시, 대표

## 140 명사 자리 _ 복합명사

해설 동사 enable 뒤에 mail과 빈칸이 있는데 mail만으로는 enable의 목적어로 어색하므로 빈칸에 mail과 함께 복합명사를 구성하는 명사가 와야 한다. 따라서 '우편 배달원'이라는 의미를 구성하는 명사 (C) carriers가 정답이다.

어휘 carrier 배달원

## 141 접속부사

해설 빈칸 앞 문장에는 많은 소규모 지방 우체국에는 충전 시설들을 뒷받침할 수 있는 전기 관련 기반 시설이 없다는 말이, 빈칸 뒤에는 주로 규모가 더 큰 지역 거점들에서 전기 트럭을 활용할 것이라는 말이 쓰여 있다. 이는 원인과 결과의 흐름이므로 '그러한 이유로 인해'라는 의미로 결과를 말할 때 사용하는 (C) For that reason이 정답이다.

어휘 for instance 예를 들어 after all 결국, 어쨌든 even so 그렇다 하더라도

## 142 문장 고르기

번역 (A) 그 변화는 대기 오염을 감소시키기 위한 것이기도 하다.
(B) 현재 전국에 그러한 시설이 30곳 존재한다.
(C) 그 차량들은 NPS의 기존 트럭에는 없는 여러 특징을 자랑한다.
(D) 가장 큰 센터들은 이미 매일 수천 건의 소포를 처리하고 있다.

해설 빈칸 앞에 전기 관련 기반 시설을 언급하면서 주로 규모가 더 큰 지역 거점들에서 전기 트럭을 활용할 것이라는 말이 쓰여 있다. 따라서 이러한 활용 방식과 관련된 문장이 이어져야 자연스러우므로 해당 시설이 전국에 몇 군데나 존재하는지 알리는 (B)가 정답이다.

어휘 be intended to ~하기 위한 것이다, ~하려는 의도이다 pollution 오염 boast 자랑하다 existing 기존의 lack 부족하다 handle 처리하다, 다루다

## 143-146 회람

수신: 멜닉 주식회사 전 직원
발신: 이반 멜닉
제목: 중요한 방문
날짜: 9월 25일

다음 주 화요일, <파함 먼슬리> 기자가 그 잡지에 필요한 제 프로필 작성을 준비하기 위해 멜닉 주식회사를 방문할 것입니다. 저를 143 **인터뷰하는 것**뿐만 아니라, 우리 회사의 운영에 관해 알아보기 위해 우리 사무실도 둘러볼 것입니다. 돋보이게 해 주는 기사는 사업에 정말로 도움이 될 수 있으므로, 이분이 우리에 대해 좋은 인상을 갖고 갈 수 있도록 144 **모두** 노력해 주시기를 바랍니다. 145 **그날은 하루 종일 업무 공간을 깔끔하게 유지해 주십시오.** 146 **기자**와 이야기를 하게 될 경우, 어떤 것에 관해서든, 심지어 우리 경쟁사에 관해서도 부정적인 발언은 피하시기 바랍니다. 또한 담당 분야가 아닌 주제에 대한 질문은 정중하게 거절해야 합니다. 이번 방문이 성공적으로 이루어질 수 있도록 협조해 주셔서 미리 감사드립니다.

어휘 correspondent 기자, 특파원 in preparation for ~에 대한 준비로, ~에 대비해 operation 운영, 영업, 가동 flattering 돋보이게 해 주는, 으쓱하게 만드는 impression 인상, 감명 avoid 피하다 negative 부정적인 competitor 경쟁사, 경쟁자 politely 정중히 refuse 거절하다 cooperation 협조, 협력

## 143 동사 어휘

해설 앞 문장에 기자가 방문할 예정이라는 말이 있으므로 기자가 방문해서 할 수 있는 일을 나타내는 어휘가 들어가는 것이 자연스럽다. 따라서 '인터뷰하다'를 뜻하는 interview의 동명사 (D) interviewing이 정답이다.

어휘 replace 대체하다 introduce 소개하다, 도입하다

## 144 대명사 어휘

해설 빈칸 뒤에 기자가 좋은 인상을 받을 수 있도록 노력하는 일이 언급되어 있는데, 이는 이 회람을 받는 전 직원이 기자가 방문할 때 해야 하는 일에 해당하므로 '모두, 모든 사람'을 뜻하는 (A) everyone이 정답이다.

## 145 문장 고르기

번역 (A) 우리의 모든 업무는 철저해야 하고 제시간에 완료되어야 합니다.
(B) 이는 홍보부의 책임입니다.
(C) 그날은 하루 종일 업무 공간을 깔끔하게 유지해 주십시오.
(D) 우리 회사는 막 10주년을 기념하려 하고 있습니다.

해설 빈칸 앞에 기자가 좋은 인상을 갖고 갈 수 있게 노력해 달라고 당부하는 말이 쓰여 있어 좋은 인상을 남기는 일과 관련된 문장이 이어져야 자연스럽다. 따라서 업무 공간을 깔끔하게 유지하도록 부탁하는 (C)가 정답이다.

어휘 thorough 철저한, 꼼꼼한 on time 제때 public relations department 홍보부 responsibility 책임 tidy 말끔한 be about to 막 ~하려 하다 celebrate 기념하다, 축하하다 anniversary (해마다 돌아 오는) 기념일

TEST 10

## 146 명사 어휘

해설 앞에 기자 방문과 관련된 주의 사항을 전달하고 있으므로 빈칸이 포함된 문장도 '기자와 이야기하게 될 경우' 주의 사항을 전달하는 내용이 되는 것이 자연스럽다. 따라서 '기자'를 뜻하는 (B) reporter가 정답이다.

어휘 candidate 후보자, 지원자 executive 임원, 이사

# PART 7

### 147-148 제품 설명

브라우어 마린
e로그북, 전자 운항 일지

브라우어 마린의 e로그북 소프트웨어 프로그램은 선박의 활동과 관련된 필수 정보를 편리하게 저장할 수 있는 방법을 제공합니다. 이것은 승무원 활동과 오일 배출, 나침반 관측 등의 세부 정보를 기록하는 전통적인 종이 운항 일지를 대체합니다. e로그북은 작성하는 데 인터넷 접속을 필요로 하지 않으며, **147 단 한 대의 컴퓨터에서 실행시킬 수도 있고, 서버에 연결된 다수의 사용자 단말기에서 이용할 수도 있습니다.**

적절한 담당자가 항목을 작성하고 승인할 수 있도록 각 사용자에게는 고유한 로그인 개인 정보가 있습니다. **148 더 쉽게 로그인할 수 있도록 개인 비밀번호가 설정될 수 있습니다.** 승인된 사용자는 운항 일지 디지털 기록을 항만 관리부에 보낼 수도 있습니다.

어휘 logbook 운항 일지, 업무 일지 convenient 편리한 store 저장하다, 보관하다 replace 대체하다 traditional 전통적인 discharge 배출, 방출 observation 관측 (정보) access 접속, 이용 user terminal 사용자 단말기 connected 연결된 unique 고유의, 독특한 log-in credentials 로그인 개인 정보 ensure that 반드시 ~하도록 하다, ~임을 보장하다 personnel 직원들, 인사(부) approve 승인하다 entry 입력 (정보) PIN 개인 비밀번호 authorized 승인된

## 147 Not / True

번역 해당 제품에 대해 언급된 것은?
(A) 다양한 곳에서 접속하도록 설정될 수 있다.
(B) 항만 관리자들이 대상 고객이다.
(C) 인터넷에서 다운로드할 수 있다.
(D) 효율적인 운송 경로를 계획하는 데 이용된다.

해설 첫 단락 후반부에 서버에 연결된 다수의 사용자 단말기에서 이용할 수 있다(made available at multiple user terminals connected to a server)고 언급되어 있으므로 (A)가 정답이다.

어휘 set up 설정하다, 설치하다 multiple 다양한, 다수의 intended 대상이 되는, 의도된 efficient 효율적인

> Paraphrasing
> 지문의 made available at multiple user terminals connected to a server
> → 정답의 access from multiple sites

## 148 세부 사항

번역 고객들은 어떤 옵션을 선택할 수 있는가?
(A) 입력 기록의 대량 승인
(B) 간소화된 로그인 방식
(C) 실시간 정보 표시
(D) 과거 기록의 디지털화

해설 두 번째 단락에 더 쉽게 로그인할 수 있도록 개인 비밀번호가 설정될 수 있다(A PIN can be set to make logging in easier)고 했으므로 간편한 로그인 방식을 뜻하는 (B)가 정답이다.

어휘 bulk 대량의, 대규모의 simplified 간소화된 method 방식, 방법 real-time 실시간의 digitization 디지털화

> Paraphrasing
> 지문의 to make logging in easier
> → 정답의 simplified log-in method

### 149-150 온라인 후기

https://www.summitresort.ca/reviews

서밋 리조트 최근 고객 후기

1월에 친구들과 긴 주말 동안 서밋 리조트를 방문했는데, **149 이 아름다운 곳으로 가는 많은 여행들 중 첫 번째가 될 것으로 예상합니다.** 이 리조트에 대해 가장 좋은 점은 바로 워커 산에 있다는 것입니다. 어떤 객실에서든 경관이 아주 멋지고, **150(C) 리조트의 뒤쪽 출입구로 나가서 곧장 슬로프에 올라 스키나 스노우보드를 탈 수 있었습니다.** 워커 산에는 모든 난이도의 슬로프가 있고, 의자식 리프트는 안전합니다. 저녁에는 **150(D) 이 리조트의 하이랜드 그릴에서 저녁 식사를 하거나** 셔틀버스를 타고 근처 마을로 갔습니다. 마지막 날에 저희 중 몇몇은 추가 요금을 지불하고 구내 스파를 방문했는데, 집에 가기 전에 **150(A) 그곳 사우나에서 지친 근육을 풀어 주어서 아주 좋았습니다.** 전반적으로, 저희는 아주 즐거운 시간을 보냈으며, 진심으로 다른 분들에게 서밋 리조트를 추천합니다.

라번 리즈, 2월 10일

어휘 stunning 아주 멋진, 굉장히 아름다운 chairlift 의자식 리프트 reliable 신뢰할 수 있는 onsite 구내의, 현장의 rest 쉬게 하다 overall 전반적으로 heartily 진심으로

## 149 Not / True

번역 리즈 씨가 자신의 후기에서 언급하는 것은?
(A) 자신의 객실이 리조트의 뒤편에 있었다.
(B) 친구가 자신에게 서밋 리조트를 추천했다.
(C) 아마 서밋 리조트를 다시 방문할 것이다.
(D) 숙박비에 대해 단체 할인을 받았다.

해설 지문 초반부에 이 아름다운 곳으로 가는 많은 여행들 중 첫 번째가 될 것으로 예상한다(I expect it will be the first of many trips to this lovely place)고 했으므로 나중에 다시 방문할 의향이 있다는 것을 알 수 있다. 따라서 (C)가 정답이다.

> Paraphrasing
> 지문의 it will be the first of many trips to this lovely place
> → 정답의 will probably visit Summit Resort again

## 150 Not / True

번역 리즈 씨가 언급한 활동이 아닌 것은?
(A) 사우나에서 휴식하기
(B) 기념품 쇼핑하기
(C) 겨울 스포츠 하기
(D) 레스토랑에서 식사하기

해설 스키나 스노우보드를 탈 수 있었다(we could ski or snowboard ~)고 한 부분에서 (C)를, 그 리조트의 하이랜드 그릴에서 저녁 식사를 했다(we had dinner at the resort's Highland Grill)고 한 부분에서 (D)를, 사우나에서 지친 근육을 풀어 주어서 아주 좋았다(it was very nice to rest our tired muscles in its sauna)고 한 부분에서 (A)를 확인할 수 있다. 하지만 기념품 쇼핑과 관련된 정보는 제시되어 있지 않으므로 (B)가 정답이다.

어휘 relax 휴식하다 souvenir 기념품 engage in ~에 참여하다, ~에 관여하다

> Paraphrasing
> 지문의 we could ski or snowboard
> → 보기 (C)의 Engaging in winter sports
> 지문의 had dinner at the resort's Highland Grill
> → 보기 (D)의 Eating in a restaurant
> 지문의 rest our tired muscles in its sauna
> → 보기 (A)의 Relaxing in a sauna

### 151-152 초대장

**[151] 피어슨 극장에서 엘라 닐의 최신 창작극 <브라이트 라인>의 초연 행사에 귀하 및 동반 손님 한 분을 정중히 초대합니다.**

3월 2일 목요일 오후 7시

1950년대의 뉴욕을 배경으로 하는 <브라이트 라인>은 미술과 삶에 대한 남다른 관점을 공유해 학생들에게 영감을 주는 한 미대 교수의 이야기를 전합니다.

플래티넘 등급의 피어슨 극장 후원자이신 [152] **귀하께 공연 후에 출연진 및 창작팀과 함께하는 만남의 시간 행사를 위해 남아 계실 것을 권합니다.** 다과도 제공될 것입니다.

2월 24일까지 555-0148번으로 전화 주셔서 두 행사 모두에 대한 참석 여부를 회신 바랍니다.

어휘 cordially 정중히, 진심으로 original 원래의, 원본의 inspire 영감을 주다 unusual 특이한, 이례적인 outlook 관점, 전망 -tier ~ 등급의 supporter 후원자, 지지자 post-show 공연 후의 meet-and-greet 만남의 시간 cast 출연진 refreshments 다과, 간식 RSVP (초대장 등에서) 참석 여부를 회신 바랍니다

## 151 추론

번역 <브라이트 라인>에 대해 암시된 것은?
(A) 학생들에 의해 상연된다.
(B) 뉴욕에서부터 투어 중이다.
(C) 닐 씨의 경험을 바탕으로 한다.
(D) 전에 무대에 올려진 적이 없다.

해설 첫 단락에 엘라 닐의 최신 창작극 <브라이트 라인>의 초연 행사에 초대한다(Pearson Theater cordially invites you and one guest to the premiere of *A Bright Line*, the latest original play by Ella Neal)는 내용이 쓰여 있는데, 초연 행사를 진행한다는 말은 처음 공연한다는 뜻이므로 (D)가 정답이다.

어휘 put on 상연하다 be based on ~을 바탕으로 하다 stage 무대에 올리다

> Paraphrasing
> 지문의 premiere → 정답의 has not been staged before

## 152 세부 사항

번역 초대장 수령인은 무엇을 할 수 있는가?
(A) 교수가 진행하는 강연 참석하기
(B) 원본 미술품 관람하기
(C) 공연자들과 이야기하기
(D) 공연에 관한 의견 설문 조사 참여하기

해설 후반부에 공연 후에 출연진 및 창작팀과 함께하는 만남의 시간 행사를 위해 남아 있어 달라(you are also encouraged to stay for a post-show meet-and-greet with the cast and creative team)고 알리고 있다. 따라서 배우들과 만나서 이야기할 수 있을 것이므로 (C)가 정답이다.

어휘 recipient 수령인, 수취인

> Paraphrasing
> 지문의 a post-show meet-and-greet with the cast
> → 정답의 Speak with some performers

### 153-154 온라인 채팅

신디 베리 (오전 11시 24분)
안녕하세요, 조나단. 당신의 최근 경비 보고서를 처리하는 중인데, 8월 7일 점심 식사 금액을 잘못 입력한 것을 발견했어요. 레스토랑 영수증에 25.76달러가 아니라 25.67달러로 나와 있습니다. [153] **그 부분과 총액을 고쳐서 보고서를 다시 제출해 주시겠어요?**

조나단 팍스 (오전 11시 26분)
아, 실수해서 죄송해요. 네, [154] **내일 아침에 가장 먼저 그걸 가져다 드릴게요.**

신디 베리 (오전 11시 27분)
[154] **마감 기한이 오늘입니다.** 그렇지 않으면, 환급 받으시는 데 한 달 더 기다리셔야 할 겁니다.

TEST 10

조나단 팍스 (오전 11시 28분)
음, 제가 오늘 재택 근무 중입니다. 그리고 이메일로는 보고서를 받지 않으시는 게 맞죠?

신디 베리 (오전 11시 29분)
맞아요. 서명된 종이 문서가 필요합니다. 좋아요, 그러시면 내일 뵙죠.

어휘 process 처리하다 expense 지출 (비용), 경비 amount 액수, 금액 receipt 영수증 fix 고치다, 바로잡다 resubmit 다시 제출하다 deadline 마감 기한 otherwise 그렇지 않으면, 그 외에는 extra 추가의, 여분의 reimbursement 환급

### 153 세부 사항

번역 베리 씨는 왜 팍스 씨에게 연락했는가?
(A) 보고서 수정을 요청하기 위해
(B) 업무상의 점심 식사를 계획하도록 제안하기 위해
(C) 영수증 제출을 상기시키기 위해
(D) 지출 한도에 대해 주의를 주기 위해

해설 베리 씨가 쓴 첫 번째 메시지에 잘못된 액수를 고쳐서 보고서를 다시 제출해 달라(Could you fix that and the total amount and resubmit your report?)고 요청하고 있으므로 (A)가 정답이다.

어휘 revision 수정, 정정 warn 주의를 주다, 경고하다 limit 한도, 제한

> Paraphrasing
> 지문의 fix that and the total amount
> → 정답의 revisions

### 154 의도 파악

번역 오전 11시 28분에 팍스 씨가 "제가 오늘 재택 근무 중입니다"라고 쓸 때, 무엇을 의미할 것 같은가?
(A) 출장을 끝마쳤다.
(B) 행사에 참석할 수 없을 것이다.
(C) 마감 기한을 맞추기 위해 노력 중이다.
(D) 베리 씨에게 문서를 갖다줄 수 없다.

해설 오전 11시 26분에 팍스 씨가 수정한 보고서를 내일 아침에 가장 먼저 갖다주겠다(I'll get that to you first thing tomorrow)고 말한 것에 대해 베리 씨가 마감 기한이 오늘(The deadline is today)이라고 밝히자, 팍스 씨가 '제가 오늘 재택 근무 중입니다'라고 대답하는 흐름이다. 이는 재택 근무로 인해 수정한 보고서를 오늘 갖다줄 수 없다는 뜻이므로 (D)가 정답이다.

어휘 conclude 끝마치다, 종료하다

### 155-157 정보

직원 능력 향상 프로그램

조직에서 특정 직무에 자격을 갖춘 지원자들을 찾는 데 어려움을 겪고 계신가요? 155 **직원 능력 향상 프로그램은 직무 능력 부족 문제를 해결할 수 있는 수습 제도를 만들 수 있도록 고용주들을 도와드립니다.** 참가하는 기관은 해당 특정 분야에 대한 전문 지식을 갖춘 교육 자문과 짝을 이루게 됩니다. 이 자문은 해당 기관의 인력 수요를 규정하고 맞춤 수습 제도를 고안하는 것을 도와드립니다. 156 **일반적으로 견습생이 해당 분야의 허가증이나 자격증을 받기 위해 필요한 외부 교육과 현장 교육을 결합합니다. 이 프로그램은 최대 12,000달러까지 외부 교육 비용을 직접 지불해 드립니다.** 157 **수습 직원이 고용되거나 기존의 직원들 사이에서 선정되어 수습 제도가 시작되는 대로, 해당 고용주와 수습 직원은 지속적인 지원을 받게 됩니다.** 해당 자문은 프로그램이 성공적으로 완료될 때까지 양측과 주기적으로 만납니다.

어휘 workforce 전체 직원들, 인력 boost 향상, 증진 organization 단체, 기관 qualified 자격을 갖춘, 적격인 candidate 지원자, 후보자 apprenticeship 수습 제도 shortage 부족 participant 참가자 be matched with ~와 짝을 이루다 advisor 자문, 상담 전문가 expertise 전문 지식 particular 특정한 define 규정하다, 정의하다 tailored (특정 목적 등에) 맞춰진 typically 일반적으로, 전형적으로 combine 결합하다 on-the-job 현장의, 실습의 external 외부의 apprentice 수습 직원 licensing 허가증, 면허증 certification 자격증, 수료증 instruction 교육, 지도 ongoing 지속되는

### 155 주제 / 목적

번역 해당 프로그램의 목적은 무엇인가?
(A) 고용주들이 직원을 교육하는 것을 돕는 것
(B) 고용주들을 숙련된 구직자들과 연결해 주는 것
(C) 고용주들에게 새 노동 관련 규정에 관해 조언하는 것
(D) 소속 직원들을 잘 대우해 주는 고용주들에게 보상을 주는 것

해설 지문 초반부에 해당 프로그램이 직무 능력 부족 문제를 해결할 수 있는 수습 제도를 만들 수 있도록 고용주들을 돕는다(The Workforce Boost Programme assists employers in creating apprenticeships to solve their skills shortages)고 언급되어 있으므로 (A)가 정답이다.

어휘 connect 연결하다, 연관 짓다 skilled 숙련된, 능숙한 regulation 규제, 규정 reward 보상해 주다 treat 대우하다

> Paraphrasing
> 지문의 assists employers in creating apprenticeships to solve their skills shortages
> → 정답의 help employers train workers for positions

### 156 추론

번역 누가 해당 프로그램으로부터 직접 돈을 받을 것 같은가?
(A) 특정한 직원 복지 혜택을 제공하는 회사들
(B) 직무 자격 요건을 위한 교육을 제공하는 기관들
(C) 인기 없는 분야에서 근무하는 데 동의하는 구직자들
(D) 추가 자격증을 취득하는 직원들

해설 지문 중반부에 허가증이나 자격증을 받기 위해 필요한 외부 교육과 현장 교육을 결합한다고 언급하면서 최대 12,000달러의 외부 교육 비용을 직접 지불한다(It typically combines on-the-job training with any external education ~. The programme pays directly for up to $12,000 of the cost of external instruction)고 알리고 있다. 따라서 그런 교육을 제공하는 기관들이

직접 돈을 받을 것임을 알 수 있으므로 (B)가 정답이다.

어휘 benefit 혜택, 이점 qualification 자격 (요건), 자격증 agree 동의하다 unpopular 인기 없는 obtain 획득하다, 얻다 extra 추가의, 별도의

## 157 문장 삽입

번역 [1], [2], [3], [4]로 표시된 곳 중에서 다음 문장이 가장 적합한 곳은 어디인가?

"해당 자문은 프로그램이 성공적으로 완료될 때까지 양측과 주기적으로 만납니다."

(A) [1]
(B) [2]
(C) [3]
(D) [4]

해설 제시된 문장에 both parties라는 단서가 있고, 자문이 양측과 주기적으로 만난다고 했다. 따라서 both parties가 가리킬 수 있는 사람들인 the employer and the apprentice를 포함해 지속적인 지원이 가능하다고 알리는 문장 뒤에 위치한 [4]에 들어가 어떻게 지원하는지 알리는 흐름이 되어야 알맞으므로 (D)가 정답이다.

어휘 regularly 주기적으로 party 당사자 completion 완료

### 158-160 공지

봄 물물교환 행사

브룩스빌 공원
5월 20일 토요일 오후 1시부터 오후 4시

BYO 브룩스빌은 제4회 봄 물물교환 행사를 선보이게 되어 자랑스럽게 생각합니다! 이 연례 행사는 사람들이 더 이상 원치 않는 가정용품, 의류, 도서를 비롯한 기타 소유물을 기증하고 다른 사람들이 기증한 물품을 가져갈 수 있는 기회입니다. 참가비는 없으며 물건을 가져올 필요도 없습니다. 158 **하지만 물품을 기증하시는 분들은 그 물품들이 진열되기 전에 주최 측에서 그것들이 깨끗하고 온전하면서 좋은 상태인지 확인할 수 있도록 반드시 "접수 테이블"로 가져오셔야 합니다.**

BYO 브룩스빌은 친환경 제품 판매점이자 청소용품, 화장품, 식품 리필 스테이션입니다. "BYO"는 "Bring Your Own"을 의미하는데, 고객이 구매한 제품을 159 **담아 갈** 용기와 가방을 직접 가져와야 합니다. 봄 물물교환 행사 같은 행사들뿐 아니라, 160 **낡은 의류 수선 같은 친환경 기술에 관한 정기 강좌도 제공하고 있습니다.**

어휘 swap 물품 교환 annual 연례적인, 해마다의 give away 기증하다, 증정하다 possession 소유물 participation 참가, 참여 requirement 필요, 필수 조건 drop-off 갖다 놓기 organizer 주최자, 조직자 retailer 소매업체 eco-friendly 친환경적인 refill station 리필 스테이션(플라스틱 등의 사용을 줄이기 위해 포장용기 없이 내용물만 판매하는 곳) stand for ~을 의미하다, 상징하다 container 용기, 그릇 mend 수선하다 worn-out 낡은, 닳은

## 158 추론

번역 공지에 언급된 테이블에 대해 암시된 것은?
(A) 행사가 끝나기 전에 치워질 것이다.
(B) BYO 브룩스빌 내에 위치해 있다.
(C) 행사 인력이 배치될 것이다.
(D) 더 이상 적절히 작동하지 않을 수 있는 물품을 진열할 것이다.

해설 첫 단락에 주최 측에서 기증 물품의 상태를 확인할 수 있도록 반드시 "접수 테이블"로 가져와야 한다(those who do give away items must bring them to the "drop-off table" so that organizers can ensure ~)고 언급되어 있다. 이를 통해 주최 측 직원이 접수 테이블을 운영한다는 것을 알 수 있으므로 (C)가 정답이다.

어휘 remove 치우다, 없애다 staff 직원을 두다 personnel 인력, 인사(부) properly 적절히, 알맞게

## 159 동의어

번역 두 번째 단락, 네 번째 줄에 쓰인 "carry"와 의미가 가장 가까운 것은?
(A) 판매하다
(B) 착용하다, 닳게 하다
(C) 운송하다, 옮기다
(D) 제공하다, 발표하다

해설 'carry'를 포함한 부분은 '고객이 구매한 제품을 담아 갈 용기와 가방을 직접 가져와야 한다(customers are required to bring their own containers and bags to carry their purchases)'라는 의미로 해석되는데, 여기서 carry는 '담아 가다, 옮기다'라는 뜻으로 쓰였다. 따라서 '옮기다'라는 의미의 (C) transport가 정답이다.

## 160 세부 사항

번역 공지에 따르면, BYO 브룩스빌은 무엇에 관한 교육을 제공하는가?
(A) 채식 음식을 요리하는 방법
(B) 손상된 의류를 수선하는 방법
(C) 자신만의 청소용품을 만드는 방법
(D) 플라스틱 용기를 재사용하는 방법

해설 두 번째 단락에 BYO 브룩스빌이 낡은 의류 수선 같은 친환경 기술에 관한 강좌도 제공한다(it offers regular classes on eco-friendly skills such as mending worn-out clothing)고 언급되어 있으므로 (B)가 정답이다.

어휘 damaged 손상된

> Paraphrasing
> 지문의 mending worn-out clothing
> → 정답의 repair damaged clothing

TEST 10

### 161-163 이메일

발신: daiju.hasegawa@dhasegawa.com
수신: r.alvarado@shermanderm.com
제목: 알림
날짜: 8월 1일

알바라도 씨께,

9월 1일부터 161 **저는 그래픽 디자인 서비스에 대해 현재 요금인 시간당 40달러 대신 시간당 45달러를 청구할 예정입니다.** 이러한 변동은 최근 상승한 우리 지역의 생활 물가를 감당하기 위해 필수적입니다. 163 **귀사의 새 이메일 소식지를 위해 제가 제작한 템플릿**과 그동안 해온 다른 작업에 대한 귀하의 만족도를 고려할 때, 162 **제 쪽으로** 프로젝트를 계속 보내 주시는 게 귀하의 병원에 그리 큰 부담이 아니기를 바랍니다. 이 변동에 대해 어떤 우려 사항이든 있으실 경우, 제게 알려 주십시오.

다이주 하세가와

어휘 effective ~부로 (시작해), ~부터 효력이 있는 charge 청구하다, 부과하다 current 현재의 necessary 필수적인, 필요한 cover (비용 등을) 충당하다 prohibitive 엄청나게 비싼 my way 내 쪽으로 satisfaction 만족(도) template 템플릿 견본, 형판

## 161 주제 / 목적

번역 하세가와 씨는 왜 이메일을 보냈는가?
(A) 자신의 업체를 광고하기 위해
(B) 서비스에 관해 문의하기 위해
(C) 예약 일정을 변경하기 위해
(D) 요금 인상을 알리기 위해

해설 시작 부분에 자신의 그래픽 디자인 서비스에 대해 현재의 요금인 시간당 40달러 대신 시간당 45달러를 청구할 것(I will be charging $45 per hour for my graphic design services instead of my current fee of $40 per hour)이라고 알리면서 그 이유 등을 설명하고 있으므로 (D)가 정답이다.

어휘 advertise 광고하다 rate 요금, 등급

> Paraphrasing
> 지문의 will be charging $45 / instead of my current fee of $40 → 정답의 a rate increase

## 162 동의어

번역 네 번째 줄에 쓰인 "my way"와 의미가 가장 가까운 것은?
(A) 제 돈으로
(B) 제가 하도록
(C) 제가 설명해 드린 대로
(D) 제 것과 유사한

해설 'my way'가 포함된 부분은 '제 쪽으로 프로젝트를 계속 보내는 것'이라는 의미로 해석된다. 이 말은 '제가 할 수 있게 프로젝트를 계속 보내는 것'을 의미하므로 '제가 하도록'이라는 의미의 (B)가 정답이다.

## 163 세부 사항

번역 해당 병원은 최근에 무엇을 했는가?
(A) 다른 지역으로 이전했다.
(B) 전공이 특별한 의사를 고용했다.
(C) 새로운 커뮤니케이션 수단을 시작했다.
(D) 그래픽 디자인 프로젝트를 위한 입찰을 요청했다.

해설 후반부에 상대방 병원의 새 이메일 소식지를 위해 템플릿을 제작(the template I created for your new e-mail newsletters)한 일이 언급되어 있으므로 병원에서 새 이메일 소식지를 시작했다는 것을 알 수 있다. 따라서 (C)가 정답이다.

어휘 relocate 이전하다 unique 특별한, 독특한 specialty 전문성, 전공 launch 시작하다 channel 수단, 경로 bid 입찰(가)

> Paraphrasing
> 지문의 new e-mail newsletters
> → 정답의 a new communication channel

### 164-167 회람

날짜: 2월 19일
수신: 전 직원
발신: 기업 본사
제목: 정보

직원 감사 주간의 일환으로, 164 **씨사이드 커피 경영진은 직원 여러분께 일 년 내내 이용할 수 있는 다양한 특혜를 상기시켜 드리고자 합니다.** 직원들께서는 교대 근무마다 식품과 음료를 하나씩 무료로 드실 수 있습니다. 미리 병에 담겨 있는 것들을 제외한 모든 종류의 음료가 이 제공 서비스에 포함됩니다. 근무하지 않을 때는, 165 **직원들은 결제 시 직원 번호를 제시하면 모든 씨사이드 매장에서 모든 제품에 대해 25% 할인을 받을 수 있습니다.** 이는 여러분께서 출퇴근 시간을 기록할 때 사용하는 번호입니다. 마지막으로, "워크 플러스" 플랫폼을 통해 식료품 매장에서부터 음악 스트리밍 서비스 회사에 이르는 여러 제휴 업체에서도 혜택을 제공합니다. 아직 해보지 않았다면, 166 **www.workplus.com/seaside에 방문하여 등록하고 혜택을 이용해 보세요.**

늘 그렇듯이, 우리 씨사이드 가족의 일원이 되어 주신 것에 대해 감사드립니다.

레이드 월든
인사 부사장

어휘 headquarters 본사 appreciation 감사(의 마음) management 경영진, 운영진 perks 특혜, 특전 available 이용 가능한 year-round 연중, 일 년 내내 shift 교대 근무 checkout 계산대 clock in and out 출퇴근 시간을 기록하다 benefit 혜택, 이점 range from A to B (범위가) A에서 B에 이르다 sign up 등록하다, 신청하다 take advantage of ~을 이용하다

## 164 주제 / 목적

번역 회람의 목적은 무엇인가?
(A) 매장 정책의 변경 사항을 설명하는 것
(B) 고객들의 불만 사항을 공유하는 것
(C) 판촉 행사에 관한 의견을 요청하는 것
(D) 직원 보상책을 개괄적으로 설명하는 것

해설 첫 단락 시작 부분에 회사 경영진이 직원들에게 일 년 내내 이용할 수 있는 다양한 특혜를 상기시키려 한다(Seaside Coffee management would like to remind employees of the variety of perks available to them year-round)고 언급하면서 몇 가지 혜택을 설명하고 있으므로 (D)가 정답이다.

어휘 policy 정책 complaint 불만, 불평 promotion 촉진, 증진 overview 개괄, 개요 incentive 보상책, 장려 정책

## 165 Not / True

번역 씨사이드 커피의 제품 할인에 대해 언급된 것은?
(A) 하루에 한 번만 이용할 수 있다.
(B) 일주일 동안만 이용 가능하다.
(C) 숫자로 된 코드를 제공해야 한다.
(D) 책임자의 재량에 따라 제공된다.

해설 첫 단락 중반부에 직원들은 결제 시 직원 번호를 제시하면 모든 씨사이드 매장에서 모든 제품에 대해 25% 할인을 받을 수 있다(employees may receive a 25% discount on any product at all Seaside locations by giving their employee number at checkout)고 쓰여 있으므로 (C)가 정답이다.

어휘 provision 제공 numerical 숫자의 discretion 재량

> Paraphrasing
> 지문의 giving their employee number
> → 정답의 the provision of a numerical code

## 166 세부 사항

번역 회람 수신인들에게 무엇을 하도록 권장되는가?
(A) 예정된 휴식 시간 갖기
(B) 온라인 등록 과정 완료하기
(C) 고객들에게 제휴 업체들에 관해 알리기
(D) 소셜 미디어 플랫폼에 게시글 올리기

해설 첫 단락 후반부에 www.workplus.com/seaside를 방문해 등록할 것(visit www.workplus.com/seaside to sign up)을 권하고 있으므로 (B)가 정답이다.

어휘 registration 등록 process 과정 post 게시글을 올리다

> Paraphrasing
> 지문의 visit www.workplus.com/seaside to sign up
> → 정답의 Complete an online registration process

## 167 문장 삽입

번역 [1], [2], [3], [4]로 표시된 곳 중에서 다음 문장이 가장 적합한 곳은 어디인가?
"미리 병에 담겨 있는 것을 제외한 모든 종류의 음료가 이 제공 서비스에 포함됩니다."
(A) [1]
(B) [2]
(C) [3]
(D) [4]

해설 제시된 문장은 특정 제공 서비스를 가리키는 this offer와 함께 어떤 음료가 그 서비스에 포함되는지 알리는 의미를 지니고 있다. 따라서 무료 음료 이용 혜택을 언급하는 문장 뒤에 위치한 [2]에 들어가 이용 가능한 음료의 종류를 알리는 흐름이 되어야 자연스러우므로 (B)가 정답이다.

어휘 beverage 음료 pre-bottled 미리 병에 담긴 include 포함하다

### 168-171 이메일

발신: 비어트릭스 메이저
수신: 앤드류 더넘
제목: 회신: 키친 회원권
날짜: 3월 30일

더넘 씨께,

켈소 키친 회원권을 재개하는 것에 관해 문의해 주셔서 감사합니다. 네, 168 **귀하께서 전에 푸드 트럭을 위한 재료를 준비하기 위해 저희 주방 공간을 이용하셨던 것을 기억합니다. 식당을 개업해서 잘 운영되고 있다는 말씀을 듣게 되어 기쁘네요.** 켈소 키친은 새로운 조리법을 169 **개발할** 수 있는 공간을 분명 제공할 수 있습니다.

현재 월 회비는 400달러입니다. 이 비용으로 최대 30시간 동안 모든 것이 갖춰진 공용 주방 중 한 곳을 이용하실 수 있습니다. 예약은 필수이며, 반드시 저희 온라인 시스템을 통해 이뤄져야 합니다. 170 **회원들께 재료를 보관할 수 있는 잠금 가능한 보관 용기가 2개 할당되며, 그중 하나는 저희 대형 냉장실에 보관될 수 있습니다.** 예정된 시간이 종료되기 전에 공간을 깨끗이 청소하시고 사용하신 모든 조리 도구를 세척하셔야 한다는 점을 기억해 주시기 바랍니다.

171 **귀하가 저희 시설에서 준비하는 음식은 고객들에게 판매되지 않을 것이므로, 저희가 필요한 유일한 서류는 책임 보험 증명서입니다.** 화요일부터 토요일, 오전 9시에서 오후 5시까지 언제든 이것을 저희 사무실로 가져오셔서 회원권을 재개하는 절차를 시작할 수 있습니다.

비어트릭스 메이저

어휘 inquiry 문의 ingredient (음식) 재료, 성분 recipe 조리법 entitle ~에게 자격을 주다 fully equipped 모든 것이 갖춰진 allot 할당하다, 배정하다 lockable 잠금 가능한 cage 보관 용기 store 보관하다 walk-in (사람이 서서 들어갈 정도로) 대형의 implement 도구 proof 증명(서), 증거 liability insurance 책임 보험

## 168 Not / True

번역 더넘 씨에 대해 언급된 것은?
(A) 요리책을 출간할 계획을 세우고 있다.
(B) 두 가지 종류의 시설을 운영해 봤다.
(C) 자신의 식당을 체인으로 확장하기를 바란다.
(D) 전에 켈소 키친의 직원이었다.

해설 더넘 씨는 이메일의 수신자로, 첫 단락에 더넘 씨가 푸드 트럭을 했던 것과 식당을 개업한 것(you used to use our kitchen space to prepare ingredients for your food truck. ~ you have opened a restaurant ~)이 언급되어 있으므로 (B)가 정답이다.

어휘 operate 운영하다, 영업하다 establishment 시설, 설립물

> Paraphrasing
> 지문의 food truck / restaurant
> → 정답의 two types of establishments

TEST 10

## 169 동의어

번역 첫 번째 단락, 네 번째 줄에 쓰인 "develop"과 의미가 가장 가까운 것은?
(A) 가져가다, 데리러 가다, 구입하다
(B) 연장하다, 확장하다
(C) ~에 대한 작업을 하다
(D) 시연하다, 설명하다

해설 'develop'을 포함한 부분은 '새로운 조리법을 개발할 수 있는 공간을 분명 제공할 수 있다(~ can certainly provide you with space to develop new recipes)'라는 의미로 해석되는데, 여기서 develop은 '개발하다'라는 뜻으로 쓰였다. 새로운 조리법을 개발한다는 것은 새로운 조리법을 위한 작업을 한다고 볼 수 있으므로 '~에 대한 작업을 하다'라는 의미의 (C) work on이 정답이다.

## 170 세부 사항

번역 켈소 키친은 회원들에게 무엇을 제공하는가?
(A) 안전한 음식 보관 공간
(B) 장기 회원 할인
(C) 청소 서비스의 선택적 이용
(D) 요리 기법에 대한 월간 강좌

해설 두 번째 단락에 회원들에게 재료를 보관할 수 있는 잠금 가능한 보관 용기가 2개 할당되며, 그중 하나는 대형 냉장실에 보관될 수 있다(Members are allotted two lockable cages for storing their ingredients in, one of which can be kept in our walk-in refrigerator)는 내용이 있으므로 (A)가 정답이다.

어휘 storage 보관, 저장 long-term 장기간의 optional 선택적인

> Paraphrasing
> 지문의 our walk-in refrigerator
> → 정답의 storage space for food

## 171 추론

번역 켈소 키친에 대해 암시된 것은?
(A) 회원들 간의 협업을 권장한다.
(B) 그곳 시설은 주중보다 주말에 더 바쁘다.
(C) 최소 하루 전에 예약해야 한다.
(D) 음식을 판매하는 회원들에게 추가 서류를 요구한다.

해설 세 번째 단락에 켈소 키친에서 준비하는 음식이 고객들에게 판매되지 않을 것이므로 필요한 유일한 서류는 책임 보험 증명서(Since the food you prepare in our facility will not be sold to customers, the only documentation we need from you is proof of liability insurance)라는 말이 쓰여 있다. 이는 바꿔 말하면 그곳에서 준비한 음식을 판매하려면 다른 서류가 더 필요하다는 뜻이므로 (D)가 정답이다.

어휘 collaboration 협업, 공동 작업 in advance 미리, 사전에 extra 추가의, 여분의

## 172-175 온라인 채팅

마슬기 (오전 9시 8분)
안녕하세요, 데빈. 172 **어제 저녁에 박물관의 주 계정으로 받은 이메일을 확인해 보셨어요?**

데빈 스튜어트 (오전 9시 9분)
확인해 볼게요.

마슬기 (오전 9시 10분)
172 **발신인 이름이 베로니카 건입니다. 어제 프램로드의 투어 중 하나에 참석했다고 말씀하시네요.**

데빈 스튜어트 (오전 9시 12분)
그리고 173 **19세기 미국 패션 전시회에 있는 격자무늬 드레스가 우리 라벨에 쓰여 있는 것보다 아마 10년 더 나중일 것이라고 생각한다고요?**

마슬기 (오전 9시 13분)
네, 소매 디자인 때문에요. 우리가 그걸 살펴봐야 할 것 같아요. 이분이 꽤 박식한 것 같아요.

데빈 스튜어트 (오전 9시 13분)
동감이에요. 제가 셀리아를 채팅에 초대할게요.

데빈 스튜어트 (오전 9시 14분)
셀리아, 우리 새 전시회에 대해 받은 이메일을 당신에게 전달할게요. 이걸 살펴보신 다음, 174 **당신이 헴필 대학교에서 만났던 패션 역사 교수님에게 의견을 받아 줄 수 있나요?**

셀리아 볼 (오전 9시 16분)
물론이죠. 175 **이 사안이 얼마나 긴급한 거죠? 가끔씩 그분이 이메일에 답장하시는 데 며칠씩 걸리거든요.**

데빈 스튜어트 (오전 9시 17분)
175 **오늘 안으로 파악해 주었으면 해요.**

셀리아 볼 (오전 9시 18분)
알겠습니다. 175 **그분께 전화해보고 알게 된 것을 말씀드릴게요.**

어휘 account 계정 plaid 격자무늬 exhibition 전시회 decade 10년 sleeve (옷) 소매 knowledgeable 박식한, 아는 것이 많은 forward 전송하다 pressing 긴급한 figure out ~을 파악하다, 알아내다

## 172 세부 사항

번역 마 씨가 언급하는 이메일은 누가 썼는가?
(A) 투어 가이드
(B) 신임 큐레이터
(C) 박물관 방문객
(D) 전시회 기부자

해설 9시 8분과 10분에 마 씨가 작성한 메시지에 어제 저녁에 박물관의 주 계정으로 받은 이메일(the e-mail that the museum's main account received)을 언급하며, 이메일 발신자가 어제 프램로드의 투어들 중 하나에 참석했다(The sender's ~ she took one of Pramrod's tours yesterday)고 했다. 따라서 이메일을 쓴 사람은 박물관 투어 참가자임을 알 수 있으므로 (C)가 정답이다.

### 173 세부 사항

번역 채팅 메시지 작성자들은 어떤 문제를 이야기하고 있는가?
(A) 박물관에 있는 한 물품의 연대가 잘못 표기되어 있을 수도 있다.
(B) 오래된 의류 한 점이 취약한 상태이다.
(C) 몇몇 전시물에 부착된 라벨이 읽기 어렵다.
(D) 복원 작업으로 인해 드레스의 디자인이 바뀌었다.

해설 9시 12분에 스튜어트 씨가 이메일 작성자가 19세기 미국 패션 전시회에 있는 격자무늬 드레스가 라벨에 쓰여 있는 것보다 10년 더 나중일 것이라고 생각한다(she believes that the plaid dress in the nineteenth-century American fashion exhibition is probably from a later decade than what our label says) 고 말하고 있으므로 (A)가 정답이다.

어휘 date 연대를 표기하다, 시기를 추정하다 incorrectly 잘못하여, 부정확하게 fragile 취약한, 깨지기 쉬운 exhibit 전시물 restoration 복원, 복구

> Paraphrasing
> 지문의 the plaid dress ~ is probably from a later decade than what our label says
> → 정답의 An item in the museum may be dated incorrectly

### 174 세부 사항

번역 볼 씨는 무엇을 하라는 요청을 받는가?
(A) 게시용 안내문 초안 작성하기
(B) 웹사이트의 한 페이지 없애기
(C) 물건을 주인에게 돌려주기
(D) 외부 전문가에게 자문 구하기

해설 9시 14분에 스튜어트 씨가 볼 씨에게 헴필 대학교에서 만났던 패션 역사 교수님에게 의견을 받아 줄 수 있는지(get an opinion from the fashion history professor you met at Hemphill University?) 물었다. 이는 외부의 전문가에게 자문을 구하도록 요청하는 것이므로 (D)가 정답이다.

어휘 draft 초안을 작성하다 remove 없애다, 제거하다 consult 자문을 구하다, 상담하다 external 외부의

> Paraphrasing
> 지문의 get an opinion from the fashion history professor → 정답의 Consult an external expert

### 175 의도 파악

번역 오전 9시 18분에 볼 씨가 "알겠습니다"라고 쓸 때, 의미하는 것은 무엇인가?
(A) 이제 전시 공간을 출입할 수 있다.
(B) 스튜어트 씨가 전달한 이메일을 받았다.
(C) 상황의 긴급함을 이해하고 있다.
(D) 할당된 업무에 도움이 필요치 않다.

해설 9시 16분에 볼 씨가 얼마나 긴급한 사안인지(How pressing is this issue?) 묻자, 스튜어트 씨가 오늘 안으로 파악해 달라(I'd like to get it figured out by the end of the day)고 요청하는 것에 대해 볼 씨가 '알겠습니다'라는 말과 함께 전화로 알아보고 말해 주겠다(I'll call him and let you know what I find out)고 대답하고 있다. 따라서 '알겠습니다'라는 말은 긴급한 사안임을 알고 한 답변임을 알 수 있으므로 (C)가 정답이다.

어휘 have access to+명사 ~을 이용할 수 있다, ~에 접근할 수 있다 urgency 긴급함 assistance 도움, 지원 assignment 할당(된 일)

### 176-180 임대 계약서+이메일

상업용 부지 임대 계약서

이 계약은 헨리에타 깁스(임대인)와 네이선 호프먼(임차인) 간에 3월 7일 체결한다. [180] **임대인은 임차인에게 4월 1일부터 12월 31일까지 호프먼 미술관 운영 목적으로 상업용 공간을 임대하는 데 합의한다.** 양측 당사자는 다음의 조항에 합의한다.

항목 1: 임대 부지
임대되는 부동산은 베이츠 가 249번지 베이츠 플라자에 위치해 있다. [176] **이 부동산은 1,361평방피트의 매장과 매장 입구 바로 앞에 있는 두 개의 주차 공간으로 구성되어 있다.**

항목 2: 임대료 및 납입금
임차인은 매달 1일에 1,500달러의 기본 임대료를 지불하는 데 합의한다. [177] **임차인은 또한 분기별로 사업체 순이익의 7%에 해당하는 비율의 임대료도 지불한다.** [178] **임차인은 베이츠 플라자의 보도 및 화장실 유지 관리 비용으로 각각 월 25달러와 월 30달러를 지불해야 한다.**

항목 3: 임차인 의무
임차인은 반드시 해당 부지를 깨끗하고 잘 관리된 상태로 유지해야 한다. [179] **모든 쓰레기는 반드시 매주 세 차례 치워야 한다.** 임차인에 의해 초래된 손상은 반드시 알려야 하며, 임차인의 비용으로 수리해야 한다.

항목 4: 계약의 갱신 또는 연장
임차인은 이 계약을 갱신하거나 연장할 수 있는 선택권을 지닌다. 이렇게 하기 위한 요청은 반드시 임대 기간 종료 최소 두 달 전에 이뤄져야 한다.

임대인: *Henrietta Gibbs*
헨리에타 깁스
임차인: *Nathan Hoffman*
네이선 호프먼
날짜: 3월 7일

어휘 commercial 상업의 lease 임대 (계약); 임대하다 agreement 계약(서), 합의(서) landlord 건물주, 임대인 tenant 세입자, 임차인 operate 운영하다, 영업하다 party 당사자 following 다음의, 아래의 terms and conditions (계약 등의) 조항, 약관 premises 부지, 구내 property 부동산, 건물 consist of ~로 구성되다 storefront (거리) 상점 rent 임대료, 월세 net profit 순이익 on a quarterly basis 분기 단위로 charge 청구하다, 부과하다 respectively 각각 maintenance 유지 관리, 시설 관리 obligation 의무 expense (지출) 비용, 경비 renewal 갱신 extension 연장, 확장 renew 갱신하다 extend 연장하다, 확장하다

TEST 10

발신: 네이선 호프먼
수신: 헨리에타 깁스
날짜: 10월 18일
제목: 임대 계약 갱신

깁스 씨께,

180 **1년 임대 계약 갱신을 요청하고자 이메일을 씁니다.** 베이츠 플라자가 미술관을 운영하기 좋은 장소였기 때문에, 그곳에서 계속 운영하고 싶습니다.

하지만 저희 계약서의 조항 중 하나를 변경했으면 합니다. 179 **쓰레기 처리 요건을 일주일에 단 한 차례로 낮출 수 있을까요?** 저희 업체는 쓰레기가 많이 나오지 않거든요. 이것이 가능한지 알려 주시기 바랍니다.

네이선 호프먼

어휘 term 기간 disposal 처리, 처분 lower 낮추다, 내리다

## 176 Not / True

번역 임대 계약서에 대해 사실인 것은?
(A) 건물 실내외를 포함한다.
(B) 두 업체 사이의 계약이다.
(C) 법률 대리인에 의해 준비되었다.
(D) 양측 당사자가 합의하면 일찍 종료될 수 있다.

해설 첫 지문 항목 1에 임대되는 부지가 1,361평방피트의 매장과 매장 입구 바로 앞에 있는 두 개의 주차 공간으로 구성된다(It consists of a 1,361-square-foot storefront plus the use of the two parking spaces directly in front of the storefront's entrance)고 제시된 것에서 실내외 공간이 모두 포함된다는 것을 알 수 있으므로 (A)가 정답이다.

어휘 encompass 아우르다, 포함하다 property 부동산, 건물 legal 법률의 representative 대리인, 대표자 terminate 종료하다

> Paraphrasing
> 지문의 a 1,361-square-foot storefront / the two parking spaces directly in front of the storefront's entrance → 정답의 indoor and outdoor property

## 177 Not / True

번역 임대료에 대해 언급된 것은?
(A) 분기마다 점차적으로 인상될 것이다.
(B) 특정한 지불 방법을 통해 송금되어야 한다.
(C) 미술관의 수익에 따라 총액이 달라진다.
(D) 늦게 납부 시에는 벌금이 있다.

해설 첫 지문 항목 2에 임차인이 분기별로 사업체 순이익의 7%에 해당하는 비율의 임대료도 지불한다(The tenant will also pay a percentage rent fee of 7% of the business's net profits on a quarterly basis)는 조건이 쓰여 있으므로 (C)가 정답이다.

어휘 incrementally 점차적으로 via ~을 통해 particular 특정한 depending on ~에 따라, ~에 달려 있는 penalty fee 벌금

> Paraphrasing
> 지문의 a percentage rent fee of 7% of the business's net profits
> → 정답의 varies depending on the gallery's profits

## 178 세부 사항

번역 임차인이 반드시 비용을 지불해야 한다고 임대 계약서에 명시되어 있는 것은 무엇인가?
(A) 임대 부지에 대한 개조
(B) 건물 손상 비용을 충당하는 보험
(C) 공공 서비스 제공업체 변경
(D) 일부 공용 공간 유지관리

해설 첫 지문 항목 2에 임차인은 베이츠 플라자의 보도 및 화장실 유지 관리 비용으로 각각 월 25달러와 월 30달러를 지불해야 한다(The tenant will be charged $25 per month and $30 per month, respectively, for maintenance of the sidewalk and restrooms of Bates Plaza)는 조건이 명시되어 있으므로 (D)가 정답이다.

어휘 improvement 개조, 개선 insurance 보험 cover (비용 등을) 충당하다 utility service (전기, 수도 등의) 공공 서비스 maintenance 유지관리

> Paraphrasing
> 지문의 the sidewalk and restrooms of Bates Plaza
> → 정답의 some common areas

## 179 연계

번역 호프먼 씨는 임대 계약서의 어느 부분에 대한 수정을 요청하는가?
(A) 항목 1
(B) 항목 2
(C) 항목 3
(D) 항목 4

해설 호프먼 씨가 쓴 이메일 두 번째 단락에 쓰레기 처리 요건을 일주일에 단 한 차례로 낮출 수 있는지(Could the waste disposal requirement be lowered to just once a week?) 묻는 말이 있다. 이는 첫 지문의 항목 3에 명시된 '모든 쓰레기는 반드시 매주 세 차례 치워야 한다(All waste must be removed three times per week)'는 조건에 대한 수정을 요청하는 것이므로 (C)가 정답이다.

어휘 revision 수정, 개정

## 180 연계

번역 호프먼 씨가 제안하는 갱신된 임대 계약에 대해 암시된 것은?
(A) 추가 조건을 포함할 것이다.
(B) 원래의 계약보다 기간이 더 길어진다.
(C) 이미 깁스 씨와 논의했다.
(D) 명시된 마감 기한 후에 요청했다.

해설 이메일 첫 단락에 1년 임대 계약 갱신을 요청하기 위해 이메일을 쓴다(I am writing to request the renewal of my lease for a one-year term)고 했는데, 이는 임대 계약서 첫 단락에 4월 1일부터 12월 31일까지(from April 1 to December 31)로 표기된 기존의 계약 기간보다 더 긴 기간에 해당하므로 (B)가 정답이다.

어휘 condition 조건 span (기간, 범위 등) ~에 걸쳐 이어지다 specified 명시된

## 181-185 기사+이메일

예술가 스포트라이트: 라바냐 굴라티

에드먼턴, 캐나다 (2월 5일)—화가 라바냐 굴라티가 아름다운 벽화로 미술계의 주목을 받고 있다. [181] **이 대규모 미술 작품들은 대부분 자연 세계를 묘사하는 것으로서**, 에드먼턴과 캐나다 전역의 몇몇 다른 도시의 거리에서 볼 수 있다.

"저는 콘크리트 벽처럼 인공적인 것을 완전히 새로운 창작품으로 바꾸는 과정을 아주 좋아합니다"라고 굴라티 씨는 말한다. "도시에 살면서도 우리는 여전히 환경과 연결될 수 있는 방법을 찾을 수 있습니다. 제 작품이 사람들에게 이 점을 상기시켜 주었으면 좋겠어요."

고객의 의견은 기획 과정에서 필수적인 부분이며, [185] **굴라티 씨는 어떤 디자인 시안이든 마무리하는 데 최소 3주의 기간을 필요로 한다.** 굴라티 씨는 최종 결과물에 대한 명확한 구상이 있으면 그림을 빠르게 완성할 수 있다고 말한다.

[182] **놀랍게도, 굴라티 씨의 고객들은 벽화가 그려질 부분을 청소하고 손질해야 한다.** 굴라티 씨는 이것이 비용을 줄일 뿐 아니라 고객들도 작업의 일부로 참여할 수 있게 해 준다고 말한다. 굴라티 씨는 이 작업에 필요한 물품에 대한 조언을 제공하며, [183] **그녀의 웹사이트 www.gulatiart.ca에는 종합적인 단계별 설명이 담긴 동영상이 올라가 있다.**

어휘 grab the attention of ~의 주목을 받다 mural 벽화 large-scale 대규모의 depict 묘사하다 process 과정 artificial 인공적인 entirely 완전히 creation 창작(품) urban 도시의 connected to+명사 ~와 연결된 input 의견 essential 필수적인 a minimum of 최소 ~의 vision 구상, 비전 treat (화학 약품 등으로) 처리하다 cut down on ~을 줄이다 advise 조언하다 supplies 물품, 용품 comprehensive 종합적인 step-by-step 단계별의 instructions 설명, 안내

수신: contact@gulatiart.ca
발신: a_rankin@omail.ca
날짜: [185] **2월 8일**
제목: 문의

굴라티 씨께,

귀하의 작품에 대해 최근에 실린 기사를 읽었으며, 온라인에서 찾은 귀하의 벽화 사진에 깊은 인상을 받았습니다. 저희 커피 매장이 이전하는데, 두 군데 벽화가 필요합니다.

1. 2층짜리 건물의 한쪽 면(스토커트 가 852, 외벽)에는 잠재 고객들이 주목할 극적이면서 시선을 끄는 벽화를 원합니다.

2. 메인 실내 좌석 공간에는 숲을 배경으로 편안한 분위기를 만들려고 합니다. [184] **현재 위치는 철거 예정인데 그곳의 나무 바닥은 남겨둘 예정이고, 그것들이 어떻게든 포함됐으면 좋겠습니다.**

이번 주에 만나서 작품에 대해 논의하고, [185] **2월 18일까지 제안하시는 디자인의 스케치를 받을 수 있을까요?** 계약서에 서명하는 대로 은행 계좌 이체로 계약금을 드릴 수 있습니다.

앨버트 랜킨

어휘 inquiry 문의 be impressed with ~에 깊은 인상을 받다 relocate 이전하다 exterior 외부의 eye-catching 시선을 끄는 potential 잠재적인 relaxing 편안한, 느긋한 atmosphere 분위기 save 따로 남겨 두다 current 현재의 site 장소, 현장 tear down 철거하다 include 포함하다 somehow 어떻게든 propose 제안하다 deposit 선금, 보증금 bank transfer 은행 계좌 이체 contract 계약(서)

### 181 Not / True

번역 기사에서 굴라티 씨의 벽화에 대해 언급하는 것은?
(A) 전 세계 각지에서 찾아볼 수 있다.
(B) 일반적으로 자연을 주제로 한다.
(C) 가치가 상승할 것으로 예상된다.
(D) 주로 대중으로부터 자금을 지원받는다.

해설 기사 첫 단락에 굴라티 씨의 벽화가 대부분 자연 세계를 묘사한다(These large-scale works of art, most of which depict the natural world)고 쓰여 있으므로 (B)가 정답이다.

어휘 feature 특징으로 하다 theme 주제 increase 상승하다 value 가치 fund 자금을 제공하다 the public 일반인들

> Paraphrasing
> 지문의 depict the natural world
> → 정답의 feature a nature theme

### 182 세부 사항

번역 굴라티 씨의 고객들은 무엇을 하도록 요청받는가?
(A) 그림을 그릴 표면 준비 작업하기
(B) 페인트 종류 선택하기
(C) 과정을 사진으로 촬영하기
(D) 완성된 벽화를 주기적으로 닦기

해설 기사 네 번째 단락에 굴라티 씨의 고객들이 벽화가 그려질 부분을 청소하고 손질해야 한다(Surprisingly, Ms. Gulati's customers are expected to clean and treat the area where the mural is to be painted)고 언급되어 있다. 이는 벽화가 그려질 표면에 대한 준비 작업을 의미하므로 (A)가 정답이다.

어휘 surface 표면 regularly 주기적으로

> Paraphrasing
> 지문의 clean and treat the area where the mural is to be painted → 정답의 Prepare the painting surface

TEST 10

## 183 세부 사항

번역 기사에 따르면, 굴라티 씨의 웹사이트 방문객들은 무엇을 할 수 있는가?
(A) 상세한 교육용 동영상 시청하기
(B) 프로젝트 비용 견적서 받기
(C) 이전 고객들의 후기 둘러보기
(D) 굴라티 씨의 배경에 관해 더 알아보기

해설 기사 마지막 단락에 굴라티 씨의 웹사이트에 종합적인 단계별 설명이 담긴 동영상이 올라가 있다(~ has a video with comprehensive step-by-step instructions on her Web site, www.gulatiart.ca)는 말이 쓰여 있다. 이는 자세한 설명을 제공하는 동영상을 볼 수 있다는 뜻이므로 (A)가 정답이다.

어휘 detailed 상세한 instructional 교육의 estimate 견적(서) browse 둘러보다 previous 이전의

> **Paraphrasing**
> 지문의 a video with comprehensive step-by-step instructions → 정답의 detailed instructional video

## 184 세부 사항

번역 랜킨 씨는 무엇을 하고 싶어 하는가?
(A) 오래된 건물이 철거되는 것을 막기
(B) 자신의 새 커피숍 바닥에 벽화 그려 넣기
(C) 자신의 매장에서 예술가가 강연하도록 하기
(D) 사용했던 재료를 미술 작품에 포함하기

해설 이메일 세 번째 단락에 랜킨 씨가 현재 위치는 철거 예정인데 그곳의 나무 바닥은 남겨둘 예정이고, 그것들이 어떻게든 포함됐으면 좋겠다(I will save pieces of the wooden floor of our current site, which is to be torn down, and I would like those to be included somehow)고 했으므로 (D)가 정답이다.

어휘 prevent 막다 include 포함하다 incorporate 포함하다 material 재료, 물품

> **Paraphrasing**
> 지문의 pieces of the wooden floor of our current site / would like those to be included
> → 정답의 Incorporate used materials

## 185 연계

번역 랜킨 씨의 어떤 제안을 굴라티 씨가 수용할 수 없을 것 같은가?
(A) 계약금 지급 일정
(B) 작품 제작에 드는 총 비용
(C) 디자인 제작 일정
(D) 벽화 하나의 위치

해설 랜킨 씨가 작성한 이메일 상단에 작성 날짜가 2월 8일(8 February)이고, 네 번째 단락을 보면 10일 후인 2월 18일까지 디자인 스케치를 받을 수 있을지(get sketches of your proposed designs by 18 February) 묻고 있다. 하지만 기사 세 번째 단락에 굴라티 씨는 어떤 디자인 시안이든 마무리하는 데 최소 3주의 기간을 필요로 한다(Ms. Gulati requires a minimum of three weeks to finalize any design plan)는 말이 쓰여 있어 디자인 작업 일정을 수용할 수 없을 것으로 볼 수 있으므로 (C)가 정답이다.

어휘 accommodate 수용하다 fee 요금 timeline 진행 일정

## 186-190 웹페이지+이메일+회의 요약본

http://www.twinklemedia.com/ps

트윙클 미디어 - 제작 서비스

[186] **실시간 행사를 녹화하는 것뿐 아니라, 트윙클 미디어는 대본이 있는 광고 및 기업 동영상 제작을 지원할 수 있습니다.** 저희는 네 가지 서비스 패키지를 제공합니다.

브론즈 - 고객이 기획하고 연기하는 콘텐츠를 촬영해 드리며, 편집과 필요시 제목 및 라이센스가 있거나 저작권 사용료가 없는 음악을 추가하는 기본적인 후반 제작 서비스를 제공합니다.

실버 - 브론즈 패키지 서비스 외에도, 영상에 시각적인 흥미를 더하거나 어려운 개념을 설명하기 위해 간단한 애니메이션을 제작합니다.

골드 - 제작 전 작업 중 일부를 저희 업무에 추가하여, 영상 및 애니메이션 구성에 관해 조언을 제공하고 [188] **대본을 작성합니다.**

플래티넘 - 특별히 전문적인 연출을 위해, 최고 수준의 영상 촬영, 후반 제작 작업, 애니메이션 및 대본 작성을 보완할 수 있도록 [188] **영상에 출연할 배우들을 섭외합니다.**

시작하려면 문의 양식을 작성하세요!

어휘 scripted 대본이 있는 commercial 상업적인, 광고의 corporate 기업의 post-production 후반 제작의, 촬영 후의 licensed 허가된, 인가된 royalty-free 저작권 사용료가 없는 visual interest 시각적 관심 illustrate 설명하다, 분명히 보여 주다 task 업무, 일 plate 일, 업무 structure 구성하다, 조직하다 presentation 연출, 표현 cast 섭외하다 complement 보완하다 top-notch 최고 수준의, 일류의 videography 영상 촬영

발신: 우정호 <jeonghow@twinklemedia.com>
수신: 서배너 브래즈웰 <s.braswell@accounti.com>
제목: 회신: 업데이트
날짜: 9월 15일

브래즈웰 씨께,

[187] **귀사의 제품 사용 설명 영상을 위한 예산 한도에 관해 새로운 소식을 알려 주셔서 감사드립니다.** [188] **귀하의 바람대로, 저희는 제공되는 서비스 규모를 축소할 것입니다. 귀사의 프로젝트가 아직 초기 단계이기 때문에 섭외 과정을 시작하지 않아서 이 변경으로 인해 누구도 불편하게 하지 않을 것이니 안심하셔도 됩니다.**

각 영상에서 다루기를 원하시는 기본 요점들의 배치를 완료하셨다는 소식을 듣고 기뻤습니다. 그 정보를 저희에게 보내 주시고 어카운티 접근 권한을 부여해 주시기 바랍니다. [188, 189] **대본을 제작하기 위해서는 저희 팀이 직접 해당 소프트웨어의 기능들을 사용해 보고, 귀하나 저희**

**의 질문에 답변해 주실 수 있는 다른 어카운티 직원을 만나야 할 것입니다**. 저희는 9월 18일 목요일 오전이나 9월 22일 월요일 오후에 시간이 있습니다. 어느 시간이 귀하께 가장 좋을지 알려 주시기 바랍니다.

우정호
고객 관리 책임자
트윙클 미디어

어휘 budget 예산 limit 한도, 제한 tutorial 사용 설명(서) in accordance with ~대로, ~에 따라 scope 규모, 범위 process 과정 inconvenience 불편하게 하다 map out 배치하다, 계획하다 cover (주제 등을) 다루다 access 접근 (권한) feature 기능, 특징 have availability 시간이 있다

회의 요약

트윙클 미디어

189 **프로젝트: 어카운티 제품 사용 설명 영상**

9월 22일 오후 1시 30분 - 4시
참석자: 우정호, 이벳 로드리게스, 189 **숀 프리먼(고객사 직원)**

프리먼 씨가 어카운티의 기능에 관한 질문에 답변해 주셨습니다(첨부된 메모 참고).

다음과 같은 일정으로 고객사 승인을 위해 영상 대본을 제출해 드리기로 약속했습니다.

"시작하기" - 9월 24일
"중요한 설정" - 9월 26일
"판매 및 거래 내역서" - 9월 30일
"지출" - 10월 2일

190 **"중요한 설정"은 진행자가 등장하는 것보다 애니메이션과 성우 더빙이 더 적합하다고 결정되어**, 그 대본이 승인되는 대로 제작을 시작할 수 있습니다. 프리먼 씨가 나머지 영상들의 촬영 일정에 대해 금요일까지 전화 주실 것입니다.

어휘 representative 직원, 대표자 attach 첨부하다 approval 승인 following 다음의, 아래의 invoice 거래 내역서 expense 지출 (비용), 경비 voice-over 성우 더빙 suitable 적합한, 알맞은 presenter 진행자, 발표자 approve 승인하다

## 186 Not / True

번역 웹페이지에서 트윙클 미디어에 대해 언급하는 것은?
(A) 대규모 촬영 스튜디오를 보유하고 있다.
(B) 제품 광고를 전문으로 한다.
(C) 직원들이 영상용 창작 음악을 작곡한다.
(D) 서비스에 행사 영상 촬영이 포함된다.

해설 웹페이지 첫 단락에 트윙클 미디어가 실시간 행사를 녹화하는 것뿐 아니라, 대본이 있는 광고 및 기업 동영상 제작을 지원할 수 있다(In addition to recording live events, Twinkle Media can assist with the production of scripted commercial and corporate videos)고 쓰여 있으므로 (D)가 정답이다.

어휘 specialize in ~을 전문으로 하다 advertisement 광고 compose 작곡하다 original 독창적인, 원래의 include 포함하다

> Paraphrasing
> 지문의 recording live events
> → 정답의 event videography

## 187 주제 / 목적

번역 이메일의 한 가지 목적은?
(A) 프로젝트 계획 변경을 확인하는 것
(B) 예산에 관해 더 많은 정보를 요청하는 것
(C) 우 씨의 이전 작업물 중 일부를 소개하는 것
(D) 촬영 과정의 단계들을 설명하는 것

해설 이메일 초반부에 예산 한도에 대한 새로운 소식을 알려줘서 고맙다(Thank you for the update on the budget limit for your product tutorial videos)고 한 후, 제공되는 서비스 규모를 축소할 것(~ we will reduce the scope of our services to be provided)이라고 알리는 말이 쓰여 있다. 이는 예산 한도 변경에 대한 소식을 듣고 그에 따라 서비스 계획을 변경하는 것을 알리는 것이므로 (A)가 정답이다.

어휘 confirm 확인하다, 확인해 주다 modification 수정, 변경 previous 이전의, 과거의

> Paraphrasing
> 지문의 reduce the scope of our services to be provided
> → 정답의 a modification to a project plan

## 188 연계

번역 브래즈웰 씨는 어떤 서비스 패키지를 받을 것 같은가?
(A) 브론즈
(B) 실버
(C) 골드
(D) 플래티넘

해설 브래즈웰 씨에게 보내는 이메일 첫 단락과 두 번째 단락에 서비스 규모를 축소한다(we will reduce the scope of our services)는 점과 아직 섭외 과정을 시작하지 않았다(we have not begun the casting process)는 점, 그리고 대본을 만드는 일(To produce the scripts)이 각각 언급되어 있다. 따라서 웹 페이지 하단에 배우 섭외 과정(we cast actors to appear in your video)이 포함된 서비스인 '플래티넘'에서 대본 집필(write the script) 서비스가 포함된 '골드' 패키지로 규모가 축소되는 것을 알 수 있으므로 (C)가 정답이다.

## 189 연계

번역 브래즈웰 씨에 대해 암시된 것은?
(A) 프리먼 씨의 동료이다.
(B) 우 씨의 요청 사항들 중 하나를 이행하지 못했다.
(C) 계획된 영상의 숫자를 늘렸다.
(D) 가급적 가장 이른 회의 날짜를 선택했다.

TEST 10

해설 회의 요약본에 프로젝트가 어카운티 제품 사용 설명 영상(Project: Accounti Product Tutorial Videos)으로 나와 있고, 숀 프리먼 씨는 고객사 직원(Shaun Freeman (client representative))으로 표기되어 있다. 따라서 이메일 두 번째 단락에 브래즈웰 씨나 질문에 답변해 줄 다른 어카운티 직원과 만나야 한다(meet with you or another Accounti employee who can answer any questions we have about it)고 한 부분에 언급된 '다른 어카운티 직원'이 숀 프리먼 씨임을 알 수 있으므로 (A)가 정답이다.

어휘 colleague 동료 (직원) fulfill 이행하다, 충족하다

## 190 세부 사항

번역 회의 요약본에 따르면, 어느 영상이 사람을 담은 장면을 포함하지 않을 것인가?
(A) "시작하기"
(B) "중요한 설정"
(C) "판매 및 거래 내역서"
(D) "지출"

해설 회의 요약본 마지막 단락에 "중요한 설정"은 진행자가 등장하는 것보다 애니메이션과 성우 더빙이 더 적합하다고 결정됐다(It was decided that animations and voice-over are more suitable than an on-camera presenter for "Important Settings,")고 언급되어 있으므로 (B)가 정답이다.

어휘 footage 장면, 동영상

### 191-195 제안서 양식+제안서 양식+이메일

제안서

| 고객 정보: | [191] **업체 정보:** |
|---|---|
| 그린웨이 회계 | **윈덤 이사 전문 회사** |
| 로비넷 길 689, 1호 | 워시 가 1150 |
| 뱅크스타운, NSW 2200 | 뱅크스타운, NSW 2200 |

프로젝트:
2인 1조로 고객 사무실의 모든 물건을 트럭에 싣고 내리는 작업과 이 화물을 약 5.2킬로미터 운송하는 작업. [195] **가구 분해 및 조립 서비스 포함.** [193] **운반용 상자와 발포 비닐 제공,** 하지만 작은 물품은 고객이 미리 포장해야 함.

업체 제안:
업체는 세금 포함 1,850달러의 금액으로 상기 프로젝트를 실시한다.
고객은 프로젝트 완료 즉시 전액 지불한다.
가격은 제안서 제출 30일 후에 만료된다.

제안서 동의
[191] **업체 담당 직원:** **함아영**
날짜: 9월 13일

고객 대표: ____________
날짜: ____________

어휘 proposal 제안(서) contractor 계약업체 crew (함께 일하는) 조, 반 transport 운송 cargo 화물 approximately 약, 대략 disassembly 분해 assembly 조립 include 포함하다 packing 포장 in advance 사전에, 미리 carry out 실시하다 immediately 즉시 completion 완료 expire 만료되다 submission 제출 acceptance 동의, 수락 representative 대표자, 대리인

닐슨 이전 서비스 회사: 제안서
퍼켓 가 560
야구나, NSW 2199

제안 대상: 그린웨이 회계
로비넷 길 689, 1호
뱅크스타운, NSW 2200

발급일: 9월 15일
유효 기간: 10월 14일
닐슨 이전 서비스 회사는 트럭을 이용해 고객의 현재 사무실에 있는 모든 물품을 레베스비, 얼스 길 77로 옮길 것을 제안한다. 이사일 전에 [195] **고객은 반드시 가구를 분해하고 필요한 포장 작업을 완료해야 한다.** [193] **판지 상자 및 보호용 패드의 대여 포함.**

비용: 1,490달러 (세금 미포함)
[192] **고객은 제안 동의 시 50%(745달러)를 보증금으로 지불해야 하며, 잔금은 이사가 완료되는 대로 지불되어야 한다.**

제안서 준비: 윌리엄 버니어
고객 서명: ____________
날짜: ____________

어휘 issue 발급하다 valid 유효한 propose 제안하다 entire 전체의 content 내용물 current 현재의 via ~을 통해 disassemble 분해하다 necessary 필수의 deposit 선금, 보증금 remainder 잔여, 나머지

수신: 그린웨이 회계 직원
발신: 로자리오 발레스, 대표
제목: 다가오는 이사
날짜: 9월 29일

새 사무실 이전 일정을 최종 확정했습니다. 포장용 물품은 월요일부터 이용할 수 있을 것입니다. 수요일 정오까지 작은 물품들을 포장해 놓으시기 바랍니다. [195] **이삿짐 회사 사람들이 도착했을 때 모든 것을 실을 준비가 되도록 몇몇 직원들이 그날 남아서 책상과 파일 캐비닛, 책장들을 분해하겠다고 자원해 주셨습니다.** 나머지 모든 직원들은 그날 오후에 쉬어도 됩니다. 하지만 [194] **이사가 진행되는 목요일에는 모든 직원이 재택 근무 계획을 세워야 합니다.** 마지막으로 금요일 아침에는 새 사무실로 출근해서 짐을 풀고 설치하는 일을 도와주시기 바랍니다.

어휘 upcoming 다가오는 relocation 이전, 이주 material 물품, 재료 available 이용 가능한 volunteer 자원하다 the rest of ~의 나머지 take apart 분해하다 rest 쉬다, 휴식하다

work from home 재택 근무하다 report to+명사 ~로 출근하다
unpacking 짐 풀기 setup 설치

## 191 추론

번역 함 씨는 누구이겠는가?
(A) 건물 검사관
(B) 발레스 씨의 비서
(C) 윈덤 이사 전문 회사 직원
(D) 그린웨이 회계 대표

해설 첫 번째 제안서 하단에 업체 담당 직원(Contractor Representative)으로 함 씨의 이름이 표기되어 있고, 상단에 업체 이름이 윈덤 이사 전문 회사(Contractor Information: Windham Movers)로 쓰여 있어 함 씨는 이 회사의 직원임을 알 수 있다. 따라서 (C)가 정답이다.

**Paraphrasing**
지문의 Representative → 정답의 employee

## 192 세부 사항

번역 닐슨 이전 서비스 회사의 고객들은 무엇을 반드시 해야 하는가?
(A) 비용 절반 미리 지불하기
(B) 자신의 이사 차량 운전하기
(C) 소지품 목록 제공하기
(D) 필요한 주차 허가증 받기

해설 닐슨 이전 서비스 회사의 제안서인 두 번째 제안서 하단에 고객이 제안 동의 시 반드시 50%(745달러)를 보증금으로 지불해야 한다(Customer must submit deposit of 50% ($745) at acceptance of proposal)는 조건이 제시되어 있다. 이는 미리 절반의 비용을 지불하라는 뜻이므로 (A)가 정답이다.

어휘 supply 제공하다 belongings 소유 물품, 소지품 obtain 받다, 얻다 necessary 필수의 permit 허가증

**Paraphrasing**
지문의 submit deposit of 50%
→ 정답의 Pay half of a fee in advance

## 193 연계

번역 두 회사 모두 고객들에게 무엇을 제공하는가?
(A) 보험 보장
(B) 야간 물품 보관
(C) 단거리 이사 할인
(D) 포장용 물품 이용

해설 첫 번째 제안서 중반부에 운반용 상자와 발포 비닐이 제공된다(Moving boxes and bubble wrap provided)고 했고 두 번째 제안서 중반부에 판지 상자 및 보호용 패드의 대여가 포함된다(Loan of cardboard boxes and protective padding included)고 했으므로 두 회사 모두 이사하는 데 필요한 포장용 물품을 제공한다는 것을 알 수 있다. 따라서 (D)가 정답이다.

어휘 insurance 보험 coverage 보장 (범위) storage 보관, 저장

**Paraphrasing**
지문의 Moving boxes and bubble wrap / cardboard boxes and protective padding
→ 정답의 packing materials

## 194 세부 사항

번역 이메일에 따르면, 그린웨이 회계 직원들은 언제 원격으로 근무해야 하는가?
(A) 이사 컨설턴트의 방문 중에
(B) 각자의 업무 공간을 치운 후 오후에
(C) 이사하는 날 하루 종일
(D) 새 사무실이 설치되는 동안

해설 이메일의 후반부에 이사가 진행되는 목요일에는 모든 직원이 재택 근무 계획을 세워야 한다(everyone should plan to work from home on Thursday during the move)고 했으므로 (C)가 정답이다.

어휘 workstation 작업 공간 set up 설치하다, 마련하다

**Paraphrasing**
지문의 work from home → 질문의 work remotely

## 195 연계

번역 그린웨이 회계에 대해 암시된 것은?
(A) 새로운 장소에 필요한 추가 가구를 구입했다.
(B) 닐슨 이전 서비스 회사가 이사 작업을 진행할 것이다.
(C) 과거에 윈덤 이사 전문 회사를 이용했다.
(D) 금요일 아침에 정상 업무 활동을 재개할 것이다.

해설 이메일 중반부에 이삿짐 회사 사람들이 도착했을 때 모든 것을 실을 준비가 되도록 몇몇 직원들이 그날 남아서 책상과 파일 캐비닛, 책장들을 분해하겠다고 자원했다(A few employees have volunteered to spend the rest of the day taking apart the desks, filing cabinets, and bookshelves so that everything is ready to be loaded up when the movers arrive)는 말이 쓰여 있다. 윈덤 사의 제안서인 첫 번째 제안서에서 가구 분해 및 조립 서비스가 포함된다(Furniture disassembly/assembly service included)고 했고, 닐슨 사의 제안서인 두 번째 제안서에는 고객이 가구를 분해해야 한다(Customer must disassemble furniture)고 했으므로 그린웨이는 닐슨 사를 이용한다는 것을 알 수 있다. 따라서 (B)가 정답이다.

어휘 extra 추가의, 여분의 carry out 실행하다, 수행하다 resume 재개하다

TEST 10

## 196-200 이메일 + 일정표 + 이메일

수신: 패링턴 통합 물류 전 직원 <staff@farringtonil.com>
발신: 벤카타 나야르 <v.nayar@farringtonil.com>
날짜: 2월 13일
제목: 예정된 계획
첨부: 확정 일정표

직원 여러분,

3월 한 달에 걸쳐, 패링턴 통합 물류(FIL)는 [196] **직원들의 능력을 향상시키고 다른 부서 사람들과 교류하는 데 도움이 될 세션을 제공하기 시작할 것입니다.** 이 시간들이 유용하고 가치 있다고 생각하시기를 바랍니다.

신입 사원과 부서장들을 위한 시간은 참석이 의무라는 점에 유의하시기 바랍니다. 불참할 것으로 예상되는 경우, 저에게 알려 주시기 바라며, 제가 사안별로 상황을 판단할 것입니다. [197] **전 직원에게 공개되는 세션의 경우, 점심 시간에 사내에서 개최되는 것들은 신청할 필요가 없지만, 저녁 시간에 열리는 것은 미리 등록하셔야 합니다.**

벤카타 나야르
운영부장, 패링턴 통합 물류

어휘 upcoming 곧 있을, 다가오는 confirm 확정하다, 확인해 주다 session (특정 활동을 위한) 시간 enhance 향상시키다, 강화하다 network 교류하다 informative 유용한 worthwhile 가치 있는 mandatory 의무적인 absent 불참한, 부재 중인 assess 평가하다 on a case-by-case basis 사례별로 sign up for ~을 신청하다 on site 구내에서, 현장에서 register 등록하다 in advance 미리, 사전에

패링턴 통합 물류 3월 프로그램

| 날짜 | 시간 | 세부 정보 | 참가자 |
|---|---|---|---|
| 3월 3일 월요일 | 오후 12:30 | 회사 구내식당, 점심 | 신입 사원 |
| 3월 13일 목요일 | 오후 12:30 | 회사 구내식당, 점심 | FIL |
| 3월 18일 화요일 | 오후 7:00 | [199] **선샤인 카페, 저녁** | **부서장** |
| [197] **3월 21일 금요일** | **오후 6:30** | **빅토리아스 비스트로, 저녁** | **FIL** |
| 3월 24일 월요일 | 오전 11:30 | 회사 구내식당, 점심 | FIL |

어휘 participant 참가자 cafeteria 구내식당

수신: 벤카타 나야르 <v.nayar@farringtonil.com>
발신: 코마키 이나바 <inabakomaki@mkmail.com>
[200] **날짜: 4월 2일**
제목: 3월 행사

나야르 씨께,

귀하의 사무실에서 세션을 진행하도록 초대해 주셔서 대단히 감사합니다. 참가자들의 참여도가 높았고, 토론이 생산적이었습니다. [199] **선샤인 카페에서 저녁 식사를 하면서 모든 직원들과 이야기 나눌 수 있어서 즐거웠고, 맥코맥 씨의 통찰력이 특히 흥미로웠습니다.** 저는 전업으로 컨설팅 분야에 진출할 계획을 세우고 있기 때문에, [200] **제 웹사이트를 위한 콘텐츠를 작업하고 있으며, 이는 다음 달 말부터 방문객들이 이용할 수 있을 것입니다.** [198] **귀하 또는 귀하의 동료들 중 한 분께서 이 사이트에 쓰일 추천 후기를 제공해 주실 의향이 있으실지 궁금합니다.** 가능한지 알려 주시면 감사하겠습니다. 제게 아주 큰 도움이 될 것입니다.

코마키 이나바

어휘 engaged 참여한 fruitful 생산적인 insight 통찰력 particularly 특히 branch out into ~로 진출하다, 확장하다 available 이용 가능한 colleague 동료 testimonial 추천 후기

### 196 주제 / 목적

번역 첫 번째 이메일의 목적은 무엇인가?
(A) 곧 있을 교육 행사에 대한 제안을 이끌어 내는 것
(B) 경영팀의 새로운 인원을 소개하는 것
(C) 직원들에게 직무 능력 개발 기회를 알리는 것
(D) 결근에 대해 새로 시행되는 정책을 설명하는 것

해설 첫 단락에 직원들의 능력을 향상시키고 다른 부서 사람들과 교류하는 데 도움이 될 세션을 제공할 것(~ offering several sessions to help our employees enhance their skills and network with people from other departments)이라는 말이 쓰여 있다. 이는 직원들의 직무 능력을 개발하는 기회를 알리는 것에 해당하므로 (C)가 정답이다.

어휘 elicit 이끌어 내다 professional development 직업 능력 개발 opportunity 기회 implement 시행하다 absence 결근, 부재

> **Paraphrasing**
> 지문의 enhance their skills
> → 정답의 professional development

### 197 연계

번역 직원들이 어떤 행사에 반드시 미리 등록해야 하는가?
(A) 3월 3일 점심
(B) 3월 13일 점심
(C) 3월 18일 저녁
(D) 3월 21일 저녁

해설 첫 번째 이메일 두 번째 단락에 전 직원에게 공개되는 세션에 대해 말하면서 저녁 시간에 개최되는 것은 미리 등록해야 한다(For the sessions open to all staff, ~ but you do need to register in advance for the evening one)고 언급되어 있다. 일정표에서 참가 대상이 전 직원(FIL)이자 저녁 시간에 개최되는 것을 찾으면 밑에서 두 번째 줄에 기재된 3월 21일 저녁 시간(Fri., March 21 / 6:30 P.M. / Victoria's Bistro, Dinner / FIL)이므로 (D)가 정답이다.

## 198 주제 / 목적

번역 이나바 씨가 나야르 씨에게 이메일을 보내는 한 가지 이유는 무엇인가?
(A) 도움을 요청하기 위해
(B) 회사 행사를 연기하기 위해
(C) 일자리 제의를 받아들이기 위해
(D) 시작 날짜에 관해 문의하기 위해

해설 두 번째 이메일 두 번째 단락에 이나바 씨가 나야르 씨에게 자신의 웹사이트에 쓰일 추천 후기를 제공해 줄 의향이 있는지 궁금하다(I'm wondering if you or one of your colleagues would be willing to provide a testimonial to be used on the site)고 했는데, 이는 도움을 요청하는 것이므로 (A)가 정답이다.

어휘 postpone 연기하다 inquire 문의하다

## 199 연계

번역 맥코맥 씨는 누구일 것 같은가?
(A) 한 부서의 책임자
(B) 새롭게 고용된 FIL 직원
(C) 선샤인 카페 주인
(D) 나야르 씨의 행정 업무 보조

해설 맥코맥 씨의 이름이 언급되는 두 번째 이메일에 선샤인 카페에서 저녁 식사하면서 이야기 나눈 것이 즐거웠다는 말과 함께 맥코맥 씨의 통찰력이 특히 흥미로웠다(I enjoyed chatting with all of your staff over dinner at the Sunshine Café and found Ms. McCormack's insights to be particularly interesting)고 언급되어 있다. 일정표에서 선샤인 카페에서 열린 행사의 참가자가 부서장(Sunshine Café, Dinner / Department Managers)으로 표기되어 있어 맥코맥 씨가 부서장임을 알 수 있다. 따라서 (A)가 정답이다.

## 200 추론

번역 두 번째 이메일에서 웹사이트에 대해 암시하는 것은?
(A) FIL을 위한 사업을 만들어 낼 가능성이 있다.
(B) 부정확한 정보를 포함하고 있다.
(C) 5월 말에 시작될 것이다.
(D) 나야르 씨의 동료에 의해 디자인되었다.

해설 두 번째 단락에 이나바 씨가 자신의 웹사이트는 다음 달 말부터 이용 가능할 것(~ my Web site, which will be available to visitors from the end of next month)이라고 했는데, 이메일 상단의 작성 날짜가 4월 2일(Date: April 2)이므로 5월 말부터 이용 가능하다는 것을 알 수 있다. 따라서 (C)가 정답이다.

어휘 generate 만들어 내다 contain 포함하다 incorrect 부정확한 launch 시작하다

TEST 10

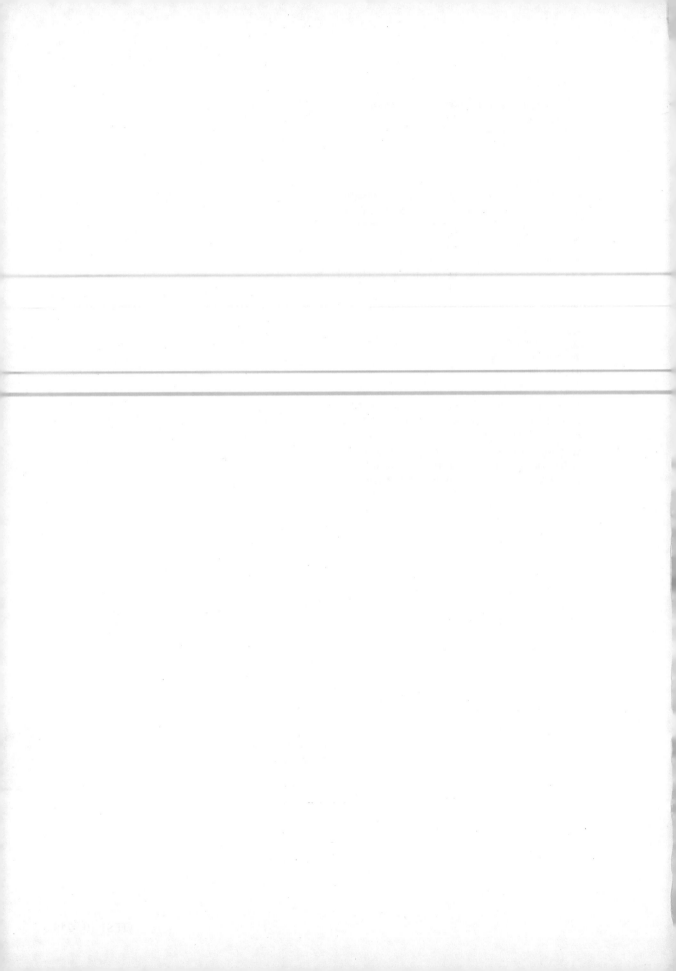

토익주관사

# YBM 실전토익 RC 1000

전면 개정판

1